The Works Of The Rev. William Jay, Of Argyle Chapel, Bath: Short Discourses To Be Read In Families. The Christian Contemplated In A Course Of Lectures. Prayers...

William Jay, Cornelius Winter, John Clark

THE WORKS

OF THE

REV. WILLIAM JAY,

OF ARGYLE CHAPEL, BATH.

COMPRISING

MATTER NOT HERETOFORE PRESENTED TO THE
AMERICAN PUBLIC.

IN THREE VOLUMES.

VOL. II.

CONTAINING

SHORT DISCOURSES TO BE READ IN FAMILIES—THE CHRIS-
TIAN CONTEMPLATED IN A COURSE OF LECTURES—
AND PRAYERS.

NEW-YORK:

PUBLISHED BY HARPER & BROTHERS,
No. 82 CLIFF-STREET.

1844.

PREFACE.

MANY persons who maintain the worship of God in their houses, wish, occasionally at least, to blend instruction with devotion. But they are not able to deliver any thing of their own, nor can they easily avail themselves of satisfactory assistance from others.

We have commentators; but expositions are designed to be consulted rather than read, and are calculated to aid sacred criticism, and promote a general knowledge of the Scriptures, rather than to enliven the exercises of social piety. We have also paraphrases; but these too often consist of a mere languid redundancy of words which, by pretending to illustrate, only oppress and encumber the sense, and generally serve no other purpose than to destroy the simplicity, weaken the force, and diminish the effect of the word of truth. "In the very best compositions of this kind," says a judicious writer, "the gospel may be compared to a rich wine of high flavour, diluted in such a quantity of water, as renders it extremely vapid." Paraphrase is useful only in cases of obscurity, but the word of God generally considered, is not hard to be understood. We do not apply the same censure to the reflections which are found at the end of the chapters or paragraphs, and which sum up their contents. These are often exceedingly valuable and useful: but it is easy to see that they are not very well adapted to the design before us. They are necessarily too refined in their coherence, too extensive in their review, too general in their remark, to leave a forcible impression on the minds of common readers or hearers.

Sermons have been often employed, and many discourses have been published, professedly for the use of families. But it has been remarked—That these discourses have not been distinguished from others, either in their length, their style, or their subjects. It has been asked, Is there no difference in circumstances between public worship and domestic devotion? It has been said, Let a minister place himself in a private family, and lead the morning or evening devotion, and he will soon find how unsuitable it would be to deliver in a parlour a sermon which he had prepared for the pulpit.

Discourses to be used on such occasions as these should be short—not commonly surpassing ten minutes; seldom more than a quarter of an hour. As children and servants often form the greatest part of the little assembly, and should never be overlooked—these addresses should be plain and apprehensible, not argumentative, nor consisting of long paragraphs—they should be easy and natural, not elaborate or highly polished—they should be entertaining and interesting, not dry and soporific

Hence they should shun the formality of method and numerous divisions; and abound with short and significant sentences, bold images, striking incidents, lively descriptions and characters. Two classes of Scriptures would furnish perhaps the best foundations for these exercises. First, the *historical*, which holds forth the duties of religion in examples and instances. And secondly, the *figurative*, which explains divine things by resemblance. There is no better method of gaining the attention and of impressing the minds of children and common people, than teaching by comparison, or illustrating spiritual things by natural. It is needless to observe how much our Saviour's discourses abound with such allusions. Wit-

3

ness the prodigal son, the strayed sheep, the mustard seed, the leaven, the lilies—all this made its way directly to the heart; it was impossible ever to forget it; his followers hung upon his lips; children cried, Hosanna! and the common people heard him gladly.

In compliance both with his own conviction and the repeated solicitations of others, the Author has ventured to undertake the present work. He does not affirm, however, that what he has done comes perfectly up to his wishes, or corresponds with the plan he has suggested. He found that it was easier to censure than to amend; to judge than to execute. But this he professes: he has attempted to be simple, without being coarse; and to be intelligible to the illiterate, without proving disgustful to the wise. He has laboured to unite perspicuity with brevity; and, in the small compass allowed him, to introduce a subject, and secure an effect. Frequently unable in a few pages to do justice to the various parts of a Scripture, he has endeavoured to seize some one more prominent view of it, and to turn it into a source of consolation, a motive to holiness, a help to devotion. His aim has been to show that faith is not a notion, but a principle; and to bring down religion from airy speculations into common life, that our piety may not be periodical, but keep us in the fear of the Lord all the day long.—He wished to make Christianity to appear lovely in its spirit, reasonable in its commands, rich in its motives and resources, and beyond expression kind and tender in its promises.

The wish of the Author to engage particularly the attention of Servants and Children, will frequently appear in his manner. For such adaptations he makes no apology. Though he does not wish to indulge a bad taste, he would ever remember that a preacher ought to have compassion on the ignorant, and on them that are out of the way. That which is too smooth, easily slides off the memory; and that which is lost in the act of hearing, will do little good. It is desirable to get something that will *strike* and *abide;* something that recurring again and again, will employ the thoughts and the tongue; and if this cannot be accomplished in certain instances but by modes of address which perhaps are not so classically justifiable, should not a minister prefer utility to fame? Paul in his noble energy adds the comparative degree to the superlative, and calls himself less than the least of all saints. He invented new words, and used quaint ones He could say, " I have made myself servant unto all, that I might gain the more. To the weak became I as weak, that I might gain the weak: I am made all things to all men, that I might by all means gain some." If a child ran away and became a profligate, a good father would be anxious to have him reclaimed; and if a person should go to him and say, " I think I could prevail upon your son to abandon his unhappy course of living"—would such a father say, " O try! but see to it that you conform perfectly to every rule of good speaking." Or should he return and announce his success, would the father deem it worth while to ask, " Did you dispose your arguments quite logically, or make use of no obsolete term or trite phrase?"— " He that winneth souls is wise."—" If a man err from the truth, and one convert him, let him know that he who converteth a sinner from the error of his ways shall save a soul from death, and shall hide a multitude of sins." What a recompense!

—The circumstances of families are perpetually varying, and what is suitable seldom fails to impress. It was not possible, however, to accommodate a lecture to every supposable case; but the Author has endeavoured to introduce a comprehensive variety, and hopes something will be found pertinent to all the more common and interesting occurrences. He has more than once noticed events of an afflictive nature. The heart is then soft and serious. He has improved the various seasons of the year. He has also provided subjects which are adapted to all the greater festivals. Members of the Established Church may read these on the appropriated days, while Dissenters can surely have no objection to read at some time or other a few reflections on the birth or ascension of Christ. " One man esteemeth one day above another; another esteemeth every day alike; let every man be fully persuaded in his own mind. He that regardeth the day, regardeth it unto the Lord ; and he that regardeth not the day, to the Lord he doth not regard it.—Why dost thou judge thy brother ? Or why dost thou set at nought thy brother ? For we shall all stand before the judgment-seat of Christ."

—Such was the Prospectus by which the Author announced the work he had undertaken. The circulation of the proposals occasioned from his friends a variety of hints concerning the plan. Some of these could not be regarded, but others have led to a little deviation from the original sketch—in two cases—The one respects the style ; the other the length.

With regard to the former it was suggested—that in families where discourses of this kind were likely to be read, there were often Youths of both sexes, of some education and improvement—that these formed a very important part of the object of such a publication—and therefore that the eye should not be too exclusively fixed on servants and children. In consequence of this, the Author has frequently paid a little more attention to the composition.

With regard to the other it was observed—that between an hour, and the time proposed, there were many intermediate degrees—and that those who had been accustomed to read discourses of the former length, would find the latter too disproportionately short. The Author has therefore rendered some of these exercises a little longer : but as far as he can judge, none of them even now will take up more than thirty minutes. This circumstance has rather reduced the number of addresses.

After all, the Author scarcely knows whether the alterations are improvements. He has found, that if in the multitude of counsellors there is safety, there is also perplexity. The work has been finished in a short space of time, under frequent indispositions and many interruptions. It might have been much better executed. But all human productions are susceptible of endless improvement ; and were an author to wait till his own mind is completely satisfied, he may linger in idle hope, till death—every moment hastening on—deprives him of all opportunity to serve his generation. The grand point at which we should aim is—to work while it is called to-day, knowing that the night cometh, wherein no man *can* work—and to gain from the Master the sentence with which he defended and applauded Mary —"Let her alone—She hath done what she could."

The Author has not placed the discourses according to any principle of arrangement ; but the INDEX will enable the reader to find the subject suited to any particular purpose.

After publishing the prospectus, a much esteemed friend sent the Author the following reflections, which he had never seen before. They are extracted from the *Monthly Review* for May 1800. In noticing " Family Sermons, by the Rev. E. Whitaker, Canterbury, 3 vols.," the writer observes,

" Prepossessed by the title of this work, we commenced our perusal of it with the flattering expectation of finding what has indeed been long wanted ; viz. a set of sermons particularly calculated for the use of families ; such as are proper for parents and masters to read on Sunday evenings to their children and servants. It is astonishing that amidst the torrent of sermons continually issuing from the press, there should scarcely be found any which answer this description : but our clergy do not sufficiently consider that compositions calculated for the pulpit are not always adapted for the purposes above specified. In our opinion Family Sermons ought to be short, plain, pious, and practical. They should not tire by length, nor perplex by profundity. The plain truths of the Christian religion, the social and personal virtues, should be their subjects, and these should be treated with a view to practical application, rather than to learned explanation.

" Our modern sermons are considerably shorter than those of the last age, but they are still too long for domestic use. Children and servants are soon tired of listening to admonitions ; and when languor prevails, the mind ceases to be in a proper state to receive instruction. Above all things, therefore, he who composes Family Sermons should avoid prolixity and dry argumentation. He should endeavour to put himself in the situation of a sensible and well-disposed master of a family, who wishes to embrace the opportunity afforded on the Sunday evening of inculcating on those under his care and authority the lessons of religion and virtue. Such a man, in making such an attempt, would select no subject of controversy, would discover no desire of display, but would strive, with all brevity, affectionately and piously to address their plain understandings, consciences, and feelings."

The Author has inserted this extract because there is such a remarkable coincidence of reflection, and because by such an authority he would strengthen his own opinion. He apprehends there is only one article in which the work now introduced will be found to differ from the plan recommended above. And it is this: He has brought forward, sometimes more fully and distinctly, and oftener still by connexion and implication, subjects which the conductors of this celebrated Review may consider as too much partaking of the controversial, and speculative, and which they would entirely exclude from such a performance. But the Author is satisfied not only of the truth, but of the importance of these doctrines: he has seen their beneficial influence practically exemplified; and he is persuaded the inculcation of them is necessary to ministerial usefulness. And as he has written from conviction, and has delivered himself without censoriousness, he expects from impartiality the same candour with which, notwithstanding difference of sentiment, his former works have been received.

The Discourse on "Death" was occasioned by the dissolution of the Rev. William Rowe, pastor of the Baptist Church in Weymouth. Though not of the Author's own denomination, he considered him equally entitled to affection and esteem; and dying at Bath, he was led to notice the event. His bereaved widow, and some of his relations and friends who were present, earnestly requested (as they understood the Author was publishing) that he would permit the Discourse to stand in the Volume, omitting what was said of the character and experience of the amiable and excellent individual. To comply with the desire afforded him pleasure.

The last Discourse is the usual length of pulpit addresses. The insertion of this the Author wishes to be considered as a small token of his respect for a female friend,* at whose application it was preached a second time; when it was secured by a professional short-hand writer. It is published with scarcely an alteration.

Percy Place; June, 1805.

* The lady of Samuel Mills, Esq. Finsbury-square.

CONTENTS.

8 CONTENTS.

CONTENTS.

AN ADDRESS

TO

MASTERS OF FAMILIES.

MASTERS OF FAMILIES!—You have often heard, and perhaps always admired the resolution of Joshua. He had gathered all Israel together in Shechem, and thus he addressed them—"If it seem evil unto you to serve the Lord; choose you this day whom ye will serve, whether the gods which your fathers served that were on the other side of the flood, or the gods of the Amorites, in whose land ye dwell: but as for me and my house, we will serve the Lord."

THIS DETERMINATION DERIVES A CONSIDERABLE FORCE FROM THE PERSON WHO FORMS IT. It was Joshua. But who was Joshua? A soldier, a hero, a commander-in-chief of the armies of the living God, the governor of Israel, the principal man in the state. He it was who in the presence of an assembled country was not ashamed to say, "As for me and my house, we will serve the Lord."

And does religion degrade talents, tarnish dignity, disparage greatness? It ennobles titles, and adds lustre to a crown. Are they only the vulgar, the foolish, the dastardly, who profess to acknowledge God? God has been served by persons of all ranks, and of all distinctions. In every age of the world some of the wise, the mighty, the noble have been called. And no where does religion shine to more advantage than in circumstances of elevation. Nothing is more pleasing than to see a combination of greatness and goodness in the same character. And nothing can be more useful. The higher classes have more opportunities and capacities for doing good than others. They are like a city set upon a hill; they cannot be hid. They are widely visible. Their influence is extensive and powerful. Their example regulates not only manners, but morals: for it would be easy to prove that morals, equally with fashions, work downwards from superiors to inferiors. If the great distinguish themselves by the profession of truth, the worship of God, the practice of virtue, they will be sure to draw others after them. Whereas if they are infidel, irreligious,

vicious, they are infected fountains, poisoning the multitudes that drink of the streams, and spreading mischief all around.

Observe also THE INDEPENDENCE WITH WHICH THE DETERMINATION IS EXPRESSED. Joshua was by no means indifferent to the welfare of others. He wished all who heard him to choose the God he had chosen, and serve the God he served. But he could not allow himself to be influenced by them. If they will not follow him, he resolves to go alone. "O ye seed of Abraham! if you forsake him, which God forbid, not I. If you will not cleave to him, I must. If there was no individual in the nation, in the world to accompany me, I would say as I now do—'As for me and my house, we will serve the Lord.'"

The case which Joshua here supposes is neither an impossible, nor an unusual one. In a thousand instances you will find yourselves alone if you are resolved to obey the dictates of truth, and the calls of duty. If "the whole world lieth in wickedness," and you will be "holy in all manner of conversation and godliness," you must be singular. If you live among fools, and are wise, you must be singular. If you live among the poor, and are rich, you must be singular. And it is presumed that you would have no great objection to be distinguished by wisdom, or wealth. And why should you be so terrified at the charge of singularity, in a cause infinitely more honourable? Nothing is so excellent as goodness, and no goodness is so praiseworthy as that which is singular. This shows a purity of motive, and a dignity of principle. This argues a grandeur of mind, a soul not meanly enslaved by custom, but asserting its own freedom, and daring to think and act for itself. Such a man does not wait for the company and countenance of others to embolden him—he can venture by himself: and despise the shame—when as he advances, abandoned crowds pursue him with their sneers and reproaches. Such was Abdiel.

11

" Faithful found
Among the faithless, faithful only he;
Among innumerable false, unmoved,
Unshaken, unseduced, unterrified,
His loyalty he kept, his love, his zeal;
Nor number nor example with him wrought
To swerve from truth, or change his constant mind
Though single. From amidst them forth he passed
Long way through hostile scorn, which he sustained
Superior, nor of violence feared aught."

On such a man the Saviour fixes his eye, and cries, " Them that honour me, I will honour. He that confesseth me before men, him will I confess before my Father and the holy angels. Be thou faithful unto death, and I will give thee a crown of life."

It may be remarked, that THE RESOLUTION IS PERSONAL. Indeed he *begins* with *himself*: " As for *me* and my house, we will serve the Lord."

Nothing can dispense with an obligation to personal piety. Nothing merely official, or relative; nothing we do for others, while we are destitute of the grace of God in our own souls, can secure us. " Many will say to me in that day, Lord, Lord, have we not prophesied in thy name! and in thy name have cast out devils! and in thy name done many wonderful works!" And indeed those who are regardless of their own souls are not likely to be very attentive to the souls of others. Mere profession and a regard to decency may carry you some way; but there is nothing like a personal experience of divine things to inflame zeal. Unless you serve God yourselves, your efforts will be transient, partial, irregular. They are also likely to be unsuccessful. A drunken master is a poor preacher of sobriety to servants. A proud father is a miserable recommender of humility to children. They will do as you *do*, rather than do as you *say*. Your example will counteract all the effect of your counsel; and all the convictions you would fix in the mind will fall like arrows from an impenetrable shield. " Thou therefore, which teachest another, teachest thou not thyself! Thou that preachest a man should not steal, dost thou steal? Thou that sayest a man should not commit adultery, dost thou commit adultery? Thou that abhorrest idols, dost thou commit sacrilege ?"

You should therefore begin " both to do, and to teach." You should be able, in a humble measure at least, to say to those who are under your care, " Be ye followers of me, even as I also am of Christ." Personal religion must precede domestic—therefore Joshua does not say *my house* shall serve him *without me.* But domestic religion must accompany personal—and therefore Joshua does not say *I* will serve him *without my house:* he includes both—

And thus, finally, the determination is RELATIVE and EXTENSIVE: " As for me and my house, we will serve the Lord."

But the question is—How could he say this? Could he be answerable for his family as well as for himself! We may consider this two ways, as expressing either his happiness or his duty.

If he could say this from a knowledge of his family; if after observation he was assured of the good and pious dispositions of all those who were under his care—we should envy his happiness. This has sometimes been the case. But the privilege is not common.

The words therefore are rather to be considered as an expression of his duty. Not that he supposed it was in the power of his resolution to make the members of his household truly pious. He knew that God alone is the author of conversion; but he knew also that God uses means, and requires us to use them: that it is only in the use of them he has promised his blessing; and therefore that it is only in the use of them we can expect it. Were we to hear a pious husbandman saying, " This year I will have wheat in *this* field, and in *yonder* I will have barley," you would not mistake him. He does not mean to intimate that he can produce the grain, but he can manure, and plough, and sow, and weed —he intends to do this—and then to look for the divine blessing to give the increase.

Thus Joshua resolves to endeavour in the wise and zealous use of all proper means to render the family he governs truly religious. He would instruct, reprove, admonish, encourage them. He would address every principle of action. He would rouse every passion in their bosoms. He would seize every favourable opportunity, improve every striking occurrence to impress the mind with seriousness. He would cherish every promising appearance. He would lead them to the house of God, and keep them from profaning his holy day. He would pray not only *for* them, but also *with* them. He would worship God not only in the closet, but in the parlour, and with his children and servants in the train.

And this, O ye masters of families! this is that which I wish to enforce upon you all. O that I could find out acceptable words, as well as words of truth! O that I knew by what arguments I could induce you to establish the worship of God in your own houses!

To render our reasoning upon this subject easy of apprehension and remembrance, let me call upon you to consider domestic religion in reference to God—in reference to yourselves—and in reference to your families.

I. Think of it IN REFERENCE TO GOD. To him family religion has a threefold relation. The first is a relation of RESPONSIBILITY. For we are required to glorify God in every condition we occupy, and in every capacity we possess. For instance: If a person be poor, he is commanded to serve God as a poor person. But suppose he should become rich. He would then be required to serve him as rich : and from the time of his acquiring this wealth, he would be tried by the rule of wealth. If a man be single, he is command-ed to serve God as single; but no sooner is he placed over a family than he is required to serve God as the master of a family: and from the moment of his obtaining this new connexion he will be judged by the duties which belong to it. God has committed to him a trust, and he expects him to be faithful to this trust. He has given him a talent, and he expects him to use this talent. In a word, he has made him a steward, and he will call him to give an account of his stewardship. When, so to speak, the man has been tried, then comes forth to be judged the master of the family! Bring forth the law of the house —Have you walked by *this* rule? What have you done for me *here?*—Nothing! Did I not assign you the government of a family: and to qualify you for this very purpose did I not give you a peculiar authority and influence? How have you employed them?— Anticipate the proceedings of this awful day, and "judge yourselves, that you may not be condemned with the world."

The second is a relation of GRATITUDE. How numerous and pressing are your obligations to his kindness and his care! He has crowned your wishes, and supplied all your wants. When you were a poor, solitary, insignificant individual, he raised you into consequence, and multiplied you into a family. Behold "thy wife, like a fruitful vine, by the sides of thy house; and thy children like olive plants round about thy table." Whose "secret has been upon thy tabernacle?" Whose providence has "blessed the labour of thy hands?" Whose vigilance has suffered "no evil to befall thee, nor any plague to come nigh thy dwelling?" And will you basely refuse him the glory which is due unto his holy Name? Will you refuse to honour him in a family in which he has scattered so many blessings? Shall thy house, which should be the temple of his praise, be only the grave of his mercies?

The third is a relation of DEPENDENCE. For can you dispense with God in your dwellings? Are not all your schemes, your exertions, and the assistances you secure, "less than nothing, and vanity," without his aid and his blessing? "Except the Lord build the house, they labour in vain that build it. Except the Lord keep the city, the watchman waketh but in vain." "It is vain for you to rise up early, to sit up late, to eat the bread of sorrows: for so he giveth his beloved sleep." The wisest course therefore is to secure his favour, who has all events under his control, and "is able to do for us exceeding abundantly above all we ask or think." And is this to be done by irreligion?

Observe his promises and his threatenings. Or rather let us observe *one* of them. "The curse of the Lord is in the house of the wicked: but he blesseth the habitation of the just."

What a dreadful look has this Scripture towards a wicked family! What a benign aspect towards a righteous one! What a tremendous thing is "the curse of God:" and this does not hover over the building, does not look in at the window, does not stand at the door—but is "in the house," spreading through every apartment, and feeding like a worm upon all the possessions. You may see the appearance of pleasure, and as you draw nigh, you may "hear music and dancing"—but "there is no peace, saith my God, unto the wicked." Magnificence may reign there; there may be rich furniture, and a table spread with dainties—but what are all these when the divine anger has said, "Let their table be made a snare, a trap, and a stumbling-block, and a recompense unto them?" And if this be the case with their good things—what will they do in the evil day? What can be expected under their disappointments and afflictions—but impatience, and rage, and despair?

But he "blesseth the habitation of the just:" and his blessing with bread and water is a good portion. If they have but little, it is sanctified. Their enjoyments are relished. Their trials are alleviated. Religion opens a refuge, when every other refuge fails, and applies a remedy to evils otherwise remediless. They have a God in trouble. His grace is still the same. His providence is making all things work together for their good. Their walls are continually before him. The voice of rejoicing and of salvation is in the tabernacles of the righteous! This brings us,

II. To consider family religion IN REFERENCE TO YOURSELVES.

And here, in the first place, you ought to be concerned for your spiritual welfare. You ought to value that which has a tendency to restrain you from sin, and to excite you to holiness. Now it is easy to see that the practice we are recommending has such an influence. Can he who is going to prayer with his family swear or be obscene? He will be upon his guard, if it be only to preserve himself from the charge of hypocrisy. Another feels no such motive. He can indulge himself in bad words, and vile tempers, without incurring the reflection of inconsistency. And because he makes no pretensions to virtue, he may imagine himself at liberty to practise vice.

And upon this principle it is that many refuse to make a profession of religion—to come to the table of the Lord—and to adopt family worship. They reason properly enough —that in consequence of this they must become more watchful and circumspect. But what can we think of the principle? What can we think of a man who fears to be restrained from the commission of sin, and to be urged to the performance of duty?

Such a practice also will secure tranquillity of mind. The omission of this duty leaves a sting in the conscience, occasions many a bitter reflection through life, and plants a dying pillow with thorns. When you see those who were placed under your care going astray, becoming the victims of error and vice and misery, it will not be easily in your power to suppress the rising, or to soothe the painful accusation—"Ah! this might have been prevented, had you discharged your duty. Does not their destruction lie at your door?" But the man who has faithfully discharged his obligations, feels an internal composure. If indeed his efforts be not crowned with success, he will lament; but this grief differs very materially from that torture which springs from self-condemnation for a trust betrayed, for opportunities neglected, for exertions omitted. He has a satisfaction under all his distress; and his rejoicing is this, the testimony of his conscience, that in simplicity and godly sincerity, not by fleshly wisdom, but by the grace of God, he has had his conversation with the world, and more abundantly to them-ward.

But surely you are not indifferent to your temporal circumstances. You wish to have peace and order in your dwelling. You wish to have your property secured, and your business well performed. You wish to see fidelity, diligence, submission. You wish to be honoured and obeyed. But do men gather grapes of thorns, or figs of thistles? Surely you cannot expect these things to be produced without principle; and what principle can so certainly and fully produce them as religion? What else can enforce them by sanctions and motives so awful, so binding, and which operate equally in all places and at all times; and thus secure the performance of duty, when you are absent as well as present? By teaching them to regard God, you teach them to regard yourselves. Piety is the firmest basis on which to build morality. To which we may add, that when religion is fairly exemplified in character, there is a majesty and a force in it: it surrounds the possessor with an awe that represses a thousand impertinences, and extorts respect. "Abraham commanded his children and his household after him"—and what a son had he in Isaac! what a servant in Eleazar!

III. Let us therefore consider this subject IN REFERENCE TO YOUR FAMILY. The members which compose it are in reality parts of yourselves: children are natural parts, and servants are civil parts of yourselves. These have therefore peculiar claims upon you; and what would people think of you were you to avow that you had no regard for them, and would do nothing that would advance their welfare? If in the cold you denied your servants warmth, if you gave them bad food, and short allowance; if you turned them out of doors as soon as they were sick, and they knew not where to lay their head—the world would execrate you. If you were to suffer your children to go naked, to beg their bread, to perish with hunger in a ditch, or take your little ones and dash them against the stones —you would be shunned as a monster. But you act a far more criminal, and a far more infamous part, by disregarding their spiritual and everlasting welfare. Doubtless Herod after killing the infants in Bethlehem was viewed and shunned with horror—but he was far less cruel than you. He only destroyed the body, you damn the soul. He only slew the children of others, but you murder your own! "If any provide not for his own, and especially for those of his own house, he hath denied the faith, and is worse than an infidel." And can you imagine you have done this, when you have endeavoured to answer the question, "What shall they eat, and what shall they drink, and wherewithal shall they be clothed?" What is the body to the soul? What is time to eternity? You may amass for them riches, you may leave them an estate; but your house is the way to hell, going down to the chambers of death.

Under this article, let us observe more distinctly two things.

The first is the importance of Religion to the individuals under your care. Is it not "the one thing needful?" Is it not "profitable to all things, having promise of the life that now is, and of that which is to come?" You cannot deny this. Can you then be indifferent to the religion of your offspring, without being indifferent to their welfare? While you say by your practice, that it is nothing to you whether they be pious or vicious—do you not at the same time, and in the most undeniable manner, declare—that it is nothing to you whether they be respectable or infamous? loved or abhorred of God? saved or lost for ever!

And the second is this—the probability of their becoming religious by your means. BAXTER gives it as his opinion, That if family religion was duly attended to, the public preaching of the word would not long be the common method of conversion. Without adopting this sentiment in all its extent, we may observe that there is certainly enough to encourage the heads of families to exert themselves, and to condemn them if they do not. If the crop be so valuable, who would not sow, especially if he could "sow in hope?" And who knows not the force of early impressions, and the strength of early habits? Who has not read, "Train up a child in the way that he should go, and when he is old he will not depart from it?" In such families there has generally been a seed to serve the Lord. And this has appeared not only in children; how often have servants had reason to say, "Blessed be God that ever I entered that family. There were the eyes of my understanding opened. There were my feet turned into the way of peace."

MASTERS and PARENTS! I have thus endeavoured to bring into a small compass the arguments for the worship of God in your families. On a subject so frequently discussed, novelty was not to be expected; but I hope that what has been said, will be found sufficient to convince your judgment, and determine your practice.

I cannot conclude the Address without lamenting that there is so little attention paid to Family Worship, in a country professedly Christian, and in a period supposed to witness an increase of godly zeal. There is no more religion in the families of some who pretend to believe the Scripture, than there would be if they were atheists. To see many attending so regularly and frequently the preaching of the Gospel, would lead to a conclusion, or at least a hope, that they were the true worshippers of God; but when we follow them home to their own dwellings, we find them no better than heathens. Heathens! forgive me this wrong—I blaspheme you by the comparison. You had your household gods, which you daily worshipped, and which nothing could induce you to resign— I only ask you to be consistent. If you are Israelites, be Israelites *indeed!*

It may be asked, whether we imagine that there is any *peculiar* deficiency with regard to family devotion in our *day?* And to this we readily answer, we are persuaded there is; and it appears both in the frequent neglect, and the superficial performance of it, especially contrasted with the commonness of profession, and the frequency of public ordinances. We wish to speak freely, but without meaning to give offence. It is easy to see in the lives of our good old forefathers, what a value they set upon the morning and evening worship of God in their houses. With them it was an object, and an object of first rate importance: they entered upon it with seriousness and preparation; they arranged their worldly business, and their household affairs, in a subserviency to it; *public* worship did not exclude it, or drive it up into a corner. But of late years an undue stress has been laid on public exercises; and opportunities of hearing have been so multiplied, as to produce a kind of religious dissipation, so that persons of a religious character, as well as persons of a worldly, are seldom at home; there is some entertainment every evening in the week, and every hour of the sabbath. And hence there is very little inclination or time for family duty. It is so much easier to go and lounge in a place of worship, and hear some new performer, than to retire into the closet to examine the heart, and call together a family, and endeavour to

instruct and impress them, that we cannot help wondering how it was ever possible for the former to be looked upon as a greater test of piety than the latter!—God forbid that we should decry public worship, or the preaching of the word: he has commanded us "not to forsake the assembling of ourselves together, as the manner of some is"—but that man is surely under a mistake, who thinks to please God by incessantly running from one public opportunity to another, while he leaves his children to run wild, to grow up in ignorance, and to profane the sabbath.

I have stated the case strongly. But where this evil does not prevail in the extreme, it operates in the degree; and I cannot help sincerely wishing that the cause of the complaint could be removed. It is very desirable that useful bodies of men should be rendered more useful; and this in the case before us could be easily done, if those who have the lead would more strenuously inculcate the importance of family religion, and regulate the length and frequency of their public services accordingly.

There is another thing which, because it has a relation to the subject before us, I notice. Of late years a considerable number of persons not in the ministry have been stimulated to go of a Saturday evening, or a Sunday morning into the towns and villages as occasional preachers. The motive was laudable; but it has also contributed to the effect we have deplored. Families are thus frequently bereaved of their head on the sabbath; and who knows not that the sabbath is the principal day in which men of business can be much in a religious sense with their families? I hardly know how to censure this; I do not in every instance. But it may be well to ask, whether God ever calls us to a course which requires us to neglect or violate those duties which he has enjoined in his word? In a general way, the ministry requires a man's whole attention. And when Providence has furnished the means of a respectable introduction to the office by institutions for improvement, it is a duty to avail ourselves of them.

But to return. Let me beseech masters of families with all imaginable importunity not to think this practice a matter of indifference, which they are at liberty to perform or neglect. It is a duty. It is a duty of unspeakable importance. Do not therefore put it off longer. Begin this very evening, and before you lie down in your beds honour God in your families.

—"But we have not time!" What time does it require? Out of four and twenty hours cannot you furnish a few moments for God, or rather for yourselves? Would you think that time lost which is best employed? "There is nothing got by stealing, or lost by praying." Surely, if you have no time at present, you could redeem a little by order, by economy, by diligence. To every thing there is a season, and a time to every purpose under the heavens.

"But I have not the capacity!" Have you ever fairly made the trial? Would not your ability increase by exercise? Is it not a want of inclination, rather than of power? "Where there is a will there is a way." And this would be the case here; for you would find that if incapable of leading the devotion of the family extemporaneously, you could furnish yourselves with excellent forms. And it is to be lamented that prejudice should ever preclude the use of them when it is needful.

"But I have neglected it so long, that I am ashamed to begin!" You ought to be ashamed of sin, but not of duty. You ought to be ashamed that you have lived so long without it; but you ought not to be ashamed that you are wiser and better than you once were. Again. You say, "If"———But I will answer no more of your objections. They are only excuses: and you know—yes, you know—that they do not satisfy your own consciences now, and will avail you nothing in the great and terrible day of the Lord.

But some of you live in the habit of family worship. It will not therefore be amiss to conclude with a few words by way of direction.

Be spiritual in the performance. There is great danger of formality, where things customarily return, and with little possibility of variation. Think of God. Remember with whom you have to do, and what you have to do with him.

Do not confine family worship to prayer. Include also reading the Scripture, and if possible sing the praises of God.

Be short. A few minutes of simple and affectionate devotion is far better than eking out nearly half an hour by doubling over the name of God, telling the Supreme Being what he is, and by vain repetitions.

Be early. Do not leave it till the family are drowsy and stupid.—But here a case of conscience occurs, and such, alas! as the inconsistencies of the present day would render too common. "When should those of us have family worship, who attend public amusements; for instance—the theatre?" I answer, by all means have it *before you go!* When you return it will be late; and you may not feel yourselves quite so well affected towards it. We have known professors who have always omitted it when they came home from the playhouse! Besides, if you have it before, you can implore the divine blessing upon it; and beseech God to assist you in redeeming time, in overcoming the world, in preparing for eternity !!

Reader! You may imagine that the Author has written this with a smile! but he has written it with shame and grief. He earnestly wishes that many would adopt Family Worship.—But he is free to confess that there are some of whom he should be glad to hear that they had laid it aside.

SHORT DISCOURSES

FOR

FAMILIES.

DISCOURSE I.

RETURNING FROM A JOURNEY.

Thou shalt know that thy tabernacle shall be in peace; and thou shalt visit thy habitation, and shalt not sin.—Job v. 24.

IN the Scripture, "God hath abounded towards us in all wisdom and prudence." There is a suitableness in it to every character, and to every situation in life. It cautions youth, and it sustains age. It soothes the poor, and it humbles the rich. It is equally useful, whether we are in a state of solitude or society. It teaches us how to behave ourselves in every connexion we form, and in all the circumstances through which we pass.

The words which I have read may be considered as a promise made to a good man—WITH REGARD TO HIS ABSENCE FROM HOME. When he goes a journey, at the call of Providence, he may leave all his concerns with the Lord whom he serves, for he will guide his steps, and suffer no evil to befall him, nor any plague to come nigh his dwelling.

The person to whom this promise is made is supposed to have A HOUSE. It is called a *tabernacle:* and it is so named in allusion to the houses of the Easterns, which, especially in the days of Job, were principally tents or tabernacles, to enable them to move the more easily from place to place, in feeding their flocks and herds. Abraham is commended for not building a fixed mansion, but reminding himself, even by his external circumstances, that he was a stranger and a sojourner, as were all his fathers, and that there is none abiding—" By faith he sojourned in the land of promise, as in a strange country, dwelling in tabernacles with Isaac and Jacob, the heirs with him of the same promise: for he looked for a city which hath foundations, whose builder and maker is God." And would it not be well for us to view our abode, however

pleasing and durable it may appear, as only a temporary residence—a shelter of accommodation for a traveller? "Soon shall I be called to leave this dwelling—I am going the way of all the earth—Soon shall I ascend these stairs for the last time, and in this bed I shall soon close mine eyes to sleep till the heavens be no more."—David therefore calls his palace *the tabernacle of his house.*

However plain the building may be, it is a mercy to have a house to live in. To be homeless, is a condition the most pitiable. Let us think of Cain, expelled from the presence of the Lord, "a fugitive and a vagabond in the earth." Let us think of those whose doom David does not implore, but foretell; "Let his children be continually vagabonds and beg; let them seek bread also out of their desolate places." Let us think of those good men who "wandered in deserts and in mountains, and in dens and caves of the earth"—of the apostles, who could say, "we have no certain dwelling-place;" and above all—of our Lord and Saviour, who, "while foxes had holes, and the birds of the air had nests, had not where to lay his head." Let us think of all this, and be thankful to the kindness of Providence for a *tabernacle* to which human skill has added so many conveniences and comforts. Hence springs the powerful idea of home, to which the wandering tribes in savage countries are strangers. We insensibly acquire a love to inanimate things, and derive no little pleasure even from local prejudices. Who can feel indifferent to a place where he received his birth—where he passed his days of infancy, and indulged in the diversions of youth—where his body has been so often refreshed with sleep, and screened from piercing cold and descending torrents—and where he has shared so many social joys, from conversation and books around the friendly fire, or in the adjoining garden!—Home has a thousand attractions.

But, dear as it is, we must sometimes

C   2*   17

LEAVE it. In those cases indeed we should always remember the intimation of the wise man, "As a bird that wandereth from her nest, so is a man that wandereth from his place." Persons who have families and callings should not be too frequently, nor too long, from home. It will cherish a roving disposition, multiply expense, injure those affairs which require inspection, and produce a nameless train of evils. But sometimes journeys are necessary. Business may call a man abroad. Friends and relations may live at a distance. Health may require a change of scene. Now when God calls us abroad, he will take care of us, and we may hope to find the proverb true, The path of duty is the path of safety.

Hence he is reminded of the WELFARE of his house and family in his absence. Thou shalt know that thy tabernacle "is in peace." Peace means PROSPERITY. "Blessed is every one that feareth the Lord, that walketh in his ways—for thou shalt eat of the labour of thy hands; happy shalt thou be, and it shall be well with thee." The Lord can keep off disease. He can render business successful. He can afford every needful supply. What peace can there be while children are crying for food, and there is none to give them! But, "fear the Lord, all ye his saints; for there is no want to them that fear him. The young lions do lack and suffer hunger, but they that seek the Lord shall not want any good thing." Suppose they have not so much as others—Philip Henry tells us that "The grace of God will make a little go a great way;" and David says, "A little that a righteous man hath is better than the riches of many wicked."

Peace is HARMONY. There can be no happiness in a family, among the members of which are found reserve, suspicions, bickerings, contentions. "Where envying and strife is, there is confusion and every evil work." What is pomp without concord! What is abundance without union and attachment! "Better is a dinner of herbs where love is, than a stalled ox and hatred therewith. Better is a dry morsel and quietness therewith, than a house full of sacrifices with strife." It has been justly said, that quietness under a man's roof is a blessing only exceeded by one thing, viz. quietness in his conscience. "O how good and how pleasant a thing it is for brethren to dwell together in unity"—where all move in concert, mutually attentive to serve and please, exchanging nothing but tender affections and kind offices!

> "How pleasant 'tis to see
> Kindred and friends agree;
> Each in their proper stations move;
> And each fulfil his part.
> With sympathizing hearts,
> In all the cares of life and love!"

Peace is PRESERVATION. To how many disasters is a family exposed if God withdraws his protection! A great wind may come and smite the four corners of the house, and it may fall and bury us in the ruins. A man may start up from his bed, and hear within the noise of thieves and robbers seizing his property and threatening his person At midnight, when deep sleep falleth upon man, he may be awakened by the cry of fire, and see the flames consuming his substance, and not leaving an avenue by which to carry off his babes—What a blessing is it to have a tabernacle in peace!

Nor shall the tabernacle only be preserved, but the OWNER too. "And thou shalt visit thy habitation, and shalt not sin." It is a mercy when we go from home to come back alive and well; for though we are too little sensible of it, we always travel in jeopardy. Let us reflect.—We might have been terrified and robbed by wicked and unreasonable men. We might have been left groaning under the pain of bruised limbs and broken bones. Our lives might have been spilt upon the ground, and we might have died among careless and mercenary strangers, and our friends have received the sad intelligence, broken to them by degrees,—that we were—no more.

And are no suitable RETURNS to be made to the God of our salvation! Surely for all this he expects from us something better than sin. But a man would sin in this case, if he visited his habitation without thankfulness, and did not fall down and adore the "Preserver of men." He would sin, if his gratitude was not lively and practical, and, "by the mercies of God," he did not present his "body a living sacrifice"—and resolve to walk within his house with a perfect heart, to set no wicked thing before his eyes, to hate the work of them that turn aside"—to watch over his conversation, and to guard his temper—and to flee passion and pride, and "the love of money, which is the root of all evil" —to be satisfied with his lot, and resigned under his trials—to behave towards his servants as one that has "a Master in heaven" —to train up his "children in the nurture and admonition of the Lord," ruling well his own house "after a godly sort"—that God may derive a revenue of glory, not only from himself, but from his family.

He would sin also, did he not confide in him in future more simply and firmly; for God, by these instances of his attention and proofs of his faithfulness, solicits us to trust in him, commands us to give up our fears, and says, "Cast all your care upon me, for I care for you."

Let us observe one thing more, and conclude. DOMESTIC PIETY CROWNS DOMESTIC PEACE. It should be our daily prayer, when we go out and when we come in,— "Lead us not into temptation, but deliver us from evil." In all our employments, and in all our enjoyments, to be preserved from sin is the greatest privilege; it should therefore be our greatest concern. Sin is a dreadful thing, for it is always the attraction of wrath. "The curse of the Lord is in the house of the wicked; but he blesseth the habitation of the just. The house of the wicked shall be overthrown; but the tabernacle of the righteous shall flourish."

Let us, therefore, keep sin out of our dwellings; and say, with Joshua, " As for me and my house, we will serve the Lord." Then neighbours, and angels, and God will say, " The voice of rejoicing and of salvation is in the tabernacles of the righteous. Peace be both to thee and to thine house, and peace be unto all that thou hast." Amen.

DISCOURSE II.

GOD THE BEST OF FATHERS.

If ye then, being evil, know how to give good gifts unto your children, how much more shall your Father which is in heaven give good things to them that ask him?—Matthew vii. 11.

THE parental relation is a very familiar and a very instructive one. It is, therefore, often employed to hold forth the union between God and his people. But while it aids our conception, it cannot do justice to the subject. Man, from whom our idea of this relation is taken, is *evil*, whereas, " our Father which is in heaven" is *perfect*. Defects appear in the dispositions and actions of every earthly father; but when the Supreme Being assumes the character of a parent, he fully exemplifies it. He does *much more* than was ever seen—ever heard of in this relation before. And hence, according to our Saviour, we may learn as much from the difference, as from the resemblance in this striking comparison.

Let us, then, see how PRE-EMINENTLY he sustains the parental office; and learn thereby the happiness of his children.

The first instance of superiority is derived from KNOWLEDGE. Men know not always what is good for their offspring. Sometimes they ignorantly yield to their wishes, and in effect give them stones instead of bread, and serpents instead of fish. Not knowing sufficiently their talents and dispositions, they may place them in a line of business which will embarrass or ensnare them, instead of one in which they would appear to advantage. From the same principle, they may advise them to form connexions which would prove their vexation through life, or hinder them from unions which would complete their happiness. They may not know how to approach their minds most successfully by instruction: to fix them, if volatile; to give

them confidence, if timid. By checking, they may chill; and by indulgence, they may not only encourage, but dissipate. All these disadvantages necessarily arise from our defective knowledge.

But our Heavenly Father is the only wise God. His understanding is infinite. It is our happiness that he knows what we really need; knows when to refuse, and when to yield; and so arranges our circumstances in life, as to make " all things work together for our good."

The second instance of superiority is derived from CORRECTION. It is thus that the Apostle distinguishes between " fathers of our flesh," and " the Father of Spirits." " They verily for a few days chastened us after their own pleasure:" often from whim and caprice; from fretfulness and passion; to relieve their feelings, rather than to comply with their convictions. Hence, if they did not rebuke us at the very moment of provocation, they could not do it at all: whereas, if they had been concerned for our welfare, the reason for correction would have remained when the irritation had subsided—" But He for our profit, that we might be partakers of his holiness." There is no tyranny in God: there are no uneasy sensations in him. If he afflicts, it is—not from passion, but principle; and this principle looks only to the advantage of his children.

We may also err on the other side. We may be too soft to the faults of our offspring, and our tenderness may degenerate into foolish fondness. Eli is an awful example of this: " His sons made themselves vile, and he restrained them not." It is said also of Adonijah, that his father David " had not displeased him at any time in saying, Why hast thou done so?"—But it is cruel to connive where we should punish: " he that spareth the rod, hateth his son." And God will not sacrifice our profit to our feelings. If our welfare requires it—he will frown—or withhold the tokens of his love—or shut us up for a time —or smite us—and severely too. Nor let us think hardly of his dealings with us, since it is written, " Blessed is the man whom thou chastenest, O Lord, and teachest him out of thy law."

Behold a third instance in which God surpasses every earthly parent. It arises from NEARNESS and OBSERVATION. They cannot be always with their children, so as to attend to their circumstances. They sleep, and are unable to watch over them. They are employed, and business draws them off, and occupies all their thoughts. They journey, and leave their little ones behind them with many an anxious feeling. There is an age when their children go from them: school or trade calls them away from home, and they are no longer under the eye of their natural guardians. It was well for the little Shunamite, when seized in the field, that he had a father by—he said unto his father, "My head, my head!" Joseph would have been preserved from the rage of his brethren, in the plain of Dothan, had his venerable father been there—but in vain he looked—and called —no father was nigh.

But here it is otherwise. If we are the children of God, we are never out of his sight —" He withdraweth not his eyes from the righteous." He who keepeth them—"never slumbers nor sleeps." Though he governs worlds, he attends as much to each individual as if nothing else engrossed his care. And wherever we go—there is he. Jeremiah found him in the dungeon. Daniel in the lions' den. John in the isle of Patmos. And Jonah and Paul in the deep. "Yea," says David, "though I walk through the valley of the shadow of death, I will fear no evil: for thou art with me; thy rod and thy staff they comfort me."

Fourthly. Parents may be UNABLE to relieve their children, if with them. I pity the mother whose ears are assailed with the cries of half-fed babes, when, alas! she has no more to give them. I feel the situation of poor Hagar; her bread consumed, and the bottle of water spent—what could she do?—" she cast the child under one of the shrubs"—and "she went and sat her down over against him, a good way off, as it were a bow-shot: for she said—Let me not see the death of the child. And she sat over against him, and lifted up her voice, and wept." "By faith, Moses when he was born was hid three months of his parents, because they saw he was a proper child"—and what could they do more? They make him a little "ark of bulrushes, and daub it with slime and with pitch—and lay it in the flags by the river's brink"—one thing more is possible—"his sister stood afar off, to wit what would be done to him." And here Providence took up the business, or what had become of the poor helpless infant? We read in the Gospel of "a certain nobleman whose son was at the point to die"—and what in this case could titles and riches do for him? Nothing. He therefore goes abroad in search of aid. O, I sympathize with the father who hears from the physician the sad hint—Sir, I can do nothing more for the child. He enters the room—we behold him standing by the side of his expiring Isaac—but unavailing are all his tears—life quivers upon the lip, and the eye is closed—for ever.

The children of God are never in a condition in which HE cannot effectually aid them. "They are the sons and daughters of the Lord Almighty." O blessed thought! our Father is Lord of heaven and earth. The silver and the gold are his: his "are the cattle upon a thousand hills; the world is his, and the fulness thereof." There is no enemy which he cannot vanquish; no disease which

he cannot cure; no want which he cannot supply.

Fifthly. Other parents are not suffered to CONTINUE by reason of death: and thus their children become ORPHANS. It matters not how heavy the affliction may be—they are left—left perhaps uneducated, unprovided for. Incapable at present of appreciating their loss, they are to learn it by bitter experience. Behold them passing through an unfeeling world, on which they are turned adrift to be overreached by artifice, oppressed by injustice, injured by violence. In vain do they visit a father's tomb with the voice of joy or grief: "his sons come to honour, and he knoweth it not; and they are brought low, but he perceiveth it not of them."

But hear David: "When my father and my mother forsake me—then the Lord will take me up." Hear the Church: "Doubtless thou art our father, though Abraham be ignorant of us, and Israel acknowledge us not." With him the relation continues for ever—he is "the everlasting Father:" and hence his children can never be destitute. In every loss they have this to comfort them —"the Lord liveth; and blessed be my rock; and let the God of my salvation be exalted."

Again. The LOVE of parents is far exceeded by the love of God. There is no affection perhaps more ardent and forcible than parental: hence God assumes it: "Like as a father pitieth his children, so the Lord pitieth them that fear him." But this marks resemblance, not equality; for the one is no more to the other than a drop to the ocean. Though the love of a father be great, it is generally, and it is justly supposed that the love of a mother is more so. We see in this the wisdom and kindness of Providence, which thus makes duty a privilege, and reconciles the woman to numberless privations, and cares, and toils, in rearing the human race, from which the man is exempted: and God avails himself therefore of this relation also: "As one whom his mother comforteth, so will I comfort you."

"Can a fond mother from herself depart,
Can she forget the darling of her heart:
The little darling whom she bore and bred
Nurs'd on her knee, and at her bosom fed;
To whom she seem'd her ev'ry thought to give,
And in whose life alone she seem'd to live?"

"Can a woman forget her sucking child, that she should not have compassion on the son of her womb? yea, they may forget, yet will not I forget thee. Behold, I have graven thee upon the palms of my hands; thy walls are continually before me. For this is as the waters of Noah unto me: for as I have sworn that the waters of Noah should no more go over the earth; so have I sworn that I would not be wroth with thee, nor rebuke thee. For the mountains shall depart, and the hills be removed; but my kindness shall not depart from thee, neither shall the covenant of my peace be removed, saith the Lord that hath mercy on thee."

Finally. Parents give good things to their offspring, HOWEVER IMPERFECTLY THEY MAKE KNOWN THEIR WANTS AND DESIRES. Behold a family of several children: Here is one who is able to come and ask for his supplies in proper language—a second begs in broken phrases—but here is a third that cannot speak at all—but he can point, he can cry. Sweet babe! thou too art a child—thou too shalt succeed—every thing pleads for thee—thy dimpled cheeks, thy little hand, thy big shining tears. And if *we* who are *evil* do this, what think we of HIM whose "tender mercies are over all his works?" Let us therefore go to him—let us go, and ask as we are able. Let us remember, that words are not necessary to inform him who knows all things, or to move him who is already "more willing to give than we are to receive." He hears the voice of our *weeping*. Our *desire* is before him, and our *groaning* is not hid from him.

He calls himself your Father, to teach you with what dispositions you should enter his sacred presence. It is to encourage you to approach him with holy confidence and humble boldness.

Admire him. Love him. Hope in him. Repair to him. "Pray without ceasing." "Pray, and not faint." "He who hears the young ravens that cry," will not refuse the importunity of children. He hears prayer. Thousands, millions, have sought him—and none ever sought him in vain. These successful suppliants, returning from his throne, encourage us to go forward, all saying, "I sought the Lord, and he heard me, and delivered me from all my fears. They looked unto him and were lightened, and their faces were not ashamed. This poor man cried, and the Lord heard him, and saved him out of all his troubles." "O taste and see that the Lord is good: blessed is the man that trusteth in him."

DISCOURSE III.

SATURDAY EVENING.

To-morrow is the rest of the holy Sabbath unto the Lord.—Exod. xvi. 23.

ANOTHER week is drawing to a close. Another period has been added to the season of God's longsuffering patience, and to the time of your preparation for an eternal world. These hours are gone to appear before God—What can they testify in your favour? They are gone, to return no more—How have you improved them? What use have you made of your trials, your mercies, your means of religious instruction and edification? On such an occasion as this, it is well to look

back and review the past. But I wish you also to look forward. "To-morrow is the rest of the holy Sabbath unto the Lord." Let us consider the sabbath as a rest, and see with what dispositions we should think of its approach.

First. The sabbath is *a rest*.

It is so even to the BRUTE CREATION. The mercies of God are over all his works: He takes care for oxen. It is pleasing to hear him say, "that thine ox and thine ass may rest as well as thou." If animals were endued with reason, they would bless God for the kind and tender design of a sabbath. But, alas! in how many instances does the wickedness of man counteract and defeat the goodness of God!

The sabbath is a rest for the BODY. Those who live in ease and idleness cannot value the day as a cessation from labour: all days are nearly alike to them. But think of the condition of thousands and millions of your fellow-creatures—think of a man sitting six days at a loom, or standing six days at a forge;—how inviting, how soothing, how useful, how necessary is a period of repose! Man is impelled to labour: "In the sweat of thy face shalt thou eat bread, till thou return unto the ground; for out of it wast thou taken: for dust thou art, and unto dust shalt thou return." But is there nothing to soften the rigour of the obligation? Who could bear everlasting drudgery and fatigue? Behold a refreshing pause: a day of relaxation. The labourer lays aside the implements of industry—changes his apparel—unbends his wearied limbs—enjoys the fresh air of heaven. The alteration of scene conduces to the preservation of health—enlivens the dull sameness of toil, and renews the waste of spirits. Who would be cruel enough and senseless enough to blot out the sabbath from the days of the year! How heavily and joylessly would time pass away without these precious intervals! How many pleasing emotions associate themselves with the idea of a sabbath!—our charming Poet therefore has not forgotten to notice the want of this in the lines supposed to have been written by Alexander Selkirk in his solitude:

> "But the sound of the church-going bell
> These valleys and rocks never heard;
> Never sigh'd at the sound of a knell,
> Nor *smiled* when a Sabbath appear'd "

But it is principally designed to be a rest for the MIND—a SPIRITUAL rest. Thus it is not a day of inactivity, but of reflection and devotion—a day in which, disengaged from the concerns of time and sense, we may attend to the things which belong to our peace, examine our state and our character, inquire where we are going, and what preparation we have made for the journey. It is almost the only opportunity some of the labouring poor have to gain religious information. It is the return of this day, that reminds them that they are men, that they are heirs of immortality. It is the worship of this day, that preserves in them a sense of that dignity and importance which they are so likely to lose while grovelling always in the earth, or toiling among the beasts that perish. A pious mind will overflow with joy to behold them under the sound of the Gospel, and to think of the accomplishment of these words, "Though the Lord give you the bread of adversity, and the water of affliction, yet shall not thy teachers be removed into a corner any more: but thine eyes shall see thy teachers; and thine ears shall hear a word behind thee, saying, This is the way, walk ye in it, when ye turn to the right hand, and when ye turn to the left." A pious mind will love to enter the cottage, and witness the Sunday scene—the Bible is taken down, and while one child is stationed between the knees, and the rest are sitting around, a portion is read of that blessed book which " brings glad tidings to the poor," and teaches us " in whatever state we are, therewith to be content."

The real Christian indeed does not confine his devotion to particular seasons: he will mingle piety with business, and endeavour to acknowledge God in all his ways. But still he finds week-days to be worldly days: he wants a retreat—he wants a time of refreshing from the presence of the Lord.

When, therefore, he awakes in the morning, he can say,

> " Welcome, sweet day of rest,
>   That saw the Lord arise;
> Welcome to this reviving breast,
>   And these rejoicing eyes!"

Blessed be his name, he has *fed* me through the week—but

> " The King himself comes near,
>   And feasts his saints to-day:
> Here we may sit, and see him here,
>   And love and praise and pray."

Here is such a day as Christians want—a day entirely for their souls and their God. They feel impressed and sacred; every thing wears a new appearance. And

> " With joy they hasten to the place
>   Where they their Saviour oft have met;
> And while they feast upon his grace,
>   Their burdens and their griefs forget."

This leads us, secondly, to inquire with what dispositions we should think of the approaching Sabbath.

We should endeavour to FINISH ALL OUR WORLDLY AFFAIRS AS EARLY AS POSSIBLE ON A SATURDAY EVENING, that we may feel free and composed. Edgar, one of our Saxon kings, passed a law, that the Sabbath should be observed from nine o'clock Saturday evening till Monday morning. I wish the custom, if not the law, was revived. How wrong is it for tradesmen, and masters and mistresses of families, to drive things off so as to create hurry and confusion on the very eve of the Sabbath, and to retire later, and with a mind less fitted for devotion, than on any other day in the week! Where something of this is unavoidable, persons are to be pitied.

We should expect the return of this season with THANKFULNESS. Let us bless God for an institution which shows his concern for our present and everlasting welfare, and marks his lovingkindness more than his sovereignty: for " the sabbath was made for man." Let us bless God, that our lives are spared, and that in a few hours we hope to hear the multitude who keep holy-day saying, " Let us go into the house of the Lord;" let us bless him, that we are in circumstances which promise us ability to join in the sacred exercises, and that we are not by accidents and diseases doomed to pass a solitary sabbath, and impelled to take up the melancholy complaint,

> " Lo! the sweet day of sacred rest returns—
> ———————— But not to me returns
> Rest with the day. Ten thousand hurrying thoughts
> Bear me away tumultuous, far from heaven
> And heavenly work: alas! flesh drags me down
> From things celestial, and confines my sense
> To pre-ent maladies. Unhappy state!
> Where the poor spirit is subdued to feel
> Unholy idleness; a painful absence
> From God and heaven, and angel's blessed work;
> And bound to bear the agonies and woes
> That sickly flesh and shatter'd nerves impose."

We should expect the return of the day with HOLY AWE. It is a solemn thought—and we should impress it upon our minds—that every sabbath, every sermon, every prayer, is a step taken, which brings us nearer heaven or hell—that the means of grace with which we are so frequently indulged will prove either " the savour of life unto life" or " of death unto death." Yes—these are privileges which will not leave us as they find us: if they are not food, they will prove poison; if they do not cure, they will be sure to kill. They are talents, for each of which we shall be called to give the strictest account, and, unimproved, they will sink us deeper in condemnation than either Jews or heathens.

We should meet the sabbath with PIOUS RESOLUTION. Here is at hand a returning season of mercy, let me embrace it. By how many will it be profaned—but "as for me and my house, we will serve the Lord." How many of these invaluable opportunities have I already trifled away! how many have I sinned away! O let me now awake, and be serious and diligent: let me not shorten the day by rising late; let me not lose it by inattention. Let it not be "a price in the hand of a fool."

But what is resolution without PRAYER? " The preparation of the heart and the answer of the tongue in man are from the Lord." Without him, we can do nothing.

Let us therefore betake ourselves to him in humble and earnest prayer. Let us beseech him to grant that we may be "in the Spirit on the Lord's day;" that his grace may be sufficient for us—that we may "worship the Lord in the beauty of holiness"—that we may "not be forgetful hearers, but doers of the word"—that, in waiting upon him, our strength may be renewed—"that we may mount up with wings as eagles—that we may run and not be weary, and walk and not faint."

Such a Sabbath will leave us prepared for the duties and trials of the week. Such a Sabbath will lead us to say, "A day in thy courts is better than a thousand: I had rather be a door-keeper in the house of my God, than to dwell in the tents of wickedness." Such a Sabbath will be a foretaste of glory, the beginning of heaven. What is heaven? "There remaineth," says the Apostle, "a rest for the people of God." It is in the margin, "a keeping of Sabbath." Such is the representation of the happiness above: and oh! how instructive, how endearing is it, to those who love sabbaths below! By-and-by your week-days will be over, and the Saturday evening of life will come. You will lie down—and fall asleep—and open your eyes on a Sabbath infinitely superior to any we can expect on earth. Here we worship with a few—there we shall join the general assembly—Here we often feel unsuitable frames, and our powers are always unequal to our work—there our faculties will be raised to the highest degree of perfection, and we shall "serve him day and night in his temple." Here our Sabbaths end, and we soon go down again from communion with God into the vexing, debasing things of the world—there the Sabbath will be eternal; and we "shall go no more out." "We shall be for ever with the Lord." "Wherefore comfort one another with these words."

But should there be in this little assembly one individual who is a stranger to the pleasures of devotion, and who dislikes the employment of God's holy day, let me ask—Is he qualified for an eternal sabbath, who is now groaning, as he passes from duty to duty, *What a weariness it is to serve the Lord! when will the Sabbath be gone?* Can he enjoy even the thought of being for *ever* engaged in religious exercises, who at present feels *a day, an hour, a few moments* employed in them disagreeable and irksome? The question is awful—may the Lord help you to lay it to heart. Amen.

DISCOURSE IV.

THE EYE OF GOD ALWAYS UPON US.

"*Thou God seest me.*"—Gen. xvi. 18.

THESE are the words of Hagar, Sarah's handmaid—and I have read them, hoping that you will individually make the reflection your own. They can easily be remembered, because of their brevity: they should be daily thought of, because of their importance.

Let us see whether this reflection be not founded in truth; and show, by taking several views of it, how instructive and edifying it may be rendered.

Hagar was convinced that God saw *her.* Indeed he found her in the wilderness of Shur, where no human eye discerned her. By an angel he admonished her to return, and humble herself under the hand of her mistress; and predicted the character and condition of her child unborn—"He will be a wild man; his hand will be against every man, and every man's hand against him: and he shall dwell in the presence of all his brethren." On this she called the name of the Lord that spake unto her, "Thou God seest me."—But how much more striking is this to us! We are able to compare the accomplishment with the prophecy. The descendants of this poor woman's child are the Arabians; and they continue to this day a wandering, uncivilized multitude. They live by treachery and plunder; they are at war with all the world; no conqueror has ever subdued them; while they spread themselves over a vast country, thirteen hundred miles in length, and twelve hundred in breadth. Can any thing be hid from Him who declareth the end from the beginning, and before a babe is born can describe with unerring exactness the disposition and circumstances of his offspring for a number of ages to come?

His knowledge of all our concerns may be inferred from his universal presence. Effects prove him to be everywhere—for everywhere life is given and sustained—and this is the work of God only. Now if he be everywhere, what can be placed out of his sight? Hence we read, "Can any hide himself in secret places, that I shall not see him? saith the Lord. Do not I fill heaven and earth? saith the Lord.

Besides, how could he judge the world in righteousness, unless he were perfectly acquainted with all our doings? He could not produce what he had never witnessed—but we know that "God will bring every work into judgment, with every secret thing, whether it be good or whether it be evil." The Scripture therefore tells us that "his eyes are in every place, beholding both the evil and the good:" that "his eyes are upon the ways of man, and he seeth all his goings:" that "there is no darkness nor shadow of death where the workers of iniquity may hide themselves. Hell is naked before him, and destruction hath no covering. Neither is there any creature that is not manifest in his sight: but all things are naked and open unto the eyes of him with whom we have to do." Human inspection is very limited, and easily interrupted. I now see you—but place between us only a screen or a curtain, and I see you no more. I now behold you—but let the sun go down, or this candle be extinguished, and for want of a medium of vision the eye seeks you in vain. Think, then, of a Being, of whom it is said, " Yea, the darkness hideth not from thee: but the night shineth as the day: the darkness and the light are both alike to thee."

What use then should we make of this undeniable truth!—"Thou God seest me," is a reflection very pleasing to good men—very dreadful to sinners—and very edifying to all.

First. It is VERY PLEASING TO GOOD MEN.—Hence, when David had been considering the omniscience of God as compassing his path and his lying down, and as acquainted with all his ways, he exclaims, "How precious also are thy thoughts unto me, O Lord! how great is the sum of them!" His meditation of an all-seeing God was sweet; and therefore it was frequent. How is it with us! If we feel a satisfaction in thinking of this attribute, it is a good evidence of our sincerity. Now this is the case with the Christian—he comes to the light, and instead of shunning scrutiny, he invites it. If I am not right, says he, I wish to be set right. I know that he will discover in me much that is amiss, but he knows that I am willing to have it cured; and as he alone can heal, why should I wish to keep my physician ignorant of any part if my complaint! "Search me, O God, and know my heart: try me, and know my thoughts: and see if there be any wicked way in me, and lead me in the way everlasting."

" Thou God seest me!" This is a pleasing reflection when I fear some hidden corruption which has hindered the answer of prayer, and often deprived me of comfort, but which I cannot, after the most faithful investigation, detect. He can discern it.—"Show me wherefore thou contendest with me."

" Thou God seest me." This is a pleasing reflection when I feel those infirmities which make me groan. He sees grace, however small; he sees the disadvantages of my situation, the influence of the body over the mind, and of sensible things over the body; he sees that the "Spirit indeed is willing when the flesh is weak." "He knoweth my frame, he remembereth that I am dust."

" Thou God seest me." This is a pleasing reflection with regard to prayer. I often know not what to pray for as I ought; but he always knows what to give. I cannot express myself properly in words, and words are not necessary to inform him who "knoweth what is the mind of the Spirit—my desire is before him, and my groaning is not hid from him."

" Thou God seest me." This is a pleasing reflection when I am suffering under the suspicions of friends, or the reproaches of enemies. "Behold, my witness is in heaven, and my record is on high. Lord, thou knowest all things, thou knowest that I love thee."

" Thou God seest me." This is a pleasing reflection when I am in trouble. He knows all my " walking through this great wilderness;" he knows where the burden presses; he knows how long to continue the trial; and by what means to remove it. In no condition am I hid from my heavenly Friend. He saw Jeremiah in the dungeon, and Daniel in the lions' den. My circumstances are perplexing—"I go forward, but he is not there; and backward, but I cannot perceive him: on the left hand, where he doth work, but I cannot behold him; he hideth himself on the right hand, that I cannot see him—But he knoweth the way that I take: when he hath tried me, I shall come forth as gold. The eyes of the Lord are upon them that fear him, upon them that hope in his mercy."

Secondly. To the WICKED IT IS A VERY AWFUL REFLECTION. Yes: what can be more awful than the thought—that God sees you rise in the morning, goes forth with you, observes you all the day long—that you have passed under his eye from infancy to youth, and from youth to manhood—that he has beheld every plan you have formed, every bargain you have made—that he has observed not only actions but motives, not only words but thoughts, not only the evil you have committed but the evil you wished to commit; all the filthiness of your imaginations as well as of your lives—all the difficulties you have had to overcome in pursuing a sinful course, every check of conscience, every rebuke of Providence—and has noticed not only the number but aggravations of all your crimes. And what renders all this still more dreadful is this—that he does not forget any thing he has seen. You have forgotten many of your transgressions, but he remembers even the sins of your youth. Sometimes persons sin from custom and habit; and know not when they do so—for instance, they know not when they lie or swear. If it were possible to secure all their evil words for one month, one year—and read it to them—what a surprise would they express! Well, not one of them has escaped the Divine notice: he has recorded them all in the book of his remembrance. And to complete the terror of this consideration—all he has seen he will publish before the whole world: and he will also punish all that he has seen "with everlasting destruction from the presence of the Lord, and from the glory of his power."

Thirdly. The reflection will be found very USEFUL TO ALL.

Useful as a check to sin. For can a person sin while he realizes this? can he affront the Almighty to his very face?—Impossible. This would restrain us even from secret faults, and make us as pure in the closet as in the sanctuary, for God is in the one as well as in the other.

> "—O may these thoughts possess my breast,
> Where'er I rove, where'er I rest;
> Nor let my weaker passions dare
> Consent to sin—for God is there."

—Useful as a motive to virtue. The presence, the eye of one who is above us, and whom we highly esteem and reverence, elevates our minds and refines our behaviour: and we desire to act so as to gain his approbation. A servant feels this when he is before his master, and a subject when he is before the king. One of the heathen philosophers therefore recommended his pupils, as the best means to induce and enable them to behave worthily, to imagine that some very distinguished character was always looking upon them. But what was the eye of a Cato compared with the eye of JEHOVAH! Who would not approve themselves unto God? "In his favour is life."—"I have kept thy precepts and thy testimonies," says David, "for all my ways are before thee."

Finally. Useful as a reason for SIMPLICITY and GODLY SINCERITY. Oh! let it banish all dissimulation from our religious exercises; and whether we read, or hear, or pray, or surround the table of the Lord, let us remember that "God weigheth the spirits." If we had to do with men only, a fair appearance might be sufficient; "but the Lord looketh to the heart." And can we play the hypocrite under those eyes which are as a flame of fire! What will a name to live, a form of godliness, avail us with him who is "a Spirit, and seeketh such to worship him as worship him in spirit and in truth?"

Let us then no longer suffer ourselves to be led by *sense*, but let us live and walk by *faith*. Let this important truth sink down into our hearts—that the eye of God is always upon us. The truth indeed remains the same, whether we regard it or not—but if we lay hold of it by faith, and keep it present in our thoughts by meditation, it will be found the noblest of all principles; it will preserve us from sin; it will excite us to duty; it will make us "sincere and without offence till the day of Christ."

DISCOURSE V.

THE DEATH OF JESUS.
(GOOD FRIDAY.)

Verily, verily, I say unto you, except a corn of wheat fall into the ground and die, it abideth alone: but if it die, it bringeth forth much fruit.—John xii. 24.

D 3

DEATH—death the most dreadful of all events, has often been rendered a blessing.

The death of a BELIEVER has been useful. It has encouraged and established those who were walking in the way to Zion with many a trembling step, and many a shivering fear how it would go with them at last. When they have viewed a dying Christian, and have seen the grace of God, they have been glad: their courage has been revived, and they have rejoiced in hope. Why may it not be so with me? "The Lord is my helper, I will not fear." His looks, his words, his experience, have also made an impression on the minds of the careless, which has never been erased. After turning their backs on a sermon, they have been convinced by a dying bed. There the evidence was too plain to be denied, too solemn to be ridiculed. They have admired and resolved to follow a Master who is so good to his servants, and who does not "forsake them when their strength faileth; but is the strength of their heart and their portion for ever."—And the death of the saint has proved the life of the sinner.

The death of a PARENT has been useful. His expiring charge has never been forgotten. The thought of separation for ever from one so loved and valued, has awakened in the son a salutary fear. Returning from a father's grave, he has met with God, saying, "Wilt thou not from this time cry unto me, My father! thou art the guide of my youth!" and, turning into his closet, he has kneeled, and said, O thou "in whom the fatherless findeth mercy, I am thine, save me."—And the death of the parent has proved the life of the child.

The death of a MINISTER has been useful. Some of the servants of God have laboured faithfully without seeing the fruit of their labours. One has sown and another has reaped. But the removal of our mercies, by showing us their value, leads us to prize them. It has been so with many a conscientious preacher. He has been little regarded while living, but when dead his word has come with power to the conscience; his addresses, prayers, and tears, have been remembered by his people; and the expectation of meeting him at the last day has forced them to exclaim, "How shall we escape?"—And the death of the minister has proved the life of the hearer.

The death of a MARTYR has been useful. His patience and fortitude; his joy and triumph; his forgiveness of injuries, and his prayers for his persecutors, have struck beholders, rendered a religion honourable that could produce such marvellous effects, led to an examination of its evidences; and faith and zeal have been the result of inquiry. "The wrath of man has praised God,"—"and the blood of the martyrs has been the seed of the Church."

But where are we now? We have an ex

ample to produce, infinitely greater than all these. Let us leave the disciples, the members of "the household of faith," and behold their Lord, "the author and finisher of faith." Jesus dies, and his death is the "life of the world." The death of the believer has been the life of the sinner; the death of the father has been the life of the son; the death of the preacher has been the life of the hearer; the death of the martyr has been the life of the beholder—But our Lord Jesus, as he was going to be crucified, exclaimed, "I, if I be lifted up, will draw all men unto me." This is the meaning of the words which I have read: "Verily, verily, I say unto you, except a corn of wheat fall into the ground and die, it abideth alone: but if it die, it bringeth forth much fruit."

Go forth and behold the process of vegetation. Take a corn of wheat—how small, how insignificant, how useless it appears! But it is extremely valuable, and with care may be made to stock a field, a country! But how does it thus multiply! Keep it in the granary, and it remains the same. It must be sown, to fructify and increase. Let it be buried under the clods, and perish as to its present form and appearance—and lo! it springs up, and brings forth in some places "thirty, in some sixty, and in some an hundred fold." And behold the mystery of the cross, around which we are this day assembled! It was equally necessary for our Saviour to suffer and die. In death he becomes the principle of our life. By this he fills heaven with praise, the Church with blessings, the world with followers. This is the "fruit" which by dying he brings forth"—an immense number of Christians.

For you know, a grain of corn multiplies by yielding other grains like itself. "That which thou sowest is not quickened, except it die: and that which thou sowest, thou sowest not that body that shall be, but bare grain, it may chance of wheat, or of some other grain: but God giveth it a body as it hath pleased him, and to every seed his own body." If therefore Jesus be compared to seed, and he be sown to multiply, he will produce others like himself. If barley be sown, barley comes up; if wheat be sown, wheat appears; if Christ be sown, Christians are brought forth.—This is a very striking and a very useful thought. For it may be asked, What are Christians? And the answer is, What was Christ? They are predestinated to be conformed to him: and as they "have borne the image of the earthy, they must also bear the image of the heavenly." Here, indeed, the likeness is not complete—but it will be perfect in due time: they "shall be like him, for they shall see him as he is"—as entirely like him as one grain of corn resembles another, from which it was derived, in substance and in figure. But let us re-

member that the likeness is now begun, and must be advancing, according to the words of the Apostle, "Beholding as in a glass the glory of the Lord, we are changed into the same image, from glory to glory, even as by the Spirit of the Lord."—He was "not of the world;" and Christians "are not of the world." It was his "meat to do the will of him that sent him;" and they also can say, "his commandments are not grievous." "He went about doing good;" and they are endeavouring to "serve their generation according to the will of God." He "was meek and lowly in heart;" and they "are learning of him." "The world knoweth them not, for it knew him not."—A Christian springs from Christ; and he is like him.

There is one thing here which we should not overlook, for it will afford the benevolent mind a delicious pleasure; I mean the largeness of the crop—This corn of wheat, by dying, bringeth forth "much fruit." "Are there few that shall be saved?" This question was once proposed to our Saviour, and it is observable that he made no reply to it; but he did say to those that asked him, "Strive to enter in at the strait gate; for many, I say unto you, will seek to enter in and shall not be able." And by this he has taught us that it is wiser to endeavour to secure our salvation individually, than curiously to inquire after or controvert the number of the saved. If, however, the question were asked properly, we could answer—No. He is leading "many sons unto glory:" and when he has collected them altogether, they will be found "a great multitude which no man can number, of all nations and kindreds and people and tongues." Of him whose soul was made an offering for sin, it is said, "The pleasure of the Lord shall prosper in his hand:" "He shall see of the travail of his soul, and shall be satisfied." And will a little good, a little success, satisfy the vastness of his benevolence! O how many must be delivered from misery, and restored to happiness, before he will say, "It is enough; I am fully repaid for the anguish I endured in the garden and on the cross!"

Now all those who will be saved, owe their spiritual being and blessedness to his death. This is fully expressed. Had he not died, he would have "remained alone"—and accordingly while alive, he was comparatively alone. He had some followers; but they were few in number, and of one nation only: the Gentiles were not addressed.—But lo! when he dies, he brings forth much fruit: he becomes considerable, and renowned as a leader: three thousand were called under one sermon: "and the Lord added to the Church daily such as should be saved." "Mightily grew the word of the Lord, and prevailed." It spread from city to city, from province to province, till it soon reached the boundaries of the Roman empire. Now this was adapted and designed to show that his sufferings were to precede his glory; and that by dying he was to have a numerous "seed to serve him, which should be accounted to the Lord for a generation."

And does not every thing that enlivens us, and conforms us to our Lord and Saviour, derive its existence and its efficacy from his death?

Is the influence of the Holy Ghost needful to convince us of sin, and renew us in the spirit of our minds? This is the purchase, the reward, the consequence of his death. "Christ hath redeemed us from the curse of the law, being made a curse for us: for it is written, Cursed is every one that hangeth on a tree: that the blessing of Abraham might come on the Gentiles through Jesus Christ; that we might receive the promise of the Spirit through faith."

Is deliverance from our spiritual enemies necessary to our "serving him without fear in holiness and righteousness before him all the days of our life? Here "he spoils principalities and powers, and makes a show of them openly. Now is the judgment of this world, now is the prince of this world, cast out."

Is it necessary for us to feel a "lively hope" by which we "draw nigh to God?" The cross inspires it. "Surely he hath borne our grief and carried our sorrow; the chastisement of our peace was upon him, and with his stripes we are healed. He that spared not his own Son, but delivered him up for us all, how shall he not with him also freely give us all things?"

Has gratitude an influence in forming the Christian character? Here, here it is inflamed. "For the love of Christ constraineth us; because we thus judge, that if one died for all, then were all dead: and that he died for all, that they which live should not henceforth live unto themselves, but unto him which died for them, and rose again. Unto him that loved us, and washed us from our sins in his own blood, and hath made us kings and priests unto God and his Father; to him be glory and dominion for ever and ever. Amen."

Finally. Is an example of holiness indispensable? Here we behold a representation of all the graces and the duties he recommended. Here we see an entire obedience and submission to the will of his heavenly Father—humility the most profound—patience the most astonishing—forbearance the most free from revenge—the love of relations and friends the most exquisitely tender.— "He suffered for us, leaving us an example that we should follow his steps."—And thus all the principles and assistances of the Christian life are furnished by the death of the Saviour. Let us conclude by three reflections.

And first. Let us render the works of nature instructive and edifying. Let us not be of the number of those of whom the prophet speaks, when he says, "seeing many things, they observe not." Nor let us contemplate the creation with the eye of a naturalist only. Let us go over it as Christians; let us hold communion with "things unseen and eternal," by means of those "which are seen and temporal." Thus our Saviour has taught us to find the influence of the Gospel in the leaven hid in the meal; the agency and comforts of the Holy Ghost in the blowing of the wind, and in rivers of living water; and the efficacy, utility, and necessity of his death in the sowing, corruption, and the revival of corn.

Secondly. "God is wonderful in counsel and excellent in working." His thoughts are not our thoughts, neither are his ways our ways." The enemy supposed he had completely succeeded when our Lord was crucified—"Now (says he) his cause is crushed, his followers will be dispersed and annihilated, and his name will be heard no more." But all this was "according to the determinate counsel and foreknowledge of God." Death was the road to life, and shame to everlasting renown. They were sowing him, to make him fruitful. In falling a victim, he conquered, and from the cross he passed to the possession of a throne, in which he reigns king of saints, and will reign king of nations.

Thirdly. What think ye of "Christ crucified?" I know what prophets and apostles thought of it. I know the importance his death occupies in the scriptures of truth. I know that when Moses and Elias appeared in glory, "they spake of the decease which he would accomplish at Jerusalem." I know an ordinance is expressly appointed to "show forth his death;" that the preaching of the Gospel is called "the preaching of the cross;" and that the praises of heaven are ascribed to him as "the Lamb that was slain, and has redeemed us unto God by his blood." But what are your views of this interesting subject? "to the Jews" it was "a stumblingblock;" to "the Greeks, foolishness;" and to thousands now it is a thing of no importance. Is it to you "the wisdom of God" and "the power of God?"—Our creed and our experience will be found very defective, unless they have much of the sufferings and death of Christ in them.

Spirit of grace and truth! take of the things of Jesus, and show them unto us. May we "know the fellowship of his sufferings." May we "be made conformable unto his death." May we be enabled individually to say, "I am crucified with Christ: nevertheless I live; yet not I, but Christ liveth in me: and the life which I now live in the flesh I live by the faith of the Son of God, who loved me, and gave himself for me."—"God forbid that I should glory, save in the cross of our Lord

Jesus Christ, by whom the world is crucified unto me, and I unto the world."

DISCOURSE VI.

CONFIDENCE IN GOD COMPOSING THE MIND.

Thou wilt keep him in perfect peace whose mind is stayed on thee.—Isaiah xxvi. 3.

In many things people differ widely from each other, but in one thing they are agreed—they all wish for satisfaction, they all desire inward tranquillity. And indeed what is every thing else without this? What is ease of circumstances, and even health of body, if the *mind* be perplexed, distracted, tormented? "The spirit of a man will sustain his infirmity; but a wounded spirit who can bear?"

Now Isaiah tells us how we may obtain and preserve a blessed composure in a miserable world. "Thou wilt keep him in perfect peace, whose mind is stayed on thee." These words require some explanatory remarks, and will furnish us with some practical reflections.

In explaining these words, it may be necessary to inquire,

First, What we are to understand by *staying the mind on God.* And to this we answer, that it simply means, relying upon him or trusting in him. Man is an indigent and a dependent creature. He is not equal to his own happiness; he feels a thousand necessities which he cannot supply from his own stores; he therefore goes abroad for succour, and looks after something to lean on—and as the world always stands nearest, upon this he always leans first. And though he finds it to be a "broken reed," which disappoints his hope, and "pierces him through with many sorrows," he returns to this miserable dependence again and again, till Divine grace brings him to his proper rest, and enables him to say—"Now, Lord, what wait I for? my hope is in thee." And thus are fulfilled the words of the prophet: "It shall come to pass in that day, that the remnant of Israel, and such as are escaped of the house of Jacob, shall no more again stay upon him that smote them; but shall stay upon the Lord, the Holy One of Israel, in truth. The remnant shall return, even the remnant of Jacob, unto the mighty God."

Now that which, in these cases, we stay the mind upon, is the word of God—consisting of information and promises—revealing his goodness and his all-sufficiency—offering himself as our portion, and even commanding us to depend upon him. Accordingly it is said, "Trust in him at all times; ye people, pour out your hearts before him: God is a refuge for us. Trust ye in the Lord for ever, for in the Lord Jehovah is everlasting strength." Here is a foundation that will not give way, a resource that cannot fail. And here we learn what is our duty: it is—not to hesitate, not to wait for fresh evidence and assurance—but to believe what God has spoken, to take him at his word, and to venture upon his engagements. In doing this, we run no manner of risk: his word is called "the faithful word;" it is said also to be "a tried word;" and those who have tried it most, have the firmest persuasion of its truth.

Now this *staying* of the mind on God, secondly, "keeps it in peace." It does this, not only as it insures the Divine blessing—for God will honour them that honour him, and by nothing is he so much glorified as by our reliance upon him—but also by a natural influence and tendency. Let us specify a few instances in which this confidence tranquillizes the mind.

This alone can calm the mind when convinced of sin, and searching in dreadful distress for pardon. "We which have believed," says the Apostle, "do enter into rest." "I am guilty," cries the awakened sinner; "but my condition is not desperate." "I wait for the Lord, my soul doth wait, and in his word do I hope." I hear a voice saying, "Behold the Lamb of God that taketh away the sin of the world." "The blood of Jesus Christ his Son cleanseth us from all sin." Here is something to stay the mind upon. He "died for the ungodly;" and such am I. Yea more, he invites "all that labour and are heavy laden to come to him," and promises to give them "rest"—*and* "mine iniquities are a burden too heavy for me to bear," and I sigh and groan, "O wretched man that I am! who shall deliver me from the body of this death?" Sometimes this confidence is very feeble; it scarcely amounts to a probability—it is merely a kind of peradventure—"who can tell?"—I may succeed. But even this is attended with some effect. Like a twig to a sinking man, it serves to keep his head above water, until something else can be brought strong enough to help him ashore. Or, to vary the image, it will keep him from giving up in despair the use of means and of prayer. "I will hang upon him till he shakes me off. If he drives me back, it is nothing more than I deserve—but I will not go back. If he is pleased to kill me, I shall have no right to complain—but I will not be my own murderer. 'If I perish, I perish;' but here I will die." In other cases this confidence rises higher; and however unworthy and helpless the man feels himself to be, he is persuaded that God will receive him graciously, and in due time appear to his joy. In consequence of this, agitation and terror subside, and he "both hopes and quietly waits for the salvation of the Lord."

This confidence also calms the mind under delays. To pray, and receive no answer; to stand knocking—not, like other beggars, for a few moments, but from day to day, and from week to week, and see no opening—this is truly discouraging—and the danger is, lest we should withdraw, saying, with the unbelieving nobleman, "Why should I wait for the Lord any longer?" But "he that believeth maketh not haste." He will say—God is a sovereign, I have no claims upon him—a delay is no refusal—perhaps he has answered me already, and I have a substitute for the blessing implored—however this may be, of one thing I am certain, I must succeed at last: 'He never said to the seed of Jacob, seek ye me, in vain."—Hence springs "the patience of hope."

This confidence composes the mind in the events of life—and this is the thing principally intended. We live in a world of changes and uncertainties. Disorder and confusion seem everywhere to reign. Vice is often triumphant, and virtue oppressed. And with regard to ourselves, our wisest schemes are frequently thwarted, our fairest hopes destroyed, our choicest comforts laid waste. Thus we are liable to be perpetually ruffled and dismayed; and there is only one principle that can sustain and solace the mind—it is, holy confidence in God. Nothing occurs by chance—God governs the world—if we could see what God sees, we should do precisely what God does—his people are his care—nothing can essentially injure them—yea, 'all things are working together for their good." These are reasons for repose. Here the mind fixes, and feels peace: the peace of a child, who has only to mind his book; the Father will manage and provide: the peace of a traveller, who has one with him to order all the journey, and to bear all the expense. It is a peace that flows from the absence of anxiety: the believer casts all his care upon the Lord, who careth for him; he reclines his head on the soft bosom of Providence, and falls asleep. This peace peculiarly regards intricate dispensations; for these are the most apt to perplex and discompose the mind. But when the mind is stayed on God, the believer is satisfied and serene, even in darkness. Though I know not whither I am going, I know with whom—my guide is infallible. I will not "charge him foolishly," but confide in his skill: "what he does I know not now, but I shall know hereafter." I see much wisdom in what is clear, but there is much more in what is obscure; it is the depth that makes it profound, and that renders it so difficult to fathom. This tranquillity is commonly preceded by many a struggle with self-will and self-conceit.

We naturally wish to have things according to our mind, and make various attempts to govern our own affairs. But by degrees we are convinced that "the way of man is not in himself; it is not in man that walketh,

to direct his steps." After repeated deceptions, both on the side of our hopes and fears, after many embarrassments into which our folly and rashness had plunged us, or to which they had exposed us; we begin to say, in earnest, "The Lord shall choose our inheritance for us. I have now done. Lord, my heart is not haughty, nor mine eyes lofty; neither do I exercise myself in great matters, or in things too high for me. Surely I have behaved and quieted myself as a child that is weaned of his mother; my soul is even as a weaned child."

But the peace that flows from this trust in God is, thirdly, said to be *perfect.* It is not indeed absolutely so, as if it were incapable of addition—but it is so, first, comparatively. What is every other peace to this? What is the delusion of the Pharisee, the stupidity and carelessness of the sinner, the corn and wine of the worldling—what is every thing else, compared with this peace? What can be so desirable, so excellent! It is "a continual feast."

It is so, secondly, In relation to this confidence. It is true, this peace rises and falls, but it is only because this confidence varies. All the disquietudes which a Christian feels, spring from the weakness or the want of faith in God. It is not from outward things. These are often blamed, and these may be very trying—but it is not the water *without* the vessel that sinks it, but that which gets in. The primitive Christians could say, "We are troubled on every side, yet not distressed; sorrowful, yet alway rejoicing." It is very possible therefore to have this peace within, while in the world we have tribulation; and Christians are so accessible to fear, so preyed upon by anxiety, so depressed by afflictions of various kinds, because they do not sufficiently rely on God: "If ye will not believe, surely ye shall not be established." It is therefore true, that *in proportion* as the mind is stayed on God, he keeps it in *perfect* peace.

Let us apply the passage thus explained to some practical purposes.

First. *How safe and how happy are real believers!* The people of the world are exceedingly mistaken respecting them. They imagine their life to be a sad, heavy, gloomy thing; whereas it is the most free, and cheerful, and placid. While others are struggling in their own strength, and managing all their concerns themselves, fretful when they meet with untoward events, and always dissatisfied even when they succeed, the Christian "casts his burden upon the Lord, and he sustains him." He leaves his affairs with God, and goes on, assured that he will order them aright. His concern is only to please and glorify God in the circumstances in which he is placed; events are the Lord's. "He is careful for nothing; but in every thing, by prayer and supplication, with thanksgiving, he makes his requests known unto God; and the peace of God, which passeth all understanding, keeps his heart and mind through Christ Jesus." "I hope in him for eternal life, and it would be shameful not to trust in him for every present supply. 'He who spared not his own Son,' will 'withhold no good thing' from me. It is comparatively a matter of little consequence what befalls me here; I am only 'a stranger and a pilgrim;' my God 'ruleth over all;' and he has promised that 'he will never leave me nor forsake me.' 'The Lord is my helper; I will not fear.' "

"He shall not be afraid of evil tidings; his heart is fixed, trusting in the Lord."—Tell him, his substance is destroyed: No, says he, my "inheritance is incorruptible and undefiled, and fadeth not away, reserved in heaven for me." Tell him such a friend or relation is dead: but, says he, "The Lord liveth, and blessed be my rock, and let the God of my salvation be exalted." And you yourself are decaying and dying: Yes, says he, I am sent for, and am going home. With regard to public calamities, he feels, and in some respects he feels more than others. Divine grace produces sensibility, and excites a public spirit. He knows the desert of sin, and the indications of approaching wrath make him shudder: "My flesh trembleth for fear of thee, and I am afraid of thy judgments." But, strange as it may appear, there is a firmness and a composure of mind blended with all these feelings. He knows that "the Lord reigneth;" that he is "doing all things," and doing all things "well;" that whatever becomes of other empires, the Gospel shall spread, the Church is safe: and these are the most important interests—these render the world valuable. He can therefore join with Luther, who said, whenever he heard of any alarming intelligence, "Come, let us sing the forty-sixth psalm—'God is our refuge and strength, a very present help in trouble; therefore will we not fear, though the earth be removed, and though the mountains be carried into the midst of the sea. God is in the midst of her; she shall not be moved; God shall help her, and that right early. The Lord of hosts is with us; the God of Jacob is our refuge. Selah.' "

Secondly. *Let us seek after this blessed condition of the godly.* Till the mind be stayed on God, it has no resting-place. It is union with God that gives the mind solidity. How light is it, detached from God; it is blown about easier than the down of a thistle in the wind. Out of him, as the sanctuary of the soul, every storm annoys, every trifle disquiets: and "man at his best estate is altogether vanity." If any thing could add force to these reflections, it would be the nature of the times in which we live. We be-

hold a "cloudy and dark day." The revolutions which have taken place, and the general aspect of things at present, are dreadful to those who have no God. O let a sense of our danger endear the only refuge, and the vanity of this world induce us to seek after the real happiness of another! Let us abandon the practice of sin, and no longer "lay up for ourselves treasure upon earth," which only serves to debase the soul and fill it with perpetual alarms—and let us ask for God "our Maker, who giveth songs in the night;" let us depend upon him, cleave to him, live in him.

On what else can we rely, that will not, instead of settling the mind, discompose it the more? Is it Honour? What so precarious and variable as the praise of man! Is it affluence? "The rich man's wealth is his strong city, and as a high wall in his own conceit." But does not every day's observation, as well as Scripture, cry, "Trust not in uncertain riches, but in the living God!" Is it Moral Philosophy; a strength of reasoning? There are circumstances in which the calmest reflections and the noblest resolutions will be only as stubble before the wind. In the time of trial, all other supports will fail: the storm increasing, will drive us from our holdings: there is only one "anchor of the soul, sure and steadfast." It is, a scriptural hope in God. This will prepare a man for all the vicissitudes of time; this will help him to go on his way rejoicing through all the troubles of life; and this will finally enable him to look "the king of terrors" out of countenance, and to exult with the apostle, "Nay, in all these things we are more than conquerors through him that loved us. For I am persuaded that neither death, nor life, nor angels, nor principalities, nor powers, nor things present, nor things to come, nor height, nor depth, nor any other creature, shall be able to separate us from the love of God which is in Christ Jesus our Lord."

DISCOURSE VII.

SPRING.

Thou renewest the face of the earth.
Psalm civ. 30.

ALL nature is a book, and the various parts of it are so many multiplied pages in which we may read and consider "the wonderful works of God." The Seasons of the year are every way interesting. They are necessary for the production of our food, and the preservation of our health. Their succession adds to the beauty of creation. Their revolutions furnish us with subjects of reflection, and lessons of importance.

The season is arrived in which we behold

the renovation of nature. Let us endeavour to render it profitable.

I. David was an attentive observer of the works of creation. Many a fine evening did he employ in " considering the heavens, the works of God's finger; the moon and the stars which he has ordained." He rose early, and beheld the "sun as a bridegroom coming out of his chamber, and rejoicing as a strong man to run a race." He looked abroad in winter, and exclaimed, "He sendeth abroad his ice like morsels; who can stand before his cold." He rejoiced when more favourable weather encouraged him to walk abroad: he observed "the birds building their nests, the springs running among the valleys, the grass growing for the cattle, and herbs for the service of man," and, hailing the revival of a faded world, lifted up his eyes and said, "Thou renewest the face of the earth."

There are few real lovers of nature; there are few who so behold its scenes as to pause and admire, till they have imbibed a sympathy with them; till they feel themselves at home in them; till they are detached from every thing human, and little, and debasing. Let us go forth into the field to meditate: meditation is often better than books. Our own thoughts will do us much more good than the opinions of others. Wisdom and truth are shy in the world; but here they are easily discovered and secured. Danger often attends our perusal of the works of men; but there is no hazard in pursuing knowledge among the works of God. People complain of the world, and confess whenever they return from its companies and diversions, that "all is vanity and vexation of spirit"—why will they not come forth, and refresh themselves here? Why will they not leave the wilderness, and enter this garden of the Lord? Here I live in a world of my own—here I feel my independence and my freedom—here I can learn how I have been overcome, and where I must place a watch and a guard—here the good thoughts, which were scattered and weak before, are collected into a powerful motive, and bear down all opposition to duty—what was wavering before, is now decided—what was timid, grows courageous. When I go into the field, I enter my closet; I shut the door about me; I admit what company I please; I exclude the vicious who would pollute, and the trifling who would interrupt; I hear not the folly of the vain, or the slander of the malicious—that world of iniquity which drops from the tongue; "I pray to my father which is in secret; mine eye poureth out tears unto God;" I have an emblem of final repose—"here the wicked cease from troubling, and here the weary are at rest."

" God made the country, and man made the town."

Nevertheless, how many are there who leave the works of the Creator to bury themselves among those of the creature; and while professing to admire the beautiful and the marvellous, disregard the wonders that are perpetually springing up around them! They will go any distance, incur any expense, to see a piece of mechanism, sculpture, painting; while in their way they pass by productions infinitely more curious, and finished. They are struck with a fine robe; but never contemplate a lily: and yet "Solomon in all his glory was not arrayed like one of these." When a man of fame announces a design to perform any thing, thousands flock around him; while God, working day by day the most astonishing effects, is unnoticed; and no one is drawn forth to attend to him, though he has said, "I will that men magnify my works which they behold."

II. It becomes us not only to observe nature, but to observe it devotionally, and as Christians. There is a difference between viewing and improving these things: there is a difference between our studying them as mere admirers and philosophers, and applying them as men formed by divine grace for a life of communion with God. It is the command of the Apostle—"Whatsoever ye do in word or deed, do all in the name of the Lord Jesus, giving thanks to God and the Father by him."

See a Christian among the works of nature. He looks after God in all—for he needs him in all: and he is enabled to find him. Though familiar with the effect, he does not disregard the cause. With him, common instrumentality does not conceal divine agency. He maintains in his mind a connexion between the author and the work; and the one reminds him of the other. He walks with him in the ways of his Providence, as well as in his goings in the sanctuary; adores him in the field as well as in the temple; and acknowledges him in the ordinary course of nature, as well as in the extraordinary displays of his power, and wisdom, and goodness.

He also makes them images to remind him of better things. The rising sun brings to his thoughts "The Sun of righteousness arising with healing under his wings;" a flowing spring, the influence of the Holy Ghost; the rain and the dew, the doctrine of the Gospel. Thus, by a holy chemistry, he extracts heaven from earth.

From these scenes he also derives motives to devotion, and encouragements to confidence. For instance: does he view a proof of divine wisdom, he cries, "O how able is this God to teach me, to manage all my concerns—how wonderful in counsel, how excellent in working!" Does he contemplate a display of Divine power, "How able is this God to preserve, sustain, deliver me! 'Is any thing too hard for the Lord?'" Does he observe instances of his bounty, he asks—"Can 'he who hears the ravens that cry,' refuse supplies to his children?"

Nor does he partake of the bounties of nature like a brute, only concerned to gratify his animal appetite, and entirely regardless of him from whom every indulgence comes. He receives them from the hand of his heavenly Father; he tastes his love in them; he cries, "'O that men would praise the Lord for his goodness, and for his wonderful works to the children of men! Bless the Lord, O my soul—who giveth me all things richly to enjoy,' and who provides, not only for my relief, but my delight.' I will live to him who lives in so many ways for me, and by 'his mercies I will present my body a living sacrifice, holy and acceptable unto him, which is my reasonable service.'"

III. Let us observe and adore this wonder-working God *in renewing the face of the earth.* How many times has he done this since the creation! He does it every year. The change is equally remarkable and pleasing. See the winter drawing off his army of winds, and frosts, and snow, and hail—and spring succeeding the monarch of desolation. Under his soft and gentle reign, all begins to smile: life in a thousand ways breaks forth: all is verdure, and fragrance, and beauty; all is joyous. What variety of colours, what harmony of sounds! "The valleys stand thick with rising corn, and the little hills rejoice on every side," while a voice from the fields and meadows calls—"Arise, and come away; for lo! the winter is past, the rain is over and gone. The flowers appear on the earth; the time of the singing of birds is come, and the voice of the turtle is heard in our land."

Let us remember, that he who renews the face of the earth, can renew the *Church.* Think of any particular cause—however depressed, he can revive it; however small, he can increase it. When his influences descend, "his word comes down like rain upon the mown grass, as showers that water the earth;" and his people are "filled with all the fruits of righteousness"—the congregation is like a field which the Lord has blessed." Or think of his cause at large. He can drive away errors, and superstition, and animosities from the nations of the globe, and bless the world with the Gospel of peace, and the means of salvation—and the "wilderness and solitary place shall be glad for them; and the desert shall rejoice and blossom as the rose. It shall blossom abundantly, and rejoice even with joy and singing: the glory of Lebanon shall be given unto it, the excellency of Carmel and Sharon; they shall see the glory of the Lord, and the excellency of our God."

He can also renew the *soul.* The Fall has reduced our spiritual powers to a state of desolation the most deplorable. Now when a sinner is led to see and feel this, he prays,

"Create in me a clean heart, O God, and renew a right spirit within me." And we read of the "renewing of the Holy Ghost;" and of "being renewed in the spirit of our minds." Thus "God beautifies the meek with salvation;" and the change in nature is an imperfect representation of the change made in the soul by divine grace. This can illuminate the darkest understanding, and soften the most rebellious will; this can tranquillize the most troubled conscience, and sanctify the most depraved affections.—After conversion, the people of God may have a winter season: their growth may be checked; every thing may appear to be dead; they may feel the chilling absence of the "Sun of righteousness," and sigh, "O when wilt thou come unto me?" But when he returns, all revives. Then the believer is quickened, then he expands, and buds, and brings forth "much fruit." "He has life, and he has it more abundantly."

Again. He can renew the *body.* Has sickness invaded thy frame—art thou "made to possess months of vanity, and are wearisome nights appointed unto thee"—art thou saying, "my purposes are broken off"—"mine eye shall no more see good?"—Remember, "he killeth and maketh alive; he bringeth down to the grave and raiseth up." Every disease is under his control, and goes at his bidding. He can re-colour thy cheeks, "strengthen thy weak hands, and confirm thy feeble knees, so that thy youth shall be renewed like the eagle's." Let the body die—even then we are not hopeless—he shall renew it. "So is the resurrection of the dead. It is sown in corruption, it is raised in incorruption; it is sown in dishonour, it is raised in glory; it is sown in weakness, it is raised in power; it is sown a natural body, it shall be raised a spiritual body." "According to this promise, we look for new heavens and a new earth, wherein dwelleth righteousness." "And God shall wipe away all tears from our eyes: and there shall be no more death, neither sorrow, nor crying, neither shall there be any more pain: for the former things are passed away."

To conclude. The Seasons of the year have often been considered as emblems of human life.—*Youth* is the *Spring.* Yes, my young friends, yours is the season of which nature, lovely nature, now reminds us. Think of this in all your walks. How pleasing and how beautiful is Spring! But how short, how fading! Yet how important! On this all the year depends. If no blossoms now appear, or if these blossoms be destroyed, no glory in summer, no abundance in autumn, no provision in winter.

My young friends, you are now forming your future destiny, and giving a character to your future years. O seize these valuable hours for purposes the most momentous—The improvement of your understanding—the correction of your tempers—the formation of your habits—the enlargement of your capacity to serve God and your generation—and, above all, diligence in "working out your salvation with fear and trembling."

And, O thou God of all grace, hear our prayer! "Let thy work appear unto thy servants, and thy glory unto their children, and let the beauty of the Lord our God be upon us: and establish thou the work of our hands upon us; yea, the work of our hands establish thou it: that our sons may be as plants grown up in their youth, and our daughters as corner-stones, polished after the similitude of a palace." Amen.

DISCOURSE VIII.

THE HAPPY FAMILY.

Now Jesus loved Martha, and her sister, and Lazarus.—John xi. 5.

THE Scripture is not filled with the creations of worlds, the revolutions of empires, the palaces of kings, the intrigues of politicians, the exploits of heroes. In perusing it, we are often led into common and private life; and are called upon largely to observe individuals who made no splendid figure in the eyes of mankind. But a character may be important and interesting without secular honours. He that is born of God is truly great, and he that is beloved of the Saviour is truly happy. Many persons of distinction who once lived in Judea are now forgotten; their names, their places of abode, their connexions, have all perished from the earth; but there is one family transmitted down to our own times with peculiar marks of regard, and which will be had "in everlasting remembrance." It resided at Bethany, and consisted of a brother and two sisters. These three happy individuals lived together in harmony and in piety—and what crowned the whole was this—"Now Jesus loved Martha, and her sister, and Lazarus." Let us consider—THE OBJECTS of this love—THE NATURE of it—and THE MANNER in which it was EXPRESSED.

I. The OBJECTS of this love were Martha, and her sister, and Lazarus.

It is worthy of our observation, that several of our Lord's immediate followers were related to each other. Peter and Andrew were brothers; John and James were brothers; so also were James and Jude. The ruler whose son our Lord cured, "believed, and his whole house." And here our Saviour had three disciples in one dwelling, when perhaps the whole village scarcely produced a fourth.

I pity the family where there is *no one* beloved of Jesus—no friend to attract the Saviour's regards—no protector to stand in the breach and keep back invading judgments—no intercessor to draw down the blessing of Heaven—no good example to reprove, encourage, stimulate. What does an angel think when he passes by such an irreligious dwelling!

It is a mercy to find even *one* pious individual in a house. And whoever that distinguished character be, I would say to him—Be thankful; be circumspect; remember, every eye observes you; and every tongue is asking, "what do ye more than others?" Labour to be the happy instrument of the conversion of the rest. Render your religion amiable: "whatsoever things are lovely, and of good report, think on these things. For what knowest thou, O wife, whether thou shalt save thy husband? or how knowest thou, O man, whether thou shalt save thy wife?" But how happy is that family "where two or three can gather together in his Name," and know that he is "in the midst of them;" where the whole number "are of one heart and of one soul;" where all are connected together by claims more endearing than those of nature—by ties which death cannot dissolve, nor eternity impair! And such was this family.

But though these three were all beloved of our Lord, they appear to have differed from each other very considerably. Of Lazarus indeed much is not said. He seems to have been a serious, solid, established professor of religion. But the two sisters are more strongly marked; more minutely characterized. Mary, it is probable, had been lately called. She was full of those pleasing, but often transient emotions which generally accompany the beginning of the Christian life. Wondering at the gracious words which proceeded out of his mouth, "she sat at the feet of Jesus." Of a devotional taste, a contemplative turn of mind, she was disposed to give more time and attention to her favourite exercises, than perhaps prudence would justify. The reverse of this was the defect of Martha. She was anxious, and eager. She was susceptible of domestic vanity; and therefore too fond of parade and expensive entertainment—"cumbered about much serving." She was also fretful, and by the loss of temper betrayed into such indiscretion as to break in upon our Lord's discourse, and petulantly to require him to send Mary to her assistance, and thus drew upon herself the rebuke of the Saviour: "Martha, Martha, thou art careful and troubled about many things: but one thing is needful: and Mary hath chosen that good part which shall not be taken away from her." But our Lord loved Martha as well as Mary. He knew her frame; he saw kindness reigned in her heart, and that she was no less attached to him than her sister, though she had mistaken the best way of showing her esteem.

E

And hence we should do well to observe two things.

First. That the real followers of Jesus may have their peculiarities, their mistakes, their imperfections. Christians are new creatures. They really differ from others, and the general tenour of their lives shows that they "have not received the spirit of the world, but the Spirit which is of God." But they feel infirmities; and too frequently give proof to those around them that they are renewed but in part. We do not mean to plead for sin; but it is obvious from the history of the first disciples of our Lord and Saviour, that while the grace of God has a holy influence, it seldom if ever changes the constitutional complexion; and that while it sanctifies the powers of human nature, it does not give us new ones. It renders the possessor open to conviction, and makes him willing to retract what he has done amiss; but it does not lay him under an impossibility of doing wrong. Hence a diversity of character in the Church of God. Hence a variety of degrees in the spiritual life. Hence blemishes mixed with excellences, and defects rendered the more observable by the neighbourhood of some very praiseworthy qualities in the same individual. And hence, while religion appears to be divine in its origin and its tendency, we can easily discern that it is human in its residence and its exercise.

Secondly. We should learn to esteem and value imperfect goodness. Yea, an old divine goes further, and says, "We should love one another, not as saints but as sinners." Not that we are to love sin, or cease to reprove it. This is not his meaning: but he would intimate, that we are to be tender and pitiful; that we are to consider ourselves, lest we also be tempted; that we are not to be indiscriminate in our censures, but to praise as far as we can; and that the strong are to bear the infirmities of the weak, and not please themselves. "For who hath despised the day of small things?" Behold "the Shepherd of Israel! he gathers the lambs with his arm, and carries them in his bosom, and gently leads those that are with young." Behold "the Lord mighty in battle! a bruised reed shall he not break, and smoking flax shall he not quench, till he send forth judgment unto victory." Behold the sufferer in the garden of Gethsemane! he compassionately apologizes for the infirmities of his followers: "What! could ye not watch with me one hour? the spirit indeed is willing, but the flesh is weak." "Be ye followers of him as dear children." Remember, "he loved Martha, as well as Mary and Lazarus."

But II. How did he love them? I answer—as a FRIEND—and as a SAVIOUR.

First. Love is a passion of human nature. It shone forth in our Saviour with peculiar partiality. This is to be accounted for in the congeniality peculiar to certain dispositions, by which they immediately attract each other and unite. Though the humanity of our Lord was real, it was also sinless; and, as his mind was perfectly free from every improper bias, doubtless nothing engaged the preference of his regard but what was virtuous and of good report. The vicious, the sceptical, the worldly-minded, we may be assured, had no charms for him, whatever were their accomplishments. There is one thing we may learn from this part of his example—it is, to justify the partiality of friendship. He would not have us to shut up our bowels of compassion against any of our fellow-creatures; for we are to do good as we have opportunity unto all men; but he teaches us by his own practice, that we are not bound to take every one into our bosom. We are at liberty to choose and select. Our Lord regarded all the Apostles; but John is called "the disciple whom Jesus loved." He was kind to all his followers; but it is said, "now Jesus loved Martha, and her sister, and Lazarus." But to "know Christ after the flesh," and to enjoy his peculiar affection under the advantage of his human nature, was a privilege confined to few.

There is therefore, secondly, another sense in which he loved Martha, and Mary, and Lazarus, and in which also he has loved us. It is, with the divine love of a Saviour; a love which existed long before we had a being; a love which sprang from no excellency in us, but was entirely self-derived; a love not only the most undeserved, but the most costly and powerful. It led him to undertake our cause, to assume our nature, to suffer and die for us. "He bare our sins in his own body on the tree, that we being dead to sin, might live unto righteousness: by whose stripes we are healed. Greater love hath no man than this, that a man lay down his life for his friends:" but he has discovered a greater: he laid down his life for enemies; he "died for the ungodly: while we were yet sinners, Christ died for us." The same love gave us the Gospel, called us by his grace, and pardoned all our sins, for his name's sake. And the same love will perform all our reasonable desires; make "all things work together for our good;" and "keep us by his power, through faith, unto salvation, ready to be revealed in the last time." But this leads us

III. To observe the manner in which he expressed his love to these three favoured individuals. Every thing is not recorded; but several circumstances are noticed, which will prove instructive and useful.

First. He visited them. This interview was doubtless often refreshing to our Lord himself. While "foxes had holes, and the birds of the air had nests, the Son of man had not where to lay his head;" he had no house nor room of his own: and we have reason to believe, that sometimes at least, after preaching much, and journeying far, he was destitute of accommodations. Once we read that "he went up into a mountain, and continued there all night in prayer to God." In another instance, we find him so wearied as to be able "to sleep in the hinder part" of a fishing vessel, "even in a storm!" But some knew his value, and ministered to him of their substance. At the house of Martha he was always welcome. And we may be assured, that he was a guest that always paid for his entertainment. He honoured them, more than they could favour him. Who can imagine the happiness of Lazarus and his sisters when they received the Lord of life and glory under their roof! Oh! to have heard him bless the food—to have heard him perform family worship—to have heard him discourse! He was "fairer than the children of men; grace was poured into his lips. Never man spake like this man." With what joy would Martha and her sister, and Lazarus think of such visits in prospect! how long would they furnish matter for conversation and remark afterwards! How unwilling would they be to lose him! how earnestly would they press his stay!—Though removed from this world, as to his bodily presence, he will be with his people essentially, spiritually, peculiarly, to the end of time. He visits them now. "He that hath my commandments, and keepeth them, he it is that loveth me: and he that loveth me shall be loved of my Father, and I will love him, and will manifest myself to him." Say not, "Lord, how is it that thou wilt manifest thyself unto us, and not unto the world!" Judas—not Iscariot—once asked him this question: and "he answered and said unto him, if a man love me he will keep my words, and my Father will love him, and we will come unto him, and make our abode with him."

Secondly. His love admitted of their suffering affliction. Disease invades the family —"Lazarus is sick." The sickness of the brother is the distress of the sisters; they are filled with anguish, anxiety, and alarm. His love could have hindered all this; and probably we should have thought that it would have done it—"Surely he will exempt friends he so highly regards from every thing trying and disagreeable." But his thoughts are not as our thoughts, neither are his ways as our ways. His love is wise; it seeks our everlasting welfare; it does not take pleasure in our pain, but it does in our profit: and though "no chastening for the present seemeth to be joyous, but grievous, nevertheless, afterward it yieldeth the peaceable fruit of righteousness unto them that are exercised thereby." You may therefore share in his affection and be severely tried, relatively or in your own persons. A Lazarus beloved of Jesus sickens and dies. "As many as I love, I rebuke and chasten. Whom the Lord loveth he chasteneth, and scourgeth every son whom he receiveth."

But, Thirdly. His love suffered him in their distress to treat them with apparent neglect. As soon as Lazarus was seized, "his sisters sent unto him, saying, Lord, behold, he whom thou lovest is sick." Yet, instead of sending an answer, or repairing instantly to Bethany, it is said, "when he heard therefore that he was sick, he abode two days still in the same place where he was." And before he sets off, Lazarus is dead! A friend is born for adversity; then we peculiarly need his presence, his assistance, his counsel, his sympathy: and Jesus was their friend. How then is this indifference to be accounted for? It was not indifference. So indeed it appeared to Martha and Mary; and no doubt it was very discouraging and perplexing; it gave rise to many unkind thoughts—"What can be the reason of this! surely he has relinquished his regard; we have presumed too much upon his friendship."—But he was not indifferent. He was only "waiting to be gracious." His delay was no refusal. Every thing is beautiful in its season. He knew that "his time was not yet come." Our extremity is his opportunity. No! He indifferent to their case! all the time he was thinking of them, and caring for them. He entered into all their feelings, and,

Fourthly, said to his disciples, "Our friend Lazarus sleepeth; but I go, that I may awake him out of sleep. Let us go unto him." Before he approaches the bereaved house he comes to the grave—"Then, when Mary was come where Jesus was, and saw him, she fell down at his feet, saying unto him, Lord, if thou hadst been here, my brother had not died. When Jesus therefore saw her weeping, and the Jews also weeping which came with her, he groaned in spirit, and was troubled, and said, where have ye laid him? They say unto him, Lord, come, and see. Jesus wept. Then said the Jews, Behold how he loved him! And some of them said, Could not this man, which opened the eyes of the blind, have caused that even this man should not have died?" Again he groaned in himself. At length, giving way to his compassion, he produced an undeniable proof of his affection, as well as of his power— "Lazarus, come forth!"—And he walks home between his sisters, who were filled with joy and gratitude. Thus all was overruled, not only for the glory of God, but for the good of Lazarus, the good of his sisters, the good of the disciples, the good of many, who, in consequence of the miracle, believed. And thus we learn that he can do us and our connexions much more service by the permission and continuance of our trials, than by preventing, or immediately removing them. He "does all things well. His work is perfect, his ways are judgment."

Let us then, satisfied that he has our welfare in view, leave the means by which it is to be promoted to himself. Let us ascertain an interest in his love, and say, "Behold, here I am; let him do to me as seemeth good to him."

Ah! some of you are ready to exclaim, This is what above all things I want to determine. Happy Martha, and Mary, and Lazarus! Jesus loved you!—Oh that he loved *me*. This would be the cordial of affliction, and the consolation of death. Loved of *him*, I could bear reproach; I could endure all things. A fellow-creature may love me, and be unable in a thousand cases to succour me; but *his* love passeth knowledge, and is attended by the exercise of infinite perfections. There is no enemy which he cannot conquer, no wound which he cannot heal, no hope which he cannot realize. "Say unto my soul, I am thy salvation." Does he love me? Can I know this? Yes; and the case is more easily decided than you imagine. The very solicitude you express shows that your indifference towards him is destroyed. And he has said, "I love them that love me, and they that seek me early shall find me."

"*I love them that love me.*"—And do you not love him? Do you not esteem him above all, for the excellences of his nature and the blessings of his goodness? Do you not most earnestly implore his favour, his image, his presence? Are you not willing to live at his disposal; to obey him; to ask daily, "Lord, what wilt thou have me to do?" Now, if you love him, be assured that he loves you. But, O blessed Saviour, what a difference, what a disproportion is there between our love and thine!

> "Our love so faint, so cold to thee,
> And thine to us so great.

> "Come, holy Spirit, heavenly dove,
> With all thy quick'ning pow'rs;
> Come, shed abroad a Saviour's love,
> And that shall kindle ours."

"*And they that seek me early shall find me.*" For there are some who cannot say, with confidence, "I do love him." But their "desire is to the Lord, and to the remembrance of his name." They mourn for sin. They hunger and thirst after righteousness. They go on praying—"Oh that I may win Christ!" These are earnestly seeking him; and they shall find him—find him as "the pearl of great price"—find him to pardon, and sanctify, and keep—find him *here* in all the supplies of grace, and *hereafter* in all the treasures of glory.

But, O ye young! the promise has the most favourable reference to you. You can seek him *early*; not only, as it implies, earnestly, but, as it more naturally means, betimes. And though all who seek him shall find, *you* shall find him *peculiarly*. It is better to have a guide at the beginning, than after we have long gone astray, and lost much of our time and strength for the journey. If invaluable privileges attend religion, the sooner they are embraced, the more advantage shall we derive from them. The Saviour is peculiarly pleased with your early devotedness to him. He considers himself more honoured by these voluntary offerings of the first-fruits, than by the constrained services of worn-out age: and "them that honour him, he will honour." In every future period of life, in every distress, in every danger, in the hour of death, and in the day of judgment, he will say—"*I remember thee, the kindness of thy youth.*"

DISCOURSE IX.

THE SIGHT OF CHRISTIAN FRIENDS ENLIVENING.

And from thence, when the brethren heard of us, they came to meet us as far as Appii forum, and the three taverns: whom, when Paul saw, he thanked God, and took courage.—Acts xxviii. 15.

THE case was this. From the malice of his countrymen, Paul had "appealed unto Cæsar." He was therefore under the necessity of going to Rome. In his voyage he was shipwrecked on the island of Melita, now called Malta, and which has been of late, as well as in earlier times, so famous. After continuing there three months, he renewed his voyage, landed at Puteoli, not far from Naples, and went towards Rome. At Rome there were *brethren;* and when they heard of his approach, they went down to "meet him as far as Appii forum, and the three taverns." This did them honour; it marked their zeal and their kindness. But observe the effect of the interview on the mind of the Apostle—"Whom, when Paul saw, he thanked God, and took courage."

This teaches us, First, THAT CHARACTERS THE MOST DISTINGUISHED IN THE CHURCH OF GOD, MAY SOMETIMES NEED ENCOURAGEMENT. What made the Apostle now droop, we cannot determine. Perhaps he had heard what a tiger Nero had lately become; perhaps he began to feel some melancholy thoughts respecting the result of his trial. To appear before the emperor of the world, in the presence of a thousand spectators, was enough to make nature shudder—and there is nature as well as grace, and there are animal spirits as well as religious principles, in the best.

Whatever was the cause, it seems the Apostle was now depressed and desponding—even he, who, in his epistle to the Romans, could say, "if God be for us, who can be against us? nay, in all these things we are more than conquerors, through him that loved us"—even *he* discovers a dejection of mind, and a failure of courage.

People often imagine that the saints recorded in the Scripture, were a race of men entirely different from modern Christians. This is a mistake. Even *they* found themselves in an enemy's country; *they* travelled also through a vale of tears, pierced with thorns and briers—without were fightings, and within were fears. Our case therefore is not peculiar—we neither sigh nor tremble alone. Where are the hands which never hang down, the knees which never become feeble? Zion said, "The Lord hath forsaken me, and my Lord hath forgotten me." Asaph said, "My soul refused to be comforted: I remembered God and was troubled; I complained, and my spirit was overwhelmed." David said, "My soul cleaveth to the dust." And Paul exclaimed, "O wretched man that I am! who shall deliver me from the body of this death?" If such was the experience of characters so pre-eminent, what wonder that we are liable to the same exercises?

Secondly. LET US OBSERVE THE BENEFIT THAT IS TO BE DERIVED FROM INTERCOURSE WITH CHRISTIAN FRIENDS. When Paul saw these brethren, he was inspired with new life; he dropped his melancholy gloom, and marched forward with confidence and joy— He "*took courage*." "Ointment and perfume rejoice the heart: so doth the sweetness of a man's friend by hearty counsel. Iron sharpeneth iron: so a man sharpeneth the countenance of his friend."

In no condition is it "good for man to be alone." Religion, instead of destroying the social principle, refines and strengthens it. Our Saviour has promised, that "where two or three are gathered together in his name, he will be in the midst of them." To cheer and animate each other, "he sent forth his disciples two and two before his face." "Two are better than one; for if they fall, the one will lift up his fellow: but wo to him that is alone when he falleth; for he hath not another to help him up."

Have you ever been in distress? How soothing was the presence of a tender and a pious friend! Such a person was "a ministering spirit"—an expositor of the promise: "The Lord will strengthen him upon the bed of languishing; thou wilt make all his bed in his sickness." Have you ever been in spiritual darkness and perplexity?—you sighed, "No one was ever like me!" But a Christian related his experience, and announced the same feelings, and you were set at liberty. Or have you in a scorching day been ready to perish for thirst? Like another angel, in the case of Hagar, "he opened your eyes, and showed you a well"—And you "*went on your way rejoicing*." God of all grace! whatever thou art pleased to deny us while in this world, withhold not from us a

Christian friend—one who will counsel us in our doubts, comfort us in our sorrows, animate us by his example, and encourage us by his confidence!

How pleasing is it, when traveling to heaven, to overtake those who will be "our companions in tribulation, and in the kingdom and patience of Jesus Christ!" How overjoyed is a Christian to find some followers of the Lamb, when he has entered a town or a village; saying, with Abraham, "Surely the fear of God is in this place!" It has enlivened him, and he has exclaimed, "Well, there are more that love and serve my Lord and Saviour than I imagined." What a glow of satisfaction does a man, called by Divine grace, diffuse in a church when he enters to ask for communion and fellowship with them —"They that fear thee will be glad when they see me, because I have hoped in thy word." How desirable is the Lord's day, and the Lord's house, in which we see so many of our brethren!

> "Lord how delightful 'tis to see
> A whole assembly worship Thee!
> At once they sing, at once they pray;
> They hear of heaven and learn the way!"

How charming will heaven be, where we shall see "a multitude which no man can number, of all nations, and kindreds, and people, and tongues, standing, before the throne, and before the Lamb, clothed with white robes, and palms in their hands!"

Thirdly. Let us remark, THAT WE MAY BE EDIFIED BY THOSE WHO ARE BELOW US IN STATION, IN TALENTS AND IN GRACE. Thus these private Christians helped an inspired Apostle—"When he saw them, he thanked God and took courage." Apollos was an eloquent man, and mighty in the Scriptures; but he was "taught the way of the Lord more perfectly," by two of his hearers, Priscilla and Aquila. Naaman the Syrian was a mighty man; but he was indebted for his cure to a little maid. She had been taken captive in war, and waited upon Naaman's wife, and "she said unto her mistress, would God my Lord were with the prophet that is in Samaria! for he would recover him of his leprosy." "The king is served by the labour of the field."

Let us learn then that there is no such thing as independence—that there is a connexion among men which embraces all ranks and degrees—and a dependence founded upon it; so that no being is above the want of assistance, and no being is useless or unimportant. It is in the world, and it is in the Church, as it is in the human frame. "God hath set the members every one of them in the body, as it hath pleased him—and the eye cannot say unto the hand, I have no need of thee; nor again, the head to the feet, I have no need of you—that there should be no schism in the body; but that the members should have the same care one for another."

Lastly. ALL THE COMFORT AND ADVANTAGE WE DERIVE FROM CREATURES SHOULD AWAKEN GRATITUDE TO GOD.—It is said, "*he thanked God.*" Doubtless the Apostle was sensible of his obligations to these brethren, and thanked *them* for their civility and tenderness in coming, unasked, so far to meet him.—But says Paul—Who made these Christian friends? Who inclined them to favour me? Who rendered them the means of restoring my soul? " Of him, and through him, and to him, are all things: to whom be glory for ever. Amen."

"Do not err, my beloved brethren. Every good gift and every perfect gift is from above, and cometh down from the father of lights, with whom is no variableness, neither shadow of turning." He uses channels to convey blessings to us; but all our springs are in him. The heathen made gods of every thing that afforded them pleasure, and we are too prone to do the same. Instruments sometimes intercept the praise that is going to be offered to God; and when this is the case, he often lays them aside or renders them useless—for the divine jealousy will not endure a rival.

And here is the difference between a carnal and a spiritual mind. The man who possesses the former, lives without God in the world. Though he divine perfections surround him, and a thousand voices continually address him, he walks on, all careless and insensible. Whereas the Christian is disposed to acknowledge God in all his ways. The stream leads him to the fountain. The gift reminds him of the giver: the instrument, of the agent. He holds communion with God in common things. He is thankful for common mercies. He sees and adores him in the springing of the earth, in the rain, and fruitful showers, in the refreshments of sleep, and in the pleasures of friendship. He grieves with Archbishop Leighton that a world so full of his mercy should be so empty of his praise. He cries with David, "O that men would praise the Lord for his goodness, and for his wonderful works to the children of men! Bless the Lord, all his works in all places of his dominion: bless the Lord, O my soul!" Which of these characters do we resemble?

DISCOURSE X.

THE CHRISTIAN INDEED!
(BEFORE THE LORD'S SUPPER.)

I am crucified with Christ: nevertheless I live; yet not I, but Christ liveth in me: and the life which I now live in the flesh I live by the faith of the Son of God, who loved me, and gave himself for me.—Gal. ii. 20.

IT has been said by an old divine, "That

if religion be any thing, it is every thing; if it be important at all, it is all important." And indeed if it be impartially considered, with regard to prosperity or adversity, life or death, time or eternity, it will appear to be, in the eye of reason, as well as in the testimony of Scripture, "*the one thing needful.*" Hence it becomes necessary to know wherein it consists—to examine its qualities—and to trace its effects.

A fuller representation of genuine religion was perhaps never given than we have in the words before us. For you will observe that the inspired writer does not here speak of himself as an Apostle, but as a Christian, and therefore, that what he describes as his own experience, will apply to all the subjects of divine grace. It leads us to consider—the TRUE CHARACTERS—the GRAND PRINCIPLE—and the ALLOWED CONFIDENCE of real religion.

I. Let us attentively observe the SEVERAL CHARACTERS here given us of true godliness, and see whether we have any thing like them in ourselves. Says Paul, "I am crucified with Christ: nevertheless I live; yet not I, but Christ liveth in me."

It has then a character of MYSTERY, of wonder, or (shall I say?) paradox. How strange is it to see a bush burning with fire, and unconsumed!" How marvellous is it to find that the poor only are rich, the sick only are well, and that a broken heart is the greatest blessing we can possess! How surprising is it to hear persons saying, We are " sorrowful, yet always rejoicing; having nothing, and yet possessing all things: as dying, and behold we live"—to hear a man say, " I am crucified," though he has the use of all his limbs—crucified with Christ, though Christ had been crucified on Calvary long before—and to add, " nevertheless I live"— then with the same breath to check himself, and deny this—" yet not I"—and to crown the whole, " Christ liveth in me,"'though he was then in heaven! What unintelligible jargon is all this to the carnal mind! " For the natural man receiveth not the things of the Spirit of God: for they are foolishness unto him: neither can he know them, because they are spiritually discerned." A Christian is "*a wonder unto many.*" How absurd, and ridiculous did all this once appear to us—but it is our mercy that the darkness is past and the true light now shineth—that we begin to perceive beauty and harmony and worth, where once nothing struck us but confusion and discord and insignificance—that we can, say, with the man in the Gospel, " One thing I know, that whereas I was blind, now I see."

It has a character of MORTIFICATION. " I am crucified with Christ." The grace of God has to pull up, as well as sow; to destroy, as well as build. It has much to slay in us —it has to slay our vain confidence, our self-righteous hopes, our pride, our depraved affections. It finds us alive to the world and to sin, and it leaves us dead to both. To die to any thing, in the language of Scripture, is to have no more connexion with it, no more attachment to it: "how shall we that are dead to sin, live any longer therein" —if we were alive to it, we might be enticed—but what are allurements presented to a dead corpse? " Knowing this, that our old man is crucified with him, that the body of sin might be destroyed, that henceforth we should not serve sin: for he that is dead is freed from sin." It has no more dominion over him; he loves it no longer.

But to crucify, is not only to destroy; it signifies a peculiar kind of death—a violent, unnatural death: and sin never dies of its own accord, nor from weakness, nor from age; it must be put to death by force. It signifies a painful death—think of a body fastened to a tree, suspended in torture, nails driven through the hands and feet, (parts so susceptible of pain, by reason of the concurrence of nerves and sinews)—who was ever crucified without anguish? Whoever was a Christian without difficulty, self-denial, sacrifices, and groans, and tears? Though crucifixion was a sure death, it was a slow and a lingering one. And our corruptions, though doomed to be destroyed, are not despatched at once. We shall have to mortify the deeds of the body as long as we are here; but sin is nailed to the cross, and shall never gain an ascendency over us again;—its death is inevitable.

It has a character of LIFE—"nevertheless I live." And life brings evidence along with it. "I compare," says the believer, "my present with my former dispositions. I was once dead to a certain class of objects; for they could no more affect me than natural things can impress a dead body; but now, for the very same reason, I know that I am alive—because they do impress me; they do interest me; they do excite in me hopes and fears; I am susceptible of spiritual joys and sorrows. I live, for I breathe prayer and praise; I live, for I feel the pulse of sacred passions; I live, for I have appetites, and do hunger and thirst after righteousness; I live, for I walk and I work; and though all my efforts betray weakness, they prove life—I live." A real Christian is not a picture—a picture may accurately resemble an original, but it wants life: it has eyes, but it sees not; lips, but it speaks not. A Christian is not a figure: you may take materials and make up the figure of a man, and give it the various parts of the human body, and even make them move, by wires; but a Christian is not moved in religion by machinery, but life—nothing is forced and artificial.

Why is religion so burdensome to many? The reason is, they have nothing in them to render these things like the functions of life,

natural and easy. Hence they drudge and toil on, often exclaiming, What a weariness it is to serve the Lord!—and drop one thing after another, till they give up the whole. But where there is spiritual life, there is an inward propensity to holiness, there is a savouring the things which be of God: there is nothing of that ignoble and slavish devotion which springs from custom, or is impelled by external motives only—they find his service to be perfect freedom; his yoke easy, and his burden light; such a burden as a pair of wings to a bird; they would be awkward and troublesome, and useless, if tied on, but, as living parts of his body, they are graceful and pleasing, and the instruments of flight towards heaven.

It has a character of HUMILITY.—" Yet not I"—This is the unvarying strain of the Apostle. " Not by fleshly wisdom, but by the grace of God, we have our conversation in the world. By the grace of God I am what I am: and his grace, which was bestowed upon me, was not in vain; but I laboured more abundantly than they all: yet not I, but the grace of God which was with me. I have learned, in whatsoever state I am, therewith to be content: I know both how to be abased, and I know how to abound; everywhere, and in all things, I am instructed both to be full, and to be hungry; both to abound, and to suffer need—I can do all things through Christ, who strengtheneth me."

Compare with this language the sentiments of the Pagan philosophers. Take one as a specimen of the rest. Cicero says, " We are justly applauded for virtue, and in virtue we rightly glory, which would not be the case if we had virtue as the gift of God, and not from ourselves. Did any person ever give thanks to God that he was a good man? No; but we thank him that we are rich, that we are honourable, that we are in health and safety." Now this argues not only the most dreadful pride, but the grossest ignorance, and it would be easy to prove that goodness is much less from ourselves than any thing else. The material creation has not such degrees of dependence upon God as the animal; the animal world has not such degrees of dependence upon God as the rational; and rational beings have not such degrees of dependence upon God as pure and holy beings —beings reconciled from rebellion, renewed from depravity, and preserved, all weakness as they are, in the midst of temptation. Penetrate heaven—there "they cast their crowns at the feet" of their deliverer, and acknowledge that if they reign at all, it is by mere favour. This disposition must enter us before we can enter heaven. " He that abaseth himself shall be exalted; but he that exalteth himself shall be abased." Dependence is the only proper condition of a creature, especially of a fallen creature, and the Gospel is designed and adapted to produce self-annihilation, that " no flesh should glory in his presence, but that, according as it is written, *he that glorieth, let him glory in the Lord.*"

Finally, it has a CHRISTIAN character—but " Christ liveth in me." This life is indeed formally in me: I am the subject of it, but not the agent. It is not self-derived, nor self-maintained; but it comes from him, and is so perfectly sustained by him, that it seems better to say—not " I live," but " Christ liveth in me."

He has a sovereign empire of grace, founded in his death, and he quickens whom he will. He is our life—not only as he procures it by redemption, but also as he produces it by regeneration; and he liveth in us as the sun lives in the garden, by his influence calling forth fragrance and fruits; or as the soul lives in the body, actuating every limb, and penetrating every particle with feeling.

II. Let us consider the GRAND INFLUENCING PRINCIPLE of this religion—" It is the faith of the Son of God." " If you ask," says the Christian, " how it is that I live so different from others, and so different from my former self, here is the secret. There is a faith which has immediately and entirely to do with the Son of God: of this faith I have been made the happy partaker, and in proportion as I can exercise this, I do well. This brings me supplies from his boundless fulness. This places me in the strong hold. This invigorates duty. This alleviates affliction. This purifies the heart. This overcomes the world. This does all. By faith I stand; by faith I walk; by faith I live—' and the life that I now live in the flesh, I live by the faith of the Son of God.' "

To explain this, it will be necessary to observe, that the communication of grace from Christ, to maintain the Divine life, depends on union with him, and that of this union faith is the medium. Let me make this plain. It is well known that the animal spirits and nervous juices are derived from the head to the body; but then it is only to that particular body which is united to it. And the same may be said of the vine: the vine conveys a prolific sap, but it is exclusively to its own branches. It matters not how near you place branches to the stock: if they are not *in it*, they may as well be a thousand miles off; they cannot be enlivened or fructified by it. " The branch cannot bear fruit of itself, except it abide in the vine: no more can we except we abide in him, for without him we can do nothing." Now he is the head, and we are the members: he is the vine, we are the branches.

And this union from which this influence flows, is accomplished by faith only: " *he dwells in our hearts by faith.*" If faith be an eye, it is only by this we can see him. If faith be a hand, it is only by this we can lay hold of him.

He is the food of our souls, but it is by faith that this food is converted into aliment: they are his own words: " he that eateth me, even he shall live by me." Place all the motives of Christianity around a man—if he does not believe them, they cannot touch him; this is the *only* medium by which they can operate. How can the threatenings of our Lord produce fear—How can the promises which he has given excite hope—but by being believed? By this the various parts of the whole system are brought to bear upon the conscience, and the practice. Therefore says the Apostle; " the life that I now live in the flesh, I live by the faith of the Son of God, who loved me, and gave himself for me."

III. This brings us to notice the confidence, THE APPROPRIATION which this religion allows. Now what we mean to establish here —is not that every real Christian can use this language as boldly as the apostle Paul. Then we should make some " *sad*," some whom God has commanded us to make " *merry:*" there are degrees in grace; and there is weak faith as well as strong faith.

But I would intimate, first, that genuine religion always produces a concern for this appropriation. It will not suffer a man to rest in distant speculations and loose generalities, but will make him anxious to bring things home to himself, and to know how they affect *him.* With regard to duty, he will say, " Lord, what wilt thou have *me* to do?" When he hears of promises and privileges, he will ask, Am *I* interested in these; may *I* claim them?—" Say unto my soul, I am *thy* salvation."

I mean also to intimate, secondly, that a Christian may attain this confidence, and draw this conclusion. Let him take God at his word, and from the general language of the Gospel, make out a particular inference. —He loved sinners, and gave himself for the ungodly. Let those who have no need of a Saviour stand and debate; I need him; and I see he is come to save sinners, and I am one: to die for the ungodly, and this is my character. I see also that the Master calls me, and invites me by name, or, which is much safer and better, by description: I am oppressed with a load; and I am tired, struggling to get free; and he says, " Come unto me, all ye that labour and are heavy laden, and I will give you rest."

To enable you to decide this business, let me ask you—Have you not had a view of your lost condition by nature, and so of your absolute need of Christ? Have you not discovered his grace and his glory, in living and dying for you, so as to feel your soul powerfully drawn towards him? Under this attraction have you not been led to apply to him, throwing yourself down at his feet, " Here is a blind sinner—be thou my wisdom; a guilty sinner—be thou my righteousness; a polluted sinner—be thou my sanctification; an enslaved, miserable sinner—be thou my redemption." And do you not feel something good as the consequence of this? Is not your mind so filled, so fixed, that you no longer rove after the world? do you not melt in godly sorrow for sin? are you not constrained by holy love to the Saviour to say, "Speak, Lord, for thy servant heareth;" and to "live not unto yourselves, but to him that died for you and rose again?" Where these things are wholly wanting, there is no real faith; where they are found, a person can be guilty of nothing like presumption, in saying, "he loved me, and gave himself for me."

Thirdly, we would intimate that nothing can exceed the blessedness which results from such an appropriation of the Saviour in his love, and in his death. All evangelical consolation is wrapped up in it. Could each of you make it your own—How would eternity be disarmed of its dread! With what composure would you look forward to death! How cheerfully would you bear your trials! How pleasant would all your worship prove! With what lively and suitable feelings would you approach this morning the table of the Lord, where a dying Jesus is not only presented to your faith, but to your very sight, "evidently set forth, crucified, among you!"

"*He loved me, and gave himself for me!*" O my soul, think of these words. The Son of God, higher than the kings of the earth, the Lord of all, he has condescended to remember me in my low estate—He has *loved* me—and oh! how marvellous the expression of this love—he gave—nothing less than *himself*—to be my teacher and example only? No, but to be my substitute, my ransom; to bear my "sins in his own body on the tree." And all this goodness regards unworthy, unlovely *me!*

Did he love me, and shall I not love him? Has he given himself for me, "an offering and a sacrifice to God, for a sweetsmelling savour"—and shall I be unwilling to give myself to him, "a living sacrifice, holy and acceptable, which is my reasonable service?"

And, O my soul, rejoice in him. What may I not expect from his hands—what will he deny, who did not withhold himself!

DISCOURSE XI.

THE FINAL CHANGE.

(EASTER.)

Behold, I show you a mystery; we shall not all sleep, but we shall all be changed, in a moment, in the twinkling of an eye, at the last trump: for the trumpet shall sound, and the dead shall be raised incorruptible, and we shall be changed.—1 Cor. xv. 51, 52.

HERE a scene opens upon us, in comparison with which every thing else becomes worthless, little, uninteresting. And let me tell you—

It is a transaction in which you will be, not merely spectators, but parties concerned.

It is an event the most certain.

It is a solemnity that is continually drawing near. For while I speak, you die—and "*after death the judgment!*" Does not this subject therefore deserve, as well as demand, your most serious attention?

The chapter before us regards the resurrection. But those only can be raised who *die* —what shall become of those, who at this awful period shall be alive? "Behold, I show you a mystery; we shall not all sleep, but we shall all be changed, in a moment, in the twinkling of an eye, at the last trump: for the trumpet shall sound, and the dead shall be raised incorruptible, and we shall be changed."

Here we may observe the union there is among the followers of the Redeemer. Christians, however distinguished from each other, are inhabitants of one country, brethren of one family, members of one body. They are influenced by the same Spirit, and are traveling the same road. Diversity of circumstances, peculiarity of religious discipline, remoteness of situation, distance of time, do not affect the relation that unites them all together. The Apostle looks forward to the end of all things, and says, *we* who are alive, and remain unto the coming of the Lord, shall not prevent them who are asleep.—"Then *we*, who are alive and remain, shall be caught up together with them in the clouds, to meet the Lord in the air: and so shall we ever be with the Lord. We shall not all sleep, but we shall all be changed."

Of the number of this universal Church, some *die*, but the representation that is given us of their death is very pleasing—"*they sleep.*" Death is often an alarming subject, even to Christians; to reduce this dread, they would do well to endeavour to view it under those images by which the Scripture has expressed it—a departure—a going home—a sleep. Man is called to labour. He goes forth in the morning, toils, with some little intermission, all the day, and in the evening retires, and lays himself down to sleep—and "the sleep of a labouring man is sweet, whether he eat little or much." And such is every Christian. They have much to do; and they must do it "while it is day: for the night cometh wherein no man can work." Death brings them repose: "They rest from their labours." Sleep is a state from which you may be easily awakened. You look at the babe in the cradle; he neither sees you,

F 4*

nor hears you; but you fee. no uneasiness on this account; by-and-by the senses will be unlocked, and he will be taken up, smiling and refreshed. "Our friend Lazarus sleepeth," says the Saviour; "but I go that I may awake him out of sleep." And he called, "Lazarus, come forth!" and, though he had been dead four days, he heard and came. From his throne in glory, Jesus, the resurrection and the life, looks down upon the mansions of the dead, and at the appointed time he will say to the heavenly hosts, Our friends are sleeping in the dust—attend—I go to awake them out of sleep: and lo! "all that are in their graves hear his voice, and come forth!"

Thus far the laws of mortality prevail. Death "is the way of all the earth;" and of all the righteous too: and this will continue to be the case to the end—but then many will be found *alive*. The language of the Apostle is instructive. The present system is unquestionably to be destroyed; but it will not wax old and perish through corruption. All the productions of the earth will be as fair as ever. The inhabitants of the earth will not be gradually consumed till none are left: the world will be full; and all the common concerns of life will be pursued with the same eagerness as before. And "as it was in the days of Noah, so shall it be also in the days of the Son of man. They did eat, they drank, they married wives, they were given in marriage, until the day that Noah entered into the ark, and the flood came and destroyed them all." Many of the Lord's people too will be found alive; and perhaps they will be much more numerous than at any former period. Now in what manner will these be disposed of? This is what the Apostle professes to teach.

"Behold," says he, "I show you a mystery." He means a secret: something unknown before; unknown to the Corinthians, and it is likely unknown to himself. But, probably, while reflecting upon this subject, and thinking what would be the destiny of those that should reach the end of time, he was informed, by inspiration, that they should not die, but be transformed.

"We shall all be *changed*." We are always varying now. We never continue in one stay: what vicissitudes do we experience in the lapse of a few years in our conditions, in our connexions, in our very frame! But what a change is here—a change from time to eternity, from earth to heaven, from the company of the wicked to the presence of the blessed God; from ignorance to knowledge; from painful infirmities to be "presented faultless before the presence of his glory with exceeding joy!" But the change principally refers to the body: "for flesh and blood cannot inherit the kingdom of God; neither doth corruption inherit incorruption."

Enoch and Elias carried their bodies along with them to heaven: but though they did not die, they passed through a change equivalent to death. The same change which will be produced in the dead by the resurrection, will be accomplished in the bodies of the living by this transformation; and of this we have the clearest assurance: "So is the resurrection of the dead. It is sown in corruption; it is raised in incorruption: it is sown in dishonour; it is raised in glory: it is sown in weakness; it is raised in power: it is sown a natural body; it is raised a spiritual body. As we have borne the image of the earthy, we shall also bear the image of the heavenly."

Further, observe the ease and despatch with which all this will be performed—"In a moment, in the twinkling of an eye." What a view does this give us of the dominion and power of God! Think of the numbers that will be alive! Think of the inhabitants of one city—of one country—of all the nations of the globe—all these metamorphosed in one instant; immortal even in body, and capable of endless misery or happiness! And "why should it be thought a thing incredible?" Who said, "let there be light; and there was light?" Who "spake, and it was done; commanded, and it stood fast?" "Is any thing too hard for the Lord?" Let the work be—what it really is—the greatest of all miracles; we have an Agent more than equal to the execution of it: "He shall change our vile body, that it may be fashioned like unto his glorious body, according to the working whereby he is able even to subdue all things unto himself."

Finally, observe the signal: "At the last trump: for the trumpet shall sound, and the dead shall be raised incorruptible, and we shall be changed!" When the Lord came down on Horeb to publish the Law, "the voice of the trumpet waxed exceeding loud." By the sound of the trumpet the approach of kings has been announced. Trumpets are used in war. Judges in our country enter the place of assize preceded by the same shrill sound. And those who have witnessed the procession well know what an awe it impresses, and what sentiments it excites. All feel: even those who are not to be tried catch a powerful sympathy. But think of the condition of the poor prisoners, whose fate hangs in suspense, and is now going to be decided!—What are their agitations, and forebodings, when they hear the judge is entering! But here is a trumpet whose clangour will be heard for thousands of miles—louder than a million thunders—which will awaken all the dead, and change all the living—cause heaven and earth to flee away—and leave us all before the Judge of the universe!

And what says Peter in reference to all this?—"Wherefore, beloved, seeing that ye look for such things, be diligent that ye may be found of him in peace, without spot, and blameless." Can you be indifferent to any of your actions, when they are recorded in the book of his remembrance, and will be published before an assembled world? What you are doing now you are doing for ever. It is a light thing to know how you are to be disposed of for a few months or a few years —What is to become of you when you go hence, and are seen no more? It signifies very little whether you class with the rich or the poor, the learned or the illiterate, the honourable or the despised. The question is —In what rank will you be found, when "before him shall be gathered all nations, and he shall separate them one from another, as a shepherd divideth his sheep from the goats?" Will that trumpet call you to "lamentation, and mourning, and wo!" or will its language be, "lift up your heads with joy, for your redemption draweth nigh!"

He who will then be the Judge, is now the Saviour. He will then say to the wicked, "Depart"—but, blessed be his name, he does not say so now to any—His language is, "Come." "Come," says he; "come unto me, all ye that labour, and are heavy laden, and I will give you rest. Him that cometh unto me I will in no wise cast out."

And this reminds me of another trumpet, of which Isaiah speaks in these striking words: "It shall come to pass in that day that the great trumpet shall be blown, and they shall come which were ready to perish in the land of Assyria, and the outcasts in the land of Egypt, and shall worship the Lord in the holy mount at Jerusalem." *This* trumpet you *have* heard. But, alas! how have you heard it? Has this "grace of God which bringeth salvation," taught you " to deny all ungodliness and worldly lusts, and to live soberly, and righteously, and godly, in the present world, looking for that blessed hope, and the glorious appearing of the great God and our Saviour Jesus Christ?" O let the judgment-trumpet awaken your attention to the Gospel-trumpet; and may the latter prepare you for the former! Amen.

DISCOURSE XII.

RELIGIOUS THINGS, PLEASANT THINGS.

(LORD'S DAY EVENING.)

Our holy and our beautiful house, where our fathers praised thee, is burned up with fire: and all our pleasant things are laid waste. Isaiah lxiv. 11.

THUS spake these pious Jews. And we may consider the words either as expressing an affliction, or as discovering a disposition.

The captivity had destroyed all their civil and sacred institutions. The temple was a magnificent building, endeared by a thousand claims; but now it exhibited to the passing eye only a scene of ruins—their "holy and beautiful house"—was burnt with fire. One circumstance could not fail to touch and impress their minds—it was the place "where their fathers praised him." What a veneration does an edifice acquire that has stood for ages the sanctuary of devotion, and in which successive generations have worshipped God! What a solemn thought is it, that we occupy seats once filled by those who have gone "the way of all the earth! The fathers, where are they? and the prophets, do they live for ever?" And we are "accomplishing, as an hireling, our day," and are making room for our children. Here they heard his word, called upon his name, sung his praise, offered up prayers and vows for us! Their example reproves and alarms us. *They* were alive in his service; does *our* devotion discover any degree of seriousness and fervour? Are we "followers of them who, through faith and patience, inherit the promises?" Shall we one day join our pious ancestors, "and sit down with Abraham, Isaac, and Jacob, in the kingdom of God?" Again: "All their pleasant things were laid waste"—the sacred utensils employed in the service of God; the ministers of the sanctuary; the altar, the table of shewbread, the ark, the pot of manna, Aaron's rod that budded, the cloud of glory, their new moons and sabbaths, the callings of assemblies. This, to the pious among the Israelites, was a far greater affliction than the loss of all their temporal privileges. Their country was dear to them, but Jerusalem was dearer; and they "loved the gates of Zion better than all the dwelling-places of Jacob."

This affliction, blessed be God, is not ours. Our civil and religious privileges are still continued, and we hope, will pass down unimpaired to the latest posterity. But the words discover a disposition which will be found to harmonize with the feelings of all the people of God. I refer to the manner in which they speak of the service of God, and the exercises of devotion: "Our pleasant things." Hence, we observe, that the means of grace, the ordinances of religion, are, to the Israel of God, PLEASANT THINGS.

And First, what are they?

In the number of their pleasant things, they include the sanctuary. To them the temple is not a prison, a place of confinement and correction; but it is the house of their heavenly Father, their "holy and beautiful house;" and *beautiful* because *holy*. "I was glad when they said unto me, let us go into the house of the Lord. For a day in thy courts is better than a thousand. I had rather be a door-keeper in the house of my God, than to dwell in the tents of wickedness. How amiable are thy tabernacles, O Lord of Hosts!"

In the number of their "pleasant things," they include Sabbaths. To many indeed God's holy day is uninviting, and even irksome: they therefore cry out, "what a weariness it is to serve the Lord! when will the Sabbath be gone, that we may set forth wheat!" pursuing their gain, or finding their own pleasures. But the Christian "calls the Sabbath a delight, and considers the holy of the Lord honourable." To him it is a time of refreshing from the presence of the Lord; a weekly jubilee; and wearied with the toils, and follies, and vexations of the world, he hails a day of seclusion from it; a day that "brings him to God's holy mountain, and makes him joyful in his house of prayer—This is the day which the Lord hath made, we will rejoice and be glad in it."

And are not the Scriptures some of their "pleasant things?" Job could say, "I have esteemed the words of his mouth more than my necessary food." David could say, "More to be desired are they than gold, yea, than much fine gold; sweeter also than honey and the honeycomb." Jeremiah could say, "Thy words were found, and I did eat them; and they were unto me the joy and rejoicing of my heart." It is the character of a good man, and the pledge of his blessedness: "his delight is in the law of the Lord, and in his law doth he meditate day and night; and he shall be like a tree planted by the rivers of water, that bringeth forth his fruit in his season; his leaf also shall not wither; and whatsoever he doeth shall prosper."

This too will apply to the preaching of the word. The Christian does not wish to be always hearing sermons, for he knows that every thing is beautiful in its season, and the claims of duty are numerous and various—but he values opportunities of hearing the glad tidings of salvation: he welcomes the message and the messenger, and exclaims, "How beautiful are the feet of them that preach the gospel of peace, and bring glad tidings of good things!" And though their trials be many, "and the Lord gives them the bread of adversity, and the water of affliction," yet they find an ample compensation and relief in this—that "their eyes behold their teachers, and their ears hear a voice behind them, saying, this is the way, walk ye in it, when they turn aside to the right hand, and when they turn to the left."

They find it a pleasant thing to approach God in prayer, and to "come before his presence with singing"—a pleasant thing to surround his table, and to refresh their minds with the memorials of a Saviour's dying love —a pleasant thing to be in the circle of pious friends, and to hear from their lips "what God has done for their souls." These are some of their "pleasant things."

Let us inquire, Secondly, how they become so POWERFULLY ATTRACTIVE? For it is certain that they are not so universally: by numbers they are not only neglected, but despised. Whence then do real Christians find them so pleasing?

First, there is in them a suitableness to their dispositions. Thus we know music charms those who have an ear for it. Money is a pleasant thing to the covetous; honour, to the ambitious; scandal, to the slanderous. In all these instances there is something that meets the taste; and that which gratifies always delights. So it is here. "That which is born of the flesh is flesh; and that which is born of the Spirit is spirit. They that are after the flesh do mind the things of the flesh; but they that are after the Spirit, the things of the Spirit." The pleasure of the Christian does not depend upon persuasion—but inclination: he is not merely told that the provisions of the Gospel are good, but he has a spiritual relish. Since he is a "new creature," he has new appetites, and "hungers and thirsts after righteousness."

Experience, however, is another source of this pleasure. We are attached to books which have afforded us peculiar satisfaction. The kindnesses of friends endear them. A spring, which in a scorching day, and when we were ready to expire, yielded us a refreshing supply, will be thought of with pleasure. The new-born babe is at first urged by a natural instinct, but afterwards it cries for the breast, not only from a sense of want, but a sense of enjoyment. So it is with the Christian. He has found these things to be good for him. Having "tasted that the Lord is gracious," his language is, "Evermore give us this bread!" Many do not know what it is to enjoy God in the means of grace; they are not attached to ordinances, because they have derived no profit from them. But Christians have striking proofs of their beneficial influence in their own experience: they know that in keeping them there is great reward: they remember how they have been owned of God—at one time, by delivering their souls from the power of temptation—at another, by filling them with "all joy and peace in believing." Some seasons and exercises they can review with singular feeling. In these they were "abundantly satisfied with the fatness of his house:" they were made to "drink of the river of his pleasures. In his light they saw light." And the memory of these peculiar communications and discoveries makes them long with David "to see his power and his glory as they have seen him in the sanctuary!"

Continual need also renders them pleasant things. Though the Christian hopes the good work is begun in him, he feels how far it is from being complete. His deficiencies are great and many. Something is lacking to his faith, his hope, his knowledge. Sometimes also he feels decays. His zeal cools into indifference. Earthly things sensualize his mind. He wants to have his convictions renewed; his impressions regenerated. And how are these deficiencies to be filled up; these decays to be repaired? Read the promise—"In all places where I record my Name, I will come unto thee, and I will bless thee. They that wait upon the Lord, shall renew their strength: they shall mount up with wings as eagles; they shall run and not be weary, and walk and not faint." Draw nigh to God, and he will draw nigh to you.

Let us review what we have said—and learn,

First, TO JUSTIFY RELIGION FROM THE REPROACHES OF THE WORLD. The world pretends that the services which religion demands of us are all slavery and gloom; and they spread this evil report of the good land to check inquiries, especially the young. But if you are willing to enter in, "let no man's heart fail him!" The Scripture assures us that "her ways are ways of pleasantness, and all her paths are peace." And "wisdom is justified of all her children." Those who have tried (and these are the only competent witnesses), instead of complaining of bondage, find the Saviour's service to be perfect freedom, and own—especially compared with the yoke of their old master—that "his commandments are not grievous."

Secondly. LET US TRY OURSELVES BY THIS RULE. A man may want assurance, and still be in a state of safety; but if he be habitually a stranger to pleasure in divine things, and can pass through all the services of religion as a mere formalist, it is an awful proof that "he has no part nor lot in the matter: his heart is not right in the sight of God." A number of speculative opinions, cold ceremonies, cheap moralities, in which the affections have no share, can never be a substitute for real devotion. "The Lord looketh to the heart." He does not value those exercises which are performed from necessity; unwillingly, grudgingly. He abhors the sacrifices of those who are glad of excuses to keep them from his worship; who would be thankful were he entirely to dispense with their services; who feel him as a task-master while they are performing the drudgery of his work. The question is—Are spiritual things your "pleasant things?" If not, you are destitute of the mark of a real Christian, and you have a poor prospect before you in eternity. God will not force you into heaven to make you miserable; but miserable you would be, even in heaven, in your present state. The nature and duration of its employments—an eternal sabbath—a temple in which you shall serve

him day and night—an intercourse only with those who are perfectly pure and holy—all this would be intolerable to an unrenewed mind, who is "saying to God, depart from us, we desire not the knowledge of thy ways."

Thirdly. What an *affliction* do Christians sustain when they are DEPRIVED OF THEIR "PLEASANT THINGS!" This may be done two ways. First, by the removal of these privileges from them. Thus persecution has sometimes forbidden them to assemble together, and has silenced their preachers, destroyed their sanctuaries, and banished all religious ordinances from a neighbourhood. God sometimes inflicts his judgments upon a place for neglect and abuse of Gospel privileges. He can send a more dreadful dearth than a "famine of bread," even "a famine of hearing the word of the Lord." He can as easily convey an evangelical ministry from one country to another, as we can carry a candle from one room into another :—" I will remove thy candlestick out of his place, except thou repent." Or, secondly, by removing Christians from these privileges. Thus business may call them away from a favoured situation, accidents or sickness may detain them prisoners from the courts of the Lord. And though in these cases he does not leave them comfortless, still they feel their loss, and can say, "When I remember these things, I pour out my soul in me: for I had gone with the multitude, I went with them to the house of God, with the voice of joy and praise, with a multitude that kept holy day."

Let us, Fourthly, be very THANKFUL THAT THESE "PLEASANT THINGS" ARE WITHIN OUR REACH—that we have been so long favoured with them—that we have them in so rich an abundance—that we have liberty to partake of them—and strength to go forth and enjoy them:—surely "the lines are fallen to us in pleasant places; yea, we have a goodly heritage. Let us enter his gates with thanksgiving, and his courts with praise."

And Finally, LET US RAISE OUR THOUGHTS AND DESIRES AFTER THE "PLEASANT THINGS" OF HEAVEN. Philip Henry often said, when he had finished the delightful exercises of the Sabbath, "Well, if this be not the way to heaven, I know not what is." Yes, these are introductory to the glory that shall be revealed: they are foretastes to endear it, and earnests to insure it. And when you come to die—if you can say, in sincerity, "Lord, I have loved the habitation of thy house, and the place where thy honour dwelleth"—you may plead with confidence, "Gather not my soul with sinners, nor my life with bloody men." No: he will not gather you, in eternity, with those you never loved in time. Being let go, you shall join your own company, and be for "ever with the Lord."—And if the streams be so sweet, what will the fountain be? "In his presence *there is ful-*

ness of joy, and at his right hand *there are pleasures for evermore!"* Let us sing—

> " These are the joys he lets us know,
> In fields and villages below ;
> Gives us a relish of his love,
> But keeps his noblest feast above.
>
> " In paradise, within the gates,
> A higher entertainment waits:
> Fruits new and old, laid up in store,
> Where we shall feed, but thirst no more."

DISCOURSE XIII.

NEARNESS TO THE CROSS.

Now there stood by the cross of Jesus his mother, and his mother's sister, Mary the wife of Cleophas, and Mary Magdalene. When Jesus therefore saw his mother, and the disciple standing by, whom he loved, he saith unto his mother, Woman, behold thy son! Then saith he to the disciple, Behold thy mother! And from that hour that disciple took her unto his own home.—John xix. 25—27.

THIS is one of the most remarkable passages in the history of our Saviour's passion. The language is peculiarly simple and affecting. The scene is exquisitely tender. The characters are in the highest degree interesting ; and the circumstances in which they are placed, altogether new and wonderful. O for a class of feelings becoming the subject! Let us fix our minds on three things. I. THE SITUATION OF THE MOTHER. II. THE ADDRESS OF THE SAVIOUR. III. THE OBEDIENCE OF THE DISCIPLE.

Women are more than once brought forward in the Gospel, and the notice taken of them is always to their honour. Thus, while others have forsaken him and fled, we here find three females rising above the fears of their sex, braving the horrors of the execution, piercing through the crowd, and approaching the foot of the cross—there to testify their sympathy with their suffering Lord —to show how willing they are to die with him—to admire his patience and his meekness—and to secure his dying words. " Now there stood by the cross of Jesus his mother, and his mother's sister, Mary the wife of Cleophas, and Mary Magdalene." What were the feelings of these three Marys! But—

I. The MOTHER OF OUR LORD IN THIS SITUATION demands a larger share of our notice. I admire in her the efficacy of Divine grace. She is able to *stand* near the cross; she does not faint away and drop down. She keeps her feelings within due bounds. Here are no outrageous exclamations, no bitter complaints flung at Heaven for not avenging him of his adversaries, no imprecations on his murderers, no rending of garments, no wringing of hands, no plucking of the hair! She feels as a mother, she endures as a Christian; and, submitting to the mysterious designs of Providence, suffers with all the dignity of an angel.

The people of God know not what they can bear, till they are tried. When the " time of need" comes, then comes " the grace to help," and it is always found to be sufficient for them. I shall never despair of the support of a Christian, in any situation, however distressing, after beholding Mary standing near the cross of her dying son. Ye tender mothers, who may be called to part with beloved children! remember, religion allows you to feel, but forbids you to faint. You are not to be swallowed up of over-much sorrow, but to preserve a calm of mind favourable to the exercises of reason and of grace. You are to endeavour to say, " It is the Lord, let him do what seemeth him good: the Lord gave, and the Lord hath taken away, and blessed be the name of the Lord." Think of Mary, and say —" What can my affliction be, compared with hers!"

For who can adequately imagine her anguish! When old Simeon saw the infant Messiah, he said to his mother, " Yea, and a sword shall pierce through thy own soul also!" And now the prediction is accomplished.—Oh! to see her son enduring *such* a death! Suspended in torture! Oh! how would she agonize when she saw the nails driven through his hands and feet! And then for *such a son* to endure all this extreme of anguish!—a child foretold by prophets, announced by angels—all goodness, excellency, perfection!—who had never displeased her, but endeared himself by every word, by every action!—A child, the glory of her house, the consolation of her age—for to crown all, she was now a widow! Joseph her husband was dead—but Jesus her son was yet alive, and in his power and kindness she was sure to find a resource. But now her remaining prop is struck away, and her " only coal in Israel is quenched!" And she is to be thrown out, a bereaved, exposed, helpless, pennyless widow, upon a selfish, unfeeling, cruel world!

II. In such a condition, and with such prospects, she attracts the eye of our Lord; and HE SPEAKS. He addresses her in a manner suited to her trying circumstances. " When Jesus therefore saw his mother, and the disciple standing by, whom he loved—he saith unto his mother—Woman, Behold thy son!" Though I die, there is one who will discharge the filial office; who will guard, and nourish, and provide for thee—*Behold thy son!* Then saith he to the disciple—" Behold thy mother! Receive her—not as a pauper, or a mere pensioner on thy bounty, but regard her, as you would the tenderest of all connexions—*Behold thy mother!"*

This is very instructive. It reminds us, first, of the indigence of our Lord and Saviour. Many talk of poverty, but he *was* poor. In ordinary cases he was sustained by alms; in extraordinary ones, by miracles. When he came to die, he had no personal property, no landed estate to leave. All he had to bequeath was his wearing apparel; and even this never came to his mother. "They parted his raiment among them, and for his vesture did they cast lots: these things therefore the soldiers did."

What becomes then of riches? Are we such fools as to fall down and worship this idol of general adoration? Does money produce—does it imply—worth? A man may be an apostle, and be moneyless. "Silver and gold have I none," says Peter. "Foxes have holes, and the birds of the air have nests, but the Son of man hath not where to lay his head"—yet he was "the brightness of the Father's glory, and the express image of his person?"—But, alas! all this will not keep numbers from thinking money the essence of all excellency. Money can add charms to ugliness: money can transform wrinkles into youth: money can fill brainless heads with wisdom, and render nonsense oracular: money can turn meanness into virtue; and, falling like snow, can cover a dunghill, and give it the appearance of whiteness and innocency!

Behold, secondly, an instance of the Divine goodness, which ought to encourage the poor and needy. When one comfort is withdrawn, another is furnished. When Jesus is removed, John is raised up. A Christian should never despair. Our heavenly Father has more than one way of providing for his children. His resources are innumerable and inexhaustible. "O fear the Lord, all ye his saints; for there is no want to them that fear him: the young lions do lack and suffer hunger; but they that seek the Lord shall not want any good thing." Let those who are dying without wealth, and have nothing to leave behind them, hear him saying, "Leave thy fatherless children; I will preserve them alive: and let thy widows trust in me." Let those who fear that by bereavement they shall be reduced and impoverished, say, with David, "When my father and my mother forsake me, then the Lord will take me up. In him the fatherless findeth mercy."

Thirdly, we learn that we should endeavour to be useful, not only living, but dying. We see the Saviour attentive to the duty of every season, and every circumstance. Never so occupied, even by his sufferings, as to forget others: he dies as he had lived; and not only when "going about," but even when nailed to the cross, we behold him—"*doing good!*"

A Christian, if he has not done it before, should now "set his house in order." He should arrange his affairs, and dispose of his effects, and secure guardians for his children —so as not to occasion perplexity and discord after his decease. He should be also attentive to the spiritual improvement of those around him. If able to speak, he should recommend the Saviour, and speak well of his ways. Dying words are impressive. This is the last time you can do any thing for your generation. "By faith Jacob, when he was dying, blessed both the sons of Joseph, and worshipped, leaning upon the top of his staff." "Now the days of David drew nigh that he should die; and he charged Solomon his son, saying, I go the way of all the earth: be thou strong therefore, and show thyself a man; and keep the charge of the Lord thy God, to walk in his ways, to keep his statutes, and his commandments, and his judgments, and his testimonies, as it is written in the law of Moses, that thou mayest prosper in all that thou doest, and whithersoever thou turnest thyself." Mr. Bolton said to his children, who stood around his dying bed, "See that none of you meet me in an unconverted state at the day of judgment." Dr. Rivet said, in his last illness, "Let all who come to inquire after my welfare be allowed to see me: I ought to be an example in death as well as in life."

Fourthly. A lesson of filial piety is clearly deducible from this subject. Children are under an obligation to succour and relieve their parents according to their ability. And this is not to be considered as charity, so much as common justice. The Apostle therefore calls it a requiting:—"Let them requite their parents." I admire the disposition of David, who, when wandering from place to place, seemed regardless of himself, if he could provide a safe and comfortable situation for his father and mother: "He went to Mizpeh of Moab: and he said unto the king of Moab, Let my father and my mother, I pray thee, come forth and be with you, till I know what God will do for me." I admire still more David's Son and David's Lord, who, even in the agony of crucifixion, commends his poor mother to the care of the beloved disciple.

And here you ask—but why did he this? Could he not have provided for her himself? —He who turned water into wine, and made a few loaves sufficient to feed a whole multitude—could not he have furnished means for the subsistence of a destitute mother? Behold, in answer to this, another reflection. He does not needlessly work miracles. The manna which followed the Israelites in the wilderness ceased as soon as they could provide themselves with the corn of the land. He generally fulfils his kind designs by common means, and in the established course of things. His care extends to the poor as well as to the rich. He has made the rich stewards, but not proprietors: he has given them an abundance, not to hoard up, but to expend and to administer. And the poor and distressed are as much consigned by Providence to the care of the affluent, as Mary was charged upon John. None of God's benefits terminate wholly on the possessor—they are means as well as mercies, talents as well as endowments. If we are enlightened, we are to "arise and shine;" if converted, we are to "strengthen our brethren;" if comforted, we are to "comfort others with those comforts wherewith we ourselves are comforted of God;" if we have "all things richly to enjoy," we are to be "ready to communicate, willing to distribute."

Suppose a master should call into his presence a servant, and say to him, "Take this money, and go, carry it to such a poor family;" and suppose the servant, as soon as he had gotten possession of it, should resolve to keep it, or lay it out on some finery or amusement; what would you think? Would you blame the master, as wanting in generosity? No—but you would say, "O thou wicked servant!" And what would the master himself say?—Surely he would punish him; and he would well deserve it: for he would be at once guilty of unfaithfulness and cruelty. Such a master indeed may never find out this villany. But the rich are going to appear before a God who "cannot be mocked," to give an account of the application of the property which he committed to their trust, for certain purposes which his word clearly specifies. It was given them to teach the ignorant, to clothe the naked, to "make the widow's heart to sing for joy"—Wo! wo be to them, if they shall be found to have frustrated the kindness of his designs, either by not using, or by wasting his goods!

Once more. John was "the disciple whom Jesus loved:" he had a peculiar friendship for him—and how does he express it? Not by diminishing his care, but by enlarging the claims of his duty; not by increasing his estate, but by giving him a consumer—consigning to him an aged female for life. You may deem this a strange proof of his affection—a strange way of honouring him! But, if you view the matter aright, you will see that there is nothing unaccountable in it. To be employed by him and for him is a dignity and a privilege. If he pleased, he could well dispense with our poor services; but he engages us—to improve our graces, and to reward our exertions. And, in proportion as we are in a good frame of mind, we shall long to be instruments in the Saviour's hands, and bringing ourselves daily to his footstool, we shall ask, "Lord, what wilt thou have me to do?" John, therefore,

III. EXECUTES THE ORDERS OF HIS DYING LORD. "From that hour that disciple took her unto his own home." He does not stand weighing things: "Can I afford to do it? Shall I not entail upon myself expenses for life? and not only so, but trouble also—yea, and reproach and suspicion, by accommodating the mother of one who was executed as a malefactor—an enemy to Cæsar?"—He obeys cheerfully, instantly, implicitly.

And let us remember, that true obedience is prompt; and will lead us to "do all things without murmuring and disputing." This is peculiarly the case with regard to charity. Real benevolence, if I may so express it, is not too longsighted and thoughtful; it will not suffer the fine impulse to cool by indulging hesitations: when an obligation strikes us, it will not allow of our eluding it by giving us either inclination or time to bring forward the hardness of the times, the slackness of trade, the increase of family, the multiplicity of cases. While we stop to investigate every particular, to make comparisons, to collect evidences, and to take great pains not to be deceived—the opportunity is gone: our neighbour may not be alive a few days hence, or we may not—and thus, by cautious and delayed beneficence, he will lose the relief, and we the honour of the action. Therefore, says Solomon, "Withhold not good from them to whom it is due, when it is in the power of thine hand to do it. Say not unto thy neighbour, go, and come again, and to-morrow I will give, when thou hast it by thee."

To return. Let us now follow the mother of our Lord to her new residence. Venerable woman, whom all generations have blessed, we rejoice in thy comfort! Thou hast "a certain dwelling-place," thou shalt not want!—With what kindness would John treat the charge of his departed Lord! With what tenderness would he nourish her! How many evenings would they pass together in discoursing of the Saviour ascended to his Father, and their Father, to his God and their God! How would they dwell upon his sermons, his miracles, his sufferings! We meet once more with this distinguished woman in the sacred history. In the beginning of the Acts of the Apostles, we find the twelve returning from the place of his ascension, and in an upper room; and it is said, "They continued with one accord, in prayer and supplication with the women, and Mary the mother of Jesus." After this she disappears, and we hear of her no more. But we shall by-and-by see her, and derive from her all the interesting particulars relative to the birth, the infancy, the youth of the child Jesus, over which, for wise purposes, a veil is now thrown.

Let me conclude by calling upon you to choose for yourselves the *situation* of these three women—they were "standing *by the cross* of Jesus. *There*, by reading the Scripture, by meditation, by the exercises of faith, by the memorials of his death—*there* you may fix yourselves. It is a blessed station:

take it, and "determine to know nothing save Jesus Christ and him crucified."

Do you wish to contemplate whatever is grand and sublime? Take this station. Behold him on the cross—See "the Sun of righteousness," as he sets, gilding the heavens with glory. See him, as he dies, exercising every grace, displaying every perfection!

Does the world prevail over thee? Take this station. Exclaim, with the Apostle, "God forbid that I should glory, save in the cross of our Lord Jesus Christ, by whom the world is crucified unto me, and I unto the world!

> "His dying crimson, like a robe,
> Spreads o'er his body on the tree:
> Then am I dead to all the globe,
> And all the globe is dead to me."

Do you feel trials and afflictions? Take this station. Behold a suffering Saviour. "Consider him that endured such contradiction of sinners against himself, lest ye be wearied and faint in your minds."

> "Thousands have found the bless'd effect,
> Nor longer mourn their lot:
> While on his sorrows they reflect,
> Their own are all forgot."

Are you oppressed with a sense of guilt? Take this station. Bruised by sin, remember him who was bruised for it. Be of good cheer. "Surely he hath borne our grief, and carried our sorrows; the chastisement of our peace was upon him, and by his stripes we are healed."

Do you wish for an example? Take this station. Behold here not only your sacrifice, but your pattern. While he atones, he instructs. "He suffered for us, leaving us an example that we should follow his steps: who did no sin, neither was guile found in his mouth: who, when he was reviled, reviled not again; when he suffered, he threatened not; but committed himself to him that judgeth righteously"—who, full of forgiveness, prayed for enemies, and said, "Father, forgive them, for they know not what they do" —who, all affection and concern for his relations, said, Woman, behold thy son!" Son, behold thy mother! Ye children, admire him. Admire him, ye friends. Admire him, ye disciples, who wear his honoured name— "nor stop at wonder—imitate and live." May we "be planted together in the likeness of his death, that we may be also in the likeness of his resurrection."

DISCOURSE XIV.

THE THRONE OF GRACE.

Let us come boldly unto the throne of grace, that we may obtain mercy, and find grace to help in time of need.—Heb. iv. 16.

PRAYER is of so much importance; it is such an honour, such a privilege, such a

means of sanctifying, relieving, enriching the soul—that he who teaches us to pray is our best friend; and there is nothing we should more highly prize than those instructions which are designed to regulate and encourage our addresses to God.

And such is the design of the Apostle in the words which I have read. He tells us of a throne of grace, and informs us in what manner, and for what purpose we are to approach it. "Let us come boldly unto the throne of grace, that we may obtain mercy, and find grace to help in time of need."

The language is metaphorical. When God enacts laws, he is on a throne of legislation; when he administers these laws, he is on a throne of government; when he tries his creatures by these laws, he is on a throne of judgment; and when he receives petitions and dispenses favours, he is on a "*throne of grace.*"

The idea of a throne inspires awe, bordering on terror. It repels rather than invites. Few of us could approach it without trembling. But what is the throne of an earthly monarch, the greatest earthly monarch that ever swayed a sceptre? The God we address is "the King of kings, and the Lord of lords." In his eye, an Alexander is a worm; yea "all nations before him are as nothing, less than nothing, and vanity. Heaven is his throne, and this earth is only his footstool." How can we enter his presence, or approach his infinite majesty?—Blessed be his name, he fills the "mercy-seat;" he is on a "throne of grace;" and we are allowed, and even commanded, to come to it *boldly.* But

I. IT IS NECESSARY FOR US TO KNOW WHAT THIS BOLDNESS IS.

And we may be assured that it is not audacity, rudeness, or a trifling freedom. We have sometimes heard persons address God, in a manner which they would not dare to use, I will not say to a superior, but even to a fellow-creature of their own level. Such persons would do well to compare Scripture with Scripture. For what is the language of the Bible in other places? "God is greatly to be feared in the assembly of the saints, and to be had in reverence of all them that are about him." "Be not rash with thy mouth, and let not thine heart be hasty to utter any thing before God: for God is in heaven, and thou upon earth, therefore let thy words be few." "Wherefore we receiving a kingdom which cannot be moved, let us have grace, whereby we may serve God acceptably, with reverence, and godly fear. For our God is a consuming fire." They would also do well to remember the nature of the business in which they are engaged; for if we are imploring "mercy and grace," common sense will tell us, that the boldness we are allowed to indulge, can be only the boldness of a penitent and a suppli-

G 5

cant. Now an encouragement to beg, is not surely a license to offend. Prayer and insolence ill accord together.

This boldness then, arises from nothing in ourselves, but purely from the goodness of the Being we address—and it consists principally in a persuasion that we are freely authorized to come, and may confidently hope to succeed.

What a change is made in the view and feelings of a person by conviction of sin! Sin was once nothing in his view; but now, awakened to consider, and enlightened to perceive its nature and consequences, he feels it to be the greatest evil: as before he could not be made to fear, he can scarcely now be induced to hope. Knowing his desert, and judging under the influence of human and guilty feelings, he finds it difficult to believe that God will receive him—But till he *does* believe this, he will not, he cannot come to him aright. God has therefore made provision to excite and sustain the confidence of self-condemned sinners.

He has revealed himself, not as implacable, but as full of pity and compassion, as "the Lord God gracious and merciful." He has "commended his love towards us, in that while we were yet sinners, Christ died for us." The conclusion is not more justly drawn, than it is infinitely encouraging: "He that spared not his own Son, but delivered him up for us all, how shall he not with him also freely give us all things? Surely he hath borne our grief, and carried our sorrow, the chastisement of our peace was upon him, and by his stripes we are healed." His blood "cleanseth us from all sin. He is the end of the law for righteousness to every one that believeth." He "suffered, the just for the unjust, that he might bring us unto God." I mention this the more fully, because we "come unto God by him:" and in proportion to our knowledge of the Mediator, and our reliance upon him, will be our enlargement and consolation in duty. It is here that our hopes take their rise: it is here that we are "filled with all joy and peace in believing." "In whom, [speaking of Christ, says the Apostle,] we have boldness and access with confidence by the faith of him. And again, having therefore, brethren, boldness to enter into the holiest by the blood of Jesus, by a new and living way which he hath consecrated for us, through the vail, that is to say, his flesh; and having an high priest over the house of God; let us draw near, with a true heart, in full assurance of faith, having our hearts sprinkled from an evil conscience, and our bodies washed with pure water."

We have also "exceeding great and precious promises"—such as these: "God so loved the world, that he gave his only begotten Son, that whosoever believeth in him should not perish, but have everlasting life."

"Let the wicked forsake his way, and the unrighteous man his thoughts; and let him return unto the Lord, and he will have mercy upon him; and to our God, for he will abundantly pardon. For my thoughts are not your thoughts, neither are your ways my ways, saith the Lord. For as the heavens are higher than the earth, so are my ways higher than your ways, and my thoughts than your thoughts."

To illustrate these promises, and to banish every fear, that springing from unworthiness and guilt, would hinder our application to him, he has been pleased to add a succession of examples. Some of these are derived from characters the most vile: but vile as they once were, "they were washed, they were sanctified, they were justified in the name of the Lord Jesus, and by the Spirit of our God." Among men, the chief offenders are always made examples of justice—but here they have frequently been made the examples of mercy. Civil governors are afraid to pardon the most criminal lest they should operate as encouragements—but here they are designed to be precedents: "for this cause I obtained mercy, that in me first Jesus Christ might show forth all long-suffering as a pattern to them that should believe on him to life everlasting." By these instances he has said—"Never despair.—See what I can do. Learn that neither the number nor the heinousness of your sins shall destroy you, if you are willing 'to obtain salvation by the Lord Jesus Christ.'"

In time also, the believer's own experience much aids his confidence. Though he has no more dependence upon himself than he once had, he learns to trust more simply and firmly in him who has never "turned away his prayer," but has been "a very present help in every time of trouble."

This boldness takes in not only a confidence of success, but also "a holy liberty in our addresses to him, expressive of intimacy and privilege." Are we Christians? We come not as strangers and foreigners, but as fellow-citizens with the saints, and of "the household of God." "We have received, not the spirit of bondage again to fear, but the Spirit of adoption, whereby we cry, Abba, Father!" Other monarchs can be approached only at certain seasons; and in certain cases; and with certain formalities. But you may call upon him at "all times;" and in all "circumstances." You may "in every thing make known your requests unto God." You may go and inform him of all that perplexes, all that alarms, all that distresses you. He deems nothing too little for you to spread before him. You may tell him what you can tell no earthly friend. And you are not required to keep at a distance, but allowed to come "even to his seat—to order your cause before him—to fill your mouth with arguments—to put him in remembrance—to plead with him"—to persevere, and not "let him go except he bless you."

II. Having considered the manner in which, let us observe THE PURPOSES FOR WHICH WE ARE TO COME TO THE THRONE OF GRACE. They are these—to "obtain mercy"—and to "find grace." These blessings are wisely connected together by the Apostle, because there are too many people who try to separate them. They would be saved from hell, but not from sin. They wish to be pardoned, but not renewed. They would have mercy, but not grace.

But be not deceived. Whom God forgives he sanctifies and prepares for his service. And both these blessings are equally important and necessary to our salvation. Let us therefore pray for both.

First. Pray for *mercy.* And pray like those who know they greatly need it. You are verily guilty. You are charged with innumerable transgressions, and your consciences tell you that many of them are attended with circumstances of peculiar aggravation. Till these are pardoned, you are in a state of condemnation: and what a doom is that which is denounced upon you by the law which you have broken! Think of "the wrath of God." Think of the "worm that dieth not, and the fire that is never to be quenched. It is a fearful thing to fall into the hands of the living God!"

And you are continually liable to the execution of this sentence. You *must* die soon, you *may* die this very night; this very hour: and then it will be too late to cry for mercy. Be prevailed upon therefore to seek it immediately and earnestly—"Have mercy upon me, O God, according to thy lovingkindness: according unto the multitude of thy tender mercies, blot out my transgressions."

But we shall need the exercise of mercy as long as we are in the body. We often contract fresh guilt. Our most holy things are defiled. "Who can say, I have made my heart clean; I am pure from my sin?" Archbishop Usher often said he hoped to die with the language of the publican in his mouth; and his biographer tells us his wish was fulfilled—he died, saying, "God be merciful to me, a sinner." What an exalted character is given us of Onesiphorus! Yet, says the Apostle, "the Lord grant unto him, that *he* may find"—not justice—but "*mercy* of the Lord in that day." He would need mercy till then, and then he would need it more than ever. And when we all come to appear before his righteous tribunal, to have our actions and our motives tried—"should he mark iniquity, who could stand?" Let us therefore say, with Job, "Though I were righteous, yet would I not answer him; but I would make supplication to my Judge."

Secondly. Let us pray for "grace to help in time of need." But is not every time a time of need with us? It is. And there is not a moment in our existence in which we can live as we ought, independently of Divine grace. We need this grace, to mortify our corruptions; to sanctify our affections; to resist temptations; to overcome the world. It is this, and this alone, that can enable us to pursue our journey; to run our race; to accomplish our warfare; to "endure to the end." We cannot pray, or sing, or hear, or read, as we ought, without the assistance of this grace helping our infirmities. "We cannot," says Bishop Hopkins, "stand one moment longer than God holds us; or walk one step further than God leads us." For a thing constantly necessary, the Apostle would teach us to pray constantly.

But there are some seasons in which we peculiarly require the aid of Divine grace. Two or three of these it may be proper to mention.

Prosperity is a time of need. Few "know how to abound." It is no easy thing to be full, and not deny God. Worldly fame and affluence have often had a baneful effect on the minds of good men; have attached them too strongly to earth, and slackened their diligence in seeking "a better, even a heavenly country." They have had less dependence upon God, and less communion with him. They have grown high minded and illiberal; and exhibited far less of the Christian in their advancement than in their poverty. Others have lost their religion entirely in passing from a cottage to a mansion. "The prosperity of fools shall destroy them." Let us therefore be wise, and remember, that the wisdom which can alone preserve us consists in our fearing always; in a diffidence of ourselves; in our praying, "hold thou me up, and I shall be safe." He indeed can keep us from falling, even in slippery places. Thus he guarded Joseph and Daniel, in situations equally high and dangerous.

Affliction is a time of need. It matters not from what quarter the trouble springs: it is a trying season; and the Christian is concerned to "come forth as gold." He not only wants support and comfort, so that he may not "faint," but he wants strength and preservation, so that he may not sin. He is concerned to be secured from impatience; from distrust of Providence; from quarreling with instruments. He wishes to glorify God in the fires; and to derive advantages from his crosses, so as to be able to say, "It is good for me that I have been afflicted." For all this he seeks the Lord; and what the Lord said to Paul he may apply unto himself: "My grace is sufficient for thee: for my strength is made perfect in weakness."

Death is a time of need. And it is an unavoidable one—other times of need *may* come, but this *will* come. It is indeed the last time of need—but it is also the greatest. It is new and untried. It settles every thing for ever. It is awful to let go our hold of earth, to give up the soul into the hand of God, to enter eternity. The enemy also now uses all his force to distress: for there are two seasons in which he is peculiarly busy: when we are coming to Christ for grace—and when we are going to him for glory. Now others may endeavour to banish this subject from their minds; but the Christian *must* think of it. And he will be concerned to die safely—as to consequences; honourably—as to religion; comfortably—as to himself; and usefully—as to others. And what can be done here without grace to help—to help in this time of need! If many Christians, who are now cast down, were but assured that their sun would set without a cloud, they would be filled with strong consolation, bear cheerfully their trials, and look forward to every future scene with pleasure. Well, grace *can* do this, and *has* done it for many; and even for many who were "once walking mournfully before the Lord!" When the time of need came, then came the grace—suffering grace for a suffering hour—and dying grace for a dying hour.

Now if this be our errand in prayer—if we are to pray—"that we may obtain mercy, and find grace to help in time of need," does it not follow, as a fair inference from the subject, that a prayerless person is destitute both of the mercy and grace of God? This is an awful truth; and it leads me, before I conclude, seriously to ask you—

First. Have you come to this throne? Have you ever prayed? Perhaps you have sometimes dragged through the duty as a task—but did you ever feel it to be your privilege and your pleasure? Perhaps you have engaged in it occasionally—but has it been your habitual employment? Perhaps you have called upon God in the hour of sickness and danger—but, as health returned, have you not discontinued prayer by little and little, till you have lived entirely without him in the world? You have frequently attended public worship—do you pray much in your closet; or, in the duties of your calling, do you send up many a desire to God, saying, "Lord, help me?" You are fond of hearing sermons—but while you so often hear from God, does God ever hear from you?

Secondly. Do you design to come? or have you resolved to "restrain prayer before him?"

Do you imagine you can acquire these blessings in any other way than by prayer? This is impossible: "For all these things," says God, "will I be inquired of:" "Ask, and it shall be given you; seek, and ye shall find; knock, and it shall be opened unto you."

Or do you imagine these blessings are not worthy of your pursuit? Alas! strange as it may appear, I suspect that this is the case. You are not prepared to estimate these advantages. You do not feel your need of mercy and grace; otherwise surely you would deem them worth asking for. If you could gain a fortune by prayer—would you not pray? Or health—would you not pray? But what are these to mercy and grace? These comprise every other blessing—and nothing else can be a blessing without them.

Or do you imagine they are not to be gained? There is no ground for such despair: he "waiteth to be gracious; and is exalted to have mercy." "Come, for all things are now ready." None are excluded. All are welcome.

Yet if one class of petitioners could be more welcome and successful than another, it would be the YOUNG: "I love them that love me; and they that seek me *early* shall find me."

DISCOURSE XV.

SUMMER AND HARVEST.

He that gathereth in summer is a wise son: but he that sleepeth in harvest is a son that causeth shame.—PROV. x. 5.

WHAT a scene of desolation was presented to the eye of Noah when he opened the door of the ark! No human face appeared. The earth was stripped of all its beauty; and no trees, no plants, no grass were to be seen. The effects of the Deluge were everywhere awfully visible; and every cloud, every wind, excited alarm. In this condition he offered a sacrifice. God accepted it—and to dissipate his fears, and to draw forth his confidence, he said, "While the earth remaineth, seed-time and harvest, cold and heat, and summer and winter, and day and night, shall not cease."

Each of these periods is not only useful, but instructive. We cheerfully part with the dreary hours of winter, to embrace the reviving spring; and as readily resign the growing hours of spring, to welcome the joyful harvest. When, under Divine Providence, this season arrives, "the year is crowned with his goodness; the earth is full of his riches;" and the husbandman is called forth to secure the golden produce. He is reasonably expected to make every concern give place to this, and to exert all his diligence to improve the short, but all-important period. Hence the reflection of Solomon: "He that gathereth in summer is a wise son; but he that sleepeth in harvest is a son that causeth shame."

Common sense readily acquiesces in this truth. But let us accommodate the subject to moral and spiritual purposes. Let us represent YOUR HARVEST SEASON; and enforce upon you the NECESSITY OF DILIGENCE IN USING IT.

I. God affords you OPPORTUNITIES FOR GOOD. He favours you with seasons which may be considered as your harvest.

In this view we may regard the whole period of life. While you are continued in this world, you have "space for repentance; and the longsuffering of our Lord is salvation."

You are blessed with a season of Gospel grace. While many are sitting in darkness, and in the region of the shadow of death, upon you "hath the light shined, to guide your feet into the way of peace." You not only live in a country where there is a written revelation, but your "eyes see your teachers, and your ears hear a voice behind you, saying, This is the way, walk ye in it, when ye turn aside to the right hand, or to the left." Though the preaching of the word is neglected by some, and despised by others, it is an invaluable privilege. By this, the Scripture is explained to the mind, and enforced on the conscience: by this, you are warned of your danger, and encouraged to flee for refuge; you are called upon to draw nigh, and assured that "all things are now ready." "Faith cometh by hearing; and hearing, by the word of God."

And this reminds us that you have a season of civil and religious liberty. You have the Bible in your hands, and are not fined for reading it. You may assemble together in public, and hear the word of life without danger. Your devotions are sanctioned by law, and you may "sit under your own vine, and under your own fig-tree, and none make you afraid." What advantages do we possess, above many of our ancestors who suffered for conscience' sake! They laboured, and we have entered into their labours. "They took joyfully the spoiling of their goods. They had trial of cruel mockings and scourgings; yea, moreover, of bonds and imprisonment. They were stoned, they were sawn asunder, were tempted, were slain with the sword: they wandered about in sheepskins and goatskins: being destitute, afflicted, tormented: of whom the world was not worthy: they wandered in deserts, and in mountains, and in dens, and caves of the earth."

Some are living in a religious family, where they have the benefit of instruction, prayer, and example. Some, like Timothy, have been trained up by a mother and a grandmother, of unfeigned faith, and, "from a child, have known the Scriptures, which are able to make us wise unto salvation."

Who, in passing through a vale of tears, has not experienced a day of trouble? From such a period, many have had to date their saving acquaintance with Divine things. Affliction is favourable to religion: it abstracts, it softens, its awes the mind: it strips the world of its attractions, and starves us out of the creature into God.

Where is the person, who does not know what we mean by a season of conviction? Conscience has sometimes forced you to a stand. Like Felix, you have trembled under the power of the world to come. You have sometimes been pleasingly affected: you have wept, and prayed, and sighed—"Now, Lord, what wait I for? my hope is in thee."

But can I forget another season? Can I forget to urge the admonition of wisdom and friendship—"Remember now thy Creator, in the days of thy *youth*, while the evil days come not, nor the years draw nigh when thou shalt say, I have no pleasure in them!"— Never, never, my young friends, will you have a season in which your hinderances are so few, or your helps so many. Every thing now invites; every thing constrains you. "Behold, now is the accepted time; behold, now is the day of salvation."

II. I would enforce upon you the NECESSITY OF DILIGENCE TO IMPROVE YOUR REAPING SEASON.

And first. Consider how much you have to accomplish. You have the work of a husbandman in harvest—Will this allow you to be drowsy and idle? Does it not require you to rise early, and be active all the day? To seize every moment, and secure every assistance? The salvation of the soul is a great and arduous concern; and many things are required of you. For though you are not left to yourselves, nor called to act in your own strength, yet religion is a race, and you must run; it is a warfare, and you must fight. The blessings of the Gospel are free, but they are to be sought and gained. It is God that "worketh in us to will and to do of his own good pleasure;" but we are commanded, notwithstanding this, yea, because of this, to "work out our salvation with fear and trembling." Spring then from the bed of sloth; shake off every impediment: you have sins to be pardoned, passions to be subdued, graces to be exercised, duties to be performed—a harvest to gather in!

Secondly. Consider the worth of the blessings that demand your attention. The advantages held forth by the prospect of harvest animate the husbandman to diligence, and reconcile him to exertion; but what are the blessings of the field, compared with the blessings of salvation! The one is perishable, the other is eternal—the one is for the body only, the other is for the soul. What is an earthly portion in a barn, to "an inheritance incorruptible and undefiled, and that fadeth not away, reserved in heaven for us!" I would address you as rational creatures. Is it not desirable to be redeemed from the curse of the law? to be justified freely from every charge brought against us at the bar of God? to be delivered from the tyranny and rage of vicious appetites and passions? Great is the happiness of those that belong to God here;

ut who can describe the exalted glory and joy that await them hereafter? Do you not wish to enter in with those who shall be for ever with the Lord? "They shall hunger no more, neither thirst any more; neither shall the sun light on them, nor any heat. For the Lamb which is in the midst of the throne shall feed them, and shall lead them unto living fountains of waters; and God shall wipe away all tears from their eyes." Will not this indemnify you for every sacrifice, and abundantly recompense all your toil?

Thirdly. Remember that your labour will not be in vain in the Lord. "Be not weary in well-doing, for in due time you shall reap if you faint not." The husbandman has many uncertainties to contend with; insects, blights, droughts, and storms—but *probability* stimulates *him*,—how much more should actual *certainty* encourage *you!* "They that sow in tears shall reap in joy. He that goeth forth and weepeth, bearing precious seed, shall doubtless come again with rejoicing, bringing his sheaves with him."

Fourthly. Remember that your season for action is limited and short. Harvest does not last long. Your time in the whole compass of it is but "a few days:" and how little of it deserves the name of life, or can be applied to any important services. When infancy, sleep, business, recreations have engrossed their share—is the remainder, think you, too long a period to acquire the kingdom of God and his righteousness? But your time is uncertain as well as short. The present only is yours—you know not what a day or an hour may bring forth. The fool in the Gospel talked of "goods laid up for many years," when he had but a few moments left: God put his finger upon his conscience, and said, "Thou fool, this night shall thy soul be required of thee." "Man knoweth not his time: as the fishes that are taken in an evil net, and as the birds that are caught in the snare, so are the sons of men snared in an evil time when it falleth suddenly upon them." Youth is no certain protection from the grave. Death does not go by age, nor does it always wait till it has sent a warning. Your time is always in motion: if you are idle, time is not; but hurrying you forwards. If you do not perceive your progress, every hour, every moment, brings you nearer to your end. And your time once gone, cannot be recalled. God has plainly told you that there is a season when he will not be found: "therefore seek ye the Lord while he may be found, call ye upon him while he is near." In vain those who despised the warnings of Noah clung to the sides of the ark when the door was shut: it was then too late. "Strive to enter in at the strait gate: for many, I say unto you, will seek to enter in and shall not be able. When once the master of the house is risen up, and hath shut to the door, and ye

begin to stand without, and to knock at the door, saying, Lord, Lord, open unto us; and he shall answer and say unto you, I know ye not, whence ye are: then shall ye begin to say, we have eaten and drunk in thy presence, and thou hast taught in our streets. But he shall say, I tell you, I know you not whence ye are: depart from me, all ye workers of iniquity. There shall be weeping and gnashing of teeth, when ye shall see Abraham, and Isaac, and Jacob, and all the prophets, in the kingdom of God, and you yourselves thrust out."

Therefore, finally. Reflect upon the consequences of negligence. Is a man blamed for sleeping in harvest? Does every one reproach him as a fool? Does he deserve to suffer famine? You act a part far more absurd and fatal who "neglect this great salvation," and will not embrace "in this your day the things that belong to your peace before they are hid from your eyes." Having made no provision for futurity—for eternity, your ruin is unavoidable. It will also be insupportable. "It shall be more tolerable for Tyre and Sidon at the day of judgment than for you." For a strict account will then be required of all your talents and opportunities: and what can you answer? O the feelings of sinners in hell who have perished under the means of grace!—How will their consciences upbraid and condemn them? O the anguish and despair of sinners, when, dropping from time into eternity, they exclaim, "The harvest is past, the summer is ended, and we are not saved?"

Let us conclude, first, by blessing God for the harvest with which he has again favoured our country. We went forth with anxious hope: we saw "first the blade, then the ear, and after that the full corn in the ear." We lifted up our eyes and saw "the fields already white unto harvest," and with tears of joy said, "Thou hast prepared of thy goodness for the poor." We only wanted "the appointed weeks of harvest"—and lo! the weather is favourable; and the precious treasure will soon be secured! "It shall come to pass in that day, I will hear, saith the Lord, I will hear the heavens, and they shall hear the earth, and the earth shall hear the corn, and the wine and oil; and they shall hear Jezreel." However numerous the means and the second causes are which concur to enrich us with plenteousness, God is the original mover, and to him our praise is to be addressed. Without his blessing, the ox would have ploughed, and the husbandman would have sowed, in vain. How easily could he have shrivelled up the grain by heat, drowned it by showers, destroyed it by insects! By his permission, an enemy might have invaded our borders, and war have spoiled "the finest of the wheat." Every thing is full of God, he lives through all life, and while seeming to do nothing, is doing all. "Every good gift, and every perfect gift, is from above, and cometh down from the Father of lights." To him let our praise ascend in a perpetual flow of affection and obedience. While we live upon Divine goodness, shall we never acknowledge it, or acknowledge it in word only! Is this our kindness to our Friend? O that our insensible hearts may be affected, and that "the goodness of God may lead us to repentance! O that men would praise the Lord for his goodness, and for his wonderful works to the children of men! Bless the Lord, O my soul!"

But let us remember, that "man liveth not by bread alone;" nor is he to "live here always." He has a soul within him, and an eternity before him; and he would be worse than a brute were he only concerned to provide for the inferior part of his nature, and the shortest period of his existence. What will these things be to us when we come to die? What are they now? We feel far greater wants now than any of these things are able to supply. We want "all spiritual blessings in heavenly places in Christ."

And, blessed be God, they are attainable. Let us therefore improve this season by making it a religious monitor. As we walk in the fields, or reflect while at home on the process of harvest, let us say, "O my soul, thou too hast thy season; and every thing forbids thee to be slothful. See 'the children of this world:' how wise they are 'in their generation:' And shall they labour so eagerly for 'the meat that perisheth,' and I be all indifference to acquire that 'meat which endureth unto everlasting life?' 'I must work the work of him that sent me while it is day: the night cometh when no man can work.'"

DISCOURSE XVI.

THE FUNERAL OF A YOUTH.

Now when he came nigh to the gate of the city, behold, there was a dead man carried out, the only son of his mother, and she was a widow: and much people of the city was with her. And when the Lord saw her, he had compassion on her, and said unto her, Weep not. And he came and touched the bier: and they that bare him stood still. And he said, Young man, I say unto thee, Arise. And he that was dead sat up, and began to speak. And he delivered him to his mother.—Luke vii. 12—15.

As we follow our Saviour in the evangelical history, we verify the words of the Apostle, when he says of him—"he went about doing good." This character marks his diligence, and the cause in which it was employ-ed. His life was one continued career of goodness. He did good to the soul and to the body. He did good by preaching, and by miracles.

Every thing recorded of him is worthy of our attention; but the narrative before us is beautiful and impressive in the highest degree. We behold grandeur blended with simplicity, and omnipotence with compassion. The circumstances progressively rise in importance; the mind is at last powerfully attracted to a single point, and all the passions remain in awful suspense, till the joyful event relieves us by a flood of tears.

The miracle requires a few REMARKS and a few REFLECTIONS.

The first thing we behold is a FUNERAL PROCESSION. This is a scene which we have all witnessed; a scene by no means unusual —but, alas! owing to its frequency and familiarity, it fails to impress. It is however an occurrence unspeakably interesting in itself, and it ought to rouse our attention. How many lessons, were we disposed to learn, would a funeral supply!

Place yourselves under a tree in a meadow, along which lies the pathway to the lonely churchyard. You say within yourself, "Here it comes, in slow and silent sadness. See! every one has some importance. Who could bear to die unmourned! What a loss is the death of some! See those who walk nearest to the corpse—these are the bereaved. The rest are friends and neighbours, and a heedless rabble drawn by the spectacle. 'Man goeth to his long home.' 'It is the end of all men, and the living should lay it to heart.' Soon the like services will be performed for me. When carried along myself, how insensible shall I be to all those things which now agitate and perplex me! Of what importance will it then be, whether I have been poor or rich, honourable or despised?—' But one thing is needful.' Oh! may I 'choose that good part which shall not be taken away from me.'—' Let me die the death of the righteous, and let my last end be like his.'"

But let us draw near, and contemplate this funeral solemnity. It was the funeral of a young man. We are not informed whether he died by disease or accident, slowly or suddenly; but he was carried off in the prime of life. "One dieth in his full strength, being wholly at ease and quiet. His breasts are full of milk, and his bones are moistened with marrow. Another dieth in the bitterness of his soul, and never eateth with pleasure. They shall lie down alike in the dust, and the worms shall cover them." "What is our life? It is even a vapour which appeareth for a little time, and then vanisheth away?" What is beauty, strength, youth! "Verily, every man, at his best estate, is altogether vanity." Think of this, ye young. Remember, the old are not the only victims of death. Enter churchyards: measure graves: read inscriptions:

> "——— What pathos in the date!
> — Few dorters preach so well!"

He was the "only son of his mother." There is an ocean of love in the hearts of parents towards their children. Witness the reluctance and exclamation of Jacob—" Me have ye bereaved of my children. Joseph is not, Simeon is not, and ye will take Benjamin away!—All these things are against me." Witness the mourning of David, even over a bad, a rebellious son. "The king was much moved, and went up to the chamber over the gate, and wept: and as he went, thus he said: O my son Absalom, my son, my son Absalom! would God I had died for thee, O Absalom, my son, my son!" But this parental affection is stronger on the side of the female, than of the male. Not only has the mother more natural sensibility and tenderness than the father, but the child, if I may so express it, is much more hers than his; it is hers by months of anxiety, and pangs of anguish; it is hers by a thousand nightly watchings and daily cares; it is hers by numberless pleasures given and received, in which neither stranger nor friend intermeddles with her joy. Thus the performance of duty is secured and sweetened. But that which renders duty a privilege, in the very same proportion increases the fear of loss, and the anguish of separation. What then were the feelings of this mother—deprived of her *only* son? Had he been one of many, the loss would have been partial, and the affliction more easily endured—but he was the only pledge of virtuous affection, the only hope of future years—her life was entirely bound up in his. Mourning for an only son is mentioned in the Scripture as the extreme of grief. "O daughter of my people, gird thee with sackcloth, and wallow thyself in ashes: make thee mourning, as for an only son, most bitter lamentation: for the spoiler shall suddenly come upon us."

But what closes the melancholy tale of this woman is—that she was a *widow!* A widow is always an affecting character, as she is liable to injustice and oppression, from those fiends who take advantage of weakness and distress; as she is deprived of the companion of her journey, and compelled to travel alone; as her anxieties are doubled, and there is none to share them with her. In this state, a child may seem an addition to her difficulties—but if he excites care, he diverts grief: he is some company in her solitary hours; in him something of the husband remains; in his face the father's image is admired. He will render himself serviceable by dutiful attentions; he will place on her the regard which he owed the deceased, and love her with a double affection. He will

also plead her cause, and become her protector and her refuge. But—such is no longer the condition of this poor widow. None is now left to support her tottering age; her last leaf is shaken down; her "last coal in Israel is quenched." And she is now, it is probable, going to bury her only son, in the same grave with his father. The opening of a husband's tomb would make her wounds bleed afresh—What would be her agony, when she would turn round, and leave the sepulchre—"There have I buried all my earthly happiness and hope—O for the day when I shall come hither too—and be gathered to my kindred dust!"

Sorrowful as the occasion was, she attended the funeral herself. And we commend her. It was following her only son as far as she could go; it was deriving from the scene all the instruction it could afford, and all the impression it could produce. But in our age of improvement, and refinement, and feeling, friends and relations seldom accompany the funeral of their connexions. A minister often buries a child, when he has no other audience to address than the few individuals who carry it to the grave! Yes, we are told—and we only wish to know some things by hearsay— that in genteel life, as soon as the patient has expired, they withdraw from the very house, and leave the dead to mercenaries— so that the minister can only meet the undertaker and his company, whose profit is entirely of another kind! Whither are these things tending? And have people now, more sensibility than formerly? No—but they have more affectation; they have more love to the world; they have more aversion to every thing serious! But are men determined to banish and to keep from their minds every intimation of their mortality! With what surprise and horror will death come upon those who never think of it! Are persons afraid of sorrow? "It is better to go to the house of mourning than to the house of mirth. By the sadness of the countenance the heart is made better." What advantages did this widow derive from her personal attendance in such trying circumstances?

—She was not alone—"Much people of the city was with her." This showed the esteem in which the family was held. But though numbers of the friends and neighbours of the widow attended her on this mournful occasion, sympathising with her under the heavy affliction and wishing to comfort her, little relief could *they* afford. They kindly commiserate her case, but cannot restore her son. Submission and patience were the only lessons they could preach or she could learn. But here comes advancing towards them another company, *the Leader of which can "save to the uttermost."* The two parties join in the suburbs of the city.— Observe our Lord and Saviour.

First, he knew all the particulars of the case. Those who were with him could only see, as they were passing by, a funeral—but he knew the corpse stretched upon the bier; he knew that it was a young man; that it was the only son of his mother; and that she was a widow!

Secondly. He did not wait to be implored. Some of his miracles were wrought in answer to the supplications of the individuals themselves; for he never refused any who applied to him—and this should teach us to pray for *ourselves*. Some of his miracles also were performed in consequence of the intercession of others: thus we find neighbours and relations were more than once honoured by obtaining a cure for their connexions—and this should encourage us to pray for *others*. But of several he could say, " I am found of them that sought me not." Sometimes, before we call he answers: such a very present help is he in trouble. In the case before us, the relief was entirely spontaneous and self-moved.

Thirdly. When he saw her, he had " compassion on her." By nothing was our Saviour more distinguished than by pity and tenderness—He was " touched with the feeling of our infirmities." His eye affected his heart. He made all the miseries he beheld his own, under the influence of this compassion.

Fourthly, he " said unto her, Weep not." How unavailing, not to say impertinent, would this have been from any other lips! Were you officiously to advance, and breaking the silence of the funeral train, to say to the chief mourner, " Woman, be happy; weep no more ;" would it not be deemed equally singular and vain? And it is more than probable that, in the case before us, the language of our Saviour would excite surprise, especially in the widow herself. Holding back her veil—she would look to see what stranger passing by thus interested himself in her grief, and gave her advice so easy to offer, and so impossible to take. When lo!

Fifthly, Jesus, without any ostentatious ceremony, " went and touched the bier—and they that bare it stood still ;" all amazement and expectation. Every eye is fixed upon him. What a moment of suspense and eagerness! At length, in a tone of uncontrolable authority, " he said to the young man, *I say unto thee, Arise!*" He does this in his own name. He claims a power which controls even the dead. And the event justifies the pretension. He never spake in vain. In a moment, in the twinkling of an eye, the blood begins to liquefy and flow through the veins and arteries; the lungs heave again; the eyes open—he " that was dead sat up and began to speak"—my soul, what did he say!

Finally, observe the application, the delicacy—what shall I call it—of the miracle: and " he delivered him to his mother !" He did not say, Go, preach the Gospel; or, Come, follow me. It was a prodigy of " lovingkindness ;" of " tender mercy." He would comfort her, and therefore he prefers *her* satisfaction to the honour *he* would have gained by the attendance of such a disciple on himself. What a present was here! " He delivered him to his mother !"

How striking the whole scene! To see a man instantly called back—from the invisible world! What awe would it produce; what wonder would it excite! Some would be ready to flee from him—but the mother—she would embrace him after this second birth, and " remember no more again her anguish, for joy that a man is born again into the world." But would the son engross all her attention? Would she not think of Jesus? this friend in trouble; this restorer of her happiness? I see her kneel and adore.

Let us conclude by three general reflections.

I. WHAT A VALE OF TEARS IS THIS WORLD! How various and numerous are the evils to which human life is exposed! " Man that is born of a woman, is of few days and full of trouble !" " Surely every man walketh in a vain show, surely they are disquieted in vain! he heapeth up riches, and cannot tell who shall gather them." His pains are great, his disappointments frequent, his cares corroding. His possessions generate alarms: and in proportion to his affections are his afflictions: his roses grow on thorns, and his honey wears a sting. Here we see a fellow-creature pining with sickness. There we hear a voice saying, " I sit, and am alone as a sparrow upon the house-top. Lover and friend hast thou put far from me, and mine acquaintance into darkness." It is impossible to walk the street, or pass along the road, without being assailed by sights and sounds of distress. And how peculiarly lamentable are some of these !—But

II. LET THE AFFLICTED REMEMBER THAT THEY ARE NOT LEFT WITHOUT RESOURCE. Let them learn where to flee in the day of trouble. It is to the Friend of sinners. Why, is the Saviour any longer on earth that we may apply to him? Unquestionably—how else could he fulfil his promise, " Where two or three are gathered together in my name, there am I in the midst of them?" His bodily presence was not necessary to his assistance " in the days of his flesh :" he could speak a cure at a distance. He is now essentially and spiritually near—near enough to hear all your complaints, and to afford you succour. He knows and observes all your distresses, and he has the same tenderness, and the same power as of old. Is your condition very trying and alarming? You have no cause for despair. " At even-tide it may

H

be light." Little did this poor woman expect to meet with such a glorious change in her circumstances at the funeral of her last comfort. "When the Lord turned again her captivity, she was like them that dream!" But he was pleased to bring her thus low before he helped her, to teach us never to think our case desperate, or to suppose that his interference can come too late.

But he does not deliver me! The time and the manner of relief are his own. There are cases in which he can do us more good by the continuance than by the speedy removal of our sorrows. But of this we may be assured, that he will not suffer us to call upon him in vain.

Let us apply this to a particular case. You say—"I share in this woman's affliction, but not in her joy. My child is dead—but no Jesus says to me, *Weep not*." Yes, Rachel—"Thus saith the Lord; refrain thy voice from weeping, and thine eyes from tears: for thy work shall be rewarded; and they shall come again from the land of the enemy. And there is hope in thine end, saith the Lord, that thy children shall come again to their own border." But he will not raise my child to this fond embrace? Yes—He who said to the young man, "Arise!" is "the resurrection and the life." Thy child shall rise again, and be delivered unto thee all over glorious; and no fear of separation shall damp the joy of your re-union.

III. WHAT THINK YOU OF CHRIST? Does not his character combine every excellency and attraction? And is the relation of all this given us merely to gratify our curiosity? Are we to peruse the life of our Lord and Saviour as we would read the history of a Cyrus or Alexander? No—it is not written for our amusement, but for our profit. And then we peruse it properly, when we admire him—love him above all—depend wholly upon him —and feel the transforming efficacy of every view we take of his character, "changing us into the same image, from glory to glory, as by the Spirit of the Lord."

Let us therefore "be followers of him as dear children." Let us cultivate benevolence, and do all the good we can, especially to the fatherless and widows. These he has peculiarly recommended to our attention, not only by his example, but by his word. "Ye shall not afflict any widow, or fatherless child. If thou afflict them in any wise, and they cry at all unto me, I will surely hear their cry; and my wrath shall wax hot, and I will kill you with the sword; and your wives shall be widows, and your children fatherless." We know you cannot work miracles—but you can show mercy. Go—"visit the widow in her affliction." We know you cannot raise her dead son—but you can preserve her living one. Go—and administer healing medicines and wholesome food; go and clothe his naked body, and inform his ignorant mind; go and endeavour to snatch him from ruin, and render him the staff of his poor widowed mother's age. Go—go, and enjoy all the luxury of doing good. "When the ear heard me, then it blessed me; and when the eye saw me, it gave witness to me: because I delivered the poor that cried, and the fatherless, and him that had none to help him. The blessing of him that was ready to perish came upon me: and I caused the widow's heart to sing for joy."

DISCOURSE XVII.

FEARS REMOVED.

And Manoah said unto his wife, We shall surely die, because we have seen God. But his wife said unto him, If the Lord were pleased to kill us, he would not have received a burnt-offering and a meat-offering at our hands, neither would he have showed us all these things, nor would he as at this time have told us such things as these.—Judges xiii. 22, 23.

SAMSON is the last of the Israelitish Deliverers recorded in this book. He differs very much from all his predecessors; for we never find him presiding over the council, or commanding in the army; but he was a tremendous scourge to the enemies of his country in his own person.

His history is full of wonders. An angel ushers him into the world. This angel first appeared to his mother, and foretold his birth. He soon after discovered himself also to his father, in company with his mother. His father immediately provided an entertainment for him—but the angel commanded him to offer it in sacrifice to the Lord. He did so— the angel ascended in the flame, and they saw him no more. By this they knew that he was a divine messenger, and in consequence of this apprehension, "Manoah said unto his wife, We shall surely die, because we have seen God. But his wife said unto him, If the Lord were pleased to kill us, he would not have received a burnt-offering and meat-offering at our hands, neither would he have showed us all these things, nor would as at this time have told us such things as these."

And what does this passage teach us? I. WHAT PECULIAR IMPRESSIONS DIVINE MANIFESTATIONS MAKE UPON THE MIND. II. THE DIFFERENCE THERE IS IN THE KNOWLEDGE AND EXPERIENCE OF THE LORD'S PEOPLE. III. THE PROFIT THAT IS TO BE DERIVED FROM A PIOUS COMPANION. IV. HOW MUCH THERE IS IN THE LORD'S DEALINGS WITH HIS PEOPLE TO ENCOURAGE THEM AT ALL TIMES IF THEY HAVE SKILL ENOUGH TO DISCERN IT.

I. See the *peculiar impressions which Divine manifestations make upon the mind.*

To a certain degree these impressions are proper. Such manifestations ought to strike our minds, to humble us, to produce reverence and godly fear. If an earthly king were to call upon us, we should be filled with awe as soon as he discovered himself—how much more should this be the case, when he approaches us, who is "*King of kings, and Lord of lords.*" Hence Jacob exclaimed, "How dreadful is this place: this is none other but the house of God, and this is the gate of heaven?" Job said, "I have heard of thee by the hearing of the ear: but now mine eye seeth thee: wherefore I abhor myself, and repent in dust and ashes." Isaiah also, in like manner cries out, "Wo is me! for I am undone: because I am a man of unclean lips, and I dwell among a people of unclean lips: for mine eyes have seen the King, the Lord of Hosts." Thus awfully were these good men impressed, as soon as they apprehended the presence and glory of God.

But impressions, good in themselves, may become excessive; and the cause producing them may be misunderstood, and even deprecated. Thus Manoah reasons: "We shall surely die, for we have seen God!" This was a common apprehension of old, and it is easy to account for it. Ever since man became a sinner, an enemy to God, every approach of the Deity has awakened in him terror and confusion. Our consciences naturally tell us that we deserve nothing but heavy tidings from the invisible world: we therefore dread every messenger thence. And even when God comes to us in mercy, the same sentiment occurs, and sometimes leads us, like Manoah, to mistake his design, and draw a fearful conclusion from it.

Thus, when he comes to convince us of sin, and to humble the pride of our hearts, we imagine that we shall now die—But we are mistaken; he is only come to prepare us for the proofs of his love. He impresses us with a sense of our danger, that we may flee for refuge; with a sense of our pollution, that we may wash and be clean, in the fountain which he has provided. "They that be whole need not a physician, but they that are sick."

Thus, when he comes in providence, and destroys our schemes, and visits us with breach upon breach; here again we imagine we are going to be undone! But we shall presently see that he came as a friend, though disguised, and only used means to wean us from the world, and bring us more entirely to himself as our exceeding joy.

Let us, II. Remark *the difference there is in the knowledge and experience of the Lord's people.* What surprises and terrifies one, is both plain and pleasing to another. What opposite conclusions do Manoah and his wife draw from the same event! He infers wrath; she mercy. The former looks for destruction; the latter for salvation. Thus,

there are degrees in grace. There is *hope*, and the *free assurance of hope.* Some have *little* faith; others are "strong in faith," "rich in faith." In the Church there are *babes;* and there are these "*of full age*, who by reason of use have their senses exercised to discern both good and evil."

And this difference is not always to be judged of by the order of nature, or external advantages. "There are first that shall be last, and there are last that shall be first." We find here the weaker vessel the stronger believer. Nor is this a solitary instance. They were women, yea widows, who ministered to our Lord of their substance. The three Marys approached the feet of the cross, when the disciples forsook him and fled. These also appeared first at the sepulchre. Nothing is said of the father of Timothy, but the Apostle celebrates the "unfeigned faith of his mother and his grandmother." He also speaks honourably to the Philippians of "those women that had laboured with him in the Gospel."

Neither does this difference in their attainments affect the reality of their religion, or the safety of their state. The infant is no less a child than the young man. Our Saviour does not despise "the day of small things." "A bruised reed shall he not break, and smoking flax shall he not quench, till he send forth judgment unto victory."

Nevertheless, it is very desirable to be matured and established Christians—not only to be alive in religion, but lively; not only to be fruitful, but to bring forth much fruit; and to be "filled with all joy and peace in believing," that we may not only have hope, but "*abound in hope*, through the power of the Holy Ghost." And this is important, not only as the glory of God, and the comfort of your own minds, depend much upon it, but also as it prepares for usefulness, and enables you the better to "serve your generation," and the more easily to "speak a word in season to him that is weary."

This leads us to notice, III. *The profit that is to be derived from a pious companion.* "Two are better than one; because they have a good reward of their labour. For if they fall, the one will lift up his fellow; but wo to him that is alone when he falleth: for he hath not another to lift him up." Man is formed for society, and religion indulges and sanctifies the social principle. And if a man be concerned for his spiritual welfare, he will be glad to meet with those who are traveling the same road, and are partakers of the same hopes and fears: he will be thankful to have one near him who will watch over him, and admonish him; who by seasonable counsel will fix him when wavering, embolden him when timid, and comfort him when cast down. And it is to be observed, that in spiritual distress we are often suspicious of our own reasonings and conclusions: we know the deceitfulness of our own hearts, and are afraid lest while they encourage they should ensnare. We can depend with more confidence upon the declarations of our fellow-Christians. Only let them relate their own experience, recall to our minds some forgotten truth, apply some promise, or give a new turn to a particular circumstance—and we are relieved and delivered.

And happy is the man who has such a friend and helper in "*the desire of his eyes.*" In various instances, the importance of the female character to the welfare of man appears. She will aid Manoah in bringing up their children: and the earlier parts of education devolve almost exclusively upon her. She will assist him in the management of his estate: "the heart of her husband doth safely trust in her, so that he shall have no need of spoil. She will do him good and not evil all the days of his life. She looketh well to the ways of her household, and eateth not the bread of idleness." "No man ever prospered in the world without the consent and co-operation of his wife." She will also help him in the preservation of his character, of his health, of his peace of mind. Her soothing voice can charm away "the evil spirit;" her soft hand can smooth the wrinkles of an anxious brow, and wipe off the mildew of an unwholesome evening. But she is found, in the noblest sense, "a help-meet for him," in aiding his piety; in adding flame to his devotion; in furnishing motive to his zeal. By prayer, by example, by conversation, she can encourage his resolutions, disperse his doubts, and "help his unbelief." Such was the happiness of Manoah: he had one who was an "heir with him of the grace of life." "But his wife said unto him, If the Lord were pleased to kill us, he would not have received a burnt-offering and a meat-offering at our hands, neither would he have showed us all these things, nor would as at this time have told us such things as these."

Whence, IV. We take occasion to observe, that there is always *enough in the Lord's dealings with his people to encourage them, if they have wisdom enough to discern it.* How well did this woman reason! How naturally, yet how forcibly! "Nay—let us not turn that against us, which is really for us. We shall not die, unless God be pleased to kill us; and surely the tokens of his favour are not the pledges of his wrath."

Her conclusion is drawn from two things. First, the acceptance of their sacrifice: "If the Lord were pleased to kill us, he would not have received a burnt-offering and a meat-offering at our hands." It is not his manner to accept the offering, and reject the person: "And the Lord had respect unto Abel and his offering; but unto Cain and his offering he had not respect." Secondly, the secrets with which he had favoured them— "Neither would he have shown us all these things, nor would as at this time have told us such things as these." This regards the birth of their son, his education, his deliverance of their country—If the accomplishment of this be certain, our destruction is impossible.

Let us leave Manoah and his wife, and think of ourselves. It is a dreadful thing for God to kill us. What is the loss of property, of health, or even of life, to the loss of the soul! Men can "kill the body," but there "is no more that they can do; but God is able to destroy both body and soul in hell." "It is a fearful thing to fall into the hands of the living God."

Hence it becomes unspeakably important to know how he means to deal with us. And, blessed be his name, there are satisfactory evidences that he is not our enemy, but our friend, and concerned for our welfare. Some of these are more general; others are more peculiar.

He has not left himself without witness "in that he has done us good, and given us rain from heaven, and fruitful seasons, filling our hearts with food and gladness."

He has borne with our provocations; and though he could easily and righteously have destroyed us, we are still in the land of the living, and we ought to "account that the longsuffering of our Lord is salvation. The goodness of God leadeth to repentance."

Had he desired the death of the sinner, would he have provided and accepted the grand sacrifice which Jesus made upon the cross for us?—But we know he provided it; we know he accepted it; we know that it was an "offering and a sacrifice to God for a sweet-smelling savour."

If he were pleased to kill us, would he have given us such exceeding great and precious promises—promises so rich, so general, so free! Would he have said, "Seek ye the Lord while he may be found; call ye upon him while he is near. Let the wicked forsake his way, and the unrighteous man his thoughts: and let him return unto the Lord, and he will have mercy upon him; and to our God, for he will abundantly pardon." "Him that cometh unto me, I will in no wise cast out."

Resolved on your destruction, would he have favoured you with such affecting discoveries? Like the man in the Gospel, though unable to tell every circumstance attending the operation, cannot you say, "One thing I know, that whereas I was blind, now I see?" Has he not "called you out of darkness into his marvellous light?" Are you not filled with wonder—does not every thing appear new! Have you not seen an evil in sin which has rendered it odious and burdensome

—a depravity in yourselves, which has led you ever since to exclaim, Behold, I am vile —and such a glory in the Saviour as makes you willing to follow him whithersoever he goeth? "Flesh and blood have not revealed this unto thee, but our Father who is in heaven."

Had his aim been your ruin, would he have produced in you such sentiments and dispositions?—So that the heart of stone is removed; you *mourn* for sin, and for the sins of others, as well as your own. You "*hunger and thirst after righteousness;*" and as much long to be sanctified as to be pardoned; and pray as much to obtain purity as peace. You love the sceptre, as well as glory in the Cross; and your dependence upon the Saviour's death is accompanied by endeavours to imitate his example; and you can never be perfectly reconciled to yourselves, till "the same mind be in you which was also in Christ Jesus." If he smiles, you are satisfied to bear the frowns of the world; and can say, as you advance in duty and reproach, "If this be to be vile, I will yet be more vile."

And under your greatest discouragements, under every temptation to go back, have you not been enabled to persevere in the use of means? Though you have been strangers to comfort and freedom in duty, you have not restrained prayer before him; but, through many a benighted season, you have waited for him "more than they that watch for the morning." On the very verge of despair, something has afresh excited hope: "then I said, I am cast out of thy sight: yet, will I look again toward thy holy temple." You have had a degree of confidence—not only that you *shall* not seek him in vain—but that you *have* not sought him in vain: "I said, in my haste, I am cut off from before thine eyes: nevertheless thou heardest the voice of my supplication, when I cried unto thee." And thus, while powerfully drawing you, he has been secretly sustaining you; as in the case of David, who said—"My soul followeth hard after thee—thy right hand upholdeth me."

Now all this is really his work. By the grace of God, you are what you are: it is "he that has made you thus to differ" from others, and from yourselves. And if "the Lord has a mind to kill you," why should he have done all this? The conclusion is as obvious as it is encouraging. He could have destroyed you without these exertions in your favour. Surely, he does not excite expectations, to disappoint us; or desires, to torment us. Surely he does not produce a new taste, a new appetite, without meaning to indulge, to relieve it. Besides—as he does nothing in vain, so he does nothing imperfect. What he begins, he is able to finish; and when he begins, he designs to finish. With regard to other agents, we cannot certainly infer the completion from the beginning: their views

alter; they meet with unexpected difficulties; their purposes are frequently broken off—but it is otherwise here. The foundation of God standeth sure, and the "top stone shall be brought forth with shoutings—grace, grace, unto it!" It shall never be said of the God of our salvation—"He began to build, but was not able to finish." "We are confident," says the Apostle, "of this very thing, that he who hath begun a good work in you will perform it until the day of Jesus Christ."

May you likewise be humbly confident of the same truth. May you be enabled to say, with David, "The Lord will perfect that which concerneth me: thy mercy, O Lord, endureth for ever: forsake not the work of thine own hands."

And "when you are converted" from your doubts, and fears, and dejections, "strengthen your brethren. Comfort the feebleminded. Support the weak. Be patient towards all men. Lift up the hands which hang down, and the feeble knees; and make strait paths for your feet, lest that which is lame be turned out of the way; but let it rather be healed."

DISCOURSE XVIII.

THE PROFANE EXCHANGE.

Lest there be any fornicator, or profane person, as Esau, who for one morsel of meat sold his birthright. For ye know how that afterward, when he would have inherited the blessing, he was rejected: for he found no place of repentance, though he sought it carefully with tears."—Heb. xii. 16, 17.

THE history of the wicked, as well as of the righteous, is useful. By their crimes we are cautioned; and we are warned by their miseries. And as the Israelites fled from the tents of Korah, when "the ground clave asunder and swallowed them up," saying, "lest the earth swallow us up also"—so should we abandon the course of the ungodly world, lest we share in their tremendous ruin.

Anxious for our welfare, the Scripture addresses our fear as well as our hope, and holds forth instances of divine vengeance, as well as proofs of divine mercy. Hence the command of our Lord: "Remember Lot's wife." And hence the admonition of the Apostle: "Lest there be any fornicator, or profane person, as Esau, who for one morsel of meat sold his birthright. For ye know how that afterward, when he would have inherited the blessing, he was rejected: for he found no place of repentance, though he sought it carefully with tears."

And what is all this to us? "Much every way." I compare your privileges with his privileges—your sin with his sin—and your doom with his doom.

I. Let us view Esau in his original state—and COMPARE YOUR PRIVILEGES WITH HIS PRIVILEGES. To stand supreme in the house of the patriarch Isaac was no trifling prerogative: his house was "the house of God, and the gate of heaven." In this family, Jehovah revealed himself; and there he was adored and served, while idolatry prevailed over all the other nations of the globe. And such was once the condition of this unhappy character. Accordingly he possessed the birthright, and stood in a fair way to obtain all the advantages flowing from it. And these were great and numerous.

To the birthright belonged pre-eminence over the other branches of the family. To the birthright appertained a double portion of the paternal inheritance. To the birthright was attached the land of Canaan, with all its sacred distinctions. To the birthright was given the promise of being the ancestor of the Messiah—the "first-born among many brethren"—the Saviour "in whom all the families of the earth were to be blessed." And to the birthright was added the honour of receiving first, from the mouth of the father, a peculiar benediction, which, proceeding from the Spirit of prophecy, was never pronounced in vain.—Such were the prospects of Esau.

And what are yours? It is true, you were not born in the house of Isaac; but you have been brought forth in a Christian country, in a "land the Lord careth for," where "the darkness is past, and the true light now shineth." You have the Bible; you have Sabbaths; you have sanctuaries; you have ordinances; you have ministers; you have the throne of grace; you have the promise of the Holy Ghost: and *all things* appertaining to your everlasting happiness *are now ready.* You possess much; but all your present advantages are not to be compared with those glorious hopes to which you are called by the Gospel. You have the prospect of becoming a "kind of firstfruits of his creatures," of joining "the general assembly and the Church of the firstborn, whose names are written in heaven"—a primogeniture whose privileges far surpass those of the son of Isaac: a birthright which comprehends a "better country" than Canaan, even heaven, where we shall reign "kings and priests unto God," where "the Lord commandeth the blessing, even life for evermore!" But this pearl is not for the swine, who, ignorant of its value, tramples it under foot; but for those who, conscious of its incomparable worth, prefer it to every thing else, and, like the wise merchant, are willing to sell all to buy it. These high advantages may be sacrificed.

II. Let us therefore view Esau in the surrender of his privileges, and COMPARE YOUR SIN WITH HIS SIN.—"*For one morsel of meat he sold his birthright.*" It is obvious that the loss was *voluntary* and *base.* First, it was voluntary. No one forced it from him—he *sold* it. He was indeed tempted to part with it by the sensation of hunger, and the sight of pottage when he was faint: an object was before him which promised the immediate gratification of his sensual appetite. But he could very soon have obtained food upon far easier terms. And surely the birthright could not have a rival in a mess of meat! Where was reason? Does the man yield to the brutes?—No: he was not compelled to sacrifice his claims. And who compels *you* to abandon your hopes of heaven? Who forces you into perdition? You say that you live in a world full of enticing objects; that the dominion of sense is strong; that it is not very easy to resist the impulse of the moment. But is it impossible to resist? Have not many overcome, though placed in the same circumstances, and possessed of the same nature with you? What is goodness untried? Have you not reason as well as appetite? Is not grace attainable by you? Is it not sufficient for you? And remember that you can never have so strong a motive to commit sin as to avoid it. The greatest difficulties therefore which you have to overcome, are those which are placed to keep you from hell. What is the applause of a fellow-creature to the frown of the Almighty? What is a momentary pleasure to endless pain? And you *know* you act freely: you know that all the men in the world cannot force you to will: you know that the tempter can do nothing more than propose—the determination rests with you. You cannot justify yourselves even now to your own consciences, and hereafter, unable to allege one excuse, *you will be speechless!* Here is the true cause of your ruin—"ye will not come unto me that ye might have life." "Ye have loved idols, and after them ye will go."

Secondly, it was equally base. For what is the price of the birthright? An empire? A crown?—A crown sparkles in the eye of ambition: a throne is the highest pinnacle of human pride:—Nothing like it—but a despicable trifle, "one morsel of meat"—"a mess of pottage"—the dearest dish, says Bishop Hall, that was ever purchased, except the forbidden fruit. But I feel ready to dispute this. Are not you more than like him? Do not you surpass him in folly? For what do you sell the treasures of the soul and eternity—but a thing of nought, a fleeting indulgence, a false point of honour, an imaginary interest? Here is your eternal infamy and disgrace! "Ye have sold yourselves," says the prophet, "for nought." For what proportion is there between the things which you thus exchange? Duly consider the "unsearchable riches of Christ;" think what it is to be "blessed with all spiritual blessings in heavenly places;" what it is to live in pleasure, to die in hope, to obtain "*glory, honour, and immortality.*" These are the blessings you give up. And what do you gain by the surrender? Solomon tells you, "*vanity and vexation of spirit.*" Worldly things are less than the soul, and cannot fill it; worse than the soul, and cannot satisfy it. They have no relation to our grand wants, or our best interests. They please, only to poison; they elevate, only to depress. They "perish in the using." You can carry nothing of them with you. You are not certain of holding them for life; and if you were, "what is your life? It is even as a vapour, that appeareth for a little time, and then vanisheth away." View them in the light of Scripture; view them under the anguish of conscience; view them from the borders of the grave; view them from the vastness of eternity,—and they are nothing. Nevertheless for these—and often without obtaining them—you sin away your everlasting portion. "What is a man profited if he should *gain the whole world and lose his own soul?*" If the whole cannot indemnify him—can a part—a particle? "O ye sons of men, how long will ye love vanity and seek after leasing?—Have the workers of iniquity no knowledge?"

III. Let us CONSIDER ESAU IN HIS MISERY, AND COMPARE YOUR DOOM WITH HIS DOOM. "*For you know how that afterward, when he could have inherited the blessing, he was rejected: for he found no place of repentance, though he sought it carefully with tears.*" Read the relation in the book of Genesis. Nothing could be more affecting than his expostulations, and his bitter cries—but to no purpose does he urge his petition or press his father to retract: the benediction is pronounced, and Isaac acquiesces in the decision of Heaven. For repentance here refers to Isaac, not to Esau: the meaning is, not that Esau humbled himself in vain for his sin, and could not obtain forgiveness—but that he could not prevail upon Isaac to change his mind, and reverse what he had spoken: that, with regard therefore to the birthright which he had sold, his loss was irretrievable.

And did God thus by his righteous judgment exclude from all his claims the profane Esau because he had despised them—"How shall we escape if we neglect so great salvation? Of how much sorer punishment suppose ye shall he be thought worthy, who hath trodden under foot the Son of God, and hath counted the blood of the covenant, wherewith he was sanctified, an unholy thing, and hath done despite unto the Spirit of grace?" Are you disposed to pity him? Yea, rather, weep for yourselves. Your loss is inestimably greater than his loss. After all his disappointments he had something left, and could entertain himself with the diversions of the field: but your condition will be destitute of all resources. And with no business to engage, no amusements to beguile,

> ———' Say, ye gay dreamers of gay dreams,
> How will ye weather an eternal night,
> Where such expedients fail?'

Then your application will be useless. You may supplicate; but you will be rejected, and no place will be found for repentance in the mind of your Judge, though you "seek it carefully with tears."

Hence we see what a difference there is between the origin and the issue of an irreligious course. "A prudent man foreseeth the evil and hideth himself, but the simple pass on and are punished." The wise will always judge of things by their end. It is the end that crowns the action. Sin is never profitable; but its beginnings are flattering. "Stolen waters are sweet, and bread eaten in secret is pleasant—but he knoweth not that the dead are there; and that her guests are in the depths of hell. Though wickedness be sweet in his mouth, though he hide it under his tongue: though he spare it, and forsake it not; but keep it still within his mouth: yet his meat in his bowels is turned, it is the gall of asps within him." "What fruit had ye then in those things, whereof ye are now ashamed? for the end of those things is death."

Again. Sin unavoidably brings a man sooner or later to lamentation and regret. "Thine own wickedness shall correct thee, and thy backslidings shall reprove thee: know therefore and see, that it is an evil thing, and bitter, that thou hast forsaken the Lord thy God, and that my fear is not in thee, saith the Lord God of hosts." And hence, if we studied our true comfort, we should never sin: we should reason thus: "If ever I am saved, I must be brought to repentance, and every sin I now commit will then give me pain: and if I have not that godly sorrow which worketh repentance unto life, what will be the self-condemnation and anguish of a dying bed and a judgment day? Sin, like Ezekiel's roll, is written, 'within and without, with lamentation and mourning and wo.'"

Let us also remark, that there is a repentance which is unavailing. Paul tells us of a "sorrow of the world which worketh death." Some are fretting because every one will not submit to their humours. Some grieve over their temporal losses, and never ask "where is God my maker, that giveth songs in the night?" Every remorse of conscience is not the effect of saving grace. Judas "repented, and went and hanged himself." The eyes which sin closes, eternity will open. But then grief comes too late. The blessing once lost, cannot be recovered.

I know that many unguarded things have been said of the loss of a day of grace. The subject is alarming. I do not pretend to do justice to it, or to answer any curious questions which may arise from it. What I think I am authorized to say from the Scripture is this. First. That while there is life, there is hope; nor can we imagine that God would prolong existence but to afford us space for repentance. This indeed he has assigned as the reason. God " is longsuffering to us-ward, not willing that any should perish, but that all should come to repentance." " The longsuffering of our Lord is salvation." Secondly. It is always dangerous to delay the work of repentance; since, by repeated acts, habits are formed, and dispositions rendered more and more unfavourable. The disease neglected, becomes inveterate; and the shrub suffered to stand, grows into a deep-rooted tree. " Can the Ethiopian change his skin, or the leopard his spots? then may ye also learn to do good who are accustomed to do evil." But we should not only consider repentance as a work to be performed by us, and the delay of which multiplies difficulties; but also—and without this our repentance cannot be saving —as a blessing and an influence to be imparted from God. Now your criminal delay in seeking this renders it less probable that you will ever find it: for though you cannot deserve grace, you may grieve it: and after so many invitations scorned—what wonder if he should say, " None of them that were bidden shall taste of my supper!" Thirdly. There are cases and circumstances in every man's life more friendly to religion than others. On these much seems to turn; and these may be lost even in this life. I have no doubt but that when Felix trembled, he felt as he never did before, and never did again. But he wilfully strove to do away the impression. And have not some of you had convictions which have for the time filled you with fear? Have you not had such relishes of good things as have led you to " call the sabbath a delight," and to " hear the word with joy?" Have not your closets occasionally seen a bended knee? Have not your walks witnessed your tears and vows? Your earthly hopes withered, and your comforts removed—have you not been constrained to turn aside from the world, deploring its emptiness, and sighing for a nobler good? Now when he *draws*, we should *run*; when he *knocks*, we should *open*. Fourthly. Death, it is certain, ends all your opportunities. After this, no pardon will be offered; no motives will be urged. Time is for sowing, and eternity for reaping; and " what a man soweth that shall he also reap." Hence the distinction always maintained in the Scripture between this world and another: the one is a state of probation, the other of decision. Hence the importance of life. Hence the wisdom of complying with the admonition, " Seek ye the Lord while he may be found, call ye upon him while he is

near." For there is a season when, if you " call upon him, he will not answer, and if you seek him early, you will not find him." And how soon you may be in this unalterable state it is impossible to determine. We know your breath is in your nostrils; you are exposed to a thousand accidents and diseases.

But your harvest is not yet past, your summer is not yet ended. Still he bears with you. Once more he invites you. It is time, it is high time, and, blessed be his name, it is not too late, to seek him. I see him now standing with the door wide open, beseeching you as you love your souls to enter in— You refuse—and he shuts to the door, saying, " *O that thou hadst known, even thou, at least in this thy day, the things which belong unto thy peace—but now they are hid from thine eyes!*"

DISCOURSE XIX.

NATHANAEL.

And Nathanael said unto him, Can there any good thing come out of Nazareth? Philip saith unto him, Come and see. Jesus saw Nathanael coming to him, and saith of him, Behold an Israelite indeed, in whom is no guile! Nathanael saith unto him, Whence knowest thou me? Jesus answered and said unto him, Before that Philip called thee, when thou wast under the fig-tree, I saw thee. Nathanael answered and said unto him, Rabbi, thou art the Son of God; thou art the King of Israel. Jesus answered and said unto him, Because I said unto thee, I saw thee under the fig-tree, believest thou? thou shalt see greater things than these.— John i. 46—50.

MUCH of the excellency of the Scripture lies in this—that it does not state things in general representations, but descends to particulars—that it does not place them before us in speculative notions, but in practical effects—that it does not describe them only, but exemplifies—so that we see them alive and in motion.

The passage of Scripture which is now to engage our attention is peculiarly interesting and instructive. It is a narrative of the interview between our Lord and Nathanael. It leads us,

First, to observe THE ADVANTAGES OF OCCASIONAL SOLITUDE.—What was Nathanael doing under the fig-tree? We are not informed. Perhaps he was reading the Scripture— perhaps he was engaged in meditation—perhaps he was praying—perhaps he was joining himself to the Lord in a perpetual covenant, saying, " Lord, I am thine, save me: and manifest thyself to me." Some purpose had allured him there which our Saviour noticed and approved; he saw him "*in secret*," and he now "*rewards him openly*." Does he see us! Are we strangers to retirement? Surely, if we are Christians, and concerned for the welfare of our souls, we shall often retire, and find that we have much to do alone. I pity the man whose life is full of action, and void of thought. I pity the professor who lives only in public; who is always hearing sermons; who pays very little attention to the duties of the family, and none to those of the closet.

It is alone that we disengage ourselves from the dominion of the world. The world conquers us in a crowd. When our senses are dazzled, and our minds amused, we are too much occupied to find out the cheat; but when we are drawn back from it, when we calmly consider it as an object of lonely contemplation, oh! how is its importance diminished, how is its influence reduced! It is then we sigh—" vanity of vanities, all is vanity." It is alone that conscience operates, that motives impress, that truth is examined and applied. It is alone that we obtain a knowledge of ourselves; it is there we can examine our condition, investigate our characters, discover our follies and our weaknesses. Alone, we can be familiar with God, and divulge to him secrets which we could not communicate to the dearest friend, or express in any public or social exercises of religion.

I love the fig-tree. I love to go forth from among the works of man, to enjoy the creation of God: to enter a wood—to walk through a field of standing corn—to follow the windings of a river—to view the playfulness of the lambs—to listen to the varied melody of the birds. Here is nothing to vex, nothing to pollute. What an innocency, what a softness does it spread over the mind! How disposed is the heart to welcome and cherish every devotional sentiment!

" O sacred solitude! divine retreat!
  Choice of the prudent, envy of the great—
  There from the ways of men laid safe ashore,
  We smile to hear the distant tempest roar:
  There blest with health, with business unperplext,
  This life we cherish, and insure the next."

Secondly. Let us remark HOW PERFECTLY ACQUAINTED OUR SAVIOUR IS WITH OUR MOST PRIVATE CONCERNS. " Whence knowest thou me ?" asks Nathanael, when our Saviour had, in few words, developed his character. Jesus answered—" When thou wast under the fig-tree I saw thee." This good man imagined himself alone there: he supposed no eye saw him. No wonder therefore he was surprised, to hear a person, who appeared only a man like himself, announcing the whole affair: no wonder he was immediately convinced of his Messiahship, and exclaimed, " Rabbi, thou art the Son of God, thou art the King of Israel." To know all persons and things infallibly, is the prerogative of God only. He therefore claims it, in distinction from all creatures: " The heart is deceitful above all things, and desperately wicked;

who can know it? I the Lord search the heart, I try the reins, even to give every man according to his ways, and according to the fruit of his doings." And what says our Lord, in his address to John? " The churches shall know that I am he who searcheth the reins and hearts; and I will give unto every one of you according to your works." In the days of his flesh, actions were not necessary to inform him, nor did he derive additional discovery from the declarations of others: " he knew all men, and needed not that any should testify of man: for he knew what was in man."

Let us remember therefore, that " the eyes of the Lord are in every place, beholding both the evil and the good." Of this he will give proof hereafter, when " he shall bring every work into judgment, with every secret thing, whether it be good, or whether it be evil." It will be in vain for the sinner then to say—when his wickedness is published to the world—" Whence knowest thou this ?"— I saw thee, says the Judge, devising mischief upon thy bed ; I saw thee walking in a way that was not good; I saw thee endeavouring to stifle every conviction of conscience, and to banish every serious reflection from the mind; thou hast always stood in my presence ; thou hast always sinned under mine eye. I beheld all thy actions, I heard all thy words, all thy thoughts were open to my view—and here they all are———

But let the righteous rejoice. He sees their situations, their trials, their dangers, their fears, their desires. He has " engraven them upon the palms of his hands, their walls are continually before him."

Let the broken-hearted penitent be encouraged. Godly sorrow affects loneliness. Into many a corner you retire to pour out tears unto God. Well, thither his eye follows you—" To this man will he look, even to him that is poor, and of a contrite spirit, and that trembleth at his word." " And the Lord said unto Ananias, Arise, and go into the street which is called Straight, and inquire in the house of Judas for one called Saul, of Tarsus: for, behold! he prayeth."

Thirdly. SINCERITY IN RELIGION IS A QUALITY WHICH OUR SAVIOUR CALLS UPON US TO OBSERVE AND ADMIRE. What an honourable character, as he approaches him, does he give Nathanael! " Behold an Israelite indeed, in whom is no guile." By calling him an " Israelite," he distinguishes him from other nations; and by calling him an " Israelite indeed," he distinguishes him from his own. For all " were not Israel, who were of Israel." From the beginning, " he was not a Jew who was one outwardly; neither was that circumcision which was outward in the flesh: but he was a Jew, who was one inwardly; and circumcision was that of the heart, in the spirit, and not in the letter;

I   6*

whose praise was not of men, but of God."
Now Nathanael was one of these true Israelites; he was in reality, as well as by profession, one of the people of God. And the evidence he gave of this was, his freedom from
guile. But our Saviour does not say he has
no guilt—a man may be freckled, or have
spots, and not be painted. A Christian is
not sinlessly pure; he has many unallowed
and bewailed infirmities; but guile he has
not: he is no hypocrite. He does not, in religion, ascend a stage to assume a character
which does not belong to him. He is what
he appears to be. There is a correspondence
between his professions and actions; his
meaning and his words. He is upright in
his dealings with himself—in his dealings
with his fellow-creatures—and in his dealings
with his God. He is all of a piece. He is the
same alone as in company: the same in his
own house as in the house of God: the same
in prosperity as in adversity.

This is the character that stands fair with
his own conscience. This is the character
that enthrones himself in the esteem of
others. This is the character that the King
of Glory delights to honour. "The prayer
of the upright is his delight." "Light is
sown for the righteous, and joy for the upright in heart." "The upright shall dwell
in thy presence." "The Lord God is a sun
and shield: the Lord will give grace and
glory: no good thing will he withhold from
them that walk uprightly." "Hast thou,"
said he to Satan, "hast thou considered my
servant Job, that there is none like him in
the earth, a perfect and upright man, one
that feareth God, and escheweth evil?" And
placing such a character before us, in a situation the most sublime and awful, he says,
"Mark the perfect man, and behold the upright, for the end of that man is peace."
There are two reasons why he calls upon us
to admire a Nathanael. The one is, THE
RARENESS OF THE CHARACTER. It is not to be
seen every day. Many make no pretensions
to religion; and many have only "a form of
godliness," while "they deny the power
thereof."

"Broad is the road that leads to death,
  And thousands walk together there;
But wisdom shows a narrower path,
  With—here and there—a traveller."

The other is, THE EXCELLENCY OF THE
CHARACTER. It is indispensably necessary, in
all religious concerns—nothing can be a substitute for this integrity—nothing that we can
say, nothing that we can do, nothing that we
can suffer. Without this, every thing else will
only render us the more vile and abominable.
Judas is called—a devil. On the other hand,
where this is found, and God sees that a man
acts conscientiously, and from a sincere desire
to please and glorify him, he will pass by mistakes, pardon imperfections, and accept him

"according to what he has, and not according to what he has not."

And this leads us to a fourth remark.
THERE MAY BE TRUE GRACE, WHERE THERE
IS AT PRESENT VERY LITTLE LIGHT. This
was the case with Nathanael. His knowledge as yet was small; his mind was contracted; and he laboured under low prejudices. He had no apprehension of a Messiah,
distinguished by poverty and suffering. And
because Nazareth was a wicked place, and a
place of obscurity, he concluded, nothing
good or great could originate thence. Nevertheless he was open to conviction—he complied with the invitation, "Come and see"—
he immediately "believed with the heart,
and confessed with the tongue"—and our Saviour, pleased with his proficiency, promises
to "lead him into all truth."

Now this may be the case with others.
And indeed, so far am I from supposing it
necessary, to evidence the reality of a man's
conversion, that he should in every thing see
clearly at first, that I commonly suspect those
that are all at once so ripe in knowledge,
and so high in doctrine. These dispropor-
tionated notionalists remind me of those unhappy children, whose heads grow so much
faster than their bodies—the effect of disease, or weakness of constitution, not of
health and vigour. I love to see knowledge,
experience, and practice advancing together
"unto a perfect man, unto the measure of
the stature of the fulness of Christ." That
which comes up in a night may wither in a
night—we dislike mushroom piety. If we
look into nature, we shall find things slower
in their growth, in proportion to their excellency. How rapidly nettles, and thistles,
and reeds, and osiers spring up to maturity!
but the oak is as much slower in attaining its
perfection, as it is more firm in its grain,
more durable in continuance, more important
in its use.

Let us not then conclude that a man is a
stranger to divine grace, because he is unable,
at present, to go all our lengths in sentiment.
It is not possible for us to determine, in certain disadvantageous circumstances, with how
much ignorance in the judgment true grace
in the heart may be connected. How little
of the plan of salvation did Peter know, when
our Saviour said, "Blessed art thou, Simon
Barjona: for flesh and blood hath not revealed
it unto thee, but my Father which is in heaven?" As the sanctification of the soul, so the
illumination of the mind is gradual; and
surely intellectual defects are no more wonderful than moral ones.

Nor let us be anxious to force upon him
doctrines which at present he is not prepared
to receive. Our Saviour said to his disciples,
"I have yet many things to say unto you;
but ye cannot bear them now." Where the
heart is right with God, a growing experience

in divine things will, after a while, make room for the admission of every important truth.

And therefore, we remark, finally, THAT WHERE GRACE IS REAL, IT WILL IN DUE TIME BE ATTENDED WITH CLEARER LIGHT. "Because I said unto thee, I saw thee under the fig-tree, believest thou! Thou shalt see greater things than these." Grace is an active principle, and leads us to use what we have—and "to him that hath shall be given, and he shall have more abundance." It disposes us to go on, "and then shall we know, if we follow on to know the Lord." It inspires reverence and humility, and a dependence on Divine teaching—and "the secret of the Lord is with them that fear him, and he will show them his covenant: the meek will he guide in judgment, and the meek will he teach his way." Let not thy deficiencies therefore cast thee down. You are under the care of one who will "not break a bruised reed, nor quench the smoking flax, till he send forth judgment unto victory." He has your welfare at heart. The convictions and desires which he has produced in you are tokens for good. He will never leave nor forsake you, "till he has done all that which he has spoken to you of: he will perfect that which concerneth you." It is now only the dawn; but the dawn is the pledge and the beginning of noon. "And the path of the just is as the shining light, which shineth more and more unto the perfect day." And whatever discoveries he has already made, remember, you shall see "greater things than these"—

First, greater in this world; more of himself, of his word, of his grace, of his providence. He can enable us to see divine things more clearly; more impressively; with more confidence, and with more appropriation. Let us not limit our desires, or our hopes.

Secondly, greater in another world. After all our attainments, this earth is only a land of obscurities. But heaven is everlasting light. In those happy regions there is "no darkness at all."—"Now we see through a glass, darkly; but then face to face: now we know in part; but then shall we know even as also we are known. And when that which is perfect is come, then that which is in part shall be done away."

Then he will fully reveal himself. "We know that Messiah who is called Christ shall come; and when he is come, he will tell us all things."

DISCOURSE XX.

THE CHARACTERS OF SIN.

What fruit had ye then in those things whereof ye are now ashamed? for the end of those things is death.—Romans vi. 21.

IT is of the greatest importance to enter-tain proper apprehensions of the evil of sin. Hence the Scriptures are so large and particular in describing it. They place it before us in every quality, and express it under every allusion that can rouse our indignation, or awaken our fear and our flight. Witness the language of the Apostle: "What fruit had ye then in those things whereof ye are now ashamed! for the end of those things is death."

Behold the enemy. Sin is here arraigned and condemned in all the periods of time: the past, the present, and the future. For the past—here is unprofitableness; for the present—here is disgrace; and for the future—here is perdition. Let us, then, consider sin under these three characters. I. As UNFRUITFUL. II. As SHAMEFUL. III. As DESTRUCTIVE.

And I. The Apostle asks, "What fruit had ye in those things!" The question implies an undeniable negative, and suggests that sin yields no real benefit, no solid satisfaction. It should be otherwise. Sin ought to produce something: for it costs much. It requires the sinner to wage war with himself, to overcome innumerable difficulties, to make the most expensive sacrifices. Now, for a man to labour and toil, to give up all the advantages of religion, to sacrifice his soul, his God, his everlasting welfare, and plunge into "the lake that burneth with fire and brimstone" —for nothing! is hard indeed!

And is not this the case! Read the history of wicked nations, families, individuals. What does the sinner ever gain or enjoy! What that is valuable and satisfactory!— What that deserves the name of "fruit!" What that even corresponds with his own expectation!—The enemy told Adam and Eve that they should "be as gods," when his design was to degrade them "below the beasts that perish." And thus we read of "*the deceitfulness of sin:*" it attracts by flattery; it destroys by delusion. It looks on with blandishing smiles, but conceals the cloven foot; it presents the bait, but hides the hook; it talks of liberty and indulgence, but this is only to favour its inroads; once admitted, slavery and desolation spread all around. It promises much, but how does it perform! "Though wickedness be sweet in his mouth, though he hide it under his tongue; though he spare it, and forsake it not; but keep it still within his mouth: yet his meat in his bowels is turned, it is the gall of asps within him." Sinful gratifications continue no longer than the actions themselves: for then, consequences begin to be thought of: reason ascends the throne, and scourges; conscience awakes and condemns. Nor is it easy for the sinner to creep along to the commission of his crimes unseen by reason, unobserved by conscience; and, oh! when they are lookers on!—how, by their warnings and reproaches, do they imbitter his enjoyment! He finds nothing of that contentment and pleasure which he looked for. As he returns home, with the stain and sting of sin, he sighs inwardly—"And is this all? If this deserves the name of pleasure, how shortlived, how worthless, how mean! O that I had hearkened to the voice of wisdom and kindness, which said, 'Turn ye not aside from following the Lord—turn ye not aside: for then should he go after vain things, which cannot profit nor deliver; for they are vain.'"

Suppose now a sinner was compelled to rise and answer this question truly—How has sin advanced your well-being? What has it done for you? What has it done for your connexions, for your bodies, for your souls, for your property, for your reputation? Suppose the swearer was to tell us what he has gained by his oaths; the drunkard by his cups; the sensualist by his uncleanness; the prodigal by his extravagance, his idleness, his evil company; yea, the proud, the envious, the malicious, by indulging their vile tempers? Suppose he was to sum up his expenses and his savings; to balance his accounts at the end of a year, of a week, of a day—surely he must find that his gains do not counterbalance his loss, his wages do not reward him for his drudgery, his pleasures do not make him amends for his pains even in the *lowest* degree.

Let any one as a man of reason consider his weary steps; his mean condescensions and compliances; his corroding anxieties and suspicions; his restless desires and tormenting fears, when under the dominion of some lust or passion—to gain a fancy or a feather; to acquire the opinion of some poor worm; to pick up a little shining dust, to enjoy some light, unsatisfying, and low indulgence—and will he not confess that these things are more than unprofitable and vain? Above all, what does a Christian think when he reviews his wicked courses? He is able now to judge between sin and holiness. He now clearly sees that the practice of sin obliged him to forego, and compelled him to endure. He now clearly sees that it constrained him to live a stranger to his true interest; that it never allowed him one taste of real joy, or one moment of real peace; that it enslaved him; stripped him; starved him. Since he has served God, he looks back with painful regret upon every hour he spent in the service of sin: it appears to him an hour of inconceivable loss and injury: and he goes on weeping, and taking shame to himself.

And this brings us, II. To consider the DISGRACEFULNESS of sin. Of these unfruitful things, says the Apostle, "ye are now ashamed." And well ye may; for there is nothing in the world so scandalous as sin. Whatever be a man's station, or office, or abilities, sin degrades all, and renders him vile. It is not a shame to be obliged to labour; it is not a shame to be poor and dependent; it is not a shame to be tried and distressed—but it is a shame to be a sinner. For is it not shameful to be a fool? Is it not shameful to be a base coward? Is it not shameful to be a traitor to the best of kings? And to be ungrateful and perfidious to the kindest of all friends? If a benefactor should receive you to his house, and afford you all the supplies of his table—would it not be shameful to steal out of his presence, blaspheme his name, and endeavour to counteract all his designs? Enlarge the number of images—select whatever may be deemed base and scandalous among men, and be assured it will apply with infinitely greater force to the evil of sin. We say again, nothing is so degrading, nothing can be so shameful as sin.

But to do justice to this part of our subject, it may be necessary to observe, that there are three kinds of shame which attend sin. The first is natural; the second gracious; and the third penal.

There is a natural shame which arises in men from the commission of sin. This it was that made our first parents hide themselves among the trees of the garden as soon as they had transgressed the Divine command—so closely did shame tread on the heels of guilt. This class of emotions may be in a great measure subdued by continuance in sin; for sin is of a hardening tendency. Accordingly we read of some who "hide not their sin like Sodom." Jeremiah says of some, "Were they ashamed when they had committed abomination? Nay, they were not at all ashamed, neither could they blush." And the Apostle speaks of some who "glory in their shame." But these characters are not general, and this shamefulness in sinning is not easily, and perhaps never was perfectly attained. "The eye of the adulterer waiteth for the twilight, saying, no eye shall see me: and disguiseth his face. For the morning is to them even as the shadow of death: if one know them, they are in the terrors of the shadow of death." Hence they not only repair to corners, and elude observation—which they would not do if there was any thing that tended to their praise; but hence also, they frame excuses and apologies. And if not ashamed of their proceedings, why attempt to deny or palliate? Why plead mistake, ignorance, surprise, infirmity? Why ascribe their sins to weakness or necessity, rather than to inclination or choice—unless they deemed them a disparagement to their character? Hence it is—that the sinner cannot endure to be alone, or bear to dwell on his own actions. Though naturally full of self-love and admiration, he slips away from his own presence, and shuns all intercourse with his greatest favourite. And why? Because he is ashamed even to meet *himself*

Upon the same principle too, when arrived at a certain pitch of iniquity, he abandons the moral world, and mingles only with those of his own quality: for here mutual wickedness creates mutual confidence, and keeps them from reproaching one another.

There is also a gracious shame which accompanies "repentance unto life." This shame does not spring from a fear of the discovery of sin, but from a sense of the pollution and odiousness of it. Some crimes are universally considered as abominable; but *all* sin appears so to the real penitent: and he is now ashamed of things which pass uncensured in the world, and which once produced no uneasiness in himself. Conversion changes not only a man's state, but his affections and his convictions. Sin appears in consequence of it exceeding sinful; and, oh! what holy self-abhorrence, and loathing, and shame are now felt! The publican standing afar off, "would not lift up so much as his eyes to heaven." "Mine iniquities," says David, "have taken hold upon me, so that I am not able to look up." Ezra said, "O my God, I am ashamed and blush to lift up my face to thee, my God: for our iniquities are increased over our head, and our trespass is grown up unto the heavens." And returning Ephraim smote upon his thigh, and confessed, "I am ashamed, and even confounded, because I did bear the reproach of my youth." And so these believing Romans were *now* ashamed of the sins even of former years. And this ingenuous shame will be in proportion to our perception of the glory and the goodness of God. The more we think of his patience in bearing with us, while we were rebelling against him, and of his mercy and grace in pardoning our sins, and adopting us into his family, after all our provocations; the more shall we be affected with our vileness in offending him.

There is also a *penal* shame, by which we mean that shame which attends sin in a way of punishment. For God has so ordered things, that if a man be not ashamed *of* his sins, he shall be put to shame *by* them. And how often, and in how many instances is the transgressor dishonoured in this world! See the professor of religion—"reproached," not "for the sake of Christ:" this would be his honour—but buffeted for his faults: suffering, *not* for well-doing, but for evil-doing. See the miser. "He is a proverb and a by-word." See the extortioner. How many "curse his habitation!" Behold the adulterer. "Whoso committeth adultery with a woman, lacketh understanding: he that doeth it destroyeth his own soul; a wound and dishonour shall he get, and his reproach shall not be wiped away." So true is the reflection of Solomon, that—"a wicked man is loathsome, and cometh to shame."

But this will be more especially the case hereafter. Of the Israel of God we read that "They shall not be ashamed nor confounded, world without end:" of Christians, that they shall "have confidence, and not be ashamed before him at his coming." But this implies the truth of the reverse; and we are assured that the wicked will "rise to shame, and everlasting contempt"—ashamed in themselves; and contemned by each other, by saints, by angels, and by the Judge of all.

And oh! when they see to what disgrace they have wilfully reduced themselves; when they hear all the wickedness of their hearts, as well as lives, published before an assembled world—what wonder is it, that they call to "the mountains and the rocks to fall on them and hide them"—not only from the wrath to come, but also from shame and confusion of face?

And thus we have, III. reached the conclusion of this dreadful course, which is—DEATH: "for the end of these things is death." And by death the Apostle includes much more than the dissolution of the body. This indeed was the produce of sin: "By one man sin entered into the world, and death by sin, and so death hath passed upon all men, because all have sinned." But besides the universal and unavoidable law of mortality which sin has established, there are many instances recorded in the Scripture, of God's inflicting death immediately upon sinners in a way of judgment. Lot's wife, Nadab, and Abihu, Ananias and Sapphira, are proofs that, even in this sense, "*the end of these things is death.*" And if we had an inspired history of present times, and could trace up to their proper causes those effects which are now confounded in the common course of things, we should perhaps find the destruction of many a transgressor originating in the same way. And what assurance have *you* that the next time you take his name in vain, or make a lie, you shall not be instantly sent from the place of sinning to the place of suffering?

Death also sometimes attends sin, not only as an immediate judgment from God, but as a natural consequence of vice. It is said that "bloody and deceitful men shall not live out half their days." How many criminals come to an untimely end at the gallows! How frequently do persons, by anger, intemperance, and such like courses, hasten on dissolution, and become self-murderers! Many might have lived longer had they lived better; and have enjoyed a good old age, had it not been for a profligate youth: but now, if they drag on a miserable existence at all, they are "filled with the sins of their youth," which will "lie down with them in the grave." An old divine says, "the board has killed more than the sword." And a physician of great repute has given it as his opinion, that scarcely one in a thousand dies a natural death.

But what the Apostle principally intends,

is—not the corruption of the body in the grave, but the destruction of both body and soul in hell. It is what the Scripture calls, the " second death." It is what our Saviour means, when he says, " He that believeth not shall be damned." It is not an extinction of being, but of happiness and of hope. Such is the end of sin. And it is a *dreadful* end ; it is a *righteous* end ; it is a *certain* end.

It is a *dreadful* end. Nothing that we can here feel or fear deserves to be compared with it. Think of the degree and the duration of this misery. Reflect upon those intimations of it which we find in the Scripture. Think of being " bound hand and foot, and cast into outer darkness, where there shall be weeping and wailing, and gnashing of teeth." Think of a place, " where the worm dieth not, and the fire is not quenched." Think of the sentence, " Depart, ye cursed, into everlasting fire, prepared for the devil and his angels." Surely there is enough in one of these representations to freeze a man with horror, and to keep him from sin all his life long! " It is a fearful thing to fall into the hands of the living God!"

It is a *righteous* end. Hence the wicked themselves will be speechless : not one of them will be able to complain " I do not deserve this ; he deals very hardly with me." Had not this doom been as just as it is dreadful, God, with whom there is no unrighteousness, would never have assigned it as the portion of sin. It is not possible for us to know all the demerit of sin ; because we know not fully the excellences it has insulted, the obligations it has violated, the effects it has produced in the creation of God. But there is One who is infinitely wise ; let us rest satisfied with the judgment of the Judge. And one thing we may observe, if the greatness of the penalty confounds us, that in proportion as beings are holy, sin appears to them evil. Thus sin appears much more evil to a saint, than to a sinner ; by the same rule it appears more evil to an angel than to a saint ; and infinitely more evil to God than to an angel.

Finally. It is a *certain* end. From what quarter can you derive a hope to escape? The power of God enables him to inflict this misery. " Hast thou an arm like God, or canst thou thunder with a voice like his?" The holiness of God excites him to inflict this misery. He " is of purer eyes than to behold iniquity. The wicked shall not stand in his sight, he hateth all workers of iniquity." The truth of God binds him to inflict this misery. The word is gone out of his mouth, and shall not return. " The Scripture cannot be broken ;" and there " the wrath of God is revealed from heaven against all ungodliness and unrighteousness of men. The wicked shall be turned into hell, with all the nations that forget God. Upon the wicked God shall rain down snares, fire and brimstone, and an horrible tempest ; this shall be the portion of their cup."

He therefore that expects any other end of his pride, his avarice, his swearing, his Sabbath-breaking, his disobedience, than death, is " sporting himself with his own deceivings ;" and is even aggravating his doom by presumption and unbelief. " And it shall come to pass, when he heareth the words of this curse, that he bless himself in his heart, saying, I shall have peace, though I walk in the imagination of mine heart, to add drunkenness to thirst. The Lord will not spare him : but, then, the anger of the Lord and his jealousy shall smoke against that man, and all the curses that are written in this book shall lie upon him, and the Lord shall blot out his name from under heaven." And is it possible for you to lie down to sleep, when you know that God is bound to punish you, and under an oath to destroy you?

What use should we make of this subject ? First, remember the particulars of this discourse ; seriously reflect upon them, and resolve to have " no more fellowship with the unfruitful works of darkness, but rather reprove them." Ask yourselves—" Since I went astray—what *have* I got but shame— and what *can* I get but death?" With this beat off all the solicitations of sin—" Away— what can you offer me? Do you think I am in love with disgrace, or in want of destruction?" Surely " the workers of iniquity have no knowledge ;" surely the heart of the sons of " men is full of madness"—or they could not be induced to continue a moment longer in a course so unprofitable, so scandalous, so fatal—especially since there is such an encouragement afforded to all who are willing to leave it : " Let the wicked forsake his way, and the unrighteous man his thoughts : and let him return unto the Lord, and he will have mercy upon him ; and to our God, for he will abundantly pardon."

Secondly, let those who are delivered from this condition be thankful. " By nature children of wrath even as others ; sometimes foolish and disobedient, deceived, serving divers lusts and pleasures, living in envy and malice, hateful, and hating one another—such—such were some of you ; but ye are washed, but ye are sanctified, but ye are justified in the name of the Lord Jesus, and by the Spirit of our God." And you are saying, " Not by works of righteousness which we have done, but according to his mercy he saved us, by the washing of regeneration, and renewing of the Holy Ghost ; which he shed on us abundantly through Jesus Christ our Saviour ; that being justified by his grace, we should be made heirs according to the hope of eternal life." Admire and adore the freeness, the efficacy, the riches of this grace, by which you are what you are. And be cautious and watchful in future.

Will you turn again to folly? Would you listen to your old seducer, now you know that shame and death always follow his steps? Do you want another taste of this infamy and hell? "And now what hast thou to do in the way of Egypt, to drink the waters of Sihor? or what hast thou to do in the way of Assyria, to drink the waters of the river? Thine own wickedness shall correct thee, and thy backslidings shall reprove thee: know therefore and see that it is an evil thing and bitter that thou hast forsaken the Lord thy God, and that my fear is not in thee, saith the Lord God of hosts."

To conclude—Mark the difference between the service of sin, and the service of God. It holds in all the articles we have reviewed. If sin be unfruitful—godliness is not: "godliness is profitable unto all things." Take a Christian, and ask him—What fruit have you had in all these duties and ordinances; in all this self-denial and separation from the world? Oh, says the Christian, much every way. "In keeping his commandments there is great reward." I have found "rest unto my soul." His "yoke is easy. His burden is light. His ways are ways of pleasantness, and all his paths are peace."

If sin is shameful—holiness is not. The work in which it employs us is honourable and glorious. I do, says the Christian, indeed blush—but not in the sense you mean. I am ashamed—but it is at what I have left undone —not at what I have done. I am ashamed, but it is of my progress, not of my course: I am ashamed, but it is of myself—not of my master. No: he has dealt well with me. As far as I have sought him, he has been found of me. As far as I have trusted in him, he has not disappointed me. I follow him from conviction; and I am not ashamed to avow my adherence to him, and my dependence upon him.

If sin ends in death—religion does not. While the possessor has his "fruit unto holiness," his "end is everlasting life." And it is the end that crowns all. We have seen that religion has many great advantages at present: but if it had not—if it were all gloom, and bondage, and hardship—it has this incomparable recommendation—it ends well: ends in "glory, honour, immortality, and eternal life." If the way be rough, it leads to heaven. If the gate be strait, it opens into the paradise of God: "Mark the perfect man, and behold the upright, for the end of that man is peace."

"Therefore thus saith the Lord God, Behold, my servants shall eat, but ye shall be hungry: behold, my servants shall drink, but ye shall be thirsty: behold, my servants shall rejoice, but ye shall be ashamed: behold, my servants shall sing for joy of heart, but ye shall cry for sorrow of heart, and shall howl for vexation of spirit."

"Wherefore do ye spend money for that which is not bread? and your labour for that which satisfieth not? hearken diligently unto me, and eat ye that which is good, and let your soul delight itself in fatness. Incline your ear, and come unto me: hear, and your soul shall live; and I will make an everlasting covenant with you, even the sure mercies of David."

DISCOURSE XXI.

ACQUIESCENCE IN THE WILL OF GOD.

And the king said unto Zadok, Carry back the ark of God into the city: if I shall find favour in the eyes of the Lord, he will bring me again, and show me both it and his habitation: but if he thus say, I have no delight in thee; behold, here am I, let him do to me as seemeth good unto him.—2 Sam. xv. 25, 26.

IT is very desirable to teach by example. This mode of tuition is the most pleasing, the most intelligible, and the most impressive. How useful to a scholar is a copy! How much does a builder aid our apprehension by giving us a model of the edifice he means to rear! In reading history, how much more are we struck with the representations of a battle, than by any rules of war!

So it is in spiritual things. The various subjects of religion are most advantageously placed before us, not in their abstraction—but embodied, enlivened, exemplified. We want instances—facts. We naturally inquire how did faith operate in Abraham, and meekness in Moses? We are anxious to know how men of acknowledged religion behaved themselves in such a season of prosperity, or in such an hour of distress?

In this, as well as in every thing else essential to the welfare of man, the Scripture comes in to our assistance, and holding up to our view a succession of characters, in diversified situations, furnishes us with warnings, encouragements, motives—as our circumstances may require.

The condition of David, when he spake the words which we have read, was severely trying. His son Absalom had commenced a powerful rebellion; in consequence of which he was compelled, with a few faithful followers, to leave Jerusalem, and pass over the brook Kidron towards the way of the wilderness. "And lo! Zadok also was there, and all the Levites with him, bearing the ark of the covenant of God: and they set down the ark of God; and Abiathar went up, until all the people had done passing out of the city."

Here he paused. And here I call upon you to observe him. In such a distressing and perplexing condition, the mind will be "driven with the wind, and tossed," unless, there be some grand principle to anchor it. This Job had. " Behold, I go forward, but he is not there; and backward, but I cannot perceive him: on the left hand, where he doth work, but I cannot behold him: he hideth himself on the right hand, that I cannot see him: but he knoweth the way that I take: when he hath tried me, I shall come forth as gold." And this David had. His religion aided him. It shone forth in this darkness: it glorified this trouble; and rendered it the occasion of exercising several pious dispositions, which we are going to remark. " And the king said unto Zadok, Carry back the ark of God into the city: if I shall find favour in the eyes of the Lord, he will bring me again, and show me both it, and his habitation: but if he thus say, I have no delight in thee; behold, here am I, let him do to me as seemeth good unto him." Behold here—his love to devotion—his dependence upon Divine Providence—his submission to the will of God.

I. Observe his ESTIMATION OF DIVINE MEANS AND ORDINANCES. The ark and the tabernacle were much more to him than his throne and his palace. And therefore he only mentions these. " Carry back (says he,) the ark of God—if I shall find favour in the eyes of the Lord, he will bring me again"—to my house and my family !—No: but " he will bring me again, and—show me both it, and his habitation"—the ark and the tabernacle. Not that he undervalued the privilege of a safe return. Religion is not founded on the destruction of humanity. We are not required to contemn the good things of nature and providence. Indeed, were we to despise them, it would not be possible for us to discover resignation under the loss of them. Then our submission appears, when we know their value, and are capable of relishing them—yet can willingly give them up at the Divine call.

Yea, when we are not sufficiently sensible of our obligations to God for temporal blessings, he often teaches us their value by their loss. In sickness the man has prized health, and has said, How little did I think of the goodness of God, in continuing the blessing so long! If I enjoy it again, " all my bones shall say, who is a God like unto thee !" Were an enemy to invade our shores; were the din of war to drive us from our dwellings, carrying our infants in our arms; were we oppressed by the exactions of tyranny—we should soon feelingly acknowledge the advantages of national safety, of civil liberty, of wise and good laws. Owing to our present connexions and circumstances, a thousand things demand a share of our attention, and ought to excite our gratitude.

But our attention and our gratitude should be wisely exercised. We should be principally affected with " the unsearchable riches of Christ;" we should supremely regard our souls, and those spiritual blessings which belong to our everlasting welfare. Minds truly gracious estimate their situations and conveniences in this world by the opportunities they give them of service for God, and of communion with him. Hezekiah asks, in distress, " What is the sign that I shall go up into the house of the Lord ?" " One thing," says David, " have I desired of the Lord, that will I seek after, that I may dwell in the house of the Lord all the days of my life, to behold the beauty of the Lord, and to inquire in his temple."

Are you like-minded ? If you are, you will not suffer a little trouble or a little expense, to keep you from the house of God. When compelled to abstain from his courts, you will feel your exclusion painful. With a mournful pleasure you will think of the seasons when you went " to the house of God with the voice of joy and gladness." With longing desire you will ask, " When shall I come and appear before God ?"

This will influence servants in the choice of their stations. They will forego a number of advantages, and put up with a number of difficulties, rather than be deprived of the means of grace.

This will actuate the man of property in fixing the bounds of his habitation. Many persons in leaving off business go down into the country; and looking around them, say —Behold, yonder is a hanging wood—There are beautiful meadows—Here is a fine stream of water. But the Christian would inquire, before he pitched his tent, Is " the tree of life" here ? Can I here have access to the " wells of salvation ?" Can I " go in and out, and find pasture ?"

II. See his FAITH IN DIVINE PROVIDENCE. David views his defeat or his success, his exile or his return, as suspended entirely on the will of God. He does not balance probabilities—" These things are for me, and those are against me. When I think on these circumstances, I feel hope; but when I dwell on those, I tremble. I know the issue turns upon the pleasure of the Almighty. ' He bringeth down, and he lifteth up. When he giveth peace, then who can make trouble ? And when he hideth his face, then who can behold him, whether it be done against a nation, or a man only ? ' "

Not that he acted the part of an enthusiast, and despised the use of means. This appears obviously from the measures he devised, especially his employing the counsel of Hushai. But while he used means, he did not trust in them. He knew that duty is ours, and that events are the Lord's. He therefore looks beyond all instruments and second causes, to an Agent, " who worketh all things after the counsel of his own will."—" If I shall find favour in the eyes of the Lord, he will bring me again, and show me both it, and his habitation."

David knew it was easy for Him to take

wisdom from the wise, and courage from the brave: and to confound all his devices.

He knew also, that it was equally easy for God to turn again his captivity. He knew that his wisdom is infinite, his power almighty, his resources endless; he knew that "his counsel shall stand, and he will do all his pleasure." It would be well for us to remember this in our difficulties, and to view a change in our distressing circumstances, as turning simply on the will of God. "If he speaks the word, I shall be healed. If he favours my cause, I am released. He 'knows how to deliver.' 'Nothing is too hard for the Lord.' It does not become his people ever to despair. He cannot come too late. Balaam may prepare altars, and offer sacrifices; but how can he 'curse whom God hath not cursed?' Nebuchadnezzar may heat the furnace, and the faithful servants of God may be even thrown in; but the God whom they serve is continually able to deliver them. Had he interposed earlier, the salvation would not have appeared so marvellous and divine. He often makes our extremity his opportunity. 'For the Lord shall judge his people, and repent himself of his servants, when he seeth that their power is gone, and there is none shut up or left."

III. He professes A FULL ACQUIESCENCE IN THE DISPOSAL OF THE ALMIGHTY. "But if he thus say, I have no delight in thee: behold, here am I, let him do to me as seemeth good to him." Here are no imprecations of vengeance against seditious subjects, and a rebellious son; no bitter complaints of instruments; no "charging God foolishly;" no "teaching God knowledge." He falls down at his feet, wishing to be raised up, but willing to remain. He mourns, but he does not murmur.

Thus Eli before him had said, "It is the Lord; let him do what seemeth him good." And thus his Son and his Lord long after, and almost on the very same spot, exclaimed, "O my Father, if this cup may not pass away from me except I drink it—thy will be done."

I have been thinking what helped to produce this disposition in David. Now there were two things in himself, and two in God, which promoted this resignation: and I mention them because they ought equally to influence us in our calamities.

There were two things in himself. The one was—a sense of his own Unworthiness. A consciousness of our desert is necessary to our submission under the afflictive dispensations of Providence. When this prevails, instead of wondering at our trials, we only wonder at our exemptions and mitigations; and say, "It is of the Lord's mercies that we are not consumed, because his compassions fail not." It was thus with David. A recollection of the ungrateful and guilty part which he had acted, stopped his mouth, and made him silent in the dust. "I have behaved more undutifully towards my father and my sovereign, than ever Absalom did towards his. 'I will bear the indignation of the Lord, because I have sinned against him. Why should a living man complain, a man for the punishment of his sin? Surely it is meet to be said unto God, I have borne chastisement, I will not offend any more. That which I see not, teach thou me; if I have done iniquity, I will do so no more.'"

The other was—his Ignorance. For while the former convinced him that he had no right to choose, this persuaded him that he had no ability. He knew that he had often been deceived; deceived both by his hopes and fears; that he had desired things which would have been his ruin, and dreaded things which had proved some of his chief mercies; that "the way of man is not in himself, it is not in man that walketh to direct his steps." Hence he referred himself to God, as to one who knew what was best for him, saying, "Lord, my heart is not haughty, nor mine eyes lofty: neither do I exercise myself in great matters, or in things too high for me. Surely I have behaved and quieted myself as a child that is weaned of his mother, my soul is even as a weaned child."

There were also two things in God which aided this acquiescence. First, his Sovereignty. "Has he not a right to do what he will with his own? Did not he find me a poor shepherd? Did not he raise me to the throne? —And if he requires me to lay down the sceptre, and reduces me back again to humble life—he is righteous: his authority is unquestionable. I have nothing that I can call my own: and he can take nothing that is not his."

Secondly, his Goodness. The authority of God awes us, and we say,

"Peace, all our angry passions then;
Let each rebellious sigh
Be silent at his *sovereign will*,
And every murmur die."

But it is something else that produces the cheerfulness of submission. It is the principle which actuates him—which is love; it is the end he has in view—which is our profit: it is a belief that however things may be determined, with regard to our feelings—they "shall all work together for our good;" it is a conviction that if we suffer, these sufferings are as necessary as the knife to the vine; as the furnace to the gold; and as medicine to the body. This, and this alone can enable us cordially to say, "Behold, here am I, let him do to me as seemeth good unto him."

Let us be followers of David in this holy resignation of ourselves to the pleasure of God. There are two reasons why you should aspire after this state of mind.

First. It will be very advantageous to yourselves. In passing through a vale of tears you must expect to weep; but as you cannot escape afflictions, surely common prudence will lead you to ask, how you are to bear them? Now this acquiescence in the will of God is the preparation of the Gospel of peace, with which you are to be shod. Thus prepared, you may travel on through the wilderness—but what will you do if barefooted, when you meet with thorns and briers? To vary and enlarge the metaphor—impatience turns the rod into a scorpion. While the yoke presses the neck, patience lines it with down; and enables the man to say, It is good for me to bear it. There is nothing so likely to obtain the removal of your afflictions, as this submissive frame of mind. In chastising a child, what would move you like this yielding; like the ingenuous confession, " My father, I deserve this; and I hope it will be useful to me through life?"—I borrow the image—" I have surely heard Ephraim bemoan himself thus; Thou hast chastised me, and I was chastised, as a bullock unaccustomed to the yoke: turn thou me, and I shall be turned; for thou art the Lord my God. Surely after that I was turned, I repented; and after that I was instructed, I smote upon my thigh; I was ashamed, yea, even confounded, because I did bear the reproach of my youth. Is Ephraim my dear son? Is he a pleasant child? For since I spake against him, I do earnestly remember him still: therefore my bowels are troubled for him; I will surely have mercy upon him, saith the Lord."

Secondly. Nothing can be more honourable to religion. To surrender ourselves to the Divine disposal is the purest act of obedience: to subdue our unruly passions, is the greatest instance of heroism. It ennobles the possessor. It renders him a striking character. Nothing is so impressive as the exercise of the passive graces. It carries conviction into the minds of beholders, and forces them to acknowledge that there is a reality, and an excellency—because there is such an efficacy in " the glorious Gospel." " The ornament of a meek and quiet spirit is in the sight of God of great price."

But you say—Is all this attainable? It is. We readily confess that it is no easy thing thus to refer ourselves to God; especially in practice. We here see the Christian in his best frame, and in his best moments. But it is practicable—it has been exemplified by thousands of the same nature and infirmities with yourselves. It is practicable—I mean by Divine grace. And this grace is sufficient for you, and is promised to you. " Ask, and it sha.. be given you; seek, and ye shall find; knock, and it shall be opened unto you. For whoso asketh receiveth; and whoso seeketh findeth; and to him that knocketh, it shall be opened."

We conclude with the remark of an old Divine. That we may not complain of the present—let us view God's hand in all events and that we may not be afraid of the future—let us view all events in God's hand. Amen.

DISCOURSE XXII.

THE CHILD JESUS.
(CHRISTMAS.)

For unto us a child is born, unto us a son is given: and the government shall be upon his shoulder: and his name shall be called Wonderful, Counsellor, The mighty God, The everlasting Father, The Prince of Peace.— Isaiah ix. 6.

To " him gave all the prophets witness." But what testimony was ever borne him like this!—Here we have a prediction at once the most clear in its application, the most glorious in its contents, the most consolatory in its design. And the return of this day renders it peculiarly seasonable. Let us therefore indulge ourselves in a few reflections—upon his Incarnation—his Empire—and his Names.

I. WE HAVE HERE HIS COMING IN THE FLESH. " Unto us a child is born, unto us a son is given."

It is remarkable, that all this should be spoken of as *present*. In the time of Isaiah, the event could only be prophecy—but it is proclaimed as history. The Church of those days could only have *expected* this blessing; but they mention it as *actually enjoyed*—a child *is* born: a son *is* given! Purpose and execution, promise and accomplishment, are the same with God. " One day with the Lord is as a thousand years, and a thousand years as one day." The divisions of time which with us mark the past, the present, and the future, are nothing to him, whose being is one continual now, and who says of himself, " I AM is my name, and this is my memorial in all generations." And faith, uniting us to God, elevates us into his views, and makes us partakers of his excellences: " faith is the substance of things hoped for, the evidence of things not seen."

But for whom is this blessing designed? Who are authorized to say, unto *us* a child is born, unto *us* a son is given? The persons to whom he was immediately sent were " the lost sheep of the house of Israel." " He came first unto his own, and his own received him not." This was not, however, universally the case. There were some " who were looking for redemption in Jerusalem." Simeon, Anna, and others, eagerly embraced him as " the consolation of Israel." Some, affected by his preaching and miracles, also believed in him. All his first followers and his twelve Apostles also were Jews. Since then, an awful blindness has happened to this singular people: and " even unto this day, when Moses is read, the vail is upon their heart. Nevertheless when it shall turn to the Lord, the vail shall be taken away. And so all Israel shall be saved: as it is written, There shall come out of Sion the Deliverer, and shall turn away ungodliness from Jacob."

But he was to be a more general blessing. "It is a light thing," says God, "that thou shouldest be my servant to raise up the tribes of Jacob, and to restore the preserved of Israel: I will also give thee for a light to the Gentiles, that thou mayest be my salvation unto the end of the earth." And hence the angel said to the shepherds, "Behold, I bring you good tidings of great joy, which shall be *to all people.*" None therefore are excluded from hope on this blessed occasion. He is come to die for the *ungodly,* for *enemies,* for *sinners.* Surely here is a sufficient warrant for personal and universal application to him. Unto you—and you—and you—" is born this day in the city of David, a Saviour which is Christ the Lord!" Some indeed will not eventually derive salvation from him: but he himself has assigned the reason, and beyond this we should not go: "Ye *will* not come unto me, that ye might have life." If people spurn the remedy, we need not inquire why they are not cured.

But what is the benefit acknowledged? Unto us "a child is born," unto us a "son is given." And is there any thing wonderful in this? Do we not hear of it every day? Is it not the privilege of almost every family? And is there indeed nothing wonderful in the birth of an infant? How marvellous is the union of soul and body! What a mysterious thing is human life! How admirable the provision made to relieve its wants, to support its weakness, and to rear its tender years!

The birth of any infant is a far greater event than the production of the sun. The sun is only a lump of senseless matter: it sees not its own light; it feels not its own heat; and, with all its grandeur, it will cease to be: but that infant beginning only to breathe yesterday, is possessed of reason—claims a principle infinitely superior to all matter—and will live through the ages of eternity!

But this child is all prodigy. He is miraculously conceived; and born of a virgin. His coming "shakes the heaven, and the earth, the sea, and the dry land." For what other child did ever the heavens assume a new star? Wise men come from the east? Angels descend from glory? Ye rulers of the earth, "I said, ye are gods;" but, with all your pride and vanity, at the birth of your first-born son—the stars roll on in their courses—angels pursue their work—the festivity is confined to human beings, and to a small circle of them—neighbouring countries scarcely hear of it.

What are other children at twelve years of age? The mind is only beginning to open; the ideas are trifling and unarranged; it is the transition from foolish into intelligent. Behold this child when twelve years old, doing his heavenly Father's business; sitting in the midst of the doctors both hearing and asking them questions. And all that heard him were astonished at his understanding and answers. After this he went down to Nazareth, and was subject unto his own parents. And here a large proportion of his life is concealed from our view. We only know that he received no learned education, and have reason to believe that he laboured with his own hands; for in one place he is called "the carpenter." But when he appeared in public, he spake "as never man spake." He healed the sick. He raised the dead. He cast out devils. "He went about doing good." "He died for our sins: he rose for our justification." And he "entered into his glory, far above all principality, and power, and might, and dominion, and every name that is named, not only in this world, but also in that which is to come." What a gift was here! But this brings us,

II. To CONSIDER HIS EMPIRE: "The government shall be upon his shoulder." The utmost that a child can be born to is to fill a throne; and we deem this an enviable honour. But if we should be fortunate enough to reach the pre-eminence, what a short time does he hold the sceptre, before it drops from his feeble hand by the decays of nature; or is forced from his grasp by the effects of violence! But the child Jesus is decreed a permanent, unchangeable authority: "His dominion is an everlasting dominion, and his kingdom is from generation to generation. And the God of heaven shall set up a kingdom which shall never be destroyed: and the kingdom shall not be left to other people, but it shall break in pieces, and consume all these kingdoms, and it shall stand for ever."

And over what a molehill does the most extensive worldly monarch reign! The Babe lying in the manger claims unbounded empire. There is not a being in the universe but is either his subject, or his slave. He has "the keys of hell and of death." All the affairs of this world are under his management. Nothing occurs by chance. "It is he that determines concerning a nation, and concerning a people," to establish, or to destroy; to enlarge, or to diminish. They are all in his hands but "as clay in the hands of the potter." He is "King of kings and Lord of lords." They are amenable to his authority; they rule by his permission; they are controlled by his power. He girds them and guides them, though they know him not. As far as they move in the direction of his purpose, they are invincible; when they oppose it, a straw checks and overthrows them. He is peculiarly King in Zion. He is "a Prince" as well as "a Saviour" to his people. They that know his name not only trust in him, but submit themselves to him. And their submission is natural and cheerful, because he puts his laws into their minds, and writes them in their hearts. While they obey his commands, they also acquiesce in his dispensations. To him they refer all their temporal concerns, and are willing that he should choose their inheritance for them. Thus he has a kingdom within a kingdom; a kingdom of grace within a kingdom of his providence —and the one is subservient to the other. "He is head over all things unto the Church, which is his body." He has every thing necessary for the defence of his people and the success of his cause. Therefore this "king shall reign and prosper. He shall have dominion also from sea to sea, and from the river unto the ends of the earth. Yea, all kings shall fall down before him; all nations shall serve him. His name shall endure for ever: his name shall be continued as long as the sun; and men shall be blessed in him; all nations shall call him blessed."

Much has been said on the subject of government, and volumes have been written to ascertain the prerogative of princes, and the duties of subjects. While men are depraved beings, absolute power lodged in the hands of an individual would be dangerous. Authority must therefore be limited; one part of government must be a balance to another; and laws must be placed above men. But could a governor be found perfect in wisdom and goodness, who in all cases knew what was proper to be done, and would be always inclined to do it, *his* power could not be too absolute, nor *his* authority too uncontrolled. Such a being is the Lord Jesus—and therefore he is "the blessed and only Potentate; and has all power given unto him in heaven and in earth."

But where does this government, thus all his own, rest? "Upon his shoulder." This may appear to some a coarse image. Ancient poetry, however, has beautified it by representing a man bearing upon his shoulders the pillars of the universe. But what was this fabled Atlas! The world with all its concerns really depends on the Redeemer— he "upholdeth all things by the word of his power." And government upon the shoulder is significant: it implies burden; difficulty. It cannot be administered without much labour and care. And this is one reason among others why we are commanded "to pray for kings, and for all that are in authority!" Who can need our prayers so much!—What a charge devolves upon a parent when Providence puts into his hands a living mercy, and says, "Take this child and nurse it for me: I constitute thee its governor, and at thy hands will I require it." What an

awful task has the tutor of youth! What a weighty undertaking has the pastor of a congregation!—But think of the affairs of a kingdom!! Ask the rulers of this world, whether government be an easy and an enviable concern. How distracted is the head that wears a crown! "I am not able," says Solomon, "to go in and out before so great a people." "I am not able," says Moses, "to bear all this people;" hence he had assistants provided him. The weight of government is too much for one person, and therefore it is divided among many. A king has his council, his ministers, his officers. He cannot be all eye, all ear, all hand; he therefore avails himself of the eyes, the ears, and hands of others. But the King of saints stands in need of no help: infinite as his empire is, he manages the amazing whole without fatigue, and without perplexity.

III. LET US REVIEW HIS NAMES. Names are designed to distinguish, to describe, and to honour. In common, a single name is sufficient for a single individual. Human excellences and accomplishments are rare and solitary. One man attends to the stars, and we call him an astronomer; a second is skilled in the species of plants, and we call him a botanist; a third speaks well, and we call him an orator. The name generally sums up all claims of each. But what a number, and what a variety of sublime titles are employed to show forth the praises of our Lord and Saviour!—"His name shall be called *Wonderful, Counsellor, the mighty God, the everlasting Father, the Prince of Peace!*"

First. He is *Wonderful.* He is so principally in the constitution of his person. Here we see combined deity and humanity; finite and infinite; all-sufficiency and omnipotence; weariness and want. This is "the great mystery of godliness" which will for ever employ the admiration of the redeemed —"God was manifest in the flesh. In the beginning was the Word, and the Word was with God, and the Word was God. And the Word was made flesh, and dwelt among us, (and we beheld his glory, the glory as of the only begotten of the Father,) full of grace and truth." Indeed his whole history appears to be unparalleled. His manner of life; his mode of teaching; his death; his resurrection; his dealings with his people in providence and grace—are all marvellous.

Secondly. He is *Counsellor.* He appears for us in court. He is "our advocate with the Father." And while he pleads our cause above, he guides our affairs below. In "him are hid all the treasures of wisdom and knowledge." He is the source of all spiritual knowledge. "I am come," said he, "a light into the world, that whosoever believeth on me should not abide in darkness. Counsel is mine!" Yes, blessed Redeemer, every wrong step we have taken through life, has been occasioned by our disregarding thy instructions.

To thee may we henceforth bring all the difficulties we feel with regard to doctrine and duty, experience and practice, our condition and our circumstances; and daily and hourly may we ask, " Lord, what wilt thou have me to do ?"

Thirdly. His name shall be called " *The mighty God.*" And he would not be called so unless he were so. Unless he were so, the attributes which are essential to deity would not be the properties of his nature, and we should never have read of him in the Scriptures of truth, as knowing all things, as omnipotent, as everywhere present, as eternal. Unless he were so, the works which are peculiar to deity could never have been performed by him, nor the worship which is peculiar to deity be claimed for him and rendered to him. We do not here consider this doctrine controversially : it stands in a situation which shows its importance, and the connexion it has with the experience and hope of believers. Thus he is mighty to save; no case, however desperate, with regard to ourselves and creatures, can be too hard for him. This principle enters into all his offices. It gives infinite value to his righteousness, and efficacy to his death. It renders all he does for us and in us, divine.

Fourthly. He is " *The everlasting Father,*" or, as it is better rendered, " the Father of the everlasting age." So the gospel dispensation is described, as being final with regard to this world, and in distinction from the temporary economy of the Jews. It is the meaning of the Apostle, when he says, "And this word, Yet once more, signifieth the removing of those things that are shaken, as of things that are made, that those things which cannot be shaken may remain." And hence he adds, " We," who embrace the gospel, " we receive a kingdom which cannot be moved." And hence the angel which John saw flying in the midst of heaven, had the " everlasting gospel to preach" unto them that dwell upon the earth. Of this dispensation he is the author, the founder. It is derived entirely from him; and therefore, in the language of a Jew, he is the " Father" of it. Hence, real Christians are considered as his children—" Behold, I and the children which God hath given me." And again, " he shall see his seed." They derive their new and holy being from his word and Spirit; and they resemble him; they are " changed into the same image from glory to glory." And as he is the Father of the everlasting age, so he is " the everlasting Father :" the relation subsisting between him and his family can never be dissolved; his offspring can never be orphans.

Finally. He is " *The Prince of Peace,*" And of all kinds of peace. Peace above us—by reconciling us to God. Peace around us —by reconciling us to our fellow-creatures,

destroying our pride and envy, and inspiring us with humility and benevolence. Peace within us—by reconciling us to ourselves: not to our sins—but to our remedy, our dependence, our duty, and condition. When this takes place, the troubled conscience is calmed; the tumultuous passions cease from their raging; tormenting fears and distracting anxieties give way; we are careful for nothing, but in every thing by prayer and supplication we make known our requests unto God, and " the peace of God which passeth all understanding keeps our hearts and minds through Christ Jesus."

It was thus that he addressed his sorrowing disciples when he was departing from them : " These things have I spoken unto you, that in me ye might have peace. Peace I leave with you, my peace I give unto you." And remember that there is no peace worth having but his. The ungodly and the people of the world may be insensible of their danger; they may banish reflection from their minds; they may live in what they call pleasure, and say to their soul, take thine ease— but " There is *no peace,* saith my God, unto the wicked." But Jesus procures, reveals, produces a peace the most valuable. " He healeth the broken in heart, and bindeth up all their wounds." Ye weary and heavy laden—let your burdens be what they may —go to him—he will " *give you rest: and his rest shall be glorious.*"

Such is the Saviour, whose arrival in our world we this day celebrate. And what think you of him ? I know what some think of him. There are some who have this morning by faith embraced the new-born Messiah, with a rapture expressive of this language; " Lo, this is our God; we have waited for him, and he will save us: this is the Lord; we have waited for him, we will be glad and rejoice in his salvation." They no longer feel a void within: they no longer rove, asking, " Who will show us any good ?" They have found the pearl of great price. His character and his claims have fixed and filled their minds. The manger, the cross, and the throne—these are their attractions. Here they feel obligations the most solemn and pleasing; here they find consolation the most refreshing and pure. It is here they can live, it is here they can die. Here it is that they can say, with David, " Thou art fairer than the children of men ;" —with the Church, " Yea, he is altogether lovely ;"—with the Apostle, " Yea, doubtless, and I count all things but loss, for the excellency of the knowledge of Christ Jesus my Lord !"

But what do *you* think of him ? Has he " no form nor comeliness; no beauty that you should desire him ?" Do you feel no love to his name ? Do you never pray, " Lord, save, or I perish ?"—What then are we to think of you? What are we to think of the blindness of your understandings, and of the depravity of your affections? Indifferent to him?—What are we to think of your regard to your own safety and happiness? Can you find salvation in any other? What will you do without him when you come to die? How will you appear before him when he is seated on his great white throne?

For—once in the end of the world hath he appeared to put away sin by the sacrifice of himself, and "to them that look for him will he appear a second time, without sin unto salvation." See the Babe of Bethlehem, the Judge of all! "Behold, he cometh with clouds, and every eye shall see him. But who may abide the day of his coming, and who shall stand when he appeareth! Happy those who have loved and followed him " in the regeneration!" He will receive them to himself, "that where he is there they may be also."

"But where shall the ungodly and the sinner appear?"

DISCOURSE XXIII.

THE DESIGN OF OUR SAVIOUR'S COMING.

(CHRISTMAS.)

And she shall bring forth a son, and thou shalt call his name JESUS: for he shall save his people from their sins.—Matt. i. 21.

It is a wonderful event which we have this day been called to commemorate. The fulness of time is arrived: the prophecies are accomplished: the promises are fulfilled: the expectations of the Church are realized: "the desire of all nations is come—and we have been with the shepherds at Bethlehem, and have seen "the babe wrapped in swaddling-clothes, and lying in a manger."

For what purpose has the son of God assumed our nature, and in circumstances of the deepest humiliation entered our world? A new star has graced his birth: "wise men" have traveled from the East to do him homage; "and a multitude of the heavenly host have praised God and said, Glory to God in the highest, and on earth peace, good will towards men!" Thus heaven and earth have borne witness to the importance of this event. But wherein does the importance of it appear? By what title answerable to his character shall we acknowledge him? Wherein lies our concern with him? And why are we so interested in his birth, as to make it the subject of our greatest joy?

Let us call to mind the address of the angel to Joseph, when he announced his conception of the Virgin Mary—"And she shall bring forth a son, and thou shalt call his name JESUS: for he shall save his people from their sins."

Here is a "name above every name:" a name which "is as ointment poured forth"—it is Jesus. This name was not only given by the order of God, but explained by the same order. Jesus signifies Saviour. But this name was not peculiar to him—others had worn it. The Hebrew name which answers to Jesus is Joshua; and two persons had this name expresaly given them under the Old Testament: the commander who succeeded Moses; and the high priest concerned in the building of the second temple. The Levites also in the days of Nehemiah confess to God; "According to thy manifold mercies thou gavest them *saviours*, who saved them out of the hand of their enemies." Such a saviour was Gideon and Samson, with many others.

The name then is common; but not the reason of the imposition—"For he shall save his people from their sins." As if he had said—"Others have been called saviours because they have rescued the body; they were temporal deliverers; they saved the Jews from the Egyptians, the Philistines, the Midianites. But this child is called a Saviour for a nobler reason—he rescues the soul—he is an eternal Deliverer. 'He saves his people from their sins.'"

By this explanation, the angel not only distinguishes Jesus from every other saviour, but opposes the favourite prejudices of the nation to which he belonged. The Jews expected a Messiah who should be called a Saviour; but by this name they understood a hero, a conqueror who should break the civil yoke, free them from the tyranny of Rome, and if not lead them to universal empire, at least restore them to all their original dignity in their own land. "But, O ye Jews," says the Angel, "the Saviour is come to restore you, not to an earthly Canaan, but a better, even a heavenly country. He is come to deliver you, not from civil bondage, but from spiritual slavery: not from Cæsar, but Satan. He is come to save you from your greatest enemies; and these are—not the Romans—but *your sins*."

Let us not pass over this. Jesus came, not to suggest improvements in agriculture; plans of commerce; theories of civil policy. He left the governments of the world as he found them: these are things which fall within the reach of our wisdom to devise, and our power to accomplish.—But who could save a soul from sin?

Let us, I. Consider sin as an enemy. And, II. See in what manner the Saviour delivers us from it.

We talk of enemies. What should we think of an adversary, who, filled with malice, and armed with power, should invade our country, ravage our fields, destroy our cottages and mansions, our palaces and temples; who should despoil us of our goods, tear us from our families, deprive us of our liberty, and lead us away in irons, to terminate a wretched existence in a dungeon or a mine! And oh! were a deliverer to arise to crush the foe, and to save the captives—how should we prize him! If he had suffered in the struggle, his wounds would be deemed scars of honour. When the ear heard him, it would bless him; and when the eye saw him, it would give witness to him. Our very children, made familiar with the story, would never see him pass along without exclaiming, "Hosannah, blessed is he that cometh in the name of the Lord!" But this enemy would be a friend, compared with sin: and such a deliverer, therefore, would be nothing, compared with the Saviour of sinners. How is it then that we feel so much indifference towards him; that we are not continually uttering the memory of his great goodness! that we are not daily praying "Let the whole earth be filled with his glory!" It is because—we do not believe the enemy to be so dreadful. The reason is—that we entertain slight notions of sin. To judge of the importance of a remedy, it is necessary to know the malignity of the disease: to ascertain the claims of a benefactor to our gratitude and love, it is necessary for us to know the evils from which he delivers us.

Every thing turns upon this. If sin be our worst enemy, it is easy to prove that he who saves us from it is our best friend. Let us then look at sin, and take three or four views of its evil and malignity.

Behold sin *with regard to God.* That must be the greatest evil, which is most opposite to the greatest good. In forming our estimate of sin, we are not to judge of it so much by the relation it bears to us, or to our fellow-creatures, as by its relation to God; for against *Him* it is committed; and every sin strikes at God as much as if no other being was affected by it; and notwithstanding its fatal effects with regard to mankind, we may say to God, of every transgression, "Against thee, thee only have I sinned, and done this evil in thy sight." Sin is enmity against God; against his attributes; against his government. God never yet revealed a design which sin hath not withstood; nor gave a command which sin has not trampled under foot. Sin deposes God from his sovereignty, abuses his goodness, abhors his holiness, vilifies his wisdom, insults and denies his omniscience, his justice, and his power. And hence nothing is so offensive to God. It is called the "abominable thing which he hates." And we read that he is "of purer eyes than to behold iniquity." It is a metaphor, taken from a person who has such a perfect abhorrence of a thing, that he cannot bear the sight; the very thought of it shocks

him. This is that which renders man, though the work of his hands, filthy and abominable; and constrains even the God of love, the Father of mercies, to say, concerning him, "The wicked shall not stand in my sight, I hate all the workers of iniquity."

Behold sin in its *names.* For what term is there, expressive of reproach or misery; what image is there, that can produce aversion or fear; that is not employed by the Scriptures to represent sin? Sin! it is disobedience: it is rebellion: it is treason: it is murder: "it is the work of the devil." Sin! it is ignorance: it is folly: it is madness. Sin! it is blindness: it is deafness: it is dumbness: it is sickness: it is poison: it is slavery: it is plague: it is death: it is hell! Now, as it is said of Nabal, "as the name is, so is the man;" the same may be observed of sin: as the name is, so is the thing. Sin is not libelled by any of these dreadful representations; they are all given us by One who perfectly understands sin, and they fall infinitely short of the subject. For if we compare sin with other evils, it will be found substantially to contain them all, and to be the cause of all. This is the fountain which has imbittered all our streams, and the seed which has so thickly sown the world with wretchedness.

Behold therefore again the *effects* of sin. How different is man from what he was originally!—But sin has made this change. Sin has stripped him of his glory, and taken the crown from his head: "wo unto us that we have sinned!"

Observe the soul of man—it is sin that has debased it, defiled it, robbed it of the image, and banished it from the presence of God—it is this that has filled it with confusion and regrets—it is this that has produced unruly passions, tormenting anxieties, a terrified conscience, a wounded spirit.

Take the body of man. This was once all immortal, without a defect, a disease, a danger. But "by sin death entered into the world," and was crowned "king of terrors." And now "man that is born of a woman is of few days, and full of trouble." At his birth he enters a labyrinth of thorns and briers, and cannot move without "piercing himself through with many sorrows." Even every comfort has its cross, and every blessing its curse. And how little of the misery of the world comes under our observation! Oh! could we witness all the pains of the diseased at this moment: could we behold all the effects of war, pestilence, and famine! Could we see the bones of all the human race, from the death of Abel to this very hour piled into one immense heap—oh! what could we think of an enemy capable of producing such mischief as this!

Behold Adam and Eve, expelled from Paradise. Behold the Deluge, sweeping away "the world of the ungodly." Behold Sodom and Gomorrah, "set forth as an example, suffering the vengeance of eternal fire." See the plagues of Egypt, the destruction of the former inhabitants of Canaan, the dispersion and misery of the Jews, a people once dear to God—in all these instances, the evil of sin is brought down to a level with our senses. And it is sin also that has reduced the material creation to vanity, and doomed it to a general conflagration. As, under the law, the very house of the leper was to be pulled down, so it is with regard to this world. You say, Can trees, and valleys, and hills, and skies, be criminal? No; but they have been the unconscious instruments of the sinner's guilt, they have been contaminated by his use of them, and the day of God cometh, wherein "the heavens shall pass away with a great noise, and the elements shall melt with fervent heat, the earth also, and all the works that are therein, shall be burned up."

Thus far we have traced the effects of sin down through the history of *this* world. But there is another world that has been running parallel with this, and which will continue when this is no more. And here the consequences of sin most tremendously appear.

Enter it and see. The first thing that strikes you, is the fall of an innumerable multitude of superior beings, hurled down from heaven—What roused the vengeance which pursues them with such severity? What is it that, in a moment, could transform angels into devils! A little of that envy, that pride, that independence of spirit which you think nothing of—"he spared not the angels that *sinned*, but cast them down to hell, and delivered them into chains of darkness, to be reserved unto judgment."—And what place is that, "the smoke of whose torment ascendeth up for ever and ever?" Sin built hell; sin produced "the worm that never dies;" sin kindled "the fire that never shall be quenched." Oh! could you lay down your ear, and hear sin spoken of in its proper dialect, by the old sons of perdition! What do you suppose Judas now says of betraying his master for thirty pieces of silver; Saul of persecuting David; Cain of killing his brother Abel! But all this regards the present degrees of their misery, not its future continuance.

Hence, you must contemplate sin in the threatenings of the Scripture. Oh! read and tremble. Read of "everlasting destruction from the presence of the Lord and the glory of his power"—read of a doom which I hope you will never hear—"Depart, ye cursed, into everlasting fire, prepared for the devil and his angels." Now I reason thus, and a child can understand me—if God can righteously threaten all this misery, he can also righteously inflict it; and if he can righteously inflict such misery, sin must deserve it—and if sin deserves it—deserves such punish-

ment!—How is it possible for us to think too highly of its guilt!!

There is yet another way of judging of the evil of sin——and it is—by considering the means employed to remove it. Now there was only one Being in the universe equal to this work—the Lord of life and glory. By no other hand could this enemy fall; a thousand attempts had been made—but the victory was reserved for him.

And there are two things here worthy our remark.

The first is, that he derives from this work his highest title. His name is the memorial of this achievement; he will henceforth be known through all worlds as the conqueror of sin! And therefore we find, that though he is a Creator and Preserver, yet he is adored under the character of a Saviour, by all the saints on earth, and by all the angels in heaven. "Worthy is the *Lamb that was slain* to receive power, and riches, and wisdom, and strength, and honour, and glory, and blessing." "Unto him that loved us, and *washed us from our sins* in his own blood, and hath made us kings and priests unto God, be glory and dominion for ever and ever. Amen.

And the second is, That even in this glorious Personage, who alone was adequate to the undertaking, it required something peculiar and extraordinary to accomplish it. He does not deliver a sinner as he performed his other works. In order to *save*—he must be humbled and exalted—he must descend from heaven to earth—and ascend from earth to heaven.

Let us enter into this, and, II. Consider IN WHAT MANNER HE SAVES HIS PEOPLE FROM THEIR SINS. Now he accomplishes their deliverance by price—and thus he redeems: and by power—and thus he renews: in other words, by his cross, and by his grace.

To save us, he must suffer: by the shedding of his blood we are ransomed, and by his death we live. The case is this. Where the command of the law is broken, the curse of the law enters. Sin renders man obnoxious to punishment; and this punishment is as certain as the justice and the truth of God can make it. Now we had sinned, and therefore must have suffered—had not the Saviour become our surety, and our substitute. But he, standing in our place, became answerable for us; "he has redeemed us from the curse of the law, being made a curse for us." Thus it is said, the Lord "laid on him the iniquity of us all." And how was it laid upon him—but by way of expiation? And for what purpose was it laid upon him?—but that we might be released from a load which would have sunk us to the lowest hell. Hence it is said, "Behold the Lamb of God that taketh away the sin of the world. Once in the end of the world hath he appeared, to put away sin by the sacrifice of himself." In this sense he is so often said to "die for us"—not only for *our good*, but *in our place*, and *as our victim*. How else could he have fulfilled the types under the law? We are assured from the writings of the New Testament, especially from the epistle to the Hebrews, that the daily and annual sacrifices offered by the Jews were typical of Christ: but if they typified him at all, it must have been in his death; and if they typified any thing in his death, it must have been the atonement which it made. They could not typify, in him, the death of a martyr, sealing his doctrine with his blood; or the death of an example illustrating the virtues which he had taught. These views of his death are true as far as they go; but they did not go far enough to reach the main thing, the thing which God determined from the foundation of the world to render prominent in his death, and which the Church has so beautifully expressed in these words—"He was wounded for our transgressions, he was bruised for our iniquities; the chastisement of our peace was upon him; and with his stripes we are healed."

And thus it is that he saves us from the guilt of sin. But, to take a full view of this part of the subject, it is necessary to observe, that by his atonement he not only removes guilt from the view of God, but also takes it from off the mind. For it is here alone that we find effectual relief. That which appeases God's wrath, can alone appease the sinner's conscience. This blood, which speaketh better things than that of Abel, addresses both God and the sinner—it says to the one, "Forbear to strike;" and to the other, "Be encouraged to hope." It answers all that justice has to say in a way of claim, and unbelief in a way of objection. Thus by believing "we enter into rest." Our fears and jealousies subside; we draw near to God with humble confidence, and feel "a peace which passeth all understanding."

But to know whether our relief be really peace, or nothing more than ease—it is necessary to consider, not only how it is obtained, but by what it is accompanied. The peace he gives has purity *with* it, yea, purity *in* it. Those whom he redeems, he sanctifies; those whom he pardons, he renews. And hence you read of our being "saved by the washing of regeneration, and the renewing of the Holy Ghost."

In attending to this process, let us remember, that he always saves us from the *love* of sin. Here is the difference between moral reformation and evangelical conversion. In the one, sin is avoided; but in the other, it is abhorred. For sin may be shunned where it is still loved; and the retreating sinner may look back, like Lot's wife, and bewail the idols he has been forced to leave. Am I addressing none who know what it is to forsake sin, only from a regard to reputation, from the

influence of connexions, and the fear of consequences? Would you not rejoice if God would take off the restraint, and allow you to live as you please? Would you not feel grateful towards him if he would permit you to live in sin, and not die in sorrow? Blessing him for the indulgence, would you not go forth, free and easy, and say, "Well, no longer will I be detained from worldly dissipation—my heart has been always in it. No longer will I avoid slander—I always found it the salt which gave a relish to conversation. I will now grind the faces of the poor, and debase myself even to hell, to get wealth—I loved money equally well before; but it was dreadful to think that no covetous man, who is an idolater, should have any inheritance in the kingdom of God—but now I can be covetous here, and safe hereafter?"

Turn we to the Christian. Of the Redeemer's subjects it is said, "Thy people shall be willing in the day of thy power;" and among other things, he is willing to part with sin—with all sin—with even his dearest sins. His present hatred is greater than his former love. He now sees, not only what sin has cost him, but also what it cost the Redeemer. "Can I ever call that sweet, which he found so bitter; or deem that light, which he found so heavy? Can I ever be a friend to his enemy?—to a monster that killed *him* who is all my salvation, and all my desire?" A Christian may be surprised by sin, but he can never be reconciled to it. He has sworn eternal hatred against it—and he took the oath under the cross.

But is this all? Is he held in bondage by a tyrant he detests? No. Jesus opens the prison to them that are bound. He saith to the prisoners, Go forth. Sin shall not have dominion over you; for ye are not under the law, but under grace. Thus sin is dethroned—not only in the heart, but also in the life. By the influence of his Holy Spirit, he increasingly mortifies their corruptions, and enables them to "lay aside all malice, and all guile, and hypocrisies, and envies, and all evil speakings, and, as new-born babes, to desire the sincere milk of the word, that they may grow thereby." The means of grace are now prized; and as they are used with a humble dependence and a holy purpose, they are not used in vain. In waiting upon the Lord, their "strength is renewed: they mount up with wings, as eagles; they run, and are not weary, and they walk, and are not faint." Losses and trials, and all the dispensations of Providence, are now also under a gracious agency, and are made to "work together for their good."

But while the reign of sin is thus destroyed, the remains of it continue: and these are deplored and felt by the Christian as his greatest distress. "O wretched man that I am! who shall deliver me from the body of

L

this death?" In these circumstances, two things relieve his mind, and animate him in the warfare. The one is, that his Saviour is "able to keep him from falling;" and the other is, that "he will present him faultless before the presence of his glory, with exceeding joy." Then will he shake himself from all his dust, and "put on his beautiful garments" of complete holiness. What a blissful change! When he examines himself, he can find no ignorance, no pride, no unbelief, no weakness—He is become a part of a "glorious Church, and has no spot, or wrinkle, or any such thing!"

But this respects only the soul—yonder still lies the poor body. Death is the consequence of sin; and while the body is in the grave, the believer is not saved from all the natural effects of sin. But Jesus comes—"the resurrection and the life. He will change this vile body, that it may be fashioned like unto his glorious body, according to the working whereby he is able even to subdue all things unto himself."

Now behold the work of the Saviour perfectly accomplished, and the deliverance of his people absolutely complete. Behold him "delivering up the kingdom to God, even the Father," and hear him saying, "All these I engaged to save from their sins; and lo! they are all sinless."

To conclude. Let us observe, First, If his name be called Jesus, because he shall save his people from their sins, how awfully deceived are those who hope to be saved in them! And yet, a degree of this confidence too commonly prevails. There are few indeed but entertain some expectation of going to heaven when they die, however unholy they may live. Hence, though conscious that they love sin, and indulge themselves in the practice of it, they feel nothing like despair or distress. But upon what principle is your hope founded? Did you never read that "without holiness no man shall see the Lord! Know ye not that the unrighteous shall not inherit the kingdom of God?" Did the Saviour come to give you a license to sin with impunity? His coming was designed to make sin appear "exceeding sinful;" his aim, as you have heard, was to save us from it. "He gave himself for us, that he might redeem us from all iniquity, and purify unto himself a peculiar people, zealous of good works. For this purpose the Son of God was manifested, that he might destroy the works of the devil." And what notion have you of salvation, unaccompanied with a deliverance from sin? This is like saving a man from drowning, by keeping him under the water which is destroying him; or like recovering a man from sickness, by leaving him under the malady which constitutes the complaint. Were it possible for you to be pardoned and not sanctified, you could enjoy no communion with

God, and God could derive no service from you: you would remain strangers to peace and pleasure; and the cause of your misery would be left behind. Sin and sorrow are inseparable. God himself cannot separate them: he can only destroy the one by removing the other. He makes men happy by making them holy.

Besides these thoughtless creatures which I have mentioned, there are some who are more systematically wrong with regard to this subject. They profess to glory in the Saviour's cross, but they will have nothing to do with his sceptre. His righteousness is their darling theme; but they mean by it—a fine robe to cover a filthy back. They are fond of the assurance of faith; but they intend by it a speculative persuasion of their safety, underived from and unconnected with any gracious operations and qualities, as evidences. They consider it as a species of unbelief even to question their being the people of God; but they retain the love of the world in their hearts, and discover the same unsubdued tempers as others. They think it would be wrong to allow sin either to distress or alarm them—sin cannot hurt a believer—indeed sin has not the same evil when found in them, as when found in others: "he hath not beheld iniquity in Jacob, neither hath he seen perverseness in Israel!" This error does not, like many others, arise from mere ignorance. And therefore the apostle Jude calls those who hold it "ungodly men, who turn the grace of our God into lasciviousness." And they would do well to remember that another Apostle says, "The wrath of God is revealed from heaven against all ungodliness and unrighteousness of men." And the Saviour himself says, "But these mine enemies, which would not that I should reign over them, bring hither, and slay them before me." The character here given of the Lord's people is, that they are saved from their sins: and this is what every truly awakened soul desires.

Therefore, Secondly, Here is relief and consolation for those who are sensible of the evil of sin, and are asking, "What must I do to be saved?" Though deliverance appears so unspeakably desirable, you feel that you are wholly unable to accomplish it yourselves. Nothing in your sufferings, or doings, can wash away the pollution, or subdue the influence of sin. Such despair as this makes way for the hope of the Gospel. The convictions, which you feel so painful and alarming, are necessary, to enable you to perceive the meaning, and to feel the importance of this glorious dispensation. And these also prepare you to welcome the approach of such a peculiar Saviour. So that to you it is not only "a faithful saying," but "worthy of all acceptation, that Jesus Christ is come into the world to save sinners." Open, then, your hearts, and let me pour into them the delightful message—"Unto you is born this day, in the city of David, a Saviour which is Christ the Lord!" He is come to "seek and to save that which was lost." He is come that you "might have life, and that you might have it more abundantly." The Sun of righteousness is arisen with healing under his wings." Exercise faith upon him. In him there is plenteous redemption. He is now asking, "Wilt thou be made whole?"

Let not the nature or the number of your transgressions keep you from him. For what is he come—but to save us from our sins! If you do not think yourselves too good, he does not think you too bad to be saved by him. Throw yourselves at his feet, and say, "O Lord, undertake for me—'Save me, and I shall be saved; heal me, and I shall be healed; for thou art my praise.'"

Finally. What should be the feelings of those who are already saved by him!—To you, all this is more than speculation: it is experience. You were once "in the bondage of corruption;" but "the Son has made you free; and you are free indeed." Not that you are freed from all service and obedience—but you now obey and serve a master whose "yoke is easy, and whose burden is light." From such an obligation you do not wish to be delivered. You can never forget what great things he has done for you. You acknowledge his goodness in saving you from indigence, from accidents, from diseases, from "wicked and unreasonable men"—but, above all, you bless him for "turning you away from your iniquities."

Thus delivered out of the hand of your enemies, see that you "serve him without fear, in holiness and righteousness before him, all the days of your life." Feel your engagements to him. Let the impressions of gratitude become every day more powerful. And to a wondering, or a despising world, say, with the Apostle, "The love of Christ constraineth us; because we thus judge, that if one died for all, then were all dead: and that he died for all, that they which live should not henceforth live unto themselves, but unto him which died for them, and rose again."

DISCOURSE XXIV.

THE UNION OF PRAYER AND WATCHFULNESS.

Nevertheless we made our prayer unto our God, and set a watch against them day and night.—Neh. iv. 9.

In this mode of defence we have an example worthy of our imitation. It is equally expressive of piety and prudence; of dependance upon God, and the use of means.

And such a union as this is equally pleasing and profitable. It forms the man, and the Christian. It blends duty and privilege together. It keeps our devotion from growing up into rank enthusiasm; and our diligence from sinking into the wisdom of the world, which is foolishness with God.

Let us not imagine that the force of this example is inapplicable to us. What did our Saviour say to his disciples in the garden? "Watch and pray, lest ye enter into temptation"—the very thing here exemplified by Nehemiah and his brethren: "Nevertheless we made our prayer unto our God, and set a watch against them day and night." Besides, one of the most common and striking images by which the life of the Christian is held forth is that of a warfare. A warfare we find it to be—"without are fightings, and within are fears." Like these builders, we also are opposed by various classes of enemies who labour to hinder our work, and are always endeavouring to get an advantage over us. What then can be more reasonable than to betake ourselves to *Prayer* and *vigilance?*

I. Let us MAKE OUR PRAYER TO GOD. On him let us place our reliance; and bring all our perplexities, afflictions, and wants, and spread them before his throne. Nothing can be done without prayer.

Prayer is recommended by God himself—"Call upon me in the day of trouble, and I will deliver thee, and thou shalt glorify me."

The very exercise of prayer is useful. It calms the mind; it drives back our fears; it strengthens the weak hands, and confirms the feeble knees.

Prayer—is the forming of a confederacy with God, and bringing down the Almighty to our assistance: and

"Satan trembles when he sees
The weakest saint upon his knees."

He knows that he cannot contend with Omnipotence; but he will never be afraid to meet you alone, however you may be armed. He will never be afraid to engage you in the field if he can keep you out of the closet. This then is our wisest course, because it is our safest—not to encounter the enemy single-handed, but when we are in danger of any sin, feel any rising passion, or perceive any approaching temptation—to say, "O Lord, I beseech thee, deliver my soul. Here is a foe, and I feel my weakness and my ignorance—O come to my succour; inspire me with strength; teach my hands to war, and my fingers to fight. 'O Lord, haste thee to help me!'"

For let us remember that every thing is under his control; and according as we please or offend him, according as he interposes in our favour or refuses his aid, we fail or prosper. "Except the Lord build the house, they labour in vain that build it. Except the Lord keep the city, the watchman waketh but in vain."

Does a nation dispense with God, and place their proud dependence on natural and acquired resources? He can "lead away their counsellors spoiled, and make their judges fools." He speaks, and the tempest roars—and a navy sinks in "the mighty waters." He sends sickness; a general is laid by—and his absence occasions the destruction of a whole army, and the devastation of a whole country.

Does a man in trade dispense with God, and rely upon the wisdom of his own understanding, the power of his own arm, or the claim he has on the friendship of others?—How easily can God convince him of his dependence upon Providence! He can touch an invisible spring, and a thousand occurrences are in motion: the man wonders to find his plans crossed, his hopes disappointed. It matters not what he gets—he gets nothing. "Ye have sown much, and bring in little; ye eat, but ye have not enough; ye drink, but ye are not filled with drink; ye clothe you, but there is none warm; and he that earneth wages earneth wages to put into a bag with holes." Or he may succeed—but his prosperity will destroy him. The God he disregards stands by, and as he drinks the poison, says, "Let him alone." He *would* be rich without consulting God—and he *is* rich—and falls "into temptation, and a snare, and into many foolish and hurtful lusts, which drown men in destruction and perdition."

Surely a Christian does not think of going on without God! Generally and habitually, he does not. "Without me," says the Saviour, "ye can do nothing; and the believer is convinced of this—but not so much as he ought to be; and sometimes he seems entirely to forget the conviction. Let us take an instance. When our Lord forewarned Peter of his danger, Peter deemed the premonition needless—"Though all men should be offended because of thee, yet will I never be offended; though I should die with thee, yet will I not deny." And he was sincere. But though warm, he was not wise. He was not aware of his own weakness. He did not consider how differently he would feel in new circumstances; he did not apprehend that a little curiosity would bring him into company, and company into danger; and that the impertinence of a maid-servant would induce him to "curse and to swear, saying, I know not the man." Had he prayed where he presumed—had he said, "Lord, thou knowest all things; thou knowest my frame, and rememberest that I am dust; I bless thee for the merciful caution; 'hold thou me up and I shall be safe,' "—he would have triumphed where he fell: and have been—not an instance of the weakness of human nature, but

of the power of Divine grace. Let his injury prove our security. "Let him that thinketh he standeth, take heed, lest he fall." "Trust in the Lord with all thy heart, and lean not unto thine own understanding: in all thy ways acknowledge him, and he shall direct thy paths." "Let us therefore come boldly to the throne of grace, that we may obtain mercy, and find grace to help in time of need."

But what is the dependence upon God which we recommend?—It is wise, it is cautious, it is active. And if vigilance be nothing without prayer, prayer is nothing without vigilance. We must therefore,

II. SET A WATCH, BECAUSE OF OUR ENEMIES, NIGHT AND DAY. This is not so much attended to as it ought to be. For the help God affords is not designed to favour indolence, but to encourage exertion; and in his wisdom he has connected the means and the end together: and therefore to expect the end, without the use of the means, is nothing but presumption.

If people would exercise the same common sense in religion which they discover in the ordinary affairs of life, it would save them from a thousand mistakes. Behold the husbandman. He knows that God gives the increase—but he also knows *how* he gives it—and therefore manures, and ploughs, and sows, and weeds. His reliance upon God tells him that favourable seasons and influences are necessary, to raise and ripen the corn—but he is never guilty of such folly as to go forth at harvest, and expect to reap where he has not sown. Yet such is the folly of many with regard to religious things. Such is the folly of a man who complains he does not profit by the word—but never tries to impress his mind with the importance of the duty in which he is going to engage; never hears with attention and application; never retires to review what he has heard, and to make it his own. Does the word of God operate like a charm, so that it is equally the same whether a man be awake or asleep? Such is the folly of a man who complains that his children are not religious, when he knows that he never trained "them up in the way they should go;" never prayed with them; never instructed them early in the principles of the Gospel; never placed before them a good example in his own temper and life. Such is the folly of those heads of families who complain of servants—not considering that kind affections, expressions, and actions, can only be returned where they are received—that a harsh, unfeeling, tyrannical master; that a haughty, niggardly, scolding mistress—can never be served by cordial attention, and cheerful obedience. By failing in their duty to their dependents, they set the consciences of their dependents easy in the breach of duty to them. A poor man may talk of casting all his care upon God, and sing Jehovah jireh—" the Lord will provide," as long as he please ; but if he become idle, wandering about from house to house ; if he omit opportunities of exertion, and lives beyond his income—let such a man remember, that he tempts God, but does not trust him— an inspired Apostle says, " if any man also will not work, neither shall he eat." God knows our dispositions, and hence he is prepared to advise us—and he has commanded us " not to be unequally yoked together with unbelievers." If we disregard this admonition, and form irreligious alliances—all the devotion in the world will never remedy the mischief or prevent the misery.

He then who, while he lives carelessly and indifferently, hopes to be delivered from evil merely by prayer, is only " sporting himself with his own deceivings." He who enjoined prayer, never intended to make it the "sacrifice of fools." Prayer, when unaccompanied by a corresponding course of action, is trifling with God ; and prayer, when contradicted by our practice, is insulting God to his face.

And therefore, not only be prayerful, but " sober and vigilant." And to enable you " to set a watch" successfully—take the following directions.

First. Impress your minds with a sense of your danger. The evil which lurks under every temptation is inexpressible. The design of it is to make you *sin*; and to sin, is to debase your nature, to defile your conscience, to rob yourselves of peace and reputation, and to destroy " both body and soul in hell." I know there is a deceitfulness in sin ; and that the enemy endeavours to represent it as a liberty and pleasure ; or, if an evil at all, as a trifling one. But take your estimate of all sin from the Scripture, from the Judge himself who is to punish it—and you will find that it is " exceeding sinful"—that its history, like Ezekiel's roll, is " written within and without, with lamentation and mourning and wo."

Think of this—and common sense being your counsellor, you will watch ; you will be willing to make any sacrifices, any efforts, rather than lie down in everlasting shame and sorrow. " If I conquer—I gain endless honour and happiness. If I am overcome—I am undone for ever. And, O my soul, is there no danger of this? Are there not temptations in every situation? In my business? In my food? In my dress? Have I not a wise and a powerful adversary, who " goes about as a roaring lion, seeking whom he may devour?" And is there not a subtle party within, carrying on a traitorous correspondence with the world and the devil without!—O my soul, awake, and watch !"

Secondly. Study your constitutional weakness and failings. Endeavour to know " what

manner of spirit your are of." Some are more inclined naturally to sloth ; others, to anger and impatience : some, to pride and vanity ; others, to wantonness and the pleasures of sense. There is a " sin that most easily besets us ;" and this demands our peculiar circumspection and care.

Thirdly. Observe how you have already been foiled or ensnared. He who would encounter an enemy successfully should be informed of his mode of fighting ; and how is this to be done but by observation and reflection ? " How was such a place taken? How did I lose such a battle? What rendered the last campaign so little efficient ?—Let me look back upon my past life ; and endeavour to derive wisdom from my old follies, and strength from my falls. By what secret avenue did sin enter? Have I not been taken by surprise, where I deemed myself most secure? And may not this be the case again? Are there not some places and companies from which I never returned without injury? Shall I turn again to folly? Let painful experience awaken me—and keep me awake."

Thirdly. Guard against the beginnings of sin. You should learn, even from an enemy ; and take the same course to preserve yourselves, as the Devil does to destroy you. Now the tempter never begins where he intends to leave off. Would he induce a man to impurity? He does not propose the crime at once—but prepares for it by degrees, by the cherishing of loose thoughts, by the indulging of improper familiarities, by the courting of favourable opportunities. If he would produce infidelity—he first reconciles the youth to read poisonous books, perhaps for the sake of the style, or some curious subject treated of ; he draws him into the company of those who entertain loose notions of religion, and ridicule *some* of its doctrines and institutions : from these, he joins the sceptic ; and *he* prepares him for the scoffer. Guard therefore against the first deviations from the paths of righteousness. Crush the cockatrice in the egg ; or it will grow up into a frightful serpent. Cut off the shoots of iniquity ; yea, nip the very buds : it will otherwise " bring forth fruit unto death."

Finally. Avoid the occasions of sin. Nothing is more dangerous than idleness, or having nothing to do. Our idle days, says Henry, are the Devil's busy ones. And, says another, When the mind is full, temptation cannot enter ; but when it is empty and open, the enemy can throw in what he pleases. Stagnant waters breed thousands of noxious insects ; but this is not the case with living water.

A prudent man looketh well to his going, and will think it at any time worth while to go round, in order to avoid a pit. " Remove thy way far from her, and come not nigh the door

8

of her house"—lest, by going nigh, you should be tempted to go in. "Can a man take fire in his bosom, and his clothes not be burnt? Can one go upon hot coals, and his feet not be burnt?" Can a man wish the weeds in his garden to wither, and daily water them? If a man prayed to be heavenly-minded, would he go and wait in a place of dissipation for the answer?

Sometimes Christians are called into situations and circumstances, in the discharge of their duty, that are very trying. When this is the case, the business is the Lord's; and he will take care of the servant employed in it. And therefore, in such instances, we have seen the weakest believers preserved. But it is otherwise when you rush into such dangers, uncalled of God. Is God bound to work miracles as often as you choose to play the fool, or to act the sinner? Are you justified in bringing yourselves into a situation where the alternative is either a supernatural deliverance, or a shameful fall?

Thus, then, let us make our prayer to God, and set a watch. Let us impress our minds with a sense of our danger—let us study our natural dispositions—let us remark in what manner we have been injured already—let us guard against the beginnings—and shun all the occasions of sin. Thus shall we "stand in the evil day; and having done all, shall stand. Yea, in all these things, we shall be more than conquerors through him that loved us."

Nor shall we be always in a state of warfare. We shall soon exchange the toil of the soldier for "the rest that remains for the people of God." Our praying and our watching will soon be needless. We shall put off the helmet, and put on the crown. "Sing, O daughter of Zion: shout, O Israel: be glad and rejoice with all thy heart, O daughter of Jerusalem! The Lord hath taken away thy judgments: he hath cast out thine enemy: the King of Israel, even the Lord, is in the midst of thee: thou shalt not see evil any more."

DISCOURSE XXV.

THE TREE OF LIFE.

In the midst of the street of it, and on either side of the river, was there the tree of life, which bare twelve manner of fruits, and yielded her fruit every month: and the leaves of the tree were for the healing of the nations.—Rev. xxii. 2.

"Yea, doubtless, and I count all things but loss, for the excellency of the knowledge of Christ Jesus my Lord." Such was the exclamation of the Apostle. Such was the judgment he formed of an acquaintance with the Saviour of sinners. He saw an excellency

in it that led him comparatively to undervalue and even despise every thing else. And no wonder.

What can be so suitable, so necessary, to creatures in our circumstances, as the knowledge of the Lord Jesus? If we are exposed —he is our refuge. If we are wanderers— he is our guide. If we are poor—he is rich. If we are nothing—he is "all, and in all."

The Christian, feeling his necessities, and enlightened from above to know the source of his supplies, often exclaims, as he reads through this sacred volume, "We have found him of whom Moses in the law, and the prophets, did write; whom David, Joseph, Isaac, pre-figured; who realizes, in his own character, the temple, the altar, the paschal lamb, the ark." He holds communion with him as the "Rock of ages," as "the Sun of righteousness," as the "Fountain of living waters," as—"the Tree of life, in the midst of the paradise of God."

Of this we have a striking representation in the words before us. John saw the new Jerusalem descending from heaven. It was a city four-square. The gates, the walls, the very foundations, were of precious stones. The pavement was of gold—for what we adore, they trample upon. Thus far the allusion is taken from the world of art—but nature also lends her combined aid—and here is a reference to Eden, the original residence of man. In this residence, it is well known, man drank pure water, and lived on fruit. Accordingly, a fine river watered the garden; and a tree, called "the tree of life," grew in the centre. Hence the water of life, and the tree of life, stand significantly for all the supplies of the spiritual life. And here we have both. "And he showed me a pure river of water of life, clear as crystal, proceeding out of the throne of God and of the Lamb. In the midst of the street of it, and on either side of the river, was there the tree of life, which bare twelve manner of fruits, and yielded her fruit every month: and the leaves of the tree were for the healing of the nations."

It will be necessary to premise, that the tree of life which John saw, was not a *single* tree: for, then, how could it grow on both sides of the river? but a *species* of tree, or many trees of one kind. There is nothing forced or unusual in this language. We should be easily understood were we to say, the cedar tree grows on both sides of Lebanon; or the apple-tree flourishes best in such a soil: and we should be understood to mean —not an individual tree, but the kind of tree. And this is confirmed by a parallel passage, taken from the visions of Ezekiel. "And by the river upon the bank thereof, on this side and that side, shall grow all trees for meat, whose leaf shall not fade, neither shall the fruit thereof be consumed: it shall bring forth new fruit according to his months, because their waters they issued out of the sanctuary: and the fruit thereof shall be for meat, and the leaf thereof for medicine." Upon the same principle, it is not necessary to suppose the tree of life in Eden was a single tree; it was more probably a number of trees of the same species, finely arranged, and bearing in abundance. This conjecture has to plead not only probability, but authority. The learned Doctor Kennicot has defended this opinion.

But however this may be—whatever the tree of life was to man in his innocency, Christ is to man in his fallen estate; what that was to Adam under a covenant of works, Christ is to man under a covenant of grace. That insured life to obedience; he insures life to faith. It is his own declaration, " God so loved the world, that he gave his only begotten Son, that whosoever believeth in him should not perish, but have everlasting life." This is the new and living way opened in the Gospel, and by which we can alone pass into a happy immortality.

Whether the tree of life in paradise was more than sacramental, affording a pledge of the continuance of life, while man remained in a state of obedience; or whether, in addition to this, it had an innate virtue to perpetuate the immortality of those who partook of it—we cannot absolutely determine. The latter has been deemed probable by many, from the words of Moses; " And the Lord God said, Behold, the man is become as one of us, to know good and evil: and now, lest he put forth his hand and take also of the tree of life, and eat, and live for ever: therefore the Lord God sent him forth from the garden of Eden to till the ground from whence he was taken. So he drove out the man; and he placed at the east of the garden of Eden Cherubims, and a flaming sword which turned every way, to keep the way of the tree of life." But we are sure that Jesus Christ has not only procured for us a title to endless life, but actually communicates life to all those who believe in him. " God hath given to us eternal life, and this life is in his Son." And therefore it can only be derived from him. And as what we live upon is previously destroyed, so that we literally live by death —the death of fruits and vegetables, and animals—so by his death we live. It is his own declaration, though it may prove as offensive to some who read it, as it did to those who originally heard it: " Then Jesus said unto them, Verily, verily, I say unto you, except ye eat the flesh of the Son of man, and drink his blood, ye have no life in you. For my flesh is meat indeed, and my blood is drink indeed. He that eateth my flesh, and drinketh my blood, dwelleth in me, and I in him. As the living Father hath sent me, and I live by the Father: so he that eateth me, even he shall live by me."

And, therefore, we cannot be made " partakers of Christ" without resembling him. We cannot receive a life-giving Saviour, and remain dead in trespasses and sins. If joined to him, we shall be quickened by him, and walk " in newness of life." And it is owing to the little communion we have with him that our religion is so languishing, and that there are so many " things in us that are ready to die:" for he came not only " that we might have life," but " that we might have it more abundantly."

The situation of this tree is worthy of our attention. Endeavour to apprehend the scenery as it appeared to the eye of John. The river softly rolled down the middle, and thus formed a street on each side of it; and in the midst of each street, in a beautiful row, grew the tree of life. So that the inhabitants could walk between the houses and the trees, and between the trees and the river, on each side. It was therefore not concealed, but obviously seen; it every where met the eye, and tempted the hand. Nor was it confined, but easy of access to all who passed along, and to persons on either side of the river— " In the *midst* of the street of the city, and on *either* side of the river, was there the tree of life."

And " the righteousness of faith speaketh on this wise, Say not in thine heart, who shall ascend into heaven? (that is, to bring Christ down from above:) or, who shall descend into the deep? (that is, to bring up Christ again from the dead.) But what saith it? The word is nigh thee, even in thy mouth, and in thy heart: that is, the word of faith, which we preach; that if thou shalt confess with thy mouth the Lord Jesus, and shalt believe in thine heart that God hath raised him from the dead, thou shalt be saved." Is Christ hidden? Exposing himself to view in every direction, he cries, " Behold me, behold me. Look unto me, and be ye saved, all the ends of the earth; for I am God, and there is none else. Come unto me, all ye that labour and are heavy laden, and I will give you rest."

Is he secluded from approach, and from participation? Few, comparatively, will partake of him—but he has told us the reason: " Ye *will not* come to me, that ye might have life." Otherwise, none are forbidden: for " there is neither Jew nor Greek, there is neither bond nor free, there is neither male nor female, for ye are all one in Christ Jesus: for the same Lord over all is rich unto all that call upon him." Is he a fountain? He is a fountain opened. Was he represented by the manna? This fell all around the camp, and all were equally welcome to go and gather it up. Was he held forth by the brazen serpent? This was suspended upon a pole fixed in the centre of the camp, and it was announced, that every one that was bitten, when he looked upon it, should live. Was he typified by the cities of refuge?

There were six of these at certain distances from each other, that, in what part soever of the country the man-slayer lived, he might soon reach a place of safety. They were situated on high hills, or on extensive plains, that the avenger of blood might not overtake him, while searching for them. The roads leading to them were fifty-eight feet four inches wide, and well repaired, that nothing should hinder his progress, or stop him for a moment. Where rivers would have checked their course, bridges were thrown over: and where crossways would have perplexed their minds, directing posts were fixed, with their extended arms pointing and crying, REFUGE, REFUGE!—The application of all this is easy. Oh! think of it, ye who are disposed to "flee for refuge to the hope set before you!" Here is strong consolation—and spiritual distress requires it.

Behold further, the *fertility* of this tree.

First. It is said that it bears "twelve manner of fruits." Other trees yield only after their kind. To a vine we go for grapes, to a fig-tree for figs. But suppose a tree that should bear both these, and ten more sorts of the most delicious fruit! Would it not excite your curiosity? Would you not even go far only to see this wonder of nature!

"Turn your eyes towards me," says the Saviour, "I am all this. I am the 'child born,' and 'the everlasting Father.' 'I am the root and the offspring of David.' 'I am alpha and omega, the beginning and the ending.' I am he 'that liveth and was dead.' I am 'the Lamb slain from the foundation of the world,' and the 'lion of the tribe of Judah.' Such a combination of perfections and blessings, O man, did thy salvation require! Though all thy miseries flow from one cause—sin; thy wants are various, and demand various relief. You are enslaved, and need redemption—and I give my 'life a ransom for sinners.' You are guilty, and need justification—and my 'blood cleanseth from all sin.' You are unholy, and need sanctifying grace—and 'a new heart will I give you, and a new spirit will I put within you.' You are weak—but 'my strength shall be made perfect in weakness.' You have tribulation in the world—but 'in me you shall have peace.'" Thus God "supplies *all* our need according to his riches in glory by Christ Jesus." Thus we are "blessed with *all* spiritual blessings in heavenly places in Christ."

Secondly. The produce is not only abundant but continual. It yielded her fruit "every month." This is not the case with our trees. They bear only once a year. And hence our spring is so important—we go out and anxiously look for the buds and blossoms; and if we find none, our hope is cut off, and for twelve months we impatiently wait for the return of the season. But this tree bears al-ways—in winter, as well as in summer—perhaps he bears most in winter, or at least more is then gathered than at any other time. Our external troubles, and our internal distresses, endear him, and urge us to make a more earnest application to him. But the Apostle tells us that he found him answerable to all his varying conditions: "I have learned, in whatsoever state I am, therewith to be content. I know both how to be abased, and I know how to abound: every where and in all things I am instructed both to be full and to be hungry, both to abound and to suffer need. I can do all things through Christ which strengtheneth me." If we prosper, he can keep us. If we fall into adversity, he can sustain us. He can bless you in social scenes; and also in solitary seasons. Joseph enjoyed him in the prison, and Daniel in the lions' den, and John in his banishment. And when nothing else looks green and fair—he affords succour and supplies. And therefore says the Christian, whose faith and hope are fixed on him; "Although the fig-tree shall not blossom, neither shall fruit be in the vines; the labour of the olive shall fail, and the fields shall yield no meat; the flock shall be cut off from the fold, and there shall be no herd in the stalls; yet I will rejoice in the Lord, I will joy in the God of my salvation." Hence, in a case more distressing to a good man than any other; I mean, when his family yields him no comfort, bears nothing, yea, discovers no marks of spiritual life—he can pluck something from this tree, which is always bending with fruit: "Although my house be not so with God; yet he hath made with me an everlasting covenant, ordered in all things and sure: for this is all my salvation, and all my desire, although he make it not to grow." And when we are taking a farewell of life, and all the powers of nature fail—he is the strength of our heart, and our portion for ever—And hence the same tried and triumphant believer exclaims, "Yea, though I walk through the valley of the shadow of death, I will fear no evil; for thou art with me: thy rod and thy staff they comfort me."

When our Saviour, as he came from Bethany, hungered, he saw a fig-tree, and went up to it, hoping to find fruit thereon, and found none, "for the time of figs was not yet." But he himself will never occasion such a disappointment in those who apply to him. Come when we will, it is always the time of fruit. The tree bears "every month." Ye young, you cannot come too soon. Ye aged, you cannot come too late. It is necessary, however, to observe that this is true only of the time of your continuance in this world. If you drop through life destitute of the blessings of his salvation, your opportunity is over, and will never return. You are therefore admonished to "seek the Lord while he may be found, and to call upon him while he is near. Behold, now is the accepted time: behold, now is the day of salvation."

Observe, finally, what is said of the leaves of this tree. They "are for the healing of the nations." Other trees have leaves, and they are by no means useless. Not only do they add to the appearance and beauty of the tree—for how would a tree look without them!—but they serve to screen the new-born naked bud from the cold by night, and the excessive heat by day; they catch the dew and the rain; retain and guide the moisture; and thus they aid the preservation and growth of the fruit. The leaves of a tree afford a comfortable shade to those who not only wish to partake of its produce, but want also to stand out of the sun. The Church therefore says, "I sat down under his shadow with great delight, and his fruit was sweet to my taste." Leaves, especially in the earlier ages of the world, were frequently applied to wounds, and many of them are to this day reckoned medicinal.

What then are the leaves of this tree, here distinguished from the fruit—but the institutions of religion, the ordinances of the Gospel, which we commonly and properly call the means of grace? These derive their being and their efficacy from him, as leaves from a tree. In the use of these he has promised his blessing: by the application of them, he brings us health and cure. What are our Sabbaths? What are our sanctuaries? What are the ministers of the word? What is this book—What are the leaves of this book?—but "the leaves of this tree, which are for the healing of the nations?"

When we are perfectly recovered, and removed to that country, "where the inhabitants shall no more say, I am sick," these means and ordinances becoming unnecessary, will be laid aside. There will be no more prayer; no more sermons; no more bread and wine, the emblems and memorials of a Saviour's death. The end of all will be fully accomplished in our happy experience.

In the mean time, they are of unspeakable importance, and we should be careful to show our regard for them two ways:

First. By being thankful that we are indulged with the means of grace ourselves. Let us hear what the saints of old said, who lived under a dispensation far inferior to ours. "How amiable are thy tabernacles, O Lord of Hosts!—Blessed are they that dwell in thy house; they will be still praising thee. Blessed is the man whom thou choosest, and causest to approach unto thee, that he may dwell in thy courts: he shall be satisfied with the goodness of thy house, even of thy holy temple.' As soon as ever our ministers end their discourses, we should remember the words of our Lord: "Blessed are your eyes, for they see; and your ears, for they hear. For verily I say unto you, that many prophets and right-

eous men have desired to see those things which ye see, and have not seen them; and to hear those things which ye hear, and have not heard them." Not only are these means instrumental in awakening us at first, but they are useful to revive, to refresh us; to strengthen our weak hands, and confirm our feeble knees, all through life. Here, like Hannah, we pour forth our sorrows, and leave them behind us. Here, with Jeremiah, we find his word and eat it, and it is the joy and the rejoicing of our hearts. Our doubts are solved. Our peace is restored. Our resolutions are invigorated. Our "strength is renewed. We mount up with wings as eagles, we run and are not weary, and walk and are not faint."

Secondly. Let us be concerned for the extension of these privileges to others. Let us exert all our influence in diffusing them. Let us endeavour to spread them, not only in our own neighbourhood, and in our own country, but in all "the regions of darkness, and of the shadow of death." O when shall these leaves be for the healing of "the nations!" How much do they need the influences of the gospel of peace! How are they enslaved; how are they bruised; by tyranny, by war, by superstition, by "the God of this world!" Hear how they groan; see how they bleed and die! How many millions of your fellow-creatures are there who never heard of the name of a Saviour! They feel the same depraved dispositions with yourselves, but know nothing of that grace that can create a clean heart, and renew a right spirit within them. They are burdened with a sense of guilt, and many of them make costly sacrifices, and go toilsome pilgrimages, to get relief—but they never heard an Apostle saying, "Behold the Lamb of God that taketh away the sin of the world!"

Let us therefore pray that God would pity the nations, and communicate to them the same means and privileges which he has bestowed upon us. It is easy to see how healing the institutions of the Gospel are to a nation, even when in numberless instances they are not effectual to salvation. Where they prevail, they civilize the multitude. They tame the fierceness of their passions, and the savageness of their manners. They tend equally to secure the prerogative of the prince, and the rights of the subject. The same may be said of all the other relations in life. They expand the affections, quicken sensibility, and promote benevolence. There was no hospital in the heathen world. The philosophers of Greece and Rome never planned an infirmary. But in this country, so highly favoured by the Gospel, it is hardly possible to move without being struck with the monuments of christianized humanity. Here the blind are led into an asylum. There orphans are snatched from ruin. There the victims of seduction are hid from infamy, and

M   8*

encouraged to repentance. And here the sick are made whole.

What then would a nation be—if all its inhabitants were christians indeed! A single sentence of the Gospel, if every one would agree to be influenced by it, would be enough to turn a country into a paradise—" Whatsoever ye would that men should do to you, do ye even so to them!"

Lord Jesus, put this law into our minds, and write it in our hearts! Increase daily the number of those who shall make it the rule of their lives! " Thou art fairer than the children of men: grace is poured into thy lips: therefore God hath blessed thee for ever. Gird thy sword upon thy thigh, O most Mighty—and in thy majesty ride prosperously, because of truth, and meekness, and righteousness. O King of saints, become the king of nations—and reign for ever and ever!" Amen.

DISCOURSE XXVI.

BACKSLIDING REPROVED.

Go and cry in the ears of Jerusalem, saying, Thus saith the Lord; I remember thee, the kindness of thy youth, the love of thine espousals, when thou wentest after me in the wilderness, in a land that was not sown.—Jeremiah ii. 2.

THIS address employs a figure of speech very common in the Scripture, especially in the prophecies. It consists in representing the state of a nation by the various ages, changes, and circumstances of a single individual.

When the Jews left Egypt, and began their journey in the desert, it was the time of their " youth." And when, in Horeb, God claimed them as his peculiar people, and they said, all that the Lord commandeth us we will do, it was the season of their " espousals." Since that interesting period, they had become more remiss and degenerate. And Jeremiah is commissioned to cry in the ears of Jerusalem—" I remember thee, the kindness of thy youth, the love of thine espousals, when thou wentest after me in the wilderness, in a land that was not sown."

Yet surely these words are not less suited to an individual than to a nation; or less true of Christians than of Jews. Let us then consider them two ways. I. As THEY FURNISH US WITH REMARKS. II. As THEY APPLY TO CHARACTERS.

These words supply us with several useful remarks.

First. Behold in God a disposition to commend, rather than condemn; to praise, rather than to censure. To a person who reads the history of the Jews, their early behaviour in the wilderness will appear very improper and blameworthy. They discovered much ingratitude and unbelief; they often complained and murmured, and sometimes talked of making themselves a leader, and returning back into Egypt. Nevertheless God here speaks of it comparatively with honour—" I remember thee, the kindness of thy youth, the love of thine espousals, when thou wentest after me in the wilderness, in a land that was not sown." He was acquainted with all the disadvantages of their situation. He considered how material things affected the body, and how the body influenced the mind. He knew their frame, and remembered that they were dust.

" He saw their flesh was weak and frail,
He saw temptations still prevail;
The God of Abraham loved them still,
And led them to his holy hill."

While we admire this tenderness, let us learn also to resemble it. Let us excuse and approve as far as we can; and in examining characters let us observe the good more largely than the evil. Let us beware of indiscriminate reflection; of speaking severely of persons in the gross; of branding a whole course of life with the reproach of a particular action. A man may redden with a blush, or turn pale with a fright—but what should we think of the painter, who in his delineation would secure this temporary incidental colour, instead of his natural and common complexion! When the angel appeared to Abraham, Sarah behaved very unbecomingly; she hid herself behind the door; she listened, she disbelieved, she laughed, and she denied the whole. There was only one good thing; one thing commendable and exemplary on this occasion—and the Holy Ghost has seized and mentioned this only to her honour: " Even as Sarah obeyed Abraham, calling him Lord, whose daughters ye are as long as ye do well, and are not afraid with any amazement." Job, in the paroxysm of his grief, cursed the day of his birth; but he is proposed only as an example of patience; " Ye have heard of the patience of Job." Notwithstanding the imperfections remarked in the seven churches of Asia—they are still called the seven " golden candlesticks."

Secondly. " God remembers the past." Our memories soon fail us. How little can we now retrace of all the busy concerns in which we have been engaged! How few of our actions, and how much fewer of our words, and of our thoughts, are we able to recover from the oblivion of time! But all of them are with God. Old impressions soon give place to new ones, and we often find it difficult to recall, without assistance, an occurrence that happened a few months, or a few weeks ago. But " a thousand years are in his sight but as yesterday, when it is passed, and as a watch in the night."

As he observes every thing, so he retains it; and what with us—is past, with him

—is present. It was a persuasion of this that led David to pray, "Remember not against me the sins of my youth." For he can easily show us that he remembers them. He can write bitter things against us, and make us possess the iniquities of our youth. He can bring back old sins by afflictions; and he can bring back old sins by convictions. He can tell us all things that ever we did. Transgressions committed forty years back, he can revive, even in their aggravations and circumstances, with all the freshness of recent guilt. And it is well to be convinced of this truth, in a way of mercy, and while we can apply for pardon. For he will certainly convince every impenitent sinner of it hereafter, in a way of justice, when he will publish to the world all the private wickedness of his heart and life, and fill him "with shame and everlasting contempt."

Thirdly. It is well to be informed of what we once were, and to be led back to our former history and experience. It is useful for a preacher sometimes to cry in our ears, and remind us of our natural state; that we may "look to the rock whence we are hewn, and to the hole of the pit whence we were digged." It is needful for him to remind us of the dispensations of Providence which have attended us in former years:

"Why should the wonders He has wrought
Be lost in wonder, and forgot?"

It is well for us to raise our Ebenezers, and to inscribe upon them, "Hitherto hath the Lord helped me." Such memorials God himself prescribes. "O my people, remember now what Balak king of Moab consulted, and what Balaam the son of Beor answered him from Shittim, unto Gilgal; that ye may know the righteousness of the Lord. And thou shalt remember all the way which the Lord thy God led thee these forty years in the wilderness, to humble thee, to prove thee, to know what was in thine heart, whether thou wouldest keep his commandments or no."— It is desirable to bring back to the mind our former frames and feelings in religion. We need every thing that is favourable to self-examination and self-knowledge. We ought to be able to judge of our progress, or of our declensions, in the divine life. The state of our souls in particular circumstances and seasons should be secured, that after the lapse of years, it may be reviewed. A comparison of our present, with our former experiences, will in some instances encourage; and in more condemn.

But we need reproof. It will be profitable for us to afflict our souls. "The sacrifices of God are a broken spirit: a broken and a contrite heart, O God, thou wilt not despise."

This brings us, II. To consider those words AS APPLICABLE TO CHARACTERS.

And First. They will apply to Christians under declensions in religion. It is said of Jehoshaphat, that he walked "in the first ways of David his father." This is an intimation that his first ways were his best: that the king never equalled the shepherd. This is awful. But the case is not peculiar to him. Backsliding is no uncommon thing. For it should be remembered that where there are no gross and scandalous deviations from the path of duty, there may be many secret alienations of heart from God; and where iniquity does not abound, the love of many may wax cold. Let us imagine the Supreme Being, by his ministers, addressing such characters as these:—

I remember thee, the kindness of thy youth —I remember thy simplicity. One motive influenced and decided you. If God was pleased and glorified, and you could enjoy his smiles and his presence—it was enough; and the applause or censure of worms was less than nothing and vanity. You rejoiced that you were "counted worthy to suffer shame for his name;" and binding the reproach of the cross as an ornament upon your brow, you said, If this be to be vile, I will yet be more vile. One thing you desired of the Lord, and that you sought after—it was a participation of the portion of his saints. Therefore, regardless of all other things, you prayed, "Remember me, O Lord, with the favour thou bearest unto thy people: O visit me with salvation; that I may see the good of thy chosen: that I may rejoice in the gladness of thy nation, and glory with thine inheritance." You did not think of stipulating for any thing else—with this, having only food and raiment, you could learn to be content. But, alas! since this period, how often have you looked aside after the friendship of the world! how often have you yielded a little of your firmness to avoid the reproach of the cross! It is not sufficient for you now to have "God for your portion"—you are miserable unless you are in a fair way of adding house to house, and joining field to field. A little disappointment in worldly things fills you with fretfulness and despondency—as if all was gone or going—and, like Jonah, you sometimes exclaim, when a gourd withers, "I do well to be angry even unto death."

—I remember thy attachment to the means of grace. O how you loved his word: it was your meditation all the day!—How welcome was the preaching of the Gospel! Then a trifling indisposition; a little rain or cold; the unseasonable calling of a friend—did not keep you from the courts of the Lord—nor did you hear half asleep. How you prized the Sabbath! How you numbered the intervening hours that should draw it on! How you hailed it when it arrived—"This is the day which the Lord hath made: we will rejoice and be glad in it!" And O how precious were those seasons in which, around the table of a crucified Saviour, you received the dear memorials of his dying love! In the reception you said—"His flesh is meat indeed! and his blood is drink indeed!" and in the review—"I sat down under his shadow with great delight, and his fruit was sweet to my taste!" Then Christians appeared like angels. How attractive, how edifying, was the communion of saints! If two of you walked towards Emmaus, you took sorrowful and sweet counsel together; the Redeemer was your theme and your companion; and when you came to the village whither you went, you said one to another, "Did not our heart burn within us while he talked to us by the way, and opened to us the Scripture!" And when alone, was not your meditation of him sweet, and therefore frequent! Could you not say, with David, "How precious are thy thoughts unto me, O Lord; how great is the sum of them! If I should count them, they are more in number than the sand: when I am awake, I am still with thee."

I remember thy holy and active zeal:—how you abounded in the duties of obedience; how you daily asked, "Lord, what wilt thou have me to do?" How dissatisfied you were in the service of God, unless you could "draw near even to his seat;" how the bitterness of repentance made you loathe sin; at what an awful distance you kept yourselves from its approach; how you shunned "the very appearance of evil;" how, when the name of God was blasphemed, you could not sit "like a man in whose mouth there are no reproofs," but spoke for God, and defended his cause; how "jealous" you were "for the Lord of hosts;" how your bowels yearned over perishing sinners; how you longed to teach transgressors the way in which you were walking; how you seized every opportunity to invite others to taste and see that the Lord is good; how to relations, friends, neighbours, you said, "Come with us, and we will do you good; for the Lord hath spoken good concerning Israel!"—I need not proceed. Such is the change.—

And has God deserved it! Have you gained by these declensions from him? Have you not compelled him to say, "Have I been a wilderness unto Israel—a land of darkness? O that they had hearkened to my commandments! then had their peace been as a river, and their righteousness like the waves of the sea!"

How dreadful is it that, when every thing requires our advancement, we should be stationary! that, when means and ordinances, mercies and trials, unite to urge us forward; that, when our obligations to God are daily increasing, and the day of account every hour approaching—we should not only stand still —but even draw back!

Surely it is high time to awake out of sleep! Declining Christian! attend to the admonitions given to the declining Churches: "Nevertheless I have somewhat against thee, because thou hast left thy first love. Remember therefore from whence thou art fallen, and repent, and do the first works; or else I will come unto thee quickly, and will remove thy candlestick out of his place, except thou repent. Be watchful, and strengthen the things which remain, that are ready to die: for I have not found thy works perfect before God. Remember therefore how thou hast received and heard, and hold fast, and repent. If therefore thou shalt not watch, I will come on thee as a thief, and thou shalt not know what hour I will come upon thee." Lay these things to heart. Say, "O that it was with me as in months past!" Carry thy case to the Scriptures; to the cross of Christ; to the throne of grace; and pray—"Create in me a clean heart, and renew a right spirit within me. Restore unto me the joy of thy salvation, and uphold me with thy free Spirit. Open thou my lips, and my mouth shall show forth thy praise. Wilt thou not revive us again, that thy people may rejoice in thee? Show us thy mercy, O Lord, and grant us thy salvation."

Secondly. The words will apply to those who promised fair in their youth, and are now become irreligious. Many a fine morning has been overspread with clouds, and followed by foul weather. Many a tree in spring has been covered with blossoms, which have never settled into fruit. And thus it has been with many a youth who has discovered amiable and pious propensities. Thus it was with the young man who came to our Lord as an humble inquirer concerning eternal life: it is said, "When Jesus saw him, he loved him." Thus Joash was remarkable for early goodness; and was preserved in it during the lifetime of the excellent Jehoiada; but, upon the death of his guardian, he was drawn aside by evil company and counsel. And, from this and various other causes, there are many young persons in the same condition now.

Perhaps you say—"But we are not vicious and profligate." So far it is well. And oh that this was true of all! but, alas! we have swearers now, who in their youth feared an oath; we have sabbath-breakers now, who in their youth revered the sacred hours; we have sceptics and scoffers now, who from a child knew and admired "the Scriptures, which are able to make us wise unto salvation." You say, "We are not like them." But they were not thus drawn aside all at once; they became wicked by degrees. This is always the course of sin. They "proceed from evil to evil:" they "wax worse and worse." The way to hell is down hill; once in motion, it is easy to go on, and you know not where you shall stop. You say, "We are not like them." But let me, my dear young friends, ask you—Are you not much less piously inclined than you once were? Have you not exchanged a lovely teachableness of mind, for conceit and self-sufficiency? a tenderness of conscience, for an insensibility of mind, which the word can seldom move? Have you not given up private prayer? Have you not lost much of your veneration for the pious and the good? Cannot you trifle with what once made you tremble? Are you not beginning to "walk in the counsel of the ungodly;" to "stand in the way of sinners;" to "sit in the seat of the scornful?"

Ah! had you proceeded in the good course in which you were once engaged, ere now you might have been far advanced and established; ere now, actions would have produced habits, and habits have yielded pleasure. What can be more distressing, than your declensions from the good ways of God, to your pious friends; to your godly ministers! how does it grieve them to see you breaking over the barriers of a good education, and resolving that the prayers, and tears, and vows of your connexions shall be all in vain! Ministers viewing you with hopeful pleasure as they buried the aged and the honourable, were saying—Well, others are coming forward, and will be the pillars of our bereaved churches: "instead of the fathers shall be the children." Your parents were beginning to say to each other—We shall soon be laid low in the dust—but these our loved offspring shall be a seed to serve him. Now a death has spread over all their hopes!—especially when they reflect, that—you are likely to go greater lengths in error and wickedness than others; and that you will be reclaimed with much more difficulty than those who never did such "despite to the Spirit of grace."

But Thirdly. There are some who in their early days are truly devoted to the service and glory of God. To you, my dear young friends, the words are applicable—not in a way of reproach, but honour—not in a way of rebuke, but encouragement. And what we wish you to observe is this—that early piety is peculiarly acceptable to the God of your lives and mercies. He takes it kind—O wonderful condescension! O touching motive!—he takes it *kind:* "I remember thee, the *kindness of thy youth,* the love of thine espousals, when thou wentest after me in the wilderness, in a land that was not sown."

You are forsaking the world, and willing to follow him whithersoever he goeth. *You* are pressing through a thousand allurements and seductions to reach him, and to say, kneeling at his footstool, "Whom have I in heaven but thee! and there is none upon earth that I desire beside thee." *You* give him the first-born of your days, the first-fruits of your reason and affections—And I say again—he

takes it as kindness—"I love them that love me, and they that seek me early shall find me." He will guide you with his counsel, and afterwards receive you to glory. Should life be spared to a late period, it will only extend your course of usefulness, and with pleasure you will look back upon a life of mercy and grace, of communion with him, and dedication to him. Found in the way of righteousness, he will view your hoary head as "a crown of glory." When the days come, in which many will say, "We have no pleasure," it shall be otherwise with you. Under the decays of nature, and the loss of friends of which time has robbed you; when every thing earthly has become distasteful; and you are made to "possess months of vanity, and wearisome nights are appointed unto you"—with humble boldness you may plead, "Cast me not off in the time of my old age; forsake me not when my strength faileth. O God, thou hast taught me from my youth: and hitherto have I declared thy wondrous works. Now also, when I am old and gray-headed, O God, forsake me not; until I have showed thy strength unto this generation, and thy power to every one that is to come." And he will answer you: "Even to your old age I am he; and even to hoary hairs will I carry you: I have made, and I will bear; even I will carry, and will deliver you."

DISCOURSE XXVII.

THE MISERY OF CONTENDING WITH GOD.

Wo unto him that striveth with his Maker!
Isaiah xlv. 9.

THE life of man is held forth by various images: and it is worthy of our observation that they will apply equally to the righteous and the wicked. For instance,

The Christian is a traveller—and so is the sinner; only the one is journeying to heaven, and the other to hell.

The Christian is a husbandman—so is the sinner. Both sow: only the one "sows to the flesh, and shall of the flesh reap corruption; while the other sows to the Spirit, and shall of the Spirit reap life everlasting."

The Christian is a soldier—and we read in the Scripture of his commander, his enemies, and his arms; of his "fightings without," and of his "fears within;" of his toil, and of his triumph.—But if the life of the Christian be a warfare, so is the life of the sinner. There is however this difference between them. The one wages a good warfare, and is crowned with glory and honour—the other is engaged in a cause the most infamous, and covers himself with shame and confusion. The one is sure of victory—the other is certain of defeat. The one fights for God—but the other against him—and "Wo unto him that striveth with his Maker!"

I. LET US MENTION SOME INSTANCES IN WHICH THE SINNER STRIVES WITH GOD.

II. CONSIDER THE *Wo* WHICH HIS OPPOSITION NECESSARILY ENTAILS UPON HIM.

And, O! let me beseech you this evening to hear, not only with seriousness, but with self-application, that while I am endeavouring to lay open this *crime*, and this *curse*, you may individually ask yourselves, in the presence of God, whether you are chargeable with the one, in order to determine whether you are exposed to the other.

I. Let me specify some INSTANCES IN WHICH THE SINNER MAY BE CONSIDERED AS STRIVING WITH GOD. And here I hardly think it worth while to mention atheism, which opposes his very being, and tries to banish him from the world which he has made. Some indeed have supposed that a speculative atheist is an impossibility. I have often thought that if such a monster can be found, he is to be found, not in a heathen but in a Christian country. How far God may give up a man "to strong delusion to believe a lie," who has despised and rejected the advantages of revelation, it is not for us to determine—but "if the light that is in thee be darkness, how great is that darkness!"

It is undeniable however that we have a multitude of practical atheists. That is; we have thousands who live precisely as they would do if they believed there was no God; and are no more influenced by his presence and perfections, than if they were persuaded the Scripture was "a cunningly devised fable." Yea, they not only live "without God in the world," but they live against him! Wherein!

First. They strive with him by transgressing his holy and righteous law. And this is done, not only by the commission of those sins which it forbids, but also by the omission of those duties which it enjoins. The man that does not love his neighbour and strive to do him good, is therefore criminal, as well as the man who robs and oppresses him. This law is also broken by the desires of the heart, as well as by the actions of the life. It is so spiritual as to apprehend murder in angry words, and adultery in wanton looks. Now every instance of disobedience is a contention with God; a daring struggle to determine whether we shall be governed by his will or by our own.

Secondly. The sinner strives with God by opposing the Gospel. The Gospel is a scheme of mercy designed to glorify God in the salvation of man, and is made known "for the obedience of faith." It calls us to repentance. It calls us to renounce our own righteousness. It calls us to flee for refuge to the Saviour of sinners. If, therefore, we go on in our impenitency; if we endeavour to establish our own righteousness, and save ourselves; if we endeavour to rear a shelter, instead of repairing to the only refuge provided—we are striving with God. In the Gospel God says, "Come and let us reason together;" but the sinner says, "Depart from us: we desire not the knowledge of thy ways." The language of the Gospel, as a token of willing submission, is, "Kiss the Son"—the language of the sinner is, "We will not have this man to reign over us." The language of the Gospel is, "Go and wash in Jordan seven times; and be clean"—the language of the sinner is, "Are not Abana and Pharpar, rivers of Damascus, better than all the waters of Israel? may I not wash in them and be clean?" No. And the reason is, that your cure can only come from God, and he has determined to save you in his own way: he has revealed only one remedy; to this the promise is made; to this he requires you to submit; and if you refuse this method, and think of becoming your own physician, you are at variance with God. And even after persons have some serious concern about their souls, they find it no easy thing to yield up themselves unreservedly to this sovereign plan. Such is the pride of reason, and the force of legality; such a difficulty is there in relinquishing all apprehension of some worthiness and strength of their own; and such a disposition have they to make themselves better before they rely on the Saviour, that they are often detained long in opposing this gracious scheme, till increasing conviction compels them to acquiesce. And, though the force of it be subdued, something of the old leaven remains in the people of God all through life.

Thirdly. The sinner strives with God by violating the dictates of conscience. Conscience is the Divinity in man. And how often, and how faithfully, has it addressed you! "'O do not that abominable thing that I hate'"—and yet you did it. "Abandon that vicious course: 'its steps take hold on hell'"—and yet you pressed forward. "Beware of that irreligious connexion: 'evil communications corrupt good manners: a companion of fools shall be destroyed'"—and yet you complied with their enticements. And O! what labour have you had to lull conscience asleep, that you might steal forth and pursue your iniquities undisturbed! How hard have you often found it to subdue the uneasinesses which have sprung from its reproaches and condemnation! And sometimes, in struggling with you alone, has it not been ready to gain the victory, till you went forth and called in to your assistance—your comrades, and your dissipations; and thus rallied and reinforced, you have renewed the contest, and again "done despite unto the Spirit of grace?"

Fourthly. The sinner strives with God by refusing to resign himself to the dispensations of his providence. By various blessings and indulgences, in his person, in his family, or in his business, God would attach his heart to himself. Hence the Apostle says, that " the goodness of God leadeth to repentance:" it ought to do so: it is the design and the tendency of it—But the sinner frustrates this design and tendency—yea, he does more—he turns it into an encouragement to sin. He is evil because God is good; and the mercies, which should serve as so many " cords of love" to draw him to God, he employs as so many weapons of rebellion against him! " Because sentence against an evil work is not executed speedily, therefore the heart of the sons of men is fully set in them to do evil. Let favour be showed to the wicked, yet will he not learn righteousness: in the land of uprightness will he deal unjustly, and will not behold the majesty of the Lord."

God tries other means. He sends a succession of disappointments and afflictions. These are designed to wean him from the world—but " he holds fast deceit, he refuses to return." They are " to hedge up his way with thorns"—but he breaks through them, and wanders on. By these God arms himself to awaken his fears, and drive him back—but " he rushes upon the thick bosses of his buckler." God strikes—and he strikes again! " O Lord, are not thine eyes upon the truth! thou hast stricken them, but they have not grieved; thou hast consumed them, but they have refused to receive correction: they have made their faces harder than a rock: they have refused to return."

He fixes the bounds of our habitations; arranges all our affairs; leaves nothing to chance. And upon this principle we " should learn, in whatsoever state we are, therewith to be content." For God cannot err. But the sinner murmurs and complains; he quarrels with the allotments of Providence; he wishes to rectify the Divine proceedings—God has not properly disposed of him, or of others—and the common sentiment is, that God has placed him too low, and others too high; indulged him too little, and others too much.

Again. The sinner strives with God by the persecution of his people. For such is the intimate and inseparable union between him and his followers, that in whatever degree you endeavour to injure them, you oppose him: he considers it as done against himself: " for he that toucheth them, touches the apple of his eye." Therefore said our Lord and Saviour, " Saul, Saul, why persecutest thou me?"

Finally. He strives with God by trying to hinder the spread of his cause. He who, by fraud or force, would keep the Gospel from entering a neighbourhood, or, by reproach or threatening, would discourage people from hearing it, is in avowed opposition to the revealed will of God, " who will have all men to be saved, and come unto the knowledge of the truth." Persons may endeavour to justify their opposition in some cases, because those who are labouring to do good are not of their community, and " walk not with them"—but, surely, it becomes them to be exceedingly cautious in their conclusion, and to weigh the admonition of Gamaliel: " Refrain from these men, and let them alone: for if this counsel or this work be of men, it will come to nought; but if it be of God, ye cannot overthrow it: lest haply ye be found even to fight against God."

And be it remembered, that men will be judged not according to their success, but according to their intention. God may overrule their rage for good, and make all their efforts to subserve the cause they oppose—but as this was not their design, it will not be their exculpation. It was " in their heart" to prevent the diffusion of truth, and the influence of the Gospel: and God deals with them accordingly. He " looketh to the heart;" and will punish them in proportion to the good they would have hindered, and the evil they would have spared, had they been successful. For " wo unto him that striveth with his Maker!"

II. No wonder such a wo is here denounced—for this striving with God is,

First, A practice the most shameful and ungrateful. What would you think of a child who should strive with his father, reproach his character, counteract all his designs, and endeavour to injure his concerns?—But such is your conduct towards God. " Is not he thy Father, that hath made thee?" What would you think of a person who would set himself against a benefactor that had never given him the least ground of provocation, and had always been doing him good? But such is your conduct towards God. He has preserved your souls in life. His air you have breathed. From his table you have been fed. He has given you all things richly to enjoy.

Has he not therefore reason to be astonished at your baseness and ingratitude? " Hear, O heavens; and give ear, O earth: for the Lord hath spoken: I have nourished and brought up children, and they have rebelled against me. The ox knoweth his owner, and the ass his master's crib: but Israel doth not know, my people doth not consider."

It is, Secondly, a practice the most unreasonable and absurd. For observe—in all the instances in which you oppose him, he is aiming to promote your good: his design is to make you wise, to make you holy, to make you happy; and the advantages of compliance will be all your own. Besides—

Can you do without him?—Can you do without him in life? In death can you do without him? Who else can pardon you?

or sanctify you? or comfort you? or give you an abundant entrance into the everlasting kingdom of our Lord and Saviour? What then can equal the folly of offending and provoking *Him* whose favour is life, and upon whom you absolutely depend for every thing essential to your happiness in time and eternity?

And therefore, Thirdly, Nothing can be more injurious and ruinous. In striving with him, you only resemble the wave that dashes against the rock, and is driven back in foam; or the ox that kicks against the goad, and only wounds himself; or the thorns and briers that should set themselves in battle array against the fire. Hence says God, " Let the potsherds strive with the potsherds of the earth." If you will contend, choose an enemy like yourselves, with whom you may claim some kind of equality. There is none between you and me. There are cases, in which it may be proper to wage war, where there is only a probability, or even a possibility of victory. But what desperate madness actuates *you! You* strive with an adversary by whom you know you *must* be conquered. For " have you an arm like God, or can you thunder with a voice like his?" Need you be told, that he can work immediately upon the mind, and in the twinkling of an eye could produce such terrors in your consciences as would be intolerable? Need you be told that he is able to destroy both body and soul in hell? Need you be told that all creatures, from an angel to a worm, are under his control, and only wait his signal to fall upon you?

This, you say, only shows what he *can* do. Let us then see what he *will* do. What has he said? Read these threatenings: " If ye walk contrary to me, I also will walk contrary to you; and will punish you seven times for your iniquity." " He shall be revealed from heaven, with his mighty angels, in flaming fire; taking vengeance on them that know not God, and that obey not the Gospel of our Lord Jesus Christ: who shall be punished with everlasting destruction from the presence of the Lord, and from the glory of his power. And Enoch also, the seventh from Adam, prophesied of these, saying, Behold, the Lord cometh with ten thousand of his saints, to execute judgment upon all, and to convince all that are ungodly among them of all their ungodly deeds which they have ungodly committed, and of all their hard speeches which ungodly sinners have spoken against him."

" But what reason have we to believe that all this is true?"—Because it is found in a book written by God himself. Because many of these threatenings have already been accomplished. Because it accords with those evils and miseries which are found to attend wickedness even in this world. And because no one ever hardened himself against God

and prospered. Did Pharaoh? Did Belshazzar? Did the Jews?

To improve this awful subject, let me ask —Whether you are for God or against him? Be not surprised—you are either his friends or his enemies: there is no neutrality here. In some cases, neutrality is allowable if not commendable. In family disputes, or in quarrels among neighbours, it may be proper to stand neuter. If we can do no good, we shall do no harm; and this is often a considerable point. In the senate of a nation a member may waive his vote; things may be balanced in his mind; and nothing for the time may cause either side of the question to preponderate. And it is the excellency of a representative to be of no party. Two nations may worry and consume each other, while a third however pressed, may remain neutral and save its wealth and its subjects. But here—we repeat it—and it cannot be repeated too often; here, there is not, and there cannot be a state of indifference. " He that is not for me is against me; and he that gathereth not with me scattereth abroad. No man can serve two masters, for either he will hate the one, and love the other; or else he will hold to the one, and despise the other. Ye cannot serve God and Mammon."

Are you then the enemies of God; and have you to this hour been striving with your Maker? O! let me admonish you. Let me address you in the words of Eliphaz to Job: " Acquaint now thyself with him, and be at peace: thereby good shall come unto thee." Let me urge you, in the language of the apostle Peter: " Humble yourself under the mighty hand of God, and he will exalt you in due time." If you are willing to return, be not discouraged. Behold him stretching forth the golden sceptre, saying, Touch, and live: " I will be merciful to the unrighteous, and their sins and iniquities will I remember no more." He is " in Christ, reconciling the world unto himself, not imputing their trespasses unto them." He has established " a ministry of reconciliation," and sends forth his ambassadors to " beseech" you to be reconciled unto God. How wonderful that he should not wait to be solicited, but make the proposal himself, and urge you to accept of it! Will not such love prevail? Do you still harbour doubts in your minds which keep you from him? Let me if possible dispel them by another illustration—for till your hope be excited, it is in vain to expect your return. A king may justly punish rebels: but suppose from his clemency he has issued a proclamation, assuring them that whoever within a given period will come in and give up his arms, shall be pardoned and released —What would you think of this prince, if, as soon as one of these rebellious subjects entered his presence to claim the privilege, he should have him immediately executed!—But you say—surely he never could do this—his honour would be at stake. Though he was originally under no obligation to save him, he is now; for he has bound himself by his word. And can God deny himself!—Venture then upon his promise. Go to him with weeping and supplication, and say, " O Lord, other lords beside thee have had dominion over us: by thee only will we make mention of thy name." But remember, you have no time to lose—the season of allowed submission is fixed, and will soon elapse. " Agree with thine adversary *quickly*, whiles thou art in the way with him; lest at any time the adversary deliver thee to the judge, and the judge deliver thee to the officer, and thou be cast into prison."

Happy are you who have abandoned the unrighteous struggle, and are now one with God. The enmity of your heart has been slain, the weapons of your rebellion have been thrown down, and many a tear shed upon them. Be as zealous for him as you have been against him. He has done much for you; and you have much to do for him. Rise up for him against the evil doers, and stand up for him against the workers of iniquity. Redeem for him the time which you have lost. Honour him with your substance. Employ in his service every power you possess, and every blessing you enjoy. Whether you live, live unto the Lord; or whether you die, die unto the Lord; so that, living or dying, you may be the Lord's.

To conclude. We have been speaking of a striving with God which is unlawful and destructive—but there is a striving with him which is allowable and necessary. It is by prayer and supplication. Such was the strife of the woman of Canaan under the several discouragements she at first received, to try her fervency and her faith. " Let me alone," said God to Moses; Moses was striving with him in prayer for the preservation of the Israelites; and God speaks as if he could do nothing against prayer. " Let me go," said the angel to Jacob; Jacob was wrestling with him; and " he said, I will not let thee go, except thou bless me. And he blessed him there."

And when Providence seems to oppose the promise; when experience seems to disagree with the word; when we are exercised with delays and rebukes too—then to persevere—to pray and not faint—this will be found nothing less than a wrestling with God. But this is a holy violence. This is a pleasing resistance. And in this strife we are sure to prevail. He never said to the seed of Jacob, Seek ye me, in vain. " Wait on the Lord; be of good courage, and he shall strengthen thine heart: wait, I say, on the Lord. The kingdom of heaven suffereth violence, and the violent take it by force."

N 9

DISCOURSE XXVIII.

COMMUNION WITH THE SAVIOUR INSEPARABLE FROM HOLINESS.

If I wash thee not, thou hast no part with me.
John xiii. 8.

If the most minute circumstances in the lives of illustrious characters be perused with eagerness and pleasure, surely we can never feel indifferent to any part of the history of our Lord and Saviour. He was fairer than the children of men: he was higher than the kings of the earth: all he did was wise and good: and we are concerned in all.

Observe the transaction to which the words before us refer—" Jesus knowing that the Father had given all things into his hands, and that he was come from God, and went to God; he riseth from supper"—Such a solemn preface raises a high degree of expectation. From such an introduction, who would not look for an illustrious display of his power and glory ?—But " he laid aside his garments; and took a towel and girded himself. After that he poureth water into a bason, and began to wash the disciples' feet, and to wipe them with the towel wherewith he was girded. Then cometh he to Simon Peter: and Peter said unto him, Lord, dost thou wash my feet?" How much was all this in character with Peter !—He was strongly attached to his Master, and deeply sensible of his own unworthiness; but forward and impetuous; rash in action, and often speaking without due reflection. Therefore " Jesus answered and said unto him, What I do thou knowest not now; but thou shalt know hereafter." " There is something more in this action than you are aware of, and by-and-by you will perceive it." The intimation refers to the design of this washing, which was twofold. First, exemplary—to enforce upon them condescension, humbleness of mind, brotherly kindness. And secondly, symbolical—to lead their minds impressively to things of a higher nature. What therefore was perhaps excusable in Peter before, became censurable now. After such an intimation he should have implicitly acquiesced; instead of which, he saith, " Thou shalt never wash my feet." Upon which, Jesus answered him in plain and awful terms, " If I wash thee not, thou hast no part with me."

Though this declaration intends nothing less than the necessity of obedience in this instance, it surely comprehends much more. He therefore now does not mention the washing of his feet, but of himself: if I wash *thee* not. And the threatening—thou hast " no part with me," seems too dreadful to be denounced against an unwillingness to comply with this ceremonial observance, which sprang from something good as well as evil in the Apostle; and was therefore a mixel action: a sin of infirmity. Besides, we know that our Saviour was accustomed to teach by facts and imagery; to pass from the body to the mind; to ascend from particular hints to general truths; and to express more than is immediately perceived, in order that it might be discovered by repeated meditation, or illustrated by subsequent events.

We deemed these few words necessary to justify ourselves from the deserved reproach of those who, as they call it, are always spiritualizing the Scriptures, and building important doctrines on historical circumstances, till the word of God becomes contemptible to the wise, and unintelligible to the simple; and seems to have no real and determinate sense left. It is high time that this trifling and mischievous mode of teaching should be discountenanced and laid aside.

Let us hasten to consider, with all the seriousness the subject requires, THAT PURIFICATION, WITHOUT WHICH ALL OUR HOPE OF AN INTEREST IN CHRIST IS VAIN. " If I wash thee not, thou hast no part with me." Of this exclusion from Christ, Let us examine THE CONDITION——THE DREADFULNESS——and THE CERTAINTY.

I. THE CONDITION—"If I wash thee not."

It reminds us that sin is of a defiling quality. When God looked down from heaven upon the children of men, it is said, they were "altogether become filthy." Hence, we read of "the filthiness of flesh and spirit." This evil hath defiled all our powers and all our actions; all we possess and all we enjoy; and while it pollutes us, it causes us also to pollute others.

Man may palliate the evil of sin, but in the view of the Supreme Judge it is unspeakably vile and hateful—" He is of purer eyes than to behold iniquity." And when the sinner himself is convinced of sin, he sees it in the same light. As a discovery of the guilt of sin awakens his fear, so a perception of the impurity of it excites his aversion and disgust. He sees, he feels that he is unclean, and deservedly excluded from communion with all holy beings. He cries, " Behold, I am vile ! wherefore I abhor myself, repenting in dust and ashes." He " loathes himself for all his abominations;" nor will he be perfectly reconciled to himself while any of the hateful defilement is found within him.

Now this enables us to determine what our Saviour means by washing us. It is the sanctification of our nature. It is what the Apostle calls "the washing of regeneration, and the renewing of the Holy Ghost." As water removes defilement and restores to purity, so the influences of Divine grace deliver us from sin and make us truly holy. Hence we find it promised in a fulness and variety of expression, "I will sprinkle clean water upon you, and ye shall be clean : from all your filthiness, and from all your idols, will I cleanse you. A new heart also will I give you, and a new spirit will I put within you: and I will take away the stony heart out of your flesh, and I will give you an heart of flesh. And I will put my Spirit within you, and cause you to walk in my statutes, and ye shall keep my judgments, and do them." We do not indeed mean to intimate that real Christians are entirely freed from all sin here—for then, who could lay claim to the character ? Unmixed purity is the privilege of heaven. There alone shall we be " presented faultless before the presence of his glory with exceeding joy." The greatest saints have now their infirmities; and groan, being burdened. But let us remember that though this work is completed in eternity, it is begun in time: that the true Christian is the subject of a glorious change, not only as to his actions, but also as to his dispositions; that he is saved from the love of every sin, and the dominion of every sin; that there is no sin unknown which he does not wish to discover; and no sin discovered which he does not resolve to destroy; and no sin which he resolves to destroy, but he strives and labours to destroy—" plucking out even a right eye, or cutting off even a right hand; denying all ungodliness, and worldly lusts, and living soberly, righteously, and godly, in the present world."

But how are we thus cleansed from our iniquities, and who has the honour of our deliverance ? He is the grand purifier: his name is called Jesus, because he saves his people from their sins. " If I wash thee not." The work is his, and whatever means are used, they derive both their being and their efficacy from him. There is no other fountain opened for sin and uncleanness than his dying wounds supplied. His " blood," says the Apostle, " cleanseth us from all sin." " He loved us," says the Church, " and washed us from our sins in his own blood."

Let us not look to him for justification only, but remember that he is " made of God unto us sanctification," also; that he delivers us not only from the curse, but the pollution of sin; that he rescues us not only from the burden of condemnation, but the bondage of corruption; and not only gives us the title to heaven, but produces in us the meetness for it— He " is all in all." To induce you to seek after this state, consider,

II. THE DREADFULNESS of the exclusion— "Thou hast no part with me." " Thou hast no real interest in me; and thou canst have no reasonable expectations from me." There is something very tremendous in this. Hear how the Apostle Paul speaks of a privilege from which you are excluded. " But what things were gain to me, those I counted loss for Christ. Yea, doubtless, and I count all things but loss for the excellency of the knowledge of Christ Jesus my Lord; for whom I have suffered the loss of all things, and do count them but dung, that I may win Christ, and be found in him, not having mine own righteousness, which is of the law, but that which is through the faith of Christ, the righteousness which is of God by faith; that I may know him, and the power of his resurrection, and the fellowship of his sufferings, being made conformable unto his death: if by any means I might attain unto the resurrection of the dead." The Apostle was a good judge, and you here see that he infinitely preferred union with Christ to every thing else. But you say, you are not like-minded; you do not thus value him; you prefer a thousand objects to an interest in him—and therefore to you there seems nothing so very dreadful in this threatening.

But the question is—whether your judgment be a righteous one. A pearl is not the less precious because the swine tramples it under foot. A toy is not more valuable than a title to an estate because an infant or an idiot may give it the preference.

And the question also is, whether you will always remain in the same opinion. Will the day of judgment, think you, operate no change in your sentiments! Will not the approach of death alter your convictions? What! when all those things which now engage and amuse you fail—will you want no better portion! If while I am speaking a messenger from the "king of terrors" should seize you, and you were carried to your bed, and compelled to look backward upon your life, and forward to your doom—what could succour and relieve you?—Yea, if conscience were to fall upon you this moment, and the terrors of the Almighty troubled you; you would soon find the truth of Solomon's words. "The spirit of a man may sustain his infirmity: but a wounded spirit who can bear!" —And then what advantage could you derive from all your worldly possessions! They would be all physicians of no value; miserable comforters. Your relief could only come from another quarter—but from that quarter you are forbidden to hope.

If our Lord and Saviour was an unimportant character, your exclusion from him would not be so fatal—but the fact is, that every thing you need is found in him, and to be derived only from him. Of what worth Christ is to us, is a question, says an old writer, which would nonplus all the saints on earth and angels in heaven to answer. One thing we are certain of—that no being in the universe can fill his place, and do for us what he is able to do. And therefore, if he will have nothing to do with us, our case is indeed miserable and hopeless. We are wanderers without a guide: we are dying patients without a physician or a remedy: we are exposed to the deluge, and have no ark. It matters not to whom we belong; if we had part with a king, he could not help us in our most important concerns—the concerns of the soul and eternity. He cannot give us the true riches. He cannot deliver us from the wrath to come. He cannot bless us with all spiritual blessings in heavenly places. And what can we do without these! "Neither is there salvation in any other, for there is no other name given under heaven among men whereby we must be saved." And if we miss salvation, we are lost for ever. "What is a man profited, if he should gain the whole world, and lose his own soul; or what shall a man give in exchange for his soul?"

To have no communion with him in whose favour is life; to hear him say, I have a family, but you are no part of it—you are not a child, nor even a servant; to hear him say, I have a plantation, but you are not in it— you are not a cedar, no, nor a shrub; to hear him say, I have in reserve for my followers, thrones of glory, rivers of pleasure, fulness of joy—but as for you—you—have "neither part nor lot in the matter, for your heart is not right in the sight of God"—if this be not dreadful, nothing can be dreadful.

Especially when we add that there is but one alternative—If you have no part with Christ and his people, you must have your portion with hypocrites and unbelievers, with the devil and his angels! You have already fixed you destiny; you have chosen the left hand; you are already mingling with the goats; you are walking the downward road —"As for such as turn aside to their crooked ways, the Lord will lead them forth with the workers of iniquity." Who believes this? Let us then see whether we cannot establish,

III. THE CERTAINTY of this exclusion. There are two ways of proving this. The one is by testimony. "If you receive the witness of man, the witness of God is greater." And, says not our Lord and Saviour, "If I wash thee not, thou hast no part with me?" One declaration from him renders a thing as certain as a thousand—otherwise I could go on quoting Scripture—and say—"They that are Christ's have crucified the flesh, with the affections and lusts." "If any man be in Christ, he is a new creature; old things are passed away, behold, all things are become new." "If any man have not the Spirit of Christ, he is none of his." But where shall I end? "Know ye not that the unrighteous shall not inherit the kingdom of God! Be not deceived; neither fornicators, nor idolaters, nor adulterers, nor effeminate, nor abusers of themselves with mankind, nor thieves, nor covetous, nor drunkards, nor revilers, nor extortioners, shall inherit the kingdom of God." The other is reasoning from principles. Let us view the Saviour, with whom we hope to have communion for ever—But he is pure and holy; his person is pure; his kingdom is pure—pure are its joys, its services, and its company. If therefore, we are not made pure and holy, we have no likeness in him; and were we in a state of union, such a heterogeneous mass of materials would form a body like the image of Nebuchadnezzar, where the head was indeed of gold, but the breast and arms of silver, and the inferior parts of baser metal, down to the feet, which were part of iron and part of clay. Can this be a representation of the Church of the living God? If Christ is the head, and Christians are the body, let us remember that the head and the body partake of the same nature: and that if Christ be the vine, and Christians the branches, the vine and the branches partake of the very same qualities.

What intercourse can there be where nothing prevails but a contrariety of inclination and an opposition of interest? "How can two walk together except they be agreed? What fellowship hath righteousness with unrighteousness? and what communion hath light with darkness? and what concord hath Christ with Belial? or what part hath he that believeth with an infidel? and what agreement hath the temple of God with idols?"

Indeed without this renovation we should be wholly incapable of deriving happiness from our connexion with him. Our being for ever in his presence would only render us miserable: there would be nothing in the praises or in the pleasures of that sacred state to fulfil our desires, or to gratify our taste. Dismiss the Bible, or suppose that God had expressed no determination to exclude "every thing that defileth" from the abodes of blessedness: in this view the case would be the same as it is now; the happiness of an unrenewed sinner is impossible upon every principle. Wherever he may be placed, *while he has sin in him, he has hell with him.*

This train of reflection informs us, First, how exceedingly those misunderstand the Gospel, and delude their own souls, who expect to be "made partakers of Christ," while they seek not to be sanctified by him. "He was manifested to take away our sin. He gave himself for us, that he might redeem us from all iniquity, and purify unto himself a peculiar people, zealous of good works." In this every real Christian rejoices; the plan meets his wants and his wishes. He gladly embraces the Saviour in all his offices, and while he glories in his cross, submits to his sceptre. He seeks after a present salvation from sin, as well as a future deliverance from wrath; and the faith which purifies his conscience, purifies his heart. But to look for comfort without holiness, is to separate what God has unalterably joined together. To depend upon Christ for pardon and acceptance, so as to encourage ourselves in sin, or reconcile ourselves to it, is "a way which may seem right

unto a man, but, be assured, the end thereof are the paths of death!"

We may, Secondly, congratulate those who are made free from sin. You have "an inheritance among them that are sanctified." Yea, you not only share with the saints, but also with the Saviour: you have part with Christ! you partake of his safety and his dignity. "When he, who is your life, shall appear, you shall also appear with him in glory. You shall sit with him upon his throne. You shall enter the joy of your Lord. If children, then heirs, heirs of God, and joint heirs with Christ."

Can you be poor?—Having nothing, you possess all things. "For all things are yours; whether Paul, or Apollos, or Cephas, or the world, or life, or death, or things present, or things to come; all are yours: and ye are Christ's; and Christ is God's."

Can you be miserable? "Rejoice in the Lord always; and again I say, rejoice." If "troubled on every side"—you are "not distressed:" if "perplexed"—you are *not* in despair: if "persecuted"—you are "not forsaken:" if "cast down," you are "not destroyed."

And if you have part with him in his glory, can you be unwilling to share with him in his reproach? If you are to "live with him;" cannot you "die with him?" If you are to "reign with him," cannot you also "suffer with him?" According to the Apostle, you ought to "rejoice, inasmuch as you are made partakers of Christ's sufferings; that when his glory shall be revealed, you may be glad also with exceeding joy."

Thirdly. Are there any here whose desires are awakened, and who are asking, Can I obtain a portion in Christ, and how is it to be obtained? Let me conclude by a word of direction and encouragement. And it is this. From a deep conviction of your need of him, apply immediately to him. "Take with you words," which he himself has furnished, and say, "Lord, take away all iniquity. Wash me thoroughly from mine iniquity, and cleanse me from my sin. Create in me a clean heart, O God; and renew a right spirit within me."

Exercise faith upon his power, and say, "Lord, if thou wilt, thou CANST make me clean." Be persuaded of his willingness. Believe that "he waiteth to be gracious, and is exalted to have mercy upon you."

What were those who are now so happy with him? They were once "far off: and children of wrath, even as others." Behold, they all rise up and address you: "O taste and see that the Lord is good; blessed is the man that trusteth in him." "That which we have seen and heard, declare we unto you, that ye also may have fellowship with us, and truly our fellowship is with the Father, and with his Son Jesus Christ."

Above all, hear their Lord and Saviour,

saying, "Him that cometh unto me, I will in no wise cast out!"

DISCOURSE XXIX.

A CHECK TO PRESUMPTION.

Let us therefore fear, lest, a promise being left us of entering into his rest, any of you should seem to come short of it.—Heb. iv. 1.

"FAITHFUL are the wounds of a friend." Hence, says David, "let the righteous smite me; it shall be a kindness : and let him reprove me; it shall be an excellent oil, which shall not break my head: for yet my prayer also shall be in their calamities."

Would you deem a man your enemy because he told you the truth ? especially if the intelligence was of importance, and your ignorance of it would be ruinous ? Would you blame a person, who seeing your house to be on fire, would endeavour to wake you from a pleasing dream ? Or would you say to one who checked you on the brink of a precipice —"Why did you not suffer me to go on ! Why did you spoil my reverie ?" Surely even a blow that saved you from such dreadful jeopardy, would be esteemed an instance of friendship.

But all allusions fail when we think of the soul and eternity. Every thing is little and trifling compared with the acquisition of endless life. Here is a subject which requires, infinitely more than any other, fidelity in the speaker ; and a disposition open to conviction and fearful of deception, in the hearer. " Let us therefore fear, lest, a promise being left us of entering into his rest, any of you should seem to come short of it."

Let us consider two things. The First regards THE BLESSING PROMISED. And the Second, THE STATE OF MIND IN WHICH WE SHOULD CONSIDER IT.

I. The Gospel is not only a revelation, but A PROMISE : and A PROMISE exceeding great and precious. It not only holds forth to our view, but it proposes to our hope eternal life ; and whatever is previously necessary to the acquisition of it. The promise was early made, and was often renewed with enlargements. Thousands in the successive ages of the world have laid hold of it, and—it is " left" for us. Yes, in this blessed book, we have " a promise left us of entering into his rest."

But what is this rest ?—We may view it as it is begun upon earth, or completed in heaven. Even while the believer is upon earth, this rest is not only ensured, but begun. Hence, says the Apostle, " We which have believed do enter into rest." Before he knew the Saviour, he was a stranger to rest ; but Jesus had said, "Come unto me, all ye that labour and are heavy laden, and I will give

you rest ;" he was enabled to believe his word ; he ventured upon his promise, made application to him, and found " rest unto his soul." Let us observe him—

View him with regard to his *understanding,*—and you will find that he has rest. He is freed from the jealousies and uneasinesses which arise from uncertainty of mind with regard to truth. He is no longer the sport of delusion : he is no longer like "a wave of the sea, driven with the wind and tossed," now urged in one direction, and now in another ; he no longer flounders in the mud and mire—he has found rock ; he stands upon it ; his goings are established. He "knows whom he has believed." He knows that he " has not followed cunningly devised fables." He knows "the doctrine" he has received " to be of God."—He "has the witness in himself."

View him with regard to his *conscience*—and you will find that he has rest. He is freed from the torment of fear, and the horrors of guilt. A crucified Saviour " has redeemed us from the curse of the law, being made a curse for us. He bore our sins in his own body on the tree. He gave himself for us an offering and a sacrifice to God, for a sweet-smelling savour." An apprehension of this truth " healeth the broken in heart, and bindeth up their wounds." In proportion as we realize it by faith, the burden, too heavy for us to bear, loosens and falls off ; and, " being justified by faith, we have peace with God, through our Lord Jesus Christ."

View him with regard to his *passions* and *appetites*—and you will find he has rest. While pride and envy, and malice, and avarice, and sensual affections, reigned within, often striving with each other, and always fighting against the convictions of his judgment, the man's breast was nothing but a scene of tumult : he was "like the troubled sea, when it cannot rest ; whose waters cast up mire and dirt : there is no peace, saith my God, unto the wicked." But sanctifying grace has delivered him from " the bondage of corruption," and from the tyranny of adverse and raging lusts : it has subdued his tempers, and regulated his desires ; it has restored order and self-government—and these have restored peace.

View him once more with regard to his "condition and circumstances"—and you will find that he has rest. He is freed from those anxieties and disquietudes which devour others who make the world their portion, and have no confidence in God. But the world is not his portion ; he has not laid up his treasure on earth. His inheritance is " incorruptible and undefiled, and fadeth not away, reserved in heaven for him." He is nobly superior to events. Nothing that occurs can materially affect him ; he is therefore easy and composed. He has also a confidence in

God which wonderfully calms the mind with regard to present occurrences. He knows that the God who loves him, reigns over all; that all his dispensations are righteous, and wise, and kind; that he will not forsake him, but " make all things," however contrary in their appearance and tendency, to " work together for his good." Hence he feels a holy indifference, a blessed resignation to the will of Providence; and committing all his concerns to his Heavenly Father, he learns " in whatsoever state he is, therewith to be content :" according to the language of the Prophet and the Apostle: " Thou wilt keep him in perfect peace whose mind is stayed on thee : because he trusteth in thee." " Be careful for nothing; but in every thing by prayer and supplication with thanksgiving let your requests be made known unto God. And the peace of God, which passeth all understanding, shall keep your hearts and minds through Christ Jesus."

But, excellent as his present condition is, compared with his former state, it is nothing compared with his future. With all his advantages here, a voice perpetually cries in his ears, " Arise and depart; for this is not your rest." However favourable the voyage, they are now on the boisterous, treacherous ocean; they are looking out for their native shore; and by-and-by they will enter the harbour—" then are they glad because they are quiet; so he bringeth them into their desired haven." At death we are told the righteous and the merciful enter into rest. And this rest is pure, undisturbed, and everlasting.

They shall rest from " their labours." Though all activity, they shall be incapable of fatigue and languor, for their powers will be fully equal to their work. " Repentance shall be hid from their eyes." Their praying days will be all over. It shall never more be said to them, " Be patient in tribulation;" or " fight the good fight of faith." Without were fightings, and within were fears : but they are for ever ended. Darkness no longer struggles with light; or faith with unbelief. " The flesh no longer lusteth against the Spirit, nor the Spirit against the flesh." They are delivered from all the temptations which were so often ensnaring or distressing them here. " There the wicked cease from troubling, and there the weary are at rest." " And there shall be no more death, neither sorrow, nor crying, neither shall there be any more pain, for the former things are passed away." And nothing remains of their trials, but a grateful remembrance of the hand that sustained them under all their difficulties, and delivered them from all their grief.

The Apostle therefore, to express heaven, often uses the word rest. And it is observable that he employs two allusions to enable us to conceive of it the more clearly : the one taken from Canaan, in which the Jews rested after the toils of the wilderness; and the other from the Sabbath, on which Christians rest after the perplexities of the week.

Ah! ye glorified saints, you can tell us what this blessed rest is. You have traversed the wilderness—where you " wandered in a solitary way; where you found no city to dwell in :" where, " hungry and thirsty, your souls fainted in you." But you have left the desert! you have passed the river Jordan; and have entered " the land flowing with milk and honey"—you are " come unto the rest which the Lord your God giveth you."

Your week days, your worldly days are now over, and you have begun your Sabbath. Here you loved the Sabbath : but here the Sabbath was soon over, and the things of the world again deprived you of the fine feelings it produced. You sometimes passed silent Sabbaths, and mourned the loss of sanctuary privileges. You always spent imperfect ones : you could not do the things that you would; and soon grew weary in the service of God, though not of it. But now your " strength is perfectly renewed." You are " for ever with the Lord." You " serve him day and night in his temple; and shall go no more out"— you have the keeping of " the Sabbath which remains for the people of God."

Such is the blessing. Let us consider, II. THE STATE OF MIND IN WHICH WE SHOULD REGARD IT—Let us therefore " fear, lest a promise being left us of entering into his rest, any of you should seem to come short of it." But what is this fear?

It is not the fear of the sluggard dismayed by difficulties, and crying, " There is a lion in the way, I shall be slain in the streets." Such a man will be sure to come short. The fearful are to have " their part in the lake that burneth with fire and brimstone, which is the second death."

Nor is it the fear of the unbeliever, who suspects that the promise shall not be accomplished; for there is not the least ground for such an apprehension : because " faithful is he that hath promised, who also will do it." This fear prevailed in the Jews, and excluded them from the land of Canaan. They thought God had undertaken more than he could perform : they asked, " Can he furnish a table in the wilderness?" they said, " The people are too strong for us :" and thus despairing, they murmured to return. Let us guard against this fear, and be fully persuaded that what God has promised he is able to perform; and that, difficult, or even impossible as it may appear in our eyes to bring a guilty, depraved, helpless sinner to glory—if he has undertaken it, he will perfect that which concerneth us.

But the fear here enjoined is a fear of caution; of vigilance; of scrutiny; a fear which leads us to examine ourselves; and allows us in this awful concern to be satisfied with nothing less than evidence; a fear that induces us to question—and therefore to inquire whether we are the subjects of divine grace; whether we are the "heirs of promise;" whether we have a title to heaven, and are in a fair way to obtain this blessedness.

Now the thought of missing this rest is surely enough to awaken in you this peculiar concern—especially when you consider two things: the possibility of your coming short; and the consequence of your coming short.

First. To excite in you this fear, remember the possibility of your coming short. And here let me mention a fact which should make you tremble. It is this—out of *six hundred thousand* Israelites, who came out of Egypt to possess the land of Canaan, *two only* entered!—But what is this to us? Hear how the Apostle applies it. "Moreover, brethren, I would not that ye should be ignorant, how that all our fathers were under the cloud, and all passed through the sea; and were all baptized unto Moses in the cloud and in the sea; and did all eat the same spiritual meat; and did all drink the same spiritual drink: for they drank of that spiritual rock that followed them: and that rock was Christ. But with many of them God was not well pleased: for they were overthrown in the wilderness. Now these things were our examples"—adds the Apostle. They are emblems and warnings to us. We here behold persons, under a dispensation of peculiar privileges, considered as the people of God, delivered from their enemies by the most wonderful displays of Divine power; clothed in garments unimpaired by wearing, or by time; and whose meat and drink were not only miraculous, but sacramental—and, after all this, we see them perishing under the wrath of Heaven. "Wherefore," says the Apostle again, "let him that thinketh he standeth" high in the Divine favour, and is perfectly secure, "take heed lest he fall." Let him not depend on external privileges; on gifts; on being baptized in his infancy; on his partaking of the memorials of the Saviour's death—or a thousand other things, which are no certain proofs of salvation. Persons may go far, but not far enough; they may be convinced, but not converted; like Saul, they may have *another* heart, and not a *new* one. And indeed nothing is more common than delusions of this kind. Oh! how many there are who say, "I am rich, and increased with goods, and have need of nothing; and know not that they are wretched, and miserable, and poor, and blind, and naked!" Oh! how many are there who entertain confident hopes of heaven, that will never see it! They are pillowed up on the bed of carnal security—die like lambs—and awake with the devil and his angels! "Let us therefore fear."

But, Secondly. Consider the consequence of coming short. Is it not dreadful to be deprived of "that fulness of joy"—of that "crown of life"—of that "everlasting kingdom which God hath promised to them that love him?" What would it be to lose your business, your health, your friends, compared with the loss of the soul?

And remember, there is no medium between heaven and hell—if you miss the one, the other is unavoidable.

And remember, also, the aggravations which will attend the misery of those who perish in your circumstances. There is nothing so healing, so soothing, as the expectation of hope; and of course there is nothing so tormenting as the disappointment of it, especially where the object is vastly important. What then can equal the regrets and horrors those will feel who shall come short of eternal life! What will be their reflections when they see that the blessing was attainable, but that their own folly had deprived them of it! And when they discover their mistake, but, alas, too late to rectify the error! —A timely fear would have prevented all this.

Yea, remember also, that you will not only be disappointed *in* coming short—but you will be punished *for* it. Your perdition will be your greatest sin. You could not be lost without contemning the *authority* of God, who commanded you to believe on the name of his Son Jesus Christ, and trampling under foot his *mercy* and his *grace*. You offend him even more by your unbelief than by your iniquity. The Gospel has its threatenings, as well as the Law; and after the one has condemned you for transgressing its commands, the other will condemn you for the rejection of its remedy. Thus, as the Apostle says, the word you hear will "prove the savour of death unto death." How then can you escape if you neglect so great salvation? If you could even elude the curse of the law, you would have to encounter the damnation of the Gospel. What then think you of both? "Can thy heart endure, or thy hand be strong, when he shall deal with thee?"—"Let us therefore fear."

And observe, how far the Apostle extends the admonition—"Let us fear, lest *any* of you *seem* to come short of it." We see that he applies it to *all:* deeming none below the benefit of caution, and none above the necessity of it—lest "*any* of you." And he applies it to all in the *greatest* degree. Lest any of you—what! should come short? No —but *seem* to come short. He not only forbids us to go back—but even to look back. He would have us not only avoid the reality —but the appearance of evil. He would have us not only possess religion, but "adorn the doctrine of God our Saviour in all things." He would not have us remit our caution and our zeal in the smallest degree, so as to render our adherence to the truth suspicious, or our declension from the ways of God probable. He would not have you to leave your eternal state in the least uncertainty; or live so as to awaken doubts in others, and to lead the people of the world to say—" Ah! they are yielding by little and little; they cannot throw off every thing at once—they will soon join us again." We are, like the patriarchs, to " declare *plainly* that we seek a country" —and not puzzle our neighbours to determine whether to consider us at home, or only as strangers and pilgrims upon earth. We are not to be doubtful characters, so that no reader can make any thing of us, or say whose hand the writing is; but we are " to be *manifestly* the epistles of Jesus Christ, known and read of all men." " Let us therefore fear, lest, a promise being left us of entering into his rest, any of you should *seem* to come short of it."

To conclude. Let us observe, first, how thankful we should be for such a promise left us of entering into his rest! For surely we could not have reasonably expected it. Had we been informed that God was about to give us a revelation from heaven, our guilty minds would have foreboded nothing but tribulation and wrath, vexation and anguish, upon every soul of man that doeth evil. This we deserved —but behold, he speaks—and his " thoughts are thoughts of peace, and not of evil, to bring us to an expected end." The address is to tell us of a remedy for our disease; a refuge from the storm; a passage from this world of misery into a better, even " a heavenly country."

O what welcome intelligence is this! How much did we stand in need of such a discovery, such an assurance as this! Our earth is a vale of tears; creatures are broken reeds and empty cisterns: our mortifications are frequent; our pains numerous; our enjoyments unsatisfying! " Surely man walketh in a vain show!"—But he is not compelled to walk so now. There are realities attainable; there is satisfaction; there is rest. " He hath showed thee, O man! what is good. Acquaint now thyself with him, and be at peace, thereby good shall come unto thee." Do not, do not resemble the Jews of old : " to whom he said, This is the rest wherewith ye may cause the weary to rest, and this is the refreshing :—yet they would not hear."

Let us, secondly, see how necessary it is in religion to avoid passing from one extreme into another. The Gospel encourages our hope: but then it enlightens it, and guards it. It tells us not to " refuse to be comforted;" but it teaches us to blend a holy jealousy with our confidence, and " to rejoice with trembling." Some people seem to consider the fear of which we have been speaking, as legality and unbelief—whereas it is promoted by an evangelical frame of mind, and is the offspring of faith. It does not question the

truth of the promise—but only makes a man anxious to ascertain whether he has any part or lot in the matter.

And should this be carelessly decided? Can a man in such a case be too safe or too certain? Is it not much better to be even needlessly distressed for a time, than to be deceived for ever? Is it not better to have a troubled conscience than a seared one? " To this man, says God, will I look, even to him that is poor, and of a contrite spirit, and that trembleth at my word." " Pass the time of your sojourning here in fear. Be not highminded, but fear. Work out your salvation with fear and trembling."

Indeed, this fear seems to be unavoidable from the very nature of the case. Whoever attends to the workings of his own mind, well knows that the proposal of any great or unexpected benefit always produces a variety of emotions. Wonder is the first: this is instantly succeeded by joy—but there is another feeling which also immediately seizes the mind and works very powerfully—and this is solicitude—care to attain and secure it—fear, lest after all we should not realize the possession of it. And this is what our Saviour means when he says, " The kingdom of heaven is like unto treasure hid in a field : the which when a man hath found, he hideth, and for joy thereof goeth, and selleth a.. that he hath, and buyeth that field." This *hiding* is not in order to secresy, but safety : for as by hiding things we commonly secure them— the one is put for the other; and this explanation accords with the experience of every awakened soul. For in proportion as you prize salvation, and desire it, and apprehend it to be necessary—will be your fear of coming short of it. Indifference does not generate fear—No—but conviction does, and so does attachment.

Lastly. What are we to say of those of you who know nothing of this salutary concern? Perhaps, if some of you were to speak what you feel, you would say, That the loss of this rest was the least of all your fears. It never disturbs your repose by night, nor embitters your enjoyments by day. Whenever the thought enters, you consider it as an intruder and soon expel it. All your fear is limited to the world and the present life. You fear for your health, and are alarmed when any unfavourable symptoms appear. You fear for your business; your fortune; your estate, and cannot deem yourselves too secure. " You ask, what shall I eat, and what shall I drink, and wherewithal shall I be clothed?" But you never inquire, " What must I do to be saved?"

And yet what is every other interest to this?—And do you imagine that this greatest of all concerns can be managed or secured without attention or care? Do you think that leaving the boat to the stream will bring

you safe—while you are asleep, or at play?
—This may do if you wish to sail down *with*
the stream and be carried into the gulf below. But the course to heaven lies *against*
the stream—and helm and oars and labour
and diligence are indispensably necessary.
"Let us therefore fear, lest, a promise being
left us of entering into his rest, any of you
should seem to come short of it." Amen.

DISCOURSE XXX.

REVIEW OF LIFE.

(LAST DAY OF THE YEAR.)

And God requireth that which is past.
Eccl. iii. 15.

WITH God, nothing is past; nothing is future. I AM is his name, and this is his "memorial in all generations." "One day with
the Lord is as a thousand years, and a thousand years are as one day."

The very reverse of this is the case with
us. For with us, nothing is present: all is
future, or past. Thus a man stands by the
side of a river, and sees something swimming
down the stream—now it is above him—and
now it is below him—but it never abides
before him—so of all the things that befall
us in this world, to use the language of the
poet,

> " We can never say, they 're here,
>   But only say, they 're past."

But when they are gone by, we have not
entirely done with them. Some consequences do remain, and others ought to remain—" And God requireth that which is
past." He demands an account of the past
—and this we shall have to render hereafter: he demands an improvement of the past
—and this we must attend to now.

Let us then apply this to a review of our
MEANS—to a review of our MERCIES—to a
review of our SORROWS—and to a review of
our SINS. We cannot have a better opportunity for this exercise, than the present season,
when we are closing another period of our
short and fleeting time. While therefore the
few remaining sands of the year are running
out, let us remember, that God requires "that
which is past"—

I. A REVIEW OF OUR PAST MEANS AND
PRIVILEGES. God judges of things as they
are: he knows that the body is nothing to the
soul, or time to eternity. He has therefore
graciously provided for our spiritual and everlasting welfare. He remembered us in our
low estate, and devised a way in which his
mercy could be exercised in harmony with
his justice. This purpose of grace, formed
before the foundation of the world, was accomplished in the fulness of time. The friend
of sinners came to seek and to save that

which was lost. He was delivered for our
offences, and was raised again for our justification. "All things are now ready." But
you are to be made ready too. Hence the
dispensation of the Gospel, and all the advantages with which you have been indulged.
By these, I mean your having been born in
a land of vision where the Saviour of the
world is known. I mean, your having enjoyed the blessings of the Reformation, which
gave each of you the Scriptures in your mother tongue;—in the original, the Bible
would have been no more to you than a fine
well of water covered by a rock, which you
could not move, or as so many beautiful pictures hung up in a dark room; but now the
stone is rolled away from the well's mouth,
and these pictures are placed in open day.
I mean, your having had the word of life, not
only to read, but also to hear. I mean, your
having had ministers to call you to repentance,
to warn you of your danger, to beseech you
in Christ's stead to be reconciled unto God.
I mean, the various ordinances of the sanctuary, and all the helps to seriousness and devotion which the goodness of God has afforded
you. These means of grace are unspeakably
important, and you have had them in rich
profusion: you have had " line upon line, and
precept upon precept." During the past year
only you have to account for fifty-two sabbaths, and perhaps more than one hundred
sermons!—What influence have all these
had upon your minds? Are you crucified
to the world? Are you denying yourselves,
and taking up your cross, and following the
Saviour? Are your affections more spiritual,
your principles more powerful, your minds
more enlightened? Must we address you as
our Lord did his disciples, " Are ye also yet
without understanding?" or as the apostle
did the Hebrews, "When for the time ye
ought to be teachers, ye have need that one
teach you again which be the first principles
of the oracles of God; and are become such
as have need of milk, and not of strong
meat?"

Oh! let me call upon you to review all
your opportunities and means of instruction
and improvement, and compare yourselves
with them. See whether the end of them
has been answered at all; and whether your
proficiency has been proportioned in any degree to the number and value of your privileges. Do not think your concern with them
is all over—" God requireth that which is
past." What is become of these advantages?
To what purposes have you applied them?
Where are the fruits of them?—They were
given you as talents to improve; and if they
have been *useless*, be assured they *will* prove
injurious. If they do not save, they will condemn; and if they are not the "savour of life
unto life," they are the "savour of death
unto death."

O

The proprietor of the vineyard said, "Behold, these three years I come seeking fruit on this fig-tree, and find none." Observe this. You see God distinctly notices *how many* seasons of unprofitableness people have passed through. And if he thought of cutting down this tree because in a favourable situation it had yielded nothing for *three* years only, what can he resolve but the immediate destruction of those individuals who have been fruitless under the means of grace for ten, twenty, perhaps forty or sixty years! Surely the vine-dresser himself cannot implore for such, one year, one month, one week more! "He that being often reproved hardeneth his neck, shall suddenly be destroyed, and that without remedy."

II. He requires a review of past mercies. When humble and attentive minds look back, their mercies appear so many that it is impossible to enumerate them. And hence divines have taught Christians to serve their mercies as botanists do flowers—to class them: or as astronomers deal with the stars —to form them into constellations. They tell them, in looking back, to think of mercies temporal and spiritual; mercies public and private; mercies personal and relative. They tell them to think of continued mercies, restored mercies; and of preventing and delivering mercies. They would have them also fix their minds on particular instances— for instances affect much more powerfully than things in a mass. They teach them also not to overlook the circumstances which enhance their blessings; such as are derived from their seasonableness, their utility. Take their advice, and pursue this plan.

How many times has he lulled you to sleep in his arms; fed you at his table; clothed you from his wardrobe! How often has he supplied your wants, and wiped away tears from your eyes! When brought low, has he not helped you? When in jeopardy, has he not defended you? When sickness has alarmed your fears, has he not led you back from the gates of the grave? When accidents have been ready to destroy, have not "all your bones said, who is a God like unto thee!" In how many cases has he given us favour in the eyes of our fellow-creatures; and blessed us with the advantages and pleasures of friendship! From what low and obscure beginnings has he raised some of us in the course of his wonder-working providence! and how well does it become us to compare the former— when with our staves we passed over Jordan, with the present, when we are become two bands, and have all things richly to enjoy!

There are few persons who in looking back are not able to perceive some very striking displays of Divine goodness. We do not wish people to be forward to publish these to the world—many of them would not be, and could not be striking to others; but they ought to observe these remarkable interpositions themselves, and to say with David, "Bless the Lord, O my soul, and forget not all his benefits." Nothing can impress or influence our minds when it is forgotten. We should therefore recall our mercies, and place them full before us, that we may feel whether we have rendered according to the benefit done us. How much of our insensibility and ingratitude springs from inattention and a bad memory! and how well may it be said of thousands, as it was of Israel, "Of the rock that begat thee thou art unmindful, and hast forgotten God that formed thee!"

As it is so necessary to keep things in the mind, and as our memories are so treacherous, it would be well for us, in every possible way, to aid our recollection, and to endeavour to preserve and perpetuate those good feelings, which our mercies produce when we receive them. Thus "Samuel took a stone and set it between Mizpeh and Shen, and called the name of it Ebenezer, saying, Hitherto hath the Lord helped us." And thus Joseph, by the very names of his children, would recall the wonders which the Lord had shown him: "Joseph called the name of the first-born Manasseh: for God, saith he, hath made me forget all my toil, and all my father's house. And the name of the second called he Ephraim: for God hath caused me to be fruitful in the land of my affliction." And hence the command given to Ephraim; "Set thee up way-marks, make thee high heaps; set thine heart toward the highway, even the way which thou wentest: turn again, O virgin of Israel, turn again to these thy cities."

If we had indulged a person year after year all through life, should we not require him to think of it; to be sensible of our kindness, and to behave towards us in a manner becoming his obligations? There is nothing perhaps we feel more painfully than the ungrateful reception of the favours we bestow: and a very few instances of unthankfulness are sufficient to induce us to discontinue our benefits. What then does God think of us? Not only are the expressions of his goodness infinitely more numerous than any favours we can show our fellow-creatures, but they are all undeserved. Our fellow-creatures have claims upon us, and we are bound, as we have opportunity, to do good unto all men. But God is under no obligation to us. All his bounty is grace; and therefore, if he is continually doing us good, and filling our hearts with joy and gladness, surely he expects that the language of our lips, and of our lives, should be, "What shall I render unto the Lord for all his benefits towards me!— He requireth that which is past." And he demands,

III. A review of our past sorrows and distresses. With all our supplies and indulgences, you nave had your hours of trouble; and have found this world to be a vale of tears. Can you forget those seasons in which your worldly comforts fled, your refreshing gourds withered, your beloved friends and relations were removed by death?——Oh! never——"the wormwood and the gall" of such ——and such an affliction——"my soul hath it still in remembrance, and is humbled within me." And be not afraid to think of it. "By the sadness of the countenance the heart is made better;" it is made more serious, and more soft; and thus the soil is improved for wisdom, and truth, and devotion to flourish in. Do not derive your morals from the school of the world. Their maxims are imperfect opposition "to the Spirit which is of God." They endeavour to banish from their minds every thing that has a tendency to do them good. Hence when troubles befall them, the design of which is to bring them to reflection, they do every thing in their power to escape a sense of them, and to prevent the remembrance of them. And thus the kind and salutary purposes of Heaven, in afflicting them, are disregarded, and they go on thoughtlessly, till the "evil day" comes upon them with all its horrors and surprise.

As our troubles are designed to do us good, not only in experience, but also in review, we should labour after a practical remembrance of them. They have been lost upon us, unless they have made us wiser, more sober-minded, and less disposed to expect a rest below the skies. We should judge of the future by the past, and conclude that life will be what it has been, a chequered scene; and that no condition, no connexion, will afford us unmixed happiness. Surely, after the experience of years of vanity, we should begin to gird up the loins of our minds, and to declare plainly that we seek a better country. Surely these disappointments and regrets urge us to say, with David, "And now, Lord, what wait I for? my hope is in thee;" or with Micah, "Therefore will I look unto the Lord, and will wait for the God of my salvation; my God will hear me!" We cannot now plead ignorance: our dreams have been disturbed: we are awake—and it is high time to arise. It is high time that the trifler should become a man, and the man a Christian.

It is an awful thing to come out of trouble: for it always leaves us better or worse than it finds us. We should therefore ask, with peculiar concern—"What benefit have I derived from such a visitation of Divine Providence? The rod spoke—did I hear its message? The physician has been employed—is my distemper even beyond the reach of medicine? I have lost the life of my friend—and have I lost his death too? My relation has entered the joy of his Lord—I have one reason for loving earth less, and do I love it

more? one reason for loving heaven more, and do I love it less?"

Past afflictions should also teach us not to be too much dejected or dismayed in prospect of future ones. For how has it been with us? We feared as we entered the cloud, but the cloud was big with mercy, and poured down blessings. What terrified us in imagination, we bore with cheerfulness. When the day of trial came, we had grace to help in time of need; and it was found sufficient for us. And our God is the same, and has promised that he will never leave us nor forsake us.

And, oh! happy is he who, in reviewing his griefs, can say, "Well, so many of my troubles are gone for ever. So many steps of my wearisome journey I have taken—and the hour is not far off that shall end the toilsome pilgrimage."—

> "O most delightful hour, by man
>   Experienc'd here below—
> The hour that terminates his span,
>   His folly and his wo!
>
> "Worlds should not bribe me back to tread
>   Again life's dreary waste;
> To see my days again o'erspread
>   With all the gloomy past.
>
> "My home henceforth is in the skies—
>   Earth, seas, and sun, adieu;
> All heaven unfolded to my eyes,
>   I've no regret for you."

IV. GOD REQUIRES US TO REVIEW OUR PAST SINS. Many of these have grown out of our privileges, our mercies, and our trials. They have been attended with singular aggravations. They are more in number than the hairs of our head. In many things we offend all.

It is well, if upon a review of the year, we can exculpate ourselves from sins committed against man——but what are these compared with the offences which we have committed against God! Indeed all sin is really committed against God. There is not a duty which we owe our fellow-creatures, but he has enjoined the observance of. He has commanded us to love our neighbour as ourselves, and therefore every deviation from this rule is a transgression of his law, and a provocation of his anger. But when we judge ourselves more immediately in relation to him, when we consider what he has righteously required of us, and reflect upon our omissions of duty, and our actual departures from him, in thought, word, and deed, we are compelled to exclaim——"Who can understand his errors?" The review is painful—but it is useful, it is necessary.

It will lead us to admire the longsuffering of God, in bearing with us year after year. Though we have proved such cumberers of the ground, he has still spared us. Though we have so often provoked him, he has not destroyed us. We may look upon each other this evening with astonishment, and say, "It is of the Lord's mercies that we are not consumed, because his compassions fail not."

It will be a call to repentance. This always commences in a conviction of sin, and is daily brought into exercise by fresh discoveries of its remaining existence. "They shall come with weeping, and with supplications will I lead them."

It will humble us. And we need every check to pride, for we are prone to think more highly of ourselves than we ought to think. But what are we? Have we lived a day without being fools, loiterers, undutiful servants, unfaithful stewards? And what reason can we have to be proud?

It will promote charity. We shall be tender towards others, in proportion as we deal honestly and severely with ourselves. The most effectual way to take us off from beholding the mote in our brother's eye, is to employ ourselves in extracting the beam from our own. We have all our infirmities, though they may not be precisely of the same kind with those which lead us so rigorously to condemn others. We are all "in the body, and should consider ourselves, lest we also be tempted."

It will be a spur to diligence. Do you ask, in what are we to use diligence? This depends, in some respects, upon the condition you are in. Perhaps to this hour some of you have been anxious about every thing, except the pardon of your sins. While these remain unforgiven, the wrath of God abideth on you, and you are every moment in danger of sinking into the lowest hell. It is obviously therefore your duty, immediately and earnestly to seek after an interest in Christ, by whom alone you can be justified freely from all things.

But diligence equally becomes those of you who hope that you are already partakers of this blessing. You can never do enough for him who has saved you by his grace. You have much lost time to redeem: and much lost ground to recover. When you ought to have been running, you have been standing still—perhaps drawing back. Some who began the divine life long after you, are now far before you on the heavenly road. You are surrounded with dangers which require incessant vigilance and prayer. You have a thousand mistakes to rectify, and numberless excellences to acquire. What is the life of a good man? What is it that distinguishes him from others—but a faithful investigation of his faults; an attention to moral improvement; an endeavour to make each day a practical criticism on the past? He observes *how* he was hindered: and remarks *where* he fell, or was *likely* to fall. And thus he levies a contribution of profit even upon his losses; and derives wisdom from his ignorance, strength from his weakness, and zeal from his indifference

To urge you to this four-fold review, Remember the intimation we gave you at the beginning of this address, and which is so fully expressed in the words of the Apostle— "So then every one of us shall give account of himself to God." Therefore, judge yourselves, that you may not be condemned with the wicked. This account will be personal, public, and impartial. "He will bring every work into judgment, with every secret thing, whether it be good, or whether it be evil." And whence will he bring them? From the book of his remembrance: there he has recorded all your means and mercies, troubles and sins. From the book of your own memory: there also they are secured. For there is a difference between remembrance and memory; the former often fails, but what is inscribed upon the latter abides indelibly, and only requires something to shine upon the letters to render it legible. Have you not observed that what seemed dead in the mind, only required circumstances to revive it? With what freshness and force have things long forgotten sprung up in the memory when recalled by occurrences! Thus all the history of man will hereafter be re-traced—retraced in order to be tried—and tried in order to be approved or condemned. "Wherefore, beloved, seeing that ye look for such things, be diligent that ye may be found of him in peace, without spot, and blameless."

With this solemn thought, let us close the period of our time that is now going to be numbered with the years before the Flood. It has seen many carried down to their graves, and has brought us so much nearer our own. "The fathers—where are they? And the prophets, do they live for ever?" "Man goeth to his long home, and the mourners go about the streets." And when a few years are come, we shall go the way whence we shall not return. We are accomplishing, as an hireling, our days; and our neighbours, our friends, our relations will soon seek us— but—we shall not be.

Let us sing:

"Lord, what a feeble piece
    Is this our mortal frame!
Our life, how poor a trifle 'tis,
    That scarce deserves the name!

"Alas, the brittle clay,
    That built our body first!
And, ev'ry month, and ev'ry day,
    'Tis mould'ring back to dust.

"Our moments fly apace,
    Nor will our minutes stay;
Just like a flood, our hasty days
    Are sweeping us away.

"Well, if our days must fly,
    We'll keep their end in sight;
We'll spend them all in wisdom's way,
    And let them speed their flight.

"They'll waft us sooner o'er
    This life's tempestuous sea;
Soon we shall reach the peaceful shore
    Of blest eternity."

DISCOURSE XXXI.

OUR IGNORANCE OF FUTURITY.

(NEW YEAR'S DAY.)

So soon as I shall see how it will go with me.
Phil. ii. 23.

I HAVE the pleasure to address you on the first day of another year. The day is only distinguished from others by human institution; but this has given it various advantages and characters, natural and civil, intellectual and moral. It is often a season of peculiar transactions; in which persons balance their accounts, commence business, form connexions. It is a period marked by humanity and benevolence. Children beseech time mercifully to spare the guides of their youth. The father and mother hope to see their dear offspring long coming around them. The husband congratulates the desire of his eyes, and the wife hails the companion of her journey. Friendship renews every lively desire; and all, however indifferent at other times, yield to custom, and wish your returns of this day to be many and happy.

It is a season of thankfulness and joy. We praise the Preserver of men, who has held our souls in life, and carried us through the unnumbered dangers of another year—while our feelings are tempered to solemnity by the reflection that many have finished their course, and that we look for some of our own relations or acquaintances in vain.

For it is a period of seriousness and recollection. It reminds us of the instability of the world, and the rapidity of time. Of this indeed, every day and every hour should remind us; but the changes made, and the losses occasioned by these variations, are too common and inconsiderable to awaken reflection. But the termination of a year rouses even the careless, impresses even the insensible. And if we do not allow the subject to operate on the mind, who does not feel for the moment the sentiment of Job, "When a few years are come, I shall go the way whence I shall not return?"

But there is another relation in which we may consider this day. When we begin a new division of time, we naturally look forward, and endeavour to penetrate our future condition. The prospect is intimately connected with many of our duties, and will become injurious or profitable, according to the manner in which it is indulged. Let us then confine our attention to this view of the subject. And consider, I. OUR INABILITY TO DETERMINE OUR FUTURE CIRCUMSTANCES. II. SHOW WHAT USE WE SHOULD MAKE OF OUR IGNORANCE. III. SEARCH FOR SOMETHING TO SATISFY AND COMFORT US, UNDER ALL OUR SUSPENSION AND UNCERTAINTY.

I. Though the endowments which distin-
guish the apostles were extraordinary, they were not absolute, but limited in their exercise by Him who gave them. In some cases Paul could discern spirits, and foretell things to come—but in others he was held in ignorance, and could only reason from probabilities. Thus he said to the church of Ephesus, "And now, behold, I go bound in the Spirit unto Jerusalem, not knowing the things that shall befall me there." He was now a prisoner at Rome.—His trial was depending, but the result of it he was unable to determine. He could therefore only form his plan conditionally, and resolve to send Timothy to the Philippians "so soon as he should see how it would go with him."

And will this not apply more fully to our circumstances?

When we look into futurity, all that meets the eye is a dark unknown. Even in those cases in which God has announced things to come, the prophecy is wrapped up in so much obscurity, that the fulfilment and the explanation generally arrive together. We can previously ascertain nothing. And how often has this been exemplified in the calculations of wise men—and some not very wise—with regard to those predictions which remain to be accomplished! Not only have they been drawn off from more useful duties, but they have frequently survived their laborious schemes, and been ashamed of the confidence with which they have published them. After gazing from the tower of their folly, they found that God had gone by in another road than that which they appointed him, and had used other instruments than those which they had put into his hands. They did not consider that the advantage of prophecy is to be derived from the completion; and that so far is a previous knowledge of it from being necessary, that it would in many instances prove hurtful, and often prevent the accomplishment. It is not for us to know the times and the seasons which the Father hath put into his own power.

In the course of a few years only, how have all our conjectures been disappointed! More than once we had imagined that we had seized the clew, and the skein of Providence seemed likely to be unravelled; but suddenly we found it more entangled than before. And would any one now undertake to determine what will be the state of the nations of the earth a few months hence?

Sometimes a cloud no bigger than a man's hand has overspread the heavens; and from apparently inadequate causes events have arisen the most astonishing: while, on the other hand, the best-concerted plans and the most powerful resources have failed. Some are offended at the word chance; but the Scripture employs it, and it is no improper term. If indeed we apply it to God, it is profane—for "known unto God are all his works from the beginning; his counsel shall stand, and he will do all his pleasure." But what counsel is to him, chance is to us. We know nothing before it arrives. The consequences of things would be known if these things themselves moved on in one even regular course, and always terminated uniformly in the same manner—but when we see them often turning up contrary to their natural tendency—when we see that "the race is not to the swift, nor the battle to the strong, nor yet bread to the wise, nor riches to men of understanding, nor favour to men of skill"—our anticipations must be always liable to uncertainty. "Time and chance happeneth to them all."

What says your own history? He has led you, but it has been by "a way which you knew not;" and perhaps you hardly know it now. How wonderful have been the removals of your habitation, and the connexions which you have formed! How strange and unlooked-for have been both your friends and your enemies! Some have acquired wealth, and others filled offices towards which they could not have formerly aspired. Had these changes a few years before been foretold, they would have appeared incredible; and the subjects of them would have said, "If the Lord should make windows in heaven, might this thing be!"

So little have we been capable of judging aright, that we have in a thousand instances mistaken our real welfare: we have desired enjoyments which would have been a snare; and have been afraid of trials which have proved to be some of our chief mercies. When he was approaching to "empty us from vessel to vessel"—to keep us from "settling upon our lees;" when he came to prune away our suckers—that we "might bring forth more fruit;" we mistook the friend for an enemy; and said, "All these things are against me," when they were "all working together for our good!"

Nor have you any information that can enable you to see how things will go with you for a single year. You know not how it will go with your health this year—what seeds of disorder may spring up in your frame; what accidents may befall your persons. You know not how it will go with your circumstances this year—what losses or successes you may experience; what new scenes of enjoyment may be opened, or what old ones may be dried up. You know not how it will go with your relations this year—whether you will be indulged with their continuance or stripped of their company. Perhaps the eye of Providence now sees the hearse standing before your door; and you trying to go in to take a last view of your happiness, before it be committed to "the house appointed for all living." The Lord preserve this family! but in what different circumstances may the members of

it assemble together on the return of this day! The wife may be seen in widowed weeds! The children may appear orphans! The sister may say, "Alas! my brother!"

Let us, II. SHOW WHAT USE WE SHOULD MAKE OF THIS IGNORANCE.

Let us learn from it our littleness; let us confess that we are nothing, and that God is all in all. "Vain man would be wise;" and there is nothing of which he is so proud as his knowledge—but there is nothing that should make him more humble. For what can we know? "Who knoweth what is good for man in this life, all the days of his vain life which he spendeth as a shadow? For who can tell a man what shall be after him under the sun?" Can he distinguish between appearances and reality? Can he see the combination, the dependences, and the effects of things? Does he "boast himself of to-morrow," when he "knoweth not what a day may bring forth?" "The way of man is not in himself: it is not in man that walketh to direct his steps." Are we then qualified to be our own guides, or to manage our own affairs? "Trust in the Lord with all thine heart, and lean not unto thine own understanding. In all thy ways acknowledge him, and he shall direct thy paths. "He shall choose our inheritance for us." "Lord, my heart is not haughty, nor mine eyes lofty: neither do I exercise myself in great matters, or in things too high for me. Surely I have behaved and quieted myself, as a child that is weaned of his mother: my soul is even as a weaned child."

Secondly. Since we cannot see how things will go with us, we should beware of presumption. "Go to now, ye that say, to-day or to-morrow we will go into such a city, and continue there a year, and buy and sell, and get gain: whereas ye know not what shall be on the morrow." The Apostle here gives us the scheme of an unsanctified tradesman. He resolves to go without delay to some place where he can carry on business to advantage. His aim is not fraud, but fair gain in the lawful way of buying and selling. And where is the harm of all this? Is not diligence laudable? Are we not commanded to provide for our own house? Wherein then does this man appear blameable? Perhaps he was actuated by avarice, and was seeking not a subsistence, but a splendid independence. Perhaps he was influenced by imprudence, and was not aware of the bad effects of roving abroad, or of changing his scene of action: for "as a bird that wandereth from her nest, so is a man that wandereth from his place:" and "a rolling stone gathers no moss." This may be true—but what this man is here condemned for is this—God is not in all his thoughts. These words, "I will," are too big for him. Regardless of God, he engages to live a year, and all the year to be successful. He seems to exclude the possibility of sickness or accidents; of unfaithful servants or insolvent debtors: of dear purchases and cheap sales: as if he foresaw and secured all the events of the year himself—While he was not sure that he should be able even to *begin* his journey, and knew not what should be even on the *morrow*. Well does the Apostle call this rejoicing "boasting," and say, that "all such rejoicing is evil."

Things may be within the reach of our knowledge and not of our power; but how can that be within the reach of our power that does not fall under our knowledge? How can we ward off dangers of which we are not apprized? How can we arrange and regulate occurrences of which we can have no foresight? Now this is our case. We know only the *present*; and what superstructure can we build on such a narrow foundation? How often, even while forming a plan, has the lapse of a few days so varied circumstances, that we have been compelled to new model it, or to abandon it altogether! "Let no man deceive himself. If any man among you seemeth to be wise in this world, let him become a fool, that he may be wise. For the wisdom of this world is foolishness with God. For it is written, "He taketh the wise in their own craftiness. And again, The Lord knoweth the thoughts of the wise, that they are vain. He leadeth counsellors away spoiled, and maketh the judges fools."

We dare not infer the future from the present. David erred here. After he had been delivered from Saul, and other enemies, he tells us that he had too much confidence. And in "my prosperity I said, I shall never be moved. Lord, by thy favour thou hast made my mountain to stand strong:" but hear what he adds—"Thou didst hide thy face, and I was troubled." The rich have been often stripped of their wealth; and the caressed of their honour. Many a fair morning has turned out a very stormy day.

Thirdly, the same considerations which should check presumption, should also prevent despair. Seeing we know not how it will go with us, why should we look only for evil? It may be far better than the foreboding of our fears. Our deliverance may be much nearer than we imagine.

> "The Lord can clear the darkest skies,
> Can give us day for night,
> Make drops of sacred sorrow rise
> To rivers of delight."

Indeed, our extremity is often his opportunity. It is often darkest just before break of day. And when the ebbing of the tide is lowest, the flowing is nearest.

Fourthly. Since we see not how it will go with us, let us draw off our attention from future events to present duties. We are to cast not our work, but our care upon the Lord. Duty and means belong to us, but events are entirely his. And he says to us, as the king did to his prime minister: "Attend you to my affairs, and I will attend to yours." "Take therefore no thought for the morrow: for the morrow shall take thought for the things of itself. Sufficient unto the day is the evil thereof. Be careful for nothing; but in every thing by prayer and supplication with thanksgiving let your requests be made known unto God. And the peace of God which passeth all understanding, shall keep your hearts and minds through Christ Jesus." Such is the temper and the business of a Christian. The child at school is not to lean his elbow on the table, and vex himself by thinking how he shall find raiment, how he shall get home, how the expense of his education is to be defrayed. He is a learner; he is to mind his book—the father requires no more of him—*he* will provide. The farmer is not to muse from day to day about the weather, "perhaps it may not be a fine season —there may be a blight—and all my labour may be lost." No: but he is to act; he goes forth bearing precious seed, commits it to the ground, and then pursues his other business— and what can his anxiety do afterwards? "So is the kingdom of God, as if a man should cast seed into the ground, and should sleep, and rise, night and day, and the seed should spring and grow up, he knoweth not how. For the earth bringeth forth fruit of herself, first the blade, then the ear, after that the full corn in the ear." The soldier is to learn his exercise, to obey the word of command, to keep his arms bright, to be always at the post assigned him; but he is not to neglect all this, by busying himself in drawing plans of the campaign, and describing the duties of the general.

Finally. Our ignorance of what may befall us should lead us to seek after a preparation for all events. Do you ask, where shall we find it? I answer, in the blessed influence of Divine grace. This drew prayer from Jacob when he went forth with a staff; and praise when he returned with a fortune. This preserved Daniel in the court of Darius and in the lion's den. This enabled Paul to say, "I know both how to be abased, and I know how to abound: everywhere and in all things I am instructed both to be full and to be hungry, both to abound and to suffer need. I can do all things through Christ which strengtheneth me." And seeing we have not the ordering of the weather, nor the choice of our food—happy is the man, whose constitution enables him to bear *any* weather, and whose appetite enables him to relish *any* food.

This leads us, III. To inquire WHAT THERE IS TO ENCOURAGE US UNDER ALL THIS DARKNESS AND UNCERTAINTY. You say, I see not how it will go with me. And it is well you do not. You know as much as it is good for you. For it is with the mind as it is with the senses. A greater degree of hearing would incommode us; and a nicer degree of seeing would terrify us. If our eyes could see things microscopically, we should be afraid to move. Thus our knowledge is suited to our situation and circumstances. Were we informed beforehand of the good things prepared for us by Providence, from that moment we should cease to enjoy the blessings we possess, become indifferent to present duties, and be filled with restless impatience. Or suppose the things foreknown were gloomy and adverse, what dismay and despondency would be the consequence of the discovery! and how many times should we suffer in imagination what we now only endure once in reality! Who would wish to draw back a vail that saves them from so many disquietudes! If some of you had formerly known the troubles through which you have since waded, you would have fainted under the prospect.

You say, You see not how it will go with you; but God does. And he is your friend, and your father, and loves you better than you love yourselves, and is far more concerned for your happiness than you can be. " Why sayest thou, O Jacob, and speakest, O Israel, My way is hid from the Lord, and my judgment is passed over from my God?" Nothing is hid from him. " He knows thy walking through this great wilderness. He knows thy soul in adversity." He sees all thy dangers and all thy wants. Nothing can surprise him whose eyes are in every place. Nothing can elude his notice who numbers the heirs of thy head. When Abraham was called to leave his own country, and his father's house, he obeyed; and " he went out, not knowing whither he went." But though he knew not " whither he went," he knew with *whom:* he knew that he followed a guide who could not lead him astray. And thus Job relieved his mind under a pressure of perplexity: " Behold, I go forward, but he is not there; and backward, but I cannot perceive him: on the left hand, where he doth work, but I cannot behold him: he hideth himself on the right hand, that I cannot see him: but he knoweth the way that I take: when he hath tried me, I shall come forth as gold."

You say, You see not how it will go with you. But you know, " that it shall be well with them that fear God." You know that if you are his, though your way may be thorny, " your shoes shall be iron and brass;" and that as " your day is, so shall your strength be." You know that love is the spring of all your trials, as well as of your comforts. And that though no " chastening for the present seemeth to be joyous, but grievous: nevertheless, afterward it yieldeth the peaceable fruit of righteousness to them which are exercised thereby." You know

that " God is faithful, who will not suffer you to be tempted above that ye are able; but will with the temptation also make a way to escape, that ye may be able to bear it." In a word, and is it not enough to know this? —you *know that " all things work together for good to them that love God; to them that are the called according to his purpose."*

You say, You see not how it will go with you. But your ignorance only regards *time:* all in *eternity* is sure. Beyond this land of darkness dwells everlasting light. Your uncertainty only regards the roughness or smoothness of the way—for you know what stands at the end of it—It is your Father's house, where are many mansions!

> " See the kind angels at the gates
> Inviting us to come;
> There Jesus the forerunner waits
> To welcome traveller's home."

Yes, you know how it will go with you there. There you will " enter into peace;" there " the days of your mourning will be ended;" there you will be " for ever with the Lord!"

> " There—shall we see his face,
> And never, never sin;
> There from the rivers of his grace
> Drink endless pleasures in."

Ah! blessed privilege—and happy they who can enjoy it! They have enough to relieve them in every distress. Their afflictions must be light and momentary indeed, when they are persuaded that they are working out for them a far more exceeding and eternal weight of glory. But this is not my case. My perplexity seems to increase in proportion as I advance. To me the other world seems darker than this; and it is a gloomy valley that leads to it. Oh! if I knew that all would *end* well!—But this is that which adds a pressure to every burden, and embitters all my comforts—I see not how it will go with me AT LAST."

My Christian friend: I designed not by what I have said, to intimate that such a persuasion is essential to your safety, but only that it is a desirable privilege; and in this we are agreed. But remember *it is attainable.* You may have " a good hope through grace," and " the full assurance of hope." You are commanded to seek it. In the mean time, I would observe, that the solicitude you feel, is no bad evidence in your favour. In proportion as the mind feels the importance of salvation, it longs for certainty, and, fearful of deception, is not satisfied with slender evidence. May the Lord, you are now following sorrowful and in darkness, shine upon your path, and " fill you with all joy and peace in believing, that you may abound in hope, through the power of the Holy Ghost."

But if we cannot begin the new year with confidence and joy, let us do it with seriousness and prayer. Let us resolve to walk before him in newness of life. Let us commit ourselves to the care of his Providence, to the word of his grace, to the agency of his Holy Spirit. And let us lift up our hearts with our voices while we sing,

"And now, my soul, another year
  Of thy short life is past;
I cannot long continue here,
  And this may prove my last.

"Much of my dubious life is gone,
  Nor will return again;
And swift my passing moments run,
  And few perhaps remain.

"Awake, my soul, with solemn care,
  Thy true condition learn;
What are thy hopes, how sure, how fair,
  And what thy great concern!

"Now a new scene of time begins
  Set out afresh for heaven;
Seek pardon for thy former sins
  In Christ so freely given.

"Devoutly yield thyself to God,
  And on his grace depend;
With zeal pursue the heavenly road—
  Nor fear a happy end."

DISCOURSE XXXII.

RELIGION MORE THAN FORMALITY.

Having a form of godliness, but denying the power thereof.—2 Tim. iii. 5.

AND what is godliness! It is the tendency of the mind towards God: and is exercised in believing in him, loving and fearing him, holding communion with him, resembling his perfections, and employing ourselves in his service. It is the introduction of God into all our concerns, our acknowledging him in all our ways, our doing all we do in his name, and with a reverence to his authority and glory, through the mediation of the Saviour, and by the influences of the Holy Spirit.

This is godliness; and nothing else deserves the name. This godliness however has its *form* and its *power;* and this distinction enables us to arrange *four classes of characters.*

For, first, *there are some who have neither the power nor the form of godliness.* They are as destitute of the pretension as they are of the reality; and often glory in this—for we read of some "who glory in their shame."

Secondly, *there are some who possess both the power and the form.* And these are the most worthy of our esteem and imitation. May their number daily increase!

Thirdly, *there are some who have the power of godliness, but not the form.* Their religion is a kind of disembodied spirit: and because some have laid too much stress upon outward things, they lay too little. They carry their notions of the spirituality of divine worship so far as to exclude social considerations; the influence of the body over the mind; and the use which the Supreme Being himself makes of our senses, to aid our graces, and which is simply the principle upon which

baptism and the ordinance of the Lord's Supper are founded. They do not remember that though the substance be confessedly the main thing, circumstances are often very beautiful and impressive and beneficial; that we are not only to possess, but to profess religion; that we are not only to serve God individually, but to unite ourselves to a body of Christians, and walk in holy fellowship, "striving together for the faith of the Gospel; and that we are bound not only to "glorify God in our spirits," but "in our bodies also, which are God's." So that the form when attached to the principle, is so far from being improper, that it is commendable and important.

But here we have reached the Fourth class to which we referred, *those who have the form, but deny the power.* These are awful characters; and therefore, says the apostle, to Timothy, "From such withdraw thyself." We should do this as much as possible with regard to their persons, but above all with regard to their state. In order to this—let us, I. CONSIDER THE POWER OF GODLINESS; and, II. INQUIRE WHENCE IT IS THAT SO MANY WHO DENY IT ARE STILL DISPOSED TO MAINTAIN THE FORM.

I. THE "POWER" OF GODLINESS IS HERE DISTINGUISHED FROM THE MERE "FORM:" and indeed it is easy to show the difference between them. The one is principally external, and deals in words—the other is internal, actuating our feelings, and governing our actions. The one is the name—the other is the thing; the one is the appearance—the other is the reality. The one is the body—the other is the soul, that inspires every member, and penetrates every particle of the frame. The one is the picture—the other is the original: the one shows us the Christian on canvass—the other presents him to us alive and in motion.

Now what I want to convince you of here is this—that real godliness is more than a show, a fancy, a form—it has an efficacy in it—there is a power attending it. For consider how it is produced and maintained. It is in its existence, as well as in its revelation, a Divine principle. Hear how the Apostle speaks of it in his epistle to the Ephesians. "God is able," says he, "to do exceeding abundantly above all that we ask or think"— "according to the power that worketh in us." I bow my knees to the Father of our Lord Jesus Christ—"that he would grant you, according to the riches of his glory, to be strengthened with might by his Spirit in the inner man." And again, he prays for them, that they may know—what is the exceeding greatness of his power to us-ward who believe, according to the working of his mighty power, which he wrought in Christ, when he raised him from the dead, and set him at his own right hand, in the heavenly places:"

where we find—that the same almighty energy which quickened into endless life the entombed body of our Lord, is actually put forth in the renovation of the believer: "that like as Christ was raised up from the dead, by the glory of the Father, even so we also walk in newness of life." Hence it is called "the life of God;" and "the participation of the Divine nature." What is the water that the Saviour promises to give to those that ask him! "Living water." "And," says he, "the water that I shall give him shall be in him a well of water springing up into everlasting life." Here is nothing stagnant and dead; but every thing is expressive of influence and activity. Thus the Apostle tells the Thessalonians that the Gospel came to them—"not in word only, but in power:" and that they received it, not as the word of men, but as it is in truth, the word of God, "which effectually worketh also in you that believe." And thus, to view the subject more separately, and in parts, we read of "the work of faith, the labour of love, and the patience of hope."

Observe the subjects of Divine grace. This principle distinguishes them from others: and is capable of producing a holy singularity. If you have only the form of godliness, there will be no practical difference between you and others; if servants—you will be as idle, as gossipping, as regardless of the property of your employers, as others: if wives—you will be as unsubmissive; if husbands—as tyrannical: if tradesmen—as grasping and overreaching as others. But if you have the power—you will resemble good Nehemiah. "The former governors," says he, "were chargeable to the people—but so did not I, because of the fear of God." Piety would not suffer him to act like them. And if you are under the influence of it, you will not, in your various relations and circumstances, be borne down by the errors and vices around you: but you will be *able* to act uprightly: you will be kept from consulting custom, and be constrained to listen to conscience: you will not be permitted to sin as do others, or "sleep as do others—you will not be conformed to this world, but be transformed, by the renewing of the mind, that you may prove what is that good, and acceptable, and perfect will of God." A dead fish can swim *with* the stream, but a live one can swim *against* it.

Yea, this principle distinguishes the man from himself. Thus, under the influence of it, the drunkard becomes sober; the swearer learns to fear an oath, and the liar a lie. He that stole, steals no more, but labours. The churl becomes liberal, and the niggard bountiful; it cannot be otherwise. If the man has been moral before, he continues to avoid the same vices, to perform the same duties, and to attend the same means of grace as before—

but from very different motives, and in a very different manner. He has now also much more to engage his attention. His regard is no longer confined to externals only, but he is taken up with "the hidden man of the heart;" and prays with David, "Create in me a clean heart, O God, and renew a right spirit within me." Hence spring exercises to which he was once a stranger; and he feels himself engaged in a warfare which often perplexes him, and leads him to exclaim, "If I am his, why am I thus?"

Behold then the life of the real Christian, and trace the operation of the power of godliness there.

It appears with regard to the ordinances of divine worship. Others who have only the form, come without expectation and prayer, and return without reflection and concern: they are satisfied with their attendance—but he is not. He is anxious to derive spiritual advantage from it: he enters the closet before he approaches the temple, and his language is, "Oh that I knew where I might find him, that I might come even to his seat!" Oh that I may be of "the circumcision who worship God in the spirit, rejoice in Christ Jesus, and have no confidence in the flesh."

It appears with regard to the dissipations of the world. He voluntarily resigns those amusements in which he once placed so much of his happiness: and he returns no more to them. And why? If he were mindful of the country whence he came, he has opportunity to return: he is surrounded with the same allurements as others—why then does he not engage in these diversions again?—Because he has found something infinitely more noble and more satisfying. And a greater good has power to abolish the impressions of a less. When the sun arises, the stars disappear. And the grapes of Eshcol cause us to forget the leeks and onions of Egypt.

You may see it in the mortification of sin. He denies himself; he crucifies the flesh with the affections and lusts; he plucks out a right eye, and cuts off a right hand. You may see it in what he is willing to sacrifice and to suffer. Read history: read the book of martyrs; read the eleventh chapter of the epistle to the Hebrews—and see what the force of this powerful principle can accomplish. There you see an Abraham at the command of God, "leaving his own country, and his father's house, and going out, not knowing whither he went:" and, in obedience to the same authority, "when tried, offering up Isaac; his son, his only son; of whom it was said, that in Isaac shall thy seed be called." There you see a "Moses, when come to years, refusing to be called the son of Pharaoh's daughter; choosing rather to suffer affliction with the people of God, than to enjoy the pleasures of sin for a season; esteeming the reproach of Christ greater riches than the treasures of Egypt: for he had respect unto the recompence of the reward. By faith he forsook Egypt, not fearing the wrath of the king: for he endured as seeing him who is invisible. And what shall I more say? for the time would fail me to tell of Gideon, and of Barak, and of Samson, and of Jephthah; of David also, and Samuel, and of the prophets: who through faith subdued kingdoms, wrought righteousness, obtained promises, stopped the mouths of lions, quenched the violence of fire, escaped the edge of the sword, out of weakness were made strong, waxed valiant in fight, turned to flight the armies of the aliens. Women received their dead raised to life again: and others were tortured, not accepting deliverance; that they might obtain a better resurrection; and others had trial of cruel mockings and scourgings, yea, moreover of bonds and imprisonment: They were stoned, they were sawn asunder, were tempted, were slain with the sword: they wandered about in sheepskins and goatskins; being destitute, afflicted, tormented; (of whom the world was not worthy:) they wandered in deserts, and in mountains, and in dens and caves of the earth."

"But we are not called to such scenes as these." Blessed be God, you are not. But every Christian, says Luther, is a piece of a martyr; "yea," says the Apostle, "and all that will live godly in Christ Jesus shall suffer persecution." There is the same malignity in human nature against vital religion as formerly; and it will operate as far as it is permitted by circumstances. And when religion is vital, it will enable a man to abide the test; and resolve to go forward, notwithstanding the ridicule of infidels, the sneer of worldlings, and the reproaches of relations and friends. And this requires a degree of the same grace as martyrdom.

The vigour of this principle appears also in other sufferings. How many are there at this moment, enduring a variety of grief in private, whose names will never be published in history, but who, in the eye of God, are greater than the admired heroes of the age! They act nobly, without the prospect, or the desire of notice, or of fame: they breathe no revenge towards instruments; they neither charge God foolishly nor unkindly in any of the disappointments and afflictions which have befallen them; they are strangers to impatience and repining; and all you hear is, "I mourn, but I do not murmur. I pray, but I do not prescribe. 'The Lord gave, and the Lord hath taken away, and blessed be the name of the Lord.' I have more reason for thankfulness than complaint. I know not what he is doing with me—but 'he knoweth the way that I take.' Whether the trial be removed or continued, increased or di-

minished, it is with him to determine—so it should be—and so it shall be. 'Behold, here I am, let him do to me as seemeth good unto him!'"

Yea, we have seen and heard the saints "joyful in glory, and shouting aloud upon their dying beds;" raised above the fear of "the king of terrors" himself, and exulting, "O death, where is thy sting? O grave, where is thy victory? The sting of death is sin, and the strength of sin is the law: but thanks be unto God, that giveth us the victory through our Lord Jesus Christ." Surely, therefore, in the religion of the blessed Jesus, there is an excellency, an efficacy, a power.

But this power, derived from a Divine influence, and distinguishing the Christian from others and from himself—this power, which enlivens him in ordinances, raises him above the world, subdues his corruptions, and supports and comforts him in all his sufferings—this power, many, alas! are ignorant of, and in works, if not in words, really deny.

II. They yet assume and maintain the form—and some of the reasons which induce them to do this, are the following:

First, because the *form* is comparatively easy. The difficulty lies in the *power*. It is an easy thing to pretend to be rich; to purchase splendid apparel and furniture; and live in style upon the property of others—which is the fashion of the day. This differs exceedingly from the economy and industry and labour of the man who in his calling gains a competency lawfully. It is an easy thing to profess to be wise: but to acquire knowledge by the weariness of study; by rising early and sitting up late; by keeping the mind always alive, and attentive to perceive, appropriate, and classify fresh intellectual stores—here is the difficulty. And thus it is in the case before us. The *form* of godliness requires no strenuous exertions; demands no costly sacrifices. It is the *power* of it that renders the Christian life a "striving to enter in at the strait gate;" a "pressing into the kingdom of God;" a "wrestling with principalities and powers;" a "running the race that is set before us;" a "fighting the good fight of faith." And it is this too that incurs opposition from the world. It will indeed be acknowledged that sometimes the very form draws forth the rancour of others: and of all people those are most to be pitied who are persecuted for what they have not; who are reproached as Christians without deserving the honour. But upon a nearer inspection of these mere formalists, the world is generally made quite easy. They see that they were mistaken in the characters; they find that they are "of their own," though wearing a religious uniform. And discovering in them their own spirit, which dispose-them to plead for their vanities and leads them to indulge in the very same practices, as far as they can safely do it—they will readily allow them their odd way of thinking, or their peculiar observances; yea, they may even consent to go with them to hear their favourite preacher, if these formalists will go with them in return to see their favourite actor. The real Christian may say to these nominal ones, as his Lord and Saviour did to the Jews; "The world cannot hate you; but me it hateth, because I testify of it that the deeds thereof are evil."

Secondly, Persons are sometimes induced to take up the form of godliness through the influence of their connexions. From some of them they feel the influence of authority; from some, the influence of friendship; from some, the influence of business. For with many, "gain is godliness;" and they assume religion because they imagine they can succeed better in the church than in the world. This often decides the place of their hearing. Some of them also pay for seats in *several* places of worship—it makes them known—and is likely to increase customers.

Though religion particularly and practically considered be obnoxious to mankind, yet viewed superficially and in the gross, it commonly obtains something like applause; and few would choose to have any thing to do with a person who avowed himself to be irreligious in principle and practice. Many therefore nicely determine the boundary of safety; and without going so far as to give offence, they will go far enough to procure respect. Hence, says Henry, "they assume a form of godliness to take away their reproach, but not the power of it to take away their sin."

Thirdly, They avail themselves of the form of godliness to preserve peace within. For without something of religion, conscience would rage and clamour; but by means of this, it is amused and quieted; and this renders it so extremely dangerous. For, engaged in a number of duties, he presumes on the goodness of his state; and feeling no fear, he makes no inquiry. The man is secure without being safe; and while "poor towards God," supposes himself to be "rich, and increased with goods, and to have need of nothing."

But "what is the hope of the formalist though he has gained?" And what does he gain? He may pass for religious in the opinion of his fellow-creatures, and lull conscience to sleep—But does he obtain the approbation of God? Can he possibly elude his discernment? "His eyes are as a flame of fire," which will pierce through every pretension, and consume every disguise. No. "He is not a Jew, which is one outwardly; neither is that circumcision, which is out-

ward in the flesh: but he is a Jew, which is one inwardly; and circumcision is that of the heart, in the spirit, and not in the letter; whose praise is not of men, but of God. The kingdom of God is not meat and drink, but righteousness, peace, and joy in the Holy Ghost. The kingdom of God is not in word, but in power."

And to draw towards a close—If such a subject as this was ever necessary, it is peculiarly so in the present day, when hearing the gospel entails so little reproach, and the profession of religion is so cheap, having become so common. Let me therefore beseech you to examine yourselves by this solemn test; and to inquire, whether you have the power, as well as the form of godliness. It is a good evidence in your favour, if you are willing to come to the light; and can even address yourselves to God in the language of David: "Search me, O God, and know my heart: try me, and know my thoughts: and see if there be any wicked way in me, and lead me in the way everlasting."

And be it remembered, that in a case of such vast importance, and where the consequences of deception are not to be repaired, we cannot be too anxious to be right. It is better to have a timorous conscience, than a presumptuous one: and to be unnecessarily distressed for awhile, and—be safe—than to enjoy a carnal confidence, and—perish for ever!

To induce you to seek after real godliness, you would do well to reflect on "the exceeding great and precious promises," which are attached to it in the Scriptures of truth. If you have the life and power of religion, you will indeed be engaged in exercises and trials which the mere formalist escapes—but then you will have privileges and hopes of which he can never partake. He does not go far enough to relish its enjoyments or amass its riches. But "for this shall every one that is godly pray unto thee, in a time when thou mayest be found: surely in the floods of great waters they shall not come nigh unto him." "The Lord hath set apart him that is godly for himself." "Bodily exercise profiteth little: but godliness is profitable unto all things, having promise of the life that now is and of that which is to come." For eternity—here is the assurance of deliverance from every evil, the possession of all good, the vision and the presence of their Lord and Saviour for ever. And for time—here is the certainty—not of health, of property, of ease and friendship—but what is far better—the *persuasion*, that "all things shall work together for good to them that love God, to them that are the called according to his purpose!"

"Look thou upon me, and be merciful unto me, as thou usest to do unto those that love thy name!"

DISCOURSE XXXIII.

AUTUMN.

We all do fade as a leaf!—Isaiah lxiv. 6.

THE inspired writers often send us to the animal, and even to the vegetable worlds for instruction: and it must be confessed, that they are wonderfully adapted to strike and to admonish us.

The misfortune however is, that " seeing many things, we observe not." The means of instruction are plentifully dispensed, but a mind to use them is rarely found.

Yet such a mind it behoves us to cultivate. And when the attention is awakened, and we are willing to learn, every thing becomes a teacher or a monitor. " The heavens declare the glory of God. All his works praise him." The ravens encourage us to trust in him for food; and the lilies for clothing. His voice is heard in the thunder: he whispers also in the breeze: and even a falling leaf preaches a lesson to man.

From our windows, or in our walks, we may now see the trees, shedding their honours.—Isaiah tells us that this is an emblem of ourselves—" For we all do fade as a leaf."

It is observable that he does not compare life to a tree. An oak by slow degrees rises to perfection, and long maintains its glory. For ages it defies the fury of the elements, and at last, after long and repeated assaults, it gradually decays, or sullenly submitting to the axe, sinks slowly and crashing upon the ground. Many trees are much less solid and durable than the oak. But man is compared to none of them—his image is " a leaf."

A leaf while it hangs on, adorns the branches and looks beautiful; it is the shelter of the fruit and the dress of the tree; it waves to the wind and murmurs to the ear. But how weak, how frail is it! By what a slender bond does it retain its situation! How small a force is required to bring it down to the ground! where it soon mixes with the earth, and is no more to be distinguished from it.

A leaf does not always endure a whole season. It is exposed to a thousand disasters. It is often crushed in its prime. Insects gnaw it off; the beasts of the field may devour it; winds may scatter it; or it may be shaken down with the fruit. And, between the diseases and accidents to which human nature is liable, few of the human race comparatively attain old age. The Jews formerly reckoned up nine hundred and three diseases; but accidents are absolutely innumerable. A vapour may cause death: our houses may bury us in their ruins: our food may poison us. When we consider the extreme delicacy of the human frame, and the multiplicity of fine and tender parts of which it is composed,

the derangement of one of which brings on the dissolution of the whole—the wonder is, that we ever live a single day to an end! Accordingly many are carried to the grave as soon as they are born. They open their eyes on a vale of tears; weep and withdraw. Others grow in stature, become lovely in form, engaging in manners, amiable in temper, and promising as to wisdom and virtue; these live long enough to engage the affections of their relatives, and then leave them mourning and " refusing to be comforted because they are not." Others advance further, form connexions, and enter on their busy schemes—but " in that very day, their thoughts perish." Sometimes wars, famines, pestilences, and earthquakes, receive a commission to destroy. These may be compared to storms, which desolate a whole forest at once, and cover the ground with foliage.

When a leaf falls it drops irrecoverably. It is otherwise with the tree: " there is hope of a tree if it be cut down that it will sprout again, and that the tender branch thereof will not cease. Though the root thereof wax old in the earth, and the stock thereof die in the ground, yet, through the scent of water, it will bud and bring forth boughs like a plant." But the leaf has no second spring: it can never be revived. And man is like it. " Man dieth and wasteth away, yea, man giveth up the ghost and where is he!—Man lieth down, and riseth not: till the heavens be no more, they shall not awake, nor be raised out of their sleep." Oh! could prayers and tears bring him back, and rejoin him to the living! But all is vain!—And equally vain are all our wishes and our endeavours to prevent the doom! " O remember that my life is wind; mine eye shall no more see good. The eye of him that hath seen me shall see me no more: thine eyes are upon me, and I am not. As the cloud is consumed, and vanisheth away; so he that goeth down to the grave shall come up no more. He shall return no more to his house, neither shall his place know him any more."

But the main thing intended in the image, is the short continuance of its being, and the still shorter duration of its vigour and verdure. Be favourable, ye winds, and, ye beasts of the field, come not to devour—let the leaf remain and flourish. How contracted the measure of its existence—and of its glory! When Jacob was asked how old he was, he answered, " The days of the years of my pilgrimage are one hundred and thirty years: few and full of evil have been the days of the years of my pilgrimage: and I have not attained unto the days of the years of the life of my fathers, in the days of their pilgrimage." But if he fell short of the age of his ancestors, we come vastly short of his. That man is old. Ask him how many annual periods of time he has passed through! " Threescore years and ten." Ask him how life looks in review?—"As a tale that is told; as a dream when one awaketh." Ask him how it passed away?—"As a flood—swifter than a weaver's shuttle." Ask him where now are the companions of his youth! How many will he reckon up, who have gone down to the grave, and have seen corruption! and how few remain to be the associates of his hoary hairs! "Behold, thou hast made my days as an hand's breadth, and my age is as nothing before thee; verily, every man at his best estate is altogether vanity."

And how often does a leaf fade, sooner than it falls! And is it not so with man! If spared, how soon does he begin to discover infirmities! "The days of our years are threescore years and ten; and if, by reason of strength, they be fourscore years, yet is their strength labour and sorrow;" labour in the preserving, and sorrow in the possessing. The body decays; the head bows down; the beauty consumes away; the hands cannot perform their enterprise; "the grinders cease because they are few, and those that look out of the windows be darkened."—The powers of the mind partake also of the declension. Sir Isaac Newton, before his death, could not comprehend one of his own axioms! The memory drops its treasures. The vigour of fancy fails. Judgment is dethroned. "Man at his best estate is altogether vanity."

Such is the representation of human nature. For this extends to all; whether old or young, poor or rich, despised or honourable, foolish or wise, yea wicked or righteous— "we ALL *do fade as a leaf.*" And who is not ready to say with David, "Wherefore hast thou made all men in vain?" But to enable us to judge properly in this case, and to vindicate the Divine perfections and providence—

Let us remember,

First, That this state of frailty and vanity was not the original state of man; but the consequence of transgression. God made man upright and immortal; but "by one man sin entered into the world, and death by sin, and so death hath passed upon all men, because all have sinned."

And, Secondly, That it is not his only state. There is another life to which the present is introductory, and in connexion with which it should always be considered. The one is the way; the other is the end. The one is the seed time; the other is the harvest. The one is a state of probation; the other of retribution.

Thirdly, The vanity and brevity of the present life, if wisely improved, is advantageous with regard to the future.

It furnishes us with no inconsiderable proof of a world to come. Every thing in such a state as this being unanswerable to our faculties, our wants, and our desires; we are constrained to look out for another.

It urges us towards it, and helps to prepare us for it. Since it is only a troublesome voyage, who would desire its longer continuance? Since all is vanity and vexation of spirit here, are we not even compelled to seek a better, a heavenly country? Since the world is our grand enemy, is it not well to find it rendered so unlovely and unseducing? Now you have only a few days to live; you have no time to trifle, but *must* attend to the things which belong to your peace, before they are hid from your eyes.

This frail life too, in the Fourth place, is continually guarded by a wise and tender Providence. All our times are in his hand. He careth for us. "A sparrow falleth not to the ground without our Heavenly Father: and the very hairs of our head are all numbered."

Let us add two additional reflections and conclude. And First, if life be like a fading leaf, let us regard it accordingly—

Let it prevent despair. If life be short, thy troubles cannot, O Christian, be long!

Let us also repress fear. It is little the most powerful can do, and before they strike they may fall. "I, even I am he that comforteth you: who art thou, that thou shouldest be afraid of a man that shall die, and the son of man that shall be made as grass?"

Let it check envy. "Be not thou afraid when one is made rich, when the glory of his house is increased: for when he dieth he shall carry nothing away: his glory shall not descend after him. Fret not thyself because of evil doers, neither be thou envious against the workers of iniquity, for they shall soon be cut down as the grass, and wither as the green herb."

Let it moderate your attachments and dependence. Make what use you can of a leaf, but do not lean upon it for support; do not hold your estate by it. Regard your present possessions and comforts as vain and vanishing; and detach your affections from things below. "Wilt thou set thy heart on that which is not?" Parents! view your children as uncertain delights. Husbands! remember how easily the desires of your eyes may be removed from you.—To-day we have friends and relations, to-morrow we are alone like a sparrow upon the house-top.

And oh! bring it home to yourselves—you are going as well as your comforts. Reflect upon your frailty—not only at a funeral, or under sickness, or in old age—but habitually —and immediately. To what purpose is it to put the evil day far off in apprehension, when it is so near in reality? "Boast not thyself of to-morrow, for thou knowest not what a day may bring forth. Go to now, ye that say, to-day or to-morrow we will go into such a city, and continue there a year, and buy and sell, and get gain; whereas ye know not what shall be on the morrow. For what is your life! It is even a vapour that appeareth for a little time and then vanisheth away."

Let me then ask you, How do matters stand with regard to another world? Are you born again? Have you a title to heaven or a meetness for it? The grand question is—not "what shall I eat, or what shall I drink, or wherewithal shall I be clothed?"—but "*what must I do to be saved?*" You should be principally concerned—not for to-morrow—but for eternity. To-morrow may never come; eternity will. May the Lord prepare us for it!—"So teach us to number our days that we may apply our hearts unto wisdom."

Let us remember, Secondly, that all is not fading. "All flesh is grass, and all the glory of man as the flower of grass. The grass withereth, and the flower thereof fadeth away; but the word of the Lord endureth for ever: and this is the word which, by the Gospel, is preached unto you."—By means of this everlasting word, you are informed of a SAVIOUR, who is the same yesterday, to-day, and for ever—of durable riches—of bags which wax not old—of a crown of life—of "an inheritance incorruptible, and undefiled, and that FADETH NOT AWAY."

"Let us therefore fear, lest, a promise being left us of entering into his rest, any of you should seem to come short of it."

DISCOURSE XXXIV.

THE DESIGN OF AFFLICTION.

Therefore, behold, I will hedge up thy way with thorns, and make a wall, that she shall not find her paths. And she shall follow after her lovers, but she shall not overtake them; and she shall seek them, but shall not find them: then shall she say, I will go and return to my first husband; for then was it better with me than now.—Hosea ii. 6, 7.

THE language of Scripture is very figurative. And herein lies much of its excellency and utility. For since we derive our knowledge through the medium of the senses, in no other way could spiritual truths so easily and forcibly lay hold of the mind.

Nothing is more common in the prophecies than to express the relation between God and the Jews of old by the alliance of marriage. He was considered as their husband. Hence they were laid under peculiar obligations to him; and hence their sins had the character of violating the marriage contract.

They were commanded to worship the Lord alone; and Him only were they to serve. But, alas! "they often declined from his ways, and hardened their heart from his fear;" or, to use the language of the metaphor: "They went a whoring after other gods; and played the harlot with many lovers." Hence the calamities which befell them. But while these calamities were the effects of sin, they were also the means of bringing them to a proper state of mind. They are therefore considered eventually as mercies; and are spoken of not in a way of threatening, but promise: "Therefore, behold, I will hedge up thy way with thorns, and make a wall, that she shall not find her paths. And she shall follow after her lovers, but she shall not overtake them; and she shall seek them, but shall not find them: then shall she say, I will go and return to my first husband; for then was it better with me than now."

But what is all this to us? Much every way. "Whatsoever things were written aforetime, were written for our learning; that we, through patience and comfort of the Scripture, might have hope." God has a people for his name in all ages. And Christians stand in the same relation to him now as the Jews did of old. And are we better than they? In no wise. And were not God's dealings with them designed to be typical of his dealings with us? They were: and in reading their history, we may peruse our own.

Let us then endeavour to explain and improve the words as applicable to ourselves.

They do not indeed require much explanation. For when God says—"I will hedge up thy way with thorns," it is obvious that he means—I will perplex them, embarrass them; pierce them through with many sorrows. There is another hedge which God raises for his people, and of which we read in the Scripture—it is the hedge of PROTECTION. Thus, speaking of Israel as a vineyard, says God, "I will take away the hedge thereof;" thereby laying it open to the intrusion of beasts and travellers. And thus, when Satan surveyed the condition of Job, he saw that he could not touch him without Divine permission—"Hast not thou made an hedge about him, and about his house, and about all that he hath, on every side?"

But the hedge here spoken of is the hedge of affliction, composed of some of those thorns and briers which sin has so plentifully produced in this wilderness world. And the metaphor is taken from a husbandman, who, to keep his cattle in the pasture, and prevent their going astray, fences them in; and the sharper the hedge the better. Thus God resolves to make our rovings difficult. If we *will* go astray, we must smart for it. "Now what hast thou to do in the way of Egypt, to drink the waters of Sihor? or what hast thou to do in the way of Assyria, to drink the waters of the river? Thine own wickedness shall correct thee, and thy backslidings shall reprove thee: know therefore and see that it is an evil thing and bitter, that thou hast forsaken the Lord thy God, and that my fear is not in thee, saith the Lord God of hosts."

But he adds—"I will make a wall, that she shall not find her paths." This is another image to convey the same truth, only with this addition—that if lighter afflictions fail of their end, God will employ heavier. They may be foolhardy enough to break through the thorns, and may go on though wounded and bleeding—but they shall not get over the wall—I have stones as well as brambles—I will present insuperable difficulties. Yes, God can deprive us of liberty; he can reduce our means; he can deprive us of health and property; he can take away the desires of our eyes with a stroke; and easily and effectually stop us in all the ardour of our schemes and enterprises.

It shows us what a variety of troubles God has to dispose of; afflictions of all kinds and of all degrees; suited to our natural disposition and our moral perverseness. It shows us also our obstinacy; that God is compelled to deal with us as with brutes, who are not to be governed by reason and ingenuous motives, but require blows and restraints. So foolish are we and ignorant, so much are we like a beast before him, that we must be hedged in with thorns, and confined in with a wall.

At length, wearied to find their paths, and unable to overtake their lovers, they are convinced of their folly, take shame to themselves, and resolve to go back. To this they are excited not only by present distress, but by former pleasure. They remember the happiness they once enjoyed in the service of God—and say, "What have I any more to do with idols? I will go and return to my first husband; for then was it better with me than now."

Thus it was with the prodigal. He had destroyed his reputation, and wasted his substance among harlots and in riotous living; he had reduced himself to the most abject condition, and lived on the husks which the swine did eat, and no man gave to him. One day—a thought of home struck him—he instantly formed a comparison between his present and his former circumstances—he recollected the honour that attended him before his wanderings; the plenty that crowned his father's board; how much was always taken away from the table, yea, how much even the servants left;—and sighed—and said—"How many hired servants of my father's have bread enough and to spare—and I perish with hunger!—I will arise and go to my father, and will say unto him, Father, I have sinned against heaven and before thee, and am no more worthy to be called thy son; make me as one of thy hired servants"— "Therefore, behold, I will hedge up thy way with thorns, and make a wall, that she shall not find her paths. And she shall follow af-

ter her lovers, but she shall not overtake them; and she shall seek them, but shall not find them: then shall she say, I will go and return to my first husband; for then was it better with me than now."

From the passage thus briefly explained, let us glance at four things. The First reminds us of OUR DEPRAVITY. The Second, of THE DIVINE GOODNESS AND CARE. The Third, of THE BENEFIT OF AFFLICTION. And the Fourth, OF THE DIFFERENCE THERE IS BETWEEN OUR ADHERING TO GOD, AND OUR DEPARTING FROM HIM.

I. We are reminded of OUR DEPRAVITY. It appears in our proneness to go astray. There is in us an "evil heart of unbelief in departing from the living God." We transfer to the creature those regards which are due only to the Creator. We fear other things more than God; we love other things more than God. We make friends, and fame, and fortune, our dependence; and withdraw our hope and confidence from Him who is the only portion of his people. Thus they become our idols.

And these are our lovers, who profess to give us "our bread and our water, our wool and our flax, our oil and our drink." These are the rivals of the Supreme Being; and, alas! they are too often successful, and draw away our hearts from God. Our backslidings are many. For let us not deceive ourselves. Let us not judge of our declensions only by gross acts, but by the state of our minds. It is indeed a mercy if we have been preserved from those scandalous falls which would disgrace our profession. But where none of these vices have appeared in the life, there have been many deviations from God in our thoughts, and affections, and pursuits. By this therefore we should try ourselves. For in proportion as we "love the world, the love of the Father is not in us." And in the same degree that we "make flesh our arm, our heart will always depart from the Lord."

II. But our depravity is not more observable than THE DIVINE GOODNESS AND CARE. For while we are thus perpetually roving from him—what does he? Does he destroy us? No. Does he abandon us to ourselves, saying, They are joined to idols; let them alone? No—but he employs means, various means to hinder and to reclaim us. "I will hedge up thy way with thorns, and make a wall, that she shall not find her paths; and she shall follow after her lovers, and shall not overtake them: and she shall seek them, but shall not find them."

And why does he make use of all these various expedients? Is it because he stands in need of us?—no—but because we stand in need of him, and can do nothing without his counsels and his comforts—because he is very pitiful and of tender mercy—because he is concerned for our everlasting welfare—

because he would not have us deceived, ensnared, destroyed—because he would not have us take up with this world as our portion, but keep our eye upon a better, even a heavenly country, and confess ourselves to be strangers and pilgrims in the earth.

And when the believer comes to himself, and considers these dealings of God with him, he exclaims, " ' Lord, what is man, that thou art mindful of him, or the son of man, that thou shouldest visit him!' What am I, to engross the attention of the Almighty! Am I worthy of all these pains! Can I ever bring forth fruit to reward this expense of cultivation! 'What is man, that thou shouldest magnify him! And that thou shouldest set thine heart upon him; and that thou shouldest visit him every morning, and try him every moment!' "

III. This brings us to remark THE BENEFIT OF AFFLICTION. This benefit might be exemplified several ways.

Afflictions are designed to be trials. They evidence the reality and the degree of our religion both to ourselves and others. When a person is surrounded with worldly possessions and enjoyments, it is not easy for him to determine whether he is leaning on these or on God. But let them be removed, and his reliance will quickly appear. If he is placing his dependence on these, he will sink when they are removed. But if while he uses them, and is thankful for them, he still makes God "the strength of his heart, and his portion for ever," he will not faint in the day of adversity; but be able to say with former sufferers, "We are troubled on every side, yet not distressed: we are perplexed, but not in despair; persecuted, but not forsaken; cast down, but not destroyed. Although the fig-tree shall not blossom, neither shall fruit be in the vines; the labour of the olive shall fail, and the fields shall yield no meat; the flocks shall be cut off from the fold, and there shall be no herd in the stalls: yet I will rejoice in the Lord, I will joy in the God of my salvation."

Afflictions are excitements. They quicken to the exercise of grace, and to the performance of duty. When Absalom wished to see Joab, he sent him a messenger, but he would not come—he sent a second time, but he still refused. Well, what was he to do now?—Says Absalom to his servants, "See, Joab's field is near mine, and he hath barley there—go and set it on fire;" and he will soon come to know the reason. And so it fell out: "Then Joab arose and came to Absalom, unto his house, and said unto him, Wherefore have thy servants set my field on fire!" Why, says Absalom, Not because I wished to do thee an injury, but wanted an interview, and could obtain it in no other way. Thus, when we become indifferent to communion with God, and disregard the suc-cessive messages of the word—"Go," says God to some fiery trial, "go and consume such an enjoyment—and he will soon be with me; soon be upon his knees, saying, ' Do not condemn me; show me wherefore thou contendest with me. Why am I thus! Lord, what wilt thou have me to do?' "

But here we particularly see that afflictions are intended to be spiritual preventions—they are " to keep man from his purpose." The people of God are not always aware of this at first, and therefore, when they meet with these obstructions, they sometimes fret, and think they do well to be angry even unto death: they think he is their enemy, while he is proving himself to be their friend; and that he is opposing their progress, when he is only hindering their wanderings. Disappointments in favourite wishes are trying, and we are not always wise enough to recollect—that disappointments in time are often the means of preventing disappointments in eternity. Our murmurings and repinings arise from our ignorances: we see not the precipice and the pit on the other side of the hedge or of the wall.

I wish you therefore, above all things, to remember, that it is a most singular mercy for God to render the pursuit of sin difficult. If we are going astray—is it not better to have the road filled with thorns than strewed with flowers! Is it not better to have it rough and uninviting, than smooth and alluring! If there are certain things in us, the destruction of which is equally necessary and difficult—is it a blessing to have them fed, or to have them starved! There are some who are now rejoicing because their plans succeed, and every thing favours their wishes, who, if they knew all, would see awful reason to weep and mourn—And there are others, who, if they knew all, would no longer be sorrowful because they cannot advance, but are checked in every path they tread. They would see that they are chastened of the Lord, that they may not be condemned with the world. They would see that the loss of creatures is to lead them to ask more earnestly for " God their maker, who giveth songs in the night." They would see that the sickness of the body is designed to be the cure of the soul. They would see that earth is imbittered, that heaven may be endeared.

Such a discovery of the design and consequences of these exercises would change the whole face of the dispensation, and lead them not only to submit but to give thanks.

But how awful is it when afflictions are useless; and even medicine is administered in vain! And there are those, who, like Ahaz in distress, sin more and more against God. When He arms himself to withstand them in their mad career, they " rush upon the thick bosses of his buckler." If they cannot pierce the hedge or the wall by which he opposes them, they will lie down in sullen obstinacy and sin " as they can"—to use the words of the prophet, rather than yield. " Thou hast stricken them, but they have not grieved; thou hast consumed them, but they have refused to receive correction; they have made their faces harder than a rock—they have refused to return."

But this shall not be the case with the people of God. The grace which employs the means will render them effectual. They shall not only feel—but reflect—and resolve. " Then shall she say, I will go and return to my first husband, for then was it better with me than now !"

IV. We observe THE DIFFERENCE THERE IS BETWEEN OUR ADHERING TO GOD, AND OUR FORSAKING HIM. Behold the declining Christian seduced by the world. When he was beginning to deviate—many a Samuel cried, " Turn ye not aside: for then shall ye go after vain things, which cannot profit or deliver;—for they are vain." But he disregarded the friendly counsel. Others had been drawn into this unhappy course; and they had all told him the confusion and regret with which it had been attended.—But he would also try for himself—and, says God, Let him try—" that he may know my service and the service of the kingdoms of the countries." By-and-by he heard a voice saying—" O that they had hearkened to my commandments! then had their peace been as a river, and their righteousness as the waves of the sea!—Have I been a wilderness unto Israel ? A land of darkness ! Wherefore say my people, We are lords; we will come no more unto thee ?"

And now he bethinks himself, and begins to compare the present with the past. " How different the scorching sands, the briers, and serpents of this desert, from the green pastures in which I once fed, and the still waters by which I once refreshed my weary soul ! ' O that it was with me as in months past.' Once I walked with God. I could behold his face with confidence. The glory of the Lord was risen upon me, and I walked all the day long in the light of his countenance— ' Then was it better with me than now !' Once I had free access to the throne of grace. I approached it with humble and holy boldness; and there are many places that can witness to the tears of joy and sorrow with which I poured out my soul before God. But now the recollection fills me with dismay. I have now little heart to pray. Conscience indeed drags me along to the duty, but I enter the presence of my God with a slavish fear or a chilling indifference—' Then was it better with me than now !' Once I had sweet communion with the Saviour of sinners. When oppressed with a sense of guilt, I saw the all-sufficiency of his sacrifice, and the perfection of his righteousness, and by be-

lieving, I entered into rest. Under every accusation, he was near that justified me. In every duty, and in every trial, he encouraged me by saying, My grace is sufficient for thee: ' I will never leave thee, nor forsake thee.' Now I only see my sins and my enemies—but where is the Saviour and the helper!— ' then was it better with me than now !' Once I experienced the gracious influences of his Holy Spirit. By these I was enlivened, refreshed, and enlightened. I saw clearly the path of duty. I could harmonize providences and promises. I claimed the privilege of a child and an heir of God. But now the Comforter, who should relieve my soul, is far from me. I have grieved the Holy Spirit of God, by which I was sealed unto the day of redemption—' Then was it better with me than now !' O what enlargements of soul had I in his ordinances ! How often did I find the sanctuary to be no less than the house of God, and the gate of heaven ! How sweet was his word to my taste, yea sweeter than honey to my lips ! What a feast did I enjoy at his table ! His flesh was meet indeed, and his blood was drink indeed !— ' Then was it better with me than now !' And oh ! with what cheerfulness I carried my cross ! I could even glory in tribulation also; for as the sufferings abounded, the consolations did also much more abound. The storm without raged in vain—for all was peace within—but now conscience knaws me like a worm—and the promises which should be my support, are neither within reach nor within sight—' Then was it better with me than now !' There was a time that I could see him not only in ordinances, but also in providences; not only in his word, but also in his works. I could enjoy him in my creature comforts. I relished his love in my daily food; I saw his goodness in all my connexions: but now I know not whether any thing I possess is sent in wrath or mercy; I can find him in nothing: ' Behold, I go forward, but he is not there; and backward, but I cannot perceive him; on the left hand, where he doth work, but I cannot behold him ; he hideth himself on the right hand, that I cannot see him !'

" I cannot fully describe my case. All I know is—and this I feel by an experience too bitter to be expressed—*that it is not with me as it—once was !*"

Some of these feelings, in a lower degree, are common to an apostate professor, who has left off to be wise and to do good. But the experience of such a man differs exceedingly from the feelings of a backsliding believer; for the judgment of the believer was never drawn over from the Lord's side, though it was not suffered for a time to be heard; and he has enjoyments to look back upon which a stranger never intermeddled with. He can remember not only the dreadfulness of a state of utter distance from God by nature, but also the blessedness of being brought nigh by the blood of Christ. He knows what it is to live under his smiles and by his influences. And now that the charm which deceived him is dissolved—now that he has leisure for reflection—now that he is separated from his very idols, no wonder he resolves if possible to return to a state in which it was better with him than now.

And let those who have been led astray and have fallen by their iniquity, adopt immediately the same resolution. While you consider the melancholy change that has taken place in your experience—remember two things—

First, that it cannot be better with you than it is till you return to God; since it is by your departure from him that you have sustained all these losses and incurred all this misery. "Set thee up way-marks, make thee high heaps; set thine heart toward the high way, even the way which thou wentest; turn again, O virgin of Israel, turn to these thy cities."

And, Secondly, while with weeping and supplications you are disposed to seek him again, guard against that despondency which would tell you that it will be in vain. It is not in vain. There is hope in Israel concerning this thing. He waiteth to be gracious, and is exalted to have mercy upon you. "Return, ye backsliding children, and I will heal your backslidings. Behold, we come unto thee; for thou art the Lord our God. Truly in vain is salvation hoped for from the hills, and from the multitude of mountains: truly in the Lord our God is the salvation of Israel."

Have any of you been restored? Turn not again to folly. Has it not cost you enough already? After all this, will not the very appearance of evil terrify you? Live near to God.—Your welfare depends upon it.

And as for those young converts who have just subscribed with their own hand and surnamed themselves by the name of Israel, let these also beware. Now perhaps you think there is very little danger of this caution. Such at present is your attachment to the Saviour and his way, that it seems to be impossible for you ever to forget the one or forsake the other. But how many who once had the same confidence with yourselves, have since denied him or followed him afar off! "Wherefore let him that thinketh he standeth, take heed lest he fall. Watch and pray, lest ye enter into temptation: the spirit indeed is willing, but the flesh is weak."

"Now unto Him that is able to keep you from falling, and to present you faultless before the presence of his glory with exceeding joy, to the only wise God our Saviour, be glory and majesty, dominion and power, both now and ever!—Amen."

DISCOURSE XXXV.

THE END OF THE SAVIOUR'S EX-ALTATION.

Him hath God exalted with his right hand to be a Prince and a Saviour, for to give repentance to Israel, and forgiveness of sins. Acts v. 31.

ELEVATION is necessary to influence. Of what advantage is "a candle under a bushel?" —but place it "in a candlestick, and it giveth light to all that are in the house." While the sun is below our earth, all is dark and cold— but when he arises, there "is healing under his wings;" and from his loftiness in the skies he scatters his enlightening and enlivening beams. When the shrub rises up out of the ground, it rather requires than affords support and assistance—"but when it is grown, it becomes a tree, so that the birds of the air come and lodge in the branches thereof." A man in the obscurity and contractedness of private life may feel dispositions prompting him to do good—but he can only pour forth benevolent wishes and shed ineffectual tears. But give him pre-eminence, place in his hands the reins of empire, and at his disposal the treasures of the state, and lo! thousands are refreshed by his shadow, protected by his power, and enriched by his bounty; his fame spreads encouragement; prayer also shall be made for him continually, and daily shall he be praised. Thus Jesus "ascended far above all heavens, that he might fill all things."

Or take another illustration. The life of Joseph is not only affecting as a history, but also important as a type. Joseph was hated of his brethren; and they sold him as a slave to a company of Ishmaelites in order to prevent the fulfilment of his dreams. But the means used to hinder his advancement terminated in the promotion of it; and in process of time he was made ruler over all the land of Egypt. And it is worthy of our regard, that his elevation was—not only the aggrandizement of himself—but also the preservation of thousands, and in a peculiar manner the salvation of his father's house. He was the only dispenser of supplies to those who were perishing with famine—and "Go unto Joseph"—was the order given by Pharaoh to every petitioner.

But a greater than Joseph is here. Thus Jesus suffered from the hands of sinners: and they acted only as enemies—but the curse was turned into a blessing. His sufferings led to his exaltation; and this exaltation was not only a personal reward—but a relative glory. He is made head over all things "unto his body the Church." He has power given him over all flesh, "that he should give eternal life to as many as the Father has given him." And him, says the Apostle, to the Jews, "him hath God exalted with his right hand to be a Prince and a Saviour, for to give repentance to Israel, and forgiveness of sins."

Thus he is advanced as mediator, to the grandeur and resources of his present station, not only to govern, but to save; and to save by governing. Some are exalted as princes who are by no means saviours. They do not study to secure the common rights of mankind.—They do not set examples of temperance, humanity, and social affection. They do not cultivate harmony and peace. They seem only raised up to oppress and to destroy. Murder and desolation mark their progress. The ruins of towns and villages, the tears of widows and orphans, are the materials of their glory. They sacrifice the lives of their subjects to save their own—yea, they frequently sacrifice them to gratify their pride, their vanity, their avarice, their revenge. But *he* sacrificed himself for the welfare of his subjects —"I give my flesh for the life of the world." They are princes of war—but he is "the Prince of peace." They are princes of death —but he is "the Prince of life." They are princes and destroyers—but he is "a Prince and a Saviour." He takes us under the wing of his protection; redeems us from the curse of the law; delivers us from the wrath to come; saves us from our sins. He makes his subjects holy and happy—For "he gives repentance unto Israel, and forgiveness of sins."

Let us take three views of these blessings. —Let us consider—THEIR MEANING—THEIR CONNEXION—and THEIR SOURCE.

I. Let us consider THEIR MEANING.—What is *repentance?* Every one will see the propriety of making this inquiry, who only reflects—that every thing excellent admits of counterfeit—that there are specious resemblances not only of every moral virtue, but of every Christian grace—and that Pharaoh, and Ahab, and Judas, and others, are said to have repented, and after all died in their sins. Perhaps a better definition of repentance was never given than by an old divine, one excellency of which is, that it is easily remembered. He tells us that "Genuine repentance consists in having the heart broken *for* sin, and *from* it."

Be it then remembered, that the subject of repentance is convinced of sin. He sees that it is the greatest evil in the universe— not only as it is the cause of his sufferings, and has exposed him to the miseries of hell —but because it is the pollution of his soul, and the degradation of his nature, and has rendered him vile and abominable in the eyes of God. Hence he feels shame, self-loathing, abhorrence, grief, and contrition—especially when he apprehends the goodness of God, which has spared him under all his offences,

provided for him a ransom, and through a suffering Saviour is willing to receive him graciously. This dissolves the heart and makes him "sorrowful after a godly sort." For the tear of evangelical penitence drops from the eye of faith; and faith while it weeps stands under the cross. "I will pour upon the house of David, and upon the inhabitants of Jerusalem, the spirit of grace and of supplications: and they shall look upon me whom they have pierced, and they shall mourn for him, as one mourneth for his only son, and shall be in bitterness for him, as one that is in bitterness for his first-born."

The pressure of these various feelings constitutes what we mean by having the heart broken *for* sin. But the man has now new dispositions and resolutions; and hence a new course of life. He is delivered from the love of sin, the love of *all* sin, however dear before. He is freed from the dominion of sin— so that it no longer "reigns in his mortal body, that he should obey it in the lusts thereof. Neither yields he his members as instruments of unrighteousness unto sin; but yields himself unto God as those that are alive from the dead, and his members as instruments of righteousness unto God." He avoids also the occasions of sin, and "abstains from all appearance of evil."—And this is what we mean by having the heart broken *from* sin."

And what is *forgiveness?* It is simply the removal of all obligation to punishment. It does not render a man innocent of the crimes which he has committed; for a man can never appear otherwise to God than he really is; and it will be everlastingly true, that Job cursed the day of his birth, and Peter denied his master. But sin contracts guilt, and guilt binds over to punishment: now, forgiveness cancels this obligation and restores the offender to safety. And frequently, at least among men, forgiveness extends no further. But it does with God. He takes pleasure in those whom he pardons as if they had never sinned, and indulges them with the most intimate friendship.

When two individuals have been at variance, the hardest to believe in reconciliation is the offender. The blame is his: and judging under a consciousness of his desert, he can hardly be persuaded that the party he has injured does not feel like himself. History informs us that when a man had offended Augustus, the emperor, to show his greatness of mind, declared that he pardoned him. But the poor creature, who expected only destruction, astonished beyond measure, and fearing the declaration was too good to be true, in all the simplicity of nature, instantly desired his majesty to give him some present as a proof that he had really forgiven him. Thus anxious is the awakened mind. Such a free and full forgiveness after all his heinous provocations seems incredible; he therefore desires a token for good: and many pledges of the most perfect reconciliation the God of all grace affords in his dealings with his people. He hears their prayer; he is with them in every trouble; he delivers them and honours them; he makes all things to work together for their good, and engages to receive them to glory.

II. Let us glance at THE UNION OF THESE BLESSINGS. Repentance and forgiveness of sins are mentioned together. Now let it be observed, that this is not a meritorious connexion between repentance and forgiveness—as if the one deserved the other—for they are both given—and how can one gift merit another?

But there is between them, First, a connexion of propriety. It would not accord with the wisdom of God to deliver from hell a man who would be miserable in heaven; to forgive one incapable of enjoying or serving him—yea, one who abhors him. Without repentance we should never value the blessing of forgiveness, and therefore we should neither be happy in nor thankful for the possession of it. If a servant or a child were to behave improperly, though goodness may incline you to pardon, you would naturally require a proper state of mind, and signs of sorrow, confession, and reformation; otherwise your forgiveness would look like connivance at the transgression, or indifference to the offence, and encourage a repetition of disobedience.

Hence there is between them also, a connexion of certainty. They are indissolubly united—no one ever really enjoyed forgiveness without repentance; and no one ever truly exercised repentance without forgiveness. And hence it follows that the best way to ascertain our state before God is—not a reference to dreams and visions, sudden impulses, and accidental occurrences of Scripture to the mind—no—but an examination of our character; a comparison of ourselves with the features of pardoned sinners portrayed in the Gospel. To know whether we are justified, let us inquire whether we are renewed in the spirit of our minds: and be assured of this, that he is not the partaker of Divine forgiveness who is not the subject of genuine repentance.

On the other hand, as there is an inseparable connexion between these, if you had been humbled for your sins; if your hearts had been broken for them, and from them; you should not despair of acceptance, but view this experience as the authorized evidence of Divine favour. "Believe in God." He cannot deny himself. And he has said, " He that confesseth, and forsaketh his sins, shall have mercy. Let the wicked forsake his way, and the unrighteous man his thoughts; and let him return unto the Lord, and he will

have mercy upon him; and to our God, for he will abundantly pardon."

III. We remark THE SOURCE OF THESE BLESSINGS—"*He gives* repentance unto Israel and forgiveness of sins."

Some think repentance a very *legal* subject, and are ready to condemn the man who preaches it, as a stranger to the Gospel. But there never was a greater mistake than this. For not to mention, that our Lord "came to call sinners to repentance," and that the Apostles "went forth preaching everywhere that men should repent"—I would observe, that repentance is a subject peculiarly evangelical. The law has nothing to do with repentance—it does not even command it—all it has to do with the transgressor is to condemn. It allows him neither liberty nor ability to repent—but the Gospel gives him both. And indeed to little purpose would it give us the one without the other. But here is our encouragement—the Gospel not only gives us *space*, but *grace* for repentance. What in one view is a duty, in another is a privilege: and what is commanded is also promised. The " broken heart and the contrite spirit" is not only a sacrifice which he will not despise, but it is also a sacrifice which he must provide!

And he does provide it. He " gives repentance unto life." For having ascended up on high leading captivity captive, " he received gifts for men, even for the rebellious also, that the Lord God might dwell among them." The chief of these was the dispensation of the Holy Ghost. By his influence the understanding is enlightened and the conscience awakened; the heart of stone is taken away and a heart of flesh given; and sinners, before weak and averse to holiness, are enabled to " walk in his statutes, and to keep his judgments to do them." Thus the word is rendered effectual; and the events of Providence are sanctified; afflictions make them "acknowledge their offence; and the goodness of God leadeth them to repentance."

And if repentance be not derived from ourselves—can forgiveness of sins? If the former be a gift—can the latter be a purchase?— "He gives repentance unto Israel, *and* forgiveness of sins." And hence two things follow.

First, if we possess these blessings—we learn to whom we are to address our praise. " Surely, shall one say, in the Lord have I righteousness and strength."

Secondly, if we want them—we see to whom we are to address our prayers. Betake yourselves to the Friend of sinners, and say, "'Lord, remember me now thou art come into thy kingdom.' 'Heal me, and I shall be healed; save me, and I shall be saved: for thou art my praise.' 'Lord, if thou wilt thou canst make me clean.'—And hast thou not said, 'him that cometh unto me, I will in nowise cast out?' Behold a sinner that wishes to have nothing more to do with sin. O save him from the bondage of corruption, as well as from the burden of condemnation. 'Have mercy upon me, O God, according to thy lovingkindness: according unto the multitude of thy tender mercies, blot out my transgressions. Create in me a clean heart, O God; and renew a right spirit within me.'"

Oh! be induced to do this, and to do this immediately. Here is a Saviour exalted to bless you with all spiritual blessings—and especially to bless you, by "turning every one of you away from your iniquities"—and there is no blessing like this. Seek him while he may be found: call upon him while he is near. For there is a time when if you call he will not answer, and if you seek him early you will not find him. The season for obtaining these blessings is short and uncertain. Surely you need not be informed that you are sinners—but "the wages of sin is death." While you are strangers to pardon, you are only "treasuring up wrath against the day of wrath." You are open to all the miseries of life, the sting of death, the torments of hell. Yea, you are exposed to a double condemnation; one from the Law which you have transgressed, and another from the Gospel which you have despised. And how is it that you do not lay these things to heart! How is it you do not fear lest every moment "the earth should open its mouth," and your souls "go down quick into hell!" How will you contrive to sleep to-night—when you know that if you die in your present state, God is under an oath to destroy you!

But "blessed is he whose transgression is forgiven, whose sin is covered. Blessed is the man unto whom the Lord imputeth not iniquity, and in whose spirit there is no guile." He is blessed in his duties, for he is assured of acceptance and assistance. He is blessed in his enjoyments, for he tastes the lovingkindness of God in them. He is blessed in his trials, for they flow from love and are designed for his profit. Now he is delivered from the curse, he can bear the cross. He will not endure his troubles long; and he does not endure them alone.

Here are some whom he has pardoned. He gave them to see and feel and confess their sins. He discovered to them the scheme of salvation revealed in the Gospel. He enabled them to come with all their unworthiness, smiting upon their breasts, and saying, "God be merciful to me, a sinner"—and believing, they passed from death unto life. They found rest unto their souls. They are now serving him, and they find his "yoke easy, and his burden light."

"And I say unto you, ask, and it shall be given you: seek, and ye shall find; knock, and it shall be opened unto you. For every

one that asketh receiveth: and he that seeketh findeth: and to him that knocketh it shall be opened." Amen.

DISCOURSE XXXVI.

RELIGION MAKES US PROFITABLE.

I beseech thee for my son Onesimus, whom I have begotten in my bonds: which in time past was to thee unprofitable, but now profitable to thee and to me.—Philemon 10, 11.

THE Epistles are of three classes. Some are addressed to Christians at large—some to particular Churches—and some to single individuals.

The Epistle before us is of the third class. —And as it is inscribed to one person, so it is limited to one subject. It furnishes none of those glaring scenes which the pencil of the historian requires: but it is full of importance to a Christian teacher. It says nothing of the intrigues of statesmen, the contentions of senators, the exploits and mischiefs of heroes; but it yields topics of reflection much more interesting and useful to a serious reader. These are concisely expressed in the words which I have read.

We will therefore STATE THE CIRCUMSTANCES OF THE CASE TO WHICH THEY REFER: and DEDUCE SOME REMARKS FROM THEM FOR OUR INSTRUCTION AND EDIFICATION.

THE CIRCUMSTANCES OF THE CASE may be thus briefly stated. At Colosse lived Philemon. He appears to have been a person of some respectability, if not distinction. The Apostle calls him a fellow-labourer. He had a church in his house; and by his liberality often "refreshed the bowels of the saints."

With this Philemon lived a servant whose name was Onesimus. Onesimus like too many servants was ungodly, though he lived in a pious family and enjoyed religious means and privileges. He robbed his master, and with the purloined property made his escape. As it is usual for such criminals to go to some large populous place to avoid detection, Onesimus hastened to Rome, the capital of the world.

Thither Paul had arrived a little before in consequence of his appealing unto Cæsar; and having hired a house, "preached the kingdom of God, and received all that came in unto him." As he was the subject of conversation in the city, Onesimus is informed of him; and from curiosity or some other motive—perhaps he had heard his name or seen his person at his master's house, he goes to the Apostle's lodgings and attends his ministry. Probably Paul preached against thievery. However this may be, "the word was quick and powerful, sharper than any two-edged sword, piercing even to the dividing asunder of soul and spirit, and of the joints and mar row, and was a discerner of the thoughts and intents of the heart." Onesimus is convinced and alarmed. He feels his guilt: and now dreads not only human but divine justice. He cannot get rid of his distress; but walks about the city crying to himself, " What must I do to be saved?"

At length he resolves to go and open his case to Paul—" He may afford me instruction and relief." He waits upon him. " Sir, I lately heard you preach, and I am one of the characters you described and condemned." —What is your name? "Onesimus."—What are you? " I was a slave."—And who was your master? " Philemon of Colosse."—Him I know. But what, Onesimus, brought you here?—Onesimus weeps—" Oh! I cannot deny it, I cannot conceal it—I robbed my master and fled hither from justice. And ever since I heard that sermon, I can find no rest. My iniquities have taken hold upon me, so that I cannot look up. My sin was the most heinous and aggravated: it was a good master I injured! How often did he admonish me! How earnestly did he pray for me!"

See here what a victory grace obtains over nature! Onesimus goes and confesses himself a thief!—For he was now remote from the scene of action; no person was there to impeach him? and if he had not acknowledged the crime himself, it could never have been known. This was no pleasant task. Nothing could be more irksome to the pride of the human heart. It is as common to cover as to commit sin. Men, such is their injustice and self-love, men wish to appear better in the eyes of their fellow-creatures than they really are; even better than they know themselves to be. But when the Holy Ghost lays a burden upon the conscience, no diversion can remove it. Divine grace produces self-abasement; and a true penitent will not only confess his sin to God, but when called by circumstances, he will own it also to men, to his fellow Christians, to Ministers. And such a disclosure may sometimes ease the mind of a load of anguish, and teach the person to whom the communication is made how to speak a word in season, and apply the remedy of the Gospel. We are therefore commanded to " confess our faults one to another, and to pray one for another, that we may be healed." Be it remembered however, that when such a penitent thus acknowledges his sins—he will not do it as if he were relating heroical deeds or even actions of indifference—he will not like some speak of his former wickedness with a kind of pleasure, arising from the apprehension that they magnify divine grace, and render his conversion the more marvellous and certain, or at least with a tone and countenance far from expressing deep humiliation and godly sorrow, but he will evidence, by his feelings and his manner, " a broken heart, and a contrite spirit which God will not despise." To return.

Persuaded of his sincerity, the Apostle would have taken Onesimus into his service, had it not looked like detaining what is deemed another man's property. He therefore conscientiously resolves to send him back to Philemon. And influenced by the same principle, Onesimus wishes to return—but fears the displeasure of his offended master; and is conscious that if he demanded reparation, it would not be in his power to make it. The Apostle therefore undertakes to plead his cause, becomes his surety, and sends along with him a letter of recommendation full of the most persuasive eloquence—and this is the principal subject —" I beseech thee for my son Onesimus, whom I have begotten in my bonds; which in time past was to thee unprofitable, but now profitable to thee and to me."

Hence let us derive the following REMARKS.

First. Observe the humility, the tenderness, the kindness of the Apostle Paul. Great as he was, he exemplifies in his own practice what he recommends in his doctrine to others, " mind not high things, but condescend to men of low estate." He does not think it beneath him to attend to the wants and wishes of this poor slave, and to write a whole epistle on his behalf. The more the mind is raised by intelligence and religion, the less will it be impressed with those adventitious distinctions which dazzle the multitude. True greatness is always condescending and sympathetic. Are we mistaken? What do we see yonder? Let us draw near. " He riseth from supper, and laid aside his garments; and took a towel, and girded himself: after that he poured water into a basin, and began to wash his disciples' feet, and to wipe them with the towel wherewith he was girded. So after he had washed their feet, and had taken his garments, and was set down again, he said unto them, know ye what I have done to you? Ye call me Master and Lord; and ye say well: for so I am. If I then, your Lord and master, have washed your feet; ye also ought to wash one another's feet. For I have given you an example, that ye should do as I have done to you. Verily, verily, I say unto you, the servant is not greater than his lord; neither he that is sent, greater than him that sent him. If ye know these things, happy are ye if ye do them." And who does them? Some imagine themselves humble because their condescension has never been put to the trial. Others have proved how very little they resemble our Lord and Saviour by declining those instances in which their condescension ought to have appeared. Alas! how many are there who " hide themselves from their own flesh;" who would think it beneath them to perform personally an office of humanity and charity for the poor and needy; who would never stoop to write a letter for a menial domestic; who treat their servants no better than brutes —and often not half so well.

But servants should be considered as fellow-creatures and as humble friends. It is a scandal to a Christian, to suffer a servant to leave his house unable to read. Are you not to do good as you have opportunity? Shall we call that contemptible which God deigns to honour? Did not He who made thee in the womb make them? Has he not endued the low-born child, the beggar, the slave, with a portion of reason and immortality? Are they not the care of his providence? Are they not the purchase of the Saviour's blood? And has he not assured us that " it is not the will of our Heavenly Father, that one of these little ones should perish?"

Secondly. Let us learn how impossible it is to hinder the work of God: or frustrate the purposes of his grace.—" Whom I have begotten in my bonds." Nothing comes to pass by chance. What appears to be chance among men is nothing less than the providence of God permitting, appointing, arranging, overruling all events. " He doth according to his own will in the army of heaven, and among the inhabitants of the earth, and none can stay his hand, or say unto him, what doest thou? His counsel shall stand, and he will do all his pleasure." And what a complication of occurrences and circumstances sometimes enters into the execution of his design: some of them apparently inconsistent with it, others seemingly subversive of it! But he grasps and guides them by an unerring hand: he harmonizes them and gives them a unity of tendency! they reach their end: none of them are superfluous; none of them could be spared.—The very wrath of man praises him, and the remainder of it he restrains.

Can a man stop the rolling tide? Can he retard the progress of the sun? The cause of God is in motion and will crush every obstacle. Nor is this all—he makes opposition an advantage: his enemies intend one thing and he another; and they serve an interest they despise and labour to repress: their schemes fulfil his plan; he turns them from their natural currents into secret channels prepared to receive them, and in which they flow along into " the fulness of him that filleth all in all."

Paul, persecuted in Judea, is driven to Rome. But though he " suffers as an evil doer, even unto bonds, the word of God is not bound." In these bonds he did wonders. His sufferings turned out to the furtherance of the Gospel. There he wrote many of his epistles. There he re-animated the timid by his example. He filled the capital with the savour of the Redeemer's knowledge. How many were called by his instrumentality we know not; but we find that his name was known " in the palace," and we read of " saints even in Cæsar's household." And, Onesimus! you will have reason to bless God for ever for his confinement and imprisonment there!

Do we lay too much stress upon this circumstance?—The salvation of one soul, the soul of a poor slave, is an event of far greater importance than the deliverance of a nation from civil bondage. " There is joy in the presence of the angels of God over one sinner that repenteth." Besides, Onesimus became a minister; the Apostle speaks of him as such in his epistle to the Colossians: Ignatius, in his epistle to the Ephesians, speaks of him as pastor of their church immediately after Timothy: and the Roman martyrology assures us that he was stoned to death in Rome under the reign of Trajan the emperor. There he entered a state of grace, and there also he entered a state of glory! How wonderful! At one time this man was there a wicked fugitive slave—and a few years after a preacher of the Gospel, a martyr for the word of God and the testimony of Jesus Christ!

Thirdly. Therefore let us learn to despair of none of our fellow-creatures. Whatever time has elapsed; whatever means have been useless; whatever lengths a man has run, let us encourage ourselves with this thought, that other seasons may prove more favourable—that other instruments may prove more successful—that he is not gone beyond the reach of the divine arm; of the mercy of God to pardon; of the grace of God to change and sanctify.

This observation is for you, O parent, whose heart is bleeding over those undutiful and ungodly offspring, who despise your authority, your prayers, and your tears. " God is able, even of these stones, to raise up children unto Abraham."

This observation is for you, O minister, whose sabbath-day evenings are imbittered by the exclamation, " Lord, who hath believed our report!"—who are looking with despondency on that hearer who, after all your faithful warnings, is rejecting the counsel of God against himself. The desire of his eyes may be torn from him. Sickness may recall him from the wanderings of health. He may go into a new neighbourhood; he may meet with very different companions; he may hear another preacher; and he may so hear as that his soul may live. Is any thing too hard for the Lord? He can vary his means. His resources are endless. We are prone to give up characters too soon. Persons have been considered as abandoned of God at the very time he was going to display his power and the riches of his grace in their conversion.

This observation is for you, O sinner, who have to this hour been unhappy, or rather criminal enough to live without God in the world, but now that you feel a willingness to return, are concluding that it will be in vain. No. "There is hope in Israel concerning this thing." And "where sin has abounded, grace shall much more abound. That as sin hath reigned unto death, even so might grace reign through righteousness unto eternal life by Jesus Christ our Lord."

Fourthly. Conversion makes a man useful. "Who was in *time past unprofitable*, but is *now profitable*." This is the case with every regenerate sinner. To render us profitable is the design of religion, and it is easy to see that it must be the effect of it. Religion is social and diffusive. According to our Saviour's language, the possessors of divine grace are the salt of the earth to keep it from corruption. They are the lights of the world to keep it from darkness; and this light is not to be concealed "under a bushel," but to be fixed "on a candlestick, that it may give light to all that are in the house." And their light is "so to shine before men, that they may see their good works, and glorify our Father which is in heaven." The talents they receive from God look beyond themselves. The blessings they enjoy they are to communicate. They are to "comfort others with the comforts wherewith they themselves are comforted of God." Of their fortune they are only stewards, not owners. —They are commanded to "bear one another's burdens." And even in their prayers they are taught brotherly love—they are to plead for others as well as for themselves; they are to say, "*our* Father—forgive us *our* trespasses; and give us this day *our* daily bread." Divine grace never leaves us as it finds us. It produces a change the most wonderful and glorious and beneficial. "The wolf also dwells with the lamb: and the leopard lies down with the kid: and the calf and the young lion and the fatling together, and a little child leads them. Instead of the thorn comes up the fir-tree, and instead of the brier the myrtle-tree. The wilderness and solitary place shall be glad for them; and the desert shall rejoice and blossom as the rose."

Divine grace destroys those vices by which we are injurious to others. For the best charity I can exercise towards my fellow-creatures, says a good man, is to leave off sinning myself. It subdues the selfishness which is so common to our depraved nature; it enlivens and expands the affections; it leads us to rejoice with them that do rejoice, and weep with them that weep. It teaches and enables us to act with propriety in every capacity and relation in life. Every company and neighbourhood is the better for us: we are as "a dew from the Lord." And thus the promise is fulfilled in every child of

R

Abraham by faith; "I will bless thee and thou shalt be a blessing."

Finally. We remark that our being useful does not depend upon our abilities and station. See Onesimus—a slave—profitable —even to such men as Philemon and Paul —profitable to "thee and me." It is with the community as it is with the body. "The body is not one member but many. If the foot shall say, because I am not the hand, I am not of the body, is it therefore not of the body? And if the ear shall say, because I am not the eye, I am not of the body, is it therefore not of the body? If the whole body were an eye, where were the hearing? If the whole were hearing, where were the smelling? But now hath God set the members every one of them in the body, as it hath pleased him. And the eye cannot say unto the hand, I have no need of thee: nor again, the head to the feet, I have no need of you." Thus we behold in the world and in the church, difference of rank, of office, of talents; but there is a connexion between the whole, and a dependence arising from it. And from this none are exempted; even "the king is served by the labour of the field."

Every man, whatever be his condition and circumstances, is of some importance in society—and we should labour to impress our minds with this reflection—especially in three cases.

Let us remember it—when we are in danger of pride and disdain with regard to any of our fellow-creatures. The idol you adore is not every thing, and the wretch you despise is something. Perhaps he is more necessary to you than you are to him.

Let us remember it—when discouraged from exertion. Oh! if I had such opportunities and means, I would serve my generation. But if great faculties were necessary, they would be more frequently bestowed. Situations calling for ten talents are rare—those which require five are more common—but those which demand only one are to be found every where and every day. And in nothing are we so likely to be mistaken as in such conclusions. He that is "not faithful in little," has no reason to believe that he would be "faithful in much."

We should also remember it—when we are tempted to do good in unlawful ways. What I mean is this. Some suppose that they can only be useful in such a particular station or office, and hence they are ready to leave their present condition to rush into it. But, says the Apostle, "Let every man abide in the calling in which he is called of God." Things are so constituted, that if *any* man wishes to do good, he *may* do it in the circumstances in which he is placed; he has some influence. For instance—and to refer to the case before us—are you a servant! Jacob was a servant, and Laban, his master, said, "I have learned by experience that the Lord has blessed me for thy sake." Joseph was employed by Potiphar, "and it came to pass from the time that he had made him overseer in his house, and over all that he had, that the Lord blessed the Egyptian's house for Joseph's sake: and the blessing of the Lord was upon all that he had, in the house and in the field." Hence, says the Apostle to Titus, "Exhort servants to be obedient unto their own masters, and to please them well in all things; not answering again, not purloining, but showing all good fidelity; that they may adorn the doctrine of God our Saviour in all things." And hence he says to Timothy, "Let as many servants as are under the yoke count their own masters worthy of all honour, that the name of God and his doctrine be not blasphemed." Here we see how much depends upon Christian servants: they may either recommend their religion or disgrace it. For the people of the world are not quite so blind as we sometimes suppose them to be: although incapable of entering into Christian experience, they can estimate the value of principles, by the goodness of their effects. And what can they think of the gospel, if the professors of it are as bad, or even worse than others; inattentive to the duties of their places, idle, gossippers, busy-bodies, heady, insolent, unfaithful to their trust? On this principle, I am sorry to say, that there are some who have expressed a determination to have nothing more to do with religious servants. But they surely mean servants who are religious only in *pretence*—who raise hopes by their profession, which they disappoint by their practice—and thus cause the way of truth to be evil spoken of:—for as to those servants who are *really* religious, they *must* be better than others—they must be "profitable."

Let us therefore conclude with two reflections.

First. If religion renders people, in all situations, valuable and useful, how deserving is it of encouragement! Let therefore all unite together to promote it.

Let governors and magistrates promote it. This is the way to have good subjects and citizens. Innumerable are the advantages which communities derive from it in civilizing, restraining, and sanctifying mankind. Human laws cannot extend far enough, in a thousand cases interesting to the peace and welfare of a nation. They can never reach the heart. But religion lays hold of the conscience, and places a man, even when alone, under the eye of God, and in sight of endless happiness or wo.

Let masters of families promote it in their households. This is the way to have obedient servants, and dutiful children. Piety is the firmest basis of morality: secure God's claims and you will not miss your own.

Let this influence those who have companions to choose; and also those who have connexions to form. Oh! young man, "favour is deceitful, and beauty is vain, but a woman that feareth the Lord, she shall be praised." Oh! young woman, devote thyself to nothing profane, sceptical, irreligious; marry, but "only in the Lord."

Secondly. If religion be profitable to others, it is much more so to ourselves. It sanctifies all our mercies. It sweetens all our trials. It teaches us "in whatever state we are, therewith to be content." "Its ways are pleasantness. Its paths are peace." "Yea, it is profitable unto all things, having promise of the life that now is, and of that which is to come."

No wonder therefore it should be called wisdom, and that Solomon should speak of it as he does. "Wisdom is the principal thing: therefore get wisdom: and with all thy getting, get understanding."

DISCOURSE XXXVII.

THE CURE OF BLIND BARTIMEUS.

And it came to pass, that as he was come nigh unto Jericho, a certain blind man sat by the way-side begging: and hearing the multitude pass by, he asked what it meant. And they told him, that Jesus of Nazareth passeth by. And he cried, saying, Jesus, thou son of David, have mercy on me. And they which went before rebuked him, that he should hold his peace: but he cried so much the more, Thou son of David, have mercy on me. And Jesus stood, and commanded him to be brought unto him: and when he was come near, he asked him, saying, What wilt thou that I shall do unto thee: and he said, Lord, that I may receive my sight. And Jesus said unto him, Receive thy sight, thy faith hath saved thee. And immediately he received his sight, and followed him, glorifying God.—Luke xviii. 35—43.

To read the Scriptures superficially will not answer the purpose of a man who is desirous of being made "wise unto salvation." He will peruse them with reverence, he will explore them with diligence, and feel all anxious and prayerful to have the end for which they were given realized in his own experience.—And what is this end? The Apostle tells us. "Whatsoever things were written aforetime were written for our learning, that we, through patience and comfort of the Scriptures, might have hope."

Our Saviour made every misery he beheld his own. "He took our infirmities, and bare our sicknesses." As he moved from place to place, he restored friends to the bereaved, and health to the diseased. He raised the dead. He made the lame to leap as an hart, and the tongue of the dumb to sing. He gave ears to the deaf, and eyes to the blind.

These things, even in a temporal view, cannot fail of exciting in us a sympathetic joy with the poor wretches who received relief, and adoring praise to the Author of their deliverance; but as intended to convey spiritual instruction, they acquire additional importance. For if these miracles are not to be considered as types, they furnish us with illustrations in explaining the disorders and cure of the mind.

Let us therefore review the circumstances of the history before us—and endeavour to derive some useful admonitions from it.

The subject of the miracle was "a blind man." We are not informed whether he was born blind, or whether the calamity had befallen him by disease or accident. This however was his melancholy condition; and a more pitiable one perhaps cannot be found. It is worthy of compassion even when found in circumstances of affluence and ease—but how much more so when it is attended with indigence and want! And this was the additional affliction of blind Bartimeus—"He sat by the way-side begging." Poor people should be thankful to God for the preservation of their limbs and senses. If they have no patrimony nor independence, they can labour; and while they have hands and eyes, they should scorn habits of beggary. But the helpless are not to starve; nor are we indiscriminately to reject every application we meet with upon the road.—Though, blessed be God, there is less need of this in our highly-favoured land than in most other countries, owing to the legal provision made in all our parishes for the poor and needy who are unable to gain a subsistence by labour.

One of the characters of our Saviour's miracles was publicity. Impostors require secrecy and darkness. There have been miracles designed to delude the ignorant and credulous—but where have they been manufactured? In cells, convents, and deserts. Before whom have they been performed? A few selected, interested witnesses. But says our Saviour, In secret have I done nothing. He wrought his miracles in the face of day; in the most open and exposed situations; before crowds of spectators; and among whom were found not only the curious, but malicious. Thus he recovered this man before a multitude in the high way, and close to the city of Jericho.

Several of our Saviour's miracles seem to have been unintentional. Thus it is said, "As he entered a certain village, there met him ten men, that were lepers, who stood afar off." Thus again we read, that "when he came nigh to the gate of the city of Nain,

behold, there was a dead man carried out, the only son of his mother, and she was a widow." And so here: "It came to pass, that as he was come nigh unto Jericho, a certain blind man sat by the way-side begging." Was then, you may ask, was his finding these objects accidental or designed? Unquestionably designed. He was not taken by surprise. He saw the end from the beginning. His plan was formed; and he was "working all things after the counsel of his own will." But he would show us that he is master not only of events, but of occasions, and of circumstances; and that though these circumstances appear loose, irregular, and contingent to us, they subserve his pleasure, and all occur in their proper time and place. Thus the bow "drawn at a venture," carried the arrow which fulfilled the purpose and the word of God in the death of the king of Israel.

The occurrence, however, was casual to Bartimeus himself; and when he rose in the morning, and was led forth by some friendly hand to the place where he was accustomed to beg, little did he imagine that before the evening he should obtain his sight, and be walking at the distance of some miles from home without a guide! This was the most successful of all his begging days. Boast not; despair not—of to-morrow, for thou knowest not, either as to evil or good, what a day may bring forth.

Imagine him then sitting under the shadow of some hedge or tree, against the side of the road—listening to apprehend if any travellers were approaching, of whom he might ask a small pittance of alms. For though he could not see, he could hear—this was an alleviation of his distress; and it has been remarked, that scarcely ever was there an instance of a man being naturally both blind and deaf. And in many cases we find the loss of one sense in some measure made up by the greater perfection of another. Blind people are generally very quick of hearing; as may be observed by those who visit their asylums. Well, while musing—a noise strikes him, and the sound draws nearer and nearer. He asks what it means—and being told that "Jesus of Nazareth was passing by"—he cried, saying, " 'Jesus, thou son of David, have mercy on me!' Though I am not deserving, my case is distressing. O pity me. O help me!"

But whenever was it known that a poor suppliant met with no hinderance in coming to the Deliverer for mercy! "They which went before rebuked him that he should hold his peace." From what principle could this proceed! Knowing that silver and gold the master had none, did they suppose that he was clamorous for alms! Did they conclude that his entreaties would be deemed noisy and troublesome! Did they deem him beneath the Saviour's notice, and suppose that the Son of David would have nothing to do with him! Alas! they discovered too little tenderness themselves, and were too little acquainted with their Lord and Saviour, who never did and never will consider such importunity unreasonable or presumptuous; never did and never will break a bruised reed, nor quench the smoking flax. Nor was Bartimeus to be discouraged. He felt wisely. "This is my opportunity, and it may never return. I have addressed thousands who could give me bread—but never did I meet with one before who could give me eyes. And, oh! in a moment he will be out of hearing—and when may he pass by again? 'He cried so much the more, Thou son of David, have mercy on me!'"

Such a cry arrests our Lord in his journey; he cannot take another step—" He stood." What cannot prayer do? Once the sun of nature stood still at the desire of Joshua, who was eager to complete his victory. And, lo! now, "the Sun of righteousness" stands still, with "healing under his wings," at the desire of Bartimeus, who begs a cure. "He stood." And has thereby taught us never to think it a hinderance in our journey to pause to do good. To do good is our *chief* business; and to this every thing else is to be rendered subordinate and subservient. "And commanded him to be brought." By this circumstance he administered reproof and instruction. Reproof—by ordering those to help the poor man who had endeavoured to check him; instruction—by teaching us that though he does not stand in need of our help, he will not dispense with our services; that we are to aid each other; that though we cannot recover our fellow-creatures, we may frequently bring them to the place and means of cure.

Our Saviour is acquainted with all our sins, but he requires us to confess them; he understands all our wants, but he commands us to acknowledge them; he is always graciously affected towards our case, but he would have us properly affected with it ourselves. He knew the desire of this man—the case was too plain to be mistaken—but he would know it from himself; and therefore when he was come near, he asked him, saying, "What wilt thou that I shall do unto thee?—And he said, Lord, that I may receive my sight. And Jesus said unto him, Receive thy sight: thy faith hath saved thee." Wherein did this man's faith appear? I answer, in his confession—calling him the Messiah, and Jesus, the son of David: and also in his application—for had he not believed in his power as able, and in his goodness as willing, to succour and relieve him—he would not have addressed himself so earnestly to him. Thus his faith honoured Christ, and Christ honoured his faith. Thus his faith excited prayer, and prayer brought him relief. Thus his faith produced a unity of design and a correspondence of disposition between the giver and the

receiver, the agent and the subject, the physician and the patient. It is in this way that so much is ascribed in the Scriptures to the influence of faith.

And what would be the feelings of this man as soon as he received sight! O what joy, what ecstasy, what gratitude, would he discover! How would he look, and gaze—all things are become new!—But the first object upon which he would fasten his eyes would be his Benefactor and Deliverer. He would admire—and weep—and adore—and kneel—and arise—and resolve never to leave him. Thus the man lame from his mother's womb no sooner received strength in his feet and ancle-bones than he, "leaping up, stood and walked, and entered" with his deliverer "into the temple—walking—and leaping—and praising God:" how exquisitely natural is all this! But what follows is no less so: it is said—"The lame man which was healed *held* Peter and John, while all the people ran together unto them, in Solomon's porch:" he *held* them, grasping their hands or their garments—it was a grasp of affection—of gratitude—perhaps also of fear, lest the malady should return, and he should not be near those who alone could cure him.

So here: as soon as Bartimeus received sight from the Lord Jesus, "he followed him in the way, glorifying God." We may view this two ways. It was first an evidence of the reality and perfection of the cure. In other cases where human skill has removed blindness by couching—the restored orbs cannot be immediately used; light is admitted into them by degrees; the man cannot measure distances, nor judge with accuracy; and he is not fit to be left to himself. But it is said, our Lord, "did all things well." His manner distinguished him—the man saw at once clearly: and was able to conduct himself. Secondly, it was an improvement of the greatness of the mercy. "I can never," says he, "discharge my obligations to such a gracious and almighty friend. But let me devote myself to his service—let me continually ask, 'Lord, what wilt thou have me to do?'"

From the narrative thus explained, I would take occasion to bring forward FOUR ADMONITIONS.

And the First is this. BE PERSUADED THAT YOU ARE ALL SPIRITUALLY IN THE CONDITION OF BARTIMEUS—and that without divine illumination, you are no more qualified for the concerns of the moral world than a blind man is for those of the natural world. It may be as difficult as it is important to convince persons of this truth. For "vain man would be wise, though he be born like a wild ass's colt;" and many, like the offended Pharisees, ask—"Are we blind also?" But to the law and to the testimony. There is no image under which the Scripture more commonly holds forth our natural condition than blindness. We read of our being "alienated from the life of God, through the ignorance that is in us, because of the blindness of our hearts;" and we are told that "the God of this world hath blinded the minds of them that believe not." Our Saviour sends Paul "to open their eyes;" the Apostle prays for the Ephesians, "that the eyes of their understanding may be enlightened;" and David prays for himself, "Open thou mine eyes, that I may behold wonderous things out of thy law."

If a blind person were to say, "I see," we should be disposed to censure or pity him; we should suspect that he was influenced either by pride or insanity; and be satisfied that if a trial were made, the result of it would prove that what he affirmed was false. "Let him work—see where he seeks for his instruments, and how he uses them. Let him walk—see whether he can escape that stumblingblock or that pitfall. Desire him to pull a mote out of a brother's eye. Show him a fine painting, and ask him to mark its beauties." Men may deny their ignorance; but their lives and actions prove it. For instance: "He that loveth not, knoweth not God." And do men love God? Is he in all their thoughts? Is their meditation of him sweet? Are they inclined to speak of him? The Saviour is "fairer than the children of men; yea, he is altogether lovely"—but they see "no form nor comeliness in him; no beauty that they should desire him." "Though destruction and misery are in their paths," they see them not; "and the way of truth, though revealed in the Scripture, have they not known." Is not this blindness?

Though Bartimeus was surrounded with landscapes, they were nothing to him. Though the sun shone upon his head, he saw nothing of its lustre. He saw not the guide that led him to and fro: he never saw his own features; and had he been possessed of the finest mirror in the world, it could not have shown him what manner of man he was. Thus blind is man; thus unacquainted is he even with himself: thus ignorant is he, under all the advantages of external helps, and even of the Bible too—without divine teaching. "The natural man receiveth not the things of the Spirit of God: for they are foolishness unto him; neither can he know them, because they are spiritually discerned. But he that is spiritual judgeth all things; yet he himself is judged of no man."

Secondly. BE PERSUADED THAT, WITH REGARD TO THE REMOVAL OF THIS BLINDNESS, YOU ARE IN AS HOPEFUL A CONDITION AS THIS POOR MAN. In all these miracles our blessed Lord holds himself forth as the all-sufficient helper of sinners. By the cures which he wrought on the body, he shows how *able* he is to save the soul; and they were performed and recorded on purpose to lead us to

him for spiritual and everlasting deliverance. Hence, says the Evangelist, speaking of the signs which Jesus did truly in the presence of his disciples—"These are written that ye might believe that Jesus is the Christ, the Son of God; and that, believing, ye might have life through his name." Rejoice, therefore, that He who raised the dead can quicken those who are dead in trespasses and sins— that He who healed the leper can cleanse the soul from all unrighteousness,—and that He who opened the eyes of the blind can lead inquirers into all truth.

Did he refuse this man? Did he ever refuse any who applied to him in distress? Had he rejected but *one* supplicant, it would have been the means of discouraging some to the end of the world; they would have feared that there was something similar in their own case. But what can we say now? We see that his actions spoke the same language with his gracious lip—"Him that cometh unto me, I will in no wise cast out."—"Come unto me, ALL ye that labour, and are heavy laden, and I will give you rest." This is to characterize him in *every* age: he is "the same yesterday, to-day, and for ever." He is therefore equally *willing*.

"But I am so poor and mean. Many of my fellow-creatures, who are only raised a little above me in circumstances, despise me. And will the King of glory concern himself in my affairs?" Yes; he condescends to men of low estate. He preached the Gospel himself principally to the poor—and to show you that your mean condition is no disadvantage in applying to him—behold him pausing, and listening to a beggar in the road. "This poor man cried, and the Lord heard him, and saved him out of all his trouble."

But you say, he is no longer here. Oh! were he now on earth, dwelling among us, how happy should we be to betake ourselves to him in all our difficulties and distresses! but the heavens have received him until the restitution of all things. Yet though no longer visible, he is still accessible; though not to be seen, he is to be found—to be found in his word, and upon his throne, and in his house: we read of "the goings of our God and King in the sanctuary;" he is now passing by, "full of pity, joined with power;" address him. Bartimeus only heard that he was passing by; he did not see him when he addressed him. Address him, then, in the same circumstances, and you will soon find that he "is nigh unto them that call upon him, to all that call upon him in truth."

Take therefore a Third admonition. BE PERSUADED TO IMITATE THE IMPORTUNITY OF THIS BLIND BEGGAR, IN CRYING FOR MERCY. For this purpose reflect upon the sadness of your present condition. Think what a degraded, uncomfortable, unsafe state you are in, and how certainly, unless you are delivered from it, you will soon pass from the darkness of sin into the darkness of hell. And then consider the happiness of those who have been delivered from the kingdom of darkness. "Blessed is the people that know the joyful sound; they shall walk, O Lord, in the light of thy countenance. In thy name shall they rejoice all the day, and in thy righteousness shall they be exalted; for thou art the glory of their strength, and in thy favour our horn shall be exalted." Pray therefore that you may be made a partaker of the inheritance of the saints in light.

And especially let your importunity, like this poor man's, appear with regard to two things. First, like him, seize the *present* moment. Let not the opportunity afforded you be lost by delay. You know not whether you will have another. Your indifference may provoke him to withdraw in anger, resolving to return no more. Your heart may be hardened through the deceitfulness of sin. You may be deprived of reason. This very night your souls may be required of you! How many are falling around you in the bloom of life! How many are called away without warning! And are you secure? "Seek ye the Lord while he may be found, call ye upon him while he is near." Secondly, like him, be not silenced by discouragement and opposition. Many may try to check you. Infidels may tell you to hold your peace—and say, "It is all delusion." Philosophers may tell you to hold your peace—and say, "It is all enthusiasm." Physicians may tell you to hold your peace—and say, "It is all nervous depression—away to company and the theatre." Even divines may warn you to be soberminded, and to avoid being righteous overmuch. Formalists may tell you, "It is needless to be so warm." Companions, friends, relations, may surround you with objections, entreaties, insults, threatenings—And you—what will you do under all this? Do!—why say, "This is a case in which another is not to judge for me. It is a personal concern—and it is an affair infinitely, everlastingly important. I must succeed or perish. Lord, help me!"

Fourthly, If he has healed you! If you can say, "One thing I know, that whereas I was blind, now I see"——LIKE BARTIMEUS, BE CAREFUL TO FOLLOW THE SAVIOUR.

This is the best way to evidence your cure. None follow him blind: but those whose eyes he has opened, see so much to admire and so much to desire in him; they feel such a dependence upon him, and such an attachment to him; that they are willing to forsake all, in order to follow him whithersoever he goeth. And every proof of your conversion, separate from this adherence to the Saviour, is fallacious and ruinous.

This is also the best way to improve your deliverance. Thus you will "show forth the praises of him who hath called you out of darkness into his marvellous light." Follow him, then, as an imitator of his example. Follow him as a servant, to obey his orders and to bear his reproach. Follow him, to spread his fame and to be a witness of his power and his goodness.

What an affecting sight must it have been in the days of his flesh, to have seen him moving about, followed by a number of persons whose complaints he had removed, and who acknowledged that to him they owed all the happiness they enjoyed—to hear one saying, He restored my son—another, He unstopped my deaf ears—and a third, He opened my blind eyes! He is not alone now in our world. There are some who are following him in the regeneration. They are the trophies of his free and almighty grace. They were once sinners, but are now renewed in the spirit of their mind. They were once darkness, but they are now light in the Lord, and are all looking to him and saying, "Not unto us, O Lord, not unto us, but unto thy name give glory, for thy mercy and for thy truth's sake!"

But what will it be, when he will be seen in company with all his people on the heavenly plains! What a day when the Redeemer will be seen with all his captives; the Physician of souls with all his patients; and all of them acknowledging that by his grace they are what they are! What a multitude! How full of joy, and how full of praise! And on his head will be many crowns! He will inhabit all the praises of Israel! "Then he shall come to be *glorified in his saints, and to be admired in all them that believe!*"

DISCOURSE XXXVIII.

WINTER.

Thou hast made winter.—Psalm lxxiv. 17.

AND he makes nothing in vain. Winter therefore is as worthy of our attention, as either of the former seasons which have passed under our review.

The scenes indeed all around us, which we lately beheld, have assumed a new and chilling appearance. The trees are shorn of their foliage. The hedges are laid bare. The fields and favourite walks have lost their attractions: and the garden, now it yields no perfumes and offers no fruits, like a friend in adversity, is forsaken. The vegetable creation looks dead. The tuneful tribes are dumb. The cattle are grave, and no longer play in the meadows. The north wind blows. "He sendeth abroad his ice like morsels; who can stand before his cold!"—We rush in for shelter.

But let us take some particular views of this subject.

And First, Winter belongs to the plan of heaven, and is a season indispensably necessary. It aids the system of life and vegetation; it kills the seeds of infection, and destroys pestilential damps; it refines the blood; it gives us vigour and courage; it confirms the nerves, and braces up the relaxed solids.

Snow is a warm covering for the corn; and while it defends the tender blades from nipping frosts, it also nourishes their growth. Isaiah remarked this long ago; and speaks of "the snow—coming down from heaven, and watering the earth, to make it bring forth and bud." The case is this. When the snow thaws, it melts into genial moisture; sinks down into the soil, and leaves the nitrous particles with which it is charged in the pores. Thus the glebe is replenished with that vegetable nutriment which will produce the bloom of spring and the fertility of autumn.

Winter therefore is only the needful repose of Nature, after her labours for the welfare of the creation. But even this pause is only to acquire new strength; or rather it is a silent and secret energy of preparation to surprise and charm us again with fresh abundance. Nor has the Creator forgotten our well-being and comfort during this period:

For Winter is, Secondly, a season which has its pleasures. I love to hear the roaring of the wind. I love to see the figures which the frost has painted on the glass. I love to watch the redbreast with his slender legs, standing at the window, and knocking with his bill to ask for the crumbs which fall from the table. I love to observe the husbandman carrying forth the provender for his harmless charge—while the creatures of his care, not with boisterous impatience, but with waiting eyes turned towards the place of their supplies, ask for their "meat in due season"— and I here see one of the many ways in which "HE openeth his hand and satisfieth the desire of every living thing."

Is it not pleasant to view a landscape whitened with snow? To gaze upon the trees and hedges dressed in such pure and sparkling lustre? To behold the rising sun labouring to pierce a fog which had enveloped the heaven and the earth, and gradually successful in dispersing these vapours—so that objects by little and little emerge from their obscurity, and appear in their own forms, while the mist rolls up the side of the hill and is seen no more?

A few things also brave the rigour of the season and remain evergreen. The box, the laurel, the yew-tree, the laurustinus, are grateful exemptions from the law of desolation. Nor should we forget the curling ivy, nor the crimson berries of the wild hawthorn.

Winter affords recreation for the understanding, as well as for the senses. If we are less abroad, we have more intercourse within. If rural pleasures are diminished, social ones are increased.

> "O Winter!———
> I love thee, all unlovely as thou seem'st,
> And dreaded as thou art!"
>
> "Compensating his loss with added hours
> Of social converse and instructive ease,
> And gath'ring, at short notice, in one group
> The family dispersed, and fixing thought,
> Not less dispers'd by daylight and its cares—
> —I crown thee king of intimate delights,
> Fire-side enjoyments, home-born happiness,
> And all the comforts that the lowly roof
> Of undisturb'd retirement, and the hours
> Of long uninterrupted evening know."

Yes, there are amusements to be found, without having recourse to noisy, public dissipations, in which health, innocency, and peace, are frequently sacrificed; where vicious passions are cherished, and persons are rendered incapable of relishing genuine pleasure.

> "—Cards are superfluous here, with all the tricks
> That idleness has yet contrived
> To fill the void of an unfurnished brain,
> To palliate dulness, and give time a shove."
>
> "Discourse ensues, yet not trivial, yet not dull,
> Nor such as with a frown forbids the play
> Of fancy, or proscribes the sound of mirth:
> Nor do we madly, like an impious world,
> Who deem religion phrensy, and the God
> That made them an intruder on their joys,
> Start at his awful name, or deem his praise
> A jarring note."

Thirdly. Winter is a season in which we should peculiarly feel gratitude for our residence, accommodations, and conveniences. Things strike us more forcibly by comparison. Let us remember how much more temperate our climate is than that of many other countries. Our winter is nothing, when we turn to the Frigid Zone. Think of those who live within the Polar Circle: dispersed; exposed to beasts of prey; their poor huts furnishing only a miserable refuge; where linger months of perpetual night and frost; and, by the absence of heat, almost absolute barrenness reigns around.

When the French mathematicians wintered at Tornea, in Lapland, the external air suddenly admitted into their rooms, seizing the moisture, became whirls of snow; their breasts were rent when they breathed it; and the contact of it with their bodies was intolerable. We read of seven thousand Swedes who perished at once, in attempting to pass the mountains which divide Norway from Sweden.

And while our Winter reigns here with great comparative mildness, how many blessings distinguish our portion from that of others around us, and demand our praise! We have a house to defend us; we have clothes to cover us; we have fire to warm us; we have beds to comfort us; we have provisions to nourish us;—"What shall we render? Bless the Lord, O my soul, and forget not all his benefits."

Fourthly. This season calls upon us to exercise Benevolence. Sympathy is now more powerfully excited than at any other period; we are enabled more easily to enter into the feelings of others less favoured than ourselves. And while we are enjoying every conveniency and comfort which the tenderness of Providence can afford—O let us think of the indigent and miserable. Let us think of those whose poor hovels and shattered panes cannot screen them from the piercing cold. Let us think of those, whose tattered garments scarcely cover their shivering flesh. Let us think of the starving poor, who, after a struggle which to relinquish, give up their small pittance of bread to get a little fuel to warm their frozen limbs. Let us think of the old and the infirm; of the sick and the diseased. When the evening draws on, let us reflect upon the scene so exquisitely touched by the pencil of sensibility—

> " Poor, yet industrious, modest, quiet, neat,
> Such claim compassion in a night like this,
> And have a friend in every feeling heart.
> Warmed while it lasts, by labour all day long
> They brave the season, and yet find at eve,
> Ill clad, and fed but sparely, time to cool.
> The frugal housewife trembles when she lights
> Her scanty stock of brush-wood blazing clear,
> But dying soon like all terrestrial joys.
> The few small embers left she nurses well:
> And, while her infant race, with outspread hands
> And crowded knees, sit cow'ring o'er the sparks,
> Retires, content to quake, so they be warm'd."

Let " the blessing of them that are ready to perish come upon us." Who would not " labour, that he may have to give to him that needeth!" Who would not deny himself superfluities, and—something more—that his bounty may visit " the fatherless and the widows in their affliction!"

Ah! ye unfeeling, ye worldly-minded, that " stretch yourselves upon your couches—that chant to the sound of the viol—that drink wine in bowls, and anoint yourselves with the chief ointments, but are not grieved for the affliction of Joseph!"—oh! ye, who can repair to every avenue of dissipation, and trample on so much distress, and shut your ears against so many groans in your way thither—on what do you found your title to humanity?"—" Thy judgment is to come." Or do you lay claim to religion? Merciless wretch, can knowledge or orthodoxy save thee?—" Whoso hath this world's good, and seeth his brother have need, and shutteth up his bowels of compassion from him; how dwelleth the love of God in him? My little children, let us not love in word, neither in tongue, but in deed and in truth. If a brother or sister be naked, and destitute of daily food, and one of you say unto them, Depart in peace, be ye warmed and filled; notwithstanding ye give them not those things which are needful to the body; what doth it profit? even so, faith if it hath not works is dead, being alone."

To conclude. Winter should improve us m knowledge.

It affords leisure, and excludes many interruptions—it is therefore favourable to application. Let us read, and study, and prepare for action and usefulness in life.

And let us not pass heedlessly by these subjects of reflection and improvement, which the very season itself yields. How instructive, for instance, is the goodness of God, not only in the preservation of the human race, but in taking care of all the millions of animals during a period which threatens to destroy them! What a number of retreats does he provide for them! Some of them, by a singular instinct, change the places of their residence. Some of them are lulled into a profound sleep for weeks and months. Some live on the fat they have replenished themselves with during the summer. Some carry their provisions beforehand, and lay them up in their cells. " God takes care for oxen; and hears the young ravens that cry."

And all this teaches us, First, to resemble him, and be kind to every being. If we learn of him, we cannot be cruel to the brute creation. We cannot be indifferent to their shelter and nourishment, when we remember, that " his mercies are over all his works."—Secondly, to trust in him. He who provides for animals, will not abandon children. " Behold the fowls of the air: for they sow not, neither do they reap, nor gather into barns; yet your heavenly Father feedeth them. Are ye not much better than they?"

The season is also instructive as an emblem. Here is the picture of life—thy flowery spring, thy summer strength, thy sober autumn are all hastening into winter. Decay and death will soon, very soon, lay all waste. What provision hast thou made for the evil day! Hast thou been laying up " treasure in heaven?" Hast thou been labouring for " that meat which endureth unto everlasting life?"

Every thing decays except Holiness. This therefore is the true character of man; and this shows us that he was designed for a religious state rather than any other. Pursue this then as " the one thing needful; and choose that good part that shall not be taken away from you."

Soon Spring will dawn again upon us, in its beauty and its songs. And " we, according to his promise, look for new heavens and a new earth, wherein dwelleth righteousness." No winter there—but we shall flourish in perpetual spring, in endless youth, in everlasting life!

> " Then let our songs abound,
> And every tear be dry;
> We're marching through Immanuel's ground,
> To fairer worlds on high."

DISCOURSE XXXIX.

CHRISTIANS NOT OF THE WORLD.

They are not of the world.—John xvii. 14.

MANY have a form of godliness while they

deny the power thereof. Many also walk very unanswerably to the demands of their holy profession. And these things very much disparage the Gospel, and perplex the minds of inquirers.

What in such a case are we to do? Let us abide by the judgment of God, which is always according to truth. Let us examine the Scriptures. There—real religion is held forth in its unbending dignity and matchless purity. And let us remember too—that in every age there have been some, though comparatively few in number, and generally little known, who have embodied their principles in their lives, and "adorned the doctrine of God our Saviour in all things." And the Saviour sees them, and knows them, and confesses them: and said to them all, in his intercessory prayer—"I have given them thy word; and the world hath hated them, because they are not of the world, even as I am not of the world."

It is the middle clause only of this passage to which we would now call your attention. —*Christians are not of the world.* Let us, I. EXPLAIN AND ESTABLISH THE TRUTH OF THE ASSERTION; and, II. APPLY THE REFLECTION TO SOME USEFUL PURPOSES.

I. When our Saviour says—"They are not of the world"—we can hardly suppose that he intends a total abstraction from the world, or rather a separation from it, in all respects. What then does he mean? A consideration of four articles will be sufficient to answer this question.

First. They are not of the world, because they are not attached to their party. We should be exceedingly mistaken were we to suppose that religion requires us to seclude ourselves wholly from society; for many of its instructions suppose various connexions with our fellow-creatures, and are designed to regulate our intercourse with them.

In many cases therefore it is lawful to associate with the people of the world. Such are cases of necessity—when we are compelled by our situations to live among them. Such are cases of business—in which we are called to trade with them. Such are cases of charity and piety—in which we endeavour to relieve their temporal distresses, or to awaken their minds to religious concerns. Such also are cases of civility and affinity—for godliness does not make us rude; nor does it banish natural affections; nor disband the relations of father and child—husband and wife—brother and sister, which have been established by nature and Providence.

But further than this a Christian will not go. He cannot choose the people of the world as his companions and friends; he cannot seek after intercourse with the world when it depends upon his own option, and none of the afore-mentioned reasons can justify the familiarity. The authority of God forbids it. "Save yourselves from this untoward generation. Have no fellowship with the unfruitful works of darkness, but rather reprove them. Wherefore come out from among them, and be ye separate, saith the Lord, and touch not the unclean thing; and I will receive you, and will be a Father unto you, and ye shall be my sons and daughters, saith the Lord Almighty." The peace of his fellow Christians forbids it. Such bold intimacies with the world would grieve the strong, and throw a stumblingblock in the way of the weak; and "when ye sin so against the brethren and wound their weak consciences, ye sin against Christ." He therefore cannot say as some do, in justifying his worldly freedoms—"I do not regard what others think of me, my own conscience does not condemn me." He considers others as well as himself; and never supposes his conduct innocent in the sight of God while it is censurable in the eyes of men. Oh! what a noble, what a delicate, what a self-denying disposition does the Gospel produce! "Wherefore," says the Apostle, "if meat make my brother to offend, I will eat no flesh while the world standeth, lest I make my brother to offend." The welfare of his own soul forbids it. "Can a man take fire in his bosom, and his clothes not be burned? Can one go upon hot coals, and his feet not be burned?" Why did God warn the Jews of old not to mingle with the surrounding nations? Because he foresaw that such intercourse would seduce them— and so it fell out—"They were mingled among the heathen, and learned their works; and they served their idols, which were a snare unto them." And it is owing to such intimacies with the people of the world, in our day, that "the love of many waxes cold;" that they are drawn off by degrees from the house of God; and yield up one thing after another, to avoid giving offence, till their profession becomes not only their disgrace, but their burden, and they completely throw off the restraint.

And here, my young friends, I would particularly address you! Beware of wicked company; beware of infidels; beware of sceptics; beware of those who deride the leading doctrines of the Gospel, or even the infirmities of the people of God. Your seducers generally begin very remotely from the place where they mean to leave off. While they are endeavouring to obtain your regards, they often conceal what, if divulged at once, would shock your feelings; but, when they have engaged your affection and confidence, they will draw you on, till you look back with horror upon the distance you have passed; or, what is worse, be given up to "a reprobate mind!" Break off therefore such connexions—your safety requires it.

S   12*

If the associate be as a right hand, cut it off; or as a right eye, pluck it out. Love nothing to the prejudice of your souls. Cultivate no friendships that will end in everlasting ruin. Join those that have abandoned the City of Destruction, and are pressing into the kingdom of God. Take David for your example, and be able to say as he did—" I have not sat with vain persons, neither will I go in with dissemblers. I have hated the congregation of evil doers; and will not sit with the wicked. I am a companion of all them that fear thee, and of them that keep thy precepts."

Indeed if you are partakers of the grace of God, your disposition will forbid all unnecessary alliance with the world. You will feel new wants and desires, and these will impel you to new associations; you will readily leave the vile and the vain, in search of those who are traveling your road, and can be helpers of your joy; you will "take hold of the skirt of him that is a Jew, saying, we will go with you, for we have heard that God is with you."

And this reminds us of a Second particular. They are not of the world, because they are not actuated by "the spirit of the world." And this is the grand thing—to have a temper of mind, a moral taste, different from the world. Indeed every thing else is vain without this. Your forsaking the world in profession; your leaving it in appearance by your apparel, your discourse, your manner of life, is nothing unless it be animated by internal principle. It is *in the heart* that the separation must take place. And when the heart is detached from the world, these two advantages flow from it.—First, even in the midst of all your secular concerns, whether in the field or in the shop, you will maintain your distinction. Though in the world, you will not be of it—because the heart is elsewhere—and God looketh to the heart. And Secondly, when the heart is withdrawn from the world, every thing else will follow of course.

Then you will not be governed by the maxims and opinions of the world. You will not ask, what are the sentiments of the multitude, but what says the Scripture? I do not wish to be "conformed to this world, but to be transformed, by the renewing of the mind, that I may prove what is that good, and acceptable, and perfect will of God." You will not be attached to its amusements and dissipations. The sun arising conceals the stars —not by spreading gloom, but by diffusing lustre. The child becoming a man, resigns without reluctance or regret the toys and trifles of infancy. It is a poor thing to be dragged out of the dissipations of the world, against inclination, while we still look back with Lot's wife, and inwardly sigh, Oh that I were permitted to enjoy them still!—But it

is a glorious thing to leave these diversions from the discovery and possession of superior entertainment and sublimer joys. You will not be led by the conversation of the world: for speech is governed by affection; "and out of the abundance of the heart the mouth speaketh." In a word, you will not "walk according to the course of this world:" the tide of your actions and pursuits will flow in a direction perfectly opposite."

Thirdly. They are not of the world, because "they are not natives there." Hear what our Lord said to the Jews—" Ye are from beneath, I am from above; ye are of this world, I am not of this world." The expressions are explanatory of each other: because they were from beneath, therefore they were of the world; and because he was from above, therefore he was not of the world. Their respective extractions determined the country to which they belonged. Now the believer may adopt the same language. He is here only as "a stranger, and a foreigner," not a native: he derives his being from heaven—if not as a man, yet as a Christian; and as a Christian we are speaking of him. And as he is born from above, no wonder that he "seeks those things which are above, where Christ sitteth on the right hand of God."

And, therefore, in the Fourth place, they are not of the world, because "they do not choose their portion." We read of some "who have their portion in this" life; and they are called, as well they may be, "men of the world." But in distinction from them, says David, "'As for me, I will behold thy face in righteousness, I shall be satisfied when I awake with thy likeness.' They lay up treasure here—but my treasure is in heaven. They make earth their home—but I regard it only as my passage. They confine all their hopes and fears within the narrow compass of mortality—I seek a country beyond the swellings of Jordan. Death ends their happiness, as well as their lives—but it secures and completes mine."

Hence it is that the Christian feels an indifference to present things, and learns in whatsoever state he is therewith to be content. This never can be the case with the man who makes the world his portion: if present things constitute his all, he cannot be moderate in his joys or sorrows. But a Christian can be moderate in both, because they are not his all. His inheritance is reserved in heaven for him. He therefore weeps as those that weep not; and rejoices as those that rejoice not; and buys as those that possess not. He feels worldly trials—but he is not miserable. He is thankful for temporal indulgences—but he is not exalted above measure. He does not want much; he does not expect much while here. All he requires of the world, as did the Israelites of the king of Edom, is permission to pursue his peaceful course towards the land flowing with milk and honey : " Let us pass, I pray thee, through thy country : we will not pass through the fields, or through the vineyards, neither will we drink of the water of the wells ; we will go by the king's highway ; we will not turn to the right hand nor to the left, until we have passed thy borders. We will go by the highway ; and if I and my cattle drink of thy water, then I will pay for it ; I will only," without doing any thing else, " go through on my feet."

Thus Christians are not of this world—for they are not attached to their party—they are not actuated by their spirit—they are not born in their country—they do not choose their portion.

II. What does this truth teach us ? Why, First, it enables us easily to account for the world's persecution of real Christians. " I have given them thy word; and the world hath hated them, because they are not of the world, even as I am not of the world; if ye were of the world, the world would love his own : but because ye are not of the world, but I have chosen you out of the world, therefore the world hateth you." They are not willing indeed to acknowledge that this is the cause of their hatred. No; they resemble their old predecessors, who, when our Saviour said, " Many good works have I showed you—for which of these works do you stone me ?" the Jews answered him, saying, For a good work we stone thee not : but for blasphemy ; and because that thou, being a man, makest thyself God." So these say now—It is not for your holiness we condemn you—but for your pride, your censoriousness, your hypocrisy.

But let me ask you—Do you not load them with these charges in order to justify your malignity ? Do you not magnify infirmities into crimes ? Do you not reproach a whole body for the faults of a few ?—Besides, while living in sin yourselves, is it possible for us to imagine that you can be grieved because professors of religion are not blameless ? And why do you not hate these things universally —why connive at them in others ? You say —Why these things are much worse in *them* by reason of their religious pretensions— There is indeed much truth in this—and we see with what circumspection should professors act, lest they should furnish cause for offence ! But, after all, this will not reach the reason of this malignity. For how is it that the most holy and zealous Christians have been the most obnoxious to the men of the world ? How is it that when they have been unquestionably free from those blemishes, and have had even the recommendations of birth, learning, liberality, amiableness —still they have been the scorn of the world ! And to remark a much stronger case—How was it that the Lord and Saviour was much more abhorred and opposed by the world than any of his followers ? Was he proud, censorious, false ? Was he not incarnate virtue— perfect lowliness ? Do we not clearly learn from his example, that real godliness, whatever endearments it possesses, can never be welcome to a " carnal mind, which is enmity against God ?" And what our Saviour said to the Jews of old will apply to many Christians—falsely so called now—" The world cannot hate you"—you are so much like it— " but me"—me " it hateth, because I testify of it that the works thereof are evil." Bear the same decisive testimony by your words and actions, and be assured a portion of the same rancour will follow.

The case is plain. Resemblance is a ground of affection ; but unsuitableness, of dislike. The people of the world wish to be in darkness—and Christians shine. They wish to sleep undisturbed—and Christians by their exertions, rouse and alarm them. One wicked man does not reproach another—but the holy example of the righteous always upbraids and condemns.

Hence, says the Apostle, " All that will live godly in Christ Jesus shall suffer persecution" of one kind or another; either the persecution of the hand, of the tongue, or of the heart. It began early; Cain slew his brother Abel; " and wherefore slew he him ?" He doubtless alleged other reasons himself— but this was the true cause—" his own works were evil, and his brother's righteous." It prevailed also in the family of Abraham; " and as it was then, so it is now : he that was born after the flesh persecuted him that was born after the Spirit." " Marvel not therefore," says our Saviour, " if the world hate you." You marvel at something new, something unexpected. But is this the case with the opposition of the world ? Have you not been apprized of it from the beginning ? Is it not the way in which all your brethren have trodden—and even your " elder Brother" too ?—Then do not murmur: you suffer in the noblest company ; and your enemies can neither hinder your present peace, nor destroy your future happiness. Yea, " blessed are they which are persecuted for righteousness' sake ; for theirs is the kingdom of heaven. Blessed are ye when men shall revile you, and persecute you, and shall say all manner of evil against you falsely for my sake. Rejoice, and be exceeding glad : for great is your reward in heaven: for so persecuted they the prophets which were before you."

Secondly. If the distinguishing badge of a Christian is this—that he is " not of the world"—then are there few real Christians to be found. Do not say, this conclusion arises from severity of mind. " The Lord our God add unto the people, how many soever they be, an hundred fold !"—But it necessarily follows from a regard to the truth of God. If we abide by the decisions of his word—is there not enough to justify our fears with regard to thousands who bear the Christian name? Look around you. It is true He who knoweth all things may discover a difference which eludes our view—but surely there ought to be a visible as well as a real difference between the citizens of earth and the citizens of heaven. Surely, Christians should "*declare plainly*" that they seek a country, and that this is not their rest.

We often judge of our fellow-creatures by a wrong standard: thus we "bless the covetous whom the Lord abhorreth; we condemn a drunkard and an adulterer, and very deservedly—but what say we against those that "mind earthly things?" Who recollects that "if any man love the world, the love of the Father is not in him?"

Judge yourselves, I beseech you, by this test. Ask yourselves wherein you differ from the men of the world: whether you are not labouring more for "the meat that perisheth than for that meat which endureth unto everlasting life;" whether you are carried down the stream by the vices or follies of the age, or whether you "rise up for God against the evil doers, and stand up for him against the workers of iniquity;" whether you are "serving your generation, or sleeping as do others;" whether any speak evil of you, or you are the favourites of those who are enemies of God?

Thirdly. See how little we should be affected with the charge of preciseness and singularity. By persons of good sense and liberal minds singularity is never valued for its own sake; and there is also an assumed, unnecessary singularity in trifling things, which is by no means praiseworthy. But there is a certain singularity which does the Christian honour, and without which you cannot belong to the Saviour; for "He gave himself for our sins, that he might deliver us from this present evil world: He gave himself for us, that he might redeem us from all iniquity, and purify unto himself a peculiar people, zealous of good works." And why then should we be so terrified at the charge? You would not be afraid of being peculiarly wise, or beautiful, or wealthy. Why then wish to escape the praise of being singular in religion? What wisdom, what beauty, what riches can be compared to this!

Fourthly. If Christians are not of the world, no wonder they are more than reconciled to a withdrawment from it. No wonder they love solitude, enter their closets, and shut to their doors—there they exchange the world for God. No wonder they prize the Sabbath —it is a day of retreat, it is an emblem of the heavenly rest. No wonder if death be no longer formidable—it is a leaving the world —but what world? a vain world, a vexing world, a defiling world. Such a departure may be painful to those who have lodged all

their happiness on earth—but the Christian is not of the world—and the wonder is, that he is not more eager to be gone out of it.

Let me conclude with an admonition. Let me address Christians. Let me call upon you "not to fashion yourselves according to your former lusts in your ignorance; nor to walk as other Gentiles walk, in the vanity of your minds." Stand on your own hallowed ground. Maintain your separation from the world. Do not venture too far, even in lawful things: the line which divides good and evil is only an hair's breadth—and may therefore be easily, and sometimes insensibly passed. Be not ambitious of worldly honours; nor covetous of worldly riches—"Seekest thou great things to thyself? seek them not." Be thankful for such a degree of temporal good as will help; but never be anxious for such a degree as will hinder. One staff is useful to a traveller: a bundle of staves would be an incumbrance. "Godliness, with contentment, is great gain. For we brought nothing into this world, and it is certain we can carry nothing out. And having food and raiment, let us be therewith content."

But what shall I say to those of you who are still "of the world?" Let me remind you, that there will soon be a full and an everlasting separation between the righteous and the wicked—yea, that the division is already made—that the parties are receding from each other—and hastening to their respective stations. Oh! be prevailed upon to leave the world before the world leaves you—for leave it you must, either by choice or compulsion; and is it not better to leave it by the allurements of grace than by the violence of death? Oh! leave the world, while it is in your power to prove that you relinquish it for conscience' sake. Oh! leave it, as you will wish you had renounced it when you enter an eternal state; and now show yourselves in the class in which you hope to appear at the day of judgment. View the world as an object of solitary contemplation. View it as an object of dying contemplation. And "arise and depart hence."—If you remain in the world, with the world you will perish.

How I pity certain individuals who seem to have their everlasting welfare at heart, but cannot once for all resolve to give up the world! They are for ever purposing, but never decide. They seem to yield to every thing we advance, until we touch the subject of separation from the world—then they immediately shrink back; and if pressed, employ all their ingenuity to excuse or palliate their attachments and compliances. Are you of this number?

Perhaps you imagine your withdrawment from the world will be a very miserable thing. Now even allowing it to be irksome, still if it can be proved to be necessary, you ought to submit to it. You act thus in other pressing cases. But we are bold to affirm that if you detach yourselves from it, you will be infinitely more happy than in connexion with it. What liberty, what satisfaction have the votaries of the world? Are they not the most pitiable of all beings? Are they not always disgusted or disappointed?—And still more peculiarly wretched is a state of suspense, between the world and religion; where you have the inconveniences of both, without the pleasure of either. But, says Solomon, "Her ways are ways of pleasantness, and all her paths are peace." "My soul," says David, "shall be satisfied as with marrow and fatness; and my mouth shall praise thee with joyful lips: when I remember thee upon my bed, and meditate on thee in the nightwatches."

Good Matthew Henry said, as he was expiring, to his friends in the room; You have heard and read the words of many dying men —and these are mine; I have found a life of communion with God the happiest life in the world. "Strait is the gate, and narrow is the way." But hear Bishop Beveridge: If the way be narrow, it is not long; and if the gate be strait, it opens into endless life.

DISCOURSE XL.

WEAK GRACE ENCOURAGED.

For who hath despised the day of small things?
Zech. iv. 10.

It is not indeed easy to determine always what is small. Things, at first apparently trivial and uninteresting, often become very great and momentous.

It is so in nature. The oak, whose branches cover the side of the mountain, and whose strength defies the storm, grows from an acorn which we could trample under foot. Broad rivers and streams, which fertilize the countries through which they roll, and become a sea, would, if retraced, be found to spring from obscure, if not imperceptible springs.

It is so in science. There was a time when Johnson was learning his letters. Sir Isaac Newton, sitting in a garden, saw an apple fall from a tree; and this lead him to speculate on the power of gravity: he saw a boy blowing bubbles, and this led him to investigate the subject of light and colours. And from such hints was derived much of the grand scheme of philosophy which distinguished this illustrious genius.

It is so in political affairs. As we read history, how often are we forced to exclaim, "Behold, how great a matter a little fire kindleth!" What an inconsiderable incident has sometimes set a whole nation in a blaze! How wonderful the difference between many of the revolutions of empires in their rise and in their effects!

It is so in moral concerns. "Know ye not that a little leaven leaveneth the whole lump?" Our Saviour teaches us that there may be murder in an angry word, and adultery in a wanton look. Hence the wisest part we can act is to stop beginnings, yea, to avoid the very appearance of evil. "Then, when lust hath conceived, it bringeth forth sin; and sin, when it is finished, bringeth forth death."

And what inference should we derive hence? Why this. A philosopher will not despise the day of small things; a statesman will not despise it; a moralist will not—and should a Christian! God forbid. "For who hath despised the day of small things?" Let us then apply this question entirely to the subject of religion.

And here it will be necessary, First, to observe, that the work of grace in the soul is frequently small in its commencement—I say frequently, for it is not always so. The various graces of the Holy Ghost seem to have been, at once, perfectly produced in the Apostle Paul: so great was his unwavering faith, his lively hope, his inflexible courage, and his unconquerable zeal.

But in a general way it is small in its beginning. The soul resembles the field, where we see "first the blade, then the ear, and after that the full corn in the ear." God could instantly produce the fruits of the earth in their maturity, but we know from the event that it does not accord with his wisdom. He therefore advances them from very small principles, and by a gradual process, to their perfection. Our Saviour spake a parable, which will apply to the grace of God in the heart, as well as the gospel in the world, and which serves to illustrate and confirm the truth of this representation. "The kingdom of heaven," says he, "is like to a grain of mustard seed, which a man took and sowed in his field: which is indeed the least of all seeds: but when it is grown, it is the greatest among herbs, and becometh a tree, so that the birds of the air come and lodge in the branches thereof."

The Christian is a soldier; and the beginning of his career is naturally the day of small things. He is a raw and awkward recruit; he can neither march well, nor easily and gracefully use his arms. And then when he has acquired the theory of his exercise, he has the practical part to learn: and it is actual experience only that can make the warrior.

The Christian is a scholar; and when he enters the school, it is of course a day of small things. He begins with his rudiments, and though he has many things to learn, "he cannot bear them now." Or to speak less figuratively. He has some light, and such as flesh and blood could never reveal; but it is indistinct. "He sees men as trees walking." It terminates for the present rather in desires and admiration than any thing else. It is " marvellous light ;" it leads him to wonder and exclaim—" Where have I been ? How was it that I did not see these things before ? Whence is it that I perceive them now ? How can I acquire them ? How can I ensure them ?" Thus he longs, and prays, and waits for the Lord more than they that watch for the morning.

He has some hope, but while it excludes despair, it also admits of doubts and fears. He does not question the power of the Saviour, but his will ; nor the truth of his promises, but their application to himself. His affections are warm, but his faith is weak. Little stumbling-blocks throw him down, as even a wrinkle in the carpet will occasion the fall of a child. He is easily perplexed and distressed. His afflictions embarrass him, and lead him to say, If I am his, why am I thus ? He cannot bear the frown of Providence ; and because God chastises him, he fears that he is going to condemn. And this, according to Solomon, is another mark of a weak state of religion : " If thou faint in the day of adversity, thy strength is small."

But Secondly, weak, unpromising, and even discouraging as all this may appear, it is not to be despised. And for this THREE REASONS MAY BE ASSIGNED.

First. Our Saviour does not despise the day of small things. Observe what is said of him in prophecy. " He shall come down like rain upon the mown grass ; as showers that water the earth. He shall feed his flock there like a shepherd :" but in this flock all are not sheep : there are lambs ; and these are weak and tender, and unable to travel fast or far. And " he shall gather the lambs with his arm, and carry them in his bosom" not on his shoulder—an emblem of strength, but in his bosom—the image of affection—" and shall gently lead those that are with young. A bruised reed shall he not break, and the smoking flax shall he not quench : he shall bring forth judgment unto truth."

Let us look after this lovely character in the Gospels. We shall soon find him.—There came " a ruler, and besought him that he would come down and heal his son, for he was at the point of death." He thought Christ could cure him—there was his faith : but he could not believe that he was able to do it by his word, or without his bodily presence—there was his weakness. What does our Saviour ? He takes him at his desire, and goes away with him. What were his own disciples after all the education which he had given them ? His cross scandalized them ; and his resurrection appeared to them like a dream. Even to the hour of his ascension they had some expectations of a temporal kingdom. But they loved him, and had forsaken all to follow him ; and he did not cast them off. He bore with their infirmities, solved gradually all their doubts ; and " loving his own who were in the world, he loved them unto the end."

He rose from the dead with the same disposition he had discovered in life. What poor wavering creatures were the two disciples going to Emmaus ! They were ready to bury their last hope, and drew melancholy conclusions from circumstances which were really in their favour. He knew their state, and joined them in their sorrowful walk. He enlightened their minds, confirmed their faith, and enlivened their affections ; so that " they said one to another, Did not our heart burn within us, while he talked with us by the way, and while he opened to us the Scriptures ?"

When he ascended, he carried the same heart with him to heaven : we " have not an high priest who cannot be touched with the feeling of our infirmities." Hear what he said, long after he had entered his glory, to the Church of Philadelphia : " I know thy works : behold, I have set before thee an open door, and no man can shut it : for thou hast a little strength, and hast kept my word, and hast not denied my Name."

O blessed Saviour ! thou receivest the weak as well the strong—thou dost not despise the day of small things. May we be followers of thee as dear children !

Secondly. We should not despise the day of small things, because it is precious. Real grace is infinitely valuable. It is the work of God ; it is the image of God ; it is the glory of God ; it is the delight of God. " The Lord taketh pleasure in them that fear him, in them that hope in his mercy." The individual who possesses it is raised in the eye of an angel, yea, in the eye of God himself, above heroes, and philosophers, and kings. When the God of heaven and earth surveys our world, " To this man," says he, " will I look, even to him who is poor, and of a contrite spirit, and who trembleth at my word." This renders the righteous more excellent than his neighbour. This gives the heirs of faith such importance, that " the world is not worthy of them." This enlightens, this frees, this sanctifies, this dignifies the soul. In prosperity, in adversity ; alone, in company ; in life, in death—this is the one thing needful. And wise and happy is he who even resigns all to make it his own. " Happy is the man that findeth wisdom, and the man that getteth understanding. For the merchandize of it is better than the merchandize of silver, and the gain thereof than fine gold. She is more precious than rubies ; and all the things thou canst desire are not to be compared unto her. Length of days is in her right hand ; and in her left hand riches and honour. Her ways are ways of pleasantness, and all her paths are peace. She is a tree of life to them that lay hold upon her ;

and happy is every one that retaineth her." A little grace then is too precious to be despised!

And Thirdly. We should not despise the day of small things, because it will be a day of great things. That child will become a man: contemn not his infancy. Suppose he is now only a babe—he is an heir, and when of age will possess an inheritance reserved in heaven for him—he is a prince, and will reign for ever and ever. What is the dawn to the day! But we do not despise it: and why do we not! Because it is the pledge and the beginning of noon. And "the path of the just is as the shining light, which shineth more and more unto the perfect day."

Yes; Divine grace shall assuredly increase. "The righteous shall hold on his way; and he that hath clean hands shall wax stronger and stronger." "He has life, and he shall have it more abundantly."—What is sown in weakness shall be raised in power. What Eliphaz said of Job may be applied with peculiar force to the Christian: "Though thy beginning was small, yet thy latter end shall greatly increase." Oh! what will that poor, meek, doubting, distressed Christian be, when God, who has already "begun the good work," will "accomplish in him all the good pleasure of his will!" In a few years he will be upon a level with the angels of God. In a few months he will be presented faultless before the presence of his glory, with exceeding joy! "It is written, eye hath not seen, nor ear heard, neither have entered into the heart of man the things which God hath prepared for them that love him."

Seeing therefore that the day of small things is so much regarded by our Lord and Saviour—is already so valuable—and will so certainly increase, "with all the increase of God;" let us beware of despising it.

We conclude the subject with A QUESTION; AN ADMONITION; AND A CAUTION.

The QUESTION is this—Is it even a day of small things with you! You have had your day of rebellion—do you know any thing of a day of reconciliation! You have wandered from God—have you ever returned to him! You have been ignorant of Divine things—can you say at last, "whereas I was blind, now I see!" You have been dead to the things of God—are you now alive to them! and do they impress and govern you! Have you any new and holy bias given to your will and affections! Do you "hunger and thirst after righteousness!" Are you praying, "create in me a clean heart, O God, and renew a right spirit within me!"

Can this be a useless inquiry! Will it be a waste of time to retire this evening, and ask yourselves—whether "you have received the grace of God in truth!"—What will you do without it!

The ADMONITION calls upon you not to overlook or undervalue imperfect religion, whether in yourselves or others. If you are upright in heart, you will be in most danger of despising it in yourselves. Judging of your grace by the degree of it, you may conclude you have the reality. Comparing yourselves with others who are more advanced in the Divine life, you may shrink into nothing, and imagine you have no part or lot in the matter.

But beware of any rash conclusions. You may be traveling in the same road, though not with equal steps. You may be of the same species, though not of the same stature. While you mourn for what you want, you should rejoice in what you have. While you ought to be humble, you ought also to be thankful; and in taking shame to yourselves, you should acknowledge what God has done for your souls. If you are not what you would be, you are not what you once were; if you are not like some of the Lord's people, you are not like the rest of the world.

But you are also in some danger with regard to others. You may think too little of a real work of grace. Yea, from inattention, or from prejudice; from the manner in which it commences, or from some peculiarities in the subject, you may suppose God has done nothing, where he has been doing much.

Guard against this. And remember also, that it is not enough that you do not despise the day of small things; you must cherish it. Ministers should cherish every promising impression made upon the minds of their hearers. Parents should cherish every tender and pious disposition in their children. Friends should cherish every favourable appearance in their acquaintances. And "ye that are strong should bear the infirmities of the weak, and not please yourselves. Wherefore lift up the hands which hang down, and the feeble knees; and make straight paths for your feet, lest that which is lame be turned out of the way: but let it rather be healed. Warn them that are unruly, comfort the feebleminded, support the weak, be patient toward all men."

But it is necessary to mention a CAUTION: it is this. Let not the subject we have been considering cause remissness in duty, or lead any "to settle upon their lees." Were you, from what has been said, to rest satisfied with any present attainments, it would be an abuse of encouragement; it would be an evidence that you know nothing of the power of Divine grace in reality. For

"Whoever says, I want no more,
Confesses he has none."

Those who have "seen the Lord," will always pray, "I beseech thee show me thy glory." Those that have once "tasted that the Lord is gracious," will always cry, "Evermore, give us this bread to eat."

Besides, more is *attainable*. There is a fulness from which you may receive, "and grace for grace." There is a command; "Open thy mouth wide, and I will fill it." There is a promise; "Ask and ye shall receive, that your joy may be full."

And more is *desirable*. There are particularly two reasons why you should seek after a growth in grace.

The first is taken from usefulness. For supposing you are safe—ought you to have no concern for the welfare of your fellow-creatures, and the spread of the Saviour's cause around you? Ought you to wish merely to creep to heaven, without doing any good upon earth? Should you not wish to recommend religion every step of the way; and to honour God, who has done such great things for you, both in the life that you live, and in the death that you die?

And the other is drawn from comfort. It is with grace as it is with other things: when little, it is not easily seen; but by growing, it becomes more visible. There are richer and higher consolations in religion which some never taste of; they see them—but are not tall enough to reach them. For these depend—not upon the existence, but the degree of grace. In a word, to use the language of an old divine, "A little grace will bring us to heaven *hereafter*, but great grace will bring heaven to us *now*." Weak faith may be compared to a small infirm leaky vessel, which does indeed carry the passenger safely over, but subjects him to many a restless anxiety, and many a dreadful fear: while strong faith is a firm and well-constructed ship, that enables him to smile at the waves, to defy the storm, and gloriously enter the desired haven.

Therefore "giving all diligence, add to your faith virtue; and to virtue knowledge; and to knowledge temperance; and to temperance patience; and to patience godliness; and to godliness brotherly kindness; and to brotherly kindness charity. For if these things be in you, and abound, they make you that ye shall neither be barren nor unfruitful in the knowledge of our Lord Jesus Christ. But he that lacketh these things is blind, and cannot see afar off, and hath forgotten that he was purged from his old sins. Wherefore the rather, brethren, give diligence to make your calling and election sure: for if ye do these things, ye shall never fall: for so an entrance shall be ministered unto you abundantly into the everlasting kingdom of our Lord and Saviour Jesus Christ."

DISCOURSE XLI.

MARTHA AND MARY.

Now it came to pass, as they went, that he entered into a certain village: and a certain woman named Martha received him into her house. And she had a sister called Mary, which also sat at Jesus' feet, and heard his word. But Martha was cumbered about much serving, and came to him, and said, Lord, dost thou not care that my sister hath left me to serve alone? bid her therefore that she help me. And Jesus answered and said unto her, Martha, Martha, thou art careful and troubled about many things: but one thing is needful: and Mary hath chosen that good part, which shall not be taken away from her.—Luke x. 38—42.

BIOGRAPHY is a species of history peculiarly interesting and useful. And in this the Bible excels. The sacred writers describe to the very life. They fear no displeasure; they conceal no imperfection; they spare no censure.

And while they discover their impartiality, they equally prove their wisdom and prudence. This appears from the examples they delineate. What are philosophers, politicians, heroes, to the generality of mankind? They may excite wonder, but they cannot produce imitation. They may indulge curiosity, but they cannot furnish motives, encouragements, cautions. But here we are led into private life; we contemplate ordinary scenes; we see goodness in our own relations and circumstances. We behold blemishes which *we* are to shun, excellences which *we* are to pursue, advantages which *we* are to acquire.

Thus the Scripture becomes not a glaring comet, but "a lamp unto our feet, and a light unto our path."

Pass we to the narrative before us.

But previous to our advancing some general reflections from the whole passage, it will be necessary to take notice of the characters here mentioned; and to see wherein the one was to be censured, and the other to be commended.

Perhaps it is needless to premise that both these females were good women. It is expressly said, that "Jesus loved Martha," as well as Mary. And we are informed that when our Saviour was coming to Bethany, after the death of Lazarus, "Martha, as soon as she heard that Jesus was coming, went and met him, but Mary sat still in the house." These two sisters did not differ in their religious character, as Jacob and Esau; Saul and David; Peter and Judas; but only one of them was less influenced by her principles in this instance than the other; for our Lord does not condemn her general conduct, but her present action; and even this he does not censure absolutely, but comparatively. Some things may be said in commendation of Martha, and others in extenuation.

She discovered a noble freedom from the fear of man—"she received him into her house;" when it was well known that he was pursued by the heads of the Jewish nation

His entrance could not be hid; he had many with him. She also discovered her kindness and hospitality in her concern to provide for our Lord and his disciples, and in deeming nothing too good for them. I like also her attention to the affairs of her own household. Though she was a woman of some consequence, she does not deem it beneath her to attend even to the economy of the table; yea, even to serve with her own hands when an emergency required. An affectation of state and of delicacy in the mistress of a family, has occasioned disorders, wastes, and embarrassments which have ended in the ruin of many houses! The mother of Lemuel, in characterizing a wife, even for a prince, in those days—tells him, among other things—that "she riseth also while it is yet night, and giveth meat to her household, and a portion to her maidens—that she looketh well to the ways of her household, and eateth not the bread of idleness!"

Some things also may be said in her excuse. She was the mistress of the house, and it was her province to provide. This appears to have been a sudden occurrence; many came in unawares; and perhaps she was unfurnished—and this would naturally create hurry, confusion, uneasiness. But, after all that can be said in justification of Martha, our Saviour reproves her. She was therefore blameworthy; for his judgment is always according to truth. He could read the state of the mind; he could weigh motives; he could distinguish circumstances.

And from what he has mentioned, we may conclude that there was in her, a considerable share of domestic vanity. I advert to that vanity which makes Religion exclaim over thoughtless profusion, "Why is this waste?" Are there no charities to sustain—are there no hungry wretches to feed—no naked ones to clothe? I advert to that vanity which descends lower than pride in dress or furniture, which commonly attends wealth newly acquired, and adheres to vulgar minds, incapable of discerning that simplicity is essential to elegance: a vanity whose empire is as large as the table; a vanity which collects all its praise from sordid appetite; a vanity which, while it entertains the body of a visiter, generally starves the mind. The Shunamite discovered much more good sense than Martha on a similar occasion. She wished to entertain Elisha; but she considered character; she would not even suppose that a prophet of the Lord required splendour or luxury; she therefore said unto her husband, "Behold now, I perceive that this is an holy man of God which passeth by us continually. Let us make a little chamber, I pray thee, on the wall; and let us set for him there a bed and a table, and a stool, and a candlestick; and it shall be when he cometh to us, that he shall turn in hither." But

Martha, instead of a plain repast, "was cumbered about much serving;" and was all anxiety to furnish an entertainment, which while it was rendered unnecessary by the plainness and piety of the visitants, allowed her no degree of leisure, and engrossed all her time and attention. Thus she deprived herself of an opportunity to hear our Saviour's discourse. This she should have prized. He was no ordinary teacher: his stay was not likely to be of long continuance; she knew not when the blessing would come again in her way.

This was not all. She rudely breaks in upon the devotion of the company, interrupts our Lord's discourse, condemns her sister as idle, and tries to involve our Saviour in the quarrel: "Lord, dost thou not care that my sister hath left me to serve alone? Bid her therefore that she help me." Here we see ill humour, fretfulness. She is "troubled about many things;" and in her haste and heat, she loses the command of her temper and the government of her tongue.

But behold Mary. All reverence, all attention, all composure, feeding on the doctrine of eternal life—she "sat at his feet." She wisely and zealously improved the opportunity given her for the good of her soul. "This is my summer, my harvest; let me redeem the time."

It must have distressed Mary to hear her sister so passionately complain of her; and many a one in her circumstances would have replied, "Why could she not have called me aside, and have spoken to me alone? Why expose me before the whole house? If I have not been so attentive to other things, surely the occasion will plead some excuse." But not a word of this nature. The calm silence of this good woman seems to say, "I leave my defence to him. 'He is near that justifieth me.'" Nor was she mistaken. He more than vindicates;—he applauds her preference: and tells Martha that he will not comply with her demand, to send Mary to her assistance, but will suffer her to remain listening at his feet, and still enjoying the privilege she had chosen. It is the meaning of his declaration when he said; "Martha, Martha, thou art careful and troubled about many things: but one thing is needful: and Mary hath chosen that good part, which shall not be taken away from her."

But what is here said of a particular instance of pious disposition will apply to religion at large. To render this passage of Scripture therefore more generally useful, let me call upon you,

I. To CONSIDER THE DILIGENCE OF THE SAVIOUR IN THE IMPROVEMENT OF TIME. He goes about doing good. His lips drop as the honeycomb. He always pays for his entertainment. In the parlour as well as the temple, he furnishes admonition and counsel

No sooner does he enter this house than we find him teaching.

Let us follow his example. Ministers should not be backward to speak unless before large and public assemblies. The Apostles, like their Saviour, not only taught publicly, but from house to house. Christians should labour to be useful wherever they are: every place, every company should be the better for them. They should render friendly, and even ordinary visits edifying. Religion is not to be confined to the Church or the Sabbath. It is not to be a dress, which you may assume or lay aside at pleasure: it is a nature; a life. It is to keep us "in the fear of the Lord all the day long:" to enter business with us; to attend us in all our common actions; and to teach us that "whether we eat or drink, or whatever we do, we should do it to the glory of God." Hence we are commanded to "comfort one another; to exhort one another; to provoke one another to love, and to good works, and—so much the more as we see the day approaching." But, alas! who does not stand reproved and condemned? "Are we not carnal, and walk as men?" Do we "redeem the time because the days are evil?" Does "no communication proceed out of our mouth, but such as is good to the use of edifying, that it may minister grace to the hearers?" Shall "vain words never have an end!"—"A word fitly spoken, how good is it! it is like apples of gold in pictures of silver!"

II. OBSERVE HOW IMPROPER IT IS FOR A FOLLOWER OF THE LORD JESUS TO BE SENSUAL AND SELFISH. Mary who hears his word pleases him better than Martha who prepares his meal: yea, Martha even grieves him by her assiduity to entertain him. He would rather feed than be fed. He pleased not himself. He shunned every kind of self-indulgence. He "came not to be ministered unto, but to minister, and to give his life a ransom for many." And calling ourselves by his name, are we fanciful? are we finical? are we fond of giving trouble? are we slaves to our appetites? are we desirous of dainty meat? "He that saith he abideth in him, ought himself also to walk even as he walked. They that are Christ's have crucified the flesh, with the affections and lusts."

Especially should ministers be like-minded with their Lord and Master. They often at least occasion excess, and draw upon themselves reflection. The preparations made to receive them would imply a fondness for extravagance, variety, delicacy. Let them attest their innocency. Let them show their people that they seek not theirs but them. Let them, by their words and actions, discountenance parade and excess. Are circumstances of this kind beneath our attention? Is it not one of the lessons which the passage before us is designed to teach? When our Saviour sent forth his Apostles, did not his admonitions turn principally upon this subject? For things in themselves of unequal importance with others, become weighty by their connexions, their influence, their indications. A feather, or a straw, may serve to discover the direction of the wind, as well as a tree. What a fatal secret does that preacher betray who shows that he minds earthly things!

III. WE SEE WHAT DIVERSITIES THERE ARE IN THE FOLLOWERS OF OUR LORD. Even the good ground brought forth in various proportion—thirty—sixty—an hundred fold. What a difference was there between the faith of the Centurion and of Thomas! Abraham and Lot were both righteous, but how imperfect does the nephew appear compared with the uncle!

Many things diversify the degree and the exercises of religion. Thus the stations in which Providence places good men differ; one shall be favourable to devotion, another shall afford less leisure and create more distraction. Constitutional complexion also has its influence. Thus some Christians are more inclined to contemplation and the shades; others are formed for the active virtues. The difficulties which chill the timid serve only to rouse and animate the bold and courageous. Religion, like water, partakes a little of the nature of the soil over which it runs. The very same truth was revealed both to Nebuchadnezzar and Daniel—the succession of the four monarchies. Nebuchadnezzar was a king and a conqueror; and admired things in proportion to their worldly grandeur. Accordingly he viewed these empires as an image whose brightness was excellent, the head of which was fine gold, and the subordinate parts of inferior metal. Daniel was a man of peace and of wisdom: and to him they appeared "as four great beasts, coming out of the sea, diverse from each other: the first a lion with wings; the second a bear with three ribs in its mouth; the third a leopard with four wings of a fowl, and four heads; and the fourth dreadful and terrible, with iron teeth." Take an illustration from it. Imagine four persons—one phlegmatic, another choleric, a third sanguine, and the fourth melancholic—drop religious truth into each of these—and do you suppose that it will not receive a tinge from each peculiar temperament? In all these cases something of the original character will remain. And I always view it as a considerable evidence of sincerity when religion, if I may use the expression, acts naturally; it shows that people are off their guard; that they have not a particular part given them to act. For were this the case, they would resemble one another much more nearly; and a dull constrained uniformity would prevail. Thus it is with pretenders. If a man of humour professes religion without possessing it, he will keep a check upon himself, and by means of this, appear grave and formal: but if he be really a partaker of religion, we should expect that his natural character will commonly show itself even in his duties; it will indeed be regulated, but not destroyed.

IV. WE MAY MEET WITH HINDERANCES IN RELIGION FROM THOSE WHO SHOULD BE OUR ASSISTANTS. Such are friends and relations. A wife should cherish good impressions, fan the flame of devotion, and be a helper to her husband in spiritual as well as in temporal concerns—but she may prove a seducer: she may lead him into vanity and the dissipations of the world. Michal ridicules the holy joy of David. A brother may discourage a brother. A sister may reproach and repel a sister. Our foes may be those of our own household.

Yea, even by religious friends and relations we may sometimes be injured. Instead of making straight paths for our feet, they may throw stumblingblocks in our way. They may press "hard sayings" before the mind is prepared to receive them. They may discourage us by their expressions of assurance and ecstasy. They may be wanting in sympathy. They may censure and condemn our actions from ignorance of our circumstances and motives.

V. How ANXIOUS SOEVER WE MAY BE ABOUT MANY THINGS, ONE THING ALONE REALLY DESERVES OUR ATTENTION:—"one thing is needful." It is hearing the Saviour's words; it is an attention to the soul; it is—RELIGION. What! is nothing else necessary? Yes; many things. But compared with this, they are less than nothing and vanity. Other things are accidentally needful—this is essentially so. Other things are occasionally needful—this is invariably so. Other things are partially needful—this is universally so —needful for prosperity and adversity; needful for the body and the soul; needful for time and eternity. Some things are needful for some individuals, but not for others; but this is needful for all: needful for kings and subjects; needful for rich and poor; needful for old and young.

If indeed we judge of it by the people of the world, we shall not think so when we look around us. The many seem to be prizing and pursuing every thing in preference to this. Instead of viewing it as essential to man, they seem only to regard it as a circumstance of his being and his welfare, which may safely be dispensed with. But let us take the testimony of God. What saith the Scripture? "Wisdom is the principal thing therefore get wisdom: and with all thy getting get understanding. Let us hear the conclusion of the whole matter: fear God, and keep his commandments; for this is the whole duty of man." Yes, says the Saviour, "One thing is needful." Hence we find David and Paul reducing every concern into one. "ONE thing have I desired of the Lord, that will I seek after; that I may dwell in the house of the Lord all the days of my life, to behold the beauty of the Lord, and to inquire in his temple." "This ONE thing I do: forgetting those things which are behind, and reaching forth unto those things which are before."

Finally. It is worthy of our remark, that REAL GODLINESS IS NOT ONLY A NECESSARY, BUT A DURABLE ACQUISITION. "Mary hath chosen that good part, which shall not be taken away from her." Permanency adds bliss to bliss. Some things are not worth preservation; but an invaluable treasure, a thing absolutely needful, will awaken all our concern, and we shall be anxious not only to possess it, but also to retain it.

And what a difference is there in this view, between religion and other advantages! Nothing that we here possess can be called our own. What we acquire with so much difficulty it is impossible to secure. If we choose honours, riches, pleasures, friendships, they will be sure to fail us, and to fail us often when we most need their aid. But the blessings we derive from godliness are our own for ever. They are not liable to those numberless accidents which so easily deprive us of earthly possessions. No violence, no fraud, can rob us of them. "Our joy no man taketh from us." Our treasure "moth and rust cannot corrupt, nor thieves break through and steal." Even the desolations of death, which strip us of every thing else, cannot touch the believer's portion: he can carry all his goods along with him into another world, where they will be for ever increasing. It is "an inheritance incorruptible, and undefiled, and that fadeth not away."

Surely religion is wisdom—and "wisdom is justified of all her children."

This review should therefore more than satisfy those who, like Mary, *have* chosen this good part. Your choice will bear reconsideration. The more you examine it, the more worthy of all your regard will it appear. Be not ashamed to own it. Let religion be your boast, as well as your comfort. What is there to excite a blush! What, in importance and continuance, are the pursuits and acquisitions of the most admired of your fellow-creatures, compared with yours!

It should also influence those who have *not* made it. And oh that I could induce you to decide, and to decide *this evening!* I say, this evening, because you are not sure of another season. I say, this evening, because every delay adds to the difficulty of your choice. I say, this evening, because there is nothing so urgent; nothing that can equally claim or reward your attention.

Should you be induced to neglect this great salvation, what will be your reflections in a dying hour, and before the bar of God! What will you think in endless misery of those follies and vanities for which you sacrificed eternal life! "What is a man profited if he gain the whole world, and lose his own soul? or what shall a man give in exchange for his soul?"

He who approved and applauded Mary's choice is here this evening to witness yours. He sees you, he hears you; he is waiting to be gracious, and exalted to have mercy upon you. You must sit at his feet as a disciple, or be made his footstool as an enemy. What is the choice you intend to make! "I call heaven and earth to record this day against you, that I have set before you life and death, blessing and cursing: therefore choose life, that both thou and thy seed may live."

DISCOURSE XLII.

GOD ABANDONS THE INCORRIGIBLE.

Ephraim is joined to idols: let him alone.
Hos. iv. 17.

NOTHING seems so absurd as idolatry. How surprising is it that a man should make a figure with his own hands, and then fall down and adore it! How wonderful is it that a being endued with reason, should worship reptiles and even vegetables! Nevertheless, this was the case for ages. "They changed the glory of the incorruptible God into an image made like to corruptible man, and to birds, and four-footed beasts, and creeping things——they changed the truth of God into a lie, and worshipped and served the creature more than the Creator who is blessed for ever."

Let us rejoice that the darkness is past, and that the true light now shineth. It is our privilege to live in a land of vision, where we are informed of a Being who made all things by the word of his power; who possesses unbounded excellences; and who deserves our supreme devotion. We know God; but, alas! we do not glorify him as God. Every unregenerate sinner is a little pagan world in himself: he has his gods, his temples, his altars, his sacrifices. And as the Jews of old were more criminal in their idolatry than the heathens, because they were favoured with a revelation of the only living and true God—so it is with those who call themselves Christians: their sin is increased by the means they possess of knowing and serving him.

What! you say, would you prove Christians to be idolaters!—Why not?—What is idolatry? Is it not the transferring to the Creator? If therefore we love or fear any thing more than God; if we make it our portion, and de-

pend upon it for our happiness, we are chargeable with idolatry.

What do you think of the man who is more ambitious to obtain the applause of dying worms than "the honour that cometh from God only?"—He is an idolater.

What do you think of the man who devotes himself to the lower gratifications of sense, or the more refined dissipations of fashion, and "loves pleasure more than God?"—He is an idolater.

What do you think of the man whose thoughts and affections daily encircle the throne of mammon; whose earth-born soul cannot pass by a particle of shining dust without kneeling and praying; who, to acquire it, rises and grinds the faces of the poor, and transgresses the laws of God; whose highest aim, and whose only business is to amass his thousands?—Such a man, to use the words of Job, "says to gold, Thou art my hope; and to fine gold, Thou art my confidence." "His wealth," says Solomon, "is his strong city, and as an high wall in his own conceit." "He trusts," says the Apostle, "in uncertain riches." The covetous man therefore is expressly called "an idolater," and stands in this book "excluded from the kingdom of God."

Nations who depend for their protection and prosperity upon navies, armies, commerce,—and forget God—are idolaters. And families are idolaters who suspend their subsistence and welfare upon one individual, and suppose that if he were removed their eye could "no more see good."

All this is "trusting in man and making flesh our arm;" and in proportion as we do this, "the heart departeth from the Lord." And this is the essence of man's apostacy. Something besides God has his admiration and attachment, his hope and dependence; and whatever this be, whether an image or an angel, it is, in the language of Scripture, "an idol."

Men may pretend to regard God, and to adore their idols too; but this is pronounced to be impossible. "No man can serve two masters: for either he will hate the one, and love the other; or else he will hold to the one, and despise the other. Ye cannot serve God and mammon." "Ye adulterers and adulteresses! know ye not that the friendship of the world is enmity with God? whosoever therefore will be a friend of the world is the enemy of God. Love not the world, neither the things that are in the world. If any man love the world, the love of the Father is not in him."

They may not adore the same idols with others, for their dispositions and circumstances are various; and they may sometimes change their idols. But while any thing detains the heart from God, the man is in a state of perdition. And such is the infatuation of the sinner, that though always deceived and often confounded, he still goes on; he holds fast deceit; and refuses to return—till God rising in displeasure resolves to abandon him—and cries—"He is joined to idols—let him alone."

There is something in this declaration uncommonly dreadful. And this will appear—

First, if you DISTINGUISH THIS DESERTION FROM ANOTHER, WHICH MAY BEFALL EVEN THE SUBJECTS OF DIVINE GRACE. Of this God speaks when he says, "I will go and return to my place till they acknowledge their offence and seek my face: in their affliction they will seek me early." Thus God sometimes leaves his people when they are becoming high-minded, to convince them of their dependence upon him. He leaves them to their own strength to show them their weakness; and to their own wisdom to make them sensible of their ignorance. By their embarrassments they are soon made to feel how unable they are to manage their own affairs; and no longer exercise themselves in great matters, or in things too high for them. Thus, to convince the child who is regardless of your counsel that it is not safe for him to go without your guiding and sustaining hand, you leave him where the danger is not great, or where you could seize him as he falls—though you would not say, "let him alone," if you saw him climbing up a ladder, or crossing a deep river on a narrow plank.

Thus God may leave his people—but this differs exceedingly from the abandoning of the incorrigible. The one is from love; the other is from wrath. The one is the trial of wisdom, varying its means; the other is the decision of justice, after means have been used in vain. The one is to reform, the other is to destroy. The one is partial; and always leaves something of God behind, which will urge us to seek after him: the other is total and final.

Consider, Secondly, that THIS LEAVING OF THE SINNER IS A WITHDRAWING FROM HIM EVERY THING THAT HAS A TENDENCY TO DO HIM GOOD.—"Let him alone."

Ministers! "Let him alone." He has complained of your fidelity. He has called you the troublers of Israel. Disturb him no more.

Saints! "Let him alone." Withdraw your intercourse. Cease your reproofs.

Thou all quickening word! "Let him alone." Rise not up in his remembrance. Place before him no promises to invite, nor threatenings to alarm.

Conscience, thou internal monitor! "Let him alone." Before the commission of sin—never warn: and after the commission of sin—never condemn. Let him enjoy his crimes. Never mention a judgment to come. Never let him hear that the end of these things is death. Never try to refute those false reasonings by which he would reconcile his creed to his practice.

Providence! "Let him alone." Ye afflictions, say nothing to him of the vanity of the world. Let all his schemes be completely successful. Let his grounds bring forth plentifully. Let him have more than heart can wish.

Does the judge order a man to be scourged, who is going to be executed?—Does the father correct the child that he has determined to disinherit?—Is the tree pruned and manured after it is ordered to be cut down, and the axe is even at the root?

Take a third view of this dreadful sentence—Consider THE IMPORTANCE OF THE BEING WHO THUS ABANDONS. It would be much better if all your friends and neighbours; if all your fellow-creatures, on whom you depend for assistance in a thousand ways, were to league together, and resolve to have nothing to do with you—than for God to leave you, "in whom you live, and move, and have your being." Oh! to be abandoned by him in whose favour is life—to hear him say, As for the others, I will teach them, but I will not teach thee; I will sanctify them, but I will not sanctify thee—thee I disown!—Oh! if the God of mercy will have nothing to do with us, who will! If the God of patience cannot bear with us, who can!

While God is with us, we can spare other things. While passing through the water and through the fire, if he be with us we need fear no evil. Yea, under the most distressing revolutions in our own affairs, and in the world around us—it is enough, if we can sing with the Church, "The Lord of hosts is with us, the God of Jacob is our refuge."

But what is every thing else without God! —how lamentable was the speech of Saul "I am sore distressed, for the Philistines make war against me, and God is departed from me!" When the enemy is approaching; when the day of death draws nigh—and you have no God!—every creature to whom you call for assistance will reply, with the king to the woman, "If the Lord do not help thee, whence shall I help thee!" When he goes, away goes all our protection, and our blessedness, and our hope. Well therefore did he say of old—"Wo unto them when I depart from them!"

For, Finally, consider WHAT WILL BE THE CONSEQUENCE OF THIS DETERMINATION. It will be a freedom to sin; it will be the removal of every hinderance in the way to perdition; and thus give the unhappy wretch an unchecked passage along the road to hell. When God dismisses a man, and resolves he shall have no more assistance from him—he is sure of being ensnared by error, enslaved by lust, and "led captive by the devil at his will," down to the regions of everlasting wo!

For what would be the consequence of saying to a blind man approaching a precipice —Let him alone! What would be the consequence of saying to a man asleep while the house is in flames—Let him alone! Their destruction. And so it is here. We are such poor insufficient creatures, that it is not necessary for God to *do* any thing—he has only to let us alone. It is not necessary for him to strike a blow—the disease is undermining our frame. We have taken poison, and all that is necessary to its killing us is not to counteract its malignity.

Such is the judgment here denounced. Let us conclude by remarking,

First, The justice of this doom. Why does he say, "Let him alone!"—Because "he is joined to idols." "My people would not hearken unto my voice; and Israel would none of me: so I gave them up unto their own hearts' lust: and they walked in their own counsels." All the punishments he inflicts are deserved; and he never inflicts them without reluctance. "O that my people had hearkened unto me, and Israel had walked in my ways! O that thou hadst hearkened unto my commandments! then had thy peace been as a river, and thy righteousness as the waves of the sea."—But may not God abandon those who have renounced him! Is he compelled to force his favours upon us! Has his patience no bounds! Is he not righteous, as well as gracious! Is there mercy with him that he may be feared! —or insulted!

Your condemnation entirely turns upon a principle that will at once justify *him* and silence *you.* "Ye *will not* come to me that ye might have life. Because I have called, and ye have refused; I have stretched out my hand, and no man regarded; but ye have set at nought all my counsel, and would none of my reproof: I also will laugh at your calamity; I will mock when your fear cometh; when your fear cometh as desolation, and your destruction cometh as a whirlwind; when distress and anguish cometh upon you. Then shall they call upon me, but I will not answer; they shall seek me early, but they shall not find me: for that they hated knowledge, and did not choose the fear of the Lord: they would none of my counsel: they despised all my reproof. Therefore shall they eat of the fruit of their own way, and be filled with their own devices."

Secondly. Let me call upon you to fear this judgment. And surely some of you have reason to be alarmed. With some of you the Spirit of God has long been striving. You have had a pious education. You have heard the admonitions of friends. You have seen good examples. You have attended the preaching of the Gospel, and have sometimes been deeply affected, and sometimes even compelled to pray. And after all this you turned again to folly; and have "done despite unto the Spirit of grace."

Now you know what he has said. "He that being often reproved hardeneth his neck shall suddenly be destroyed, and that without remedy." And you know what he has done. You know that, provoked by the continual rebellions of Israel, "he sware in his wrath that they should not enter into his rest." And you know the master of the feast, incensed by the ungrateful refusal of his kind invitations, gave his servants a new commission, and said, "none of the men that were bidden shall taste of my supper." And what if after all your disobedience and perverseness he should say this of you! What if remaining the same after all the methods employed for your conversion, he should say, "He that is unjust, let him be unjust still; and he that is filthy, let him be filthy still!"—"He is joined to idols: let him alone."

If you say you have no forebodings of this, the symptoms are so much the worse. Spiritual judgments are the most awful, because they are insensibly executed. It is a principal part of them to take away feeling; to lull us to sleep in the very lap that kills; to make us cry, Peace, peace, when destruction is coming upon us; to dispose us to embrace error easily; and to delude us so strongly as to believe a lie.

Thirdly. Perhaps some of you are saying, "I am afraid this is my doom already. My convictions seem to have been stifled. The serious impressions I once experienced are worn off—nothing seems to do me any good— I derive no advantage from the Sabbath—or the word."

Perhaps this is true. And if so, God forbid that I should say any thing to hinder or weaken your alarm. If any thing can save, it must begin with this reasonable and salutary terror.

But it may be also a groundless apprehension. And should this be the case, as the most safe are always the most anxious, I would observe—First, that this fear is a good sign that he has not *yet* said this. Secondly, that it will be a good means to keep him from *ever* saying it. Thirdly, to use the words of an old writer, it is a blessed proof that God does not let you alone, if you cannot let him alone; but continue to pray; and though discouraged by delays, "wait for him more than they that watch for the morning; I say, more than they that watch for the morning."

And if this be not your unhappy case, be thankful; and cheerfully acquiesce in his dealings with you. Christians! he who has given you so many proofs of his care will never leave you nor forsake you. His eye is upon the righteous. His ear is open unto their cry. All his saints are in his hands. He will guide them with his counsel, and afterwards receive them to glory. Perhaps many things have been taken away—but he has not withdrawn himself. Perhaps you have been left alone of friends and relations—but with the Saviour you can say, I am not alone: because the Father is with me.

Do not therefore groan under your exercises—if I am his, why am I thus? You are thus because you are his. He chastens you because he loves you. He will not let you alone because you are not bastards, but sons! He destroys the cisterns to bring you nearer to himself—the fountain of living waters. He hedges up your way with thorns, that you may not pursue those paths which lead you astray from him, your "exceeding joy."

And rather than you should stop short of the prize of your high calling; rather than you should sit down satisfied with a portion in this world—he will spoil your prospects—turn every pleasure into a pain—and imbitter or dry up every spring of comfort.

Heavenly Father! who knowest what things we have need of before we ask thee, express thy concern in what way thou pleasest; but never treat me with neglect! Chide me if I err; take peace from me when I sin; fill me with painful reflections and apprehensions when the world is drawing me away from thee; but never—never say—"He is joined to idols: LET HIM ALONE!"

DISCOURSE XLIII.

THE ASCENSION OF OUR SAVIOUR.

Go to my brethren, and say unto them, I ascend unto my Father, and your Father; and to my God, and your God.—John xx. 17.

IT is not necessary to inquire—Whose language is this? No sooner do we hear it than we exclaim, with one of his followers on another occasion—"It is the Lord!"

The words are addressed to Mary Magdalene, as a reward for her constancy in adhering so firmly to him, and for her affection in seeking so early after him. He appeared to her before he showed himself to his Apostles. The relation is singularly interesting. But we have only to remark, that she was so transported with the sight of her Lord and Saviour, that she was going to embrace his feet and bedew them with tears of joy. But he said unto her, "'Touch me not; for I am not yet ascended to my Father'—but shall soon; and there is no time to lose—private satisfaction is to be relinquished for public service—I employ you immediately as my herald; what you have seen I wish others to hear—use no delay; but 'go to my brethren, and say unto them, I ascend unto my Father, and your Father; and to my God, and your God.'"

There are two things in the words which require our attention. I. THE PERSONS TO WHOM THE MESSAGE IS ADDRESSED. II. THE SUBSTANCE OF THE INTELLIGENCE.

I. It may be asked—Why was not this information sent to the scribes and pharisees and chief priests? Why did he not thus convince his enemies, and render his resurrection undeniable? Because—"whosoever hath, to him shall be given, and he shall have more abundance; but whosoever hath not, from him shall be taken away even that he hath. The meek will he guide in judgment, and the meek will he teach his way. The secret of the Lord is with them that fear him; and he will show them his covenant." He never refused explanation to any humble inquirer—but he was surely not obliged to force information upon those that "hated knowledge." To what purpose is it to adduce evidence to those that shut their eyes and will not see? They had seen him heal the sick with a touch, and raise the dead with a word. They knew the report of the guards, and had given them money to propagate a known falsehood, "saying, his disciples came by night and stole him away while we slept."

But his own followers only laboured under infirmities. They loved him, and had forsaken all to attend him. They wished to be established in the truth; they were willing to come to the light, and had doubtless been praying, "That which I see not, teach thou me." And, "then shall we know if we follow on to know the Lord: his going forth is prepared as the morning: and he shall come unto us as the rain, as the latter and former rain unto the earth." And thus enlightening, and thus refreshing was this message to the perplexed and desponding disciples.

But what I wished to observe here was not only his sending this message exclusively to his disciples, but also his addressing them under a particular name—"my brethren." This is more than he could have said of angels. He is only their Lord; but he is our brother. "He took not on him the nature of angels, but he took on him the seed of Abraham." Thus he is "bone of our bone, and flesh of our flesh." "Both he that sanctifieth, and they who are sanctified, are all of one; for which cause he is not ashamed to call them brethren, saying, I will declare thy name unto my brethren, in the midst of the church will I sing praises unto thee. Wherefore in all things it behoved him to be made like unto his brethren; that he might be a merciful and faithful high priest in things pertaining to God, to make reconciliation for the sins of the people." Many an elder brother has stood between the affections of the father and the rest of the children, by engrossing the whole of the inheritance has reduced the younger branches to dependence, if not to want; but Jesus pitied those who were less happy than himself, pleaded for them, shared with them in all their miseries, and determined to make them partakers of all his honours and riches. Thus they have fellowship with him; they are "heirs of God, and joint heirs with Jesus Christ."

By using this name he would show that his elevation had not made him forgetful of those he was to leave behind. Though he was now rich, and they were poor; though he had now a glorious body, and they were groaning under the burden of the flesh; though he had now all power in heaven and in earth, and they were weak, despised, and persecuted—he calls them brethren. Yea, he will not be ashamed to do this even in the great day when he shall sit upon the throne of his glory, and before him shall be gathered all nations. In the presence of men, of angels, and of God, he will say, "Inasmuch as ye have done it unto one of the least of these my brethren, ye have done it unto me."

His addressing them in this message, as brethren, would comfort his disciples. One had denied him; the rest had forsaken him and fled. They had acted a very unworthy part, and their consciences made them uneasy. And had they heard only of his resurrection, it would have filled them not merely with surprise, but with terror; and afraid of his rebukes they would have hid themselves from him rather than have approached him. When therefore he sends them word that he is risen from the dead, he calls them " brethren; and by this he seems to extend his arms to embrace them again; by this he seems to call after them, and say, " ' Return, ye backsliding children ;' I am ready to pity the weak, and to pardon the penitent." Thus he dispels their anxiety, and fills them with hope. And thus he realizes his illustrious type when he made himself known to those who had treated him with baseness and cruelty. Joseph saw what confusion, and anguish, and dread, the discovery of himself had produced in those who were now in his power, and at his mercy; and therefore with his name he is eager to mention his relation, and to give them encouragement to trust in him. " He said unto his brethren, I am Joseph; doth my father yet live ? And his brethren could not answer him; for they were troubled at his presence. And Joseph said unto his brethren, Come near to me, I pray you. And they came near. And he said, I am Joseph your BROTHER, whom ye sold into Egypt. Now therefore be not grieved, nor angry with yourselves, that ye sold me hither: for God did send me before you to preserve life."

And did not our Lord, by using this endearing name in these circumstances, convey to them an intimation of duty ? "Since I do not disown the relation in which you stand to me; since I acknowledge you as brethren notwithstanding your imperfections, follow my example; acknowledge each other as brethren; 'love as brethren; let there be no strife between you, for ye are brethren.' Disclaim me for your brother, or receive as such every follower of mine. Whether strong in the faith or weak; whether young men or babes—they all stand in the same relation to me, and in the same relation to you."

II. Hence he adds, "Go to my brethren, and—say unto them, I ascend unto my Father, and your Father; and to my God, and your God."—LET US TAKE SOME VIEWS OF THIS INTERESTING INTELLIGENCE.

It may be necessary to premise that this ascension was real and local. He had a body, and this he assured his disciples after his resurrection, had flesh and bones, and could not only be seen, but touched and handled. With this he ascended. Heaven therefore is a place, as well as a state; his body cannot be every where; but wherever it be, there is heaven, at least—there is the Christian's heaven. Let us now consider this ascension —in reference to HIMSELF—HIS ENEMIES—and HIS PEOPLE.

If we view it in reference to HIMSELF, we may observe—that in ascending he returned to the place whence he came, and assumed the glory which he had laid aside, or rather obscured. Did you never observe with what ease and freedom from surprise he always spoke of heaven? Prophets and Apostles seemed to labour for expressions when they spoke of it—to them heaven was new as well as vast; but *He* speaks of it familiarly —as one to whom there was nothing in it novel or wonderful. And this *was* the case. He *was* the Prince of heaven—and the palace was only his home. "What," says he, "and if ye shall see the Son of man ascending up where he was before !—I have glorified thee on the earth : I have finished the work which thou gavest me to do. And now, O Father, glorify thou me with thine own self, with the glory which I had with thee before the world was."

He also ascended to enjoy the reward of his humiliation and sufferings. For our sakes he became poor. He was born in a stable, and laid in a manger. As he grew up he appeared "a man of sorrows and acquainted with grief." After a life of contradiction and anguish, he "became obedient unto death, even the death of the cross. Wherefore God also hath highly exalted him, and given him a name which is above every name." His humiliation and death are not to be opposed to his glory—they were the road that led to it. There was "a joy set before him, for which he endured the cross, despising the shame :" and what he died to procure he now ascends to possess. What a change in his condition ! Ye who have sympathized with him in the garden, come rejoice with him upon the throne. "He dieth no more : death hath no more dominion over him." The head that once wore a "crown of thorns," is now "crowned with glory and honour !"—The hands once nailed to a tree now wield the sceptre of universal empire. And he who was once surrounded by blaspheming men is now worshipped by all the angels in heaven !

We may consider the ascension of our Lord in reference to his ENEMIES. Thus he is a conqueror. He had foes, but he vanquished them; "and having spoiled principalities and powers, he made a show of them openly." "He triumphed over them." It was customary for a Roman general, after a successful and glorious termination of a war, to return to the capital of his country. This he entered in triumph. He rode in a lofty car. Some of the spoils were suspended from on high. A number of the captives were fastened to the axle-tree of the chariot wheels. Myriads gazed and shouted; while the conqueror scattered largesses among the admiring and applauding multitude.

Behold the triumph of our Redeemer! "Thou hast ascended on high, thou hast led captivity captive: thou hast received gifts for men: yea, for the rebellious also, that the Lord God might dwell among them." He has conquered the conquerors, and bound those who had enslaved us. Sin, the devil, the world, death—these are the enemies he has overcome. And to-day he enjoys his triumph. "Lift up your heads, O ye gates; and be ye lift up, ye everlasting doors; and the King of glory shall come in. Who is this King of glory? The Lord strong and mighty, the Lord mighty in battle. Lift up your heads, O ye gates; even lift them up, ye everlasting doors; and the King of glory shall come in. Who is this King of glory? The Lord of hosts, he is the King of glory. God is gone up with a shout, the Lord with the sound of a trumpet. Sing praises to God, sing praises: sing praises unto our King, sing praises."

O Christians! what have you to fear? You behold your chief in triumph, and your enemies in chains. We can easily imagine how a Roman could fear the enemy while they waged the war, and before the victory was obtained—but would he tremble, think you, when he saw these foes defeated, spoiled, and exposed to view, to prove the reality of their subjection? What emotions were excited in all parts of England, through which the Spaniards were led, after the destruction of their invincible armada, and when the instruments of their cruelty were carried along with them! How fearless of enemies now taken captive—what joy at having escaped from their teeth! And shall not we rejoice in him who has "saved us from our

enemies, and from the hand of them that hate us?" How certainly would they, and how nearly had they proved our destruction!

But as he triumphs, he also bestows upon us various and inestimable blessings. "Wherefore he saith, when he ascended up on high, he led captivity captive, and gave gifts unto men. And he gave some, apostles; and some, prophets; and some, evangelists; and some, pastors and teachers; for the perfecting of the saints, for the work of the ministry, for the edifying of the body of Christ." There is another gift, without which we should still have perished, and this also descends from a glorified Saviour. "Therefore, being by the right hand of God exalted, and having received of the Father the promise of the Holy Ghost, he hath shed forth this which ye now see and hear." He hath said to his disciples, "Nevertheless I tell you the truth; it is expedient for you that I go away: for if I go not away, the Comforter will not come unto you; but if I depart, I will send him unto you." This promise was soon fulfilled, not only in miraculous, but also in saving and sanctifying operations; and continues to be accomplished in the enlightening, conversion, and establishment of every real believer.

But this has led us to anticipate the Third view we are to take of the Saviour's ascension. It regards his PEOPLE.

And thus he ascended as the High Priest of their profession. "If he were on the earth," says the Apostle, "he should not be a priest." He means that had he continued here, he could not have completely fulfilled the office that typified him. To understand this, it is necessary to observe, that the high priest was not only to offer sacrifice: when he had slain the atoning victim, he took the blood into the holy place, and sprinkled it upon the mercy-seat, and also burned incense. Whether on this occasion he used any words we are not informed—but the action spake loud enough. Thus Jesus having suffered on earth, produces and pleads his sufferings in heaven: "Christ being come an high priest of good things to come, by a greater and more perfect tabernacle, not made with hands, that is to say, not of this building; neither by the blood of goats and calves, but by his own blood he entered in once into the holy place, having obtained eternal redemption for us. For Christ is not entered into the holy places made with hands, which are the figures of the true; but into heaven itself, now to appear in the presence of God for us." There he maintains our cause; there, as our intercessor, he offers much incense with the prayers of all the saints, and obtains for us both the acceptance of our persons and services. "Wherefore he is able also to save them to the uttermost that come unto God by him, seeing he ever liveth to make intercession for them.

U

Who is he that condemneth? It is Christ that died, yea, rather that is risen again, who is even at the right hand of God, who also maketh intercession for us." How eloquent are his wounds! How vocal is his sacrifice! "Blood of sprinkling, which speaketh better things than that of Abel!" speak not only to God, but to our souls, that hearing thy voice we may enter into rest; and, though unworthy and imperfect in all our duties, we may have "boldness and access with confidence, by the faith of thee!"

He ascended as their head and representative. Two characters had ascended before, Enoch and Elias. But they ascended as private individuals; and it did not follow because they ascended, that others would ascend too: they were not so connected with others as to move them by their influence. But he attracts, he draws millions. His glory is the pledge of our own. By virtue of an intimate and inseparable union which no event can destroy, no distance can weaken—because he lives, we shall live also. He is the master, and we are the servants; he is the head, and we are the body. We are therefore said to be "raised up and made to sit together with him in heavenly places." The apostle, speaking of the Christian's hope, says, "Which hope we have as an anchor of the soul both sure and steadfast, and which entereth into that within the vail; whither the forerunner is for us entered, even Jesus, made an high priest for ever after the order of Melchisedec." You see even heaven would be no refuge for us, if he were not there. When our hope penetrates heaven, there is nothing on which our hope can fix but himself. But he has entered, and not for himself only but for us—to procure a passage—to prepare a place for us—and to insure our following after. When he entered his glory he opened the kingdom of heaven to all believers. And the gates he left open—saying, "More are coming. I am only the forerunner of a 'multitude which no man can number, out of all nations, and kindreds, and people, and tongues.' I saw them loosening from the world and asking for a better country. Some were coming from agreeable scenes, and many from great tribulation. They are now upon the road, at unequal distances. I have made provision for their guidance and safety, and here in due time will they all arrive."

He ascended as their protector and governor. "He that descended is the same also that ascended up far above all heavens that he might fill all things." His situation and capacity are sufficient to relieve all the wants, and accomplish all the hopes of those that are under his care. He has universal sovereignty and boundless resources—and he has all this for them. "He is head over all things unto his body the Church." Their

present and everlasting welfare is secured; since he has all creatures under his control, and can make all things work together for their good?

And now what remains but that we translate this article of our creed into our lives, express his government in our subjection, and by being the most obedient of all servants, declare him to be the greatest of all masters?

And First, follow him where he now is. "If ye then be risen with Christ, seek those things which are above, where Christ sitteth on the right hand of God." Is not he your portion and your treasure? Why then are you so attached to earth? Why seek ye the living among the dead? "He is not here: he is risen; he is ascended." Far above this vain world is your Saviour and your exceeding joy. How strange is it that you do not more long to depart to be with him! When a most beloved friend has removed from you to a distant part of the kingdom, has it not weakened your attachment to your own situation, and made you think much of his? You have buried a relation; you have a child in heaven. How you follow him thither in your thoughts and desires! You have something to render heaven more endearing and attractive. And oh! how much less has the world to charm and to chain you! But the body is deposited in yonder grave—thither you go—feel an interest, and claim a property in the dust—this was—it is—mine. But nothing of the Saviour remains here—Not even his dust—for he saw not corruption: his body forsook the tomb, and was "received up into glory." Away then from earth—and follow after him to heaven.

Secondly. "Seeing that we have a great High Priest that is passed into the heavens, Jesus, the Son of God, let us hold fast our profession." Let not those who know where he is, be ashamed of their connexion with him or dependence upon him. Boldly avow his truth, and openly employ yourselves in his service. If you disown him, you are far worse than Peter. Peter denied him—but he was then at Pilate's bar, and going to be crucified. But you deny him now he is Lord of all, and coming to judge the world!

Thirdly. What encouragement can you want to rejoice in him! You have a brother at court. He says to you, as Elisha said to the Shunamite, "Wilt thou be spoken for to the king?" In every difficulty you can go to him and say, "Lord, I am oppressed; undertake for me." His ear is open to your prayer; his eye views all your walking through this great wilderness; his arms are underneath you; he will make you more than conquerors over all your enemies. And by-and-by he will "come again and receive you to himself, that where he is, there you may be also."

"But where will the ungodly and the sinner appear?" Beware of opposing. Beware of neglecting him! It is unreasonable. It is ruinous. He is now "exalted to be a Prince and a Saviour, to give repentance unto Israel, and remission of sins." If you seek him, he will be found of you. But if you make light of these things, how can you escape? Remember that he is ascended to be *your* Judge. "Behold, he cometh with clouds, and every eye shall see him. But who may abide the day of his coming, and who can stand when he appeareth?"

DISCOURSE XLIV.

THE PRAYER OF NEHEMIAH.

O Lord, I beseech thee, let now thine ear be attentive to the prayer of thy servant, and to the prayer of thy servants, who desire to fear thy name: and prosper, I pray thee, thy servant this day, and grant him mercy in the sight of this man. For I was the king's cupbearer.—Nehemiah i. 11.

THIS book partially records the history of the children of the captivity after their return from Babylon, in consequence of the decree and proclamation of Cyrus. The Persian empire now flourished in all its grandeur; and Greece and Rome were rising to eminence in the world. But "the Lord's portion is his people: Jacob is the lot of his inheritance."

We find therefore the attention of the Scripture principally confined to the Jews; and the affairs of the surrounding nations are no otherwise mentioned than as they have some connexion with the concerns of the Israel of God. And Nehemiah, in the view of the Supreme Being, was a far more illustrious character than Demosthenes the orator, Zenophon the commander, or Plato the philosopher who lived about the same time.

The eye affecteth the heart, and so does the ear. Nehemiah was at too great a distance to see the ruinous condition of Jerusalem—but he heard of it, and the effect it had upon his mind did him honour. "It came to pass in the month Chisleu, in the twentieth year, as I was in Shushan the palace, that Hanani, one of my brethren, came, he and certain men of Judah; and I asked them concerning the Jews that had escaped, which were left of the captivity, and concerning Jerusalem. And they said unto me, The remnant that are left of the captivity there in the province are in great affliction and reproach: the wall of Jerusalem also is broken down, and the gates thereof are burned with fire. And it came to pass, when I heard these words, that I sat down and wept, and mourned certain days, and fasted, and pray-

ed before the God of heaven." And thus he concludes his humiliation and devotion: "O Lord, I beseech thee, let now thine ear be attentive to the prayer of thy servant, and to the prayer of thy servants, who desire to fear thy name: and prosper, I pray thee, thy servant this day, and grant him mercy in the sight of this man. For I was the king's cupbearer." These words furnish us with the following remarks.

I. GOD HAS HIS SERVANTS IN ALL CONDITIONS AND OCCUPATIONS OF LIFE. In his Church "there is neither Jew nor Greek; there is neither bond nor free; there is neither rich nor poor." We behold Zenas the lawyer, Erastus the chamberlain, Paul the tent-maker, Luke the physician, Zaccheus the publican, Peter the fisherman, Joseph the carpenter, Amos the herdsman, Daniel the minister of state, Nehemiah the cupbearer—all standing in the same relation, swayed by the same influence, rejoicing in the same hope, and destined to live together in the same everlasting kingdom.

This is by no means a useless remark. Let it teach us two things.

First, not to condemn bodies and professions of men indiscriminately. All such reflections are not only illiberal, but dangerous, and often produce very mischievous consequences. For too many are governed by opinion, rather than principle; and what they know they are commonly supposed to be, they are very likely to become; concluding that since they are doomed to wear the scandal of the character, they may as well have the profit of it. There may be exceptions; but in general we shall find, that if we honour those with whom we have to do with our confidence, they will feel a responsibility, and be concerned to repay us. But when we indulge suspicions, and behave towards our fellow-creatures as spies and enemies—is it likely that they will feel towards us as friends?

Secondly; let us not make our business an excuse for ungodliness. Some lines of life are indeed much less favourable to morality and religion than others; they afford fewer helps, or more hinderances than others—and this consideration should powerfully influence those who have the disposal of youth. But where the providence of God places us, the grace of God can keep us. And hereafter you will see many of the glorified taken from the same employments with yourselves. "These," says God, "these had the same nature, were partakers of the same infirmities, and placed in the same circumstances with yourselves. But they 'escaped the corruption of the world through faith.' They found time to serve me. They distinguished between the duties and the vices of their calling, and so performed the one as to avoid the other. They 'followed me in the regeneration, and I appoint unto them a kingdom.'—' Well done, good and faithful servant; thou hast been faithful over a few things; I will make thee ruler over many things: enter thou into the joy of thy Lord!'"

II. IF WE HAVE ACCESS TO SUPERIORS, WE SHOULD USE IT FOR GOOD. Many of the Jews could not approach Artaxerxes; but the office of Nehemiah gave him an introduction: and he resolves to intercede for his country and his people. In this way some have opportunities of usefulness which are denied to others: they have the eye, the ear, the favour of the rich and great. And they should lay hold of these opportunities—not to indulge and aggrandize themselves—but to mention truths which persons in elevated circumstances seldom hear; to recommend religion, of which they generally entertain mistaken notions; to place before them scenes of distress, which are not often noticed in the high places of the earth.

Should it please God to call them by his grace—though their souls are no more valuable than those of the meanest slaves, they can be more extensively exemplary and beneficial than others: or, if not—it is well to remove their prejudices; it is well to moralize them; it is well to derive from them external assistance in relieving the poor, and maintaining the cause of God.

Let us remember that we are answerable for all our talents, and one of them is—the influence which in various degrees we have over others. How are we using it? Are we followers of him " who went about doing good?" He made this the grand business of life. It was his leading aim in every situation and company. To this he rendered every thing subservient. May the same mind be in us which was also in Christ Jesus!

III. THE BEST WAY TO SUCCEED IN ANY ENTERPRISE WITH MEN IS TO COMMEND THE MATTER TO GOD. So did Nehemiah: " Prosper, I pray thee, thy servant this day, and grant him mercy in the sight of this man." And the propriety of this action fully appeared in his management of the undertaking, and the success with which it was crowned. Every thing is sanctified by the word of God and prayer. Nothing is too little to bring to the throne of grace. Our intercourse with God will best prepare us for our dealings with men. It will repress every unhallowed purpose; it will give decision and vigour to good resolutions; it will inspire rectitude and dignity in action; it will enable us to bear disappointment or success.

When we have thus commended a concern to God, the mind is set at liberty, and feels satisfaction and composure. Hence, says Solomon, " Commit thy works unto the Lord, and thy thoughts shall be established:" as if he had said, " An enterpr se will neces-

sarily give rise to much thought and solicitude, but when we carry it to God, and leave it with him, the mind is fixed, and no longer driven hither and thither, troubled and perplexed." And in unison with this is the admonition of the apostle : " Be careful for nothing : but in every thing, by prayer and supplication with thanksgiving, let your requests be made known unto God. And the peace of God which passeth all understanding shall keep your hearts and minds through Christ Jesus."

When we have thus addressed ourselves to God, difficulties vanish. We know that if the affair be injurious, he can easily hinder it; and if it be good for us, he can as easily pomote it. " His kingdom ruleth over all." Every event is under his direction, and every character under his control. When Herod had imprisoned Peter, the church assembled together to obtain his enlargement—But what did they? Did they draw up a petition, and address it to the king, signed with their names? No, they applied at once, not to the servant, but to the master : they applied to One who had Herod completely under his check: " Prayer was made, without ceasing, of the church unto God for him."

And what was the consequence? What were bars and fetters to God? " When Herod would have brought him forth, the same night Peter was sleeping between two soldiers, bound with two chains: and the keepers before the door kept the prison. And behold, the angel of the Lord came upon him, and a light shined in the prison: and he smote Peter on the side, and raised him up, saying, Arise up quickly. And his chains fell off from his hands."

Solomon has told us, and not without reason, that " the king's heart is in the hand of the Lord, as the rivers of water; he turneth it whithersoever he will." Eastern monarchs were absolute : they consulted nothing but their own pleasure: yet God had them more under his command than the husbandman has a direction of the water in a meadow. Now the husbandman can easily give it a new current by digging a new channel—and in this case it is worthy of our observation that the nature of the water remains the same, and no violence is offered to impel it along— it flows as freely as before. Admirable image this, of God's overruling providence in making use of princes and heroes and politic ans, to accomplish his own designs, while their dispositions are unchanged and unrenewed, and they willingly follow the leadings of their pride, avarice, or revenge!

There is a two-fold dominion which God exercises over the mind of man. The one is by the agency of his grace. Thus he can enlighten the most ignorant understanding, and subdue the most rebellious will; he can take away the heart of stone, and give a heart of flesh. We see this exemplified in the conversion of Saul of Tarsus, in his way to Damascus. From a furious persecutor, he becomes at once a disciple and an apostle, and from that hour the language of his life was, "Lord, what wilt thou have me to do!" But there is another empire which he exercises over mankind—it is by the agency of his providence. History is full of this. He can give another heart, when he does not give a new one. Where he does not convert, he can check; he can raise up a diversion; he can indispose the mind by dejection; he can disorder the body: and in consequence of the movement of one of those circumstances which are all dependent upon his pleasure—the whole state of an affair will be changed. Jacob was convinced of the dominion and influence of God over the affairs, and even the dispositions of men: and therefore when he was returning home, and had to meet his exasperated brother Esau—though he used all the means which prudence could suggest, he trusted in God for his safety and success: he therefore retired and prayed—he earnestly committed the whole concern to God—and behold the result! Though Esau set off with a determination to kill his brother, his heart was softened upon the road, and he fell upon Jacob's neck, kissed him, and wept. For "when a man's ways please the Lord, he maketh even his enemies to be at peace with him."

IV. It is worthy of our notice, HOW NEHEMIAH SPEAKS OF THE GOVERNOR OF ONE HUNDRED AND TWENTY-SEVEN PROVINCES—"*This man.*" Artaxerxes, it is probable, seldom thought of himself in a manner so humiliating. Grandeur threw a lustre which dazzled him; and a thousand flatterers were employed to make him believe he was more than human. But he was really no more than a "man." He had only five senses; he was made of the same dust with his slaves; he was vulnerable, frail, mortal—a pain in the least member would tell him so; an accident or a sickness would speak out; death and worms would end the dispute. "I said, ye are gods; but ye shall die like *men.*"

It would be well for those who are placed above others in circumstances, to remember in how many respects, of far greater importance, they are only upon a level with them. And it would be well for us all to remember it; for we are prone to idolatry: we are always making flesh our arm: and this leads to a succession of disappointments, by which God says to us, "Cease from *man* whose breath is in his nostrils, for wherein is HE to be accounted of?"

Let us not however suppose that Nehemiah "despised dominion," or "spoke evil of dignities." We are far from supposing that the destruction of the various ranks in society would increase human happiness; and it is certain that the Scripture takes these distinctions as they are, and even requires us to "render to all their due; honour to whom honour is due, fear to whom fear, and tribute to whom tribute." It commands us to "fear God, and honour the king;" and to be "subject not only for wrath, but also for conscience sake." But Nehemiah was now before the God of heaven and earth; and what is the greatest monarch in the world compared with him? Less than nothing and vanity. This is the way to reduce worldly impressions: the world strikes and conquers you when it meets you absent from God. Bring it into his presence—view it there—and what is it? What are the smiles of men to the favour of God? What are their frowns to his anger? What can drive you back from duty, while he is near to support you? "I, even I, am he that comforteth you: who art thou, that thou shouldest be afraid of a *man* that shall die, and of the son of man, which shall be made as grass? And forgettest the Lord thy Maker, that hath stretched forth the heavens and laid the foundations of the earth? And hast feared continually every day because of the fury of the oppressor, as if he were ready to destroy? and where is the fury of the oppressor?" When Ahab and Jehoshaphat were going up to Ramoth Gilead to battle, they sat each upon his throne, arrayed in their robes. Four hundred prophets appeared before them—but the god of this world had blinded their minds; they could not see afar off; they only beheld these two monarchs, and therefore feared and prophesied smooth things. But Michaiah is called in—and he dares to speak the truth; and what emboldened him? He "saw the LORD sitting on HIS throne, and all the host of heaven standing by him on his right hand and on his left." And in view of him—what were these two *men?* Had Moses seen only Pharaoh armed with power and rage, he would have shrunk from the execution of his commission—but he saw a greater than Pharaoh: "by faith he forsook Egypt, not fearing the wrath of the king, for he endured as seeing him who is invisible." And what was this *man* to him? "And I say unto you, my friends, be *not* afraid of them that kill the body, and after that *have no more* that they can do. But I will forewarn you whom ye shall fear: fear *him* which, after he hath killed, *hath power to cast into hell;* yea, I say unto you, *fear him.*"

Finally, OBSERVE HOW THIS GOOD MAN CHARACTERIZES HIMSELF AND HIS BRETHREN—THY SERVANTS WHO DESIRE TO FEAR THY NAME."

This is striking—and it teaches us, that modest, diffident language best becomes us, especially before God. Even as Abraham says, "I that am but dust and ashes have taken upon me to speak unto the living God." Jacob says, "I am not worthy of the least of all thy mercies." David says, "So foolish was I, and ignorant, I was like a beast before thee." And Paul, "I am less than the least of all saints: I keep under my body, and bring it into subjection, lest, having preached to others, I myself should be a cast-away." I would rather hear a person expressing a humble hope, than a towering assurance. Zion's travellers are represented as coming " with weeping and supplication." We are now in a world of action and of trial—not of rapture and triumph. " Blessed is the man that feareth always." Even Nehemiah only speaks of his "desiring" to fear God's name.

Indeed there are many who must derive their satisfaction from their desires, rather than any thing else. They cannot say they *do* fear him, or love him, or depend upon him—but they know they "*desire*" to do it. But for all such there is a most encouraging promise: " Blessed are they that do hunger and thirst after righteousness, for they shall be filled." These desires are proofs of something good, and pledges of something better. They are evidences of grace, and forerunners of glory. Desires are the pulse of the soul, by which we may judge of our spiritual life and health. In some respects they are more decisive than actions. Actions may be counterfeited, desires cannot; we may be forced to act, but not to will. And therefore let us have recourse to this. Let us observe the prevailing bias of our minds; the direction in which, and the objects towards which our desires move.—Let us examine whether we are not restless after the friendship and image of God. Let us see whether we cannot make the language of David our own: " As the hart panteth after the water-brooks, so panteth my soul after thee, O God. My soul thirsteth for God, for the living God: when shall I come and appear before God? Remember me, O Lord, with the favour that thou bearest unto thy people: O visit me with thy salvation; that I may see the good of thy chosen, that I may rejoice in the gladness of thy nation, that I may glory with thine inheritance."

We may add, that all the people of God while here, must place their religion in desires rather than action. Let me not however be misunderstood. I do not mean to intimate that the desires of the Christian are not active ones—for they are; and in proportion to their degree they will necessarily excite him to strive, to wrestle, to fight, and to use all the means which lead to the end he has in view. And, I am sorry to say, that, for want of knowing this, many individuals are deceived, to their everlasting ruin—imagining that they have gracious desires, while they are strangers to Christian diligence. Balaam could say, " Let me die the death of the righteous, and let my last end be like his:" but he had no concern to live their life.

Herod wished to see our Saviour work a miracle, but would not take a journey for the purpose. Pilate asked, what is truth? And would not stay for an answer. There are many languid, occasional, temporary desires, which are far from indicating the existence of Divine grace in the heart. The desire of many is like that of the sluggard, of whom it is said, " The desire of the slothful killeth him; for his hands refuse to labour." Desires then are nothing without endeavours.

But our meaning is this—That what a Christian *does* in this world is very little, compared with what he *ought* to do, and even *would* do. If you view his dispositions; if you judge of him by his desires, he would attend on the Lord without distraction;" he would " run and not be weary, and walk and not faint;" he would equal a seraph in the service of heaven. But if you view his executions; if you judge of him by his attainments, he cries out, " The' flesh lusteth against the Spirit, and the Spirit against the flesh: and these are contrary the one to the other: so that I cannot do the things that I would. When I would do good, evil is present with me, and how to perform that which is good I find not. O wretched man that I am! who shall deliver me from the body of this death?"

Christian! This will not be the case always. He who has given you the *will*, which once you had not, has promised, in due time, to give you all the *power* you now want. You will soon drop every burden, and escape every impediment. You will soon appear before his throne, and serve him day and night in his temple: " When that which is perfect is come, then that which is in part shall be done away."

"Grace will complete what grace begins,
To save from sorrows or from sins:
The work that wisdom undertakes
Eternal Mercy ne'er forsakes."

DISCOURSE XLV.

AN ADDRESS TO YOUTH.

(THE FIRST DAY OF THE YEAR.)

Wilt thou not from this time cry unto me, My Father, thou art the guide of my youth?— Jer. iii. 4.

IT is a lovely view which the Supreme Being has given us of himself in the words of Ezekiel, " As I live saith the Lord, I have no pleasure in the death of the wicked." His mercies are over all his works. But if there be any of his creatures for which he seems more peculiarly concerned than another— they are you, my dear children—they are you, my young friends!

Hence, to engage you in his service betimes, he has laid hold of every principle of action; he has addressed every passion of your nature—your hope and fear—your joy and sorrow—your honour and disgrace. He *commands* you as a sovereign—"Remember now thy Creator in the days of thy youth." He *promises* you as a God—"I love them that love me, and they that seek me early shall find me." He *expostulates* with you as a father—"Wilt thou not from this time cry unto me, My Father, thou art the guide of my youth?"

These words teach us—I. THAT YOUTH NEED A GUIDE. II. THAT GOD IS WILLING TO TAKE THEM UNDER HIS DIRECTION. III. THAT THE WAY IN WHICH THEY ARE TO ENGAGE HIS ATTENTION IS BY PRAYER. And IV. THAT THERE ARE PARTICULAR SEASONS IN WHICH HE EXPECTS TO BE SOUGHT BY THEM, and from which he dates the expostulation—"Wilt thou not from this time cry unto me, My Father, thou art the guide of my youth?"

I. Yes, my dear youth, you need many things. For whatever amiableness and attractions you may possess, you are fallen creatures. You are guilty—and want pardon. You are depraved—and need to be renewed in the spirit of your minds. And you are wanderers—and NEED A GUIDE. Let me try to convince you of this.

Now we are expressly assured by the prophet, "That the way of man is not in himself; it is not in man that walketh to direct his steps." And if this be true of old travellers, who have long been moving Zion-ward, how much more is this the case with those who are only beginning to start! There is nothing we are so unwilling to own as our ignorance—but though "vain man would be wise, he is born like a wild ass's colt. He goes astray from the womb, speaking lies." The human mind is naturally dark. We bring no knowledge of any kind into the world with us—it is all originally external, and drawn in through the senses. It is the consequence of instruction, and is obtained by slow degrees. And as to religious knowledge, we should have been entirely destitute, but for a revelation from God. And when this light is given, it is like the sun shining on a blind man: it affords the medium, but not the faculty of vision. Another work therefore is necessary to make us wise unto salvation—and hence David prays for himself: "Open thou mine eyes, that I may behold wondrous things out of thy law:" and hence the Apostle prays for the Ephesians; "That the God of our Lord Jesus Christ, the Father of glory, may give unto them the spirit of wisdom and revelation, in the knowledge of him; the eyes of their understanding being enlightened; that they may know what is the hope of his calling, and what the riches of the glory of his inheritance in the saints."

Again. There is one kind of knowledge, in which you must be deficient—that which is derived from trial, and which we call experience. You have not had opportunities to observe, to compare, and to distinguish things. You have not remarked the difference there is between appearances and reality; between the beginning and the end of enterprises. You are therefore liable to imposition and delusion. The less experience we have, the more needful is a guide—but, alas! that which ought to make youth diffident renders them presumptuous:

For they are full of confidence. We read of "the meekness of wisdom." And it is certain that intelligence produces modesty: it brings to view difficulties which never strike the superficial observer; it shows us that so far are we from all claim to infallibility, that we are not only liable but likely to err. For advancing in knowledge is like sailing down a river, which widens as we proceed, until the prospect expands into an ocean, and we see no land. But ignorance and inexperience generate and cherish rashness and forwardness. A quickness of growth is often in proportion to the shallowness of the soil, as we see in the stony ground—but young people often mistake a readiness of apprehension for a depth of judgment and a comprehensiveness of mind. Hence they will speak with decision on subjects which perplex others; are positive where the wise are uncertain; and flounder on where talents and years are afraid to step.

Now, too—the passions and appetites begin to rage in their violence. These becloud the understanding, and prevent reflection; and rendering them averse to reproof and impatient of control, urge them on, and plunge them into a thousand improprieties and embarrassments.

Let us also remark their situation and circumstances "in this present evil world." If thus ignorant and inexperienced; if thus full of confidence and eagerness of desire, they had to travel through a smooth and safe country—it would not be so dangerous. But they have to journey through regions full of pits and snares; where enemies are concealed in ambush; where by-paths perpetually present themselves; where seducers "lie in wait to deceive;" and where fruits grow on the sides of the road fair to the eye, but deadly in the taste. And here—what can be done here—without a guide?—Who will cry, "Forbear—There is danger—These 'steps take hold on hell.' 'This is the way, walk ye in it!'"

And to close the whole—Let us remember the consequences which will arise from wrong steps taken in youth. Some of these will make work for bitter repentance hereafter. With regard to others, repentance itself will be unavailing: you must endure the connexions you have formed; and carry the infirmities you have entailed upon yourselves down to the grave. What you now do will give not only a colouring but a character to the whole of your future life.

Youth then needs a guide. But whom will you choose?—We have to remind you,

II. THAT GOD IS READY TO BECOME YOUR LEADER, and that it is your duty and privilege to place yourselves under his direction. He would have you cry unto him, saying, "Thou art the guide of my youth."

The Israelites of old, in passing through the wilderness to Canaan, found in God all that their situation required. They were exposed to danger—and he was their defence. They were destitute of provisions—and he furnished them with supplies. They were in a trackless desert—and knew not the way they should take—and he was their guide. By the fiery cloudy pillar he determined all their encampments and journeyings: as this rose they rose; as this turned they turned—till by a right way it led them to a city of habitation. And he is equally the leader of his people now. "A good man's steps are ordered by the Lord."—"In all thy ways acknowledge him, and he shall direct thy paths." And who can express the satisfaction of mind which arises from such a reflection as this!—"Well, I have a dangerous world to pass through, and I wish to pass through it safely and usefully, and to reach heaven at last. This is my aim as well as desire: and I am not a lonely, nor an uncertain traveller. God is with me. I am under the care of his providence. I have the Scripture for my rule. I have also the promise of the Holy Spirit to lead me into all truth—'and as many as are led by the Spirit of God, they are the sons of God.'"

And this is surely enough to incite you to apply to him. For, my dear young friends, what properties could you wish for in a guide, that are not to be found in God? He is infinitely wise, and cannot lead you astray. He has conducted millions; and "the wayfaring man, though a fool, has not erred" under his direction. He is infinitely powerful. He can support you under the heaviest burdens, deliver you from every adversary, and "make all things work together for your good." He is infinitely kind. He will bear with your infirmities, and sympathize with you in all your troubles. And he is infinitely faithful: not a word shall fail of all that he has spoken; and you may say with David, "This God is our God for ever and ever, he will be our guide even unto death."

Thus "he leads his people, to make himself a glorious name." And thus all who have been under his guidance have extolled their leader—especially after they had finished their course. When they looked back upon his dealings with them, the review furnished them with peculiar songs of wonder and of praise; and their language has been, "To him that led his people through the wilderness —for his mercy endureth for ever."

And this is he who is willing to become your guide; and who proposes himself as your guide—only,

III. Remember, How YOU ARE TO ENGAGE HIS ATTENTION—you are to "cry to him." "Wilt thou not from this time cry unto me, My Father, thou art the guide of my youth?"

This familiar expression intends prayer and supplication; and it prevents you from using as an excuse for the omission of the duty— that you are not masters of words, and cannot deliver yourselves in proper language. For what is prayer? Is it not the desire of the heart towards God?—If you cannot pray —cannot you cry unto him? He can hear the voice of your weeping. He knows the meaning of a sigh; of a look. "My desire," says David, "is before thee, and my groaning is not hid from thee."

And let me here remark two things—the first is—that you are not to expect this guidance without prayer. His own declaration is sufficient to decide this—"For all these things," says he, "will I yet be inquired of by the house of Israel, to do it for them." And the second is—that you are not to despair of this guidance with it. It is God's way to produce in us conviction of our need, and to draw forth our desires after the influences and blessings he has to bestow; but he that commands and inclines us to call upon him will not suffer us to call upon him in vain. "Ask, and it shall be given you; seek, and ye shall find; knock, and it shall be opened unto you. For every one that asketh receiveth, and he that seeketh findeth; and to him that knocketh it shall be opened."

Therefore "let the heart of them rejoice that seek the Lord." And if unhappily you have lived without him in the world; if other lords have had dominion over you—but you are now willing to abandon them, and to make mention of his name only, saying, "Lord, I am thine, save me;"

"Grant me thy counsels for my guide,
  And then receive me to thy bliss;
  All my desires and hopes beside
  Are faint and cold compar'd with this"—

—be assured he will in no wise cast you out; but will receive you graciously, and love you freely. We have therefore only to observe,

IV. THAT THERE ARE PARTICULAR SEASONS IN WHICH HE EXPECTS TO BE SOUGHT AFTER BY THE YOUNG, and from which he dates the expostulation—"Wilt thou not from this time cry unto me, My Father, thou art the guide of my youth?"

And first—this is the case when they leave the house of their friends, and the wing of their relations. Behold a youth removing from home—to go to school—to learn a business—to travel. He departs. The fond mother views him from the window—and turns away—to weep. The father accompanies him to a distance—having left him—looks back again—and prays—" The God which fed me all my life long unto this day, the angel which redeemed me from all evil, bless the lad, and let my name be named on him, and let him grow into a multitude." Though in such circumstances he still engrosses affection and solicitude, he is no longer immediately under the notice of parents. They have given him instruction; they can maintain a correspondence by writing—but they are no longer near him; and he may fall into mistakes, which will decide his condition before they can know the danger or offer advice. To such a youth God says, " Wilt thou not *from this time* cry unto me, My Father, thou art the guide of my youth !"

Secondly. When the young are bereaved of their parents, and will see their faces and hear their voices no more for ever. This is no uncommon affliction—but it *is* an awful one—and sometimes the most distressing consequences ensue. There dies a father—and—behold, the widow descends from the sopha of ease to the oar of labour—and the children lose the caresses of the neighbourhood; are scattered; oppressed; injured. For few in our world act according to the laws of genuine friendship, or inquire, like David, " Is there any left of the house of Saul, that I may show him kindness for Jonathan's sake !" But the moral hazards of such bereavements are still more dreadful. Deprived of a correcting, restraining, and directing hand—left to himself with evil propensities, and surrounded with error and vice —what wonder is it that the young traveller is drawn aside, and led the downward road ! Are there any here this evening who have been deprived of their relations, and are thus exposed ! Say with David—" When my father and my mother forsake me, then the Lord will take me up." Yes—if you cry to him—he will not leave you orphans: he will be to you all that you need; and you shall prove " that it is good for a man to bear the yoke in his youth." Returning therefore from such a grave—hear him saying, Wilt thou not from " *this time* cry unto me, My Father, thou art the guide of my youth !"

Thirdly. This is the case at the commencement of a new period of life. Such is the day on which I now address you. God has preserved you through all the perils of another year, and has thereby laid you under a thousand fresh obligations to love and serve him. You now stand on the threshold of a new division of time—and are you determined to enter it without God ? Would you think of living another year of vanity, of irreligion, and of danger ! Let this day be distinguished by the surrender of yourselves to him who cries, " My son, give me thine heart." Then you will begin the year with every advantage his presence and favour can

afford; then he will say to you as he did to the Jews of old, when they had laid the foundation of the temple, " From this day will I bless you." From this first day of the year he asks you—" Wilt thou not *from this time* cry unto me, My Father, thou art the guide of my youth !"

Fourthly. This is the case when the young see any of their friends and companions carried off by a premature death. Every death is instructive and impressive—but the death of one cut down in the flower of his days is peculiarly so—especially to the young themselves. And the reason is this. It attacks their presumption; it expels them from their favourite refuge of lies. For there are very few of the young who resolve to have nothing to do with religion at all; but they leave the concern to a future season, and in the mean time make no doubt of their safety. They expect to live to old age, and then—when they have carried various points, and their relish for liberty and pleasure is abated—then they resolve to mind the salvation of the soul, and to dedicate to religion a season good for nothing else. Now, not to observe the baseness of this conduct, and how likely it is to provoke God to cast you off—not to observe how few are ever called in old age—not to remind you that your disinclinations to religion will grow with your years, that the disease by continuance will grow inveterate, and that as soon may " the Ethiopian change his skin, and the leopard his spots, as those learn to do good who are accustomed to do evil"—let me refer you to an early grave, to convince you of the absurdity of your hope and resolution. Here you see—that " *all* flesh is *grass ;* and the *goodliness* thereof as the flower of the field :" that life is a vapour that appeareth for a little time, and then vanisheth away; that youth is no security from the stroke of death; and therefore that nothing can be more unwise than to depend in a business so momentous on events so precarious.

Now you glory in your vigour and strength; and promise yourselves many years—when perhaps this night your soul may be required of you; when perhaps there is but a step between you and death; when perhaps the feet of them that have carried out your associate are ready to carry you out. " For man also knoweth not his time: as the fishes that are taken in an evil net, and as the birds that are caught in the snare; so are the sons of men snared in an evil time, when it falleth suddenly upon them."

Again. This is the case at a season when the young have peculiar convictions and impressions. And where is the youth who has not !—Have you not sometimes, like Felix, trembled when you have heard of the powers of the world to come ! Have you not sometimes deplored feelingly the poverty of earthly plea-

X   14*

sures and resources, and sighed and asked for a better country? When you have seen believers tranquil in affliction, and happy even in dissolution, have you not prayed, "How goodly are thy tents, O Jacob, and thy tabernacles, O Israel! Let me die the death of the righteous, and let my last end be like his!"

These are cords of love, by which he would draw you to himself—and will you cut them off? These are so many ways in which he addresses you—and will you refuse him that speaketh from heaven? Oh! cherish these emotions. "*To-day* if ye will hear his voice, harden not your hearts." "Wilt thou not from *this time* cry unto me, My Father, thou art the guide of my youth?"

In a word: this is the case with the season of youth in general. For if you ever mean to attend to the things which belong to your peace—the time of youth is unquestionably the best season. Let me mention only two things. First. If you wish to befriend others, it is the best season. "One sinner destroyeth much good." His example and his influence in a course of years will produce injuries to society, which if brought to repentance, he will deplore, but will not be able to repair. And how painful will it be when he is advancing to heaven to see some of his fellow-creatures going down to hell, and reflect that he was the means of leading them astray! If a thought could imbitter the happiness of heaven, it would be this.

On the other hand, one real Christian may do much good, especially if he begin young. And here let me quote a passage from that devoted man of God, Richard Baxter. In the place where God made him most useful, which was at Kidderminster, "My first and greatest success," says he, "was among the young: and so it was, that when God had touched the hearts of the young with a love of goodness, in various instances their friends, their fathers, their grandfathers, who had lived in ignorance and sin before, became religious themselves, induced by their love to their children, who now appeared so much wiser, and better, and more dutiful than before. In a little time religion spread through many families, and after a few years there was scarcely a house in which the worship of God was not maintained."

Secondly. If you wish to befriend *yourselves*, this is the best season. For "godliness is profitable unto all things, having promise of the life that now is, and of that which is to come. Its ways are ways of pleasantness, and all its paths are peace. Should you succeed in the world—it will keep your prosperity from destroying you. Should you meet with disappointments—it will comfort you in all your tribulation: for to "the upright there ariseth light in the darkness." Should it be said to you as it was to one of old, "This year thou shalt die"—death will be your eternal gain. Or should your time be lengthened out to a number of years—life will be a blessing, and your "hoary head will be a crown of glory, being found in the way of righteousness." Indeed a preparation for death is the only preparation for life; and were you sure to live the age of Methuselah, it would be your wisdom and interest to commence the course here recommended immediately, and to enjoy as soon as possible all those incomparable advantages which can be derived only from divine grace. And therefore—"Wilt thou not from this time cry unto me, My Father, thou art the guide of my youth?"

Such is the question with which God addresses you this evening. And what answer do you return?————I cannot imagine any thing more awful than this moment of suspense. Your relations; your Christian friends; the enemy of your souls; the angels of God, and God himself—are all waiting to hear what reply you will make to the solemn inquiry. Whether your pious connexions shall rejoice or be miserable; whether you shall be the plagues or the blessings of society; whether you shall add to the safety or danger of your country; whether there shall be joy in heaven or hell; whether you shall be saved, or perish for ever—all—all depends upon the nature of the answer you return!

But solemn as all these circumstances are, I forebode from many of you a negative reply. For such efforts as these have already been made in vain. "The heart is deceitful above all things, and desperately wicked."—Already perhaps some of the desires of the flesh and of the mind have gained an ascendency over you. Already perhaps you have armed yourselves with sceptical principles, or loose notions of religion. The temper of the times in which we live is peculiarly discouraging; for the days are come, foretold by the Apostle, when "men shall be lovers of their ownselves, covetous, boasters, proud, blasphemers, disobedient to parents, unthankful, unholy, without natural affection, trucebreakers, false accusers, incontinent, fierce, despisers of those that are good, traitors, heady, high-minded, lovers of pleasure more than lovers of God." To all this we may add that the heads of families do not second the endeavours of ministers by adding private instructions, discipline, admonition, and example to public means of religion.

Hear then the answer of these youths to this all-important question—"Wilt thou not from this time cry unto me, My Father, thou art the guide of my youth?" Some, less daring, hesitate a little, and say, "I pray thee have me excused." But others, more bold, reply—No. They "say unto God, Depart from us: we desire not the knowledge of thy ways." Such is the language of your dispositions, pursuits, and lives. Ah! who could have thought that you could act such a disingenuous, such a foolish, such a shameful, such a destructive part?

But so it is. You have refused the terms of peace. The armistice is broken—and from this hour God and you are at war. And who will prevail? " Who ever hardened himself against him, and prospered? Hast thou an arm like God? Or canst thou thunder with a voice like him?"

But are all here like minded? No. While the generality are gone in another direction—I see some "asking the way to Zion, with their faces thitherward." Here, O Lord, they are, ready to "join themselves to thee in a perpetual covenant that shall not be forgotten." Take them under thy guidance; and say unto their souls, " I am thy salvation. O satisfy us early with thy mercy; that we may rejoice and be glad all our days. Make us glad according to the days wherein thou hast afflicted us, and the years wherein we have seen evil. Let thy work appear unto thy servants, and thy glory unto their children. And let the beauty of the Lord our God be upon us: and establish thou the work of our hands upon us: yea, the work of our hands establish thou it."

DISCOURSE XLVI.

THE UNBELIEF OF THOMAS.

(EASTER.)

But Thomas, one of the twelve, called Didymus, was not with them when Jesus came. The other disciples therefore said unto him, We have seen the Lord. But he said unto them, Except I shall see in his hands the print of the nails, and put my finger into the print of the nails, and thrust my hand into his side, I will not believe. And after eight days again his disciples were within, and Thomas with them: then came Jesus, the doors being shut, and stood in the midst, and said, Peace be unto you. Then saith he to Thomas, Reach hither thy finger, and behold my hands; and reach hither thy hand, and thrust it into my side: and be not faithless but believing. And Thomas answered and said unto him, My Lord and my God. John xx. 24–28.

WHETHER the sacred writers be themselves the characters they record, or whether they describe the lives and actions of others—in all their relations we discover an impartiality that cannot fail of being highly acceptable to a lover of truth. Every thing is expressed without prejudice. The failings of good men are exposed as freely as their excellences; and we are equally instructed and edified by their wisdom and folly, by their faith and their unbelief.

Witness the history of Thomas contained in the narrative which I have read, and from which I would derive a few reflections suited to a season which commemorates the Saviour's victory over his enemies, his deliverance from the reproach of the cross, and his acknowledged glory as "the resurrection and the life."

Following the order of the words, we shall consider, I. THE INCREDULITY OF THOMAS. II. THE MEANS EMPLOYED TO ESTABLISH HIS FAITH. III. THE NOBLE CONFESSION HE MAKES IN CONSEQUENCE OF HIS CONVICTION. May he who favoured these disciples with his bodily presence, be in the midst of us, by the influences of his Holy Spirit! May he reveal himself to us, not as the object of sense, but of faith; and enable us to receive the kingdom of God as a little child, that we may share in the blessedness of those who have not seen and yet have believed!

I. Let us consider THE INCREDULITY OF THOMAS.

The occasion which drew it forth was this. Our Lord rose early in the morning of the first day of the week. In the evening he suddenly appeared to his disciples. The disciples were assembled together, and had shut the door for fear of the Jews. But it was easy for our Lord and Saviour, who had all power in heaven and in earth, to open himself a passage. He did so, and came unobserved, and stood in the midst of them, and having blessed them, withdrew. "But Thomas was not with the disciples when Jesus came." We are not informed of the reason of his absence—but no sooner had he returned, than his fellow-Apostles said unto him, with a rapture becoming the discovery: "We have seen the Lord!"

Upon hearing this, who would not have expected that Thomas, after some inquiry, would have exclaimed, "Happy you who have been privileged with the sight of a risen Saviour! Oh that I had been with you! Could I have foreseen that he would have honoured this place with a visit, nothing should have induced me to quit the sacred spot." But in place of these emotions which were so natural, he cries out, "Except I shall see in his hands the print of the nails, and put my finger into the print of the nails, and thrust my hand into his side, I will not believe." Thus he will not only have the evidence of sense, but he will trust no one's senses but his own. He is not even satisfied with the sight of his eyes—his very hands must minister to the wants of his faith. He not only disbelieves himself, but he seems willing to shake the confidence of his brethren. He accuses them, not indeed of lying, but of mistake: he supposes that they had not exercised proper caution, but had been deceived by a phantom, which their imaginations had taken for a reality; or rather by an apparition, which they had supposed to be the body of our Saviour. Two things it is probable made him think so. First, the Jews had adopted the notion, that souls occasionally appeared after death, clothed in subtle bodies. From whatever quarter this prejudice originally came, or whatever degree of truth was to be attached to it—it seems the disciples, as well as their countrymen, had embraced the belief. Hence, when our Lord walked upon the water, they believed that they had "seen a spirit," and were filled with fear; and hence also these very disciples drew the same conclusion when our Lord appeared to them after he was risen from the dead: "And as they thus spake, Jesus himself stood in the midst of them, and saith unto them, Peace be unto you. But they were terrified and affrighted, and supposed that they had seen a spirit." Secondly, what strengthened the prejudice of Thomas was, that he showed himself to them in the night—the very season in which ghosts and spectres were supposed to appear.

If we pass from the occasion of this unbelief to the evil of it, we shall find that the behaviour of Thomas at this season was rash and foolish and obstinate—and every way blameable. For consider only the importance of the truth disbelieved. It was the foundation of the Christian religion—and of all our hopes—for "if Christ be not risen, our faith is vain: we are yet in our sins." Consider also the greatness and force of the evidence he had to resist. Jonah had typified his resurrection; David had clearly foretold it; Job had rejoiced in it; and our Saviour himself had more than once affirmed that he should not only be crucified, but be "raised again the third day."—Here was a number of witnesses—for not to mention that Mary Magdalene had seen him, that Peter had seen him, that the two disciples going to Emmaus had seen him—here were ten united testimonies; and these witnesses were his companions, and fellow-Apostles, of whose integrity and capacity he was conscious: and their witness was eye-witness and ear-witness; and the disciples had doubtless told him, that they had not only heard and seen him, but that he had shown them the marks of his passion, and had even eaten with them: for this was the fact, as another Evangelist has informed us. "And he said unto them, Why are ye troubled? and why do thoughts arise in your hearts? Behold my hands and my feet, that it is I myself. Handle me, and see: for a spirit hath not flesh and bones, as ye see me have. And when he had thus spoken, he showed them his hands and his feet. And while they yet believed not for joy, and wondered, he said unto them, Have ye here any meat? And they gave him a piece of a broiled fish, and of a honeycomb: and he took it, and did eat before them."

Yet after all this—says unbelieving Thomas, "Except I shall see in his hands the print of the nails, and put my finger into the print of the nails, and thrust my hand into his side, I will not believe." But all this is very instructive. Let us learn from it—

The value of Christian fellowship. With this the Apostle was well acquainted; and therefore he exhorts us "not to forsake the assembling of ourselves together as the manner of some is." He does not only refer to a total forsaking of social devotional exercises, but to a partial and an occasional one. Circumstances will sometimes arise to prevent our attendance; but we should be careful that they are *reasons*, and not *excuses*, that detain us. What an injury did Thomas sustain in consequence of his absence—and had he not been with the Apostles the Lord's day following, he might have continued still in his unbelief. We know not what we lose by neglecting even one opportunity of going to the house of God when it is in our power. There might have been perhaps something in the sermon peculiarly suited to our condition: something which might have scattered our doubts or relieved our distress. Has not the Saviour said, "where two or three are gathered together in my name, there am I in the midst of them?" Is he not "known in his palaces for a refuge?" Do you not long to see his power and glory, so as you *have* seen him in "the sanctuary?"

We learn, also, how prone we are to establish improper criterions of truth. How often do we judge of things exclusively by our experience, our reason, our senses! But what can be more foolish than this? To how small a distance do these powers extend! How many things are certainly true, the truth of which falls not within the compass of either! How many things can a man relate which appear impossible to a child! Tell the inhabitant of the sultry climes that, at a certain season of the year, water, which they have only seen in a fluid state, becomes solid; and hard enough to walk upon—and it will seem to him an idle tale: he has witnessed no such thing; and, reasoning from what he knows, he deems it incredible. If Thomas had constantly judged according to the rule he professed, how little could he have believed at all! He could not have believed that ever there was such a lawgiver as Moses, or such a prophet as Isaiah. He could have believed nothing recorded in the Jewish Scriptures—for nothing of all this had he seen and heard. And it is worthy of inquiry, whether many of the objections commonly urged against several of the leading doctrines of the Gospel do not very much arise from a similar source. It would be easy to prove that they are clearly revealed; but ignorance and pride rise up and ask, "How can these things be?" It is improbable; impossible.

THE UNBELIEF OF THOMAS.

Whereas having ascertained the Bible to be the word of God, we should implicitly embrace all its contents. Our belief should not be rendered easy or difficult by the probability or improbability, by the plainness or the abstruseness of the subject; but be always and simply determined by " the authority of the revealer." This obtains even with regard to human testimony : and if we believe the testimony of man, the testimony of God is greater. To believe no more than we can comprehend, or reduce to some of our modes of knowledge—is not to honour the authority of God at all—yea, it is a reflection upon his wisdom and his veracity: upon his wisdom—— as if he could tell us no more than we know; and upon his veracity—as if he were not to be trusted, if he could.

We also remark, that it is possible for a good man to be overtaken in a fault. He is " sanctified but in part." He may be checked in his course, and chilled in his zeal. His hope may decline; his faith may stagger through unbelief. Indeed, where is the believer who has not reason to cry out with the father of the child, " Lord, I believe, help thou my unbelief?" The Apostles themselves prayed, " Lord increase our faith." But there is a difference between impressions and principles; between a wrong step and a wrong course. Let us not judge of a character by a single action. Thomas had true faith, notwithstanding this instance of unbelief. And he soon recovered from his infirmity.

Yea, it was overruled for good. It ended in the humiliation and zeal of this disciple; and in the greater confirmation of thousands ever since. For if those who have attested the things reported unto us in the gospel had been men of easy and hasty persuasion, their deposition would have been suspicious—but we find that they were men full of pertinacious doubts; they admitted nothing, till evidence extorted conviction. His unbelief therefore is the means of strengthening our faith. To which we may add, that it serves also to honour our Lord and Saviour, not only by evincing more fully the truth of his resurrection, but also in discovering the excellency and amiableness of his character.

II. OBSERVE THE MEANS EMPLOYED TO ESTABLISH HIS FAITH. " And after eight days again his disciples were within, and Thomas with them. Then came Jesus, the doors being shut, and stood in the midst, and said, Peace be unto you. Then said he to Thomas, Reach hither thy finger, and behold my hands; and reach hither thy hand, and thrust it into my side: and be not faithless, but believing."

It is hence observable, that though Thomas did not believe the declaration of the disciples, he still associated with them, and thus placed himself in the way of Divine manifestation. This was well. Let us remember it. And bad as our present frame may be, let us always resolve to repair to the means of grace. For " they that wait upon the Lord shall renew their strength." How often have the people of God been pleasingly disappointed in holy exercises! How often, before they have been aware, have they passed from darkness to light, and from fears and sadness to confidence and joy! Therefore " wait on the Lord; be of good courage, and he shall strengthen thy heart: wait, I say, on the Lord."

Eight days however elapse before Thomas is released from his perplexity. And what days of dreadful suspense were these—while he was uncertain all the time whether Jesus was the Messiah or an impostor—whether the curse of the law was removed or left in all its force!—But " he will not contend for ever, neither will he be always wroth, lest the spirit should fail before him, and the soul that he has made." He comes—again—not armed with vengeance—but crying " Peace." Thomas would doubtless be afraid—and he had reason to expect a severe rebuke—but Jesus instantly forbids all uneasy apprehensions, saying, " ' Peace be unto you.' I am not come to destroy, or to condemn—but to save and to reclaim; to restore and to comfort."

Behold the condescension and kindness of our Lord and Saviour in dealing with this man. Instead of abandoning him, he pities his errors and infirmities: " the bruised reed he does not break, and the smoking flax he does not quench, but brings forth judgment unto victory." He seeks after the poor strayed sheep, and with unspeakable tenderness brings it back. He suffers Thomas to prescribe, and complies with his unreasonable demand: " Reach hither thy finger, and behold my hands; and reach hither thy hand, and thrust it into my side: and be not faithless, but believing."

But while all this marks the compassion of our Lord and Saviour, it also serves to show his all-pervading knowledge. Thomas little thought that Jesus knew his offence, or had heard the language of his incredulity; but our Lord here reminds him that he was perfectly acquainted with his disposition, and that though unseen, he had heard all which had passed. He therefore answers him word for word—yea, he repeats the very terms which Thomas had used. He had said, " Except I shall see in his hands the print of the nails, and put my finger into the print of the nails, and thrust my hand into his side, I will not believe;" and lo! Jesus, the moment he appears, though no one had informed him of this, says—" Thomas, reach hither thy finger, and behold my hands; and reach hither thy hand, and thrust it into my side: and be not faithless, but believing." Let us also remember, that his eyes are in every place, beholding the evil and the good; that "he compasseth *our* path and our bed, and is acquainted with all our ways; and that there is not a word in *our* tongue, but he knoweth it altogether."

We have only to observe further, that it hence appears evident, that our Lord retained after his resurrection the memorials of his passion—there were the marks of the nails and of the spear. And did his ascension erase them? John saw him as "a lamb that had been slain." These not only served at first to prove the truth of his resurrection, and the materiality of his body, but will for ever remind us of the way in which our happiness was procured; and will excite us to everlasting adoration and praise. He challenges the complete salvation of his people: "Father, I will that they which thou hast given me be with me where I am to behold my glory." Do any ask for the justice of his claim? See his appearance; behold the proofs of his sufferings and death: "neither by the blood of goats nor calves, but by his own blood, he entered in once into the holy place, having obtained eternal redemption for us." See how he delights in the deliverance of his people! Had he looked back upon his sufferings with regret, he would have abolished the impressions of them: but he reviews Calvary with pleasure; he "sees of the travail of his soul, and is SATISFIED." And shall we be ashamed of the marks of the dying of the Lord Jesus!— The scars of a general, wounded in the defence of his country, are viewed by his fellow-citizens with admiration and applause. And "God forbid that I should glory, save in the cross of our Lord Jesus Christ, by whom the world is crucified unto me, and I unto the world."

III. Let us pass to the consequence of all this. It produced a full persuasion of mind in the wavering disciple. It does not appear that Thomas complied with the liberty the Saviour gave him to handle him and see— and which had been required before as an absolute condition of faith. No. Conviction flashed into his mind. He is satisfied with the evidence afforded, and is ashamed of his own perverseness and unbelief. He weeps for joy as well as sorrow, and he not only believes with the heart but confesses with the mouth. "And Thomas answered and said unto him, My Lord and my God!" Few words, but very interesting.

It is the language of dedication and devotion—"my *Lord.*" By calling him his Lord, what does he but acknowledge him as his master, and resign himself to his service— saying, "'What wilt thou have me to do?' Thou hast an undeniable right to my obedience. At thy disposal I am resolved to live. And if I have offended and dishonoured thee—the more concerned will I be to please and to serve thee."

It is the language of faith; of faith, not only in his resurrection, but in his divinity; of faith, not only in his dominion, but in his deity—"my Lord and my *God.*" How is this evidence to be baffled? The title was given him by "a good man"—and what good man upon earth ever did or ever will call a magistrate, a teacher, an angel, his *Lord* and his *God?* Besides Thomas was brought up in the Jewish religion, and could not be ignorant of the unity of the Divine nature: he knew what Moses and the prophets had said against idolatry; and how solemnly God himself had declared, "My glory will I not give to another, nor my praise to graven images." As *he* would have been backward to give this title, so our *Lord* would have been backward to receive it, unless it had been his due; yea, he ought peremptorily to have refused it; and to have reproved him for it—as the apostles rebuked those who spoke of them as "gods" come down from heaven, and would have done them homage. This was the more to be expected, because he was the prophet that should come into the world to bear witness to the truth, and to guide our feet into the way of peace. But he accepts—he commends the confession! One resource is left. It is to consider this confession as an exclamation produced by a sudden surprise or fright—"O Lord God—it is he!" But this is making Thomas not devout but profane. Besides it is remarked, that it was an *answer,* and that he did not exclaim *about* him but spake *to* him; "Thomas *answered* and said *unto him,* My Lord and my God!" He was therefore the object of his address.

While therefore others dispute and doubt, let us adore and rejoice. Let us give him the glory which is due unto his holy name. Let us say with confidence, "I know whom I have believed, and am persuaded that he is able to keep that which I have committed unto him against that day." For we should not be satisfied with a speculative belief of this truth. Thomas uses the language of appropriation: "*My* Lord, and *my* God." Were it not for this possessive pronoun *my,* the devil may use the creed as well as the Christian. For he "believes and trembles." He knows that he is Lord and God—but not *his,* either to serve or to enjoy. And without this, such a Being is terrible, especially when we know that unless he is our friend, he is our enemy. But to hear him saying, "I am thine, and all that I have;" to take hold of his covenant and say, All these blessings are mine; to "encourage ourselves in the Lord our God," and say, "thou art my portion and refuge in the land of the living: whom have I in heaven but thee, and there is none upon earth that I desire beside thee"— what peace! what joy must such a blessed confidence inspire!

"My beloved is mine, and I am his. He loved me, and gave himself for me"—what then can trouble me! What can alarm me! What can I want! He is able to do for me exceeding abundantly above all that I ask or think. His perfections are mine, his providence is mine, his promises are mine—mine is the promise of the life that now is, and of that which is to come.

Till we attain this blessed hope we are strangers to some of the most pleasing parts of the Christian life. But how can we attain it?—Be his, and he will be yours. Call him your Lord in a way of service, and he will own himself to be your God in a way of privilege. For there is a connexion between these—if you have chosen him, be assured he has chosen you; and if you love him, be assured he has loved you. For the one is the consequence, and therefore the evidence of the other.

Many are ready to call him their God, who do not honour him as their Lord: they boast of communion with him, but do not live in a state of subjection to him. This is awful. For if you are not his to serve, you have no reason to conclude that he is yours to save.

This is the way—to ascend from that which is more clear, to that which is less obvious. The Christian cannot always say he is mine—but when is it that he cannot say I am thine! Thine to seek thee and obey thee —thine only and wholly—and for ever thine? If for the present you are unable to say, with David, "Thou hast given me the heritage of them that fear thy name"—go on—praying as he did—and you shall not pray in vain—"Remember me, O Lord, with the favour that thou bearest unto thy people: O visit me with thy salvation: that I may see the good of thy chosen, that I may rejoice in the gladness of thy nation, that I may glory with thine inheritance"

DISCOURSE XLVII.

CONTENTMENT WITH LITTLE.

And having food and raiment let us be therewith content.—1 Tim. vi. 8.

WHEN Jacob was going from Beersheba to Haran, he was indulged with a very remarkable vision. It was designed to encourage him in the dangers and difficulties of his journey. It deeply impressed his mind, and drew forth his devotion; and on this occasion we are told that "He vowed a vow, saying, If God will be with me, and will keep me in this way that I go, and will give me bread to eat, and raiment to put on; so that I come again to my father's house in peace: then shall the Lord be my God. And this stone, which I have set for a pillar, shall be God's house: and of all that thou shalt give me, I will surely give the tenth unto thee."

What we now admire is the moderation of Jacob's desire with regard to temporal supplies. He does not stipulate for affluence, power, honour, splendid equipage; he does not ask for delicacies or dainties—but only for conveniences; but only for necessaries—"bread to eat, and raiment to put on."

His example holds forth a rule by which every good man's disposition should be governed with regard to the things of this life. It is the admonition of the Apostle: "Having food and raiment let us be therewith content."

Is it then unlawful for a Christian to be rich? Is he bound to refuse worldly advantages when they come fairly in his way? By no means.

But he is not to be worldly-minded—he is not to seek great things for himself—he is not to toil and grasp, and covet like others— he is not to be fretful and miserable when certain enjoyments are denied him. A Christian is to guard against extravagant desires, and to be satisfied with little. To inspire you with this moderation, let me lead you to contemplate a few objects which have a tendency to enforce it.

I. LET US CONSIDER THE NECESSITIES OF NATURE. These are few, and simple, and easily satisfied. For we should distinguish between real and artificial wants. Civilization has rendered the latter far more numerous than the former; and more of our fellow-creatures are employed in providing for the one than the other. We are inspired with false maxims of living; we deem a thousand things indispensable which our welfare does not require. The trial is often made; there are many who pass through life destitute of those things which are commonly supposed to be requisite to our well-being: but do they not live as long, as healthily, and as happily as the heirs of abundance? Yea, do they not in general live longer, and healthier, and happier? Especially are they not free from those maladies which arise from indulgence, variety, repletion, ease, and the want of labour? Hence you will find that the rich, if wise, live as much as possible like the poor, confining themselves to the simplicity of nature, and doing many things voluntarily, which the lower classes are constrained to do from necessity.

In reference to happiness, a man only *has* what he can *use*. If he possesses a thousand pounds which he cannot use, it matters not, as to the benefit he derives from it, whether it be in his coffer or in the bowels of the earth. When his wants are supplied, all that remains is only to keep or to give away, but not to enjoy. What is more than serviceable is superfluous and needless; and the man is only rich in fancy. Nature is satisfied with little; it is vanity, it is avarice, it is luxury, it is independence, it is "the God of this world" that urges us to demand more.

II. WE SHOULD DO WELL TO CONSIDER THE INSUFFICIENCY OF THE CREATURE. When we see men dissatisfied with what they have, and all anxiety and exertion to amass an abundance of this "world's goods," we should imagine there was a superlative excellency in these things, and that our happiness absolutely depended upon them. But it is not only our Saviour who has told us, that "a man's life consisteth not in the abundance of the things which he possesseth." Happiness is an internal thing. "A good man shall be satisfied from himself." He has a source of pleasure, independent of external events, and which shall survive the dissolution of the globe. It is not the water without the vessel that sinks it, but that which is admitted in. Paul and Silas could sing praises at midnight in the inner prison, when their feet were made fast in the stocks, and their backs bruised with the scourge. The world promises only to deceive, and fails us when we most need its aid. People have risen to affluence and splendour—but their desires increased with indulgence: and they found themselves no nearer satisfaction than before. Yea, they learned what common sense would have told them before, that hills were more exposed than valleys—that the larger space we occupy, the wider mark are we for the arrows of disappointment—that the longer our robes are, the more likely they are to be torn or soiled. Care is an evil spirit that haunts fine houses and large estates: "in the fulness of his sufficiency he shall be in straits." Solomon had more than food and raiment. A thousand streams emptied themselves into his cup of prosperity. He withheld his heart from no joy. And what is his conclusion? "Vanity of vanities: all is vanity, and vexation of spirit!" What can the greatest abundance do for a man? A pain in the foot or the tooth will destroy all the sense of pleasure the good things of this world can afford. None of them can reach the soul; and the mind is the man. None of them can calm the conscience; purify the passions; fill the desires. None of them can raise us above the fear of death, nor the dread of eternity. "Riches profit not in the day of wrath."

What inference do we draw from hence? Why, seeing these things are so insignificant and worthless as to our chief interest, we should not make them our portion; we should not hang our hopes and fears upon them; we should not suffer them to engage our solicitude. It is the reflection of the wise man: "Seeing all these things but increase vanity, what is man the better?"

III. TO INDUCE YOU TO BE SATISFIED WITH SUCH THINGS AS YOU HAVE, CONSIDER YOUR UNWORTHINESS. You murmur because you have not more—but should you not be thankful for what you have! If a man owes you a debt, you ought to have your demand; and if you do not receive the whole, you may justly complain. But it is otherwise with a beggar who asks alms. You would think it strange were he to prescribe the measure of his benefactor's bounty—or were you to hear him pettishly exclaim, as soon as his friend from pure generosity had relieved him—"This will not do—this is not enough—I must have much more than this—I must have an abundance."

Such is the man who is not satisfied with what God has given him. There is indeed a difference here, but it makes against us. We are under obligation to relieve. Our fellow-creatures have claims upon us from the command of God and the brotherhood of human nature. But is God under any obligation to confer favours upon us? Have we any claims upon him? Whence do we derive them? Have we not eaten of the forbidden tree? Have we not transgressed the holy laws of God times without number? Would it not be a righteous thing with God to take vengeance? Are we not compelled to say, with David, "Thou art justified when thou speakest, and clear when thou judgest?" How much more therefore are we bound to say, with Jacob, "I am not worthy of the least of all thy mercies?" Cease complaining, Christian. If you have not what you desire, you have infinitely more than you deserve. Hide your blushing face, and hate your ingratitude. You were a traitor against the King of kings—you strove to dethrone him; you were tried, found guilty, and condemned to die. He of his clemency reprieved you—pardoned you—and gave you a promise that no one should harm you, and that you should not want food, or raiment, through life. And you—after all this—you will turn away disgusted? and say—Is this all?—Why does he not give me a mansion? A palace?

IV. OBSERVE WHAT YOU HAVE ALREADY IN POSSESSION, OR IN REVERSION. When I view the Christian—when I see him blessed with all spiritual blessings in heavenly places—when I see him a son of God, an heir of immortality—loved with an infinite love; redeemed by the blood of the everlasting covenant; called out of darkness into marvellous light; justified freely from all things; holding communion with God; claiming all the exceeding great and precious promises—looking forward to "an inheritance incorruptible and undefiled, and that fadeth not away:" and as certain of all this as if it were actually bestowed upon him already—when I see all this, and find him dissatisfied, and hear him murmuring—because he has not a little more thick clay; because a few pins and straws are denied him—I wonder and I weep. What must angels think! What a scandal is all this to religion! O why do not these blessings absorb us!

Once they did. When we were first induced to seek them—we thought of nothing else. We then said, If I succeed and obtain these—how willingly can I leave every thing else—if I have only food and raiment, I shall be therewith content. And are these blessings less in possession than in expectation? Is not the Saviour the same? Is there not enough in his fulness to fill the mind always?

V. Consider the providence of God. Suppose now a voice from heaven were to assure you—that a little was best for you.— You answer, I would try to acquiesce. And cannot God speak by actions as well as words? And does not his providence tell you all this?—By the subversion of your schemes? by the disappointment of your hopes? by the situation and circumstances in which you are placed?

Does any thing come to pass by chance? "Are not the very hairs of your head all numbered?" Does God take care for oxen; does he feed the fowls of the air; does he clothe the grass of the field? And does he abandon friends—children? No: he appoints, arranges, overrules all your concerns. This consideration repressed the ferment of unsanctified passion in David—"I was dumb; I opened not my mouth, because thou didst it." This calmed Job: though the Chaldeans, the Sabeans, and the elements of nature had deprived him of all, he looks beyond them to One whose agency hushed all his passions,— "The Lord gave, and the Lord hath taken away; and blessed be the name of the Lord."

Realize this principle. See the providence of God determining the bounds of your habitations; the age in which you were to live; the stations you were to fill; the comforts you were to enjoy; and the trials you were to endure. And if you have not much of the world—ask—Whence is it? Is it because my heavenly Father is not able to give me more?—No: "The silver and the gold are his. The earth is the Lord's, and the fulness thereof: the world, and they that dwell therein." Is it because he has no inclination to indulge me? No: "He takes pleasure in the prosperity of his servants." It is therefore to be resolved into the wisdom and kindness of his administration. His wisdom tells him how much I can bear—and his kindness will not suffer him to give me more. His aim is my welfare. The same disposition which leads him to give induces him to deny. He corrects, and he crowns with the same love. This loss is to enrich me; this sickness is to cure me. I know that all things work together for good, to them that love God, to them that are called according to his purpose.

And to his government in providence, as well as grace, I once solemnly, and have since repeatedly given myself up. Too ignorant, too impatient, too carnal to choose properly myself, I said, "Thou shalt choose my inheritance for me." And shall I find fault with his decisions, after beseeching him to decide? And with his guidance, after desiring him to guide?

VI. Consider how much safer you are with little than with much. Honey does not more powerfully attract bees than affluence generates temptations. Did you never see men ruined by prosperity? Did you never read the verse following our text —"But they that will be rich fall into temptation and a snare, and into many foolish and hurtful lusts, which drown men in destruction and perdition: for the love of money is the root of all evil: which while some coveted after, they have erred from the faith, and pierced themselves through with many sorrows." Did you never hear our Saviour saying, "How hardly shall they that have riches enter into the kingdom of God!" And do you wish to make the way to heaven more difficult than it is, and to render your salvation almost an impossibility? If desirous of subduing depraved principles and tempers, what madness makes you try to nourish them? Why do you wish to have fewer motives to live by faith? And to have stronger ties of attachment to earth? If you pray to be preserved from evil, why wish to be led into temptation? Why would you cross the mouth of hell upon a narrow plank? What makes you think that you can sail where others have been wrecked? What confidence must you have in your own strength to imagine that where so many have fallen you can conquer!

Have you duly considered the duties as well as snares of a prosperous condition? "Where much is given, much will be required." We think it a fine thing to be rich —but we do not consider the awful account the rich will have to give, not only of the manner in which their wealth was obtained, but also of the manner in which it was expended! We do not consider that they will be responsible for all the good they could have done in spreading the Gospel, and in relieving the poor, but which they neglected.

For they are not proprietors of these goods, but only stewards; and the great Lord of heaven and earth will soon say, "Give an account of thy stewardship, for thou mayest be no longer steward."—Produce your account, O ye rich. You had so much intrusted to your care—Have you employed it? And how has it been employed?—Oh! the embarrassment, the misery of some! "So much has been wasted in dress. So much in amusements. So much in extravagance of table and furniture." "Depart!"

Finally. Consider the brevity of your continuance upon earth, where alone you will need any of these things. "What is your life? It is even a vapour that ap-

Y   15

peareth for a little time, and then vanisheth away!" And how much of this fleeting period is already consumed! There may be but a step between you and death. Now—

If time be short, your trouble cannot be long. "Weeping may endure for a night, but joy cometh in the morning." These "light afflictions are but for a moment." Behold the pilgrim. He meets with many disagreeable occurrences; he expects storms; he looks for a traveller's fare—but says he, "Why should I vex myself! These inconveniences are only for a time: I have better accommodations at home."

Were you ever so prosperous, it is only the sunshine of a day—the evening shades are beginning to spread, and will hide all your glories from your view. Read the verse before the text: "For we brought nothing into this world, and it is certain we can carry nothing out." Yes, we must leave it all behind; and what will it be to us then? "Behold!" said Esau, "behold! I am at the point to die: and what profit shall this birth-right do to me!" So should you say: I am hastening off the stage; the graves are ready for me—of what importance will it be in a few days, perhaps in a few hours, whether I have been rich or poor; whether I have been honourable or despised!

"Be not thou afraid when one is made rich, when the glory of his house is increased: for when he dieth, he shall carry nothing away: his glory shall not descend after him. Though while he lived, he blessed his soul; and men will praise thee, when thou doest well to thyself. He shall go to the generation of his fathers; they shall never see light. Man that is in honour, and understandeth not, is like the beasts that perish."

Now of that which we have spoken, this is the sum: "Let the brother of low degree rejoice in that he is exalted; but the rich in that he is made low: because as the flower of the grass he shall pass away; for the sun is no sooner risen with a burning heat, but it withereth the grass, and the flower thereof falleth, and the grace of the fashion of it perisheth: so also shall the rich man fade away in his ways. Be careful for nothing: but in every thing, by prayer and supplication with thanksgiving, let your requests be made known unto God. And the peace of God, which passeth all understanding, shall keep your hearts and minds through Christ Jesus." "Two things have I required of thee; deny me them not before I die. Remove far from me vanity and lies; give me neither poverty nor riches; feed me with food convenient for me: lest I be full, and deny thee, and say, Who is the Lord? or lest I be poor, and steal, and take the name of my God in vain." "Lord, my heart is not haughty, nor mine eyes lofty: neither do I exercise myself in great matters, or in things too high

for me. Surely, I have behaved and quieted myself as a child that is weaned of his mother: my soul is even as a weaned child. Let Israel hope in the Lord from henceforth and for ever."

Christians, we have been admonishing you to be content with a little of the things of this life. But God forbid you should be satisfied with a little religion—a little grace. Here you should be ambitious. Here you should be covetous. It is a holy ambition. It is a heavenly covetousness. You are allowed to seek more. You are commanded to seek more. More is attainable. More is necessary. Therefore be not alive only in religion—but be lively—do not only bring forth fruit—but much fruit—that your heavenly Father may be glorified, and that you may appear to be his disciples. Let your faith grow exceedingly, and the charity of every one of you towards each other abound. And say, with the Apostle, "I count not myself to have apprehended: but this one thing I do, forgetting those things which are behind, and reaching forth unto those things which are before, I press toward the mark, for the prize of the high calling of God in Christ Jesus."

DISCOURSE XLVIII.

OUR DUTY IN RELATION TO THE SPIRIT.

(WHIT-SUNDAY.)

Quench not the Spirit.—1 Thes. v. 19.

THE works of nature and the works of grace spring from the same Author; and the former are designed to explain and exemplify the latter. We can scarcely perceive any thing in the whole compass of creation which will not easily supply us with an emblem, or a monitor of some religious truth.

The Holy Ghost, whose ministry comes this day under our review, is held forth by various images. In our Lord's conversation with Nicodemus—by the operation of the wind: "The wind bloweth where it listeth, and thou hearest the sound thereof, but canst not tell whence it cometh, or whither it goeth: so is every one that is born of the Spirit." In his address to the woman of Samaria—by the refreshments of water: "If thou knewest the gift of God, and who it is that saith to thee, Give me to drink, thou wouldest have asked of him, and he would have given thee living water." For "this he spake of the Spirit, which they that believe on him should receive." In the words before us, the Apostle derives the comparison from fire: "Quench not the Spirit."

All the properties and effects of fire are strictly applicable to the Spirit. Does fire penetrate and search?—How piercing and painful are some of his discoveries and influences! Does fire destroy?—He consumes our errors and our corruptions. Does fire refine?—He purifies and sanctifies. Does fire produce both light and heat?—He not only illuminates, but warms. Does fire conduce to our comfort?—He fills us "with all joy and peace in believing."

It is hardly necessary to observe, that the Holy Ghost is not spoken of personally, but in reference to his agency and operations. Now these are twofold. First, extraordinary and miraculous—these were confined to the apostolical age. Secondly, common and saving; and these will continue to be experienced to the end of the world. And be it remembered, that while these are no less real in their existence than the former, they are far more glorious in their effects. Though they do not heal bodily diseases, they cure the disorders of the mind. Though they do not qualify us to "discern spirits," they lead us to "prove ourselves," and to "examine whether we be in the faith." Though they do not furnish us with "other tongues," they enable us to comply with the admonition: "Let no corrupt communication proceed out of your mouth, but that which is good to the use of edifying, that it may minister grace unto the hearers."

These influences of the Spirit are rendered necessary by our depravity and inability. Some of the wiser heathens confessed the need of divine assistance to enable a man to commence and continue a virtuous course. But what unenlightened reason imperfectly discerned, the book of God has fully established. There we find all real religion traced up to a divine agency. If there be a Christian grace to be exercised, it is called "the fruit of the Spirit." If there be a Christian duty to be performed, it is to be done in "the Holy Ghost." We are said to "live in the Spirit;" and "to walk in the Spirit." And that the Spirit is still possessed for these all-important purposes appears undeniable—if we appeal to the testimony of the Scripture. Witness its decisions—"Ye are not in the flesh, but in the Spirit, if so be that the Spirit of God dwell in you. Now if any man have not the Spirit of Christ, he is none of his. Know ye not that ye are the temple of God, and that the Spirit of God dwelleth in you?" Witness its promises—"I will put my Spirit within you, and cause you to walk in my statutes." "If ye, being evil, know how to give good gifts unto your children, how much more shall your heavenly Father give the Holy Spirit to them that ask him!" Witness its commands—"Be filled with the Spirit. Grieve not the Holy Spirit, whereby ye are sealed unto the day of redemption. Quench not the Spirit." Let us examine this admonition.

FIRE MAY BE QUENCHED MANY WAYS. The most direct way is, BY CASTING WATER UPON IT. And this I compare to actual, wilful sin. By this Christians are sometimes seduced, and the consequences with regard to religion are mournful. An example is better than a description. Let us take David as an instance, and see the injurious effects of his fall. Read his penitential psalm. Some have told us that sin cannot hurt a believer. I am sure it injured David. His fall produced several fractures, and occasioned him the most acute pain and anguish. This is what he means when he says, "Make me to hear joy and gladness; that the bones which thou hast broken may rejoice!" He is filled with awful apprehensions of being cast away—"Cast me not away from thy presence; and take not thy holy Spirit from me. He is deprived of the joy of the Lord, which was once his strength—"Restore unto me the joy of thy salvation, and uphold me with thy free Spirit." He was struck dumb, and could not speak of God, or to God, or for God, as he once did—"Open thou my lips, and my mouth shall show forth thy praise." Finally, he had made by his fall breaches and ravages in the Church—"Do good in thy good pleasure unto Zion: build thou the walls of Jerusalem." For in this case it may be truly said that "one sinner destroyeth much good." The sins of a professor cause "the enemies of the Lord to blaspheme; justify and confirm the wicked in their iniquity; and lead the world to suspect that religion is only the covering of hypocrisy. Nor do they only "affect them that are without:" they also prove a stumblingblock to the weak, and a distress to the strong; and discourage the heart, and weaken the hands of those who minister in holy things. Thus they check the cause of God in general, as well as injure the welfare of the individual.

Let us therefore beware. Let us never imagine ourselves beyond the reach of temptation. We carry about us passions and appetites which are not completely subdued. "The sin that dwelleth in us" renders us susceptible of danger from external circumstances. Indeed there is nothing with which we have to do, however harmless in itself, that may not prove an occasion of sin. "Wherefore let him that thinketh he standeth take heed lest he fall." Let us "watch and be sober." Let us "watch and pray." Let us "pass the time of our sojourning here in fear," and daily and hourly come to "the throne of grace, that we may obtain mercy, and find grace to help in time of need."

Secondly. FIRE MAY BE QUENCHED BY SPREADING EARTH UPON IT. And observe to what we apply this. We do not here speak, as in the former article, of things grossly, and unquestionably criminal—but we speak of "minding earthly things; of the cares of this world; and the deceitfulness of riches, which choke the word, so that it becometh unfruitful." We speak of an excess of business, which not only employs, but "entangles a man in the affairs of this life." A man seldom, if ever, feels this, in simply pursuing the path of duty; but it results from false aims and wrong dispositions. The man "will be rich:" he deems a superior style of life necessary; he *must* gain a rapid independence in order to retire and live in a state of ease and idleness, for which God never designed any man. Hence he not only labours, but toils; grasps; schemes; speculates. And what is the consequence? The powers of the soul are limited, and when full—whatever fills them—can hold no more. And as the water partakes of the quality of the soil over which it rolls, so our minds soon acquire a sameness with the object of our affection and pursuit. When the man immersed in secular concerns hears the word—"his heart is going after his covetousness;" he is still planning and getting. When he prays, a number of worldly thoughts rush in, and, by dividing his attention, damp his ardour. He cannot "attend upon the Lord without distraction."

I speak of certain vanities and amusements, in which, after all the wise and warm have urged, some professors, even of evangelical religion, occasionally indulge themselves. Such characters prove the embarrassment of their teachers, and erase the boundary line which should obviously separate the church from the world, by their frequent passing from one into the other. And if they will not admit that these diversions are unlawful in themselves—will they, can they deny that they have a tendency to destroy spirituality of frame, to impair a taste for devotion, to alienate from a life of communion with God, and of preparation for eternity?

I speak of worldly and political conversation, which, so far from tending to "the use of edifying," frets the mind, and genders strife; draws off the attention from the divine agency to second causes; attaches us to a party, and commits us to approve of all their proceedings; and cools religious ardour. If we talk most of that which we love best; if from the abundance of the heart the mouth speaketh—where habitually are the thoughts and affections of many professed Christians? Surely it becomes us to live so as to "declare plainly that we are strangers and pilgrims upon earth:" surely we should show to all around us, that we only deem "one thing needful," and this is the care of the soul. With regard to many things which properly enough belong to others, but would impertinently engage us, we should resemble the devoted Nehemiah—"I sent messengers unto them, saying, I am doing a great work—so that I cannot come down: why should the work cease, while I leave it, and come down to you?"

Thirdly. FIRE MAY BE QUENCHED BY THE SEPARATION OF THE PARTS. And this you will apply to our divisions.

With what earnestness does our Apostle enforce connexion and co-operation among Christians! "Now, I beseech you, brethren, by the name of our Lord Jesus Christ, that ye all speak the same thing, and that there be no divisions among you; but that ye be perfectly joined together in the same mind, and in the same judgment, endeavouring to keep the unity of the Spirit in the bond of peace. There is one body and one Spirit, even as ye are called in one hope of your calling: one Lord, one faith, one baptism, one God and Father of all, who is above all, and through all, and in you all. If there be therefore any consolation in Christ, if any comfort of love, if any fellowship of the Spirit, if any bowels and mercies, fulfil ye my joy, that ye be like-minded, having the same love, being of one accord, of one mind." The enemy knows the importance of union and harmony; he therefore labours to separate; and, unhappily, he finds too much to favour his wishes in our ignorance, prejudices, bigotry, and infirmities. How comfortable and edifying is it, when believers meet together, not only "in one place," but "with one accord;" when, of "one heart, and of one soul," they look upon each other with cheerfulness, and embrace each other in holy friendship. "Behold, how good and how pleasant it is for brethren to dwell together in unity!" It is fragrant as the richest perfume: and refreshing and fertilizing as the dew of heaven. It peculiarly attracts the Divine blessing. Hence, says the Saviour, "if two of you shall agree on earth as touching any thing that they shall ask, it shall be done for them of my Father which is in heaven. For where two or three are gathered together in my name, there am I in the midst of them." But how changed is the scene where there are whisperings, swellings, antipathies, disorders in a Christian Church! Its beauty is defaced—its worship is perverted—its strength is impaired—and

"The Spirit, like a peaceful dove,
　Flies from the realms of noise and strife."

There are some families who are quarreling all day, and then go to prayer in the evening—but this is not "lifting up holy hands without wrath and doubting." It were to be wished that some persons would adopt the important duty of family worship—but it would be well for others to lay it aside: and indeed this is likely to be the case in time. Such mixtures and inconsistencies are too shocking to be long continued. If prayer does not induce people to avoid passion, and brawling, and contentions, these evil tempers will make them leave off prayer, or perform it in a manner worse than the neglect of it. The Apostle Peter exhorts husbands and wives to discharge their respective duties, "as being heirs together of the grace of life, that their prayers be not hindered."

We may take another view of this part of our subject. One truth aids another truth; and one duty another duty. Detach private devotion from public, or public worship from private, and both sustain an injury. Separate practice from principle, or principle from practice; faith from works, or works from faith; promises from commands, or commands from promises—and in the same proportion you diminish and destroy the effect of the whole. The flame burns by keeping these things together.

Fourthly. FIRE MAY BE QUENCHED BY WITHHOLDING FUEL. A real Christian will soon feel the disadvantage of disregarding the means of grace. Were he indeed a mere professor of religion, he would be sensible of no such injury; he has no divine principle to watch over and to cherish. You may keep in a painted fire without fuel—but a real one cannot be maintained without it, unless by a miracle. But we have no reason to expect miracles! Is the Divine assistance intended to sooth our sloth, or to encourage our exertion? Is it to be expected in a state of remissness and indifference, or in the use of means?—"The hand of the diligent maketh rich." "For all these things will I be inquired of by the house of Israel to do it for them." "Blessed is the man that heareth me, watching daily at my gates, waiting at the posts of my doors." "They that wait upon the Lord shall renew their strength: they shall mount up with wings as eagles; they shall run and not be weary; and they shall walk, and not faint." Thus directed and encouraged, believers repair to his word, to his throne, to his house, and to his table; and are not disappointed. They find him in his ordinances, and they know by blessed experience, that he attends to their complaints, enlivens their devotion, "helps their infirmities, and supplies all their need from his riches in glory by Christ Jesus." They who desire soul prosperity, who would not only have life, but have it more abundantly, will be found most regular, and serious, and diligent, in the use of those means which God has appointed for this very purpose, and by which he increases their faith, confirms their hope, and makes all grace to abound towards them.

We cannot quench what we have not. The exhortation therefore, supposes the possession of the Spirit, and, therefore, I have thus far considered it in reference to Christians. Yet the words may be taken in a more general way. There is a common work of the Spirit that accompanies the preaching of the word, the effect of which may be entirely lost. Thus we read that when Herod "heard John, he did many

things, and heard him gladly." But he cherished a criminal passion which destroyed all these fair beginnings. Felix heard Paul. It was his own desire. He wished to be gratified by a relation of the peculiarities of "a sect everywhere spoken against." But Paul, instead of indulging his curiosity, addressed his conscience. He "reasoned of righteousness, temperance, and judgment to come." And "Felix trembled." The judge on the bench trembled before the prisoner at the bar. It was not the Apostle's eloquence *alone* that produced this effect. But instead of aiding this impression, the trembler dismisses the preacher—"Go thy way for this time; when I have a convenient season, I will call for thee." This season never arrived. He afterward saw the Apostle, and conversed with him often, but he never experienced again the feelings he had subdued.

Let the hearers of the gospel remember this. Beware how you stifle your convictions, and "do despite unto the Spirit of grace." Seek ye the Lord while he may be found, call ye upon him while he is near. He has said, "my Spirit shall not always strive with man. Behold, now is the accepted time; behold, now is the day of salvation."

DISCOURSE XLIX.

THE ASCENSION OF ELIJAH.

And it came to pass, as they still went on, and talked, that, behold, there appeared a chariot of fire, and horses of fire, and parted them both asunder; and Elijah went up by a whirlwind into heaven.—2 Kings ii. 11.

"By one man sin entered into the world, and death by sin, and so death hath passed upon all men, because all have sinned." Death is called "the way of all the earth;" and the grave, "the house appointed for all living." No distinction of age, of rank, of character has secured the possessor from the stroke of mortality. The young as well as the old, the rich as well as the poor, the honourable as well as the obscure, the learned as well as the illiterate, have successively gone down to the dust and seen corruption. Yea, the righteous themselves die. Though infinitely dear to God, and distinguished by inestimable privileges, even *they* are not exempted from the afflictions of life, or the necessity of dissolution.

This invariable law of mortality has however been dispensed with in two cases. Enoch lived before the Flood. "By faith Enoch was translated, that he should not see death; and was not found, because God had translated him; for before his translation he had this testimony, that he pleased God." Two thousand one hundred and twenty-one years after, we behold, in like manner, Elijah the Tishbite received up into glory. "And it came to pass, as they still went on, and talked, that, behold, there appeared a chariot of fire, and horses of fire, and parted them both asunder; and Elijah went up by a whirlwind into heaven."

Observe, First, How he was employed at the time of his removal: they were "going on and talking." Without this information, many would have concluded, that after he had received the intimation of his speedy departure, he was engaged alone in meditation and prayer. But it is a mistaken sentiment, that a preparation for heaven is to be carried on only by abstraction, contemplation, devotion. No inconsiderable part of it consists in diligence in our stations and endeavours to be useful to our fellow-creatures to the last. "Blessed is that servant whom his Lord, when he cometh, shall find so doing." It is observable that our Saviour ascended, while he was addressing his disciples. "He led them out as far as Bethany; and he lifted up his hands, and blessed them. And it came to pass, while he blessed them, he was parted from them, and carried up into heaven."

A little of the conversation is recorded. "And it came to pass, when they were gone over, that Elijah said unto Elisha, Ask what I shall do for thee, before I be taken away from thee. And Elisha said, I pray thee, let a double portion of thy spirit be upon me. And he said, Thou hast asked a hard thing: nevertheless, if thou see me when I am taken from thee, it shall be so unto thee; but if not, it shall not be so." A vail is thrown over the remainder of this interesting discourse. Perhaps it turned upon the heavenly world; perhaps it respected the state of the church he was going to leave; perhaps it furnished instruction and consolation to his successor in office. However this may be, the conversation was doubtless such as became the solemnity of the occasion. For what could be more awful and impressive! He knew that he was standing on the verge of eternity, and expected every moment the signal of his leaving this world. And could he be vain! Could he trifle? And since "you know not the day nor the hour in which the Son of man cometh, what manner of persons ought you to be in all holy conversation and godliness! Let no corrupt communication proceed out of your mouth, but that which is good to the use of edifying, that it may minister grace unto the hearers. If any man offend not in word, he is a perfect man, and able also to bridle the whole body."

Secondly. Observe how he was conveyed from earth to heaven. "There appeared a chariot of fire, and horses of fire, and parted them asunder; and Elijah went up by a whirlwind into heaven." Was he removed by the instrumentality of a luminous cloud approaching and enclosing him, and then rising with a rapid curling motion? Or was he removed by the ministry of angels, disguised under these brilliant forms? This seems more probable. For "are they not all ministering spirits, sent forth to minister unto them that shall be heirs of salvation?" Is it not said that "He shall send forth his angels and gather together his elect from the four winds, from the one end of heaven to the other?" Is it not said that Lazarus died, "and was carried by angels into Abraham's bosom?"

Though these glorious beings "excel in strength, they do his commandments, hearkening unto the voice of his word." And we know that they have been often held forth under the allusions here employed. "Of the angels he saith, who maketh his angels spirits, and his ministers a flame of fire. The chariots of God are twenty thousand, even thousands of angels: the Lord is among them as in Sinai, in the holy place."

Let us hasten to something less questionable and more important. Let us take several views of this wonderful transaction.

I. Let us consider it as A GRACIOUS RECOMPENCE OF SINGULAR PIETY. Not that Elijah was perfect. We are expressly told that he was a man of like passions with us. And we read that once he was afraid, and fled, and wished in himself to die. But in judging fairly of a person, you are to bring forward the whole of his character; and to remember that casual infirmities no more destroy the effect of general excellency than the hills and valleys of the earth destroy its globosity, or a few motes or clouds a solar day. The circumstances also in which he lives should be fairly weighed; for the power and degree of religion are to be often estimated by the unfavourableness of our situation, and the difficulties we have to overcome.

Elijah was a man whose religion was uncommon. "He was jealous for the Lord of Hosts:" and faithful and steadfast in his adherence to the true worship of God, in times of peculiar defection and degeneracy. He was indeed mistaken, when he said, "I am left alone:" there were seven thousand men who had not bowed the knee to the image of Baal, and whose lips had not kissed him. But though this was a considerable number, compared with his conclusion, it was nothing compared with the bulk of the country. The nation was gone astray from God; idolatry universally prevailed; all classes pleaded for idols.

He had therefore to oppose numbers. And numbers take off the two common restraints, of fear and shame; and constantly present to the eye familiar and seducing examples. It is no easy thing to avoid following a multitude to do evil.

He had also to oppose superiors, whose influence is peculiarly corrupting. He lived under the reign of the worst of all the bad kings of Israel. "For Ahab, the son of Omri, did evil in the sight of the Lord, above all that were before him. And Ahab made a grove. And Ahab did more to provoke the Lord God of Israel to anger, than all the kings of Israel that were before him."

He had also to oppose the established ministers of religion. Behold him encountering the whole priesthood of Baal. Behold him challenging to a public trial four hundred and fifty of his sycophant prophets—and with unparalleled firmness, ordering them all to be put to death—though he knew the altar was defended by the throne. "Elijah said unto them, Take the prophets of Baal: let not one of them escape. And they took them. And Elijah brought them down to the brook Kishon, and slew them there."

All this naturally drew upon him reproach. Ahab called him "the troubler of Israel." Jezebel abhorred him, and bound herself in an oath to slay him. But God often appeared for him: he gave him the keys of the clouds; he fed him with ravens; he commanded strangers and foreigners to entertain him; he destroyed captains and their men for his sake—and at last he made an exception in his favour, and took him to heaven without dying: carrying him more than a conqueror in a chariot of triumph through the air. And thereby said to a careless and depraved age, and to us also—upon whom the ends of the world are come—"Them that honour me I will honour, but they that despise me, shall be lightly esteemed. Have no fellowship with the unfruitful works of darkness, but rather reprove them. Bear your faithful testimony to my cause by your words and actions. Contend earnestly for the faith once delivered to the saints. Dare to be singular. Come out from among them, and be ye separate, and touch not the unclean thing; and I will receive you, and will be a Father unto you; and ye shall be my sons and daughters, saith the Lord Almighty. If you are losers in my service, you shall not be losers by it. Verily I say unto you, there is no man that hath left house, or parents, or brethren, or wife, or children, for the kingdom of God's sake, who shall not receive manifold more in this present time, and in the world to come life everlasting. Verily, there is a reward for the righteous; verily, he is a God that judgeth in the earth."

II. Let us consider it as AN INTIMATION OF THE FUTURE HAPPINESS THAT IS RESERVED FOR THE SERVANTS OF GOD. Instances and facts strike the mind much more powerfully than abstract reasonings. By the example of Elijah's ascension it was seen that there was another state of being after this life—that there was another place of residence and of happiness besides this earth—that it was to be obtained by leaving this world—and that even the body was to share in it.

This was a circumstance of importance. Nothing of the kind could be inferred from nature. Men were seen to perish by accidents and diseases and decays. They were laid in the grave: cold and silent they remained there. Wives had gone to the tombs of their husbands; children to the tombs of their mothers—but in vain had they implored their return. In time the body became a mass of putrefaction; and dissolving into its original element, could no longer be distinguished from other dust.

But man is an incarnate being. The body is a constituent and an essential part of human nature. Man *was* embodied in his primeval state, and *will* be embodied in his final state. A state of separation, therefore, is a state of imperfection; and whatever happiness may be enjoyed in a disembodied state, it will not be, it cannot be complete before the morning of the resurrection. To this therefore the sacred writers lead us forward: and while they clearly allow an intermediate separate existence, they tell us that we "shall be recompensed at the resurrection of the just;" that "when the chief Shepherd shall appear, we shall receive a crown of glory that fadeth not away." When Paul would relieve the minds of bereaved Christians, he reminds them that their connexions will rise again: and in reference to himself he says, "If by any means I might attain unto the resurrection of the dead."

Yes, the body will be a partaker of endless happiness with the soul; and even "in our flesh shall we see God." And here was a specimen of it. Here they saw a man carried up into heaven embodied. Here they saw what transformation of the body was capable of experiencing—it could become light, agile, unsusceptible of danger; it could retain identity, and yet drop those properties which render it a prison and a burden; and become a fit companion for the skies. This was a beaming forth of that glory which has been more fully revealed under the gospel dispensation, and especially in the glorification of the body of our Saviour, which is to be the model of our own. "For he shall change our vile body, that it may be fashioned like unto his glorious body, according to the working whereby he is able even to subdue all things unto himself. So also is the resurrection of the dead. It is sown in corruption; it is raised in incorruption. It is sown in dishonour; it is raised in glory. It is sown in weakness; it is raised in power. It is sown a natural body; it is raised a spiritual body. There is a natural body, and there is a spiritual body."

III. We may consider this translation as a SUBSTITUTE FOR DEATH. In some such way as this, it is probable, would men have passed from earth to heaven had they never sinned. In some such way as this will those living at the last day be qualified for glory. "Behold, says the Apostle, I show you a mystery: we shall not all sleep, but we shall all be changed, in a moment, in the twinkling of an eye, at the last trump: for the trumpet shall sound, and the dead shall be raised incorruptible, and we shall be changed." Elijah died not, but he was changed. And in whatever way we pass into heaven, a change analogous to death and the resurrection must pass upon us. The reason is obvious. "Flesh and blood cannot inherit the kingdom of God; neither doth corruption inherit incorruption." Were the body removed with its present animal properties, it would require food and sleep and medicine even in heaven. The eye would be unequal to the splendour of the glory, the ear to the melody of the sounds, the taste to the exquisiteness of the joy, the powers to the constancy of the work. Our senses and organs are adapted to our present state, but not to our future condition. We now see how little we can bear. When an angel appeared to Daniel, he was instantly seized with a stupefaction which he could not resist. When John in his exile saw Jesus, though he had been familiar with him, and had leaned on his bosom, he "fell at his feet as dead." And by the way, this regulates the dealings of God with his people, while they are in the body. Moses asked for a sight of God, which would have proved his death—"Thou canst not see my face; for there shall no man see me and live." The disciples, in the mount of transfiguration, "fell asleep." It was not so much a moral, as a natural infirmity: the animal frame was overpowered with the glory of the scene. Were He to afford to his people such discoveries and communications as they may sometimes desire, it would unhinge them from earth, indispose them for the duties of their stations, and disorder their whole frame.

IV. We may regard it as A MODE OF TRANSITION MUCH TO BE DESIRED. Death is not a pleasing subject of meditation. It is called "an enemy." It is said to be "the king of terrors." Even exclusive of the future consequences, there is much to render it formidable. Nature cannot be reconciled to its own dissolution. Who loves to be taken to pieces?

> "The pains, the groans, the dying strife,
> Fright our approaching souls away;
> Still we shrink back again to life,
> Fond of our prison and our clay."

Its forerunners and its attendants are dismaying. I have heard of a very good man, who often said he was not afraid of death, but of dying—he was chilled with the thought of corruption and worms. If we saw a viper, and knew that the poisonous fang was extracted, and that it was perfectly harmless—who could put it into his bosom without shuddering?

Let it be remembered, that such feelings as these do not argue an inferior degree of religion. Even the apostles themselves were not strangers to these sensations. "For in this, said they, we groan earnestly; desiring to be clothed upon with our house which is from heaven. If so be that being clothed, we shall not be found naked. For we that are in this tabernacle do groan, being burdened; not for that we would be unclothed, but clothed upon, that mortality might be swallowed up of life." They wished to enter heaven without dying.—But to us this is impossible. To death as an inevitable doom we all look forward. It is the way, and the only way to the city of habitation.

Let us not however blaspheme death. Let us rather see what there is to reconcile us to it. Let us compare Elijah's mode of removal with our own, and see whether the difference be so marvellously great.

You have to die. But consider the names attached to death by him who perfectly knows the nature of it. He tells us, "If a man keep my sayings, he shall never see death"—it ought to be called something else—so qualified and softened is it with regard to him. Call it a departure—the departure of a prisoner from his prison, of a traveller from his inn, of a scholar from his school—"The time of my departure is at hand. I long to depart." Call it a sleep—sleep is inviting to the wearied labourer, who has borne the burden and heat of the day.

> "They sleep in Jesus and are blest:
> How sweet their slumbers are;
> From suff'ring and from sin releas'd,
> And freed from every care!"

"Our friend Lazarus sleepeth."

You have to die. But the sting of death is removed—for "the sting of death is sin"— "and he bore our sins in his own body on the tree." Death stung him; but, as it is fabled of the bee, left his sting in him. It is harmless now. It may terrify, but it cannot injure.

You have to die. But God promises to be with you there. "For he hath said, I will NEVER leave thee nor forsake thee"—and therefore be assured he will not leave you in this time of need. To this the promise is peculiarly made: "I will be with him in trouble." Hence David triumphs, "Yea, though I walk through the valley of the shadow of death, I will fear no evil: for thou art with me; thy rod and thy staff they comfort me."

You have to die. But the soul will be immediately disposed of infinitely to your advantage. Death will carry you from the same vain world, the same vexing world, the same defiling world—as Elijah's chariot car ried him. Death will carry you to the same rest, to the same fulness of joy, to the same glorious company as Elijah's chariot carried him. Absent from the body, you are present with the Lord.

You have to die. But the body will certainly follow. Though you do not take it along with you, but leave it in the grave, it shall not be lost there. He will come and inquire for your dust. It is redeemed. "If Christ be in you, the body is dead because of sin, but the spirit is life because of righteousness. But if the Spirit of him that raised up Jesus from the dead dwell in you, he that raised up Christ from the dead shall also quicken your mortal bodies by his Spirit that dwelleth in you."

You have to die. But by death you may glorify God, more than by such a removal as Elijah's. It affords opportunity to display the influence of divine grace under suffering, to bear witness to the goodness of the Master you serve; to commend the ways of godliness; to convince some, to encourage others. One dying Christian has often made many in love with death. While witnessing such a scene, they have been ready to say, "Let us go away that we may die with him."

It matters therefore little *how* the believer departs from this world to a better.

But the event is always worthy of our observation. "Mark the perfect man, and behold the upright; for the end of that man is peace."

And whether he ascend to heaven in a whirlwind, or be removed by a fever or a dropsy, "Let me die the death of the righteous, and let my last end be like his!"

DISCOURSE L.

THE PUNISHMENT OF ADONI-BEZEK IMPROVED.

But Adoni-bezek fled; and they pursued after him, and caught him, and cut off his thumbs and his great toes. And Adoni-bezek said, Threescore and ten kings, having their thumbs and their great toes cut off, gathered their meat under my table: as I have done, so God hath requited me.—Judges i. 6, 7.

DESTRUCTION had long been denounced upon the inhabitants of Canaan for their sins. At length the measure of their iniquity is full; and the Jews are appointed to be the executioners of the Divine vengeance. Moses dies before they enter on the dreadful task; but Joshua succeeds him, and becomes the scourge of this devoted race. But even he dies before the complete reduction of the promised land. Immediately after his death, Judah and Simeon assemble their forces, and attack the enemy at Bezek, and gain a dreadful victory.

Z

They slew a thousand men, and took Adoni-bezek prisoner. On this bloody tyrant they inflict a punishment, as singular as it was severe—"They cut off his thumbs and his great toes." This drew from him the words which you have heard. "Adoni-bezek said, Threescore and ten kings, having their thumbs and their great toes cut off, gathered their meat under my table: as I have done, so God hath requited me."

This passage of Scripture is a picture. Let me hold it up to view, and call upon you to mark the principal contents of the representation.

I. See in it THE INSTABILITY AND UNCERTAINTY OF WORLDLY GREATNESS. Look at this man—and behold in what slippery places God sets the mighty and noble. How great was he in the field—where armies fled before him! how great in the palace—where a number of vanquished princes fed under his table! But behold him now—dethroned, insulted, dismembered; and his present extremity of wretchedness imbittered by the recollection of the prosperity that once crowned his head. "And seekest thou great things to thyself? Seek them not. Boast not thyself of to-morrow; for thou knowest not what a day will bring forth."

From the eagerness with which mankind pursue the distinctions of life, we should conclude, not only that they were very valuable in themselves, but that no kind of precariousness attached to them. We should suppose that they were able to ensure durable possession—and God, who in his word always gives language to actions, tells us, "Their inward thought is that their houses shall continue for ever, and their dwelling-places to all generations: they call their lands after their own names." But let not the strong be secure; let not the honourable be vain; let not the rich be high-minded. Connect certainty with the motion of the wind, or with the waves of the sea—but do not trust this treacherous, this changeable world. "Lay not up for yourselves treasures upon earth, where moth and rust doth corrupt, and where thieves break through and steal." "Riches make to themselves wings and fly away." "Man being in honour abideth not; he is like the beasts that perish." What is all history but a narrative of the reverses to which all earthly things are liable, however firmly established they once appeared to be: of the revolutions of empires; the destruction of cities; of the mighty put down from their seats; of counsellors led away spoiled, of politicians disgraced, generals banished, and monarchs put to death!

II. See in it JUDGMENT OVERTAKING THE SINNER IN THIS LIFE. Nor does Adoni-bezek stand alone as an instance of the *present* punishment of sin. Behold Adam and Eve driven out of Paradise. See the Flood sweeping away the world of the ungodly. See the smoke of the Cities of the Plain. Remember Lot's wife—she looked back, contrary to the divine command, and "she became a pillar of salt." The servant of Elisha enters his master's presence—tells a lie—and goes out "a leper as white as snow." Ananias and Sapphira utter a known falsehood before the Apostle, and are both instantly numbered with the dead. And of such importance is truth to the welfare of the community—and so hateful is it to the Supreme Being—that not only are all liars to have their portion in the lake which burneth with fire and brimstone, which is the second death—but in these instances we see "hell from beneath moved to meet them at their coming!"

It may however be necessary to observe that this is not always the case. The misery of the sinner is principally reserved for a future world, and we are now in a state of probation. But God would confirm our faith in his adorable providence. If *all* sin was punished here, we should look no further; if *no* sin, we should not easily believe in the power, the holiness, the truth of God. He therefore sometimes signally interposes; and will be known by the judgments which he executeth: "so that a man shall say, Verily there is a reward for the righteous; verily he is a God that judgeth in the earth."

Present punishment, too, is less frequently executed under the gospel than under the law; and the reason is—that a future state of retribution was not so clearly and fully revealed to them as to us. Hence their threatenings are often filled with expressions of temporal evils, while ours only announce miseries beyond the grave. Then an adulterer was to be stoned; now he is to be—damned.

We may add that the punishment of sin in this world is sometimes unavoidable. Thus, if nations are punished at all, they must be punished in time—for they have no existence in eternity; there men exist only as individuals. And nearly the same may be said of a family. Hence we read "the curse of the Lord is in the house of the wicked: but he blesseth the habitation of the just."

Yea, the present punishment of sin is in some measure natural. For how frequently do men's sufferings arise from the very sins they commit! Extravagance breeds ruin—indolence, poverty—intemperance, disease. "Who hath wo? Who hath sorrow? Who hath contentions? Who hath babbling? Who hath wounds without cause? Who hath redness of eyes? They that tarry long at the wine; they that go to seek mixed wine." Why are men so unhappy—but because they are unholy. They walk contrary to God, and God walks contrary to them. They transgress his commands, and expose themselves to his wrath; and then they are alarmed with fear. They yield to vile passions. and appetites, and then they groan by reason of bondage. They violate all the rules which conduce to the welfare of the community, and then they are expelled from the esteem and regard of their fellow-creatures. And what can hinder all this?

So that sin does not recompense or even indemnify the sinner here. "The *way* as well as the *end* of transgressors is hard." As the righteous here have some foretastes of their future happiness, so the wicked have here the beginnings of sorrows. As godliness has the promise of the life that now is, as well as of that which is to come, so sin has the curse of this world, as well as of another.

III. See in it PUNISHMENT INFLICTED AFTER LONG DELAY. Behold the career of this sinner! "Threescore and ten kings" he had thus inhumanly mangled. Thus he repeated his crime again and again—even until seventy times! What a lengthened course of iniquity was here!—"So long and so often had I done this, that I thought God had not seen, or did not remember. But he has found me out; and I live long enough to be a miserable instance of this awful truth—that however long punishment may be delayed, it will at last be inflicted—As I have done, so God hath requited me."

The wonder is—not that he was overtaken so soon—but that he was spared so long; and seemed to be allowed to triumph in his iniquity. The flourishing condition of sinners for a time, and especially for a long time, unchecked by calamity, is an event which has often perplexed even pious minds. Thus Jeremiah exclaims "Righteous art thou, O Lord, when I plead with thee; yet let me talk with thee of thy judgments: wherefore doth the way of the wicked prosper? Wherefore are all they happy that deal very treacherously?" David also tells us: "As for me, my feet were almost gone; my steps had well nigh slipped; for I was envious at the foolish, when I saw the prosperity of the wicked."

But what is more to be lamented is, that hereby the unhappy creature himself is frequently deluded. He is apt to mistake forbearance for connivance; and what God does not immediately punish, he concludes that he entirely neglects. "He hath said in his heart, I shall not be moved; for I shall never be in adversity." "Because sentence against an evil work is not executed speedily, therefore the heart of the sons of men is fully set in them to do evil." But we should remember the end of providence in such a dispensation. He frequently spares the ungodly for the sake of the godly: the extraction of the tares would injure the wheat. By forbearing the blow, he would give space for repentance: "the longsuffering of our God is salvation." He has therefore ends to answer worthy of himself. But be convinced of this

—that he never designed to cherish in you a hope of impunity. His patience is not forgiveness. "Be sure your sins will find you out. He that being often reproved hardeneth his neck, shall suddenly be destroyed, and that without remedy." He is patient; but he is faithful, and the Scripture cannot be broken. He is patient: but patience has its limits; and the year of trial granted to the barren fig-tree will expire, and then, if unfruitful, it shall be cut down, and cast into the fire. He is patient: but if his patience end not in your conversion, it will be glorified in your destruction. "These things hast thou done, and I kept silence: thou thoughtest that I was altogether such an one as thyself; but I will reprove thee, and set them in order before thine eyes. Now consider this, ye that forget God, lest I tear you in pieces, and there be none to deliver."

IV. See in it A CORRESPONDENCE BETWEEN SIN AND SUFFERING. "What I have inflicted upon others, is now inflicted upon me: and in my very punishment I read my crime—as I have done, so God hath requited me!" Our Saviour has said, "With the same measure ye mete, it shall be measured to you again." And Eliphaz tells us, that he had particularly remarked this even in his days. "I have seen they that plough iniquity, and sow wickedness, reap the same." From the nature of their suffering, men may often learn the character of their sin. God sometimes sends our troubles with a label upon them—it seems impossible to mistake their design. We are commanded to "hear the rod;" it says many things—but it frequently tells us the very sin for which we smart: it thunders or whispers, "this is the duty you have neglected. This is the idol you have adored. Hast thou not procured this unto thyself?"

Between sin and punishment there is sometimes a *comparative* conformity. This is the case when we suffer things which have some resemblance to our crimes. Thus the Jews, for serving strange gods, were compelled to serve strange masters. Forty days the spies were employed in exploring the land of promise, and forty years the people are condemned to wander in the wilderness for believing them.

Sometimes there is also between them a *direct* conformity. This is the case when we suffer in the same way and in the same things in which we sin. Thus it is said of the Chaldeans, "Because thou hast spoiled many nations, all the remnant of the people shall spoil thee." Thus it is said of the Church of Rome. "For they have shed the blood of saints and prophets, and thou hast given them blood to drink; for they are worthy." What was the subject of David's sin? The numbering of his people. In this he suffers: a pestilence carries off seventy thousand of his subjects. What was the design of wicked Haman? "Then said Zeresh his wife and all his friends unto him, Let a gallows be made of fifty cubits high, and to-morrow speak thou unto the king that Mordecai may be hanged thereon; then go thou in merrily with the king unto the banquet. And the thing pleased Haman, and he caused the gallows to be made." What was his doom? "And Harbonah, one of the chamberlains, said before the king, Behold also the gallows, fifty cubits high, which Haman had made for Mordecai, who had spoken good for the king, standeth in the house of Haman. Then the king said, Hang him thereon. So they hanged Haman on the gallows that he had prepared for Mordecai. And to mention no more, in the very place where Jezebel caused the dogs to lick the blood of Naboth, the dogs licked her blood?

But there is a *future* conformity still more dreadful; and of which the Apostle speaks when he says, "Be not deceived; God is not mocked; for whatsoever a man soweth, that shall he also reap. For he that soweth to his flesh, shall of the flesh reap corruption; but he that soweth to the Spirit, shall of the Spirit reap life everlasting." The man who sowed thistles, and expected to reap wheat, would be deemed a fool. But are we not equally foolish? What are the principles we imbibe, the dispositions we cultivate, the pursuits in which we are engaged, that we are concluding they will issue in glory, honour, and immortality? Is there any relation between these? Do not the steps of the road we travel take hold on hell? Misery is not only the reward of our works, but the very tendency of our sin. Hear this, ye covetous and unfeeling. Your hard-heartedness is not punishable by any human tribunal—but see your crime meeting you at the bar of God: "he shall have judgment without mercy, that showed no mercy." Think of this, ye despisers of the Gospel—he now addresses *you* in vain; "Because I have called, and ye refused: I have stretched out my hand, and no man regarded; but ye have set at nought all my counsel, and would none of my reproof."—And hereafter you shall address *him* in vain: "I will also laugh at your calamity: I will mock when your fear cometh; when your fear cometh as desolation, and your destruction cometh as a whirlwind; when distress and anguish cometh upon you: then shall they call upon me, but I will not answer; they shall seek me early, but they shall not find me."

Finally. See in this Scripture THE HAND OF GOD ACKNOWLEDGED, WHILE MEN ONLY ARE EMPLOYED—"God hath requited me." But who saw any thing of him? Did not the sons of Judah and of Simeon cut off his thumbs and his great toes? Yes—but "is there an evil in the city, and the Lord hath not done it?" "I form the light, and create darkness: I make peace, and create evil. I, the Lord, do all these things." War is as much a judgment from God, as famine or pestilence. And not only are lawful princes and magistrates the ministers of God, but he makes use of robbers and tyrants; as it is written: " Out of him came forth the córner; out of him the nail; out of him the battle-bow; out of him every oppressor together."

But admitting this to be true—how came Adoni-bezek, a very wicked man—a heathen —how came *he* to acknowledge it ?—The case is this—" The Gentiles who have not a written law," says the Apostle, " are a law unto themselves: their thoughts also in the mean time accusing or else excusing one another." There is a conscience in every man; the principle belongs to human nature; and no wickedness is able completely to banish it. And calamity has always been observed to have a powerful effect to enliven it. So that the man who, in the days of prosperity and ease, banished reflection, never thought of God; or if he did, considered himself perhaps as the favourite of Heaven, because he was so much indulged on earth—is now abstracted; impressed; softened: he is left alone with his conscience: this tells him of his desert; this awakens all his fears. Hence sickness, accidents, death are dreadful—they stir up the apprehension of Deity. He suspects more in the storm than thunder and lightning—God is there. The shaking of a leaf seems to say, " What is this that thou hast done ?"

A good man perceives the hand of God in all events, and he *wishes* to see it. " The Lord," says Job, " gave, and the Lord hath taken away: what! shall we receive good at the Lord's hand, and shall we not receive evil ?" This calmed him. And this discovery of God is the Christian's relief and comfort in affliction—because he knows that God is his father and friend, and will not, cannot injure him. But it is otherwise with the sinner. His apprehension of God is forced upon him; he would gladly get rid of the conviction: it is all terror and dismay to him—for he knows that God is his adversary, and he may now be coming to lay hold of him—he knows that he has a long account to give, and this may be the time of reckoning. Hence the bitterness of affliction: it is regarded not only as a trial, but as a punishment. The sinner's distress seems to be the effect of chance; but he feels it to be the consequence of design. He discerns in it the injustice of men; and yet is compelled to confess that it is the righteous judgment of God. And thus, by the medium of this penal consciousness, God maintains his moral empire in the world, without deviating from the usual course of events, or breaking in upon the stated laws of nature. He works

no miracle, yet his agency is believed. He does not render himself visible, yet his presence is felt and acknowledged; and common calamities are made to operate like positive tokens of divine displeasure.

Though the subject has been very instructive and practical, I wish to add two exhortations.

First. ABHOR CRUELTY. It is equally disgraceful to religion and humanity. It renders you unpitied of God and man. I hope none of you would be so dreadfully savage as this monster, to torture and mangle your fellow-creatures, if you had it in your power. But let me speak a word for the poor brutes, who cannot speak for themselves, though unhappily they have the power of feeling. My dear little friends, never torment animals. Never sport with the misery of insects. Never cut off their legs or wings. God's " tender mercies are over all his works." " He hears the young ravens that cry." " Be followers of God as dear children." But what are we to say in another case ?

Adoni-bezek was merciful compared with those who endeavour to draw their fellow-creatures into sin. This is not only to injure the body, but to cast the soul into hell: and what is any present suffering compared with endless misery !

Secondly. IMPROVE THE CASE OF EXAMPLES. If they were not particularly adapted to do us good—the word of God would not be so full of them. Never read them carelessly. Lodge them in your memory. Often reflect upon them.

And make use of the dreadful as well as the pleasing. It is necessary that sin should be made hateful. It is necessary that we should be awakened to flee from the wrath to come.

And do not suppose that such a character as Adoni-bezek is alone exposed to danger— " Except ye repent, ye shall *all* likewise perish."

" For we must all appear before the judgment-seat of Christ, that every one may receive the things done in his body according to that he hath done, whether it be good or bad. Knowing therefore the terrors of the Lord, we persuade men: but we are made manifest unto God; and I trust also are made manifest in your consciences."

DISCOURSE LI

THE CHEERFUL PILGRIM.

Thy statutes have been my songs in the house of my pilgrimage.—Psalm cxix. 54.

How different are the views and feelings of men in the review of life ! How dismal and terrifying is it to look back on years bar ren of good and filled with wickedness; to look back upon time wasted, opportunities misimproved, faculties perverted, mercies abused, character destroyed; to look back and find nothing from which the mind can derive a future hope, or acknowledge a past satisfaction!

But it is pleasing and edifying to look back—I will not say upon a well-spent life—but upon those years in which we have known God, or rather have been known of him; in which we have loved and endeavoured to serve him; in which we have enjoyed something of his presence and his smiles. It is delightful to call to remembrance places and seasons made sacred by communion with him; and to think over the advantages and pleasures we have derived from his ordinances, and from his blessed word.

David does this. "Thy statutes have been my songs in the house of my pilgrimage."

Hence we observe three things. I. A GOOD MAN VIEWS HIS RESIDENCE IN THIS WORLD AS ONLY THE HOUSE OF HIS PILGRIMAGE. II. THE SITUATION, HOWEVER DISADVANTAGEOUS, ADMITS OF CHEERFULNESS. III. THE SOURCES OF HIS JOY ARE DERIVED FROM THE SCRIPTURE.

I. When David speaks of THE HOUSE OF HIS PILGRIMAGE, he may literally design to express his exile and wanderings when banished by the persecution of Saul, or the rebellion of Absalom. But he intends it more generally, as significant of the whole course of his life on earth. For being a partaker of divine grace, he would say this in a palace as well as in a prison; he would say it when surrounded with all the ensigns of majesty, as well as when stripped of all his possessions. If a Christian had the dominion of Alexander, and all the treasures of the Indies, yet in all this abundance, and with all this greatness, he would feel himself poor, feel himself from home, feel himself a stranger and a sojourner—and seek a better country, that is an heavenly.

At first indeed the world is far from appearing to us in this reduced and insignificant point of light. Its maxims and pursuits fall in with our depraved dispositions. And unacquainted with its vanity and vexation, we rush forth filled with high and eager expectations. We think to find it a paradise—but thorns and briers, sand and drought, tell us it is a wilderness. We dream that we are eating, but awake and feel that we are hungry—and looking around us, we see that there is nothing to feed us.

Various are the disappointments and the calamities that imbitter life; and "many are the afflictions of the righteous." Yet we are mistaken if we suppose that it is wholly or principally owing to these that he views himself now in a house of pilgrimage. The spirit of the world no longer reigns in him. He renounces the world, not only because it is unfriendly, but because it is unsuitable: not because he cannot carry every thing before him, but because he no longer loves it. He forsakes the world when it smiles, as well as when it frowns. He is not violently torn from it, but resigns it in consequence of the discovery and apprehension of something infinitely better. The eyes of his understanding are enlightened, and he sees what is the hope of his calling, and what is the glory of the riches of his inheritance in the saints: and this henceforth becomes his prize. Having discerned by faith another world, he makes a true estimate of this—he sees that the present is not a state to fix in, but only a region to pass through; and therefore finds that he is not at home, but journeying.

He is born from above, and therefore naturally aspires after his native land. Does not every thing tend to the place of its original?

His portion is above. The inheritance incorruptible, and undefiled, and that fadeth not away, is reserved in heaven for him. There his hope is laid up; there is his treasure—and what wonder if there his heart be also! There he is to gain deliverance from all his errors; perfection of holiness; a glorious body; the possession of all the promises. Can he be satisfied to live at a distance from all this?

His kindred dwell above—there are to be found his father, his elder brother, the younger branches of the household of faith. Thither many of his once dear connexions on earth are gone, and thither all the wise and good are going; and he can now only get a glance of them upon the road, or exchange a few words as they pause for refreshment at the inn. There they shall all unite and be for ever with each other, and for ever with the Lord. Here he is in motion, then he will be at rest; he is now traveling, he shall then reach home, and "sit down with Abraham, and Isaac, and Jacob in the kingdom of God."

Inferior, however, as his present situation is, compared with the future—we are reminded,

II. THAT IT WILL ADMIT OF CHEERFULNESS: he can sing—"thy statutes have been my songs in the house of my pilgrimage."

Genuine religion excites and interests the feelings. It is equally absurd and dangerous to place it in cold ceremonies, or external performances in which the affections have no share. The same may be said of reducing it merely to an intellectual system. The principles of revelation are addressed, not only to the understanding, but to the heart. Ought I to believe that Jesus Christ died for my sins, and that two and two make four, with the same indifference and insensibility? Impossible. That Jesus Christ came into the world to save sinners is not only "a faithful saying," but a saying "worthy of all acceptation:" it contains all that is great and good and suitable and necessary—and can never be properly received, if it meets only with a frigid speculative assent.

We do not indeed plead for ignorant and unaccountable feelings : but we contend that the light of Christianity is like that of the sun, which, while it illuminates, also enlivens and fructifies. We do not admire the zeal which burns up the brain; but we plead for the fervour that warms the heart: and we say, and saith not the Scripture the same? that "it is good to be always zealously affected in a good thing." And wherefore is every thing like warmth in religion branded with the name of enthusiasm? Warmth is expected in the poet, in the musician, in the scholar, in the lover—and even in the tradesman it is allowed, if not commended—why then is it condemned in the concerns of the soul—a subject which, infinitely above all others, demands and deserves all the energy of the mind? Would a prisoner exult at the proclamation of deliverance—and is the redeemed sinner to walk forth from his bondage, unmoved, unaffected, without gratitude or joy? No. "Ye shall go out with joy, and be led forth with peace : the mountains and the hills shall break forth before you into singing, and all the trees of the field shall clap their hands!" Shall the condemned criminal feel I know not what emotions, when instead of the execution of the sentence he receives a pardon; and is the absolved transgressor to be senseless and silent?—No. "Being justified by faith, we have peace with God through our Lord Jesus Christ. By whom also we have access by faith into this grace wherein we stand, and rejoice in hope of the glory of God. And not only so, but we glory in tribulations also. And not only so, but we also joy in God, through our Lord Jesus Christ, by whom we have now received the atonement."

Other travellers are accustomed to relieve the tediousness of their journey with a song. The Israelites, when they repaired from the extremities of the country three times a year to Jerusalem to worship, had songs appointed for the purpose, and traveled singing as they went. And of the righteous it is said, "They shall sing in the ways of the Lord. The redeemed of the Lord shall return, and come to Zion with songs, and everlasting joy shall be upon their heads". Religion therefore is productive of many pleasing feelings. And we make use of this fact two ways.

First, we say that those who are habitually strangers to pleasure in divine things have reason to suspect their condition. Persons may want the joy of confidence, and yet have the joy of hope: and they may have very little, if any, of the pleasures of hope, while yet they find pleasures in religious exercises and dispositions. They may love the place where God's honour dwelleth, and be glad when it is said to them, "Let us go into the house of the Lord;" they may "call the Sabbath a delight;" and say, "It is good for me to draw nigh to God." But it is awful if you find the Sabbath a weariness, the house of God a prison, and the presence of God irksome—it is awful if you find religious duties a task instead of a privilege. It is one of the characters of the true circumcision—that "they rejoice in Christ Jesus."

Secondly, those are mistaken who shun religion under the apprehension that it is unfriendly to their happiness, and prescribes a joyless course, engaged in which they must bid adieu to pleasure. Man needs present gratification, and religion provides for it. The Master he serves does not require him to live only in expectation : he has much in possession, though he has more in hope. There the clusters grow, but hither some of them are sent.

> "The hill of Zion yields
> A thousand sacred sweets
> Before we reach the heav'nly fields,
> Or walk the golden streets."

Surely you will allow that happiness depends upon God, and that he is able to make a man happy at present—and is it likely that he will suffer an enemy in rebellion against him to be happier than a servant who is endeavouring to serve him! If such be your conclusion—what a monstrous notion of God do you entertain! Besides, has he not assured you in his word that his "yoke is easy, and his burden light"—that his "ways are ways of pleasantness, and that all his paths are peace!" And does not the experience of all those who have made the trial confirm the truth of the representation! Have not his followers found that "to the upright there ariseth light in darkness!" have they not sung in seasons and circumstances which would have filled others with misery and dismay! Behold Paul and Silas. At midnight in the inner prison, their feet made fast in the stocks, their backs bleeding with the recent scourge—they not only prayed—but "sung praises unto God!" Behold the Church. She views every earthly resource as dried up—but can say, "Although the fig-tree shall not blossom, neither shall fruit be in the vines; the labour of the olive shall fail, and the fields shall yield no meat; the flock shall be cut off from the fold, and there shall be no herd in the stalls: yet I will rejoice in the Lord, I will joy in the God of my salvation." Behold David. He bids fare well to life; his heart and his flesh fail him—but he exclaims, "Yea, though I walk through the valley of the shadow of death, I will fear no evil: for thou art with me; thy rod and thy staff they comfort me."

III. Whence did David, and whence does every Christian derive this joy? I answer, From the Scriptures. "Thy statutes have been my songs in the house of my pilgrimage." The discoveries and the promises of this blessed book are adapted to rejoice the pilgrim's heart.

What are these discoveries? They tell him of the *end* of his faith, even the salvation of his soul—they remind him continually of his country; they place it before him in every engaging form, and prove how far it surpasses every thing here—while it will infinitely indemnify him for all his losses, and reward him for all his difficulties.

They show him clearly and unerringly the way. Thus they give him the peace and satisfaction of certainty: he knows that he is not journeying at random—not a step is taken in vain—each brings him nearer home.

They assure him that he is not alone in his trials and exercises. They call upon him to observe way-marks thrown up by former pilgrims, where he began to think no pious foot had ever trod. "'The same things,' say they, 'happened to your brethren who were before you in the world.' 'Be ye followers of them who through faith and patience inherit the promises.' 'Take the prophets, who have spoken in the name of the Lord, for an example of suffering affliction, and of patience. Behold, we count them happy which endure. Ye have heard of the patience of Job, and have seen the end of the Lord: that the Lord is very pitiful and of tender mercy.'" How suitable, how animating, how blessed are such discoveries as these!

But promises are something more than discoveries; and with these the Scripture abounds. They are "exceeding great and precious." And what can the pilgrim want or desire that is not insured by them?—A freedom of motion? This is insured. "Thou shalt walk in thy way safely, and thy foot shall not stumble." An ability to hold on?—This is insured. The "righteous shall hold on his way; and he that hath clean hands shall wax stronger and stronger." Victory over enemies?—This is insured. "Thou shalt tread upon the lion and adder; the young lion and the dragon shalt thou trample under foot." All needful supplies?—These are insured. "O fear the Lord, ye his saints; for there is no want to them that fear him. The young lions do lack and suffer hunger; but they that seek the Lord shall not want any good thing." Is not all this sufficient to induce him to go on his way rejoicing?

We have been speaking of the experience of David, and of the experience of all the Lord's people. Are you like-minded with them? There are only two sorts of people in the world. All are citizens of earth or of heaven. And naturally all are of the first class—but some are by divine grace obeying the command; "Arise ye and depart hence: for this is not your rest."

Are you men of the world—do you feel yourselves at home—would you be satisfied to live here always—provided you could succeed according to your wishes? Are you looking only to those things that are seen and temporal? The man who takes up with this world as his portion is worse than a brute. He is unworthy of the soul he carries within him. He starves his mind. He makes no provision for the evil day. It matters not what he has—he is in a miserable condition—he has nothing that can either satisfy or save. A man going to execution is for the present very well off: he has a carriage to ride in; a guard to attend him; officers to accompany him, and a number of followers. But what would you think of the man if he deemed all this the token of his honour, rather than the forerunner of his punishment; and should only consider how he is accommodated, but never ask whither am I going? Alas! how many such fools are there! They only think how it is with them at present, but never inquire what will become of them hereafter. But "the end of these things is death."

There are others who are delivered from the present evil world, and are heirs of the kingdom which God has promised to them that love him. As strangers and pilgrims, let me give you three admonitions, founded on the several parts of the discourse which you have heard.

First. Always regard your present condition as a state of pilgrimage—and never view it as any thing more. This will regulate your desires, and moderate your wishes after earthly things. This will keep you from being too much elated when you meet with prosperous scenes. Not that you will disparage the bounties of Providence—you will even be thankful for them, as conveniences by the way—but you will consider them *only* as accommodations; and not mistake them for the advantages and glories of home—you will not therefore sit down, but still press forward. This will enable you to endure with fortitude and resignation the hardships you may encounter. You will say, "As a traveller, I expect such things; they are only the inconveniences of a journey—it will soon be over—'and I reckon that the sufferings of this present time are not worthy to be compared with the glory which shall be revealed in us.'"

Second. Cherish a humble and a holy joy. Consider this not only as your privilege—but duty. Enforce it upon your minds by the authority of God, who commands you to rejoice always, and by a consideration of the importance of it to others. Nothing will honour and recommend your religion more than this. It will show those around you, that you have found what they are seeking after. Surely you do not, you cannot wish to travel to heaven alone—but habitually cheerful—singing as you go—you will be constantly inviting and alluring your relations, friends, neighbours, to join you. You will address them, as Moses addressed Hobab, the son of Raguel—"We are journeying unto the place of which the Lord said, I will give it you: come thou with us, and we will do thee good: for the Lord hath spoken good concerning Israel."

Third. Love and study the Scriptures. He that avoids reading a portion of them daily forsakes his own mercy; and is so far regardless of his safety, welfare, and comfort. Therefore "bind them continually upon thine heart, and tie them about thy neck. When thou goest, it shall lead thee; when thou sleepest, it shall keep thee; and when thou awakest, it shall talk with thee. For the commandment is a lamp: and the law is light; and reproofs of instruction are the way of life."

Precious Bible! like thy blessed Author, our sun and our shield, thou giver of grace and glory, thou conductor through all this gloomy vale to our everlasting home, how many advantages have we already derived from thee! Thou hast often solved our doubts, and wiped away our tears. Thou hast been sweeter to our taste than honey and the honeycomb. Thou hast been better to us, in our distresses, than thousands of gold and silver. Unless thou hadst been our delight, we should have perished in our affliction.

No wonder Job "esteemed thee more than his necessary food." No wonder David chose thee as his heritage for ever, and found thee to be the rejoicing of his heart. No wonder the noble army of martyrs parted with their estates and with their blood, rather than with thee. May we value thee as our richest jewel, may we love thee as our dearest good, may we consult thee as our surest counsellor, may we follow thee as our safest rule!

And oh! thou eternal Jehovah, "send out thy light and thy truth: let them lead me! let them bring me unto thy holy hill, and to thy tabernacles. Then will I go unto the altar of God, unto God, my exceeding joy; yea, upon the harp will I praise thee, O God, my God!"

DISCOURSE LII.

SIN RUINS A KINGDOM.

(FOR A FAST-DAY.)

Only fear the Lord, and serve him in truth with all your heart: for consider how great things he hath done for you. But if ye shall still do wickedly, 'ye shall be con-

sumed, both ye and your king.—1 Sam. xii. 24, 25.

SUCH was the language of Samuel to the Jews. The words have a peculiar force in them. It arises from the wisdom of the address. How could he have given them a better representation of their duty? And how could he have more powerfully recommended it?

He requires of them nothing superstitious; nothing merely ritual and ceremonious; nothing only external and temporary—but the exercise of piety flowing from the fear of God, and accompanied with a sincerity and fervour in serving him. This is all. "Only fear the Lord, and serve him in truth with all your heart." This he enforces by two motives; the one drawn from gratitude, and the other from interest. He has been your friend; he can be your enemy. He has done great things for you; and he will do great things against you. Consider this—"Consider how great things he hath done for you. But if ye shall still do wickedly, ye shall be consumed, both ye and your king."

Already I hope you have dropped Judea, and fixed your attention on your own country. The words could never have been more applicable to the Jews than they are to us. And hence we have been led to choose them on this solemn occasion, when we are called to assemble together to acknowledge our sins and to implore the Divine mercy.

To render the Scripture useful, we must consider persons in former ages as specimens of human nature in general; and the dispensations of Providence towards them as holding forth the unchangeable perfections of Jehovah. Thus individuals, families, churches, nations, become exemplary, and by their welfare or ruin, encourage our hope, or awaken our fear.

Among all the nations of the earth there is no one to which we can so properly refer as the Jews—not only because their history is true, and events are traced up to their proper causes—but because there is a greater correspondence between them and us than between us and any other people. They only of all the nations of antiquity worshipped the same God with us. They only, like us, were under the reign of grace as well as providence, and enjoyed religious and spiritual privileges blended with civil and natural. Let us attend to this.

Samuel tells them that "the Lord had done great things for them." David could not review their history without admiration. "What one nation in the earth is like thy people, even like Israel, whom God went to redeem for a people to himself, and to make him a name, and to do for you great things and terrible, for thy land, before thy people, which thou redeemest to thee from Egypt, from the nations and their gods?"

Moses, at a much earlier period, gave them a pre-eminent blessedness. "Happy art thou, O Israel! who is like unto thee, O people, saved by the Lord, the shield of thy help, and who is the sword of thy excellency! and thine enemies shall be found liars unto thee, and thou shalt tread upon their high places."

Abraham lived in Ur of the Chaldeans. God, in his sovereign grace, "called him to his foot," and commanded him to depart from his own country and his father's house, in search of a place which he should afterwards receive for an inheritance. He told him he should be the ancestor of a nation, numerous as the stars of heaven, and that one of his posterity should finally bless all the families of the earth. He multiplied and increased him. With Isaac and Jacob, the heirs with him of the same promise, he was a stranger and a pilgrim upon earth. "When they were but a few men in number; yea, very few, and strangers in it; when they went from one nation to another, from one kingdom to another people: he suffered no man to do them wrong; yea, he reproved kings for their sakes; saying, Touch not mine anointed, and do my prophets no harm."

Their deliverance from the land of Egypt and the house of bondage is well known. He brought them forth with a strong hand and an outstretched arm. Creatures of every rank espoused their cause, and punished their enemies. When in jeopardy from their pursuers, the sea opened, and they passed through, as on dry ground, which the Egyptians assaying to do, were drowned. Then they sang his praise. And the deliverance was the food of their faith, and hope, long afterwards. "Thou didst divide the sea by thy strength; thou breakedst the heads of the dragons in the waters. Thou breakedst the head of Leviathan in pieces, and gavest him to be meat to the people inhabiting the wilderness."

Forty years wandered they in the desert. They knew not their way—he was their guide. They were exposed to dangers—he was their defence. They had no supplies—he rained down manna; the rocks poured out water; and their clothes waxed not old upon them. Had they unwholesome damps by night? The pillar of cloud became a fire and absorbed them. Were they open by day to the heat of a burning sky? The pillar of fire became a cloud and diffused an immense shade over them. Thus "the sun did not smite them by day, nor the moon by night."

By-and-by Jordan rolled back its streams, and they took possession of a land, where were wells which they digged not, houses which they builded not, vineyards which they planted not: a land flowing with milk and honey; wherein there was no scarceness; and upon which the Lord's eye was from the beginning even to the end of the year.

But they had unspeakably greater advantages than all these. What says David! "He showeth his word unto Jacob, his statutes and his judgments unto Israel. He hath not dealt so with any nation: and as for his judgments, they have not known them." What says Paul! "Who are Israelites; to whom pertaineth the adoption, and the glory, and the covenants, and the giving of the law, and the service of God, and the promises; whose are the fathers, and of whom as concerning the flesh Christ came, who is over all, God blessed for ever."

And has he not done great things for us! —It is not foolish partiality, but truth that compels us to say, "The lines are fallen to us in pleasant places; yea, we have a goodly heritage." O England! "blessed of the Lord be thy land, for the precious things of heaven, for the dew, and for the deep that coucheth beneath. And for the precious fruits brought forth by the sun, and for the precious things put forth by the moon. And for the chief things of the ancient mountains, and for the precious things of the lasting hills. And for the precious things of the earth, and fulness thereof; and for the good will of Him that dwelt in the bush." Have we not a land of woods and rivers, of fields and of meadows, "of wheat and of barley?" Are not "our oxen strong to labour;" and do not "our sheep bring forth thousands, and ten thousands in our streets?" Are we not placed in a climate whose temperature equally secures us from scorching heat and intolerable cold? What advantages do we possess as an island! In consequence of this, we have been preserved from invasion; and our country has not been made a field of slaughter. What do we know of war? We have only witnessed its remote preparations and effects. We have not heard the "confused noise of warriors," nor seen "garments rolled in blood." Nor have our nurses, terrified at the sound of battle, fled with our infants and lamed our Mephibosheths for life. Commerce has filled our rivers with ships, and poured the produce of the four quarters of the globe upon our tables. We have a constitution which displays the sober, improved, tried wisdom of ages. We have laws, distinguished by their justice, their mildness, their impartiality. The poor are equally protected with the rich; and character and talents can rise to eminence from the cottage, as well as from the mansion. Humanity and benevolence have distinguished the national character; and around us rise institutions of charity to embrace the sons and daughters of every kind of wretchedness.

Capernaum, though a little mean fishing town, was said to be "exalted unto heaven" —and the reason was—because our Lord and Saviour had honoured it with his presence, and had preached in it the kingdom of God,

From the moment the Gospel enters a country, the importance of it commences in the eye of angels; and then—then it is said—"Arise, shine, for thy light is come; and the glory of the Lord is risen upon thee." And when it withdraws from a place, "Ichabod!" may be written upon the walls—"The glory is departed." At a very early period this inestimable blessing reached our highly favoured isle. And while it has been withdrawn from countries once blessed with the same privilege, it has been continued to us, notwithstanding all our unworthiness and provocation. Popery had indeed obscured the glory of the Gospel, locked up the Scriptures in an unknown language, and sacrificed thousands of victims to superstitious rage. But the Reformation gave us the Bible; and said, Read, and live! And the glorious Revolution fixing liberty on a firm and legal basis, said, Assemble together; Preach and hear; Worship God according to the dictates of your own consciences, and "he that toucheth you toucheth the apple of mine eye!" Thus ever since we have sat under our own vine and fig-tree, and none have made us afraid. We have filled our sanctuaries; we have enjoyed our Sabbaths; and though he has given us the bread of adversity and the water of affliction, yet has he not removed our teachers into a corner, but "our eyes behold our teachers, and our ears hear a voice behind us, saying—This is the way, walk ye in it, when we turn aside to the right hand or to the left."

Ah! think of the want of all this!——"But blessed are your eyes, for they see; and your ears, for they hear: for verily I say unto you, that many prophets and righteous men have desired to see those things which ye see, and have not seen them; and to hear those things which ye hear, and have not heard them."

And to secure all these civil and religious advantages—how often has he made our cause his own! How seasonably and signally has he interposed to save us from the designs of our enemies! When brought low, he has helped us: "at even-tide it has been light."

Can we be insensible to all this?—If there were any ingenuousness in us, this motive alone would be sufficient.

But fear has its use—and it is necessary to tell you not only that you are bound by gratitude—but interest. "If ye shall still do wickedly, ye shall be destroyed, both you and your king." This is dreadful.—Think of a king you love, as well as honour, and "whose life is a lesson to the land he sways"—driven from his throne. Think of liberty exchanged for slavery. Think of property rapaciously plundered, or devoured by tyrannical exaction. Think of your private dwellings affording those who are dearer to you than yourselves no security from brutal passions. Think of the temples of God burnt up, or converted to other purposes. Think—But let us not pursue this lamentable train of reflection—but consider a few remarks, tending both to illustrate and confirm the danger of a wicked kingdom, and then to inquire after the state of our own.

And First. If there be a moral governor of the universe, sin must provoke him. A righteous God must love righteousness; a holy God, holiness; a God of order, order; and a God of benevolence, benevolence: and accordingly he must abhor all that is opposite to these. And hence it is said, that "God is angry with the wicked every day; the wicked shall not stand in his sight: he hateth all workers of iniquity." And this is essential to every lovely and reverential view we can take of God. For who could adore a being who professed to govern the world, and suffered the wicked to go on with impunity?

Second. If sin provoke God, he is able to punish it. He is the Lord of hosts, the Lord strong and mighty, the Lord mighty in battle. All the elements are his. Every creature obeys his nod, from an archangel to a worm. How idle is it, in a case like this—to talk of armies and navies, and alliances—how absurd is it to compare force with force, and to say, after flattering calculations, "Oh! the enemy cannot come!" He cannot come unless God send him; but he can come easily enough if he should. Is any thing too hard for the Lord—when he would either show mercy or execute wrath?

Third. Bodies of men are punishable in this world only. In eternity there are no families, churches, nations. If therefore a country is to be destroyed, it is tried and condemned and executed here. When we see an individual sinner prospering in the world, and not immediately punished—our faith is not staggered; for we "know that his day is coming." But if a wicked people were allowed to escape—we should be confounded—we should ask, "Where is the God of judgment?" For in this case, they *are* not punished now. And they *cannot* be punished hereafter.

Fourth. There is a tendency in the very nature of sin to injure and ruin a country. It violates all the duties of relative life. It destroys subordination. It relaxes the ties which bind mankind together, and makes them selfish and mean. It renders men enemies to each other.—Social welfare cannot survive the death of morals and virtue.

Fifth. God's dealings with guilty nations are confirmed by his word, and indeed by all history. He has invariably punished them in due time. Witness the state of Nineveh, Babylon, and others. Thus the nation Samuel addressed put his declaration to the trial—and found it true. A succession of severe judgments befel them—till at last wrath came upon them to the uttermost, and "the Romans came and took away both their place and nation."

Finally, to enable us to draw the conclusion, he often—he always—gives previous intimation of his displeasure—so that were not men blind and deaf they must see and hear his coming. When you see the body wasting away by disease, and every complaint growing more inveterate, you suspect that death will be the consequence—it is already begun. "When the fig-tree, and all the trees, put forth leaves, we know that summer is nigh." Our Saviour said unto the people, "When ye see a cloud rise out of the west, straightway ye say, There cometh a shower; and so it is. And when ye see the south wind blow, ye say, There will be heat; and it cometh to pass. Ye hypocrites, can ye discern the face of the sky and of the earth; but how is it that ye do not discern this time?" And how is it that we do not perceive that God is angry with us—that he is contending with us?—Are none of his forerunners arrived?—Has he not more than spoken?—Has he not smitten us—and more than once? And if lighter judgments do not reform, will not heavier ones destroy? The consequence is infallible. "If ye still do wickedly, ye shall be consumed, both you and your king."

But you ask—Have we any cause to fear this?—I answer, just in proportion to the degree of our sin. Now there are two ways by which we may judge of our national guilt. The first is to enumerate the sins which reign predominant among us. To do this would not only be shocking, but endless. For what vice can be named that is not constantly committed through the land?—The other method is to lay down criterions, by which we may estimate the prevalency and the aggravations of sin in a country. And what test has ever been devised that is not alarming when applied to ourselves?

Divines have told us—That if God has favoured a nation with the revelation of his will, their sins are aggravated by means of this light—For "where much is given, much will be required; and he that knew his Lord's will, and did it not, shall be beaten with many stripes." Thus a heathen country, committing the very same sins with a country enlightened with the Gospel, is far less criminal. Thus, a country overspread with superstition, where the Bible is scarcely known, and its contents can be only viewed through a depraved and disfiguring medium—such a country, committing the very same sins, would be far less guilty than a country favoured with a purer worship, and where evangelical instruction is open to all. And does not this apply to us?

They have told us, That when God has distinguished a people by singular instances of his favour, that people will be proportionably criminal, unless they distinguish themselves by their devotedness to him. Thus God from time to time aggravated the sins of the Jews. "He made him ride on the high places of the earth, that he might eat the increase of the fields; and he made him to suck honey out of the rock, and oil out of the flinty rock; butter of kine, and milk of sheep, with fat of lambs, and rams of the breed of Bashan, and goats, with the fat of kidneys of wheat; and thou didst drink the pure blood of the grape. But Jeshurun waxed fat and kicked: thou art waxen fat, thou art grown thick, thou art covered with fatness; then he forsook God which made him, and lightly esteemed the Rock of his salvation. Hear, O heavens, and give ear, O earth: for the Lord hath spoken, I have nourished and brought up children, and they have rebelled against me." And is not this our case?

They have told us, That when a nation is under the corrections of the Almighty, they are eminently sinful if they disregard the tokens of his wrath, and go on careless and insensible. Hence, says Isaiah, "In that day did the Lord God of hosts call to weeping and to mourning, and to baldness, and to girding with sackcloth; and behold, joy and gladness, slaying oxen, and killing sheep, eating flesh, and drinking wine: let us eat and drink; for to-morrow we shall die. And it was revealed in mine ears by the Lord of hosts, surely this iniquity shall not be purged from you till ye die, saith the Lord God of hosts." In like manner, says Jeremiah, "Thou hast stricken them, but they have not grieved; thou hast consumed them, but they have refused to receive correction: they have made their faces harder than a rock; they have refused to return."—And what impressions have his judgments made upon us? Have they restrained us from any of our pride and luxury? Have they reduced the number of worldly amusements; or chilled the ardour of dissipation? If a stranger were to come among us and observe our manners, would he think we were in any distress, or had received any unfavourable omens?"

They tell us—to mention no more—That shamelessness in sinning is a sure proof of general corruption. And where is the man among us who is not more afraid of a threadbare coat, than of a dishonest action? To fail in business, and defraud innocent sufferers of their lawful property, is no longer scandalous; never excites a blush. Impurity is gloried in—and a young man, in most companies, who should profess himself virtuous, would be turned into ridicule! Much—everything depends upon the character of females. See how many of the barriers of virtue they have permitted to be removed! Behold the experiments which fashion has tried upon their reserve, their decency, their purity— See how they have adorned themselves in modest apparel, with shamefacedness and sobriety!

If such tests prove the degree of national guilt—our guilt is great; and if sin destroys kingdoms—I say, we have reason to fear.

It is not indeed for us to determine when the iniquity of a nation is full: and it seems that God sometimes prolongs the duration of a country for some providential purposes. They may be instruments in his hand of mercy or of wrath. But such a destiny does not hinder their final ruin. Though they are his instruments, they are not his favourites. He may use them and still punish them.

There is one thing of which we hear very much, and many seem to consider it as a counterpoise to all our fears, that there are so many good people among us. Blessed be God this is true, and they certainly afford us encouragement. Ten righteous men would have saved Sodom. And God says of the Jews, "I sought for a man among them that should make up the hedge, and stand in the gap before me for the land, that I should not destroy it; but I found none. Therefore have I poured out mine indignation upon them. I have consumed them with the fire of my wrath; their own way have I recompensed upon their heads, saith the Lord God." Let us therefore rejoice in this encouragement. But let us rejoice with trembling. Let us remember that it is a hopeful circumstance— but that it does not absolutely insure the salvation of a country. Let us recollect that there was a time when God used the following language to Jeremiah and Ezekiel concerning the Jews: "Therefore pray not thou for this people, neither lift up cry nor prayer for them, neither make intercession to me: for I will not hear thee. Then said the Lord unto me, Pray not for this people for their good. Though Moses and Samuel stood before me, yet my mind could not be toward this people: cast them out of my sight, and let them go forth. Though these three men, Noah, Daniel, and Job were in it, they should deliver but their own souls by their righteousness, saith the Lord God." What learn we from all this?—That there are cases in the history of nations—when the Divine forbearance is exhausted, and then the cries of the righteous will avail no more than those of the wicked. Were there not in Judea some of the best men that ever lived when the Babylonians invaded and conquered them? Have there not been pious people in every Christian country when destroyed? Does God love his followers now better than formerly, when he suffered them to share in a thousand public calamities?—While he punishes his enemies, may he not correct his friends? Or cannot he indemnify them? Or hide them? Or deliver them? He *must*

fulfil his word to his servants upon which he has caused them to hope—but he is also engaged to render vengeance to his adversaries—" he will not spare the guilty."

"What then, would you have us despair?" I would—*If* we are resolved still to do wickedly. *If* we are not brought to national repentance, I would wish every individual to *expect* that we shall be destroyed, both we and our king. "At what instant I shall speak concerning a nation, and concerning a kingdom, to build and to plant it; if it do evil in my sight, that it obey not my voice, then will I repent of the good wherewith I said I would benefit them."

But the reverse is true. "At what instant I shall speak concerning a nation, and concerning a kingdom, to pluck up, and to pull down, and to destroy it; if that nation against whom I have pronounced turn from their evil, I will repent of the evil that I thought to do unto them." Blessed be God for this welcome intelligence. For by this he assures us—and the Scripture cannot be broken—that not only innocence and righteousness will save a country—but also repentance and reformation. Oh that our country may be led to make trial of this encouraging truth! May we search and try our ways, and turn again unto the Lord. May we seek him while he may be found, and call upon him while he is near—" for he is gracious and merciful, slow to anger, and of great kindness, and repenteth him of the evil."

We learn therefore who is the worst enemy of his country—*the sinner*; and who is the best friend—*the Christian*. "By the blessing of the upright, the city is exalted; but it is overthrown by the mouth of the wicked!"

Let us all therefore seek after divine grace to renew our own souls, and to sanctify our own lives; and do all in our power to promote godliness around us. Let us endeavour to hinder all the sin we can—in our families and neighbourhood—by prayer, by example, by influence. As much sin as we hinder, so much misery and danger shall we prevent.

Let us prize those institutions which are favourable to the morality and sanctification of mankind. Especially let us value the GOSPEL. It is the grand, and the only effectual means of "teaching men to deny all ungodliness and worldly lusts, and to live soberly, righteously, and godly in the present world."

We are called upon to confess and bewail our national wickedness, and on such an occasion as this we should feel ourselves to be parts of one great whole. But no man will ever be properly affected with the sins of others till he is impressed with *his own.* Here then our concern is to begin. We are individually to look backward—and inquire, "What have I done?"—and to look forward— and ask, "Lord, what wilt thou have me to do?" We find the builders, in Nehemiah, "labouring every one over against his own house." And it is a plain but an expressive image, of an old writer—"that the best way to have a clean street is for every one to sweep before his own door."

Let us therefore personally "cease to do evil, and learn to do well." Let us fear the Lord and serve him. Let us mourn and weep for the abominations that are done in the land—and if we are not the repairers of the breach, the restorers of paths to dwell in—let us remember, it shall be well with *us*. If we suffer *with* others, we shall not suffer *like* them. And we shall soon reach Immanuel's land, where the din of war will be heard no more!

And oh! remember, if your country should be saved, and you as an individual continue impenitent—*you*—*you* will be certainly destroyed! And what is any national calamity to "everlasting destruction from the presence of the Lord, and the glory of his power!"

DISCOURSE LIII.

THE SAVIOUR COMFORTING HIS DISCIPLES.

(AFTER A FUNERAL.)

In my Father's house are many mansions; if it were not so, I would have told you. I go to prepare a place for you. And if I go and prepare a place for you, I will come again, and receive you unto myself; that where I am, there ye may be also.—John xiv. 2, 3.

NEVER man spake like this man! Grace was poured into his lips! And in him were accomplished in the highest sense the words of the prophet—"He hath given me the tongue of the learned, that I should know how to speak a word in season to him that is weary."

Having assembled with his disciples in an upper room, and administered to them the memorials of his death—he announced his approaching departure. Sorrow filled their hearts. Perhaps they expressed it in words; perhaps it was visible in their countenances. However this may be—he perceived it, and said, "Let not your heart be troubled."

But what can bear them up under such a loss?—We grieve when we lose a good man, a friend, a common benefactor. But they were to lose their Lord and Saviour, their teacher, the resolver of their doubts, their comforter in every affliction. How then would he relieve them? What is the remedy he applies?—It is faith!—The discoveries of faith are the best support under the evils of sense. "I had fainted," says David, "unless I had believed to see the goodness of the Lord in the land of the living."—"Ye believe in God," says our Saviour, "believe also in

me." But what would he have them believe? You have heard—"In my Father's house are many mansions: if it were not so, I would have told you. I go to prepare a place for you: and if I go and prepare a place for you, I will come again, and receive you unto myself; that where I am, there ye may be also."

Let us consider the various particulars of this intelligence; and the certainty of the whole.

I. THE DECLARATION OF OUR SAVIOUR CONTAINS EVERY THING THAT CAN FEED THE CONTEMPLATION, AND ENLIVEN THE HOPE OF THE CHRISTIAN.

In describing heaven, he calls it his "Father's house"—as much as to say, I am only going home. Now he is not ashamed to call his people brethren. "Behold," says he, after his resurrection, "behold, I ascend to my Father and your Father, and to my God and your God." Heaven therefore is their home also. The world knoweth them not—it knew him not. They are only strangers and pilgrims on earth. They take many a weary step; and often meet with rough usage and trying weather. But when tempted to complain, they are prevented by the reflection that this is not their home—better entertainment awaits them at their journey's end—heaven will make amends for all. Dr. Rowland Taylor, when drawing near the tower of Hadley, in Suffolk, where he had been a minister, and was now going to be a martyr—being asked how he did—answered, "Never better; for now I know that I am almost at home!"—And looking over the meadow between him and the place where he was to be immediately burnt, he said, "Only two stiles more to get over, and I am at my Father's house." And when the venerable Mr. Mede was asked how he did, replied, "I am going home as fast as I can, as every honest man ought to do when his day's work is over; and I bless God I have a good home to go to."

Yes—a *good* home indeed! Think of a building *of* God and *for* him; think of an edifice in which he resides; and which is worthy of his infinite Majesty!—We have seen splendid palaces. We have read of others, the magnificence of which seems to exceed belief. The Scripture tells us that Solomon's palace was the wonder of the earth; and that when the queen of Sheba had surveyed it, "there remained no more spirit in her." But what is all this to heaven! "The palace of the great King." No man could see it and live. But all this is your home—it is your "Father's house."

Our Lord tells us that in this house there "are many mansions." No inconsiderable number will be required. For if it be asked, are there few that shall be saved?—taking them all, eventually and collectively, we answer, No. The Captain of our salvation is leading "many sons" unto glory. And John saw before the throne "a great multitude which no man could number," from all the diversities of the human race. But there is room enough in the house of God to accommodate all his immense family. There is therefore nothing to justify monopoly. There is enough and to spare.

But the expression implies not only multiplicity, but variety. Though the house is one, the apartments are many. There is something in the heavenly state suited to the circumstances, and character, and taste of every inhabitant. The land of Canaan was given to the Jews; but each tribe had its own division, and the lots of no two of them were in all respects alike. In the world of nature we see "one glory of the sun, and another glory of the moon, and another glory of the stars; for one star differeth from another star in glory." Among the angels we read of thrones and dominions; principalities and powers: they have their orders and degrees. This also we have reason to believe will be the case with glorified saints. We see endless diversity in all God's works and ways. And will heaven be an exception? All will be perfectly blessed—but why should all be similarly employed; or equally endowed? Plunge a number of vessels into the sea—they are all alike filled—but, various in their dimensions, they hold unequal proportions.

Further; he tells them, "'I go to prepare a place for you.' You are coming too—but I must go first—to remove every impediment; to perform every condition; to secure every advantage."

For this happiness is not such as Adam would have obtained after a proper trial of his obedience in Paradise. It is the happiness of a lost creature, in whose restoration difficulties were found which the Saviour alone could remove. And before *He* can remove them—see how much it was necessary for him to accomplish! It was necessary for him to come down from heaven to earth, and return from earth to heaven. To your complete happiness—his death was necessary—his resurrection was necessary—his ascension and intercession were necessary—his universal empire, and his dispensation of the Holy Ghost were necessary.

He went away, not only to possess a personal reward, but to assume a relative dignity—not only to live a life of glory, but also a life of office; and hence says the Apostle, "If when we were enemies we were reconciled to God by the death of his Son, much more being reconciled, we shall be saved by his life!" Hence he said to his disciples, "It is expedient for you that I go away; for if I go not away, the Comforter will not come unto you: but if I depart, I will send him unto you." With his own blood he entered into the holy place, having obtained eternal redemption for us. He appeared in the presence of God for us, pleading his sacrifice, and claiming the purchase of the Cross: "Father, I will that they also whom thou hast given me be with me where I am, that they may behold my glory which thou hast given me: for thou lovedst me before the foundation of the world." He has taken possession of heaven in our name, and he holds it for us. And we read that he entered within the vail as our forerunner, whose office it is to prepare for the reception, and to announce the approach of those to whom he belongs.

Again. "If," says the Saviour, "I go and prepare a place for you, I will come again, and receive you to myself. This is fulfilled in two cases. He comes again at death. And this is infinitely desirable. It is an awful thing to die. And many a Christian has found himself in such a frame of mind as to say—

> "Oh! if my Lord would come and meet,
> My soul should stretch her wings in haste;
> Fly fearless through death's iron gate,
> Nor feel the terrors as she pass'd!"

He does this. He is peculiarly near to his people in their expiring moments. Many of them have confessed his presence in words; while others who have not had the same degree of rapturous confidence, have equally proved it by effects. Yes, he comes to irradiate the dark valley; he comes to establish their faith, and to enliven their hope, and to make all grace to abound towards them in this time of need. He comes to take them in from this world of storms to their everlasting refuge—to receive them to himself—as you would go to the door to receive a beloved friend from a distance, or hasten to embrace a dear child returning, after a long absence, from school.

He also comes again at the last day to receive them to himself. And this coming differs very much from the former. The one is spiritual, but the other will be personal. The one is private, and invisible; the other will be public and obvious, for every eye shall see him. The one is to receive his people individually; the other will be to receive them collectively. The one is to receive their souls, but the other is also to receive their bodies. This is a grand article of our faith and hope. "To them that look for him, will he appear a second time, without sin, unto salvation. Our conversation is in heaven; from whence we also look for the Saviour, the Lord Jesus Christ: who shall change our vile body, that it may be fashioned like unto his glorious body, according to the working whereby he is able even to subdue all things unto himself."

Finally he adds, "That where I am, there ye may be also." Whatever situation were prepared to receive the Christian, he would feel himself more than disappointed if when he came he could not see *him*, enjoy *him*, be for ever with *him*. For he has learned to place all his happiness in him, and it is only in proportion as he can experience his presence, that he can say, of any situation, "It is good to be here."

There is in heaven company of the first sort; society the most delicious. There we shall join the innumerable company of angels. There we shall mix with all the truly wise and good. There we shall be introduced to martyrs, apostles, patriarchs. We shall sit down with Abraham, Isaac, and Jacob in the kingdom of God. We shall see those who have gone before us, with whom we were once connected by the tender ties of nature or of friendship. But Jesus is "the chief of ten thousand." Whom have we in heaven but him!—And he cannot be satisfied unless we shall be with him to share in all his honour and happiness. "To him that overcometh will I grant to sit with me in my throne, even as I also overcame, and am set down with my Father in his throne. Where I am there shall also my servant be."—Such are the contents of this gracious declaration.

But the more important and interesting any intelligence be, the more anxious are we for its certainty. Our Saviour therefore,

II. MEETS THIS STATE OF MIND IN THE DISCIPLES, AND SAYS—"If it were not so, I would have told you." How friendly and familiar! And yet how convincing and forcible is this address! Take it thus.

First. If it had not been so—he *could* have told them. For he knew all from the beginning. He was perfectly acquainted with the situation of his Father's house; with the works and enjoyments of heaven; with the character of the persons who were to possess it; with the way in which it was to be obtained.

Secondly. If it had not been so—he *should* have told them. As their professed teacher. it was his office to rectify their mistakes, and to save them from delusion.

Here you will also observe, that he had always laid a peculiar stress upon a future state in his doctrine. He had endeavoured to induce them to give up the present for the future—to abandon treasures on earth, in expectation of treasure in heaven. Now if there were no such state of blessedness and recompence—ought he to have suffered them to give up every thing that was dear to them here, for the sake of a fool's paradise? He knew that they had forsaken all to follow him; and he knew that in consequence of their adherence to him, they would endure persecution and death—and if there was nothing to indemnify them, should he not have told them?

Thirdly. If it had not been so—he *would* have told them. This follows from the former. For what was proper for him to do, he always did

Besides—on all other occasions, when they had apprehended things to be otherwise than they really were, he had set them right. We see this with regard to his sufferings, and the nature of his kingdom.

He had kept back nothing that was profitable for them. "Henceforth," says he, "I call you not servants: for the servant knoweth not what his lord doeth: but I have called you friends; for all things that I have heard of my Father I have made known unto you." And surely he would not have held them in darkness and error in a case of so much consequence as this!

What room was there for suspicion? Could they question his love? Had he not abundantly proved his readiness to serve them? Was he not even then going to lay down his life for them?—What could be more awful than the circumstances he was now in? He was now ready to be offered: and do men feel inclined to deceive when—dying?

Conclude we therefore by remarking, First, How unlike our Saviour is the "god of this world." The god of this world "blindeth the minds of them that believe not." He is afraid of the entrance of light. He reigns by delusion. He knows that the end of these things is death. He knows that even now the pleasures of sin are not equal to the sorrows of religion. His servants indulge expectations, every one of which will issue in disappointment. He knows this—but he refuses to tell them so: till, from the blindness of sin, he plunges them into the darkness of hell.

Second. We shall never go on well in religion till our Lord and Saviour has gained our confidence. And this he surely deserves. He is often better than his promise, but never worse. Let us in all cases run to his word, and consider what he has spoken—if he has not said such a thing, it matters not who has —but if he has spoken it—believe it to be more sure than heaven or earth—for heaven or earth may pass away, but his word shall not pass away. If you were not welcome to come and take of the water of life freely, he would tell you—if future happiness were a fancy, or a dream, he would undeceive you; and not suffer you to run and strive in vain. Settle it therefore in your minds that he will not— that he cannot delude you.

It is expected therefore that the believer's confidence in him should be in proportion to his acquaintance with him. Hence it is said, "They that know thy name will put their trust in thee." And hence, says the Apostle, "I know whom I have believed"—my faith is not a blind, rash confidence—I am sure of my ground, therefore I tread firm—I have proved the character I depend upon, and therefore I unreservedly commit myself to him—he is an old friend, a tried friend. How many evidences have I had of his kindness, veracity, and power! How reproachful would it be if I could not trust him now! "I know whom I have believed, and am persuaded that he is able to keep that which I have committed to him against that day." If ye will not believe, surely ye shall not be established.

Third. What a Master, what a Saviour do we serve! How sincere! How kind! "His heart is made of tenderness; his bowels melt with love." How concerned is he not only for the safety, but also for the comfort of his followers! With what a soft hand does he wipe away their tears! How graciously does he reward them—how infinitely does he provide for them! "This is my beloved, and this is my friend, O ye daughters of Jerusalem!"

Fourth. Are you to fill any of these mansions?—Is there a place above prepared for you?—How people long to rise in the state! How they envy the great! How happy would they deem themselves if they could get into such—and such places! To what humiliations will they submit; what sacrifices will they be ready to make, to attain such fleeting, unsatisfying honours! But what are they—what can they be to "heavenly places!"—in which you are "blessed with all spiritual blessings in Christ?"

For whom then are they prepared! I answer, for those who are prepared for them. God makes his people "meet for the inheritance of the saints in light." The vessels of mercy are "afore prepared unto glory." Others would be only miserable there; even if God had not determined to exclude them. But "The wicked shall not stand in his sight, he hateth all workers of iniquity: without are dogs, and sorcerers, and whoremongers, and murderers, and idolaters, and whosoever loveth and maketh a lie." Here nothing that defileth can ever enter. For such as love sin there is another place prepared. "For Tophet is ordained of old; yea, for the king it is prepared: he hath made it deep and large: the pile thereof is fire and much wood; the breath of the Lord, like a stream of brimstone, doth kindle it." The place indeed was prepared, as our Saviour says, "for the devil and his angels;" but sinners, by their rejection of his grace, will make it their own!—It is therefore said that Judas, when he died, went to his "*own place.*"

Lastly. Let us rejoice in hope. Let us lay open our minds to these everlasting consolations which our Saviour here reveals and insures. Let them fill us with a joy unspeakable and full of glory in all our present trials, and especially under the loss of dear and valuable friends.

Let us remember that when no longer visible to us, they are not lost. They have reached their Father's house. They are disposed of infinitely to their advantage. And this should subdue the selfishness of our grief. If we love them, we ought to rejoice in their promotion.

We have no reason to believe that they are acquainted with our circumstances, or can employ themselves for our welfare—yet for us they languish, and for us they die. We may improve their removal; it should draw us away from earth, and attach us the more to heaven. And thus their going away will be for our welfare. When we lose the lives of our friends, we should be careful not to lose their deaths too.

They will not come to receive us to themselves—but they will welcome us when we enter their everlasting habitations. The separation is temporary. A time of re-union will come. We shall see their faces, and hear their voices again in the flesh. O cheerful consolation!—how suitable—and how sure! "I would not have you to be ignorant, brethren, concerning them which are asleep, that ye sorrow not, even as others which have no hope. For if we believe that Jesus died and rose again, even so them also which sleep in Jesus will God bring with him. For this we say unto you by the word of the Lord, that we which are alive and remain unto the coming of the Lord shall not prevent them which are asleep. For the Lord himself shall descend from heaven with a shout, with the voice of the archangel, and with the trump of God: and the dead in Christ shall rise first: then we which are alive and remain shall be caught up together with them in the clouds, to meet the Lord in the air: and so shall we ever be with the Lord. Wherefore comfort one another with these words."

DISCOURSE LIV.

THE DISCIPLES IN A STORM.

And when he was entered into a ship, his disciples followed him. And, behold, there arose a great tempest in the sea, insomuch that the ship was covered with the waves: but he was asleep. And his disciples came to him, and awoke him, saying, Lord, save us: we perish. And he saith unto them, Why are ye fearful, O ye of little faith? Then he arose and rebuked the winds and the sea; and there was a great calm. But the men marvelled, saying, What manner of man is this, that even the winds and the sea obey him!—Matt. viii. 23—27.

A STORM at sea is one of the sublimest appearances in nature. Hence it has often employed the painter's pencil and the poet's pen. David, whose genius was very vivid and distinct in its conceptions, has given us an admirable representation of this impressive scene. "They that go down to the sea in ships, that do business in great waters; these see the works of the Lord, and his wonders in the deep. For he commandeth and raiseth the stormy wind, which lifteth up the waves thereof. They mount up to the heaven, they go down again to the depths: their soul is melted because of trouble. They reel to and fro, and stagger like a drunken man, and are at their wits' end. Then they cry unto the Lord in their trouble, and he bringeth them out of their distresses. He maketh the storm a calm, so that the waves thereof are still. Then are they glad because they are quiet: so he bringeth them unto their desired haven."

Let us repair this evening to the lake of Galilee, and behold a vessel in a storm, containing the twelve apostles and the Lord of all. The narrative is every way instructive and useful. And was written for our learning. The circumstances are six. They are these—THE STORM AROSE WHILE THE DISCIPLES WERE FOLLOWING OUR LORD. WHILE THEY WERE ALARMED, HE WAS ASLEEP. IN THEIR DISTRESS THEY IMPLORE HIS ASSISTANCE. HE REPROVES THEIR FEARS. HE COMMANDS THEIR DELIVERANCE. HE DRAWS FORTH THEIR ADMIRATION AND PRAISE.

They sailed in a calm, and soon encountered a storm. It is the emblem of life; at least the life of many. They launched forth into the world with fair appearances and high-raised expectations; but they had not proceeded far before the clouds gathered blackness, the sky was overspread, the winds howled, the waves roared, and they said, with Hezekiah, "Behold, for peace I had great bitterness." It is the emblem of many a particular enterprise; for so unanswerable often is the end of a thing to the beginning of it, that prudence as well as Scripture, seems to say, "Boast not thyself of to-morrow, for thou knowest not' what a day may bring forth."

But we are not only taught that we may sail in a calm, and meet with a storm;—we may encounter one even when sailing with Christ. This was the case here. They were acting in obedience to his authority and in compliance with his example: " When he was entered into a ship, his disciples followed him; and, behold, there arose a great tempest in the sea, insomuch that the ship was covered with the waves." How is this? He could have prevented the fury of the elements, and have given them a peaceful and pleasant passage over. But then he would not have taught us so much. Particularly we should have wanted a confirmation of this truth—that prosperous gales do not always attend us in the prosecution of duty. And yet this is a very important lesson. It is of great utility to the young, who are just beginning a religious course. It will prevent their expecting exemption from trials and difficulties; it will lead them to believe that these things may occur, will occur: and thus when the evil day comes they will not think it strange, or grow weary and faint in

their minds; but rather be emboldened and confirmed. "O my soul, did He not tell me this! Did he not assure me that in the world I should have tribulation—that, as a traveller, I must look for some unfavourable weather and disagreeable road—that there would be a slough, a hill of difficulty, a valley of humiliation—and here they are! I am right. Here David sighed. Here Paul groaned. These are way-marks which they have thrown up. I am journeying the same way; 'the way everlasting.'"

For want of having this truth present to the mind, many Christians who are more advanced in the divine life, have been confounded and dismayed. All misery wears the character of sin, of which it is the consequence; it naturally therefore reminds us of it. God is the source of all light and joy; and when we see nothing of the one, and feel nothing of the other, it is not easy to believe that he is present with us. We are ready to say, with Gideon, "'If the Lord be with us, why then is all this evil befallen us?' Surely he would have hindered all this. Surely, if he had it in his power, a father would keep a child from every thing hurtful; and a benefactor, a friend. How then can God be my benefactor and father, when, though he could by a single volition cure all my complaints, he suffers me from week to week to struggle with poverty, pine in sickness, and groan under disappointment! If I am his, why am I thus?" But here we err. We do not consider that his thoughts are not our thoughts, nor his ways our ways—that though his love be real, it is also wise—that though no chastening for the present seemeth to be joyous, but grievous, nevertheless afterward it yieldeth the peaceable fruit of righteousness to them that are exercised thereby. Hence it is not said, Blessed is the man that escapes, but "blessed is the man that endureth temptation; for when he is tried, he shall receive a crown of life." Afflictions are the same to the soul as the plough to the fallow ground, the pruning-knife to the vine, and the furnace to the gold. Let none, on the other hand, conclude that they are right because they are prosperous. Success is flattering not only to our wishes, but to our pride; and when we are very warm in any cause, we are prone to consider every favourable circumstance as expressive of divine approbation. But did God approve of Jonah's flight because, when he came down to the sea-shore, he found a ship just ready to sail? What says poetry?

> "God's choice is safer than our own:
>   Of ages past inquire
> What the most formidable fate?—
>   To have our own desire."

What saith the Scripture? "He gave them their heart's desire, but sent leanness into their soul."

2 B   17

Secondly. WHILE HIS DISCIPLES WERE PERPLEXED AND ALARMED, "HE WAS ASLEEP." O sleep, thou soft, downy enemy! how much of our time, our short, our uncertain, our all-important time dost thou rob us of!—*His* whole life was an illustration of his remark—"I must work the works of Him that sent me while it is day: the night cometh, wherein no man can work." He never spoke an idle word; never spent an idle hour. He was in watchings often: we read of his teaching early in the temple; of his rising a great while before day and praying; of his going up into a mountain, and continuing all night in prayer to God. Now for once we read of his sleeping. We may take three views of it.

It was a sleep of *refreshment*. Wearied nature required repose in him as well as in us. For though he was divine, he was also truly and properly a man, and was possessed of all our sinless infirmities. At one time we find him upon the road begging a draught of cold water; at another, he hungered and found no food on the fig-tree. He was now heavy to sleep, and like a labouring man—such he was—his sleep was sweet; and regardless of delicate accommodations, he could lie down and enjoy it even in a fishing ship, and in a storm!

This renders the sleep *wonderful*. There could have been no fear, no uneasiness within: all was secure and serene. Some of you, it is probable, could not sleep in a storm. Judas was now on board. I dare say Judas could not sleep. What a hell would his avarice produce in his guilty conscience! But see Jacob. He is journeying alone; the shades of the night descend; yet he "takes the stones of the place for a pillow, and lays himself down to sleep!" David abroad in the field, in the rebellion of Absalom, and when he had few troops with him, said, "I will both lay me down and—sleep, for thou, Lord, only makest me dwell in safety." Peter, in the night preceding his designed execution, was "sleeping between two soldiers" so soundly, that the angel was obliged to strike a blow, as well as a light, in order to awake him. "So he giveth his beloved sleep!" Happy they whose minds are tranquillized by the blood of sprinkling. Happy they, who, though sensible of daily infirmities, can say, "Our "rejoicing is this, the testimony of our consciences that in simplicity and godly sincerity, not with fleshly wisdom, but by the grace of God, we have had our conversation in the world." Happy they who can this evening retire, and feel a comparative indifference to life or death; who can say, If I live, it will be to serve thee; and if I die, it will be to enjoy thee.

Again. The sleep was *designed*, and our Saviour had a particular end to answer by it. He would try the disposition and dependence of his disciples, and show us that he may be with his people in a storm, and yet seem to be indifferent; seem to see nothing, hear nothing, feel nothing. Thus it was with Abraham: his deliverer did not interpose to say, Forbear, till the hand had grasped the knife, and was stretched out to use it. Thus it was with the Jews in Egypt. He had engaged, at the end of four hundred and thirty years, to deliver them; but he seemed to have forgotten the promise: the very last day of this long period was arrived—but he awoke in time; and before the returning dawn all the host of the Lord had escaped!—He defers these interpositions to render them the more divine and wonderful. His glory never shines so brightly as on the dark ground of human despair. When creatures have withdrawn, and the eye sees nothing all around but desolation, then, if he approaches us, he must be seen, and be welcomed with peculiar joy and praise: while by such a dispensation he says to his people in all future ages—" Never despond; I can turn the shadow of death into the morning; at eventide it shall be light."

" Just in the last distressing hour
The Lord displays delivering power;
The mount of danger is the place
Where we shall see surprising grace."

In the mean time he exercises our faith and patience, and calls forth our desires after him. He knew that his disciples would soon apply to him; and so they did.—

It is the Third circumstance in the relation. "THEY CAME TO HIM AND AWOKE HIM, SAYING, LORD, SAVE US: WE PERISH." It has been said that those who would learn to pray, should go to sea; and one would suppose that danger so imminent and sensible would produce this effect. But, alas! many have returned from sea without learning to pray. Perhaps indeed they prayed while the storm continued—but their devotion sunk faster than the winds and waves. How many are there who consider prayer as a task to be performed in perilous circumstances, but not their daily duty, their constant privilege! We read of some birds that never make a noise but at the approach of foul weather: and there are persons who never cry to God but "when his chastening hand is upon them." —What would you think of a neighbour, who never called upon you but when he wanted to borrow or beg? Would you not say, What a selfish wretch! he has no regard for me; he thinks of nothing but his own convenience? And what can God think of your religion, if you never seek him but in trouble?

And yet we are authorized to say, that trials have frequently been the means of bringing a man to God: he and God first met in affliction; but a friendship for life was the consequence. I cannot therefore but look hopefully towards a man who is brought into trouble; just as when I see a smith putting a bar of iron into the fire, I conclude that he is going to do something with it, to form out of it some useful implement, which could not be done while it was cold and hard. In his affliction Manasseh sought the Lord. Upon the same principle, thousands have had reason to say, " It is good for me that I have been afflicted."—We may also observe, that as trials are useful to begin, so they are employed to assist a life of prayer. For Christians themselves sometimes grow too careless and insensible. God hears from them less frequently, less fervently than before. Other things amuse them and engage them. But how differently do they feel in the hour of mortification and disappointment! " Where is God my Maker, that giveth songs in the night? Therefore will I look unto the Lord, I will wait for the God of my salvation, my God will hear me."

> " Now I forbid my carnal hope,
> My fond desires recall;
> I give my mortal interest up,
> And make my God my all."

By this you may judge whether your storms are blessings or curses. Do they make you passionate or prayerful? Are you quarreling with the winds and waves, or spreading the case before the Lord? Are you looking to creatures, or to him who has them all under his command, and " in all our affliction is afflicted?" " I would seek unto God, and unto God would I commit my cause : which doeth great things and unsearchable; marvellous things without number."

Fourthly. OUR LORD REPROVES HIS DISCIPLES. But observe, I beseech you, for what it is that he censures them. It is not for breaking in upon his repose. Some of you may remember the confinement of one hundred and forty-six Englishmen in what is called the black hole at Calcutta. It would harrow up the feelings of your souls were I to relate the sufferings of these brave men, driven into a dungeon, which was a cube of eighteen feet, walled up eastward and southward, the only quarters whence refreshing air could come, and open westward by two small windows barred with iron—all this under a melting sky—and many of the men wounded! But what I refer to is this. The cries of these sufferers at last were such as to prevail on one of the enemy's soldiers to go and implore relief of the Suba or Chief. But he soon returned, saying that the Suba was asleep, and that it was upon pain of death any one dared to awake him before the time—and before he awoke many of them had expired! —But it is not so with thee, O blessed Jesus, thou Saviour of the world! Thou despisest not thy prisoners. We cannot by our continual coming weary thee. Thou hast always an ear to which misery is welcome. The groans of a broken heart are as delightful to thee as the songs of angels. No: he does not reprove them for their prayer—but their fear. They were in a needless panic. They talked of perishing, not considering who was with them; and that they could not sink without his sinking too. His safety proved their security. Therefore he saith unto them, " Why are ye fearful, O ye of little faith?" And hereby he shows us—that our alarms originate in the want of faith—that faith may indeed be real where it is little—but that being little, it renders us liable to apprehensions and dismay—and that if a small degree of faith will be sufficient for fine weather sailing, a greater is necessary in a storm—a faith assured of our union with him; clear in its views of his power and love; and firm in its dependence upon his promise.

But oh! in what manner did our Lord utter this reproof? It is impossible to do justice to those lips into which grace was poured, and which spake as never man spake. But had we heard him, I am persuaded his tone of voice would have been more expressive of kindness than severity. It would have been the address of one who pitied while he blamed; who was touched with the feeling of their infirmities; who knew their frame, and remembered they were but dust; who knew the influence outward things have upon the body, and the influence the body has upon the mind. He would not therefore keep them in suspense, but

Fifthly: it is said, " THEN—HE AROSE AND REBUKED THE WINDS AND THE SEA, AND THERE WAS A GREAT CALM." What a scene was here! I see him opening his eyes—but not with surprise. Nothing astonished him through life. I see him going upon deck—not in haste. Haste is the effect of confusion—he had always too much to do to be ever in haste. I see him facing the storm.—But what said he? He " rebuked" the winds and the sea. To rebuke is a word that we apply to intelligent creatures only. We talk of rebuking a servant or a child—but not a tree or a stone. Thus the storm is personified and addressed as if it could hear him; and it did hear him and obey. And " there was a great calm!" Those who are acquainted with the sea know that after a storm is hushed, the deep continues for a considerable time to rise and fall and fret. But the sea now immediately subsided from its raging, and spread into a smooth surface. For his work is perfect. He doth all things well. And the execution honours him as much as the design.

But Finally. What effect had all this upon his disciples? They are not only convinced, but impressed: they not only " believe with the heart," but " confess with the tongue:" and, filled with ADMIRATION AND PRAISE at such a peculiar and unexampled display of perfection, " they marvelled, saying, What manner of man is this, that even the winds and the sea obey him!" Some persons if known would be abhorred; others would decline upon acquaintance; and where intimacy does not reduce our esteem, it commonly diminishes our admiration. In other cases, ignorance is the cause of wonder: but here it is knowledge; for the character is perfect, and the object infinite. The more we know of the Saviour's attributes and works and ways, the more we shall admire and adore. And we are told that when he has ended all our storms, and made all things to work together for our good—then "he shall come to be glorified in his saints, and to be admired in all them that believe." We admire him indeed now. He has already fixed and filled our minds. We already see in him such various and numberless excellences, that the world has faded into nothing by the comparison. We see in him every thing to feed our contemplation, every thing to encourage our hope, every thing to excite imitation, every thing to command attachment and praise. But how small a portion is known of him!

> "—Nor earth, nor seas, nor sun, nor stars,
>   Nor heaven his full resemblance bears:
>   His beauties we can never trace,
>   Till we behold him face to face."

Let me conclude, First, by a word to the disobedient. He who addressed the wind and the sea, has often addressed you. He has addressed you by sickness, by affliction, by delivering mercy, by conscience, by friends, by ministers, by his law and by his gospel, by threatenings and by promises. But more insensible, more rebellious than the wind or the sea, you have not heard or obeyed him. And yet you pretend to possess reason! But wherein do you show it? "A prudent man foreseeth the evil and hideth himself, but the simple pass on and are punished." And this will be your case. You are not only his creatures, but his subjects; he has not only given you privileges, but rendered you accountable for them, and he is coming to try you by them. And can you be ignorant of the result? "As for these mine enemies that would not that I should reign over them, bring them forth and slay them before me."

Secondly. Let me call upon those of you who love the Saviour, to familiarize him to your minds as present with you in all your difficulties. You need not say, Oh! if he were on earth, I would go to him, and tell him my grief, and ease my burdened mind. You may do so now; for though he is no longer visible, he is still accessible; and if you call, he will answer, and say, "Here I am." He is a very present help in trouble.

Look to him to tranquillize a stormy world. The nations are angry—but He who stilleth the raging of the sea can also calm the tumults of the people.

Look to him, to pacify a troubled conscience. In the midst of the most painful distress and anguish within, he can say unto your soul, "I am thy salvation." Fear not.

Look to him in all your trials. Surely, in a storm, there ought to be a difference between you and others. They have made no provision for the evil day: but you have a friend, a kind friend, an almighty friend with you. You have tried him. You know "whom you have believed;" and he knoweth them that trust in him, and will "never leave them nor forsake them."

Have you evils in prospect? Does a dispensation of Heaven approach you, that, instead of opening like a fine morning in May, seems setting in like a winter's night, with "dark waters and thick clouds of the sky?"

> "Ye fearful saints, fresh courage take;
>   The clouds ye so much dread
>   Are big with mercy, and shall break
>   In blessings on your head.
>
> "Judge not the Lord by feeble sense,
>   But trust him for his grace;
>   Behind a frowning Providence
>   He hides a smiling face."

DISCOURSE LV.

FAMINE.

Behold, the days come, saith the Lord God, that I will send a famine in the land.—Amos viii. 11.

Sin is said to be "an evil and a bitter thing." It is evil in its nature, and bitter in its consequences. It is evil with regard to God, and bitter with regard to us. It "brought death into the world, and all our wo." Numberless are the miseries to which it has reduced individuals, families, nations, and the whole human race.

Among these, one of the most dreadful is Famine. It would not be easy even for the imagination to do justice to a calamity so tremendous. What must it be to view "the heavens over us as brass, and the earth beneath us as iron!" What must it be, from the appearances of nature, to exclaim, "Is not the meat cut off before our eyes, yea, joy and gladness from the house of our God? The seed is rotten under the clods, the garners are laid desolate, the barns are broken down; for the corn is withered. How do the beasts groan! the herds of cattle are perplexed because they have no pasture; yea, the flocks of sheep are made desolate." What must it be to make observations like these: "The tongue of the sucking child cleaveth to the roof of his mouth for thirst: the young children ask bread, and no man breaketh it unto them. They that did feed delicately are desolate in the streets: they that were brought up in scarlet embrace dunghills. They that be slain with the sword are better than they that be slain with hunger, for these pine away, stricken through for want of the fruits of the field."—"Can a woman forget her sucking child, that she should not have compassion on the son of her womb? Yea, she may forget." Yes! even mothers have dressed and devoured their own offspring. The horrible fact is mentioned three times in the history of a people once peculiarly dear to God. In the siege of Jerusalem by Titus, Josephus tells us that the daughter of Eleazer had fled from beyond Jordan to the metropolis, in the general distress: she had been wealthy, but was now reduced to the last extremity : after a heartrending address, she killed her infant at the breast for food—and when some ruffians entered the house, and demanded whatever provision she had, she presented a dish, and throwing by the napkin—showed them the remains of her child—the other part she had eaten! Referring to the siege of Jerusalem by Nebuchadnezzar, says the prophet Jeremiah : " The hands of the pitiful women have sodden their own children : they were their meat in the destruction of the daughter of my people." In the siege of Samaria, by Benhadad the Syrian, we read : " As the king of Israel was passing by upon the wall, there cried a woman unto him, saying, Help, my lord, O king. And he said, If the Lord do not help thee, whence shall I help thee ? out of the barnfloor, or out of the winepress ? And the king said unto her, What aileth thee ? And she answered, This woman said unto me, Give thy son, that we may eat him to-day, and we will eat my son to-morrow. So we boiled my son, and did eat him : and I said unto her on the next day, Give thy son, that we may eat him : and she hath hid her son. And it came to pass when the king heard the words of the woman, that he rent his clothes ; and he passed by upon the wall, and the people looked, and, behold, he had sackcloth within upon his flesh."

Who is not ready to say—Let us turn from these scenes of horror, and falling upon our knees, pray, " O Lord, correct us, but with judgment ; not in thine anger, lest thou bring us to nothing."

And yet there is a famine infinitely more dreadful than all this : and to keep you no longer from our subject, it is the very judgment here denounced : " Behold, the days come, saith the Lord God, that I will send a famine in the land, not a famine of bread, nor a thirst for water, but of hearing the words of the Lord. And they shall wander from sea to sea, and from the north even to the east ; they shall run to and fro to seek the word of the Lord, and shall not find it."—We need not inquire to what periods the prophecy immediately refers. It was to be accomplished at different times, and in various degrees.

We divide our reflections into three parts : the First of which regards THE NATURE OF THIS JUDGMENT. The Second, ITS DREADFULNESS. And the Third, ITS INFLICTION. " To-day if ye will hear his voice, harden not your hearts."

I. Let us consider the NATURE OF THIS JUDGMENT. It takes in the loss of the Gospel, as a judgment administered by preaching. It is a famine, not of reading, but " of hearing the words of the Lord."

We may consider this famine as *eternal.* The means of grace, and the ordinances of religion, are exclusively confined to this life. If you die strangers to the power of godliness, so you must continue. Your mistake will indeed be discovered, but cannot be rectified. *There* no throne of grace. *There* no messengers of mercy. *There* no invitations to turn and live. *There* no sabbath smiles upon you ; no temple opens to receive you ; no altar spreads before you the hallowed emblems of the Saviour's death. " Behold, now is the accepted time ; behold, now is the day of salvation." Hence it is that we urge you to " seek the Lord while he may be found, and to call upon him while he is near :" and remind you of our Lord's admonition, " Strive to enter in at the strait gate : for many, I say unto you, will seek to enter in, and shall not be able. When once the master of the house is risen up, and hath shut to the door, and ye begin to stand without, and to knock at the door, saying, Lord, Lord, open unto us ; and he shall answer and say unto you, I know you not whence ye are : then shall ye begin to say, We have eaten and drunk in thy presence, and thou hast taught in our streets. But he shall say, I tell you, I know you not whence ye are ; depart from me, all ye workers of iniquity. There shall be weeping and gnashing of teeth, when ye shall see Abraham, and Isaac, and Jacob, and all the prophets, in the kingdom of God, and you yourselves thrust out."

We may consider this famine as *spiritual.* And thus it refers to the state of the mind ; and takes place when souls are reduced to such indifference and insensibility as to be morally or judicially incapable of improvement by the institutions of religion, even should they be continued among them. When a man can no longer use food, or turn it into nourishment, it is the same with regard to himself as if all provision was denied him—death must be the consequence. The case of many who have long been favoured with the Gospel, is, according to this view of the subject. alarming. Much has been said, very incautiously, of the termination of a day of grace. In a sense every day is a day of grace ; and " God is longsuffering to us-ward, not willing that any should perish, but that all should come to repentance." While therefore there is life, there is hope. But surely this hope diminishes, as impenitency becomes inveterate. Surely favourable opportunities may elapse and return no more. Surely convictions may be stifled, and impressions worn off never to be renewed. Surely, by unsanctified attendance, year after year, the most important truths may become so familiar as to lose all their effect. Surely, by incessant trifling with divine things, God may be provoked to recall his influence from his ordinances—and thus will be fulfilled the prophecy of Esaias, who saith, "Hearing ye shall hear, and shall not understand; and seeing ye shall see, and shall not perceive: for this people's heart is waxed gross, and their ears are dull of hearing, and their eyes they have closed; lest at any time they should see with their eyes, and hear with their ears, and should understand with their heart, and should be converted, and I should heal them."

We may consider this famine as *doctrinal*. It may then be occasioned by the removal of faithful ministers, and the succession of others of different principles. This is sure to cause a declension in the number and in the zeal of the members of churches. For the grace and the truth of God always go together. And in this case the gospel is really taken away, and something is made a substitute that will be found ineffectual for all the purposes of conversion and consolation. As light recedes, darkness in the same proportion follows. Every system has some parts in it that are essential. When the leading doctrines of the gospel are denied or concealed, the gospel is withdrawn; and when this is withdrawn, "Ichabod" may be inscribed upon the walls of the building.—"The glory is departed."

This famine may be considered as *literal*. This is the case when a people are deprived of the very institutions of religion, and are forbidden the assembling of themselves together according to their convictions. This may be done by the inroads and oppression of an enemy; by the encroachments of tyranny; by the loss of liberty of conscience. Our forefathers could explain this.

II. Let us pass from the nature of this judgment, to examine THE DREADFULNESS OF IT. To some men indeed this famine would be a very little grievance. Probably it would prove a pleasure rather than a pain. If the gospel was removed, they would be less incommoded and alarmed. They would rather have no prophets, unless they would "prophesy smooth things." Of a Micaiah they exclaim, "I hate him; for he doth not prophesy good concerning me, but evil." "Yea, they say,"—how dreadful are actions put into words,—"yea, they say unto God, Depart from us; we desire not the knowledge of thy ways." But do we take the value of learning from the opinion of a fool? Do we estimate the jewel from the swine, that, igno-

rant of its worth, tramples it under foot? Do we cease to admire Handel because some have no ears for his harmony and melody, or may choose to be perverse and fastidious?—But what do we? We disregard ignorance and prejudice, and seek after a proper standard by which we may obtain the decisions of truth. Let us apply the same rule to the subject before us. To know the dreadfulness of this judgment, let us,

First; dwell upon the advantages derivable from the preaching of the gospel. The generality of those that are called by divine grace are saved by this instrumentality.— "Faith cometh by hearing, and hearing by the word of God." And the usefulness of it continues through the whole of the Christian life. "He gave some, apostles; and some, prophets; and some, evangelists; and some, pastors and teachers; for the perfecting of the saints, for the work of the ministry, for the edifying of the body of Christ: till we all come, in the unity of the faith, and of the knowledge of the Son of God, unto a perfect man, unto the measure of the stature of the fulness of Christ." Some are unable to read, and many have little time to search the Scriptures. Particular errors and vices are continually arising and prevailing, that require the application of particular doctrines, and the inculcation of particular duties: and a minister will study these in the choice and in the discussion of his subjects. How often in his palaces have some of you found God for a refuge! How often have your perplexities been solved, your fears banished, your hearts filled with all joy and peace in believing!— Could you be reconciled to the thought of losing all the pleasure and profit you have found by experience to be connected with the means of grace?

Secondly; let us think of the importance of the soul and eternity. The body is the meanest part of our nature; and time is the shortest portion of our duration, by a decree no less than infinite. The chief question therefore should never be, "What shall I eat, and what shall I drink, and wherewithal shall I be clothed?"—but "What must I do to be saved?" The chief care ought to be, to gain spiritual wealth, spiritual honour, spiritual food—for these regard man in his most essential claims and necessities. Every thing should be considered as good or evil, according to its connexion with the soul and eternity: and from this principle, which a child can understand, we infer, that, beyond all comparison, the famine most to be dreaded is that which regards not the body, but the soul; not time, but eternity.

Thirdly; observe the design of such a dispensation. Some judgments, though painful, are still profitable. They remove the human arm; but it is to lead us to a dependence on the Divine. They take away the desires of our eyes; but it is that we may ask, "Where is God my Maker, that giveth songs in the night?" How blessed was the humiliation that reduced Manasseh from the throne into a prison, where he sought and found the Lord God of his fathers! How kind was the famine that drove the prodigal to his father's house! "O God, chastise me, but do not abandon me. Try me as thou pleasest, but do not withdraw from me the proofs and the mediums of thy grace. Say any thing but this —'He is joined to idols, let him alone.'" Other judgments are in mercy, but this is in wrath. Other judgments are parental, but this is penal. Other judgments may urge us into heaven; but this is the way to hell, "going down to the chambers of death."

Fourthly. In estimating this curse, let us appeal to the sentiments of the righteous. Their conviction, in a case like this, far outweighs the opinion of the politicians and philosophers of the age. The question is a religious one, and "the spiritual judgeth all things, though he himself is judged of no man." In what terms does David deplore the loss of divine assemblies? "When I remember these things, I pour out my soul in me: for I had gone with the multitude, I went with them to the house of God, with the voice of joy and praise, with a multitude that kept holy day. O God, thou art my God; early will I seek thee: my soul thirsteth for thee, my flesh longeth for thee in a thirsty land, where no water is; to see thy power and thy glory, so as I have seen thee in the sanctuary." Take those who are confined from the ordinances of God by disease or accident—though God does not leave them comfortless, neither are they unsubmissive, yet with the recovering Hezekiah they are asking, "What is the sign that I shall go up to the house of the Lord?"

We can rise but one step higher, and there we meet with God himself. His people *may* err: but his understanding is infinite; he *cannot* be deceived. What does *he* think of this judgment? You may infer it from his benediction; "Blessed are the people that know the joyful sound." You may infer it from his promise; I will give them pastors after my own heart, that shall feed them with knowledge and understanding. Though the Lord give you the bread of adversity, and the water of affliction, yet shall not thy teachers be removed into a corner any more, but thine eyes shall see thy teachers: and thine ears shall hear a word behind thee, saying, This is the way, walk ye in it, when ye turn to the right hand, and when ye turn to the left." You may infer it from his threatening; "Behold, the days come, saith the Lord God, that I will send a famine in the land, not a famine of bread, nor a thirst for water, but of hearing the words of the Lord."

III. We have to reflect on THE EXECUTION OF THIS SENTENCE. For some may be ready to say, How can such a thing be? It is very improbable; and, considering the divine promise, it seems to be impossible. For has he not said—"This is my covenant with them, saith the Lord; my Spirit that is upon thee, and my words which I have put in thy mouth, shall not depart out of thy mouth, nor out of the mouth of thy seed, nor out of the mouth of thy seed's seed, saith the Lord, from henceforth and for ever. Upon this rock will I build my church, and the gates of hell shall not prevail against it." But a distinction instantly removes this difficulty. God has engaged to establish his church universally; but this does not regard any particular body of professors. He has engaged that the gospel shall never be removed from the world; but this does not hinder the withdrawment of it from particular places. If after all you are slow of heart to believe; if you are still thinking that such language as this never can, or never will be accomplished with regard to us; let me ask you,

First. Is not He who utters this threatening almighty, and so able to fulfil it? If he has infinite resources, from which he can bless his friends, he has the same power, the same dominion to furnish him with arms against his enemies. He can never be at a loss for instruments to do his pleasure; nor can these instruments, however weak in themselves, prove feeble in the hand of Omnipotence.

Secondly. Is not He who utters this threatening just, and so disposed to fulfil it? Men may draw God as they please; they may imagine him all patience and pity; but they will find themselves mistaken. "A God all mercy is a God unjust." He is an equitable Governor, as well as a tender Father. He is holy in all his ways, and righteous in all his works. If sin is the abominable thing that he hates—if it be aggravated by light and knowledge—if the servant that knew his Lord's will and did it not shall be beaten with many stripes—if the abuse of the greatest privilege be the greatest guilt—can God see all this without concern, without provocation? If at an infinite expense he has sent the gospel among us, and we make light of it; refuse to read or to hear it; or make the hearing of it a matter of mere curiosity or entertainment; applying it to no one purpose for which it was given, or turning it into licentiousness—is it *conceivable* that we can do this with impunity? *Can* God connive at such wickedness? *Must* he not prove that he is "of purer eyes than to behold iniquity?" Mercy sent forth the messengers to invite to the marriage-feast: but what said Justice of those that refused? "None of the men that were bidden shall taste of my supper."

Thirdly. Is not he that utters this threatening, faithful, and so bound to fulfil it? Even a Balaam could say, " The Lord is not a man that he should lie, or the son of man that he should repent. Hath he said, and shall he not do it! Hath he spoken, and shall he not make it good?"—He has evinced his truth in his denunciations as well as his promises. If Joseph found his word true, so did Pharaoh; and Saul was constrained to believe it as well as David.

Fourthly. Has not he who utters this threatening fulfilled it already in various instances? Here we appeal from principles to facts. The gospel *has* been removed from a country; a people *have* been unchurched. The Jews are an eminent example. While they enjoyed their ceremonial services, they had the gospel in type; and when the Saviour was among them, they had the gospel in reality: but the kingdom of God was taken from them, and given to a people " bringing forth fruit in its season." When we consider the names by which they were called; the miracles, the ordinances, the privileges that distinguished them; and see this garden of the Lord laid waste, this people a reproach and a byword—with what force comes the admonition of the apostle: " If he spared not the natural branches, take heed also lest he spare not thee." What became of the Church of Rome, so famous as to be " spoken of throughout the whole world?" It was made " a cage for every unclean bird." Where are the seven churches of Asia? The places that once knew them, know them no more for ever. The blasphemies of the Koran sound where once the name of Jesus was as ointment poured forth; and the banners of an infamous impostor wave where once was erected the standard of the Cross, to draw all men into it. All these had a time wherein to know the things that belonged to their peace—and then they were hid from their eyes. " Wherefore let him that thinketh he standeth take heed lest he fall."

The subject demands *gratitude*. We have reason to bless God that we have not had a famine of bread; that he has crowned the year with his goodness; and fed us with the finest of the wheat. But still less has he visited us with a famine of hearing the words of the Lord. Why did the gospel reach us at such an early period? Why, when it was denied to so many, was it imparted to us? Why, since it has been withdrawn from numbers once favoured with it, is the blessing yet continued to us—and in such purity and plenty? —" Not unto us, O Lord, not unto us, but unto thy Name give glory, for thy mercy and for thy truth's sake."

Again. Let us be concerned to improve it while we possess it. It is our Saviour's application of the same doctrine. " Then Jesus said unto them, Yet a little while is the light with you. Walk while ye have the light, lest darkness come upon you: for he that walketh in darkness knoweth not whither he goeth. While ye have the light, believe in the light, that ye may be the children of the light." With gospel means, be concerned to obtain gospel grace; and earnestly pray that the ministry of the word may become the ministration of the Spirit. " Be ye doers of the word, and not hearers only, deceiving your own selves. For if any be a hearer of the word, and not a doer, he is like unto a man beholding his natural face in a glass: for he beholdeth himself, and goeth his way, and straightway forgetteth what manner of man he was. But whoso looketh into the perfect law of liberty, and continueth therein, he being not a forgetful hearer, but a doer of the work, this man shall be blessed in his deed."

Finally. As it is so dreadful to be destitute of the gospel, think how many of your fellow-creatures are found in this deplorable condition. They would be glad with the crumbs that fall from your table. They never hear of a Saviour. They feel depraved propensities, but know nothing of that grace which can create in us a clean heart, and renew in us a right spirit. They feel guilty fears, but know nothing of that blood which cleanses us from all sin. Pray that the Scriptures, and that missionaries may speedily reach them. Pray that the Sun of righteousness may arise, with healing under his wings, and comfort them with the knowledge of salvation. " God be merciful unto us, and bless us; and cause his face to shine upon us. That thy way may be known upon earth, thy saving health among all nations. Let the people praise thee, O God; let all the people praise thee. O let the nations be glad and sing for joy: for thou shalt judge the people righteously, and govern the nations upon earth."

DISCOURSE LVI.

CONVERSION.

Verily I say unto you, Except ye be converted, and become as little children, ye shall not enter into the kingdom of heaven.—Matt. xviii. 3.

THE disciples were such dull scholars, that after all the education our Lord and Saviour had given them, they were yet imagining that his kingdom " was of this world." They supposed that he would deliver them from the Roman yoke; advance them as a nation to the high places of the earth; and lead them forth conquering and to conquer. In this secular empire they believed there would be degrees of power and glory, as in any other; and expecting that these places would be filled by some of their own body, after a dispute among themselves, they inquire of their Master which of them should be the greatest?

How does our Lord reprove and instruct them? Instead of delivering a lecture on the abstract nature and advantages of a state of mind with which they appeared to be almost entirely unacquainted; "he called a little child unto him, and set him in the midst of them—and said, Verily I say unto you, Except ye be converted, and become as little children, ye shall not enter into the kingdom of heaven."

Let us consider,

I. THE TEMPER THAT DISTINGUISHES THE SUBJECTS OF DIVINE GRACE.

II. THE WAY IN WHICH WE ARE TO ATTAIN IT.

III. THE IMPORTANCE OF POSSESSING IT.

I. THE TEMPER THAT DISTINGUISHES THE SUBJECTS OF DIVINE GRACE. It is infantile. We must be "as little children." But it is not to be inferred that we are to resemble them in every thing—

We are not to be like them in ignorance: "Be ye not children in understanding." A grayheaded babe would be an unnatural and a shocking sight: and yet there are persons who have been many years in the religious world, who have never cultivated their minds, nor improved their privileges and opportunities; and who may be addressed in the words of the apostle, "When for the time ye ought to be teachers, ye have need that one teach you again which be the first principles of the oracles of God; and are become such as have need of milk, and not of strong meat. For every one that useth milk is unskilful in the word of righteousness: for he is a babe. But strong meat belongeth to them that are of full age, even those who by reason of use have their senses exercised to discern both good and evil."

We are not to resemble them in fickleness: "That we henceforth be no more children, tossed to and fro, and carried about with every wind of doctrine, by the sleight of men, and cunning craftiness, whereby they lie in wait to deceive." Children are extremely versatile. Though they are impressed with a thousand things, and seem for the time incapable of growing weary of them, they pursue nothing with certainty and constancy. And there are men, there are professors like them. They have no determinate sentiments; they have no fixed plan; they live extempore; they wander from party to party, they rove from preacher to preacher; you can place no dependence upon them; their attachment and behaviour to-day are no proofs of their attachment and behaviour to-morrow. Let not such think to rise to eminence. Consistency, steadiness, is essential to character. "Unstable as water, thou shalt not excel."

We are not to resemble them in sullen-ness, in waywardness, in pettishness. Have you never met with persons whom it is impossible to please? Or whose importance and vanity are gratified by the perplexity of your attempt? It is not because you employed the wrong expedient that you were not successful; any other would have met with the same fate. The more you allure, the further are they off—the very thing to which our Saviour refers. "Whereunto shall I liken this generation? It is like unto children sitting in the markets, and calling unto their fellows, and saying, We have piped unto you, and ye have not danced; we have mourned unto you, and ye have not lamented."

In all this we are forbidden to be found like little children. And yet we are enjoined by our Saviour to resemble them. How is this? I answer, metaphors employed by the sacred writers are not to be taken universally, but in connexion with the subject that requires illustration. It is sufficient that there be a real and striking resemblance in the article of comparison. And this is unquestionably the case here.

For we may observe, that as soon as children are ushered into the world, they cry for the nourishment God has prepared for them. And as it is in nature, so it is in grace. The new creature has wants to be relieved, and appetites to be indulged: and there is provision suited to them in religion. Hence we read, "As newborn babes, desire the sincere milk of the word, that ye may grow thereby."

Again. Little children are teachable, and ready of belief. They receive with unsuspecting confidence the declaration of their father. If any doubt arises, if any dispute occurs, they run to him, and his testimony decides every thing. Thus should it be with us. We are to receive the kingdom of heaven as a little child. I was going to say, We cannot be too credulous when God speaks. He cannot be imposed upon himself, and he cannot deceive us: his wisdom forbids the one, and his truth the other. What one party believes, and another denies, should have little influence over us; while we have the judgment of God, to which we can appeal. "To the law and to the testimony: if they speak not according to this word, it is because there is no light in them." When we find any thing revealed in this book, we are not to hesitate in admitting it; we are not to reason upon it, "How can these things be?" but with a ready mind yield up ourselves to the "obedience of faith; and do all things without murmuring or disputing."

Little children also are distinguished by a freedom from anxieties. Though they possess nothing adequate to their own support, and see not the resources from which their supplies come, they feel no uneasiness; they rely with cheerfulness on the father to provide for them; and never question his ability or his

2 C

will. And shall we despond because we are not affluent? Shall we be miserable because we are called to live by faith on the providence of God? Shall we disobey that gracious command, "casting all your care upon him, for he careth for you?" Shall we never regard the address of our Lord to his disciples? "Consider the ravens: for they neither sow nor reap; which neither have storehouse nor barn; and God feedeth them: how much more are ye better than the fowls!" "And which of you with taking thought can add to his stature one cubit? If ye then be not able to do that thing which is least, why take ye thought for the rest? Consider the lilies how they grow: they toil not, they spin not; and yet I say unto you, that Solomon in all his glory was not arrayed like one of these. If then God so clothe the grass, which is to-day in the field, and to-morrow is cast into the oven; how much more will he clothe you, O ye of little faith? And seek not ye what ye shall eat, or what ye shall drink, neither be ye of doubtful mind. For all these things do the nations of the world seek after: and your Father knoweth that ye have need of these things. But rather seek ye the kingdom of God; and all these things shall be added unto you."

Little children are devoid of malignity. The trifling resentments they sometimes feel and discover are soon over, and they are "at one again," and as friendly as before. There is nothing implacable in them: they easily forgive, and perfectly forget. For which reason the Apostle says, "In malice be ye children;" which is the same as saying, in another place, "Be ye angry, and sin not: let not the sun go down upon your wrath: neither give place to the devil. Let all bitterness, and wrath, and anger, and clamour, and evil speaking, be put away from you, with all malice: and be ye kind one to another, tenderhearted, forgiving one another, even as God for Christ's sake hath forgiven you."

But the thing principally, though not exclusively intended, is the humility of little children. Hence our Saviour adds, "Whosoever therefore shall humble himself as this little child, the same is greatest in the kingdom of heaven." Little children have no ideas of distinction till they are given them. They do not assume state, or stand up for points of honour. If they were not taught otherwise by their hopeful parents, they would be satisfied with the simplest fare and the plainest raiment. Left to themselves, the children of a nobleman would play familiarly with the child of a peasant. They have no great aims; no towering projects; they are pleased with little and common things.

And Christians are required not only to wear humility, but to be "clothed" with it. They are to be sensible of their insufficiency;

they are to "condescend to men of low estate." They are not to be ambitious of preeminence; they are not to be "desirous of vain glory; provoking one another, envying one another." They are not to "seek great things for themselves;" they are to "learn in whatsoever state they are, therewith to be content:" and, longing to be good rather than to be great, feel the sentiment of David: "Lord, my heart is not haughty, nor mine eyes lofty: neither do I exercise myself in great matters, or in things too high for me. Surely I have behaved and quieted myself, as a child that is weaned of his mother: my soul is even as a weaned child." Having considered the nature of this temper,

II. Let us inquire THE WAY IN WHICH WE ARE TO ATTAIN IT. It is by conversion. We must be "converted," and "*become as little children.*" And this teaches us two things, which ought to be remembered.

First. The temper we are required to possess is not in us naturally, but is the consequence of a divine change. Innate depravity is, alas! too fully established by Scripture, observation, and experience, to be denied. A man that knows himself will readily subscribe to the mortifying confession of David: "I was shapen in iniquity, and in sin did my mother conceive me;" and acknowledge, with Paul, "In me, that is in my flesh, dwelleth no good thing." This being admitted, it follows, that we are not *made* Christians, but *become* such; that it is the effect not of a natural but a spiritual birth. Ye must be "*born again.*" As creatures we are in Adam; but if any man be in Christ, "he is a new creature: *old things have passed away; and, behold, all things are become new.*" In order to be religious, we must be saved—"saved by the washing of regeneration, and the renewing of the Holy Ghost."—And since this conversion is designed to produce in depraved beings such a character as our Saviour describes, it also follows that this conversion implies much more than a change of opinions, or a mere reformation of manners. It is a renovation in the state of the heart; in our principles, motives, and dispositions. It turns the whole bias of the soul another way, and proves by its tendency that it is divine, according to the promise; "Then will I sprinkle clean water upon you, and ye shall be clean: from all your filthiness, and from all your idols, will I cleanse you. A new heart also will I give you, and a new spirit will I put within you: and I will take away the stony heart out of your flesh, and I will give you an heart of flesh. And I will put my spirit within you, and cause you to walk in my statutes, and ye shall keep my judgments, and do them."

Secondly. This change is to be judged of by its effect. Here many people err. They endeavour to ascertain the time and the manner, and the instrument of their conversion—and distress themselves because they cannot determine. But the grand thing is to inquire—whether the work be done; whether we have passed from death to life; whether we can say, "One thing I know, that whereas I was blind, now I see!" On the other hand, persons may talk of a change that took place in them at such a period, under such a minister—of the reality of which it would be difficult to find any *present* evidence. But what has your supposed conversion done for you? In what state, in what temper has it *left* you? Wherein do you differ from *others* and from *yourselves?* Whom do you *now* resemble? The picture here pourtrayed?—Do you resemble little children by your spiritual desires, your faith in God's word, your reliance on his providence, the kindness of your disposition, the humbleness of your mind? And is your want of more conformity to this model your chief distress? And are you praying, as if nothing comparatively had been yet done, "Create in me a clean heart, and renew a right spirit within me?"

III. Let us observe THE IMPORTANCE OF POSSESSING THIS TEMPER. "Except ye be converted, and become as little children, ye shall not enter into the kingdom of heaven" —An exclusion the most awful; the most unavoidable; the most universal.

First. The most *awful.* Many things court our attention that are by no means essential to our safety or welfare. We ought to be ashamed of the impressions they make upon our minds; they are unworthy of our hopes or fears; it is of little consequence whether we gain or lose them; and it will be our wonder hereafter that we could ever have been so much influenced by them. But to be deprived of the blessings of the Gospel dispensation; to be excluded from all the treasures of grace and glory; to see infinite riches, honours, and pleasures, and to hear a voice saying, They are not for thee?— "There shall be weeping and gnashing of teeth, when ye shall see Abraham, and Isaac, and Jacob, and all the prophets, in the kingdom of God, and you yourselves thrust out." If you do not deem these blessings of importance *now*, it is because you never reflect upon them—but you will not always be able to banish thought: it is because you have substitutes for them, and these divert, though they do not satisfy—but all of them will soon be torn from you: and what in a dying hour, and in a judgment-day, will you do without an interest in this heavenly kingdom?

An exclusion, Secondly, the most *unavoidable.* If God has said in the Scripture that "without holiness no man *shall* see the Lord;" if God *must* be true, and the Scripture cannot be broken; if there *must* be a suitableness between the faculty and the ob-

ject before there can be enjoyment; if those distinctions *must* be maintained which preserve the moral order and harmony of the world; if we *must* be like God, before we can hold intercourse with him; if light *can* have no communion with darkness, and righteousness have *no* fellowship with unrighteousness—then, upon every principle to which either reason or religion conducts us, every unrenewed sinner stands inevitably excluded from the kingdom of heaven.

An exclusion, Finally, the most *universal.* There are few things in the world so invariably established as not to allow of some deviations. Every general rule has its exceptions. Even the fixed laws of nature have been changed; iron has been made to swim, and flames have been forbidden to burn. But be not deceived; our Saviour here reveals a law that admits of *no* change; and lays down a rule that allows of *no* exception. There never has been, there is not, there never will be, there never can be an instance even to qualify this assertion: "Except ye be converted, and become as little children, ye shall not enter into the kingdom of heaven."

Let us conclude with these additional reflections.

First. From our Saviour's address, you learn to improve from the various objects we behold in the world of nature. If you wish to hold communion with God, you may be reminded of him all the day long; if you wish to learn, you never need be at a loss for a teacher: "Ask now the beasts, and they shall teach thee; and the fowls of the air, and they shall tell thee." Hast thou a garden? And dost thou never walk in it but as a creature—delighted with its flowers and its fruits? Dost thou never think of that garden in which Adam fell; or of that garden in which Jesus suffered? Hast thou children? They *are* cares; they *may* be comforts; but they *must* be instructers and admonishers, unless we are careless and stupid in the most criminal degree.

Secondly. We see what a difference there is between the opinion of the world and the judgment of God. The natural man admires the temper that will endure no insults; he applauds the successful votary of wealth and power; he talks of a becoming pride, a noble pride; to him it is a paradox that "all pride is an abomination to the Lord;" that "the meek shall inherit the earth;" that "the slow to anger is better than the mighty; and he that ruleth his own spirit than he that taketh a city." He wonders to hear, that if "he would be wise, he must become a fool that he may be wise;" that to sink in his own esteem is the way to rise in the esteem of Heaven; that he who "exalteth himself shall be abased, and he who abaseth himself shall be exalted." But such is the testimony of God; and his judgment is always according to truth. Oh that we may take our views of excellency alone from him; and make his estimate our own. "For not he that commendeth himself is approved, but whom the Lord commendeth."

Thirdly. We congratulate those who have the Spirit of Christ. The world knoweth you not: you think meanly of yourselves, and you ought: for you are encompassed with infirmity—but you are heirs of the kingdom which God hath promised to them that love him; an everlasting kingdom; a kingdom in comparison with which the renowned empires of the earth vanish into smoke—the kingdom of heaven! What can you desire more? How thankful, how satisfied, how happy you should live!

And how holy!—

Be concerned to maintain a behaviour answerable to your state and expectation. You are princes. "Walk worthy of God, who hath called you unto his kingdom and glory."

DISCOURSE LVII.

THE LOSS OF CHILDREN.

And he said, While the child was yet alive, I fasted and wept: for I said, Who can tell whether God will be gracious to me, that the child may live? But now he is dead, wherefore should I fast? can I bring him back again? I shall go to him, but he shall not return to me.—2 Sam. xii. 22, 23.

THERE is much to censure in David. Yet He, whose understanding is infinite, and whose judgment is always according to truth, has pronounced him "a man after his own heart;" and told us, that "he did that which was right in the eyes of the Lord, and turned not aside from any thing that he commanded him all the days of his life, save only in the matter of Uriah the Hittite."

The narrative of his crime has, it is to be feared, been the occasion of hardening ungodly men in their iniquity. But this has been the consequence of perversion. It was written not for encouragement, but for caution. It cries, "Let him that thinketh he standeth take heed lest he fall;" it shows the readiness of God to pardon the truly penitent who confess and forsake their sin; and it exemplifies not only the efficacy, but the nature of genuine repentance.

You will not wonder that I have referred to this awful event in David's history, since the subject of our present meditation is derived from it. Let us consider—HIS AFFLICTION—HIS BEHAVIOUR UNDER IT—AND THE EXPLANATION HE GIVES OF HIS CONDUCT.

I. His AFFLICTION was the death of his child. The death of a child is by no means an uncommon event. If our offspring are spared, and appear like olive plants around our table, we ought to be thankful, and to rejoice; yet to rejoice with trembling. When we reflect on the tenderness of their frame, and consider to how many accidents and diseases they are liable; and that many of their earliest complaints cannot be perfectly ascertained, and may be injured by the very means employed for their relief—the wonder is that they ever reach maturity.

Near half of the human race die in a state of infancy. Some have the allotment which Job so passionately wished had been his own: "Why died I not from the womb? Why did I not give up the ghost when I came out of the belly? Why did the knees prevent me? Or why the breasts that I should suck?" Others are dressed and appear on the stage of mortal life; but, long before the close of a single scene, withdraw, and are found no more. Others are spared longer, and multiply attractions and endearments. Some begin to open their powers, as well as charms. You saw rising up the seeds of instruction you had sown; the child was forming into the companion—but you looked, and, lo! he was not—and you sighed, "Childhood and youth is vanity!"—Some lose one child from among many; and even this can ill be spared. What then must it be to lose an only one: and perhaps not the only one in possession, but the only one in hope! What a mortality is there in some families. How often have some fathers and mothers been visited with breach upon breach. Here, as I walk over the mansions of the dead, I find two buried in the same grave, and inscribed above them, "They were pleasant in life, and in death not divided." There I find six slumbering in the same bed of dust, and the stone thus vents the anguish and submission of the parental heart—

> "The dear delights we here enjoy,
> And fondly call our own,
> Are but short favours borrow'd now,
> To be repaid anon."

The death of David's child was predicted by Nathan, and was the consequence of the father's sin. "Because by this deed thou hast given great occasion to the enemies of the Lord to blaspheme, the child that is born unto thee shall surely die." But how is it that the guilty father continues, and the innocent babe is cut off? "The landlord," says an old writer, "may distrain on any part of the premises he chooses." We would rather say, that there are many cases in which he requires us to walk by faith, and not by sight: that he does all things well, even when clouds and darkness are round about him: we would say, that he indemnified this child by taking it to himself—while the father was punished, and suffered more relatively than if he had died himself.

The execution follows the sentence. "The

Lord struck the child that Uriah's wife bare unto David, and it was very sick."

II. Observe THE BEHAVIOUR OF DAVID WITH REGARD TO THE AFFLICTION.

It takes in prayer—" He besought God for the child." What was so likely to enable him to gain his wishes, or to bring his mind into a state of preparation for a denial of them? Prayer is always proper: but how seasonable, how soothing, how sanctifying, in the day of trouble! Blessed resource and refuge! may we always make use of thee. " From the end of the earth will I' cry unto thee, when my heart is overwhelmed! lead me to the Rock that is higher than I."—" Is any afflicted, let him pray."

He also humbled himself: " He fasted, and went in, and lay all night upon the earth." There was doubtless something peculiar in this case: the child was the offspring of adultery. Much of David's distress arose from reflection on his sin: his grief was the grief not only of affliction, but of penitance. And when are our losses and trials purely afflictions? Is there nothing in our sufferings to bewail but the smart? Is it not sin that has made this world a vale of tears? Is it not our remaining depravity that constrains a merciful God to employ such painful dispensations? Are we not guilty of idolizing or undervaluing the blessings we are going to resign? May we not charge God foolishly in the trouble we are going to enter? Is it not desirable to know wherefore he contends with us? Humiliation is as necessary as prayer.

We have seen David's behaviour before the death of the child; let us remark his behaviour after it. His servants feared to tell him of the event; for they said, " Behold, while the child was yet alive, we spake unto him, and he would not hearken unto our voice: how will he then vex himself if we tell him that the child is dead? But when David saw that his servants whispered, David perceived that the child was dead: therefore David said unto his servants, Is the child dead? And they said, He is dead." And what does he!

Some disregard their persons, and affect a slovenliness in grief. But David "arose from the earth, and washed, and anointed himself, and changed his apparel."

Some remain invisible; and even the temple sees nothing of them during the season that peculiarly requires their attendance: for " God is known in his palaces for a refuge." But David " came into the house of the Lord and worshipped." It was to acknowledge the hand of God in his affliction; it was to say, with Job, " The Lord gave, and the Lord hath taken away; and blessed be the name of the Lord:" it was to praise him, that his sin, though chastised, was forgiven; and to beseech him to proceed no further.

Some disregard the duties of their stations and connexions in life; and weeping hinders sowing. But David knew he had a family that demanded his attention, and whom it behoved him to convince that the exercises of religion can relieve and refresh the mind: " and when he required, they set bread before him, and he did eat."

Believers are " men wondered at;" and they who are estranged from the life of God cannot comprehend the principles upon which the actions of believers turn. They consider forgiveness of injuries as a proof of cowardice. They mistake deep humiliation and fervent prayer for an inordinate attachment to creatures; and view acquiescence and thankfulness under trials as senseless indifference. " Then said his servants unto him, What thing is this that thou hast done? Thou didst fast and weep for the child when it was alive; but when the child was dead thou didst rise and eat bread."

" But he that is spiritual judgeth all things, though he himself is judged of no man." His service is a reasonable service; his conduct results from conviction and motive. David therefore explains himself: " And he said, While the child was yet alive, I fasted and wept: for I said, Who can tell whether God will be gracious to me, that the child may live? But now he is dead, wherefore should I fast? can I bring him back again? I shall go to him, but he shall not return to me."

This brings us to the

III. part of our subject.—" And he said, While the child was yet alive, I fasted and wept: for I said, Who can tell whether God will be gracious to me, that the child may live?"—He deemed the event uncertain. It is obvious that he did not consider the threatening as absolute and irreversible. He knew that many things had been denounced conditionally; and he knew also that the goodness of God was beyond all his thoughts.

As there seemed a possibility of success, so the desirableness of the blessing led him to avail himself of it. One might have supposed that the death of a child so young would not have been a very considerable affliction, especially as he would have been always a memorandum of his sin, and he could not have questioned his future happiness; but he speaks of his recovery as an instance of God's grace to himself—so great is the force of parental affection. His attachment indeed seems to have been extraordinary; and this was doubtless permitted of Heaven to render his correction the more severe. Such is the import of his reasoning: " I should have deemed it a peculiar favour had God spared my child; and while life remained, the indulgence of hope was not improper, nor the use of means unlawful. Submission follows the event."

But what led him to assuage his grief? What made him—I will not say insensible, but resigned? Attend, ye who have sustained bereaving providences, and behold your model. " But now he is dead, wherefore should I fast? can I bring him back again? I shall go to him, but he shall not return to me."—The unavailableness of grief—the certainty of his own dissolution—the hope of a union in heaven—these were the sources from which his resignation flowed.

First. Continued grief was unavailing. " Now he is dead, wherefore should I fast? can I bring him back again?" Ah, no! says one; but this is the very accent of my loss. " There is hope of a tree if it be cut down, that it sprout again, and that the tender branch thereof will not cease; but man lieth down and riseth not." I have seen my child asleep, but I could awake him at pleasure; but no call can pierce the ear of death. I have taken leave of my child for a journey, but the pain of parting was alleviated by the hope of meeting again; but now I shall see his face, and hear his voice no more. I am reminded of his presence throughout the long day; he meets me no more in my favourite walk; at table his *seat is empty*—and the places that once knew him will know him no more for *ever*. But, upon this very principle, grief is proved useless; and what cannot be prevented or removed, must be endured. Such is the appointment of Heaven; and his determination is not only sovereign, but righteous and good. To alter it is therefore not only impossible in the execution, but rebellious in the attempt.

Secondly. He contemplates his own death as certain: "I shall go to him." By this he intends the grave; and this part of our subject is common to *all* mankind. As sure as any of your connexions are gone, you are going after, and will soon join them " in the house appointed for all living." And has not this a tendency to moderate your grief? Does it not remind you of the vanity of life? Does it not proclaim that " time is short; and therefore it remains that they that rejoice be as though they rejoiced not, and they that weep as though they wept not?" If we were to live here always, or to live here long, we should be justified in feeling a deeper interest in its events; but we are only like a wayfaring man that turns aside to tarry for a night, and in the morning goes on his way.— And does it not show me that my chief business is to prepare for my own removal, rather than to lament the departure of others? I have no time for unprofitable sadness—I am just going to take a journey of infinite importance—

" Awake, my soul, with solemn care
   Thy true condition learn;
   What are thy hopes? how sure, how fair?
   And what thy *great concern?*"

How natural, how beautiful, how solemn is the reflection of a pious man[*] after burying his child:—" And now one of our family is gone to take possession of the sepulchre in all our names. Ere long I shall lie down with my child. Perhaps many of the feet that followed it shall attend me thither. It is a warning of Providence, that these concluding days of my life may be more regular, more spiritual, more useful, than the former."

Thirdly. He expects to follow his child not only into the grave, but into glory; and anticipates a renewed union with him in heaven. This was unquestionably David's case; but *this* part of our subject must be limited. When we see people in affliction, it seems hard to deny them consolation; but we dare not administer every kind of comfort to every kind of character—it would be only deceiving and destroying their souls. This part of our subject then must be limited two ways.

First, as to *the dead*. We cannot join those in heaven who are not gone there; and all do *not* go there when they die. We are not called to pronounce positively upon their misery; but what hope can we entertain, without offering violence to the Scripture, of the salvation of those who lived without prayer, who profaned the Sabbath, who were slaves to avarice and pride? In many other cases, if we *have* a hope concerning the deceased, it must be weak, and ought to be concealed: weak, from the deficiency of evidence; and concealed, from the fear of mischief.

But of others, when they die, we have a scriptural and a pleasing persuasion. And why should we mourn for them? They have overcome and are crowned. They have done with trouble, and have entered " the rest that remains for the people of God." Now this consolation extends to all children who die in a state of infancy. I know there are some who believe in the damnation of infants. They have no higher a notion of a God of love, the Father of mercies, the God of all grace, than to suppose that he will punish eternally creatures whom the Scripture itself calls innocent as to personal and actual transgression, and whose condition depended entirely upon himself. Admitting this barbarous notion; could such a Being ever be trusted in? or loved? But the God we worship is not Moloch; neither is the punishment we contend for in a future state separate from the effects of conscious guilt, regret, self-accusation—of all which those who die in infancy are incapable. We listen not to unfeeling and system-hardened divines, but to that Saviour " who gathers the lambs with his arms, and carries them in his bosom," and who, having invited our own souls to rest, cries, " Suffer little children to come unto me, and forbid them not, for of such is the kingdom of heaven."

The second limitation regards *the living*.

* Dr. Doddridge.

You cannot join those who are gone to heaven, if you do not go there yourselves. And if you are not " new creatures;" if you do not "deny yourselves, and take up your cross and follow the Redeemer," you must join another assembly, to whose taste you are now conformed, and whose portion you have here chosen. Death separates the precious from the vile, and unites only those of similar dispositions. But where we entertain a hope concerning our connexions, and concerning ourselves, the bitterness of death is passed.

Let us close. What parents are the most afflicted? Those who have children living— but living in sin and—walking according to the course of this world. Where is the father who would not a thousand times rather follow his son to the grave than see him growing up an enemy to God by wicked works? There is no hope of meeting such a child again. And yet instances like these are by no means unusual. But surely they should become subjects of serious inquiry— surely parents should ask themselves whether they have faithfully discharged the trust committed to them. And while we ought to be tender of those whose hearts are bleeding over undutiful and ungodly offspring, we should not overlook the word that says, "Train up a child in the way that he should go, and when he is old he will not depart from it."

As for those who have buried early hopes; remember that by their removal you have an opportunity afforded of exercising the grace of submission, and are left more free to attend to other duties. Guard against an excess of sorrow, which will drink up the spirits and work death. Comfort one another with the assurance that their death is their everlasting gain. Here they were in an enemy's country surrounded with snares; and who can tell how soon they might have fallen the victims of temptation? They are infinitely happier than it is possible for you to conceive, and their blessedness is secured beyond the power of injury.

Remember they are not separated from you for ever—you are going to them. They are waiting to receive you into everlasting habitations. On your arrival there, you will know them, and they will know you; even they will know you there, who never knew you here.

And may you not indulge the expectation, not only that you will know them, but be serviceable to them—be employed in forming and in teaching them? Oh! the pleasing work of a mother, to rear a child in that better country, free from sin, perverseness, pain; without anxiety, and without fear!

Nor imagine that in the mean time they are disregarded or overlooked, because of their tender age, or their inferiority of any other kind. Selfishness and pride only reign here.

That world is a world of condescension, of kindness, of love. There are pious friends. There are angels who attended them here. There is "your Father and their Father, your God and their God." " Thus saith the Lord; a voice was heard in Ramah, lamentation, and bitter weeping; Rachel weeping for her children, refused to be comforted for her children, because they were not. Thus saith the Lord; Refrain thy voice from weeping, and thine eyes from tears: for thy work shall be rewarded, saith the Lord; and they shall come again from the land of the enemy. And there is hope in thine end, saith the Lord, that thy children shall come again to their own border."

DISCOURSE LVIII.

THE BREAD OF LIFE.

And Jesus said unto them, I am the bread of life: he that cometh to me shall never hunger; and he that believeth on me shall never thirst.—John vi. 35.

" Yea, doubtless, and I count all things but loss for the excellency of the knowledge of Christ Jesus my Lord." Such is the exclamation of Paul. And he does not despise what he could not possess, or undervalue what he did not understand. He was a man of genius and of learning. He had examined the claims of human science, and knew how little it could do for man in his most important interests. He was also no stranger to the knowledge of his Lord and Saviour. The Son of God had been revealed in him; and from that blessed hour his acquaintance with him had been constantly increasing. He knew whom he had believed; and such was the efficacy of this knowledge, in purifying his passions, in tranquillizing his conscience, in refreshing and delighting his heart, that he was led comparatively to depreciate every thing else; and determined " to know nothing save Jesus Christ and him crucified."

And is not this the determination of every Christian? And is it not justifiable? Is it not wise? Need we wonder that his Saviour is every thing *with* him, since he is every thing *to* him?—his sun and shield—his guide and guard—his physician and friend—his righteousness and strength—his clothing and his food. " And Jesus said unto them, I am the bread of life: he that cometh to me shall never hunger; and he that believeth on me shall never thirst."

Observe, I. A REPRESENTATION OF THE SAVIOUR. II. THE WAY IN WHICH WE ARE TO DERIVE ADVANTAGE FROM HIM. III. THE HAPPINESS HIS FOLLOWERS SHALL ENJOY.

I. A REPRESENTATION OF THE SAVIOUR. "I am the bread of life." All life is valuable, and there are several degrees of it rising above each other. There is vegetable life: this is superior to dead matter, as a tree is more excellent than a stone. There is animal life: this is superior to vegetable, as a bird is more excellent than a tree. There is rational life: this is superior to animal, as a man is more excellent than a beast. His form and his powers proclaim his pre-eminence, and prove him lord of this lower world. But there is a life superior to human, and which "the natural man understandeth not, because it is spiritually discerned." It is called "the life of God." Of this man was originally possessed; from this he has fallen by sin; to this he is restored by divine grace.

And there are some who are proofs of the possibility of this restoration. They have "passed from death unto life." Though alive to other things, they were once dead to the things of God. They had no spiritual sensibility: but they now feel. They had no spiritual appetite; but they now "hunger and thirst after righteousness." They had no spiritual senses, "to discern both good and evil;" but they now hear his voice, see his glory, and "taste that the Lord is gracious." They had no spiritual energy or action; but they now "strive to enter in at the strait gate, walk in the way everlasting," and "labour, that, whether present or absent, they may be accepted of him." These dispositions may be imperfect, and these exertions may be weak; but they could not make the one, nor be conscious of the other—unless they were alive.

The Scripture loves to present religion to us under the notion of *life*; and it is a very important and distinguishing one. In a picture there is likeness, and how striking does the resemblance sometimes appear! But what a difference is there between the shadow and the substance; between the image and the original. It seems to speak; but it is silent. The "breathing canvass" is not life. A figure may be formed equal to the size of a man; and ingenuity may add motion to likeness: but it is not self-moved; its movements, few and senseless, result from foreign force or skill. And mechanism, however fine or finished, is not life. How many things that look like religion fall short of it. How many have the form of godliness, while they deny the power thereof. How many, destitute of all inward principle, are actuated in duty by external motives only; and whose devotion begins and ends with the operation of the circumstances producing it! But God puts his Spirit within us, and causes us to walk in his ways, and to keep his statutes.

Now observe the relation in which the Lord Jesus stands to this life. "I am," says he, "the bread of life." Bread often stands for all that nourishes and sustains our bodies; and hence we read of the "staff of bread:"

the meaning is, that life leans on it for support. And our Saviour is all that is necessary to the life of God in the soul;" "I am come," says he, "that they might have life, and that they might have it the more abundantly. For the bread of God is he which cometh down from heaven, and giveth life unto the world."

Bread corn is bruised. The grain passes through a process which seems likely to destroy it before it becomes our food. And what means our Saviour when he says, "The bread that I will give you is my flesh, which I will give for the life of the world!" Some tell us that he refers to his doctrine only. It is admitted that instruction may be called the food of the mind—but why does our Lord refer to his *flesh?* And what master ever spake of his disciples eating *himself?* "My flesh is meat indeed, and my blood is drink indeed. He that eateth my flesh and drinketh my blood, dwelleth in me, and I in him." What can this imply but a truth so fully revealed in the Scripture—That he becomes our Saviour by being our sacrifice, and that we live by his death!

His language leads us to another reflection, which is not the less important because it is common. It is this: Bread is nothing to us however prepared, or presented, or possessed, unless it be eaten. You may perish with bread in your house, and even in your hand—it is only by admitting it into the animal system that it can become nourishment. "I am the living bread that came down from heaven; if any man *eat* of this bread he shall live for ever. Except ye *eat* the flesh of the Son of God, and *drink* his blood, ye have no life in you. He that *eateth* me, even he shall live by me." Is not this saying that a Saviour unapplied will profit you nothing? He may have in himself every thing you need; he may be nigh you; he may be proposed to you in the gospel—and all this is true; but he must be received by faith. For to vary the image, "To as many as received him, to them gave he power to become the sons of God, even to them that believe on his name."

This brings us to remark,

II. THE WAY IN WHICH WE DERIVE ADVANTAGE FROM HIM. It is by coming to him; by believing on him. "He that *cometh* to me shall never hunger; and he that *believeth on* me shall never thirst." And here we are not to suppose that two different characters are intended, of which the one comes to our Lord, and the other believes on him. The expressions designate the same person; and are explanatory of each other. So that if you ask, What is coming to him? you are told, that it is believing on him. And if you ask, What is believing on him? you are told, it is coming to him.

The case is this. Since so much depends

on real faith, it is necessary for us to know what it is: but as we have more to do with the uses of things than with their nature; and as they are more obviously known by their operations and effects, than by their physical and abstract qualities, the Scripture holds forth faith by its office, and in its actings. It tells us what faith *does* in the man who is the possessor of it: it "works by love;" it "overcomes the world;" it "purifies the heart;" it brings a man to Christ. He that believeth on him, comes to him. This representation of faith is very instructive.

First. It reminds us that the Lord Jesus is accessible. In the days of his flesh he was approachable in his bodily presence; and many went to him and implored relief; and none ever implored in vain. In this sense we can no longer approach him; in this sense he is "no more in the world." But unless he is accessible under another and a higher view, how can he verify the promise; "Where two or three are gathered together in my name, there am I in the midst of them?" Did he appoint his disciples to meet him in Galilee after his resurrection; and did they go down and find him there? So he has ordained means, in the use of which if *we* are found, *he* will be found. For he is present among the assemblies of his people, and in his house, and at his table, and in his word, and upon his throne; there dispensing mercy and grace to help us in every time of need.

Secondly. It teaches us that faith is not a notion, but a principle; and is always attended with an application of the soul to the Redeemer. Under the influence of it I cannot rest without him; but from a conviction of my perilous and perishing case, and a persuasion of his power, appointment, and readiness to succour and to save me, I go to him and address him. I throw myself at his feet, and cry, "Lord, save, I perish." I see him as the only refuge, and I seek to enter him. I view him as the Lord my righteousness and strength, and pray to be found in him. On this foundation I begin to build: from this "fulness I receive, and grace for grace."

And let it be remembered, that this application which always distinguishes genuine faith from false, is not a single address, but a renewed, a continued exercise. He that believeth on him is not one that *came* and transacted an affair with him, and then had nothing more to do with him—no—but one that *cometh.* Peter has the same thought, and equally excludes those whose religion is an action; instead of a course of action, instead of a habit, instead of a life—"to whom *coming* as unto a living stone." He will be necessary to the last: as long as we contract fresh guilt; as long as we are called to bear new trials and discharge new duties; as long as we are in the body of this death—so long must we come to him.

Let us notice,

III. THE HAPPINESS HIS FOLLOWERS SHALL ENJOY: "He that cometh to me shall *never hunger,* and he that believeth on me shall *never thirst.*" This assurance admits of several explanations.

First. The follower of Jesus shall never hunger nor thirst again after the world. This distinguishes him from all unrenewed men; for they hunger and thirst after nothing else. And this was once his own case. But having tasted the provisions of God's house, his language now is, " Lord, evermore give me this bread." Having seen the glory of the only begotten of the Father, full of grace and truth, nothing else allures or charms: " Whom," says he, " whom have I in heaven but thee? and there is none upon earth that I desire beside thee." Endeavours will be made to draw off the soul from this sovereign good. The world will present its riches, honours, pleasures, and prospects; and often ask, " What is thy Beloved more than another beloved?" But these syren songs will be sung in vain. All believers indeed are not equally mortified to earthly things; but as far as grace prevails in the soul, they will, they must lose their influence: as far as we are " after the Spirit," we shall "mind the things of the Spirit." And no real Christian, who walks by faith, and not by sight, can so seek after the world again as to make it his portion, or to place his happiness in it. A covetous, ambitious, sensual, pleasure-taking Christian is a character the Scripture knows nothing of.

Secondly. He shall not hunger and thirst in vain. The new creature has wants and appetites, but ample provision is made to relieve and indulge them; and the believer knows where to go for those blessings; and is not liable to disappointment in seeking for them. He no longer runs to and fro, asking, Who will show me any good? He has found the source of satisfaction, and derives supplies from it. It is adequate to the immensities of his desires. More *than* the " consolation of Israel " he does not long for, though he does long for more *of* it. But

Thirdly. He shall not hunger and thirst always. The days of imperfect enjoyment will soon be over. Then every power will be filled; every hope accomplished; every wish realized. Then, says David, " I shall be satisfied when I awake with thy likeness."

The subject thus briefly explained, is—

A standard by which we may estimate *Christ.* What a life have we been speaking of! But the higher and nobler this life is, the more does it glorify him—for he is "the bread of life." There is nothing men so value as life. Even this vain life, which we spend as a shadow—even this suffering life, which we find to be a series of cares, losses, pains, and troubles—how we cleave to it! how con-

2 D   8*

cerned we are to secure and continue it; how readily we pay the physician that recovers it; how highly we prize the food that sustains it; and pressed with want, what exertions and sacrifices are we not willing to make to obtain relief! Surely we are not sensible of our spiritual necessities; surely we have no desires after the life of our souls, eternal life, or we should above all esteem *Him* by whom *alone* it is to be attained; and not urge his compassionate heart to complain, " Ye will not come unto me that ye might have life."

The subject is a standard by which we may estimate *faith*. Why does the apostle call faith *precious?* Because " he that believeth on the Son hath everlasting life: and he that believeth not the Son shall not see life; but the wrath of God abideth on him." It is indispensable to our salvation. It is the medium of all our intercourse with the Redeemer of sinners. If faith be nothing without Christ, Christ is nothing without faith.

The subject is a standard by which to estimate the *Christian*. The world knoweth him not: it knew not his lord and master—and why should the servant wish to be above his master, or the disciple above his lord? He may be poor and afflicted; but a man is not to be judged of by outward things, but by the state of his mind, and by his future state. A Christian without pride, may pity philosophers and kings. He is safe. He is happy. His happiness is not only insured but commenced. He hears nothing but complaints in the world; and no wonder, since they are seeking the living among the dead;—but he has *found* rest; he feels satisfaction. He has much in hand, and more in hope. The Saviour is now with him; and soon he will be for ever with the Lord.

" Blessed are the people that are in such a case."

" Look thou upon me, and be merciful unto me, as thou usest to do unto those that love thy name." Amen.

DISCOURSE LIX.

THE SCRIPTURE DESPISED.

I have written to him the great things of y law, but they were counted as a strange thing.—Hosea viii. 12.

THE history of the Jews is not only wonderful but instructive. It shows us what God is, and what man is. In every page we see the goodness of the one, and the wickedness of the other.

For it is in vain to imagine that the depravity of this people was peculiar to themselves. They were fair specimens of human nature; and we have no reason to believe that we should have been better than they,

under the same dispensation—yea, under superior advantages, we *are* no better than they.

When Hosea exercised his ministry, the volume of Scripture was not complete. The additions of several of the prophets, and of all the New Testament writings, were wanting—whereas we have these additions; the system of revelation is now perfect; and the man that adds to the words of this book is accursed, as well as the man that takes away from it. Thus our privilege is much enlarged, and, alas! our guilt is increased along with it; and what God said of Ephraim applies to us with equal truth, and with greater aggravation; " I have written to him the great things of my law, but they were counted as a strange thing." These words lead us to consider three things with regard to the Scriptures. I. THEIR AUTHOR. II. THEIR SUBJECT. III. THEIR RECEPTION.

I. Observe THEIR AUTHOR.—" I," says God, " I have written to him the great things of my law." This fact it would be well for us to remember whenever we read or hear it; for the manner in which the Scripture affects us will always depend upon our persuasion of this truth. If we consider it as a cunningly devised fable, we shall treat it as a delusion. If we believe it to be the word of man, we shall receive it as a human production. But if we are convinced that it is indeed the word of God, we shall feel it to be divine, and it will work powerfully in us, as it does in those who believe.

Now in favour of these writings we advance a *Divine* claim. " All Scripture," says the apostle, " is given by inspiration of God." So that whoever was the penman, he was the author. I hope I need not labour to prove this. I hope you have not found it necessary to deny it, by indulging in a vicious course of life. " For this is the condemnation, that light is come into the world, but men love darkness rather than light, because their deeds are evil." They are infidel because they are wicked, and pretend to quarrel with the doctrines of revelation because they hate the practice. The character of its enemies has always been a strong recommendation of the Scripture.

We pass by the proofs derived from prophecies and miracles; from the number and competency of the original witnesses of the Gospel; from its success in the world; from the convictions of the wise, and the sufferings of the good—and remark only at present, the internal evidence there is to prove that this book was written by God. When we survey the works of nature, we discern impressions of perfection and effects of contrivance, so as to urge the examiner to exclaim, " This is the finger of God." Now opening these leaves, we find a resemblance that reminds us of the same agent. We perceive in the book of Scripture, as in the book of Creation, the same degree of plainness and obscurity intermixed; the same difference between the nature and the use of things, the one eluding research, and the other level to common apprehension; the same order, and the same sublime irregularity; some parts peculiarly prominent, while the whole equally rejects all attempts completely to systematize it. We see that the Scripture is adapted to the actual state of man; that it is suited to his wants and weaknesses in every period, whether he be young or old; in every condition, whether he be prosperous or afflicted; in every relation, whether he be a master or servant, a father or child, a citizen of this world, or an heir of immortality. The book understands my fears, and meets my hopes; and were I to find it by accident, and had never read it before, I must, upon perusing it, confess, that it could only have been produced by one who perfectly knew my misery, and was infinitely concerned for my welfare—that is, GOD. "I have written to him"—What! Observe,

II. THE CONTENTS—"the great things of my law." We naturally judge of an author by his work; but there are cases in which we judge of a work by the author. What I mean is this; we have such a knowledge of some men, and such a confidence in them, that we are sure they cannot write improperly; and conclude even beforehand, that what *they* send forth must be worthy of our purchase and our perusal. And as soon as we learn that God himself is the author of this book, we may approach it confidently, expecting to find in it a *greatness* becoming his glorious Name.

Nor shall we be disappointed. We here find great things.

Great in *number*. What other book ever laid open such a boundless multiplicity of subjects, and gave rise to such an infinity of thoughts?

Great in *profundity*. What other book could bear thousands of writers and preachers to be always explaining and improving it! What other book would bear daily and hourly reading and reviewing!—Yet we always find something fresh and interesting; and the subjects so far from being exhausted, lead us to pray, "Open thou mine eyes, that I may behold wondrous things out of thy law." "Eye hath not seen, nor ear heard, neither have entered into the heart of man, the things which God hath prepared for them that love him. But God hath revealed them unto us by his Spirit: for the Spirit searcheth all things, yea, the deep things of God."

Great in *importance*. Here we see the way in which God harmonizes all his perfections in the salvation of man. Here we see how he delivers a perishing sinner from the curse of the law and the bondage of corruption; how the guilty are made righteous; how the unholy are made pure; how the weak are rendered equal to every duty and difficulty of the Christian life.—The subjects are not addressed to our fancies and opinions, but to our consciences. They relate to the soul, to eternity. They include "exceeding great and precious promises;" and which infinitely surpass all the offers of the world.

Great in their *efficacy*. They have awakened the most secure consciences; they have softened the hardest hearts; they have comforted the greatest sufferers; they have enabled them to glory in tribulation, and to triumph in death. Plato complained that he could not bring over the inhabitants of even one village to live by the rules of his philosophy. But how many millions have been reformed and renewed by the doctrines of the Cross! "The words that I speak unto you," says our Saviour, "they are spirit, and they are life." "I am not ashamed of the gospel of Christ," says Paul, "for it is the power of God unto salvation to every one that believeth." It bringeth salvation, not only as to the discovery, but the experience of it; and teaches us what nothing else ever did, or ever will teach, to "deny all ungodliness and worldly lusts, and to live soberly, righteously, and godly, in the present world; looking for that blessed hope, and the glorious appearing of the great God and our Saviour Jesus Christ." And where it does not save, it civilizes; and it has done more in taming the fierceness and savageness of the multitude, in raising the tone of morals, in securing the welfare of the community, than all the civil institutions in the world.

In a word, the greatest thing we have upon earth is the Gospel. It dignifies every country in which it is found; and the poorest cottage that contains a Bible is rendered unspeakably more valuable than a heathen palace. This gave the Jews their pre-eminence over all other nations; "to them were committed the oracles of God." No wonder therefore that the prophet should consider the loss of this mercy as the greatest judgment that could ever befall a people. "Behold, the days come, saith the Lord God, that I will send a famine in the land; not a famine of bread, nor a thirst for water, but of hearing the words of the Lord."

III. Let us consider THE RECEPTION WHICH THIS DIVINE COMMUNICATION MEETS WITH. "I have written to him the great things of my law, but they were counted as a strange thing." A *strange thing* here means a thing foreign to us; a matter of indifference; a thing that does not concern us, and cannot affect us; by which we shall gain nothing if we observe it, lose nothing if we despise it; a thing unworthy of our attention: the very reverse of what Moses said, "It is not a vain thing for you; because it is your life." And that men thus in reality treat the Scriptures of truth, is the charge here advanced. Let us examine it.

First; it is a charge the most *wonderful*. We should naturally suppose that a book written by God himself would engage attention. We should reasonably conclude that it would excite no little interest if it only professed to be his work; how much more if the probability of this fact was strong; but who would think it possible to disregard it, if the evidences in its favour were numerous and undeniable!—All other books, being human, betray the imperfections of their authors; yet they are eagerly bought and read, admired and relished: but here is a book neglected, that is proved to be divine!

People are naturally attracted to a work that regards themselves. If I were to announce that a book was published which only mentioned your name, it is questionable whether you would be able to sleep till you had seen it. If you were poor, or if you were sick and dying, and a publication could inform you how to obtain riches, or health, and cure—you would surely obtain it, and examine it with singular solicitude. But the Scripture speaks of *you*; it describes *your* character; it contains the charter of *your* privileges; it reveals a deliverance from all *your* woes; and by a method that awakens your wonder, while it relieves your wants. The angels desire to look into these things, and study them with intense application; yet angels need no repentance, no redemption. And will you—you who are immediately and eternally interested in them—will *you* make light of them!

A charge, Secondly, the most *criminal*. We often err in our estimate of things, especially those of a moral nature. We have frequently a wrong standard by which to judge of what is good; hence that which is highly esteemed among men, is an abomination in the sight of God. In the same way we deceive ourselves with regard to what is evil. We judge of sin by outward appearances, or by the grossness of the action. But God takes into view not only the injury that is done to our neighbour, but the dishonour that is done to himself; not only what is done, but what is omitted: he weighs the state of the mind, the motives that determine us, the good we oppose and hinder; the difficulties we have to overcome, the convictions we have to stifle, the reasons that render us inexcusable. And by this rule, nothing can be more wicked, than to treat with contempt or neglect the means God has provided and revealed in his infinite goodness and wisdom for our everlasting welfare. It cannot therefore, while any thing like justice remains in the world, be done with impunity.

Hence, Thirdly, the charge is the most *dreadful*. If indeed God was to deal with you after your desert, he would not bear with you a day or an hour. But he is a God of patience; and is longsuffering to us-ward, not willing that any should perish. Yet, lest you should suppose that forbearance is connivance, and that, because he does not immediately reckon with you, he will never call you to account, hear, I beseech you, the following threatenings which he stands solemnly pledged to execute:—"And if it come to pass, when he heareth the words of this curse, that he bless himself in his heart, saying, I shall have peace, though I walk in the imagination of mine heart, to add drunkenness to thirst: the Lord will not spare him, but then the anger of the Lord and his jealousy shall smoke against that man, and all the curses that are written in this book shall lie upon him, and the Lord shall blot out his name from under heaven." "Then shall they call upon me, but I will not answer; they shall seek me early, but they shall not find me: for that they hated knowledge, and did not choose the fear of the Lord: They would none of my counsel: they despised all my reproof. Therefore shall they eat of the fruit of their own way, and be filled with their own devices." "How shall we escape if we neglect so great salvation!" "He that despised Moses' law died without mercy under two or three witnesses: of how much sorer punishment, suppose ye, shall he be thought worthy, who hath trodden under foot the Son of God, and hath counted the blood of the covenant, wherewith he was sanctified, an unholy thing, and hath done despite unto the Spirit of grace!"

We could add to the number of these tremendous denunciations. But surely more than enough has been repeated to rouse all your anxiety, and to lead you to inquire, "Lord, is it I!"

Yet, Fourthly, the charge is very *commonly deserved*. Few pay a due regard to the blessed word of God.—Take infidels, who openly reject it, and endeavour to make others believe what it would seem impossible for them to believe themselves, that a system so wise in its contrivance, so beneficial in its tendency, so holy in its influence, is the work of foolish or wicked men!!—Take apostates. How many, even in our own day, have we seen, who once made a flaming profession of religion, whose hearts have turned back, and whose steps have declined from his ways; who can laugh at that which once made them tremble, and are "so bewitched"—I use the words of the Apostle, "that they cannot obey the truth."—Take nominal Christians, some of whom would be much offended if you refused to consider them as real ones. Yet how seldom do they read it! How rarely do they hear it! And of those that hear it, often hear it, hear it dispensed with fidelity and affection, how many are there who are curious hearers, captious hearers, forgetful hearers,

hearers only deceiving their own selves! Did you never observe the complaint that God addressed to Ezekiel? "Son of man, the children of thy people speak one to another, every one to his brother, saying, Come I pray you, and hear what is the word that cometh forth from the Lord. And they come unto thee as the people cometh, and they sit before thee as my people, and they hear thy words, but they will not do them: for with their mouth they show much love, but their heart goeth after their covetousness. And, lo, thou art unto them as a very lovely song of one that hath a pleasant voice, and can play well on an instrument: for they hear thy words, but they do them not." Does this apply to none of us? It characterizes thousands who attend even where the Gospel is preached in its purity. We say therefore again, that, *few* pay a due regard to the word of God; few imbibe its spirit; few fear its threatenings; few embrace its promises; few obey its commands; few practically own its authority.

But to conclude. The charge is not *universally true.* Blessed be God, there are some exceptions; and we trust in the number of exceptions some of *you* are found. I hope some of you are daily kneeling before this sacred volume and praying, "Teach me thy way, O Lord; I will walk in thy truth: unite my heart to fear thy name." Good men have always been attached to their Bibles! Many have shed their blood, rather than even conceal their regard to it. We read in the book of martyrs of a husbandman who gave a whole load of hay for one leaf of one of the epistles! BOYLE, that great philosopher, said, speaking of the Scripture, "I prefer a sprig of the tree of life to a whole wood of bays." Judge HALE, that ornament of his profession and country, said, that "if he did not honour God's word by reading a portion of it every morning, things went not well with him all the day." Job said, "I have esteemed the words of thy mouth more than my necessary food." David exclaimed, "O how love I thy law! it is my meditation all the day! More to be desired are they than gold, yea, than much fine gold; sweeter also than honey and the honeycomb."

Can you express yourselves in similar language? Are these your sentiments? You ought to be thankful—and to be thankful not only that you possess such an invaluable blessing as the Scriptures, but that you have been taught to prize it, and enabled to use it. You have found it to be, in your own happy experience, a compass to guide you; a remedy to heal you; a sword to defend you; a balm for every wound, a cordial for every fear.

But let me urge upon you a still greater attention to the word of God. Let it not only "dwell" in you, but dwell in you "richly," and "in all wisdom." Pray for the spread of it, that it may have "free course and be

glorified." Long for the day when the Scripture shall be found in every family. Be concerned to furnish those around you with the Bible who may be destitute of it. Take peculiar care early to awaken in those whom God has graciously given you, an affectionate and a familiar regard to it. It is the order of Heaven. "These words, which I command thee this day, shall be in thine heart: and thou shalt teach them diligently unto thy children, and shalt talk of them when thou sittest in thine house, and when thou walkest by the way, and when thou liest down, and when thou risest up. And thou shalt bind them for a sign upon thy hand, and they shall be as frontlets between thine eyes."

O precious Bible! I could for ever enlarge in thy praise.—Read it, ye mourners in Zion: it will wipe away your tears. Read it, ye bereaved: it will assure you that a father of the fatherless, and a husband of the widow, is God in his holy habitation. Read it, ye poor: it will soothe you under your privations. Read it, ye rich: it will sanctify your abundance. Ye old, read it: it will support your tottering age. Ye young, read it: it will preserve your giddy steps. "Bind them continually upon thine heart, and tie them about thy neck. When thou goest, it shall lead thee; when thou sleepest, it shall keep thee; and when thou awakest, it shall talk with thee. For the commandment is a lamp; and the law is light; and reproofs of instruction are the way of life."

DISCOURSE LX.

THE ADVANTAGE OF HAVING GODLY PARENTS.

A good man leaveth an inheritance to his children's children.—Prov. xiii. 22.

WHAT so interesting as children? Children are pledges of mutual and hallowed affection. Children recall the early scenes of our own lives; they renew our image; they embalm our memory; they multiply and perpetuate ourselves. Other attachments lose their influence over us with age, but love to children warms the heart in death. It is the source of numberless and unutterable hopes and fears, and pains and pleasures.

What is the emblem of divine compassion? "Like as a father pitieth his children, so the Lord pitieth them that fear him." Rachel weeps for her children, and "will not be comforted, because they are not." Who does not feel for the venerable patriarch as he exclaims, "Me have ye bereaved of my children: Joseph is not, and Simeon is not —and will ye take Benjamin away? All these things are against me." Who can refuse to mourn with the king of Israel as he retires from the shouts of a victory that had saved his own life; and, as he goes up into his chamber over the gate, weeping, exclaims, "O my son Absalom! my son, my son Absalom! would God I had died for thee, O Absalom, my son, my son!" When the woman came to our Lord on the behalf of her daughter grievously vexed with a devil, how does she express herself! "Thou Son of David, have mercy on *me*." The mother suffered as much by sympathy as the daughter by disease; and the deliverance of the one would have been the relief of the other.

But if parents are affected by the condition of children, children are affected by the conduct of parents. Thus we read that God "visits the iniquities of the fathers upon the children unto the third and fourth generation of them that hate him." "Which is certainly unjust," some are ready to exclaim; "and is sufficient to condemn the book in which the assertion is found." And yet we constantly see children, in ways innumerable, suffering for the vices of their ancestors. By the idleness and drunkenness of one father, his infants are reduced to rags and ruin. By the licentious guilt of another, disease carries off his newborn babe—the babe is not criminal, yet it is tortured with pain and dies. The fact is undeniable; and deism has to encounter the same difficulty with revelation. Religion is no more chargeable with it than the course of nature. If the Bible be not the word of God, the world is the work of God; and where is the difference between his announcing such a rule, or his acting upon it? On the other hand, goodness operates powerfully and beneficially in descent; and we read that "God showeth mercy unto thousands of them that love him and keep his commandments:" that "his mercy is from everlasting to everlasting upon them that fear him;" and "his righteousness unto children's children." And among the various subjects that come under the observation of Solomon, is that of a godly father entailing blessings on his family. "A good man leaveth an inheritance to his children's children."

Let us premise three things.

I. THE CHARACTER IN QUESTION IS A GOOD MAN. Some persons are prejudiced against the very use of the term: but they would do well to remember that it is one of "the words the Holy Ghost teacheth." It is needless to repeat passages to prove this; but it may be necessary to observe that the term is to be taken with limitations. None are good *perfectly*: for "there is not a just man upon the earth that doeth good and sinneth not." Paul confessed that *he* had not attained—that *he* was not already perfect; but only pressing towards the mark. None are good *naturally*: for as we are all derived from the same source, and this is a depraved one, "who can bring a clean thing out of an unclean?" We

are not *born* Christians, but are *made such*. "If any man be in Christ, he is a new creature." But some are *saved* by the washing of regeneration, and the renewing of the Holy Ghost. God has begun "a good work in them;" and the work denominates the subjects of it. Such is the *origin* of the character. But what are the features of it?

In a good man we must have *piety*. He trusts in God, and submits to him; he loves and fears him. He keeps holy the Sabbath of the Lord his God. He enters his house; he reads and hears his word; he comes to his table; he approaches his throne for mercy and grace to help him in time of need. And while others live without God in the world, he is actuated by a desire to please and glorify him in all his actions. Unless the heart be right with God, we are nothing. Without principle and motive, whatever noise we make in religion, we are but "sounding brass and a tinkling cymbal."

In a good man we must have *sincerity*. You would not think of applying the word to a mere pretender; to one whose actions were always at variance with his words and his heart; to one who was all form and varnish in religion; a whited sepulchre, which looks fair outwardly, but is within full of death and corruption. But you feel no reluctance to appropriate the term to one, even though he has not much light, and is not free from infirmities, who *is* what he *appears* to be; and of whom our Saviour would say, "Behold an Israelite indeed, in whom there is no guile."

In a good man we must have *uniformity*. He is not one thing alone, and another in company. He is not a meek follower of the Lamb in the house of God, and a tyrant in his own. He is not prayerful in sickness, and prayerless in health. He is not humble in adversity, and proud and rigorous in prosperity. He is the same essentially in all the varieties of human condition: the changes of life serve only to prove his character, and to develope it. They are trials, and often severe ones; but they meet with gold; and it will "appear unto praise and glory and honour at the appearing of Jesus Christ."

In a good man we must have *benevolence* and *beneficence*. It is not enough to be barely moral; and to render to all their due. A good man does not keep just within the precincts of legal obligation; but goes forth where no human statute would punish him for neglect; and having freely received, he freely gives. The love and gratitude which he cannot extend to God, overflow upon his fellow-creatures. He has imbibed the Spirit of him who went about doing good; and as he has opportunity, *he* does "good unto all men, especially unto them that are of the household of faith." This part of his character the Scripture makes a test of the reality of every other part: "He that loveth not his brother whom he hath seen, how can he love God whom he hath not seen? Whoso hath this world's good, and seeth his brother have need, and shutteth up his bowels of compassion from him—how dwelleth the love of God in him?" It is this that attaches others so firmly and inviolably to him: "scarcely for a righteous man will one die, yet peradventure for a good man some would even dare to die." It is this that draws so peculiarly the gracious notice of God himself. "To do good and to communicate, forget not, for with such sacrifices God is well pleased. A good man showeth favour and lendeth: he will guide his affairs with discretion. Surely he shall not be moved for ever: the righteous shall be had in everlasting remembrance. He shall not be afraid of evil tidings: his heart is fixed, trusting in the Lord."

Secondly. Solomon supposes that such a good man may be found in connected life. And what is there in his goodness that is likely to hinder this? what is there in his goodness that does not render it the more probable? His religion will improve all those views and feelings that tend to make him social and useful. Some have attached I know not what kind of holiness and preeminence to celibacy; but the Scripture knows nothing of it. There we read that "marriage is honourable in all." There we find the doctrine—of forbidding to marry, branded with infamy. Jesus graced a wedding with his own presence, and wrought his first miracle to aid even the festivity of the scene. God himself in paradise instituted marriage; and said, "It is not good for man to be alone." And who will rise up and give his Maker the lie? Enoch married earlier than his cotemporaries, and begat sons and daughters; and yet "he walked with God; and was not, for God took him." Compare this man, early surrounded with family connexions, with a wretched, sordid monk in a cell, or with any of those poor, selfish, coldhearted beings who refuse to serve their generation according to the will of God—and which of them rises or sinks in your estimation?—Yea, it is supposed that this good man has offspring too—another natural conclusion, and sanctioned generally by the promise of God. "Blessed is every one that feareth the Lord; that walketh in his ways. For thou shalt eat the labour of thine hands: happy shalt thou be, and it shall be well with thee. Thy wife shall be as a fruitful vine by the sides of thine house: thy children like olive plants round about thy table. Behold, that thus shall the man be blessed that feareth the Lord. The Lord shall bless thee out of Zion: and thou shalt see the good of Jerusalem all the days of thy life. Yea, thou shalt see thy children's children, and peace upon Israel."

Thirdly. Though the subject is spoken of in reference to the man, the woman is by no means excluded. Though she moves less publicly and visibly, her influence, like that of the more primary and hidden springs in a machine, is certainly great and efficient. To a family, a good mother, no less than a good father, is an invaluable blessing. To whom under God did the Jewish Church owe a Samuel? To a wise and pious Hannah. To whom did the Christian Church owe a Timothy? "From a child he had known the Scripture, which is able to make us wise unto salvation;" and the secret is laid open: "When," says the Apostle, "I call to remembrance the unfeigned faith that is in thee, which dwelt first in thy grandmother Lois, and thy mother Eunice, and I am persuaded that in thee also." It is not to Jesse, but to Jesse's wife, that David so tenderly and devoutly refers, when he says, "O Lord, truly I am thy servant; I am thy servant, and the son of thine handmaid: thou hast loosed my bonds. O turn unto me, and have mercy upon me; give thy strength unto thy servant, and save the son of thine handmaid."

These things being premised, let us examine what that inheritance is, which a good man leaves to his offspring.

I. It comprehends RELIGIOUS INSTRUCTIONS. There are some who are unfriendly to the practice of infusing into children any doctrinal principles; and plead for leaving their minds quite free and unbiased, till they are able to judge for themselves. But can a parent forbear to impart to those who are peculiarly dear to him what he knows to be of unspeakable importance, and of immediate necessity? Will the mind of his child remain free and unbiased through infancy and youth? If empty of good, will it not be filled with the evil that so pressingly surrounds it in a world like this? Will the enemy check his march, and leave the passes unoccupied till you choose to possess them yourselves?—If our children do not remember God in the days of their youth, they are not very likely to remember him at all. The promise is, "I love them that love me, and they that seek me early shall find me:" but can they love him without knowing him? Do they seek him by instinct, or from motive? We are commanded to use means even by him who works in us both to will and to do of his good pleasure: and if we regard his authority, the dispute is ended: "Train up a child in the way he should go: and when he is old, he will not depart from it." Fathers, provoke not your children to wrath: but bring them up in the nurture and admonition of the Lord." Hear how Moses charges the Jews: "And these words, which I command thee this day, shall be in thine heart: and thou shalt teach them diligently unto thy children, and shalt talk of them when thou sittest in thine house, and when thou walkest by the way, and when thou liest down, and when thou risest up. And when thy son asketh thee in time to come, saying, What mean the testimonies, and the statutes, and the judgments, which the Lord our God hath commanded you? Then thou shalt say unto thy son, We were Pharaoh's bondmen in Egypt; and the Lord brought us out of Egypt with a mighty hand: and the Lord showed signs and wonders, great and sore, upon Egypt, upon Pharaoh, and upon all his household, before our eyes: and he brought us out from thence, that he might bring us in, to give us the land which he sware unto our fathers. And the Lord commanded us to do all these statutes, to fear the Lord our God, for our good always, that he might preserve us alive, as it is at this day. And it shall be our righteousness, if we observe to do all these commandments before the Lord our God, as he hath commanded us."

Here the duty is not only enjoined, but explained: and we see in the performance of it nothing harsh, nothing formal; it is a familiar, a domestic employment. The father goes not before the child, but follows him; he answers; and the inquiries of the child remind him of the information he needs, and show him the state and opening of the mind on which he is called to attend. How has God the father of all taught us? What is the Old Testament but a collection of imagery, of maxims, and proverbs? but a narrative of great and interesting events, the creation of the world, and the operations of Providence from age to age. What is the Gospel? A body of divinity? A system of theology? No. It is history. It consists of facts and reflections. It is in this way alone that the young can be interested and taught to purpose.

A good man will withhold no useful information from his children: but while he does not overlook them as inhabitants of the present world, he views them as the awful heirs of immortality; and is principally concerned that they should know the things that belong to their everlasting peace. What is every other acquisition, if they are not wise unto salvation!

A good man will cherish in the minds of his children a belief of divine truth, however mysterious; and maintain in them a sense of the limitation and weakness of human reason; but he will not lead them to metaphysical subtleties, and " doubtful disputations, that gender strife rather than godly edifying." He will even distinguish in his endeavours between what *may* be true, and what *is* important. "Secret things belong unto God; but things that are revealed belong to us and to our children." And unto man *he* said, Behold, the fear of the Lord, *that* is wisdom; and to depart from evil, *that* is understanding."

A good man will not fail to present to the minds of his offspring the more lovely and alluring aspects of Christianity; and patiently teach them other things as they are able to bear them.

And as there are seasons when the heart is open and impressible; as the young have moments of seriousness, in which they melt and weep; as even they are not free from sorrow and trials—a good parent will be ready to sow his seed during the shower; and to administer the comforts of the Gospel when the mind seems to turn from all other relief.

II. This inheritance takes in PIOUS EXAMPLE. " Let your light," says the Saviour, " so shine before men, that they may see your good works, and glorify your Father which is in heaven." Here we have the testimony of One who knew what was in man, to prove the value and efficacy of example in general. But in the case before us there are peculiar probabilities that it will not be in vain in the Lord. When the image is derived from a relation so near; when it is presented so early; when it is seen so constantly during a tender period; when it is associated with so many recollections to render it interesting—the impression it makes will not, cannot, be easily worn off. Even when going astray, in a solitary hour, the young man will recall the season when, embosomed in his native home, it was better with him than now; when his father, the minister too of the household, read the Scripture, led his charge daily to the family altar; maintained order and harmony without violence or severity; was devout, but equally cheerful; exemplifying " whatsoever things are true, whatsoever things are honest, whatsoever things are just, whatsoever things are pure, whatsoever things are lovely, whatsoever things are of good report, whatsoever things have any virtue or any praise in them." And what is mere occasional and often morose admonition, compared with such an example? What are rules pressed by mere authority, compared with a temper, a life so inviting! Children are more likely to practise what their parents do than what they recommend. They are much more led by the eye than by the ear. And it would be well for some children if they saw more of religion, and heard less. It would be well for them if they lived in a mild religious region, instead of being placed by fits of irregular and passionate zeal in religious stocks. We are no enemies to active and direct efforts; but we are persuaded that where few of these are made, impressions will be left by a consistent and amiable life; and that the effect of example will be more deep and durable than those of precept and reproof.

III. It takes in BELIEVING PRAYERS. A good man is a man of grace and supplication; and if he prays for his fellow-creatures at large, can he forget those of his own body? With what earnest appropriation will he think of them when the minister in the sanctuary is interceding for the young! With what ardour will he pray for them, when he is praying with them in the family! How often when kneeling—when walking alone, will he sigh, "O that Ishmael might live before thee!"

When children grow up and go forth, at the call of education or business, the hour of separation is trying, is painful: then their parents resign them, and follow them with devotional anxieties. In the world they are exposed to scenes of temptation and danger; then their parents resemble Job, who was praying while his children were feasting: "for he said, It may be that my sons have sinned and cursed God in their hearts: thus did Job continually." But when, casting off the fear of God, they become victims of vice—O the feelings of a prodigal's father!—— A minister said to Monica, the mother of Augustine, weeping over him in his profligate youth; "A child of so many tears and prayers cannot perish." This is going too far. But prayer has power with God, and prevails when offered for others, as well as for ourselves. The effectual fervent prayer of a righteous man availeth *much*. "I bless God," says Mr. Flavel, "for a religious tender father, who often poured out his soul to God for me: and this stock of prayers I esteem above the fairest inheritance on earth."

IV. It consists of SANCTIFIED SUBSTANCE. Some good men have not much to leave behind them: and this is frequently best. It is often disreputable for a Christian to die very wealthy: it implies that he has not been generous enough in his day and generation. And as it is no honour to his character, so it is seldom a benefit to his offspring: it renders them independent of motives to diligence, and makes "provision for the flesh to fulfil the lusts thereof." It is a large stock laid up for their pride and luxury; and it is soon squandered away. But "he that provideth not for his own, especially those of his own house, hath denied the faith, and is worse than an infidel." There are few good men but have something to leave behind: for religion "has the promise even of the life that now is:" it renders a man diligent and frugal; and gains him confidence and esteem. What is piously acquired is likely to be usefully expended. A few years ago a religious officer called his son to his dying bed, and addressing him by name, said, "My son, I have not much to leave you; but what I have, will wear well; for not a mite of it has been taken from the bodies of my men." All could not make such an avowal. There are even professors of the Gospel who have laid *up* what ought to have been laid *out*. The hoard they leave has been taken from the cause of God

and of the poor—perhaps much of it has been the effect of positive fraud or oppression; the cries of many have been lodged with it, and these "cries have entered the ears of the Lord God of Sabaoth."—Thus unclean and accursed it descends, and the children receive it as the Israelites the quails—at once gratified and undone. "A little that a righteous man hath is better than the riches of many wicked:" and this is as true with regard to his family as with regard to himself. He that multiplied the oil and the meal of the widow and son; of a servant that feared him; often wonderfully provides for those his people leave behind them. "I have been young, and now am old," says David; "yet have I never seen the righteous forsaken, or his seed begging bread."

Shall I mention, Fifthly, the DEATH of a good man as another part of this inheritance? In some cases nothing is said by a saint in his last moments. His testimony and advice are prevented by the nature of his disease, or the suddenness of his removal. Yet even then a dying father may do what a living one could not. The blessing may be valued when lost. But the dying experience of a good man is sometimes rendered peculiarly impressive. The expressions of his faith and hope recommend religion by showing that it can bear up the mind when every thing else fails. His supplies and consolations prove that he serves a good master, who never leaves him, nor forsakes him. But a dying admonition from a father—added to all this! "See," said Mr. Bolton to his children, "that none of you meet me in an unregenerate condition at the day of judgment!" David called Solomon, and said, "And thou Solomon my son, know thou the God of thy father; and serve him with a perfect heart and with a willing mind. For the Lord searcheth all hearts, and understandeth all the imaginations of the thoughts: if thou seek him, he will be found of thee; but if thou forsake him, he will cast thee off for ever." Who can rebel against this? "Shall I trouble his rest by departing from truth and integrity? Shall I unkindly frustrate the strong desire of his departing spirit? Can I wish to see him no more? To part with him for ever? I am now a stranger in the earth. I will seek unto God—he is my father's God. I will go in search of heaven—it is my father's house."

Finally. GOD BEARS A REGARD TO THE DESCENDANTS OF HIS FOLLOWERS. As David asked, "Is there any left of the house of Saul, that I may show him kindness for Jonathan's sake;" so by the same noble rule of friendship does God act. "The children of thy servants shall continue, and their seed shall be established before thee. Blessed is the man that feareth the Lord, that delighteth greatly in his commandments. His seed shall be mighty upon earth: the generation of the upright shall be blessed." From the beginning God has done good to some for the sake of others. Though Ishmael was denied the blessing of Isaac, "yet," says God to Abraham, "I will make him a nation, because he is thy seed." Moses tells the Israelites that they were not preferred to national privileges for *their* righteousness; "only the Lord had a delight in thy fathers to love them, and he chose their seed after them, even you above all people, as it is this day." "I will defend this city for my own sake and for my servant David's sake," said God to Hezekiah, when the Assyrian besieged Jerusalem. Many other instances might be mentioned in which we find God bestowing favours from a regard to good men, even ages after their death.

It is neither possible nor necessary to determine how far this regard extends, or in what particular ways it may sometimes operate: but the fact is beyond dispute. And how morally instructive and encouraging is it! What an appeal does it make to the heart of a parent! "If you would fill up that tender and important relation to advantage; if you would be useful even when you are no longer in this world; be concerned to please and glorify God. Devote yourselves to him whose promise is to you and to your children. The way to bless your offspring is to be religious yourselves." "A good man leaveth an inheritance to his children's children."

What an inheritance then does the sinner leave to his offspring!—No instructions—except such as regard the present evil world; no example—but of folly and wickedness; no prayers—but recorded in their place, oaths and lies; no sanctified substance; no triumph in death; no providential alliance—nothing but what will lead the children to rise up in the judgment against their parents, and cause them to be put to death!

How unhappy the condition of those children whose parents are ungodly! Let us pity them. "Let us pray for them. Let us also encourage them. "Let not the son of the stranger," says Isaiah, "that has joined himself to the Lord, say, He has utterly separated me from his people." He will cast out none that come to him. And, partakers of his grace, you may be the means of saving those who ought to have endeavoured to save you.

Let us hail those who are happy enough to claim godly parents. You ought to be more thankful than if you had been born of nobles or princes. Your obligations to God are inexpressible. But your responsibility rises with your advantages. "To whom much is given, from them be much required." And remember that nothing can be a substitute for personal religion. Pious relationship cannot save you. The rich man in hell called Abraham father. "There are last that shall be first, and there are first that shall be last.—Many shall come from the east and the west, and shall sit down with Abraham, and Isaac, and Jacob, in the kingdom of heaven; but the children of the kingdom shall be cast into outer darkness; there shall be weeping and gnashing of teeth."

The subject addresses the young, with regard to a very momentous concern, which should always be entered upon with prayer and deliberation: I mean, the choice of companions for life. Much should be looked for in the individuals themselves; but connexions are of consequence, and should not, if possible, be overlooked. You should consider not only *whom*, but *whose* you are about to choose. An intercourse will of necessity take place with their families—Is it likely to be respectable and improving? or injurious and contaminating? There is also a retrospective influence to be valued or feared—What do they inherit? What is entailed upon them from ancestors—a blessing or a curse?

There was a time when your forefathers made this a subject of serious reflection. In those better days, children never thought of acting without the advice of their parents; and their parents, like the patriarchs, never thought of sending them to the daughters of the land, but to the houses of their own people. Thus pious families combined; and while religion was befriended by marriage, it amply repaid the respect shown it by perpetuating a godly seed. This pious prudence has long been set at nought by children and parents; and the effects are too obvious to be denied, and too serious not to be deplored.

"O God, satisfy us early with thy mercy, that we may rejoice and be glad all our days. —Make us glad according to the days wherein thou hast afflicted us, and the years wherein we have seen evil.—Let thy work appear unto thy servants, and thy glory unto their children. And let the beauty of the Lord our God be upon us; and establish thou the work of our hands upon us; yea, the work of our hands establish thou it."

DISCOURSE LXI.

DIVINE KNOWLEDGE.

God, who commanded the light to shine out of darkness, hath shined in our hearts, to give the light of the knowledge of the glory of God in the face of Jesus Christ.—2 Cor. iv. 6.

THE original production of the world is a striking subject of contemplation. It exhibits a marvellous display of Divine power; and serves to distinguish the works of God from the operations of man. Man can do little; God can do every thing. Man can only act in consequence of a capacity given him; God has an all-sufficiency in himself. Man does nothing without labour and toil; God acts with infinite ease: "he speaks, and it is done; he commands, and it stands fast." Man's workmanship must resemble the materials from which it is derived; but it is the prerogative of God to bring order out of confusion, and good out of evil.

Hence the sacred writers frequently speak of the creation. They sometimes adduce it as a sovereign consideration to relieve the fears of God's people, arising from their dangers and difficulties, "Who art thou that thou shouldest be afraid of a man that shall die, and the son of man which shall be made as grass; and forgettest the Lord thy maker, that hath stretched forth the heavens, and laid the foundations of the earth?—Our help is in the name of the Lord that made heaven and earth."

At other times they allude to it as holding forth an image of Divine agency, in the renovation of our nature. With this view the Apostle, in one place, says, "We are his workmanship, created in Christ Jesus unto good works." In another, he enjoins us to "put on the new man, which after God is created in righteousness and true holiness." And in the words that await our meditation, he tells us; "God, who commanded the light to shine out of darkness, hath shined in our hearts, to give the light of the knowledge of the glory of God in the face of Jesus Christ."

It is commonly and reasonably supposed that the Apostle refers to a sentence recorded by Moses in his account of the creation: "He said, let there be light, and there was light." Longinus, the heathen, having met with this sentence, mentions it as an instance of the true sublime. The reason is obvious. It combines simplicity and grandeur; facility of operation, and immensity of effect. Paul, brought up at the feet of Gamaliel, and versed in the poetry of Greece, was no stranger to the "excellency of speech;" but he lays hold of this passage, not to illustrate the nature of style, but to exemplify the doctrine of divine grace. "God, who commanded the light to shine out of darkness, hath shined in our hearts, to give the light of the knowledge of the glory of God in the face of Jesus Christ."

The saving knowledge of God is our subject: and we are here led to consider—I. THE NECESSITY OF IT. II. THE MEDIUM OF IT. III. THE RESIDENCE OF IT. IV. THE AUTHOR OF IT.

I. THE NECESSITY OF IT. Nothing can be done without it; and yet we are naturally destitute of it.

When God viewed the earth, it was formless and void, "and darkness was upon the face of the deep;" and he produced what he did not find. So, when he comes to the soul, he sees it full of disorder and ignorance. Thus we read, that "darkness covered the earth, and gross darkness the people:" and the Apostle, referring to the state of the Gentiles, before they received the benefit of the gospel, describes them as "alienated from the life of God through the ignorance that was in them, because of the blindness of their hearts." The exemplifications of this truth are numerous and awful.

There is only one God, the Former of all things: but the world had lost the knowledge of him so early, that it is hard to determine at what period idolatry commenced. But they "had lords many, and gods many." The least exceptionable kind of idolatry seemed to be the adoration of the heavenly bodies: yet even this betrayed their ignorance, that they would worship and serve any of his creatures, however great and useful, "more than the Creator, who is God over all blessed for evermore." But they descended much lower; and "worshipped birds, and four-footed beasts, and creeping things." A dog was adored: a fly was deified.

As the object of worship was misunderstood, so the service rendered him was no longer a reasonable service. Even human blood streamed upon their altars; and the "fruit of the body was frequently offered for the sin of the soul." Innumerable other usages prevailed, which, though less cruel, were not less absurd. Indeed it is scarcely possible for us to imagine to what a degree the human mind was imposed upon and degraded. But all history bears testimony to it. —Such were the practices of mankind from age to age; and such are the delusions of mankind even now in countries unblessed with revelation.

There are persons who acknowledge this to be a just statement of the heathen world; but will not allow the application of our charge to those nations that enjoy the advantages of the Gospel. These advantages we cannot too highly value. But is there no difference between the possession of means and the proper use of them? Are men secure from error and delusion in a land of vision? Do we not often see their ignorance—in their views of the evil of sin? in their apprehensions of the way of salvation? in their indifference to the things that belong to their everlasting peace? in their subjection to the world? in their disaffection to God? For this is the decision of the Scripture; "He that loveth not, knoweth not God, for God is love." "If we say we have fellowship with him, and walk in darkness; we lie, and do not the truth." "He that saith he is in the light, and hateth his brother, is in darkness even until now." The rays of the sun may shine around a man, and upon him, while yet, because of his blindness, he may grope in darkness at noon-day: "the light shineth in darkness, and the darkness comprehendeth it not."

We may be delivered from gross idolatry

and yet indulge in a more refined species of it, and which is equally destructive to the soul. Many would be shocked to bow down before a stock or a stone, and yet they transfer to some creature the dependence and service they owe to the Lord of all. They make " gold their hope, and fine gold their confidence." The " covetous" man " is an idolater ;" so is he that " loves the praise of men more than the praise of God." Education may dispose us to revere the Sabbath, and to yield a customary attention to the ordinances of religion ; but grace alone can so act upon the heart as to enable us to worship " him who is a Spirit, in spirit and in truth."

But this knowledge of which we are destitute, is not a matter of indifference. It is of indispensable importance. " For the soul to be without knowledge," says Solomon, " it is not good." The soul without knowledge, is like the body without the eye, or the earth without the sun. The devil maintains his empire by error ; but God maintains his cause by truth. One reigns in a kingdom of darkness, the other in a kingdom of light. The one blinds all his followers, and all their works are works of darkness, the other enlightens his subjects: he engages them by choice ; and they " are all the children of the day ; they are not of the night, nor of darkness." Ignorance is not the mother of their devotion: they know whom they worship, and why they worship him. In a word, all God's operations in his people are begun and carried on in the illumination of the mind. Take repentance, faith, patience, courage, love,—what are these? If they do not result from, and are not influenced by just views of things, which supply what we call motives, they are not Christian graces, nor even moral virtues.

II. Observe THE MEDIUM OF THIS KNOWLEDGE : we have the light of the knowledge of God " in the face of Jesus Christ." " No man hath seen God at any time ; the only begotten Son, which is in the bosom of the Father, he hath declared him." And how did he declare him? Not only by the doctrines he taught, but by the work to which he was appointed ; and by his temper, his life, his character. If we would know what God is, we must learn of him " who went about doing good :" and who said to Philip, " He that hath seen me hath seen the Father ; and how sayest thou then, Show us the Father?" Hence he is called " The image of the invisible God ; the brightness of his glory, and the express image of his person."

Much of God is indeed displayed in the works of nature. Impressions of his perfections appear in the largest, and in the least. The heavens declare his glory ; and so does every blade of grass. But these works are more adapted and designed to aid us when we know God, than to produce our return to him. We do not find that those who are most familiar with the wonders of the creation are the most devoted to him. Some of them feel an overpowering admiration of a Being so wise ; and may discover an awful reverence for a Being so great ; but they know nothing of the sentiments resulting from reconciliation and friendship. The Scripture leads us back to God by the cross. " We have boldness to enter into the holiest by the blood of Jesus, by a new and living way, which he has consecrated for us through the vail, that is to say, his flesh. He has once suffered for sins, the just for the unjust, that he might bring us unto God." If he had not assumed the office of mediator, and lived and died for us, we should never have obtained any acquaintance with him that would operate as the principle of our recovery.—We might have known that there was a God, but not that he was our God. We might have known his power and righteousness, by the wrath we should have suffered ; but we could have known nothing of his giving us eternal life, for " this life is in his Son."

It is in him that we see the union and harmony of the divine perfections. It is in him that we see " the just God and the Saviour." It is in him that we see the glory of God without being dazzled to death by the effulgence. There it is softened ; there it is approachable ; there it is inviting. There we have the only discovery of him that could meet our case—the immensity of his compassion ; the exceeding riches of his grace ; the pledge of his readiness to admit us to favour and forgiveness. This alone can divest us of that fear which follows guilt, and necessarily produces enmity and flight when there is no prospect of reconciliation. " We are saved by hope :" and here it must be inspired : " he that spared not his own Son, but delivered him up for us all, how shall he not with him also freely give us all things?"

III. We are led to THE RESIDENCE OF THIS KNOWLEDGE. It is the heart ; he hath shined " in our hearts," to give us the light of the knowledge of the glory of God in the face of Jesus Christ. It is an awful truth that we may perish not only by ignorance, but by knowledge. There is a knowledge possessed by many who hear the Gospel, that will only aggravate their sin and enhance their condemnation.

We are far from pleading for a zeal without knowledge ; but let us not rest in a knowledge without zeal. We read in the Scripture of " a form of knowledge," as well as " a form of godliness." Our creed may be orthodox, while our affections are worldly. The head may be clear while the heart is cold. But the religion of Jesus is addressed to the heart ; and as the heart is, so is the man ; so is his state ; so is his character.

The knowledge of which the Apostle here speaks is very distinguishable from mere opinion and speculation; it has to do with the heart. It affects it first in a way of godly sorrow. There is a "broken heart" which "God will not despise:" and here it is produced. "They shall look upon him whom they have pierced, and they shall mourn for him, as one mourneth for his only son; and shall be in bitterness for him, as one that is in bitterness for his first-born."—Secondly; it affects the heart in a way of desire. The man longs to appropriate what he discovers. Such earnestness he feels to obtain nothing else. It is called "hungering and thirsting after righteousness." And it is as durable as it is powerful. Instead of being satisfied, it is increased by indulgence: and the prayer constantly is, "I beseech thee, show me thy glory."—Thirdly: it affects the heart in a way of complacency. The believer not only submits, but acquiesces. He submits indeed to this plan of salvation from necessity—for there is no other: but if other methods of salvation were possible, he would reject them all; he would enter no other refuge; he would build on no other foundation; he would walk in no other way. His necessity is his choice. He is not only relieved, but delighted: and so far from being ashamed, he glories: as it is written, "Blessed is the people that know the joyful sound: they shall walk, O Lord, in the light of thy countenance. In thy name shall they rejoice all the day: and in thy righteousness shall they be exalted." It also affects the heart in a way of gratitude. We see, we feel that we are not our own, but bought with a price, and bound to glorify God in our body and in our spirit, which are God's. We love him because he first loved us; and cannot but ask, what shall we render unto the Lord for all his benefits towards us? This disposition becomes the source of all cheerful obedience, and animates him in every exertion, and in every sacrifice he is called to make.

> "Were the whole realm of nature mine
> That were a present far too small;
> Love so amazing, so divine,
> Demands my soul, my life, my all."

IV. We are led to THE AUTHOR OF THIS KNOWLEDGE. It is God himself. "He who commanded the light to shine out of darkness, hath shined in our hearts, to give the light of the knowledge of the glory of God in the face of Jesus Christ." When Peter had made a good confession, our Lord said unto him, "Blessed art thou, Simon Barjona; for flesh and blood hath not revealed this unto thee, but my Father which is in heaven." The same may be said of every enlightened sinner. The same is said. "All thy children shall be taught of the Lord." "The secret of the Lord is with them that fear him; and he will show them his covenant. The

meek will he guide in judgment: and the meek will he teach his way." The same must be said. "For the natural man understandeth not the things of the Spirit of God: neither can he know them because they are spiritually discerned." The nature, the efficacy, the blessedness of this knowledge prove it to be of a divine original. And to this every believer readily subscribes. He may often question whether he is the subject of this illumination; but he never doubts whether God is the source of it. He acknowledges that by his grace he is what he is: and on him who has begun this good work he is depending for the progress and completion of it: "Open thou mine eyes, that I may behold wondrous things out of thy law. Lead me in thy truth, and teach me: for thou art the God of my salvation; on thee do I wait all the day."

O that you would think of this! Till God has revealed his Son in you, you know nothing as you ought to know. Many are proud of their attainments who are mere fools in the view of Heaven. "Vain man would be wise, though he be born like a wild ass's colt."—And here he is ruined. He goes on without prayer, relying upon himself, and supposing that he is equal to his own direction; and in the greatness of his delusion he eternally goes astray. Whereas the man that is convinced of his ignorance, and feels his insufficiency to understand divine things without a divine teacher, falls upon his knees, and immediately finds an Interpreter, who will lead him into all truth. "This is the way, walk ye in it." The wise and the prudent may sneer at the supposed enthusiasm of such a course; but we know the authority that has prescribed it: "If any of you lack wisdom, let him ask of God, that giveth to all men liberally, and upbraideth not; and it shall be given him."

Are there none here in whom this revelation has been made? Cannot you, with humble confidence, say, "'Whereas I was once blind, now I see!' I was living without God; God was not in all my thoughts: but I sought and I found him, found him in Christ 'reconciling the world unto himself, not imputing their trespasses unto them.' I was turned 'from dumb idols to serve the living and true God; and to wait for his Son from heaven.' No longer asking, Who will show me any good? 'The Lord is my portion,' said my soul, 'therefore will I hope in him.' And Oh! what a different life have I since led! I have not only heard that a life of communion with God, and of devotedness to him, is blessed, but I have found it so; and I am rejoicing in the hope, in the earnests, in the foretastes of the glory that shall be revealed."

What a mercy that the doctrine you have been hearing is not an unexperienced truth, nor a truth you have to confess with regard to others. *You* can say, "God, who commanded the light to shine out of darkness, hath shined in *our* hearts, to give *us* the light of the knowledge of the glory of God in the face of Jesus Christ!"

And for what purpose has he done this! But that you should "show forth the praises of him who hath called you out of darkness into his marvellous light. Ye were darkness, but now are ye light in the Lord: walk as children of the light."

DISCOURSE LXII.

THE BARREN FIG TREE.

(NEW YEAR'S DAY.)

Lord, let it alone this year also.—Luke xiii. 8.

It is impossible to do justice to the character, or even manner of our Saviour as a preacher. But even his enemies exclaimed, "Never man spake like this man." Much of the singular interest that he always excited in his hearers arose from his perfect acquaintance with human nature; from the tenderness of his feelings; from his improvement of present occurrences; and from his command of imagery. We have often remarked a difference between our Lord and men of erudition. When the latter avail themselves of allusions, they are ambitious of selecting those that do not so much illustrate their subject, as serve to display their reading and science: they are classical and artificial, rather than familiar and natural; and by being unintelligible to the generality of mankind, are unimpressive and useless. But all the comparisons of the latter are derived from the common scenes and operations of nature. They are such as all, however ignorant, can understand and feel. They are constantly to be met with; they become a substitute for books and teachers; they enable people, wherever they are, to teach themselves, and to find in a field, a garden, a vineyard, nothing less than the house of God, and the gate of heaven.—"He spake also this parable; A certain man had a fig tree planted in his vineyard; and he came and sought fruit thereon, and found none. Then said he unto the dresser of his vineyard; Behold, these three years I come seeking fruit on this fig tree, and find none: cut it down; why cumbereth it the ground! And he answering said unto him, Lord, let it alone this year also, till I shall dig about it, and dung it: and if it bear fruit, well: and if not, then after that thou shalt cut it down."

In this parable Four things require attention. THE PLANTATION OF THE FIG TREE. THE COMPLAINT OF THE PROPRIETOR. THE SENTENCE OF DESTRUCTION. THE INTERCESSION OF THE VINE-DRESSER TO SUSPEND THE STROKE.

I. "A CERTAIN MAN HAD A FIG TREE PLANTED IN HIS VINEYARD." This "certain man" denotes God. To him every thing belongs. "The earth is his, and the fulness thereof; the world and they that dwell therein." But the Church is peculiarly *his*, as it is called by his name, and formed to show forth his praise. It is often held forth in the Scripture by a vineyard, while the wide world is as frequently represented by a wilderness. This church, in its external and visible state, is a mixed community; so that among God's people are found wicked men; men who have indeed "a name to live, but are dead;" and wear "the form of godliness, but deny the power thereof."

This circumstance enables us to answer a question of great importance—Who is intended by the "fig tree" planted in this vineyard?—It cannot be a real Christian. All the truly regenerate are fruitful. They are not indeed *equally*, but they are *really* fruitful. The good ground brought forth in one place thirty, in another sixty, in a third a hundred fold: but though it yielded in different proportion, every part of it was productive soil. —The character here intended is a man placed in the external and visible church, and enjoying all the privileges of such a favoured situation. It was once the highly favoured Jew, to "whom pertained the adoption, and the glory, and the covenants, and the giving of the law, and the service of God, and the promises; whose were the fathers, and of whom as concerning the flesh Christ came, who is over all, God blessed for ever. Amen." It is now the highly favoured Christian, blessed with all the religious advantages of Judaism, multiplied, improved, perfected: it is now the highly favoured Briton, born not only in a land of freedom and science, but of Gospel grace. It is thou who wast brought up in a godly family, and favoured with the prayers, the instructions, the examples, the tears of pious parents. It is thou who hast a name and a place in his sanctuary, from Sabbath to Sabbath, where "thine eyes see thy teachers: and thy ears hear a voice behind thee, saying, This is the way, walk ye in it, when you turn to the right hand, and when you turn to the left." "Blessed are your eyes, for they see; and your ears, for they hear. For verily I say unto you, that many prophets and righteous men have desired to see those things which ye see, and have not seen them; and to hear those things which ye hear, and have not heard them." Few are aware of the value of such privileges.

Few consider themselves as accountable for the use of them. Few, few indeed! are concerned to improve them.—And thus we find this fig tree, though planted in a rich soil, and where nothing was wanting to make it fruitful, was all barrenness. For observe,

II. THE COMPLAINT OF THE PROPRIETOR.— "Behold," says he to the vine-dresser, "these three years I come seeking fruit on this fig tree, and find none." Every thing here is worthy of our notice. His observation, his disappointment, his patience.

His observation : "I come seeking fruit." It marks the attention which God pays to those who are favoured with religious advantages. Indeed, he investigates all his creatures to see what is in them. "His eyes are in every place, beholding the evil and the good. His eyes are upon the ways of man, and he pondereth all his goings. There is no darkness nor shadow of death where the workers of iniquity can hide themselves." What think you of this scrutiny? Is it not an awful consideration that you always move in the view of God? That "he is about your path and your lying down, and is acquainted with all your ways? That there is not a word in your tongue but he knoweth it altogether? That he searcheth all your hearts, and understandeth all the imaginations of your thoughts?"

God comes among you to see how you are carrying on your business; to see what you are doing with your mercies and your trials; to mark the manner in which you are filling up your relations in life; to observe the formation of your principles, and the cultivation of your tempers.

And remember, he is not, he cannot be mistaken in his conclusion. You may err in judging yourselves; you may err in judging your fellow-creatures; but his judgment is always according to truth. You judge after outward appearance, and depend on the declaration of others: but he looketh to the heart, and "needeth not that any should testify of man, for he knows what is in man." Distance of time and of place add to our embarrassment in the decision of a disputed fact: but all this is inapplicable to a Being that fills heaven and earth, and "with whom one day is as a thousand years, and a thousand years are as one day." What does *He* think of you?

His disappointment : "I come seeking fruit, and *find none*." This shows us that God not only searches for fruit, but expects it from those who receive religious benefits. He knows the goodness of the soil in which you are fixed; and the degrees of culture you have received. He forgets none of your privileges, nor his pains. In his book are written all your talents, and all your opportunities. He has recorded when the Gospel came to you, and how many sermons you have heard. For these are not only mercies which you are required to acknowledge, but means which you are expected to improve: they are given for this purpose, and by this purpose you will be judged. But though his expectation be so righteous and reasonable how often is it frustrated! For what does he look after? If it were lies, oaths, slanders, drunkenness, avarice—he would find enough. If it were

leaves, the leaves of profession and appearances—he would find many. If it were blossoms the blossoms of conviction, resolution, attendance on the ordinances of religion, he would discern not a few. But it is fruit— "the fruits of righteousness, which are by Jesus Christ unto the glory and praise of God, the fruits of the Spirit, which are love, joy, peace, longsuffering, gentleness, goodness, faith, meekness, temperance." And where will he find these?

His patience : "These *three years* I come seeking fruit, and find none." Why did he not complain the first year? Why did he not destroy it the second year? Why does he bear with it to the end of the third? Why? —To teach us that judgment is his strange work—that he delighteth in mercy; that he waiteth to be gracious; that he is longsuffering to us-ward, not willing that any should perish, but that all should come to repentance. He has no pleasure in the death of him that dieth. He therefore spares as long as his perfections will allow him, and even then seems to proceed with reluctance; and his dispensations, like his word, say, "How shall I give thee up?" Yet this will be the case. For observe,

III. The sentence of destruction : "Cut it down; why cumbereth it the ground? Here we see, First, that they who derive no benefit from the means of grace are detrimental. Barren trees not only yield no fruit, but encumber the ground. They take up the room of better trees, and draw off the moisture from others. All of them do this; but the injury is in proportion to their age and their size. Who can tell all the mischief resulting from a long-continued course of worldly-mindedness or wickedness! Who can imagine how much evil men of ability and authority occasion by their influence; or how much good they prevent by their omissions! But every unholy professor of religion, every mere hearer of the word, is an enemy to the welfare of mankind and the cause of the Redeemer, as he himself has determined: "He that is not with me, is against me; and he that gathereth not with me, scattereth." He impedes the success of the Gospel; he causes the adversaries of the Lord to blaspheme; he grieves the godly; he discourages ministers; he justifies the wicked, and makes them conclude that religion is either hypocrisy or a dream. He deprives others of spiritual advantages. He hears in vain the sermons that would convert others. He engrosses the means which would otherwise be employed upon persons who would bring forth their fruit in its season. "If the mighty works which have been done in thee," says our Saviour, speaking of Capernaum, "had been done in Tyre and Sidon, they would have repented long ago, sitting in sackcloth and ashes."

Secondly. Unprofitableness under the means of grace is exceedingly provoking to the Most High. And can we wonder at this when we consider what a waste it is of time; what an abuse it is of privilege; what a contempt it is of the divine goodness; what a disregard it is of the soul and eternity! Sin is to be estimated not by its grossness, but its guilt. And what aggravates guilt? The light we possess; the obligations we are under; the restraints we break through. "He that knoweth to do good, and doeth it not, to him it is sin. And that servant, which knew his lord's will, and prepared not himself, neither did according to his will, shall be beaten with many stripes. But he that knew not, and did commit things worthy of stripes, shall be beaten with few stripes. For unto whomsoever much is given, of him shall be much required: and to whom men have committed much, of him they will ask the more." Upon this principle it is easy to see that there is not, there cannot be a wretch upon the globe so guilty as the man that enjoys the privileges of the Gospel, and remains unrighteous still. He has no cloak for his sin: its commission is without excuse; and its punishment will be without alleviation. It will be more tolerable for Sodom and Gomorrah in the day of judgment than for such. The hell of a heathen, or of a Jew, will be nothing, compared with that of a Christian.

Thirdly. God possesses justice as well as mercy; and though he bears long, he will not bear always. "Sentence against an evil work is not executed speedily;" and, as the consequence, the heart of the sons of men is often fully set in them to do evil. But how absurd, as well as dangerous, is such perverse reasoning! Is forbearance forgiveness? No—nor even connivance. God is of purer eyes than to behold iniquity; and in due time he will rise and prove it. "These things hast thou done, and I kept silence; thou thoughtest that I was altogether such an one as thyself: but I will reprove thee, and set them in order before thine eyes. Now consider this, ye that forget God, lest I tear you in pieces, and there be none to deliver." The husbandman at length orders the spade to be laid down, and the axe to be brought.—Cut it down, why cumbereth it the ground? But we have,

IV. THE INTERCESSION OF THE VINE-DRESSER imploring a limited suspension. "Lord, let it alone this year also, till I dig about it, and dung it: and if it bear fruit, well: and if not, then after that thou shalt cut it down." Whose language is this?—It is the language of a Christian in favour of an irreligious relation—of a father pleading for a child; a sister for a brother; a wife for a husband; all saying with Esther, "How can I bear the destruction of my kindred?"—It is the language of a minister pleading for his people. Such

a man not only preaches, but prays. He can say with Paul, I seek not yours but you. He knows what it is to weep in secret places for their pride and unbelief, and so far is he from desiring the evil day, that he longs to avert the dreadful blow he foresees; and fearing lest any indifference of his should have caused their unprofitableness, he engages to use renewed and increasing diligence in future.

But, above all, it is the language of Jesus, the mediator of the new covenant; the mediator between God and man. He makes intercession for the transgressors; he prayed for his murderers even in death: "Father, forgive them: for they know not what they do."

First. He pleads for the suspension of the stroke. "Let it alone this year also." Thou hast borne with it long, I own, already; oh! bear with it a little longer.—And why is he so desirous of sparing the sinner a little longer in this world? Because, in order to our having the grace of repentance, it is necessary that we should have space for repentance: because while there is life there is hope; but, "when once the master of the house is risen up, and hath shut to the door," opportunity is over, importunity vain.

Secondly. He engages to use additional means to produce fertility. "Till I dig about it and dung it." The word shall be preached with more fervour than before. The minister shall be particular in describing his case, in alarming his fears. Friends shall warn, admonish, invite. Conscience shall awake and reprove. Disappointments shall show him the vanity of the world. Sickness shall invade his frame. Death shall enter his family and smite a connexion by his side. The day in which he lives shall be dark and cloudy. He shall hear of "distress of nations with perplexity; the sea and the waves roaring; men's hearts failing them for fear, and after looking for those things which are coming on the earth: for the powers of heaven shall be shaken." And can he retain his ungodliness through such a year as this?

Third. Here is the supposition of future produce. "If it bear fruit, well." The word well is not in the original: there we find nothing but an awful pause. If it bear fruit ——— Then, it might be said, thy design will be fulfilled, my prayer will be answered, the tree will be continued. Our translators have properly enough supplied the word—well.—Well for the owner: "for herein is my Father glorified, that he bear much fruit." —Well for the vine-dresser, as his labours will be rewarded.—Well for the vineyard: it will be adorned, and enriched, and replenished, where it was cumbered before.—Well for the tree itself, as it will escape the punishment of barrenness, and obtain the blessing of fruitfulness.

Fourthly. Here is the doom of final impenitence. "If not—then—after that thou shalt cut it down." It not only announces the certainty of the event, but expresses his own disposition with regard to it. He even craves but one year more; and confesses that, after this fresh instance of the Proprietor's patience and his own pains, he cannot—he will not oppose the execution of the sentence. He will interpose no longer.

There is something in this tremendous beyond all expression! We see in it even the patience of the Saviour exhausted; and his mercy not indeed delighting, but acquiescing in our misery. The refuge open to us before, in every danger, is now closed. While *he* was our friend, we always had a resource; bet the "Lamb of God is become the Lion of the tribe of Judah;" the "great day of his wrath is come; and who shall be able to stand?"

Here the parable breaks off. We want to know more, but in vain. Particularly we want to know whether another year was granted in answer to this importunity. But all is silence; wise, righteous silence; quite in agreement with the whole Scripture, which nowhere tells you that God will give you another year—another week—or even another day.

We want also to know whether, if the boon was granted, the tree became fruitful—but all is silence. If we judge from facts in general, it remained the same. If the Gospel does not succeed at first, it frequently never succeeds at all. There is a hardening of the heart through the deceitfulness of sin; and there is also a hardening of it by the means of grace. The latter perhaps is the most dreadful and hopeless of the two! Truths never heard *may* meet with the former and alarm him: but the other *can* hear nothing now; the cross, heaven, hell, eternity, the threatenings of the law, the promises of the Gospel—all these have expended their force upon him in vain. We know that with God all things are possible. Oh! seize this last, this trembling hope, and, seeking the Lord, "while he *may* be found," say, "Lord, save; I perish!"

The subject leads me to address even those of you, who are not only planted in the vineyard, but are alive unto God through Jesus Christ our Lord. It is a mercy that you are not wholly barren; but must you not acknowledge that you have brought forth very little fruit? Will it bear any comparison with your profession and your advantages? To lead you back no farther than the year we have just closed. How have you redeemed your time? What additions have you made to your knowledge? What faults have you corrected in your tempers? What good have you accomplished by your influence or by your example? How have you served your generation? How have you glorified God in your bodies

2 F

and spirits! Alas! who can take a farewell glance of the departed period of time, without many a tear and many a sigh—

"What have I done for him who died
 To save my wretched soul?
How have my follies multiplied,
 Past as my minutes roll!

"Lord, with this guilty heart of mine,
 To thy dear cross I flee;
And to thy *grace* my soul resign,
 To be renew'd by thee."

But I must address those of you in particular who have begun a new year without a new heart. Let me expostulate with you. You have long enjoyed the means of grace. The husbandman came three years to inspect this fig tree—but God has come twenty—thirty—forty—fifty—sixty—is it possible that we can go further?—Yes, even seventy years—to some of you, and yet after all has found no fruit!—You have heard of the danger of unprofitableness under religious advantages; you have heard that "the axe is now laid to the root of the tree; and every tree that bringeth not forth good fruit is hewn down and cast into the fire." Many have been cut down during the past year in their sins: many, oh dreadful exchange! have been sent to hell from the very house of God: some perhaps less guilty than you, and to whose destruction you were the means of contributing. But you are spared, and you live to enter on another year. Ah! perhaps this is the year, the very year, for which the vine-dresser has been pleading. Perhaps he has said, Grant this, and I will not ask for another hour! Perhaps upon this revolution of time all your eternal interest is suspended—and if you are not saved *this* year, you are lost for ever! Perhaps at the end of *this* year, if you are not removed from this world, you may be abandoned of God, who, as you would have none of him, will give you up to your own heart's lust, to walk in your own counsel.

One thing is certain: "there is no work, nor device, nor knowledge, nor wisdom, in the grave whither thou goest; and therefore, whatsoever thy hand findeth to do, do it with thy might." And since you know not what will be even "on the morrow," pray, with David, "Lord, so teach us to number our days, that we may apply our hearts unto wisdom."

And what is wisdom? Wisdom is a relative thing; and this is so true, that what would be wise for one man to do, would be folly in another. The question then is, What would be a wise part to act, considering the circumstances in which you are placed? Now what does common sense teach us in other cases? If a man has an important journey to take, his wisdom consists in preparing for it. If a man be in imminent danger from an overhanging precipice, he would do wisely to flee. If a man be labouring under a threatening disease, he would be reckoned a fool not to inquire after a remedy and a physician.—Avoid this folly. Betake yourselves to the Friend of sinners. Fall at his feet and say, "Heal me, and I shall be healed; save me, and I shall be saved; for thou art my praise." In him seek the justification of your persons, the sanctification of your natures; a title to heaven, and a meetness for it, with all the diligence the importance of these blessings demands; and "so much the more, as ye see the day approaching." Dedicate yourselves unreservedly to him who loved us and gave himself for us.

And then, should the news, "This year thou shalt die," be addressed to you, as it was to one of old, you may hear it without consternation; it will only announce your deliverance, your triumph, your eternal gain. And if your life should be continued through the year we have begun, and through many following years, his grace shall be sufficient for you, rendering your trials supportable, and your duties practicable and pleasant. "Whether you live, you will live unto the Lord; or whether you die, you will die unto the Lord: so that, living or dying, you will be the Lord's." Amen.

DISCOURSE LXIII.

SAUL OF TARSUS PRAYING.

And there was a certain disciple at Damascus, named Ananias; and to him said the Lord in a vision, Ananias. And he said, Behold, I am here, Lord. And the Lord said unto him, Arise, and go into the street which is called Straight, and inquire in the house of Judas for one called Saul, of Tarsus: for, behold, he prayeth.—Acts ix. 10, 11.

WE live in a world of changes. Seed time and harvest, cold and heat, summer and winter, day and night, succeed each other. Human affairs are as variable as the seasons. We have seen the rich impoverished and the poor enriched. We have seen the noble debased and the vulgar exalted. We have seen thrones demolished and empires formed.

But no changes are so important in their nature, and interesting in their consequences, as those of a moral nature—because these relate to the soul and eternity. It is painful to see a fellow-creature, under the infatuation of error and vice, proceeding from evil to evil; and waxing worse and worse, till he has proved that "the way of transgressors is hard," and that "the end of these things is death." But, oh! how pleasing is it to see a sinner plucked as a brand from the burning! How pleasing to trace in him the operation of an agency that opens his eyes, and turns him "from darkness unto light, and from the power of Satan unto God; that he may receive forgiveness of sins, and an

inheritance among them that are sanctified." Then is fulfilled the language of the prophet: "Instead of the thorn shall come up the fir tree, and instead of the brier shall come up the myrtle tree: and it shall be to the Lord for a name, for an everlasting sign that shall not be cut off."

To one of these remarkable changes we are referred by the words we have read. It took place in Saul of Tarsus. He was a young man who had been brought up at the feet of Gamaliel, and was now employing his time and talents in the infamous work of persecution. He was in a journey of iniquity, and near the end of it, when God, who is rich in mercy, called him by his grace, and revealed his Son in him. "Suddenly there shined round about him a light from heaven: And he fell to the earth, and heard a voice saying unto him, Saul, Saul, why persecutest thou me? And he said, Who art thou, Lord? And the Lord said, I am Jesus whom thou persecutest: it is hard for thee to kick against the pricks." By this he reminds him that his conduct was as ruinous as it was unreasonable, and only inflicted wounds and death upon himself.—Behold the tiger reduced to a lamb, so that a little child may lead him. "And he trembling and astonished said, Lord, what wilt thou have me to do? And the Lord said unto him, Arise, and go into the city, and it shall be told thee what thou must do. And the men which journeyed with him stood speechless, hearing a voice, but seeing no man. And Saul arose from the earth; and when his eyes were opened, he saw no man: but they led him by the hand, and brought him into Damascus. And he was three days without sight, and neither did eat nor drink."

Then follows the passage we have selected for our present meditation: "And there was a certain disciple at Damascus, named Ananias; and to him said the Lord in a vision, Ananias. And he said, Behold, I am here, Lord. And the Lord said unto him, Arise, and go into the street which is called Straight, and inquire in the house of Judas for one called Saul, of Tarsus: for, behold, he prayeth." From these words we are led to remark,

I. THAT THE LORD KNOWS WHERE WE ARE, AND HOW WE ARE ENGAGED. What was this house of Judas? Was it an inn to which Saul repaired for lodging? If so, it was a sad situation for a man in spiritual distress; and never did an inn before or since accommodate such a passenger. Perhaps it was a private dwelling, and belonged to one of his friends or acquaintances. If so, what would be the emotions of the family as he entered! One would think him mad; another would eagerly listen to the report of his companions; all would wonder; and some we should hope would be seriously impressed.

But however this may be, we find that the Lord knew *where* Saul was—the street—the very house in which he was; and he also knew *what* he was doing there.

It would be easy to multiply similar instances and proofs of his perfect acquaintance with the children of men. He knew how to guide Cornelius in sending to Joppa for Peter—"he lodgeth in the house of one Simon, a tanner, whose house is by the sea side." Nathanael had retired to a place where no human eye was likely to observe him: "but when thou wast under the fig tree," says our Lord, "I saw thee." Zaccheus ran before and climbed up into a sycamore tree, little imagining that the wonderful stranger who was to pass under would know or notice him—but he looked up and said, "Zaccheus, make haste, and come down; for to-day I must abide at thy house." When Paul was afar off upon the sea, tossed with waves, the night dark, and not a star appearing, the Lord unerringly directs a messenger to his prisoner: "There stood by me this night the angel of God, whose I am, and whom I serve, saying, Fear not, Paul; thou must be brought before Cæsar: and, lo, God hath given thee all them that sail with thee." And what said he of Sennacherib! "I know thy abode, and thy going out, and thy coming in, and thy rage against me." Well therefore says the Scripture, "The eyes of the Lord are in in every place, beholding the evil and the good."

It was this truth that David applied to himself in a manner so solemn and affecting, when he said, "O Lord, thou hast searched me, and known me. Thou knowest my downsitting and mine uprising, thou understandest my thought afar off. Thou compassest my path and my lying down, and art acquainted with all my ways. For there is not a word in my tongue, but, lo, O Lord, thou knowest it altogether." Let us follow his example, and bring home this truth to ourselves. Let sinners think of it; and never dream of secrecy in their guilt; but wherever they are, and however privately engaged, remember that "his eyes are upon the ways of man, and he pondereth all his goings; there is no darkness nor shadow of death where the workers of iniquity may hide themselves: hell is naked before him, and destruction hath no covering."—Let hearers think of it; and remember that he is privy to all they think of their ministers when alone, to all they say of them when they are in company, to all the dispositions with which they come to his house, to all the workings of their minds while in his worship, to all their disregard of instructions when they return home and enter into common life: "Thou son of man, the children of thy people still are talking against thee by the walls and in the doors of the houses, and speak one to another, every one to his brother, saying, Come, I pray you, and hear what is the word that cometh forth from the Lord. And they come unto thee as the people cometh, and they sit before thee as my people, and they hear thy words, but they will not do them: for with their mouth they show much love, but their heart goeth after their covetousness."—Let the righteous believe this; and remember, that though they are poor and needy, yet the Lord thinketh upon them; that he knoweth all their walking through this great wilderness; that their walls are continually before him. "Then they that feared the Lord spake often one to another: and the Lord hearkened and heard it, and a book of remembrance was written before him for them that feared the Lord, and that thought upon his Name."—And oh! thou dejected penitent, anxious to return with weeping and supplications to him from whom thou hast revolted—oh! think of this and be comforted. You naturally turn from a vain world, in which you find nothing congenial with your present views and wishes; you seek the shades: and are often alone—but he follows you—whether you are in the chamber or the field, his eye sees all your tears, his ear hears all your sighs. These are his promises, and he will not fail to verify them in your experience: "He looketh upon men, and if any say, I have sinned, and perverted that which was right, and it profited me not; he will deliver his soul from going into the pit, and his life shall see the light. To this man will I look, even to him that is poor and of a contrite spirit, and trembleth at my word."

II. However the Lord may try them, he will not suffer praying souls to call upon him in vain. "Go," says he to Ananias, "Go and find him out; for, behold, he prayeth, and I can withhold information and comfort no longer from him." Three days indeed he remained in a very awful state; and the period would seem an age. Everything was calculated to add to the impression. He was deprived of sight; and thus nothing could divert him without, but all his gloomy thoughts turned inward upon himself. He was also without food; the anguish of his mind was such, that he probably *could* eat nothing. All that he had heard was this, "It shall be told thee what thou must do:" but this was general, and capable of various explanations; and his dismal and guilty feelings would incline him to the less favourable conjecture.

But says the Church, "Come, and let us return unto the Lord: for he hath torn, and he will heal us; he hath smitten, and he will bind us up. After two days will he revive us: in the third day he will raise us up, and we shall live in his sight." And here we see this literally accomplished. The third day arrives, and the messenger of mercy knocks at the door and inquires for one Saul of Tarsus. This was saying, "I have not abandoned or forgotten him: though I cause grief, yet will I have compassion; I 'never said to the seed of Jacob, Seek ye me in vain.'" Who is not here reminded of one of the most beautiful and moving passages in the Old Testament? "I have surely heard Ephraim bemoaning himself thus; Thou hast chastised me, and I was chastised; as a bullock unaccustomed to the yoke: turn thou me, and I shall be turned; for thou art the Lord my God. Surely after that I was turned, I repented; and after that I was instructed, I smote upon my thigh: I was ashamed, yea, even confounded, because I did bear the reproach of my youth. Is Ephraim my dear son? Is he a pleasant child? For since I spake against him, I do earnestly remember him still: therefore my bowels are troubled for him; I will surely have mercy upon him, saith the Lord."

Joseph was a type of the Redeemer. His behaviour towards his brethren was for a time rough, and apparently very unkind. But it was more painful to him than to them. He was constrained to leave the room, and turned aside to weep. But the trial was necessary: and at length giving way to the compassion which his prudence had restrained before, he said, "I am Joseph your brother, whom ye sold into Egypt—but be not grieved."—Thus he, "whose heart is made of tenderness, whose bowels melt with love," leaves Saul three days without comfort; but it was in order to bring him to reflection, to convince him of sin, to make him feel his need of mercy, to prepare him for the displays of divine grace; and to dig low, and lay deep the foundation of a superstructure that was to rise so high. And all the time as Saul was praying, he was hearing; and longing to succour and relieve him.

What is the use you ought to make of this?—to persevere, waiting on the Lord and keeping his way, though you are not indulged with immediate success. His delays are not denials. He is as wise as he is kind. He has reasons for what we often deem indifference or severity, and reasons founded in a regard to our welfare, as well as his own glory. Hence it is said, "Therefore will the Lord wait, that he may be gracious unto you; and therefore will he be exalted, that he may have mercy upon you: for the Lord is a God of judgment: blessed are all they that wait for him." You cannot be in a worse condition than David was: but hear him. "I waited patiently for the Lord; and he inclined unto me, and heard my cry. He brought me up also out of an horrible pit, out of the miry clay, and set my feet upon a rock, and established my goings. And he hath put a new song in my mouth, even

praise unto our God: many shall see it, and fear, and shall trust in the Lord."

Say not therefore, "My hope is perished from the Lord—why should I wait for him any longer?" If you draw back, you are sure of destruction; but if you go forward, you are certain of success. "The vision is yet for an appointed time, but at the end it shall speak and not lie: though it tarry, wait for it; because it will surely come, it will not tarry." You have his word to rest upon, confirmed by the experience of all his people: "Ask, and it shall be given you; seek, and ye shall find; knock, and it shall be opened unto you." And the longer you have been praying, the nearer is deliverance. Perhaps some messenger of mercy is now on his way; perhaps the next Christian you meet may speak a word in season; perhaps the next sermon you hear may let in the light of heaven upon your gloom, and turn "the shadow of death into the morning. Wait on the Lord; be of good courage, and he shall strengthen thine heart: wait, I say, on the Lord."

III. THOUGH THE LORD CAN ACCOMPLISH HIS WORK WITHOUT HUMAN INSTRUMENTALITY, HE IS PLEASED TO MAKE USE OF IT. The voice from heaven that called him by his name, and accused him of persecution, could have told Saul at once what he must do—but a messenger shall be employed. He could have sent an angel—but Ananias shall be engaged. He shall learn it from the lips of a man; a man of like passions with himself.

His terror would not make him afraid. With *him* he could hold free intercourse and familiar conversation.

He could speak to him from his own experience; and therefore sympathize with him. He had himself exercised repentance towards God, and faith towards our Lord Jesus Christ. He had felt the heart's bitterness peculiar to religion, and had intermeddled with its joy.

It would be also useful to Ananias as well as to Saul—and this is another reason why men are employed in doing the Lord's work. By doing good to others we benefit ourselves. What do we most admire in people? What constitutes their excellency? Not their fine equipage, nor their wealth; not even their genius or learning; no, but the tender heart, the melting eye, the hand ready to relieve, the tongue that speaks a word in season, the feet that run to the door of the fatherless and widows in their affliction, a conformity to him who went about doing good. But who needs to be told that knowledge is improved by communication; that the disposition is confirmed by exercise; that the habit is formed and perfected by action? There is no way in which God could instruct us, impress us, honour us more than by making us the me diu , and distributers of those blessings of which he is the sole author.

It certainly was designed to prevent our undervaluing means, under a notion of depending on divine agency. These are not incompatible; neither does the one detract from the other. Was this communication less from God because it was made by Ananias?— Saul did not think so. Neither should we in all cases of the same nature.

Here let us however beware of two extremes. Let us not, on the one hand, overlook instruments in relying on God; nor, on the other, overlook God in using instruments. For as he uses means, so he gives them their value and their efficacy. It is not the sun that warms us, but He by the sun: it is not food that sustains us, but He by food. "Who then is Paul, and who is Apollos, but ministers by whom ye believed, even as the Lord gave to every man? I have planted, Apollos watered; but God gave the increase. So then, neither is he that planteth any thing, neither he that watereth; but God that giveth the increase. We have this treasure in earthen vessels, that the excellency of the power may be of God, and not of us."

IV. THINGS DONE IN OUR OWN APPREHENSION, AND IN THE OPINION OF OTHERS, ARE FREQUENTLY NOTHING IN THE JUDGMENT OF GOD. "Behold, he prayeth!" And what was there strange—what was there new in this? Had he never prayed before? Never.

But was he not a pharisee, and of the straitest sect of the pharisees? Were not these people held in such estimation, that it was proverbially said, If two men only enter heaven, a pharisee will be one of them? And were they not more distinguished by their prayers than by any thing else? Yes. They prayed often and they made long prayers, and they prayed even at the corners of the streets. —Yet Saul had never prayed till now.

Such is the difference between the prayer of a pharisee and of an awakened sinner! See the difference drawn by an unerring judge. "Two men went up into the temple to pray; the one a Pharisee, and the other a Publican. The Pharisee stood and prayed thus with himself, God, I thank thee, that I am not as other men are, extortioners, unjust, adulterers, or even as this Publican. I fast twice in the week, I give tithes of all that I possess. And the Publican, standing afar off, would not lift up so much as his eyes unto heaven, but smote upon his breast, saying, God be merciful to me a sinner." And he only prayed. "I tell you, this man went down to his house justified rather than the other. for every one that exalteth himself shall be abased; and he that humbleth himself shall be exalted." Such a difference is there between praying in the corner of a street to be seen of men, and withdrawing to pour out the heart before God where no eye can see us. "But thou,

when thou prayest, enter into thy closet, and when thou hast shut thy door, pray to thy Father which is in secret; and thy Father which seeth in secret shall reward thee openly." Such a difference is there between praying and saying our prayers with a form or without one. Prayer is the desire of the soul towards God, and words are not essential to the performance of it: words are nothing but as they express the state of the mind. A single sentence, or a groan that cannot be uttered, arising from a broken heart and a contrite spirit, "God will not despise:" while a fine and orderly address may be rejected, because in the exercise we draw nigh to him with the mouth, and honour him with the lip, while our heart is far from him. "God is a Spirit: and they that worship him must worship him in spirit and in truth." It is an awful consideration; but there are many who attend several sermons a week, and never hear in reality; who often join in the devotions of the sanctuary and the family, and never serve God at all: their praise and prayer are nothing to him: and as religious characters, he will disown them at last: "I know you not whence ye are."

Finally. PRAYER IS A GOOD EVIDENCE OF CONVERSION. "Go, Ananias; he is ready to receive you. Go, and be not afraid of him— the man is changed—he is become a new creature—'for, behold, he prayeth.'"

"The spirit of grace" is always a spirit "of supplications." It brings a man upon his knees. It leads him to speak to God rather than to talk of him. And much will he see, much will he feel, to urge him to seek the Lord. A hell to escape—a heaven to obtain —sins to be pardoned and subdued—duties to be performed—trials to be endured—and God to be glorified—His generation to be served —His own wants and the necessities of others! —All these are enough to induce him to pray —and to pray without ceasing.

Be it remembered however that this mark is better applied exclusively than inclusively. What I mean is this. A man may pray, and not be in a state of salvation; but he that does not pray, cannot be in a state of salvation. A man may have convictions of conscience; he may be impressed by a sermon; he may be alarmed by sickness; and be led to pray when there is no gracious principle that operates in his heart. Such a principle indeed may be safely inferred where prayer is not only public, but private; where it is not only occasional, but habitual and constant, where it is earnest and accompanied by corresponding exertions; where it is not only performed as a duty, but valued as a privilege.—But, without any distinction or qualification, we can apply it by way of exclusion. No man can be a partaker of divine grace that lives without prayer. —We are certain that a prayerless person—is a graceless person.

20

What then is the condition of many! They live without God in the world! They acknowledge him not, lying down or rising up, going out or coming in! God is not in all their thoughts! The duty of prayer they never discharge. The privilege of prayer they never enjoy!

Is this your state! If it be—oh that this day may be rendered memorable by your joining "the generation of them that seek him!" From this hour may the Lord take knowledge of you, and say, "Behold, he prayeth." Then you will enter the way everlasting. The righteous shall compass you about with songs of deliverance. "And there shall be joy in heaven over one sinner that repenteth."

DISCOURSE LXIV.

THE PARALYTIC; OR, SICKNESS IMPROVED.

And he entered into a ship, and passed over, and came into his own city. And, behold, they brought to him a man sick of the palsy, lying on a bed: and Jesus seeing their faith said unto the sick of the palsy; Son, be of good cheer; thy sins be forgiven thee. And, behold, certain of the scribes said within themselves, This man blasphemeth. And Jesus knowing their thoughts said, Wherefore think ye evil in your hearts? For whether is easier, to say, Thy sins be forgiven thee; or to say, Arise, and walk? But that ye may know that the Son of man hath power on earth to forgive sins, (then saith he to the sick of the palsy,) Arise, take up thy bed, and go unto thine house. And he arose, and departed to his house.— Matt. ix. 1—7.

WHO "went about doing good." Such is the representation given us by the apostle Peter of "Jesus of Nazareth, whom God anointed with the Holy Ghost and with power." And never was there a life more concisely or more justly drawn. All, even of the preternatural exemplifications of his character in the days of his flesh, have not come down to us. "Many other signs truly did Jesus in the presence of his disciples, which are not written in this book: but these are written, that ye might believe that Jesus is the Christ, the Son of God; and that believing ye might have life through his name."

Our Saviour had just arrived from the opposite side of the lake of Galilee, the country of the Gergesenes. While there, he had proved his power over unclean spirits; and had dispossessed two demoniacs who had been long the terror of the place. The devils, such was their mischievous disposition, and such their subjection to the control of our Lord, asked leave to enter a large herd of swine; he permitted them; "and, behold, the whole herd ran violently down a steep place into the sea, and perished in the waters." This was an exertion of authority and justice, as well as of power; the trade was unlawful, and constantly exposed them to temptation.

But see the worldly-mindedness of these people. Instead of being struck with his goodness in delivering their neighbours from such a wretched state, and in removing the occasions of sin from themselves, "the whole city came out to meet him; and when they saw him, they besought him that he would depart out of their coasts!" And "let him that is without sin among you cast the first stone" at them. Pause and inquire. Has he not approached you as a reprover—by conscience, by friends, by ministers, by providence? And have you not disliked the remonstrance; and wished to be allowed to go on undisturbed? And what if he who knows your meaning should gratify your wish! What if he who is not obliged to force his favours upon you should say, "They are joined to idols; let them alone!"

This was the case here. He takes these people at their word: "he entered into a ship, and passed over, and came into his own city."

Indeed your desires, with regard either to his presence or absence, will be accomplished. If you desire his presence, and pray that he will be with you in all your troubles and duties, he will answer and say, "Here I am. I will never leave thee nor forsake thee." When Moses said, "If thy presence go not with me, carry us not up hence;" he said, "My presence shall go with thee, and I will give thee rest." When the two disciples going to Emmaus reached their abode, and he made as if he would have gone further, "they constrained him, saying, Abide with us: for it is toward evening, and the day is far spent. And he went in to tarry with them." When the Samaritans, allured by the woman's report, were come to the well, "they besought him that he would tarry with them; and he abode there two days." But if you wish his absence; if you say, "Depart from us: we desire not the knowledge of thy ways," he will renew the expression of his severity, which the Jews suffered as our examples: "My people would not hearken to my voice; and Israel would none of me. So I gave them up unto their own hearts' lust: and they walked in their own counsels." And *wo unto us when he departs from us!* What is a man when left of him? What is a man left to himself! Oh! welcome him, in whatever character he condescends to come to you. Welcome him, even when he comes as a reprover: for "as many as he loves, he rebukes and chastens." Welcome him, even when he comes as a destroyer: your swine are not your souls; your *sins* must die, if you would live; and "it is better for thee to enter into life halt and maimed, rather than having two hands, or two feet, to be cast into everlasting fire."

No sooner had our Saviour entered Capernaum than another opportunity was presented of displaying his goodness and power.

For, "behold, they brought to him a man sick of the palsy, lying on a bed."—How numerous, how various, are the objects of human wretchedness! What proofs of the evil of sin are perpetually striking our very senses. What daily calls have we, in the distresses of others, to be thankful for our exceptions and indulgences. What room is there for the daily exercise of pity and benevolence. How happy was our Saviour, who never saw a misery that he was not able to alleviate, to remove.

The subject of this narrative was the victim of a distemper that rendered life useless and burdensome, though not immediately dangerous. The palsy is a partial death, depriving the limbs affected of sensibility and motion. The poor creature, therefore, when he heard of the fame of Jesus, was unable to go to him for relief. But it was his happiness to have those around him who were disposed to acts of humanity and compassion. The impotent man at the pool of Bethesda complained that "he had no one, when the water was troubled, to put him in." But this paralytic had some neighbours, friends, or relations, who brought him.

And it is said, our Lord "saw their faith." There was faith in the poor man; or he would have refused their assistance, and have said—Trouble not yourselves—my case is hopeless—let me alone to exhaust the remains of a miserable existence. But there was a co-operation; they also had faith, or they would not have taken the journey, and the trouble. They had a persuasion of our Lord's ability and mercy; and therefore they agreed to bring the helpless patient, and place him under the Saviour's view. And thus they, in a very material sense, became instrumental of his cure.

And herein they are an example to us. We should endeavour to do good. The ways in which we may render ourselves useful are numberless. Who is so limited as to be able to do nothing for a fellow-creature? Silver and gold you may have none. You may not have the resources of office, of genius, of learning. But who cannot advise? Who cannot speak a word in season? Who cannot sympathize? Who cannot pray? Who cannot bring to the throne of grace—the ignorant, the guilty, the afflicted, the perishing, and say, "Lord Jesus, have mercy on them! And in doing this let us remember for our encouragement, that our Saviour never turned a deaf ear to prayer—not only when it was offered for the petitioner himself, but

also when it implored relief for others. Did the leper obtain a cure for himself? So did the nobleman for his son. So did the centurion for his servant.

We are not told that the man said any thing. Nor was it necessary. His situation, lying motionless on his bed; his features, his looks—all pleaded loud enough for him. Nor did they plead in vain. "Jesus said unto the sick of the palsy; Son, be of good cheer; thy sins be forgiven thee." But did not the man come for a bodily cure? Was any thing said of his guilt? Why then does our Saviour reverse the order, and begin with the pardon of sin?

First.—To display his sovereignty. Has he not a right to do what he will with his own?—Is it not becoming in us, who have no claims upon him, to leave the time and the way of communicating his favours to the good pleasure of his will; and be thankful if he blesses us at all? We may pray, but we must not dictate.

Secondly.—To show that the soul is of more importance than the body, and should be principally cared for, even in sickness. We never need a physician so much as we do a Saviour.

Thirdly.—Perhaps the man was convinced of sin. Perhaps he suffered more from spiritual distress than from bodily pain. Perhaps he desired a pardon more earnestly than a cure; though he might have had no apprehension of our Lord's authority to bestow it. Words are not necessary to inform the Redeemer. He knows what is in man. Our desire is before him, and our groaning is not hid from him.

Fourthly.—It would serve to emit a ray of his glory, and prove a test to try the dispositions of the company. And, accordingly, so it fell out.

For, "behold, certain of the scribes said within themselves, This man blasphemeth." What, could not He do good without censure, and shall we wonder at reproach, or be deterred by it from the course of duty? It is enough that the servant be as his master, and the disciple as his Lord. Is it sinful to harbour suspicions and surmisings; and to condemn actions unknown and unexamined? It is. Does he arraign men even for their thoughts? He does. And he is acquainted with them: and "there is no creature that is not manifest in his sight: for all things are naked and open unto the eyes of him with whom we have to do." "Jesus knowing their thoughts, said, Wherefore think ye evil in your hearts?"

This indication of his being privy to sentiments, which, though they harboured, they had not expressed, would serve to raise his character, and vindicate the prerogative he claimed. But he does more. He makes use of a sensible argument, and suited to their carnal minds, which at the same time was a-very decisive one, and such as could not fail to produce immediate conviction. If he could not forgive sins without a divine authority, neither could he work miracles without a divine energy : and the exertion of the one would substantiate the possession of the other, or render it credible. " For whether is easier, to say, Thy sins be forgiven thee; or to say, Arise, and walk? But that ye may know that the Son of man hath power on earth to forgive sins, (then saith he to the sick of the palsy,) Arise, take up thy bed, and go unto thine house. And he arose, and departed to his house."

Here several things are worthy of notice. The cure was effected by a word—and in an instant! We think much, by the application of medicine, or the use of means, of easing a pain, or gradually removing it. If the constitution be renovated, it must be the work of time; strength is renewed by degrees, and requires food, and air, and exercise. But this man in a moment, in the twinkling of an eye, feels himself enlivened; and becomes a new creature.

It may be asked why he is commanded not only to walk, but to take up his bed? Was it to show more fully the reality and the completeness of the cure, in that he could not only use his limbs, but carry a burden? —Was it to teach him not to be wasteful; as in another case, after the miraculous abundance which fed the multitude, he said— " Gather up the fragments, that nothing be lost?"—Or was it to be a memento of his disease and deliverance? The mind is approached through the medium of sense. We need every assistance. " Samuel took a stone, and set it between Mizpeh and Shen, and called the name of it Eben-ezer, saying, Hitherto hath the Lord helped us." This man could never see his bed without thinking, " There I lay, when he took pity upon me. 'And I said, My strength and my hope is perished from the Lord: remembering mine affliction and my misery, the wormwood and the gall. My soul hath them still in remembrance, and is humbled in me. This I recall to my mind, therefore have I hope. It is of the Lord's mercies that we are not consumed, because his compassions fail not.'"

Again. He was ordered to return home. A man who sought his own glory would have detained him to swell the number of his followers, and to produce a trophy of his power. There is little benevolence in all our beneficence. There is often more vanity than kindness in what we do for our fellow-creatures. But he only thinks of us; and selfishness deducts nothing from his benefits.—This man had a house, and it was the sphere of his duty. " Go, and there rejoice thy friends. Go, and there fill up every relative duty. Go, and there shadow forth a spiritual cure. Go and prove that conversion is designed not to draw a man off from his calling, but to teach him therein to abide with God." " If any provide not for his own, and specially for those of his own house, he hath denied the faith, and is worse than an infidel." A man is really in religion what he is relatively : and he is more to be judged of by what he is in *his own house* than by what he is in *the house of God.*

It is easy to imagine what an affecting scene his return would produce. How far or how long he had been from home we cannot conjecture; but his connexions would be anxious for the success of the trial. Perhaps in this cottage was an old withered mother, who waited only to know the event before she departs in peace. Perhaps a wife—perhaps children were there! They are looking out between hope and fear. By-and-by they see him—not borne of four—but walking—and carrying his bed—his neighbours walking by his side. He enters. Who has not known what it is to receive back a dear friend or relation from the grave! How much more vivid is the joy arising from the recovery of a blessing, than the pleasure of continued possession!—His first concern is to adore, with his family, the Preserver of men. —But the principal thing in his extraordinary case was, that, like the publican, he has returned to his house justified—divinely pardoned and assured of it; as sure of the salvation of his soul as of the cure of his body.

Let us, in drawing towards a close,

First, fix our eyes on Jesus; the most prominent figure in every piece of evangelical history. What a wonderful, what a peculiar, what a lovely, what a glorious character does he sustain! Wherever we open the memoirs of his life, as given us by the evangelists, we find in him an originality, as free from all affectation and eccentricity, as it is from commonness. We discern the brightness of *his* glory, and the express image of *his* person, whose grandeur is his goodness, and who has named himself the " God of love." We always see him employed in revealing some truth, in conferring some benefit, in working some miracle. We always see him acting in harmony with himself, and in conformity to the design of his coming into the world, which was to seek and to save that which was lost.—Behold him the physician of soul and body; behold him the friend of man, for time and for eternity; behold him casting out none that come unto him; behold him doing " for them exceeding abundantly above all they are able to ask or think !"—And shall we peruse his life as we would the history of a Cyrus or an Alexander? Shall we read it only to amuse our minds, or merely to inform our understandings? Oh! let the blessed relation interest our hopes and our affections. Let it render him precious to us, as he is to those that believe. Let us, "beholding as in a glass his glory, be changed into the same image, from glory to glory, as by the Spirit of the Lord!"

Secondly. Think of this man; and suffer me to inquire how far his case represents your own. I would address you under a fourfold supposition.

First. Are any of you distressed in mind, and body too; oppressed at once with disease and guilt? It is a sad case; but the best thing you can do is to go to him, and address him in the language of one who has been in the same state before you. "Have mercy upon me, O Lord, for I am weak: O Lord, heal me; for my bones are vexed. My soul is also sore vexed: but thou, O Lord, how long? Return, O Lord, deliver my soul: oh save me for thy mercies' sake. For in death there is no remembrance of thee: in the grave who shall give thee thanks? Look upon mine affliction and my pain; and forgive all my sins."

Secondly. Has he healed thy body, and not said to thy soul, "I am thy salvation?" O be not satisfied with the inferior blessing. Rest not till you are justified by faith, and have peace with God through our Lord Jesus Christ. It would be infinitely better to have the forgiveness of sins, and be left languishing under incurable disease, than to be released from the most dreadful malady, and left under the guilt of sin. What are fifteen years added to our life, to go on treasuring up wrath against the day of wrath, and the revelation of the righteous judgment of God! Thousands have been recovered from the borders of the grave, and have afterwards seen not only the pit of corruption, but of destruction. What are the nine ungrateful lepers the better for their cure now! Many never think of this. They are only concerned to escape from a bed of sickness. Whether their souls are blessed or injured by the visitation, is no inquiry with them. But it is an awful thing to have an affliction removed and not sanctified.

Thirdly. Has he spoken peace to thy conscience, and is thy body still under the influence of disease? Be thankful that the greater work is accomplished, and submit to his pleasure with regard to the less. You may pray for ease and deliverance from your affliction: but it must be conditionally; "Not my will, but thine be done." He may have ends to answer by keeping you in affliction after he has pardoned you. He may design to endear to you the scriptures and the throne of grace; to wean you from a vain world; to afford you opportunities to prove the tenderness of his care, and the supports of his presence. Bodily infirmities, like breaks in a wall, says Watts, have often been avenues through which the light of heaven has enter-

ed to the soul, and made the imprisoned inmate long for release.

He has done enough to secure your welfare and happiness, whatever your outward condition may be: for "blessed is the man whose transgressions are forgiven, whose sin is covered." Your trials are without a sting, and will soon be removed for ever; and "the inhabitant shall no more say, I am sick."

Fourthly. Are there none here who are freed from sickness and condemnation too? Such was the distinguished privilege of this poor man. Thus it was with Hezekiah. In *his* mercy, assurance of pardon and recovery from disease were combined. "Behold, for peace I had great bitterness: but thou hast in love to my soul delivered it from the pit of corruption: for thou hast cast all my sins behind thy back." If this be your case, resemble him. Say, "The living, the living, he shall praise thee, as I do this day: the father to the children shall make known thy truth." Say with David, after his remarkable salvation, "Return unto thy rest, O my soul; for the Lord hath dealt bountifully with thee. For thou hast delivered my soul from death, mine eyes from tears, and my feet from falling. I will walk before the Lord in the land of the living." Publish his praise, and constrain others to come to him. Say to your neighbours and friends, "O taste and see that the Lord is good: blessed is the man that trusteth in him."

DISCOURSE LXV.

THE WORK *OF* THE DAY DONE *IN* THE DAY.

As the duty of every day required.
Ezra iii. 4.

TIME, with regard to many—I use the words of Solomon, is "a price in the hand of fools." They know not its value, nor the importance of the things they could purchase with it, if properly laid out; and therefore they barter it away upon trifles, or heedlessly lose it. But the talent is the same, notwithstanding the ignorance of the possessor.

Yes—time—time is unspeakably precious. And this is readily acknowledged by all those who know the worth of it by the loss. O what would the miserable in hell give for a little of that time which many consume in doing nothing, or worse than nothing! O what thoughts of time has a dying sinner, who has lived without God in the world! If heaven would lengthen his days, he would accept the boon on the hardest condition that could ever be proposed. Could he only but live, he would be content to labour in a mine, or beg his bread from door to door. Ah! how feelingly then does he admonish children,

2 G 20*

friends, and neighbours to number their days, and "apply their hearts unto wisdom!"

No wonder, therefore, that the Apostle should call upon us to "redeem the time;" that is, to improve it, by devoting it to the purposes for which it was given. In doing this, there is no one rule of greater importance that that which we may lawfully draw from the words before us; in which we are informed that the pious Jews returned from Babylon, having erected an altar, kept also the feast of tabernacles as it is written, and offered the daily burnt-offerings by number, according to the custom, "as the duty of every day required." It is in the margin, "the matter of the day in his day." This has grown into a proverbial saying among those who love Scripture phraseology; and teaches us that we should do the work *of* the day *in* the day.

I. WE MAY APPLY THIS TO LIFE IN GENERAL. This is called "a day"—and it is a single day—a short day—a day which it is impossible to lengthen. And what is the language of reason; of Scripture? "To-day if ye will hear his voice, harden not your heart. Behold now—is the day of salvation." And what will be your language if the same mind be in you which was also in Christ Jesus? "I must work the works of him that sent me while it is day; the night cometh, wherein no man can work."

II. IT WILL APPLY TO PROSPERITY. This is called "a day;" and Solomon tells us what is the duty of it. "In the day of prosperity be joyful." He cannot, we may be assured, intend to countenance extravagance and excess. The good creatures of God's providence are not given to be consumed upon our lusts, or to degrade a man below the beasts that perish. We are to use this world, but we are to use it as not *abusing* it.

The wise man would teach us to enjoy the comforts our circumstances afford, in opposition to that self-denial that arises, not from religious motive, but from anxiety; from a disposition to live comparatively poor and destitute at present, in order to hoard up for the future. Whereas the Apostle tells us, that "God gives us all things richly to enjoy." Those men are to be pitied who possess much and enjoy little; who have the blessings of life in abundance, but no heart to use them. These generally promise themselves great enjoyment hereafter when they shall have obtained so much. But what is the result? Their souls are often required of them before the expected season, "and then whose are those things which they have provided?"— When they do reach this period, they feel the infirmities of nature, or the assaults of disease; many of their connexions, who would once have shared their joys along with them, are lodged in the cold grave, while those that remain are praying for their death: and when to all this we add, that they carry

into these new scenes old habits that cannot be changed; what wonder is it that they "have no pleasure in them?" We should never sacrifice present happiness to future imaginations. God, like a generous friend, is pleased to see his presents enjoyed—"to enjoy is to obey." Yea, such is the goodness of our heavenly Benefactor, that he does not desire us, even by a sense of our unworthiness, to lessen our relish of his favours. But let us be always joyful *in him;* let us enjoy all *in God,* and *God in all.*

For, behold another thing that the duty of this day requires. It is *gratitude.* The more you have received from God, the greater is your obligation to him; and your language should be, "Bless the Lord, O my soul, and forget not all his benefits." In order to this, you must never sacrifice unto your own net, nor burn incense unto your own drag, because by them your portion is fat, and your meat plenteous; but "remember the Lord thy God: for it is he that giveth thee power to get wealth. The blessing of the Lord, it maketh rich, and he addeth no sorrow with it." Compare your circumstances with those of others, whose plans are equally wise, and whose dependences seemed equally sure.— Compare your present with your former condition; the "two bands" with the "staff." Compare your indulgences with your deserts: —and how can you be unthankful?

And surely the duty of this "day" requires liberality. He had others in view as well as yourselves, in all that he has done for you. He has made you stewards, and not proprietors; and he will soon call you to give up your account. This is your rule: "Let every one lay by him in store, as God hath prospered him. Charge them that are rich in this world that they do good, that they be rich in good works, ready to distribute, willing to communicate."

III. IT WILL APPLY TO ADVERSITY. This also is called "a day;" and it is said, "in the day of adversity, consider." This is the grand duty of the season. Whatever be your affliction, it is a solemn call to consider your ways; to examine your hearts and lives; to inquire wherefore he contends with you; and what he would have you to do. You are also to consider the alleviations of your suffering; how much worse it might have been; and to compare your resources with your difficulties.

Another part of the duty this "day" requires is submission. This is what the apostle Peter prescribes, with promise: "Submit yourselves under the mighty hand of God, and he shall exalt you in due time:" and this is that which the apostle Paul so beautifully enforces—"Furthermore we have had fathers of our flesh which corrected us, and we gave them reverence: shall we not much rather be in subjection unto the Father of spirits, and live? For they verily for a few days chastened us after their own pleasure; but he for our profit, that we might be partakers of his holiness." This subjection does not exclude feeling, but regulates it; keeping us, while sensible of the affliction, from quarreling with Providence, from charging him foolishly or unkindly, and leading us to say, "It is the Lord, let him do what seemeth him good." This, says an old divine, turns the stroke of the rod into a kiss.

The duty of this day also requires prayer. "Call upon me in the day of trouble. Is any afflicted? Let him pray." The very exercise of it will soothe him, while the answer of it will deliver him. Indeed, prayer is the privilege, rather than the duty, of sufferers. Who ever tried it in distress and could not say, "It is good for me to draw near to God?"

IV. WE MAY APPLY IT TO THE SABBATH. This is called "the Lord's day" because it is consecrated to the memory of his resurrection, and is employed in his service. But as to advantage, it is *our* day. It "was made for man." It is a day in which we enjoy a solemn repose from worldly employment; in which we lay in a store of spiritual supplies for the week; in which we meet God in his ordinances, and see him in the sanctuary.

Such a season has peculiar claims upon us, and we are commanded "to sanctify it, calling the Sabbath a delight, the holy of the Lord, honourable; not doing our own ways, nor finding our own pleasure, nor speaking our own words." Some profane it. Some trifle it away. And let me remind you, that it may be trifled away even in divine things. If you go to the house of God, but "leave your souls behind;" if with your mouth you show much love, but your heart goeth after your covetousness; if you hear his words, however frequently, and do them not—in vain do you worship him.

Can this be doing all the duty of the day? Our obligation does indeed take in public worship; and a Christian will say,

"With *early* feet I love t' appear
Among thy saints—"

"How amiable are thy tabernacles, O Lord of hosts! A day in thy courts is better than a thousand. I had rather be a doorkeeper in the house of my God, than to dwell in the tents of wickedness." He knows that "faith cometh by hearing, and hearing by the word of God." He will therefore gladly hear; and he will take heed *what* he hears, and *how* he hears. But this is not all. He will retire. He will indulge in private reflection. He will apply the truths which have been delivered to his own soul. He will pray that the Holy Spirit may bring these things to his remembrance, and enable him to reduce his knowledge to experience and practice. And surely something more should be done in the family on this day, than at other times; not only in keeping servants from work, and children

from play; but in rendering instruction more personal and minute, by some kind of examination and inquiry. In doing this, it is neither necessary nor proper to make the service long and irksome. It may be serious, and yet short and interesting too.

"What a dismal day have you described! 'It is a hard saying; who can hear it!'"—But hard to whom?—To you? If so—what can we think of your disposition!—And what can you think of spending an eternity in religious exercises?—Hard! To whom? Not to a Christian. These are his "pleasant things." He does not say, "What a weariness it is to serve the Lord; when will the Sabbath be gone!" He resigns it with reluctance; and in the enjoyment of its privileges he begins to enter "the rest that remains for the people of God." When once a regard for the Sabbath is gone, every thing serious goes with it. Have we to learn this?

Lastly. IT WILL APPLY TO EVERY DAY. No day comes without its appropriate duty. There is something to be done for God; our fellow-creatures; ourselves: something religious, and something secular. We are not even to neglect any of the duties of our civil concerns. We are to be diligent in our respective callings. And not only so—but we are to do every thing in its season; to do the work *of* the day *in* the day; and not leave it till to-morrow.

First, because we may not live till to-morrow. "We know not what a day may bring forth."

Secondly. Each day will have its own engagements, and it is wrong to surcharge one period with the additional work of another: "Sufficient for the day is the evil thereof." Note. It is unlawful to encumber to-day with the *care* of to-morrow; and to encumber to-morrow with the *work* of to-day.

Thirdly. Because, by this temporary negligence, we have nothing to do, or too much; whereas, by doing the work *of* the day *in* the day, we are never unoccupied, never oppressed; we keep our affairs under easy management, and never suffer them to accumulate into a discouraging mass.

Fourthly. Because by this means the mind is kept cool, and tranquil, and cheerful; and we shall know nothing of the perplexities and ill temper of those who are always in confusion and haste.

To verify this important maxim, let me lay down three rules.

First. Rise early.

Secondly. Grasp not so much business as to "entangle yourselves in the affairs of this life."

Thirdly. Arrange a plan of life, and firmly adhere to it. This will furnish you with means and resources which they know nothing of who go on as accident determines, or humour inclines. You will find that "to every thing there is a season, and a time to every purpose under the heaven."

"If you look abroad into the world, you may be satisfied at the first glance, that a vicious and infidel life is always a life of confusion. Thence it is natural to infer, that order is friendly to religion. As the neglect of it co-operates with vice, so the preservation of it must assist virtue. By the appointment of Providence, it is indispensably requisite to worldly prosperity. Thence arises a presumption that it is connected also with spiritual improvement. When you see a man's affairs involved in disorder, you naturally conclude that his ruin approaches. You at the same time justly suspect, that the causes which affect his temporal welfare operate also to the prejudice of his moral interests. " Let every thing therefore," says the apostle, " be done decently and in order."

Thus you will resemble the greatest and best of Beings, who condescends to propose himself as your model. He is the God of order. " He has fixed the bounds of the earth, and given to the sea his decree, that the waters should not pass his commandment. The day is his, the night also is his. He has made summer and winter. He appointeth the moon for seasons, and the sun knoweth his going down." And under his government, every thing arrives in its proper time and place.

May we be followers of him as dear children, and carry away with us this reflection, as one of the most important maxims of life and religion—That it highly concerns us—and becomes us to be found doing as the duty of every day requires!

And as of ourselves we can do nothing, but " our sufficiency is of God," on him let us depend, and to him let us apply, that we " may obtain mercy, and find grace to help in time of need."

DISCOURSE LXVI.

THE MARTYRDOM OF STEPHEN.

And they stoned Stephen, calling upon God, and saying, Lord Jesus, receive my spirit. And he kneeled down, and cried with a loud voice, Lord, lay not this sin to their charge. And when he had said this, he fell asleep.— Acts vii. 59, 60.

THE words and actions of dying persons are peculiarly impressive. If we have not been present to witness the interesting event of their departure, we anxiously inquire how they behaved themselves; what they did, and what they said.

We often surround the cross, and contemplate the dying of the Lord Jesus; and it is impossible to do it too often. No death is to be compared with his; whether we consider the advantages derivable from it, or the graces

which it displayed. But perhaps no death, recorded in history, approaches so nearly to it as the martyrdom of Stephen. He finished his course with joy, a few weeks after his Lord and master; and near the spot where the one was crucified was the other stoned. Let us bring the whole of his short history under our review.

Stephen was the first of the Christian Church that fell a victim to the rage of persecution. He led the van in the noble army of martyrs—that army, that " resisted unto blood striving against sin;" that army, that rose triumphantly to fame, not by the sufferings of others, but their own; that army, that conquered, but conquered by dying! Stephen was employed in administering the alms of the church. The people had been influenced in their choice of him as a deacon by his acknowledged piety and prudence: " he was full of the Holy Ghost and of wisdom." And such qualifications should alone recommend to all sacred offices. For a proper behaviour in a lower and a private condition is the best pledge of, and the best preparation for, a proper conduct in a higher and official situation. He " that is not faithful in little," is not likely to be faithful in much: " but to him that hath shall be given, and he shall have more abundantly, while from him that hath not shall be taken away even that which he seemeth to have."

Advancement in the state commonly produces envy; as it gives a man wealth, power, authority, influence. But promotion in the church only places him more forward in the battle, and exposes him to greater danger. " Then there arose certain of the synagogue, which is called the synagogue of the Libertines, and Cyrenians, and Alexandrians, and of them of Cilicia and of Asia, disputing with Stephen." Though they seem to have challenged him to this debate, and were certain of victory, they are completely foiled. " They were not able to resist the wisdom and the spirit by which he spake." Argument fails them—but malice does not. " Then they suborned men, which said, We have heard him speak blasphemous words against Moses, and against God. And they stirred up the people, and the elders, and the scribes, and came upon him, and caught him, and brought him to the council, and set up false witnesses, which said, This man ceaseth not to speak blasphemous words against this holy place, and the law: for we have heard him say, that this Jesus of Nazareth shall destroy this place, and shall change the customs which Moses delivered us. And all that sat in the council, looking steadfastly on him, saw his face as it had been the face of an angel !"

It is no unusual thing for the judge and the spectators to observe the countenance of a prisoner at the bar. It is frequently an indication of guilt or of innocency. Stephen's countenance would bear remark. It was neither flushed with passion, nor pale with fear. There reigned in it an unshaken confidence, an undisturbed serenity; meekness and majesty combined. Perhaps there was something preternatural in the case. Thus we read of our Saviour, that " as he prayed, the fashion of his countenance was changed, and his raiment became white and glistering." And it is remarked of Moses, that when he came down from communion with God in Horeb, " his face shone so that the Israelites, could not steadfastly behold him for the glory of his countenance."

But the effect does not disarm or soften his adversaries. " Then said the High Priest, Are these things so?" We must pass over the speech of Stephen; only observing what has frequently and justly been remarked, that it seems not the whole of what he intended to deliver. He was more anxious to save his audience than himself; he thought a dying testimony would be preferable to a train of reasoning, which they were in no temper of mind to receive; he saw they were full of impatience, and would not suffer him to proceed further; he therefore judged it wise to draw towards a conclusion, by a short but faithful address to their consciences. " Ye stiffnecked and uncircumcised in heart and ears, ye do always resist the Holy Ghost: as your fathers did, so do ye. Which of the prophets have not your fathers persecuted? And they have slain them which showed before of the coming of the Just One; of whom ye have been now the betrayers and murderers: who have received the law by the disposition of angels, and have not kept it."

This was intolerable. " When they heard these things, they were cut to the heart, and they gnashed on him with their teeth." " The word of God is quick and powerful, and sharper than any two-edged sword, piercing even to the dividing asunder of soul and spirit, and of the joints and marrow; and is a discerner of the thoughts and intents of the heart." And it is a poor sermon that produces no resentment, either against the preacher, or against the hearer. Who can tell what rage and malice people sometimes feel against a faithful minister? They wish to remain asleep, and he rouses them; they wish to remain in darkness, and he flashes conviction into their minds; he demonstrates their duty, and they hold fast deceit and refuse to return. Were it not for the laws of the land, such a man would often be dragged from the pulpit to the stake. But it is well when people are made enemies to themselves; when they go home at war with their pride, their avarice, their indifference; when they determine even " to crucify the flesh with its affections and lusts." It was a fine eulogium the French monarch Louis XIV.

pronounced on one of his chaplains: " When," says he, " I hear my other preachers, they always lead me to admire them; but Masillon always makes me dissatisfied with myself."—Convinced against their wills, and having nothing to answer, these wretches discover the very dispositions of the damned, who are represented as " wailing and gnashing their teeth." In *them* we see hell pourtrayed and begun. But let us observe Stephen, and behold in *him* the meekness and gentleness of Jesus Christ.

But he—" he being full of the Holy Ghost." He was replenished with his influences and joys. It was this that preserved and sustained him. A Christian is not alone in his trials and difficulties: there is something *divine* that bears him up, when the world expects him to sink. For the world can see his afflictions, but not his succours. These are invisible, but they are real; and they are wisely proportioned to his exigences, so that as the sufferings of Christ abound, the consolations abound also.

He " looked"—not upon the council, to see if any was disposed to favour his cause; nor around the hall, to see if there was any way of escape—but he " looked up steadfastly into heaven"—as one that had already his conversation there, longed to spring from his mole-hill earth, and to begin the song of Moses and the Lamb! What said that look? " Saviour, it is thy cause in which I am engaged. It is for thy dear name I suffer. On thee I depend, to thee I appeal. O carry me through this trying hour, and be magnified in my body, whether it be by life or by death!"

" And saw the glory of God, and Jesus standing on the right hand of God." Three things are here observable. First. He did not see God. No man hath seen God at any time. He is as invisible as immortal—but he beheld a splendour, the symbol of his presence, and that intimated the place where he resides and reveals himself—he " saw the *glory* of God." Secondly. When of old the prophets saw the glory of God, it was always attended with *angelical* appearances. Thus we find seraphim in Isaiah's vision, and cherubim in that of Ezekiel. These were then his agents; ministers of his to do his pleasure. " But to the angels hath he not put in subjection the world to come, whereof we speak?" Angels, with every other class of creatures, are placed under our Redeemer's feet. He is head over all things unto his body the church. All power is given unto him in heaven and in earth. And this is the source of the Christian's consolation and triumph, that his Saviour is now at the right hand of God. Hence he knows that his sacrifice is accepted, that his enemies shall lick the dust, and that all those who put their trust in him shall be saved to the uttermost. " Who is he that condemneth? Is it Christ that died, yea rather, that is risen again, who is even at the right hand of God, who also maketh intercession for us." Thirdly. In every other passage of scripture where our Saviour is spoken of, he is represented as *sitting* at the right hand of God. Sitting is a posture of rest, of dignity, and of dominion; but here he appeared *standing*—a posture of attention. The sight of Stephen touched his heart. He could no longer keep his seat—he rose to animate, sustain, receive, crown his suffering servant.

This vision he immediately makes known. This shows the animating impression it produced upon his mind. And it may also be considered as a testimony borne to the cause for which he was going to die. "You condemn me for saying that he whom you crucified lives and reigns above. But I *see* him. *There* he is. 'Behold, I see the heavens opened, and the Son of man standing on the right hand of God.'"

Their fury now can no longer be restrained. "Then they cried out with a loud voice, and stopped their ears, and ran upon him with one accord, and cast him out of the city, and stoned him." Yet in this infamous transaction, they pay some regard to the forms of justice. They do this, pretendedly, in execution of a law enacted by Moses against blasphemers. In this law, the "hands of the witnesses" were to be first upon the offender to put him to death, and afterward the hands of all the people. This circumstance explains what is here added—"the witnesses laid down their clothes at a young man's feet, whose name was Saul."

Here first comes in view an individual destined to be the most extraordinary character in the Church of God. Had a prophet stood near on this occasion and said, "Ah! Saul, you will by-and-by be stoned for the same profession, and die a martyr in the same cause;" he would have been filled with surprise and indignation, and have exclaimed, "What! is thy servant a dog, that he should do this thing?" O how wonderful are the ways of Divine Providence!—God had his eye upon him at this hour: he had watched over him through life; he had separated him from his mother's womb; and all this with a view to call him by his grace, and reveal his Son in him. He was a chosen vessel unto him, to bear his name before the Gentiles, and kings, and the children of Israel. For a time Saul seemed beyond the possibility of a reclaim. Even those who had experienced the efficacy of divine grace themselves, seemed unanimously to have despaired of him. When they heard of his conversion, they were astonished even to incredulity; and when he assayed to join himself to them, they were afraid of him. Let us despair of none. He has a mighty arm; strong is his hand, and high is his right hand. "I obtained mercy," says this monument of divine grace, "that in

me first Jesus Christ might show forth all longsuffering, for a pattern to them which should hereafter believe on him to life everlasting."

But oh! with what pain, even after a lapse of years, does he acknowledge the guilt he contracted by his connivance and assistance at this murder. "And when the blood of thy martyr Stephen was shed, I also was standing by, and consenting unto his death, and kept the raiment of them that slew him!'"

Stoning was a painful, a dreadful death. Who can think of it without shuddering?—The flesh bruised, the bones broken, the skull fractured perhaps in several places, before the soul escapes! But how died he, morally! This is the question. Archbishop Usher said, he hoped to die with the language of the publican, "God be merciful to me a sinner;" and his wish was indulged. The devotional Mrs. Rowe was found dead on her knees. And "blessed is that servant, whom his Lord when he cometh shall find so doing." Stephen died "calling upon God." And the two petitions he offered are recorded.

The first regards himself. "Lord Jesus, receive my spirit." Some people are afraid to honour the Son as they honour the Father. But we are commanded to do this. And we have here an instance of it; a prayer addressed to our Saviour, and by a man who was in circumstances to render his example unexceptionable; full of the Holy Ghost, and dying too.—What does this prayer teach us!

It teaches us that there is a separate state between death and the resurrection. Had Stephen believed that the soul would either die or sleep with the body, would he have uttered such language as this; "Lord Jesus, receive my spirit?"

It teaches us that Stephen considered our Saviour as the Lord of glory, and as possessing supreme power and authority in the other world. "I know," as if he had said, "whom I have believed, and am persuaded that he is able to keep that which I have committed to him against that day."

It shows us that Stephen was principally concerned for the security and welfare of his soul. He thought little of the body. The reverse of this is commonly the case. The body engrosses all the attention. There are many who even seem to *die* as regardless of their souls as if they had none. They only think and talk of the physician and lawyer; of their disorder and their temporal concerns. One is sometimes surprised to hear with what composure persons who cannot possibly possess a good hope through grace speak of their dissolution; and arrange the circumstances of their funeral. You would conclude they had no souls to be disposed of or provided for. Not a word escapes them concerning these! But the soul is the man. This is the immaterial, the immortal part.

"What is a man profited, if he shall gain the whole world, and lose his own soul? or what shall a man give in exchange for his soul?" Oh! says the Christian, I feel comparatively indifferent as to the destiny of my body. Let wild beasts devour it; let the flames consume it, let the winds scatter it—if I may but conclude that my soul shall be saved in the day of the Lord Jesus!

And, be it remembered, this is his concern in life as well as in death. From the hour of his conviction, the chief inquiry with him has been, not what shall I eat, or what shall I drink, or wherewithal shall I be clothed?—But, "what must I do to be saved?" How are my sins to be pardoned? How to be subdued?—Is this your concern?—If he does not receive your departing spirits at death, they will be seized by the powers of darkness, and become the prey of devils. But if you receive him in life, he will receive you at death; receive you to glory; receive you to himself, that where he is there you may be also.

Oh! that when we come to die we may feel the sentiments of Stephen, and be able to say, "Lord Jesus,

"Since the dear hour that brought me to thy foot,
And cut up all my follies by the root,
I never trusted in an arm but thine,
Nor hoped but in thy righteousness divine."

Thou art all my salvation and all my desire. In every difficulty thou hast been my guide; in every danger my refuge; in every distress my consolation. My happiest moments have been passed in communion with thee. I cannot look back upon a well-spent life. Every view I take of myself is humbling. But I review with thankfulness the instances of thy goodness. By thy grace I am what I am. And now I come to thee; and this soul of mine, which thou hast redeemed with thy blood, and won by thy love, I surrender.

"A guilty, weak, and helpless worm,
On thy kind arm I fall;
Be Thou my strength and righteousness,
My Jesus and my all."

The second petition regards his enemies; and seems to have been offered up with peculiar solemnity and earnestness: for he now "kneeled down, and cried with a loud voice, Lord, lay not this sin to their charge." Behold here a proof of the grandeur of soul real religion inspires: "It is the glory of a man to pass by a transgression." Behold an example of obedience to a command, wh'ch infidels have ridiculed, and which thousands look upon to be impracticable: "I say unto you, love your enemies, bless them that curse you, do good to them that hate you, and pray for them which despitefully use you, and persecute you." Behold an instance of conformity to the temper of a dying Saviour, who prayed, "Father, forgive them, for they know not what they do." The same spirit actuates the Master and his disciples. The difference only lies here: he received the Spirit without measure, while we possess it in a limited degree. In him the exercise of it met with no counteracting depravity; but in us it is resisted by adverse powers: and hence a perpetual warfare; "the flesh lusting against the Spirit, and the Spirit against the flesh: and these are contrary the one to the other: so that we cannot do the things that we would." But, if we have not the Spirit of Christ, we are none of his. The same principles that resided in him must be found in us; and as far as they prevail, they will produce the same effect.

Having said this, "he fell asleep." Sleep has nothing formidable in it. A weary man, after a day of toil, feels no reluctance to lie down in his bed. The disease of the babe awakens all the anxiety of the mother, and she cries, "Let me not see the death of the child;" but it is otherwise when she views him asleep. She knows that it is in her power to awake him at pleasure; and to embrace him refreshed and improved. And this is the soft representation given of the believer's death in the Scriptures; and it is so essentially just, that we here find a death of violence and anguish expressed by it. When David had served his generation, he "fell asleep"—but he died in a palace, in a fine bed, and surrounded with every indulgence. Stephen dies under a shower of stones; but he, even he fell asleep!

I see his body left on the ground, mangled with blows, and covered with gore. But let it not be despised. That body is the workmanship of God: it is the purchase of the Redeemer; it is the temple of the Holy Ghost; it shall be renewed, and fashioned like the Saviour's own glorious body.—Accordingly we find that "devout men carried Stephen—to his burial," says our translation; but this is not in the original: they carried him from the place of execution to his house, and from his house to his grave; "and made great lamentation over him."

Honour is to be valued according to the quarter whence it comes. Who would like to be deemed the favourite of Satan! And why should we wish to be admired and caressed by the world—the very world that "crucified the Lord of glory," when he was on earth; and would willingly do it again! You do not wish to stand high in the estimation of vagrants, traitors, idiots, and madmen—and what, as to religious concerns, are numbers better—and yet how many things you often conceal, or sacrifice, or pursue, to gain their favour! But "devout men;" "the saints that are in the earth"—these are "the excellent, in whom is all my delight." To belong to them; to hear them coming around me and saying, "My brother;" for them to rejoice when I rejoice, and to weep when I weep; to be loved and esteemed by them in life, in death;—this is delightful; it is, to use the words of a beautiful writer, " like walking in an eastern spice grove."

And such were the men who testified their regard to Stephen; and bedewed his sepulchre with their tears. In no other way could they mourn for him. They knew that death was his gain; but it was their loss. And the removal of such a man is a loss; a loss to the world, and a loss to the Church: the loss of a protector, an intercessor, a benefactor, an example. As they retire, we feel the earth poorer; and if all of them were withdrawn, who would wish to live here another day! Our world would be a cage of unclean birds, a den of dragons, an emblem of hell. Oh! how the death of such a friend " cools our brainless ardours!" How it detaches us from

" These low grounds where sorrows grow,
And every pleasure dies !"

How it induces us to say, with Thomas, " Let us go away, that we may die with him!"

Do we pass through the world so as to draw forth the blessings while they live, and the tears of many when we die! Are tyrannical masters, are selfish neighbours, are hard-hearted and close-fisted professors of religion thus lamented?—" When the wicked perish," says Solomon, " there is shouting." —This is dreadful.—For a man to think that there is no individual upon earth that wishes his continuance; that if he were removed, no one being would sigh; and could he endeavour to come back, he would find the door of life bolted against him—why there is something in this more chilling than death, and more cruel than the grave. And yet how many are there, who, if they were carried to their burial to-morrow, would excite no lamentation over them—unless indeed a lamentation that they had not died sooner. One perhaps would be ready to say—" O that the wretch had died before: by his wanton speculations he had ruined the substance that was to rear my babes." Another—" O that the wretch had died before he had seduced my daughter, the glory of my family." A third—" O that the wretch had died before, by his infidel principles he had poisoned the mind of my darling son."

Let us hasten to conclude by inquiring— Whether an inflexible adherence to the cause of God be not wisdom; and whether wisdom be not justified of all her children?— How amply was Stephen indemnified by the glory he immediately enjoyed in heaven—by the usefulness which his example has produced on earth—by the testimony of Divine approbation—by the satisfaction of his own mind!

Who could help feeling interested in such a character! Who would not rather have been in the condition of the martyr than of the persecutor! Surely his enemies were compelled to venerate him, and inwardly to pray, " Let me die the death of the righteous, and let my last end be like his!"

We may be losers, says Mr. Henry, in the service of God, but we cannot be losers by it. And says our Saviour, " There is no man that hath left house, or parents, or brethren, or wife, or children, for the kingdom of God's sake, who shall not receive manifold more in this present time, and in the world to come life everlasting."

Though he does not crown his servants on this side Jordan, he owns them: and he will be sure to stand by those that stand by him. The world may frown upon them, but he will smile. They may be reproached and "persecuted for righteousness' sake;" but he is near that justifieth them;" and " he that toucheth them, toucheth the apple of his eye." They may expect a succession of personal and relative trials; but "he will be with them in trouble," and deliver them and honour them. They must die; but they need not shudder at the approaching event. He will be " the strength of their heart, and their portion for ever," when every worldly resource fails. As " the earthly house of this tabernacle dissolves, they will have a building of God, a house not made with hands, eternal in the heavens." Though invisible to the eye of sense, they know that he is pleading for them within the vail; yea, by faith " they see the heavens opened, and the Son of man standing at the right hand of God." And while looking down upon them, though inaudible to the ear of sense, by faith they hear his voice saying, " Be thou faithful unto death, and I will give thee a crown of life !"

DISCOURSE LXVII.

A CHRISTIAN IS NOT A FAVOURITE WITH THE WORLD.

Yea, and all that will live godly in Christ Jesus shall suffer persecution.—2 Tim. iii. 12

WHO can help admiring the frankness of the Scripture!

We find nothing like this in the methods employed by the enemy of our souls. He deceives in order to destroy. He keeps his followers in ignorance. He allures them on by flatteries and lies. He conceals from them the dreadfulness of the end, and the hardships of the way: he cries, " Peace, peace: when there is no peace."

But the Gospel hides nothing. It shows us the difficulties as well as the enjoyments of religion; the sacrifices it requires, as well as the rewards it insures. Now this is perfectly just; and it is every way profitable. It serves to discriminate between the false, the timid, the worldly-minded; and those who are in earnest; those who know that they *must* advance or perish, and who will not flinch whatever they may feel. It also prevents surprise and confusion when the evil day comes; and keeps us from being discouraged because of the way. Yea, it even tends to confirm and establish our faith and hope, by showing us in ourselves the truth of God's word, and the experience of his people.

Upon this principle is founded the declaration of the Apostle, in which, having mentioned the sufferings he had himself endured, he adds, "To suffer is not peculiar to me: let my son Timothy, and believers universally reckon upon the same treatment: the cup is common to all, though some are called to drink a larger draught of it: 'Yea, and all that will live godly in Christ Jesus shall suffer persecution." In these words let us consider two things.

I. THE LIFE THEY DESCRIBE. II. THE CONDITION THEY ANNOUNCE.

I. THE LIFE THEY DESCRIBE. It may be taken with two distinctions.

First. It is not merely a *moral* life, but a *godly* one. The religion of many people consists only in certain regards to their fellow-creatures; and if they "do justly," and "love mercy," they are not concerned to "walk humbly with their God." We by no means depreciate morality. The Gospel demands it; and makes provision for it. A man cannot be religious without being moral; but he may be moral without being religious. It is well to be a good master, a good neighbour, a good subject—but how are you disposed towards God? Are you honest? Are you liberal? It is well. But I have another question to ask. Are you "renewed in the spirit of your minds?" Are you holy? Are you godly?—Nothing but that disposition towards God, which is implied in godliness, can give principle to our actions; induce us to avoid every sin however secret; engage us to make conscience of every duty however private; and carry us through every discouragement that lies in the way everlasting. Virtue without godliness may gain us a fair character among men, and variously subserve our temporal advantage; but whatever it may do for us as to this world, it will not be sufficient with regard to another.

Secondly. It is not merely a godly life, but a Christian one. We are not only to live godly, but to live godly "in Christ Jesus." This is a very interesting addition, and it will be necessary to examine it.—What is it to live godly "in Christ Jesus?" It is in all our religious concerns—To be governed by the revelation of Jesus Christ—To be conformed to the example of Jesus Christ—To be actua-

ted by the grace of Jesus Christ—And to depend on the mediation of Jesus Christ.

We cannot live godly in Christ Jesus, unless we are influenced by "the revelation" of Jesus Christ. "No man hath seen God at any time; the only begotten Son, which is in the bosom of the Father, he hath declared him:" and he hath declared him in such a manner as he was never known before. He has displayed him not only as making the world, but as "reconciling the world unto himself, not imputing their trespasses unto them." Hence we are to go to him, not as innocent creatures, but as guilty; feeling our need of redemption, and exercising faith on him "who suffered, the just for the unjust, that he might bring us unto God."—He has displayed him more affectionately; as "the God of all grace," as "the Father of mercies;" as love itself. Hence we are to regard him as children, not slaves; "receiving not the spirit of bondage again to fear; but the Spirit of adoption, whereby we cry, Abba Father." Shall I say he has revealed him after a more spiritual manner; as looking at the heart, and not attaching himself to particular places and forms? He has: and at the same time taught us the use we are to make of it. "The hour cometh, and now is, when the true worshippers shall worship the Father in spirit and in truth: for the Father seeketh such to worship him. God is a Spirit: and they that worship him must worship him in spirit and in truth."

We cannot live godly in Christ Jesus, unless we are conformed to the example of Jesus Christ. His godliness was not only real, but perfect. His soul was full of God; all his actions, words, and purposes referred entirely to him. He trusted in God, and never desponded under the darkest dispensations: "Behold, the hour cometh, yea, is now come, that ye shall be scattered, every man to his own, and shall leave me alone: and yet I am not alone, because the Father is with me." He loved him supremely: nor was this love cooled by the dreadful sufferings he was appointed to endure. Instead of avoiding his tremendous passion, he went forth to meet it, and said, "That the world may know that I love the Father; and as the Father gave me commandment, even so I do. Arise, let us go hence." His devotedness to his honour was invariable: "I seek not mine own glory, but the glory of him that sent me. My meat is to do the will of him that sent me, and to finish his work." His attachment to his worship was so great, that he could say, "The zeal of thine house hath eaten me up." How often do we read of his devotion! He prayed in the wilderness. He prayed in the garden. He rose up a great while before day, and went out, and departed into a solitary place, and there prayed. He went up into a mountain, and continued all night in prayer to God. It is impossible for us, while encompassed with infirmities, to equal him: but we must resemble him. "He that saith he abideth in him ought himself also to walk even as he walked." "If any man have not the Spirit of Christ, he is none of his." He had the Spirit without measure; but the same mind must be in us which was also in Christ Jesus.

We cannot live godly in Christ Jesus, unless we are actuated by the grace of Jesus Christ. It is a truth taught us in the Scripture, and of which we need to be constantly reminded, that "from him is our fruit found." Though we bear it, he enables us to yield it. "We live; yet not we, but Christ liveth in us: and the life that we live in the flesh we live by the faith of the Son of God." Does the branch flourish independently of the tree, or by means of the sap derived by union from it? "As the branch," says the Saviour, "cannot bear fruit of itself, except it abide in the vine; no more can ye except ye abide in me: for without me ye can do nothing."

The engagements to which we are called in the Scripture, seem fitter for angels than for frail and depraved men. How are they to be accomplished—how are these enemies to be conquered—how are these trials to be borne—how are these duties to be performed? How are we to live "with our conversation in heaven;" to walk by faith, and not by sight;" to "forgive those that trespass against us until seventy times seven?" Who would not shrink back, and lie down in despair, but for the voice that cries, "My grace is sufficient for thee: for my strength is made perfect in weakness?" The charge of enthusiasm has been frequently advanced against this doctrine—but would it not be easy and just to retort the charge? What enthusiasm is like that which expects such mighty effects without an adequate cause? Upon our principle, a Christian has a resource equal to all the claims of his high calling; and may without presumption say, "I know both how to be abased, and I know how to abound: every where and in all things I am instructed both to be full and to be hungry, both to abound and to suffer need. I can do all things through Christ who strengtheneth me."

We cannot live godly in Christ Jesus, unless we depend on the mediation of Jesus Christ. There are many who find it an easy thing to hope in God: they confidently presume on the acceptance of their performances; and seem even to challenge a reward. But it is otherwise with a Christian. He sees, he feels the poverty and unworthiness of his duties. He confesses that when he has done all, he is an unprofitable servant; and instead of being recompensed for the excellences of his obedience, he wonders that he is not rejected for its defects. His sabbaths

humble him as much as his week-days. He even looks off from his holy things, to find a better foundation to rely upon; a better righteousness to appear in before God. And where is this to be found? He has boldness and access with confidence, by the faith of Him who was delivered for our offences, and raised again for our justification, and ever lives to make intercession for us. He is the great High Priest over the house of God; he represents and introduces us; and "we are accepted in the Beloved."

II. Let us attend to THE CONDITION these words announce, as the consequence of the life they describe. Yea, and all that will live godly in Christ Jesus "shall suffer persecution."

This doctrine is frequently observable in the Scripture. Our Lord preached it to his immediate disciples when he said, "In the world ye shall have tribulation." It is strongly implied in the declaration, "If any man will be my disciple, let him deny himself, and take up his cross, and follow me." It is recognised even in the promise, "There is no man that hath left house, or brethren, or sisters, or father, or mother, or wife, or children, or lands, for my sake, and the Gospel's, but he shall receive an hundredfold now in this time, houses, and brethren, and sisters, and mothers, and children, and lands, with persecutions; and in the world to come eternal life." Paul held the same sentiment; and, therefore, as he visited the churches, he not only exhorted them to continue in the faith, but reminded them that "they must, through much tribulation, enter into the kingdom of God." Suffering in the Christian life he always takes for granted: "If children, then heirs; heirs of God, and joint-heirs with Christ; if so be that we suffer with him, that we may be also glorified together." Events perfectly answered to these intimations. In the Acts of the Apostles we see what Christians endured from Jews and Gentiles, priests and people; and history spreads before us examples of the same truth in every successive period.

But how is this! It seems wonderful, if not incredible, that persons whose lives are harmless, and holy, and passed in endeavours to do good, should experience treatment like this. But the wonder ceases if we observe

That ever since the Fall there has been an irreconcilable enmity between the "seed of the woman and the seed of the serpent;" that "man being alienated from the life of God," loves nothing that reminds him of God, or that resembles him; that the tempers and actions of the righteous necessarily reprove and upbraid the wicked; that their endeavours to save, disturb them in their sins; that the Gospel condemns the worldly as well as the vicious, and the formal, as well as the negligent; that as there is nothing in Christianity that flatters sin so there is nothing that flatters self; and that every man is naturally as self-righteous as he is depraved.

To this we may add another source of the inevitableness of persecution. It is taken from the Christian himself. Suffering is necessary for his trial and his triumph. Without this, how could he prove that he loves God better than friendship, reputation, wealth, or life? How could he overcome evil with good? How could he love his enemies, bless them that curse him, and pray for them that despitefully use him and persecute him?—It is warfare that makes a good soldier. A Christian is like the firmament, and it is the darkness of affliction that makes his starry graces to shine out. He is like those herbs and plants that best effuse their odours when bruised.

But you say—though this was true formerly, is it not far otherwise now? And if the truth be applied to us at all, must it not be taken with limitations? And what are they?

Here let us admit with gratitude the difference between our own times, and the days of those "who through faith and patience inherit the promises." We should not talk like martyrs. Owing to the justice and mildness of our laws, what perils do we run? We can "sit under our own vine and fig tree, none daring to make us afraid." The greater part of our sufferings are not distinguishable from the common afflictions of life; and many of the trials that some foolish professors frequently charge on religion, religion would teach them to avoid, if its admonitions were regarded. But on the other hand it must be allowed,

First; that human nature is essentially the same in every age; and that a tiger may be chained and not changed. Under every form of government "the heart is deceitful above all things, and desperately wicked." And where there is a strong active propensity against any thing, (as in this case, there *must* be against real godliness) it will show itself as opportunity offers; and such opportunity there must be in a world like this.

Secondly; that persecution admits of various degrees. It includes every kind of injury or vexation, from a fiery stake to a scornful sneer; and is not to be estimated always by the bulk of the suffering only, but by the grace, the temper, and the state of the individual that endures it. It commonly operates *now* in a way of reproach; and frequently this is no less trying than bodily pain. We know who said, "Reproach hath broken my heart." This reproach endeavours to turn their faith into folly; their hope into presumption; their meekness and forgiveness of injuries into meanness and cowardice; their sanctity into singularity or hypocrisy. It will take the blemishes of an individual,

and charge them upon the whole body. It will magnify the common infirmities of human nature into crimes. Let the young man swear and challenge; let him be a companion of them that drink, and make merry, and mock at sin; and he shall be applauded as a young man of spirit: but no sooner is he convinced that "the end of these things is death, and that the way of transgressors is hard;" and "comes out from among them, and is separate;" than he is "had in derision of all around him, and is as one mocked of his neighbour." How often has genuine religion produced the loss of friendship, or chilled the warmth of attachment into cold civility. Where power is possessed, it is frequently exerted as far as safety or a regard to appearances will allow. This is seen in the attempts of husbands, parents, and masters, to restrain from following their religious convictions their wives, their children, and their servants. With regard to relations, a Christian will sometimes find a greater trial in their affections than in their frowns. Here is a mother, in all other respects tender and kind; she takes her daughter aside, and weeps to think she should favour a doctrine "every where spoken against," and draw upon herself some opprobrious name:—she beseeches her not to grieve the heart of one who bore her—and "bring down her gray hairs with sorrow to the grave." Now, to withstand all this, and to break loose from such an embrace—not from a want of filial regard—this religion increases at the very time, but from obedience to the voice that cries, "He that loveth father or mother more than me, is not worthy of me."—What a trial is here!

Thirdly. If modern Christians frequently escape persecution, may it not be asked, whether, in many instances, it does not arise from their less fully exemplifying the spirit of their religion than the primitive Christians did? Many professors, it should be observed, seem to make it their whole concern to elude the reproach of the Cross; and we may notice two methods employed by them for this purpose, both of which will tend to prove the truth of the Apostle's assertion, even with regard to ourselves.

The one is *concealment.* This is dastardly and mean. We should never be drawn out of a corner by the praise of man, nor be driven into a corner by the fear of man. We should be ashamed of nothing we embrace upon conviction. We are required to "confess with the mouth," as well as "to believe with the heart:" and to *appear* Christians as well as to *be* such. But if we hide our peculiar character, we cannot of course provoke notice and opposition in that peculiar character.

The other is *accommodation.* And it is awful to think how one doctrine and usage after another has been given up! Christianity, says one, will never be received by Jews and Mahometans, while you "honour the Son as you honour the Father." It will never be acceptable, says another, to men of taste and learning, till you abandon the barbarous notion of the atonement, and of original sin. Now, upon this plan, what would be left after all the objectors were satisfied? How much would the residue resemble the Gospel as it now stands? And admitting that this pruned system *was* unexceptionable, and even admired by the generality of mankind, would this be a proof of its truth? If so, why was the preaching of "Christ crucified to the Jews a stumbling block, and to the Greeks foolishness;" and only to them that were "called, Christ the wisdom of God, and the power of God?" Was Paul mistaken when he said, "The natural man receiveth not the things of the Spirit of God, for they are foolishness unto him; neither can he know them, because they are spiritually discerned?"

In practice as well as principle, professors have conceded one thing after another, in order to take off prejudice, and to make themselves the more rational, and liberal, and agreeable to the men of this generation. One thing is obvious from all this trimming and changing their way; and it is this—that either Christianity or the world must be altered, before they can be rendered agreeable to each other. But Christianity allows of no alteration. It needs none. The change required therefore is, where it ought to be, in the world. Hence, says the Apostle, "Be not conformed to this world : but be ye transformed by the renewing of your mind, that ye may prove what is that good, and acceptable, and perfect will of God."

Think of this, ye God-and-Mammon men; ye would-be-friends of the world, and of God too. If your aim be to elude opposition and reproach, as far as ye are " of the world, the world will love its own :" but as far as you dissent from them, they will dissent from you ; as far as you oppose them, they will oppose you. Our Saviour may say to many Christians as he did to the Jews; "the world cannot hate you : but me it hateth, because I testify that the deeds thereof are evil."

This subject is fruitful in reflections.

First. There are some who suffer persecution—that do not live godly in Christ Jesus. For it is not the cross, but the cause that makes the martyr: men may go weeping to hell, as well as to heaven. But to whom does our observation apply? It applies to pretenders; who have "a name that they live, but are dead." The people of the world cannot easily distinguish between "the form of godliness and the power," and therefore the pretending and the sincere frequently are alike. It is a sad thing for a man to

share in the sufferings of religion, while he is a stranger to its supports, and unentitled to its privileges. But so it is; the hypocrite loses heaven for the sake of earth, and earth for the sake of heaven; and is of all creatures the most miserable.—It applies also to those whose conduct is exceptionable. If you will speculate; live beyond your income; involve yourselves in difficulties, and defraud others; and as you go along hear the reflection, "There goes a religious cheat;" bear it as well as you can: the world speaks truth: by your profession you are religious, and by your practice you are unrighteous. "What glory is it, if, when ye be buffeted for your faults, ye shall take it patiently? but if, when ye do well, and suffer for it, ye take it patiently, this is acceptable with God." Your sufferings are not Christian sufferings, unless they are unmerited by *immoral*, and even *imprudent* conduct. "If ye be reproached for the name of Christ, happy are ye; for the spirit of glory and of God resteth upon you: on their part he is evil spoken of, but on your part he is glorified. But let none of you suffer as a murderer, or as a thief, or as an evil-doer, or as a busy-body in other men's matters."

Secondly. With what caution and prayer should we assume a profession of religion! God forbid we should discourage any; even any of you, my young friends, who are disposed to join yourselves to the Lord's people in a perpetual covenant, that shall not be forgotten: we would rather invite you to cast in your lot among them, and assure you, that in religion you will find a portion infinitely better than all the pleasures of sin, and the vanities of the world—But at the same time we would not deceive you. We would follow the example of our Lord in addressing those who spoke of following him. You are going, said he, to build: "Sit down first and count the cost." Your religion will be an expensive thing. Can you bear its charges? You are going to declare war. "Sit down first and count the dangers." Have you equal forces? Good alliances? A rich treasury? "So likewise, whosoever he be of you that forsaketh not all that he hath, he cannot be my disciple."

"And who after this can think of following him?" Why all who are truly wise. Such a course, notwithstanding every sacrifice, is *wisdom;* "and wisdom is justified of all her children." If God would open your eyes as he did Balaam's, you would look upon this poor despised people, and say, "How goodly are thy tents, O Jacob, and thy tabernacles, O Israel! Let me die the death of the righteous, and let my last end be like his." If Moses, the son of Pharaoh's daughter, was here, and a palace was offered him, he would "choose rather to suffer affliction with the people of God, than to enjoy the pleasures of sin for a season; and esteem the reproach of Christ greater riches than the treasures in Egypt, having respect unto the recompense of the reward.'

Thirdly. If any man suffer as a Christian, let him not be ashamed; but let him glorify God on this behalf. It gives you an opportunity to prove your thankfulness for his goodness, and your adherence to his Gospel. Your cause is noble: it is the cause of truth and holiness; it is glory to God in the highest, and on earth peace; good-will towards men. Your companions are glorious; the same afflictions happened to your brethren who were before you in the world, patriarchs, prophets, apostles, and Jesus himself, your elder brother. Your crown is invaluable; and you may say with Paul, "I reckon that the sufferings of this present time are not worthy to be compared with the glory that shall be revealed in us."

But what shall we say to persecutors? If you feel enmity against the godly, and would injure them were it in your power, it is "a token of perdition." You may now be placed above them in circumstances; and may love to misrepresent and to vilify them. But "their Redeemer is mighty." He is "near that justifieth them." He "will plead their cause." He that "toucheth them, toucheth the apple of his eye." They shall "have dominion over you in the morning of the resurrection; and condemn you at the last day." "Know ye not that the saints shall judge the world?"

DISCOURSE LXVIII.

HOW WE ARE TO HONOUR GOD IN TROUBLE.

Glorify ye the Lord in the fires.
Isaiah xxiv. 15.

"WHETHER ye eat, or drink, or whatsoever ye do, do all to the glory of God." What an extensive admonition is this! It demands of us nothing less than an universal regard to God;—a reference to his honour in all our actions, not only religious, but civil and natural.

And yet even this does not include the whole of God's claim upon us. We are required to honour him, not only in all we *do*, but in all we *suffer*. Witness the words which I have read: "Glorify ye the Lord in the fires." Let us consider,

I. THE STATE HERE SUPPOSED. II. OUR DUTY WHEN IN IT. III. THE REASONS BY WHICH IT IS ENFORCED.

I. THE STATE HERE SUPPOSED—"In the fires." The language is figurative. It is common for the sacred writers to hold forth trouble and affliction by fire, and frequently in connexion with its opposite, water. Thus the Church triumphant looks back and exults;

"We went through fire and through water, but thou broughtest us out into a wealthy place." Thus runs the Divine promise: "When thou passest through the waters, I will be with thee; and through the rivers, they shall not overflow thee: when thou walkest through the fire, thou shalt not be burned; neither shall the flame kindle upon thee." And the Apostle Peter exhorts Christians not to "think it strange concerning the fiery trial."

Stripped of metaphor, the passage before us supposes a state of suffering.

In this state we may be found as *men:* for "although affliction cometh not forth of the dust, neither doth trouble spring out of the ground, yet man is born to trouble as the sparks fly upward."

In this state we may be found as *Christians:* for "many are the afflictions of the righteous." This fact may seem strange to the natural man, who concludes that the favourite of Heaven is entitled to every indulgence upon earth: and it has often proved a source of temptation to the people of God themselves, who have been led, from their sufferings, to suspect their safety.

But why such an inference? Their Lord and Saviour was made perfect through suffering; he was a man of sorrows and acquainted with grief; and they are fore-ordained to wear his image. There must be a conformity between the head and the members: "it is enough for the servant to be as his master, and the disciple as his Lord."

Why such an inference? "Whom the Lord loveth he chasteneth, and scourgeth *every* son whom he receiveth." "As many," says our heavenly Father, "as I love, I rebuke and chasten." The history of the Church furnishes no exceptions to this truth. And can you see good men, and men of the most eminent goodness, invariably suffering—and refuse to drink of the cup they drank of, and to be baptized with the baptism they were baptized with!

In what condition could we view them, should we now find many of those who are infinitely dear to God!—Depressed with weakness, fear, and much trembling; pining with disease; "made to possess months of vanity and wearisome nights;" disappointed in their worldly schemes and exertions; perplexed and straitened in their circumstances; bereaved of their dearest connexions; "lover and friend put far from them, and their acquaintance into darkness;" opposed and persecuted by their neighbours and relations; and finding by bitter experience that "a man's foes are those of his own household."

And what, under all this, should we find them doing?—Hardening themselves by infidel reasonings, by stoical apathy? Endeavouring to banish all sense of their sorrows, by repairing to the dissipations of the world?

21*

—They would rather die at their Saviour's feet, saying, " Carest thou not that we perish ?"—They invite feeling; but this is their language:

" What should I wait or wish for then
    From creatures, earth, and dust ?
  They make our expectations vain,
    And disappoint our trust."

" Where is God my maker, who giveth songs in the night ? Therefore will I look unto the Lord, I will wait for the God of my salvation, my God will hear me. From the end of the earth will I cry unto thee, when my heart is overwhelmed: lead me to the rock that is higher than I." This is well. It is therefore enjoined, " Call upon me in the day of trouble." But it is not enough to *seek* God in our afflictions—we must *serve* him. It is,

II. THE DUTY HERE ENJOINED. " Glorify ye the Lord in the fires."

The glory of God is essential or declarative. We cannot add to the former. In this sense, he is " exalted above all blessing and praise. Our goodness extendeth not to him." But " the heavens declare the glory of God : all his works praise him." How ? By the impressions and displays of his perfections: by showing us what he is, and what he deserves.

Thus Christians are appointed to " show forth the praises"—virtues—excellences— " of him who hath called them out of darkness into his marvellous light:" which is done by their language and by their lives. Hence it is easy to see that we glorify God in our afflictions, when we verbally and practically acknowledge

His *agency*—that nothing comes to pass by chance—that his providence is concerned in all our trials—that " there is not an evil in the city, and the Lord hath not done it." Many walk all through life and never meet with God. Whatever occurs, whether it be pleasing or painful, never reminds them of him. When they experience a distressing event, they stop at second causes; they are kept from God by the very instrumentality he employs. They exclaim, " Oh! It was that unlucky servant; it was that perfidious friend; it was that malicious enemy." But, if Eli had met with it, he would have said, " It is the Lord, let him do what seemeth him good:" Job would have said, " The Lord gave, and the Lord hath taken away: What! shall we receive good at the Lord's hand, and shall we not receive evil ?"—We glorify God in our afflictions, when we verbally and practically acknowledge

His *rectitude*. " He is righteous in all his ways, and holy in all his works ;" and none of our troubles can deny this. Let us always be concerned to keep God free of all blame. Let all our reflections turn upon ourselves. Let us own that he is justified when he speaketh, and clear when he judgeth; that we have no reason to complain, whatever we suffer, for he has punished us infinitely less than our iniquities deserve. In this way Daniel gave him glory : " O Lord, righteousness belongeth unto thee, but unto us confusion of face, as it is this day." So did David: " I know O Lord, that thy judgments are right, and that thou in faithfulness hast afflicted me." We glorify God in our afflictions, when we verbally and practically acknowledge

His *wisdom*. " He is a God of knowledge;" and this regulates his corrections, and even every circumstance attached to them. It may not be easy always to see this, because we do not fully know ourselves, our defects, and our maladies; and therefore we cannot judge properly of the means employed to cure and improve us. But of this we may be assured, that he never errs in the time, the place, the continuance, the instrument, the kind of affliction—it is precisely the very thing we need; and nothing could be altered without injury. We glorify God in our afflictions, when we verbally and practically acknowledge

His *goodness*. For this is really the principle from which proceeds every sorrow that wrings the heart. Severity is often evidential of care and of regard. If God was not concerned for your welfare, why does he employ means to do you good ? Does the husbandman prune and manure the tree that he is going to cut down ? No—but that which he wishes to save and to fructify. Is it kind to rebuke a friend, or to countenance his faults ? Is it kind in a father to suffer the child to have his own will, or to impose upon him salutary restraints, and to urge his attention to things which will qualify him for future life ? " We have had fathers of our flesh which corrected us, and we gave them reverence: shall we not much rather be in subjection unto the Father of spirits, and live ? For they verily for a few days chastened us after their own pleasure; but he for our profit, that we might be partakers of his holiness. Now no chastening for the present seemeth to be joyous, but grievous: nevertheless, afterward it yieldeth the peaceable fruit of righteousness unto them which are exercised thereby." If his aim in your afflictions be to prevent that which is your disgrace and ruin; if it be to promote that which is your glory and happiness; if it be to make you wise, humble, tender-hearted, spiritually-minded; to wean you from earth and fit you for heaven—how obvious is the love of God in sending them! But his love is to be acknowledged not only in the *design* of affliction, but in its *alleviations*. These are numerous, and a grateful mind will look after them. " It is trying—but it might have been worse. I have lost one comfort—but some have lost all. I am in trouble—but I have the sympathy of friends; I have the promises of Scripture; I have the presence of Him who said, Fear not."—We glorify God in our afflictions, when we verbally and practically acknowledge

His *power*. This regards our support and deliverance, and is to keep us from all hasty and dismal conclusions. For by nothing do we dishonour God more than by our despondency. Is any thing too hard for the Lord? However dark the scene may be, he can turn the shadow of death into the morning. If when he comes to save us, he finds no way of escape, he can easily make one. Read the history of Joseph, and of David. Observe the relief of Elijah in famine; and the deliverance of Daniel in the lions' den—and learn to trust in your almighty and wonder-working Friend. You say perhaps many of these things were supernatural.—They were. And that we are not to expect a repetition of miracles.—It is acknowledged. But he who performed these wonders is still alive, and the same yesterday, to-day, and for ever. He is as near to you as he was to his people of old; and you are as dear to him as they were. But, alas! we are not "strong in faith, giving glory to God." Israel "limited the Holy One of Israel," and so do we; and like them we do it after the wonders he has shown us. We forget "the years of the right hand of the Most High," and every fresh difficulty chills our hope, and forces our confidence to a stand. But this is wrong. We ought to be peculiarly concerned to "glorify God in the fires."—

III. We proceed to examine THE REASONS. There are three. The first is derived from *opportunity*—the second from *obligation*—the third from *hope*.

First. You ought to glorify God in the fires, because you have the finest *opportunity*. The scene naturally awakens attention, and fixes observation upon you. Nothing preaches like a fact. Nothing is so impressive as the graces of a Christian in trouble. Infidels have been convinced, the wicked have been reclaimed, the weak have been strengthened, the timid encouraged by what they have seen and heard in the hour of affliction. How much, therefore, should you prize such a useful providence, and how anxious should you be to improve such an opportunity, to illustrate your principles, to exemplify the advantages of religion, to recommend the master you serve! Let it not be a price in the hand of fools. It will be painful to look back upon such a season neglected. It will be dreadful to review such a season perverted. Yet this is often done by improper behaviour, by ungracious tempers, by passionate words.

Secondly. The *obligations* you are under to the blessed God, should induce you to glorify him in the fires. Once you had no being. He called, and you came—not in the contemptible nature of a worm—but "a little lower than the angels." What wonders are there in thy body! Yet this is the baser part. You have conscience, reason, immortality. He has taught you more than the beasts of the earth, and made you wiser than the fowls of the air. There is a spirit in you, and the "inspiration of the Almighty giveth it understanding." And is all this to enable you to labour for shining dust with the covetous? To run after air with the ambitious? To dive into mud and mire with the sensual and vicious? Should you not "worship and fall down, and kneel before the Lord your Maker?" By whom have you been upheld from the womb? At whose table have you been daily fed? From whose wardrobe have you been clothed? There is not a comfort in life but gives God a title to thy praise. But he has greater, dearer claims. Go to the manger, the garden, the cross. See him not sparing his own Son, but delivering him up for us all. See him exalting this Sufferer "to be a Prince and a Saviour; to give repentance unto Israel and remission of sins." What has he done for thee in the application of this free and full redemption? Has he opened thine eyes, and turned thy feet into the path of peace.—What has he done for thee since thou hast known him? He has ever left thee? Has he ever turned away thy prayer from him, or his mercy from thee? And is it for you to be wrapped up in selfishness? How unworthy a creature; but how much more unworthy a Christian! When a man is writing a book, says an old divine, he ought often to look back to the title, and see whether he is conforming to it, or deviating from it; and so he tells us we should often turn back and inquire the end of our creation and our redemption, in order that we may regulate ourselves by it. We ought—we ought—to "reckon ourselves to be dead indeed unto sin, but alive unto God, through Jesus Christ our Lord."

Thirdly. *Hope* should influence you. Such a disposition to glorify God in the fires is productive of your own advantage. God is a good master. Though we owe him all the obedience we render, and it is impossible for any of our works to be meritorious, yet his grace *has* made them rewardable—and "*verily* there is a reward for the righteous." We *cannot* be losers by any thing we do for him. You may often study the wishes, and promote the interests of men, and meet with no suitable return. But he renders love for love, service for service, in a proportion infinitely increased. "Them that honour me I will honour, and they that despise me shall be lightly esteemed."

One of these two things is certain, as the consequence of sanctifying the Lord in your afflictions.

First: the removal of them. For when the end is answered, the dispensation will cease. As soon as we are silent, and submit, the rod drops out of our heavenly Father's hand, and he cries, "Is Ephraim my dear son! is he a pleasant child! for since I spake against him, I do earnestly remember him still: therefore my bowels are troubled for him; I will surely have mercy upon him, saith the Lord."

Or, Secondly: Indemnification for them; so that the continuance shall subserve our welfare more than the withdrawment. And this can easily be done by the internal supports of grace, and the future recompenses of glory.

Such are the arguments to enforce this duty. But I hear you say—

> "Lord, can a feeble, helpless worm
> Perform a task so hard?
> Thy grace must all the work perform,
> And give the free reward."

It must. And there are two things I wish you to learn with regard to this grace.

The one is, the necessity, the absolute necessity of it. Without this you can do nothing, suffer nothing as you ought.

The other is, the sufficiency of it for every purpose in the divine life. It is shameful to hear Christians talking as if their duties were impracticable, or their crosses intolerable. It is disgraceful to hear them excusing their improper carriage in affliction on the ground of weakness; O! who could help it; it was so trying! What do you mean by weakness? Your own strength separate from the succours of the Gospel? Of this you cannot have too deep a sense. But are you not a Christian? Are you not in union with one who says, "My grace is sufficient for thee?" Are you ever required to "be strong" in yourselves? No—but "in the grace there is in Christ Jesus." And "in him all fulness dwells." View, therefore, your difficulties in connexion with your supplies. View his commands in connexion with his promises, and courageously face all—saying with Paul; "I know both how to be abased, and I know how to abound: every where and in all things I am instructed both to be full and to be hungry, both to abound and to suffer need. I can do all things through Christ which strengtheneth me."

DISCOURSE LXIX.

THE CONNEXION BETWEEN CHRISTIANS AND ANGELS.

We are come—to an innumerable company of Angels.—Heb. xii. 22.

How numerous, how various are our obligations to the Scriptures of truth! How they rouse, how they extend, how they enlarge, how they refine our views and our sentiments! They lead us backward; and we behold the fair frame of nature springing out of chaos. They draw us forward; and we see the heavens passing away with a great noise, the elements melting with fervent heat, the earth also, and all the works that are therein burnt up. They tell us to look inward; and under this burden of flesh, this perishing clay, we discern a spirit in man, immaterial, immortal, and able to subsist independent of the body. They call us to look upward; and drawing back the vail, they show us an order of beings, far above human, and with which Christians have the honour to be already connected. It is the testimony of the Apostle in the words before us. "Ye are come to an innumerable company of angels."

We are come to them five ways. We are come to them as FRIENDS—as ATTENDANTS—as WITNESSES—as PATTERNS—as ASSOCIATES.—As friends, from whom we were separated by the Fall—as attendants, whose care is to follow us through life—as witnesses, whose observation we are to reverence—as patterns, whose example we are to imitate—as associates, with whom we are to blend our future being, and from whom we shall derive no inconsiderable portion of our happiness.

I. WE ARE TO THEM AS FRIENDS, from whom we have been separated by the Fall.

Men and angels, in their original creation, formed but one family; and though they differed in nature and in residence, they had one father, and there would have been a free and pleasing intercourse between them. But sin destroyed the harmony of the world. Sin disunited heaven and earth. Sin separated not only between God and men, but between angels and men. When man revolted from his lawful Sovereign, they remained in their allegiance: and as sin rendered God our enemy, so it rendered angels our enemies too. Accordingly we read of their being the executioners of the Divine vengeance. As soon as Adam and Eve were expelled from Paradise, an angel rushed to the gate with a flaming sword, to keep the way to the tree of life. An angel of the Lord smote all the first-born in Egypt. An angel of the Lord, to punish David for numbering the people, goes from Dan to Beer-sheba, and seven hundred thousand victims seal his angry commission. An angel of the Lord in one night enters the camp of Sennacherib, and destroys one hundred and eighty-five thousand men. An angel of the Lord smote Herod, that he died. We pretend not to understand the prophecies in the book of the Revelation, but it is certain, that when the nations are angry, the angels are to pour out the vials of the wrath of Almighty God upon the earth. And perhaps, says a judicious expositor, if an inspired history of our own eventful times were written, the defeat of many a haughty worm would be traced up to such an awful agency. —Hence, when they have appeared to man, they have been objects of terror.

But in consequence of the mediation of our Lord and Saviour, the breach is healed. We are reconciled not only to God, but to the angels. It is the meaning of the Apostle, when he says, "Having made peace through the blood of his cross, by him to reconcile all things unto himself; by him, I say, whether they be things in earth, or things in heaven. That in the dispensation of the fulness of times he might gather together in one all things in Christ, both which are in heaven, and which are on earth; even in him." So that the angels now view us again with delight. They call themselves our fellow-servants, our fellow-worshippers, our brethren. Men and angels form again one family: *they* remained in their original state; *we* are restored to it; and such is the disposition of those celestial beings, that they do not repine, like the elder brother, at the return of the prodigal, but rejoice to welcome the younger branches of the family home; "There is joy in the presence of the angels of God over one sinner that repenteth."

II. WE ARE COME TO THEM AS ATTENDANTS, whose care is to follow us through life. The alarm that some religious people have taken at this doctrine, as if it interfered with the glory of God in their preservation, is absurd. God is the author of all good. He is the guide, the guard, the strength, the consolation of his people: but does this imply that he does not employ means in doing them good? And may we not in this case argue from analogy? He "spreads a table before us in the wilderness," but not immediately. He commands his sun to shine, and his rain to descend; yea, he requires our own exertions to prepare the supplies of nature for our use. He employs us to aid each other. We are at once the subjects and the instruments of his goodness; *he* gives, and *we* diffuse. Have you never been in sickness; never laid on a bed of languishing? And has no friend by sympathy, by kindness, by attention, reminded you of the promise—"I will strengthen him upon the bed of languishing: I will make all his bed in his sickness!" Thus too he makes use of ministers to "turn us from darkness to light;" to be "helpers of joy; to comfort us concerning our faith." Why then should it be deemed a thing absurd, or incredible, that God should employ the ministrations of angels for the welfare of his people?

Neither is it an argument against this doctrine, that the proofs of it fall under the observation of our senses. We walk by faith, and not by sight. How many things do we admit as real, that are not visible! How little is the babe aware of the fond attentions of her who bare him; and how long is it before he can estimate his obligations to a mother's vigilance! She can afterwards inform him how she denied, and exposed herself for his sake; how she watched over him by day and by night; fled with him to a purer air, or snatched him from a burning couch: but he was not sensible of it at the time. And should he happen to be blind, how much would be done for him all through life, which, though he would enjoy in the effects, he could never see. If we had organs of perception adapted to the spiritual world, what striking scenes should we constantly witness! But our incapacity does not render them less true. The king of Syria had sent an army to Dothan to secure Elisha. And when the servant of the man of God was risen early, and had gone forth, behold, an host compassed the city, both with horses and chariots. He therefore cried out, "Alas, my master, what shall we do!" He *saw* the danger; this was material. But Elisha knew the defence was as real as it was invisible. "Fear not," says he, "for they that be with us are more than they that be with them." Where? says the servant. "And Elisha prayed, and said, Lord, open, I pray thee, his eyes, that he may see. And the Lord opened the eyes of the young man; and he saw: and, behold, the mountain was full of horses and chariots of fire round about Elisha."

Thus the believer is safe in the midst of danger, "kept by the power of God through faith unto salvation." And though he may be despised, and overlooked by his fellowmen because he is poor and needy, yet has he more glorious attendance than any worldly monarch. God's noblest creatures are his children's servants. "Such honour have all the saints."

The Scripture is express upon this subject. An angel fed Elijah under the juniper tree. An angel brought to Daniel an explanation of prophecy. An angel of the Lord released Peter from prison; and comforted Paul in the storm. Angels carried the soul of Lazarus into Abraham's bosom. "The angel of the Lord encampeth round about them that fear him, and delivereth them. For he shall give his angels charge over thee, to keep thee in all thy ways. They shall bear thee up in their hands, lest thou dash thy foot against a stone. Take heed that ye despise not one of these little ones: for I say unto you, that in heaven their angels do always behold the face of my Father which is in heaven. Are they not all ministering spirits, sent forth to minister for them who shall be heirs of salvation?"

III. WE ARE COME TO THEM AS WITNESSES, whose observation we are to reverence.

It would be well for us to remember that we are always in sight. The eyes of our fellow-creatures are *often* upon us; and if

21

they were always upon us, they would restrain us from a thousand sins. But invisible beings *always* behold us. No consideration indeed is like the omniscience of God; "Thou God seest me!" We should, therefore, "set the Lord always before us." But motives do not always impress according to their real importance. We are like children, upon whom various motives operate, according to their age and disposition: the thought, therefore, that we are come to an innumerable company of angels, may strike us even more than a sublimer consideration. Now this is the fact.

We are a spectacle to angels as well as to men. The Apostle enforces a proper behaviour in religious assemblies, "because of the angels." And charges Timothy not only "before God, but his elect angels."

The angels are our observers, and what they witness they will be called upon hereafter to report. For the proceedings of the great day will be judicial; we must "give an account of the deeds done in the body, whether they be good, or whether they be evil;" and we read that the books will be opened, and witnesses called to depose. You despise my teaching, said our Saviour to the Jews, but you shall hear of it again. "The men of Nineveh shall rise in judgment with this generation, and shall condemn it: because they repented at the preaching of Jonas; and, behold, a greater than Jonas is here. The queen of the south shall rise up in the judgment with this generation, and shall condemn it: for she came from the uttermost parts of the earth to hear the wisdom of Solomon; and, behold, a greater than Solomon is here." And thus will it be with others.

I see hearers brought forward as evidence against their ministers—"You never warned us to flee from the wrath to come. You never convinced us of the depravity of our nature, and our need of 'the washing of regeneration, and the renewing of the Holy Ghost.' You made lies our refuge, and lulled us to sleep on the brink of ruin. Cursed watchman, you gave us no warning till it was too late. Cursed physician, you withheld the only remedy; you administered poison!"

I see ministers brought forward as evidence against their hearers. "Lord, I addressed them from sabbath to sabbath, with affection and fidelity. I thundered the terrors of the Law, and whispered the promises of the Gospel. I am clear from their blood. I warned and I wooed them, but they would not hear."

I see parents brought forward as witnesses against children. Ah, cruel, but necessary task! "Lord, we established thy worship in our family. We led them early to know the Scriptures. We often prayed for them, and with them. We bedewed them with our tears. We set forth the blessedness of thy ways, and rendered religion lovely. But they

would none of our counsel, they despised all our reproof."

I see children brought forward as witnesses against their parents. Oh! how dreadful to hear them say, "You taught us to swear, but not to pray. You led us into the dissipations of the world, but you never fixed in our minds the principles of the Gospel. In your lives we saw nothing but instances of levity, inconsistency, irreligion. Unnatural monsters, to bring us into existence, and leave us exposed to eternal ruin!"—Thus children shall rise up against their parents, and cause them to be put to death.

But angels will be some of the principal witnesses, in that great and terrible day of the Lord. They have inspected you perfectly. They can distinguish between the circumstances which confound us. There are cases in which two guilty individuals are implicated. They accuse each other; and no human being was privy to their wickedness. But angels saw Abel and Cain when they were alone together in the field. They can decide in an intrigue, who was the seducer, and who the seduced. What a world of private wickedness will they develope!

IV. WE ARE COME TO THEM AS PATTERNS, whose example we are to imitate. To these models our Saviour himself leads us in the form of devotion he gave to his disciples: in which he teaches us to pray, "Thy will be done on earth as it is done in heaven." And even now, this prayer is accomplished. Between believers and angels there is a resemblance, though not an equality. Wherein does it appear?

It appears in the nature of their obedience. We are told that the angels, however great, find it their privilege to serve. Though they "excel in strength, they do his commandments, hearkening unto the voice of his word." And their obedience is ready, without delay; cheerful, without reluctance; constant, without intermission; and impartial, without choice. The reason is, they love God, and it is his will alone they regard; whether, therefore, he calls them to come, or orders them to go; whether he requires them to ascend, or descend; they are equally satisfied, as they have equally an opportunity of showing their submission to him. And whatever low idea you may form of a Christian, such is, and such must be, his leading desire; and his prevailing endeavour.

It appears in their union. These beings have various degrees among them. We read of "angels and archangels; of thrones and dominions; principalities and powers. Yet these produce no contempt, no envy, no eagerness to dictate, no backwardness to co-operate. They perfectly harmonize. They have but one spirit, one wish. The Scripture represents them as uniting their voices, and answering to each other in their sacred songs.

"One cried unto another, and said, Holy, holy, holy, is the Lord of hosts, the whole earth is full of his glory." Shall I say that Christians do resemble all this! Alas! there is too little of it in our churches and assemblies. We meet together, and apparently unite in the same exercises; but if our voices accord, our hearts disagree. One hears with humility, another with captiousness. One finds the word and eats it, another goes after his covetousness. One "worships God in spirit and in truth," another in form and pretence. What a scene of confusion must one of our congregations present to the eye of Him that searcheth the heart! Even among those who are Christians indeed, there is too little of this blessed harmony and concurrence. Yet there is a degree of it. God has given them "one heart and one way." They agree "touching the things they should ask of their heavenly Father." They "magnify his Name together;" and in a little time their mutual prejudices will be done away, and they shall see eye to eye; they "shall all come in the unity of the faith, and of the knowledge of the Son of God, unto a perfect man, unto the measure of the stature of the fulness of Christ."

It appears in the subject of their study. The angels are proverbial for knowledge: we read of being "wise as an angel of God." Had we heard only of such exalted beings, we should be anxious to know what things they deemed most worthy of their attention. But we are informed. They are "the sufferings of Christ and the glory that should follow—which things the angels desire to look into." We never read of their being politicians, philosophers, naturalists, astronomers. Doubtless they contemplate the works of creation and providence, and trace the appearances of God in them. But as the redemption of the world by our Lord Jesus Christ is the greatest display of the divine perfections, their eyes seem taken off from every other object, and fixed upon this. And they are not satisfied to take a transient, superficial view of it, but gaze and examine; and the more they know, the more they wish to know. Are you like-minded? Is this the most welcome subject to your hearts? The most important to your minds? Or are you engrossed with trifles! Can you climb the skies, number the stars, fathom the ocean, penetrate the bowels of the earth, and—"neglect this great salvation!" In the eye of an angel you are a trifler. You disregard what they above all things esteem. You are no Christian—a Christian is like an angel. *This* constitutes his attraction; and he exclaims, "I determine to know nothing save Jesus Christ and him crucified: God forbid that I should glory, save in the cross of our Lord Jesus Christ, by whom the world is crucified unto me, and I unto the world."

It appears in their worship. They adore the incarnate Redeemer. When he bringeth his first begotten into the world, he saith, "Yea, and let all the angels of God worship him." When he was born there was "suddenly a multitude of the heavenly host, praising God, and saying, Glory to God in the highest, and on earth peace, good-will towards men." John heard them saying with a loud voice, "Worthy is the Lamb that was slain to receive power, and riches, and wisdom, and strength, and honour, and glory, and blessing." And is there a Christian upon earth that does not delight in the same praise —that does not sing,

"Jesus is worthy to receive
Honour and power divine:
And blessings more than we can give
Be, Lord, for ever thine."

They are his most heavenly moments, in which he is fullest of this interesting theme, and can breathe out his very soul in saying, "Unto him that loved us, and washed us from our sins in his own blood, and hath made us kings and priests unto God, and his Father, to him be glory and dominion for ever and ever. Amen."

V. WE ARE TO COME TO THEM AS ASSOCIATES, with whom we are to blend our future being, and from whom we shall derive no inconsiderable part of our happiness.

It is not good for man to be alone. He is formed for social enjoyment; and it is a great source of his present pleasure. The representation of heaven meets this propensity. We are assured that it is a state of society. And there are two classes of beings that will contribute much to our satisfaction and improvement.

The one is endearing.—It takes in those you loved in life, with whom you took sweet counsel together, and went to the house of God in company, your pious friends and relations, who now sleep in Jesus. With what reluctance you yielded them up!—Sorrowing most of all that you should see their face, and hear their voice no more! Memory from month to month renews the anguish, and opens afresh the wounds which time was beginning to heal. But wipe away your tears. They are not lost. Their separation from you is but temporary. You shall see and hear them again. You shall know them; and shall together review all the way by which the Lord has led you in the wilderness.

The other is dignifying.—It comprehends patriarchs, prophets, apostles, martyrs—*angels.* You shall be introduced to company of the very first sort. Angels are the flower of the creation; and the poorest, meanest believer shall enjoy it; and be prepared for it. There are many now whose excellences you venerate, but their pre-eminence confounds and embarrasses you. You long to be in their presence, but shrink from the interview. You could wish to be with them without being seen or heard, such a sense have you of their wisdom and your weakness; their goodness and your unworthiness. But nothing of this perplexity which now often robs us of half our social enjoyments, shall hereafter be known. Whatever sense we have of our inferiority, it will not be disagreeable; we shall feel no fear, no reluctance. These glorious beings are all generosity, tenderness, and love. They will receive us with joy. We shall find ourselves perfectly free and happy. With what pleasure will they communicate their knowledge! And with what ecstasy will you receive it! How instructive, how sublime will our intercourse be! How delightful to find ourselves translated from this bedlam-world, this Mesech,

> " From these low grounds where sorrows grow
> And every pleasure dies—"

to that better, that heavenly country: and to exchange the society of men, vain men, vexing men, sinful men, for "an innumerable company of angels."

Let us conclude with two questions.

First. How can it be said that "we *are* come to" this blessed assembly? Are Christians already in heaven? Is it possible to conceive how we *are* come to this innumerable company of angels, as *friends* who are reconciled to us, as *attendants* who care for us, as *witnesses* to observe, and as *examples* to stimulate us? All this regards the present state; but to be with them as our eternal *associates*, from whom we are to derive so much of our happiness—this regards a future state. How then are we said to be already come to this glorious community?—By the certainty of the event. By promise—and "the Scripture cannot be broken." By hope —and "hope maketh not ashamed." By anticipation, by earnests, by foretastes of this exalted felicity. A real Christian needs not to be informed that "he that believeth hath everlasting life." He is often reminded of the words of the Apostle, He "hath raised you up, and made you to sit together with him in heavenly places." In the closet, in the temple, in the communion of saints he knows that heaven is not entirely future; it is already commenced. And whatever the people of the world may think of religion, he can look them in the face, and say,

> " The men of grace have found
>   Glory begun below;
> And heavenly fruits on earthly ground
>   From faith and hope may grow.
>
> " The hill of Zion yields
>   A thousand sacred sweets
> Before we reach the heavenly fields,
>   Or walk the golden streets."

Secondly. To whom are *you* come? I shudder as I proceed to press this inquiry. I have been speaking of heaven: but remember, there is another society—a society of wicked and miserable beings—a society of which the devil is the head—a society that is constantly labouring to multiply its victims, and bring them into the same place of torment. How many are hastening to mix with it! To how many will the Judge say, "Depart, ye cursed, into everlasting fire, prepared for the devil and his angels?" Will this be your destiny in the great day? What! instead of going with the righteous, will you "be led forth with the workers of iniquity?" Instead of joining God and his angels, will you have your "portion with the devil and *his* angels?"

There cannot be a more awful question. And one would naturally conclude that you could "not give sleep to your eyes, or slumber to your eyelids," till you had endeavoured to answer it. But you ask, Is it possible to answer it? It is: and observe, I beseech you, the rule of judgment. It is not an arbitrary one. It is founded in justice and reason. It is not impulse, but character. It is not some unaccountable impression, but the principles that govern you, the dispositions of the heart, the habits of the life. By these you are to try yourselves. To know what you will be in another world, you must inquire what you are in this. To decide with whom you will have your portion in eternity, you must determine who are your companions in time. "Be not deceived, God is not mocked, for whatsoever a man soweth, that shall he also reap: for he that soweth to the flesh shall of the flesh reap corruption; but he that soweth to the Spirit shall of the Spirit reap life everlasting."

Whom then do you most admire?—Are they "the saints, the excellent of the earth, in whom is all your delight?" Have you taken hold of "the skirt of him that is a Jew, saying, I will go with you, for I have heard that God is with you." Look forward and rejoice. As sure as you can appeal to God when you come to die, and say, "Lord, I have loved the habitation of thy house, and the place where thine honour dwelleth," you may with confidence and success plead— "Gather not my soul with sinners, nor my life with bloody men." Being let go, you will repair to your own company.

But are you vain? Are you ambitious? Are you lifted up with pride?—You will "fall into the condemnation of the devil." Can you vilify and reproach the good? Can you rejoice in discovering their blemishes, and magnifying their infirmities?—Are you regardless of truth?—Do you indulge in falsehood and hypocrisy?—Do you hate your neighbour, and harbour in your bosom malice and revenge?—Do you endeavour, by your influence or example, to poison the principles, and sap the morals of those around you? There is already a connexion established, that death will only discover and complete; your resemblance points out your party and your doom—you are devils by anticipation, and must have your portion with him who is the "accuser of the brethren; a liar; a murderer from the beginning; a roaring lion, going about seeking whom he may devour."

Oh! to be—for ever a companion with Robespierre, with Nero, with Judas, with Pharaoh—with the devil—and his angels!! Surely there is enough in the thought, to keep any man in his senses all his life long from the paths of the destroyer, and to induce him to pray every moment, "Hide thy face from my sin, and blot out all my transgression. Create in me a clean heart, O God, and renew a right spirit within me. Save me, and I shall be saved; heal me, and I shall be healed; for thou art my praise." May God inspire you with these desires, and to him be glory. Amen.

DISCOURSE LXX.

THE AGED SAINT COMFORTED.

And even to old age I am he; and even to your hoar hairs will I carry you: I have made, and I will bear; even I will carry, and will deliver you.—Isaiah xlvi. 4.

SUCH was the address of God to his peculiar people, the Jews. He has a peculiar people now; and we need not ascend up into heaven, and examine the book of life, to know who they are. We have a copy of this book of life in our possession. It is the Scripture. There we have not only their portion secured, but their characters described. Let us take one exemplification only. "We are the circumcision," says the Apostle, " who worship God in the spirit; and rejoice in Christ Jesus, and have no confidence in the flesh."

Do you "*worship God*"—in public? Alone! Habitually! Do you worship God "*in the Spirit?*" Have you only "a form of godliness while you deny the power thereof?" Do you "draw nigh to him with your mouth, and honour him with your lips, while your heart is far from him?" Or do you pray, "Unite my heart to fear thy name?"

Do you "*rejoice?*" Are you grateful for your mercies; or full of murmuring and complaining? Is the service of God your pleasure, as well as your employment? Your privilege as well as your duty? Do you "rejoice in *Christ Jesus?*" Do you find consolation in him when the world is a vale of tears? When creatures fail you? Are you encouraged by the thought that there is such a Saviour? That he is so suitable to your case? So sufficient to save? Do you, even while unable to claim him, rejoice in hope; and under every dejection, throwing yourself at his feet, say,

"Should worlds conspire to drive me hence,
Moveless and firm this heart shall lie;
Resolved, for that's my last defence,
If I must perish, here to die!"

Have you "*no confidence in the flesh?*" No dependence upon your own resources, for your happiness? No dependence upon your own righteousness, for your justification? No dependence on your own strength, for your sanctification? No dependence upon your own wisdom, for your guidance?

These questions we ask so early in the discourse—that if you find yourselves to be strangers to the character of the Israel of God, you may be affected with your condition; and that, while you hear of their blessedness, you may sigh after it:—and if you are able to determine in your favour, and humbly hope, that you have avouched the Lord to be your God, and joined yourselves to him in a perpetual covenant, you may sit and hear, with gratitude and joy, that you have chosen that good part which shall not be taken away from you.

I. WHAT HAS GOD DONE? *He has made you.*

II. WHAT WILL HE DO? *Carry and deliver you.*

III. How LONG? How FAR? *To old age; to gray hairs.* "And even to your old age I am he; and even to hoar hairs will I carry you: I have made, and I will bear; even I will carry, and will deliver you."

I. WHAT HAS GOD DONE FOR YOU ALREADY? "*I have made.*" This brings him very near. It presents him to us as our Creator; as the Fountain of life. Others have claimed us as children; and we early learned to say, My father; my father. But to *them* we owe our being subordinately, and instrumentally: to *Him* we owe it supremely and efficiently. They were "fathers of our flesh:" but *He* is "the Father of our spirits."

I love to realize this relation. Is my body fearfully and wonderfully made? Do I possess reason and immortality? Are matter and spirit, clay and thought, strangely united together, to render me the being I am? "His hands have made me and fashioned me." I behold, I feel his wisdom, power, and goodness; and at once embrace him and adore! The view is instructive; it is encouraging. The constitution I possess, limited as it is in capacity, and subject as it is to infirmity, he gave me. The degree of health and strength I enjoy, he assigned me. He knows my frame; and remembers that I am but dust. He sees that to will is present with me, though how to perform that which is good I find not: he knows that the spirit indeed is willing, though the flesh is weak." Why does Peter admonish those that suffer according to the will of God to commit the keeping of their souls to him in well doing, "as unto a faithful Creator?"—Because he who made me is perfectly acquainted with all I feel; because he who made me is able to save me—

because he who made me has a benign propension to the work of his own hands. Do I form a garden, or plant a tree? I feel a propriety in it. That upon which I expend my exertion and care will soon be interesting and endeared. If a fine piece of statuary could be possessed of intelligence, the figure would find much less satisfaction in the workman than the workman in the figure. A real benefactor feels more pleasure in doing a kindness than the beneficiary feels in receiving it. What a strength of attachment has God produced in all creatures towards their young! And will the author, and the model, of all these sympathies abandon those who live, and move, and have their being in him?

But there is another and a higher operation of which the Scripture speaks. "This people have I formed for myself; they shall show forth my praise." We are his workmanship, created in Christ Jesus unto good works. "If any man be in Christ, he is a new creature." He has a new nature; new powers; a new heart; new eyes; new ears—not physically, but morally new: not new as to substance, but as to transformation and use. It is the production of a Christian out of a man: it is the change not only of that which was vicious into virtuous, but of that which was earthly into heavenly; and that which was natural into spiritual. It is of this the Apostle speaks when he says to the Philippians; "I am confident of this very thing, that he who has begun a good work in you, will perform it until the day of Jesus Christ." Whence it appears, that this operation is not only certain in its issue, but *divine* in its origin and progress; and, therefore, *excellent* in its nature. All God's works are good; but this is called *good* by way of distinction. O Christian! it is the *best* work God ever did for thee. His making thee a man was far less than his making thee *a new man*. The one brought thee into the world of nature; the other into the world of grace. The one made thee a partaker of a life full of vanity and sorrow; the other commenced in thee "the life of God!" As the creature of his power, thou art encouraged to hope in him; but this relation alone does not secure thee from his displeasure—for it is written, "Because they are a people of no understanding, therefore he that made them will not have mercy on them, and he that formed them will show them no favour." But, as the subject of his grace, a foundation is laid for everlasting confidence and joy in him. He "taketh pleasure in them that fear him, in them that hope in his mercy." He has said, "I will never leave thee nor forsake thee:" therefore they may boldly say, "the Lord is my helper; I will not fear;" and plead with him, like David; "Perfect, O God, that which concerneth me: thy mercy, O Lord, endureth for ever; forsake not the works of thine own hands." Our

promise echoes back the prayer, and leads us,

II. To consider WHAT GOD WILL DO. "*I will carry. I will deliver.*"

First. He will carry. This implies something more than to guide and to lead them. It supposes helplessness and inability on their side; and tender support and assistance on his. If a man has any thing very valuable, and peculiarly esteemed, he would not willingly leave it, or intrust it to another. God's people are his jewels. They are precious in his sight, and honourable, and he has loved them. A father carries his child, and the burden is a pleasure. Moses, in his improper expostulation with God, says, "Have I conceived all this people? Have I begotten them, that thou shouldest say unto me, Carry them in thy bosom, as a nursing father beareth the sucking child, unto the land which thou swarest unto their fathers?" The imagery is here taken from a journey. A family is traveling. But the babe cannot go alone. The father is mentioned as being the stronger parent of the two; or, rather, it intimates—that the mother is dead, perhaps she expired in giving life—she is left behind—the father therefore becomes the nurse, lays the bereaved babe in his bosom, now doubly endeared, and goes forward. God has a large family; but, as Bishop Hall observes, none of his children can go alone. Yet they are not left to perish in their weakness. He will render them equal to the difficulties and duties of the Christian life. He will afford them seasonable and adequate succour. His grace shall be sufficient for them; and his strength shall be made perfect in their weakness. "Fear not," says he, "for I am with thee; be not dismayed, for I am thy God: I will strengthen thee; yea, I will help thee; yea, I will uphold thee with the right hand of my righteousness."

Secondly. He will deliver. This implies that they are exposed to danger; but that they shall not become a prey.

He delivers them *from* trouble. Who can imagine from how many evils you are *preserved* in a world like this—every day and every hour? From how many afflictions have you been *released* in your passage through life? How has he appeared for you when there seemed no possibility of escape? But he turned the shadow of death into the morning. He brought your souls out of prison—and compassed you about with songs of deliverance.

He delivers them *in* trouble. A state of suffering is a state of trial; and it is mentioned as a moral prodigy in the affliction of Job, that "in all this he sinned not, nor charged God foolishly." Rebellion against divine providence; distrust of God's goodness; impatience; envy at the exemptions and indulgences of others—to these and many other kindred sins, we are peculiarly liable in the day of adversity; and it is a distinguished privilege to be preserved from them, even if the distress should be continued.

He delivers them *by* trouble. But for "the thorn in the flesh, the messenger of Satan to buffet him," Paul would have been "exalted above measure." "Before I was afflicted," says David, "I went astray, but now have I kept thy word." It was "the hedge of thorns" that restrained the church from "finding her paths, and following her lovers." Who is not more indebted to his trials, than to his enjoyments?

And this leads us to another view of the deliverance here promised. Our bodily dangers are nothing to our spiritual. We should be chiefly concerned for the safety and welfare of the soul. Now what are our moral hazards? Is not "our adversary, the devil, like a roaring lion, going about seeking whom he may devour?" Do we not live in a world of error? Are we not surrounded with evil examples? Are there not "fleshly lusts that war against the soul?" Is there not "in us an evil heart of unbelief in departing from the living God?"—Who then can be saved? Who can hope to endure to the end?—No one but the Christian; and even *his* expectation would be no better than presumption, were it not that he has an Almighty Deliverer who is pledged to secure him. To him he looks: on him he relies. His defence is of God, that saveth the upright in heart. He "*is* able to keep him from falling, and to present him faultless before the presence of his glory with exceeding joy;" and he says to him, as David did to Abiathar, "Abide with me, for he that seeketh thy life seeketh my life, but with me thou shalt be in safeguard."

III. But how long? How far will his tenderness and care extend? *To old age; to hoar hairs.* "And even to your old age I am he; and even to hoar hairs will I carry you: I have made, and I will bear; even I will carry, and will deliver you."

This is a period in which a man is deprived of many of his relations and friends; is gazed on by a new generation; feels a thousand infirmities, anxieties, and distresses; and is reduced to dependence upon those around him. "When thou wast young," says our Saviour to Peter, "thou girdedst thyself, and walkedst whither thou wouldest: but when thou shalt be old, thou shalt stretch forth thy hands, and another shall gird thee, and carry thee whither thou wouldest not." Owing to the nature of this period Barzillai refuses the offers of a palace: "I am this day fourscore years old: and can I discern between good and evil? Can thy servant taste what I eat or what I drink? Can I hear any more the voice of singing men and singing women? Wherefore then should thy servant be yet a burden unto my lord the king?" Such also was the view David took of the same season: "The days of our years are threescore years and ten: and if by reason of strength they be fourscore years, yet is their strength labour and sorrow; for it is soon cut off, and we fly away." But Solomon has given us an enlarged representation of the decline of life; and he mentions the disadvantage of it to enforce an important duty: "Remember now thy Creator in the days of thy youth, while the evil days come not, nor the years draw nigh when thou shalt say, I have no pleasure in them." Then will you be unable to discharge the duties of religion; then will you require all its comforts; then how dreadful to encounter the remorse of reflection, and the horror of anticipation! "While the sun, or the light, or the moon, or the stars, be not darkened, nor the clouds return after the rain; in the day when the keepers of the house shall tremble, and the strong men shall bow themselves, and the grinders cease because they are few, and those that look out of the windows be darkened, and the doors shall be shut in the streets, when the sound of the grinding is low, and he shall rise up at the voice of the bird, and all the daughters of music shall be brought low; also when they shall be afraid of that which is high, and fears shall be in the way, and the almond-tree shall flourish, and the grasshopper shall be a burden, and desire shall fail: because man goeth to his long home, and the mourners go about the streets: or ever the silver cord be loosed, or the golden bowl be broken, or the pitcher be broken at the fountain, or the wheel broken at the cistern. Then shall the dust return to the earth as it was: and the spirit shall return unto God who gave it. Vanity of vanities, saith the preacher; all is vanity."

Such is the period to which the promise extends; and two things may be observed concerning it.

First. The promise does not necessarily suppose that you will reach this period. Immensely the majority of mankind die before time can snow upon their heads. There are few comparatively who "come to their grave in a full age, like as a shock of corn cometh in his season." The wonder is that there are so many.

> "Dangers stand thick through all the ground,
>   To push us to the tomb;
> And fierce diseases wait around,
>   To hurry mortals home.

> "Our life contains a thousand springs,
>   And dies if one be gone;
> Strange, that a harp of thousand strings
>   Should keep in tune so long!"

But the meaning is, that if you should reach this period, you need not be afraid of it; he will be with you, and "a very present help in trouble."

Secondly. It is only said that he will be with you "*to* old age, and *to* hoar hairs." He will be with you all *through* "the months of vanity; and the wearisome nights appointed you;" he will be with you even when "your heart and flesh fail you." This is implied. But it was not necessary to mention it—old age and death are so near each other—they touch. This subject displays

In the First place, The patience of God. Ye aged, are you not a wonder to yourselves! Are you not compelled to exclaim, "It is of the Lord's mercies that we are not consumed, because his compassions fail not!" What a number of provocations has he had to bear with from you in the course of sixty, seventy, eighty years! How soon would a fellow-creature, however kind and longsuffering have abandoned you! But he is God and not man. Even he has asked, "How long shall I be with you? How long shall I suffer you!" And his providence and grace have answered the question—" Even to your old age I am he; and even to hoar hairs will I carry you: I have made, and I will bear; even I will carry, and will deliver you."

The subject affords Secondly, Encouragement for those who are descended into the vale of years. Doubts may assail the mind of a believer to the last. And there are things that may peculiarly produce them at this period. Such as a consciousness of guilt arising from faithful reviews of life; and a sense of unworthiness resulting from present unprofitableness. They can now no longer actively serve God. The loss of animal spirits deprives them of those lively emotions they once enjoyed. The feeble body enervates the mind; trifles distract them; and they easily misjudge themselves.

But be of good comfort, ye aged servants of God. He will not turn you out of doors now your labour is over. He remembers "you, the kindness of your youth." He accepts of your desires and designs. He pities your infirmities. He is "the strength of your hearts, and your portion for ever." If the world is weary of you, he is not. If "lover and friend have been put far from you, and your acquaintances into darkness, the eternal God is your refuge, and underneath are the everlasting arms.

Your salvation is nearer than when you believed. "The night is far spent, the day is at hand." You are riding at anchor off the fair havens; and the next wind or tide will waft you in.

And cannot you trust him, after all the proofs you have had of his power, faithfulness, and love! Cannot you make this language your own! "By thee have I been holden up from the womb: thou art he that took me out of my mother's bowels: my praise shall be continually of thee. Cast me not off in the

time of old age; forsake me not when my strength faileth. My mouth shall show forth thy righteousness and thy salvation all the day; for I know not the numbers thereof. I will go in the strength of the Lord God: I will make mention of thy righteousness, even of thine only. O God, thou hast taught me from my youth: and hitherto have I declared thy wondrous works. Now also when I am old and grayheaded, O God, forsake me not; until I have showed thy strength unto this generation, and thy power to every one that is to come."

Thirdly. What shall I say to the hoary-headed sinner! I do not pretend to inform you that the world is vain: with this you *must* be already acquainted. But is it not strange that you continue to retain such a tenacious hold of it, "trembling at once with eagerness and age!" It seems less necessary to tell you that death is near—the young *may* die, the old *must*. But like Ephraim, gray hairs are here and there upon you, and you perceive it not. You promise yourselves time to come, when there is but a step between you and death. You have lived longer than thousands of your fellow-creatures; but to what purpose? The longsuffering of God was designed to lead you to repentance. Has it done so? Look back. What a scene! Time trifled and sinned away; faculties perverted; privileges neglected and abused! Nothing done for God or your generation!— Thy gray hairs are only a fool's cap.—Thou art ripe for ruin. And would it not be righteous in God to cut thee down instantly as a cumberer of the ground! If there be an object of pity on earth, thou art the man. There is nothing at present that can afford thee comfort. But thou art not excluded from hope. "He yet waits to be gracious, and is exalted to have mercy upon you." Go to him, heavy laden with years and sins. Late repentance is seldom true, but true repentance is never too late. O that I could hear you saying, Lord, save, I perish!

Finally. What a motive is there here to induce us all to become the Lord's followers! "A friend is born for adversity:" yet very little of this friendship is to be found. How many who possess a warm regard in prosperous and earlier life, cast us off in affliction and declining years! But he will be principally with us when we principally need his aid. We may live upon him when we cannot live for him.

Here are two suppositions.

You may die; and you may die soon. In this case, you "will be for ever with the Lord."

You may live, and live to old age. In this case, he will be continually with you. "And even to your old age I am he; and even to hoar hairs will I carry you: I have made, and I will bear; even I will carry, and will deliver you."

What remains?—Let the best of all masters have the most dutiful of all servants. As he is never weary in doing us good, may we never be weary in well-doing. "But be steadfast, unmoveable, always abounding in the work of the Lord, and, bringing forth fruit in old age, be fat and flourishing, to show that the Lord is upright. He is my rock, and there is no unrighteousness in him."

DISCOURSE LXXI.

GEHAZI.

But Gehazi, the servant of Elisha the man of God, said, Behold, my master hath spared Naaman this Syrian, in not receiving at his hands that which he brought: but, as the Lord liveth, I will run after him, and take somewhat of him. So Gehazi followed after Naaman. And when Naaman saw him running after him, he lighted down from the chariot to meet him, and said, Is all well? And he said, All is well. My master hath sent me, saying, Behold, even now there be come to me from Mount Ephraim two young men of the sons of the prophets: give them, I pray thee, a talent of silver, and two changes of garments. And Naaman said, Be content, take two talents. And he urged him, and bound two talents of silver in two bags, with two changes of garments, and laid them upon two of his servants; and they bare them before him. And when he came to the tower, he took them from their hand, and bestowed them in the house: and he let the men go, and they departed. But he went in, and stood before his master. And Elisha said unto him, Whence comest thou, Gehazi? And he said, Thy servant went no whither. And he said unto him, Went not mine heart with thee, when the man turned again from his chariot to meet thee? Is it a time to receive money, and to receive garments, and olive yards, and vineyards, and sheep, and oxen, and menservants, and maidservants? The leprosy therefore of Naaman shall cleave unto thee, and unto thy seed for ever. And he went out from his presence a leper as white as snow.—2 Kings v. 20—27.

As the sun in nature enlightens valleys as well as hills, and so diffuses its influence that nothing is hid from the heat thereof—so it is with the Scripture, the luminary of the moral world. It does not confine its attention to the great; but gives directions to all ranks and degrees of men. It describes not only the excellences and defects of kings but of subjects. It represents not only the virtues and vices of masters but of servants. It gives us instances of good servants; such as Eleazar, Joseph, Obadiah. And it gives us examples of bad ones—of which number none is

2 K   22*

more strikingly awful and improving than that of Gehazi.

Let us enter a little into the history, and see what instructions it will afford.

It is supposed that Gehazi had lived with Elijah, and that at the translation of his master, he was taken into the service of his successor. However this may be, we know that he was the servant of Elisha, who it is probable had been hitherto ignorant of his real character. For the prophetical spirit was given him by measure, and the exercise of it was limited by the will of God; and till this event occurred, the true character of the man was not developed.

A person may go a long time before he meets with his own proper trial, intended to show what "manner of man he is." Indeed none of us know much of ourselves till we are tried. While the water is calm and clear, we are not aware how much mud there is at the bottom; but the winds and waves throw up the mire and dirt. If the weather be unfavourable the ants are invisible, but let the sun shine forth and they appear. Undisturbed, we see nothing of them; but remove the stone, and stir the brood only with a straw, and swarms are in motion and all alive. When our prophet had predicted the future vileness of Hazael, Hazael shocked at the intelligence exclaimed, "Is thy servant a dog, that he should do this thing?" He was probably at the time sincere; but he knew not how differently he should feel in new and untried circumstances; he knew not the seducing corrupting power of wealth and dignity upon the human heart. Hence he soon became the monster he had abhorred. These things had not even budded in winter; but spring soon calleth them forth; summer saw the blossoms turned into fruit: and autumn ripened them. And it is probable that had all this wickedness of Gehazi been foretold a few months or weeks before, he would have been equally surprised. Pray we, therefore, as directed by Him who knows what is in man, "Lead us not into temptation, but deliver us from evil."

Elisha had healed Naaman, and Naaman in his gratitude for the blessing pressed the man of God to receive a present. "But he said, As the Lord liveth, before whom I stand, I will receive none. And he urged him to take it; but he refused." Not that he deemed the gold of the Syrian impure; or did not stand in need of assistance, for he was poor; or supposed it unlawful to take a gratuity: he thankfully accepted the hospitality of the Shunamite, who furnished him with a room, with a table, a stool, and a candlestick. But he spared his purse in love to his soul; he would teach this new convert that true godliness can find its reward in its work. He would teach us to do good for its own sake; to use discretion in what is allowable; to distinguish times and cases; to know when to adhere to general rules, and when to deviate from them. In all this, " wisdom is profitable to direct."

But the servant had not looked upon the offered treasure like his master. If Elisha dispensed with it, so would not Gehazi. He therefore resolves by some means to obtain a share. "Behold," says he, "my master hath spared Naaman this Syrian, in not receiving at his hands that which he brought: but, as the Lord liveth, I will run after him, and take somewhat of him."—Naaman seeing him running, stops, descends from his chariot, and meets him with a question that shows he was fearful some evil had happened to his friend and benefactor; "Is all well? And he said, All is well. My master hath sent me, saying, Behold, even now there be come to me from Mount Ephraim, two young men of the sons of the prophets: give them, I pray thee, a talent of silver and two changes of garments." What a falsehood was here!—It was not the effect of surprise, but framed deliberately for the purpose!

The disposition of this Syrian was as noble as his rank. He was delighted to comply with this supposed desire, and to leave something behind him. "And Naaman said, Be content, take two talents. And he urged him, and bound two talents of silver in two bags, with two changes of garments, and laid them upon two of his servants; and they bare them before him. Thus he exceeds the demand; and makes some of his own train porters to Gehazi.

But where did he lodge the treasure? At "the tower" says the common translation; "the secret place," says the margin; some place separated from the dwelling-house of the man of God, and into which he could enter without being seen. Here he dismisses the two Syrian attendants, hides the load, and blesses his good fortune; and looking demurely, "he went in and stood before his master."

Elisha does not throw himself into a passion, but calmly convinces, and righteously punishes him.—"Gehazi," says he, "whence comest thou?" We are required to condemn the guilty—yet who does not pity the criminal in the hour of detection?—What a melancholy spectacle he exhibits—deprived of his innocency—his courage failing him—his countenance changing—incapable of defence —and the lies he made his refuge leaving him speechless!—"Thy servant went no whither. Then said he unto him, went not my heart with thee, when the man turned again from his chariot to meet thee?" Did he meet thee *no where?* Did he speak to thee *no where?* "Is this a time to receive money, and garments, and oliveyards, and vineyards, and sheep, and oxen, and menservants, and maidservants?"

By this question Elisha convinced him, not only that he was privy to this base action, but that he knew the very thoughts and purposes of his heart. Gehazi had already in imagination laid out the substance he had so unjustly acquired; such things he would purchase; in such a style he would live; he would improve and enlarge his means, till rising from a private to a splendid station, he could command the homage he had been accustomed to pay.

But punishment follows detection; "The leprosy therefore of Naaman shall cleave unto thee, and unto thy seed for ever. And he went out from his presence a leper as white as snow."—The punishment had three characters.

First. It was *extensive:* and took in his family as well as himself. He derived from his offspring probably, one of the motives that produced this fatal action; he would "lay up for the children; but instead of entailing a large estate, he has entailed a loathsome disease from generation to generation. If he had any affection for his offspring, how must he have been cut to the heart to see these innocent objects the victims of his vice!

Secondly. It was *scandalous* and *obvious.* He was thus excluded from the tabernacle, and carried with him marks of his fraud and sacrilege: wherever he went, his sin was read in his face and family.

Thirdly. It was *immediate:* and seizing him in a moment, without any previous symptoms or tendencies, proved that it was inflicted not by revenge, but by a supernatural impulse.

It is hoped that in due time Naaman was disabused, and informed of the vileness of the man, and the generosity of the master. But let us hasten to derive a few general and useful reflections from the whole narrative.

I. PERSONS MAY BE VERY WICKED UNDER RELIGIOUS ADVANTAGES. The means of grace, and the grace of the means are very distinguishable from each other, and are frequently found separate. Of the four portions of ground sowed with the same seed, by the same hand, and at the same season, one only was productive soil. Children trained up "in the nurture and admonition of the Lord," have been known to turn aside into "the paths of the destroyer," and to "bring down a parent's gray hairs with sorrow to the grave."

There are servants who see good example, hear daily instruction, attend morning and evening worship, yet have no fear of God before their eyes; yea they can return from these exercises and treat them with contempt, and become ten-fold more the children of hell than others! Thus we here find a bad servant living with a godly master. Some of those who resided at a distance from the man of God honoured him, and derived advantage from him, while one that stood continually before him, and heard his wisdom, and saw his miracles, and witnessed his holy life, seems to have been only corrupted and hardened by them!

But wherever such awful characters are found, let them remember that they cannot sin so cheap as others; they will be left without excuse; they will have to answer for abused privileges; their guilt will be in proportion to their advantages, and their punishment in proportion to their guilt. For "to him that knoweth to do good, and doeth it not, to him it is sin." "And that servant which knew his Lord's will, and prepared not himself, neither did according to his will, shall be beaten with many stripes. But he that knew not, and did commit things worthy of stripes, shall be beaten with few stripes. For unto whomsoever much is given, of him shall be much required: and to whom men have committed much, of him they will ask the more."

II. HERE IS A WARNING AGAINST THE LOVE OF MONEY. "Take heed and beware of covetousness."

What did Gehazi acquire by his wealth? His gain was loss. He lost his health. He lost his honour. He lost his peace. He lost his place. And without repentance, he lost his soul for ever. Was he not much happier before? He has indeed increased his substance; but he enjoys it with the abhorrence of God; the scorn of men; disease of body; the affliction of his family; the scourges of his conscience; the foretastes of hell.

What a commentary is the history of this man, and of Balaam, and Achan, and Judas, and Demas, and full one half of the modern professors of religion on the following passages of Scripture! "The getting of treasures by a lying tongue, is a vanity tossed to and fro of them that seek death." "In the fulness of his sufficiency he shall be in straits: every hand of the wicked shall come upon him. When he is about to fill his belly, God shall cast the fury of his wrath upon him, and shall rain it upon him while he is eating. He shall flee from the iron weapon, and the bow of steel shall strike him through." "But they that will be rich fall into temptation and a snare, and into many foolish and hurtful lusts, which drown men in destruction and perdition. For the love of money is the root of all evil: which while some coveted after, they have erred from the faith, and pierced themselves through with many sorrows."

"Let your conversation therefore be without covetousness. Be content with such things as you have." For, God has said, "I will never leave thee nor forsake thee. You brought nothing with you into the world, and it is certain you can carry nothing out."

"Man wants but little here below,
Nor wants that little long."

Money implies no excellence, and confers none. Neither does "a man's life consist in the abundance of the things that he possesseth." But oh! the moral hazards—the difficulties in the way of salvation attending it! This is the most dissuasive view we can take of it. "How hardly shall they that have riches enter into the kingdom of God!" Again I say, take heed, and beware of this insinuating, this detestable, this destructive passion. Meet every temptation to it with the question of our Saviour; "What is a man profited if he gain the whole world, and lose his own soul; or what shall a man give in exchange for his soul?"

III. SEE THE ENCROACHMENTS AND PROGRESS OF SIN, AND LEARN HOW DANGEROUS IT IS TO GIVE WAY TO ANY EVIL PROPENSITY.

Here is avarice leading on to lying, and one lie followed up by two more. One transgression breaks down the fence, and then others like cattle go in more easily, and by a kind of licence. One sin often renders another necessary to its execution; one sin often renders another necessary to its concealment. The obligation the sinner lays himself under, in order to proceed in an evil course, is frequently endless; while every step of the progress he makes, blinds and hardens him still more. When a child leaves his house clean in his apparel, he is afraid to soil even his feet; but the first stain he contracts makes him less regardless of the second, and the second of the third; till he thinks himself so bad, that caution is needless, and he treads any where.

Thus we read that men "proceed from evil to evil;" that "they wax worse and worse;" that these "things eat as do a canker;" that when "lust hath conceived, it bringeth forth sin, and sin, when it is finished, bringeth forth death."

And is it only in the Scripture that this truth is asserted? Do we not see it confirmed in actual instances every day? Over how many of late years have we had to mourn! But which of these unhappy characters became either infidel or vicious at once? They endured evil company, and then chose it. They trifled with the Sabbath, and then profaned it. One thing after another was given up, till they "said unto God, Depart from us; we desire not the knowledge of thy ways."

Can we then be too early in our precautions? Can we be too much afraid of our beginnings? Is it not better to crush the egg before it breaks forth into a fiery flying serpent?

IV. HOW ABSURD IS IT TO SIN WITH AN EXPECTATION OF SECRECY! "There is no darkness nor shadow of death where the workers of iniquity can hide themselves." When going forth to commit iniquity, goes not your own conscience with you? Goes not the eye of God with you? Does not He see all, and record all, and with a view to bring all into judgment! But even with regard to others it may generally be said, "Be sure your sin will find you out." There are often eye and ear witnesses of whom you have no suspicion. Strange circumstances frequently occur to awaken inquiry, and lead to detection. You may divulge your iniquity by inadvertency in conversation; by dreams when asleep; by delirium when distracted. You may be compelled to acknowledge it by the anguish of a guilty mind. Men have sometimes turned their own accusers long after the fact, and when no suspicion attached to them, and have sought shelter in a legal death.

Lastly. ABHOR AND FORSAKE LYING. It is in common peculiarly easy to detect falsehood. Hence it is said that every liar should have a good memory. And what an odious character is a liar! How shunned and detested when discovered! To every mortal upon earth, the appellation of a liar is the most detestable. A liar is the emblem of "the devil, who was a liar from the beginning, and abode not in the truth."

God, of such importance is it that we should speak the truth one to another, has sometimes remarkably interposed, not only to detect, but to punish lying. Did Ananias and Sapphira escape? Did Gehazi? The mouth of them that speak lies shall be stopped. Lies may be their refuge now. But "all liars, it is said, shall have their portion in the lake that burneth with fire and brimstone, which is the second death." For "without are dogs, and sorcerers, and whoremongers, and murderers, and idolaters, and whosoever loveth and maketh a lie."

Do not say of such a discourse as this, it is not evangelical. We know the main thing is to make you acquainted with the Lord Jesus Christ, and to bring you to him. But there are various truths which we are required to lay open; and which we find in the book of God for this purpose; they are written for our admonition, and are to be improved. And nothing can be done till men are convinced of sin. But by instances of sin, we may be led to a sinful course; from a sinful life, to a sinful nature—and so feel the necessity of an application to him, whose name is Jesus, because he saves his people from their sins; and is raised up to "bless us, by turning every one of us away from our iniquities."

DISCOURSE LXXII.

DYING REGRETS.

And thou mourn at the last, when thy flesh and thy body are consumed, and say, How have I hated instruction, and my heart despised reproof!—Proverbs v. 11, 12.

RELIGION has one undeniable advantage to recommend it—whatever it calls us to sacrifice, or to suffer, it always ends well. "Mark the perfect man," says David, "and behold the upright: for the end of that man is peace." And even Balaam exclaims, "Let me die the death of the righteous, and let my last end be like his!"

On the other hand, sin has one undeniable evil to excite our aversion and horror. Whatever sensual pleasures and imaginary profit attend its course, it always ends dreadfully. We are far from allowing that the sinner has *present* happiness; for Scripture and history, observation and experience, unite to prove that "the way of transgressors is hard." But if it were not so—if it were easy and smooth and flowery—yet, who would walk in it—since "the end of these things is death!"

Behold the representation of a sinner closing his sad career.—"He mourns at the last, when his flesh and his body are consumed, and says, How have I hated instruction, and my heart despised reproof!" Let us consider,

I. The SUBJECT of these regrets.—II. The PERIOD of these regrets.—III. The NATURE of these regrets.

I. The SUBJECT of these regrets. It is a man who has disregarded through life the means employed to preserve or reclaim him: it is one who has "hated instruction, and whose heart has despised reproof."—What instructers and reprovers has man! I mean, a man living in a country like this; I mean, a man possessing advantages like ours. These instructers and reprovers may be ranked in six classes.

In the First, we place your connexions in life.—You reside in a family, the head of which, like Joshua, has said, "As for me and my house, we will serve the Lord:" and of whom God has testified, as he did of Abraham, "I know him that he will command his household and his children after him, and they shall keep the way of the Lord, to do justice and judgment."—You have had a pious father, who has often with tears said, "My son, if thou be wise, my heart shall rejoice, even mine"—perhaps, after an example the most powerful, with his dying breath he said, "I go the way of all the earth: and thou, Solomon, my son, know thou the God of thy father, and serve him with a perfect heart and a willing mind; for if thou seek him he will be found of thee, but if thou forsake him he will cast thee off for ever."—Has not she who bore thee sometimes taken thee aside; and in eloquence, such as can only come from the heart of a woman and a mother, addressed every feeling of thy nature? "What, my son! and the son of my womb! and the son of my vows!"—If parents have never discharged the duty their office requires, have you not had an instructer and a reprover in a brother? In a sister? In a wife? In a husband? If relations have all neglected you, have you met with no pious friend? No godly acquaintance? No religious neighbour?

In the Second, we place the Scriptures. These you have in your own language, and are not forbidden the use of them. You can read them; and by the perusal bring around you Moses, and David, and Isaiah, and Paul; the prophets and the apostles; with all their warnings and invitations. And I may apply to you the words that were originally addressed to Timothy: "From a child thou hast known the holy Scriptures, which are able to make thee wise unto salvation, through faith which is in Christ Jesus. All Scripture is given by inspiration of God, and is profitable for doctrine, for reproof, for correction, for instruction in righteousness."

In the Third, we place ministers. In the name of God, whose they are, and whom they serve, they place before you your duty in the various conditions of life, and alarm and allure you to the performance of it. They proclaim the threatenings of the Law, and the promises of the Gospel. They announce your danger, and call upon you to flee for refuge to the hope set before you. "Many prophets and righteous men have desired to see the things that you see, and have not seen them; and to hear the things that you hear, and have not heard them. But blessed are your eyes, for they see; and your ears, for they hear."

In the Fourth, we place conscience. This instructer and reprover you have always with you; always in you. How often has this divine messenger, when you have been venturing on a sinful action, cried Forbear! How often has it arraigned and condemned your proceedings, and filled you with anguish and terror! How often has it told you that you are in the gall of bitterness, in the bond of iniquity; and that your heart is not right in the sight of God!

In the Fifth, we place irrational creatures. Can you hear the melody of the birds, and not be ashamed of your sinful silence! Can you see the heavenly bodies perform unerringly their appointed course, and not reflect on your own numberless departures from duty! "Go to the ant, thou sluggard; consider her ways, and be wise; which having no guide, overseer, or ruler, provideth her meat in the summer, and gathereth her food in the harvest." "Hear, O heavens, and give ear, O earth: for the Lord hath spoken, I have nourished and brought up children, and they have rebelled against me. The ox knoweth his owner, and the ass his master's crib: but Israel doth not know, my people doth not consider." "Be ye wise as serpents, and harmless as doves."

In the Sixth, we place the dispensations of providence. All events have a voice, especially those of an afflictive kind. Hence we are commanded to hear the rod. And who has not been addressed by it? He has chastened you with sickness. You drew nigh unto the grave, and looked over the brink of life into an awful eternity. He has visited you with disappointments in your worldly affairs; and told you not to lay up treasure on earth, where moth and rust do corrupt, and thieves break through and steal. You have seen your neighbours carried to their long home. You have witnessed dying beds. Your own dwelling has been made the house of mourning—"lover and friend has he put far from you, and your acquaintance into silence." The very day in which you have lived has been full of awful admonitions. When his "judgments are abroad in the earth, the inhabitants of the world should learn righteousness."

Yet now many are there who "regard not the work of the Lord, neither consider the operations of his hands!" How many are there who disregard all these instructers and reprovers! Let us turn from the subject, to

II. The PERIOD of these regrets. It is a dying hour. It is "at the last, when thy flesh and thy body are consumed."

Such a period is *unavoidable*. There is no prevention of it, nor escape from it. However long life may be, it will have an end: the last breath *will* expire; the last Sabbath *will* elapse; the last sermon *will* be heard. The sparkling eye *must* be closed in darkness; the busy tongue *must* be silenced for ever; the hands *must* forget their enterprizes; and those idolized frames, that exhausted so much time and attention in pampering and adorning them, *must* be consigned to rottenness and worms.

Such a period *cannot be far off.* "For what is our life? It is a vapour that appeareth for a little time, and then vanisheth away." It is a flood. It is a flower. It is a tale that is told. It is a dream.—It is a hand's breadth. It is nothing before God— "surely every man at his best estate is altogether vanity."

Such a period *may be very near.* The general limitation of human life is three score years and ten; but few reach it, and come to the grave in full age. Indeed when we consider of what a multiplicity of delicate organs our system is composed, and how liable they are to injury; and add to this the numberless diseases and accidents that lie ambushed in our path; the wonder is, that we live a week, a day, an hour, to an end.

Such a period is *sometimes prematurely brought on by sin.* Solomon here intimates this; and it is a supposition illustrated and confirmed by facts. How many die by the hand of civil justice; and acknowledge at the place of execution, the disregard of instruction and reproof, in which the fatal career commenced! How many of those who die what is called a natural death, might have been now living, had not their " bones been filled with the sins of their youth, that lie down with them in the dust!" How many yet living, but diseased, emaciated figures, exhibiting the appearances of decay and age, might have been sound in constitution, and healthy and strong, had they listened to that wisdom which has " length of days in her right hand," as well as in " her left hand riches and honour!" How many reduced and worn down by hard labour and living, to which they had been unaccustomed, who have pined away in want, or dragged on a miserable being in prison, might have still enjoyed liberty and ease, had they followed that godliness which " has the promise of the life that now is, as well as of that which is to come!" As to " bloody and deceitful men," they do not often " live out half their days."

But such a period as this, if it be not prematurely produced by irreligion, is always imbittered by it. " You will mourn at the last, when your flesh and your body are consumed, and say, How have I hated instruction, and my heart despised reproof!" Such self-reflection and condemnation are unavoidable—unless prevented, first, by your being cut off suddenly, and not having a moment given you for thought. Secondly, by your being deprived of reason, and thus rendered incapable of any mental exertion. Or, thirdly, by your having annihilated all moral feeling, and completely subdued the power of conscience—and who can tell how far a man may be hardened " through the deceitfulness of sin," and by trifling with the means of grace, and die in peace, though he is sure to awake in torment! Would you desire such preventions as these? Are they not more dreadful than the effect? Yet you must hope—either for sudden death—or the suspension of reason—or the loss of conscience; or you *must* expect a dying hour to be imbitterred with regrets.

III. Let us consider the NATURE of these regrets. " And thou mourn at the last, when thy flesh and thy body be consumed, and say, How have I hated instruction, and my heart despised reproof!" In other cases, " Blessed are they that mourn, for they shall be comforted." But this mourning has two attributes to distinguish it.

First. It is dreadful. A dying hour has been called an honest hour. The world then recedes from your view, demonstrating its incapacity to succour; and acknowledging that it attracted you only to show its emptiness, and elevated only to depress. The delusions of imagination give way. Criminal excuses vanish. Memory goes back, and recalls the guilt of former life: and conscience

sets your most secret sins in the light of God's countenance. With what ingratitude, folly, madness, will you charge yourselves! What reflections on opportunities lost! on faculties perverted! What fear of mercy abused; and of judgment approaching! What anticipations of hell, where the worm dieth not, and where the fire is not quenched!— Many of the sinner's dying confessions and horrors are never made known. Relations and friends conceal them. They often indeed mistake them, and ascribe these exclamations to the phrensy of the disorder. And, perhaps, were it not for the composing draught, it would be impossible, in many cases, to secure the attendance of any in the room. " It is a fearful thing to fall into the hands of the living God!"

Secondly. It is useless. I do not mean as to others—it may serve to convince them what " an evil and bitter thing it is to sin against God," and awaken in them a salutary, because a seasonable, fear. But with regard to the individuals themselves, says God himself: " Because I have called, and ye refused; I have stretched out my hand, and no man regarded; but ye have set at nought all my counsel, and would none of my reproof: I also will laugh at your calamity; I will mock when your fear cometh; when your fear cometh as desolation, and your destruction cometh as a whirlwind; when distress and anguish cometh upon you. Then shall they call upon me, but I will not answer; they shall seek me early, but they shall not find me: for that they hated knowledge, and did not choose the fear of the Lord: they would none of my counsel: they despised all my reproof. Therefore shall they eat of the fruit of their own way, and be filled with their own devices." What! Is this dying grief, always, and invariably unavailing?—I answer; we are to describe things according to their natural and common course, and not according to occasional and very unusual exceptions. And in the case before us—are not exceptions very unusual? Do not men commonly die as they live? And with regard to those dying regrets, to which so many look forward as a final refuge, and from which so many instantaneous saints are furnished for our magazine-calendars—what degree of dependence is to be placed upon them? In reply to this, let the following remarks be examined.

The First regard the Scripture. There we find *one*, and *only one* called at this hour. It was the dying thief. He implored and obtained mercy when the heaven was covered with blackness, and the earth trembled, and the rocks rent, and the graves were opened, and a suffering Saviour would crown the prodigies of nature with a miracle of grace —a case in all its circumstances so amazingly peculiar, that were not men infatu ated by sin, it could never be drawn into a precedent.

The Second is derived from observation. We have often attended persons on what was deemed their dying bed; we have heard their prayers and their professions; we have seen their distress and their relief; and had they died, we should have presumed on their salvation. But we have never known one of these, who on recovery lived so as to prove the reality of his conversion? We have often asked ministers concerning the same case; and they have been compelled to make the same awful declaration.

The Third regards the force of habit. "As well may the Ethiopian change his skin, and the leopard his spots, as they learn to do good who have been accustomed to do evil." Diseases which if taken in time are curable, by becoming inveterate are rendered desperate. "But there is no desperate case here," you are ready to say. "With God all things are possible. His grace is almighty." Acknowledged: and you shall have all the encouragement derivable from a miracle of grace. But what probability is there, that an extraordinary dispensation of grace will be adopted, after all the ordinary means of salvation have been despised and neglected? And despised and neglected too in hope of this!

Hence our Fourth remark regards the influence of such examples. If persons who live without God in the world were as frequently called in their last hour as too many seem to admit, would not the frequency of the occurrence influence persons to procrastinate their religious concerns, and to say to every present application, "Go thy way for this time, when I have a convenient season I will call for thee?" But does God by his conduct contradict his commands? And having said, "To-day if ye will hear his voice harden not your heart;"—"now is the accepted time, now is the day of salvation;"—"seek ye the Lord while he may be found, and call upon him while he is near;"—would he supersede the necessity or weaken the impression of all this, by his constantly receiving sinners when they can insult him no longer, and showing that forced regret is as acceptable to him as genuine repentance?

For Finally, observe the uncertainty the individual must feel in determining the reality of his religious feelings. How is he to know whether they are the cries of nature, or the desires of grace? whether they flow from the Spirit of God, or result from his tremendous situation, and his depressed and disordered frame? And has he not enough to bear without this cruel perplexity? Now that he needs the comforts of religion, is he incapable of deciding whether he is entitled to its promises? Now that he needs confidence, must he expire in darkness and in doubt?—

Yet, by the way, we should have more hope of such a man, if he died uncertain and distressed, than were we to see him dying in "the full assurance of hope." For though God is a sovereign, and we are not to limit the Holy One of Israel, it is not surely reasonable to expect, that a man who has given his whole life to the world, the flesh, and the devil, and is only driven to God by dying regret, should be able to say with a Simeon, who has been waiting for the consolation of Israel; "Lord, now lettest thou thy servant depart in peace, for mine eyes have seen thy salvation!" Let us conclude by three reflections.

First. *How good is God!* He is much more attentive to our welfare than we ever have been, or ever can be. He originally made man upright; and when by transgression he fell away from him, he did not avail himself of the rights his justice had acquired over him; nor did he even treat him with neglect. He remembered us in our low estate, and "so loved the world as to give his only-begotten Son, that whosoever believeth on him should not perish, but have everlasting life." He has sent us the information, with numberless means and motives to awaken our attention to it. And these he is continually reaping. So true is it, that he is "long-suffering, not willing that any should perish, but that all should come to repentance and live." So justly may he complain, "What could have been done more to my vineyard, that I have not done in it? wherefore, when I looked that it should bring forth grapes, brought it forth wild grapes?" For,

Secondly. *How fallen is man!* Some deny his depravity, contending that we are naturally virtuous, or at least as much inclined to good as evil. But if this be the fact, why do we need so many hinderances to restrain us from evil, and so many endeavours to excite us to good? And why are they ineffectual too? They ought upon this principle to be successful with the majority, or at least an equal number of mankind. But are they? Do we not see men generally breaking through every restraint, and disregarding every kind of instruction and reproof? And are not they who walk by the rule of God's word, "a peculiar people?"

Thirdly. *How important is serious thought!* In this religion commences: "I thought on my ways, and turned my feet unto thy testimonies. I made haste, and delayed not to keep thy commandments." Could men go on as they do, if they considered their ways, comparing them with the word of God, and examining their consequences? Impossible. It is thoughtlessness that ruins them. They never faithfully inquire, How will this close? Will it bring me peace at the last? How will it appear when reviewed from the borders of the grave? "A prudent man foreseeth the evil, and hideth himself; but the simple pass on, and are punished." "O that they were wise, that they understood this, that they would consider their latter end!"

DISCOURSE LXXIII.

DEATH CONQUERED.
(ON THE LOSS OF A CHRISTIAN FRIEND.)

Our conversation is in heaven; from whence also we look for the Saviour, the Lord Jesus Christ: who shall change our vile body, that it may be fashioned like unto his glorious body, according to the working whereby he is able even to subdue all things unto himself. Phil. iii. 20, 21.

THE present is not the principal state in which man is to be found; and it shoud never be viewed separate from another; to which it bears the same relation as infancy to manhood, as spring to autumn, as seed-time to harvest. Who, in nature, having scattered one kind of grain in his field, would think of filling his barn with another? And in religious concerns "be not deceived; God is not mocked: for whatsoever a man soweth, that shall he also reap; for he that soweth to his flesh, shall of the flesh reap corruption; but he that soweth to the Spirit, shall of the Spirit reap life everlasting."

This consideration stamps an awfulness on human nature; and teaches us the true importance of the present period. It is comparatively a matter of little concern what is to become of us, and where we shall reside, for a few weeks or years. The grand question is, Where are we to reside for ever? And what is to become of us when the trumpet shall sound, and all the dead, both small and great, shall stand before God, and receive of the things done in the body, whether they be good, or whether they be evil?

Some never afford this subject a moment's thought. Others remain in a state of uncertainty. But the primitive Christians gave all diligence to make their calling and their election sure; and conscious of the reality of their religion, and the blessedness of their condition, could say; "Our conversation is in heaven; from whence also we look for the Saviour, the Lord Jesus Christ: who shall change our vile body, that it may be fashioned like unto his glorious body, according to the working whereby he is able even to subdue all things unto himself." Let us consider—
THE CHRISTIAN'S STATE—THE CHRISTIAN'S EXPECTATION—THE CHRISTIAN'S DESTINY.

I. His present STATE. It is thus expressed: "Our conversation is in heaven." The original term is used two ways. Sometimes it signifies a certain alliance, and means citizenship: and sometimes it denotes a peculiar behaviour. Our translators have preferred the latter; and rendered it *conversation*. And they have done so, not only in the passage before us, but in several other places, meaning however by the term, not discourse only, but the whole tenor of our conduct. We need not disunite these two senses. The one will infer and explain the other.

Be it remembered therefore, in the First place, that the believer stands in connexion with another and a nobler world; he belongs to "a better country, even a heavenly." He is a citizen of no mean city: "a city which hath foundations, whose builder and maker is God," and which abounds with laws, honours, riches, pleasures, immunities, and intercourse, the most valuable and glorious. How did a man boast in being a citizen of Rome! When the centurion heard that Paul was a Roman, "he went and told the chief captain, saying, Take heed what thou doest: for this man is a Roman. Then the chief captain came, and said unto him, Tell me, art thou a Roman? He said, Yea. And the chief captain answered, With a great sum obtained I this freedom. And Paul said, But I was free-born." Think, then, what a privilege it is to belong to a state concerning which it is said, "Eye hath not seen, nor ear heard, nor have entered into the heart of man, the things which God hath prepared for them that love him!"—Hence our Saviour teaches his disciples to prefer their being registered among the living in Jerusalem to the power and fame of working miracles: "Notwithstanding, in this rejoice not, that the spirits are subject unto you; but rather rejoice because your names are written in heaven."

Now, Secondly, as the Christian is allied to such a country, a suitable mode of living becomes him. A citizen of Rome could live elsewhere, even in any of the distant provinces. A citizen of heaven resides on earth for a season; but he is a stranger and a foreigner. Though in the world, he is not of it. And while certain purposes detain him here, his principles, his habits, and his speech, show that he belongs to "a peculiar people." He is a citizen of glory. He prefers his fellow-citizens. He loves to speak of the glory of his kingdom. He will correspond with it; and as cold water to a thirsty soul, so will good news be from this far country. His body is here, and his business is here—but his soul is there—there is his treasure; there his inheritance; there his thoughts fix; there his affections rest;

" There his best friends, his kindred dwell;
    There God his Saviour reigns."

He acts habitually under an impression of heaven, and with a reference to it. His chief care is to gain it. He often fears that he shall miss it at last; and the apprehension stimulates his vigilance, self-examination, and diligence. He concurs in the prayer, "Thy will be done on earth, as it is done in heaven:" he mourns over his want of conformity to the servants of God above; and is seeking after an increase of those blessed tempers and joys, which are possessed by them in all their perfection. He is not only longing, but preparing for heaven. And he is hastening towards it, not only as a place of release from trouble, but as a state of freedom from sin, and communion with God.

II. His high expectation. "Our conversation is in heaven, from whence also we look for the Saviour, the Lord Jesus Christ."

This reminds us of the present abode of our Redeemer: he is now in heaven. And hence we need not wonder that Christians should have their conversation in heaven. For he is their treasure; and where "the treasure is, there will the heart be also."— The removal of a very dear friend into another neighbourhood will frequently render a place indifferent to us; and we change our residence to be near him. The death of a delightful relation will turn a paradise into a wilderness. How often do we look up, and follow our departed connexions in our thoughts! But something of them remains. The body we have laid in the grave. We go to the place to weep there. We feel a propriety in the very dust we tread. But nothing of our Saviour remains to attach us to earth: his very body is gone from us. "I am no more," said he, "in the world"—a sentence sufficient to render the world dreary; we feel his attraction as he ascends; and "rising together with Christ, we seek those things that are above, where he sitteth at the right hand of God. We set our affection on things above, not on things on the earth. For we are dead, and our life is hid with Christ in God. And when he who is our life shall appear, we shall also appear with him in glory."

Again. Though our Redeemer is now in heaven, he will come thence. The time is indeed a secret: but the thing is sure. He does not forget his friends while he is absent; he communicates with them, and supplies them: and has promised to "come again and receive them to himself, that where he is there they may be also." But how wonderful the difference between his former and his future coming! Then he was seen of few; now "every eye shall see him."— Then his glory was veiled, and "the world knew him not;" now we shall "see him as he is." Then "he was despised and rejected of men;" now he "shall come in the clouds of heaven, with all the holy angels!" Then he was born in a stable, and nailed to a cross; now "he shall sit upon the throne of his glory, and before him shall be gathered all nations." He was "once offered to bear the sins of many; and to them that look for him will he appear the second time without sin unto salvation."

Observe also the state of the Christian's mind with regard to this appearance. He looks for him.

He believes his coming; and this distinguishes him *from infidels*. They ask, "Where is the promise of his coming?" and having rendered it their interest that he should not come, persuade themselves that he will not. Their unbelief is the offspring of their vices and their fears. But with the Christian it is not a matter of opinion or conjecture; he does not say, He may come; but He will come: and by means of that "faith which is the evidence of things not seen," he beholds him already marshaling his angels —and traveling down.

But do not all believe this truth? It is an invidious task to call men infidels. But suppose they prove themselves so? Now we know from observation and experience that belief sways the mind, and governs the conduct. Even when our persuasion is founded on our own imagination, or the testimony of our fellow-creatures, it produces some effect. How much more operative should be our confidence in the testimony of God, who cannot be deceived, and who cannot lie! Now if men live precisely like others; as bold in sin; as remiss in duty; can they really believe? Do not actions speak louder than words?

The true believer therefore pays attention to his coming, and thus he is distinguished from *nominal* Christians, who, if we must allow that they believe it, are not influenced by it. What we look for we prepare for in proportion as we attach importance to it. We prepare for the reception of a friend. How much more should we prepare for the reception of a king. But here the personage expected is the King of kings; the Governor of the universe; the Judge of all!—And does the Christian, who is looking for *Him*, immerse himself in the cares of this life? Does he "sleep, as do others?" Does he play and trifle? Does he smite his fellow-servant, and eat and drink with the drunken? No; but "seeing he looks for such things, he is diligent that he may be found of him in peace, without spot, and blameless." He waits with his "loins girded, and his lamp burning;"— and "denying ungodliness and worldly lusts, he should live soberly, righteously, and godly in the present world," and is thus looking for that blessed hope, "and the glorious appearing of the great God and our Saviour Jesus Christ."

For, Finally, remark the character under which the Christian waits for him: "from whence we look for the Saviour." This was the name given him at his birth, and for the most important of all reasons, because he should "save his people from their sins." This work he has not only undertaken, but will completely accomplish. He is coming to finish it; and to fulfil all that the name imposes upon him, or implies. He will create new heavens and a new earth, wherein dwelleth righteousness. He will gather together in one the children of God that were scattered abroad. "O Death! he will be thy plagues. O Grave! he will be thy destruction: repentance shall be hid from his eyes." "For this corruptible must put on incorruption, and this mortal must put on immortality. So when this corruptible shall have put on incorruption, and this mortal shall have put on immortality, then shall be brought to pass the saying that is written, Death is swallowed up in victory. O Death, where is thy sting? O Grave, where is thy victory? The sting of death is sin; and the strength of sin is the law. But thanks be to God, which giveth us the victory through our Lord Jesus Christ."

III. His final DESTINY. "Who shall change our vile body, that it may be fashioned like unto his glorious body, according to the working whereby he is able even to subdue all things unto himself." Three things are observable.

First. The subject changed. "This vile body." Much of the wisdom and power of God is displayed in the formation of the human frame. And when we consider the multiplicity and delicacy of its parts; the connexion of its members; the proportion and adaptation of its organs to each other, and to the whole; we need not wonder that David should say, "I will praise thee; for I am fearfully and wonderfully made: marvellous are thy works; and that my soul knoweth right well. My substance was not hid from thee, when I was made in secret, and curiously wrought in the lowest parts of the earth. Thine eyes did see my substance, yet being unperfect; and in thy book all my members were written, which in continuance were fashioned, when as yet there was none of them. How precious also are thy thoughts unto me, O God! How great is the sum of them!" In this sense, it is not a vile body.

But when we view it as degraded by the Fall; as prostituted to the purposes of sin; when we think of the sordidness and lowness of its appetites and infirmities; when we view it under various kinds and degrees of disease, requiring all the interest of reward or vigour of friendship, to discharge towards a fellow-creature the common duties of humanity; when we are compelled by the approach of putrefaction to bury our dead, however once loved and valued, out of our sight; when we go and open a grave, and witness the intolerable disgrace of our nature; we acknowledge with what propriety it is called "the body of our humiliation." But this body is not to be annihilated, though reduced—it will be only *changed.* "So also is the resurrection of the dead. It is sown in corruption; it is raised in incorruption: it is sown in dishonour; it is raised in glory: it is sown in weakness; it is raised in power: it is sown a natural body; it is raised a spiritual body. There is a natural body, and there is a spiritual body."

Secondly. Here is the model to which it will be conformed: "It shall be fashioned like unto his glorious body." The comparison does not regard his body in "the days of his flesh." It was then possessed of all our sinless qualities and feelings. But, after his resurrection and ascension, it was deprived of every thing animal and humiliating. It was incapable of hunger or weariness. It could move with the ease of thought, and was invulnerable and eternal as the soul. It was glorified. A glimpse of this glory was given by way of anticipation to the disciples, in the transfiguration, when "his face shone as the sun, and his raiment was white as the light." In this glory he appeared to Saul: he shone "above the brightness of the sun," and struck him blind. When John saw him, "his countenance was as the sun shineth in his strength," and though he had been once familiar with him, and had leaned often on his bosom, he fell at his feet as dead. How glorious must that body be in which he now governs the world! In which he will judge the universe! In which we shall hold all our intercourse with Deity for ever! Yet a conformity to this glory is not a privilege too great for our hope. As sure as we now resemble the Saviour in disposition, we shall be like him in person: and the same mind will be followed with the same body.

Thirdly. We are informed of the omnipotent agency by which the work is to be accomplished; "according to the working whereby he is able even to subdue all things unto himself." It is obvious that such a renovation is nothing less than a miracle, and the most stupendous of all miracles; and therefore that it demands in him, who is to effect it, something more than kindness. "We cannot by taking thought add one cubit to our stature." We cannot replace a leaf; or revive a blade of grass. Oh! if love could bring back the dead—if cries and tears could be heard—how soon would our breaches be repaired, and our wounds healed!—Such power is not ours; it is not ours by nature; it is not ours by dispensation. But it belongs to the Saviour. "He is the mighty God." He has "power given him over all flesh. He is Lord of the dead, as well as of the living." And he fainteth not, neither is weary. The reanimation and organization of millions of dead bodies will not exhaust him. He could do infinitely more. He is "able even to subdue all things unto himself."

From this subject we should learn, First, to be thankful for the discoveries of revelation. The notions of the heathen philosophers, even concerning the immortality of the soul, were very confined and confused; and it is to be observed that they never laid stress upon it, as a principle and a motive. But the resurrection of the body never entered their minds. The history and experience of mankind had furnished no ground for such an expectation. They had always followed the body to the grave, and had seen it return to its original element. The doctrine of its revival and transformation was so new at Athens, that the preaching of it by the Apostle was turned into mockery. But the poorest and most illiterate Christian can open his Bible, and say, "I know that my Redeemer liveth, and that he shall stand at the latter day upon the earth: And though after my skin worms destroy this body, yet in my flesh shall I see God: whom I shall see for myself, and mine eyes shall behold, and not another; though my reins be consumed within me."

Secondly; observe the importance the Scripture attaches to the doctrine of the resurrection. With what severity does the Apostle speak of those who endeavour to explain it away metaphorically; and "said the resurrection is past already, and overturned the faith of some." The Gospel certainly admits of an intermediate state between death and the resurrection; but whenever the blessedness of the future world is spoken of, it is, with few exceptions, placed not immediately after death, but after the resurrection. "Thou shalt be recompensed at the resurrection of the just. If by any means I might attain unto the resurrection of the dead. I am persuaded that he is able to keep that which I have committed to him against that day. A crown of righteousness, which the righteous Judge shall give me at that day, and not to me only, but to all them that love his appearing." It would be unnecessary to multiply passages to prove the remark. But does not all this imply, that whatever the intermediate state may be, compared with the present, it is a defective one compared with the final state of the believer?—And it cannot be otherwise. Man was imbodied in his original creation; and so he will be in his ultimate condition. Till the resurrection, he wants an essential part of human nature; and a medium of connexion and intercourse with material things, from which a large proportion of the happiness of our compound being results.

Thirdly. Let this truth be always combined with the thought of death. Remember it in view of your own dissolution; and as you look towards the grave, and tremble, take courage, and drink in the heavenly intelligence which the Saviour communicates: "I am the resurrection and the life: he that believeth in me, though he were dead, yet shall he live. And whosoever liveth, and believeth in me, shall never die."

Remember it when you are called to lose your pious friends and relations. You have not parted with them for ever. Thy brother, thy sister, thy child, thy mother will rise again. "Be not ignorant concerning them which are asleep, that you sorrow not, even as others which have no hope. For if we believe that Jesus died, and rose again, even so them also which sleep in Jesus will God bring with him."

Lastly. Are you children of the resurrection? Let me earnestly entreat you not to elude the inquiry. For though the resurrection, as an event, is universal; as a privilege it is limited. "All that are in their graves shall hear his voice, and come forth; they that have done good unto the resurrection of life; but they that have done evil unto the resurrection of damnation." And can that be called a deliverance that raises a man from a bad state, and consigns him to a worse? This, will be the case with the wicked and the worldly; this will be the case with all those who have not been raised from the death of sin to the life of righteousness. The pit of corruption will resign its charge into the pit of destruction. O dreadful doom! Those bodies for which you have disregarded your souls; those bodies upon which you have expended all your time and attention; those bodies which you have nursed in sickness, and pampered in health—those bodies —*death* will surrender to the. *worms*; and— the *resurrection* to the *flames*.

DISCOURSE LXXIV.

DANIEL; OR, CONSTANCY IN RELIGION.

Now when Daniel knew that the writing was signed, he went into his house; and his windows being open in his chamber toward Jerusalem, he kneeled upon his knees three times a day, and prayed, and gave thanks before his God, as he did aforetime.—Dan. vi. 10.

In a day of rebuke and blasphemy, in which we see so many of an infidel and profligate character, and so few, even of those who profess the Gospel, adorning the doctrine of God our Saviour in all things, it is peculiarly pleasing and useful to be able to contemplate an instance of genuine, decisive, impartial, persevering, unrebukable religion before God and the Father.

And such an one we have in the example of Daniel. He had doubtless his infirmities: "for there is not a just man upon earth that doeth good and sinneth not:" but nothing is alleged against him. This is the more remarkable, since the sacred writers freely mention the faults as well as the excellences of good men; and I do not remember that any other individual, recorded in the Scriptures, has entirely escaped censure.

But let us attend to the words which I have read, and in which we have to consider—THE EMPLOYMENT OF DANIEL—THE CIRCUMSTANCES OF THE ACTION—AND THE KNOWLEDGE THAT ENHANCED THE VALUE OF THE PERFORMANCE.

I. THE EMPLOYMENT OF DANIEL. It was pious. He prayed and gave thanks before his God. He was not one of those who are satisfied with morality without godliness. He well knew that our greatest connexions are with God; and that *with him* we have principally to do. He was a good neighbour, a good citizen, a good master, and a good magistrate; but this did not excuse him from the worship of God. " He prayed—and gave thanks—before his God."

First. He *prayed.* Prayer is the breathing of the desire towards God. Words are not essential to the performance of it. As words may be used without prayer, so prayer may be used without words: he that searcheth the heart " knoweth what is the mind of the spirit;" and when we cannot command language like some of our fellow-christians, it is well to be able to say, " Lord, all my desire is before thee, and my groaning is not hid from thee."

The expediency, the necessity of prayer, results from our indigent and dependent state. We have enemies to overcome—and how are we to conquer them! we have trials to endure—and how are we to bear them! We have duties to accomplish—and how are we to perform them! We need mercy and grace to help us—and how are we to obtain them? God has determined and revealed the method in which he will communicate the blessings he has promised. " For all these things will I be inquired of by the house of Israel. Draw nigh to God, and he will draw nigh to you. Ask, and it shall be given to you; seek, and ye shall find." And, as he is a sovereign, and under no obligation to favour us at all, he has surely a right to appoint the way in which he will be gracious: but, in this appointment, his wisdom appears as conspicuous as his sovereignty; and his goodness as clearly as his wisdom. Nothing can be so beneficial to us as prayer is, not only by the relief it obtains, but by the influence it exerts; not only by its answers, but by its energy. Beyond every thing else that is instrumental in religion, it improves our characters, it strengthens our graces, it softens and refines our tempers, it contributes to our spirituality, and promotes our holiness. The more we have to do with God, the more we shall resemble him. " It is therefore good for us to draw near to him."

Secondly. He *gave thanks.* This should always attend prayer. Whenever we go to God for new favours, we should be careful to acknowledge old ones: while we implore deliverance, we should be grateful for alleviations and supports. I am sorry to say, that this is too commonly neglected. We are very selfish; and it appears even in our devotional services. We are too backward to every duty of religion; we are backward to pray, but still more to praise. Pressed by our difficulties, and urged by our wants, we are constrained to pray; but when we have succeeded, we become unmindful of our benefactor. Thus of the ten lepers that were cleansed, " one only returned to give glory to God." And even of good Hezekiah it is said, when his health was restored, and his adversaries destroyed, that " he rendered not according to the benefit done him." A sad blemish! " Oh," says David, " Oh that men would praise the Lord for his goodness, and for his wonderful works to the children of men !" And that he did not wish to enforce upon others what he neglected himself, appears from his own resolution: " I will bless the Lord at all times; his praise shall continually be in my mouth. And let us not think that he was undertaking more than could ever be accomplished: for the injunction of the Apostle is, " In every thing give thanks." There is no state that does not require gratitude. There is always much more to be grateful for than to complain of, however afflicting our circumstances may be. Yea, even those things which seem the most unfriendly to our wishes and our welfare, did we know all, would probably draw forth our highest praise. For who has had not reason to say, " It is good for me that I have been afflicted !" Daniel, you would naturally conclude, had much to *pray* for—but though a captive, in a strange land, and labouring under the most cruel persecution, he did not forget to *give thanks.*

Thirdly. He did all this *before his God.* By which we are to understand, that he placed himself, in his religious exercises, under the eye of Jehovah, and realized his presence. Abraham was commanded to " walk before God :" and it would be well for us to remember, that wherever we go, and whatever we do, God is with us, as our observer, our witness, our judge. But when we engage in devotional services, whether public or private, we are considered as withdrawn from the world, and appearing more immediately before God. And to impress our minds with this truth is the way to secure our profit. It will banish hypocrisy, and formality, and carelessness; and unite our hearts to fear God's name.

II. THE CIRCUMSTANCES OF THE ACTION.

The First regards the *place.* He " went into his house." God does not confine his regards to the great congregation; but " where two or three are gathered together in his name, there he is in the midst of them." He dwelleth not in temples made with hands;

"Where'er we seek him he is found,
And every place is holy ground."

And every house not only may be, but should be, a house of prayer; and in every family there ought to be an altar, to offer up spiritual sacrifices, acceptable to God by Jesus Christ. Daniel worshipped God in his house, and with his family—but this is not all. He worshipped God alone: he was now—not in the parlour, but in his chamber—the very circumstance enjoined by our Saviour upon all his followers, and who will find it to be their privilege as well as their duty to observe it. "When thou prayest, enter into thy closet, and when thou hast shut thy door, pray to thy Father which is in secret; and thy Father which seeth in secret shall reward thee openly."

The Second regards his *posture*. "He kneeled upon his knees." God is a spirit; and the great thing is, to worship him in spirit and in truth. This may be done under an endless variety of forms and modes. We have always reason to fear that men are drawn off from the weightier matters of the law, in proportion as they are taken up with the external and circumstantial parts of religion. The Gospel has a nobler aim in view, than to stoop to regulate by positive law the minute ceremonial order of divine worship. There are many things left very safely at large, and which may be determined by circumstances variously, and yet prove equally acceptable to God, and useful to the worshipper himself.

But though bodily exercise profiteth little, God is "to be glorified in our bodies," as well as "in our spirits:" and we are free to say, that where it can be indulged, kneeling seems to be the most proper and advantageous posture of devotion. It preserves us more from distraction; it is more expressive of reverence, humility, and submission. It was not only the posture of Daniel, but of Paul: "I bow my knees unto the God and Father of our Lord Jesus Christ." It was our Saviour's posture: "he kneeled three times, praying and saying the same words." It is the posture we all seem unavoidably to adopt, in private and in family worship.

The Third regards the *direction* in which he performed his devotion: his windows were open "toward Jerusalem." Here we see the love a pious Jew bore to his native land, and the city of his solemnities. Though it was now in ruins, "he took pleasure in her dust, and favoured the stones thereof." Though he himself was advanced and provided for, yet said he, "if I forget thee, O Jerusalem, let my right hand forget her cunning. If I do not remember thee, let my tongue cleave to the roof of my mouth; if I prefer not Jerusalem above my chief joy."

When the temple was dedicated, Solomon, in his address to God, had thus expressed himself: "If thy people sin against thee, and thou be angry with them, and deliver them to the enemy, yet if they shall bethink themselves in the land whither they were carried captives, and repent, and make supplication unto thee in the land of them that carried them captives, saying, We have sinned, and have done perversely, we have committed wickedness; and so return unto thee with all their heart, and with all their soul, in the land of their enemies, which led them away captive, and pray unto thee toward their land which thou gavest unto their fathers, the city which thou hast chosen, and the house which I have built for thy name: then hear thou their prayer and their supplication in heaven thy dwelling-place, and maintain their cause." Daniel had read this prayer: he had also read the prophecy of Jeremiah; "Thus saith the Lord, after seventy years be accomplished at Babylon, I will visit you, and perform my good word toward you, in causing you to return to this place. For I know the thoughts that I think toward you, saith the Lord; thoughts of peace, and not of evil, to give you an expected end." And thus encouraged, he hoped and believed that in due time they should be released and restored. Hence in his prayers he always remembered Zion, and would give God no rest till he established, and till he "made Jerusalem a praise in the earth." A public spirit is a great excellency: and we ought, even in our private devotions, to be social; to be concerned for our country; and the Church of God.

The Fourth regards the *frequency* of the exercise. He did it "three times a day." And surely this is little enough, considering the command, "Pray without ceasing." You all refresh your bodies three times a day. Can your souls require less? A few moments of retirement in the middle of every day would much tend to keep you in the things of God, and preserve you from the evil of the world.

I know that habitual devotion is what we should seek to maintain; but with many people at least, that which may be always done, is often never done; and if it be not proper in some cases to *bind* conscience, it will be useful, in all cases, to *remind* it: regular and appointed exercises of piety are of great importance.

David, as well as Daniel, was aware of this, and therefore says he, "Evening and morning, and at noon will I pray, and cry aloud: and he shall hear my voice."

The last circumstance is the *constancy* and invariableness of the practice—"as aforetime." There was therefore nothing *new* in it. It was not an *extraordinary* fervour, produced by the spur of the occasion; it was not occasional impulse; but the regular effects of principle and disposition. It was a plan he had laid down, a rule to which he always conformed. He did it when a young man, and he does it now he is an old one. He did it when he was in private life, and he does it now he is in public office.

Many of you, perhaps, complain that you cannot find time for duties, the importance of which you are constrained to acknowledge. But who are you? and what are your circumstances and engagements, that you cannot secure a little time for God and your souls? Daniel was a man of business; of vast business; a prime minister; having to inspect and manage the affairs of an enormous empire: yet he retired three times a day; and not for one day only, but every day. "He went into his house, and his windows being open in his chamber toward Jerusalem, he kneeled upon his knees three times a day, and prayed, and gave thanks before his God, as he did aforetime." Remark,

III. THE KNOWLEDGE THAT ENHANCED THE VALUE OF THE PERFORMANCE.

We all know that an action we admire would not discover the same degree of principle in other circumstances. When a man is surrounded with honour and applause—then—to think of himself soberly—this evinces his humility. When a man is insulted and injured—then—to rule his own spirit, and to render blessing for cursing—this marks his patience and meekness. When a man sees his danger—but says, "None of these things move me"—this is the trial and the triumph of his conviction and his resolution. Had Daniel been ignorant of the king's decree, his decision and courage would not have appeared. But he knew that the writing was signed, and was aware of the consequences of disobedience—yet he determined to stand his ground; and proved, that he loved his duty more than life; and that he who fears God fears no other fear.

Whence we learn, that no danger should hinder a good man from doing his work.

It is natural to conclude, that some would press Daniel to yield; nor is it difficult to conjecture the reasons or excuses they would urge.

Some would plead loyalty. "The command was from the king his master, and in honour of him too; and would he disobey the order of his sovereign, and when his glory was at stake!"—But Daniel knew how to distinguish between civil and religious concerns. He knew that in the former, we are to obey the powers that be; in the latter we are held by a higher homage: and if the commands of any superior contradict the commands of God, we are pre-engaged; and must "obey God rather than man." Thus children are only required to obey their parents "in the Lord."

Some would plead usefulness. "His life was in danger; and it was valuable. What a loss would the world and the Church sus-

tain!" But Daniel knew that we are to go on in the path of duty, whatever we meet with; that we are not allowed to decline a command of God, by reasoning from remote or probable consequences; that we are to cast our care upon the Lord; and that we are most useful when in simplicity and godly sincerity, "not with fleshly wisdom, but by the grace of God, we have our conversation in the world."

Some would have recommended a plan of accommodation. "He could have withdrawn into the country, and concealed himself for thirty days. He might have discontinued the exercise of prayer, though not the inclination. He might have prayed inwardly and secretly, and thus have preserved his character and his conscience too." But Daniel knew that if he had done this, it would have appeared to his friends, and much more to his enemies, that he had thrown up the duty for the sake of his secular advantage, and was afraid to trust the God of his salvation; it would have dishonoured his religion, and have justified others in temporizing and cowardice. Whereas by acting this noble and open part, he rendered himself peculiarly useful, and obtained the most distinguished honour.

I said he rendered himself by this example peculiarly *useful*. Who can imagine what an attention would be excited; what inquiries would be made; how many would become proselytes to the Jewish religion, and adore a God that, unlike their abominations, was able to save those that served him. Even an edict was passed in honour of Daniel's Deliverer. "Then king Darius wrote unto all people, nations, and languages, that dwell in all the earth; Peace be multiplied unto you. I make a decree, That in every dominion of my kingdom men tremble and fear before the God of Daniel: for he is the living God, and steadfast for ever, and his kingdom that which shall not be destroyed, and his dominion shall be even unto the end. He delivereth and rescueth, and he worketh signs and wonders in heaven and in earth, who hath delivered Daniel from the power of the lions."

Why are we required to "hold forth" the word of life; to hold fast "the profession of our faith;" to "confess with the mouth," as well as believe with the heart; to "let our light shine before men, that they may see our good works?"—Why! Because our religion is to be visible as well as real; and must be fairly and fully exhibited, in order to be impressive and profitable. It is not by trimming and yielding, but by amiable, consistent, firm, and uniform deportment, that we are to strike and convince beholders.

When Sir Thomas Abney was mayor of London, he made no scruple at the lord mayor's feast to rise in the evening and inform the company that he was going to with draw, to perform the worship of God in his family; after which he would return again. It is not every one that *could* have done this. In many it would have appeared a part over-acted; it would have appeared sanctimoniousness. But where it was a sample, and not an exception; where it was an action of a life, the whole of which corresponded with it, it is easy to conclude what effect it would produce. Even those who affected to ridicule would inwardly venerate; some would be led to reflection; some would be stung with reproach; some would be determined; and some encouraged.

Christians! how many opportunities have you of saying, with Nehemiah, " so do not I, because of the fear of God." Are you asked to go to a place of dissipation? What an opportunity is afforded you of bearing a verbal and practical testimony against a worldly life! Slander creeps into conversation. What a call have you to enter, though in a proper manner, your testimony against evil speaking!—Avow your principles. Live answerable to your profession. " Be steadfast, unmoveable, always abounding in the work of the Lord; forasmuch as ye know that your labour shall not be in vain in the Lord."

I said, he obtained by this example the most distinguished honour.

A miracle was wrought in his favour. " Then the king arose very early in the morning, and went in haste unto the den of lions. And when he came to the den, he cried with a lamentable voice unto Daniel: and the king spake and said to Daniel, O Daniel, servant of the living God, is thy God, whom thou servest continually, able to deliver thee from the lions? Then said Daniel unto the king, O king, live for ever. My God hath sent his angel, and hath shut the lions' mouths, that they have not hurt me: forasmuch as before him innocency was found in me; and also before thee, O king, have I done no hurt. Then was the king exceeding glad for him, and commanded that they should take Daniel up out of the den. So Daniel was taken up out of the den, and no manner of hurt was found upon him, because he believed in his God."

His enemies are punished. He is also advanced. He " prospered in the reign of Darius, and in the reign of Cyrus the Persian."

What sublime consolation filled his mind while he saw the divine power securing him in the very jaws of death! As he is drawn out of the den how would every eye be attracted towards him! How would the multitude follow him to his own dwelling! Whenever he appeared in public, how would every tongue be ready to extol him! What weight would attach to his character! What force would be acknowledged in his advice and his reproof!

" Them that honour me," says God, " I will honour." Whatever the world may think, there is a reality in religion; and it more than indemnifies its followers: " Godliness is profitable unto all things, having promise of the life that now is, and of that which is to come." " Verily," says the Saviour, " there is no man that hath left house, or parents, or brethren, or wife, or children, for the kingdom of God's sake, who shall not receive manifold more in this present time, and in the world to come life everlasting."

DISCOURSE LXXV.

THE UNSPEAKABLE GIFT.

(CHRISTMAS.)

He that spared not his own Son, but delivered him up for us all, how shall he not with him also freely give us all things?—Rom. viii. 32.

FEAR naturally follows guilt. When a breach has taken place between two parties, the hardest to be won is always the offender. *He* has all the consciousness of blame, and judges of the person offended under the influence of his own uneasy feelings.

But if it be hard to believe that he whom I have provoked will forgive me, how much harder is it to believe that he will indulge me—that instead of being my enemy he will be my greatest friend—and that instead of employing his power against me, all his resources shall be held at my disposal! For friendship does not necessarily succeed reconciliation, nor the munificence of kindness the forgiveness of injuries: as we see in the case of Absalom, who was permitted to return to the capital, but " lived three whole years in Jerusalem without seeing the king's face."

From these reflections it will follow, that it is no easy thing for a sinner to place his " faith and hope in God."

But difficult as this confidence in God is, it is necessary. We fell by losing it; and we can only be recovered by regaining it. We shall never serve him, never love him, never go to him, till we can see that " he is good, and ready to forgive, and plenteous in mercy to all that call upon him."

Difficult as this confidence in God is, it is attainable. He has proclaimed his name, " the Lord God, gracious and merciful, long-suffering, and abundant in goodness and truth." He has caused his goodness to pass before us. He has given us his word; and " whatsoever things were written aforetime were written for our learning, that we through patience and comfort of the Scriptures might have hope."

But in the redemption of the world by our Lord Jesus Christ every objection seems silenced for ever; and the despairing soul rises from its dungeon, and reasons itself into light and comfort from the words which I have read; "He that spared not his own Son, but delivered him up for us all, how shall he not with him also freely give us all things?"

The words contain two things.

I. A WONDERFUL FACT. II. AN UNDENIABLE INFERENCE.

I. God "spared not his own Son, but delivered him up for us all." This is THE FACT —to which we have well prefixed the term WONDERFUL. "For ask now of the days that are past, which were before thee, since the day that God created man upon the earth, and ask from the one side of heaven unto the other, whether there hath been any such thing as this great thing is, or hath been heard like it!"

Various wonders distinguish the works of God. There are marvellous displays of his power, of his wisdom, of his truth, of his holiness; but the miracle we are now led to contemplate is a miracle of love. Every other perfection is indeed apparent in the dispensation; but hear how the Scripture speaks of it: "God so loved the world, that he gave his only begotten Son, that whosoever believeth in him should not perish, but have everlasting life. In this was manifested the love of God towards us, because that God sent his only begotten Son into the world, that we might live through him. Herein is love, not that we loved God, but that he loved us, and sent his Son to be the propitiation for our sins." To magnify this goodness, observe,

First: the boon he did not withhold. He "spared not his own Son." How many things could you resign before you spared a child! Nothing is so strong as paternal affection. A man's wife is himself divided; a man's child is himself multiplied. How unwilling was Jacob to spare Benjamin, though he had many children, and it was only for a season, and to save him alive! How unwilling was David to give up even a rebellious Absalom! "Deal gently with the young man for my sake," said he in his orders to Joab; and when he heard of his well-deserved death, the father vanquished the man, and the king, if not the saint. "He went up to the chamber over the gate, and wept: and as he went, thus he said, O my son Absalom, my son, my son Absalom! would God I had died for thee, O Absalom, my son, my son!" In the famine of Samaria, the woman, by promising to make a similar sacrifice, persuaded her neighbour "to boil her son:" but when her own turn came, "lo, she hid her son!" History mentions a poor family in Germany, who were ready to perish in the time of famine. The husband proposed to the wife to sell one of their children for bread. At length she consents. But—here—here is the difficulty—which of them shall it be? The eldest was named—

but refused. This was their first-born, and the beginning of their strength. The second was named—but refused. He was the living image of the father. The third was named—but refused. In him the features of the mother breathed. The last was named—but refused. He was their youngest, the child of their old age. And so they consented to starve together rather than sacrifice one. What was the severest trial of Abraham's regard for God? "Now I know that thou fearest me, seeing thou hast not withheld—thy son—thine—only son from me." How dignified was God's Son! "For to which of the angels said he at any time, Thou art my son, this day have I begotten thee? And again, I will be to him a Father, and he shall be to me a son? And again, when he bringeth in the firstbegotten into the world, he saith, And let all the angels of God worship him." How dear was God's Son! The Son of his love; who always did the things that pleased him; in him his soul delighted! Yet he withholds him not!—He "spared not his own Son."

Secondly. Observe the state into which he surrendered him. He "delivered him up."—To what? "Be astonished, O Heavens; and wonder, O Earth!"—To a world that disowned him. "He was in the world, and the world was made by him, and the world knew him not." To a people that abhorred him, though prepared by miracles, and ordinances, and prophecies, to receive him. "He came to his own, and his own received him not." To obscurity and indigence. He was born in a stable, and laid in a manger; and as he passed through life "he had not where to lay his head." To infamy and scorn. He was reviled as a glutton and a wine-bibber; as a friend of publicans and sinners; as a madman, as a demoniac, and a rebel: "Reproach," said he, "hath broken my heart." To pain and anguish. "He was a man of sorrows, and acquainted with grief." To be betrayed by Judas; to be denied by Peter; to be forsaken of all his disciples. To Caiaphas—who insulted him; to Herod—who set him at nought; to Pilate—who condemned him; to the Romans—who crucified him.—To an agony, that before the hand of man had touched him, made him "sweat as it were great drops of blood falling to the ground;" and exclaim, "My soul is exceeding sorrowful, even unto death—If it be possible, let this cup pass from me!" "Behold, and see if ever there was sorrow like unto his sorrow. Yet it pleased the Lord to bruise him. He hath put him to grief. The Lord hath laid upon him the iniquity of us all." Surely here is love for which we want a name! Especially when we remark,

Thirdly, the persons for whose advantage he was given.—"He delivered him up"—for whom? For *us*. And who are we? Not angels; but men. Not *men* only; but *sinners*. Not sinners humbled under a sense of our misery, and applying for mercy; but sinners regardless of their deliverance, and abusing the Divine goodness: "herein God hath commended his love towards us, in that while we were yet sinners, Christ died for us. For when we were yet without strength, in due time Christ died for the ungodly." To love our parents and our children is natural. To love our friends is just and grateful. To do good to strangers is humane. To relieve the poor and needy is kind and generous. But to love our enemies, to do good to them that hate us and injure us, is divine. It is not only commanded by God, but exemplified in the highest degree—in all its perfection.

And not for a few of these rebels, but for many; not for Jews only, but for Gentiles also; not for persons of one condition and character, but of every condition and character; not for some who seek him, but for all: under whatever discouragements they may labour. Such was the indefinite and unlimited message of the angel to the shepherds: "Fear not; for, behold, I bring you good tidings of great joy, which shall be to all people." And such is the extension of the Apostle: "He spared not his own Son, but delivered him up for us *all*."

II. Let us examine THE INFERENCE to be drawn from the fact we have explained.—Shall " he not with him also freely give us all things?" Here it may be necessary to remark,

First: The *way* in which he communicates his favours. He gives them *freely*. And were it not for this, we could have no hope: for we are not worthy of the least of all his mercies. But if we are not worthy, we are welcome. If we find ourselves without money, we are called to buy without price. If the blessings are great, they are equally gracious: and we are invited to come and "take of the water of life freely."

Adam could not have merited in Paradise. Angels do not merit in heaven—their obedience is *due;* and *duty* can never be meritorious. How well, therefore, does it become sinful creatures like us, to acknowledge, when we have done all, "that we are unprofitable servants;" and have done no more than was our duty to do! And how have we done this? By a power not our own; and with numberless imperfections that deserve condemnation rather than reward. With what indignation did Peter speak to Simon Magus, who supposed the gift of the Holy Ghost was to be purchased with money! Are any of you endeavouring to buy what you ought to beg! "Repent of this thy wickedness, and pray to God, if haply the thought of thine heart may be forgiven thee."

Secondly. Observe the extent of his liberality. He will freely give us "all things." It intends whatever is needful to our salvation and welfare: pardon, to remove our guilt; strength, to aid us in the performance of duty; consolation in distress; guidance in perplexity; "a land flowing with milk and honey" beyond Jordan, and supplies for the wilderness on this side of it. It provides for soul and body. For time and eternity. "The Lord God is a sun and shield: the Lord will give grace and glory: no good thing will he withhold from them that walk uprightly. The young lions do lack and suffer hunger, but they that seek the Lord shall not want any good thing." The grant has only one limitation—the *goodness* of the things conferred: of this, God only is the judge; and therefore with him the determination must be left.

Thirdly. The *reasonableness* of our most enlarged expectation. "He that spared not his own Son, but delivered him up for us all, *how shall he not with him* also freely give us all things?" The conclusion is not only undeniable, but so simple and obvious, that it seems needless to enlarge; otherwise we might observe, that the force of the reasoning lies in this: That he was designed to prepare the way for all the blessings we need; that he is superior to them all; and that they are all really in him.

He was designed to prepare the way for the communication of all the blessings we need. Sin had stopped the effusion of the divine goodness, and forbidden God to hold communion with man. But he "devised means that his banished should not be expelled from him." He furnished the sacrifice he required. "He sent his own Son into the world, not to condemn the world, but that the world *through him* might be saved." He came to remove every obstruction, and to render the exercise of divine favour consistent with the honour of divine government. And is not this a powerful consideration, that now, if we go to God, there is nothing to hinder his mercy; nothing even in his truth, nothing even in his righteousness, nothing even in his law, to restrain him from relieving and blessing the guilty? Yea, that he can relieve and bless us in a way even glorious to all his perfections; that he can be even "faithful and just to forgive us our sins, and to cleanse us from all unrighteousness?"

He is superior to every other blessing. You are sometimes dismayed at the thought of your demerit: but if your demerit restrained the Divine goodness, the Saviour would never have appeared. You are sometimes dismayed at the greatness of the blessing you ask: but if the greatness of the blessing restrained the Divine goodness, he would have denied giving his own Son. If a man had sacrificed for you his own and his only son, you could hardly think he would withhold

2 M

from you a common instance of his bounty; for the one, you say, has no proportion to the other. What God has already given is infinitely more precious than any thing we can in future implore.

Yea, he *is* in reality every other blessing: and we *have* all with him. "He that hath the Son hath life." "He is made of God unto us, wisdom and righteousness, sanctification and redemption. He is all and in all." He, and his influences and blessings, cannot be divided. When we receive him all things are ours.

Are we not constrained to admire the Supreme Being? Can we survey the dispensation we have reviewed, and not acknowledge that he well deserves the name of "the Father of mercies, the God of all grace!" Can we think of it, and not exclaim, "Is this the manner of man, O Lord God!" No. We have heard of benefactors; but they all shrink into nothing from a comparison with him. "God is love."

Where do you study the Divine character? There are many who view God in the beauties of Nature, and the bounties of Providence; they are thankful that he does not "leave himself without witness in doing them good, and giving them rain from heaven, and fruitful seasons, filling their hearts with joy and gladness." But this is hardly rising above heathenism. Christianity seems to afford them no advantages. They never regard God in his highest, noblest work of redemption! Yet this is the dispensation by which he intends to make himself known, according to the words of the Apostle: "That in the ages to come he might show the exceeding riches of his grace, in his kindness towards us by Christ Jesus." Here the primitive Christians beheld him. "He hath shined, said they, in our hearts, to give the light of the knowledge of the glory of God, in the face of Jesus Christ." Paul did not overlook any of God's favours: but this—this drew forth all the ardour of his soul. "Thanks be unto God for his unspeakable gift. Blessed be the God and Father of our Lord Jesus Christ, who hath blessed us with all spiritual blessings in heavenly places in Christ."

But a barren consideration of a subject so important and interesting is as unworthy as indifference. The subject should always produce three effects.

First. It should inspire you with *encouragement.* Never entertain any harsh and gloomy notions of God when you go to him: but remember, that you are going to address a Being whose heart is set upon your welfare; a Being who, after all that you have done, waits to be gracious; a Being who says, "Let the wicked forsake his way, and the unrighteous man his thoughts, and let him return unto the Lord, and he will have mercy upon him, and to our God, for he will abundantly pardon." Were you to ask, "What sign showest thou, that we may believe?" Behold, says he, the garden, and the cross. See my own Son dying that you may live. I sacrifice him, and save you.

Secondly. The subject should impose upon you *submission.* Is any thing denied you that seems desirable? He distinguishes between your welfare and your wishes; between the present and the future; between appearances and reality. The blessing *is* not withheld from a want of power; nor *can* it be withheld from a want of love. If it were proper and profitable for you, he *could* bring down the kings of the earth to lick the dust of your feet; he *could* possess you with an abundance of this world's goods; he *could* free you from bodily pain, and retain your dear connexions around you: and if it were proper and profitable for you, he *would* do it. Cannot you trust him? "He that spared not his own Son, but delivered him up for us all, how shall he not with him also freely give us all things?"

Thirdly. The subject should inflame you with *gratitude.* You can never discharge your obligation to such an infinite friend; but ought you not to be sensible of it? And ought you not to convince all around you that you are alive to his glory? Should you not constantly ask, "What shall I render to the Lord for all his benefits towards me?" He spared not his own Son for you: and will you spare nothing for him? Will you not spare a little of your time? One day in every week? Some part of every day? Will you not spare a little of your substance—to spread his word, and to relieve his poor?

You ought to say—

> "Were the whole realm of nature mine,
> That were a present far too small:
> Love so amazing, so divine,
> Demands my soul, my life, my all."

DISCOURSE LXXVI.

DIVINE CORRECTION.

Furthermore we have had fathers of our flesh which corrected us, and we gave them reverence: shall we not much rather be in subjection unto the Father of spirits, and live? For they verily for a few days chastened us after their own pleasure; but he for our profit, that we might be partakers of his holiness.—Heb. xii. 9, 10.

SUPPOSE a person should prescribe a course, by following which he would promise you an escape from death. The scheme could only excite a momentary wonder; and you would not waste your time even to examine it. Scripture, history, and observation, would convince you, that "in this war there is no discharge ;" and, lifting up your eyes to heaven, you would sigh, and say, "I know that thou wilt bring me to death; and to the house appointed for all living." But it would be otherwise if he should recommend a preparation for it. This would be wise; this is necessary.

The same may be said with regard to affliction. "Although affliction cometh not forth of the dust, neither doth trouble spring out of the ground; yet man is born unto trouble, as the sparks fly upwards." No expedient has yet been discovered as a preservative from calamity. Power, wealth, honour, learning, prudence, morality, have all been unable to find a pathway through life free from sorrow. And religion, even the religion of the Bible, does not promise us security; yea, it asserts that "many are the afflictions of the righteous."

But if there is no exemption from trouble, there is a preparation for it. And since it is impossible for us to escape suffering, it is of high importance to know how we may endure it—so as never to be injured by it—and always to derive advantage from it. Our case is truly alarming, when even medicine is administered in vain. It is bad, says Bishop Hopkins, to lose the lives of our friends, but it is worse to lose their deaths. It is a serious thing, says Henry, to lose a calamity. And we ought, says Owen, as much to pray for a blessing upon our daily rod, as upon our daily bread.

How ought we then to suffer? The Apostle tells us. For, speaking unto us as unto children, he says, "Furthermore we have had fathers of our flesh which corrected us, and we gave them reverence: shall we not much rather be in subjection unto the Father of spirits, and live? For they verily for a few days chastened us after their own pleasure; but he for our profit, that we might be partakers of his holiness." Let us consider two things.

I. THE DUTY OF AFFLICTION.—II. THE REASONS BY WHICH IT IS ENFORCED.

I. THE DUTY is *subjection.* "Shall we not be in subjection?" This is not opposed to insensibility. To be insensible under affliction is not only unnatural, but immoral; and subverts the very purpose of the dispensation. Health and happiness, pleasure and pain, the life or death of our connexions, are not to be absolutely indifferent to us, we are allowed a preference with submission. We see this exemplified in the Son of God himself. "Now is my soul troubled; and what shall I say! Father, save me from this hour—I would, if it were allowable—But for this cause came I unto this hour." With strong cryings and tears he prayed: and you may say as he did, "Father, if it be possible, let this cup pass from me," if you add as he did, "Nevertheless, not as I will, but as thou

wilt." Yea, so far is this very subjection from excluding sensibility, that it necessarily requires it. There is no virtue in the senselessness of a stone. There is no patience, no resignation in bearing what we do not feel. If you do not prize what you give up at the call of God, there can be no value in your obedience.

But it is the repression of every thing rebellious—in our *carriage*—in our *speech*—and in the *temper of our minds.*

Every thing rebellious in *carriage.* It is said of Ahaz, that, in his affliction, "he sinned yet more against God." Jeremiah complains of the Jews; "Thou hast stricken them, but they have not grieved; thou hast consumed them, but they have refused to receive correction: they have made their faces harder than a rock; they have refused to return." There are some who repair to worldly company and dissipation to banish all sense of sorrow; like those in Isaiah, who said, "Let us eat and drink, for to-morrow we die." Many, under the grasp of Providence, do not ask for release, but struggle to get free; and have recourse to any unhallowed means to deliver themselves.— This is wrong. Trouble is in Scripture compared to a prison: and you are not to attempt to burn down the house, or to force open the door, or to escape by the window— but if you see him passing by who placed you there, you may address him as one did before you: "Bring my soul out of prison, that I may praise thy name; the righteous shall compass me about: for thou shalt deal bountifully with me."

Every thing rebellious in *speech.* Aaron, under the loss of his sons, "held his peace." So did David under sickness of body; "I was dumb, I opened not my mouth, because thou didst it." Job was so fearful of offending, that he determined to be silent: "Behold, I am vile: what shall I answer thee? I will lay mine hand upon my mouth. Once have I spoken: but I will not answer: yea, twice; but I will proceed no further." An example which Solomon recommends to our imitation, when he says, "If thou hast thought evil, lay thy hand upon thy mouth;" endeavour to check it: for though it be bad to feel it, it is worse to express it; it dishonours God more, and scandalizes others more. "In a multitude of words there wanteth not sin;" and there is such peculiar danger when we suffer, that it is necessary to pray continually, "Set a watch, O Lord, before my mouth; keep the door of my lips."

Every thing rebellious in the *temper of the mind.* For the Lord looketh to the heart, and if this be full of impatience and resentment, though we may do nothing and say nothing amiss, we are refractory; and though men may applaud us, God will condemn us. But we should always distinguish between a rebellious state of mind, and a rebellious emotion. The most humble and dutiful may feel at times an unruly thought suddenly rising up—but it will not be encouraged, and finding no entertainment there, it will withdraw. The disposition of the soul appears in this, that it is shocked and distressed by such a sentiment: while it longs and strives after acquiescence. We are to judge of ourselves, not by what is unavoidable, but by what is voluntary: not by what is occasional, but by what is habitual and prevailing. The rest will be readily pardoned by Him, who "knoweth our frame, and remembers that we are dust, and spares us as a man spareth his own son that serveth him." How beautifully is this state of mind characterized and expressed in the following lines!

> "Peace all our angry passions, then;
> Let each rebellious sigh
> Be silent at his sovereign will,
> And every murmur die.

And again,

> "I charge my thoughts, be patient still,
> And all my carriage mild;
> Content, my Father, with thy will,
> And quiet as a child.

> "The patient soul, the lowly mind
> Shall have a large reward;
> Let saints in sorrow lie resign'd,
> And trust a faithful Lord."

II. Let us consider THE REASONS BY WHICH THIS DUTY IS ENFORCED.

Nothing can be more pleasing and convincing than the language of the Apostle. "Furthermore we have had fathers of our flesh which corrected us, and we gave them reverence: shall we not much rather be in subjection unto the Father of spirits, and live? For they verily for a few days chastened us after their own pleasure; but he for our profit, that we might be partakers of his holiness." Here are four motives.

The First is derived from the relation in which God stands to us. He is our *Father*. This is the common name by which he has revealed himself in the Gospel; and it is equally lovely and venerable. There is indeed another being you have honoured with this title. But he is not your father in the same sense with God. The former is your father subordinately, the latter is so absolutely. The one is the father only of your *flesh*, the other is the Father also of your *spirit*—and *this* is the man; this is the principal part of human nature. The body is the case, the soul is the jewel; the one is the habitation of clay, the other is the inspired resident. By the one we resemble worms, by the other we are allied to angels; the one is mortal, the other is immortal; "the dust returns to the dust whence it came, the spirit returns to God who gave it." In whatever way the spirit unites with the flesh, in the production of it human agency has no share, and God

claims the creation of it as his prerogative. He is called "the God of the spirits of all flesh;" and is said to have "formed the spirit of man within him."

But to what does this lead? The conclusion, says the Apostle, is obvious. If he preeminently fills this relation, his claims to duty are proportionably great. You gave the fathers of your flesh reverence. Look back to the period of infancy and childhood. Were all your wishes gratified, whether wise or foolish? whether good or evil? Were no restraints laid upon you, the reasons of which you were unable to discover? Were you not compelled to apply yourselves to various exercises, which your vain and roving minds would have gladly passed by? But you regarded the authority that enjoined them; and submitted. You sometimes provoked the rod, and incurred rebuke. And you have better apprehensions of the whole system of discipline now, than you had then. But even *then* you did not strike again—your arm would have been unnerved. You did not snatch the rod out of your father's hand and break it to pieces—you would have shuddered at the thought. You did not fly from the house, and refuse to return. You did not say to him, I despise thy strokes—and will do so again. You did not even dare to ask, What right hast thou to deal thus with me? And shall a man obtain more obedience than God? "Shall you not much rather be in subjection unto the Father of spirits?" It is to be feared that the children of Jonadab will not only rise up in judgment against the Israelites, but against ourselves. Hear what God says of *them*: "Go and tell the men of Judah and the inhabitants of Jerusalem, Will ye not receive instruction to hearken to my words? saith the Lord. The words of Jonadab the son of Rechab, that he commanded his sons, not to drink wine, are performed; for unto this day they drink none, but obey their father's commandment: notwithstanding I have spoken unto you, rising early and speaking; but ye hearkened not unto me. Because the sons of Jonadab the sons of Rechab have performed the commandment of their father, which he commanded them; but this people hath not hearkened unto me: therefore thus saith the Lord God of hosts the God of Israel; Behold, I will bring upon Judah and upon all the inhabitants of Jerusalem all the evil that I have pronounced against them."

This brings us to the Second reason of submission. It is taken from the *danger of resistance*. "Shall we not much rather be in subjection to the Father of spirits, and live?" Clearly intimating that disobedience will end in death. It did so among the Israelitish children, to whom the Apostle alludes. Under the Law, rebellion after parental correction was a capital crime; it was death by statute. And thus the statute runs: "If a man have a stubborn and rebellious son, which will not obey the voice of his father, or the voice of his mother, and that, when they have chastened him, will not hearken unto them: then shall his father and his mother lay hold on him, and bring him out unto the elders of the city, and unto the gate of his place; and they shall say unto the elders of his city, This our son is stubborn and rebellious, he will not obey our voice; he is a glutton, and a drunkard. And all the men of his city shall stone him with stones, that he die: so shalt thou put evil away from among you; and all Israel shall hear, and fear." In such a case there was no alternative but submission or destruction.

And so it is here. Resistance is not only unreasonable, but ruinous. "Who ever hardened himself against Him and prospered? Wo be to the man that striveth with his Maker!" There cannot be a more awful presage of future misery than to counteract the afflictive dispensations of divine Providence, and "despise the chastening of the Almighty." It provokes the anger of God, and operates penally in one of these two ways. Either, first, it induces God to recall the rod, and, giving a man up to the way of his own heart, to say, as he did of Ephraim, "He is joined to idols; let him alone;"—or, secondly, he turns the rod into a scorpion, and fulfils the threatening; "If ye will not be reformed by me, by these things, but will walk contrary unto me; then will I also walk contrary unto you, and will punish you yet seven times for your sins." Thus he strikes at first more distantly, and less severely. He takes away a part of the man's estate. He then bereaves him of a friend or relation. He next visits him with some bodily disease. After this he strikes his conscience, and he has "a wounded spirit" that he cannot bear; he is afraid to die, and he is unable to live. At length God casts him into hell, with these words, "He that being often reproved hardeneth his neck, shall suddenly be destroyed, and that without remedy."

At the thought of this, a Christian trembles in every particle of his frame, and falling on his knees, cries, "Do not condemn me. Chasten me as thou pleasest with thy people, but let me not be condemned with the wicked. Make use of the rod of a father, but let me not feel the sword of the judge. "Search me, O God, and know my heart: try me, and know my thoughts: and see if there be any wicked way in me, and lead me in the way everlasting."

If this be your desire; if your soul bows to his authority, and subscribes to his wisdom and goodness; if you can say, "I have borne chastisement; I will not offend any more: that which I know not, teach thou me; if I have done iniquity, I will do so no more"—it

is a blessed omen; and whatever affliction you may suffer, you may say with David, "I shall not die, but live."

The Third motive is taken from *the brevity of the discipline.*—They verily chastened us, but it was only for "a few days." The child soon became a man, and the course of restriction and preparation resulted in a state of maturity. This is to be applied to our heavenly Father, as well as to our earthly ones; and contains an encouraging intimation, that the whole season of trial, when opposed to our future being and blessedness, is but a short period. Indeed the argument is much stronger in this case than in the former. There is some proportion between the days of minority and manhood, but there is none between time and eternity; there is none between the introductory and the final state of Christians. If life be short, and it is "a vapour that appeareth for a little time, and then vanisheth away," trouble cannot be long. The Scripture seems to labour for expressions to diminish any apprehension of length, as an attribute of our grief. Ye shall have "persecution ten days:" but what are ten days?—Weeping may "endure for a night;" but what is a night?—I will keep thee from "the hour of temptation:" but what is an hour?—This light affliction is but "for a moment:" but what is a moment?—Yet this is not short enough to answer, I was going to say, the impatience of our Deliverer. "For a *small* moment have I forsaken thee, but with great mercies will I gather thee."

The Last motive is derived from *the principle and design of affliction.* Men are imperfect, and their actions are like themselves. Hence, when as their children they chastened us, it was frequently "for their pleasure." They *would* do it. It was to give ease to their passions; to vent their feelings. It was from a peevish humour; a false point of honour. It was to show their authority, or maintain their consequence, regardless of our welfare.

But this is not the case with God. "*He* does not afflict willingly, nor grieve the children of men." He does it only "if needs be" —He does it "for our profit." This is his aim in all his dispensations. If he keeps you in a low and impoverished condition; if he removes lover and friend far from you; if he makes you to possess months of vanity and wearisome nights—whatever you may be tempted to think of all this—it is "*for your profit.*"

What profit! A profit that infinitely weighs down every other advantage, and which above all things, yea, and by "any means," you should be anxious to secure: spiritual profit; divine profit—"that you might be partakers of his holiness."

It is the essence of religion and happiness to resemble God: but observe in what the re-

24

semblance is principally to consist. Not in our imitation of the natural, but moral perfections of Deity. Here men perpetually mistake. They wish to be as God, knowing good and evil: they wish to be independent of others; they wish to be like the Most High in exalting their throne above the stars; they wish to govern with an arm, and to thunder with a voice like his. A Nebuchadnezzar could desire this—Adam desired this, and fell—angels desired it, and were driven from their first estate. But who wishes to be *true* like God, *patient* like God, *merciful* like God, holy—*holy* like God? Yet this is the design of the Gospel; it is to create us after the image of God "in righteousness and true holiness." It is the design—let it never be forgotten—it is the design of every affliction with which you are exercised:—"but he for our profit, that we might be partakers of his holiness." Reflect on four things when you retire, for we have not time to enlarge. If God chastens us to make us holy—we learn,

First; the *importance* of holiness, and the value of it in the eye of a Being who cannot be mistaken.

Secondly; we learn how *defective* we all are in this attainment; seeing God deems such trying means necessary, in order to promote it.

Thirdly; we learn that if any thing can promise *a happy deliverance from trouble*, it is the sanctification of it: when the end is answered the rod is laid by.

Fourthly; we learn that whatever our afflictions may do for us, they have not fulfilled the Divine purpose, *unless they have made us more holy.* It is not enough that our trials have made us more wise and cautious with regard to business; more sedate and regular in our deportment; more dissatisfied with society. Is sin more abhorred? Are our corruptions more subdued? Are we more devotional? Are we more heavenly-minded? Are we more like a pure and a holy God?

We conclude the whole with one general reflection. It regards the manner in which the sacred writers teach us. They simplify every subject they touch. They exemplify it by comparisons; and these images are not taken from the arts and sciences, but from familiar scenes; from those relations which all fill; from those occurrences which all meet with. All therefore can understand them; all can feel them. And while these images serve to illustrate religious subjects, they also instruct us in the duties of civil life.

Take an instance from the words before us. The Apostle refers to the conduct of children, to illustrate the disposition of a suffering Christian, but the very reference inculcates a dutiful behaviour in children themselves. They should give their parents reverence; the reverence of obedience to their commands, and of submission to their corrections. A child

commits one fault in rendering correction needful, but he commits another and a still greater, in neglecting and despising it. Parents have not only authority, but a charge to correct.

Again. The Apostle refers to the conduct of parents, to illustrate the character of God in chastising us; but the very reference gives him an opportunity to show parents how they ought to correct. They should not do it for their own pleasure, but the child's profit. He should see that they are not actuated by passion, but conviction; that they do it not willingly, but from a sense of duty. This being the case; would it not be better to defer punishing till provocation has subsided? This would allow of your judging impartially of the offence; of proportioning the degree of penalty to the crime; of adapting the kind of discipline to the criminal. In this case instruction would unite with correction. If rebuke be really necessary, it will be equally so an hour after; but many, if they do not chastise immediately, cannot do it at all: a sure proof that irritation, and not religion, is the principle that actuates them.

What reason have we all, masters and servants; children and parents; for deep humiliation before God!

Oh, Thou supreme, Thou infinite Excellency! enable us to make Thee our only model, and be perfect, even as our Father which is in heaven is perfect!

DISCOURSE LXXVII.

THE RULER'S DAUGHTER RAISED TO LIFE.

And he put them all out, and took her by the hand, and called, saying, Maid, arise. And her spirit came again, and she arose straightway: and he commanded to give her meat. —Luke viii. 54, 55.

It must have been very gratifying to a mind possessed of tenderness and benevolence to have accompanied our Lord and Saviour from place to place, as " he went about doing good." How delightful to have seen him, at one time, feeding a multitude of hungry people upon the grass; at another, stopping to open the eyes of a blind man, that sat by the way-side begging; at a third, restoring a poor paralytic to the use of his limbs, and enabling him to return home, carrying the bed upon which he himself had been brought; at a fourth, repairing the losses of those who had been bereaved of their connexions, and were sorrowing most of all that they should see their face, and hear their voice, no more! —Who is not ready to envy his immediate followers! Who does not wish that he had seen one of the days of the Son of man!

But no small degree of the same pleasure may be enjoyed in perusing the *history of* these interesting scenes. It is secured to us in the Gospels; it is written with a simplicity the most exquisitely natural and striking; and the events themselves are much more instructive to us than they were to those who witnessed them.

We are now going to bring under review the resurrection of the daughter of Jairus.

Jairus was "a ruler of the synagogue;" probably a magistrate: obviously a man of some eminence and consequence. "Not many wise men after the flesh, not many mighty, not many noble, are called." It was asked by our Lord's enemies, "Have any of the rulers believed on him?" They were the common people that heard him gladly; and very few in higher life were either his followers, his friends, or his suppliants. But there were some. Joseph of Arimathæa was a rich man, and a counsellor. Nicodemus was a ruler of the Jews. A centurion besought him on behalf of his servant. A nobleman besought him on behalf of his son. And Jairus besought him on account of his daughter.

That which brought him to the Redeemer was an event that reduces the high to a level with the low, and proves the insufficiency of wealth and honour. Can a higher station in the world secure peace of mind? can it ward off the common vexations of life? can it prevent sickness? can it protract the approach of death? Does it not rather multiply our fears and anxieties: and render us more widely vulnerable? does it not produce many evils, which others escape? and make every affliction less tolerable, by previous and softening indulgence?

Behold this man. Disease invades his family, and seizes a daughter; his only daughter; a daughter twelve years of age; a period of peculiar attraction, when the mind begins to move, and the character to bud; when the heart is all alive, and confidence is unchilled; when the parent begins to feel esteem blending with tenderness, and to hail a companion in a child!—She "lay a dying!" The aid of medicine had doubtless been called in: and no expense had been spared to obtain relief. But all is in vain—the disease increases—and hope begins to fail. Yet the distressed father cries, "'Let me not see the death of the child.' I have heard of the fame of Jesus of Nazareth. He is not far off. I will go to him. I will try his goodness and his power." And to him should we bring all our distresses, whether temporal or spiritual; personal or relative. They are intended to remind us of a friend born for adversity, and who is too generally forgotten in the hour of prosperity: and if they have led to an interview with him, or increased our intercourse, we have reason to bless the rod, and can acknowledge, "It is good for me that I have been afflicted."

This man had some faith in our Saviour, or he would never have taken a journey to apply to him; yet it seems to have been weak and wavering. Compare him with the Centurion. When Jesus offered to go with him, the Centurion said, "Lord, I am not worthy that thou shouldest come under my roof: but speak the word only, and my servant shall be healed." But Jairus deems his bodily presence necessary to the cure; and, therefore, falling down at his feet, he beseeches him to go to his house. The Friend of sinners would not break the bruised reed, nor quench the smoking flax. He adapted himself to the views of the petitioner; and immediately complied with his wishes.

But as they went, a messenger from the house met them, and said, "Thy daughter is dead; trouble not the Master." It is easy to conceive what a shock this would prove to the father's feelings. While there was life there was hope, however weak; but who can recall the dead? I see him turning aside to weep—struggling to say, like David, "I shall go to her; but she shall not return to me;" —or, with Job, "The Lord gave, and the Lord hath taken away; blessed be the name of the Lord;"—then, thanking the Saviour for the kindness of his intention, and for coming so far; but, like the servant, deeming all further application both useless and tiresome, Jesus, the hope of Israel, the Saviour thereof in the time of trouble, answers him, saying, "Fear not: believe only, and she shall be made whole."

May we not remark hence, First, that sometimes while dealing with the Saviour, the storm becomes darker than before? We cry for pardon, and feel a growing sense of guilt. We pray for sanctification, and the power of corruption seems to revive. We hope for deliverance, and our difficulties multiply. Thus he tries those whom he intends to succour, in order to wean them from every false dependence, and to render his interposition the more wonderful and endeared. And the trial is commonly very humbling, as it shows us the weakness of our confidence in him.

Secondly. Let us never deem importunity in prayer *troublesome*. By our continual coming we may weary the best of earthly benefactors: but it is otherwise with God our Saviour. His power is almighty; his understanding is infinite. He listens to the cries of a world of creatures dependent upon his care; and yet he can regard our affairs as much as if he had no other affairs to regard. And as to his disposition—this is such, that our prayer is his delight; and the oftener we come, and the more we ask, the more welcome we are.

Thirdly. It is never *too late* to apply to the Lord. Though means fail us, and the case is desperate as to help from creatures, yet our extremity is his opportunity; he is able to do for us exceeding abundantly, above all we can ask or think; and "at even-tide it shall be light."

And therefore, Fourthly, the way to obtain present ease, and certain relief, is to exercise faith under every discouragement. How well are, "Fear not," and "Believe only," coupled together! "Thou wilt keep him," says Isaiah, "in perfect peace, whose mind is stayed upon thee: because he trusteth in thee." But in another place he tells us, "If ye will not believe, surely ye shall not be established."

Our Saviour could have healed the child at a distance, and with a word, but he chooses to go "to the house of mourning"—to teach us to go there. A family in such a condition, is a very affecting and improving object. We instantly feel a sympathy with the distressed. We melt into pity as we see the emblems of death. The world loses its hold of our minds. By the side of the breathless corpse we see the vanity of human life; we think of the mortality of our friends—and of our own. Who can see death, and not think of eternity! We sigh—we pray. "By the sadness of the countenance the heart is made better." A visit to the house of mourning affords an opportunity of doing good, as well as of gaining good. At no other season is instruction so likely to be impressive. The ground is now prepared to receive the seed. The value of the Gospel is now felt; and you can introduce religion as—a friend; as—a comforter.

Behold our Saviour approaching the scene of sorrow. Many attended him to the door; but he would not suffer any of them "to enter in, save Peter, and James, and John, and the father and mother of the maiden." The admission of a large crowd would have produced inconvenience: and have violated the sacredness of grief. Our Lord wished not for ostentatious display; yet the truth of the miracle would require a competent number of persons to attest it; and in the mouth of two or three witnesses every word shall be established. But in vain we ask why Peter, and James, and John, were selected for this purpose? The circumstances would have been less remarkable had it not been exemplified on two other extraordinary occasions: I refer to his transfiguration, when these same three individuals were chosen to witness his glory; and to the garden, when they were admitted to witness his agony. He does not always explain himself; but of this we may be assured, that, though he acts sovereignly, he never acts arbitrarily: whatever he does, he does it "because it seemeth good in his sight;" and what *seems* good to *him, must be* so: he always has reasons to influence him; and when he shall divulge them, they will not only bring glory to him, but yield satisfaction to us.

How many little touching circumstances does the narrative incidentally mention! Thus far we have heard of the father only; now we learn that the diseased had *a mother* living. The mother had been torn with anguish twelve years ago, to give her birth; had carried her in her bosom; had fed her at her breast; had watched over her by day and night; had given "no sleep to her eyes, or slumber to her eyelids," while the disease was preying upon her child's tender frame. What her confidence in the Saviour was we are not able to determine; but informed probably, by the previous and hasty return of the servant, of his approach, and of what he had said to her husband, she also had gone forth to meet him. Thus did Martha, when he was drawing near to Bethany: "As soon as she heard that he was coming, she went forth and met him; and said, Lord, if thou hadst been here, my brother had not died!"

We have seen the few with which he entered the house; but he found many in it; and all wore the appearance of sorrow: "all wept and bewailed her." Her death was unquestioned: and we find the mourners, and the minstrels, usually employed on such occasions, already called in; and performing their lamentations.—How then could he say, "Weep not: she is not dead, but sleepeth?"

He spake modestly. Another would have said, "Come; examine this patient; see, there are no remains of life in her—you will witness before I begin, that there is nothing to aid my operations." But he would not magnify the action he was going to perform. He sought not his own glory.

He spoke figuratively. Sleep is the term commonly, in the Scripture, applied to the death of all believers: and it is peculiarly just. Sleep is the pause of care—the parenthesis of human wo. Sleep is a short death; and death is but a long sleep; during which the body rests from its toils, and at the end of which it will awake, refreshed and renewed in the morning of the resurrection.

He spake in reference to his present intention. They were preparing for her interment, and performing the funeral rites: but he would gradually intimate, that there was no need of this, since, instead of a burial, she was going to be raised to life.

He said this also to try his hearers. Accordingly it showed their disposition. For though the occasion was solemn; though they must have heard of his miracles; and were informed of the wisdom and holiness of his character; they treated his words with contempt, and indecently "laughed him to scorn." "Is he a dreamer? Are we blind? Did we never see a corpse before?—Is not the breath gone; and the flesh cold and stiff?"—

Here we are led to note two things. First. How much more are men governed by their natural views and feelings than by the word of truth; and how easily are they befooled in divine things by their sense and reason! Because their sense and reason are competent judges in some cases, they are prone to imagine they are so in all; forgetting that faith has an office, and a province, as well as sense and reason: faith adds the knowledge of God to our own; faith acquiesces in his declarations, however mysterious; and looks for the accomplishment of his promises, however improbable.

Secondly. We observe that a serious state of mind is the best preparation for divine truth. "A scorner," says Solomon, "seeketh knowledge, and findeth it not." And no wonder: he is not in earnest in his inquiries. He is under the bias of his prejudices and his passions. The mind and will of God are nothing to him: he' neither regards his grace, nor his glory. He would rather meet with argument, to countenance his error. He rejoices to discover any thing that can furnish materials for ridicule and reproach. He has a proud confidence in his own talents, and never thinks of asking wisdom of God. Every serious inquirer is a prayerful and practical one; and he will be sure to succeed. "The meek will he guide in judgment: and the meek will he teach his way. The secret of the Lord is with them that fear him; and he will show them his covenant. Then shall we know, if we follow on to know the Lord: his going forth is prepared as the morning; and he shall come into us as the rain, as the latter and former rain upon the earth."

But our Saviour does not indulge a bantering Pilate with an answer. He does not gratify an anxious Herod with a miracle. When he rose from the dead, he does not appear to those who had seen him work miracles, and ascribed them to Beelzebub. What is one of the reasons he assigns for speaking in parables? "Therefore speak I to them in parables: because they seeing see not; and hearing they hear not, neither do they understand. And in them is fulfilled the prophecy of Esaias, which saith, By hearing ye shall hear, and shall not understand; and seeing ye shall see, and shall not perceive: For this people's heart is waxed gross, and their ears are dull of hearing, and their eyes they have closed; lest at any time they should see with their eyes, and hear with their ears, and should understand with their heart, and should be converted, and I should heal them." What was the consequence of this mode of tuition? Those who loved the truth, and longed to be acquainted with it, applied to him for an explanation; and were in no case refused: while the obstinate and self-sufficient, the vicious and inattentive, stumbled and fell, and had only to thank themselves for their injury and ruin. So true is it that, "To him that hath shall be given; and he shall have more abundantly: but from him that hath not, shall be taken away even that he hath."

Hence these scoffers shall not remain in the room. After they had made a declaration,

which they could not retract, concerning the certainty of her death, "he put them all out," and, as the resurrection and the life, he "took her by the hand, and called, saying, Maid, arise." When, lo! the fountain of life is warmed, the blood begins to liquify and flow, the pulse beats again; she breathes; she looks—"her spirit came again, and she arose straightway: and he commanded to give her meat." This order was to show

The *reality* of the miracle, by the use of her faculties.

It evinced the *perfection* of the miracle; she was not restored to the state in which she died—that was a state of sickness, in which food was rejected: but to the state she was in before her disease; a state of health and appetite.

It was also to mark the *limitation* of the miracle; nothing further was to be done preternaturally; but her life, which had been restored by extraordinary agency, was to be preserved as before, by ordinary means.

It also distinguished this miracle from that of the final resurrection. The resurrection will produce a spiritual body, requiring neither sleep nor food: but this damsel was raised only to a natural life, subject to the same infirmities as that of other people, and liable to die again.

But have we not here an image of the restoration of man from the death of sin to the life of righteousness?—The Lord's hand goes with his word; and he lays hold of those he calls.—We immediately arise, and spiritual motion follows spiritual life.—We "hunger and thirst after righteousness," and the food we desire is furnished: and we are nourished up unto the measure of the stature of the fulness of Christ.

The scene must have been inexpressibly interesting.—Jesus stands in all the charms of compassion, enjoying the luxury of doing good.—The child clasps the fond father and mother, and looks around with surprise and awe upon this wonderful Stranger in the room.—The parents embrace her, and adore Him, giving vent alternately to the feelings of natural affection, and religious praise. "Her parents were astonished;" they seemed like men that dream; they could hardly believe the reality of their blessedness, while they broke forth in expressions of wonder, at the display of such power and kindness, such omnipotence and mildness; and were ready to run forth, and publish abroad their obligations to one who had done such great things for them.

But his hour was not yet come. He would furnish us with an example, not only of beneficence, but of humility. He would teach us to be content to do good, for its own sake, and like the sun to shine, and bless without noise—"but he charged them that they should tell no man what was done."

2 N   24*

Let us conclude.

If our Saviour so amazed the spectators, and honoured himself by the revival of one body newly dead; what will it be when he shall come to be glorified in his saints, and to be admired in all them that believe: when he shall speak, and "all that are in the graves shall hear his voice, and shall come forth; they that have done good, unto the resurrection of life; and they that have done evil, unto the resurrection of damnation!"

Again. It is worthy of remark, that of the three persons whom our Lord raised from the dead, Lazarus was the loved and *only* brother of Martha and Mary; the young man was the *only* son of his mother; and the damsel the *only* daughter of Jairus: so touched is he with the feeling of our infirmities; so much regard does he show to relative affection; so well does he remember that we are dust; so perfectly does he "consider our trouble, and know our souls in adversity!"

The subject leads me to address those who are parents. You say, God only knows the anxieties you feel on behalf of your rising charge. But he does know. He inspired you with the tenderness you feel, and produced the relation in which you stand. It is not consistent with the designs of his providence, that you should regard your children as burdens and torments. Nor is it his pleasure, on the other hand, and on this side the greatest danger commonly lies, that you should idolize them. You should hold them with a loose hand, as you know not how soon your "dear delights" may be taken from you, and pierce you through with many sorrows.

Have your children been blessed with health and strength? and are they now blooming like olive plants round about your table? Remember, the continuance of a blessing demands your praise no less than the recovery of it.

Have you been tried by seeing your children, "at the point to die," and did he send his word and heal them? Have you received them back, though not from the grave, yet from the borders of the grave? Dedicate them afresh to their Deliverer. "Train them up in the nurture and admonition of the Lord." And let the sickness which has not been unto death, be for the glory of God.

But others weep for their children, and refuse to be comforted, because they are not.— You no longer see, while repeating their morning and evening prayers, their little hands suspended on your knees. You no longer hear their broken, artless language, more affecting than all the eloquence of words. And you say, There is no Saviour now on earth—or I would hasten to him, and pour out my heart before him—

Yet let me ask, not unfeelingly to condemn your sorrow, but to regulate and alleviate your distress;—

Had not He who has removed your child a right to take it away? Was it not his own? Did he ever relinquish his claim to it? Did he enter your house as a robber, or as a proprietor?

Cannot he sanctify the loss, and more than make up any deficiency in creature-enjoyment, by the comforts of the Holy Ghost? So that you shall not faint in the day of adversity, but in every thing give thanks?

Is not your lamb lodged in the Shepherd's bosom? Said not the Saviour to you, as he was languishing and dying, and you wished to keep him back, "Suffer this little child to come unto me, and forbid him not, for of such is the kingdom of heaven!"

Will not the very body that is now mouldering in the dust be changed and fashioned like the Saviour's own glorious body?

Will you not soon meet? And never part? "Wherefore comfort one another with these words."

DISCOURSE LXXVIII.

THE PROFITABLE PURSUIT.

But seek ye first the kingdom of God, and his righteousness; and all these things shall be added unto you.—Matthew vi. 33.

"Man that is born of a woman is of few days and full of trouble." To the numberless real evils of life he adds imaginary ones; and of all his afflictions, none oppresses him more than care. The heathens confess this, and their philosophers endeavour to remove the burden; but they could only lighten it. They saw the disease preying upon his vitals, and they pitied and prescribed; but they could only abate the paroxysm of the pain, while the root of the distemper continued.

Let us be thankful for Revelation. Let us sit at the feet of Jesus.—How does he enforce a freedom from anxiety? Never man spake like this man. "Take no thought for your life, what ye shall eat, or what ye shall drink; nor yet for your body what ye shall put on. Is not the life more than meat, and the body than raiment? Behold the fowls of the air: for they sow not, neither do they reap, nor gather into barns: yet your heavenly Father feedeth them. Are ye not much better than they? Which of you by taking thought can add one cubit unto his stature? And why take ye thought for raiment? Consider the lilies of the field, how they grow; they toil not, neither do they spin: and yet I say unto you, That even Solomon in all his glory was not arrayed like one of these. Wherefore, if God so clothe the grass of the field, which to-day is, and to-morrow is cast into the oven, shall he not much more clothe you, O ye of little faith?

Therefore take no thought, saying, What shall we eat? or, What shall we drink? or, Wherewithal shall we be clothed? (for after all these things do the Gentiles seek:) for your heavenly Father knoweth that ye have need of all these things." We have not time to examine the beauty and the force of this reasoning. Suffice it to observe, that in the words which I have chosen for our present meditation, he finishes his admonition by opposing care to care; he would draw us off from inferior concerns by the attractions and impressions of a superior interest—an interest which demands our principal regard, and will more than indemnify us for every sacrifice we make in the pursuit of it. "But seek ye first the kingdom of God, and his righteousness; and all these things shall be added unto you." The words lead us to ask, and enable us to answer three questions.

I. What are we to seek? II. How are we to seek? III. Why are we to seek?

I. What are we to seek? "The kingdom of God, and his righteousness."

The children of this world are wiser in their generation than the children of light. If I had to propose an estate, I should easily engage your attention; how much more if I could offer a province!—a kingdom! A crown sparkles in the eye of ambition. A throne is the pinnacle of human pride. What exertions have been made, what blood has been shed, to grasp a sceptre that rules a few miles of territory, and soon drops from the hand that wields it! But here you behold "the kingdom of God:" a kingdom of which he is the founder, the governor, the owner, the giver; a kingdom announced by prophets, established by miracles, prepared before the foundation of the world; a kingdom that cannot be shaken, but remains for ever; a kingdom, in comparison of which, all the renowned empires of the globe vanish into nothing, and in the possession of which you may mourn over an Alexander as a groveling worm.

Grace and glory are not so much different states, as different degrees of the same state. Hence Christians are even *now* made partakers of this kingdom: but their present participation is imperfect. *Here* they are princes; but princes in disguise; the world knoweth them not. They are like David, anointed, but not proclaimed; and through much tribulation are entering the kingdom. Their royalties are above. There—are their robes, their crowns, their palaces; and they shall reign for ever and ever. Nothing less than this will satisfy the infinite goodness of God towards them: though they were once his foes, and by a frown he could have annihilated them, he spares them, he pardons them, he exalts them: "He raiseth up the poor out of the dust, and lifteth the needy out of the dunghill; that he may set him with princes, even with the princes of his people."

Let it however be observed that there is something inseparably connected with this kingdom of God. It is "the righteousness of God." There are some who, instead of proving their schemes by the Scripture, are always bringing the Scripture to their schemes. Having attached a favourite meaning to a particular word, they give the term the same signification wherever they meet with it, regardless of the connexion in which it stands, or the purpose for which it was introduced. We make no scruple to say, that the righteousness of God in this passage intends real holiness; the renovation of our nature; the sanctification of our lives. And we say not this from our disbelief of another very interesting doctrine of the Gospel, and which holds forth our justification as flowing from the merits of the Redeemer; and while we know that our obedience is defective, and feel that in many things we all offend, and come short of the glory of God, we humbly look for the acceptance of our persons and of our services in the Beloved; and repose the confidence of our weary souls under the shadow of his cross, "not having our own righteousness, which is of the law, but that which is through the faith of Christ, the righteousness which is of God by faith."

But this reliance is always accompanied with true holiness. The same principle that calms the conscience always purifies the heart. A title to heaven is always attended with a meetness for it. And to this our Saviour refers. No righteousness, no kingdom! The one is essential to the other. And the other is not arbitrary: it is founded in the nature of things; in the nature of man; in the nature of heaven. "Except a man be born again, he cannot see the kingdom of God." The enjoyment is impossible. To look therefore for glory without grace, or heaven without holiness, is treason against Scripture, and rebellion against common sense. It is to make God a liar; to abolish all the distinctions which preserve the harmony of the world; and to reduce the creation to a chaos. "What fellowship hath righteousness with unrighteousness? And what communion hath light with darkness? Know ye not that the unrighteous shall not inherit the kingdom of God? Be not deceived: neither fornicators, nor idolaters, nor adulterers, nor effeminate, nor abusers of themselves with mankind, nor thieves, nor covetous, nor drunkards, nor revilers, nor extortioners, shall inherit the kingdom of God."

These are the blessings we are to seek. But

II. How are we to seek them? First:

"seek ye *first* the kingdom of God and his righteousness." First, in *time :* and first, in *attention.*

We are to seek them first, in *time.*

It should be the first concern in life. Here I have an opportunity to address those of you whose reason is opening, and whose affections are beginning to glow. How encouraging is the promise: "I love them that love me, and they that seek me early shall find me! Remember therefore your Creator in the days of your youth:" hereafter you may not have time for this work: and how dreadful would the consequence of prevention be! If you die before you finish a journey you intend to take, a building you intend to rear, a connexion you intend to form, it is comparatively of little moment; you will then have done with every thing below the sun for ever. But if you die before you have secured the salvation of the soul, it would have been good for you if you had never been born: for if you are not saved, you are lost—and lost for ever! And is there no danger of this? Are any of you so young as not to have followed to the grave persons younger than yourselves? There is but a step between you and death. "For man knoweth not his time: as the fishes that are taken in an evil net, and as the birds that are caught in the snare: so are the sons of men snared in an evil time, when it falleth suddenly upon them."—But godliness is as necessary for time as for eternity. If I were sure of your living to the age of Methuselah, I should still say, "Seek ye *first* the kingdom of God, and his righteousness." You must enter the world with God, if you would pass wisely, and safely, and happily through it.—And never, my young friends, will you have such a favourable opportunity of knowing the things that belong to your everlasting peace as you now have. Of the year of life, this is the spring; of the day, this is the morning. How many are now bewailing the waste of this precious season, and vainly endeavouring to redeem the time, and repair the loss!

What applies to youth, falls with redoubled force upon age. Have you, my aged friend, been criminal enough to neglect this concern till now? Surely *you* have no time to lose. Let it be your *next* concern. It should have been your care sixty, seventy years ago. Every thing now cries with a voice louder than thunder, "Seek ye first the kingdom of God, and his righteousness."

What has been said, respecting time at large, will apply to every period of it in particular.

Seek the kingdom of God and his righteousness *first* every week; by sanctifying the first day of the week; "calling the sabbath a delight; the holy of the Lord, honourable; and honouring him, not doing thine own ways, nor finding thine own pleasure, nor speaking thine own words."

Seek them *first* every day; by securing in the morning a season for the closet and the family. Such previous devotion will best fit you for the duties and events of the day. Such intercourse with God will best prepare you for all your dealings with men.

Again. We are to seek them first in *attention.* They are to be supremely regarded, because they are supremely valuable. Many acquisitions are desirable, and some are useful, but religion is the one thing needful. It fixes its residence in the soul, and strikes its influence through eternity. If it be any thing, it is every thing: if it be important at all, it is all important. It is not therefore to be a secondary business, which is to give place to every other interest; every other interest is to give place to this; to this every other pursuit is to be rendered subordinate and subservient. Thus David, in the Old Testament, and Paul, in the New, speak of godliness as their *only* concern. "One thing," says the former, "have I desired of the Lord, that will I seek after, that I may dwell in the house of the Lord all the days of my life, to behold the beauty of the Lord, and to inquire in his temple." And, says the latter, "This one thing I do, forgetting those things which are behind, and reaching forth unto those things which are before, I press toward the mark."

Are you likeminded with them? To determine this, let me ask you two questions.

First. What are your *desires?* Every man has some languid and lazy wishes. Balaam wished to "die the death of the righteous," but was not concerned to live their life. Herod wished to see our Saviour work a miracle, but he would not stir out of doors for the purpose. Pilate asked, What is truth? and stayed not for the answer. If a few powerless, inoperative wishes would carry persons to heaven, none would ever be turned into hell. But if you are in earnest, your desires accord with the strong language of Revelation; you "hunger and thirst after righteousness:" you "wait for the Lord more than they that watch for the morning:" "your soul breaketh for the longing it hath unto God's judgments at all times." And upon a review of your anxieties, you will be able to say,

"Give me thy counsel for my guide,
And then receive me to thy bliss;
All my desires and hopes beside,
Are faint and cold compared with this."

Secondly. What are your *exertions?* For something in this case will necessarily be done. This in the Scripture is held forth by "pressing into the kingdom of God," "taking the kingdom of heaven by violence," "fighting the good fight of faith," "running the race that is set before us," "labouring to enter into his rest." Now explain these expressions as you please, deduct from them far more than the laws of metaphorical language require; yet, will not the remainder be more than enough to condemn thousands who assume the name of Christian? Will it not imply much more than that speculative, indolent, formal, time-serving, costless religion, which satisfies many of our modern professors; a religion that requires of them no sacrifices, and allows the retention of every worldly passion and indulgence?

What then are you doing? What is your prevailing and habitual course of action? Are you applying the Sabbath to the purposes for which it was consecrated? Do you read in the Scripture and hear the Gospel with reverence and attention? Do you take pains to go to the house of God with constancy, and to worship him when you are there, "in spirit and in truth?" Do you pray without ceasing? And in every thing give thanks?—You toil for the meat that perisheth—do you labour for that meat which endureth unto everlasting life? You forego ease, you give up your time, you "rise early and sit up late, and eat the bread of carefulness," to please the world, to gain a name, to increase your hoard of shining dust —are you laying up treasure in heaven? Do you deny yourselves, and take up your cross and follow the Saviour, in obeying his commands. in imbibing his spirit, in copying his example? Are you, by patient continuance in well-doing, seeking for glory, honour, and immortality? Are you steadfast, unmoveable, always abounding in the work of the Lord?—But

III. WHY ARE WE THUS TO SEEK THESE BLESSINGS? Here are two motives to animate and encourage us: the one implied; the other expressed. We shall succeed in our principal aim, which is to secure the kingdom of God and his righteousness—this is implied: and in addition to these, all other things shall be given us—this is expressed. "Seek ye first the kingdom of God, and his righteousness; *and all things shall be added unto you*;" as a kind of surplus, over and above the contract. What can we desire more.

First. Though destitute as we naturally are of his kingdom and righteousness, if we seek them in the manner here required, we shall obtain them. Such an assurance is necessary to excite attention and diligence. No man will undertake an enterprise that he deems useless and impracticable, especially if it be attended with difficulty and expense. Hope is the mainspring of motion in all the concerns of the world. The soldier wars, the scholar studies, the merchant trades, the husbandman ploughs, in hope. It is the same in religion. Here indeed, so infinite is the prize, if there was only a probability, or a possibility of success, we ought to seek it, and to seek it *first*. But we have not only

possibility, but probability; we have not only probability, but certainty to actuate us—a certainty derived from the promise of God, who cannot lie; from the gift of his own Son; from the experience of all his people. Here is no peradventure—"Ask, and it shall be given to you; seek, and ye shall find; knock, and it shall be opened unto you. They that sow in tears shall reap in joy. He that goeth forth and weepeth, bearing precious seed, shall doubtless come again with rejoicing, bringing his sheaves with him. They that know thy name will put their trust in thee: for thou, Lord, hast not forsaken them that seek thee."

Secondly. Besides gaining this kingdom and righteousness, all other things shall be added unto us. This is designed to meet an objection, by no means unusual, in the experience of Christians. It arises from their natural and civil condition in the world; from their businesses; their families; their children; their bodies. They cannot be entirely dead to those things. If they wish not to "make provision for the flesh, to fulfil the lusts thereof;" its wants must be relieved; and the honour of their profession is concerned in their "providing things honest in the sight of all men." They often find it harder to trust God in their temporal, than in their spiritual interests. This thought will, sometimes at least, enter their minds, though it be not lodged and entertained there; "If I always make religion my first concern, may I not be a loser by it? Will it not frequently stand in the way of my secular advantage?" He who knows our frame, and remembers that we are dust; he who often meets the fears of his people before they have expressed them, He cries—"No. Mind my affairs, and I will manage yours. "Them that honour me, I will honour." All these things, while you regard them, in the order wherein I place them, shall be added unto you."

It would be an unwarrantable conclusion to suppose hence, that a Christian can never expect any difficulties in life; but it does authorise us to hope for such a proportion of the good things of this world as shall be needful for us: only, of this, He who dispenses them is the judge. It is the office of a father, before a child comes to years of discretion, to choose for him; and it is the happiness of the child to have such a guide. Hence we are so much disposed to pity an orphan deprived of such a director, and thrown upon the wide world. Poor little traveller! What wonder if he mistakes his way?—Now this can never befall the children of God: He will not leave them orphans. This is their privilege, that while incapable of judging for themselves, they have a Father in heaven, infinitely wise and good, to choose for them. If they can bear prosperity without injury, they shall have it. If fulness will make them forget God, he will reduce them. He has engaged to give us whatever is conducive to our welfare—and we could have asked no more. " O fear the Lord, ye his saints: for there is no want to them that fear him. The young lions do lack and suffer hunger: but they that seek the Lord shall not want any good thing."

We also learn, from this part of our subject, that religion has a friendly influence over secular affairs. It would be cruel to intimate that every instance of failure in trade originates in vice; but it may not be going too far to say, that the generality of these deficiencies, even in good men, are not pure afflictions; but have been preceded by the neglect of some of its duties, or the violation of some of its proprieties. We have not time to enlarge here, otherwise we might show how real religion makes a man punctual, and diligent, and economical; how it makes him liberal—and " he that soweth plentifully, shall reap plentifully;" how it cuts him off from expensive vices and amusements; how it raises his character by the exercise of the moral virtues, and gains him the confidence of his fellow-creatures; how it contributes to his health, and to the improvement of his understanding, and thus helps him both to judge and to execute; how it secures him the favour of Providence—and " the blessing of God maketh rich and addeth no sorrow;" in all which instances it would appear, that it " has the promise of the life that now is, as well as of that which is to come."

What use should we make of this subject! I fear the words I have endeavoured to explain, will suit some of you in a way of exhortation only. For can you say that you resemble this portrait and have complied with this admonition? Can I bless God at the close of this exercise, that for once I have been addressing an audience who " seek *first* his kingdom and righteousness," and leave the addition of all other things to him? Ah! these other things—these engross you—and destroy. Heaven is hid from your view. Earth contains all your esteem. Your hopes and fears, desires and pursuits, are all confined within the narrow limits of time and sense! You came into the world you know not why, and are going out of it you know not whither. You are dead while you live. You have souls; but you never ask, " What must I do to be saved?" You " know not what a day will bring forth;" yet you live as if you were to live here always. You have been brought up in a Christian country; but your god is your belly, your glory is in your shame, you mind earthly things. And therefore your end will be destruction. For no man ever dropped into heaven by chance; nor does God ever force a man into heaven against his will. He always makes it the object of his solicitude; and brings him

thither, to accomplish his wishes, and to crown his services. There is a sober sense, in which, Win and wear it, is the motto inscribed on the prize for which we run.

I hope some of you are disposed to follow the advice, the command of our Lord and Saviour, founded in a regard to your everlasting welfare. Retire, and say, O God, I bless thee that thou hast not cut me off during my guilty negligence. May thy goodness lead me to repentance! May thy long suffering be my salvation! Give me a token for good that thou hast received me graciously, and henceforth rank me with thy willing people.

Some of you have weighed both worlds, and have given the future preference.

Nevertheless—these other things occupy too much even of *your* time and attention: and render it necessary for us to admonish you to reduce your regard. For this purpose you will do well to remember two things.

First. This undue solicitude injures your spiritual welfare. These suckers occupy the sap that should enter the boughs. These weeds exhaust the nourishment the ground requires for the plants. These cares of the world, and this " deceitfulness of riches, choke the word," and it becometh unfruitful.

Secondly. It is hurtful even to your temporal welfare. The surest way to have any temporal blessing is to be satisfied witnout it. When we *must* have certain things, God sees that our hearts are too much set upon them for us to be indulged with safety. On the other hand, when we refer ourselves to his pleasure, he loves to surprise and gratify us. A remarkable instance of which we have in the case of Solomon. " God said unto him, Because thou hast asked this thing, and hast not asked for thyself long life; neither hast asked riches for thyself, nor hast asked the life of thine enemies; but hast asked for thyself understanding to discern judgment; behold, I have done according to thy words: lo, I have given thee a wise and an understanding heart; so that there was none like thee before thee, neither after thee shall any arise like unto thee. And I have also given thee that which thou hast not asked, both riches, and honour; so that there shall not be any among the kings like unto thee all thy days." And what a dreadful contrast have we in the history of Eli! " There came a man of God unto Eli, and said unto him, Thus saith the Lord, Did I plainly appear unto the house of thy father, when they were in Egypt in Pharaoh's house? And did I choose him out of all the tribes of Israel to be my priest, to offer upon mine altar, to burn incense, to wear an ephod before me? And did I give unto the house of thy father all the offerings made by fire of the children of Israel! Wherefore kick ye at my sacrifice and at mine offering, which I have commanded in my habitation; and honourest thy sons above me, to make yourselves fat with the chiefest of all the offerings of Israel my people? Wherefore the Lord God of Israel saith, I said indeed, that thy house, and the house of thy father, should walk before me for ever: but now the Lord saith, Be it far from me; for them that honour me I will honour, and they that despise me shall be lightly esteemed." " But seek ye first the kingdom of God, and his righteousness; and all these things shall be added unto you."

DISCOURSE LXXIX.

GOD THE SANCTUARY OF THE AFFLICTED.

Thus saith the Lord God; Although I have cast them far off among the heathen, and although I have scattered them among the countries, yet will I be to them as a little sanctuary in the countries where they shall come.—Ezek. xi. 16.

PHILOSOPHERS have frequently remarked, what may be called, the doctrine of compensation: by which they mean, the tendency there is in nature and providence to keep things in a kind of equality; so that while, on the one hand, there are defects to counterbalance advantages, there are, on the other hand advantages to counterbalance defects. Nothing can exceed the weakness and helplessness of a new-born babe. But provision is made for the relief of its earliest wants; and the strength of maternal affection renders every exertion and sacrifice its welfare requires, a pleasure. The blind are generally superior to other men in the senses of hearing and feeling. If the poor are denied the elegances and luxuries of riches, they are not corroded with their cares, nor endangered by their perils. The labourer toils; but he is free from the languor and infirmities of the idle and disengaged: and "his sleep is sweet, whether he eats little or much."

In what condition can we be found that possesses no advantages? These a grateful mind will always look after; and, however severe the affliction, endeavour to say, " It might have been worse. I have lost much; but I am not deprived of all. He has chastened me sore; but he has not given me over unto death. The stroke is painful: but it will be profitable. ' Tribulation worketh patience; and patience, experience; and experience, hope: and hope maketh not ashamed; because the love of God is shed abroad in our hearts by the Holy Ghost which is given unto us.' " What is the emblem of the Church from the beginning of the world? A bush burning with fire, and not consumed.

And what is the motto? " We are troubled on every side, yet not distressed; we are perplexed, but not in despair; persecuted, but not forsaken; cast down, but not destroyed: always bearing about in the body the dying of the Lord Jesus, that the life also of Jesus might be made manifest in our body."

In harmony with these remarks is the language with which Ezekiel was commanded to address the Jews: " Thus saith the Lord God; Although I have cast them far off among the heathen, and although I have scattered them among the countries, yet will I be to them as a little sanctuary in the countries where they shall come." Let us consider,

I. THE CALAMITY. II. THE ALLEVIATION.

I. THE CALAMITY: " I have cast them far off among the heathen, and have scattered them among the countries."

Upon this part of our subject I am not going to speak as a historian. Then it would be necessary for me to show how this dispersion took place; the different times and degrees in which it was accomplished; the numbers that were successively carried away; and endeavour to solve many questions which have more of curiosity in them than profit. But I shall speak only as a moralist, concerned to improve the fact by rendering it instructive. The event serves to display,

First, The *agency* of God. He therefore, in the words before us, claims the work as his own: " *I* have cast them off among the heathen; *I* have scattered them among the countries." Nor is it an unusual thing for him to assert his dominion and influence over all the sufferings of nations, families, and individuals. " Shall there be evil in a city, and the Lord hath not done it? I form the light, and create darkness; I make peace, and create evil. I the Lord do all these things."

In the dispersion of the Jews he employed instrumentality, and wicked instrumentality: but neither of these detracts from his agency. What does God, without the intervention of any cause between him and the effect? He blesses us by means: he warms us by the sun; he refreshes us by sleep; he sustains us by food; and he even requires us to prepare, for our use, the supplies he gives us. In a similar way he inflicts evil. And hence an irreligious mind is detained from God by the persons or the events that injure him. He thinks only of the flood, or the fire; of the heedless servant, the uncertain friend, the cruel enemy. Because the hand that holds them is invisible, he accuses the lance, and the scourge. But a pious man can say, " It is the Lord," and will try to say, " Let him do what seemeth him good." " Let him alone," says David of the insulting Shimei. " Let him alone, and let him curse; for the Lord hath bidden him." Job, said, " The Lord gave, and the

Lord hath taken away," though they were the Chaldeans and Sabeans that plundered him. God did not carry away the Jews by miracle, but by the effect of war: by the invasion and success of unprincipled and wicked conquerors. What did Tiglath-Pileser, or Shalmaneser, or Sennacherib, or Nebuchadnezzar, think of God? They were only following the calls of vanity, and of revenge. Yet, says God, " O Assyrian, the rod of mine anger, and the staff in their hand is mine indignation. I will send him against an hypocritical nation, and against the people of my wrath will I give him a charge, to take the spoil, and to take the prey, and to tread them down like the mire of the streets. Howbeit he meaneth not so, neither does his heart think so; but it is in his heart to destroy and to cut off nations not a few." Whence we learn, that we are not to conclude that God has nothing to do in any work, because of the vileness of those who are engaged in it. He adapts his instruments to their employment, overrules the natural tendencies of human actions, to subserve his designs, and makes the very wrath of man to praise him. The event,

Secondly, displays the *truth* of God. It had been clearly foretold; it had been threatened, as early as the days of Moses: " The Lord shall cause thee to be smitten before thine enemies: thou shalt go out one way against them, and flee seven ways before them: and shalt be removed into all the kingdoms of the earth. And thou shalt become an astonishment, a proverb, and a byword, among all nations whither the Lord shall lead thee." It would be needless to prove how every successive prophet in the name of God renewed the threatening. But, in consequence of these denunciations, the calamity was identified with the divine veracity, and became surer than heaven and earth: for " it is easier for heaven and earth to pass, than one tittle of the law to fail." The Jews imagined that they had nothing to fear: they thought that such a mighty judgment was improbable, if not impossible; and presumptuously cried, " The temple of the Lord, the temple of the Lord, the temple of the Lord are we: they leaned upon the Lord, and said, Is not the Lord among us? None evil can come upon us. But the Lord is not a man that he should lie, nor the son of man that he should repent: hath he said, and shall he not do it? Or hath he spoken, and shall he not make it good?"

Thirdly. The event displays the *holiness* of God. His holiness is most strikingly seen in his abhorrence of sin. He is " of purer eyes than to behold iniquity. The wicked shall not stand in his sight. He will not spare the guilty." His conduct towards this people seems severe; and it was severe. But the provocation was peculiar. Much was

given, and much was required. Their offences were aggravated by their privileges. Sin is not to be judged of by its grossness, but by its guilt; and guilt arises from knowledge possessed, from obligations violated, from advantages abused. God has not " dealt so with any land." What wonder therefore that he should say, " You only have I known of all the families of the earth: therefore I will punish you for all your iniquities."

Fourthly. The event displays the *wisdom* of God. By their dispersion the Scriptures were diffused; and the Desire of all nations was announced and expected. The pious Jews would be in " the midst of many people as a dew from the Lord." We have reason to believe many miracles were wrought by them. We know that some were: witness the preservation of Shadrach, Meshech, and Abednego, in the fiery furnace; and Daniel in the lions' den. These prodigies, accompanying a good conversation, would doubtless induce many to become proselytes to their religion, and to " take hold of the skirt of him that was a Jew, saying, We will go with you, for we have heard that God is with you."

Lastly. The event displays his *goodness*. In the midst of judgment he remembered mercy. Though he punished them it was not to destroy, but to correct and reform: and therefore he said, " Though I make a full end of the nations, yet will I not make a full end of thee: but I will correct thee in measure." The dispensation, therefore, was temporary and limited. Hence he said, " After seventy years be accomplished at Babylon I will visit you, and perform my good word toward you, in causing you to return to this place. For I know the thoughts that I think toward you, thoughts of peace, and not of evil, to give you an expected end. Then shall ye call upon me, and ye shall go and pray unto me, and I will hearken unto you. And ye shall seek me, and find me, when ye shall search for me with all your heart. And I will be found of you, saith the Lord: and I will turn away your captivity, and I will gather you from all the nations, and from all the places whither I have driven you, saith the Lord; and I will bring you again into the place whence I caused you to be carried away captive." Hence, even in the mean time, he did not leave them comfortless. It was a calamity unspeakably awful and painful to be driven from their native land, and deprived of all their civil and sacred privileges; but it was softened. And observe,

II. The ALLEVIATION. " Thus saith the Lord God; Although I have cast them far off among the heathen, and although I have scattered them among the countries, yet will I be to them as a little sanctuary in the countries where they shall come." He undertakes to secure and accommodate them. He engages to afford them the advantage of a refuge and a temple: so that wherever they sought him, he would be found of them; and they should see his power and his glory, so as they had seen him in the sanctuary.

The doctrine to be drawn from this part of our subject is this—That God is never at a loss to serve his people; and that he will compensate them for the want of those very things that seem essential to their welfare.

Let us consider two cases in which this truth may be exemplified.

The first is, in *the loss of outward comforts.* God does not require us to be indifferent to our substance, to our health, to our friends and relations: yea, under the removal of them he allows us to feel. But it is the duty and privilege of a Christian, to be able to say with the Church, "Although the fig tree shall not blossom, neither shall fruit be in the vines; the labour of the olive shall fail, and the fields shall yield no meat; the flock shall be cut off from the fold, and there shall be no herd in the stalls: yet I will rejoice in the Lord, I will joy in the God of my salvation."

The believer may well display a superiority over those events that keep others constantly alarmed or distressed, since God is his portion; and in His unchangeableness and all-sufficiency he has a stock of happiness independent of the body and its diseases, time and its vicissitudes, the world and its dissolution.

The design of affliction is to wean us from creatures, and to bring us more entirely to make use of God. At first we are often ready to murmur and repine, imagining we are undone: but when we find, that, in consequence of the failure of the streams, we have been led to the fountain of living waters, we can be thankful for the exchange; and acknowledge that it is good for us that we have been afflicted.—Is not he better to us than ten sons; better than thousands of gold and silver? Is not he "the father of the fatherless, and the husband of the widow?" How pleasing in this view is the promise, "Therefore, behold, I will allure her, and bring her into the wilderness, and speak comfortably unto her. And I will give her her vineyards from thence, and the valley of Achor for a door of hope: and she shall sing there, as in the days of her youth and as in the days when she came up out of the land of Egypt." When Moses was wandering with the Israelites in "the wilderness, in a solitary way, and found no city to dwell in," he familiarised God under the image of a home; and said, "Lord, thou hast been our refuge and dwelling-place in all generations." When David was driven from his palace by the rebellion of Absalom, and was obliged to keep the field, he said, "Be thou my strong habitation, whereunto I may continually resort." A

pious female in the most distressing bereavement was able to say,

> "Thou dost but take *the lamp* away,
> To bless me with *unclouded day.*"

And a good man, who had endured the wreck of fortune, being asked how he bore the change in his condition so cheerfully, replied; "When I had these good things, I enjoyed God in all; and now I am deprived of them, I enjoy all in God."

How many can bear witness, that He has made that condition comfortable which they once deemed insupportable; that "as the sufferings abound, the consolations abound also;" and that the light of his countenance, the joy of his salvation, the comforts of the Holy Ghost, are effectual substitutes for every deficiency in creature-good!

Secondly. In *the want of gracious ordinances.* The preaching of the word, and the observance of public worship, will always be deemed a privilege by the godly: they will therefore repair to them, not only because they are commanded, but because they are inclined. They are glad when it is said to them, Let us go into the house of the Lord: upon the same principle, the loss of them will be their grief. "When," says David, "I remember these things, I pour out my soul in me: for I had gone with the multitude, I went with them to the house of God, with the voice of joy and praise, with a multitude that kept holy day."

God will never countenance the neglect of the means of grace; but he will make up for the want of them. And those should remember this remark, who by accident, or sickness, or the care of young children, or the duties of servitude, are wholly or partially denied the privileges of the sanctuary. When we cannot follow him, He can follow us. I have known Christians placed by Providence in situations that had very few spiritual advantages—and yet they have surpassed others who were much more favoured.

The superstitious should remember this as well as the afflicted. He dwelleth not in temples made with hands: as saith the prophet; "The heaven is my throne, and the earth is my footstool: where is the house that ye build unto me? And where is the place of my rest? For all those things hath mine hand made, and all those things have been, saith the Lord: but to this man will I look, even to him that is poor, and of a contrite spirit, and trembleth at my word." He can meet with his people in any place; and wherever he holds communion with them, the place becomes sacred. "And Jacob awaked out of his sleep, and he said, Surely the Lord is in this place; and I knew it not." Though there was no building near, "He was afraid, and said, How dreadful is this place! This is none other but the house of God, and this is the gate of heaven." To which we may add, the assurance of our Saviour to the woman at the well. "The hour cometh, when ye shall neither in this mountain, nor yet at Jerusalem, worship the Father. But the hour cometh, and now is, when the true worshippers shall worship the Father in spirit and in truth : for the Father seeketh such to worship him. God is a Spirit: and they that worship him must worship him in spirit and in truth."

What a place then is heaven!

There we shall need none of these outward advantages. What a *natural* world must that be, where we can dispense with such an essential blessing as the sun ! "And there shall be no night there ; and they need no candle, neither light of the sun ; for the Lord God giveth them light: and they shall reign for ever and ever."—There we shall need none of these spiritual helps. What a *moral* world must that be, where we can dispense with Sabbaths, with preaching, with temples! Even religion will cease there, and nothing of it remain, but the dispositions it formed, and the state to which it led. "And I saw no temple therein : for the Lord God Almighty and the Lamb are the temple of it."

What a being then is God!

He enables us to realize and to begin this blessed state, even in this world. *There* we shall be perfectly happy, because he will be *all in all :* and *here* we are happy, in proportion as we live a life of dependence upon him, and communion with him. There are some individuals who are of importance to many around them. They are eyes to the blind, and feet to the lame ; they are a father to the poor ; the blessing of him that is ready to perish comes upon them ; and they cause the widow's heart to sing for joy. But the circle is limited ; their power is contracted ; and in numberless cases, pity and prayer is all the succour they can yield. But God is the fountain of life ; he is an infinite good. "He is able to do for us exceeding abundantly above all we can ask or think." There is no want but he can relieve ; no hope but he can accomplish.

Let us rejoice that he is accessible. Though sin carried us to such a distance from him, we are "made nigh by the blood of Christ, who once suffered for sin the just for the unjust, that he might bring us unto God." Let us come unto God by him ; saying, "Return unto thy rest, O my soul, for the Lord hath dealt bountifully with thee." While many ask, Who will show us any good? may we pray, "Lord, lift thou the light of thy countenance upon me:" and feel a gladness to which the man of the world is a stranger, even when his corn and wine increase.

Happy the man, wherever he resides, or whatever is denied him, who can say with David ; "I am continually with thee : thou hast holden me by my right hand. Thou shalt guide me with thy counsel, and afterward receive me to glory. Whom have I in heaven but thee ? and there is none upon earth that I desire beside thee. My flesh and my heart faileth : but God is the strength of my heart, and my portion for ever."

"Give what thou canst, without thee we are poor,
And with thee rich, take what thou wilt away."

DISCOURSE LXXX.

OBEDIENCE THE FRUIT OF REDEMPTION.

What? know ye not that—ye are not your own ? For ye are bought with a price : therefore glorify God in your body, and in your spirit, which are God's.—1 Cor. vi. 19, 20.

It cannot be denied that the death of our Lord Jesus holds a very large and distinguishing place in the Scripture : but the importance attached to it is frequently diminished, or misunderstood.

There are some who contend that he died not to put away sin by the sacrifice of himself, but only to give us an example of patience, and to seal the truth of his doctrine with his blood. This is an error peculiarly at variance with the types and prophecies of the Old Testament, and the language and spirit of the New ; with the relief of an awakened sinner ; and the consolation of the believer who "joys in God through our Lord Jesus Christ, by whom he has received the atonement."

But there is another heresy. It consists in believing that the Son of God died not to save us *from* our sins, but *in* them ; not to render us *holy*, but *to dispense with our being so.* This, though not always avowedly professed, too generally prevails ; and alarms us with regard to many of those who are very tenacious of the doctrines of the Gospel.

Against this delusion we would warn you in the words of the Apostle : "God is not only your Saviour, but your Sovereign: and from the Cross he demands of you nothing less than a life of praise. 'What? know ye not that—ye are not your own ? For ye are bought with a price : therefore glorify God in your body, and in your spirit, which are God's.'"

Let us consider,

I. YOUR STATE.   II. YOUR DUTY.   III. THE CONNEXION BETWEEN THESE, OR THE DERIVATION OF THE ONE FROM THE OTHER.

I. YOUR STATE. Paul expresses it in the form of a question. "What? know ye not that—ye are not your own ?" Such a mode of address is very common with our Apostle ; and it always implies either the obviousness or the importance of the principle he is establishing ; and so is designed to reprove either our ignorance or our inattention. How much do we need reproof with regard to each of these! How little do we know! How little do we consider!

But let us attend to the truth of the statement. "You are not your own"—you are not the masters of your own actions, the framers of your own condition, the proprietors of your own persons: you are not at your own disposal, but entirely at the Lord's command. And if it be asked, On what principle is the claim founded, and whence does the title spring? We answer, It is a claim you cannot deny; it is a title you cannot dispute—you are redeemed—you are paid for. "Know ye not that ye are bought with a price?"

No being can be his own, unless he be supreme, absolute, independent, self-existent. In *this* view, therefore, you are not your own. He made you and fashioned you. He formed your body out of the dust of the earth, and breathed into your nostrils the breath of life. Show me one day, one hour, in which you can live without God; and that day, that hour, shall be reckoned your own. If you refuse to acknowledge his right, why do you live at his table? why are you clothed by his bounty? why are you mean enough to be indebted to him for all your enjoyments, as well as supports? Tell him to take back all that is his, and leave you nothing but what is your own. —And where is the earth you tread? the air you breathe? the light you behold?—All are vanished. And where are you?—Annihilated.

Strong however as this claim is, it is not the principal one. The Apostle alleges another. You are God's, says he, not only because he made you and preserves you, but because he has bought you—"bought you with a price."

What price! He deemed it needless to describe it. He knew every Christian could exclaim, "He hath redeemed us from the curse of the law, being made a curse for us. In him we have redemption through his blood, even the forgiveness of our sins. We are redeemed—with the precious blood of our Lord Jesus Christ, as of a lamb without blemish and without spot." Having finished the work that was given him to do, "neither by the blood of goats, or of calves, but by his own blood, he entered in once into the holy place, having obtained eternal redemption for us." What a ransom is here offered and accepted! What a redemption is here made and pleaded! Now we are his by a more awful, a more endearing, a more powerful, claim than creation. Redemption delivers us from far greater evils than creation. Redemption confers upon us far greater blessings than creation. Redemption was much more difficult than creation. Our Maker had only to speak; our Saviour had to suffer. He made us—at the expense of his breath; he redeemed us—at the expense of his blood.

II. Your DUTY. It is to "glorify God in your body, and in your spirit, which are God's." It reminds us,

First, Of our complex nature. Some by a kind of voluntary humility would strip us of our glory, and reduce us to mere matter. But "there is a spirit in man, and the inspiration of the Almighty giveth him understanding." We are fearfully and wonderfully made. We combine clay and thought. On the one side we unite with angels; and on the other with the beast that perish. We are mortal in life, and immortal in death. "Then shall the dust return to the earth as it was; and the spirit shall return to God who gave it."

Secondly. The body is not to be excluded or undervalued in religion. It is the workmanship of God, and displays much of his perfection. His providence appears in preserving and supplying it. He has redeemed it; and will glorify it. And therefore the body, as well as the soul, is to be employed in glorifying him. Religion is not only a real, but a visible thing. It flows from principle, but is to be exemplified in practice. We are not only to approve ourselves to the eye of God, who seeth in secret, but we are to convince, to impress, to encourage, others. "Let your light so shine before men that they may see your good works, and glorify your Father which is in heaven."

The form of godliness is nothing without the power; but when the form is produced by the power it is comely, and useful, and necessary. They who disregard the Sabbath and the sanctuary, (under a notion that all times and places are to be alike to Christians, and under a pretence of superior spirituality despise the exercises of devotion, and the means of grace,) show little regard to the revealed will of God, and little acquaintance with the constitution of human nature. For man is an imbodied creature; his soul is to be approached through the medium of sense; and his communion with things unseen and eternal is to be maintained by means of those that are seen and temporal. How is the Scripture to be read but by the eye? How is the Gospel to be heard but by the ear? Is not the ordinance of the Lord's supper founded on the principle, that the body may be helpful to the mind?

But our greatest danger lies not here. Many are satisfied with their state in religion, because they regularly observe its forms, and abound in bodily exercise, which, when alone, profiteth little. We therefore remark,

Thirdly, that in all the duties of religion we are indispensably bound to glorify God in our spirit, as well as in our body. This is his demand: "My son, give me thine heart." Keep this back, and every thing else you render him will be unacceptable. Actions and professions may satisfy a fellow-creature, because they may delude him: but God is not mocked—he views our principles and motives; he looketh at the heart. "God is a Spirit: and they that worship him must worship him in spirit and in truth." The Jews never insulted our Saviour more than when they bowed the knee before him, and said, "Hail, king of the Jews!" Judas gave him lip-service, and betrayed the Son of man with a kiss. If you pray without desire, sing without gratitude, hear without reverence and obedience; if you approach his table, and rest in the outward and visible signs, not discerning the Lord's body, or showing forth his death, "you draw nigh to him with your mouth, and honour him with your lips, but your heart is far from him:" and, therefore, in vain do you worship.

Fourthly. We are to glorify God in our corporeal and spiritual powers respectively, by exertions peculiar to each.

As to the *body*—we are to glorify God in guarding our health; in watching our senses; in regulating our appetites; in opposing idleness and intemperance; in "yielding our senses and our members as instruments of righteousness unto holiness;" in rendering our natural refreshments and our secular callings subservient to religion, according to the injunction, "Whether therefore ye eat or drink, or whatever ye do, do all to the glory of God."

As to the *spirit*—we are to glorify God in the understanding, by exploring his truth; in the memory, by retaining his word; in the conscience, by fearing to offend him; in the will, by submitting to his commands, and acquiescing in his dispensations; in our affections, by loving him above all; in our dependence, by "rejoicing in Christ Jesus, and having no confidence in the flesh."

All these subdivide themselves into branches of duty too minute and various to be specified. What the Apostle requires is nothing less than an entire consecration of ourselves in all our faculties and actions to God, according to his comprehensive words in another of his Epistles; "For none of us liveth to himself, and no man dieth to himself. For whether we live, we live unto the Lord; and whether we die, we die unto the Lord: whether we live therefore, or die, we are the Lord's."

III. Let us consider the CONNEXION BETWEEN YOUR STATE AND YOUR DUTY, OR THE DERIVATION OF THE ONE FROM THE OTHER. "Know ye not—that ye are not your own? For ye are bought with a price: *therefore* glorify God in your body and in your spirit, which are God's." The inference is natural. The force of it appears in four things.

First. Does not justice demand this dedication? He has not only procured a title for you, but a title to you: and unless you devote yourselves to his service, you rob him of his right. What a man has bought he deems his own; and especially when the purchase has been costly. And has not God bought you with a price—of infinite value? And would you rob him of a servant from his family: of a vessel from his sanctuary? To take what belongs to a man is robbery, but to take what belongs to God is sacrilege.

Secondly. If we do not glorify God, are we not chargeable with the vilest ingratitude? You ought to be thankful for the common bounties of his providence; but how much more for his unspeakable Gift! How ready are you to censure a fellow-creature, whom you have served and indulged, when he appears insensible to your welfare. Yet had he some claims upon you; and the favours you conferred were small, and attended with no painful sacrifices—what then should you think of yourselves? Has not God done enough to gain your hearts, and engage you in his service for ever? In what state did he find you? To what blessedness has he raised you! In what way—by what means—has the deliverance—the elevation been accomplished? "He spared not his own Son, but delivered him up for us all. He commendeth his love toward us, in that, while we were sinners, Christ died for us."

"By these cords of love, these bonds of a man, how am I drawn! How am I bound! 'What shall I render unto the Lord for all his benefits toward me? O Lord, truly I am thy servant; I am thy servant: thou hast loosed my bonds.' I am not my own: I cannot be my own: I would not be my own. Had I ten thousand bodies and spirits, they should be only and eternally thine."

This is the language of a man properly penetrated with the subject. And how necessary it is, will appear by asking,

Thirdly. Is not this glorification of God the very end of your redemption? Were you rescued from bondage to be lawless! Or to become your own masters? Does this amazing work terminate in your mere escape from deserved punishment? What says Zechariah in his song of praise? "Blessed be the Lord God of Israel; for he hath visited and redeemed his people."—"That he would grant unto us, that we, being delivered out of the hand of our enemies, might serve him without fear, in holiness and righteousness before him, all the days of our life." What says Peter? "Who his own self bare our sins in his own body on the tree, that we being dead to sins, should live unto righteousness: by whose stripes ye were healed." What says our Apostle? Let him explain the inference he has here drawn—"Who gave himself for us, that he might redeem us from all iniquity, and purify unto himself a peculiar people, zealous of good works. For the love of Christ constraineth us; because we thus judge, that if one died for all, then were all dead: and that he died for all, that they which live should not henceforth live unto themselves, but unto him which died for them, and rose again."

Lastly. How can you determine your actual interest in this redemption, unless you have dedicated yourselves unto God? Who are the persons our Saviour will render eternally happy by his death? Not the righteous, but sinners. This is true. But what sinners? Those that remain in their unbelief and impenitence?—Can the profligate; can the sensual; can they who mind earthly things, however orthodox; can such men say, "I know that my Redeemer liveth; and that in my flesh I shall see God?—They that are Christ's have crucified the flesh with its affections and lusts.—He is the Author of eternal salvation to all them that obey him." He groaned, and bled, and died: but this does not, cannot render it less true, that "without holiness no man shall see the Lord."—"This," says John, "is the message which we have heard of him, and declare unto you, that God is light, and in him is no darkness at all. If we say that we have fellowship with him, and walk in darkness, we lie, and do not the truth: but if we walk in the light, as he is in the light, we have fellowship one with another, and the blood of Jesus Christ his Son cleanseth us from all sin." What is the experience of a man who can claim all the benefits of the cross, and who will never be confounded? "I am crucified with Christ: nevertheless I live; yet not I, but Christ liveth in me: and the life which I now live in the flesh I live by the faith of the Son of God, who loved me, and gave himself for me."

Thus if we consider the claims of justice and of gratitude; if we would meet the design of God in the dispensation, or know that we have eternal life abiding in us as the consequence of it; the inference strongly results —"ye are not your own, but bought with a price—*therefore* glorify God in your body and spirit, which are God's."

If I had been addressing persons, who, like the Athenians, can only be charmed in hearing some new thing, I should not have chosen the subject on which I have been speaking. It pretends to no novelty: but it possesses importance; and to those who are in a proper state of mind, it will always prove interesting.

It clearly shows us that the doctrines of Christianity are derived from its facts; and that its duties arise from its doctrines. These doctrines therefore are not, as some would suppose, mere opinions, or speculations, but are necessarily connected with experience and practice. The Christian's consolations and motives are supplied and maintained by his principles. Is it not therefore astonishing, that the preacher who inculcates these principles is to be considered an enemy to holiness,

or as taking an improper method to produce it? *He* values his system because of its practical bearing; because of its sanctifying influence; and affirms constantly, that they which have believed in God, be careful to maintain good works. He abhors the imputation of doing evil that good may come; or of sinning that grace may abound. But he does not rear a superstructure without a foundation; neither does he lay his foundation in the sand. He does not expect spiritual motion without spiritual life. He does not look for good fruit from a bad tree. His concern is, that the spring may be healed, and then he knows the streams will be wholesome.

Oh! Christians, let it appear from your practice, as well as from your argument, that the doctrine we preach is according to godliness. Let your lives furnish us with our best defence. "Be our epistles known and read of all men." The eyes of many are upon you, not that they may find reason to remove their unhappy prejudices against the Gospel, but to confirm them; and though we quote Scripture, they will appeal to you; and perhaps all the notions they form of evangelical religion will be taken from the representations you give, and the impressions you make. May these representations be accurate! May these impressions be just! May you "put to silence the ignorance of foolish men," and "adorn the doctrine of God our Saviour in all things." —"And this I pray, that your love may abound yet more and more in knowledge and in all judgment; that ye may approve things that are excellent; that ye may be sincere and without offence till the day of Christ; being filled with the fruits of righteousness, which are by Jesus Christ, unto the glory and praise of God."

As for those who are living without God in the world, and who feel no concern to glorify him, let them remember that God will be glorified even in them—though not willingly, yet by compulsion; though not intentionally, yet by his overruling providence; though not *in their salvation*, yet *in their destruction.* His power, his truth, his holiness, and his justice will be displayed in their misery. The grace that should have been the savour of life unto life, will become the savour of death unto death. It cannot be otherwise. They are exposed to a twofold condemnation; one from the law which they have transgressed, and another from the Gospel which they have neglected. And how can they escape? "He that despised Moses' law died without mercy under two or three witnesses: Of how much sorer punishment, suppose ye, shall he be thought worthy, who hath trodden under foot the Son of God, and hath counted the blood of the covenant, wherewith he was sanctified, an unholy thing, and hath done despite unto the Spirit of grace?"

DISCOURSE LXXXI.

LIFE ENJOYED AND IMPROVED.

I know that there is no good in them, but for a man to rejoice, and to do good in his life. Eccles. iii. 12.

"I LEAD," says Wisdom, not only—" in the way of righteousness," but—" in the midst of the paths of judgment:" that is—between the extreme on each side of the road, and into which we are so liable to run. Indeed, moral duty always lies in the middle of two opposites. Patience is equally remote from stupidity and excessive sensibility: it is alike destroyed by feeling too little or too much. True courage is ashamed of rashness as well as of fear. Real economy shuns parsimony and meanness, as well as profusion and waste.

Let us apply this to the subject before us. It is desirable and necessary to form a proper estimate of our present condition; so that we may use this world as not abusing it. We are prone to value it too highly; to acquire too keen an appetite for its pleasures; to lay too great a stress upon its riches; and to rest in that, as our home, which was only designed for our passage. Yet it is possible to err on the other side; and we may neglect to secure and enjoy all the advantages which our residence on earth is capable of affording.

There are some whose liberality trenches on their allowed enjoyment. The case, indeed, is not very common; and there is something noble in the principle, when it *does* arise from principle,—for it may arise from vainglory, when a man denies himself for the sake of usefulness. Yet it should be remembered, that God " giveth us richly all things to enjoy;" that, as Christians, we are not to suffer " our good to be evil spoken of;" that, if we refuse ourselves such accommodations and comforts as our station in life permits, we shall appear sordid and avaricious to those who, while they witness our savings, are not acquainted with the use we make of them; and, that what is expended upon ourselves, in the hire of servants, the employment of workmen, and the purchase of articles in trade, is one of the ways in which we can " serve our generation." This, however, though a mistake, is an error on the right hand: the greatest danger lies on the left; and arises from the self-indulgence that trenches upon the claims of charity. For there are persons who give way to so much needless gratification, as to have no ability with which to answer the calls of misery: they are wrapped up in selfishness, looking every man on his own things, and not on the things of others; while their conscience gives them no alarm, and their very religion is bribed to acquiesce in the hardness of their hearts.

Let us see whether life will not yield sources of enjoyment and beneficence too. Solomon saw no inconsistency between these; but recommends both in the words of our text. " I know that there is no good in them, but for a man to rejoice, and to do good in his life." That is, all our temporal possessions are only valuable, as they are expended upon ourselves, or others; either as they aid our own comfort, or advance the welfare of our fellow-creatures. Let me then call upon you,

I. To REJOICE IN THEM. II. To DO GOOD WITH THEM.

I. Let me call upon you TO REJOICE IN THEM. This part of our subject requires remarks, not so much of a stimulating as of an explanatory and qualifying nature. Let me begin with two cautions.

The first regards *justice*. See that what you enjoy is your own. " Owe no man any thing," says the Apostle. You would deem it shameful to purloin from a neighbour's garden, or shop, any thing you deemed agreeable; but what is the difference between stealing, and ordering what you are conscious, at the time, you are unable to pay for? Yet there are those, who are determined, that, whoever may suffer, they will enjoy themselves; who have not only every thing comfortable, but often luxuriant, in food, in apparel, in furniture: while their tradesmen's bills give them not a moment's uneasiness; or the prospect of failure, the least sentiment of disgrace. It was well said by Lord Mansfield, that " for one cruel creditor, there were a hundred cruel debtors." Upon this head our laws are far too lenient for the support of the public welfare. But what can we think of professors of religion who can gratify themselves at the expense of others, and involve themselves in debt, rather than exercise the least self-denial! There may be honesty without religion; but it is a strange kind of religion that can subsist without honesty. A real Christian should blush, not to be seen in a threadbare, mended garment, that is *his own*; but in a goodly and splendid one, that belongs to *his tradesman!* Poverty is not disgraceful; but sin is. Jesus and his Apostles were poor; but they were not unjust: otherwise, *He* might have had where to lay his head, and *they* would not have complained of nakedness and hunger.

The second regards *moderation*. You can never suppose that God requires, or even allows intemperance. Reason does not allow it; health does not allow it; enjoyment does not allow it: for it is verified by experience, that the moderate use of all earthly good, is productive of the greatest degree of pleasure. " Let your moderation, therefore, be known unto all men;" and, while alive to the beauties of nature and the bounties of Providence, beware of losing the heart of a stranger. The danger lies on the side of gratification. Therefore, " Watch and pray, lest ye enter into temptation." Never be so absorbed in any present indulgence, as to be careless of the voice that will summon you to "arise and depart hence, for this is not your rest, because it is polluted."

After having cautioned you, allow me to admonish.

And First. If you would rejoice in the good things which God gives you under the sun,—

Cherish a grateful sensibility. Some receive all their mercies like the beasts that perish. The animal only is gratified in them. There is nothing to refine the grossness of appetite, or to increase the relish of possession, derived from the mind and the heart. How much in passing through life, does he lose who regards all its blessings as the effects of chance, and is not led by them to an intelligent Author, and an indulgent Benefactor! He has the secret of adding a hundred-fold to his enjoyment who connects all his advantages with the agency of his God, and feels his obligations to his bounty. He has the highest relish of every thing who, instead of " sacrificing to his own net and burning incense to his own drag," realizes the sentiment of Solomon, " The blessing of the Lord it maketh rich, and he addeth no sorrow with it." Gratitude is a lively and cheerful feeling, even where it regards a creature only ; how much more when it respects the God of love ! The man who lives a stranger to it can never rejoice in his mercies, and is comparatively a wretch in all his abundance.

Secondly. *Guard against habitual discontent.* To possess is not to enjoy. Many possess much and enjoy nothing. We cannot judge of a man by outward appearances. His grounds may bring forth plentifully. He may fare sumptuously every day; he may have servants to anticipate all his wants; he may have more than heart can wish ; and yet if we could look within, we should see his soul a prey to dissatisfaction. An ability to relish our mercies is considered by Solomon as the gift of God: " Also that every man should eat and drink, and *enjoy the good of all his labour,* it is the *gift of God.*" But this gift of God comes to us like other gifts, in the use of means, and is increased by them. You should, therefore, sanctify reason and exercise thought. You should compare your circumstances with the state, not of those above you, but of those below. As soon as you are placed in a condition, you should shut your eyes and ears against all its disadvantages, and dwell only on the good and improvable. You should often inquire, what it is that keeps you from taking comfort in your portion ; and be ashamed to think, that one trial should make you insensible to a thousand

favours ; that one trifling event not according to your mind, but upon which your real welfare has no dependence, should deprive every thing else of all power to interest you! Did you never think Haman a fool ? " He called for his friends, and Zeresh his wife. And Haman told them of the glory of his riches, and the multitude of his children, and all the things wherein the king had promoted him, and how he had advanced him above the princes and servants of the king. Haman said moreover, Yea, Esther the queen did let no man come in with the king unto the banquet that she had prepared but myself; and to-morrow am I invited unto her also with the king. Yet all this availeth me nothing, so long as I see Mordecai the Jew sitting at the king's gate." It is to no purpose to exempt some even from real evils; they will be sure to conjure up imaginary ones. It matters not what is done for them ; they are incapable of being pleased. It matters not where they are placed; it is impossible to make them happy. How must it shock an angel, to see a man, notwithstanding his unworthiness, surrounded with every wish, every comfort, and yet made up of fretfulness and complaint, a torment to others, and a burden to himself! He is far worse than his brethren in the field: " Doth the wild ass bray when he hath grass ? or loweth the ox over his fodder ?"

Thirdly. *Shun avaricious and distrustful anxiety.* This will produce excessive exertion, and make you forget that " the life is more than meat, and the body than raiment." Diligence is a duty, and employment is a privilege. But this cannot be said of drudgery or bondage ; these are incompatible with comfort. And why *is* the man a slave and a drudge ? Has he not often prayed " Give us day by day our daily bread ?" Has not God promised that he shall eat the labour of his hand ? Yes—but he must make haste to be rich ; he must gain, not a substance, but a fortune; he must, not continue in his calling with God, but, retire from it, to live in a state of independence and inaction: hence, he has not a moment that he can call his own ; hence he denies not only recreation, but rest, to body and mind ; hence he is afraid of every present expense and gratification ;, and loses the best part of life, in providing for the worst ! He may never reach the period that flatters him, and if he does, he may be incapable of relishing what he has laid up, owing to bodily infirmities and disease, the removal of relatives and friends, and the force of habits deprived of their proper objects.

Fourthly. *Entertain no harsh and superstitious views of Religion.* " Touch not, taste not, handle not: which things have indeed a show of wisdom in will-worship and humility, and neglecting of the body ; not in any honour to the satisfying of the flesh.

But where has God prescribed bodily flagellations? Where does He require us to withdraw from society? to turn mendicants? to live in deserts and caves? to go barefooted? and sleep on the cold ground? Is God pleased only as we are tormented? does He surround us with enjoyments only that we may not taste of them? To enjoy is to obey, because it corresponds with the obvious will of God. What says Paul of those who "forbid to marry, and command to abstain from meats which God hath created to be received with thankfulness, of them which believe and know the truth? They preach the doctrine of devils." And what says the wise man in this book? "Let thy garments be always white; and let thy head lack no ointment. Live joyfully with the wife whom thou lovest all the days of the life of thy vanity, which he hath given thee under the sun, all the days of thy vanity: for that is thy portion in this life, and in thy labour which thou takest under the sun."

Some Protestants have had a tinge of Popery, and have enjoined themselves austerities which God has never required. Their motive, perhaps, in some cases, has been good; and they adopted these mortifications, not to recommend them to God, so much as to promote their sanctification. But God knows our frame. His own means are the best; and we ought not to distinguish ourselves by morals and self-denial of unscriptural devisings; but, remembering that we serve a good master, gratefully use what his providence supplies. "For every creature of God is good, and nothing to be refused, if it be received with thanksgiving: for it is sanctified by the word of God and prayer."

Lastly. *Seek after a knowledge of your reconciliation with God.* It is your mercy that you know how this is to be obtained. Jesus is the only Mediator, and he made peace by the blood of his cross. He "once suffered for sins, the just for the unjust, that he might bring us unto God." Through him, "God now waits to be gracious, and is exalted to have mercy upon you." You are allowed, you are invited, you are commanded to "seek him, while he may be found, and to call upon him, while he is near." And can you be happy without any well-grounded hope of your pardon and acceptance with God? Could a man enjoy a feast if a sword was suspended over his head by a hair?— Could he be charmed with the finest music if he knew he was hanging over a bottomless pit by a rotten thread? Can you enjoy life while you know—that death is certain—that it cannot be far off—that it may be very near —that after death is the judgment—and after the judgment—the sentence, "Depart from me, ye cursed, into everlasting fire, prepared for the devil and his angels?" You may, indeed, banish the thought; but forgetfulness is not safety. And the thought cannot be always banished; it will sometimes intrude, and mar all your peace and pleasure. "But blessed is the man whose transgression is forgiven, whose sin is covered." The curse is removed from all his trials. He has a covenant right to all his mercies. God is his father— death is his friend—heaven is his home—the Bible is his treasure—he has nothing to do with events. Providence is engaged to make "all things work together for his good." All his interests are secured—not a hair of his head is unnumbered—he dwells safely, and is "in quiet from the fear of evil." *This* is the man to enjoy life; every thing smiles when God smiles. "Go thy way, eat thy bread with joy, and drink thy wine with a merry heart; for God now accepteth thy works."

Having called upon you to rejoice, let me exhort you also, with the royal preacher,

II. To DO GOOD. "I know that there is no good in them, but for a man to rejoice, and to *do good* in his life." Here let us inquire, What is the good these things will enable us to do? How we are to perform it? and, Why we should be concerned to accomplish it?

What good can these things enable us to do?—It is of three kinds.

They enable us to do *religious* good. This is the chief. No charity equals that which regards the souls of men; and what an honour is conferred upon property, that by means of it you can be instrumental in the salvation of sinners, in the diffusion of the Scriptures, in the preaching of the Gospel, and the establishment of the Redeemer's empire! But so it is; and every thing, under God, depends upon the pecuniary resources of his agents. What, at this hour, hinders, or limits, a thousand exertions in the cause of truth and of righteousness—but the want of "silver and gold," to replenish the funds of wisdom and zeal? "Pray ye therefore the Lord of the harvest, that he will send forth labourers into his harvest:" by which we mean, not ministers only, but men of independence, who will say, Lord, I am thine, and all that I have: men of trade and commerce, who will gain, not to squander away in extravagance, or hoard up in the miser's bag; but to honour the Lord with their substance, and to realize the prediction concerning the deliverance and conversion of Tyre: "And her merchandise and her hire shall be holiness to the Lord: it shall not be treasured nor laid up; for her merchandise shall be for them that dwell before the Lord, to eat sufficiently, and for durable clothing."

They enable us also to do *intellectual* good. This takes in education: and whatever the advocates for mental darkness suppose—who plead that because a man is born to poverty he is born to ignorance, and will fill his place the better the less he knows; no property can be better expended than that which is laid out in the instruction of the young. A little education gives a poor child the use of his understanding. It opens to him a thousand sources of pleasure, to alleviate his condition. It prepares him to support himself, and to be useful to others. While it is friendly to religion, by teaching him the nature and grounds of his duty, and enabling him to read the word of truth.

They enable us to do *corporeal* good: by which we mean, that which immediately regards the body, though the mind will also derive comfort from it. Here we can never be at a loss. We are surrounded with the defenceless, the hungry, the naked, and the sick. We live in a world full of misery, and whatever be our situation, it is impossible to elude cases of distress. But are we to elude them? Are we to hide ourselves from our own flesh? "Pure religion and undefiled before God and the Father is this, To visit the fatherless and widows in their affliction, and to keep himself unspotted from the world."

Secondly. In *what manner* are we to do it? We are to do good

Immediately, and with diligence. "Withhold not good from them to whom it is due, when it is in the power of thine hand to do it. Say not unto thy neighbour, Go, and come again, and to-morrow I will give, when thou hast it by thee." He may be dead before to-morrow, or you may be dead; and thus the action will be lost for ever. For the saints on earth have one privilege above the saints in heaven; it is the opportunity of doing good; but this opportunity, we should always remember, is as short and precarious as it is precious: "Whatsoever thy hand findeth to do, do it with thy might; for there is no work, nor device, nor knowledge, nor wisdom, in the grave, whither thou goest." We are to do good

Extensively, and with impartiality. Some cases indeed will have stronger claims than others, and the most generous ability cannot reach every case. But it is only preference—not exclusion, it is only want of means—not in disposition, that must limit our exertions. We are not to be restrained by relationship, or country, or religion, or even personal injury—yea, says our Saviour, "Love your enemies, bless them that curse you, do good to them that hate you, and pray for them which despitefully use you, and persecute you; that ye may be the children of your Father which is in heaven: for he maketh his sun to rise on the evil and on the good, and sendeth rain on the just and on the unjust."—We are to do good

Perseveringly, and without declension. We must reckon upon encountering much, very much, that will try us. We shall often meet with very unworthy returns. We shall frequently seem to labour in vain. The

2 P

harvest will very slowly follow the seed-time. Zeal, without patience, will do nothing. "Cast thy bread upon the waters: for thou shalt find it after many days. In the morning sow thy seed, and in the evening withhold not thy hand: for thou knowest not whether shall prosper, either this or that, or whether they both shall be alike good. Let us not be weary in well doing, for in due time we shall reap, if we faint not."—Let us inquire,

Thirdly. *Why* we should be concerned to accomplish it.

Why? Because the bounties of Providence were conferred upon us for this very purpose. The Donor looked beyond ourselves in communicating them. He designed them to be not only indulgences, but talents; he constituted us not so much the proprietors as the stewards; "and it is required in a steward, that a man be found faithful."

Why? Because God hath commanded it. He is our sovereign master; and if we are servants rightly disposed, we have often asked, "Lord, what wilt thou have me to do?" And has he left us ignorant of his will? Did you never read, "as we have opportunity let us do good unto all men, especially unto them that are of the household of faith?" Can any reason be assigned why he is to be obeyed, when he commands us to believe on the name of his Son Jesus Christ, and when he enjoins us not to forsake the assembling of ourselves together—and despised, when he issues the charge, "Charge them that are rich in this world that they do good, that they be rich in good works, ready to distribute, willing to communicate?"

Why? Gratitude requires it. How much has God done for us, notwithstanding all our unworthiness and guilt! What an instance of unparalleled goodness does the Apostle of love mention with rapture; and how natural, how forcible, the inference he draws from it, while teaching us to derive Christian morals from evangelical motives; "Herein is love, not that we loved God, but that he loved us, and sent his Son to be the propitiation for our sins. Beloved, if God so loved us, we ought also to love one another." Gratitude consists in a disposition to return a favour received: and from man to man, it may be so expressed, as that a compensation may be made, yea, and even more than an equivalent be returned. But we can never discharge the obligations we are under to God. Let us, however, show that we are sensible of them. Let us ask, "What shall I render unto the Lord for all his benefits towards me?" And if He is exalted above all blessing and praise, and our goodness extendeth not to him, let it extend to those who are appointed to receive, as his substitutes, the acts of our beneficence. He will judge of our disposition towards himself, whom we have not seen, by our conduct towards his creatures, and his children, whom we have seen. "To do good and to communicate forget not, for with such sacrifices God is well pleased." The Redeemer at the last day will acknowledge,. "Forasmuch as ye did it unto one of the least of these my brethren, ye did it unto me."

Why? Profit requires it. What is it that attaches one man so powerfully to another—and gives him a resource in the tears, the prayers, the attentions, of his fellow-creatures in the day of evil? Power may cause the possessor to be feared; wealth, to be envied; genius, to be admired; righteousness, to be respected: but, "for a good man some would even dare to die." Yea, goodness secures a man much higher resources than human. "Blessed is he that considereth the poor: the Lord shall deliver him in time of trouble. Blessed are the merciful; for they shall obtain mercy." But it would be needless to mention all the promises made to beneficence by a God that cannot lie, and is never at a oss to perform.

Why? Pleasure requires it. If you are strangers to the pleasures of benevolence, you are to be pitied; for you are strangers to the most pure, the most durable, the most delicious, the most satisfactory, the most God-like pleasures to be enjoyed on this side heaven.

And here I unite the two parts of our subject into one. I have called upon you to rejoice in your portion, and to do good with it: but it is possible to rejoice in doing good. The most beneficent life is the most happy life. We talk of pleasure! What are the feelings of the most successful and indulged worldling compared with those of Job! "When the ear heard me, then it blessed me; and when the eye saw me, it gave witness to me. Because I delivered the poor that cried, and the fatherless, and him that had none to help him. The blessing of him that was ready to perish came upon me: and I caused the widow's heart to sing for joy." O the delight of resembling Him, "who went about doing good!" O the joy of being followers of God, at once the greatest and the best of Beings!" GOD IS LOVE: AND HE THAT DWELLETH IN LOVE DWELLETH IN GOD, AND GOD IN HIM."

DISCOURSE LXXXII.

THE NEW CREATURE.

For in Christ Jesus neither circumcision availeth any thing, nor uncircumcision, but a new creature.—Gal. vi. 15.

IF religion be, as it is commonly acknowledged, the one thing needful; if it be absolutely indispensable to every character, and in every condition; if it be "profitable unto all things, having promise of the life that now is, and of that which is to come;" it must be desirable to know wherein it consists, what are its peculiar attributes, and how it may be distinguished from every thing that would speciously usurp its place.

To afford us this necessary satisfaction is the aim of the Apostle, in several parts of his writings; and as he wrote under the inspiration of the Holy Ghost, his decisions are infallible. "We are the circumcision, who worship God in the Spirit, rejoice in Christ Jesus, and have no confidence in the flesh. The kingdom of God is not in word, but in power. The kingdom of God is not meat and drink, but righteousness, peace, and joy in the Holy Ghost. For in Christ Jesus neither circumcision availeth any thing, nor uncircumcision; but faith that worketh by love." "*For in Christ Jesus neither circumcision availeth any thing, nor uncircumcision, but a new creature.*"

The negation extends, by a parity of reasoning, to a thousand other things. In Jesus Christ neither episcopacy, nor dissenterism; a liturgy, or prayer without a form; kneeling, or sitting at the Lord's-supper; sprinkling in baptism, or immersion; availeth any thing. We say not, that all these are equally true and proper in themselves, and that no degree of importance is attached to them; but that real religion is not essentially involved in them: real religion may subsist without them, and they may subsist without real religion.—Neither will mere orthodoxy, knowledge, gifts, profession, avail—What then? "A new creature." "For in Christ Jesus neither circumcision availeth any thing, nor uncircumcision, but a new creature." Let us endeavour to explain and improve this subject,

I. BY EXAMINING WHAT IS IMPLIED IN "A NEW CREATURE." II. WHAT IS TO BE INFERRED FROM ITS UNRIVALLED IMPORTANCE.

I. LET US EXAMINE WHAT IS IMPLIED IN "A NEW CREATURE."

Four explanatory questions may be asked upon this subject,

First. In *what sense* is a Christian a new creature? Is it a physical or a moral one? It is only a moral one. New faculties are not given him; but his faculties have new qualities and applications. Hence the original complexion, or constitutional peculiarity, remains; and the *man* is seen even in the Christian. His very religion takes a kind of hue from his natural character, whether it be sanguine or phlegmatical, tending to severity or mildness. And this is no inconsiderable proof of sincerity: for it is custom, it is formality, it is hypocrisy, that produces sameness; that constrains the lively to revolt from cheerfulness; the talkative to keep silence; and the young to look demurely, and speak and move with the gravity of old age. Had I known the individual turn and temper of Martha and Mary before our Lord entered their house, I should have viewed them as hypocrites had Mary acted as Martha did, or Martha acted as Mary did: but when I see the one "sitting at his feet," and the other "cumbered about much serving," I see a difference; but it is principle, operating according to character. To proceed. The man, therefore, continues the same as before, and yet is a new creature. His soul, and all its powers, are the same; he has not another understanding, another memory, another imagination, another genius: but these are changed in their use, and sanctified. His body is the same, and all its senses: grace does not give him another tongue, or other eyes and ears; but they are now sacred to new purposes. His condition is the same: he is not another husband, another father, another master; but he is a different one: he is godly in each of these relations. He carries on the same business: but now he abides with God in his calling. He eats and drinks as before: but now, whether he eats or drinks, or whatever he does, he does all to the glory of God. If the covetous become liberal, the proud humble, and the prayerless devout; they are new creatures as to religious purposes—and this is the subject in question. Compare Paul after his conversion with Paul before his conversion: his body and soul, his learning and abilities, and the ardour of his disposition, continued the same; and yet, was there ever a being so different?

Secondly. *How far* does this change extend? The reason of this question is obvious; it is to keep persons from resting in things, which, though good in themselves, come short of it. A man may be baptized, and not regenerated. A new creed, or a new denomination, does not make a man a new creature. It is pleasing to see a man reformed externally; but he may abandon a course of profligacy, and live soberly and righteously, and yet not live *godly* in the present world. The new creation is not a change from vicious to virtuous only; but from natural to spiritual, from earthly to heavenly, from walking by sight to walking by faith. To go still farther: a man may be convinced, and not converted; he may be alarmed, and not have the fear of God in his heart; he may receive the word with joy, and be a stranger to the comforts of the Holy Ghost. Let us hear Paul. "If any man be in Christ, he is a new creature: old things are passed away; behold, all things are become new."

His conceptions are new. His views of himself are changed. He discovers that he is a guilty creature, and deserves to perish; that he is a depraved creature, and that his heart is infinitely worse than his life; "wherefore he abhors himself, and repents in dust and ashes:" nor does he ever again recover those lofty thoughts of himself he once had. His views of the Saviour are changed. He once neglected, or despised him: but now he cries, How great is his goodness, and how great is his beauty! and deems only those happy, who enjoy and serve him.

His desires are new. He no longer asks, "Who will show us any good?" but he "hungers and thirsts after righteousness." "Yea, doubtless," says he, "and I count all things but loss for the excellency of the knowledge of Christ Jesus, my Lord. That I may win Christ, and be found in him, not having mine own righteousness, which is of the law, but that which is through the faith of Christ, the righteousness which is of God by faith: that I may know him, and the power of his resurrection, and the fellowship of his sufferings, being made conformable unto his death." These are the desires of the new creature.

His pleasures are new. The pleasures of sin he abhors. The dissipations of the world he despises; but it is his meat to do the will of his heavenly Father. He calls the sabbath a delight. He is glad when they say unto him, Let us go into the house of the Lord. He finds his word and eats it, and it is unto him the joy and the rejoicing of his heart.

His pains are new. He once felt the sorrow of the world that worketh death; but he now understands that godly sorrow, which worketh repentance unto life. He is not insensible under the afflictions of life; but says he, What is every other loss, to the loss of the soul? O this evil heart of unbelief! O this ingratitude towards the God of my mercy! O this unprofitableness under the means of grace! O this insensibility under the corrections of his Providence! "O wretched man that I am, who shall deliver me from the body of this death!" These are the groans of the new creature.

His life is new. In simplicity and godly sincerity, not with fleshly wisdom, but by the grace of God, he now has his conversation in the world. How shall he that is dead to sin, live any longer therein? If he was not vicious before, he now abhors, from disposition, what he once only shunned from selfish motives: if moral before, his morality is now evangelized; and whatsoever he does "in word or deed, he does all in the name of the Lord Jesus."—After all, this is only a specimen; the proposition is universal in its reference: old things are passed away; behold, all things are become new!" This, however, regards the extent, not the degree of this change. We therefore ask,

Thirdly. Is this work produced *instantaneously*, or is it *gradually* advanced to perfection? Were we to affirm, that it is completed at once, we should offend against the generation of God's children; for, though believers often question the reality of their religion, they never doubt the imperfection of it. We should lose the evidence of analogy. If we examine the world of nature, we shall see God producing nothing in immediate perfection; but from imperceptible beginnings carrying them, by numberless degrees, to maturity. Look into the field—there is first the blade, then the ear, and after that the full corn in the ear. Look into the fold—there are lambs as well as sheep. Look into the family—there are babes as well as young men: even our Saviour himself "increased in wisdom, and in stature, and in favour with God and man." We should lose the authority of Revelation. For what are the commands of Scripture? "Grow in grace." "Be filled with the Spirit." What are its promises? "They shall grow as the vine. The righteous shall hold on his way, and he that hath clean hands shall wax stronger and stronger." What are its representations? It describes Christians as going "from strength to strength:" as "renewed day by day:" as "changed into the same image, from glory to glory." Who then would reject the bud, because it is not the flower; or contemn the dawn, because it is not the day? "Who has despised the day of small things?" Of whom is it prophesied, "a bruised reed shall he not break, the smoking flax shall he not quench, till he bring forth judgment unto victory?"

Fourthly. Who is the *Author* of this new creation? The question seems answered by the very terms employed. Creation is a work of omnipotence, and belongs exclusively to God. This is not denied in any other instance. Men will allow, that God alone can make a blade of grass; they will allow that in him we live, and move, and have our *natural* being; and yet, with marvellous inconsistency, they would be their own saviours, and derive from themselves that *spiritual* life, which is emphatically called "the life of God," not only to show its resemblance, but its origin. If the stream can rise no higher than the fountain; if no effect can exceed its cause; if no one can bring a clean thing out of an unclean: how is it to be accounted for, that those who were once so depraved as to need a universal change, should be in the possession of real holiness? of spiritual excellency? If we appeal to the Scripture, the case is explained. There we shall find this work, in the perfection, the progress, and the commencement, ascribed to the agency of God. We are said to "live in the Spirit: to walk in the Spirit; to be born of the Spirit." "You hath he quickened," says the Apostle, "who were dead in trespasses and sins. You are his workmanship, created in Christ Jesus unto good works, which God hath before ordained that we should walk in them."—Having shown what is implied in a "new creature," let us,

II. OBSERVE WHAT IS TO BE INFERRED FROM ITS UNRIVALLED IMPORTANCE. And, "if in Christ Jesus neither circumcision availeth any thing, nor uncircumcision, but a new creature," this should regulate your inquiries —your prayers—your praise—your esteem —and your zeal.

First. It should regulate your inquiries. You are commanded in the Scripture to examine yourselves; and, therefore, the examination is necessary. But on what is it to turn? Not on the place, the time, the manner, the means of your conversion, but the reality. Can you say, "one thing I know, that whereas I was blind, now *I see?*" On what is it to turn? On that which is of the highest moment. What is it to know that you are right in every thing else; in your opinions of church government, in your views of Divine ordinances, in your notions of Gospel grace, if your heart is not right in the sight of God? Are you "saved by the washing of regeneration, and the renewing of the Holy Ghost?" This is the question. "For in Christ Jesus neither circumcision availeth any thing, nor uncircumcision, but a new creature."

It should regulate your *prayers*. If you are strangers to this work, an experience of it should be your immediate, your prevailing, your supreme concern. You should lay your unhappy condition to heart. You should reflect on what has been done for millions of your fellow-sinners, who are by nature children of wrath, even as others. You should consider, that what is impossible to man, is easy with God. You should remember, that his power is under the direction of his goodness; and that he is not only the Lord God Almighty, but the God of all grace, and the God of all comfort. You should remember, that he has provided for your weakness and depravity, as well as your guilt and danger, and that "if ye being evil know how to give good gifts unto your children, how much more will your Father that is in heaven give his Holy Spirit to them that ask him." At his dear footstool, you should plead and pray as David did, "Create in me a clean heart, O God, and renew a right spirit within me." Without this, you are undone for ever. Compared with this, every thing else you want, is a trifle. "For in Christ Jesus neither circumcision availeth any thing, nor uncircumcision, but a new creature."

Thirdly. It should regulate your *praise*. You ought to be thankful for every thing you enjoy: and in a proper frame of mind you will say, with Jacob, "O Lord, I am not worthy of *the least* of all thy mercies, and of all the truth which thou hast showed to thy servant." But gratitude should be wise, and measure out its favours according to the value of the blessing acknowledged. You should be thankful if you are favoured with civil freedom; if you have the comforts of life; if your body is free from pain and disease: but you should be much more so if the Son has made you free;

if you have the comforts of the Holy Ghost; if your soul prospers, and is in health. What are temporal good things, compared with all spiritual blessings in heavenly places in Christ? The Disciples, on their return, rejoiced in their miraculous powers; but their Master corrected them, and said, "In this rejoice not, that the spirits are subject unto you: but rather rejoice, because your names are written in heaven." If God has convinced you of sin, given you the spirit of grace and of supplication, and enabled you to believe on the Lord Jesus Christ, he has done much more for you, than if he had enabled you, with Balaam, to prophesy, or with Judas, to cast out devils. One of these endowed mortals was slain fighting among the enemies of God's people, and the other went and hanged himself, that he might go to his own place; but he has sealed you with that holy Spirit of promise which is the earnest of our inheritance. Here, therefore, call upon your souls, and all that is within you, to bless and praise his holy name. "Giving thanks unto the Father, which hath made us meet to be partakers of the inheritance of the saints in light; who hath delivered us from the power of darkness, and hath translated us into the kingdom of his dear Son. For in Christ Jesus neither circumcision availeth any thing, nor uncircumcision, but a new creature."

Fourthly. It should regulate your *esteem*. It is said of a citizen of Zion, "In his eyes, a vile person is contemned; but he honoureth them that fear the Lord." And what are all adventitious distinctions, or bodily or mental accomplishments, compared with the grace of God? The righteous is more excellent than his neighbour: a man's real worth is his religious worth. But in judging of this, do not inquire after his particular opinions, his mode of worship, or the denomination to which he belongs; but the evidence he gives of being a partaker of the Divine nature. "If any man have not the Spirit of Christ, he is none of his:" and if he has, let this be sufficient to endear him. "For in Christ Jesus neither circumcision availeth any thing, nor uncircumcision, but a new creature."

Finally. This should regulate your *zeal*. You ought to be concerned to do good: but let it always appear, that your aim is, to win souls to the Redeemer, and not to a party; not to proselyte, but to christianize. To bring men into the way everlasting, is something, is every thing; but what is it to detach them from one place of worship, and fix them in another, where the same truth is already preached? When, therefore, a person who gave *little* evidence of her being under the power of godliness, one day, said to an eminent minister, now with God, "Sir, I am going to turn from the Dissenters to the Church;" "Madam," replied he, who knew her disposition, "you are turning from no-

thing, to nothing." And says not the Apostle the same? "For in Christ Jesus neither circumcision availeth any thing, nor uncircumcision, but a new creature."

But if our text should regulate our zeal, it should also enliven and increase it. "Brethren," says James, "if any of you do err from the truth, and one convert him; let him know, that he which converteth the sinner from the error of his way shall save a soul from death, and shall hide a multitude of sins." Here is an object worthy of all our powers. And is the attainment practicable? Can we convert a sinner, save a soul, hide a multitude of sins? Yes, the honour, the pleasure,—unspeakable and full of glory,—is placed within our reach. O ye who are the subjects of his grace, be anxious to become the instruments too! Let David's prayer and resolution be your's— "Restore unto me the joy of thy salvation; and uphold me with thy free spirit. Then will I teach transgressors thy ways; and sinners shall be converted unto thee."

Surely, if there was only a probability, yea, a possibility of this success, in one instance only, it should be enough to awaken all your powers, and employ all your efforts, for life!

"Pleasure and praise run through God's host
   To see a sinner turn;
Then Satan hath a captive lost,
   And Christ a subject born."

DISCOURSE LXXXIII.

THE HAPPY PARENT.

My son, if thine heart be wise, my heart shall rejoice, even mine.—Prov. xxiii. 15.

No person can read the works of Solomon without observing how frequently he addresses the young. Two considerations not only justify his conduct, but render it exemplary. The first is, The probability of success. This, indeed, is only comparative; for owing to the depravity of human nature, many attempts to promote the welfare of mankind will fail at every age. How often have the young themselves been "wooed and awed," admonished and encouraged, in vain! Yet, surely, the hope of usefulness is greater, before the heart is hardened through the deceitfulness of sin, and the offender is entrenched in long-established habits of iniquity, which he has learned to defend by those erroneous reasonings which vice always renders necessary. "Can the Ethiopian change his skin, or the leopard his spots? then may ye also do good, that are accustomed to evil." The second is, The importance attached to it. For who can view the young without concern? Who knows not that they are to fill all future offices? that they are the sources of families and churches? that the nation and the world will be influenced by the character with which they grow up!

In doing good it is always wise to make those peculiarly our aim by whom, if good is received, it is likely to be multiplied, diffused, perpetuated. Now this is the case with the young. If you do good to an old man it is of importance to himself; but it is *confined* to himself, and dies with him. But communicate right views and dispositions to a child, and it will be impossible to calculate the degree of his usefulness: for as he rises up and spreads abroad, he exemplifies and extends them; and in time, thousands may be improved and blessed by his instruction, his example, and his influence.

Solomon well knew all this: hence he so often bespeaks the attention of youth. And what motive has he not seized and employed in this all-interesting service? Is it the certainty of eternal judgment? "Rejoice, O young man, in thy youth; and let thy heart cheer thee in the days of thy youth, and walk in the ways of thine heart, and in the sight of thine eyes: but know thou, that for all these things God will bring thee into judgment." Is it old age as the most unfavourable season for commencing a religious course, when infirmities and afflictions, instead of allowing exertion, call for consolation? "Remember now thy Creator in the days of thy youth, while the evil days come not, nor the years draw nigh, when thou shalt say, I have no pleasure in them." Is it the peculiar regard of Him, in whom are hid all the treasures of wisdom and knowledge? "I love them that love me; and those that seek me early shall find me." Is it the condescension of God, in asking for a surrender which he might demand; and addressing not our fear, but our affection? "My son, give me thine heart, and let thine eyes observe my ways." Is it the poignant anguish, or the delightful satisfaction, a child is capable of yielding to those who have the tenderest claims upon him; according as he chooses the way of folly, or of life? "The father of the righteous shall greatly rejoice; and he that begetteth a wise child shall have joy of him. Thy father and thy mother shall be glad, and she that bare thee shall rejoice. My son, if thine heart be wise, my heart shall rejoice, even mine."

Let us enter into our subject. Solomon was a parent himself; Rehoboam was his son; and probably the very person here addressed. You know what a foolish, rash, improvident, irreligious character he proved; yet was he the son of Solomon! And if Solomon perceived these rising evils when he wrote this passage, with what feelings did he utter the words, "My son, if thine heart be wise, my heart shall rejoice, even mine."

Let us consider Solomon as the representative of every father and mother, and as speaking in their name. Not that all parents are concerned for the spiritual welfare of their children: some have no more regard for the souls of their offspring than if they had none, and were to die like the beasts that perish; but this is what every parent ought to feel, and what every godly parent will feel. Let us consider,—I. THE ATTAINMENT REQUIRED: II. THE CONSEQUENCE ANTICIPATED.

I. THE ATTAINMENT REQUIRED. "My son, if thy heart be wise." A pious youth is said to be wise in heart—

First, to show us that religion is wisdom. I know, my young friends, that some will endeavour to make you think that it is folly, and at your time of life, many who have not been *reasoned*, have been *ridiculed* out of every serious notion; for a laugh with you often does more than an argument. But hear what the Judge of all says, "Behold, the fear of the Lord, that is wisdom; and to depart from evil is understanding. The fear of the Lord is the beginning of wisdom: a good understanding have all they that do his commandments. Wisdom is the principal thing; therefore get wisdom: and with all thy getting, get understanding."

And though our faith standeth not in the wisdom of man, but in the power of God, reason, as well as Scripture, is on our side. Men, the most pre-eminent in every department of genius and learning; men, who perfectly understood the value and force of evidence; men, the last in the world to be the dupes of delusion; these men have expressed a conviction of mind with regard to the truth and importance of Revelation, such as they felt upon no other subject.

Yea, and even those who are so wise in their own conceit, and even treat the godly as visionaries and madmen, will, in a very little time, change their sentiments and their language, and exclaim, "We fools counted their lives madness, and their end to be without honour! Now are they numbered with the children of God, and their lot is among the saints!"

It is a fine representation which the apostle John gives us of vital Christianity, when he says, "we have an unction from the Holy One, and we know all things." Not that a Christian is taught the secrets of nature, the inventions of art, the mysteries of politics and trade: in all these he may be inferior to a man of the world. But he knows all that is essential to his safety and welfare. He is made "wise unto salvation." He is "wise towards God." He knows himself. And he knows the Saviour of sinners. He that is ignorant of *Him* knows nothing: he that knows Him knows every thing.

Secondly. That this wisdom is not notional; but consists principally in dispositions and actions. Speculative knowledge is, indeed, necessary to experimental and practical; but does not always produce it. We often find accurate and strong convictions exerting no influence, beyond the understanding. Nothing is so certain as death; and "the living *know* that they shall die," and yet do they live as those who expect it? A man knows that the body is nothing to the soul, or time to eternity: and yet, the grand question with him is, not "What must I do to be saved?" but, "What shall I eat, and what shall I drink, and wherewithal shall I be clothed?" How many are there, who hear the Gospel, and even acquiesce in the doctrine of the Fall, and our recovery, and yet never fall at the feet of the Recoverer, crying, "Lord, save, I perish!" They are Christian in their creed; and infidel in their conduct. Religion has to do "with the heart;" and a knowledge that does not reach the heart, and govern the heart, is nothing. Knowledge is to be viewed in the order of means, and when it does not answer its end, it is considered by the sacred writers, as ignorance. Because he that does not know him to purpose, does not know him savingly; they will not allow that a man knows God at all—who does not trust in him and love him and obey him. "They that know thy Name, will put their trust in thee."—"He that loveth not, knoweth not God. He that saith, I know him, and keepeth not his commandments, is a liar, and the truth is not in him." To believe these things, and to feel them; to know these things and to do them —this is to be wise in heart: and nothing less than this is the promise of the new covenant; "I will give them an heart to know me, that I am the Lord: and they shall be my people, and I will be their God: for they shall return unto me with their whole heart."

II. THE CONSEQUENCE ANTICIPATED: "My son, if thine heart be wise, *my heart shall rejoice, even mine.*" Pious children afford their parents pleasure, on three principles:

1. A principle of *benevolence.* They rejoice in the salvation of every sinner. They would rejoice to hear of the conversion of an enemy. There is no room for envy in the Church, for there is enough and to spare, however multiplied the partakers: and nothing is so remote from a Christian's disposition as a wish to exclude or monopolize. Instead of repelling, he invites: "O taste, and see, that the Lord is good: come with us, and we will do thee good, for the Lord hath spoken good concerning Israel." And can he be indifferent to the spiritual welfare of those to whom he is united by the ties of flesh and blood? Does religion prohibit relative affection? Yea, it requires, it enlivens, it sanctifies it; and causes the possessor to cry, "How can I endure to see the destruction of my kindred?"

2. A principle of *piety.* God is peculiarly pleased and glorified by the sacrifices of early religion, in which choice, and not compulsion, influences the offerer. An old man regards devotion as a refuge, rather than a temple; and takes hold of the horns of the altar, not to bind his victim there, but to escape from being a victim himself. He only forsakes the world—when he can enjoy it no longer; and leaves his sins when they leave him.—Does he present to God his soul? All its powers are wasted and destroyed. Does he yield his body? It is a worn-out instrument in the service of sin. But the young do not insult him with the leavings of the world, the flesh, and the devil. They do not put him off with the refuse of life; they consecrate to him the first born of their days, the first fruits of their reason and affections; they give him the prime of their being, and while others too are powerfully soliciting their regards. And can a Christian be devoid of the love of God! Can he be indifferent to efforts, by which his Divine Benefactor is so signally delighted and honoured? Can he see a soldier so early entering his army, a servant so early engaging in his service, a worshipper so early approaching his altar—and see in this soldier, this servant, this worshipper of God, his own offspring—and not glow with the sentiment, "My son, if thine heart be wise, my heart shall rejoice, even mine."

3. A principle of *self-interest.* We must distinguish between self-interest and selfishness; and between a sinful self-love and a righteous self-love. "Thou shalt love," says the Law, "thy neighbour as thyself." This clearly allows and requires a proper love to ourselves; and with this the design of religion falls in, which is the advancement of our welfare. Now on this ground the piety of children delights parents, because,

First. It affords them evidence of the answer of their prayers, and the success of their endeavours. How mortifying is it to run in vain, and labour in vain! How painful to see an object of peculiar solicitude and attention baffling every effort and disappointing every expectation! But how pleasing is it to sow, and then reap! to plant, and water, and prune, and then gather the increase! How delightful to a parent to see that his instructions have not been lost; that his tears have not flowed in vain; that his God has not turned a deaf ear, when his big heart cried, "O that Ishmael might live before thee?" And what a blessed stimulus and encouragement is this to future supplication and zeal!

Secondly. Because it becomes the means of their usefulness. It is by such children parents hope to serve their generation according to the will of God. "What a pleasure is it," says the father, "that I am not sending into the neighbourhood and the nation a number of mischiefs and curses, children that are corrupters, such as will lead many to wish that the wretch who had begot them had been childless; but such as will attach the purest honour to my name, and lead numbers to say, as they witness the amiableness and beneficence of my offspring, ' Blessed is the womb that bare thee, and the peps which thou hast sucked.' "

Thirdly. Because it insures the proper returns of duty. It is natural for a parent to wish for reverence and affection; for gratitude and obedience; for assistance and comfort; especially when they feel the infirmities of nature, or meet with the afflictions of life. Who does not say, "Hearken unto thy father that begat thee, and despise not thy mother when she is old!" Who does not tremble at the threatening, "The eye that mocketh at his father, and despiseth to obey his mother, the ravens of the valley shall pick it out, and the young eagles shall eat it!" But pious principle is the best security for moral practice. He who fears God and confides in him is the only one that will feel the authority of the command and the truth of the promise; "Honour thy father and thy mother, that thy days may be long in the land which the Lord thy God giveth thee." And, my young friends, be assured of this, there can be no piety, where morality is wanting. An undutiful child can never be a partaker of divine grace.

Fourthly. Because it will free them from a thousand bitter anxieties. Here let me suppose a few of the cases in which children peculiarly interest the feelings and fears of their parents; and in which nothing but a hope of their piety can set their hearts at rest.

Such is *their removal from home.* Children, in common, are soon sent to school, or articled to business; or, in humbler life, placed abroad as servants. When this is the case, they are no longer under the eye and the wing of their parents; and frequently their intercourse with them is very slender. Some places and situations are more dangerous than others; but none are free from moral hazards to youth: and what can relieve the anxiety of a parent, but a confidence in the religious principles and dispositions of his child; that these, when he has no other witness, will remind him of an omnipresent Inspector, "the Judge of all;" and lead him to exclaim, "How can I do this great wickedness, and sin against God!"

Such is *their taking any important step in life.* Nothing awakens the concern of parents more than the settlement of their children in marriage: and nothing can delight them more than to find them disposed to " marry in the Lord;" for such a connexion only can secure the discharge of all mutual duty, and draw down the blessing of God; enable them to "walk together as heirs of the grace of life, that their prayers be not hindered;" and "seek a godly seed." But what, except the power of religion, can gua-

rantee them against the influence of beauty or talent or wealth or honour; and induce them to look after godliness as the one thing needful?

Such is *the nature of their condition in the world.* A parent cannot be insensible to the temporal estate of his children, whether they be regarded or despised; rich or poor; comfortably provided for, or struggling with the hardships of life. But *this* can comfort him, in all circumstances—" My child is only a stranger and pilgrim upon earth. He has a better country. God is his portion and his guide. He possesses that grace which, if he prospers, will preserve him; or, if he be afflicted, will support him. He has the wisdom which is from above, and knows how to be abased, and how to abound; and can do all things through Christ, who strengthens him!"

Such is *their being bereaved of their dearest relatives.* How often are parents distressed at the thought of leaving their offspring behind them, especially as the hour of their dissolution draws near! " Ah! soon their guardian and comforter will be removed far from them, and they may become a prey to cunning or oppression. Soon their cries, if injured, will not reach my ears; or the news, if well treated, gladden my heart. What a world I am leaving them in! What errors, what vices, what examples, will assail them! ' Holy Father, keep, through thy own name, those whom thou hast given me.' " If, in the midst of all this, he knows that they have chosen God as "the guide of their youth," and hears God saying, " Leave thy fatherless children, I will preserve them alive," the shadow of death is turned into the morning. "I shall not leave them orphans. He will take them up; and more than supply the place of every creature."

But let us suppose *another case.* In the order of nature, parents die before their children: but this order is sometimes reversed; and parents are called to close the eyes of those on whom they relied to close their own. But who can imagine the anguish of a father or mother, at the death of an ungodly child! Whose heart does not bleed for David? " And the king was much moved, and went up to the chamber over the gate, and wept: and as he went, thus he said, O my son Absalom, my son, my son Absalom! would God I had died for thee, O Absalom, my son, my son!" But the bitterness of death is past, when the pious father, as he views his earthly hope closing in the grave, can say, " Well, thou art hastening away from the evil to come. My loss is thy eternal gain. Thou hast not been born in vain, nor in vain have been my labour and expense in rearing thee. Thou art an immortal now. Thou art equal to the angels. Our separation is but short. Soon shall I overtake thee, and ' we shall be for ever with the Lord!'" No; that parent is not half so much to be pitied who has buried a young saint, as he that is mourning over a living sinner. Pointing to the grave, in which he had just lodged the remains of a pious youth, a father was one day heard to say, though with a quivering lip—"I do not weep for *that* dear child—he *was* my comfort and *is* my comfort—but for him, who is still alive, and is 'bringing down my gray hairs with sorrow to the grave.'"

Let me conclude:

First. By addressing those who, instead of being a joy to their parents, are only their grief. And with what vile ingratitude are you chargeable! Need I tell you what claims your parents have upon you? With what tenderness did they treat you in your infancy! What nights of watching, what days of confinement, what instances of self-denial, have they passed through in training you up to youth! What pains and cost have they incurred in furnishing you with food and raiment; and affording you an education which, perhaps, their circumstances with difficulty allowed! And do you thus requite them?— You may one day have children of your own; and "with the same measure ye mete, it may be measured to you again!" Undutiful children commonly meet with undutiful children. "I knew," says Dr. Doddridge, "a son; in his passion he struck his father down, and dragged him by the hair of his head. When he had drawn him a certain distance, he cried out, Drag me no further—for *here* I let my father go when I dragged him!" For this reason, oh! young man, never choose for a wife a daughter that has been a disrespectful daughter. And, oh! young woman, never choose for thy husband a son who has been a disobedient son. Bad behaviour in a private condition is a preparation for bad behaviour in a public one; and the curse of God is likely to attend such disreputable companions.

We read of murderers of fathers, and murderers of mothers! a charge at which you revolt; a crime that makes you shudder. But, remember, there are more ways of destroying a parent than by poison, or a blow! You may destroy their reputation; you may break their peace of mind; you may undermine their frame, and bring on premature decays, by the corrosions of anxiety and fear. We lately read in a foreign journal of an advocate who was desired to undertake the defence of a young man, charged with a serious crime. He went to his prison to obtain documents—and—in the criminal he instantly recognized—his own son, of whom he had not heard for a length of time! The sight upset his reason; and he went home, and put an end to his existence. Hast thou a father or mother in the grave, whose heart was broken by thy vice and disobedience? How deeply shouldest thou humble thyself, and repent in dust and ashes, under a consciousness of thy guilt! Hast thou a parent yet alive, to whom thou hast been only a trial and a torment? Oh! hasten to make what atonement thou canst, by confession and amendment, and become the consolation of those who are saying, "My son, if thy heart be wise, my heart shall rejoice, even mine." And here allow me the liberty of introducing two anecdotes: the one, to awaken your fear; the other, to operate, if you have any, upon your tenderness.

A pious father, in writing to his friend, says, "I lately dreamed that the day of judgment was come. I saw the Judge on his great white throne, and all nations were gathered before him. I and my wife were on the right hand—but I could not see my children. I said, 'I cannot bear this—I must go and seek them.' I went to the left hand of the Judge, and there found them all, standing in the utmost despair. As soon as they saw me they caught hold of me, and cried,—'Oh, father, we will never part!' I said, 'My dear children, I am come to try, if possible, to get you out of this awful situation.' So I took them all with me; but when we were come near the Judge, I thought he cast an angry look, and said, 'What do thy children with thee now? They would not take thy warning when on earth, and they shall not share thy happiness in heaven. Depart, ye cursed.' At these words I awoke in agony and horror."

But you say, "this was only a dream." Admitted. But a reality, equally dreadful, will be exemplified in many. Oh! what cruel separations will the last day witness. It was but a dream; yet the relation of it was the means of impressing serious conviction on the minds of several of the children.

A minister from England, happening, some time since, to be at Ed—b—gh, he was accosted by a young man in the street, with an apology for the liberty he was taking: "I think, Sir, said he, I have heard you at —— Chapel." "You probably may, Sir; for I have sometimes ministered there." "Do you remember, said he, a note, put up by an afflicted widow, begging the prayers of the congregation, for the conversion of an ungodly son?" "I do very well remember such a circumstance." "Sir," said he, "I am the very person; and, wonderful to tell, the prayer was effectual. Going, with some other abandoned young men, one Sunday, through ——, and passing by the chapel, I was struck with its appearance. We agreed to go in and mingle with the crowd, and stop for a few minutes, to laugh and mock at the preacher and the people. We had just entered, when you, Sir, read the note, requesting the prayers of the congregation for an afflicted widow's profligate son. I heard it with a sensation I cannot express. I was struck to the heart: and though I had no idea that I was the very individual meant, I felt that it expressed the bitterness of a widow's heart, who had a child so wicked as I felt myself to be. My mind was instantly solemnized. I could not laugh: my attention was riveted on the preacher.—I heard his prayer and sermon with an impression very different from that which had carried me into the place. From that moment, the truths of the Gospel penetrated my heart; I joined the congregation; cried to God in Christ for mercy, and found peace in believing; became my mother's comfort, as I had been her heavy cross, and, through grace, have ever since continued in the good ways of the Lord. An opening having lately been made for an advantageous settlement in my own country, I came hither with my excellent mother, and for some years past, have endeavoured to dry up the widow's tears, which I had so often caused to flow, and to be the comfort and support of her age, as I had been the torment and affliction of her days."

Secondly. Let me address parents. Perhaps here are some who are strangers to the pleasure of which we have been speaking. Will you allow me to ask—Whether your affliction has not been your fault? Have you discharged your duty towards your children, I will not say perfectly, but conscientiously? God works by means. And do men gather grapes from thorns, or figs from thistles? It would be little less than a moral miracle, if the children of some professors of religion were pious—such inconsistencies are they called to witness, which, in their influence, are worse than absolute neglect.

But if, "in simplicity and godly sincerity, not with fleshly wisdom, but by the grace of God, you have had your conversation in the world, and more abundantly to them-ward," and your "house is not so with God" as you desire,—yield not to despair. Never cease to pray and to admonish. Some shower of rain may cause the seed which has long been buried under the dryness of the soil, to strike root, and spring up. Manasseh had a pious education, and yet went great lengths in transgression: but in his affliction he sought the Lord God of his fathers, and he was found of him.—"Blessed are ye that sow beside all waters, that send forth thither the feet of the ox and the ass."

But all hail, ye highly favoured of the Lord, who enjoy this felicity! What satisfaction can equal that which a parent feels in seeing his children growing up intelligent and amiable, and pious and useful: approved of God, and acceptable to man! If there be a sight on earth sufficient to detain an angel in his passage, it is a father and mother surrounded with the pledges of their mutual affection, endeared by grace as well as nature, rising up and calling them blessed!

Parents! God grant you this heaven, till you are removed to another—where, presenting yourselves at his throne, you will say, "Behold, I and the children thou hast given me!" Amen.

DISCOURSE LXXXIV.

THE LOVE OF CHRIST.

And to know the love of Christ, which passeth knowledge, that ye might be filled with all the fulness of God.—Ephes. iii. 19.

As the minister addresses the people on the behalf of God, so he addresses God on the behalf of the people. Preaching and prayer are parts of his office, equally indispensable; and there is an encouraging relation between them. The one is the resource of the other. For a good minister of Jesus Christ does not look for success, as the consequence of his own reasoning or eloquence or energy; he is convinced of the depravity of human nature, and has observed how often the most powerful instruments have failed. What then animates him? Why this—He knows that the means are of Divine appointment; that God giveth the increase; that nothing is too hard for him. He, therefore, invokes his aid, and pleads the promise; "For as the rain cometh down, and the snow from heaven, and returneth not thither, but watereth the earth, and maketh it bring forth and bud, that it may give seed to the sower, and bread to the eater: so shall my word be that goeth forth out of my mouth: it shall not return unto me void, but it shall accomplish that which I please, and it shall prosper in the thing whereto I sent it."—Paul is here praying for the Ephesians, in language the most sublime and significant. "For this cause I bow my knees unto the Father of our Lord Jesus Christ, of whom the whole family in heaven and earth is named, that he would grant you, according to the riches of his glory, to be strengthened with might by his Spirit in the inner man; that Christ may dwell in your hearts by faith; that ye, being rooted and grounded in love, may be able to comprehend with all saints what is the breadth, and length, and depth, and height; and to know the love of Christ, which passeth knowledge, that ye might be filled with all the fulness of God."

In the words which we have selected for our present improvement, three things demand our attention.

I. An interesting subject.—It is *the love of Christ.* II. A desirable attainment.—It is *to know it.* III. A blessed consequence.—It is "*to be filled with all the fulness of God.*"

I. A VERY INTERESTING SUBJECT.—It is the "*love of Christ.*" The love of Christ would furnish us with a thousand sources of reflection; but we shall confine ourselves to one view of it only. It is the incomprehensibility of this love. This is the view of it which the apostle himself here takes. He tells us it "passeth knowledge." This is the noblest commendation he could have pronounced; and it would be easy to prove, that it is as just as it is glorious.

Witness the *number of its objects.* It is but a few that the bounty of a human benefactor reaches and relieves. We pity an individual. We take up a family. We explore a neighbourhood. The liberality of a THORNTON flows in various channels, through different parts of a country. The compassion of a HOWARD visits the miserable in other lands, after weeping over the dungeoned victims of his own. But a "multitude, which no man can number, out of every nation, and people, and tongue, and kindred," will for ever adore the riches of the Redeemer's love. We shall hereafter see that his love has not been circumscribed by the piety of our fears, by the uncharitableness of our censures, or the mistakes of our creed. "All nations shall be blessed in him, all generations shall call him blessed. As the stars of heaven, and as the sand on the sea shore, so shall his seed be." This is indeed Christ, the Saviour of the world.

Witness the *value of its benefits.* You feel your obligation to some of your fellow-creatures, and let them not be forgotten: they have pleaded for your reputation; they have befriended your business; they have relieved your distress; they have preserved your life: but which of them has restored you to the favour of God? Which of them has obtained eternal redemption for you? It is impossible, while we are here, sufficiently to estimate the effects of his love. We know but imperfectly the evils from which he has delivered us. What do we know of the vileness of sin, the sting of death, the curse of the Law, the wrath of God! We know but imperfectly the contents of those exceeding great and precious promises, to which he has entitled us. We know but imperfectly the import of the hope "laid up for us in heaven;" the meaning of "a crown of glory that fadeth not away;" of "beholding his face in righteousness;" of "awaking up after his likeness;" of "a glorious body like his own." "Eye hath not seen, nor ear heard, nor have entered into the heart of man, the things which God hath prepared for them that love him." "Oh how great is thy goodness, which thou hast laid up for them that fear thee; which thou hast wrought for them that trust in thee before the sons of men!"

Witness *the unworthiness of the partakers.* Whatever others may think of themselves, a Christian will readily acknowledge that he had done nothing to recommend himself; that he had done every thing to provoke and justify the Divine displeasure; that he was not only miserable, but guilty, and criminal even in his distress. Oh! this magnifies the love of Christ—it was entirely self-moved! Love, among creatures, originates from some excellency, real or imaginary. In our alms we look after something that seems to deserve what we profess to give. Mere want and wretchedness are not sufficient for our compassion, without some plea. Persons, therefore, endeavour to convince us that they have been unfortunate rather than criminal; they know that more is won from us by extenuation than confession. We wait for application. We refuse till the suppliant owns his dependence, and feels our consequence. There is little—little, indeed, of true charity among men! But "*He* is found of them that sought him not." He awakens our attention. He presses us to receive. "Scarcely for a righteous man will one die, yet, peradventure, for a good man some would even dare to die." But we were ungodly. We were enemies by wicked works—yet "for the vilest of the vile he dies!"

Witness *the expensiveness of its sacrifices.* The only quality in the love of many is its cheapness. It will endure no kind of self-denial. If they embrace an opportunity of doing good, they will never seek one. They may dip their hand into a full purse, and give a trifle of what they are convinced they cannot expend upon themselves; but they shun the trouble of inquiry, and the pain of sympathy: they will not visit the fatherless and the widows in their affliction. Few resemble the poor woman in the Gospel, who, while others gave of their abundance, and could go home to a well-spread table afterward, gave all that she had, even all her living for the day; determined that her charity should be sure, however uncertain her subsistence. But *His* love drew him from heaven to earth. He who was rich, for our sakes became poor; a man of sorrows and acquainted with grief.— Trace him in the humiliation of his life. Behold him in his agony in the garden. See his soul exceedingly sorrowful, even unto death. See him nailed to the cross, exclaiming, "My God, my God, why hast thou forsaken me!"

> "See from his head, his hands, his feet,
> Sorrow and love flow mingled down."

Saviour Jesus! never was sorrow like thine, and, therefore, never was love like thine! It "passeth knowledge."

Witness the *perpetuity of its attachment.* How rare is a friend that loveth at all times. How many fail, especially in the day of trouble. Who has not leaned on a broken reed, and bled for his dependence? Who has not had reason to complain, with Job, "My brethren have dealt deceitfully as a brook, and as the stream of brooks they pass away; which are blackish by reason of the ice, and wherein the snow is hid: what time they wax warm, they vanish: when it is hot, they are consumed out of their place?" But loving his own who are in the world, he loves them unto the end, and will afford them proof of it whenever they need his aid. He has said, "I will never leave thee nor forsake thee." "For this is as the waters of Noah unto me: for as I have sworn that the waters of Noah should no more go over the earth; so have I sworn that I would not be wroth with thee, nor rebuke thee. For the mountains shall depart, and the hills be removed; but my kindness shall not depart from thee, neither shall the covenant of my peace be removed, saith the Lord that hath mercy on thee." Nothing appears to the Christian more wonderful than this. "O," says he, "how have I tried him! How incorrigible have I been under affliction! How ungrateful for all my mercies! How unedified by means and ordinances! How often have I charged him foolishly and unkindly, while he was displaying his wisdom and goodness; and blamed him for doing the very things I had a thousand times implored! O, had he human passions! Were he a creature only! I had long ago been forsaken. But he is God, and not man; therefore I am not consumed."

Witness the *tenderness* of its regards. To know this you must be familiar with the language of the Scripture; your very souls must melt into such expressions as these: "He shall come down like rain upon the mown grass. He shall gather the lambs with his arm, and carry them in his bosom, and gently lead those that are with young. A bruised reed will he not break, and smoking flax will he not quench. In all their affliction he was afflicted. He that toucheth them toucheth the apple of his eye. He is touched with the feeling of our infirmities." You must be—I was going to say, a father, and a tender one—"Like as a father pitieth his children, so the Lord pitieth them that fear him. For he knoweth our frame; he remembereth that we are dust." You must be—I was going to say, a mother, and the tenderest that ever breathed—"As one whom his mother comforteth, so will I comfort you." You must hold communion with him, you must be intimate with him, in order to know—the mildness of his censures; the gentleness of his reproofs; the kindness of his communications; the delicacy of his encouragements. O ye models of sensibility: ye Josephs! ye Jonathans! ye Davids! ye Rachels! be ashamed of your tears! Your hearts are flint compared with his: "his heart is made of tenderness; his bowels melt with love!"

Blessed Jesus! we know thou hast loved us, but we know not how much—and angels know not how much—It "passeth knowledge."

II. HERE IS A DESIRABLE ATTAINMENT. It is *to know it*.

But does not the Apostle say, that his love "passeth knowledge?" How then does he pray, that we may know it? Can we know that which is unknowable? I answer, we may know that in one respect which we cannot know in another; we may know that by grace which we cannot know by nature; we may know that, in the reality of its existence, which we cannot know in the mode; we may know that, in the effects, which we cannot know in the cause; we may know that, in its uses, which we cannot know in its nature; we may know that increasingly, which we cannot know perfectly.

Let us apply this to the subject before us. Though the love of Christ passeth knowledge, we may know much more of it than we do. The knowledge of a Christian is gradual, and growing. He is always a learner. He will know many things in eternity of which he is ignorant in time. He will know many things as he advances in the divine life of which he is ignorant at the commencement. There are many things which, for a time, he cannot receive; but in proportion as divine grace works in him, to humble the pride of his heart; to render him willing to be saved in the Lord's own way; and to place himself under his guidance; crooked things are made straight, and rough places plain. Thus his path resembles "the shining light, that shineth more and more unto the perfect day." Thus it is promised: "Then shall ye know, if ye follow on to know the Lord." An instance of which we have in Nathanael: he had little knowledge; but he was "an Israelite indeed, in whom was no guile;" he was open to conviction, and willing to come to the light; and therefore, says our Lord, "Because I said unto thee, I saw thee under the fig tree, believest thou? thou shalt see greater things than these. And he saith unto him, Verily, verily, I say unto you, Hereafter ye shall see heaven open, and the angels of God ascending and descending upon the Son of man." We therefore observe, with regard to your knowledge of this love,

First. Your ideas of it may be more clear and consistent. There is a kind of mistiness which envelops the minds of some people: they see every thing dimly; or, like the man, when his eyes were half-opened, who saw men as trees walking. A confusion seems to reign in all their religious conceptions: they have no distinguishing views of the difference between the Law and the Gospel; justification and sanctification; the ground of the one, and the means of the other. They cannot reconcile duty and privilege; dependence and activity; a sense of our unworthiness, with a confidence of our acceptance. It is impossible for us to determine, with how much ignorance in the judgment real grace may be found connected; yet it is very desirable to have judicious and consistent views of divine things; a clear and full knowledge of the Gospel. "It is a good thing," says the Apostle, "that the heart be established with grace."

Secondly. Your views of it may be more confidential and appropriating. Your doubts and fears, with regard to your own interest in it, may yield to hope; and that hope may become the full assurance of hope. The Saviour you now admire you may be able to claim as your own; and to exult, "This is my beloved, and this is my friend. I will greatly rejoice in the Lord, my soul shall be joyful in my God; for he hath clothed me with the garments of salvation, he hath covered me with the robe of righteousness, as a bridegroom decketh himself with ornaments, and as a bride adorneth herself with her jewels."

Thirdly. Your views of it may be more impressive, more influential. It is to be lamented, that our speculative religion so far exceeds our experimental and practical. How often does the will refuse to bow to the dictates of the judgment. What a war is there often in our bosoms, between conscience and inclination. Who knows not the difference there is between a principle slumbering in the head, and alive in the heart, and at work in the life? "The living know that they shall die," that their time here is short and uncertain, and that "what a man soweth, that shall he also reap." But where is the efficacy of the belief? And though they look for such things, how few are there who live in a state of holy preparation for them! We find no difficulty in admitting that God does all things well, in the government of the world, and in the management of our individual concerns. The natural consequence would be, to preserve us from murmuring and envying; to induce us to cast all our care upon Him who careth for us; and to feel a peace "which passeth all understanding, keeping our heart and mind through Christ Jesus." But whose creed gets into his temper, and actuates his conduct?—The grand thing is, so to know the love of Christ, as to walk becoming it; to be what it requires; for all our feelings to echo back the language of the Apostle: "I am crucified with Christ: nevertheless I live; yet not I, but Christ liveth in me: and the life which I now live in the flesh I live by the faith of the Son of God, who loved me, and gave himself for me." For our whole life to be a kind of shout—"Unto him that loved us, and washed us from our sins in his own blood, and hath made us

kings and priests unto God and his Father; be glory and dominion for ever and ever. Amen."

III. This leads us to remark, A BLESSED CONSEQUENCE: That ye may be filled with all the fulness of God." If we consider man in his natural state, he is empty of God; if in his glorified state, he is full of God, or as the Apostle says, "God is all in all;" but in his gracious state, he has a degree of both his original emptiness and his final plenitude. He is not what he was; neither is he what he will be. His state is neither night nor day; but dawn: the darkness is going off, and the splendour is coming on. He is thankful for what he has; but he wants more of the presence and the image of God. He wants to be "filled (I use the language of Scripture) with the Spirit;" to be "filled with all joy and peace in believing;" to be "filled with all the fruits of righteousness, which are by Jesus Christ unto the glory and praise of God." This is what the apostle Peter recommends, when he says: "Giving all diligence, add to your faith virtue; and to virtue knowledge; and to knowledge temperance; and to temperance patience; and to patience godliness; and to godliness brotherly kindness; and to brotherly kindness charity. For if these things be in you, and abound, they make you that ye shall be neither barren nor unfruitful in the knowledge of our Lord Jesus Christ." This is what Paul exemplified in his own person: "Not as though I had already attained, either were already perfect: but I follow after, if that I may apprehend that for which also I am apprehended of Christ Jesus. Brethren, I count not myself to have apprehended: but this one thing I do, forgetting those things which are behind, and reaching forth unto those things which are before, I press toward the mark for the prize of the high calling of God in Christ Jesus." And this is what he here means by "all the fulness of God."

But what has the knowledge of the love of Christ to do with this? It is indeed easy to see how it will add to the plenitude of our comfort: how it will inspire us with "a joy that is unspeakable and full of glory." And need you be told, that "the joy of the Lord is our strength:" and that the Christian is never so active in duty as when he enjoys a sense of his privileges?

But take it with regard to holiness. Some would suppose that the knowledge we have been speaking of is a mere notion; or, if it has any tendency, it is of a licentious, rather than of a sanctifying nature; that it must tend to set men loose to duty, rather than to make them practical Christians. Hence they imagine the Christian an Antinomian, where, if they could read his heart, they would find in him most of the devotedness of real piety.

But so it is: we cannot make these things plain and easy and unexceptionable to the natural man: for "the natural man receiveth not the things of the Spirit of God: for they are foolishness unto him. neither can he know them, because they are spiritually discerned. But he that is spiritual judgeth all things, yet he himself is judged of no man." He knows others, though others know not him. The reason is, he has been in their state, but they have never been in his. They are not, therefore, acquainted with the nature and force of those principles and motives which are peculiar to him as a new creature. But he feels and glories in them. Paul knew that the only way to be filled with the fulness of God, is "to know the love of Christ, which passeth knowledge." It was this that *fully* possessed and governed himself and his fellow-labourers: "The love of Christ constraineth us; because we thus judge, that if one died for all, then were all dead: and that he died for all, that they which live should not henceforth live unto themselves, but unto him which died for them, and rose again." "And my experience," says the Christian, "confirms it. If my heart is contracted, this love enlarges it; if cold, this love inflames it; if burning, this love adds fuel to the fire. This makes difficult things easy, and bitter ones sweet. This turns all my duty into delight. This determines me to confess him before men, and emboldens me to go forth to him without the camp, bearing his reproach. This induces me, not only to avoid, but to abhor sin. This disarms temptation of its power, and weans me from a world that crucified my Lord and Saviour.

"His dying crimson, like a robe,
Spreads o'er his body on the tree,
Then am I dead to all the globe,
And all the globe is dead to me."

What remains then, but to make this love your lesson, and your study? For this purpose, daily impress your minds with the importance of knowing it. Remember that all other knowledge is dross, compared with this gold. A man may know much, to his own pride, and the admiration of others: he may be familiar with the secrets of nature; he may have the knowledge of the arts and sciences; he may be a deep politician, and a profound linguist; he may know the Scripture, in the history; and Christianity itself, in the theory—and live and die a fool. A man may go to hell, silently, by hypocrisy; openly, by profaneness: he may go self-righteously, with the pharisee; or learnedly, with the scholar! A man knows nothing with regard to his soul and eternity, if he knows not the love of Christ, which passeth knowledge—"This is life eternal."

If you would make proficiency in this knowledge, the following things are necessary:

Retirement is necessary. "Through desire, a man, having separated himself, seeketh and intermeddleth with all wisdom." This is peculiarly the case here. This subject is not for the crowd, but the closet. Friendship deals much in secrecy; especially the friendship between the Saviour and the soul. "I will allure her, and bring her into the wilderness, and there will I speak comfortably unto her." It is thus that he manifests himself to his people, and not unto the world.

Application is necessary. You must not only retire, but place the subject before your mind. You must survey it in its attributes and relations. You must learn to meditate, and meditate till the exercise becomes habitual and delightful. Then you will be able to say, "My meditation of him shall be sweet. How precious also are thy thoughts unto me, O God! how great is the sum of them! If I should count them, they are more in number than the sand: when I awake, I am still with thee."

Intercourse is necessary. There are Christians far superior to you in age and attainments; and these are not confined to your own level in the world. Many below you in condition may be above you in experience; and have much to tell you of a Saviour's grace. By mingling with them your doubts may be removed, your confidence strengthened, and "your hearts comforted, being knit together in love, and unto all riches of the full assurance of understanding, to the acknowledgment of the mystery of God, and of the Father, and of Christ; in whom are hid all the treasures of wisdom and knowledge."

Reading is necessary. We forbid not other books; but the Scripture is the word of Christ, which is to "dwell in you richly in all wisdom." This testifies of Him; and of nothing so much as his unexampled love.

Hearing is necessary. If the minister be a Christian minister, (and it is at your peril to place yourselves under any other—for you are to take heed not only *how* you hear, but also *what* you hear)—he will "determine to know nothing among you, but Jesus Christ and him crucified."

Prayer is above all things necessary. In other schools the pupils learn sitting; but in the school of Christ they all learn upon their knees. "If any of you lack wisdom, let him ask of God that giveth to all men liberally, and upbraideth not; and it shall be given him." Hence Paul prayed for the Ephesians —Hence your ministers pray for you—God help you to pray for yourselves—"*That you may know the love of Christ, which passeth knowledge and be filled with all the fulness of God.*"

DISCOURSE LXXXV.

BLESSINGS UNIMPROVED RESUMED BY THEIR OWNER.

For she did not know that I gave her corn, and wine, and oil, and multiplied her silver and gold, which they prepared for Baal. Therefore will I return, and take away my corn in the time thereof, and my wine in the season thereof, and will recover my wool and my flax.—Hosea ii. 8, 9.

IF you are accustomed to reflection, two subjects must often present themselves to your minds. They are—the goodness of God, and the wickedness of man. These subjects are equally obvious and common; and though the one is as painful as the other is pleasing, we must not turn away from it. Nor must we, in the exemplification, so think of our fellow-creatures as to forget ourselves. We frequently condemn the Jews for their unbelief, ingratitude, and rebellion; yet, instead of casting stones, it would be better to kneel and confess—

"Great God, how oft did Israel prove
By turns thy anger, and thy love;
There in a glass our hearts may see
How fickle, and how false they be."

They were fair specimens of human nature, and we have no reason to believe that we should have been better than they, had we been placed under the same dispensation: yea, have we not proved ourselves worse, under superior advantages? Let us consider,

I. THE SOURCE OF OUR MERCIES.

II. OUR GUILT IN THE USE OF THEM.

III. THEIR REMOVAL. "For she did not know that I gave her corn, and wine, and oil, and multiplied her silver and gold, which they prepared for Baal. Therefore will I return, and take away my corn in the time thereof, and my wine in the season thereof, and will recover my wool and my flax."

I. THE SOURCE OF OUR MERCIES. I gave her—"I gave her corn, and wine, and oil, and multiplied her silver and gold."

Here we do not refer to those blessings, which we call spiritual. These it should be our principal concern to obtain: for these alone can afford satisfaction to the soul, and yield us a hope beyond the grave. If the inquiry concerned these, I trust we should be prepared to join in the acknowledgment of the Apostle: "Blessed be the God and Father of our Lord Jesus Christ, who hath blessed us with all spiritual blessings in heavenly places in Christ." But we now speak of temporal good things. He who is the Saviour of the soul has provided also for the body; and his bounty ministers, not only to our support, but our delight. "He giveth us," says the apostle, "richly all things to enjoy." "He daily,"

says David, "loadeth us with his benefits." In these declarations we see, not only the plenitude of these mercies, but the author of them. To establish in your minds the conviction, that God is the giver of all you possess, I could add a number of testimonies from the sacred writers; and remark, in particular, that our Saviour has taught us to pray for them—"Give us day by day our daily bread." But it is needless to enlarge. There is one thing, however, concerning which it is of importance to admonish you. "Never suffer instruments to keep your thoughts from God."

There is, First, *unconscious* instrumentality. This takes in what we call nature. The sun, the air, the rain, the earth, the seasons, are all essential to the welfare of man. But how could this do us any good, without God? Their operation, and their very being, depend upon him. "*He* maketh *his* sun to rise on the evil and on the good. The day is *his*, the night also is *his*. *He* hath made summer and winter. *His* paths drop down fatness."—"It shall come to pass in that day, I will hear, saith the Lord, I will hear the heavens, and they shall hear the earth; and the earth shall hear the corn, and the wine, and the oil; and they shall hear Jezreel."

There is, Secondly, *voluntary* instrumentality. Thus our fellow-creatures may do us good in a thousand ways; and are we to feel towards them, only, as we do towards a bridge that carries us over a river, or a spring that refreshes us in our journey? *They* act knowingly and freely in relieving us, and display the noblest principles of their nature. And we are not only allowed, but required to be grateful towards them. And a man that is destitute of gratitude has no good principle that we can rely upon. But here again, God has higher claims upon us:—for, who placed these friends and benefactors in our way? Who endowed them with their ability? Who inspired them with their disposition? Who gave us favour in their eyes?

There is, Thirdly, *personal* instrumentality. Few of the good things of this life are obtained without some exertions of our own. Indeed, if they were, they would not be half so sweet: it is what a man gains by his own skill and diligence that is so peculiarly dear and precious—"Thou shalt eat the labour of thy hand." But are we then to turn Chaldeans? of whom it is said; "They take up all of them with the angel, they catch them in their net, and gather them in their drag: therefore they rejoice and are glad. Therefore they sacrifice unto their net, and burn incense unto their drag; because by them their portion is fat, and their meat plenteous." But from whom have we derived our natural talents and the prudence which results from experience and observation? "Give ye ear, and hear my voice; hearken and hear my speech. Doth the plowman plow all day to sow? doth he open and break the clods of his ground? When he hath made plain the face thereof, doth he not cast abroad the fitches, and scatter the cummin, and cast in the principal wheat and the appointed barley and the rie in their place? For his God doth instruct him to discretion, and doth teach him. For the fitches are not threshed with a threshing instrument, neither is a cart wheel turned about upon the cummin; but the fitches are beaten out with a staff, and the cummin with a rod. Bread corn is bruised; because he will not ever be threshing it, nor break it with the wheel of his cart, nor bruise it with his horsemen. This also cometh forth from the Lord of Hosts, which is wonderful in counsel, and excellent in working." Whose providence fixed us in a situation favourable to our efforts; and ordered those opportunities, without which our attempts might have been in vain? Where is the wisdom of a man, who sees not that his plans depended upon a multitude of events over which he had not the least control; any one of which might have rendered foolish that scheme which now appears so wise—and that undertaking fatal which now appears so flourishing? Where is the piety of the man who does not own the agency of God in his most successful endeavours, and say with Solomon, "The blessing of the Lord, it maketh rich, and he addeth no sorrow with it?" This is the grand lesson which Moses gave to the indulged Israelites: "Lest, when thou hast eaten and art full, and hast built goodly houses, and dwelt therein; and when thy herds and thy flocks multiply, and thy silver and thy gold is multiplied, and all that thou hast is multiplied; then thine heart be lifted up, and thou forget the Lord thy God, which brought thee forth out of the land of Egypt, from the house of bondage; and thou say in thine heart, My power and the might of mine hand hath gotten me this wealth. But thou shalt remember the Lord thy God: for it is he that giveth thee power to get wealth."

II. This brings us from the source of our mercies, to OUR GUILT IN THE USE OF THEM. "For she did not know that I gave her corn, and wine, and oil, and multiplied her silver and gold, which they prepared for Baal." Here are two charges: *ignorance*, and *perversion.*

First. *Ignorance.* "She knew not that I gave her corn, and wine, and oil, and multiplied her silver and gold." God does much more good in this world than is ever known. He has done each of you countless acts of kindness, of which you have never been aware. For instance—From how many evils have you been preserved, by night and by day, abroad and at home, of which you were not sensible, because the danger was hidden, by the very interposition that hindered it. But sometimes you have seen your danger.

The fire had begun to consume your property. The disease had suspended you over the grave. The accident had scarcely missed the child's life; and the Lord, in delivering, made "bare his arm." And yet, perhaps, you were only struck with the wonderfulness of the event; or your gratitude was a mere notion, vanishing "as the morning cloud, and early dew."

For a distinction is here necessary. There are two kinds of knowledge; the one speculative, the other practical. The former is nothing without the latter: it is no better than ignorance; and as such it is always considered in the Scripture. Thus the apostle John tells us, "He that loveth not, knoweth not God." And again, "He that saith, I know him, and keepeth not his commandments, is a liar, and the truth is not in him." When a man is really convinced of sin, and is taught the truth as it is in Jesus, though he had often read of it, and heard of it, he naturally says, "I never knew this before." It is said, the sons of Eli were sons of Belial, "and knew not the Lord;" it cannot mean that men of their education and office were unable to distinguish the God of Israel from idols; but they did not act as those who were acquainted with him, and professed to serve him. "Know them that labour among you," says the apostle: that is, own them, and conduct yourselves properly towards them.—It is in vain, therefore, to say, this charge does not apply to us: we are not ignorant; we know that God gives us all we enjoy. Yes; but do you know, so as to be impressed and influenced by it? This is the accusation; they know not, so as to feel, and speak, and live as if they knew. "The ox knoweth his owner, and the ass his master's crib; but Israel doth not know, my people do not consider."

But here is a second charge. It is *perversion.* "She knew not that I gave her corn, and wine, and oil, and multiplied her silver and gold, which they prepared for Baal." Instead of using them in the service and for the glory of God, they appropriated them to the use of idols! This is worse than the former, as insult exceeds indifference, and opposition, neglect. What would you feel more provoking, than for a man to borrow of you, in order to publish a libel upon your character? What would you have thought, if, when Jonathan gave him his sword and his bow, David had instantly wounded him with his own weapons? Yet is not God thus perpetually affronted and dishonoured? Does not the swearer employ the very breath he continues, in blaspheming him? Does not the drunkard take what was designed for his nourishment and refreshment, and offer it in sacrifice to his vile appetite, to the injury of his health, and disgrace of his reason? Is not the raiment, given to cover and screen us, made to minister to pride, and to excite unhallowed passions? Genius and learning are valuable in themselves, and may be applied to purposes the most useful: yet how often have they pandered for lewdness and infidelity! The tongue, "wherewith bless we God, even the Father, often curses men, who are made after the similitude of God! And the tongue is a fire, a world of iniquity: so is the tongue among our members, that it defileth the whole body, and setteth on fire the course of nature; and it is set on fire of hell."

III. Observe THE REMOVAL. "Then will I return, and take away my corn in the time thereof, and my vine in the season thereof, and will recover my wool and my flax." What a number of reflections arise from this part of our subject!

First. We see how precarious every thing earthly is! "Riches make to themselves wings and flee away:" they are called "uncertain riches." Honour hangs upon the wavering tongue of the multitude; and our laurels wither as we wear them. Children often disappoint our fondest hopes. Friends die. Our strength is not the strength of stones. Who knows how soon he may be "made to possess months of vanity, and have wearisome nights appointed unto him?" "Truly the light is sweet, and a pleasant thing it is for the eyes to behold the sun: but if a man live many years, and rejoice in them all; yet let him remember the days of darkness; for they shall be many. All that cometh is vanity."

Secondly. God withdraws our comforts as well as gives them. "*I* will return and take them away," says God. "I form the light and create darkness; I make peace and create evil: I the Lord do all these things." Job knew who had robbed him of his substance; but he said, "the Lord hath taken away." We exclaim, "O, it was that unlucky servant; it was that perfidious friend; it was that malicious enemy:" but old Eli would say, "It is the Lord; let him do what seemeth him good." Our Lord knew that Peter would deny him, and Judas betray him, and Herod insult him, and Pilate condemn him, and the Jews crucify him: yet he speaks only of God: "The cup which my Father hath given me, shall I not drink it?"

Thirdly. We learn that God does not relinquish his propriety in any of his blessings, when he bestows them: "I will take away *my* corn, and *my* wine, and will recover *my* wool and *my* flax." Still they are his: and therefore, when he comes for them, he comes not to rob, but to resume:

> "The dear delights we here enjoy,
> And fondly *call* our own,
> Are but short favours *borrow'd* now,
> To be *repaid* anon."

Fourthly. He often removes our blessings

and comforts when they seem most attractive, most necessary; when their loss is least expected, and we are rejoicing to see them flourish!—"I will take away my corn *in the time* thereof, and my vine *in the season*." So it was with Jonah. His gourd was not only removed, but in the very time thereof. "The Lord God prepared a gourd, and made it to come up over Jonah, that it might be a shadow over his head, to deliver him from his grief. So Jonah was exceeding glad of the gourd. But God prepared a worm when the morning rose next day, and it smote the gourd that it withered. And it came to pass, when the sun did arise, that God prepared a vehement east wind; and the sun beat upon the head of Jonah, that he fainted, and wished in himself to die, and said, It is better for me to die than to live."

Again. God does not deprive us of our enjoyments without a cause. "*Therefore*," says he, "because they acknowledged not that I indulged them: and employed my mercies for Baal: therefore will I return, and take them away." God gives freely; but he takes away justly: he is a sovereign in the one, but not in the other. "Why," says he, "will you be stricken any more?" And he himself answers the question: "Ye will revolt more and more." "My strokes are continued only because your provocations are renewed." "He does not afflict willingly, nor grieve the children of men: but our own wickedness corrects us, and our backslidings reprove us." It is our non-improvement, it is our abuse of our mercies, that endangers them. And upon this principle, who has not reason to tremble? who would have a right under bereavement to complain? Which of our blessings have we not frequently forfeited? which of them has not caused us "to go a whoring from God?"—"It is of the Lord's mercies that *we* are not consumed; because his compassions fail not."

Finally. His conduct, in the removal of our joys, looks forward, as well as backward; he is not only the righteous Governor, but the tender Father: he punishes, not for our destruction, but advantage; and the very consequences of sin are made the cure. Thus you here find these losses inflicted because we have departed from God; but, at the same time, they are the merciful means to bring us back to him. "Therefore, behold, I will hedge up thy way with thorns, and make a wall, that she shall not find her paths. And she shall follow after her lovers, but she shall not overtake them; and she shall seek them, but shall not find them: then shall she say, I will go and return to my first husband; for then was it better with me than now. For she did not know that I gave her corn, and wine, and oil, and multiplied her silver and gold, which they prepared for Baal. Therefore will I return, and take away my corn in the time thereof, and my wine in the season thereof, and will recover my wool and my flax." And observe what follows: "I will also cause all her mirth to cease, her feast days, her new-moons, and her sabbaths, and all her solemn feasts. And I will destroy her vines and her fig trees, whereof she hath said, These are my rewards that my lovers have given me: and I will make them a forest, and the beasts of the field shall eat them. And I will visit upon her the days of Baalim, wherein she burned incense to them, and she decked herself with her earrings and her jewels, and she went after her lovers, and forgat me, saith the Lord. Therefore, behold, I will allure her, and bring her into the wilderness, and speak comfortably unto her. And I will give her her vineyards from thence, and the valley of Achor for a door of hope: and she shall sing there, as in the days of her youth, and as in the day when she came up out of the land of Egypt." It was for their sin, that he sent the Jews into Babylon; yet it was for their *good:* "Thus saith the Lord, the God of Israel; Like these good figs, so will I acknowledge them that are carried away captive of Judah, whom I have sent out of this place into the land of the Chaldeans for their good." "Who is a God like unto thee?"

But while this subject leads us to magnify the Lord, it should afford instruction and encouragement to those who are afflicted. No affliction will ever do us good unless it excite in us both fear and hope. It can do nothing unless it lead us to condemn ourselves, and to acknowledge that God is justified when he speaketh, and clear when he judgeth. At the same time, we must apprehend not only his justice in the dispensation, but his goodness. Without this we shall feel a sullen despair, or be hardened into impenitency. Remember, therefore, that "though he cause grief, yet will he have compassion according to the greatness of his mercy:" and that your severest trials may become your greatest blessings. Many are beginning to see this already—yea, they perceive it so plainly, that they are now praising God for providences which once tempted them to entertain the most harsh and unworthy thoughts of him.

But it is a sad thing when the lamp is extinguished, and there is no Sun of Righteousness near! When creatures are lost, and He is not found, nor even sought after! When this is the case, God will either withdraw the affliction in wrath, and say, "Ephraim is joined unto idols: let him alone;" or he will increase the severity of his measures, and after chastising us with whips chastise us with scorpions. So he threatens—"And if ye will not for all this hearken unto me, but walk contrary unto me; then I will walk

contrary unto you also in fury; and I, even I, will chastise you seven times for your sins!"

The day of trouble, therefore, is a period peculiarly eventful and important. Your salvation, or destruction, may hinge upon it. God then comes near, and if you do not receive him, you may miss him for ever!—Who thinks of this! Who is sufficiently impressed with the awful consequences of *losing an affliction!* In general, you ask for our prayers when you come into trouble, and our thanksgivings when you come out. But sometimes we hardly know what to do. If we were to regard the result, we should often be far from hailing you upon your recovery from sickness, or your emerging from penury; we should see your deliverance, as you call it, wearing away every serious thought of God, renewing your worldly spirit, and leading you to violate the vows your souls made when you were in trouble. It is best, perhaps, to invite our praise when you come into affliction, and our prayers when you come out. I say, our praise when you *come into affliction*—for this is a token for good: it is a proof that God has not as yet cast you off: it is an evidence that the husbandman has not yet resolved to cut down the tree, while he digs about it and manures: the physician does not entirely despair of the patient while he orders medicine, or even amputation—I say, our prayers when you *come out*—that you may never forget the things your eyes saw, and your ears heard; never lose the lessons you received in the school of correction; but be able to say, in every review, "it is good for me that I have been afflicted, that I might learn thy statutes. Before I was afflicted I went astray; but now have I kept thy word."

To conclude. There is no subject under which we cannot teach and preach Jesus Christ. How is it that any blessings are communicated to us but through the mediation of Him, who is the way, the truth, and the life!

> "He sunk beneath our heavy woes
> To raise us to his throne;
> There's not a gift his hand bestows
> But cost his heart a groan."

What wood is it that, thrown in, heals the waters of Marah? It is the tree on which he died that takes the curse out of all our comforts, and all our crosses too. He has redeemed us from the curse of the law, being made a curse for us. While faith views the rod, however dry and barren before, it then enlivens, and blossoms, and bears: and "though no chastening for the present seemeth to be joyous, but grievous: nevertheless afterward it yieldeth the peaceable fruit of righteousness unto them which are exercised thereby." Amen.

DISCOURSE LXXXVI.

DIVINE FORGIVENESS.

——*A God ready to pardon.*—Neh. ix. 17.

God is absolutely incomprehensible, and the highest archangel cannot "find him out unto perfection." Yet we are not called to worship "an unknown God." He has furnished us with all the information necessary to bring us to himself. "All his works praise him;" but his word, "which he hath magnified above all his name, peculiarly reveals him.

In this sacred volume, indeed, some clouds and darkness are round about him. Subjects are occasionally intimated which lie far beyond the reach of our present faculties; and concerning which we may safely follow the advice of the poet: "Wait the great teacher, Death. But the Scripture renders things plain and obvious in proportion as they are important and necessary; so that he may run that readeth them. Some truths are written as with a sunbeam—such are those which regard our state as sinners, and are calculated to draw forth our faith and hope in God. For "we are saved through faith: we are saved by hope." Man fell by losing his confidence in God; and he is only to be recovered by regaining it. For which purpose we read, not only that there is forgiveness with him—but that "he is A GOD READY TO PARDON."

We shall divide our reflections into three parts. In the First we shall show WHAT IS NECESSARY TO RENDER THE SUBJECT INTERESTING. In the Second we shall ADDUCE THE PROOFS WHICH ESTABLISH THE TRUTH OF IT. And, in the Third, WE SHALL POINT OUT THE WAY IN WHICH IT *may be abused*, AND THE MANNER IN WHICH IT *ought* TO BE *improved*.

I. WHAT IS NECESSARY TO RENDER THE SUBJECT INTERESTING? THREE THINGS.

First. *A conviction of guilt.* "They that are whole need not the physician, but they that are sick." "The full soul loatheth the honeycomb: but to the hungry every bitter thing is sweet." In vain we present alms to the affluent, or offer pardon to the innocent; our kindness will offend rather than gratify. Suffer me then to ask, Are you not sinners? Have you ever lived a day, or an hour, as you ought? Have you not, at least, been chargeable with sins of omission?—But a servant's disobedience appears in neglecting to do what the master enjoins, as well as in doing what he forbids. If your conduct has not been grossly wicked, what has been the state of your heart? For the law of God is spiritual, and each command comprehends under it not only the outward acts, but our very desires and thoughts.

By the law, therefore, is the knowledge of sin. The law begins with the object of all adoration, and requires that we serve God alone. But have you never transferred to the creature that supreme regard—that love—that fear—that confidence—which are due to the Creator, God over all, blessed for evermore? If you have never worshipped wood or stone; never cried, "O Baal, hear us!" never sacrificed to devils; have you not made gold your hope, and fine gold your confidence? have you not made flesh your arm? have you not "had men's persons in admiration, because of advantage?" If you have often, if you have daily, worshipped the Supreme Being, has it been in spirit and in truth, or only with the form of godliness? Have you never taken "His Name in vain," either in profane swearing, or in idle conversation, or in those prayers and praises, which have "mocked him with a solemn sound, upon a thoughtless tongue?" Have you sanctified the "Sabbath-day, to keep it holy?" Have you not squandered away many of its precious hours in idleness, in dress, in visitings, in pleasure-taking? Have you suffered your ox and your ass, your man-servant and your maid-servant, to rest, as well as you? Have you called the Sabbath a delight? and have you honoured it by a devout attention to the purposes for which it was instituted?— But you are sure you are no *murderer!* Is there then no one dead, in whose removal you have rejoiced? Is there no one alive, at whose continuance you have inwardly repined? Have you never been angry with your brother without a cause?—You think you are no *adulterer!* But the infallible Expositor has said, "Whosoever looketh on a woman to lust after her, hath committed adultery with her already in his heart."—You repel with indignation the charge of *theft!* But is it not pride, rather than principle, that has sometimes restrained you; or the fear of the consequences, rather than a sense of the sin? Are you a stranger to all unjust gain and excessive profit in trade? Have you never taken advantage of ignorance, or confidence? Have you fully paid your servants for their toil; and never kept back the hire of your labourers, by fraud? Have you never robbed the poor of what was due to them? In a word, "Have you done unto others as you would they should do unto you?"

I have not examined you by every command of the moral law; but I have endeavoured to convict you of transgressing those of which you were most likely to deem yourselves blameless. Examine yourselves by the remainder: they are before you, and they are all "holy, and just, and good." Try yourselves by them; try your conduct by them; try your dispositions by them; and "every mouth must be stopped, and all be found guilty before God. "I was alive," says Paul, "without the law; but when the commandment came, sin revived, and I died."

Hence, a Second thing needful to render our subject interesting is *an apprehension of our danger as transgressors.* Sin exposes us to the wrath of God; for it is written, "Cursed is every one that continueth not in all things which are written in the book of the law, to do them." The tremendousness of this curse exceeds all the power of language to express, or of imagination to conceive. It is the curse of a God! The present effects of transgression show that it is an evil and a bitter thing to sin against God; and are sufficient to lead a reflecting mind to exclaim, "Who knoweth the power of thine anger? Even according to thy fear, so is thy wrath!" But these are only the beginning of sorrows —What then must the completion of them be? Who among you can dwell with the devouring fire? Who among you can dwell with everlasting burnings? If there was only a possibility of incurring a doom so infinitely dreadful, common sense, if consulted, would tell you to agonize with the question, "What must I do to be saved?" till the cruel uncertainty was over. But in your present state, there is no uncertainty. "The soul that sinneth it shall die." And how can you escape? Can you grapple with Almighty Power? Can you conceal yourselves from Infinite Wisdom? Can you flee from Him who is every where; and every where the sin-avenging God?—There is only one way of deliverance. It is forgiveness!

Thirdly. Our subject is rendered interesting by *a discovery of the privileges of a pardoned state.* We talk of happiness. Oh! what a change to be delivered from the wrath to come—to know that God's anger is turned away—that from an enemy, he is become a friend—a friend giving us cordial access to all the rights of innocency, and entitling us to a felicity superior to the happiness of Adam in Paradise, and even of an angel in glory! Well might Paul say, "Being justified by faith we have peace with God, through our Lord Jesus Christ. Yea, we joy in God, through our Lord Jesus Christ, by whom we have now received the atonement!" Well might David exclaim, "Blessed is the man whose transgression is forgiven, whose sin is covered!" Such a man has the true notion of blessedness—and he has the reality. His blessedness is insured—and it is begun. He is blessed with assistance and acceptance, in all his duties: "for he is not under the law, but under grace." He is blessed in all his mercies, and tastes a sweetness, which others know not of, derived from a covenant claim, and the love of his heavenly Father.

And what has he to fear?—Is it affliction? —His troubles, however severe, have no curse in them. They are not the effects of wrath, but tokens of love, and blessings in disguise. He will be supported under them. He will be sanctified by them. He will be delivered out of them.—Is it death? The sting of death is sin; but that sting is extracted. To die is gain. Is it the grave? The grave is no longer the condemned hole, in which the criminal sleeps the night before execution; but the chamber, in which, after refreshment, he dresses for his interview with the King of Glory. Is it the judgment? The judgment only proclaims his absolution, and ushers him into the joy of his Lord. Is this credible? Is such a blessedness attainable? Yes, and

II. We proceed TO ADDUCE THE PROOFS WHICH ESTABLISH THE TRUTH OF THE DOCTRINE—"*a God ready to pardon.*" And do you ask for evidence?

See it *in the provision he has made for the exercise of it.* For it *became* him—we use his own language; "it *became* him" to administer this pardon in a peculiar way. It was necessary that nothing like a connivance at moral evil should be suspected in the Divine government. It was necessary that sin should be condemned in the flesh, even while it was forgiven. It was necessary that God's law should not appear so rigid as to require relaxation, or so changeable and weak as to admit of dispensation; but be magnified and made honourable. It was necessary that God's truth should be seen, as well as his grace; and his righteousness, as well as his mercy. Here were difficulties which he alone could remove. Here was a plan which he alone could devise. Here was a sacrifice which he alone could provide. But, of his own self-moved compassion, "He has reconciled us unto himself by Jesus Christ. He has made him to be sin for us, who knew no sin, that we might be made the righteousness of God in him. Herein is love, not that we loved God, but that he loved us, and sent his Son to be the propitiation for our sins."—Rather than not pardon—he spares not his own Son, but delivers him up for us all. Do you ask for evidence?

See it *in the promptitude with which he pardons on our return.* "And it shall come to pass," says God, "that before they call I will answer, and while they speak I will hear." Was the father backward to receive the prodigal, when famine and misery drove him home? Disobedient and vile as he had been, "when he was yet a great way off, the father saw him, and had compassion, and ran, and fell on his neck, and kissed him. And the son said unto him, Father, I have sinned against heaven, and in thy sight, and am no more worthy to be called thy son. But the Father said to his servants, Bring forth the best robe, and put it on him; and put a ring on his hand, and shoes on his feet; and bring hither the fatted calf, and kill it; and let us eat and be merry: for this my son was dead, and is alive again; he was lost, and is found. And they began to be merry." Do you ask for evidence?

See it *in his earnestness to excite us to seek after the blessing.* It would be enough to prove that a man was ready to pardon, if he yielded immediately upon the offender's submission and application; but God does more. He not only "waits to be gracious," but he comes forward—He begins—He cries "Come, and let us reason together: though your sins were as scarlet, they shall be white as snow, though they were red like crimson, they shall be as wool." He urges: he entreats; yes—by the uneasiness of conscience, by the afflictions of life, by the importunity of friends, by the addresses of ministers—it is, as the apostle says, "as though God did beseech you—to be reconciled unto God!". Do you ask for evidence?

See it *in the character of those who have received pardon.* Some of these have been the chief of sinners; sinners of long standing; sinners whose crimes have been not only numberless, but attended with every aggravation. You have read of Manasseh; of the dying thief; of the murderers of Christ; of the Corinthian converts: yet all these obtained mercy! Do you ask for evidence?

See it, finally, *in the number of those who obtain forgiveness.* Let us not reduce them. There are thousands more than we are aware of, even when we send forth Candour to reckon them; and when they shall be all "gathered together out of every kindred and nation and tongue and people, they will be found a multitude which no man can number."—Thus real, and thus obvious, is the glorious character of Jehovah—as "A GOD READY TO PARDON."

III. But it will be requisite TO POINT OUT THE WAY IN WHICH THIS SUBJECT *may be abused,* AND THE MANNER IN WHICH IT *ought* TO BE *improved.*

The subject is abused when it leads us to deny any disposition in God to punish. God is not only to be viewed as a tender father, but a moral governor. His mercy cannot be too much extolled, provided we allow that "he is holy in all his ways, and righteous in all his works: and of purer eyes than to behold iniquity." We do not approve of the word *vindictive* justice; but *punitive* justice is essential to his character; and, without it, we could neither venerate nor love him: for how could we esteem a being, especially in the relation of a ruler, who should feel alike disposed towards the liar and the man of truth, the cruel and the kind, a Robespierre and a Howard—and treat them alike? The Scriptures do not "bid mercy triumph over God himself, undeified by such opprobrious praise:" even when he said to Moses, "I will make all my goodness pass before thee, and I will proclaim the name of the Lord before thee," he recorded himself, "The Lord God merciful and gracious, longsuffering, and abundant in goodness and truth; keeping

mercy for thousands, forgiving iniquity and transgression and sin; and *that will by no means clear the guilty.*"

The subject is abused when it encourages us to hope for pardon in ways not warranted by the word of God. For instance—

Thus—unwarranted is our hope when we expect it *without a reference to the mediation of Christ.* It is acknowledged that God's love is unpurchased; and that of his own nature he is disposed to be merciful and gracious. But the question is, Whether he has not a right to exercise his mercy and grace in his own way; and whether, if he has appointed and revealed such a way, any thing but criminal ignorance and pride can lead me to oppose it; or any thing but disappointment and wretchedness can result from my neglect of it! We are "justified freely by his grace;" and it is "through the redemption that is in Christ Jesus." "I am the way," says the Redeemer: "no man cometh unto the Father but by me."

Thus—unwarranted is our hope when we expect pardon *without repentance.* Show me a single Scripture where the bestowment of the one is unconnected with the exercise of the other. "If we confess our sins, He is faithful and just to forgive us our sins." "He that confesseth and forsaketh them, shall have mercy." "He is exalted to be a Prince and a Saviour, to give repentance unto Israel, and forgiveness of sins."

Thus—unwarranted is our hope when we expect this pardon *by delaying an application for it to the close of life.* We can never merit the Divine goodness: but it is in our power to provoke his wrath—and I would ask, What can be so likely to induce him to reject us as our being evil, "because he is good;" our "continuing in sin, that grace may abound"—while animated by the hope that a dying petition will save us, when we have sinned till we can sin no longer? He is a God ready to pardon; but he will not make this pardon "the minister of sin."

Finally. Thus—unwarranted is our hope when we expect *to find this pardon in another world, if we fail to obtain it in this.* He is ready to pardon—but it is in time only. At death "the door is shut." "Then," says God, "shall they call, but I will not answer; they shall seek me early, but they shall not find me." "Seek ye, therefore, the Lord while he may be found, call ye upon him while he is near."

But what is the proper improvement we should make of this delightful subject?

It should yield encouragement to the broken hearted. It is often as hard to persuade such persons as these to hope as it was formerly to induce them to fear. They are commonly tempted to conclude that their case is peculiar, or that the greatness of their guilt excludes them from mercy.—Is this thy case?

Art thou, my fellow-sinner, ready to say, " I am cast out of his sight !" Look again towards his holy temple. Once more turn back, and address his throne ; once more cry,

" Yet save a trembling sinner, Lord,
Whose hope, still hovering round thy word,
Would light on some sweet promise there,
Some sure defence against despair !"

And behold this sure defence ; behold this sweet promise—" a God ready to pardon !"

The subject should afford consolation to those who have believed through grace. Believers are enemies to sin, and long to be delivered from it ; but while they are in the body they are imperfect. They find it impossible to live without contracting fresh guilt. Their duties are defiled ; and among their holiest exercises they must exclaim, " If thou, Lord, shouldest mark iniquity, O Lord, who should stand ?" But are they, while they mourn, to refuse to be comforted ? Are they, while they are humble, to be hopeless ! " If any man sin, we have an Advocate with the Father, Jesus Christ the righteous ; and he is the propitiation for our sins ; and not for ours only, but also for the sins of the whole world." Instead of keeping away from God under a sense of our unworthiness, as the enemy of souls would urge us, " let us," with ingenuous feelings, " come boldly to the throne of grace, that we may obtain mercy, and find grace to help in time of need." He is " a God ready to pardon !"

The subject demands our admiration and praise. There is no character we esteem and extol so much as that of the merciful, the tender, the placable, the forgiving : " It is the glory of a man to pass by a transgression." How glorious then must God appear ! " Who is a God like unto thee, that pardoneth iniquity, and passeth by the transgression of the remnant of his heritage ? he retaineth not his anger for ever, because he delighteth in mercy."

But the subject calls upon us not only to admire, but to imitate. Is he a God ready to pardon ? " Be ye followers of God as dear children. Let all bitterness, and wrath, and anger, and clamour, and evilspeaking, be put away from you, with all malice : and be ye kind one to another, tenderhearted, forgiving one another, even as God for Christ's sake hath forgiven you."

DISCOURSE LXXXVII.

THE LORD THE UNERRING CONDUCTOR OF HIS PEOPLE.

And he led them forth by the right way, that they might go to a city of habitation.—Psalm cvii. 7.

In these words, it is not easy to ascertain the persons immediately intended. Thus they are spoken of in the preceding verses : " Let the redeemed of the Lord say so, whom he hath redeemed from the hand of the enemy : and gathered them out of the lands, from the east, and from the west, from the north, and from the south. They wandered in the wilderness in a solitary way ; they found no city . to dwell in. Hungry and thirsty, their soul fainted in them. Then they cried unto the Lord in their trouble, and he delivered them out of their distresses." Does the sacred writer refer to travellers in general ! Much of the Lord's goodness is to be seen in long and perilous journeys : but the language here employed seems too strong to justify such an application. Does he allude to the Israelites, when marching through the desert to Canaan ? Of this we are naturally reminded by some things in the description : but a part of it does not harmonize with fact. They were taken from Egypt ; but not " gathered from the lands, from the east, and from the west, from the north, and from the south." Does he refer to the return of the Jews from Babylon to Judea, in consequence of the decree of Cyrus ! We knew that Ezra, who led back a portion of them, says, " Then I proclaimed a fast there, at the river Ahava, that we might afflict ourselves before our God, *to seek of him a right way* for us, and for our little ones, and for all our substance :" and after this, we also know, they arrived safe at Jerusalem, " through the good hand of their God upon them." But what evidence have we that this Psalm was written after this event ! Or that it was not written by David ! Or, if written by him, that it is to be considered as prophetical rather than historical !

But the difficulty there is in determining the persons immediately designed is a circumstance not to be lamented. It is even an advantage ; it constrains us to a more spiritual and evangelical interpretation of the subject. And thus the whole representation is fully and easily imbodied. For the people of God are *redeemed*—redeemed from the curse of the law, the powers of darkness, and the bondage of corruption. They are *gathered*—gathered by his grace out of all the diversities of the human race ; " out of all nations and kindreds and people and tongues." Whatever this world is to others, they find it to be " a wilderness ;" where they are often tried ; but their trials urge them to prayer, and prayer brings them relief. And being divinely conducted, they at length reach their destination : and this is the conclusion of the whole, and it applies to each of them ; " And he led them forth by the right way, that they might go to a city of habitation."

Let us consider—THE LEADER—THE WAY—and THE END.

I. THE LEADER. *He* led them. The

land to be given them is said to be "very far off;" and in a journey of such extent, such difficulty, and of such importance, who would venture alone? But the believer is not alone. He travels under the conduct of Jehovah; and can say, and sometimes he can even sing too; "This God is my God for ever and ever, he will be my guide even unto death."

In the everlasting covenant, ordered in all things and sure, the engagement runs, "They shall be my people, and I will be their God." As if he should say, "I dedicate myself to their welfare. I hold myself at their call." As he undertakes to be nothing less than "*their God*," there is divinity in every relation in which he stands to them. If he is their friend, he is not only a perfect, but a *divine* friend, and therefore an *infinite* one. If he is their guide, he is not only a perfect, but a *divine* guide, and therefore an *infinite* one. Let us more particularly examine this privilege. Let us connect it with his omnipresence; his patience; his power; and his wisdom.

Let us connect this guidance with his omnipresence. As his people travel from all countries, and are remote often from each other, no creature, if their leader, could be with them all at the same time: while he approached some, he would withdraw, in the same proportion, from others. But God is everywhere. He fills earth, as well as heaven; he is constantly at hand, and to each of his people a very present help in trouble. They shall never perish for want of seasonable aid: "It shall come to pass, that before they call, I will answer; and while they are yet speaking, I will hear."

Let us connect this guidance with his patience. No other being in the universe would be able to bear with our imperfections and provocations. The meekest man upon earth, and the most merciful angel in heaven, if intrusted with us, would soon abandon his charge. A Christian has sometimes such views of his depravity; of his omissions of duty; of his distractions in it; of his ingratitude, his unbelief, his perverseness—that he cries with Job, "Behold, I am vile," and abhors himself, repenting in dust and ashes. He then wonders that God does not cast him off. But his Leader is the God of all grace: he is longsuffering; he does not break the bruised reed, nor quench the smoking flax. "Like as a father pitieth his children, so the Lord pitieth them that fear him. For he knoweth our frame; he remembereth we are dust." And while, under a recollection of his past guilt, and a sense of his present unworthiness, he prays, "Cast me not away from thy presence, and take not thy Holy Spirit from me;" his Leader replies, "I will never leave thee nor forsake thee."

Let us connect this guidance with his power. No other leader could defend them; for the country through which they pass is full of snares and dangers: and

"A thousand savage beasts of prey,
Around the forest roam."

And what emboldens them? The voice of him who cries; "Fear thou not; for I am with thee: be not dismayed; for I am thy God: I will strengthen thee; yea, I will help thee; yea, I will uphold thee with the right hand of my righteousness. I am with thee, and will keep thee in all places whither thou goest. Thou shalt walk in thy way safely, and thy foot shall not stumble. Thou shalt tread on the lion and the adder; the young lion and the dragon shalt thou trample under foot."

Let us connect this guidance with his wisdom. Who knows what is good for a man in this life? Who can distinguish between appearance and reality? Who can determine that what he wishes to shun is not a blessing? Or that what he covets is not a curse? The way of man is not in himself. Hence the admonition and the promise; "Trust in the Lord with all thine heart; and lean not unto thine own understanding. In all thy ways acknowledge him, and he shall direct thy paths. I will bring the blind by a way that they knew not; I will lead them in paths that they have not known: I will make darkness light before them, and crooked things straight. These things will I do unto them, and not forsake them." Some possess great talent, and have acquired much knowledge and experience: yet, no creature is infallibly wise, and therefore we cannot implicitly resign ourselves to him; but we may absolutely commit ourselves to God. His understanding is infinite. He sees the end from the beginning. He perfectly knows what we are, and what we want: and "though clouds and darkness are round about him, and justice and judgment are the habitation of his throne; mercy and truth go before his face."

II. THE WAY. "He led them forth by the *right way*." Many things seem inconsistent with this acknowledgment; especially the various trials with which they are exercised, and which often lead them to say with Gideon, "If the Lord be with us, why then is all this evil befallen us?" Are they persecuted by enemies, and betrayed by friends? Are they stripped of their substance; bereaved of their kindred; invaded by sickness; made to possess months of vanity, and have wearisome nights appointed for them? And, Is this the "*right* way?" In answer to this, it will be necessary to ask two questions:

First. According to what principle is it "right?" For a thing may be wrong in one view, and right in another. It is sinful to take away life; but there are cases in which it is lawful and praiseworthy: as in self-defence and the execution of judicial policy. In the system of nature, winter is as necessary as summer, and night as day; though for some purposes they are not equally good. A way that winds about may not be valued for its shortness, but it may be preferable for its safety, or for the sake of avoiding a hill, or for touching at several places where the traveller may do business. The correction which may appear cruel, if considered only with regard to the feelings of the child, appears very differently when connected with his profit. We do not extol medicine for the pleasure of taking it, but for the effect resulting from it, in the restoration of health. So it is here. Many of the dispensations of Providence, if viewed separately and partially, would be objectionable; but right when considered in connexion with their designs, and relatively to the glory of God's name and the spiritual welfare of his people. This is the rule by which they are to be tried.

Secondly. According to whose judgment is it right? And to this we immediately answer, The judgment of God. He alone is capable of judging; and his judgment is always according to truth: what seems good in his sight, must be really good: for he cannot be deceived. But we are so ignorant, and can grasp so little of the plan—so occupied, and full of prejudices—we are so selfish, so carnal, so impatient—and are such very inadequate judges, that we often call evil good, and good evil.

Four things, however, may be observed, in reference to this case.

First. It will be right, according to the judgment of the Christian himself, in another world. "What I do," says his Leader, "thou knowest not now, but thou shalt know hereafter." When in God's light he shall see light, he will join the acclamations of those to whom the mysteries which once perplexed them are explained; and say, "Marvellous are thy works, Lord God Almighty; just and true are thy ways, thou King of saints!"

Secondly. The Christian is not wholly without satisfaction even now. There are some openings into the dispensations of Heaven which more than enable him to acquiesce. When the noise of the passions is subsided, and he can hear the small still voice; when he has wiped away the tears which bedimmed his light; "I can now," says he, "perceive the reason of such a defection of friendship— I was making flesh my arm. I see why the vessel was broken—I was forgetting the fountain. He planted thorns in my tabernacle, for I was in danger of saying, This is my rest. 'I know, O Lord, that thy judgments are right, and that thou in faithfulness hast afflicted me.'"

Thirdly. We should be more satisfied with the rectitude of the Divine proceedings if we were more dutifully attentive. "Whoso is wise, and will observe these things, even they shall understand the lovingkindness of the Lord." But we too often get down from our watch-tower, or fall asleep there; and the interpreter passes by unaddressed and unseen.

Fourthly. There is one way of obtaining complete satisfaction even while we are in this vale of tears. It is to rely on his word when we cannot explain his conduct; it is to walk by faith when we cannot walk by sight. And what is it that you are required to believe in order to bring this heaven into your souls? Why, only, that He who spared not his own Son will deny you nothing that is really good for you; that he takes pleasure in the prosperity of his servants, and knows how to advance it better than you do; that he doth all things, and "doth all things well." "Who is among you that feareth the Lord, that obeyeth the voice of his servant, that walketh in darkness, and hath no light? let him trust in the name of the Lord, and stay upon his God. Thou wilt keep him in perfect peace, whose mind is stayed on thee: because he trusteth in thee." "If ye will not believe, surely ye shall not be established."

III. THE END: "He led them forth by the right way, *that they might go to a city of habitation.*" "It doth not," says the apostle John, "yet appear what we shall be; but this we know, that when he shall appear, we shall be like him, for we shall see him as he is." From these words we learn that the glory to which the believer is advancing, is not wholly developed, and yet it is not entirely concealed. Indeed, some revelation is necessary; for we cannot desire what we are ignorant of and have no sympathy with. There are, therefore, some mediums through which we may catch a glimpse. Such are the evils to which we are now exposed. Imagine all these removed. "And God shall wipe away all tears from their eyes; and there shall be no more death, neither sorrow nor crying, neither shall there be any more pain: for the former things are passed away." Such are the imperfections we now feel. Imagine all these annihilated. Then, "that which is perfect is come, and that which is in part, in knowledge, holiness, and bliss, shall be done away. We shall be presented faultless before the presence of his glory with exceeding joy." Such is the imagery the Scripture employs; and as our souls are now incarnate, and we acquire knowledge by sensation and reflection, our future condition will more powerfully impress us when it is held forth by things seen and temporal. Hence it is expressed by "rivers of pleasure; trees of life; crowns of glory; a house not made with hands, eternal in the heavens; a city of habitation."

This suggests *magnificence*. It is not a village, or a town, but a *city* of habitation. A city is the highest representation of civil community. There have been famous cities; but what are they to all this? "Glorious things are spoken of thee, O city of God!" It is the city of the living God. It is the city of the great King. It is the city which hath foundations, whose builder and maker is God. The foundation is of precious stones. The pavement is of pure gold. The gates are of pearls. "I saw no temple therein; for the Lord God Almighty and the Lamb are the temple of it. And the city had no need of the sun, neither of the moon, to shine in it; for the glory of God did lighten it; and the Lamb is the light thereof." But who can estimate the honours, the provisions, the pleasures of the place? As it is written, "Eye hath not seen, nor ear heard, nor have entered into the heart of man, the things which God hath prepared for them that love him." It is to display the munificence of his goodness, and to prove to men and angels, that he has not called himself their God in vain. "But now they desire a better country, that is an heavenly: wherefore God is not ashamed to be called their God, for he hath prepared for them a city."

Not a city of *inspection!* Many—(Eternal God! will it be any of this company!—) will look in; and "there shall be weeping, and wailing, and gnashing of teeth, when they shall see Abraham, Isaac, and Jacob in the kingdom of God, and they themselves shut out." Not a city of *visitation.* Christians shall not only enter, but abide. They shall go no more out—It is "a city of *habitation.*"

This conveys the idea of *repose.* The Christian is now a traveller; then he will be a resident: he is now on the road; he will then be at home: "there remaineth a *rest* for the people of God."

It reminds us of a *social state.* It is not a solitary condition; we shall partake of it with an innumerable company of angels, with all the saved from among men, with patriarchs, prophets, apostles, martyrs, our kindred in Christ.—"These are fellow-citizens of the saints, and of the household of God."—

The subject requires from us an admiration of God. "His greatness is unsearchable." "He dwells in the light which no man can approach unto." "Heaven is his throne and the earth is his footstool." "Thousands minister unto him, and ten thousand times ten thousand stand before him." And what are we!—"Of yesterday, and know nothing. Our habitation is in the dust. We are crushed before the moth." Numbers will not relieve our meanness; all nations before him are as nothing, and they are counted to him less than nothing, and vanity—And will *He* make *our* concerns his care? His condescension admits of no comparison. A king deigning to lead a poor beggar; a philosopher stooping to teach an infant his alphabet—is a

very inadequate image of his grace. We sometimes see persons who "condescend to men of low estate;" but they are only men themselves, deriving their nature from the same original, inheriting the same infirmities, and doomed to the same corruption. God even condescends to behold the things that are done in heaven: well, therefore, when we meet with him on earth, may we exclaim, "Lord, what is man, that thou art mindful of him! and the son of man, that thou visitest him?"

We congratulate those of you who have reason to conclude that you are the people of God. We hail you, on the ground of your *present privileges.* You are under a Divine guide; and you are in the right way. One of these necessarily results from the other. If you are under the Lord's direction, though he may lead you in a strange and a thorny way, it will be—it must be—it is, a right one: and you cannot indulge too firm a confidence. You know his name; and should put your trust in him. What have you to do with to-morrow! Events are his. Duty only is yours; and in the performance of this, he allows, he commands you, to rely upon him for wisdom and strength. "Be careful for nothing: but in every thing, by prayer and supplication with thanksgiving, let your requests be made known unto God. And the peace of God, which passeth all understanding, shall keep your hearts and minds through Christ Jesus."

But still greater reason have we to hail you, on the ground of your *future expectation.* Though you have much in hand, you have more in hope. He is *now* guiding you by his counsel, but he will *afterwards* receive you to glory. He is leading you by the right way; but the way, whatever may be said in praise of it, is not the city of habitation. But there—there the journey ends.

> "See the kind angels at the gates,
> Inviting us to come;
> There Jesus the forerunner waits,
> To welcome travellers home."

Unhappy sinners! How much are you depriving yourselves of while sacrificing all the present, and all the future advantages of religion! You may banish thought, and remain insensible of your loss for a while—but it can be for a while only—you must soon be convinced of your folly; and how dreadful, if you should learn your error when it is too late to be rectified! As yet, however, this is not your state. Your harvest is not yet past; your summer is not yet ended. You are yet in the number of those who are within the reach of mercy. May you "seek the Lord while he may be found, and call upon him while he is near."

And what says all this to you, my young friends! Will you not "from this time cry unto him, My father, thou art the guide of my

2 S

youth?" You are entering a world full of temptation. You are beginning life without the advantage of experience, and yet in all the strength of passion. How liable are you to err! And yet how much depends upon every wrong step you take. Would you be wise, and safe, and happy? Yield yourselves unto God; saying, "Lord, I am thine, save me. Lead me in thy truth, and teach me: for thou art the God of my salvation; on thee do I wait all the day."

DISCOURSE LXXXVIII.

FELLOWSHIP WITH THE RIGHT-EOUS.

Be merciful unto me, as thou usest to do unto those that love thy name.—Psalm cxix. 132.

MAN is the subject of numberless wants and desires. He feels himself unhappy, and is therefore restless for a change. He supposes the future to be better than the present, and is therefore alive to hope. He imagines the condition of others superior to his own, and hence the spirit that is in him lusteth to envy.

And how many are there who only envy those upon whom the world smiles; or who, if ever they pray, are saying, "Lord, rank me with the healthful, the rich, the honourable?" But there are some who have the knowledge of the holy, and are made wise unto salvation. These no longer ask, "Who will show us any good?" But their language is, "Lord, lift thou up the light of thy countenance upon us." "There is only," says such a man as this, "there is only one class of persons I envy. They are those whom the world overlooks and despises. They are the redeemed; the pardoned; the sanctified. They are those who are ' blessed with all spiritual blessings in heavenly places in Christ.' *These*, and these *alone*, I envy: not that I grudge them their privileges, or wish to deprive them of their portion; but I long above all things to share with them. "Remember me, O Lord, with the favour that thou bearest unto thy people: O visit me with thy salvation; that I may see the good of thy chosen, that I may rejoice in the gladness of thy nation, that I may glory with thine inheritance! Be merciful unto me, as thou usest to do unto those that love thy name."

From these words we observe—

I. THERE ARE SOME WHO LOVE GOD'S NAME. The word *name*, in Scripture, is significant of person. Thus we read of "a few names in Sardis," which had not defiled their garments; and when Peter stood up in the midst of the disciples, it is said, "the number of the names was about an hundred and twenty." As names distinguish, and make known, and recall to our minds, the characters to whom they are attached, it is hardly a figure of speech to make them stand for the individuals themselves. Thus it is with God. His name means his perfections, his nature, his being, himself; and they who love his name mean those who love himself.

Such there have been in every age of the world; for he has never left himself without witness. But do not all men love God? So far from it, that we read in the Scripture of the "haters of God:" a charge which, however dreadful, we have reason to fear will apply to the generality of mankind. Will it apply, my dear hearers, to you? In answer to this question, it is in vain for you to say that you are not haters of God, because you never *speak* against him: for there are works, as well as words, of enmity; yea, actions speak louder than words; and you are accustomed to lay more stress upon them, in judging of the disposition of a fellow-creature towards you. We read of our "being enemies to God by wicked works." And there is a "carnal mind, which is enmity against God, because it is not subject to his law." Is it true, that "God is not in all your thoughts?" That you do not like to retain him in your knowledge? That the conversation is uninteresting which turns upon his glory? That you have no desire to enjoy his presence? That you never strive to please him?—In vain also, you say, that you join in his worship, and do not find your attendance irksome. For, not to inquire whether this is true; whether your heart never rises up against the doctrine of the Gospel, the strictness of God's commands, and the spirituality of his service—let me ask, How do you feel towards the same Being, *alone?* Do you relish *private* devotion? If you were with a person you dislike, in a large and entertaining company—though even then, you would rather he was absent; the hour would pass off less disagreeably,—perhaps, even pleasantly, —because you would have other attractions and engagements: but suppose all the rest were withdrawn, and you left with this individual only—your situation would then be intolerable, and your only wish would be to escape. The application is easy. It is little proof of your regard for God, to intermingle with a large and respectable congregation in the sanctuary, especially where all the exterior of devotion is inviting; where the pulpit is distinguished by talent and eloquence, and the preacher is "as one that hath a pleasant voice, and can play well on an instrument." The question is, How do you feel towards God in the want of all this? Do you love to meet him in solitude? There are those who do.

There are those who can say, "My soul shall be satisfied as with marrow and fatness; and my mouth shall praise thee with joyful lips: when I remember thee upon my bed, and meditate on thee in the night watches.

How precious also are thy thoughts unto me, O God! how great is the sum of them! If I should count them, they are more in number than the sand: when I awake, I am still with thee." They admire his excellences, and feel his goodness. They have seen him in the sacrifice of the cross; and on Calvary have complied with a demand so long resisted before: "My son, give me thy heart." There are many dear to them on earth, and more in heaven; but they can say, "Whom have I in heaven but thee, and there is none upon earth that I desire beside thee!" For though they do not love him perfectly, they love him supremely. There is no one they so fear to offend. There is no one whose favour they so long to enjoy: "His lovingkindness is better than life." Their eyes run down with tears because men keep not his law. They delight to speak good of his name, and recommend him to others; while they glory in the success of his cause; and holding themselves at his disposal, ask, "Lord, what wilt thou have me to do?"

II. His MERCY IS THE SOURCE OF ALL THE GOODNESS THEY EXPERIENCE. It is not necessary so set aside compulsion; for Deity can suffer no impression from external power: and what is constrained has no value in it. But the great opponent of mercy is merit: and for this, man, who is naturally as proud as he is poor, will always strive to find a place. And yet where will he find it? Only in the creed of ignorance, and presumption: not, I am sure, in the testimony of the Scriptures, or in the language of believers. They "look to the rock whence they were hewn, and to the hole of the pit whence they were digged." They know that it was the mercy of God alone that brought them in the state which now attracts his regard, and inspired them with all those dispositions in which he delights: "not by works of righteousness which we have done, but according to his mercy he saved us; by the washing of regeneration, and renewing of the Holy Ghost." Nor is their consciousness of unworthiness confined to their natural condition; but since they have known God, or rather have been known of him, they see enough in their daily walk and temper, in their non-improvement of means and privileges, yea, in their very duties, to convince them that mercy is the principle of God's conduct towards them. Hence, as they are spared from year to year, they exclaim, "It is of the Lord's mercies that we are not consumed, because his compassions fail not." Hence, in their sufferings, they see that they have no right to complain; but much reason to acknowledge under the severest trials, "He has not dealt with us after our sins, nor rewarded us according to our iniquities." If they pray, it is with the sentiment of Daniel: "We do not present our supplications before thee for our righteousness, but for thy great mercies." If they hope, it is a "looking for the mercy of our Lord Jesus Christ unto eternal life."

What a character does Paul give of Onesiphorus; of his charity, and fortitude, and zeal; yet he prays, "The Lord grant that he may find mercy of the Lord in that day!" Even he needed mercy, and would need it to the last, and then more than ever. And where is the man, however holy, that would think of "that day," and not sink into despair and horror, but for the prospect of mercy! "If thou, Lord shouldest mark iniquities, O Lord, who shall stand?"

III. THE LORD HAS BEEN ALWAYS ACCUSTOMED TO DEAL MERCIFULLY WITH THEM. It is not a single, casual, occasional exercise; but a well known and invariable dispensation, to which David refers: "Be merciful unto me, as thou usest to do unto those that love thy name."

It cannot be otherwise, if his word is the faithful word; for he has promised it. He has said to every believer, "I will surely do thee good. All the ways of the Lord are mercy and truth unto such as keep his covenant and his testimonies. For the Lord God is a sun and shield: the Lord will give grace and glory: no good thing will he withhold from them that walk uprightly." Here is the rule by which he has bound himself to act towards his people. And that his conduct has been conformable to these assurances even their enemies have been judges. They have frequently been so struck with the displays of his goodness, as inwardly to venerate the godly, and to commend their condition. "Verily, there is a reward for the righteous." "How amiable are thy tents, O Jacob, and thy tabernacles, O Israel! Let me die the death of the righteous, and let my last end be like his." Thus it is said, "All that see them shall acknowledge them, that they are the seed which the Lord hath blessed." But they themselves are the best judges of the Divine conduct towards them. They can judge spiritually; and see mercy in dispensations which may appear to the world as the effects of wrath.

With what pleasure do they look back, and compare the words of his mouth with the works of his hands; "as we have heard, so have we seen, in the city of our God!" What Ebenezers have they reared as they passed along: inscribing on each, "Hitherto hath the Lord helped me!" How often, among all their complaints of themselves, have they looked up, and said; "Thou hast dealt well with thy servant, O Lord!" Time would fail me, to specify all the instances in which he has been used to deal mercifully with them. —He has been accustomed to appear for them in their temporal exigences; and though they have not had the miracle of the ravens, and the meal, they have had the mercy: "Their bread has been given them, and their water has been sure; and he has blessed their bread and their water."—He has been accustomed to indulge them, peculiarly with his own presence, when creatures have failed them by death, or weakness, or perfidy: so that they could say, "Nevertheless the Lord stood by me: I am not alone, because the Father is with me."—He has been accustomed to counteract their fears, and surpass their expectations When they said in their haste, "I am cut off from before his eyes;" he has "heard the voice of their supplication, when they cried unto him: at even-tide it has been light: he has turned the shadow of death into the morning." What appalled them in apprehension they endured with cheerfulness: "as the sufferings abounded, the consolations" more than counterbalanced them; and their greatest gains sprang from their greatest losses.—He has been accustomed to bear with their ignorance and weakness; to "help their infirmities;" to "uphold them with his free Spirit;" to "show them his power and glory in the sanctuary;" to say to their souls, "I am thy salvation." But where shall I stop?

> "My Saviour, my Almighty Friend,
> When I begin thy praise,
> Where will the growing numbers end,
> The numbers of thy grace?"

All his dealings with his people have been nothing but mercy. He was merciful to them when he frowned, as well as when he smiled. When he denied, as well as when he indulged. When he took away, as well as when he gave. What use ought we to make of this?

IV. His, MERCY TOWARDS THEM SHOULD ENCOURAGE US TO IMPLORE MERCY FOR OURSELVES. "Be merciful unto me, as thou usest to do unto those that love thy name." "I ask nothing but what thou hast been in the constant practice of giving. I come after millions, every one of whom has said, 'It is good for me to draw near to God. O taste and see that the Lord is good: blessed is the man that trusteth in him.'"

Beggars naturally love to go to a door where others have been successful, especially where none have ever been sent empty away. This, indeed, is never the case among men. No earthly benefactor, however disposed, can afford universal relief. But we have every thing to inspire our application at "a throne of grace." In what he has done through every age, we see his resources and his bounty. We see "the same Lord over all, and rich unto all that call upon him."—And we know that he is unchangeably the same. "His hand is not shortened that it cannot save, nor his ear heavy that it cannot hear." —And we know that all those who have been saved and blessed by him, had no more to recommend them to his regards than we have, but originally stood before him "wretched and miserable, and poor, and blind, and naked."—We go a step further, and we say, that one end God had in view in showing them mercy was to excite our application, and to pull up despair by the roots. And hence the characters of many of those who have found mercy. In acts of grace among men, the principal offenders are always excepted; and the reason is, not only because they are more deserving of punishment, but their pardon would be dangerous, by being so exemplary: but God has, in every age, called and saved some of the vilest of the vile; and so far from his wishing to conceal it, one of these ringleaders, in his name, says, "Howbeit for this cause I obtained mercy, that in me first Jesus Christ might show forth all longsuffering, for a pattern to them which should hereafter believe on him to life everlasting." When convinced of sin, and feeling our desert, and urged to seek for the greatest of all blessings, from him whom we have offended and provoked; it is not a little encouragement we need. And have we not everlasting consolation and good hope through grace? Let us think of the gift of his dear Son. Let us remember the promises and invitations of the Gospel. Let us reflect upon the examples of his grace. Let us consider the invariableness of his regard to prayer— "*This* poor man cried, and the Lord heard him, and delivered him out of all his trouble" —"*They* looked unto him, and were lightened, and their faces were not ashamed."— "He *never* said to the seed of Jacob, Seek ye me in vain." But,

V. WE SHOULD BE ANXIOUS TO SECURE THE MERCY THAT IS PECULIAR TO THEM; and not be satisfied with his common kindness. "Be merciful unto me, as thou usest to do unto those that love thy name."

God is good to all; and his tender mercies are over all his works. The sun is called his sun; and he makes it to shine upon the evil and upon the good; and sendeth his rain upon the just and upon the unjust. David had received from God a crown—and so had Pharaoh long before him. David had genius— so had Ahithophel, who hung himself. Natural talents and earthly possessions and enjoyments are *common* to the righteous and the wicked; and no man can infer the love or hatred of God from them—David prays for those benefits which are tokens for good and *pledges* of Divine friendship.

Again. He knew that as ordinary mercies were not *distinguishing*, neither were they *satisfying*. The greatest abundance of them cannot fill the void within; and tell the immortal mind to rove no more. There is no true peace nor joy but as we are able to say of the God of all grace, "Thou art the strength of my heart, and my portion for ever."

Yea, temporal blessings may even draw us astray, and become our sin and ruin. How many are there now in hell cursing their success in business, because it set their affections on things below; their honour, because it flattered their pride; their plenty, because it fed their passions and lusts—" The prosperity of fools shall destroy them."

To which we may add, that these outward blessings, however good in themselves, are not *durable.* They are " the meat that perisheth." They are " the treasure that moth and rust can corrupt, and thieves break through and steal." They are "but for a moment." " O give me," says the man like-minded with David, "give me the meat that endureth unto everlasting life. Give me the 'treasure in heaven, where neither moth nor rust can corrupt, nor thieves break through and steal.' Tell me that ' the eternal God is my refuge, and that underneath are the ever-lasting arms.' What are the wants of my body to the necessities of my soul! Not only is every thing here going, but—I am going! I am a dying creature; I have nothing, if I have not a hope beyond the grave. I want pardon. I want holiness. I want the ear-nests of the Spirit. I want a better country. There are those who feel a peace which passe-eth all understanding; and rejoice in hope of the glory of God.

> ' Where is the shadow of that Rock
> That from the sun defends *thy* flock?
> Fain would I feed among *thy* sheep,
> Among *them* rest, among *them* sleep.'

' Be merciful unto me, as thou usest to do unto those that love thy name.' "

Lastly. WE SHOULD BE CONTENT IF GOD DEALS WITH US AS HE HAS ALWAYS DEALT WITH HIS PEOPLE. While he could not be satisfied with any thing less than their por-tion, David asks for nothing better; he im-plores no singular dispensation in his favour, no deviation from the accustomed methods of his grace. " Be merciful unto me, as thou usest to do unto those that love thy name." This was the disposition of Paul: " if by any means I might attain unto the resurrection of the dead." He did not prescribe, but submit. The *end* was every thing; the *way* he left, with a holy indifference, to God. And it is always a good proof that your convictions and desires are from the operation of the Spi-rit when you are willing to conform to God's order. What is this order? It is to dispense his blessings connectedly. It is never to jus-tify without sanctifying; never to give a title to heaven without a meetness for it. Now the man that is divinely wrought upon will not expect, or desire the one, without the other.—Therefore he will not expect or de-sire the blessing of God without obedience: because it is always God's way to connect the comforts of the Holy Ghost with the fear of the Lord; and, if his children transgress his laws, to visit their transgressions with a rod. Therefore he will neither expect nor des're his blessing without exertion: for it has al-ways been God's way to crown only those

that run the race that is set before them, and fight the good fight of faith. Therefore he will not expect, nor desire, the Divine bless-ing without prayer: for it has always been God's way to make his people sensible of their wants, and to give in answer to prayer. Therefore he will not expect nor desire to reach heaven without difficulties: for his people have always had to deny themselves, and take up their cross. If they have not been chosen in the furnace of affliction, they have been purified. God had one Son with-out sin, but he never had one without sorrow: " he scourgeth every son whom he receiv-eth." " Yes," says the suppliant before us, " secure me their everlasting portion, and I am willing to drink of the cup they drank of, and to be baptized with the baptism they were baptized with. I want no new, no by-path to glory. I am content to keep the King's high road. " Be merciful unto me, as thou usest to do unto those that fear thy name—I ask no more."

I conclude by observing, that with regard to some of you this prayer has been answered. You are not able, perhaps, to ascertain pre-cisely how it was at first awakened in your bosom: but it *was* awakened; and made you to differ from others, and from yourselves. From that hour it has been the prevailing pe-tition; nor has it been offered in vain—He has looked upon you, and been merciful unto you, as he useth to do unto those that love his name. Be not afraid to acknowledge it. Be humble, but be grateful; and say, to the praise and glory of his grace, " Thou hast given me the heritage of those that fear thy name."

I hope some of you are beginning to make this prayer your own. The world does not appear to you now as it once did; your con-nexion with it is loosened, and you long to form an alliance with a better. You wish to be companions of them that fear God. And what should hinder you? They will receive you with delight; they are all saying, " Come with us, and we will do you good; for the Lord hath spoken good concerning Israel." " And *I* will receive you, and be a Father unto you, and ye shall be my sons and daugh-ters, saith the Lord Almighty." If he is not with us, he is not far off; for " the Lord is nigh unto them that call upon him, to all that call upon him in truth." But he *is* with you. It is he that has excited the desire you feel; and " He will fulfil the desire of them that fear him: he also will hear their cry, and will save them. Blessed are they that do hunger and thirst after righteousness, for they shall be filled."

But what can we say to those who never yet in earnest made the prayer of David their own! In a little time, you must leave all your possessions and enjoyments, relations and friends, to enter an eternal world, and to stand before the judgment-seat of Christ. Then you will see the value of what you now despise. Then the mercy peculiar to his people will appear the one thing needful. Then the saved of the Lord will shout, "O give thanks unto the Lord, for he is good, for his mercy endureth for ever!" While you will exclaim, O that we had prized that mercy, and sought after it when it was attainable!

Then, alas! it will be too late. But it is not too late at present. You are yet in the land of the living. With the Lord there is mercy; and with him there is plenteous redemption. Be prevailed upon to seek him while he may be found, and to call upon him while he is near.—You will not say, I know not how to seek him. Jesus is the way. Prayer is the breathing of desire. Even words are not necessary to inform Him who searches the heart, and knoweth what is the mind of the spirit. But you are furnished with words. Borrow language that has never been refused; avail yourselves of petitions which have been crowned with infinite success. Pray, with the prodigal, "Father, I have sinned against Heaven, and before thee, and am not worthy to be called thy son; make me as one of thy hired servants." Pray, with the publican, "God be merciful to me a sinner." Pray, with sinking Peter, "Lord, save: I perish." Pray, with the king of Israel, "Be merciful unto me, as thou usest to do unto those that love thy name."

DISCOURSE LXXXIX.

THE WATER OF LIFE.

The water that I shall give him shall be in him a well of water springing up into everlasting life.—John iv. 14.

It is a mark of true wisdom to value objects according to their real worth. It is childish, it is foolish, to be taken with toys and trifles. And yet who has not incurred this reproach? How many things not only invite, but, alas! engross our attention, which are by no means essential, or even important to our welfare! We ought to be ashamed of the impression they make upon us. They are unworthy of our hopes and fears; joys and sorrows: and angels must blush to see what exertions and sacrifices rational and immortal beings make, in order to gain vanity and vexation of spirit.

My dear hearers! many things are desirable, and some things are useful; "*but one thing is needful,*" absolutely needful; needful to every character; needful in every condition and in every period; needful for life and needful for death; needful for time and needful for eternity. It is genuine religion;

it is the grace of God; it is the water of which our text speaks—"The water that I shall give him shall be in him a well of water springing up into everlasting life."

Observe, I. Its DONOR: "*I* shall give him." II. Its RESIDENCE: "It shall be in him." III. Its ACTIVITY: "a well of water springing up." IV. Its TENDENCY: "into everlasting life."

I. And who is THE DONOR? Yonder poor man, who has not where to lay his head; who is relieved by the alms of widows; who is seen weary with his journey, and asking the refreshment of a cup of cold water! And does *He* profess to have the disposal of the blessings of salvation?—Yes; the water that "*I* shall give him."

And it is not profession only. Nothing disgraces a man more than his undertaking what he is unable to accomplish, and promising what he cannot bestow. But our Saviour raises no visionary expectations. He can more than realize every hope he excites. He is mighty to save. He is able to save to the uttermost. He was delivered for our offences, and raised again for our justification. He obtained eternal redemption for us; and, as the reward of his obedience unto death, he was invested with the whole dispensation of the Spirit: "For it pleased the Father that in him should all fulness dwell."

What a complex character is here! How abased, and yet how glorious! How poor, and yet how rich! How dependent, and yet how all-sufficient!—Yes; by him who is now saying to the woman of Samaria, "Give me to drink," are all the regions of heaven peopled! All that are brought into the glorious liberty of the sons of God, acknowledge that he redeemed them. All that are saved, own that in him they have righteousness and strength. All that are replenished, whether living under the Law, or under the Gospel, look to him as the *only* source of their supplies, and exclaim, "Of his fulness have all we received, and grace for grace." And be it remembered, that after all he has communicated he remains the same. For his fulness is not the light of a lamp, which, however large, shines, not far, and is soon extinguished; but the light of the sun, which, after shining for ages, and blessing so many myriads with his beams, shines with undiminished vigour. His fulness is not the resource of a vessel, which, however capacious, will by frequency of application be soon exhausted; but the fulness of a fountain, which, though always running, is always full.

In addition to this sufficiency, we may remark his appointment. He has not only a fulness to relieve all our wants, but he has it for this very purpose. "Having ascended up on high, he received gifts for men, even for the rebellious also." "Him hath God exalted with his right hand, to be a Prince and a Saviour, for to give repentance to Israel, and forgiveness of sins."

We must also notice his disposition. In the gifts which God bestows upon his creatures, he has in view, not only the good of the receiver, but the welfare of others. Our talents, therefore, whatever be their nature or degree, are to be considered as so many obligations to usefulness. For instance—a man has wealth; but of this wealth he is the steward, and not the proprietor: he has it to feed the hungry; to clothe the naked; to instruct the ignorant; to spread the Scriptures; to send forth missionaries: "Charge them that are rich in this world, that they be not highminded, nor trust in uncertain riches, but in the living God, who giveth us richly all things to enjoy; that they do good, that they be rich in good works, ready to distribute, willing to communicate"—But he is selfish and ungenerous: he refuses to give, or he gives with reluctance; while he expends his money in extravagance, or hoards it up in the miser's bag; and thus the wise and kind design of Providence is eluded. But donation falls in with the Saviour's disposition. He is fit to be intrusted with unsearchable riches. He has a heart to give—"his heart is made of tenderness; his bowels melt with love." He is in his element, as well as in his office, while he relieves the distressed. This ability to succour was "the joy set before him:" for this, "he endured the cross, and despised the shame." He was willing that his soul should be made "a sacrifice for sin"—if he could "see the travail of his soul." Accordingly he was assured that his death would not be in vain; that his benevolence should be completely gratified: all nations being blessed in him, and all nations calling him blessed.

And did any, in the days of his flesh, address him in vain? Had one suppliant only been repulsed or sent empty away, the rejection would have been a source of despondency in every age of the world; we should have feared that our case resembled his. But what pretence has any one now to perish in despair; when he says, by his conduct as well as by his word, "Him that cometh unto me, I will in no wise cast out. Whosoever will, let him come, and take of the water of life freely!"

Here then, we see, to whom in all our necessities we are to betake ourselves. It is to Him, who is able, who is appointed, who is willing, who is delighted to supply us. And how much better is it to proclaim such a Source of relief as this, than to lead men to rely upon themselves!—And what, but pride, can make me revolt at such a doctrine? Why should I wish to be my own saviour any more than my own creator? Why am I not satisfied, in grace as well as in nature, to "live and move and have my being," in another?

—Especially in one so dear. It is indeed painful to be under obligation to an enemy, but not to a friend. To one we love, the burden of gratitude is a pleasant load. Saviour Jesus! we love thee above all—to Thee we owe all our salvation, and all our hopes. And we rejoice to think that through eternal ages we shall be bound to serve thee, and exclaim, "Unto him that loved us, and washed us from our sins in his own blood, and hath made us kings and priests unto God and his Father; to him be glory and dominion for ever and ever. Amen."

II. Its RESIDENCE. "The water that I shall give him, *shall be in him*."

The internal principle of religion is not to be opposed to external practice. Some tell us, as they are out of sight, that their hearts are good; though their lives are not quite what they ought to be. But a good heart will be accompanied and evinced by a good life: "a good man, out of the good treasure of his heart, bringeth forth good things." It is in vain to tell us of your experience; and refer us for proofs of your religion to a number of views and feelings beyond our reach —your religion is to be visible; your light is so to shine before men that they may see your good works, and glorify your Father which is in heaven.

Yet, divine things must be known and felt before they can govern us. Christian experience, therefore, precedes Christian practice; and internal principle is essential to real godliness. Without this there will be no course of consistent, unvarying obedience; and if there was, yet there would be no value in it; for the action devoid of the motive is nothing. Here, therefore, God begins: he begins with the heart; and I admire the way he takes to secure holiness and good works. To purify the streams he cleanses the fountain; and to make the fruit good he makes the tree good. You cannot gather grapes from thorns, or figs from thistles: you may, indeed, tie a cluster of grapes, or figs, to a thorn, or a thistle—but they do not look natural there—they do not live there: and both the ligature and the fruit will in time rot off. You may fasten feathers to a wing, and a wing to a bird: but the bird can only fly by wings growing out of his body, and feathers growing out of his wings. Surely a man is never so likely to avoid all sin as when he is mortified to it; or to obey God, as when he delights in his law after the inward man. The religion of some people is all external; and we may arrange them in four classes.

The religion of the first depends on *external occurrences*. It may be compared to a stream produced by a storm, instead of being supplied by a spring. The man is seized with sickness, and is alarmed—he sends for the minister: he prays; he resolves; he promises—but he recovers, and his devotion departs with the danger and the disease. He is poor and afflicted; and he worships God in his family, and he loves to attend the preaching of the word of life;—he succeeds in business, and becomes rich and worldly—and has no time for the one, or relish for the other.

The religion of the second consists in *external performances*. They do a thousand things; but the heart is not in them. They would gladly give up the whole of their irksome task if they could do it with safety. Obedience is not enjoyed as their meat, but taken as their medicine. All their care is to make clean the outside of the cup and of the platter: they have no concern about inward purity; no struggles with innate depravity; no anxiety to have the heart right in the sight of God. But we know who has said, "He is not a Jew, which is one outwardly; neither is that circumcision, which is outward in the flesh: but he is a Jew, which is one inwardly; and circumcision is that of the heart, in the spirit, and not in the letter; whose praise is not of men, but of God."

The religion of the third is found in their *connexions*. They never examine or judge for themselves; but leave their ministers to think for them. Their own knees never bend before God; but they desire the prayers of others. They take shelter under the wing of godly parents, like the Jews, who thought they could not be destroyed because "they had Abraham to their father:" yet we read of one in hell, who said, "*Father, Abraham!*" Religion is a personal thing; and we can no more be saved by the piety of another than we can be nourished or refreshed by another's sleeping or eating.

The religion of the fourth is ALL IN CHRIST. These ridicule the very notion of a work of grace *in* us: to look after any thing *in ourselves*, though not self-derived, is legal and pharisaical. *They* have all in Christ—and so have we; but with this difference—we have all in him so as to seek all *from him*. We believe that when he died all was finished *for* us—and we are now praying that all may be finished *in* us. It is a glorious truth that in him we have sanctification as well as righteousness: but he cannot be our sanctification by suffering us to remain in sin—he is our sanctification, not by being a substitute for our sanctification, but by sanctifying us. Wo to the man who pleads for a religion, of which even Christ is the author, but of which he himself is not the subject! David prays, "Create *in* me a clean heart, O God, and renew a right spirit *within* me." And the promise of the new covenant runs; "A new heart also will I give you, and a new spirit will I put within you; and I will take away the stony heart out of your flesh, and I will give you an heart of flesh. And I will put my Spirit within you, and cause you to walk in my statutes, and ye shall keep my judgments, and do them." If such prayers and promises are to be accomplished, we must look after something *in ourselves*—and, as the apostle enjoins, *examine* not Christ, but ourselves, to know "whether we are in the faith."

III. ITS ACTIVITY. "The water that I shall give him shall be in him *a well of water springing up*." Observe the representations given us of real Christians; mark the design of the Gospel; take any of the graces of the Holy Spirit, or the images of Divine influence: all, all of them will convince you, that genuine religion is something more than notion; that it does not consist in a dormant creed, or a dead confidence; but is a principle, full of life, of energy, and of influence.

How are real Christians represented?—As those whose strength is to sit still?—No: but they are held forth by those whose profession calls for the most strenuous exertion—they are husbandmen; they are reapers; they are warriors; they are racers.

What is the design of the Gospel? These are the words of an infallible Judge: "The grace of God that bringeth salvation hath appeared to all men, teaching us, that, denying ungodliness and worldly lusts, we should live soberly, righteously, and godly, in this present world; looking for that blessed hope, and the glorious appearing of the great God and our Saviour Jesus Christ; who gave himself for us, that he might redeem us from all iniquity, and purify unto himself a peculiar people, zealous of good works."

How are the graces of the Holy Spirit described? What is faith? Is it a conviction that rests in the judgment? It overcomes the world; it purifies the heart. "With the heart man believeth unto righteousness." What is love? We read of the labour of love. What is hope? We read of a lively hope: "we are saved by hope." What is repentance? "Behold this selfsame thing, that ye sorrowed after a godly sort, what carefulness it wrought in you, yea, what clearing of yourselves, yea, what indignation, yea, what fear, yea, what vehement desire, yea, what zeal, yea, what revenge!"

All the images of Divine influence imply the same thing. Sometimes it is compared to leaven, which operates in the meal till the whole mass be leavened. Sometimes it is compared to fire, which penetrates and consumes every thing combustible within its reach. Sometimes it is likened to the force of vegetation; the seed sown is quickened and springs up, first the blade, then the ear, and after that the full corn in the ear.

No wonder, therefore, it is here expressed, not by a pool; not by dead, but living water—the water of a bursting spring: the water that I shall give him shall be in him "a well of water springing up"—into what? "into everlasting life."

IV. We have to observe—Its TENDENCY. It weans us from the world, and constrains us to set our affections on things above. It elevates our thoughts, our desires, and our pursuits, in a manner inconceivable to the groveling sons of time and sense; and enables us, even while our bodies are below, to live with our conversation in heaven.

The difference between grace and glory is not so great as some may imagine. They differ only in degree. The state is the same; the nature is the same. Grace is glory in the bud, and glory is grace in the flower. The one is the child, the other the man : the one the dawn, the other the day. For what is heaven? Is it a condition, in which all worldly distinctions will be done away, and only those remain which resulted from character? The Christian is rising towards it now. "In his eyes a vile person is contemned; but he honoureth them that fear the Lord." Is it a condition in which all the differences which now divide the religious world will be abolished; in which no inquiry will be made *where* we worshipped, but only *how*? He is tending to it now : "Grace be with all them that love our Lord Jesus Christ in sincerity. Whosoever shall do the will of my Father which is in heaven, the same is my mother and sister and brother." Does it consist in perpetual blessing and praise? He is entering it now. "I will bless the Lord at all times, his praise shall continually be in my mouth." Are the glorified happy in being ever with the Lord? He now cries, "O that I knew where I might find him!" As the hart panteth after the water-brooks, so panteth my soul after thee, O God. My soul thirsteth for God, for the living God: when shall I come and appear before God?"

A Christian, therefore, has something of heaven now : he has it in its source; in its elements; in its earnests; in its foretastes. Is he in the temple? He is "made joyful in God's house of prayer:" he "sees his power and glory in the sanctuary." Is he alone? "My soul," says he, "shall be satisfied as with marrow and fatness; and my mouth shall praise thee with joyful lips; when I remember thee upon my bed, and meditate on thee in the night watches." Is he in tribulation? He can "glory in tribulation also, knowing that tribulation worketh patience, and patience experience, and experience hope: for as the sufferings of Christ abound in him, his consolation also aboundeth by Christ." Yes: "We speak that we do know, and testify that we have seen: and that which we have heard and seen declare we unto you, that ye also may have fellowship with us, and truly our fellowship is with the Father and his Son Jesus Christ."

And yet all we possess, all we enjoy, all we experience, all we know, here, is not worthy to be compared with the glory that shall be revealed in us. If a transient visit be so delightful, what will the constant vision be! If it be so satisfactory to behold through a glass darkly, what will it be when we shall see face to face! Ah! says the Christian, grateful yet still aspiring, "In thy presence, there is fulness of joy, and at thy right hand there are pleasures for evermore. I will behold thy face in righteousness: I shall be satisfied when I awake with thy likeness."— And such is the assured blessedness of the Christian; for the tendency of this Divine principle is not liable to frustration. It cannot issue in hell. Grace is nothing, unless it conquers, as well as fights. But,

"Grace will complete what grace begins,
   To save from sorrows, or from sins."

They that believe on Christ, are said to believe on him "to life everlasting." You have often heard how to distinguish between false grace, and true: but of this you may rest assured—that what is Divine will be durable; what comes from heaven will lead to it. "We are made partakers of Christ, if we hold the beginning of our confidence stedfast unto the end." "The water that I shall give him shall be in him a well of water springing up into everlasting life."

We may say reversely the same of sin. There is a connexion between sin and hell. They only differ in degree. In the present experience of the wicked, hell is not only insured, but begun. He is miserable already in the strife between his convictions and his inclinations; in the reproaches of his conscience; in the tyranny of his passions; in the contempt of the wise and good; in the vexations of life; in the fears of death. What he now suffers is sufficient to prove a tendency in sin to produce misery: and the only reason why he is not completely miserable at present, is, because he has now the advantage of diversions; because he lives in a mixed state of things; because he is under a dispensation of forbearance and mercy—but all these preventions will soon give way, and the perfect result of sin will be—read it in the Scripture, and tremble.

May God deliver you from a course, the way of which is hard, and the end of which is death: "that being made free from sin, and become servants unto God, you may have your fruit unto holiness, and the end everlasting life."

DISCOURSE XC.

PETER'S CURIOSITY AND PRESUMPTION.

Simon Peter said unto him, Lord, whither goest thou? Jesus answered him, Whither I go, thou canst not follow me now; but thou

shalt follow me afterwards. Peter said unto him, Lord, why cannot I follow thee now? I will lay down my life for thy sake. Jesus answered him, Wilt thou lay down thy life for my sake? Verily, verily, I say unto thee, The cock shall not crow, till thou hast denied me thrice.—John xiii. 36—38.

No kind of writing is so entertaining, instructive, and useful, as biography; and for this species of composition, there is no book like the Bible. We have, indeed, no complete lives given us; but we have sketches of character, remarkable for their discrimination and effect: we have no full-length and finished portraits, but we have bold outlines and touches, which instantly and powerfully recall the originals.

Here, also, we have no "faultless monsters." When I am reading of a person, and the writer labours to represent him as perfect, I feel more than dissatisfied: I am imposed upon: I have fable given me instead of fact: I feel no moral sympathy with the subject; he does not belong to the order of humanity. In the Scriptures we have men pourtrayed as they were: their defects, as well as excellences, are placed before us; and we see what we have to shun, as well as to pursue.

Peter always appears in the sacred story, like himself. The individuality of his character is supported with wonderful propriety and consistency. We always find him eager, forward, impetuous; always zealous, but his zeal not always according to knowledge; equally rash and affectionate; speaking first and thinking afterward; bold in profession, but failing in execution—yet open to conviction, and deriving profit from his very failings. Observe the words which we have read: "Simon Peter said unto him, Lord, whither goest thou? Jesus answered him, Whither I go, thou canst not follow me now; but thou shalt follow me afterwards. Peter said unto him, Lord, why cannot I follow thee now? I will lay down my life for thy sake. Verily, verily, I say unto thee, The cock shall not crow, till thou hast denied me thrice." These words consist of two parts. In the first, our Saviour checks his CURIOSITY. In the second, he confounds his PRESUMPTION.

I. Simon Peter said unto him, "Lord, whither goest thou?" The question was occasioned by what our Saviour had said in a former part of his discourse: "Little children, yet a little while I am with you. Ye shall seek me: and as I said unto the Jews, Whither I go, ye cannot come; so now I say to you." Though he said many things after this, yet *this* impressed the mind of Peter—he resolved it again—and again; and as soon as our Saviour paused, he suddenly asks, "Lord, whither goest thou?" Now, here is something which, if we cannot commend, we

know not how entirely to censure. It has been said, that the very imperfections of good men are peculiar, and betray their excellences. Here we see Peter's love to his Lord, and concern for his presence. It is always trying to part with a dear relation or friend. Rachel weeps for her children, and refuses to be comforted, because they are not. When Elijah was going to be taken up from the earth, we see how his disciple Elisha followed him from place to place, and would not go back. When Jonathan and David were about to separate, they fell upon each other's neck and wept, until each exceeded. When, at Miletus, "Paul kneeled down and prayed with the brethren, they all wept sore, and fell on his neck, and kissed him; sorrowing most of all for the words which he spake, that they should see his face no more." But think of Christ! What a benefactor, what a master was he! How had he endeared himself to his Disciples—how essential must he have appeared to their happiness and welfare? Could Peter then view his continuance with them, or removal, with indifference?

But if our Saviour blames Peter, Peter was blameworthy; for *He* always judges righteous judgment. Peter was a little too curious—a fault, I fear, by no means uncommon. For how many are there, who are more anxious to know secret things, which belong unto God, than to improve the things revealed, which are for us, and for our children. How much attention has been employed in fruitless inquiries, concerning the Divine decrees, the downfall of antichrist, the future state of heathens, the place of judgment, the employments of the glorified state! We are all fonder of speculation than practice. Whereas, we ought to remember, that this is a world of action rather than science; that things which principally concern us are the most easily found; that in a state where we have so much to do, and so little time to do it in, we should secure ourselves as much as possible from all superfluous engagements. How many diversions, alas! have we already; necessary diversions by sleep; unavoidable diversions by business; accidental diversions by company and occurrences: and shall we add to all these—trifling and needless diversions?

The Bible is not designed to indulge our curiosity, but to be the guide of our faith, and the rule of our life: like the pillar given to the Israelites; which was not intended to amuse them as naturalists, but to conduct them as travellers, through a trackless wilderness, to the land flowing with milk and honey.

Our Saviour, therefore, never encouraged this principle. When a man asked him, "Lord, are there few that shall be saved?" He would not answer the inquiry: yea, he did not even notice the poor empty trifler at all: he said unto *them*, "Strive to enter in at the strait gate: for many, I say unto *you*, shall seek to enter in, and shall not be able." When he had told Peter his duty and destiny, Peter saw John approaching; and asked, "Lord, and what shall this man do?" But our Saviour said, "What if I will that he tarry till I come, what is that to thee? Follow thou me." So here, he shows his judgment of the inquiry by eluding it. But though he does not gratify him, he instructs him. "Jesus answered him, Whither I go, thou canst not follow me now; but thou shalt follow me afterwards." In two senses, Peter was to follow him, in due time—to the *throne*, and to the *cross*: but at present he could follow him as to neither.

First, Peter was to follow him to *glory*. It was what our Lord prayed for, and what he promised. "Father, I will that they whom thou hast given me be with me where I am, that they may behold my glory. Where I am, there shall also my servant be." This is true of all Christians. They are to be for ever with the Lord. He is gone to prepare a place for them. He is their forerunner; their trustee; and has taken possession of heaven in their name. Already he has drawn their hearts after him; and he will by-and-by draw their persons. But for every thing there is a season. He could not follow him now—because, though our Saviour's hour was come, Peter's was not; though the Master had finished the work given him to do, the servant had scarcely begun his—and "we are all immortal till our work is done." Enemies cannot hasten, nor friends retard, our departure, before the time appointed of our heavenly Father. Christians are sometimes impatient, and long to be gone; but this is wrong. "The best frame we can be in," says Henry, "is to be ready to go, and willing to stay:" if God has any thing for us to do, or to suffer, for his sake. We have three good men in the Scripture who wished for death: but they knew not what they said; and are all blamed for it. The eagerness is not only wrong, but useless. What would it avail the husbandman to fret and rave? Would this bring harvest the sooner? There must be months of winter, and weeks of cold; and nights of frost, and days of rain and sunshine. He cannot reap in May, or June: the order of nature forbids it. There is also an order in grace. Why cannot you follow him now? Perhaps you have an aged mother to support. Perhaps you have an infant charge to rear. Perhaps you are destined to give birth to an institution of charity. Perhaps you are to exemplify religion in your temper and practice. Perhaps to recommend the Gospel by your sufferings.—We must run, before we can conquer. We must fight, before we can triumph. What a length of time

are some detained in life after their connexions have fallen off; after disease and infirmity have rendered them unfit for active employment: and they seem to themselves as incumbrances, instead of helps. But there are some reasons for their detention, connected with the glory of God, and their own welfare; though, as to the knowledge of them, we must walk by faith and not by sight.

Secondly. Peter was to follow him to the *cross*. He was to suffer for him, and like him—he was to die the same kind of death—"When thou shalt be old, thou shalt stretch forth thy hands, and another shall gird thee, and carry thee whither thou wouldest not. This spake he, signifying by what death he should glorify God." But he could not follow him now, because he had not sufficient faith and resolution to suffer. The Saviour, therefore, forbears to call him to a task for which he was inadequate. This is very instructive. It shows us that our Lord's dealings with his people are founded not only in kindness, but in wisdom and prudence. He adapts the burden to the shoulder, or fits the shoulder to the burden; he smooths the road, or prepares the foot—so is the promise; "Thy shoes shall be iron and brass; and as thy day, so shall thy strength be." Some of you can look back and remember how you dreaded such and such trials. You thought, that if they should befall you *then*, you must sink under them—and so you would. But he gradually prepared you for them; and when they actually came, your mind was in a different state—you had other views and feelings—your faith was more strong, and your hope more lively. Gideon, while threshing in the barn, had not, and did not want, the degree of prowess which was necessary when he took the sword, and placed himself at the head of the army; but when, in obedience to the Divine will, he entered the field, the Spirit of the Lord came upon him. It does not become you to cast down your souls by imagining future difficulties, and comparing them with your present strength. You should not say, "O, if I was called to prison, or a fiery stake, how could I endure!" See that you are the Lord's servant: endeavour to hold yourself at his disposal; attend willingly to the duty of the day; and leave the morrow with him. Cast thy burden upon the Lord, and he shall sustain thee; he will never suffer the righteous to be moved. Sufficient for the day is the evil thereof—and what is better, sufficient for it too will be the grace. This was our Saviour's meaning; and Peter understood by his following him—his following him to suffer. He, therefore, said unto him, "'Lord, why cannot I follow thee now?' I do not want courage or zeal: Lord, 'I will lay down my life for thy sake'—and what can I do more?"

II. "Jesus answered him," with a countenance and voice more expressive of pity than severity—"'Wilt thou lay down thy life for my sake?' Ah, Peter, this is sooner said than done. Life is not so easily parted with. You trembled upon the water, and beginning to sink, you cried out, 'Lord, save, I perish.'—Be not so confident now—'Verily, verily, I say unto you, the cock shall not crow, till thou hast denied me thrice.'" Let us remark the sin; and derive some reflections from the melancholy statement.

First. The crime was heinous. To deny his Master was unfaithfulness: to deny his Friend was perfidy: to deny his Benefactor was ingratitude: to deny his Redeemer was impiety. It was, for the time, to break off all connexion with him; it was saying, I neither wish to serve him, nor to be saved by him. I know him not, nor wish to know him—"Away with him—Crucify him."

This, too, was the conduct of one who had been called from a low condition in life to the high honour of apostleship—of one who had seen his miracles—of one who was with him in the Transfiguration, and in Jairus's chamber, when he raised the dead—of one who had confessed him, and said, "To whom shall we go? Thou hast the words of eternal life: and we believe and are sure that thou art Christ the Son of the living God." Three aggravations are here mentioned. First, he was warned and admonished—he could not plead ignorance. Secondly, the sin was immediately committed. Things soon wear off from the mind; but here was no time for forgetfulness—the voice of the Saviour had hardly left his ear—his own resolution had scarcely dropped from his lips—he had said, "I will *never* be offended," and was offended *that very night:* "The cock shall not crow, till thou hast denied me *thrice*"—which is the last aggravation—here is repetition. A man may be surprised and overtaken in a fault; but the moment after, reflection may return; and he may wonder, and shudder, and flee. But Peter, after his first offence, feels nothing—he renews it again—and even again—yea, and each time he waxes worse and worse, till a lie ends in an oath—and an oath in a cursing!

From this affecting statement let us, Secondly, derive some profitable remarks.

And, first: behold the foreknowledge of our Saviour. Whoever attentively reads the four Gospels must perceive that there was always something to relieve his humiliation, and to convince us that his abasement was not original, and constrained; but assumed and voluntary: that "he made himself of no reputation; and for our sakes became poor." The soldiers in the garden apprehended him, and led him away; but not till they went backward and fell to the ground, in consequence of his presenting himself, and saying,

"I am He!" He was now to be disowned and forsaken; but he proves that he was able to read the heart, and to foresee certainly and minutely what would happen, contrary to every degree of probability. For what appearance was there that Peter would deny him—deny him just three times—and three times that very night—and that very night before the cock crew—and with the most profane language? Of all the apostles, he seemed the most determined—the least likely to yield to fear—and had at this very time engaged to die with him, rather than disown him—when, lo! at the very moment of giving this assurance of his attachment and fidelity, Jesus declares, that in two or three hours, he would falsify every thing he had said and thought! This was a proof that he "needed not that any should testify of man, for he knew what was in man."

This foreknowledge, however, does not justify or extenuate Peter's sin. Peter was perfectly free and voluntary in what he did. Foreknowledge supposes, not renders things certain: it does not compel men to sin: their sins are committed not because they are foreknown, or foretold; but they are foreknown and foretold because they will be committed.

Secondly. What reason have we to exclaim, with David, "Lord, what is man!" Survey him under the greatest advantages and obligations. Look—not at *heathens*, but at *Jews*—a people distinguished and indulged above all the families of the earth. Look—not at *Jews*, but at *Christians*, with all the privileges of the *Jews* increased and perfected. Look—not at those who are only Christians *in name*, and live under the dispensations of the Gospel; but at those who are "*partakers of the grace of God in truth*." Look at these—not only as chargeable with *infirmities;* with drowsiness of attention, or wandering thoughts in divine things; but overcome with temptation, and betrayed into the *grossest guilt*—and no longer wonder that a man after God's own heart should pray, "Keep back thy servant also from presumptuous sins: let them not have dominion over me." No longer wonder that our Saviour should say, even to his disciples, "Take heed to yourselves, lest at any time your hearts be overcharged with surfeiting and drunkenness, and cares of this life, and so that day come upon you unawares." There is nothing too vile for us to fall into, if we are left of Him who alone can keep us from falling.

Thirdly. We see how little we are acquainted with ourselves. When Peter said, "I will lay down my life for thy sake," he spoke according to his feelings. But sincerity is not constancy. There is a goodness, compared to the morning cloud and early dew, that soon passeth away. Peter did not consider the difference between an impulse and a principle; between an hour of ease and a moment of trial. We are now in health; but we know not how it would be with us if we were removed to a climate much warmer, or colder, than our own: and we know less of ourselves morally than physically. There are excellences which we may presume upon our possessing, only because we have never been called to display them. There are provocations with which we have never been tried, the effect of which would render us a wonder to ourselves. Events increase our self-acquaintance, by showing us what there is in the heart: as the waves cast up mire and dirt in the pool that was clear, because calm, before. Hazael's case is a strong one; but it will apply, in various degrees, to ourselves. He was shocked at the prophet's representation of himself when he should become a king—and exclaimed, "Is thy servant a dog, that he should do this thing?" And yet, as an old writer says, the dog did it. God only knows how much of our innocency has been owing to principle, or the absence of temptation; or what we should have been in conditions the reverse of those which have sheltered our weakness.

But, Fourthly. Here is the grand lesson you and I have to learn—That the most confident are the most exposed; and the most humble the most safe. "When I am weak, then am I strong." Why? Because the deep consciousness of my weakness will induce me to shun scenes of temptation; keep me from aspiring after high and responsible stations; and to pray, without ceasing, "Hold thou me up, and I shall be safe."

No: we do not wonder at this strange and sad revolution in Peter. He is proud and self-sufficient. He places himself above his brethren, and considers himself as much less likely to fall than they—"Though all should be offended because of thee, yet will I never be offended." He talks away about sacrificing his life—without one word like this: "By thy grace helping me: for without thee I can do nothing." A Pharisee could hardly have held more vainglorious language.—Is it any marvel, then, that he should be permitted to learn, by bitter experience, that he was nothing, and could do nothing, without that Holy Spirit whose influences he had forgotten to acknowledge? "Pride goes before destruction, and a haughty spirit before a fall." I never saw a professor of religion full of confidence in himself, and speaking censoriously of others, but who fell into some gross crime, or into some great calamity. "Be not highminded, but fear. Blessed is the man that feareth always." Let us sing the words of our incomparable Cowper:

"To keep the lamp alive,
　With oil we fill the bowl;
'Tis water makes the willow thrive,
　And grace that feeds the soul.

"The Lord's unsparing hand
　Supplies the living stream;
It is not at our own command,
　But still derived from Him.

"Beware of Peter's word,
　Nor confidently say,
'I never will deny thee, Lord,'
　But—'Grant I never may.'

"Man's wisdom is to seek
　His strength in God alone;
And ev'n an angel would be weak
　Who trusted in his own.

"Retreat beneath his wings,
　And in his grace confide;
This more exalts the King of kings
　Than all your works beside.

"In Jesus is our store:
　Grace issues from his throne;
Whoever says, 'I want no more,'
　Confesses he has none."

DISCOURSE XCI.

THE THORN IN THE FLESH.

And lest I should be exalted above measure through the abundance of the revelations, there was given to me a thorn in the flesh, the messenger of Satan to buffet me, lest I should be exalted above measure. For this thing I besought the Lord thrice, that it might depart from me. And he said unto me, My grace is sufficient for thee.—2 Cor. xii. 7—9.

Where the subject is himself, it is a delicate and a difficult thing for a man to speak properly. And, whether it be from constitutional reserve, or a fear of hypocrisy, or a sense of unworthiness and imperfections, it is certain, that those who feel most, and do most, in religion, generally talk the least about it. It is the shallow stream that cannot flow; it is the empty vessel that cannot be—touched without telling it.

Yet a reference to a person's own history and experience is sometimes not only allowable, but commendable and useful; and a man of talent and real godliness, and whose character is placed above suspicion, is often peculiarly interesting and edifying when he speaks of things concerning himself. Such a man was Paul; and the narrative he here gives us has relieved the minds, and called forth the gratitude of millions. It contains,

I. His DANGER. II. His PRESERVATION. III. His PRAYER. IV. His SUCCESS.

I. His DANGER. "Lest I should be exalted above measure by the abundance of the revelations." By "the abundance of the revelations," he refers to some extraordinary discoveries with which God had favoured him; and particularly a trance, recorded in the preceding verses: "It is not expedient for me doubtless to glory. I will come to visions and revelations of the Lord. I knew a man in Christ above fourteen years ago, (whether in the body, I cannot tell; or whether out of the body, I cannot tell: God knoweth;) such an one caught up to the third heaven. And I knew such a man, (whether in the body or out of the body, I cannot tell: God knoweth ;) how that he was caught up into paradise, and heard unspeakable words, which it is not lawful for a man to utter." On the nature and circumstances of this transaction I am not called to enlarge. I shall only remark what is necessary to our immediate purpose. It is the modesty and diffidence of the Apostle, who had concealed this privilege for more than fourteen years. How unlike him are those who sound a trumpet before them, to awaken attention to all their religious movements! who are forward to publish to the world accounts of their conversion and deliverances, depressions, and raptures—Not that it is improper to take notice of any of God's dealings with us: "Whoso is wise, and will observe these things, even they shall understand the lovingkindness of the Lord." But while we remark these things for our own profit we need not plague the public, or suppose that every body must feel interested in our concerns. Had many been indulged like Paul, they would not have contained themselves for a single day, but have announced in every company, and probably in print, that they had been in the third heaven, and heard unspeakable words! But, it is likely, Paul would never have divulged this distinction unless he had been compelled by his enemies, in vindication of his office; and when he *does* mention it he frankly acknowledges that it nearly proved too much for him —I was in danger, says he, of being "exalted above measure."

That is, First. He was in danger of being raised too high for the usefulness as a minister. A minister is to have compassion on the ignorant; to comfort the feebleminded; to sympathize with the afflicted; and to speak a word in season to him that is weary—He is to enter into all the circumstances, and melt into all the feelings of his people. Now there are things which, instead of preparing him for this accommodation, may disqualify him. He may be raised above it. That which promises the preacher usefulness, by adapting him to the state of his hearers, is not something peculiar to himself, but that which he experiences in common with them. Paul was growing too wise; he was in danger, so to speak, of shooting over the people's heads. He had to do with poor mortals upon earth—What was the language of paradise to them; It could only make them stare, or exclaim, "How fine, how wonderful a preacher! Why, no one can understand him!" But when he spake to them of thorns, and afflictions, and prayer, and sustaining grace, he was on their level; and they could apprehend and feel him.

Secondly. He was in danger of being elevated too high for his present condition as a Christian. When Peter saw Moses and Elias in glory, and our Saviour transfigured before them, he exclaimed, " Master, it is good for us to be here; let us make three tabernacles, one for thee, one for Moses, and one for Elias."—He wished to abide there: but, says the Holy Ghost, he "knew not what he said." For, admitting his wish had been indulged, what would have become of his wife and family? Peter, in his transport, had forgotten these. But these may be forgotten too soon—these must not be forgotten at all. As the Saviour does not pray that his followers, before the appointed hour, should be taken out of the world by death, so neither does he improperly draw them out of it by religion. It is their allotted residence for a season; and many relative and civil claims demand a subordinate share of their attention. He could so indulge his people, that their manifestations and joys would unhinge them from earth, take all interest out of their present connexions, and render them listless to all the duties of their stations and callings. But he is a God of judgment; and fits us for the way, as well as the end.

Thirdly. He was in danger of rising too high in his own estimation, as a favourite of Heaven. Christians, while here, are sanctified but in part. They are not like the Holy One of God, or whom it is said, "The prince of this world came, and found nothing in him." He met with nothing inflammable in him, and therefore he could kindle none of his unhallowed fires; there were no evil appetites and passions, for temptation to operate upon. But it is otherwise with us. Owing to the sin that dwelleth in us, we are in danger from every thing around us; and therefore must walk circumspectly, and watch and pray lest we enter into temptation. There are dangers in our dress; and dangers in our table; and dangers in our friends; and dangers in our children. Things innocent in themselves may become injurious; things even good in themselves may become evil. Knowledge may puff up: our enlargements in duty, and even our attainments in religion, may—through our remaining corruption—gender, or at least feed, self-sufficiency and highmindedness.

Do you wonder at *your* danger? See Paul himself in hazard, from the influence of vanity and pride. Even he was beginning to rise and swell, from the distinguishing honours that had been shown him. "Why this is a very astonishing privilege—Who was ever caught up into heaven, while on earth? This is really placing me above the prophets; yea, above Moses himself. He spake with God, it is said, face to face; but he was never admitted into the third heaven. The glorious prerogative belongs to me only." No creature, perhaps, discovered in him such a tendency towards self-exaltation; and Paul himself was probably unconscious of his danger. But it was his mercy that he had one to watch over him who discerned his exposure in time; and employed means,

II. For HIS PRESERVATION, which we proceed to consider. "There was given to me a thorn in the flesh, the messenger of Satan to buffet me, lest I should be exalted above measure." This thorn has exceedingly perplexed expositors; and they knew not, after all their conjectures, what to do with it. It would be a waste of your time, to attempt to determine what is among the secrets of the Almighty; and which, if discovered, would be of no importance. We even admire the wisdom that has left it in uncertainty. If you knew what it exclusively was, those of you who are in affliction, but not afflicted in the same thing, would be ready to say, "Ah! Paul never knew my heart's bitterness—He never had my thorn!" But now, none of you can say this; for you are ignorant of what it was. Let then a Baxter, who for thirty years endured the stone, imagine that it was his torment; let a Watts, moving in weakness, and in fear, and in much trembling, conclude that it was a nervous malady; let a third infer, that it was a slanderer; a fourth, a trying companion; and so of the rest.—If such a supposition tends to soothe the mind under irritation, and leads the sufferer to believe that it is sent to "keep man from his purpose, and to hide pride from man;" the supposition can never be improper. Thus the Scripture teaches us, by what it conceals, as well as by what it discovers; and our ignorance, as well as our knowledge, is rendered useful.

All we learn is, That this thorn in the flesh was some sharp and piercing affliction; in which the enemy of souls had a peculiar influence: for it was "the messenger of Satan to buffet him." And to buffet him was all his aim. But his intention was overruled; and the curse turned into a blessing. Thus the leech adheres to the flesh, and fills himself with blood, and looks no further: but the hand of the Faculty guides it to the place of contact, and the relief of the patient is the consequence. Thus we have seen men in a boat, looking one way, and rowing another. Thus all creatures are in the Lord's hand, and under his control: he gave Joseph favour in the sight of the jailer; brought Elijah food by ravens; and sent Paul safety by Satan himself!

But you will observe, that Paul does not say, "There was given me a thorn in the flesh, the messenger of Satan to buffet me, because I was exalted above measure," but "lest I should be." I wish you to remark this, in order to see, that affliction is designed to prevent, as well as to recover. This is a case of great importance in the experience of Christians. You say, perhaps, "After the most faithful examination of myself, I am not able to discover any duty that I have knowingly neglected; any sin that I have indulged in the practice of; any idol that I have adored." But God saw the future in the present: and the effect in the cause. No: you had not adored such a creature—but he saw that your admiration would soon have become idolatry, and that you were ready to kneel. No: you were not vain and worldly—but he saw a train of prosperous circumstances had commenced, which would flatter you into self-importance, and make you forget that this is not your rest.

He therefore determined to prevent the evil; and it is commonly said, Prevention is better than cure; and it is truly said, and never so truly—as with regard to sin. Let us take, for instance, Joseph and David, with respect to adultery. Joseph was preserved, and David was restored. But observe the difference. The one was useful, as an example, to excite and encourage; the other hardened and justified the ungodly, turned religion into a jeer, and "caused the enemies of the Lord to blaspheme." The one retained his peace of mind; the other was torn with anguish, and his sin was ever before him. The one was crowned with glory and honour, the other, in his reputation, suffered a dreadful eclipse. A blot and a dishonour did he get, and his reproach shall not be wiped away. Take Hezekiah and Paul, with regard to pride. Hezekiah was lifted up; and when he humbled himself he was forgiven: but this did not repair the many sad effects of his ambition—for "wrath came upon him and upon all Judah." But Paul was taken earlier; the God of his mercy prevented him—or who can imagine what consequences might have resulted from sin in such a character, both with regard to himself, the church, and the world!

Ah! said David, when he had been hindered from effecting a purpose of revenge; "Blessed be the Lord God of Israel, which sent thee this day to meet me: and blessed be thy advice, and blessed be thou, which hast kept me this day from coming to shed blood, and from avenging myself with mine own hand." Who is not under obligation to praise God for the same preventing goodness! One ought to say, "Blessed be God for that event, which took me out of a situation in which I now see I should have been corrupted and destroyed." Another ought to say, "Blessed be God, for that breach of friendship; it saved me from a pleasing, but irreligious companion, who would have undermined my principles." Another ought to say, "Blessed be God for such a brotherly reproof: it seems severe, and many a tear it cost me; but it checked me on the very brink of ruin." Another ought to say, "Blessed be God, I should have made flesh my arm, and gold my hope, but disappointment has turned my eye upward, and 'now, Lord, what wait I for, my hope is in thee?'"

III. How was he employed under this trying dispensation? HE GAVE HIMSELF UNTO PRAYER. "For this thing I besought the Lord thrice, that it might depart from me."

Prayer is the refuge of the afflicted. It is, therefore, recommended by Infinite Wisdom and Goodness. "Is any afflicted? let him pray." Prayer cannot be offered in vain; for, says the promise, "Call upon me in the day of trouble, and I will deliver thee." Yea, the very exercise of prayer, as well as the answer, brings succour. There is some relief even in tears. You have heard of the luxury of weeping. It is soothing, in distress, to pour our tears into the bosom of a friend, who, rejoicing when we rejoiced, will now weep when we weep. But oh! to turn aside, as Job did, and say, "Mine eye poureth out tears unto God!" To tell *Him* all that distresses us, and all that alarms, with a confidence in his compassion and sympathy and power and wisdom, all of which are infinite! Here is an asylum, from which no enemy can cut us off; here is a sanctuary, that no evil can invade; here the repose of the grave, and of glory, begins—here "the wicked cease from troubling," and here "the weary are at rest." I do not wonder that David should say, "It is good for me to draw nigh to God;" or that Hannah, when she had poured out her soul before God, should go her way and eat and drink, and her countenance be no more sad.

Prayer was the effect of Paul's suffering. Is it the result of yours? How does your affliction operate? Does it make you a suppliant, or a fury? Does it lead you to quarrel with instruments, or to commit your cause unto God? It is by their influence you are to know whether your afflictions are sanctified. If they lead you to the throne of grace; if you can say,

"Trials make the promise sweet:
Trials give new life to prayer;
Trials bring me to his feet;
Lay me low—and keep me there,"

then the thorns have done something for you; and will do more.

A man under sanctified affliction, will not pray carelessly, but "continue *instant* in prayer." He will say, with Jacob, "I will not let thee go, except thou bless me." Thus Paul besought the Lord *thrice*. Our Saviour, "in his agony, prayed most earnestly; he kneeled down and prayed three times, saying the same words." But I do not understand the expression of our apostle numerically: it imports, that he prayed fervently and frequently. But was this necessary? Is not the God he addressed "a God hearing prayer? Merciful and gracious? A very present help in

trouble?" The case is this: The prayer of faith is always immediately heard, but not always immediately answered. The reason is, not that he is wanting in kindness, but, that he exercises his kindness wisely: he is a God of judgment, and therefore he waits that he may be gracious unto us. He will take away all hope in ourselves and in creatures. He will make us sensible of the value of the blessing; and prepare us to sing aloud of his mercy when it comes. We are like children; we wish to gather the fruit while it is yet unripe; that is, before it has acquired the fine complexion and the rich flavour, and while the use of it is even dangerous. But he pulls back our impatient hand; he is resolved that it shall ripen before it is eaten. Nor will he yield for our crying.

The time of delay is often peculiarly trying. When he seems to shut out our prayer; when we stand at the door and knock, and hear nothing like an opening, especially if the weather be foul too; there is danger of our withdrawing, with the complaint of the unbelieving nobleman, "Why should I wait for the Lord any longer?" But "he that believeth, maketh not haste." He will check his murmuring and his despondency, by reflecting, that God is a sovereign upon whom he has no claims; that his own time of acting must be infinitely the most proper; and, above all, that he cannot seek him in vain. For "the vision is but for an appointed time; in the end it will speak," and its contents will be more than satisfactory. Thus Paul at length obtained,

IV. AN ANSWER. "And He said unto me, My grace is sufficient for thee." Observe two things.

First. The answer does not apparently correspond with the petition. Paul prayed to have the thorn removed: to this, God says nothing; but assures him of something equally good; yea, unspeakably better. Let us not overlook this circumstance. With regard to temporal things we cannot be too general in our prayers, or refer ourselves too much to the pleasure of God. We can hardly with safety say more than this—"O Lord, grant me such a deliverance, or such an indulgence, if it be good for me; but, if not, favour me with a denial. Not my will, but thine be done." For our prayers, like ourselves, are imperfect: nature sometimes speaks, without our being aware of it, in the tone of grace; and we are really pleading only for our pride, or impatience, or unbelief. We know not what to pray for as we ought: but the Lord knows what to give; and he gives, perfectly acquainted with the case, in all its bearings, and in all its consequences; and with a love towards us that passeth knowledge. Hence he sometimes denies a request entirely; at other times he separates the good from the evil, and grants us a part;

while frequently he answers by way of exchange. If a child was to ask of a father a fish, and he should give him a serpent, we should be shocked at the deed. But suppose the child, by reason of his ignorance, should ask for a serpent instead of a fish: we should then admire the father, if he refused what he asked, and gave him what he did not ask. We applaud not only the judgment, but the kindness of the parent, who, in the education of his son, regulates his conduct, not by his *wishes*, but by his *wants*. He may *wish* for holidays, while he *wants* schooling; he may *wish* for delicacies, while he *wants* medicine. Our heavenly Father always gives according to what we *ought* to ask;—and according to what we *should* ask,—if we had the same views with himself, and the same regard for our welfare—for our welfare governs all his dealings with us.

Secondly. The answer is yet blessed and glorious. "My grace is sufficient for thee!" —not *thy* grace, but *mine :* not that which thou hast in thy possession, but that which I have in my keeping, and will seasonably communicate, in the supply of the Spirit of Jesus Christ. Nothing in thyself, I will be always near; always within call; always within reach. "My grace is *sufficient* for thee." Sufficient for what? Write all thy wants underneath. Sufficient for what!

Sufficient for thy *work ;* which often discourages thee, and is enough to discourage thee, if it is to be performed in thine own strength. But it is not. "As thy day, so shall thy strength be. My strength shall be made perfect in thy weakness." Sufficient for what? Sufficient for thy *warfare ;* which often alarms thee, and is enough to alarm thee, if thine enemies only are seen. But look at me. "More are they that are for thee, than they that are against thee."— "Greater is he that is in thee than he that is in the world." Sufficient for what?

Sufficient for thy *affliction ;* which often depresses thee, and is enough to depress thee, if thou art to struggle with it alone. But thou art not to be alone. "When thou passest through the waters, I will be with thee; and through the rivers, they shall not overflow thee ; when thou walkest through the fire, thou shalt not be burnt, neither shall the flame kindle upon thee."

This was Paul's case. I will not remove the thorn in the flesh, says the Saviour—but while suffering—my grace shall be sufficient for thee. Whatever therefore, Christian, be your affliction, remember, here is your sufficiency ; and be persuaded, that this grace is sufficient for two purposes, which you should be more concerned to have accomplished than to have your thorns extracted. It is sufficient, First, to sanctify your afflictions : so that though "no chastening for the present seemeth to be joyous, but grievous; never-

theless, afterward it yieldeth the peaceable fruit of righteousness unto them which are exercised thereby." Secondly, it is sufficient —to render them supportable. What am I saying? I have marked the effect too low— It is sufficient to enable you to "glory in tribulation also." "Yes," says the Church, "having nothing, and yet possessing all things."—"Although the fig tree shall not blossom neither shall fruit be in the vines; the labour of the olive shall fail, and the fields shall yield no meat ; the flock shall be cut off from the fold, and there shall be no herd in the stalls: yet I will rejoice in the Lord, I will joy in the God of my salvation." And what says the experience of some of you, my fellow Christians? Have you not, when they arrived, borne with patience, with cheerfulness, with peace, with joy—trials which, in the prospect, made you tremble ! Spilsbury was a sufferer for conscience' sake. He had been once imprisoned, and released; and when apprehended a second time, he said—as they were conveying him away— his wife and children weeping around him; "Weep not for me ; I am not afraid to go to prison now, for I found God there the first time." Ah! says many a sufferer, awaking from despondency, in a situation where he thought no ray of heaven could enter, "Surely God is in this place, and I knew it not!" The people of the world often wonder that Christians are not only patient, but blessed in those circumstances which make *them* turbulent and miserable—as Isaiah finely expresses it, "like a wild bull in a net." The reason is this. They can see their losses and sufferings, but not their supports and consolations. Did they see all—did they see how *underneath were the everlasting arms ;* they would not wonder that they do not sink. Did they see how they are fed with the hidden manna, they would not wonder that they do not faint. Did they see how, in the mud-walled cottage, and lying on the half-straw bed of languishing, the kingdom of God was within them ; they would not wonder that they can "rejoice with joy unspeakable and full of glory !" But many know nothing of the blessedness of this promise; and even those who are the heirs of it know but very little.

With one reflection we conclude ; and it is a necessary application of the whole subject. To what purpose should I have proved that this grace was sufficient for Paul, and for all the people of God, since—sufficient for their work, their warfare, and their trials,—if it be not, my dear hearers, sufficient for *you ?* But it is. There is the same fulness and efficacy in it as ever; and what it has done, it can do.

But you say, Is it attainable? It is.

By whom! Every one that feels his need and implores it. "For EVERY ONE that asketh receiveth: and he that seeketh findeth: and to him that knocketh, it shall be opened."

DISCOURSE XCII.

THE REGULATION OF THE TONGUE.

Set a watch, O Lord, before my mouth; keep the door of my lips.—Psalm cxli. 3.

PRAYER is not only a duty, but the manner in which it is commanded shows it to be a duty of universal obligation. " Continue instant in prayer. Pray without ceasing. In every thing, by prayer and supplication, with thanksgivings, let your requests be made known unto God."

With these demands, the experience of a man attentive to his spiritual welfare harmonizes. He knows, he feels prayer to be always seasonable; always necessary. There is much to employ him at the throne of grace with regard to *others;* for, in his intercourse with God he does not forget the world, the nation, the church, the family; his friends, or even his foes. But when he considers *himself;* and reflects on the grace that is needful to preserve him in prosperity; to support him in adversity; to renew his heart; to govern his life; and to regulate his tongue—no wonder he says with David—"But I give myself unto prayer."

"Set a watch, O Lord, before my mouth; keep the door of my lips." These words remind us of four things—Importance—Danger—Inability—Application. A man would not use such language as this unless he was convinced—I. OF THE IMPORTANCE OF THE SUBJECT: II. THE DANGER HE IS IN OF TRANSGRESSION: III. HIS INABILITY TO PRESERVE HIMSELF: IV. THE WISDOM OF APPLYING TO GOD FOR ASSISTANCE. Let us examine and exemplify each of these four convictions.

I. A man would never use this language, without a conviction of THE IMPORTANCE OF THE SUBJECT. This conviction, I fear, does not very generally prevail. The use of speech is seldom considered morally. Unless on some very particular occasions, people imagine, that it is perfectly optional with them, what they speak, and how they speak, —saying, with those in the time of David, " Our lips are our own, who is Lord over us?" Hence numberless words are daily uttered with indifference, and never thought of again; and if ever people confess, or pray, speech never makes an article either in their confessions or prayers.

Such is the common sentiment. And, to crush it at once; to inspire you with a holy dread; to bring you upon your knees with this supplication, " Set a watch, O Lord, before my mouth; keep the door of my lips;" —let me lead you to a few passages of Scripture—a book to which you all professedly appeal. Let us consult the apostle James; he seems more than any other of the sacred writers to have enlarged upon the subject. There are many declarations in his epistles which you would do well to read, at least once a week, before you leave your retirement.

For instance, " If a man among you seem to be religious, and brideth not his tongue, but deceiveth his own heart, this man's religion is vain."

> " Religion ! what treasure untold
> Resides in that heavenly word !
> More precious than silver and gold,
> And all that this earth can afford."

Religion ! It is profitable unto all things; having promise of the life that now is, and of that which is to come. Without it, we have no hope beyond the grave, no comfort in death, no solace in affliction, no God with us in the world. But the careless use of the tongue annihilates all title to the possession, and stamps the man who assumes the profession, as a self-deluder. What a charge ! What a decision ! How many thousands does this righteous sentence unchristian and condemn ! " If any man among you seem to be religious, and brideth not his tongue, but deceiveth his own heart, this man's religion is vain."

Again; the same writer tells us, " If any man offend not in word, the same is a perfect man, and able also to bridle the whole body." A Christian, it seems, should not be stationary, but advancing. It is his duty and privilege to " grow in grace, and in the knowledge of our Lord and Saviour." And what is the consequence of this progression? What is the evidence? There is not a better test than the government of the tongue. There is nothing that implies a higher degree of wisdom and goodness; of self-attention; of the power and prevalence of holy principles. Such a man may be consulted in any enterprizes; he may be entrusted with any secret; he may be left in any trying situation; he will betray no friendship; he will punish no confidence: the very discipline and grace he must have exercised before he could have reached his present attainment are securities for every future duty, and pledges of every future excellency. Whoever has accomplished this victory need despair of no other; and it is not a figure of speech, but the language of truth and soberness—" If any man offend not in word, the same is a perfect man, and able also to bridle the whole body."

Again; says the inspired author, " Behold, we put bits in the horses' mouths, that they may obey us: and we turn about their whole body." Do you perceive the force of the image? He who has not the government of his tongue, is like a person riding a horse without a bridle—the consequence of which, especially if the beast be spirited and fierce, may be easily conjectured.—" Behold also the ships, which though they be so great, and are driven of fierce winds, yet are they turned about with a very small helm, whithersoever the governor listeth." Do you see the force of the comparison? The man that has not the control of his tongue is like a passenger on board a vessel without a rudder, rolling as the waves direct, and in constant peril of shipwreck. " Even so the tongue is a little member, and boasteth great things. Behold, how great a matter a little fire kindleth! And the tongue is a fire, a world of iniquity: so is the tongue among our members, that it defileth the whole body, and setteth on fire the course of nature : and it is set on fire of hell." As if he should say, Every thing is transacted by speech, in natural, civil, and religious concerns —how much, therefore, depends on the good or evil management of the tongue! What an ardour of holy love and friendship, or of anger and malice, may a few words fan into a flame! The tongue is the principal instrument in the cause of God : and it is the chief engine of the devil—give him this, and he asks no more—there is no mischief or misery he will not accomplish by it. The use, the influence of it, therefore, is inexpressible; and words are never to be considered only as *effects*, but as *causes*; the operation of which can never be fully imagined. Let us suppose a case ; a case, I fear, but too common. You drop, in the thoughtlessness of conversation, or for the sake of argument, or wit, some irreligious, sceptical expression—it lodges in the memory of a child, or a servant—it takes root in a soil favourable to such seed—it gradually springs up, and brings forth fruit, in the profanation of the sabbath.; the neglect of the means of grace ; in the reading of improper books ; in the choice of dangerous companions ;—Who can tell where it will end? But there is a Being who knows where it began. It will be acknowledged that some have it in their power, by reason of their office, talents, and influence, to do much more injury than others; but none are so insignificant as to be harmless.

But I must lead you from the servant to the master. Hear the language of the faithful and true Witness, and who knows the nature of the judgment, because he will be the Judge : " I say unto you, that every idle word that men shall speak, they shall give account thereof in the day of judgment. For by thy words thou shalt be justified, and by thy words thou shalt be condemned." Did you ever hear this before, and do you believe it now? What! are not only your actions, but your words—every idle word—recorded in the book of God's remembrance, to be called forth before the whole world, as evidences of your character, and of the righteousness of the sentence to be passed upon you? This surely is sufficient to convince you of the importance of the subject, and to induce you to cry, " Set a watch, O Lord, before my mouth ; keep the door of my lips."

II. A man would never use this language without a conviction that HE IS IN DANGER OF TRANSGRESSION. And if David was conscious of a liableness to err, shall we ever presume on our safety?

Our danger arises from the depravity of our nature. " The heart is deceitful above all things, and desperately wicked ; and who can bring a clean thing out of an unclean?" The stream will always resemble the fountain.

Our danger arises from the contagion of example. There is nothing in which mankind are more universally culpable than in the disorders of speech. Yet with these we are constantly surrounded ; and to these we have been accustomed from our impressible infancy.

We are in danger from the frequency of speech. " In the multitude of words there wanteth not sin." We must of necessity speak often : but we often speak without necessity. Duty calls us to intermingle much with our fellow-creatures; but we are too little in the closet, and too much in the crowd —and when we are in company we forget the admonition—" Let every man be swift to hear, and slow to speak."

We are in danger from the extent of our obligation. The laws of speech are so numerous and various, that it must be difficult indeed, not to neglect or violate some of them. Observe these laws.

There is the law of *prudence*. This condemns silliness and folly—for no one has a license to talk nonsense. This condemns all that is impertinent, and unsuited to the place, the company, and the season: " A wise man's heart discerneth both time and judgment. A word fitly spoken, O how good is it! it is like apples of gold in pictures of silver." " All foolish talking and jesting" are forbidden by the Apostle ; while he enjoins, " Let your speech be always with grace, seasoned with salt, that ye may know how ye ought to answer every man."

There is the law of *purity*. This forbids all ribaldry : and not only every thing that is grossly offensive, but all indecent allusions and insinuations, however artfully veiled: " But fornication, and all uncleanness—let it not be once *named* among you, as becometh saints."

There is the law of *veracity*. This condemns every thing spoken with a view to deceive ; or spoken so as to occasion deception: and which may be done by a confusion of circumstances ; by an omission of circumstances ; by an addition of circumstances: " Wherefore, putting away lying, speak every man truth with his neighbour; for we are members one of another."

There is the law of *kindness*. This condemns all calumny and tale-bearing; the circulation of whatever may be injurious to the reputation of another. This requires, that if you must speak—if you *must* speak—of another's fault, you do it without aggravation; that you do it, not with pleasure, but pain; and that if you censure, you do it as a judge would pass sentence upon his son. "Let all bitterness, and wrath, and anger, and clamour, and evil-speaking, be put away from you, with all malice."

There is the law of *utility*. This requires that we should not scandalize another, by any thing in our speech; but contribute to his benefit, by rendering our discourse instructive, or reproving, or consolatory. "Let no corrupt communication proceed out of your mouth, but that which is good to the use of edifying, that it may minister grace unto the hearers."

There is the law of *piety*. This requires that we should never take God's name in vain; never speak lightly of his word, nor his worship; never charge him foolishly; never murmur under any of his dispensations. It requires that we extol his perfections, and recommend his service: "Praise the Lord, call upon his name, declare his doings among the people, make mention that his name is exalted. Sing unto the Lord; for he hath done excellent things: this is known in all the earth. Cry out and shout, thou inhabitant of Zion: for great is the Holy One of Israel in the midst of thee." So will you render the calves of your lips.

Who can reflect upon all this, and not see his daily, his hourly danger? "Set a watch, O Lord, before my mouth; keep the door of my lips."

III. A man would never use this language, without a conviction of INABILITY TO PRESERVE HIMSELF.

This conviction is well founded. There is no subject the Scripture more fully teaches than our natural weakness and insufficiency. It assures us that we are left by the Fall, not only without righteousness, but without strength. "Without me," says the Saviour, "ye can do nothing." The Bible teaches us this truth, not only doctrinally, but historically. The examples of good men, and men eminent in godliness, confirm it, and confirm it in the very article before us. Moses, the meekest man in the earth, "spake unadvisedly with his lips." You have heard of the patience of Job; but he "cursed the day of his birth:" and Jeremiah, the prophet of the Lord, did the same. Peter said, "Though all men should be offended because of thee, I will never be offended—though I should die with thee yet will I not deny thee." But how did he use his tongue a few hours after?

Then began he to curse and to swear, saying, I know not the man!"

> "Beware of Peter's word;
> Nor confidently say,
> 'I never *will* deny thee, Lord;'
> But—'Grant I never may.'"

This conviction is continually increasing. As the Christian, in the course of his experience, is learning to cease from man, so is he also taught to cease from himself. He knows the truth of Solomon's words, "He that trusteth in his own heart is a fool." He has seen how little his practice has kept pace with his knowledge; he has verified the vanity of his purposes and resolutions; his warmest frames and feelings have varied, and left him a wonder to himself; he has fallen, where he once deemed himself most secure—and is *now* persuaded—though he will be more strongly persuaded of it ten years hence—that if he stands, he is kept by the power of God.

It is a conviction the most happy. You need not be afraid of it. This self-acquaintance will only reduce you to the proper condition of a creature, and prepare you for the reception of Divine supplies. Our misery is from our self-sufficiency; it is pride that ruins us. "He filleth the hungry with good things, while the rich he sends empty away. He that humbleth himself shall be exalted. If any man will be wise, let him become a fool, that he may be wise. Let the weak say, I am strong."

IV. A man should never use this language, without a conviction of THE WISDOM OF APPLYING TO GOD FOR THE ASSISTANCE WE NEED. Prayer is the effect of our weakness, and the expression of our dependence. It confesses the agency of God. They who pray and yet deny the doctrine of Divine influence, offer the sacrifice of fools; but those who believe that God works in us to will and to do, and strengthens us with all might by his Spirit in the inner man, act wisely in addressing him as David does—"Set a watch, O Lord, before my mouth; keep the door of my lips."

For, in the first place—God is equal to our preservation. However great our danger, he can keep us from falling. Whatever difficulties we have to encounter, or duties to perform, his grace is sufficient for us. "I can do all things," says Paul, "through Christ who strengtheneth me."

Secondly. His succours are not to be obtained without prayer. He has a right to determine in what way he will communicate his own favours; he is infinitely capable of knowing what method is most consistent with his own glory, and conducive to our good—and he has revealed it: and however freely he has promised his influences, he has said, "Nevertheless, for all these things, will I be inquired of by the house of Israel, to do it for them."

Thirdly. Prayer always brings the assistance it implores. "Ask," says he, "and it shall be given you: seek, and ye shall find." So it has always been: "He never said to the seed of Jacob, Seek ye me in vain."

"What a dry, uninteresting subject!"—It may be so to *you!* but it was not so to the man after God's own heart. He sung, indeed, of the mercy of the Lord for ever; and exclaimed, "Blessed are the people that know the joyful sound." But he never disregarded the practical influence of religious principles. He prayed—"Set a watch, O Lord, before my mouth; keep the door of my lips."

And suppose, my dear hearers, you were now to examine yourselves by this subject? Would you find nothing to induce you to exclaim, "Who can understand his errors?" Nothing to humble you in the dust before God?—Nothing to draw forth your penitential grief?—Nothing to urge you to a Mediator, whose blood cleanses from all sin, and in whom alone our unworthy persons, and our imperfect services, can be accepted?

Let this subject awaken and engage much of your attention in future. Make the resolution of David your own: "I said, I will take heed to my ways, that I offend not with my tongue." But let it be an enlightened resolution; while it makes you diligent—be humble; while it makes you watchful—be also prayerful. It is the Saviour's own combination; "Watch and pray, lest ye enter into temptation."

David not only prayed, "Set a watch, O Lord, before my mouth; keep the door of my lips:" but he prayed also, "Open thou my lips, and my mouth shall show forth thy praise." Religion is not made up of negatives. There is not only a time to keep silence, but a time to speak. It is not enough, that we are harmless and blameless in our speech; we must do good with it. Pray therefore, that you may be "strong in the grace that is in Christ Jesus, and be filled with the Spirit." Burnet, in the History of his own Times, speaking of the incomparable Leighton, says, "In a free, and frequent conversation with him, for twenty-two years, I never heard him utter an idle word, or a word that had not a direct tendency to edification." But what does he add besides? "And I never saw him in any other frame of mind, than that in which I wish to die!" This justifies the eulogium, and accounts for it. For,

As the man is, so is his strength. "A good tree bringeth not forth corrupt fruit; neither doth a corrupt tree bring forth good fruit. For every tree is known by his own fruit. For of thorns men do not gather figs, nor of a bramble bush gather they grapes. A good man out of the good treasure of his heart bringeth forth that which is good; and an evil man out of the evil treasure of his heart bringeth forth that which is evil: for

of the abundance of the heart his mouth speaketh."

DISCOURSE XCIII.

SPIRITUAL SUCCOUR DERIVED FROM APPOINTED MEANS.

Who, when he was come, helped them much which had believed through grace.—Acts xviii. 27.

THE God of nature is the God of grace; and his influence in the one strikingly corresponds with his agency in the other. In the world of nature, God not only brings creatures into life, but provides for their support; and, in the regular economy of his Providence, opens his hand, and "satisfieth the desire of every living thing." So it is in the world of grace. Christians are new creatures: but they are not perfect at once; they require attention and supplies. And "He who giveth to the beast his food, and to the young ravens which cry," will not overlook the wants of his own children. He taketh pleasure in them that fear him, in them that hope in his mercy. Hence they may boldly say, "The Lord is my helper, I will not fear. The Lord will perfect that which concerneth me: thy mercy, O Lord, endureth for ever: forsake not the works of thine own hands."

In harmony with this reflection are the words which we have chosen for our present improvement. They were spoken of "a certain Jew named Apollos, born at Alexandria." He was "an eloquent man, and mighty in the Scriptures;" and had come to Ephesus. "This man," it is said, "was instructed in the way of the Lord; and being fervent in the spirit, he spake and taught diligently the things of the Lord, knowing only the baptism of John." Here we remark, that natural talent, and actual knowledge, are very distinguishable from each other; and that the heart may be right with God, while the judgment, in divine things, is defective. It is well, however, to see a man using the light he has. It shows that he is sincere and in earnest; and "to him that hath shall be given, and he shall have more abundantly." This was the case here. "And he began to speak boldly in the synagogue: whom when Aquila and Priscilla had heard, they took him unto them, and expounded unto him the way of God more perfectly."

This honours both parties.

It commends Aquila and Priscilla. Though they found Apollos in Christian knowledge, inferior to themselves, yet, as he was truly pious and zealous, and had good and useful endowments, they did not despise or disparage him, saying, "He may do for others; but such a young, raw, inexperienced preacher is not deep enough for us:"—so many a *gifted* brother, and many a *gifted* sister, in our day, would have said—but they encouraged him, by their attendance; and watched and cherished the ripening of the fruit. For they also communicated to him of their own experience. But observe—They did it not superciliously, nor in public; but, with a delicate regard to his feelings, alone, in their own house.

And it looks well in Apollos, that he so willingly received their instruction. He was a young man of great parts and learning; a preacher exceedingly cried up and followed —and it was not an apostle that undertook to teach him; nor even a brother minister; but two of his hearers, and mechanics too—but he listens to them with pleasure and gratitude. And thus he shows us his good sense, as well as his humility. For those who are below us in some qualities, may yet be above us in others; and there is no such thing as independence. In the mystical body, as well as in the natural, "the eye cannot say unto the hand, I have no need of thee; nor again, the head to the feet, I have no need of you."

Apollos was willing to go where there was least help, and most probability of usefulness. But no preacher ought to be countenanced till he is accredited by some authority better than his own. When, therefore, Apollos was "disposed to pass into Achaia," he traveled with letters of recommendation: for "the brethren wrote, exhorting the disciples to receive him;" and he fully answered to their contents: "for, when he was come, he helped them much which had believed through grace."

Whence we observe—that CHRISTIANS ARE BELIEVERS—That THEY BELIEVE THROUGH GRACE—That THEY NEED HELP; and—That ASSISTANCE IS AFFORDED BY THE MINISTRY OF THE GOSPEL.

I. CHRISTIANS ARE BELIEVERS. To believe is to have a persuasion of the truth of a thing submitted to our attention.

It is obvious, however, that the credence which characterizes the subjects of divine grace, does not rest in the judgment, without producing a correspondent state of the heart; "for with the heart man believeth unto righteousness. Purifying their hearts by faith. Faith worketh by love. This is the victory that overcometh the world, even our faith." Such is the influence ascribed to the faith of the primitive Christians. That these are not the invariable effects of believing, it is evident from fact; and the advantage the apostle James took of such a fact, in his days, was to show the inutility of that faith which admits the truth into the understanding, while the possessor is not sanctified by it. "What doth it profit, my brethren, though a man say he hath faith, and have not works? Can faith save

him? If a brother or sister be naked, and destitute of daily food, and one of you say unto them, Depart in peace, be ye warmed and filled; notwithstanding ye give them not those things which are needful to the body; what doth it profit? Even so faith, if it hath not works, is dead, being alone."

If a man believe any thing with certainty, it is his own mortality; and yet, though he cannot, does not, doubt for a moment, that he is a dying creature, the conviction is completely counteracted by his passions and sins; and he lives as if he were to live here always; and according to the prayer of Moses, God alone can so teach us to number our days, that we shall apply our hearts unto wisdom. Ungodly characters may, therefore, give credit to the Scriptures in general, and to the most interesting doctrines of the Gospel, and yet retain their wickedness—"Holding the truth in unrighteousness."

The hazard of deception, to which we are exposed, arises from the near resemblance there often is between a counterfeit and a genuine faith; and the tendency there is in men to be satisfied with the assent of the mind, which costs nothing, without "obeying from the heart the form of doctrine which is delivered us; and being changed into the same image, from glory to glory, as by the Spirit of the Lord." But such is the disposition of every one that believes to the saving of the soul. See it in his conviction of the exceeding sinfulness of sin; his abhorrence of himself; and his humiliation before God. See it in his consciousness of the need of a Saviour; his reception of him; and his dependence upon him. See it in his profession of his name; and in his adherence to his ordinances. See it in the love he bears to his people; and the reproach he is willing to submit to for his sake. See it in his readiness to "deny himself, and take up his cross, and follow him." See it in the little account he makes of things seen and temporal, and the strength of his attachment to those things which are unseen and eternal.

A faith operating in such effects as these, proclaims itself to be of the operation of God's Spirit: and prepares us to observe,

II. That they who believe, BELIEVE THROUGH GRACE.

Here we may observe, that from this source comes the very object of faith, as a revelation. This principally consists in the "record, that God hath given to us eternal life, and that this life is in his Son." The Gospel assures us that the Lord Jesus is the only foundation of a sinner's hope; that "he was delivered for our offences, and raised again for our justification;" that "in him we have righteousness and strength;" that "he is able to save to the uttermost them that come unto God by him, seeing he ever liveth to make intercession for them." These are the things with which faith has to do: and how came we by the knowledge of them? They are the result of a supernatural communication: "As it is written, Eye hath not seen, nor ear heard, neither have entered into the heart of man the things which God hath prepared for them that love him. But God hath revealed them unto us by his Spirit: for the Spirit searcheth all things, yea, the deep things of God." And what influenced him to send us such glad tidings of great joy? How often is the Gospel itself called the *grace* of God! "The grace of God which bringeth salvation hath appeared unto all men.—This is the true grace of God wherein ye stand."

From this source is also derived the *existence* of faith, as a production. This may be inferred from our moral inability, or that state into which sin has brought us. Of this the Scripture gives us a mortifying, but a faithful account. "The heart," says Jeremiah, "is deceitful above all things, and desperately wicked." And "who," says Job, "can bring a clean thing out of an unclean? Not one." "When we were without strength," says the Apostle, "in due time Christ died for the ungodly." "Without me," says the Saviour, "ye can do nothing." No man can come to me, except the Father which hath sent me draw him."

But we are not left to infer the fact: we have, in the word of God, the most express ascriptions of it to a Divine influence. Upon Peter's profession of faith, our Lord said, "Blessed art thou, Simon Barjona: for flesh and blood hath not revealed this unto thee, but my Father which is in heaven." And so far was this from being peculiar to him, that it is said of the Philippians, "To you it is given on the behalf of Christ, not only to believe in him, but also to suffer for his sake;" and of the Ephesians, "By grace are ye saved, through faith; and *that not of yourselves, it is the gift of God.*" Connecting himself with them, the Apostle speaks of the "exceeding greatness of his power to usward who believe, according to the working of his mighty power, which he wrought in Christ, when he raised him from the dead, and set him at his own right hand in the heavenly places." What an accumulation of terms to express the omnipotent exertion of God!—And to what does this exertion refer? Our final resurrection from the dead? So the enemies of the present truth would have it—for what power, say they, is necessary to draw forth our bodies from the tomb, and make them like the Redeemer's own glorious body! This is true—But the Apostle refers to an energy which has already operated in believers, and by which they were made believers; an energy—not which *shall* draw forth their bodies from the corruption of the grave, but which *has* delivered their souls from the bondage of corruption, into the

glorious liberty of the sons of God; an energy—which has drawn them from rebellion to obedience; from pride to humbleness of mind; from the power of darkness into the kingdom of God's dear Son; an energy—which combines the glory of all our Saviour's miracles: at once opening the eyes of the blind, unstopping the deaf ears, causing the dumb to sing, the lame to walk, and the dead to live; an energy—that, in some sense, surpasses the creation of the world:—for in producing this, if there was no co-operation, there was no resistance; whereas here, "the carnal mind is enmity with God, for it is not subject to the law of God, neither indeed can be."

Again. From the same source is derived the *exercise* of faith as a principle. This faith must be exerted in every condition; in prosperity, and in adversity: in sickness, and in health; in solitude, and in society; in devotion, and in trade. We are to walk by faith; and by faith we are to live. But as there is nothing of so much importance as this faith, in the whole of our Christian course, there is nothing so much opposed, by all the hidden evils of the heart, and all the powers of darkness. And how is it to be maintained? "I have prayed for thee," says our Saviour, "that thy faith fail not." "Lord," said the apostles, "increase our faith." Thus the continuance and the progress of the principle depend upon the same grace which produced it; and He who is the *author*, is acknowledged also the *finisher* of our faith.

III. THEY NEED HELP. This they all feel; and this they always feel. They are not without fears whether the work is begun in them; but though they often question the reality of their religion, they never question the deficiency. This is too obvious to elude the most superficial examination of their hearts and lives. Paul himself, after all the proficiency he had made in his Christian course, was not ashamed to say, "I have not yet attained, neither am I already perfect." The Christian feels a deficiency in his knowledge which requires help. A full and judicious acquaintance with the things of God is a great advantage: but the views of some are very limited; the word of Christ does not dwell in them richly in all wisdom. Some have such obscure and confused notions, that they resemble the man under the process of illumination, who "looked up, and saw men as trees walking." Yet, before this he could see nothing; and another application enabled him to see every thing clearly.

Some ought to be ashamed of the remaining degree of their ignorance, considering the advantages they have enjoyed, and the season they have been under tuition. We may address them as our Saviour did his disciples, "Are ye also yet without understanding?" Or as Paul did the Hebrews, "When for the time ye ought to be teachers, ye have need that one teach you again which be the first principles of the oracles of God."

The Christian feels a deficiency which requires help, in his *sanctification*. He is renewed in the spirit of his mind, so as to delight in the law of God after the inward man: but "the flesh lusteth against the Spirit; and when he would do good, evil is present with him." His graces are imperfect. Something is wanting—and oh! how much—to his patience, his love, his hope, his faith. He is far from being what he ought to be in his duties. God demands of him a spiritual worship; but how little of this does he render him, when kneeling at his throne, or sitting at his table! He finds too little of the Christian in his temper; too little of the Gospel in his walk. And yet "what manner of persons ought we to be, *in all holy conversation and godliness!*"

A Christian feels a deficiency in his *comfort*, that requires help. This arises from the former. Injured in his work, and hindered in his advancement, he cannot but grieve. It is inconsistent with his disposition, to see his infirmities, and not sigh, "O wretched man that I am! who shall deliver me from the body of this death?" He is not in the possession of his inheritance; but an heir. And an "heir, as long as he is a child, differeth nothing from a servant, though he be lord of all." How often is his peace interrupted! How often is he constrained to groan, "The enemy hath persecuted my soul; he hath smitten my life down to the ground; he hath made me to dwell in darkness, as those that have been long dead. I remembered God, and was troubled: I complained, and my spirit was overwhelmed. Will the Lord cast off for ever? and will he be favourable no more? Is his mercy clean gone for ever? doth his promise fail for evermore? Hath God forgotten to be gracious? hath he in anger shut up his tender mercies?" Whatever the world may be to others, it is to him a vale of tears. In addition to the common troubles of life, he has trials peculiar to his religion; and from the union of these, "many are the afflictions of the righteous."

IV. But ASSISTANCE IS AFFORDED BY THE MINISTRY OF THE GOSPEL. "Who, when he was come, helped them much which had believed through grace." It is necessary, however, to observe, that he did this only through the blessing of God attending his labours. Hear the apostle: "Who then is Paul, and who is Apollos, but ministers by whom ye believed, even as the Lord gave to every man? I have planted, Apollos watered; but God gave the increase. So then neither is he that planteth any thing, neither he that watereth; but God that giveth the increase." This being premised, we remark that Apollos helped the believers three ways: and the same will apply to every minister of the Gospel now.

First. By his *prayers*. This was done by his praying *with* them. How much instruction and relief did they often derive from his devotional exercises. How encouraging and delightful, to hear their own wants and desires offered up officially, in all the fervour and solemnity of divine worship! But he did not only pray *with* them, but *for* them: and he prayed for them, not only in public, but in private. And was this in vain? "The effectual fervent prayer of a righteous man availeth much."

Secondly. He helped them much, by *preaching*. Preaching is an ordinance peculiar to the Gospel; and it *is* an ordinance. It would be easy to prove that there is a natural suitableness and tendency in preaching to do good: but we are to view it as a divine institution, and to infer the blessing from the appointment. When the Saviour ascended up on high he gave gifts unto men; and established the ministry, "for the edifying of the body of Christ: till we all come in the unity of the faith, and of the knowledge of the Son of God, unto a perfect man, unto the measure of the stature of the fulness of Christ." Thus the apostle tells the Romans, "For I long to see you, that I may impart unto you some spiritual gift, to the end ye may be established." And to the Thessalonians he says, "Wherefore when we could no longer forbear, we thought it good to be left at Athens alone; and sent Timotheus, our brother, and minister of God, and our fellow-labourer in the Gospel of Christ, to establish you, and to comfort you concerning your faith." Thus "faith cometh by hearing, and hearing by the word of God."

Every religion, of old, had its rites; and its votaries were accustomed to assemble together at stated times and on various occasions, in their temples and at their altars; but they never came to receive instruction. What instruction had their leaders to communicate? What could they publish, with the evidence of truth, the force of importance, or the joy of hope? But when your ministers meet you they have every thing that is interesting to announce. They can send you "help from the sanctuary, and strengthen you out of Zion." Their messages are "the savour of life unto life"—you go away new creatures. Which of you has not realized the support—the compensation of the prophet: "Though the Lord give you the bread of adversity, and the water of affliction, yet shall not thy teachers be removed into a corner any more, but thine eyes shall see thy teachers: and thine ears shall hear a word behind thee, saying, This is the way, walk ye in it, when ye turn to the right hand, and when ye turn to the left."

Thirdly. He instructed them by *example*. Example illustrates and confirms and enforces doctrine; and is deservedly said to be more influential than precept. And though we ought to consider *what* is said, rather than *who* says it, yet it is not in the power of human nature to disregard the *practice* of a *moral* and *religious* instructer: and a drunkard is not likely to preach with effect against intemperance; or one that is greedy of gain, against covetousness. The physician is not likely to gain the confidence and submission of the patient, when he prescribes for a disease under which he labours himself—but will be reminded of the proverb, "Physician, heal thyself." Therefore says Paul to his son Timothy, "Let no man despise thy youth; but be thou an example of the believers in word, in conversation, in charity, in spirit, in faith, in purity." And of Levi, says God, "My covenant was with him of life and peace; and I gave them to him for the fear wherewith he feared me, and was afraid before my name. The law of truth was in his mouth, and iniquity was not found in his lips: he walked with me in peace and equity, and did turn many away from iniquity."

To conclude. Suffer me, First, to ask the question which our Lord addressed to the man born blind, "Dost thou believe on the Son of God?" Do not put off, or elude this inquiry, which is pressed, purely from a regard to your everlasting welfare. It is of infinite importance to each of you. The salvation or damnation of the soul depends upon it. It is useless to attend to other things, while you overlook the *state* you are in before God. "He that believeth on the Son hath everlasting life: and he that believeth not the Son shall not see life; but the wrath of God abideth on him."

Secondly. If faith comes from the grace of God, they are mistaken who place it in the virtue of man. And such there are: but you have not so learned Christ. All men have not faith: you were once destitute; and if now enriched with the benefit, you are not at a loss to determine how you obtained it. You disclaim your own goodness and power, and exclaim, "By the grace of God, I am what I am." Let the same truth which excludes boasting prevent despair. Let it encourage the hope of those who fear they are strangers to this precious faith, and let it guide their application. Let it also lead those to the God of all grace who desire an increase—praying like the father of the child, who "cried out with tears, Lord, I believe, help thou my unbelief."

Thirdly. Do not despise the day of small things. Despise it not in others. Observe and cherish every serious conviction, every pious sentiment; and resemble Him who does "not break a bruised reed, or quench the smoking flax; but brings forth judgment

2 X

unto victory."—Despise it not in yourselves. The life of God is progressive, and the commencement is often no more to the completion than the mustard seed to the mustard tree. That you are not what you ought to be, should humble you; that you are not what you would be, should stimulate you; but that you are not what you once were, should encourage you. The dawn and the blade are too precious to be disregarded: they are not only beginnings, but pledges: that blade shall become the full corn in the ear; and that dawn shall shine more and more unto the perfect day. "Being confident of this very thing, that he which hath begun a good work in you, will perform it until the day of Jesus Christ."

Fourthly. Pity those who are destitute of your religious advantages. Many of your fellow-creatures have not even a Bible. Others are destitute of a gospel ministry. By their condition they cry, "Come and help us." They would be thankful for the crumbs which fall from your spiritual table; and would go any distance, and make any sacrifices, to hear with rapture—what you often attend upon with indifference.

Finally. Be grateful for the privileges you enjoy, and be concerned properly to improve them. Attend regularly and conscientiously the pastor who feeds you with knowledge and understanding. "Laying aside all malice, and all guile, and hypocrisies, and envies, and all evil speakings, as new born babes, desire the sincere milk of the word, that ye may grow thereby; if so ye have tasted that the Lord is gracious." Repair to the house of God, influenced by the command, "Forsake not the assembling of yourselves together, as the manner of some is." Go with lively expectation, founded on the promises upon which he has caused you to hope. "I will abundantly bless her provision: I will satisfy her poor with bread. I will also clothe her priests with salvation; and her saints shall shout aloud for joy. Even the youths shall faint and be weary, and the young men shall utterly fall: but they that wait upon the Lord shall renew their strength; they shall mount up with wings as eagles; they shall run, and not be weary; and they shall walk, and not faint."

DISCOURSE XCIV.

THE STAR GUIDING THE WISE MEN TO THE BABE IN BETHLEHEM.

Now when Jesus was born in Bethlehem of Judæa in the days of Herod the king, behold, there came wise men from the east to Jerusalem, saying, Where is he that is born King of the Jews? for we have seen his star in the east, and are come to worship him.—Matt. ii. 1, 2.

In the productions of Jehovah we behold immensity and minuteness; complexness and simplicity; obscurity and luminousness; an effulgence that dazzles and repels, and a softness that composes and allures. If this be true of the wonders of creation, it equally applies to the work of redemption; and shows us that nature and grace have one and the same Author. If we examine the character and the history of our Lord and Saviour, we shall discern a marvellous union of grandeur and humility; of independence and subjection; of indigence and riches. Observe his death. He suffers every kind of indignity; he is scourged, buffeted, spit upon, numbered with transgressors, crucified through weakness. But the sun is enveloped in darkness, the earth shakes, the rocks rend, the graves open, the dead arise: the centurion exclaims, "Surely this man was the Son of God;" the dying thief adores him as the disposer of the heavenly world; and cries, "Lord, remember me when thou comest into thy kingdom." See him in the ship. He sleeps—there is his infirmity. He awakes, and rebukes the wind and the sea—there is his omnipotence. Weary with his journey, he sits at the well of Sychar, and asks for a cup of cold water—but at the same time, proclaims himself the Giver of the water of eternal life.

Nothing could be more expressive of the deepest abasement than the circumstances of his birth. To read the narrative is enough to scandalize all the worshippers of the god of this world. "She brought forth her firstborn son, and wrapped him in swaddling clothes, and laid him in a manger; because there was no room for them in the inn." But the period of his birth is called the fulness of time. All heaven is awakened by it. One angel of the Lord appears to Joseph, and informs him of the dignity of the child. Another flies to the shepherds in the fields, and cries, "Fear not; for, behold, I bring you good tidings of great joy, which shall be to all people." When, lo! "a multitude of the heavenly host praising God, and saying, Glory to God in the highest, and on earth peace, good will toward men." The Spirit of inspiration, after a lapse of ages, rests upon Simeon and Anna; and they prophesy. Some are waiting for the Consolation of Israel, and looking for redemption in Jerusalem; and embrace him with a joy that loosens all the ties of life.

But in him, as the seed of Abraham, "all the families of the earth" were to be blessed. He was to be "a light to lighten the Gentiles," as well as "the glory of his people Israel." And behold a star appearing to persons in a remote clime, and leading strangers in search of the infant Messiah. "Now when Jesus was born in Bethlehem of Judæa in the days of Herod the king, behold, there came wise men from the east to Jerusalem, saying, Where is he that is born King of the Jews? for we have seen his star in the east, and are come to worship him?"

Various questions might be asked concerning these wise men, which it is not in our power to answer. We could entertain you, indeed, with the opinions of the learned concerning their profession, the country from which they came, and the star which guided them. But we hasten to make a practical improvement of the subject, only remarking, with as much brevity as possible, two or three things, in explanation of the passage.

When it is said, "We have seen his star in the *east*," you are not to suppose that they saw the star shining in an easterly direction, for it appeared to them in the very opposite quarter; and the words mark, not the situation of the object, but of the spectators, when they viewed it.

What is called a *star* could not mean any thing like those heavenly bodies which go under this name; but a luminous meteor in the middle region of the air; near enough to guide them, and at last dropping down so low, as even to signalize the very house which contained the child.

It is worthy of notice, that by a similar instrument, God formerly conducted his people through the wilderness. It was by a pillar of fire he led them to the holy hill of Zion.

But how could they infer, from this celestial appearance, that the King of the Jews was born? What relation was there between the sign and the event? All mankind originally had a revelation in the family of Noah, by whom the new world was peopled; and imperfect traces of it were found many ages after in the various nations of the globe. And though this revelation, as secured in writing, was committed to the Jews, it was not confined to them. Copies were occasionally taken away by foreigners, as objects of research, and even of religious information. Thus, we know, the queen of Sheba came to prove Solomon with hard questions, when she heard of his "fame concerning the name of the Lord." Also, by the dispersion of the Jews, their scriptures were scattered, and their prophecies as well as miracles were read; so that a general expectation was excited in the east of the birth of some very extraordinary character. It is needless to adduce proof of this; but we may observe, that Balaam, who was himself from the east, had predicted the Messiah under the very image of a star. But as the case before us was confessedly supernatural, why may we not extend the miracle a little further, and suppose, that while the sign engaged their attention God impressed their minds with a conviction of its relation and design. Could not he do this as easily as he afterwards "warned them in a dream," that they should not return to Herod, but go back into their country by another way?

He was born King of the Jews. This awakened the alarm of Herod—but it was needless; though a king, he was not a temporal prince. In this character the Jews looked for him, and, not finding in him a hero who should deliver them from the Roman yoke, they despised and rejected him. But he had other enemies to conquer, and another empire to gain. "Jesus answered, My kingdom is not of this world. If my kingdom were of this world, then would my servants fight, that I should not be delivered to the Jews: but now is my kingdom not from hence. Pilate therefore said unto him, Art thou a king then? Jesus answered, Thou sayest that I am a king. To this end was I born, and for this cause came I into the world, that I should bear witness unto the truth. Every one that is of the truth heareth my voice."

But let us offer a few remarks upon this subject; "profitable for doctrine, for reproof, for correction, and instruction in righteousness." CHRIST IS OWNED BY SOME IN THE HIGHER ORDERS OF LIFE—THEY WHO ARE REALLY DESIROUS OF FINDING HIM SHALL NOT ERR FOR WANT OF DIRECTION—WE SHOULD DEEM NO DIFFICULTIES TOO GREAT TO ENCOUNTER IN SEEKING AFTER HIM—WE ARE TO BE CONCERNED TO HONOUR CHRIST, AS WELL AS TO BE SAVED BY HIM.

I. CHRIST IS OWNED BY SOME IN THE HIGHER ORDERS OF LIFE. "Not many wise men after the flesh, not many mighty, not many noble are called; but God hath chosen the foolish things of the world to confound the wise; and God hath chosen the weak things of the world to confound the things that are mighty; and base things of the world, and things that are despised, hath God chosen; yea, and things which are not, to bring to nought things that are." Such are they who have generally constituted the majority of our Lord's followers. His more immediate disciples, when he was on earth, were Galileans, fishermen, publicans, and sinners. This was urged as a reproach by his adversaries: "Have any of the rulers, or of the Pharisees, believed on him?—But this people who knoweth not the law are cursed." And the same matter of offence has attended his cause in all ages. Had we the disposition of the Son of God, instead of being scandalized at such a dispensation, we should more than acquiesce in it; we should rejoice in spirit, and say, "I thank thee, O Father, Lord of heaven and earth, that thou hast hid these things from the wise and prudent, and revealed them unto babes. Even so, Father: for so it seemed good in thy sight." But his followers are not taken exclusively from those of low estate. There have always been some who have vanquished the difficulties of their station; and "going forth without the camp," have thrown down their distinctions at the foot of the cross, glad to part with all to purchase the pearl of great price. Zaccheus was rich. Joseph of Arimathæa was a counsellor. Nicodemus was a ruler of the Jews. We read of a nobleman "who believed, with all his house;" and "of honourable women, not a few." A man who feared God rode in the second chariot of Egypt. A prime minister of one hundred and twenty-seven provinces prayed three times a day. Kings have been nursing fathers, and queens nursing mothers. And as to talent, we are able to bring forward on the side of Christianity persons superior in every department of genius and science to its adversaries.

By all of which we do not mean to intimate that the great bring any real honour to the Gospel by embracing it—though they derive honour from it—but we wish to show what the power of Divine grace can accomplish; to rescue from despair the minds of those who are placed among the perils of elevation; and to remove the prejudice so often entertained, that Christianity is only limited to the taste of the vulgar, the illiterate, and the ignorant.

II. THEY WHO ARE DESIROUS OF FINDING CHRIST WILL NOT MISS HIM FOR WANT OF DIRECTION. "I will bring the blind by a way that they knew not; I will lead them in paths that they have not known; I will make darkness light before them, and crooked things straight; these things will I do unto them, and not forsake them. In all thy ways acknowledge him, and he shall direct thy paths." And is he unable to accomplish what he has promised? In how many ways can we ourselves convey information to a fellow-creature, even when no audible voice is heard! And how limited is human perfection: "To whom," says God, "will ye liken me, or shall I be equal, saith the Holy One? He that planted the ear, shall not he hear? He that formed the eye, shall not he see?" He who made us has access to every power of our souls. He who governs us has all the resources of nature and providence at his command. He who saves us can turn any object or event into an instrument to fulfil the purposes of his grace. Let us leave the poor heathen to Him who could make a star to conduct those who were destitute of a Bible; and who, without the intervention of a preacher, could convey to their minds a knowledge of the use of it; and let us not limit the Holy One of Israel either in his love, his power, or his wisdom. And let us remark, that where common means are withholden, God often has recourse to unusual ones. "Faith cometh by hearing:" yet it is reasonable to hope that he has awakened many who were never blessed with an opportunity of hearing evangelical preaching; he has awakened their consciences to the importance of eternal things, and taken them under his more immediate tuition: and "none teaches like him."

But as for you, my dear hearers, who live in a Christian country, and are privileged with the ordinances of religion, you can never want a star to guide. Your danger lies not on the side of ignorance, but of knowledge—knowledge unprized, neglected, perverted, abused. This is the condemnation—that you have light, but refuse to follow its leadings, and cause the Saviour to complain, "Ye will not come unto me, that ye might have life."

For you have the Scripture, "which is a lamp unto our feet, and a light unto our path." This is the word of Christ. And what part of it is there that does not lead to him? Is it the predictive? "The testimony of Jesus is the spirit of prophecy. To him give all the prophets witness." Is it the ceremonial? The altar, the tabernacle, the temple, the showbread, the sacrifices, and the incense; all were "shadows of good things to come, of which the body is Christ." Is it the miraculous? Who can help looking towards him from the ark of Noah; the deliverance of the Jews out of Egypt; the manna that fell in the desert; the waters that flowed from the smitten rock?—for "that rock was Christ." Is it the legal? The law, by convincing us of sin, worketh a sense of wrath, and annihilates all hopes of salvation by our own obedience: "The law," says the Apostle, "was our schoolmaster, to bring us unto Christ." Is it the doctrinal? All the doctrines of the Gospel are derived from his history—from his incarnation, his sufferings, and his glory; and all lead to him, as streams that flow from a fountain enable us to find it. "Who is he that condemneth? It is Christ that died, yea rather, that is risen again, who is even at the right hand of God, who also maketh intercession for us."

You have the ministry of the word. And what does every preacher of the truth but proclaim. with the forerunner, "Behold the Lamb of God that taketh away the sin of the world!" Is he asked by an anxious inquirer, "What must I do to be saved?" He would be a misleader of souls, and chargeable with their ruin, if he gave any other direction than that of Paul and Silas to the jailer; "Believe on the Lord Jesus Christ."—"These are the servants of the most high God, which show unto men the way of salvation."

You have the Spirit of promise: "Howbeit when he, the Spirit of truth, is come, he will guide you into all truth; for he shall not speak of himself; but whatsoever he shall hear, that shall he speak: and he will show you things to come. He shall glorify me; for he shall receive of mine, and shall show it unto you." Though these words had a

peculiar relation to the apostles, they have a real, and a very encouraging reference to Christians in every age of the world—"who walk not after the flesh, but after the Spirit: and as many as are led by the Spirit of God, they are the sons of God." Avail yourselves of all these advantages, and, like these men from the east, "then shall ye know, if you follow on to know the Lord." This brings us to observe:

III. WE SHOULD DEEM NO DIFFICULTIES TOO GREAT TO ENCOUNTER, NO SACRIFICES TOO GREAT TO MAKE, IN SEEKING AFTER CHRIST. Behold your example. These wise men did not say as they were setting off, "But will not our neighbours and friends condemn us?" They do not ask, "But what will the learned think of us? Will they not reproach us, as engaged in a visionary enterprise, unworthy of the professors of philosophy?" No. They did not consult the many, or the few, but the star. There is a striking difference between men, individually and socially considered. Alone, they often feel well; conscience has a moment of leisure; truth speaks, and in the absence of lies is heard; and now, convinced and impressed, they resolve to walk before God in newness of life: but all this resolution is ruined as soon as they intermingle with others. To avoid the laugh of one, and the frown of another; the coolness of friendship, or the enmity of power; they swerve from the known path of duty, and "hold the truth in unrighteousness." Public opinion is one of the greatest obstacles the grace of God has to overcome; especially in two cases—With regard to the young, who are so impressible to flattery and ridicule—And the intellectual, who pride themselves on the reputation of knowledge, and to whom the words of our Saviour may be applied; "How can ye believe who receive honour one of another, and seek not the honour that cometh from God only?" How many are there who believe on him, but fear to confess him, lest they should be put out of the synagogue, "for they love the praise of men more than the praise of God." Let us, therefore, like these Magi, choose our guide, not from below, but from above. Let us simply ask, What does God say—what does God require? It is a light thing to be judged of man's judgment. He that judgeth us is the Lord—How shall I appear before him?

Again. These men were willing to leave their country, their connexions, their families; and disregarded all the expenses, inconveniences, and dangers of a distant and difficult journey. And you know the decision: "Whosoever he be of you that forsaketh not all that he hath cannot be my disciple." Some things must be absolutely renounced. This is the case with sin of every kind, and every degree.—Bosom lusts must all be sacrificed —the right hand cut off, the right eye pluck ed out. Other things must be *conditionally* parted with. These are our temporal interests. Duty and advantage may lie the same road; but when a separation is necessary we must show, by our choice, what we deem the one thing needful. Thus Moses "refused to be called the son of Pharaoh's daughter, and chose rather to suffer affliction with the people of God than enjoy the pleasures of sin for a season." Thus, between a human and a Divine command, Peter and John said, "We ought to obey God rather than man."

If, however, the Gospel requires us to labour, and strive, and fight, it more than deserves all our exertions. If it demands sacrifices, it more than indemnifies us. "There is no man that hath left house, or parents, or brethren, or wife, or children, for the kingdom of God's sake, who shall not receive manifold more in this present time, and in the world to come life everlasting. Godliness is profitable unto all things, having promise of the life that now is, and of that which is to come." But, alas! what a difference is there between the disposition of these followers of the star, and the conduct of mankind at large—may I not add, of many of you? Though you have no such lengths to go, but the kingdom of God is nigh you; though you know more of the end of the Saviour's coming, and through the vail of his humanity can behold his glory, "the glory as of the only begotten of the Father, full of grace and truth;" though you have been invited, and pressed, times without number, to go and partake of the fulness that resides in him— what effect has all this had upon your hearts and lives? What solicitude have you discovered to "win Christ, and be found in him?" Of what importance should we deem salvation were we to judge of it by your concern to obtain it? How many will the wise men of the east rise up in the judgment against and condemn?

IV. WE ARE TO BE CONCERNED TO HONOUR HIM, AS WELL AS TO BE SAVED BY HIM. The first thought of a sinner when he seeks him is to obtain relief from him in a case wherein all other assistance must fail. He is guilty, and needs forgiveness. He is depraved, and needs renovation. He is all ignorance and weakness, and needs wisdom and strength. He therefore cries, " Lord, save, I perish !" And for this very purpose he is commanded to look to him: " Look unto me, and be ye saved, all the ends of the earth." But whenever there is a real work of grace in the heart, there will be a disposition not only to seek him, but to serve him; and we shall say with the wise men, " We are come to worship him."

What was the worship they rendered him? Some have ascribed to these men a higher degree of knowledge than we have any reason to believe they possessed. It is not to be supposed that they knew his divinity; but they viewed him as an extraordinary personage; and as they were accustomed to prostrate themselves before a superior, and offer him presents, so when " they were come into the house, they saw the young child with Mary his mother, and fell down and worshipped him : and when they had opened their treasures, they presented unto him gifts · gold, and frankincense, and myrrh."

But what worship are *you* to render him? —You are to render him the homage of the *mind*. This is done by entertaining the most exalted conceptions of him. And can you think of him too highly, after searching the Scripture, and finding him " fairer than the children of men : the King of kings, and Lord of lords : the Sun of righteousness : the Saviour of the world : the brightness of the Father's glory, and the express image of his person ?"—You are to render him the homage of the *heart*. This is done by giving him your confidence; and " blessed are all they that put their trust in him." This is done by yielding him your supreme affection; and be it observed—you do not love him at all, unless you love him above all.—You are to render him the homage of the *lip*. This is done by extolling his excellences, and recommending him to others. And can your tongue, which is your glory, be ever so well employed?—You are to render him the homage of the *life*. This is done by obeying his commands; by holding yourselves at his disposal; by submitting to his dispensations; by devoting yourselves to his cause—honouring the Lord with your substance, and, in the true spirit of a moral, or rather Christian martyr, saying—

" All that I have, and all I am,
    Shall be for ever thine ;
Whate'er my duty bids me give,
    My cheerful hands resign."

Yea,

" Were the whole realm of nature mine,
    That were a present far too small ;
Love so amazing, so divine,
    Demands my soul, my life, my all !"

Are you afraid of rendering him such homage, lest you should incur the charge of idolatry? Behold your authority: " As the Father raiseth up the dead, and quickeneth them ; even so the Son quickeneth whom he will. For the Father judgeth no man, but hath committed all judgment unto the Son ; that all men should honour the Son, even as they honour the Father. He that honoureth not the Son honoureth not the Father which hath sent him. God also hath highly exalted him, and given him a name which is above every name ; that at the name of Jesus every knee should bow, of things in heaven, and things in earth, and things under the earth ; and that every tongue should confess that Jesus Christ is Lord, to the glory of God the Father." Here is an authority which not only allows, but demands the honours we pay him.

I hope you are not confounded at the thought of yielding this homage—in the stable, and kneeling—before the manger. The wise men, it is probable, judging from the prodigy of the star, expected to find the new-born king surrounded with magnificence; but his abasement hindered not their adoration. And shall it hinder your ardour! Yea rather, shall it not inflame your love! For what has brought him down; what has placed him here! Compulsion! No:—but compassion—a love "that passeth knowledge." He who was in the form of God, took upon him the form of a servant. He made himself of no reputation. You know it, Christians! You know it:—"Ye know the grace of our Lord Jesus Christ, that though he was rich, yet for our sakes he became poor: that ye through his poverty might be rich." And is dignity lessened by condescension! Shall his goodness rob him of his glory! So far was Paul from being ashamed of his humiliation, that he exclaimed, "God forbid that I should glory, save in the cross of our Lord Jesus Christ." And when does God require all the highest orders of his creatures to adore him! When he has not where to lay his head. "WHEN HE BRINGETH THE FIRSTBEGOTTEN INTO THE WORLD, *he saith, And let all the angels of God worship him.*"

And when John heard the voice of many angels round about the throne, and the beasts, and the elders,—and the number of them was ten thousand times ten thousand, and thousands of thousands,—they cried with a loud voice, saying, "Worthy is the *Lamb that was slain* to receive power, and riches, and wisdom, and strength, and honour, and glory, and blessing."

DISCOURSE XCV.

GOD THINKS UPON HIS PEOPLE.

I am poor and needy; yet the Lord thinketh upon me.—Psalm xl. 17.

THE life of a Christian is a very chequered scene. If it be said of others, "They have no changes, therefore they fear not God;" he can say, with Job, "changes and war are upon me." However attractive this world may appear to those whose disposition is congenial with it, and who make it their portion, *he* feels that it is not his rest. He is a stranger and a sojourner, as were all his fathers: and there are seasons when he sighs, "Wo is me that I dwell in Meshech, and make my tents in Kedar. Oh that I had wings like a dove! for then would I fly away and be at rest."

But let us not view his present condition on the dark side only. It admits of relief. Under all his disadvantages and trials, he is furnished with everlasting consolation and good hope though grace. Though a soldier, he fights the good fight of faith; and does not go a warfare at his own charges. Though a stranger and a pilgrim, he has accommodations and refreshments by the way. This is his emblem—a bush burning with fire and not consumed. This is his motto—"We are troubled on every side, yet not distressed; we are perplexed, but not in despair; persecuted, but not forsaken; cast down, but not destroyed."—This is his experience—"I am poor and needy, yet the Lord thinketh upon me." It would be fastidious to refuse the divisions which these words naturally afford. They contain,

I. A HUMBLE CONDITION.
II. A BLESSED ASSURANCE.

I. A HUMBLE CONDITION. "I am poor and needy." A man may be in such a state —spiritually—experimentally—comparatively—temporally.

All men are by nature poor and needy, as to their spiritual condition. Sin is very properly considered a fall; and it has reduced us to a low estate. It expelled us from paradise; it stripped us of our original righteousness and strength; it robbed us of the image, the favour, and the presence of God; it left us no worthiness, no hope—nothing but a certain fearful looking-for of judgment, and fiery indignation to devour us.—This is what we mean by being poor and needy, spiritually.

But the conviction of our natural state is not easily fixed in the mind; and hence, far from acknowledging it, many, like the Laodiceans, are saying, "I am rich, and increased with goods, and have need of nothing; and know not that they are wretched and miserable, and poor, and blind, and naked." But the subjects of divine grace are all acquainted with their condition. The Holy Spirit has convinced them of sin; and humbled them before God. They now see, that their recovery cannot spring from any goodness or power of their own; they are convinced, that if ever they are saved, it must be by another, in whom, at once, they can find wisdom and righteousness, sanctification and redemption. Hence they become beggars at the door of mercy, and are willing to live on alms; feeling their dependence, and thankful for their supplies.—This conviction, though self-abasing, is necessary and profitable. Till we apprehend our danger, we shall not inquire after a refuge; till we are sensible of our disease, we shall not prize the physician, or submit to the remedy; till we know that we are guilty and helpless, we shall never cry with the publican, "God be merciful to me a sinner;" or with Peter, "Lord, save; I perish."—But, "Blessed are the poor in spirit: for their's is the kingdom of heaven. Blessed are they who hunger and thirst after righteousness: for they shall be filled."—This is what we mean by being poor and needy, experimentally.

As all believers feel this to be their condition, so we may observe no difference is made in their sense of it by their worldly circumstances. David was a king; yet this did not alter the view he had of himself, as a fallen, sinful, perishing creature before God. His palace was not a substitute for heaven, nor even caused him to forget it. He had fame, and armies, and riches; yet these could not supply the place of all spiritual blessings: he therefore prays, "Remember me, O Lord, with the favour that thou bearest unto thy people: O visit me with thy salvation; that I may see the good of thy chosen, that I may rejoice in the gladness of thy nation, that I may glory with thine inheritance." "I am poor and needy," says the believer, "unless as I obtain the true riches, the unsearchable riches of Christ: and I often fear I have none of them. But if I am a possessor—O how small a portion do I possess! How little, compared with what I want and wish! How little, compared with the infinite fulness there is in the Redeemer! How little, compared with the acquisitions of others! They have received from him fulness, and grace for grace. But I have not attained: I am not already perfect. How weak is my faith; how wavering my hope; how flameless my zeal. How far—O how far am I from being filled with all the fulness of God!—I am less than the least of all saints! I am nothing!"—This is what we mean by being poor and needy, comparatively.

But David was liable to affliction; and there had been periods when he was low in his outward estate. He was originally a shepherd, and often acknowledged, with equal humility and gratitude, his elevation in life. Even after he had the throne of Israel promised him, and the holy oil had been poured upon his head, he was driven out from his inheritance, and was an exile in other lands; pursued from place to place, "like a partridge upon the mountains;" reduced to the necessity of imploring of a foreign prince an asylum for his father and mother; and compelled to beg a sword and even bread for himself at Nob. Years after he was enthroned he was betrayed and opposed, and forced by a rebellion the most unnatural to leave his palace and his capital! Some believers, through life, have had very little of this world's goods. They have found it hard to provide things honest in the sight of all men. We sometimes censure and condemn; as if men were the absolute masters of their secular condition: but they are not. It does not depend upon every man to rise and prosper: "I returned, and saw under the sun that the race is not to the swift, nor the battle to the strong, neither yet bread to the wise, nor yet riches to men of understanding, nor yet favour to men of skill; but time and chance happeneth to them all." There are those who have met with losses which no talent could have prevented. Every time they have attempted to row, the wind and waves have been contrary. Is this the case with any of you? Are you set back in life? Are your visions fled? Are your purposes broken off? Remember, this has been the case with multitudes of your brethren who were before you in the world. Your elder brother had not where to lay his head; was a man of sorrows and acquainted with grief. Your condition is not the result of chance, but appointment. Your safety and welfare required it. In more easy and flattering circumstances, you would have had less love to the Scriptures; less business at a throne of grace; less longings after a better country; less proof of the tender care of Providence and the all-sufficiency of Divine grace. This is what we mean by being poor and needy, in a temporal sense. Let us,

II. Examine THE GLORIOUS ASSURANCE— "I am poor and needy; *yet the Lord thinketh upon me.*" This is,

First, the language of confidence. David speaks without hesitation, and so may every Christian; for there is nothing of which they can be more certain than this—That God thinks upon them.

It is proved by his relations. He calls himself their deliverer; their friend; their husband; their father; and as a divinity is attached to these relations, they must all therefore be perfectly exemplified. His beneficiaries, his bride, his children therefore, can never be forgotten.

It is proved by his promises. "Remember these, O Jacob and Israel; for thou art my servant: I have formed thee; thou art my servant: O Israel, thou shalt not be forgotten of me."—"I will never leave thee, nor forsake thee." These are words found in a book we know to be divine. They are the words, not of a man, that may lie, or the son of man, that may repent, but of the God of truth. Talking and doing may be two things with creatures, but they are the same with him. He is often better than his word; but who ever found him worse?

It is proved by his works. What has he not done, O Christian, to justify your hope! He remembered you in your low estate.— Without your desert, and without your desire, he raised up for you a Saviour; and seemed to love your souls better than his own Son. "He spared not his own Son, but delivered him up for you all; and shall he not with him freely give you all things?"—He found you wandering the downward road, and turned your feet into the path of peace. He has admitted you into his service, and adopted you into his family. Had he a mind to kill you, he would not have shown you such things as these. You have had your fears, but he has shown you their folly. You have said, "I am cast out of his sight;" but you have been enabled to look again towards his holy temple, and the shadow of death has been turned into the morning. You have not advanced as you ought to have done, and you mourn it; but you can say, to the praise of the glory of his grace, "Our heart is not turned back, neither have our steps declined from thy way: though thou hast sore broken us in the place of dragons, and covered us with the shadow of death."

How many things are there worthy of particular review in your history. Though they have been less marvellous, they have not been less merciful than his dispensations towards his people of old. Have you not been delivered "from the land of Egypt and the house of bondage, by a strong hand and an outstretched arm?"—I mean have you not been "delivered from the power of darkness, and translated into the kingdom of God's dear Son!" Have you not had the bitter waters of Marah healed by casting a tree into them? —I mean, have not your sufferings been sweetened by the cross of Christ? Have you not been fed by ravens?—I mean, have not the most unlikely instruments befriended you? Have not the oil and the wine multiplied?—I mean, have not inconsiderable resources been rendered sufficient for your exigences; so that, while you had nothing to depend upon, you have lacked nothing!— "Whoso is wise, and will observe these things, even they shall understand the loving-kindness of the Lord;" and be able to say, "I am poor and needy—yet the Lord thinketh upon me."

Secondly. It is the language of wonder. It is said by the apostle Peter, that God calls his people out of darkness into his marvellous light; and one of the things which fill them with surprise, and continue to fill them with surprise through life is, that God fails not to regard such creatures as we are.

It is rendered truly wonderful by the "conduct of men." This we continually witness; and we are prone to judge from what falls under our own observation. How many, alas! of those with whom you have to do, prove either frail or treacherous! How many have abandoned you, after the warmest expressions of friendship and kindness! How often have you heard the voice saying, "Cease from man! Cursed is the man that trusteth in man, and maketh flesh his arm!" In this way you have been peculiarly tried when reduced; for people reverse the maxim of Solomon, and suppose a friend born for prosperity. The flower that, while fresh and green, is put into the bosom, is thrown away when shriveled and dry. But it is otherwise here.

"I am poor and needy; yet the Lord thinketh upon me."

It is rendered wonderful by the *greatness of God.* What a trifling elevation leads one man to overlook another! How generally are the lower ranks disregarded by those who have a few acres of land, a little shining dust, or an empty title to distinguish them—while they are only worms themselves, and are crushed before the moth. "But behold, God is great, and we know him not. All nations are before him as nothing.' Well, therefore, did David, when he surveyed the universe, exclaim, "Lord, what is man, that thou art mindful of him, or the son of man, that thou visitest him!" This is nothing less than Infinite Power and Majesty stooping to weakness and meanness.

It is rendered wonderful by *our unworthiness.* The more holy any being is, the more must he be offended with sin. How then must God be provoked by it, who is of purer eyes than to behold iniquity! "And yet how much has he seen in me," says the Christian, "to try him, not only before I knew him, but since I have been called by his name. I cannot take the most superficial review of myself without seeing that it is of the Lord's mercies I am not consumed. Where is there any other benefactor that would have continued his regards, or have given me another thought, after such instances of perverseness and vileness as I have been chargeable with from year to year towards God!"

Thirdly. It is the language of consolation. "I am poor and needy; yet the Lord thinketh upon me." This is enough: this will more than counterbalance every thing that is defective or distressing in my condition. There are three things in God's thinking upon us that are solacing and delightful.

Observe the *frequency* of his thoughts. Indeed they are incessant. You have a friend whom you esteem and love. You wish to live in his mind. You say, when you part and when you write, "Think of me." You give him, perhaps, a token to revive his remembrance. How naturally is Selkirk, in his solitary island, made to say;

" My friends,—do they now and then send
　A wish or a *thought* after me?
O tell me I yet have a friend,
　Though a friend I am never to see!

" Ye winds, that have made me your sport,
　Convey to this desolate shore
Some cordial, endearing report
　Of a land I shall visit no more."

But the dearest connexion in the world cannot be always thinking upon you. Half his time he is in a state of unconsciousness;. and how much, during the other half, is he engrossed! But there is no remission in the Lord's thoughts. He never slumbers: and though he manages worlds, and calls the stars by their names, he numbers the hairs of thy head, and regards thee as much as if thou wert his only care.

Observe, in the next place, the *wisdom* of his thoughts. You have a dear child absent from you, and you follow him in your mind. But you know not his present circumstances. You left him in such a place—but where is he now? You left him in such a condition—but what is he now? Perhaps, while you are thinking of his health, he is groaning under a bruised limb, or a painful disorder. Perhaps, while you are thinking of his safety, some enemy is taking advantage of his innocency. Perhaps, while you are rejoicing in his prudence, he is going to take a step that will involve him for life. But when God thinketh upon you, he is perfectly acquainted with your situation, your dangers, your wants. "He knows all your walking through this great wilderness"—and can afford you the seasonable succour you need.—For again,

Observe the *efficiency* of his thoughts. You think upon another; and you are anxious to guide, or defend, or relieve him. But in how many cases can you think only! Solicitude cannot control the disease of the body; cannot dissipate the melancholy of the mind. But with God all things are possible. He who thinks upon you is a God at hand, and not afar off; he has all events under his control; he is the God of all grace. If, therefore, he does not immediately deliver, it is not because he is unable to redress, but because he is waiting to be gracious. "The Lord is a God of judgment, and blessed are all they that wait for him."——Let us conclude.

Here we see how it is that the believer stands while others sink. He has supports peculiar to himself; and when creatures frown or fail, he encourages himself in the Lord his God. "Although my house be not so with God, yet he hath made with me an everlasting covenant, ordered in all things, and sure: for this is all my salvation, and all my desire, although he make it not to grow. Although the fig tree shall not blossom, neither shall fruit be in the vines; the labour of the olive shall fail, and the fields shall yield no meat; the flock shall be cut off from the fold, and there shall be no herd in the stalls: yet I will rejoice in the Lord, I will joy in the God of my salvation. I am poor and needy; yet the Lord thinketh upon me."

Is this your portion? How anxious are men to gain the notice of their fellow-creatures, especially if they are a little raised above themselves in condition! "Many will entreat the favour of the prince, and every one is a friend to him that giveth gifts." But in this case you are never sure you shall succeed; and you have gained nothing if you do. Whereas here—the success is sure, and the success is—every thing. Pray therefore, with Nehemiah, "Think upon me, O my

God, for good. Seek the Lord, and ye shall live."

O believer! If God thinks upon you, ought you not to think upon him? David did. "How precious also are thy thoughts unto me, O God! how great is the sum of them! If I should count them, they are more in number than the sand: when I awake I am still with thee." If he minds your affairs—Be not you forgetful of his. Ever ask, "Lord, what wilt thou have me to do?" Ever cry, "Speak, Lord, for thy servant heareth."

DISCOURSE XCVI.

THE FOUNTAIN OF LIFE.

In that day there shall be a fountain opened for sin and for uncleanness.—Zech. xiii. 1.

THERE are many curious things in nature; and there are things useful and necessary. But we have things, shall I say, of the same kind, in the world of grace, far superior; and superior, because they regard the soul and eternity. How is the rising of the orb of day surpassed by "the Sun of righteousness, who arises with healing under his wings!" How are the meekness of the lily, and the fragrance of the rose, excelled by "the rose of Sharon and the lily of the valley!" It is pleasing to behold a number of trees adorned with blossoms, or bending with fruit—but we have in the Church "trees of righteousness, the planting of the Lord, that he might be glorified." It is delightful to view a river refreshing and fertilizing the meadows through which it murmurs—but we read of "the river of the water of life, clear as crystal, proceeding out of the throne of God and of the Lamb." There are fountains. We hear of remarkable ones abroad. We have some very valuable ones in our own country. One of these bubbles up in the place of our residence; and to which multitudes repair for relief. But I have to invite your attention this evening to a fountain infinitely more wonderful and efficacious, and of which Zechariah speaks, in the words which I have read: "In that day there shall be a fountain opened for sin and for uncleanness."

For, my brethren, to what can he refer, but the exclamation of John, the forerunner of the Messiah—"Behold the Lamb of God, that taketh away the sin of the world!" Nothing less will be found sufficient to justify, or imbody the language. Even allowing that Zechariah had not the same distinct and explicit views of the Saviour that we have who possess the explanations of the New Testament writers; it does not follow that this was not his object; for we know that the prophets often delivered predictions which they did not completely understand;

and therefore studied them after they had announced them: "searching what, or what manner of time the Spirit of Christ which was in them did signify, when it testified beforehand the sufferings of Christ, and the glory that should follow. Unto whom it was revealed, that not unto themselves, but unto us, they did minister the things, which are now reported unto you by them that have preached the Gospel unto you with the Holy Ghost sent down from heaven; which things the angels desire to look into."

I am not unmindful of the day* which has assembled us together; but my choice of a subject shows that I consider it of little importance, to dwell upon the crucifixion of Christ, as a wonderful, or a tragical scene. I am aware that such a pathetical representation might be given of the history as would draw tears from every eye—while the mind remained uninformed of, and the heart unaffected with, the nature and design of the event. The grand thing is, to know why the dispensation was necessary; and, realizing its accomplishment in ourselves, to be able to say, "He was wounded for our transgressions, he was bruised for our iniquities: the chastisement of our peace was upon him; and with his stripes we are healed."

I have two things in view.—I. To explain the promise.—II. To improve the truth it contains.

I. In the explanation of the promise, three things are observable. The *fountain*—the *opening*—and the *end*.

First. The *fountain*. This image holds forth the Redeemer. In distinction from creatures, which "are cisterns, broken cisterns, that can hold no water," he may well call himself the fountain of living waters." The Jews were accustomed, on the last, which was called the great day of the feast, to fetch water from the pool of Siloam, singing the words of Isaiah, "Therefore with joy shall ye draw water out of the wells of salvation." On that very occasion, we find our Saviour preaching; and he takes advantage of the ceremony to proclaim himself to the multitude as the true source of blessedness: "In the last day, that great day of the feast, Jesus stood and cried, saying, If any man thirst, let him come unto me, and drink. He that believeth on me, as the Scripture hath said, out of his belly shall flow rivers of living water." To the woman of Samaria he had said before, "The water that I shall give him, shall be in him a well of water springing up into everlasting life."—He shall possess a plenitude himself: but the fulness of the Christian is limited; is derived; is the fulness of a vessel. This vessel is supplied from the fulness of a fountain—and this fountain is the Lord Jesus. His fulness is original and boundless. It is the fulness of a spring; always flowing,

* Good Friday.

and yet undiminished. He is in himself an infinite and everlasting source of all the influences and blessings we need: "In him dwelleth all the fulness of the Godhead bodily: and of his fulness have all we received, and grace for grace."

Secondly. This fountain was to be *opened*. If a fountain was shut up, and sealed, though the contents would be equally precious in themselves, they would be useless to us; yea, they would only provoke our desire, to torment us. And what would the Saviour's excellences and benefits be to us, if unattainable and inaccessible? But they are placed within our view, and within our reach. This fountain was actually opened in his sufferings. His blood flowed in the garden, and upon the cross. His back was wounded by the scourge; his temples with the crown of thorns; his hands and his feet with the nails; his side with the spear. Then was the fountain opened; and one, hard by, beheld it—

" The dying thief rejoiced to see
That fountain, in his day ;"

And oh! that each of us, with humility and confidence, may be able to add;

" And there have I, as vile as he,
Wash'd all my sins away !"

The apostles laid it open doctrinally, in their preaching. Paul could appeal to the Corinthians, and say; "I determined not to know any thing among you, save Jesus Christ, and him crucified." And referring both to the subject of his preaching, and the plain and lively manner in which he had delivered it, he could say to the Galatians, "Before your eyes Jesus Christ hath been evidently set forth crucified among you."

It was, unquestionably, open, when the apostles wrote their epistles; for thousands were rejoicing in the efficacy of this fountain, and could say, "We are come to the blood of sprinkling—We are redeemed with the precious blood of the Lord Jesus Christ. The blood of Jesus Christ his Son cleanseth from all sin!"—And is it closed since? No: it stands open now—open, in the means of grace—open, in the invitations of the Word—open, in the nearness, the power, and the grace of the Saviour—how open while he says, "Him that cometh unto me I will in no wise cast out !"

Thirdly. This fountain is "opened *for sin and for uncleanness.*" There had been provisions for ceremonial pollution, under the Mosaical economy. There was the brazen sea, fifty feet in circumference, and ten in depth; in which the priests were to wash their hands and feet. There were also ten lavers, in which the things offered in sacrifice were washed, and whence the water was taken to sprinkle the offerers. There were also fountains for bodily diseases—the pool of Siloam to which our Saviour sent the man born blind; and the pool of Bethesda, where lay a great number of sufferers, waiting for the troubling of the waters. These probably had a preternatural quality imparted to them, about this period, to rouse the mind to expectation, and to prepare it to contemplate the approaching Recoverer of the human race. He differed from all these, as a fountain for moral and spiritual defilement—"for sin and for uncleanness."

And sin *is* uncleanness. Its very nature is contamination. The moment it touched a number of angels in heaven, it turned them into devils, and expelled them from their first estate. It is so contagious, that it infects every thing in contact with it, so that, as the house of the leper was to be taken down because of the inhabitant, "the heavens shall pass away with a great noise, and the elements shall melt with fervent heat, the earth also, and all the works that are therein, shall be burned up"—not because they are guilty; but because they have been the witnesses, the instruments, the abodes of sin.

Sin is a pollution the most deep and diffusive: it stops not at the surface, but penetrates the inner man of the heart; it spreads through every power, from the highest intellectual faculty, down to the lowest animal appetite. If any part were left uninjured, it would seem to be the conscience—but no; *the very conscience itself is defiled:* and nothing has been too vile to be perpetrated under its permission, and in obedience to its dictates. It is a pollution the most horrible and dangerous, as it disfigures us before God; and renders us odious in his sight. And nothing else does this. Poverty does not; meanness does not; disease does not—Lazarus full of sores, begging at the rich man's gate, and Job, covered with biles, among the ashes, were dear to God, and lay in his bosom. But sin is the *abominable thing* which his *soul hates.* Men often roll it, as a sweet morsel, under their tongue; but it is more poisonous than the gall of asps. They think lightly of it; but can *that* be a trifling thing which causes God to hate the very work of his own hands—"my soul loathed them!"—and induce the very "Father of mercies" to say at last, "Depart, ye cursed, into everlasting fire, prepared for the devil and his angels."

Have you, my hearers, such views of sin! Does it appear to you, as it does to the Judge of all, *exceeding sinful?*

Such is certainly the sentiment of every man who is "convinced of sin." The Holy Spirit leads him to see, not only its guilt, but its defilement; and while the one excites his fear, the other calls forth his aversion. Self-complacency is then ruined for ever. He no longer wonders that he stands excluded, in his present state, from the presence of a holy God. He feels that he deserves to perish—and cries with the leper, "Unclean, unclean."

And as things strike us most forcibly by contrast, the more he is enlightened to see the purity and glory of God; and especially his grace and love in the person, work, and sufferings of his dear Son; instead of being reconciled to himself, the more will he feel of the temper of Job, who exclaimed, "Behold, I am vile; what shall I answer Thee? wherefore, I abhor myself, and repent in dust and ashes."

But there is a fountain that washes out even the stains of the soul—and of sin! And it was opened for this very purpose: "In that day there shall be a fountain opened for sin and for uncleanness." And I proceed,

II. To IMPROVE THE TRUTH CONTAINED IN THE PROMISE. And should I dwell longer on this part of our subject than on the former, it will not appear wonderful to those who reflect, how much more ready people are to hear than to apply; and how seldom practice keeps pace with speculation. In order to commend myself to every man's conscience in the sight of God, I arrange the assembly in five classes; each of which has a relation to the truth before us. The first are *ignorant.* The second *presumptuous.* The third *self-righteous.* The fourth the *fearful.* The fifth the *believing.*

First. The *ignorant.* The Apostle speaks of some who cried, Peace, peace, while sudden destruction was coming upon them—such a difference is there between confidence and security. Our Lord tells us of some who are "whole, and need not the physician"—so necessary is a conviction of our spiritual state to excite a proper regard to the Saviour. And, to vary the metaphor, some are not defiled, and need not this fountain opened for sin and uncleanness. We do not mean that there are any *really* in this condition, and the reason is involved in the inquiry, "Who can bring a clean thing out of an unclean?" It is a law pervading all nature, that "like begets like." A viper brings forth a poisonous brood. Swine produce something that loves the mire. The skin of an Ethiopian will be black. What but depraved offspring can descend from sinful parents? Therefore, says Job, "What is man, that he should be clean, or he that is born of a woman, that he should be righteous?" The Scripture assures us that "all have sinned and come short of the glory of God." It teaches us, that "the heart is deceitful above all things, and desperately wicked." It assures us that it is not the life which defiles the heart; but the heart the life: "For from within, out of the heart of men, proceed evil thoughts, adulteries, fornications, murders, thefts, covetousness, wickedness, deceit, lasciviousness, an evil eye, blasphemy, pride, foolishness: all these evil things come from within, and defile the man." It requires no less than a change of nature, to show that our nature is depraved; and it requires this change in every man, to show that this depravity is universal.

Yet there are those who deny this mortifying fact; and though they live in a land of vision, are so unacquainted with the Bible, and ignorant of themselves, as to imagine that *they* are pure. "There is a generation that are pure in their own eyes, but are not washed from their filthiness." We may conclude the reception our subject will meet with from you. You cannot understand it, because you know nothing of the state to which it refers; and you cannot value it, because you feel nothing that can render it interesting. The whole system of the Gospel is founded in the fact of our guilt and depravity; and till a man is convinced of this, he will be like the deaf adder, that stoppeth his ear against the voice of the charmer, charm he never so wisely. Pardon offered to the innocent will be deemed an insult. Alms presented to the affluent will be rejected with disdain. O what a mercy, to feel our need of mercy!—Beg of God to open the eyes of your understanding, and lead you into an acquaintance with yourselves; that, seeing what you are, and feeling what you deserve, and what you need, you may be prepared to welcome the glad tidings of salvation, and deem it a faithful saying, and worthy of all acceptation, that, There is "a fountain opened for sin, and for uncleanness."

Secondly. The *presumptuous.* Antinomian perversion is far worse than mere ignorance of the Gospel. We should be cautious in applying hard names; but the Scripture makes no scruple to call those "ungodly men, that turn the grace of our Lord God into lasciviousness." And yet there are men, whose very religion leaves them *personally* unchanged: who dream of mercy while they live in sin; and claim eternal life without "the washing of regeneration, and the renewing of the Holy Ghost." But there is no salvation without cleansing: "He that hath this hope in him, purifieth himself, even as he is pure." For sin separates between God and the soul; and that wall of division must be removed before we can meet. There must be agreement before there can be intimacy. "How can two walk together, except they be agreed? What fellowship hath righteousness with unrighteousness? And what communion hath light with darkness? And what agreement hath the temple of God with idols? for ye are the temple of the living God; as God hath said, I will dwell in them, and walk in them; and I will be their God, and they shall be my people. Wherefore come out from among them, and be ye separate, saith the Lord, and touch not the unclean thing; and I will receive you, and will be a Father unto you, and ye shall be my sons and daughters, saith the Lord Almighty"

Were we even pardoned for contracting the disease, yet, while it continues uncured, we can have no ease within. If we entered heaven with an unsanctified disposition, we should be incapable of relishing its enjoyments. A title to glory can never give us a meetness for it. Wherever we carry sin in us, we carry hell with us. The Lord Jesus is a Saviour, because he "saves his people *from* their sins."—"He gave himself for us, that he might redeem us from all iniquity, and purify unto himself a peculiar people, zealous of good works." Beware of deceiving yourselves. To be washed in this fountain, is the one-thing needful. "If I wash thee not, thou hast no part with me."

Thirdly. The *self-righteous.* I mean those who hope to cleanse themselves in some other way than by this fountain. Some would wash away their sins by the tears of repentance. Some would cover them by charity: for "charity" (by the mistake of a passage of Scripture) "covers a multitude of sins." Some would pay off the old score by ceremonial and superstitious observances—And here, what an article could religious folly furnish! What is there to which men have not had recourse while asking, "How shall I come before the Lord, or bow before the high God!"

Even when people are in a measure awakened, and begin to feel their need of salvation, it cannot but be remarked, how inclined they are to some plan, some services, some sacrifice, of their own. The simple provision of God offends them; and they resemble Naaman. Naaman was a leper. He had come with a splendid train; and more full of pride than of disease, he stood, with his horses and his chariot, at the door of the house of Elisha. Hence, when Elisha sent a messenger unto him, saying, "Go and wash in Jordan seven times, and thy flesh shall come again unto thee, and thou shalt be clean, Naaman was wroth, and went away, and said, Behold, I thought, He will surely come out to me, and stand, and call on the name of the Lord his God, and strike his hand over the place, and recover the leper. Are not Abana and Pharpar, rivers of Damascus, better than all the waters of Israel? may I not wash in them, and be clean? So he turned, and went away in a rage." And would have remained a leper had not the servants been wiser than the master. Here was his error. He came for a cure, and it was, therefore, for him not to prescribe, but to submit. So it should be with you. You are not to go about to establish your own righteousness, but to submit yourselves to the righteousness which is of God. You are not to reason and speculate; but follow the Divine will. You are lost, and ready to perish. The Gospel reveals a method of salvation, and you should cheerfully and thankfully bow to it—you should *implicitly* acquiesce in it; remembering that you have no claims on the sovereign Donor; and that the plan is the effect of his wisdom, as well as of his goodness.

And would he, at an infinite expense, have provided, and made known, this way of salvation, if any other had been sufficient? Would he have called the attention of the universe to the opening of this Fountain, for the ablution of souls, had other streams been available? Our having recourse, therefore, to any other plan of salvation, is not only useless, and sure to end in disappointment; but it is criminal. There is nothing than can render us more guilty before God. It is disobedience; it is opposition. It robs him of his peculiar glory. It degrades his understanding, as well as detracts from his mercy. It "frustrates the grace of God, and makes Jesus Christ to be dead in vain."

Fourthly. The *fearful*. It is no easy thing to satisfy the conscience of awakened sinners: *they* need strong consolation who are "fleeing for refuge to lay hold of the hope set before them."—And is it not provided? Wherefore do you doubt? We acknowledge the blood of bulls and of goats could not take away sin. Neither could blood merely human. But the blood of which we speak is the blood of a Divine Sufferer; and we know the all-sufficiency of it, because it has been accepted by Him who required it on our behalf. And if *He* has heard the voice of the blood of sprinkling, and is satisfied; if his law is magnified and made honourable; and he can be faithful and just, as well as merciful and gracious, to forgive us our sins, and to cleanse us from all unrighteousness— *we* may well believe—and enter into rest.

But you say, it is not the efficiency of the Fountain you question. What then? Why, whether *I* have liberty to make use of it? Let us examine this case. And for whom is this Fountain opened? The innocent and the clean? No—It is opened "for sin and uncleanness." Guilt, therefore, constitutes no exclusion. We are told, he "came into the world to save sinners;" and that "he died for the ungodly." As I can only at first apply to him in the character of a sinner, it is obvious, that the warrant which authorizes me to apply must be addressed indiscriminately to *all* sinners. And so it is. All who have the Gospel have such a warrant—a warrant that will not only justify *any man* from presumption who acts upon it, but will be sure to condemn all those who do not. Come, therefore, come, whoever you are.

> " This Fountain unsealed
> Stands open for all
> Who long to be healed—
> The great and the small."—

But I have nothing to pay. And you need nothing:

> " This Fountain, though rich,
> From charge is quite clear;
> The poorer the wretch,
> The welcomer here "

I know that such language has been deemed altogether exceptionable; as if we encouraged sin, while we only encourage the sinner. And how are we to encourage a sinner? Is it by requiring of him, as the ground of his hope, conditions which he cannot perform? Or is it by keeping him back from Christ, while waiting for qualifications which he can never derive from himself? Are men to be warmed before they go to the fire, to entitle them to the heat, and to prepare them for it? Are patients to be recovered, or, at least, considerably mended, before they apply to the physician? The sick and the dying are his charge. Do not wait, therefore, for qualifications to recommend you—We do need a mediator between God and us, but not between us and Christ. What said Paul and Silas at once to the jailer's question? "Believe on the Lord Jesus Christ, and thou shalt be saved."

> " Let not conscience make you linger,
> Nor of fitness fondly dream:
> All the fitness he requireth
> Is to feel your need of him."

Finally. There is one class more who have a relation to our subject; and it consists of those who by faith have applied to this Saviour: and who know, by *experience*, that there is indeed a fountain opened for sin and uncleanness. *You* are witnesses. You can vouch that it is accessible and free. Were you refused? Were you required to wait? Was your claim questioned? Rather, were you not welcomed with a smile, which showed, that the backwardness had only been on your side; and with a voice, that kindly anticipated your approach, and said, "Wilt thou be made whole?"

You can vouch for its efficacy too. You *know* that it can relieve a troubled mind; that it can heal the broken in heart, and bind up all their wounds. You *know* that, while it deeply humbles before God, it can inspire a holy freedom: for you "*have* boldness and access with confidence, by the faith of Him." You *know* that, while it renders the curse harmless, it makes sin odious; and not only tranquillizes, but "purifies the conscience from dead works, to serve the living God."

When persons, labouring under a malady, have found relief, a grateful disposition leads them, as opportunity offers, to commend the physician; while a benevolent feeling urges them to recommend his remedy to others, who are suffering under the same complaint. "Praise ye the Lord. Declare his doings among the people. Make mention that his Name is exalted." Go, and divulge—not only what you have read and heard, but— what you have known and felt. Are there not thousands perishing around you? And are they not your brethren; bone of your bone, and flesh of your flesh? What was ence your promise, your vow, if you were snatched from the jaws of death yourselves?—

> " Then will I tell to sinners round
> What a dear Saviour I have found;
> I'll point to his atoning blood,
> And say, Behold the way to God!"

Pray that this way may be known on earth; this saving health among all nations. Send, where you cannot go yourselves—aid the Bible Society, in diffusing the Scriptures; and Missionary Societies, in sending forth missionaries. Employ your personal influence. Make use of your talents; make use of your tongue. Let your temper, your conduct, your life, your character, speak.

Indeed, it will be in vain for you to applaud a remedy that has done you no good. When you recommend it, with all the symptoms and effects of your disorder upon you, they will naturally say, "You have an end to answer, regardless of our welfare. You do not believe in the virtue of the medicine, or you would have used it yourself." If, therefore, you are vain, and proud, and revengeful, and selfish, and covetous; if your family is the scene of discord and strife; if your shop is famed for cunning, overreaching, and injustice; if, under the profession of Christianity, you have not the honesty of a heathen—you had much better say nothing: for people will immediately judge of your religion by you—And will your conduct impress it? Will this endear it!

But, blessed be God, allowing for human infirmities, and imperfections, inseparable from the present life; blessed be God, there are some who are emphatically the better for the Gospel: they are spiritually convalescent; they are other creatures than they once were: they are renewed in the spirit of their minds; they live soberly, righteously, and godly in the present world; and they walk worthy of the vocation wherewith they are called; they are followers of him who went about doing good. They are also increasing; and though, as yet, they are few, compared with the world that lieth in wickedness, there are enough to show the reality and power of the Saviour's grace, and to leave those without excuse who will not come to him, that they might have life.

But oh! what, what will it be when all, "out of every kindred, and nation, and people, and tongue"—all that he has ever saved, shall be assembled together, as the trophies of his cross—while he, engaging every eye, and enrapturing every heart, shall hear from the countless throng; "Unto him that loved us, and washed us from our sins in his own blood, and hath made us kings and priests unto God, and his Father; be glory and dominion for ever and ever!!"

DISCOURSE XCVII.

RELIGIOUS INDECISION.

Ephraim is a cake not turned.—Hosea vii. 8.

BAKED on one side only—neither soft nor hard—neither bread nor dough—disagreeable—unserviceable. "A very homely comparison, a very vulgar image," you say. But the sacred penmen are above our fastidiousness. They write for the common people; and what are little delicate allusions, discerned and relished only by a refinement of taste, while they are lost upon the majority of readers? *They* want something plain, and yet forcible; something to rouse the conscience, and to lodge in the mind. And "the words of the wise," says Solomon, "are as goads, and as nails;" *goads* to wound, and *nails* to fasten. If the image be vulgar, it is striking; and if the comparison be homely, it is much too flattering for the persons it is intended to express.

Let us divide our subject into three parts. I. WE SHALL INQUIRE AFTER THE CENSURED CHARACTERS. II. WE SHALL EXPOSE THEIR CONDUCT AND THEIR CONDITION. III. WE SHALL ENDEAVOUR TO BRING THEM TO A DECISION; or, as our text would authorize us to say—see if we cannot turn these cakes.

I. WHO ARE EPHRAIMITES? In answering this question, as the preacher ought to proceed with great caution, so you ought to hear with peculiar seriousness; and may the God of the spirits of all flesh empower an inward monitor to say, as we proceed, "Thou art the man."

There are three classes of persons, as far as our subject requires us to distinguish them. There are real Christians, who are entirely for God. There are the profligate, who make no pretensions to religion. And there are some who stand between both, and seem to partake of each; and *these* are the characters we are in search of.

Few are totally regardless of Divine things. Some, indeed, wear no disguise, and encumber themselves with no forms. They never call upon God's name—unless to profane it; never observe the sabbath, or hear the word preached; they explicitly avow their ungodliness, always in actions, and often in words: and, "I am for hell," is written in capitals on their forehead. But these are not the mass: there are not many who can shake off *all* religious concern. Their education, their relations, reason, conscience, reputation, even their worldly interest—all these induce them to pay *some* attention to religion. But the lamentation is, that they are only formal, external, partial—at best, but half-hearted, in their regards. "Ephraim is a cake not turned."

Who then are the characters intended? If

we look into the Scripture, we shall find some of them represented by the successors of Israel. When the king of Assyria had carried away the ten tribes from Judea, he "brought men from Babylon, and from Cuthah, and from Ava, and from Hamath, and from Sepharvaim, and placed them in the cities of Samaria instead of the children of Israel: and they possessed Samaria, and dwelt in the cities thereof. And so it was at the beginning of their dwelling there, that they feared not the Lord: therefore the Lord sent lions among them, which slew some of them. Wherefore they spake to the king of Assyria, saying, The nations which thou hast removed, and placed in the cities of Samaria, know not the manner of the God of the land: therefore he hath sent lions among them, and, behold, they slay them, because they know not the manner of the God of the land. Then the king of Assyria commanded, saying, Carry thither one of the priests whom he brought from thence; and let them go and dwell there, and let him teach them the manner of the God of the land." And so they did; and, with a mongrel devotion, they served both Jehovah and their idols; the one from affection, and the other for fear of the lions: " They feared the Lord, and served their own gods, after the manner of the nations whom they carried away from thence." We shall find some of them in a Balaam—unable to go beyond the word of the Lord; and yet loving the wages of unrighteousness; delighting in what he declined; sacrificing his conscience to his fame; blessing Israel, and showing how to curse them; praying, " Let me die the death of the righteous, and let my last end be like his," and perishing in battle against them. We shall find some of them in a young man, so promising, so wise, so humble, as to inquire after eternal life, kneeling; and so amiable, as to engage the affection of the Saviour; but who went away sorrowful, because he could not resign an earthly possession at the command of Him, who would more than have repaid the sacrifice. We shall find some of them in a Herod, who "heard John gladly, and feared him, and did many things," but retained his Herodias, and murdered his admired preacher, for the sake of an unlawful passion. We shall find some of them in an Agrippa, who, pressed by the eloquence and truth of the Apostle's reasoning, exclaimed, "Almost thou persuadest me to be a Christian."

And cannot we find, nearer home, individuals, alternately in the temple and the tavern! now in the house of prayer, and now in the place of dissipation! repairing to the one from conviction, and to the other from inclination! refusing to the passions what may trouble the conscience, and to conscience what may trouble the passions! equally remote from the ardours of the pious, and the excesses of the profane! free from gross vices, and yet indulging in graceless tempers! wearing " a form of godliness, but denying the power thereof! having a name to live, and yet dead!"

Some of these characters are to be met with in connexion with the more evangelical modes of religion. Such persons will attend only on the preaching of the Gospel. They are orthodox in their views. With their mouth, they show much love. Their feelings are sometimes powerfully excited. They receive the word with joy. They have another heart; but not a new one.

We have read of a bishop, formerly in Spain, whose clergy had long been carrying on a controversy, concerning the condition of Solomon: some pleading for his salvation, and others for his perdition. To accommodate both parties, the good bishop ordered a representation of him to be drawn on the walls of his chapel, half in hell, and half in heaven. And what better could a moral painter do with numbers in our day? We know not whether to set them down as children of wrath, or heirs of glory. Their inconsistencies are such, that each side seems to disown them; and they continue to agitate both the hopes and fears of those who have any regard for their eternal welfare. But our fears must prevail: and we proceed,

II. To EXPOSE THEIR CONDUCT, AND THEIR CONDITION. And this may be done, by observing Four things.

First. This indecision is *unreasonable*. What is there that will not convince you of the truth of this remark?—Think of God. Is he such a friend, such a father, such a master, such a sovereign, as to deserve only a languid devotion, a divided heart? " Cursed be the deceiver, which hath in his flock a male, and voweth, and sacrificeth unto the Lord a corrupt thing: for I am a great King, saith the Lord of hosts, and my name is dreadful among the heathen."—Look at the Saviour of sinners. How did he engage in the work of your deliverance? Did indifference bring him from heaven to earth; and induce him, who was rich, for your sake to become poor; and die, that you might live? He loved us, and gave himself for us: and one feeling only can correspond with his infinite kindness, a feeling of universal consecration:

" Were the whole realm of nature mine,
That were a present far too small;
Love so amazing, so divine,
Demands my soul, my life, my all!"

Look at the hell you have to escape; the glory you have to obtain; the brevity and uncertainty of the time allowed you for success. Does a state of slumber become the awfulness of your situation and prospects? " Escape for thy life: look not behind thee; neither stay thou in all the plain; escape to the mountain, lest thou be consumed."

" Whatsoever thy hand findeth to do, do it with thy might; for there is no work, nor device, nor knowledge, nor wisdom, in the grave, whither thou goest." Look at religion. Is there any medium between the truth, and importance of the subject? If you do not believe this Book to be true, you are an infidel; if you do, and disregard its contents, you are worse. Can lukewarmness ever perform the duties of religion? Is prayer only the bending of the knee? Is praise only " a solemn sound upon a thoughtless tongue?" Can lukewarmness ever conquer the difficulties of religion? Will this enable you to run the race that is set before you, or to fight the good fight of faith?—Look at your fellow-creatures. They rise up early, and sit up late, and compass sea and land, to gain a little shining dust, or the smile of the great; and yet, what a disparity is there between your zeal and their zeal, their sacrifices and your sacrifices?—Look at the uselessness of all your half measures. Have you suffered so much in vain, if it be yet in vain? Are ye so foolish, having begun in the Spirit, are you now made perfect by the flesh? If the course in which you have been engaged is not worthy of your regard, why did you go so far? If it be, why not go further? If resolved to perish, could you not have perished without resisting any sin; without performing any duty?

Secondly. This indecision is *dishonourable*. Such a man is never regarded. In vain you say, " Why, he is the very man the people of the world approve"—and suppose he was—Are they to be our judges? He that judges us is the Lord. But you are mistaken. The people of the world may like such a temporizer so far as by resemblance he justifies them; but as to real veneration and respect for him, they have none—nor can they have any. No; such a man is never regarded. He is no character. He has neither the value, nor solidity of gold: lead is his image—worthless, and easily receptive of any impression. " Unstable as water, thou shalt not excel." Uprightness and consistency are always admired. The possessor after a while lives down reproach, and enthrones himself in the judgment and esteem of his fellow-creatures. " Well," say they, " he is sincere and honest; he is all of a piece." But base is the man who changes with the times; varies with his situations; conforms to the company he is in; is always worldly with the worldly, and sanctified with the saints—Who likes " a cake not turned?"

Thirdly. Such indecision is *wretched*. Can any thing be more miserable than to have two businesses to carry on at the same time; two parties to consult in every action and in every look; two masters to serve who hate each other, and whose designs are perfectly opposite? What but distraction, confusion, and drudgery, and strife must ensue? These half Christians, owing to the light they have in the understanding, and the checks of conscience, cannot enjoy the vanities of the world and the pleasures of sin: while religion, as regarded by them, is no source of joy; they do not enter into the spirit of it, and, therefore, cannot relish its satisfactions. The real believer enjoys the light of God's countenance, the comforts of the Holy Ghost, and has meat to eat which others know not of; and the professed votary of sin and the world enjoys the delights which arise from time and sense: but the character before us enjoys neither. He gives up the creature for God, and God for the creature. He loses heaven for the sake of earth, and earth for the sake of heaven; and is of all men the most miserable.

Fourthly. Such indecision is *dangerous*. I wish to be understood to mean—*peculiarly dangerous*. Observe, in the first place: such characters are not easily converted. For though they have not religion enough to ensure their safety, they have sufficient to make them insensible of their danger. Though they have not enough to keep them awake, they have sufficient to lull them to sleep. Conscience has nothing very criminal, in their view, to reproach them with. Their exemption from immorality gives them confidence and peace. Their attention to the exterior of piety, and the decency of their general demeanour, attract from men the praise which is due to real godliness; and this flatters and confirms the good opinion they entertain of themselves. Their satisfaction with themselves is also strengthened by contrasts with the character and conduct of others, who are outwardly and openly wicked. Their very convictions, too, in time are altered; their practice has bribed their judgment; and what formerly appeared wrong is now deemed a vain scruple, the effect of education, or a contracted mind. Secondly: they are not very likely to continue always in this state. Duties never relished, in time disgust. Prayer never performed in earnest, may be wholly given up. Doctrines never known in their vital influence, may be discarded as speculations. Errors more congenial with their present feelings, and necessary to justify the course they take, may be adopted. God may withdraw his restraining and assisting grace, and leave them to their own lusts. The principles of sin, being unmortified, may gather strength by having been so long repressed, and may break forth with greater violence. And when such persons as these fall, they generally become despisers, revilers, persecutors. " When the unclean spirit is gone out of a man, he walketh through dry places, seeking rest, and findeth none. Then he saith, I will return into my house from whence I came out; and when he is come, he findeth it empty, swept, and garnished. Then goeth he, and taketh with himself seven other spirits more wicked than himself, and they enter in and dwell there: and the last state of that man is worse than the first. Even so shall it be also unto this wicked generation. For it is impossible for those who were once enlightened, and have tasted of the heavenly gift, and were made partakers of the Holy Ghost, and have tasted the good word of God, and the powers of the world to come, if they shall fall away, to renew them again unto repentance; seeing they crucify to themselves the Son of God afresh, and put him to an open shame." Thirdly: however this may be—though they hover between truth and error, holiness and sin, the world and the church, heaven and hell, through life—this will not be the case in death. They will then be developed, and have their portion with the vile and the profligate; with swearers, drunkards, thieves, and murderers; with the devil and his angels.

Ah! says the Saviour to the Laodiceans, " I know thy works, that thou art neither cold nor hot: I would thou were cold or hot. So then because thou art lukewarm, and neither cold nor hot, I will spue thee out of my mouth." And yet, oh! how he waits to be gracious, and is exalted to have mercy! Yet, even these characters, hateful as their state is, and sure, if continued in, to bring upon them the utmost destruction, he does not treat with neglect—but counsels them—" Because thou sayest, I am rich, and increased with goods, and have need of nothing; and knowest not that thou art wretched, and miserable, and poor, and blind, and naked : I counsel thee to buy of me gold tried in the fire, that thou mayest be rich; and white raiment, that thou mayest be clothed, and that the shame of thy nakedness do not appear; and anoint thine eyes with eye-salve, that thou mayest see." I cannot, therefore, conclude without endeavouring,

III. To BRING YOU TO A DECISION. I therefore address you in the language of Joshua, " Choose you this day whom you will serve:" or in the words of Elijah, " How long halt ye between two opinions? if the Lord be God, follow him: but if Baal, then follow him." The reason of the address, if you believe the Scripture, is obvious: for " no man can serve two masters: for either he will hate the one, and love the other; or else he will hold to the one, and despise the other. Yè cannot serve God and mammon." " Ye adulterers and adulteresses, know ye not that the friendship of the world is enmity with God? whosoever therefore will be a friend of the world is the enemy of God. Love not the world, neither the things that are in the world. If any man love the world, the love of the Father is not in him."

2 Z   31

Which then of these states will you take? What is your answer?

Shall it be the language of the convinced, penitent, returning Israelites, spoken of by the prophet; " Behold, we come unto thee; for thou art the Lord our God. Truly in vain is salvation hoped for from the hills, and from the multitude of mountains: truly in the Lord our God is the salvation of Israel." O that this were indeed your reply! To whom can you go but unto him: he has the words of eternal life. He is able, he is willing—to pardon, to renew, to satisfy, to delight—to bless you with all spiritual blessings in heavenly places in Christ."

Or will you say, with the rebels among the Jews, who, when admonished, " Withhold thy foot from being unshod, and thy throat from thirst," said, " There is no hope: no: for I have loved strangers, and after them will I go." Ah! think again. Listen not to the dictates of despair—" There is hope in Israel concerning this thing"—" Come and let us reason together, saith the Lord; though your sins were as scarlet, they shall be white as snow; though they were red like crimson, they shall be as wool." The bridge is not yet drawn. The door is not yet shut. Think again. Will you turn your back upon such an opening of deliverance? Can you mean what you say? Are you resolved to follow your idols, and to forsake the God of love? How shocking, how dreadful—to bid farewell to God!

Or will you take a middle course, and, neither actually complying or refusing, say to the man who importunes you, with Felix; " Go thy way for this time, when I have a convenient season I will call for thee." But we cannot admit of this reply; it is evasion. Our commission requires an immediate determination: " To-day, if ye will hear his voice, harden not your hearts." And does not your safety require the same? Boast not thyself of to-morrow; for thou knowest not what a day may bring forth. Now is the accepted time; now is the day of salvation." How long have some of you hesitated already! How wonderful is it that God has borne with you to this day, when he might justly have considered your excuses and delays, ten, twenty, forty years ago, as a rejection; and have sworn " in his wrath, that you should not enter into his rest." Surely, after this fresh proposal, God may resolve, consistently with all the riches of his goodness, to address you no more; to order away all the means and influences that can benefit your souls, and to say, " He is joined to idols, let him alone." It is certain that the longer you waver, the more difficult you will find it to decide; for the world tyrannizes the more it is obeyed; and the heart is hardened through the deceitfulness of sin. And what is it to determine that you cannot decide at once?

there any comparison between the respective claimants? Between hell and heaven? Between the bondage of corruption and the service of God? Between the way of transgressors, which is hard, and Wisdom's ways, which are all pleasantness and peace? "What fruit had ye then in those things whereof ye are now ashamed? for the end of those things is death. But now, being made free from sin, and become servants to God, ye have your fruit unto holiness, and the end everlasting life."

But the grand prevention is the world—To give up the world!—But you must give it up soon—and who is most likely to resign it with ease and pleasure; the man who idolizes it, or he that is weaned from it?—To give up the world! But how are you required to give it up? Not as to your station in it, your business, or your duty; but only as to what is evil and injurious to yourselves. Giving up the world is not giving up happiness. Did it ever make you happy? Has it not left your heart cold and void; and, even in its best estate, led you to ask, "Who will show us any good?" And who enjoys the world most in its lawful pursuits and innocent indulgences? The man who is reconciled unto God by the death of his Son, and renewed in the spirit of his mind. To him the sun shines fairer, and the rose is more fragrant than before. "OLD THINGS ARE PASSED AWAY; BEHOLD, ALL THINGS ARE BECOME NEW."

DISCOURSE XCVIII.

RETIREMENT.

And he said unto me, Arise, go forth in the plain, and I will there talk with thee.—Ezek. iii. 22.

THE pleasures and advantages of solitude have been often admired and recommended. All love the world; yet all complain of it: and whatever schemes of happiness are devised, the scene is always laid in a withdrawment from it. "It is there," says the victim of perfidy and malice, "it is there the wicked cease from troubling, and there the weary are at rest." It is there the warrior feeds his courage, and arranges the materials of victory. It is there the statesman forms and weighs his plans of policy. There the philosopher pursues his theories and experiments. There the man of genius feels the power of thought and the glow of fancy, and roves in a world of his own creation. "Through desire a man, having separated himself, seeketh and intermeddleth with all wisdom."

I have to consider solitude in reference to the Christian: it has a very interesting connexion with religion.

Ezekiel was now by the river Chebar, with the captives of Israel, to whom he had been sent: and says he, "The hand of the Lord was there upon me." This expression always marks an impulse of inspiration. What kind of impression it was that moved them in these cases we cannot determine; but they knew it to be *divine.* And we observe here—that no *place* can exclude God from approaching his servants, or holding intercourse with them.

But he is a sovereign; and may manifest himself when, and how, and *where* he pleases. Yet his sovereignty is never to be confounded with arbitrariness—He has reasons for his conduct; and though all places are alike to him, they are not the same with regard to us. To receive, therefore, the intended communication, he is ordered to *withdraw.* "And he said unto me, Arise, and go forth into the plain, and I will *there* talk with thee."

If we consider Ezekiel as a prophet, the order applies peculiarly to ministers: and says to them—"Appear, but *live* not in public. Be not too companionable. Retire much for study and devotion. It is there you will obtain an unction from the Holy One, and know all things." Look ye out, said the Apostles to the churches, deacons to manage your temporal affairs: but "we will give ourselves unto prayer, and the ministry of the word." And to Timothy, Paul said, "Meditate upon these things; give thyself wholly to them; that thy profiting may appear to all."

But the address will apply to Christians at large: and we may derive from it this observation—RETIREMENT IS FRIENDLY TO COMMUNION WITH GOD. Let us consider,

I. THE DUTY—And II. THE PRIVILEGE.

"—Call me away from flesh and sense;
One sovereign word can draw me thence:
I would obey the voice Divine,
And all inferior joys resign.

Be earth, with all her scenes, withdrawn;
Let noise and vanity be gone—
In secret silence of the mind,
My heaven, and *there my God I find.*"

I. THE DUTY enjoined—"And he said unto me, Arise, and go forth into the plain." It may be necessary to premise two things. First: The *place* is indifferent. It matters not whether it be a private room, or the open field. The thing required is to be alone. And, Secondly, It is not a state of absolute retirement that God enjoins. Man was made for society, as well as solitude: and so is the Christian. A great part of our religion regards our fellow-creatures, and cannot be discharged but by intermixture with them: and what our Saviour thought of resigning business, abandoning our connexions, and hiding ourselves in woods and cells, appears obviously, from the language which he addressed to his own disciples; "Ye are the light of the world. A city that is set on a hill cannot be hid. Neither do men light a candle and put it under a bushel, but on a candlestick; and it giveth light unto all that are in the house. Let your light so shine before men, that they may see your good works, and glorify your Father which is in heaven." It is, therefore, possible for a Christian to be alone, when he *ought* to be abroad; and to be indulging a favourite inclination, when he should exercise self-denial, in order to meet the calls of Providence. It may be much more pleasing often to sit alone, reading or reflecting, than to be called forth to give advice, or to visit the afflicted—but, as we "have opportunity, we must do good unto all men, especially to them that are of the household of faith."

But what our subject demands is, comparative and occasional secession for moral and spiritual purposes. This will be found a duty; and God says to you, as he did to Ezekiel, "Go forth, and I will talk with thee."

And says he not this by express commands? I hope you acknowledge his authority; and in the true spirit of obedience ask, "Lord, what wilt thou have me to do?" And can you be ignorant that he has said, by the mouth of his servant and of his Son, "Stand in awe, and sin not: commune with your own heart upon your bed, and be still. Enter into thy closet; and when thou hast shut thy door, pray to thy Father which is in secret, and thy Father which is in secret shall reward thee openly."

And says he not this by example? "Isaac went out into the field at eventide to meditate. Jacob was left alone, and there wrestled with him a man, until the dawning of the day." "Then went king David in, and sat before the Lord, and he said, Who am I, O Lord God! and what is my house, that thou hast brought me hitherto? And this was yet a small thing in thy sight, O Lord God; but thou hast spoken also of thy servant's house for a great while to come. And is this the manner of man, O Lord God!" Daniel retired three times a day. Peter went up to the house-top to pray about the sixth hour, and received a Divine communication. Of our Saviour, whose life has the force of a law, it is said; "In the morning, rising up a great while before day, he went out, and departed into a solitary place, and there prayed." At another time "he went out into a mountain to pray, and continued all night in prayer to God."

Says he not this by the institution of the Sabbath? We are not to consider the appointment of the Sabbath as a display of the Divine prerogative only: "the Sabbath was made for man." It has a merciful reference, even to his body; by conducing to cleanliness, comfort, and health; but the provision principally regards the welfare of the soul. The Sabbath comes, and tells us, that while we are not slothful in business, among all our cares, one thing is needful; and admonishes us to choose that good part which shall not be taken away from us. It brings us more immediately into the presence of God: and gives us an opportunity to examine our character and our condition. It renews those pious impressions which our intercourse with the things of time and sense is continually wearing off. It is in this view the believer prizes it; calling the Sabbath a delight, the holy of the Lord, honourable.

"Now from the crowd withdrawn away,
    He seems to breathe a diff'rent air;
Compos'd and soften'd by the day,
    All things another aspect wear."

The light he beholds is the Lord's. The ground he treads is sacred. Even the public worship is a seclusion from the world: it is the exchange of secular employment for religious; of civil society for spiritual; of the ledger for the Bible; of the shop for the sanctuary. But it affords him a season for the more large and particular exercises of private devotion—and the return of every Saturday evening cries, "To-morrow is the rest of the holy Sabbath unto the Lord." "Go forth into the plain, and there will I talk with thee."

And says he not this by the dispensations of his Providence? Affliction often at once disinclines us to social circles, and disqualifies us for them. Sickness separates a man from the crowd, and confines him on the bed of languishing, there to ask, "Where is God my maker, who giveth songs in the night?" A reduced condition will diminish your associates. It will drive off the selfish herd, who think that a friend is born for *prosperity*; but it will bring you Christians and ministers, whose religion teaches them to comfort those that are cast down; and they will bring God. "Lover and friend hast thou put far from me, and mine acquaintance into darkness"—is a groan that is, in time, wrung from every heart. What a solitude—what a dreariness—does the death of relations for a time produce! The death of a child will desolate the world in feeling, if not in fact. "He sitteth alone, and keepeth silence:" or sighs, "I watch, and am as a sparrow alone upon the house-top."—Some have been deserted by weakness and perfidy: Job could say, "My brethren have dealt deceitfully as a brook, and as the stream of brooks they pass away; which are blackish by reason of the ice, and wherein the snow is hid: what time they wax warm, they vanish: when it is hot they are consumed out of their place." "At my first answer," says Paul, "no man stood by me, but all men forsook me"—but, adds he, "nevertheless the Lord stood by me, and strengthened me." For the Christian is often never less alone than when alone. When Joseph was sent to prison, and he tells us *God* sent him there, " the Lord was with Joseph." When John was banished to the isle of Patmos, he was indulged with the manifestations of the Almighty. Paul, in prison, wrote many of his Epistles: and there many others, whose works praise them in the gate, composed their most admired and useful publications—They were ordered out of the world, that God might talk with them!

Says he not this by the influence of his grace? This agency always produces in its subjects certain sentiments and dispositions, which urge and attach them to retirement. I will mention four of these.

The First is a devotional temper. Whoever delights in prayer will delight in retirement; because it is so favourable to the frequency and freedom of the exercise. There we can divulge what we could not communicate in the presence of the dearest earthly friend. There words are unnecessary—" our desire is before him; our groaning is not hid from him :" the eye poureth out tears unto God; and he hears the voice of our weeping.

The Second is a desire to rise above the world. This will induce a man to retire. How often does the Christian lament that his conversation is so little in heaven, and that he is so much governed by things that are seen and temporal! But where is the world conquered? In a crowd? No: but—alone. In the midst of its active pursuits? No—but viewed as an object of solitary contemplation; viewed in the presence of Jehovah; viewed in the remembrances of eternity. Then its emptiness appears—Then the fascination is dissolved—Then we look upward and say, "Now what wait I for? my hope is in thee?"

The Third is a wish to obtain self-knowledge. This will induce a man to withdraw. It is only alone that he can examine his state; that he can estimate his attainments; that he can explore his defects; that he can discern the sources of his past dangers or falls; and set a watch against future temptation.

The Fourth is love to God.—This will lead a man to retire. When we are supremely attached to a person, his presence is all we want; he will be the chief attraction, even in company; how desirable then to meet him alone, where he seems wholly ours, and we can yield and receive undivided attention. Friendship deals much in secrecy; kindred souls have a thousand things to hear and to utter that are not for a common ear. This is pre-eminently the case with the intimacy subsisting between God and the believer. There is a peculiarity in every part of the Christian's experience. " The heart knoweth his own bitterness, and a stranger intermeddleth not with his joy :" but both his pains and pleasures bring with them evidence that they are from God—for they dispose the soul to hold communion with him. " Come," says the Church, " come, my Beloved, let us go forth into the fields, let us lodge in the villages." And says God of his people, " Behold, I will allure her, and bring her into the wilderness, and there will I speak comfortably unto her."

II. Let us consider THE PRIVILEGE promised—" And I will there talk with thee."

Mark, First—The condescension of the Speaker. We admire the nobleman that kindly notices a peasant; and the sovereign that deigns to converse with one of his poorest subjects. But who is it that here says— "There *I* will talk with thee?" And with whom does he hold this converse? It is the Creator talking with the creature. It is the God of heaven and earth, holding communion with man that is a worm, and the son of man that is a worm.

Nor is this all—annexed to our meanness are our unworthiness, and our guilt. Here is, therefore, the condescension not only of goodness, but of mercy and grace. " Lord, what is man, that thou art mindful of him, or the son of man, that thou visitest him?"

Secondly. Observe the happiness of the believer. By what scale can we judge of blessedness so rightly as the degree of nearness to God, the supreme good, the fountain of life? In his presence there is fulness of joy, and at his right hand there are pleasures for evermore. How blessed, then, is the man whom God chooses, and causes to approach unto him now. Yet " such honour have all his saints." How would a man be envied if the king was to favour him with his presence and intimacy! Especially if he was known to meet him by appointment, from time to time, alone. Yet is this no more than every Christian expects and enjoys. He has insured interviews with the blessed and only Potentate. Some of us cannot aspire after intercourse with many of our fellow-creatures, by reason of our condition and our talents. We may wish to be in their company, yet shrink from their notice: we may long to hear them talk, yet could not talk with them—we should be swallowed up—we should deem it impossible for them to listen to our weakness. But, whatever be our condition, or our talents, we have a free and invited access to God—we have boldness to enter into the holiest by the blood of Jesus—He hears our praises and complaints—and " there," says he, " will I talk with thee!"

Thirdly. What is the subject of communication? It is variously expressed in the Scripture. It is called his secret, and his covenant: " The secret of the Lord is with them that fear him, and he will show them his covenant." It is called judgment, and his way: " The meek will he guide in judgment, and the meek will he teach his way." It is peace: " He will speak peace unto his people." It regards every thing that is important to their welfare, or interesting to their feelings and hopes. It takes in what he has done for them, what he is doing, and what he will do. He speaks concerning them for time and eternity; he gives them exceeding great and precious promises; and adds to his word his oath, that "by two immutable things, in which it is impossible for God to lie, they might have strong consolation who have fled for refuge to lay hold upon the hope set before them."

Fourthly. What is the mode of address? He does not talk with us in a preternatural manner, as he did sometimes of old with his people. He came down and spake with Moses as a man talketh with his friend. Moses saw his glory, and heard his voice. But it is enthusiasm in us to expect dreams, and visions, and sudden impulses, and audible sounds. There are no new communications from God now: I mean, new in themselves, and such as were not to be found in the Bible before; for as to us they may be, and will be often new. If a man born blind was to be restored to sight, the sun, which he never saw before, would be new to him; but it would not be a new sun. We may begin to feel truths which we never thought of before; yet the truths themselves are as old as the revelation of God to man. But he opens our eyes to see wondrous things out of his law. He opens our understandings that we may know the Scriptures. He leads us into all truth. He applies the doctrines and promises of his word by his Spirit; and by enabling us to realize our own interest in them, he says to our souls, I am thy salvation.

Finally. What is the evidence of the fact? How shall we know that *he does* talk with us? Remember the two disciples going to Emmaus. Our Lord joined them as they journeyed, and inquired after the subject of their conversation and concern. "And beginning at Moses, and all the prophets, he expounded to them in all the Scriptures the things concerning himself." Yet all this time they took him for a stranger. But at supper their eyes were opened, and they knew him, and he vanished out of their sight. And this was the reflection they made on the occurrence; "Did not our heart burn within us while he talked with us by the way, and while he opened to us the Scriptures?" As if they had said—"Is it not astonishing that we did not know him earlier? That we did not discover him upon the road—For who could have conversed with us as he did? Who could have made such impression on the heart?"

Determine the Divine converse with you in the same way. Judge of it by its influences and effects. Three effects will always arise from it.

First. It will produce a deep and solemn sense of our vanity and vileness. Communion with God, instead of gendering and en-

couraging unhallowed freedoms, gives a man such intimate views of the peculiar glory of God as fill him with godly fear. Thus it was with our prophet. It was the same with Jacob, with Moses, with Elijah, with Job, with Isaiah, with Peter.

Secondly. It will draw forth unquenchable desires after additional indulgence. That which contents the believer makes him also insatiable. From his intercourse with him he desires no more than God; but he will desire more of him; and from every fresh discovery the prayer will arise, "I beseech thee, show me thy glory."

Thirdly. It will produce likeness. "He that walketh with wise men shall be wise." We soon acquire the tone and the manner of those who converse much with us, especially if they are our superiors, and we very highly love or revere them. Some boast of being much with God; but so censurable are their conduct and temper, that few of their fellow-creatures would like to be much with *them*. If you are selfish, and covetous, and censorious, and revengeful, some other being has been talking with you: this spirit cometh not from him who calleth you: it is from beneath; and is earthly, sensual, devilish. "But the wisdom that is from above is first pure, then peaceable, gentle, and easy to be entreated, full of mercy and good fruits, without partiality, and without hypocrisy. And the fruit of righteousness is sown in peace of them that make peace."

From this subject—Some are to be censured.

Such are those who call themselves Christians, and are regular in their attendance on public ordinances, but are seldom alone. They who hear much, and reflect little, are always found very imperfect characters—for it is not what we devour, but what we digest, that aids health and supports life.

Others never retire—and what is the reason? "O, we have not time; so numerous and pressing are the cares and avocations of life." Have you more engagements than David, who had to govern a large and distracted empire, surrounded with enemies—yet could he say, "Evening, and morning, and at noon, will I pray, and cry aloud; and he shall hear my voice. Seven times a day do I praise thee, because of thy righteous judgments." Do you not trifle away more time every day of your lives than is required for the purpose of devotion? Could you not, by order, and diligence, and rising earlier, secure more leisure than you now command? Where there is a will there is a way. Disinclination loves to shelter itself behind difficulties. The slothful cries, "There is a lion in the way;" and so there is; but he puts it there. Zeal clears the road, and will often convert hinderances into helps.

Let me ask whether you do not decline

being alone, because you are afraid to awaken or to meet inquiry? If so—Are you not ashamed of a peace of mind that is only preserved · by shunning reflection?—And will you be always able to shun it?—If you cannot meet conscience, how will you meet God? If you live in company, remember this—you must *die alone.*

But he whom you have neglected and contemned has yet thoughts towards you, and they are thoughts of peace. He has opened a new and living way to himself. He waits to be gracious, and is exalted to have mercy upon you. Return to him through an atoning and interceding Saviour, and live. Acquaint now thyself with him, and be at peace; thereby good shall come unto thee.

The subject requires us to comfort others.

Perhaps you approve of all we have said—but you are so straitened in your circumstances that you have not a room to retire in—and are so necessarily engrossed with the difficulties of life, that it is scarcely possible to secure a moment for devotional solitude in the field.

See that this is not your fault, but your affliction, and you may hope that God will indemnify you in some other way.

But others are more favoured. You not only love retirement, but you are able to enjoy it. Yet you find it much easier to withdraw the body than to separate the mind from earthly things. The world follows you, and invades and defiles the very sanctuary of silence. You value the presence of Him who manifests himself to his people and not unto the world; and wherever he meets with you, the place is none other than the house of God and the gate of heaven. You would gladly pass in such enjoyment the hours that duty requires to be devoted to inferior claims. Your intercourse with God, therefore, is short and interrupted; but it is refreshing and instructive. It shows you what heaven is, and makes it desirable. "Ah," you say, "if these views, these feelings, were but perfect and permanent!" Well, soon, *very soon,* they will be perfect and permanent; and you will be *for ever with the Lord.*

DISCOURSE XCIX.

DAVID'S FEAR AND FOLLY.

And David said in his heart, I shall now perish one day by the hand of Saul: there is nothing .better for me than that I should speedily escape into the land of the Philistines.—1 Sam. xxvii. 1.

THE memoirs of David occupy a large proportion of the Old Testament; and we need not wonder at this, when we consider,

not only his relation to the Messiah, but the peculiar providences that distinguished him. He is one of the most interesting characters recorded in all history. His life was singularly eventful; and as in nature we do not wish for a continuity of level, or an uniformity of aspect, but are most gratified with hill and valley, and wood and lawn, and intermixtures of the beautiful and sublime: so we are most attracted to the lives of those who have been placed in a variety of scenes, especially in conditions so opposite and extreme, that we marvel by what kind of process they could have passed the gulph between. Had we seen David a stripling in the field of Bethlehem, keeping his father's sheep, who could have thought that he would emerge from obscurity, and become the champion of Goliath, the terror of the Philistines, the conqueror of the Ammonites, and Moabites, and Edomites; and one of the most renowned heroes, monarchs, legislators, and writers of the East!

His religious experience is as interesting as the events of his life. Indeed much of the one grew out of the other, and was diversified by them. Many of his psalms, as we see by the titles, were composed in consequence of his dangers and afflictions. His trying situation produced the language I have read. It consists of two parts—His FEAR—and his FOLLY.

I. His FEAR—"David said in his heart, I shall now perish one day by the hand of Saul."

II. His FOLLY.—"There is nothing better than that I should speedily escape into the land of the Philistines."

O Thou by whose inspiration all Scripture is given, render these words profitable for doctrine, for reproof, for correction, and instruction in righteousness!

I. Observe HIS FEAR.

It was the language, not of his lips, but of his feelings—he "said *in his heart,* I shall now one day perish by the hand of Saul." He does not seem to have uttered it in words —restrained probably by prudence and kindness. It is not necessary, or proper, to trouble others with all our uneasy feelings. It is a noble and magnanimous mind that can suffer without complaint. Indeed, if a man hawks about his trouble from door to door; if he loves to talk of his trials in every company he meets, we may be assured he will never die of grief. Profound sorrow, like the deep river, flows noiseless: the man wounded at heart, like the smitten deer, leaves the herd for the shade—"He sitteth alone, and keepeth silence: he putteth his mouth in the dust, if so be there may be hope."

Religious people should be concerned peculiarly to appear peaceful and cheerful. Nothing recommends godliness more, or is more necessary to counteract the prejudice so commonly and injuriously entertained against it, as the mother and nurse of mopishness and melancholy. We would not wish you to be hypocrites, avowing joys to which you are strangers: but you are not required to publish all your painful emotions, especially before those who cannot understand, and are likely to misinterpret, them. I have often admired the holy delicacy of Ezra, when returning to Jerusalem from Babylon with a number of his countrymen. "Then I proclaimed a fast there, at the river of Ahava, that we might afflict ourselves before our God, to seek of him a right way for us, and for our little ones, and for all our substance. For I was ashamed to require of the king a band of soldiers and horsemen to help us against the enemy in the way: because we had spoken unto the king, saying, The hand of our God is upon all them for good that seek him; but his power and his wrath is against all them that forsake him." There was *really* no inconsistency between his profession of confidence in God, and asking for a convoy: for God works by means. But so it might have appeared to a heathen prince: he would therefore rather expose himself to peril than bring a cause, dearer to him than life, not only under reflection, but under suspicion.

When we see persons filling up their stations in life with diligence, and declining no duty in their power, how little can we often imagine what they feel, at the very time, within!—Truly "the heart knoweth his own bitterness." While David appeared cheerful and courageous, lest by his deportment he should confound or dismay his followers, his very soul was cast down within him.

And was this the case with a man of such superior attainments?—Where are the hands that never hang down: and knees that never tremble? We are prone to think that many of our feelings are peculiar, and to cry, If I am his, why am I thus?—Here we see the advantage of pious intercourse. The communication of Christian experience will convince us that nothing has befallen us that is not common to the partakers of divine grace; and thus, things that were stumbling-blocks before become way-marks, and marks of our being in "the way everlasting." We sometimes think that the saints recorded in Scripture were a class of beings very different from ourselves; but the Spirit of God has taken care to show us that there was nature in *them*, as well as grace; and that while they were made *holy*, they were left *human*. We see their sorrows, as well as their joys; their conflicts, as well as their victories. David, who, in the triumphs of faith, had exulted, "The Lord is my light and my salvation; whom shall I fear? the Lord is the strength of my life; of whom shall I be afraid?" now said in his heart, "I shall one day perish."

By perishing, he means dying. There is a perdition of a more dreadful import. It means not annihilation, but misery; not the destruction of being, but of all comfort and hope. This perdition the sacred writers never pretend to define. They tell us that it is "a fearful thing," but not *how* fearful a thing "to fall into the hands of the living God." Indeed they *could* not; for who knoweth the power of his anger?" From this destruction a Christian is secured: he is redeemed from the curse of the law; he is delivered from the wrath to come; and there is nothing penal in all the sufferings he endures. Yet he is not always free from apprehension, but feels many a shivering thought how it may go with him at last. Is there a Christian present that has not sometimes, if not often, said, "I shall one day perish?" And you could have drawn no other conclusion while you considered only your own ignorance and weakness, and the enemies that were seeking your soul to destroy it: but having obtained help of God, you continue to this day the living, the living to praise him. You are now saying, to his glory, "Our heart is not turned back, neither have our steps declined from thy way; though thou hast sore broken us in the place of dragons, and covered us with the shadow of death." And what is the Saviour saying? "My sheep hear my voice, and I know them, and they follow me: and I give unto them eternal life; and they shall never perish, neither shall any pluck them out of my hand."—But, by perishing, David means dying.

"I shall one day perish by the hand of Saul." And suppose he had? This was all the injury he could have done him: and we are forbidden to fear those that kill the body, and after that have no more that they can do. He must have died according to the course of nature, in a few years: and what is death in any form, to a good man, but falling asleep, or going home? He ought then, you say, to have risen above the fear of death. But the fear of death is a natural principle; and there is nothing in it more sinful than in hunger or thirst. Adam had it in a state of innocency; or there would have been no threatening in the words, "In the day that thou eatest thereof thou shalt surely die." Our Lord himself felt it, and "with strong cryings and tears made supplication to him who was able to save him from death." There was no want of resignation in this; it was the effect of a natural aversion to suffering, and which rendered his submission the more illustrious —when he said, "Nevertheless, not my will, but thine be done." Had we no appetite for food, there would be no virtue in fasting. Death is not always desirable even to a good man

When Hezekiah was ordered to set his house in order, he turned his face to the wall, and wept sore, and prayed for recovery. And if you take a man better acquainted with the way of salvation and a world of glory, yet his evidences of a personal interest are not always satisfactory—And can he be willing to go in a state of uncertainty? He may also have peculiar attractions, and detentions, in his connexions: the benefactor may feel these in his dependents; the father in his children; the minister in his people. It was this that placed Paul in a strait between two: he longed to depart to be with Christ, which was far better; but to abide in the flesh was more needful for those among whom he laboured.—David had a father and a mother who fled with him, and depended upon him for support.

But David was in no danger of perishing by the hand of Saul. Saul was indeed a malicious and powerful enemy; but he was chained, and could do nothing against him except it was given him from above. And the Lord was on David's side. And he had the promise of the throne, which implied his preservation. And the holy oil had been poured upon his head. And he had already experienced many wonderful deliverances. And he should have reasoned from the past to the future, as he had done before—"The Lord that delivered me out of the paw of the lion, and out of the paw of the bear, he will deliver me out of the hand of this Philistine." But here we see how hard it is to trust in God in the hour of difficulty.

I am far from thinking that it is an easy thing to trust in God at any time. Some, I know, are accustomed to say, "O, it is easy enough to trust in God in prosperous scenes." But they are mistaken; and mistaken because they probably never made the trial; or, at least, never made it in earnest. In such scenes it is difficult to see God, and realize him. When we have health, and peace, and affluence, and friends, it is difficult to determine whether we are relying on these, or on God. When they are removed, then our dependence is obvious. If God was the strength of our souls, he will be our support: if the creature was our portion, we shall faint in the day of adversity. The nests appear in the trees and hedges when stripped of their leaves; the winter discovering what was done in the summer, but hid before by the foliage. And thus it is with us: adversity betrays the resting-places we had in prosperity.

But to return.—It is hard to repose, and maintain a becoming confidence in God in the hour of difficulty. When means fail—and we are forbidden to look for miracles; when our way is hedged up with thorns, and we dare not break through the fence; when Providence opposes the promise, and God himself seems to be fighting against us; it is not every Job that can say, "Though he slay me, yet will I trust in him." In these cases our diffidence often extends to the power of God, as well as his goodness. People, indeed, think that they only question his will; but if they did not doubt his all-sufficiency too, why does their faith waver as difficulties multiply? Does God know any thing about difficulties? Why are they disheartened as means fail? Cannot God furnish means if he does not find them? What was the language of the Israelites?—Will he? No—But can he furnish a table in the wilderness? Can he give bread to his people? What is the commendation of Abraham's faith?—That he believed God's goodness? No—but his power: "He staggered not at the promise of God through unbelief, but was strong in faith, giving glory to God—being fully persuaded that what he had promised he was able also to perform."

You would, therefore, do well to take the advice of an old writer. "Never," says he, "converse with your difficulties alone." How is it when you suspect that a man wishes to entangle you in your talk, or to take advantage of your weakness? Fearing that he will prove too much for you, and induce you to commit yourself, you take with you a third person, a wise and an able friend. When your difficulties wish to parley with you, let God be present; God in promise, or God in experience—then they may tell you any thing. "God is our refuge and strength, a very present help in trouble: therefore will not we fear, though the earth be removed, and though the mountains be carried into the midst of the sea. The Lord of hosts is with us; the God of Jacob is our refuge."—But we are,

II. Reminded of David's FOLLY. "There is nothing better for me than that I should speedily escape into the land of the Philistines." But nothing could have been worse. For by this step—he would alienate the affections of the Israelites from him—he would justify the reproaches of the enemy—he would deprive himself of the means of grace and the ordinances of religion—he would grieve his soul with the vice and idolatry of the heathen—he would put himself out of the warrant of Divine protection—and lay himself under peculiar obligation to those whom he could not serve without betraying the cause of God.

I cannot enlarge on these: but I would remark two or three of the evil consequences naturally arising from this measure. For how could he expect to gather grapes from thorns, or figs from thistles?

First. The king of Achish gave him Ziklag for his residence. Thence he invaded the Geshurites, and the Gezrites, and the Amalekites; "David smote the land, and left neither man nor woman alive, and took away the sheep, and the oxen, and the asses, and the camels, and the apparel, and returned, and came to Achish." But when questioned concerning this business by the king, he used a dissimulation unworthy his character; inducing him to believe that he had destroyed Israelites only, and gaining his confidence by falsehood. "Achish said, Whither have ye made a road to-day? And David said, Against the south of Judah, and against the south of the Jerahmeelites, and against the south of the Kenites. And Achish believed David, saying, He hath made his people Israel utterly to abhor him; therefore he shall be my servant for ever."

Another embarrassment attends him. War breaks out between the Philistines and Israel; and Achish orders David and his men to accompany him to the battle. Now if, when the armies engaged, he should retire, or betray his post, he would be chargeable with cowardice, and treason, and ingratitude towards the king, who had been his friend, and honoured him with the command of his lifeguards.—On the other hand, if he should fight against his own people, under the banners of the uncircumcised, he would be justly considered an enemy to the Israel of God, a betrayer of his country, and would render his ascension to the throne more difficult. Out of this strait, God, who does not deal with us after our desert, delivers him. The lords of the Philistines are dissatisfied with David's going along with them, and insist upon his dismission.

But behold a third result of this wrong measure. He returns; but little does he imagine what had befallen him at home. By accompanying Achish he had left Ziklag, where his substance and his relations were defenceless. The Amalekites took advantage of his absence, and burned the town, after carrying away the spoil, and making his friends and his wives captives. Informed of all this, David was greatly distressed; and the anguish of loss was embittered by self-accusation, and the reproaches of the people: for "the people spake of stoning him, because the soul of all the people was grieved, every man for his sons and for his daughters."

See, First: How much depends on one improper step. The effects may be remediless, and give a complexion to all our future days. Our reputation, our comfort, our usefulness, our religion, our very salvation may hinge upon it.

Secondly. Let us learn how incompetent we are to judge for ourselves. "The way of man is not in himself; it is not in man that walketh, to direct his steps." Who has not found this to be true, in his own experience! Who can look back upon life, and not see how often he has been mistaken, both in his hopes and fears! If things had been according to our mind, should we not have been cursed by many an indulgence? and should we not have shunned those trials which enable us now to say, "It is good for me that I have been afflicted? Who knoweth what is good for a man in this life?" We cannot distinguish between reality and appearance; between the present and the future. We look forward into new and untried conditions with our actual views and feelings; not considering that new and untried conditions will draw forth new views and feelings; and that, like Hazael, we may become the very characters we abhor. Lot thought he could do nothing better than choose the land of the plain, the vale of Sodom, well watered as the garden of the Lord. But in doing so, he separated himself from intercourse with his uncle Abraham—his soul was vexed from day to day with the filthy conversation of the ungodly—he was taken a prisoner by the confederate kings—he was driven out of the place by fire and brimstone—his wife became a pillar of salt—his daughters plunged him into unheard-of infamy.

Take care, therefore, how you say, "There is nothing better for me," than to do this, or that. Venture on nothing rashly. Move with all your moral senses alive and awake. In your connexions for life; in removing your residence; in giving up, or changing your employment, "ponder the path of your feet, that your goings may be established." Let your eyes look on, and your eyelids straight before you. Pray, as you are directed, "Lead us not into temptation, but deliver us from evil." "Trust in the Lord with all thine heart; and lean not unto thine own understanding. In all thy ways acknowledge him, and he shall direct thy paths." We may acknowledge God in words, while we deny him in works. But it is a practical acknowledgment that is required of us; and it consists in three things. First: in our taking no step without asking counsel of the Lord. Secondly: in refusing to take one, when he calls us. Thirdly: in not charging him foolishly, when having taken a step, in compliance with his command, it proves unanswerable to our wishes and expectation: for we may be in the will of God, and meet with very painful exercises; but we must justify him in all that befalls us.

To conclude. See the dangers and mischiefs of unbelief, or the want of confidence in God. It is the worst counsellor we can ever consult: the most perilous guide we can ever follow. What did Moses and Aaron lose? "Because," says God, "ye believed me not, to sanctify me in the eyes of the children of Israel, therefore ye shall not bring this congregation into the land which I have given them:" and no entreaty could induce God to revoke the sentence. From how many gratifications, and advantages, does unbelief

3 A

cut us off, even when it does not destroy! It robs the mind of stability—" If ye will not believe, surely ye shall not be established." It withholds from it peace—" Thou wilt keep him in perfect peace, whose mind is stayed on thee, because he trusteth in thee."

Without faith, the soul is like a ship, deprived of the rudder, driven of the winds, and tossed. By believing in God, we shall find that our strength is to sit still; instead of running from one creature to another. "It is good for a man, both to hope, and quietly wait for the salvation of the Lord;" instead of conferring with flesh and blood, and adopting unhallowed expedients for relief. Them that honour God he will honour; but they that despise him shall be lightly esteemed. " For thus saith the Lord God, the Holy One of Israel; In returning and rest shall ye be saved; in quietness and in confidence shall be your strength: and ye would not. But ye said, No; for we will flee upon horses; therefore shall ye flee: and, We will ride upon the swift; therefore shall they that pursue you be swift. One thousand shall flee at the rebuke of one; at the rebuke of five shall ye flee; till ye be left as a beacon upon the top of a mountain, and as an ensign on a hill."

" Now, the God of hope fill you with all joy and peace in believing, that ye may abound in hope, through the power of the Holy Ghost."

DISCOURSE C.

THE SAVIOUR'S GRACE IN ITS FREENESS AND EFFECTS.

And the grace of our Lord was exceeding abundant with faith and love which is in Christ Jesus.—1 Tim. i. 14.

PERHAPS some of you are come from motives of curiosity, and expect to hear something new. But I have nothing new to communicate. There is only one way of salvation, and this is older than Adam: for " he hath saved us, and called us with an holy calling, not according to our works, but according to his own purpose and grace, which was given us in Christ Jesus before the world began."

You will therefore, probably, be disappointed; but this will be of little importance if you are benefited. It is at your profit I aim; and nothing is more likely to secure it than the subject we have chosen; for God only gives testimony to the word of his grace. And as for those who have tasted that the Lord is gracious, they are saying, Evermore give us this bread. Let us,

I. CONSIDER THE GRACE OF OUR LORD JESUS CHRIST. II. SHOW HOW EMINENTLY IT WAS DISPLAYED IN THE CONVERSION OF PAUL. III. PROVE THAT IT IS ALWAYS PRO-DUCTIVE OF SUITABLE INFLUENCE AND EFFECTS.

I. I may address you, my dear brethren, in the language of the apostle to the Corinthians, " Ye know THE GRACE OF OUR LORD JESUS CHRIST, that, though he was rich, yet for your sakes he became poor, that ye through his poverty might be rich."

It was this that led him to remember you in your low estate; to interpose on your behalf; to assume your nature, and to give his life a ransom for many. " Surely he hath borne our grief and carried our sorrow. He was wounded for our transgressions, he was bruised for our iniquities: the chastisement of our peace was upon him; and with his stripes we are healed."

Behold, how he loved him, said the spectators around the grave of Lazarus, when they saw only his tears. Behold, how he loved them, was surely the exclamation of angels, when, at his cross, they beheld his blood. Here is a love which passeth knowledge.— For was he compelled to submit to this undertaking? No.—Did we deserve it? " When we were yet without strength, in due time Christ died for the ungodly. Scarcely for a righteous man will one die; yet peradventure for a good man some would even dare to die. But God commendeth his love toward us, in that, while we were yet sinners, Christ died for us."—Did we desire it? It was accomplished ages before our existence. And therefore, when we were awakened, and began to seek after these things, we found them already provided: we had them not to procure, but to enjoy; and the voice cried, " Behold redemption for the enslaved, pardon for the guilty, sanctification for the unholy, strength for the weak, health for the sick, and consolation for the miserable—Come, for all things are now ready!"

In the application, as well as the procuring of our salvation, the grace of the Lord Jesus appears. Means were used; but they derived all their efficacy, and their very being, from him. Go as far back as you please, you will find him there before you; predisposing instruments, awakening and encouraging your application, preventing you with the blessings of his goodness. A friend, by his conversation, enlightened your mind—but who made this friend? Who placed him in your way? Who inclined him to seek your welfare? You hunger and thirst after righteousness: you wait for the Lord more than they that watch for the morning. But whence sprang this desire? From conviction. What produced this conviction? Reflection. And what produced this reflection? A train of events. And what are events? *Providence.* And what is providence? God in action: and God, acting for the welfare of the unworthy, is *grace.* " Of him, and through him, and to him are all things; to whom be glory. We love him, because he first loved us. I am sought of them that asked not for me; I am found of them that sought me not: I said, Behold me, behold me, unto a nation that was called by my name."

The progress is equally from the same source. He who quickens us, when dead in trespasses and sins, renews us day by day; and enables us to hold on our way, and wax stronger and stronger. Which of you, whatever be his attainments, would ever reach the end of his faith, the salvation of his soul, were he to discontinue the supply of his own Spirit? But he does not. We live in the Spirit and walk in the Spirit. His grace is sufficient for us; and in this grace we are commanded to be strong. As this laid the foundation, so it will raise the superstructure; and *he* shall bring forth the top-stone thereof, with shoutings, crying, *Grace, grace,* unto it!

And on his head were many crowns. The expression refers to the universality of his empire: for he is King of kings, and Lord of lords. But it will be also exemplified in the praises of all the redeemed from the earth. For if those, who are called under the preaching of the word, are said to be the joy and crown of the ministers, who are only the instruments of their conversion; how much more will they be so to him, who is the Author! O what a multitude of praises will adorn his head—since every believer ascribes to him the undivided glory of his own salvation; when he shall come to be glorified in his saints, and to be admired in all them that believe! and from every tongue he will hear the exclamation—"Unto him that loved us, and washed us from our sins in his own blood, and hath made us kings and priests unto God and his Father; to him be glory and dominion for ever and ever. Amen."

But, though all are saved by this grace, some individuals seem to be, in a peculiar manner, the trophies of it: and were it necessary, we could make, even from the records of Scripture, a marvellous selection of instances. We could mention Manasseh; the dying thief; the murderers of the Son of God; the Corinthian converts: but it is needless to go beyond our subject.—We are reminded,

II. THAT THIS GRACE IS EMINENTLY DISPLAYED IN THE CONVERSION OF PAUL; "And the grace of our Lord," says he, "was *exceeding abundant.*" Never did his heart pity a more undeserving wretch; or his hand undertake a more desperate case.

Perhaps you say, this made the Apostle so humble. It did. But humility is not ignorance and folly. Christians are often ridiculed for speaking of themselves in depreciating terms; especially when they call themselves the vilest of the vile, or the chief of sinners. It is admitted and lamented that such language may be insufferable affectation; and is sometimes used by persons who give ample evidence of their not believing it. When show is a substitute for reality, it is generally excessive. Many fish for praise with the bait of humility; and say things against themselves in hopes that you will contradict them—but be sure never to gratify them. It is otherwise with a real Christian: he speaks according to his real views and feelings. He does not, however, mean that he has been the greatest profligate: but he knows that sin is to be estimated by its guilt, not by its grossness; and he knows more of himself than he can know of others. He can only see the actions of others, and not the greater part even of them; but he can look into his own heart. He knows not but the sins of others will admit of extenuation; and he ought to be willing, as far as possible, to excuse; but he knows against what light, and advantages, his *own* transgressions have been committed.

But, even without this justification of his language, Paul may well refer to himself as a very signal display of the riches of the Saviour's grace. To see the exceeding abundance of it, observe

What he *once was.* He tells Timothy that he was a *persecutor,* a *blasphemer,* and *injurious.* The first time he appears in the sacred history is in connexion with the murder of Stephen; when, it is said, the witnesses laid down their clothes at a young man's feet, whose name was Saul. He, probably, reproved their slackness, and said, "Strip, and stone him—I'll take care of your raiment." How did this circumstance pain his mind, in review; and how feelingly does he mention it: "When the blood of the martyr Stephen was shed, I also was standing by, and consenting unto his death, and kept the raiment of them that slew him!" In this cause he continued: "Many of the saints did I shut up in prison, having received authority from the chief priests; and when they were put to death, I gave my voice against them. And I punished them oft in every synagogue, and compelled them to blaspheme: and being exceedingly mad against them, I persecuted them even unto strange cities." And could he have dismissed their souls to hell as easily as he deprived them of property, liberty, and life, he would have done it gladly. So unparalleled was his ferocity, that he seemed beyond the possibility of reclaim. They who knew the extent of the Saviour's grace seemed unanimously to despair of *him;* and when he assayed to join himself to them, they were afraid of him, and drew back, like sheep from the wolf.

Again. Observe how *he was engaged at the very time of his conversion.* Perhaps he has repented, and reformed: perhaps he is begging forgiveness; and is thus preparing himself for the Divine regards. Some have been called under the preaching of the Word, when they were far from expecting it. They have been apprehended under a minister, whose doctrine they came to insult, and whose person they came to injure. The word has reached the heart, and turned the stone to flesh: they have thrown down the weapons of their rebellion; and weeping over them, acknowledged the presence of all-conquering grace.—Paul was now in a journey of iniquity: he was engaged in open defiance of the Son of God, crucifying him afresh, and putting him to an open shame, at the very moment, when the Lord took knowledge of him!

Observe, also, The *manner of his call.* He is not saved in an ordinary way; but his conversion is illustrated with marvellous and miraculous circumstances. Jesus personally comes down from heaven for the purpose. But how? Flashing the lightning and rolling the thunder? No. He comes down low enough to be visible—but no terror clothes his brow. He approaches near enough to be heard—he speaks—in wrath surely?—" O thou child of the devil—I have found thee, O mine enemy." No.—Nothing but the tender expostulation, " Saul, Saul, why persecutest thou me? For three-and-thirty years I lived in thy nation—I went about doing good—I opened the eyes of the blind—to parents I gave back their children from the grave—I healed all manner of sickness and diseases among the people. I am *Jesus* whom thou persecutest—the *Saviour*—of others—and of THEE!"

Trace, finally, what *followed.* He trembles and is astonished; but this is not all. His heart is changed. He had fallen to the ground —but he now kneels. Behold, he prayeth! and to the very Being he had so often blasphemed—" Lord, what wilt thou have me to do!" He consecrates his life to his service. The lion is turned into a lamb; and a little child leads it. The persecutor is an apostle. He is straightway in the synagogue, and preaches the faith that once he destroyed. Consider the journeys he took; the sufferings he endured; the sermons he delivered; the epistles he wrote; the churches he planted and watered: see him, at the close of a life the most laborious and unexampled, the willing martyr—" I am now ready to be offered, and the time of my departure is at hand." Contemplate all this, and see, whether "the grace of our Lord was not exceeding abundant:" and also if we are not authorized,

III. To observe, that THIS GRACE IS ALWAYS PRODUCTIVE OF SUITABLE INFLUENCES AND EFFECTS. " In faith and love," says the apostle, " which are in Christ Jesus." Many effects followed; but nothing appeared more certainly and powerfully than these: *faith*— in opposition to his former unbelief; and *love* —in opposition to his former hatred and ma-

lice. He thus resembled the blind man recovered, in the Gospel: "immediately he received his sight, and followed Jesus in the way."

And First. Divine grace produces *faith.* Faith is the belief of the Gospel; a firm and lively persuasion of the truth of the record that God has given of his Son, accompanied with acquiescence, dependence, and application. It will lead me to have recourse to him for all I want. It will induce me to make use of him for every purpose he is revealed to accomplish: to enter him as my refuge, to build on him as my foundation, to follow him as my guide; to regard him as my prophet, to teach me; my high priest, to put away my sin, by the sacrifice of himself; my king, to rule me; my shepherd, to feed. This representation will hardly satisfy those whose minds are speculative; but it is Scriptural. The sacred writers describe faith, rather than define it. They hold it forth, not in the nakedness of abstraction, but in attributes and actings, by which it is more subject to apprehension. It is, in their language, looking to Christ; coming to him; committing the soul into his hands against that day.

Secondly, Divine grace will equally produce *love.*—To whom? To the Saviour himself; his name, his word, his day, his service, his ways.—To whom? To all his people; as branches of the same household of faith; as parts of the same body, having communion with each other; so that, if one member suffers, all the members suffer; and if one member be honoured, all the members rejoice. —To whom? All mankind, so as to desire their welfare, and to do them good as opportunity offers—determining the exercise of this affection by their necessities; instructing them if ignorant; reproving them if vicious; feeding and clothing them if destitute; always remembering that we are to love, not in word and in tongue, but in deed and in truth. " Whoso hath this world's good, and seeth his brother have need, and shutteth up his bowels of compassion from him, how dwelleth the love of God in him!"

Thirdly. Divine grace will produce *both* these in the *same* subjects. In five other places, as well as in the passage before us, we find faith and love in Christ Jesus connected together. This must be more than sufficient to show, that the combination is not accidental. In fact, there cannot be a more natural, or a more noble union.

Faith, according to the Apostle's order of statement, goes *before* love: for faith precedes every thing in religion: it is an original principle; it is the spring from which flow all the streams of pious temper and practice: it is the root, from which grow all the fruits of Christian obedience and affection. Using another metaphor, it is considered a foundation; and we are required to " build up ourselves on our most holy faith;" and Paul admonishes Timothy to affirm alway, that they " who have believed" in God, be careful to maintain " good works."

But love *follows* after faith. We are told that "faith worketh by love." And how should it be otherwise?' Is it possible for me to believe the compassions of the Saviour, and to realize as my own the blessings of his death, and not feel my heart affected? and my gratitude constraining me to embrace *him*, and my fellow-christians, and my fellow-creatures, for *his* sake?

By the latter of these, therefore, you are to evince the reality and genuineness of the former. " Show me," says the apostle James, to a man who imagined he had one of these, while he was a stranger to the other—" Show me thy faith without thy works, and I will show thee my faith by my works. What doth it profit, my brethren, though a man say he hath faith, and have not works? can faith save him? If a brother or sister be naked, and destitute of daily food, and one of you say unto them, Depart in peace, be ye warmed and filled; notwithstanding ye give them not those things which are needful to the body; what doth it profit? Even so faith, if it hath not works, is dead, being alone." It is admitted that faith justifies the soul, but works justify faith; and what God has joined together, let no man put asunder. Faith cannot be *divine* unless it operates in a way of holy and benevolent affection: " Beloved, let us love one another: for love is of God; and every one that loveth is born of God, and knoweth God. He that loveth not, knoweth not God; for God is love. If a man say, I love God, and hateth his brother, he is a liar: for he that loveth not his brother whom he hath seen, how can he love God whom he hath not seen? And this commandment have we from him, That he who loveth God love his brother also."

O God! we can never be completely blessed, till we love thee supremely, and our neighbour as ourselves. Put this precious law into our minds, and write it in our hearts: " for he that dwelleth in love dwelleth in God, and God in him!"

The subject, in the first place, admonishes Christians. It calls upon you, like Paul, to *review* the grace of our Lord Jesus Christ. Remember where you were, and what you were, when he said unto you—Live. Look unto the rock whence ye are hewn, and to the hole of the pit whence ye are digged. This will prove the destruction of pride and ingratitude. It will ask *you*, Who made thee to differ from another? And lead *you* to ask, What shall I render unto the Lord for all his benefits towards me?—It requires you, also, like Paul, to *acknowledge* as well as review this grace. Review it for your own sakes: acknowledge it for the sake of others. Let

the humble hear thereof, and be glad. Let the fearful hear thereof, and be encouraged. They need strong consolation, who are fleeing for refuge, to lay hold upon the hope set before them. Let them see, in example as well as in doctrine, that with the Lord there is mercy, and that with him there is plenteous redemption.

Secondly. The subject comforts the despairing. It gives the wine of the Gospel to them that are ready to perish; without diluting the strength of it away, by requiring conditions to be performed, or qualifications to be possessed, to authorize us to trust in his Name. It cries, Behold the Redeemer! How mighty to save—and how willing! Neither the number nor the heinousness of your sins exclude you from hope, if they do not keep you from him; and why should they keep you from him?

Ah! says Paul, his grace was exceeding abundant to me-ward: and it was designed, not to be a wonder, but an ensample: " For this cause I obtained mercy, that in me first Jesus Christ might show forth all long-suffering, for a pattern to them which should hereafter believe on him to life everlasting."

Sinner! Look at this pattern, and despair if you can. Rather say, Am I unworthy? So was he. My case is aggravated, and is difficult? So was his. Yet he obtained salvation? So may I—and so *I must*—if his word be true.—" Him that cometh unto me I will in no wise cast out."

Thirdly. The subject attacks the presumptuous—not those who venture to come to him as they are: this would contradict our former article, as well as the whole language of the Gospel: but those who think they *have* come to him, while they are yet in their sins. If any man be *in* Christ, he is *a new creature.* We must judge of the cause by the consequences.

We have sometimes been surprised to hear persons speak of their being converted so many years ago, and under the ministry of some good man whom they have named. What they were *before* their conversion we cannot say; it is undeniable what they are *since*— vain and worldly; proud and envious; covetous and selfish; quarrelsome and revengeful: if carried to their grave to-morrow, no widow nor orphan would shed a tear for them; neither would the cause of God or of man sustain the least loss. What could they have been before their conversion who are all this since? If such is their regenerate state, what was their natural?

Be not deceived. To the law and to the testimony. Observe the nature of conversion as it is described in the Scripture: and remember, that Divine grace is not changed by time or place. It is not only free, but powerful. It never leaves you as it finds you; it never finds you in love with holiness, and it never leaves you in love with sin; it never finds you with your conversation in heaven, and it never leaves you cleaving to the dust. It turns you from darkness unto light; and from the power of Satan unto God. It causes you to pass from bondage into liberty, and from death unto life. And though the operation may be gradual, and produce not every thing at once, yet, even in its beginning, it decides *the state*, and gives a *bias to the whole character.*

Whatever peculiar circumstances may distinguish one conversion from another, the essence and the effects are the same; and you cannot possess the grace of God in truth, if you are strangers to faith and love that are in Christ Jesus.

DISCOURSE CI.

THE DEATH OF DEATH.

Our Saviour Jesus Christ hath abolished death.
2 Tim. i. 10.

"To them that believe he is precious." But *how* precious the sacred writer does not determine. And, my brethren, is it too much to say, he could not! He is more precious than light is to the eye, or melody to the ear, or food to the taste, or wisdom to the mind, or friendship to the heart. All words and images are too poor to hold forth the estimation in which the believer holds the Saviour of sinners.

But there is one thing we may remark concerning it—The attachment is not only supreme, but reasonable. He is altogether worthy of it; and the wonder is, not that we admire and love him so much, but that we love and admire him no more. We have had benefactors, and we have heard of benefactors; but they are all nothing compared with him.—One thing alone ought to render him infinitely dear to us—It is, our deliverance from the king of terrors. For, O proclaim it to the ends of the earth, and let all the dying sons of men hear it—*He has abolished death!*

Let us consider the enemy and the victory: I. The evil in question—death. II. The destruction of it—he hath abolished death.

I. The evil in question—It is death. We should suppose that this subject was very familiar to the thoughts of men, were we to judge from the importance and frequency of the event. But, alas! nothing is so little thought of—So true are the words of Eliphaz; "They are destroyed from morning to evening: they perish for ever, without any regarding it." The subject is irksome and awful; and the whole study of the multitude is to banish and keep it from their minds.

Let us examine what *Nature* teaches us concerning death; and then go to the Scripture for additional information.

Suppose then there had been no revelation from God—what does *Nature* teach us concerning death? It sees plainly enough that it is a cessation of our being. The lungs no longer heave: the pulse ceases to beat; the blood pauses and congeals; the eye closes; the tongue is silent; and the hand forgets her cunning. We are laid in the grave, where worms feed upon us, and over the spot friendship inscribes;

"How loved, how valued once, avails thee not;
To whom related, or by whom begot:
A heap of dust alone remains of thee;
'Tis all thou art, and all the proud shall be."

So says Nature.

It also teaches us the universality of death. This is a thing that falls under the observation of our senses. It is heard and seen that all die: the rich as well as the poor; kings as well as subjects; and philosophers as well as fools. It is known that a century sweeps the globe, and dispossesses of their inhabitants every cottage, and mansion, and palace, and temple. It has never been otherwise. One generation passeth away, and another cometh. So says Nature.

Nature teaches us that death is unavoidable. After the lapse of so many ages, and the disposition there is in man to shun it, if he could,—"for all that a man hath will he give for his life,"—we may easily and fairly infer, that every expedient has been tried; and that there *can* be no discharge in this war; that this enemy can neither be bribed off, nor beaten off. It is obvious too that the human frame is weak, and not capable even of prolonged duration. Its powers, however they have been spared or cherished, soon exhibit in all proofs of declension: "the days of our years are threescore years and ten; and if by reason of strength they be fourscore years, yet is their strength labour and sorrow; for it is soon cut off, and we fly away. The keepers of the house tremble, and the strong men bow themselves, and the grinders cease because they are few, and those that look out of the windows are darkened; and the doors shall be shut in the streets, when the sound of the grinding is low, and he shall rise up at the voice of the bird, and all the daughters of music shall be brought low; also then they shall be afraid of that which is high, and fears shall be in the way, and the almond tree shall flourish, and the grasshopper shall be a burden, and desire shall fail: because man goeth to his long home, and the mourners go about the streets."—So says Nature.

Nature sees also that death is irreparable. It cannot produce a single specimen of posthumous life. In vain we linger by the corpse —the countenance will no more beam upon us. In vain we go to the grave—it will not, deaf to our cries, deliver up its trust; and the expectation of the revival of our dearest connexions will be deemed absurdity and madness. "There is hope of a tree, if it be cut down, that it will sprout again, and that the tender branch thereof will not cease. Though the root thereof wax old in the earth, and the stock thereof die in the ground; yet through the scent of water it will bud, and bring forth boughs like a plant. But man dieth and wasteth away: yea, man giveth up the ghost, and where is he? As the waters fail from the sea, and the flood decayeth and dryeth up: so man lieth down, and riseth not: till the heavens be no more, they shall not awake, nor be raised out of their sleep." All have journeyed this way; but from the bourn no traveller has returned.—So says Nature.

We may also learn from it that death is uncertain in its circumstances; and that no man knows the place, the time, the manner, in which he shall expire.—So far Nature goes; but not a step farther. So much it tells us; but it can tell us no more. Here the *Scripture* takes up the subject, and furnishes all the additional aid we need.

If it be objected, that the generality of the heathen have had some other views of death than those which we have conceded, and had even notions of an existence beyond the grave —let it be observed, that the world always had a revelation from God; and that when mankind dispersed from the family of Noah, they carried the discoveries along with them: but as they were left to tradition, they became more and more obscure; yet they yielded hints which led to reflections that otherwise would have never occurred. And if wise men, especially from these remains of an original revelation, were led into some speculations bordering upon truth, it should be remembered, that in a case like this, as Paley observes, nothing more is known than is proved; opinion is not knowledge, nor conjecture principle. We, therefore, need not hesitate to say that, separate from revelation, nothing either would or could have been known concerning death—but that it ends our being—and is universal in its prevalence —unavoidable by any means in our power— irreparable in its effects—and uncertain as to the time and mode of its approach.

But how much more does the *Scripture* teach? Here we learn,

First. Its true nature. To the eye of sense death appears annihilation; but to the eye of faith it is dissolution. Faith knows that there is a spirit in man; and that when the dust returns to the dust, whence it was, the spirit returns to God who gave it.

Secondly. Its true consequences. Very little of death falls under the observation of the senses; the most awful and interesting part is beyond their reach. It is the state of the soul; it is the apprehension of it by devils or angels; it is the transmission of it to heaven or hell. Luke tells us of the death of a rich man, who was clothed gorgeously, and fared sumptuously every day; and also of a beggar, full of sores, at his gate. In any other book nothing more would have been said, or could have been said, than the fact itself: unless the mean burial of the one, and the splendid funeral of the other. But the Scripture draws back the vail; and we see the beggar lodged in Abraham's bosom, while the rich man lifts up his eyes in hell, and calls for a drop of water to cool his tongue.

Thirdly. Its true cause. The Scripture shows us that man was not created mortal; and that mortality is not the necessary consequence of our original constitution; but is the penal effect of transgression: "In the day that thou eatest thereof, thou shalt surely die." "By one man sin entered into the world, and death by sin, and so death hath passed upon all men, because all have sinned." In Adam all die."

Fourthly. The true remedy. What! Is there a remedy for death? "What man is he that liveth, and shall not see death? shall he deliver his soul from the hand of the grave? No man can redeem his brother, nor give to God a ransom for him; (for the redemption of their soul is precious, and it ceaseth for ever;) that he should still live for ever, and not see corruption." And is there then a cure for death? What is it? Where can it be found?—Who was the Mercy promised to the fathers? Who is called the "Consolation of Israel?" Who is our hope? Who said, "I am the resurrection and the life: he that believeth in me, though he were dead, yet shall he live: and whosoever liveth, and believeth in me, shall never die?" Who said to his hearers, "If a man keep my sayings he shall never see death? He hath abolished death."—But let us,

II. Consider this DESTRUCTION—For does not death continue his ravages? Does he not fall upon the people of God themselves? Where then is the proof of this abolition? Or how is it to be understood?

It is undeniable that Christians themselves are subject to the stroke of death as well as others. God might have translated them all to heaven, as he did Enoch and Elias. But it does not comport with his wisdom: and it is easy to see that it would have made the difference between the righteous and the wicked too visible; it would not have accorded with a mixed state of obscurity and trial, where "all things come alike to all, and no man knoweth love or hatred by all that is before him." If translation had been the substitute for dissolution, there would have been no *dying in faith*; which is one of the noblest exercises and triumphs of divine grace.

I am unwilling to forego any exemplification of the subject: and, as Bishop Horne justly observes, "What we call the various senses of a Scriptural expression are, in reality, but the various parts of the complete sense." We may consider the Lord Jesus as abolishing death, spiritually—miraculously—in his own person—penally—comparatively—and absolutely. Whatever seems obscure, from the brevity of the statement, will I hope be made plain in the process of illustration: and the whole taken together must show that the Apostle's language, though bold, is not more bold than just.

First. He abolishes death, spiritually; that is, in the souls of his people. To all these, without exception, it may be said, in the words of Paul to the Ephesians, "You hath he quickened who were dead in trespasses and sins." Not that they were dead in every sense of the word: for the Apostle speaks of their walking, at the very time, according to the course of this world; but they possessed no spiritual faculties, felt no spiritual sensations, performed no spiritual actions. They were insensible and indifferent to the favour, and image, and presence, and service of the blessed God. But quickened by the Spirit of life in Christ Jesus, now they breathe the breath of prayer, and of praise. They feel the pulse of sacred passion. They hunger and thirst after righteousness. They see his glory: they hear his voice: they taste that the Lord is gracious. They walk in the way everlasting: fight the good fight of faith: and labour, that whether present or absent, they may be accepted of him. "The body is indeed dead, because of sin; but the spirit is life, because of righteousness."

Secondly. He abolished death by his miracles, while he was on earth. We find this among the proofs of his Messiahship, addressed to the disciples of his forerunner, in prison: "Go and show John again those things which ye do hear and see: the blind receive their sight, and the lame walk, the lepers are cleansed, and the deaf hear, *the dead are raised up*, and the poor have the Gospel preached to them."

He displayed his power over death in the case of the ruler's daughter. She was at the very interesting age of twelve years old. While her distressed father was gone to implore the Saviour's aid, she expired; and a messenger was sent after him to communicate the dismal tidings, and to prevent his troubling the Master, now it was too late. While there is life there is hope: but who can raise the dead? O, says Jesus, it is never too late to apply to me—*only believe.* When he arrived, the offices of death had commenced. Tho body was laid out; and the minstrels were making a noise. "And all wept, and bewailed her: but he said, Weep not; she is not dead, but sleepeth. And they laughed him to scorn, knowing that she was dead. And he put them all out, and took her by the hand, and

called, saying, Maid, arise. And her spirit came again, and she arose straightway: and he commanded to give her meat."

Another instance of this dominion was in the case of the widow's son of Nain. This young man was older than the ruler's daughter, and had been longer dead; for they were carrying him to his burial; and the widowed mother of an only child would not have allowed this, we may be assured, before the time. Our Saviour met the procession; and before any prayer was addressed to him, he saw who was weeping behind—"and he had compassion on her, and said unto her, Weep not." At the sound of which, she draws back her vail, to see what stranger interested himself on her behalf, and, with more kindness than wisdom, enjoined upon her an impossibility. "But he came and touched the bier: and they that bare him stood still. And he said, Young man, I say unto thee, Arise. And he that was dead sat up, and began to speak. And he delivered him to his mother." What a present!

Behold Lazarus. Our Saviour loved him; but suffers him to fall sick; and leaves him to the natural effect of the disease. Two days he abode still in the same place, after hearing that he was dead. When he reached the suburbs of Bethany, the process of putrefaction was supposed to have begun. "Then when Mary was come where Jesus was, and saw him, she fell down at his feet, saying unto him, Lord, if thou hadst been here, my brother had not died. When Jesus therefore saw her weeping, and the Jews also weeping which came with her, he groaned in the spirit, and was troubled, and said, Where have ye laid him? They said unto him, Lord, come and see. Jesus wept."—He ordered the stone to be rolled away, and in a tone of uncontrolable authority, he cried with a loud voice, "Lazarus, come forth. And he that was dead came forth, bound hand and foot with grave-clothes: and his face was bound about with a napkin. Jesus saith unto them, Loose him, and let him go."

Once more: we are told that as the Redeemer expired, "the vail of the temple was rent in twain from the top to the bottom; and the earth did quake, and the rocks rent; and the graves were opened; and many bodies of the saints which slept arose, and came out of the graves after his resurrection, and went into the holy city, and appeared unto many."

Thirdly. He abolished death in his own person. *His own* rising from the dead is very distinguishable from all the former instances of resurrection. The ruler's daughter, the widow's son, Lazarus, and the saints in Jerusalem, were raised by the power of another; but he rose by his own power. Of his dominion, even over his own death and revival, he had spoken before—"No man taketh my life from me; I lay it down of myself; I have power to lay it down, and I have power to take it again. Destroy this temple," said he, "and in three days I will raise it up:" and he spake of the temple of his body. *They* rose as private individuals; but *He* as the head and representative of his people: and because he lives, they shall live also. *They* only rose to a temporal life, and were again subject to disease and mortality; but "he being raised from the dead, dieth no more, death hath no more dominion over him." Hence he is called "the first-begotten of the dead; the first-born from the dead; and the first that should rise from the dead;" referring not to the order of time, but to peculiarity, supremacy, and influence.

Fourthly. He abolished death penally. Thus he has destroyed death as to its sting. The sting of death is sin—because sin exposes us to the wrath of God, and binds us over to suffer: and the strength of sin is the law—for cursed is every one that continueth not in all things written in the book of the law to do them. But Christ has redeemed us from the curse of the law, being made a curse for us. *One died for all*, says the Apostle. His death was equivalent to the destruction of all the redeemed: there was such value in his suffering, derived from his dignity, that in lieu of our perdition it was accepted as "an offering and a sacrifice to God of a sweet-smelling savour." Every moral purpose that could have been answered by the punishment of the sinner has been better subserved by the death of the Saviour. "We are ambassadors for Christ, as though God did beseech you by us: we pray you in Christ's stead, be ye reconciled to God. For he hath made him to be sin for us, who knew no sin; that we might be made the righteousness of God in him." And did he himself bear our sins in his own body on the tree? Was the chastisement of our peace laid on him, and by his stripes are we healed? Well may those who believe enter into rest: well may they sing,

"If sin be pardon'd, I'm secure;
Death has no sting beside:
The Law gives sin its damning power—
But Christ my ransom died!"

He has not abolished *going home; and falling asleep; and departing:* but he has abolished *death*. This leads us to observe that he has,

Fifthly. Abolished death comparatively: I mean, as to its terror. This is not the same with the foregoing particular. *That* regards all the people of God, and extends even to those who die under a cloud of darkness, and a load of depression: it belongs to a Cowper, who died in despair, as well as to a Hervey, who said, "Lord, now lettest thou thy servant depart in peace, according to thy word; for mine eyes have seen thy salvation." *All* believers die *safely;* there is no curse for them after death, or in death. In *this sense,*

their end is peace; peace in the result, if not in the passage. But their end is generally peace in experience as well as in result. There are, however, cases of constitutional infirmity that may not only exclude joy, but even hope. Sometimes the nature of the disorder is such as to hinder sensibility, or expression. Sometimes, too, God may allow the continuance of fear, even in those he loves, as a rebuke for loose or irregular walking; and as a warning to others. It is a great mercy, as the time draws on, to be raised above the torment of fear, and to be able to say, *The bitterness of death is past!*

And this is commonly the case with those who die in the Lord. It has been the case even with those who have had to encounter a death of torture. Martyrs—men, women, children, have embraced the fiery stake, with all joy and peace in believing. It has been the case with those who have had every thing agreeable in their condition, and attractive in their connexions. They have said to those they were leaving, "You are dear—but I am going to him, who is all-wise, all-kind, all-fair." And such have been their views of opening glory, and such their earnests and foretastes of it, that they have not only been resigned to go, but have longed to depart to be with Christ, which is far better. Yea, we have often observed this to be the case with those who all their lifetime were subject to bondage through fear of death. When the hour has arrived, they have had mercy and grace to help in time of need; and, amazed at their former apprehensions, and their present feelings have said;

"Tell me, my soul,
Can *this* be *death?*"

"Yea, though I walk through the valley of the shadow of death, I will fear no evil: for thou art with me; thy rod and thy staff they comfort me."

"I have tasted Canaan's grapes;
And now I long to go
Where the Lord his vineyard keeps,
And where the clusters grow."—

While spectators have been ready to envy them their condition, and have seen our doctrine explained and verified—"He hath abolished death."

Finally. He will do this absolutely. He will abolish the very state: "He must reign till he hath put all enemies under his feet. The last enemy that shall be destroyed is death. So also is the resurrection of the dead. It is sown in corruption; it is raised in incorruption: it is sown in dishonour; it is raised in glory: it is sown in weakness; it is raised in power: it is sown a natural body; it is raised a spiritual body. There is a natural body, and there is a spiritual body. As we have borne the image of the earthy, we shall also bear the image of the heavenly."

This amazing change, this infinite consummation, will be accomplished by *his* agency—I "will raise him up at the last day." He "shall change our vile body, that it may be fashioned like unto his own glorious body, according to the working whereby he is able even to subdue all things unto himself."

> "His own soft hand shall wipe the tears,
>   From every weeping eye;
> And pains, and groans, and griefs, and fears,
>   And DEATH ITSELF SHALL DIE.

Let it not be said, but this is a future event; and the Apostle speaks of the past—he *has* abolished death. His recompense is as certain as his sufferings. Purpose and execution are the same with him. His promise is fulfilment. One day with the Lord is as a thousand years, and a thousand years as one day. "He that sat upon the throne said, Behold, I make all things new. And he said unto me, Write: for these words are true and faithful. And he said unto me, IT IS DONE. I am Alpha and Omega, the beginning and the end."— These reflections should relieve us in the loss of pious connexions. And how many have bereaving dispensations constrained, in speaking of their relations, to look back and say—I *had* a child—a parent—a wife—a husband! Who has lived a few years in this vale of tears, and not had reason to sigh, "Lover and friend hast thou put far from me?" And is sensibility forbidden us? "Our tears become us, and our grief is just."—Yet may a departing saint say, with a dying Saviour, "Weep not for me, but weep for yourselves and for your children." Yes, we are objects of pity—not they. We who are still in the wilderness—not they who have entered the land of promise. We who are still in the conflict—not they who have gotten the victory. We who rise in the morning to cares that corrode us, fears that alarm us, infirmities that press us down—not they who have obtained joy and gladness, and whose sorrow and sighing are fled away. Did they die? No—*death* is abolished.

> "Why do you mourn departing friends,
>   Or shake at death's alarms?
> 'Tis but the voice that Jesus sends,
>   To call them to his arm."

Are they *dead*? No.—Their spirits are now with God: and their "flesh rests in hope. He will not leave their souls in hell, neither will he suffer his holy ones to see corruption" for ever. "I would not have you to be ignorant, brethren, concerning them which are asleep, that ye sorrow not, even as others which have no hope. For if we believe that Jesus died and rose again, even so them also which sleep in Jesus will God bring with him. Wherefore comfort one another with these words."

Again. Should not this subject raise the minds of Christians above the fear of dissolution?—You dread it—but what is it you dread? According to Paul—*nothing*—for he has *abolished* death. Yea—this is only one part of your consolation. This is all negative comfort. But remember, he has turned the curse into a blessing: he has made of the enemy a friend. Instead of robbing you, it relieves; it enriches—it is the making of you for ever.—TO DIE IS GAIN!

Behold the recommendation of religion; by which I mean the religion of the Gospel; for there is no other that reaches the case of fallen man. The people of the world often affect to despise Christians; but there are moments in which they really envy them. When conscience has a wakeful moment, and they are led to reflect on the believer's final safety and privileges, they exclaim, with Balaam, "Let me die the death of the righteous, and let my last end be like his." And no wonder; for he alone is the happy man whose chief interest is provided for; who is safe for the soul and eternity—not he who has health, but he who is prepared to lose it—not he who prospers in life, but he who has hope in death—not he who lays up treasure on earth, but he who in heaven has a better and an enduring substance—he who can say, with Job, "I know that my Redeemer liveth, and that he shall stand at the latter day upon the earth: and though after my skin worms destroy this body, yet in my flesh shall I see God: whom I shall see for myself, and mine eyes shall behold, and not another; though my reins be consumed within me." Ignorance may conceal from a man his danger: wickedness may harden his heart against a sense of it: vain reasonings may stupify the conscience with an opiate—but there is no true victory over death but that which is derived from the cross and grace of the Redeemer. Happy ye who are found in him! It is not presumption, but becoming confidence, in you, to dare every thing—and to triumph over all. "Nay, in all things we are more than conquerors through him that loved us. For I am persuaded, that neither death, nor life, nor angels, nor principalities, nor powers, nor things present, nor things to come, nor height, nor depth, nor any other creature, shall be able to separate us from the love of God, which is in Christ Jesus our Lord."

To conclude. What then is the duty of a sinner? It is, to remember that it is appointed unto men once to die, and after this the judgment; that his breath is in his nostrils; that if he leaves the world a stranger to the Lord Jesus, temporal death will only be the passage to eternal—but that there is hope in Israel concerning this thing: that God has sent his only begotten Son into the world, that we might live through him; that he came, not only that we might have life, but have it more abundantly—and that we cannot escape, if we neglect so great salvation.—It is, to pray, with Moses, "So teach us to number our days, that we may apply our hearts unto wisdom." It is, to "seek the Lord while he may be found, and to call upon him while he is near." All else, for creatures circumstanced like you, is folly or trifling. "This is the work of God, that ye believe on him whom he hath sent. He that believeth on the Son hath everlasting life: and he that believeth not the Son shall not see life; but the wrath of God abideth on him."

Say then—"I am mortal—yet an heir of eternity. Every breath I draw brings me nearer the hour when this world will recede from my view, and proclaim its vanity and vexation. Then, O solemn thought! these states of changeless existence will open on my view in all their tremendous grandeur and importance. Then, dreadful alternative! the glories of heaven, or the damnation of hell, will be my portion.—To which of these am I hastening?—What am I? A sinner.—What then is my doom? The wages of sin is death.—But is there no escape? 'With the Lord there is mercy, and with him there is plenteous redemption.' O cheering hope! But is it for me? He came into the world to save sinners; he died for the ungodly; and why not for thee?—And can he save me? He is able to save to the uttermost. And will he save me? 'Him that cometh unto me I will in no wise cast out.' O heavenly intelligence! 'Tis a saying worthy of all acceptation—I am saved by hope—To the throne of grace will I flee—on the Friend of sinners will I rely—and in the exercise of faith, love, patience, and obedience, 'all the days of my appointed time will I wait'—till —it will be nothing more—till my *change* comes." Amen.

DISCOURSE CII.

THE TWO INTERCESSORS.

He ever liveth to make intercession for them.
Heb. vii. 25.
The Spirit itself maketh intercession for us.
Rom. viii. 27.

ONE of the ways—"for we are not ignorant of his devices," one of the ways, in which the enemy of souls destroys men, is by joining together what God has separated. Hence the alliance between the world and religion; and hence the awful declarations; "No man can serve two masters: for either he will hate the one, and love the other; or else he will hold to the one, and despise the other. Ye cannot serve God and mammon. Love not the world, neither the things that are in the world. If any man love the world, the love of the Father is not in him. Ye adulterers and adulteresses, know ye not that the friendship of the world is enmity with God? whosoever therefore will be a friend of the world is the enemy of God. If God had told us that we cannot walk on the sea, or flee in the air, we should have believed him, without risking life by experiment: but here—in declarations equally express, men are not content without trying whether his word will come to pass or not.— And, were it not for the dreadfulness of the result, we should say—"And let them try! But 'God will be true, and every man a liar!'"

Another mode by which he destroys, is to separate what God has joined together; such as principle and practice; doctrine and duty; pardoning mercy and renewing grace: the water and the blood—for he came by water and blood; not by water only, or blood only, but by water and blood: these were not severed in their effusion from the cross, and they cannot be divided in their application to the soul. That man is not yet truly awakened and enlightened from above, who does not see and feel his equal need of —the Saviour and the Sanctifier—the Son of God and the Spirit of God—the work of the one *for* him, and of the other *in* him.

To such a connexion I am going to lead you. For be it remembered, every Christian has two Advocates, two Intercessors; and they should be viewed relatively to each other. "Jesus ever liveth to make intercession for them. The Spirit itself maketh intercession for us." We have therefore three things in view. And,

I. Let us consider THE INTERCESSION OF CHRIST. Dr. Owen, long ago, complained, and there is much truth in the remark, that we do not dwell enough, in our thoughts, on the present life of Christ: for he is living, not a life of glory only—though even this should delight those that love him; but a life of office. It was expedient for *us* that he went away. It was for our welfare that he ascended into heaven, as well as descended into the grave. "He was delivered for our offences, and was raised again for our justification." "Because he lives, we shall live also." "If, when we were enemies, we were reconciled to God by the death of his Son; much more, being reconciled, we shall be saved by his life."

When our Saviour left our world, he ascended up *far above all heavens;* and frailty might have feared, that his concern for us would have ceased with his residence among us. When a friend is going far away, we sometimes painfully think of the proverb, "Out of sight out of mind." Men, as they rise, too commonly lose much of their recollection; and forget even those to whom they were under obligation before.—"Yet did not the chief butler remember Joseph, but forgat him." But, says Paul, though Jesus the Son of God be passed into the heavens, "we have not an high priest who cannot be touched with the feeling of our infirmities." The ligature which unites us remains—and is all sensibility and life. Had we seen him as he was going up, we should have prayed, with the dying thief, " Lord, remember me when thou comest into thy kingdom." And does he not? Yes; " he ever liveth to make intercession for us."

Volumes might be written on the subject; but we must be brief. It has been questioned whether this intercession be *vocal*. Why should it not? He is " clothed in a body like our own." Certainly the common reason assigned—that it would be inconsistent with his present dignity, is not valid. For do we not know that dignity is never injured by condescension?—That true greatness is tender and sympathizing? That his goodness is his glory?—" Do we forget the grace of our Lord Jesus Christ, who, when he was rich, for our sakes became poor, that we through his poverty might be rich?"—And that he does not give up the kingdom to God, even the Father, *till* he has put down all rule, and all authority, and power?

But, not to intrude into things which we have not seen, it is enough for us to know,

First. That his intercession is *real*. It consists in his personal appearance; in the presentation of his sacrifice, and claiming the benefits arising from it. Æschylus was strongly accused, and likely to be condemned. His brother Amyntas engaged to be his advocate. Amyntas had done much for the commonwealth, and in a certain action, in their service, had lost a hand. He came into the court. The court was uncommonly crowded; and all were eager to hear him plead on so interesting an occasion. But he said nothing—he only held up his dismembered arm!! The audience and the judges were so moved, as immediately to order his brother's release. It does not appear that the High Priest *said* any thing when he entered the holy place: but what he *did*, spake loud enough. He wore the names of the twelve tribes of Israel on his breast-plate; he took the blood of the slaughtered victim in a basin, and sprinkled the mercy-seat, and burned incense before the golden altar, and then came forth and blessed the people. Abel's blood *spake* to God from the ground; that is, it demanded vengeance: the blood of Jesus is equally vocal; but it speaketh better things than that of Abel—it calls for mercy. How did John see him in the vision? As a lamb that had been slain; that is, with the wound in the neck, and the blood on the wool. Without a figure—he retains in his glorified body the marks of his sufferings and death. The saints and the angels behold them, and exclaim, " Worthy is the Lamb that was slain!" God views them, and says, " Ask of me, and I will give thee the heathen for thine in-

heritance, and the uttermost parts of the earth for thy possession." So the Saviour said himself.—THEREFORE " doth my Father love me, because I lay down my life for the sheep."

Secondly. It *extends to all our important interests*. We may look upon his prayer for his disciples, on the night in which he was betrayed, as a specimen of his continued intercession before the throne. And for what does he not there plead? Is it their preservation? " Keep through 'thine own name those whom thou hast given me. I pray not that thou shouldest take them out of the world, but that thou shouldest keep them from the evil." Is it their renovation? " Sanctify them through thy truth: thy word is truth." Is it their union? " That they all may be one; as thou, Father, art in me, and I in thee, that they also may be one in us: that the world may believe that thou hast sent me. And the glory which thou gavest me I have given them; that they may be one, even as we are one." Is it their glorification? " Father, I will that they also whom thou hast given me be with me where I am; that they may behold my glory, which thou hast given me: for thou lovedst me before the foundation of the world."

Thirdly. It is *successful*. " I know," says he, " that thou hearest me always." This conclusion is derivable from the grandeur of his character, and his nearness to God. He is called God's own Son, his only begotten Son, his dear Son, in whom his soul delighteth. It is derivable from the ground of his demand. By his obedience unto death, even the death of the cross, he has rendered the communication of the blessings we need consistent with the truth, and righteousness, and law of God. It is derivable from Divine fidelity. He who is faithful to his saints, cannot be unfaithful to his Son: the joy that was set before him, as the recompense of his sufferings, he *must* possess. He " shall see his seed; he shall prolong his days, and the pleasure of the Lord shall prosper in his hands. He shall see the travail of his soul and shall be SATISFIED."—To which we may add, the interest he feels in his people. What he asks on their behalf, he asks for himself; for they are one and " he is glorified in them."

II. Let us examine THE INTERCESSION OF THE SPIRIT: for the Spirit " itself maketh intercession for us."

In entering on this part of our discourse, it is necessary to observe, that, subjectively and instrumentally considered, religion is our *own* work: *we* run the race set before us; and fight the good fight of faith: *we* believe, and repent, and pray—But, owing to our natural ignorance, and weakness, depravity, and aversion, it is God that worketh in us to will and to do of his good pleasure. To his Spirit, therefore, all our renovation is ascribed: we

THE TWO INTERCESSORS. 381

are said to be "born of the Spirit;" to be "led by the Spirit;" to "live in the Spirit;" to "walk in the Spirit;" and to "worship God in the Spirit."

Let us see how this general reflection bears upon the subject before us. "I will pour," says God, "upon the house of David, and the inhabitants of Jerusalem, the Spirit of grace and of supplication." "Because ye are sons," says the Apostle, "God hath sent forth the Spirit of his Son into your hearts, crying, Abba, Father." And Jude exhorts Christians to "pray in the Holy Ghost." And how are we to understand this? There is only one way in which the Spirit itself maketh intercession *for* us; and that is, by making intercession *in* us: it is, by teaching, and enabling us to make intercession for ourselves: for the Apostle adds, "he maketh intercession for us, with groanings which cannot be uttered." Let us see, then, how this Divine agency brings the sinner upon his knees, and keeps him there.

First. The Spirit leads us to an acquaintance with ourselves. He removes the vail of ignorance and delusion that concealed our state, our wants, and our desert: and the man who once said, I am rich, and increased with goods, and have need of nothing, now sees, that he is wretched, and miserable, and poor, and blind, and naked. He no longer denies his guilt; or palliates his offences; or goes about to establish his own righteousness: but, filled with self-abhorrence, condemnation, and despair, cries, "God be merciful to me a sinner." For,

Secondly. The Spirit fixes upon the mind a concern to be delivered and relieved, too great to be shaken off. Many persons are followed with some general notions of their being in an unconverted state; and feel some superficial apprehensions of the unhappiness and danger of such a condition: but they have no burden too heavy for them to bear; they are not weary, and heavy laden; they can sleep, and eat, and drink, and trade, and trifle, as well as before. But it is not so with the man whom God is bringing along to his footstool. He sows in tears. His sin is ever before him. Neither business, nor company, nor amusement, can ease the anguish of his broken heart; or divert him from the inquiry, "What must I do to be saved?"

Thirdly. The Spirit enables us to apprehend and believe the mercy and grace revealed in the Gospel. Hence arises a hope that maketh not ashamed. This hope enters the soul, as the sun does a garden in spring; calling forth, by a genial influence, the leaves and the buds, after the dreariness of winter. We are sweetly, yet powerfully, excited and encouraged to make known our requests unto God. We see that our case, however deplorable, is provided for; that all things are now ready; that the blessings we need are as free as they are suitable. Particularly we see Jesus as the Mediator of the new covenant; as once suffering for sin, the just for the unjust, that he might bring us unto God; as the way to the Father—and "have boldness and access with confidence by the faith of him." Thus these words of the Saviour are fulfilled, "He shall glorify me, for he shall receive of mine, and shall show it unto you."

Finally. The Spirit renews our souls, removes our alienation from the life of God, and produces in us those principles and dispositions which cause us to delight in approaching him; and even to give thanks at the remembrance of his holiness. Thus our duty is converted into a privilege; and we find it too good to draw near to God ever again to restrain prayer before him.

Here I would observe, That this influence is afforded us all through life, and is not confined to the commencement of a religious course: neither is it limited to persons of inferior attainments only—What says the Apostle? *We* know not what to pray for as we ought; but the Spirit helpeth *our* infirmities. The wisest, if left to themselves, would often ask for scorpions, instead of fish—but he maketh intercession for the saints, according to the will of God. The most zealous sometimes grow careless and formal—but he quickens their souls, when they cleave unto the dust. The holiest contract fresh guilt, and when they remember God, are troubled —but he revives their confidence by the application of the blood of sprinkling: and brings them into the presence of God again as their Father and their Friend.

Therefore, grieve not the Holy Spirit, whereby ye are sealed unto the day of redemption. It would be, not only the vilest ingratitude, considering what he has done for you; but the greatest folly. How much, how entirely, do you depend upon his agency— you cannot even pray without him—and what can you do without prayer? Would you grieve a friend, and induce him to give up his correspondence, and his visits; and constrain him to withhold his assistance, and to look another way, if he meet you in the road—when you every moment need his smiles and his aid?

Shall I also say, Beware that you do not abuse this encouraging truth? It is abused, when you neglect prayer till, you say, the Spirit moves you. For we are to stir up ourselves to take hold of God. We are to cry for aid, as the Church does: "Awake, O north wind; and come, thou south; blow upon my garden, that the spices thereof may flow out." By tacking about, the mariner gets wind—not by lying still. God helps us, not in the neglect—but in the use of means—"Draw nigh to God, and he will draw nigh to you." The more dull and dead we feel ourselves the more we need these exercises, which are appointed to help us; and which, for this very reason, are called the *means* of grace. And Christians well know what a change they have often experienced, even *in* the performance of the duty! They have kneeled down, dark, and cold, and contracted; but have risen up enlightened, and inflamed, and enlarged; and have exemplified the promise; "They that wait upon the Lord shall renew their strength; they shall mount up with wings as eagles; they shall run, and not be weary; and they shall walk, and not faint."—Having considered the intercession of Christ, and explained the intercession of the Spirit, let us,

III. View them IN THEIR RELATION TO EACH OTHER.

It is easy to *distinguish* these Intercessors. The one makes intercession above; the other below: one in the court of heaven; the other in the conscience. The one makes intercession for us, the other in us. The sanctifying Intercessor produces the petition; the atoning Intercessor introduces it: the one is the notary that indites the case; the other is the counsellor that pleads it before the jury and the Judge.

But there is a connexion between them; and it is threefold. First: a connexion of derivation. The one flows from the other. If the Son of God had not made intercession *for* you as a sinner, the Spirit itself would never have made intercession *in* you, as a believer. Christ hath redeemed us from the curse of the law, being made a curse for us: "that the blessing of Abraham might come on the Gentiles through Jesus Christ; that we might receive the promise of the Spirit through faith." Secondly: a connexion of dependence. The one needs the other. Is not the work of the Spirit pure and holy? *Can* that which he produces be imperfect and polluted? You must distinguish between the same work as it is his, and as it is ours. What comes from him is pure and complete; but as far as it is done by us it is defective and defiled, like water, which, however clear from the spring, rolling over a muddy bottom, or running through an impure channel, will be soiled and injured. Hence all need, as long as they are here, the continued mediation of the Saviour: and he is the great high priest over the house of God, for this very purpose, and offers with much incense the prayers of all saints. We need not be afraid to pray, since all our services pass through his hands, and he presents and perfumes them. Thirdly: a connexion of evidence. The one proves the other. As to some of you, how long have you been praying, "Say unto my soul, I am thy salvation? Show me a token for good, that I may rejoice in thee? What happy beings would you go away at the end of this exercise, if you could ascertain one thing: namely,

that the Redeemer thinks upon *you* for good—and appears in the presence of God for *you.*

Well; the proof does not lie far off—it is nigh thee, even in thy *mouth* and in *thy heart.* It is prayer—not fine prayer—not well-arranged language; the proof does not require language at all. No—but a broken heart; a contrite spirit; tears; sighs; groanings—groanings which cannot be uttered.

Of this therefore rest assured, that if the Spirit itself is thus making intercession *in* you, Jesus is ever living to make intercession *for* you.

And what can you desire more? It was the privilege of David, that he had a friend at court—and this was Jonathan the king's son. It was the privilege of Jacob's sons, that they had a friend at court—and this was Joseph their brother. Christians! both these advantages are united in your portion. You have a Friend at court; you have an Advocate with the Father, Jesus Christ the righteous—and he is the King's Son; he is your Brother. "Who is he that condemneth? It is Christ that died, yea rather, that is risen again, who is even at the right hand of God; who also maketh intercession for us. Who shall separate us from the love of Christ? shall tribulation, or distress, or persecution, or famine, or nakedness, or peril, or sword? Nay, in all these things we are more than conquerors through him that loved us."

And while he represents you in heaven, may you, Christians, represent him on earth. While he pleads your cause, may you plead his; and henceforth live, not to yourselves, but to Him who died for you and rose again '

DISCOURSE CIII.

THE GRAND INQUIRY.

Lovest thou me?—John xxi. 17.

SOME of the greatest works of God seem to have been the effects of accidental occurrences, rather than the results of design. The reason is, because God is the sovereign Master of occasions, as well as of their consequences. He foresees them; he procures them; and what is contingency with us, is purpose with him.

The same may be said of his Word. Many parts of it were produced by particular events; but they were intended for universal and perpetual use; and therefore, in reading them, we should be concerned to bring what is said of others to bear upon ourselves. Many of the Psalms of David were composed by the author under the influence of peculiar circumstances; but these peculiar circumstances were comprehended in the Divine arrangement, and have been rendered subservient to the welfare of the Church of God in all ages of the world. When Joshua was going to cross the river Jordan, at the head of the Jewish tribes, to take possession of the land of Canaan, God addressed him, and said, "I will not fail thee, nor forsake thee; be strong and of good courage." The promise was personal; yet, after a lapse of near two thousand years, the Apostle applies it to all believers, whose minds need the same support, and whose confidence is derived from the same assurance; "Let your conversation be without covetousness; and be content with such things as ye have: for he hath said, I will never leave thee, nor forsake thee. So that we may boldly say, the Lord is my helper, and I will not fear what man shall do unto me."

This reflection fully justifies the plan we have in view this evening—The words which I have read were originally addressed to Peter; and you are familiar with the circumstances of the history. I will not detain you a moment in referring to them. But, my dear hearers; imagine the Saviour of the world looking down from his throne, and applying this question to you—to each of you—young or old—rich or poor—learned or illiterate—while heaven and hell are in suspense, anxiously waiting for your reply—LOVEST THOU ME?

The question is REASONABLE.
The question is IMPORTANT.
The question SUPPOSES DOUBT.
The question ADMITS OF SOLUTION.

LOVEST THOU ME?

I. The question is REASONABLE. And why is it reasonable? Because we *ought* to love him, and the affection is *just*. This part of our subject engages us in a train of reflection, at once difficult, mortifying, and apparently presumptuous. Difficult—not from the fewness of materials, but from the necessity of making a selection, where proofs are so numberless. Mortifying—not because the theme is irksome; but it is painful to think, that any should want conviction of his worth, or even need to have their minds stirred up by way of remembrance. Apparently presumptuous—for what are we, worms of the earth, to take upon us to investigate his merits, and to determine whether he is deserving of the regard he requires. Oh! let not the Lord be angry while we thus speak, and, for the sake of those that hear us, attempt to lay open a few of the sources of his claims.

And, First, my brethren, we call upon you to contemplate his *person*. Go, read his history. Look at his likeness as it is sketched in the Gospel. Survey his features: behold the beauty of the Lord, and inquire in his temple. *What* is he? In himself he is the most amiable of all beings. He "is the chief of ten thousand; yea, he is altogether lovely. He is fairer than the children of men:" fairer than the children of God: as much above an-

gels as he is above mortals: comprising in himself all the graces of time, and all the perfections of eternity; all the attractions of humanity, and all the glories of Deity. Bring forward all the excellences the world ever saw: add as many more as the imagination can supply: render them all complete: combine them together—yet this is not He that here demands thy affection; all this aggregate is no more to him that asks, "Lovest thou me?" than a ray of light to the sun, or a drop of water to the ocean: compared with the Saviour, it is nothing, less than nothing, and vanity.

Secondly. Observe his *doings*.

Look *backward*, and consider what he *has* done. He remembered thee, O Christian, in thy low estate: and, without thy desert, without thy desire, he interposed between thee and the curse of the Law, and said, "Deliver from going down to the pit: I have found a ransom." He came and preached peace. He established the Gospel dispensation. He gave apostles, prophets, evangelists, pastors, teachers; for the work of the ministry. He sent the word of life to this country, and brought it to thy door. He preserved thee through years of ignorance and rebellion by his power: and at length called thee by his grace; so that thou art no longer a stranger and a foreigner, but a fellow-citizen with the saints, and of the household of God.

Look *upward*, and consider what he *is* doing. He has taken with him to heaven the same heart of tenderness that he possessed on earth. He remembers thee, now that he is come into his kingdom. He ever liveth to make intercession for thee. He is moving the wheels of nature, and ordering the dispensations of Providence, for thy welfare: he is making all things to work together for thy good. There is not a prayer you offer up but he hears it. There is not a duty you discharge but he enables you to perform it. There is not a trial you endure but he sustains you under it. There is not a blessing you taste but he sweetens and sanctifies it.

Look *forward*, and consider what he *will* do. For he has made known the thoughts of his heart, and bound himself by promise. He is engaged to be with you in trouble; to render your strength equal to your day; and to make his grace sufficient for you. He is engaged to comfort thee upon the bed of languishing; to receive thy departing spirit to himself; to change thy vile body into a resemblance of his own glorious body; to confess thee before an assembled world; and to say of those services over which thou hast so often blushed and groaned—" Well done, good and faithful servant; thou hast been faithful over a few things, I will make thee ruler over many things; enter thou into the joy of thy Lord."

Thirdly. Mark his *sufferings*. For, to

enable him to be our best friend, something more was necessary than the wishes of benevolence, or the exertions of power. To obtain eternal redemption for us, he submits to a scene of humiliation and anguish, such as no tongue can express, or imagination conceive. For our sakes, he who was rich, became poor—so poor, that while foxes had holes, and the birds of the air had nests, the Son of man had not where to lay his head. For our sakes, the King of glory was numbered with transgressors; had his name cast out as evil; was treated as a glutton, a winebibber, a friend of publicans and sinners, a madman, a demoniac, a rebel, a traitor. For our sakes, he, who was blessed for evermore, became a man of sorrows, and acquainted with grief. Before the hand of man had touched his body, we find him in the garden exceeding sorrowful, even unto death: we see him sweating as it were great drops of blood falling down to the earth; we hear him praying, "Father, if it be possible, let this cup pass from me." As we follow him from Gethsemane to Golgotha, he gives his back to the smiters, and his cheek to them that plucked off the hair; he hides not his face from shame and spitting. The thorns enter his sacred temples. They pierce his hands and his feet; he hangs upon the cross, suspended by the soreness of his wounds, and as he dies—and well he may—he appropriates to himself the language of the prophet; "Is it nothing to you, all ye that pass by? behold, and see if there be any sorrow like unto my sorrow!" No; blessed Saviour! Never was there sorrow—and, therefore, never was there love—like thine!—

But we must observe, not only what he suffers *for* us, but what he suffers *from* us. The more holy any being is, the more does he abhor sin. Sin is, therefore, more offensive to a saint than to a man; it is more intolerable to an angel than to a saint; and it is more grievous to God than to an angel. How infinitely provoking it is to *him*, may be inferred from his own expostulation and complaint, with regard to his people Israel; "Oh, do not this abominable thing that I hate. Is it a small thing for you to weary men, but will you weary God also? Thou hast made me to serve with thy sins; thou hast wearied me with thine iniquities." And yet, how much of this has he had to bear with from us, even since we have known him, or rather have been known of him! O, what unprofitableness under the instructions of his word and the ordinances of his house! what insensibility and ingratitude under all his mercies! what incorrigibleness under all his rebukes! what murmuring and repining under the dispensations of his providence! what charging him foolishly, and unkindly, even when his wisdom and kindness were performing the very things which we had a

thousand times implored him to accomplish! —And all this, from day to day—from year to year—in lengthened provocation!—While he, with all his patience, seemed urged to ask, "How long shall I be with you? how long shall I suffer you?" O, if he were swayed by human passions! if he were a mere creature like ourselves—where, at this hour, should we have been found? In the whole universe, where is the benefactor that would have continued his regards a moment longer, after meeting with such instances of indifference, of perverseness, of vileness—as we have been continually displaying towards the Lord that bought us?

Even this is not all. We must not only observe, what he suffers *for* us, and *from* us, but also what he suffers *in* us. "For we have not an high priest who cannot be touched with the feeling of our infirmities." Such is the intimate union between him and his people, that, as the Head, he feels afresh what every member bears. He that persecutes them persecutes him. He that toucheth them toucheth the apple of his eye. In all their affliction he is afflicted—

"O, for this love, let rocks and hills
Their lasting silence break!
And all harmonious human tongues
The Saviour's praises speak."

"Angels! assist our mighty joys,
Strike all your harps of gold:
But when you raise your highest notes,
His love can ne'er be told."

LOVEST THOU ME?
II. The question is IMPORTANT. And why is it important? Because we *must* love him; and the affection is not only just, but necessary. To illustrate this, you will observe—

That this love is even necessary to our sanctification. Love is a powerful and a transforming principle. By constant residence in the mind, the image stamps and leaves its own resemblance; so that every man is in reality the same with the supreme object of his attachment. If he loves any thing sordid and mean, he will become so too; while his intercourse with purity and grandeur will be sure to refine and elevate his mind. And hence it is easy to see what will be the effect of the love of Christ: for, as he is the centre of all excellency, the source of all perfection, it follows, that, in proportion as our love to him prevails in us, it will renew us; it will exalt us; it will change us into the same image, from glory to glory, as by the Spirit of the Lord.

This love is necessary to give us delight in all our religious services. We shall never proceed to advantage in any cause, especially if much opposed and tried, unless we feel an interest in it: conviction may carry us some way, but affection much farther. It is the nature of love to render difficult things easy, and bitter ones sweet. What was it that turned the seven years of hard bondage, that

Jacob served for Rachel, into so many pleasant days! The affection he bore to her who inspired him. What is it that more than reconciles that mother to numberless nameless anxieties and privations, in rearing her baby charge? "Can a woman forget her sucking child, that she should not have compassion on the son of her womb?" It is love that does all this. But there is no love like that which a redeemed sinner bears to his Redeemer; and, therefore, no pleasure can equal that which he enjoys in pleasing him. While others say, What a weariness it is to serve the Lord! *he* finds his service to be perfect freedom; he calls the Sabbath a delight; he is glad when they say to him, Let us go into the house of the Lord; he finds his word, and he eats it, and it is the joy and the rejoicing of his heart. Religion renders all this our duty; but it is love alone that can make it our privilege; it is love alone that can bring the soul into it; it is love alone that can make it our meat to do the will of Him that sent us, and to finish his work.

This love is necessary, to render our duties acceptable. To a renewed mind nothing can be more desirable than the approbation of his Master; nothing more delicious than the testimony that he pleases him. The humility of the Christian, however, renders the attainment no easy thing. He feels the poverty and the unworthiness of his services; and, instead of supposing that his obedience merits a recompense for its excellences, he rather wonders that it is not rejected and disdained for its defects. But the Lord looketh to the heart; and when this is given up to him, he values the motive, though we err in the circumstances; he regards the intention, when we fail in the execution; and says as he did to David, "It is well that it was in thine heart." In judging of our services, he admits into the estimate, not only what we do, but what we desire to do. He judges by the disposition; he acknowledges liberality where nothing is given; and applauds heroism where nothing is suffered. "For where there is first a willing mind, it is accepted according to that a man hath, and not according to that he hath not." But it is equally true, that "in vain we draw nigh to him with our mouth, and honour him with our lip, while the heart is far from him."

Finally. This love is necessary, to ascertain our interest in the Saviour's regards. His followers are not described by their knowledge, their gifts, their creed, their profession; but by their cordial adherence to him. We may do many things materially good; we may abound with external privileges; we may eat and drink in his presence, and he may preach in our streets; we may prophesy in his name, and in his name cast out devils, and do many wonderful works; and yet at the great day he may profess unto us, I never

knew you. But hear Paul: "Grace be with all them that love our Lord Jesus Christ in sincerity;" and remember that this is a decision, as well as a wish; a promise as well as a prayer—Grace *shall* be with them, adequate to all their exigences. I am far from saying that our love to him is the cause of his love to us: but it is unquestionably the consequence, and therefore the evidence. His love produces ours; but our love evinces his: "I love them that love me." And when we consider the attributes of his love—a love so tender, so active, so gracious, so durable, so changeless—what are we not authorized to expect from an assured interest in it?

LOVEST THOU ME?

III. The question SUPPOSES DOUBT. And, my brethren, is there nothing in you to render this love suspicious? Let us fairly and honestly examine.

And First. Is there nothing to render it doubtful to the *world?* You are not only to *be* Christians, but to *appear* such. You are required not only to believe with the heart, but to confess with the tongue; and to hold fast, not only the reality, but the profession of faith, without wavering. Like the primitive saints, you are to be *manifestly* the epistles of Christ, known and read of all men; and not render it impossible, or even difficult, to determine whose hand has inscribed you. Like the patriarchs, you are to declare *plainly* that you seek a country; and not perplex all around you to decide whether you are settling here, or only strangers and pilgrims upon earth. To them that are in darkness it is said, "Show yourselves."

Have you always done this? Have you risen up for Him against the evil doers, and stood up for Him against the workers of iniquity? Have you never denied his name?—Never concealed his truth? Never been ashamed to avow your principles and your connexions? Have you never made concessions, in presence of the vain and the vicious, to escape a reproach which it would have been your glory to have deserved; and concerning which, binding it as a garland around your brow, you should have said, If this is to be vile, I will yet be more vile? Have your temporizing carriage and conversation never inspired men of the world, whom you had professedly left, with the hope that you were coming round again; and would in time rise above all your scruples, mingle in their dissipations, and run with them to the same excess of riot?

Secondly. Is there nothing to render it doubtful to the *Church?* Nothing can be more opposite to the spirit of the Gospel than a dark and distrustful temper. We should not harbour a misgiving mind; we should not even take advantage of the infirmities of our brethren, to conclude that their hearts are not right in the sight of God. Charity suffereth long, and is kind; charity hopeth all things, believeth all things, endureth all things. Yet it must be acknowledged that candour has its difficulties as well as duties. It has its bounds, beyond which it cannot pass. We must not be induced, by any tenderness of judgment, to violate the express decisions of the word of God. There are many, and, perhaps, never more than in our day, of whom, as the Apostle says to the Galatians, "We stand in doubt." They keep our hopes and our fears equally awake through life. When we pray for them, we are at a loss whether to consider them as in the flesh or in the Spirit. We receive them to the Lord's table, not because we are convinced of their state, but know not how to refuse them: and we continue them in communion upon the same principle. But, my brethren, these things ought not so to be. Your ministers and your fellow-members are entitled to satisfaction concerning, if not the degree, the reality of your religion.

Thirdly. Is there nothing to render it doubtful to *yourselves?* "indeed," say some of you with a sigh, "Indeed there is." Hence I go mourning all the day. How happy should I be, if I could but make out this awful case.

> " 'Tis a point I long to know;
>   Oft it causes anxious thought;
>   Do I love the Lord or no?
>   Am I his? or am I not?"

"I am a wonder as well as a grief to myself. If there are things that sometimes make me hope I am not in a state of nature, there are others—and these, alas! are far more numerous—that make me fear I am not in a state of grace. O my soul, surely this state implies much more than I have experienced: surely there is a secret that has not been revealed to me. *If* I loved him—could I ever read without pleasure the book that unveils his glories! *If* I loved him—could I ever fear to die, and shrink back from the only event that can bring me into his presence? *If* I loved him—could I feel so impatient under those reproaches and afflictions that make me a partaker of the fellowship of his sufferings?

> "*Could* my heart so hard remain;
>   Prayer a task and burden prove;
>   Every trifle give me pain;
>   If I knew a Saviour's love?
>
> "If I sing, or hear, or read,
>   Sin is mix'd with all I do:
>   You that love the Lord indeed,
>   Tell me—is it thus with you?"

Lastly. Is there nothing to render it doubtful to *the Saviour!*" There is a sense in which this is impossible. His eyes are in every place, beholding the evil and the good. No disguise can screen us from his penetration. We are all transparency before him. But we are to distinguish the question of right from the question of fact. With regard to right, he may, and he often does complain in his word, as if he was disappointed and surprised at the conduct of his professing people. And is there not a cause? You would think it strange if a husbandman should expect fertility from the dry sand or the barren rock: but it would be otherwise if he had a vine planted in a rich soil, and attended with every kind of culture. Then, surely, his expectation of fruit would be natural; and he would have reason to complain if nothing was produced. And is not this, at least in an awful degree, true of many of us? Estimating our proficiency by our advantages, *ought* he not to have found in us what he has yet sought for in vain? *Ought* he not to have seen something in our tempers and lives much more perfect; something in our conduct so unequivocal, something in our exertions and sacrifices so decisive, as to lead him to say, Now I know that thou lovest me; as God said to Abraham, "Now I know that thou fearest me, seeing thou hast not withheld thy son, thine only son, from me."

LOVEST THOU ME?

IV. The question ADMITS OF SOLUTION. It is not only possible, but comparatively easy to know whether we love another. And here it will be in vain for you to allege, that though this is generally true, the case before us is a peculiar one, because the object is invisible. For this furnishes no objection to our remark. Who knows not what it is to love a being he never saw? Many of us never saw Howard: but who does not feel veneration at the mention of his name? Who does not glow at the perusal of his journeys of mercy? Who does not melt at the sight of his statue. I envy not the heart of that man who can enter St. Paul's Cathedral, and view, unmoved, the mild compassion that beams and breathes even through the cold marble image. I never saw Cowper; but can I think of this amiable, this celestial spirit; can I read his matchless Letters, and his immortal Task, and not feel a thousand tender sympathies that attach me to him, and render inviting that part of the universe in which his piety and his genius range undepressed and uncontrolled? With regard to those with whom you are familiar, that which you love them for is not that which you see, but that which you cannot see. It is their mind, their heart, their intellectual qualities, their moral principles. Honesty, virtue, dignity; these are all invisible: it is true you have seen their actings, and their effects; but you never saw them—Yet we hope you love them.

It is also useless to urge, as an exception to the justice of our remark, that the love of which we have been speaking is a principle, and not a passion. We readily acknowledge the propriety of the distinction, and hope it will always be remembered. Had it been duly considered, many things would never have been published that have caused the way of truth to be evil spoken of: and many Christians would have escaped the despondency into which they have been plunged by judging of their state, not by the habitual and prevailing bias of their soul, but the flow and rise of their animal spirits. While, however, we allow the distinction, we deny the inference that might be supposed to result from it. For if we call this love esteem, rather than attachment—still it *is* esteem: if we call it a principle, and not a passion, still it *is* a principle—a principle that has a real being—and with whose operations and effects we are all acquainted. How then will this love show itself?

It will show itself by our *thoughts*. These naturally follow the object of our regard, and it is with difficulty we can draw them off. The current may be diverted by force; but the prevention removed, it soon flows in its wonted channel, and finds its former destination. Where the carcase is, there will the eagles be gathered together. David could say, "I love thee, O Lord, my strength." And what was the consequence? "How precious are thy thoughts unto me, O God! how great is the sum of them! if I should count them, they are more in number than the sand: when I awake, I am still with thee." If, then, I love the Saviour, I shall surely think of him. I shall reflect upon his character, his glory, and his grace. I shall dwell much upon his humiliation and sufferings. My thoughts will cling and cluster around his cross like bees around the hive—and my "meditation of him will be sweet." Even when my hands are employed in the common affairs of life, my mind will often ascend, and take a view of the Lamb that was slain: and I shall feel the refreshing and enlivening influence of these thoughts—for they are not thoughts of speculation, but of affection.

This love will show itself by our *speech*. "Out of the abundance of the heart the mouth speaketh." When Peter and John were ordered by the council to speak no more in the name of Jesus, what was their reply? "We cannot but speak the things which we have seen and heard." How was it with a certain woman in the company when his preaching had touched her heart? "She lifted up her voice, and said, Blessed is the womb that bare thee, and the paps which thou hast sucked." When the multitude cried, "Hosanna, Blessed is he that cometh in the name of the Lord," the Pharisees besought him that he would rebuke and silence them. What said the Master? "You are strangers to their views and feelings, or you would know that you require an impossibility: 'for if these should hold their peace, the stones would immediately cry out.'"

So great are the Saviour's charms: so powerful are the impressions of his grace! "One generation shall praise thy works to another, and shall declare thy mighty acts. They shall abundantly utter the memory of thy great goodness, and shall sing of thy righteousness. All thy works shall praise thee, O Lord; and thy saints shall bless thee. My mouth shall speak the praise of the Lord: and let all flesh bless his holy name for ever and ever."

It will show itself by desire after intimacy. Do we love another? We long to be with him. Separation is a grief. Distance is a torture. We wish to annihilate the space that intervenes. We meet him at the time appointed, and feel a pleasure in the interview that words can no more express than paint can do justice to light or heat. Our Lord and Saviour has promised to be found of them that seek him; in his word, in the assemblies of his people, on his throne, and at his table. To these, therefore, if I regard him, shall I repair, and with a disposition expressive of this language, "As the hart panteth after the water brooks, so panteth my soul after thee, O God. My soul thirsteth for God, for the living God: when shall I come and appear before God?" Is he withdrawn from me? I shall "lament after the Lord." And turning to those who are better acquainted with him, and know his resting-places, I shall anxiously ask, "Saw ye him whom my soul loveth?"

Once more. This love will show itself by *devotedness to the service and glory of its Master*. And here, my brethren, I wish to lay a peculiar stress. Nothing, be it ever remembered, can authenticate the existence of this principle in our hearts, detached from this regard to his will. It is in this way that he himself requires us to place our love beyond all dispute: "He that hath my commandments, and keepeth them, he it is that loveth me. If ye love me, keep my commandments." Am I then an enemy to his enemies? Am I a friend to his friends? Do I espouse his cause? Do I pray for the extension of his empire? Do I rejoice in the success of his affairs? Do I weep over the dishonours of his name? Am I sorrowful for the solemn assembly, and is the reproach of it my burden? Do I daily and hourly inquire, "Lord, what wilt thou have me to do?" Do I present myself at his footstool, saying,

"All that I have, and all I am,
   Shall be for ever thine;
Whate'er my duty bids me give
   My cheerful hands resign.

'Yet if I might make some reserve,
   And duty did not call,
I love my God with zeal so great,
   That I should give him all."

—When God had addressed David, and given him the choice of war, pestilence, or famine, he pressed for a decision, and said—"Consider now, and see what answer I shall return to him that sent me."

Men, Brethren, and Fathers! Allow me to close with a similar demand. What answer shall I give to Him in whose name I have addressed the solemn question—LOVEST THOU ME! or, What answer will *you* give! For I would rather you should deliver it yourselves. It would distress every feeling of my soul to return a negative answer—How could I tell him, on your behalf, "No, I do not love him?" And yet, what other reply could many of you make; at least, if you made a true one? And to what purpose would it be to return a falsehood? He is not mocked.

—What would *you* say—*you* love him?—No: you dare not. You *know* that his love is not in you. You *know* that you daily prefer a thousand objects to his favour, and image, and service. You *know* that you constantly ask with the world, "Who will show me any good?"—But you never pray, "Lord, lift thou up the light of thy countenance upon me. O remember me with the favour thou bearest unto thy people. O visit me with thy salvation." *You* love him!—"What meaneth then this bleating of the sheep in my ears, and this lowing of the oxen which I hear!"—Your whole lives contradict your avowal, and render it your folly as well as your guilt. Actions speak louder than words; and these are the exceptions they compel you to make. "Yes, O Lord, I love thee—but I never think of thee. I love thee—but I cannot endure the conversation that turns upon thy praise. I love thee—but I wish to shun thy presence: 'depart from me, I desire not the knowledge of thy ways.' I love thee—but thy law is not my delight; and I resolve to follow the way of my own heart."

And what—if this be your answer, what are we to think of you? What are we to think of your taste? What are we to think of your temper? How low! How vile! What a compound of stupidity and depravity is thy wretched soul, to be even capable of indifference towards greatness and goodness so infinite! If you had no love to the creation, no love to the beauties of spring; if you had no love to him that begat you; no love to her that bore you; no love to her that lieth in thy bosom: it would be infinitely less disgraceful than to declare, you have no love for Him who died for you, and rose again.

And is this your answer?———Deliver it yourselves. Look up, and if you have courage, tell him; tell him, by your lips, what you have constantly told him by your lives—"No: I do not love thee. I deem thee unworthy of my regards. Whoever becomes thy follower, I will not." And is this your language?—If we lived in a period of temporal judgments, I would instantly desire this congregation to withdraw: I would say, Flee from the tents of these men, lest the earth open its mouth, and swallow them up. But you believe that no such doom awaits you; and therefore you imagine yourselves secure. But spiritual judgments are much more dreadful than temporal; and wrath the longer it is delayed, becomes the larger in the aggregate, and the heavier in the fall. "If," says the Apostle, "if any man love not the Lord Jesus Christ, let him be Anathema Maran-atha." Oh! to be excluded, when the Lord comes, from his favour, from communion with his people: to be sealed up, under his curse, in hopeless misery, when he appears! Who can describe the horrors of such a scene! Who can dwell upon it!—We are not going to attempt it—it is too awful for declamation.

But let me observe—There is no *unrighteousness* in the sentence. The very victims of this justice will be compelled to feel, if not acknowledge, its equity; and hence they will be speechless.

Neither is there any *uncertainty* in the execution of it. If the word of God is true, this *will* be the portion of every man, whatever be his condition or character, that dies a stranger to the love of Christ. Such a disposition of mind *must* terminate in perdition. There is no other part of the universe to which you are suited: and there will be the same propriety in shutting you up in hell, when you die, as in confining a madman in Bedlam, or a rebel in prison. Were you even allowed to enter heaven, the state of your mind would destroy all the happiness of the place. And if you would consult, in religious concerns, the same common sense that guides you in secular life, you could not withstand the conviction for a moment. For *could* you be happy in being for ever the companions of those with whom you now feel no congeniality, and whose intercourse you now so anxiously shun? Could you be happy in being for ever in the presence of One you always disesteemed; and in hearing for ever the praises of a Being you never loved!

Yet I will not, I cannot conclude such a subject as this with the language of terror. While I feel a horror at the crime, I would gladly save the criminal. While I condemn, I pity. And if there is an object worthy our compassion in this assembly.—Who claims it? —It must be—not the man that is stripped of his substance, that is bereaved of his friends, that has been through life saying, "I looked for light, and behold darkness"—No—He may be dear to Heaven, and the valley of Achor may be given him for a door of hope. But it is the man that sits yonder, and in whose soul there is not one sentiment of love to him whom all the angels adore!

"Ah!" art thou saying, "this is my condi-

tion—What is the duty of a wretch like me?"
—It is, to get a full conviction of the fact. It
is, to reflect with shame and sorrow on the
fault. It is, to guard against despair, which
will only harden thee into enmity, while a
hope of mercy—after all!—will tend to soften
and allure. It is, to pray that the heart of
stone may be turned to flesh, and the promise
accomplished—"I will pour upon them the
spirit of grace and of supplications: and they
shall look upon him whom they have pierced,
and they shall mourn for him as one mourneth for his only son, and shall be in bitterness
for him, as one that is in bitterness for his
first-born."

But there are some here who ought to be
able to answer the question in the affirmative.
Come forward, Christians, and let us hear
your reply.—Why do you draw back? We
are called upon to fear, "lest, a promise being left us of entering into his rest, any of us
should seem to come short of it." It is true:
but the Scripture justifies confidence, as well
as awakens caution.—Why are you afraid
to speak! " O, it is an awful thing to determine; and if, after all, I should be mistaken!" The very apprehension is a good
evidence in your favour.—"I have nothing to
boast of."—Acknowledged.—"I ought to be
very humble." And ought you not to be very
thankful too? And is not this impossible,
while you refuse to own what he has done
for your souls!—"I would then hesitate no
longer.—I hope—I may—I can say, with Peter; LORD, THOU KNOWEST ALL THINGS,
THOU KNOWEST THAT I LOVE THEE."

All hail, ye highly favoured of the Lord!
This is your distinction; this is your privilege—your noblest distinction, your richest
privilege,—that you love him! But there
are two things which you ought to remember:
the one, to hide from you pride; the other, to
excite in you diligence.

Though you love him *now*, you did not love
him *always*. There was a time (and with
some of you it was a long time) before you
saw any form or comeliness in him, or beauty
that you should desire him. " Ah!" says
Augustine, "ah, my Lord, I began to love
thee too late!"

Though you love him *really*, you do not love
him *sufficiently*. Your love is nothing, compared with the zeal of many of your brethren,
less indebted to him than you. It is nothing,
considering how long you have known him.
It bears no proportion to your means, your
obligations, your professions. Yet this love is
all the return he expects; all he requires
from us!—Let us, therefore, sing the words
of Dr. Watts:

" Dear Lord, and shall we ever live
    At this poor dying rate;
Our love so faint and cold to thee,
    And thine to us so great!

" Come, Holy Spirit, heavenly Dove,
    With all thy quick'ning powers:
Come, shed abroad a Saviour's love
    And that shall kindle ours."

THE END OF SHORT DISCOURSES.

THE

CHRISTIAN CONTEMPLATED,

IN A

COURSE OF LECTURES.

PREFACE.

CUSTOM seems to have rendered it almost necessary, for an Author never to appear before the Public without a Preface; in which something, if not concerning himself, yet concerning his work, is looked for, as a respect due to his readers. Yet Rousseau says, it is a part of the book never read, unless by women and children. The Author however indulges a hope that this is not very extensively true; since, in writing the following introductory remarks, he certainly intended, as will appear from their length, something more than a ceremonious conformity to example.

The design of this Series of Lectures was—to diversify a little the ordinary course of ministerial instruction—to excite and secure attention by a degree of allowable novelty and curiosity—and to bring together various things pertaining to the same subject; so that they might aid each other in illustration and improvement, by their arrangement and union.

—But why are they published? The writer is aware what an abundance of religious works is perpetually issuing from the press: and he would not wonder, if some should think that *he* has too often appeared before the Public already. Yet he trusts an author is not necessarily supposed to say to his readers, "Now attend only to me.' Surely many publications may be serviceable for different purposes, and in different degrees; and a writer may be allowed to conclude, that the production of his pen may obtain a measure of welcome and useful attention—without the vanity of supposing that it is superior to *every* other, or the folly of expecting that it is to supersede *any* other. If too the author be a public teacher, and has met with acceptance, it is natural to suppose that he will secure a considerable number of connexions more immediately his own, and who will be rather partial to the writer, for the sake of the preacher. Such was the case here. In two or three days after this Course of Lectures was finished, a large number of copies was called and subscribed for by those who had heard them. Many of these applicants were persons whose opinion and desire would have had weight with any one who knew them; while all of them had claims upon the Preacher, as stated, or occasional parts of his audience.

The Author can truly say that he yielded to publish with a reluctance which only an *ascertained* earnestness could have overcome. Yet he is now glad, especially with regard to his own audience, that the importunity was expressed, and has been complied with. For near thirty-five years he has been labouring to serve his present charge, in the unity of the Spirit, and in the bond of peace, and he hopes he may add, in righteousness of life: and though he commenced his connexion young, yet such a period strikes far into the brevity of human life, and calls upon him to think, and feel, and act, with increasing seriousness and diligence, knowing that the night cometh wherein no man can work; and to be concerned that after his decease, his people may be able to have the things he has spoken always in remembrance. The work therefore, as a brief epitome of his preaching, will serve as a kind of ministerial legacy, to be perused, particularly by the younger members of his church and congregation, when the clods of the

3

valley will be sweet about him; and by which, though dead, he may yet speak—perhaps, in some cases, to more purpose than while living. The work may tend to correct some pious mistakes both on the right hand and on the left. It contains many of the Author's views on important subjects after considerable experience and observation. For such remarks his station has been favourable, and his opportunities numerous; especially from the variety and latitude of his religious intercourse. This has never been confined to Christians of his own denomination. He has not suffered prejudice so to magnify—what his convictions might have led him to consider the mistakes or imperfections of any who differ from him, as to make him overlook their excellencies as individuals or communities; or to prevent his mingling with them in company, and co-operating with them in services; or to deprive him of that pleasure and profit which he knows may be derived from those who cannot frame to pronounce exactly the Shibboleth of a spiritual tribe. He has always preferred to study religion, not in its abstractions, but in its subjects; not in its speculative opinions, but in its practical principles; not in its distant generalities, but in its appropriated and particular influences. He has always endeavoured to follow it out, from its too common confinement in certain notions, seasons, and services, into actual and ordinary life; and to esteem and applaud it only in proportion as it exerts and displays itself in that " wisdom which is from above, which is first pure, then peaceable, gentle, and easy to be entreated, full of mercy and good fruits, without partiality and without hypocrisy."

This may in some measure account for the desire which has given rise to the publication. For it is to be presumed, that there will be some considerable conformity between the views of a minister and the people of his charge after a voluntary, long, and perfectly affectionate connexion. It is certain that these Lectures would not have been completely congenial with the taste of some hearers. *They* would in *any course* of religious discussion have said, " We want more of doctrine, and more of Christ." Now we are far from treating these terms *themselves* with contempt or disrespect. We love the doctrines of the Gospel; and believe that it is a good thing that the heart be established with grace. We attach importance to evangelical truth; and have no notion of piety without principle, or of good fruit but from a good tree—This is our creed: " By grace are ye saved through faith; and that not of yourselves; it is the gift of God: not of works, lest any man should boast. For we are his workmanship, created in Christ Jesus unto good works, which God hath before ordained that we should walk in them." Yet, we cannot be ignorant that the complaint we have supposed, is too often the whining and seditious jargon of a party; and the very last party in the world we should ever consult with regard to preaching. These desperate adherents to something not easily fixed and definable in sentiment, but always accompanied with a spirit as well known and invariable in its operation as any of the laws of nature, are, in spiritual things, what some discontented zealots are in political; and as the latter render the cause of rational liberty suspicious and despicable, so the former disserve and disgrace the cause of evangelical religion—They are gospel radicals They are not always even moral: they are never amiable. They neither pursue nor think upon the things that are lovely, and of good report. They set at nought all sacred relations, proprieties, and decencies; while many of them abandon family worship, and leave their children without any attempts to bring them into the way everlasting, not knowing but they may be some of those against whom God " has sworn to have indignation for ever," and not daring to go before Him, or to be profane enough to take the work out of His hands. Self-willed are they; self-confident; presumptuous; censorious; condemnatory of all that are not initiated into their temper and exclusions. With regard to their ministers, they are not learners, but judges; and often make a man an offender for a word. In hearing, all is fastidiousness. Appetite has given place to lusting. They go to the House of God, not for wholesome food, but for something to elevate and intoxicate. The preacher is nothing, unless he can make them drink and forget their duty, and remember their danger no more. Their religion is entirely an impersonal thing, any further than as it consists in belief and delusion. They look for all in Christ, not as the only source from which it can be received into us—this is truth: but as the only residence in which it is to remain, while they themselves continue the same. They are complete in Him—not as to the all-sufficiency provided in Him for their actual and entire recovery; but without their being new creatures. They look after nothing in themselves—and nothing in themselves should be looked for as the ground of their acceptance with God, or as self-derived or self-sustained: but they look after nothing in themselves even as the effect of divine agency and communication—forgetful of the inspired prayer, "Create in me a clean heart, O God, and renew a right spirit within me:" regardless of the assertion, "It is God that worketh in you to will and to do of his good pleasure:" subverting the promise, "Then will I sprinkle clean water upon you, and ye shall be clean; and from all your filthiness and from all your idols will I cleanse you: a new heart also will I give unto you, and a new spirit also will I put within you; and I will put my Spirit within you, and cause you to walk in my statutes, and ye shall keep my judgments and do them." Their state is not a condition to be submitted to any process of trial—as those enemies to Christian comfort would have it, who admonish persons to examine themselves whether they are in the faith; and to prove their ownselves; and to give all diligence to make their calling and election sure. Their peace requires that all this should, without hesitation, be taken for granted; while every thing is to be cried down as unbelief that would dare to lead them to question, for an instant, their security, or to keep them from being at ease in Zion. The sinner is not only guilty but diseased—but they are concerned only to remove the sentence of condemnation, while the disorder is left. They absolve, but not heal: they justify, but not renovate. The king's daughter is all glorious within, while her clothing is of wrought gold—with them the righteousness of Christ is a fine robe to cover a filthy body. All their sin, past, present, and future, is so completely done away, that it were folly to feel anguish on the account of it. Their miscarriages are not theirs; but those of sin that dwelleth in them. Their imperfections are regretless, because unavoidable—no man can keep alive his own soul.

Now we are willing to concede that *all* those from whom we occasionally hear complaints, do not go into these lengths; and we are persuaded that were these worthier individuals perfectly informed concerning the men we have very truly but inadequately sketched, they would exclaim, " My soul, come not thou into their secret; and mine honour, to their ' system' be not thou united." Yet *they* sometimes murmur, as if in sympathy with them; and borrow their language, unconscious whose technicality it is: and are in danger that their good should be evil spoken of. To be strenuous for evangelical preaching is commendable; but they view the desideratum in too confined an import. They think it, if not improper, yet needless, for a minister to inculcate many things which he *must* feel to be binding upon him. " Oh!" say they, " the grace of God will teach people all this." The grace of God will incline, and enable us to do all this: but it is the Bible that teaches. This contains all our religious information; and we only want to be led into all truth. The sacred writers never left these things to be taught by the grace of God, without instruction. They never intrusted them to *inference.* They particularized and enforced them. There is not one of Paul's Epistles, a large proportion of which might not have been spared as impertinent, upon this plea: for as surely as the former parts lay the foundation doctrinally, the latter labour to build us up on our most holy faith. But these would restrain a public teacher from the extensiveness of the Gospel itself. They would oblige him to hold forth Christianity only in the first rudiments, not in the advanced science. They would confine him to a kind of abstract inculcation of a small class of principles; which principles are indeed unspeakably important, yet lose much of their importance, by being accompanied with certain alliances, and developements, and applications. Yea, they would not willingly allow him to do more than constantly iterate, from Sabbath to Sabbath, a few well-known and favoured sentiments, in a manner the most undeviating, and in phraseology the most hackneyed. They prefer a scheme of divinity drawn up by some fallible fellow-creature, to the Scripture at large, which, like God's other works, no one can perfectly systematize; but in which, as in Nature, we have, instead of mechanism, infinite freshness, and richness, and variety, and irregularity: that is, order beyond our reach. They are sure, if not to oppose, yet not to aid; if not to stigmatize, yet not to countenance and applaud any attempt the preacher shall make to extend the views of his hearers; to improve their understandings; to lead them through the whole land of Revelation in the length and breadth thereof; in a word to do any thing that would follow up the recommendation of the Apostle, " Leaving therefore the principles of the doctrine of Christ, let us go on unto perfection."

Here the Lecturer is unspeakably happy in being able to say to the people he addresses, " Ye have not so learned Christ." He therefore felt no embarrassment in the study or in the delivery of these discourses. He had only to consult his own convictions, and was not necessitated to think of the likings or dislikings of a sickly fancy, a perverted orthodoxy, a party spirit, or an anathematizing bigotry. Neither would he ever consent to officiate in any congregation where he could not stand fast in the liberty wherewith Christ has made him free. This freedom he thinks a preacher cannot too highly value and assert in the discharge of his work—A freedom from the fear of man that bringeth a snare—inducing and enabling him to say, as he rises from his knees to enter the pulpit,

> Careless, myself a dying man,
> Of dying men's esteem;
> Happy, O God, if thou approve,
> Though all beside condemn."

—A freedom (whatever advantages they may afford him by their collectiveness and arrangements) from the fetterings and exclusiveness of human systems of theology—A freedom from the least sense of any obligation requiring him, in the interpretation and improvement of any passage of Scripture before him, to force its natural and obvious meaning into any frame of Arminian or Calvinistic theory or authority—A freedom also from spiritual favouritism, and which might lead him, from *partiality*, to shun to declare all the counsel of God, as well as from timidity.

May the Author be permitted to plead for a freedom of another kind—an exemption from a wish to gratify the few, at the expense of the profit of many: an exemption from fastidiousness of composition and address: an exemption from such a primness of diction, as admits of the introduction of no anecdote, however chaste, and shuts out the seizure of all hints suggested by present feelings and occurrences: an exemption from the too serious apprehension of little faults in seeking to secure great impressions? Here, to the intimidation and checking of the preacher, how often is he told of the dignity of the pulpit—as if there was any worthy, or *real* dignity in a case like this, separate from utility! What *is* the highest, and *should* be the most admired dignity in the preacher—but an apparent forgetfulness of every claim, but his object; and such an absorbing solicitude for the attainment of it, as leaves him, *unable* to notice inferior things? Without such an impression, no man can do a great work gracefully; for if in the execution he is observed to be alive and attentive to any littleness, it will revolt the beholder, instead of pleasing him. An officer in the midst of action, will be all occupied in urging and completing the conflict—what should we think of him if he turned aside after a butterfly, or showed himself at liberty to mind and adjust his ring, or his dress? Let a preacher be as much as possible correct; but let him think of founding his consequence upon something above minuteness and finesse. Let him never imagine that his *influence*, or *dignity*, will ever be impaired by his feeling and displaying a noble elevation; an indifference to every thing else—while the love of Christ bears him away, and he is *lost*, in endeavouring to save a soul from death, ánd to hide a multitude of sins. There is nothing with which a preacher should be less satisfied than a tame correctness, or his producing something that will bear criticism, but which is as devoid of excellency as it is free from defect. He that winneth souls is wise. What is every other praise of an instrument, if it does not answer its end? What is every other commendation of a preacher, if he be useless? unimpressive? uninteresting? What is it, that nothing is complained of, if nothing is applauded? What is it, that nothing offends, if nothing strikes? What is the harangue that dies in the hearing, and leaves nothing for the hearers to carry away, to think of in solitude, and to speak of in company? What but a fault is the smoothness of address, that prevents every excitement that would rend by terror, or melt by tenderness? A sermon may resemble a French drama, that observes inviolably all the unities, and challenges severity as a finished piece; but excites no sentiment, and produces no effect. But give us rather the Shakspeare, who, with blemishes which a less shrewd observer than Voltaire may detect, actually succeeds; arrests; inspires; and enchants. We need not plead for coarseness or faults. A speaker may be animated, yet decorous and orderly too: but in popular addresses, if either fails, it is far better to sacrifice correctness to impression, than effect a nicety of endeavour. Let the squeamishly hypercritical remember that he is labouring to little purpose while consuming his time and attention in subtle accuracies, and polished dulness. And let the man who is in earnest about his work never yield to an under anxiety resulting from the possibility of a trifling mistake; and which, as Gray says of penury, would repress his noble rage and chill the genial current of his soul. Let him feel his subject, and follow his ardour, recollecting that great excellences or impressions will redeem small failures; and even prevent their being noticed—unless by the little and perverseminded, who only sit to discover and remark any minute impropriety—adders to every thing else in the charmer, charm he never so wisely.

There is also some difference between the heat of delivery and the coolness of review; between the leisure and discrimination of readers—and hearers. More freedom therefore will be permitted in preaching than in publishing: ánd what the press may forbid, the pulpit may tolerate. Yea, the pulpit may require it, especially for the sake of a large part of the congregation. For these, though they have not the advantage of culture, yet have souls as well as others, and their moral wants must be attended to. Now a preacher need not grovel down to the lowest level of the vulgar; yea, he should always take his aim a little above them; in order to raise and improve their taste: but he must not soar out of their sight and reach. Yet he may be tempted to this by the presence of others. But let him remember, that those who are more educated and refined, ought, not only to endure, but to commend his accommodation; yea, and they will commend, instead of censuring him, if they are really concerned for the welfare of their brethren less privileged than themselves. If they are benevolent and pious as well as intelligent, they will always be more pleased with a discourse suited to general comprehension and improvement, than with a preparation, which, in other circumstances, they might relish as an intellectual treat for themselves. To which we may add, that there is not so great a difference here as some mistaken and elaborate orators imagine. Genuine simplicity knows a mode, which while it extends to the poor and unlearned, will equally please their superiors. For—

> "So it is when the mind is endued
> With a well-judging taste from above;
> *Then*, whether *embellished* or *rude*,
> 'Tis *nature* alone that we love.

> "The *achievements* of *art* may *amuse*,
> May even our *wonder* excite,
> But *groves*, *hills*, and *valleys* diffuse
> A *lasting*, a *sacred delight*."

In one of his charges, Archbishop Usher says to his clergy, "How much learning and wisdom, my brethren, are necessary to make these things plain!" Could he have said any thing more fine and judicious than this? Here is the proper direction and exertion of a minister's talents, whether natural or acquired. They are not to unfit him for any part of his office—which they may easily do, at the stimulation of vanity or pride; but to qualify and aid him the better to perform it. It is to be feared that some do not employ *their* abilities to make things plain—if they do, we can but lament their deplorable want of success. But it would seem as if their aim was to dazzle, rather than enlighten; to surprise, rather than inform; to raise admiration at their difficult composition, rather than with the Apostles to use great plainness of speech. Even their claim to originality often regards only the mode of representation. The ideas they wish to pass off as new, when examined, are found only common-place sentiments. The well is not really deep; but you cannot see to the bottom, because of their contrivance to make the water muddy. They are not really tall; and so they strain on tiptoe. They have not a native beauty that always appears to most advantage without finery: and so they would make up the deficiency by excess, and complexity, and cumbersomeness of ornament. He who cannot rise in the simple grandeur of a morning sun, can excite notice by the gaudy brilliancy of manufactured fireworks; and flame and sparkle down, as well as up. To notice in *some respects* a style that has been constructed (for it could hardly have been involuntary) so inverted, involved, obscure, difficult—half blank verse; might seem to be going out of the Author's province. He leaves, therefore, others to remark, that this style, though it may be extolled by the lower orders of professional men; and half-educated artisans: and excitable youth, with a smattering of science and a bad taste; it will never obtain the approbation of the really judicious and discerning. He leaves others to remark, that it is disdained by scholars, and at war with classical purity. Lord Kaimes tells us, that in every language, clearness of expression and simplicity of thought are the first marks of elegance. Milton observes, that nothing accords with true genius but what appears easy and natural when once it is produced. Agreeably to which, Addison says, that the secret of fine writing is, for the sentiments to be natural, without being obvious; and contends, that what produces surprise without being simple, will never yield lasting pleasure to the mind. Hume, in his Essay on Refinement and Simplicity in Style, comes soon to this conclusion; that it is better to err in the *excess* of simplicity, than in the excess of refinement; the former extreme being more beautiful and less dangerous than the latter. He observes, that the works read again and again with so much pleasure, all lean more to the one side than to the other—that it is increasingly needful to be guarded against the extreme of refinement when learning has made much progress, and good writers appear in every species of composition: as men will then be the more tempted to endeavour to please by strangeness and novelty, and so fill their writings with affectation and conceits—and that simplicity may be lost not only in subtlety, but in effort and straining; and nature and ease be buried under an artificial load of laborious diffusion.

But while the preacher leaves others to speak upon this subject as a literary question, it cannot be improper for him to notice it in another and far more important connexion; and to deprecate the adoption of such a style *in divinity*, and to warn his younger brethren against every approach and tendency towards it. For how perfectly is it unlike the language of inspiration! What an entire contrast does it form with the simplicity there is in Christ Jesus! And how useless must such hard and unintelligible diction be to ordinary minds! And who are the mass in almost every audience?—They, who are often comparatively neglected, if not despised, there. Leighton, and Watts, and a thousand other names, whose works praise them in the gate, and are now useful to *all*, might have so written, as to be useless to *many*. Had our Saviour felt the low ambition of some, he might easily have been beyond the comprehension and the attraction of the multitude. In Him were hid all the treasures of wisdom and knowledge. He spake as never man spake. But was it a proof against his manner, or the highest recommendation of it, that the *common* people heard him gladly; and that *all* bare him witness and wondered at the gracious words which proceeded out of his mouth? The Author would not for the world be in the condition of that preacher whose attendants do not, cannot say, "Here the poor have the Gospel preached unto them." They not only need it; and should excite our compassion by their temporal privations and sufferings, as well as by their spiritual condition; but they are capable of understanding, and receiving, and admiring it. Learning is not necessary here. The doctrines of the Gospel are not the result of research, but testimony. There are funds of good sense and good feeling in the common people, as well as in others: and they are even capable of appreciating what is truly superior in preaching, if it be properly presented and *illustrated*. The fault is always much more with the preacher than with them. He does not adapt himself to those he professes to teach: he does not make them his aim; he does not study them; he does not throw himself into their modes and habits of thinking and feeling; he has nothing simple and natural in his official being. They understand and relish the Pilgrim's Progress, and the history of Joseph; and the parable of the lost sheep, and of the prodigal son. They are easily informed and impressed by the sayings of our Lord, and the language of the Scriptures. But nothing is to be done in *them* without excitement; and they are addressed without emotion. Their very understandings must be approached through their imaginations and passions; and they are lectured as if they had none. They are never to be starved into a surrender; and they are circumvallated and trenched at a distance. They are only to be taken by an assault; and they are slowly and formally besieged. They want familiar and seasonable imagery; and to show the preacher's learning, they are furnished with allusions taken from the arts and sciences. They want striking sentences, and the words of the wise, which are as goads and as nails; and they have long and tame paragraphs. They only want truths to be brought home to their consciences, for they admit them already; and they are argued and reasoned into confusion or doubt. They want precedents; and are furnished with precepts. They want instances; and are deadened by discussions. They want facts; and are burdened with reflections.

The Bible adapts itself to the state of our nature: and knowing how little all are, and how little many *can* be affected with abstract representations of virtues and duties, it blends religion with history and biography; so that while we read the rule, we may see the exemplification; and be reproved, excited, and encouraged, while we are informed. It is not a series of logical definitions, like dead bodies well laid out and dressed—all is life and motion. It gives us actions rather than words. We view the fruits of righteousness growing on the tree. We have, not the pilgrimage, but the pilgrim; and go along with him from the city of destruction to the shining city. We are not spectators only; we are his companions; we are interested in all he meets with; we weep when he weeps, and rejoice when he rejoices. It is not Christianity that is set before us, but the Christian; and we attend him following his Saviour, denying himself, taking up his cross, resisting temptation, struggling with unwearied patience through a thousand difficulties, braving with fortitude every danger, and emerging out into glory, honour, and immortality. By nothing can the attention of children be so effectually caught as by facts and narratives: and "men are but children of a larger growth." What is the greater part of the Old Testament, but history? There is scarcely a Psalm, but refers to some fact in the experience of the composer. What are the prophets, but historians by anticipation? Many of them state various past, and cotemporary events. The book of Jonah has only one prediction in it; but it describes in a most vivid and interesting manner the actual and wonderful occurrences that befell the bearer himself. How pleasing and striking are the short and simple annals of Ruth! What is the book of Job but the matchless dramatic story of a good man in his affluence, his adversity, and his deliverance? In the book of Genesis we are present at the creation, the destruction, and the re-peopling of the world ; we live, we travel, we worship with the patriarchs : we stand round their dying beds. It is needless to add, that the remainder of the Pentateuch, with the books of Joshua, Judges, Samuel, Kings, Chronicles, Ezra, Nehemiah, and Esther, are all of the narrative kind, including general and individual sketches of the most wonderful people on earth. But what is the Gospel itself, according to Matthew, Mark, Luke, and John ? Is it any thing like our treatises and bodies of divinity ? It is the history of the Son of God. While the Acts are a portion of the history of the Apostles: and the Epistles are evermore enlivened with characters, incidents, and allusions. Is this the work of God ? Does he know perfectly what is in man, and necessary to him ? Has he herein abounded towards us in all wisdom and prudence ? Is it not then surprising that religious instructers should not think it necessary or desirable to resemble him ? And can any thing be more unlike this inspired, and attractive, and irresistible and impressive mode, than the structure of many of the discourses that are delivered in our public assemblies ? Hence, they awaken so little attention ; and yield so little pleasure ; and take no firm hold on the mind and feelings, especially of the young and the common people—

" And drowsy tinklings lull the distant folds."

General declamations and reflections do little in a popular audience. The preacher must enter into a detail, and do much by circumstances. Nothing can penetrate, but what is pointed. Every indictment must particularize and specify. The eye may take in a large prospect, but we are affected by inspection. We must not stand long with our people on the brow of the hill, showing them a wide and indistinct expansion, but take them by the hand, and lead them down to certain spots and objects. We are to be characteristic—not only with regard to persons, though this is of great importance ; but also with regard to vice and virtue, faults and excellences. To what purpose is it to admonish servants to be good ? The question is, in what is their goodness to appear ? Therefore says the Apostle, " Exhort servants to be *obedient* to their own masters, and to *please them well* in all things ; not *answering again* ; not *purloining*, but showing *all good fidelity* ; that they may *adorn* the *doctrine* of God our Saviour in all things." Does Solomon only condemn drunkenness ? What is there in the wretched crime ; in its excitement, progress, evil, danger, misery, that he does not strike ? " Who hath wo ? who hath sorrow ? who hath contentions ? who hath babbling ? who hath wounds without cause ? who hath redness of eyes ? They that tarry long at the wine ; they that go to seek mixed wine. Look not thou upon the wine when it is red, when it giveth his colour in the cup, when it moveth itself aright : at the last it biteth like a serpent, and stingeth like an adder. Thine eyes shall behold strange women, and thine heart shall utter perverse things : yea, thou shalt be as he that lieth down in the midst of the sea, or as he that lieth upon the top of a mast. They have stricken me, shalt thou say, and I was not sick ; they have beaten me, and I felt it not : when shall I awake ? I will seek it yet again."

A preacher also must indulge in a certain degree of diffusiveness. He who passes rapidly from one thing to another is not likely to impress, or indeed even to inform the majority of his audience. To affect *them*, he must commonly dwell upon the thought a little ; and sometimes more than a little ; even with an enlargedness that may seem needless ; and with a repetition in other words and exemplifications, that may go for tautology, with persons of quicker apprehensiveness. Hints will please the scholar, and set his own mind pleasingly in motion ; and he can instantly add from his own stores. But many have nothing but what they receive. Besides, some are more struck with one species or instance of illustration and confirmation, and some with another : and he whose mind was wandering or heedless at first, may haply be seized afterward. For precept must be upon precept, line upon line ; here a little, and there a little. And the preacher will often see by the look and manner of a hearer that what he failed to accomplish by a first stroke, has been done by a second.

The Author is perhaps furnishing materials with which to condemn himself. And let him be condemned, as far as he deviates from these rules. He is fully persuaded of their goodness and truth. He can only say, it has long been his endeavour to conform to them. Upon the same principles he has acted with regard to a few other things, in which, if he has erred, he has erred from design.

Such is the large use he has made of Scripture language. If holy men spake as they were moved by the Holy Ghost, we should prefer the words the Holy Ghost useth. They are surely, on their own subjects, the most definite and significant. They are also well known: and it is a great advantage in addressing hearers that we are not perplexed with terms and phrases; but have those at hand which they understand—What a difficulty do we feel in dealing with those who are ignorant not only of the doctrine, but the letter of the Scripture! It is probable that a very judicious critic and eloquent divine* would censure the author as in an extreme here : yet *he* seems to allow it to be an error on the safer side ; and thinks that a great and original writer has condemned the copious use of Scripture language with too much severity. We avail ourselves of his striking remarks in his review of Mr. Foster's Essays. " To say nothing of the inimitable beauties of the Bible, considered in a literary view, which are universally acknowledged ; it is the book which every devout man is accustomed to consult as the oracle of God ; it is the companion of his best moments, and the vehicle of his strongest consolation. Intimately associated in his mind with every thing dear and valuable, its diction more powerfully excites devotional feelings than any other ; and when temperately and soberly used, imparts an unction to a religious discourse, which nothing else can supply. Besides, is there not room to apprehend, that a studied avoidance of the Scripture phraseology, and a care to express all that it is supposed to contain in the forms of classical diction, might ultimately lead to the neglect of the Scriptures themselves, and a habit of substituting flashy and superficial declamation, in the room of the saving truths of the Gospel ? Such an apprehension is but too much verified by the most celebrated sermons of the French ; and still more by some modern compositions in our own language, which usurp that title. For devotional impression, we conceive that a very considerable tincture of the language of Scripture, or at least such a colouring as shall discover an intimate acquaintance with those inimitable models, will generally succeed best."

If it be allowed from all these considerations, that the language of the Bible has such claims, will it not follow that the frequent use of it will tend to bring the preacher's own language into some degree of keeping with it ? Surely that style is best for religious instruction which most easily and congenially incorporates the composition of the Bible with it. This is not the case with some modes of writing and speaking. But if there be unsuitableness, and difficulty, and discordancy, in the junction ; which is to blame ? and which requires to be altered in order to their readier coalescence ? the language of Scripture, or our own ? Knox has affirmed, that no writer or speaker will ever be so tender, and pathetic, and touching, as he whose diction is most imbued with the manner and phraseology of the sacred authors.

It will be perceived that the Lecturer has not unfrequently made use also of the language of poetry. This is sometimes condemned ; but a sentence of this kind will often relieve, and often revive the attention ; while it serves to fix a sentiment more firmly in the memory. And is it not in this very way that God has addressed men ? How much of the Bible is poetical! How curiously constructed are some of its divisions ! In one case a whole Psalm is divided into as many sections as there are letters in the Hebrew alphabet : every division contains an equal number of verses ; and each verse begins with the same letter. " I," says inspired Wisdom, " dwell with *prudence*, and find out knowledge of witty inventions." And will a man inquire—not whether an usage accords with God's condescension, and is likely to be useful, especially to the middle and lower classes—but whether, after a poetical quotation, his style will not seem to sink ; or whether the thing be

* Mr. Hall.

sanctioned by any first-rate authority—and this too—this weighing of trifles; while he is doing the work of eternity, and has souls perishing in view! Paul knew the end would not sanctify sinful means; but he knew it justified the use of any lawful ones; and therefore, with a nobleness of mind that raises him infinitely above the intellectually proud and unaccommodating, he could say, "Though I be free from all men, yet have I made myself servant unto all, that I might gain the more. Unto the Jews I became as a Jew, that I might gain the Jew; to them that are under the law, as under the law, that I might gain them that are under the law; to them that are without law, as without law (being not without law to God, but under the law to Christ,) that I might gain them that are without law. To the weak became I as weak, that I might gain the weak: I am made all things to all men, that I might by all means save some. And this I do for the gospel's sake, that I might be partaker thereof with you."

In the following documents, some things may be found looking rather inconsistent with each other. This arises from a wish the Author felt strongly to represent and recommend—whatever it was—the *present* subject. And he is greatly mistaken if this be not the method of the sacred writers. They never seem afraid of expressing themselves too forcibly at the time. They never stop to qualify the things they are delivering. There *are* qualifications to be found; but these are brought forward in other places, and where they are themselves the subjects enforced. Our Saviour makes no limitations or exceptions, when he is enjoining confidence in the care and providence of God—"Take no thought for your life, what ye shall eat, or what ye shall drink; nor yet for your body, what ye shall put on. Is not the life more than meat, and the body than raiment?—Take therefore no thought for the morrow: for the morrow shall take thought for the things of itself. Sufficient unto the day is the evil thereof." But the same authority says elsewhere—"Go to the ant, thou sluggard; consider her ways, and be wise: which having no guide, overseer, or ruler, provideth her meat in the summer, and gathereth her food in the harvest." "How long wilt thou sleep, O sluggard? when wilt thou arise out of thy sleep?" "Let thine eyes look right on, and thine eyelids straight before thee." "He becometh poor that dealeth with a slack hand; but the hand of the diligent maketh rich." He must be a spiritless teacher who never produces the surprise of paradox; who never alarms the timid and cautious; and whose strength of statement and urgency does not furnish some seeming contradictions.

The Author is not sure the same thought, or expression, may not occur more than once in these Lectures; or that he may not have used them before in some of his other publications; for writers are often the least acquainted with their own works; being afraid to read them, lest they should discover faults too late for correction, and be only rendered miserable by the discovery. Should this be the case, it is not only hoped that they may be excused on the ground of inadvertence; but also that they may prove not wholly unuseful, being found in different connexions, and applied to different purposes.

The subjects were commonplace in themselves; and could be only rendered novel in any degree by their order and treatment. They were also very extensive subjects, and the difficulty of the preacher arose from the necessity of selection and concentration. He was obliged to reject much that offered, and to confine himself in each instance to two or three views. These ought to have been the most leading, and comprehensive, and profitable. But here the Author can only be answerable for intentions and endeavours.

To conclude. No thought was entertained of any thing more than the delivery of these Lectures from the pulpit till many of them were preached. They were therefore only distinguishable from his ordinary public addresses by their length. Into this he was led by a wish to do some justice to the subject without a second discourse upon the same topic, which always divides and impairs the impression. Till a desire began to be expressed for their publication, he had only short notes from which they could be written out. But he then began to secure them, especially by hints and mementos after preaching : and he is persuaded his friends will find the Lectures more than substantially the same they heard with so much candour and acceptance. They will also observe, that he has secured as far as possible even the style in which they were delivered.

One thing will be perceived in each of the discourses. He has largely treated the subject in a way of application. He did not intend to hold up the Christian to barren contemplation. His aim was to make his hearers fellow-heirs, and of the same body, and partakers of the promise of Christ by the Gospel.

"Behold the awful portrait and admire :
Nor stop to wonder—imitate and live."

WILLIAM JAY.

Percy Place; Sept. 10th, 1826.

CONTENTS.

14

CHRISTIAN CONTEMPLATED.

LECTURE I.

THE CHRISTIAN, IN CHRIST.

" I knew a man in Christ."—2 Cor. xii. 2.

" A CHRISTIAN is the highest style of man :
And is there, who the Cross wipes off,
As a foul blot, from his dishonour'd brow ?
If angels tremble, 'tis at such a sight !"

So sings, with his accustomed energy and excellence, our admired Young. It is not, however, with the poetry of this passage we now have to do, but with the sentiment contained in it.

Yes—" a Christian *is* the highest style of man." Inspiration itself pronounces him to be " more excellent than his neighbour, however that neighbour may be distinguished. Who, on a fair trial, can bear a comparison with him ?—The rich ? But he has " the true riches ;" durable riches, with righteousness; " the unsearchable riches of Christ."—The honourable ? But he is " great in the sight of the Lord :" he has " the honour that cometh from God only."—The learned ? But he is made " wise unto salvation ;" he has " an unction from the Holy One, and knoweth all things."—The sons of heroism ? But, " He that is slow to anger is better than the mighty, and he that ruleth his own spirit than he that taketh a city." He subdues enemies that vanquish all other victors: he is more than a conqueror; and the Captain of his salvation thus eulogizes and rewards him : " Him that overcometh will I make a pillar in the temple of my God, and he shall go no more out; and I will write upon him the name of my God; and the name of the city of my God, which is New Jerusalem, which cometh down out of Heaven from my God, and I will write upon him my NEW NAME."

It was a high encomium our Saviour pronounced on his forerunner: " Among them that are born of women, there hath not risen a greater than John the Baptist." But observe the addition: yet " he that is least in the kingdom of Heaven is greater than he." Even Adam in his original state, was nothing to a Christian. Redemption delivers us from far greater evils than creation: the one rescues us only from non-existence; the other, from sin, and death, and hell. The blessings of grace are far superior to those of nature. What was the garden of Eden to " the new heaven and the new earth wherein dwelleth righteousness ?" What was the tree of life to Him, the true source of immortality, who came, " not only that we might have life, but have it more abundantly ?" We were made by an exertion of wisdom and power ; but we are saved by the " manifold wisdom of God ;" and by " the exceeding greatness of his power, according to the working of his mighty power, which he wrought in Christ when he raised him from the dead, and set him at his own right hand in the heavenly places."

When therefore a man, ashamed of such an infinite distinction, endeavours to free himself from the imputation as a reproach, it *is* credible that

" If angels tremble, 'tis at such a sight !"

For however deluded *we* are, *they* judge of things according to their real value and importance.—The world may shout at a victory that has slain its thousands, and filled domestic life with " the fatherless and the widow ;" but " there is joy in the presence of the angels of God over one sinner that repenteth." Men may disesteem and neglect " the sufferings of Christ, and the glory that should follow ;" but " the angels desire to look into these things." Christ crucified was to the Jews a stumblingblock, and to the Greeks foolishness; but John " heard the voice of many angels round about the throne, and the beasts and the elders; and the number of them was ten thousand times ten thousand, and thousands of thousands, saying, with a loud voice, Worthy is the Lamb that was slain to receive power, and riches, and wisdom, and strength, and honour, and glory, and blessing."

Your preacher, therefore, is more than justified in a plan, the design of which he has already intimated, and which he now proceeds to lay before you. It is to hold up the CHRISTIAN to your view, in some very important and comprehensive conditions and relations. To this design, we dedicate Twelve Lectures.

The First will lead you to contemplate the Christian, in CHRIST.

The Second, in the CLOSET.
The Third, in the FAMILY.
The Fourth, in the CHURCH.
The Fifth, in the WORLD.
The Sixth, in PROSPERITY.
The Seventh, in ADVERSITY.
The Eighth, in his SPIRITUAL SORROWS.
The Ninth, in his SPIRITUAL JOYS.
The Tenth, in DEATH.
The Eleventh, in the GRAVE.
The Twelfth, in GLORY.

"Consider what I say, and the Lord give you understanding in all things."

We are this morning to behold the Christian,

In CHRIST.

If this Lecture is more general than the remaining ones, let it be remembered that it is fundamental to the whole series; and with the subject of it, every thing in religion begins. All in your Christian character is derived from Christ. You cannot *be* a Christian unless you are *in* him.

Of this state the Apostle here speaks. "I knew a man," says he, "in Christ." The mode of expression is humble and modest; but by this "man" he unquestionably intends himself. We all have known some in Christ; and this should awaken our joy and praise. But religion is a personal thing. We cannot be saved by the grace of others. Yet their experience should encourage and induce us to apply to the same source. For they were once destitute; and He who enriched them is able to supply us, and is equally willing. He even *intends* that every instance of his mercy should be a plea against despair. Hence the "man" before us could say, "Howbeit, for this cause I obtained mercy, that in me first Jesus Christ might show forth all longsuffering for a pattern to them that should hereafter believe on him to life everlasting."

To come nearer our subject. There are three states mentioned in the Scripture with regard to Christ.

The first is to be *without* Christ. "At that time," says the Apostle, to the Ephesians, "ye were without Christ." This is true of the heathen; and it is true of all those who are living in sin, even in the land of vision. "The light shineth in darkness, and the darkness comprehendeth it not." This is the state of Nature.

The second is to be *with* Christ. "I long," says Paul, "to depart and to be with Christ, which is far better." "And so," says he, "shall we be for ever with the Lord." This is the state of Glory.

The third is to be *in* Christ. This is the state of Grace. I need not remark how frequently the Scripture speaks of this condition. Let us reduce its declarations to some easy and brief arrangement. Of this state let us consider,

I. The NATURE.
II. The IMPORTANCE.
III. The EVIDENCE.

I. The NATURE.—What is it to be *in* Christ? It is to be a Christian. Paul, speaking of certain individuals, says, "who were in Christ before me:" that is, they embraced Christianity before he did. "The churches," says he, "which are in Christ;" that is, Christian churches, in distinction from those which were Heathen and Jewish. "Salute," says he, "Apelles approved in Christ:" that is, an approved Christian.

It is needless to multiply examples, as the thing is undeniable. But admitting the fact, there must be some reason, and some very powerful reason, not only for the frequency of the expression, but for the expression itself. The language is perfectly peculiar. There are indeed various relations and connexions in life; and some of our fellow-creatures are much attached to others, and very dependent upon them: yet we never say, a patient is *in* his physician; or, a servant *in* his master; or, a disciple *in* his teacher. But we constantly read of our being *in* Christ—and, "If any man speak, let him speak as the oracles of God." New terms imperceptibly make way for new doctrines; nor has any subtlety of the enemy of souls succeeded better in corrupting the mind from the simplicity there is in Christ, than modernizing the language of divinity. When men are shy of the "words the Holy Ghost teacheth," we are always afraid they are beginning to be ashamed of the things.

The expression means a state of union with Christ. This union may be considered as visible and professional; or real and vital. This is not a distinction without a difference: there is a foundation for it, in reason; and it is even necessary, to harmonize the testimonies of divine truth. Thus our Saviour says, "Every branch in me that beareth not fruit, he taketh away. If a man abide not in me, he is cast forth as a branch, and is withered; and men gather them and cast them into the fire, and they are burned." Thus a man may be in him, and be *fruitless;* and be in him, and *perish.* But can either of these be true, when applied to those who are Christians indeed; and of whom, by a change of metaphor, it is said, "I will put my Spirit within them, and cause them to walk in my statutes, and to keep my judgments and do them?" and "I give unto them eternal life, and they shall never perish, neither shall any pluck them out of my hand?" We therefore must admit, that a person may be in him by profession, when he is not in him, in reality: in him, by a form of godliness, while he denies the power thereof; in him, by an external alliance with his church, and by the use of his ordinances, while he is a stranger to the renewing of the Holy Gost, and the grace of God in truth. As religion ceases to be persecuted, and becomes respectable, such pretensions will be frequent; and they may for awhile impose upon men, and even good men: but God is not mocked—and what is the hope of the hypocrite though he hath gained, when God casteth away his soul?

But there is another union with Christ: and *this* union is not only real and vital, but the most intimate, and entire, and indissoluble; independent of the changes of time, unaffected by the diseases of the body, uninjured by death, untouched by the destructions of the last day.

Let us look at it—But how shall we do this? Here the sacred writers lead the way: and were we like-minded with them, our senses would minister to our faith, and every thing would admonish us of the Lord of all. The sun would tell us that there is a nobler orb above him, "with healing under his wings." The wind would remind us that "so is every one that is born of the Spirit." We should think of Christ, and of Christians as one with him, whenever we saw a foundation and a building; a fountain and a stream; a shepherd and his sheep; a king and his subjects; an advocate and his client. None of these indeed can do justice to the subject; the subject being so peculiar in its nature, and so boundless in its extent. The sacred writers feel this, and therefore, to increase their efficacy, they throw off from the images they employ every imperfection in their kind; they add to them attributes which are not naturally inherent in them; and they multiply their number, that they may accomplish by combination what could not be done by individuality: and thus, though these allusions fall short of the glory they are applied to illustrate, they aid our meditations. With many of these we are furnished in the Scripture. Let us glance at a few of them; and let us be thankful that instead of their having any thing novel in them, they are well known and familiar.

We are in Christ as we are in Adam. "In Adam all die: so in Christ shall all be made alive." From the first we derive our natural being, and from the second our spiritual. By the one we fell, by the other we rise again. By the disobedience of one, many were made sinners; and by the obedience of one, shall many be made righteous. From the one, sin reigned unto death; by the other, grace reigns through righteousness unto eternal life. "The first man is of the earth, earthy; the second man is the Lord from heaven. As is the earthy, such are they also that are earthy; and as is the heavenly, such are they also that are heavenly; and as we have borne the image of the earthy, we shall also bear the image of the heavenly."

It is commonly supposed that the ark was designed to be a type of Christ: it certainly affords a striking image of him. A deluge was coming on, and Noah and his family were exposed to the flood, as well as others. But they escaped uninjured; for they availed themselves of the shelter mercy had provided. They entered it in time; and the Lord shut them in: and they could not have been safer had they been in heaven. Not a drop of the torrents from above, or of the deep below, touched them; and through the universal wreck they sailed out into fair weather and into a new world. But there was no other mode of deliverance. Swimming was useless; a boat was a vain thing for safety; and truly in vain was salvation hoped for from the hills and the multitude of mountains. All were overwhelmed that contemned the Divine appointment; for though there were abysses of destruction everywhere, there was only one ark. "Neither is there salvation in any other; for there is no other Name given under heaven among men whereby they must be saved," than the name of Jesus. "I am," says he, "the way, the truth, and the life. No man cometh unto the Father but by me."

A peculiar provision under the Law was also an emblem of our subject. The man committing casual murder was exposed to the avenger of blood, who had a right to kill him wherever he should be found, unless in one of the cities of refuge. The place of immunity was situated on an eminence, to be visible from afar. The road to it was open, and wide, and prepared; and when there was any danger of mistake, a direction pointed— "Refuge, Refuge." To this, therefore, the offender, incapable of trifling or tarrying, fled for his life; and it is easy to imagine what were his feelings, his anxiety, his anguish, till he had entered the asylum; and the calm and confidence he enjoyed as soon as he could turn and face the foe, and say, "Thou canst not touch me here." To this, the Author of the Epistle to the Hebrews, who would well understand the allusion, refers, when he speaks of those "who have fled for refuge to lay hold of the hope set before them."

Christians are in Christ as the branches are in the tree. It matters not how near a branch is to a tree—yea, if it lean against it; yea, if it be corded to it, or even nailed, it can neither flourish or live, unless it be in the stock. But when it is in the tree, the very same sap that pervades the one, flows into the other, and sustains and fertilizes it. And says our Saviour, "As the branch cannot bear fruit of itself unless it abide in the vine, no more can ye, except ye abide in me; for *without* me ye can do nothing."

And to mention nothing more—They are in Christ as the members of the human body are in the head. For he is called "the head of his body the Church:" and believers are

C

said to be "members of his body, of his flesh, and of his bones." They are real and living parts of him. As the head governs and directs the body, they are under his guidance and authority: and as the body is actuated by the head, and depends upon ligatures with it, and influences from it, so they live by him; and of his fulness they all receive, and grace for grace. Let us,

II. Consider the IMPORTANCE of this state.

We often, in determining the worth of a thing, *appeal to authority:* and we are much influenced in our decision by the competency of the judge. Here it must be confessed the multitude are not a safe guide, nor yet many of those who by their rank and attainments may seem entitled to take the lead in society. They rise early and sit up late, and eat the bread of sorrow, and deny themselves, and compass sea and land, for fortune and for fame. But their urgency in the things of time and sense, forms a deplorable contrast with their insensibility and negligence with regard to the things that belong to their everlasting peace. So that were we to estimate the value of the prize by the zeal of the candidates, we could not deem it worth a moment's thought. But we do not appeal to the blind and the deaf in questions of colour and of sound. How can the votaries of the god of this world appreciate a kingdom that is righteousness, peace, and joy in the Holy Ghost? "The world knew him not" when on earth: and it is not wiser now. But the spiritual judgeth all things, though he himself is judged of no man. Let us turn to Paul. Paul was a man of learning and wisdom. He had been the greatest enemy to the cause of the Gospel, and had, from the most irresistible and perfect conviction, become its adherent and advocate. He was not a novice in experience, but had been for many years acquainted with the Saviour, studying him as a Minister, as well as believing in him as a Christian, when he wrote to the Philippians. Yet what was his language? "Yea, doubtless, and I count all things but loss for the excellency of the knowledge of Christ Jesus my Lord, for whom I have suffered the loss of all things, and do count them but dung, that I may win Christ, and be found IN HIM." Thus *he* was fully persuaded that a union with Christ was a state infinitely desirable: and that his estimation was well founded will appear—

If we survey the state *in connexion with the advantages inseparable from it, but never to be enjoyed without it.* And here I must make a selection. For I find myself in a garden abounding with productions, all of which I wish to commend; but I have only time to lead you to notice a *few* of the flowers and the fruits; and in doing this, order is not necessary.

But is it desirable to be delivered from captivity and bondage—a bondage the most degrading; a captivity the most oppressive? Here you enjoy it. "If the son therefore shall make you free, ye shall be free indeed." "In whom we have redemption through his blood, even the forgiveness of sins."

Is it desirable to be safe from condemnation? Condemnation is to be judged of by the doom to which it consigns us. Now "Cursed is every one that continueth not in all things written in the book of the law to do them." And who can appreciate the misery of this curse? Who knoweth the power of His anger? It is a fearful thing to fall into the hands of the living God. But "there is now no condemnation to them that are in Christ Jesus." That is, none that will affect their security. Conscience may condemn; the world may condemn; Satan, the accuser of the brethren, may condemn—but these are not the Judge. "Who shall lay any thing to the charge of God's elect? It is *God* that justifieth. *Who* is he that condemneth? It is *Christ* that died; yea, rather, that is risen, who is even at the right hand of God, who also maketh intercession for us."

Is acceptance with God desirable? Here we have it—"This," says God, "is my beloved Son, in whom I am well pleased." The complacency extends to us, as well as to himself. "Thou hast loved them," says the Saviour, "as thou hast loved me." He hath made us accepted in the Beloved: and this is true both of our persons and our services. "He gave himself for us, an offering and a sacrifice to God for a sweet-smelling savour;" and we could not have been originally so dear to God as we now become, through his mediation.

Tell me, ye who delight in communion with God, and are so often constrained to repair to him for mercy and grace to help in time of need, Is it good to draw nigh to God? And can you go to Him freely as your Father? at all seasons? on all occasions? and in every thing by prayer and supplication make known your requests unto God, with an assurance of success? "In whom we have boldness and access with confidence, by the faith of him."

In him we have all our supplies and endowments. "We are complete in him." Where can I find righteousness? In vain I look even to my duties and to my holy things. These are all defective and polluted; and if they *deserve* any thing, it is condemnation: and if he *thus* enters into judgment with us, no flesh living can be justified. But Christ is the end of the law for righteousness to every one that believeth. Thus I appear before him, "not having my own righteousness which is of the law, but that which is of faith:" and this not only justifies me from all things, but gives me a title to eternal life.—And where but in him can I find strength? The journey I have to take, the race I have to run, the warfare I have to accomplish; the duties I have to perform; the trials I have to bear: all these are not only above my natural powers, but even above the grace I possess, without fresh and constant supplies of the Spirit of Jesus Christ. But he cries, " *my* grace is sufficient for thee, for *my* strength is made perfect in weakness." Surely therefore shall one say, " In the Lord have I righteousness and strength."

Where shall we end? " If children, then heirs, heirs of God and joint heirs with Christ." But *he* is heir of all things: therefore, says the Apostle, " All things are yours: whether Paul, or Apollos, or Cephas, or the world, or life, or death, or things present or things to come, all are yours; and ye are Christ's, and Christ is God's." You are united to him, and he is united to God. You are in him, and he is in God. How secure, then, is the happiness of believers! Their life is hid—with Christ—in God! How incapable of rupture is the connexion between them and God, unless the medium that unites them can fail! But " I am persuaded that neither death, nor life, nor principalities, nor powers, nor things present, nor things to come, nor height, nor depth, nor any other creature, shall be able to separate us from the love of God which is in Christ Jesus our Lord."

We may also view the importance of this state *in connexion with certain seasons when it must be peculiarly felt.* There are four of these.

The first is the hour of *conviction.* What is the reason that many of you read and hear of this state with such indifference? that you make light of the invitation to enter it! and go your way, one to his farm and another to his merchandise? You do not feel yourselves in the wretchedness and jeopardy it implies and is designed to relieve. One question forced from a wounded spirit—" What must I do to be saved?" would magnify this state more than all the arguments your preachers can ever employ. When a man is awakened to serious consideration; when he examines his character and condition; when he looks and sees what he is, what he wants, what he deserves: when he perceives the vastness and certainty of his danger; when he finds himself perfectly unable to effect his own deliverance, and knows also that the help of men and angels united could not reach the desperateness of his case—then, how inexpressibly desirable appears a connexion with him who is able to save to the uttermost! who was delivered for our offences, and raised again for our justification! in whom it hath pleased the Father that all fulness should dwell! Then how delightful to hear him say, " Come unto me, all ye that labour and are heavy-laden, and I will give you rest!"

Then how blessed, by believing, to enter into rest, and " joy in God through our Lord Jesus Christ, by whom he has now received the atonement!"

The second is the day of *trouble.* And this may always be expected; for man is born to trouble as the sparks fly upwards. And what, in the wreck of property, in the loss of relations and friends, in the failure of health and comfort—what will you do without " the consolation of Israel?" While your cisterns are broken, the fountain of living water is far off; while your lamps are extinguished, no Sun of righteousness is nigh. But if you had an interest in him who is the hope of Israel, the Saviour thereof in the time of trouble, your trials would be all sanctified and alleviated: at what time you were afraid, you would be able to trust in him: in the multitude of your thoughts within you, his comforts would delight your soul. " I am cast down, but not destroyed. I feel my losses, but I am not lost. The waters are bitter, but this tree heals them. The Cross takes away the curse. Yea, the curse is turned into a blessing. It is good for me that I am afflicted. I know this shall turn to my salvation, through prayer and the supply of the Spirit of Jesus Christ."

The third is an hour that awaits you all. The day of trouble may come—the hour of *death* must come. The one is probable, the other is absolutely certain. For what man is he that liveth and shall not see death? The living know that they shall die. But though death be a universal event, it is not a universal privilege. It would be the most dreadful delusion in many of you to say, " It is better for me to die than to live;" for however severe your present sufferings may be, they are only the beginning of sorrows. If death find you out of Christ, it would be good for you if you had never been born. There will be nothing to screen you from the power with which it is armed by sin. It will deprive you of all you hold most dear. It will terminate your space for repentance. It will close all your opportunities of mercy. It will put a seal upon your character and condition for ever. It will arrest, and deliver you to the judge, and the judge will deliver you to the officer, and you will be cast into prison, and you shall not come out thence till you have paid the uttermost farthing. But hear the voice from heaven: " Blessed are the dead that die *in the Lord.*" He in whom they are found, has abolished death, by the final destruction of the state, and the present removal of the sting; by the change of its nature and office; by turning it into a departure, a sleep; by making it endless gain. If death finds you in Christ, it will be the angel of the covenant; it will wipe away all your tears; it will lead you to the altar of God, to God your exceeding joy.

You may continue to neglect and despise

the Friend of sinners *now*, but you will have other thoughts soon. Death will discover and display the errors of life. How will you then wonder that the trifles and vanities which now engross you should ever have acquired such an ascendency! How will you be amazed that you constantly disregarded him who alone can befriend you when all other helpers fail! *Then* you will learn, but in vain, that an interest in Christ is the one thing needful. Cannot you look forward? Cannot you foresee this, before the knowledge can result only in despair?

For, fourthly, There is another day, and from which the former derives its greatest dread—it is appointed unto men once to die, and after this the *judgment*. I do not ask you what are your thoughts now?—but what will they be, when the heavens shall pass away with a great noise? when the elements shall melt with fervent heat? when all that are in their graves shall come forth? when the dead, small and great, shall stand before God, and the books shall be opened? What will you then do without a friend, an advocate? Then the tribes of the earth will mourn and wail because of Him. Then they who have despised Him, and rejected Him, will cry to the rocks and mountains to hide them from the wrath of the Lamb. But the believer in Jesus lifts up his head with joy, for his redemption draweth nigh. Here he looked for the mercy of our Lord Jesus Christ unto eternal life, and now he enjoys it. He is found *in* him, and therefore he is found *of* him in peace—and hears him say, " Come, ye blessed of my Father, inherit the kingdom prepared for you from the foundation of the world." To which we may add, that all this admits of anticipation by faith; and now, even *now*, he can say—" I am not ashamed; for I know whom I have believed, and am persuaded that he is able to keep that which I have committed to him against that day."—Let us, therefore,

III. Consider the EVIDENCE of our being in Christ.

There is no doubt but it is very desirable to know this; and it would be strange to suppose that it is impossible to ascertain it; especially since we are not only required to examine ourselves, and prove whether we are in the faith, but also to rejoice in the Lord always. Paul, we see, was assured of this— " I knew a man in Christ:" and he knew himself to be so, not as he was an Apostle,—for a man might have been an Apostle, and not in Christ: this was the case with Judas,—but, as a believer. Official service is very distinguishable from personal experience, and gifts do not pledge the existence of grace. John does not say, we know that we have passed from death to life because we can prophesy or speak with new tongues, but " because we love the brethren."

When, however, we speak of this confidence, a little explanatory caution may be necessary. People often call it the full assurance of faith. This is indeed a scriptural expression, but it occurs only once; and then it is used to denote, not a certainty of appropriation and experience, but a full persuasion of our being allowed, by the new and living way which He has consecrated, to enter the presence of God in prayer, and partake of all the blessings of his salvation. There is, therefore, an expression we prefer to this—it is " the full assurance of hope." Our present confidence is the confidence of hope, and of hope only. This hope may be considered in a state of conflict with doubts and fears; or in a state of victory and triumph over them: in the one case, there will be anxiety and uneasiness; in the other, joy and repose: but the degree does not alter the nature of the thing itself.

On what, then, is this confidence founded? Dreams? Visions? Voices in the air? Sudden impulses? Passages or promises accidentally presented on opening the Bible? and applied, regardless of the connexion from which they are taken, or the characters of those by whom they are adopted? On what strange, what dubious, what unauthorised evidences do some rest their eternal hope! " To the law and to the testimony: if they speak not according to this word, it is because there is no light in them."

All the errors, however, in judging ourselves, are not on one side. There are mistakes on the right hand as well as on the left: and though they are not so dangerous, they may be distressing and even injurious; and therefore we must guard against them.

In deciding your condition, you should not make the experience of others too much the standard of your judgment; for though, as in water, face answereth to face, so the heart of man to man; yet, along with a general conformity, there is frequently much difference, especially in the degree and duration of those spiritual exercises which commonly precede the joy of God's salvation, and attend the part of divine doctrine that first seizes our attention.

Neither should you be too minute in your inquiries. The blind man, who was not able to answer every question pertaining to his case, could yet say, " One thing I know: whereas I was blind, now I see." A man may be sure of his natural life, though he knows not when it commenced; and he actually possessed the boon, long before he was able to prove it to himself, though he always evinced it to others. What we have to look after should be influences and effects; and these may be undeniable, without the knowledge of the time, the means, and the manner of their production. A slow and gradual operation is less striking than a sudden and instantaneous; but the increase of the corn sown, is as real, and as divine too, as the multiplication of the barley loaves, in the Gospel.

When we are deciding our Christian state, we should not try ourselves by attainments. The reality of divine grace is one thing; the degree is another. We may be of the same species with a fellow-creature, though not of the same stature: and though not equally advancing, we may be in the same way. This I know is liable to some abuse; and we are always afraid, when we thus speak, lest people should avail themselves of it, "to settle," as the Scripture has it, "upon their lees;" or, in other words, to be content with a hope of their safety, while they are careless of religious progression. Thus it is said, Cromwell having asked a minister "What was the lowest evidence of regeneration," said, on receiving an answer, "Then I am safe." And yet there are moments of gloom and depression, in which the question must be—not have I much grace? but have I any? When the house is on fire, the tradesman does not think of taking stock; his only concern *then* is to save.

It is a good evidence in your favour, if you *value the thing:* and, while the multitude ask, "Who will show us *any* good?" can say—*One* good only can serve my purpose; and the language of the Apostle, and of the martyr, is not too strong for me—"None but Christ, none but Christ!" "That I may know him, and the power of his resurrection, and the fellowship of his sufferings, being made conformable unto his death." "Blessed are they that hunger and thirst after righteousness; for they shall be filled."

It is a token for good, when you *feel much concern and anxiety about this state.* It has been said, that it is easy to believe what we wish; but, Paley remarks, that the experience of every man gives the lie to this maxim. We all know, that in proportion as we attach moment to a thing, and find our happiness involved in it, we find it hard to persuade ourselves that we have a firm hold of it; we are alive and awake to every supposition of uncertainty: we still want stronger proof and confirmation. Does the miser feel it easy to believe that his money, the god of his idolatry, is safe? A mother hears that the vessel in which he sailed is wrecked on a foreign shore, but that her son is rescued from the deep. There is nothing in the world she so much desires to be true: yet is it easy for her to banish her solicitude and doubt? She will peruse every document; and examine every witness; and scarcely be able to think he is living, till she presses him in her arms. Now we may reason from the less to the greater. A man who feels the infinite importance attached to the soul and eternity, will always find it difficult to consider himself a child of God, and an heir of glory; and

will never cease saying, "Give me a token for good, that I may rejoice in thee. Say unto my soul, I am thy salvation." Smoke is not fire, yet there is no smoke where there is no fire—doubts and fears are not faith, but they are gendered by it.

They who are united to Christ are characterized by the *change* which they have experienced. This change is not only real, but entire—entire, not in the degree, but extent. It is complete in nothing; but it is begun in all the Christian's views, and sentiments, and dispositions, and dependence, and taste, and motives, and pursuits. Hence, says the Apostle, "If any man be in Christ, he is a new creature: old things are passed away; behold, all things are become new."

They are also distinguished by *the principle which governs them.* Hence we read, "They that are in Christ Jesus, walk not after the flesh, but after the Spirit." The former will excite as well as the latter; but they do not yield to it: and his servants we are, whom we obey. The one is opposed, the other is encouraged. The one enters into the mind by fraud or force like a robber, producing alarm and misery, and allowing of no peace, till he is expelled. The other is invited; and when he comes, is welcomed and entertained as a friend. "They that are after the flesh do mind the things of the flesh; but they that are after the Spirit, the things of the Spirit. For to be carnally minded is death, but to be spiritually minded is peace. Because the carnal mind is enmity against God: for it is not subject to the law of God, neither indeed can be. So then they that are in the flesh cannot please God. But ye are not in the flesh, but in the Spirit, if the Spirit of God dwell in you. Now if any man have not the Spirit of God, he is none of His."

And this leads us to remark, that all they who are in him *resemble* him. "He that saith he dwelleth in him, ought himself also to walk even as he walked." Not only gratitude and consistency require this, but evidence. "If," says the holy Saviour, "I wash thee not, thou hast no part with me." There must be likeness in order to fellowship. "For what fellowship hath righteousness with unrighteousness, and what communion hath light with darkness? Or what concord hath Christ with Belial? Christ and Christians are, not like Nebuchadnezzar's statue: the head of which was of gold, while the subordinate parts were of inferior metal; down to the feet which were partly iron and partly clay. "He that sanctifieth, and they who are sanctified, are all of one." He is a partaker of their nature; and they are the partakers of his. They are not of the world even as he is not of the world. They have the same mind which was also in Christ Jesus: a sameness of sentiment and feeling; a oneness of heart and of soul—"he that is joined to the Lord, is one spirit."

Men and Brethren—Are you in Christ?

Perhaps you have never yet asked yourselves this question. You have been careful of your property; and every legal doubt has led you to call in the lawyer. You have been anxious for your character, and every whisper of slander has led you to vindicate your reputation. You have been all alive to your health, and every symptom of disease has instantly led you to consult the physician. But to this very hour—and you know it—to this very hour—never once in your lives have you retired, and seriously asked yourselves—Am I in Christ? And yet you acknowledge—that your eternal happiness depends upon it—and that this life is your only opportunity to attain it—and that this season is not only short, but uncertain—and that "in such an hour as ye think not, the Son of man cometh!" Yet you call yourselves rational creatures! Yet you allow that "a prudent man foreseeth the evil, and hideth himself; but the simple pass on, and are punished!"

My dear Hearers. You admire one and another of your fellow-creatures, and think how happy you should feel if you could make their advantages your own. And what are these advantages? Are they not things that perish in the using? that afford no satisfaction in the enjoyment? that profit not in the day of wrath? that cannot deliver from death? And are these the things for which you envy men of the world, who have their portion in this life? Is it not time, especially for some of you, to grow wiser; and to form your estimates by the judgment of God, which is always according to truth? "Search the Scriptures." There you will find that they, and they alone, are wise, and safe, and happy, who can say, to "the praise of the glory of his grace, we know that the Son of God is come, and hath given us an understanding, that we may know him that is true: and we are in him that is true; even in his Son, Jesus Christ. This is the true God, and eternal life." Envy these—not by grudging them their blessedness, but by longing for a participation of it; and pray with one, who though a king himself, yet overlooking all his earthly advantages, kneeled and said, "Remember me, O Lord, with the favour thou bearest unto thy people: oh visit me with thy salvation; that I may see the good of thy chosen, that I may rejoice in the gladness of thy nation, and glory with thine inheritance."

Let this be your concern—let it be your *supreme* concern—"Seek ye *first* the kingdom of God, and his righteousness."—And let it be your *immediate* concern. You cannot be happy too soon. While you hesitate, and linger, the opportunity may be irrecoverably lost. Therefore "Seek ye the Lord while he may be found; and call upon him while he is near." And for your encouragement, be persuaded that you will not, cannot

seek him in vain. All things are now ready. Rise, he calleth thee—and says, "Him that cometh unto me, I will in no wise cast out."

How ought we to conduct ourselves towards those that are in Christ? Surely, if they have little of earthly distinction, they should be judged of by their treasure in heaven. Whatever they are in themselves, their destination, their rank, their *relation*, should ensure them respect. They are to be valued for *his* sake with whom they are one; and *shall* be one for ever. In consequence of this union, if we slight and injure them, *he* feels it as if done to himself: "He that touches them, touches the apple of his eye." In the same way, he regards our attentions and kindnesses to them, as if they were favours conferred upon himself: "Inasmuch as ye did it unto one of the least of these my brethren, ye did it unto me."

Finally. How ought they that are in Christ to conduct *themselves?* How cheerfully, how gratefully ought you to feel! Once far off, and now nigh! Once strangers and enemies, and now fellow-citizens with the saints, and of the household of God! Once having nothing, and now possessing all things! You have had much forgiven—you should love much. He has done great things for you—you should largely inquire what you can do for him; and, "by the mercies of God, present your body a living sacrifice, holy and acceptable, which is your reasonable service." O you who live by this Saviour, make him known. Recommend him. Begin with your own family. You are concerned to provide for your children. But how is your love operating? Is it not in laying up for them treasure on earth? or seeking great things for them in the world? It would be infinitely better to leave them in Christ, than to leave them with thousands of gold and silver; or to leave them with kings upon the throne. Forget not your friends, and your neighbours. Hold forth the word of life impressively and invitingly to all around you. Teach transgressors his ways, and let sinners be converted unto him. What says the Poet?

" Oh! 'tis a Godlike privilege to save
And he that scorns it is himself a slave.
Inform the mind: one beam of heavenly day
Will heal the heart, and melt his chains away."

What says the Apostle? "If a man err from the truth, and one convert him, let him know that he which converteth a sinner from the error of his ways, shall save a soul from death, and shall hide a multitude of sins." Amen.

LECTURE II.

THE CHRISTIAN, IN THE CLOSET.

" *Enter into thy closet.*"—Matt. vi. 6.

THE curiosity and attention of men are

awakened by very different excitements, according to their temper, and education, and habits in life; and what is despised by some as worthless, is studied by others with peculiar delight.

But there is really a gradation in the value of objects themselves. The works of art display great skill and ingenuity; but the productions of nature are much more deserving of our inspection: witness the remark of our Saviour concerning the lilies of the field—"Solomon in all his glory was not arrayed like one of these." But the operations of grace far surpass the results of nature; for they regard the soul and eternity: and display more of the perfections of Deity. Therefore, says David, "Thou hast magnified thy word above all thy name." Therefore He himself says, "Behold, I create new heavens and a new earth: and the former shall not be remembered, nor come into mind."

The subjects of divine grace, therefore, are the most interesting characters in our world. Many indeed neglect and despise them; but there is one class of persons—always dear to a minister of Christ, who feel them the most powerfully attractive. They are those, who, roused to a sense of their danger, are exclaiming, "What must I do to be saved?"—who, longing to return to Him from whom they have revolted, are inquiring, "How shall I come before the Lord, and bow before the high God?"—who, bound for the glory to be revealed, are "asking their way to Zion, with their faces thitherward." If you were going a journey of great difficulty, and yet of unspeakable importance; and were in company with a multitude of individuals; he amongst them all, who had travelled the road himself, would be the man of your preference; and you would endeavour to get near and converse with him. To a suffering patient, the most engaging person he could meet with, next to the physician—for none would bear a comparison with him—would be the man who had himself laboured under the same complaint, and could tell of the manner in which the remedy is applied; and whose own recovery would be a living voucher not only of its safety, but of its efficacy and success.

In a series of discourses, to bring the CHRISTIAN before you, for your admiring and practical contemplation, last Lord's Day we viewed him IN CHRIST; we are this morning to consider him—

In the CLOSET.

Wonder not, my Brethren, that we bring forward this view of the Christian so *early*. By this he is distinguished from the commencement of his religious concern. He soon turns aside from the vile and the vain, and bewails himself alone. *They* cannot enter into his feelings *now*. They know nothing of a broken heart and a contrite spirit, unless

as a subject of wonder or contempt. He feels his sin to be a burden too heavy for him to bear, and longs for ease; but the "wide world" cannot relieve him, cannot sympathize with him, cannot direct him to "the rest and the refreshing." All great sorrow seeks solitude and secrecy: "He sitteth alone, and keepeth silence, because he hath borne it upon him; he putteth his mouth in the dust, if so be there may be hope." Did ever language describe the experience of the penitent so beautifully, so feelingly, as the words of our heavenly Bard?

> "I was a stricken deer, that left the herd
> Long since. With many an arrow deep infix'd
> My panting side was charged, when I withdrew
> To seek a tranquil death in distant shades.
> There was I found by one, who had himself
> Been hurt by the archers. In his side he bore,
> And in his hands and feet, the cruel scars.
> With gentle force soliciting the darts,
> He drew them forth and heal'd, and bade me live.
> Since then—
> With few associates, and not wishing more,
> Here much I ruminate, as much I may,
> With other views of men and manners now
> Than once; and others of a life to come."

Yes, his chief business *now* is with God; and this is not to be managed in a crowd: and as this business continues and increases through life, abstraction and retirement will always be desirable, always necessary. His religion cannot flourish—cannot live—without it.

Our theme is very extensive. Let us detach from it four articles. Let us review the Christian in his Retirement, with regard to

I. PLACE.
II. TIME.
III. ENGAGEMENT.
IV. MOTIVES.

I. With regard to PLACE.

Our Saviour says, "Enter into thy *closet*." The word signifies any retired apartment; and some imagine that he employs a term of such latitude, that we might have no excuse for omission, if we are unfurnished with a place appropriated more expressly to pious use.

The connexion requires this extension of meaning. Our Lord applies the word "closet" obviously in opposition to the "corner of the street;" and in distinction from the openness of the "synagogue," where persons could be "seen of men," and for which purpose these situations were chosen by the Pharisees. But *He* would have his disciples to avoid all appearance of ostentation; and perform their devotions where they would be concealed, unless from a witness in Heaven. Yet if the end, which is privacy, can be answered, the place would be indifferent.

> "*Where'er we seek Him, he is found;*
> And *every* place is holy ground."

"I will that men pray *everywhere*," says the Apostle, "lifting up holy hands, without wrath, and doubting." God said to Ezekiel, "Go forth into the plain, and there I will talk with thee." Isaac made a closet of the field. Daniel, of the river-side. Nathanael, of the fig-tree. Peter, of the housetop.

A variety here must be admitted, or the duty cannot be performed by many, at all. For what numbers are there who are unable to command a convenient room for religious engagement. This is a trying case: and especially to those who have been accustomed to enjoy such an advantage. The Preacher knew a pious female, who had been reduced from a mansion, and compelled to occupy a hired and contracted apartment; yet nothing in the humiliating and distressing change seemed to affect her, but her want now of a a place of seclusion, in which to indulge her private devotion. For the "peculiar people," even in common circumstances, fail not to give proof of their distinction: "They that are after the flesh, do mind the things of the flesh; but they that are after the Spirit, the things of the Spirit." If, my Christian friends, you have the privilege of accommodation, be grateful for it, and use it well: and if you have not, remember, your Heavenly Father knoweth it, and that where "there is first a willing mind, a man is accepted according to what he hath, and not according to what he hath not." Be as retired as you *can*, since you cannot be so retired as you *would*; and if your circumstances will not allow of your being hid, and some of your family must witness your exercises, be not afraid of opposing the Saviour's pleasure. Though you are seen of men, you are not seeking to be seen by them.

It is possible to retire mentally, even in company; and many an act of devotion is performed by the Christian without the formality of the exercise, when he is busied in his ordinary concerns. Nehemiah worshipped secretly, without retirement; and, while, as a cup-bearer, he was performing his office in attending on the king, "prayed to the God of Heaven."

The Jews had their Proseuchæ, oratories, or praying-houses, in secluded situations, by streams of water, and in woods, and on the sides of mountains. The Scripture more than once refers to such places. In one of these it is probable our Saviour passed the night he spent in devotion; and in one of these Paul seems to have addressed his hearers in the vicinity of Philippi. They were a pleasing and a wise provision; as persons could here indulge themselves in private devotion whenever they were prompted by disposition, and opportunity; and especially those who had scarcely any other sacred retreat. We have not such accommodations: but Nature itself, during a large portion of the year, affords us advantages; and it is wonderful that persons do not oftener avail themselves of these interesting spots of retirement. We have known some who, whenever the season and the weather allowed, often retired thus, to perform their morning and evening devotions. Instead of their minds being diverted, and their thoughts dissipated, by the scenery, the works of God refreshed and impressed them, and furnished them with excitements and assistance. And there are those, now living, who, if ever they feel devout, feel it in a garden, or a field, or a meadow. The bubbling spring; the apple-tree, among the trees of the wood; the rose of Sharon; the lily of the valley; the purple rising and the golden setting of the sun; aid their communion with Him who is all in all. The sowing of the grain; the blade; the ear; the full corn in the ear; the mower filling his hand, and the binder of sheaves his bosom; the husbandman and the gleaner—all these teach them to think and feel devoutly. They love the creatures of their God, and feel them their friends; and while the herd grazes at their feet, and the sheep repose at their side, and the lambs sport in sight, a voice seems to say, "Thou shalt be in league with the stones of the field; and the beasts of the field shall be at peace with thee." They hear God in the breeze; they sing his praise in the note of the bird; they make every scene a book; every object a preacher; every place a temple.

We only add, what an advantage is the omnipresence of devotion, in that solitude which is not chosen, but brought upon us by the necessity of circumstances: when lover and friend are put far from us by death, and the heart within us is desolate; when traveling, and we droop in the loneliness that is felt in the midst of strangers; when, by distance or condition, our connexions are beyond our reach, and we are inaccessible to them! Ah! says Jonah, in the midst of the sea, "I will look again towards thy holy temple." "From the ends of the earth," says David, "will I cry unto thee, when my heart is overwhelmed." Cowper has not overlooked this consolation, in the language he has put into the mouth of the lonely islander—

> "But the sea-fowl is gone to her nest,
>   The beast is laid down in his lair;
> E'en here is a season of rest,
>   And I to my cabin repair.
> There's mercy in every place;
>   And mercy, encouraging thought!
> Gives even affliction a grace,
>   And reconciles man to his lot."

We consider it,

II. With regard to TIME.

When are we to enter our closet? and how *long* are we to remain there? You are not to be there *always*. You will hear, as we proceed, that the Family, the Church, the World, have all claims upon you. Every duty has its season, in which alone it is beautiful and acceptable. "No duty," says Bishop

Hopkins," will be approved of God, that appears before him stained with the murder of another duty." Yea, a Christian sometimes forces himself away from the delights of solitude, to engage in services far less pleasing than lying down in these green pastures, and feeding beside these still waters. But self-indulgence, even when the enjoyment is religious, must yield to the will of his Heavenly Father, as soon as it is known.

Retirement, however, should be *frequent*. Yet, if you ask *how* frequent? I do not pretend absolutely to determine. The Scripture does not decide: it was needless to decide—as needless as the prescribing how often you should eat and drink. Your wants will regulate the one; and your love will regulate the other. Love is the Christian's grand principle; and love does not require to be bound: it is ingenuous; it is urging; it is contriving; and will get, with all possible expedition, to its object. Besides, no rule *can* be laid down that will apply equally to all. There is a great difference in our conditions, and our callings. At different periods too, the Providence of God may vary our duties. Thus good people formerly, spent much more time alone, than the peculiarities of the day in which we live will allow us. It does not follow that they had more piety than Christians now: their religion was more compressed, and flowed in a deeper channel; but that of modern Christians, though shallower, is more diffusive and rapid. They had not those openings for activities abroad—those calls to extensive and manifold beneficence and exertions, which the followers of Christ now have. *These*, therefore, cannot gratify themselves by spending hours together in their loved seclusion. *They* hear a thousand voices crying, "Come, and help us." They see that "the fields are already white unto harvest:" they know that "the harvest is great;" that "the labourers are few;" that the season is short; that the weather is uncertain; and the consequences of negligence, not only incalculable, but remediless.

Christians, however, should get as much leisure for the Closet, as they are able. And in order to this, they should guard against the waste of time; they should economize time; they should redeem time from indecision, and trifling, and especially from the vile and wretched consumptions of unnecessary sleep. David mentions three times a day: "Evening and morning, and at noon, will I pray, and cry aloud." Daniel observed the same rule: "He went into his house; and his windows being opened in his chamber towards Jerusalem, he kneeled upon his knees three times a day, and prayed, and gave thanks before his God, as he did aforetime." This was a custom much recommended, and observed by many of our forefathers: they thought, and they wisely thought, that a few

moments of retirement in the middle of the day, as well as morning and evening, tended to check temptation and vanity, and to keep the mind in the things of God. But *twice* a day, at least, the Christian will withdraw. Less than this will not surely keep us "in the fear of the Lord all the day long"—and for this, the morning and evening will be deemed the most suitable periods. Under the Law, a lamb was offered every morning and every evening. How much is there in each of these returning seasons to excite and to impress! "It is a good thing," says the Psalmist, "to give thanks unto the Lord, and to sing praises unto thy name, O Most High: to show forth thy lovingkindness in the morning, and thy faithfulness every night."

As to the particular hour, this must be a matter of discretion: only it should be as early as possible, both in the morning and evening, to avoid disturbance in the one, and drowsiness in the other. I will put amusements out of the question. But if you return late from visiting, it is better to retire even late than not at all. Yet in many of these cases would it not be preferable to retire a few moments before you go? Would you be less prepared for company? Would you be less safe? Would you be less edifying?

What may be done at any time, is often done at no time: and while we have no plan or purpose, we are open to every casualty that may seize us, and turn us aside. It is therefore necessary to have *appointed* seasons for Retirement; and desirable to adhere to them as invariably as we can.

There are also *occasional* and *extraordinary* calls to private devotion, when more than usual time should be allowed, that the mind may be affected with the event, and obtain the peculiar assistance the case requires. I should have a poor opinion of that Christian, who would not employ more than common retirement, when going to change his residence, his calling, his condition in life; or to take any important step, the consequences of which may affect not only his comfort, but his conduct and character for ever. When Jacob was going to meet his exasperated brother Esau, who was coming against him with four hundred men, he was found alone wrestling with the Angel. When our Saviour was going to ordain his twelve Apostles, the day following; "He went out into a mountain to pray; and continued all night in prayer to God." And when his hour of suffering was drawing near, we find him in the Garden of Gethsemane, and retiring three times even from his selected disciples, and praying.—Let us,

III. Consider this Retirement with regard to its ENGAGEMENTS.

Many retire. But the tradesman retires to cast up his accounts, and to plan his

D

schemes; the statesman, to enjoy his relaxation and ease; the philosopher, to pursue his theories and experiments; the poet, to rove among the aspects of nature, or to lose himself in creations of his own—and perhaps God is not in all their thoughts. So far from inviting *Him* into their solitude, when they apprehend his approach, they repel the impertinent intruder; and say unto God, "Depart from us; we desire not the knowledge of thy ways." But we are speaking of religious retirement. The Christian withdraws for three purposes.

First, He is engaged in *Reading.* This enlarges his views, and impresses his mind, and furnishes him with aids to devotion. But *what* does he peruse? Principally the Scriptures. I say principally, because other books may be occasionally read to advantage, and we have a plenitude of excellent works for the closet. Yet I confess, the Scriptures alone appear to be the best reading in retirement, especially for the poor, and those who have little leisure. They are the fountain; other books are streams, and streams are seldom entirely free from something of the quality of the soil through which they flow. Who would not draw the water of life for himself from the spring-head? The Scriptures come immediately from God, and lead immediately to Him! There is a boundless variety and fulness in them. They are always new. They entertain, while they teach; and profit while they please. There is always something in them that bears upon our own character and condition, however peculiar it may be. "They are profitable for doctrine, for reproof, for correction, and for instruction in righteousness, that the man of God may be perfect, throughly furnished unto all good works." I would recommend, generally, a regular reading of this sacred Volume: for every word of God is pure: and whatsoever things were written aforetime, were written for our learning; that we, through patience and comfort of the Scripture, might have hope. But "let him that readeth understand." It is better to peruse a paragraph with attention and reflection, than carelessly, and without observation, to run over several chapters.—For,

Secondly, He is engaged in *Meditation.* And my Brethren, it is desirable that you should employ your own powers; for you will be more affected and benefited by the efforts of your own minds, than by the thoughts of others. The faculty will be improved and increased by exercise; and cannot be acquired without it, any more than a man can learn to swim by never entering the water. And surely you cannot be at a loss for subjects. If your reading does not supply you immediately with materials, there are the seasons of the year, the state of the world, the condition of your family, your own individual circumstances, temporal and spiritual. Two subjects are always at hand—your own depravity and unworthiness, of which fresh proof is given every day and every hour: and—"the love of Christ, which passeth knowledge." In *his* sufferings and glory, the angels always find enough to attract and engage their profoundest thoughts; and shall these be less interesting to *you*—to whom they are not only true, but important; not only wonderful, but infinitely necessary? They are all your salvation; let them be all your desire: and say, with David, "My meditation of him shall be sweet,"—"My soul shall be satisfied as with marrow and fatness, and my mouth shall praise Thee with joyful lips, when I remember thee upon my bed, and meditate on thee in the night watches,"—"How precious are thy thoughts unto me, O God! how great is the sum of them! If I should count them, they are more in number than the sand. When I awake, I am still with Thee." Whatever the subject of your meditation may be, content not yourselves with considering it generally and abstractedly; but take some particular view of it, and bring it home to yourselves. "Is the Lord *thy* portion, O my soul? Dost *thou* hope in him? Art *thou* an heir of this promise? Dost *thou* stand in the way of this threatening? Art *thou* living in the performance or neglect of this duty? Say not, 'And what shall this man do?' but, 'Lord, what wilt thou have *me* to do?'"

Thirdly, He is employed there in *Prayer.* This is the special design of it. This is what our Saviour here enjoins: "Enter into thy closet; and when thou hast shut thy door, *pray.*" If ever you are at a loss to meditate, surely you can never be at a loss to pray! How numberless are your wants How much have you to implore for yourselves and others! How much to confess at the foot of the Cross! How much to call forth your thanksgivings and praise! And all this is included in Prayer.

And the manner need not discourage you. For here the excellency does not consist in the mode of expression—the desire is all in all. "The sacrifices of God are a broken spirit: a broken and a contrite heart, O God, thou wilt not despise." Even words are not necessary here. God reads deep meaning in the tear; and hears heavenly eloquence in the sighs of those that seek him: and often the most acceptable and successful intercession is made "with groanings which cannot be uttered."

These are the engagements of the Christian in his retired moments. But it is not necessary that he should perform all these exercises always: though it is very desirable that they should be all included; or that he should observe them precisely in the order we have stated them. They may, sometimes, alternately precede each other; and they may sometimes be intermingled. We have an instance of the blending together of these exercises in the retirement of David, with the recital of which we shall conclude this division of our discourse. For, as soon as Nathan had waited upon him, and had delivered the words of the vision—" Then went king David in and sat before the Lord, and he said, Who am I, O Lord God, and what is my house, that thou hast brought me hitherto? And this was yet a small thing in thy sight, O Lord God; but thou hast spoken also of thy servant's house for a great while to come: and is this the manner of man, O Lord God? And what can David say more unto thee? for thou, Lord God, knowest thy servant. For thy word's sake, and according to thine own heart, hast thou done all these great things, to make thy servant know them. And now, O Lord God, the word that thou hast spoken concerning thy servant, and concerning his house, establish it for ever, and do as thou hast said. For thou, O Lord of Hosts, God of Israel, hast revealed to thy servant, saying, I will build thee an house: therefore hath thy servant found in his heart to pray this prayer unto thee. And now, O Lord God, thou art that God, and thy words be true, and thou hast promised this goodness unto thy servant: therefore now let it please thee to bless the house of thy servant, that it may continue for ever before thee: for thou, O Lord God, hast spoken it: and with thy blessing let the house of thy servant be blessed for ever."—Let us consider Retirement,

IV. With regard to its MOTIVES.

The obligation might be enforced from the authority of God, whose will is supremely binding on the consciences of all those who are informed of it; and whose language ought always to be, " Speak, Lord, for thy servant heareth." It might also be enforced by example. We could show, how the most eminent saints, and the most *busy* too, have abounded in this employment—and at the head of all, we could present the Lord Jesus himself, whose conduct has the force of a law upon his followers, who in vain profess to abide in him unless they also walk even as he walked. How often do we read of his withdrawing himself, to be alone with his Heavenly Father! And can any of you dare to intimate, Ah! he needed retirement; but I can dispense with it!—But while it is enjoined by the highest authority and sanctioned by the highest example, it comes recommended by the highest advantage: and every thing unites to prove that it is a reasonable service. Mrs. Berry says in her Diary, " I would not be hired out of my closet for a thousand worlds. I never enjoy such hours of pleasure, and such free and entire communion with God, as I have here: and I

wonder that any can live prayerless, and deprive themselves of the greatest privileges allowed to them." If the twelve Apostles were living in your neighbourhood, and you had access to them, and this intercourse drew you away from the Closet, they would prove a real injury to your souls; for no creature can compensate for the want of communion with God.

We may connect Retirement with *the acquisition of knowledge.* " Through desire, a man having separated himself, seeketh and intermeddleth with all wisdom." This is peculiarly true of one kind of wisdom, and which the Heathen Oracle pronounced to be of heavenly descent—Self-Knowledge. For how can those, who are for ever engaged in company, and engrossed by business, become acquainted with their character and their state? How can they compare themselves accurately with the word of truth; and look after the workings of the hidden man of the heart; and weigh their motives; and measure their deficiencies; and detect the sins of their holy things; and " walk humbly with their God?"—like those who retire with Him, and in his " light see light!"

Retirement is necessary to *reduce the force of secular influence.* When is it the world deceives us, allures us, overcomes us? Not when we are alone. Not when it is contemplated in the presence of our Bible and our God. There the fascination drops off. There we see that whatever successes we have gained, we are still losers, without " the one thing needful." There we feel that the favour of man, who is a worm, is less than nothing and vanity, compared with the friendship of God. There we wonder that we have ever submitted to be the slaves of folly; and vow against the tyrant in future.

> " When I can say, my God is mine ;
> When I can feel his glories shine ;
> I tread the world beneath my feet,
> And all that earth calls good or great."

Is the *resemblance of God* a trifle? *This* results from our intimacy with Him. " Evil communications corrupt good manners." But while " a companion of fools shall be destroyed, he that walketh with wise men, shall be wise." We soon assume the manners, and imbibe the spirit of those with whom we are familiar, especially if the individual be a distinguished personage, and we pre-eminently revere and love him. Upon this principle, the more we have to do with God, the more we shall grow into his likeness, and " be followers of him, as dear children." When Moses descended from communion with him, his face shone: and although he was not aware of the lustre himself, the people could not steadfastly behold him for the glory of his countenance; and he was constrained to hide it under a veil. The Christian, too, may be insensible of his excellences and proficiencies; but his profiting will appear unto all men; all will take knowledge of him that he has been with Jesus.

Retirement prepares us for all other services. Judge Hale, in his Letters to his Children, makes no scruple to say, " If I omit praying, and reading a portion of God's blessed word, in the morning, nothing goes well with me all the day." Dr. Boerhaave said, that " his daily practice of retiring for an hour in the morning, and spending it in devotion and meditation, gave him firmness and vigour for the business of the whole day." He who goes forth from God, after inquiring his will, and committing himself to his care, is the best fitted for all the successes or disappointments of life. It is alone with God, that the Minister best qualifies himself for his work: it is there that he is wrought into the due temper of his office; it is there he rises above the fear of man, that " bringeth a snare," and resolves not " to shun to declare *all* the counsel of God; it is there he is inspired to say,

> " Careless, myself a dying man,
> Of dying men's esteem :
> Happy, O God, if thou approve,
> Though all beside condemn."

He is the last man in the world who should be " to be had." He should learn to resist, with the firmness of a martyr, all encroachments on his holy solitude. His hearers will soon learn, by the want of savour in his ministrations, that he loves to be more abroad than at home, and is fonder of the parlour than of the closet. Whereas the man that issues from frequent and long retirement, will ascend the pulpit as Aaron entered the Tabernacle of the Congregation, when the holy oil had been poured upon his head, and the fragrance filled the place.—To speak of the Christian's preparation for public worship, may be deemed legal or superstitious by some; but the Scripture speaks of it, and the godly have always found their account in it. Previous retirement detaches the mind from earth; it composes the thoughts; it tends to prevent distractions in waiting upon God; and aids to produce that seriousness of spirit, which is essential to our edification by the means of grace. They will always profit most by the sanctuary, who are much in the closet.

It furnishes also *a good evidence of our state.* Do not judge of yourselves by what you are before men—What are you with God? Your sincerity is chiefly evinced by your regard to the *unseen* duties of religion. These show that you are actuated by pious principle, and not by any of those inferior motives which produce appearances. In public duties you are open to the observation of others. Hypocrites may lift their hands and eyes; and affect great fervour and zeal. Curiosity may prompt our repairing to the ordinances of the Temple; and the dispensation even of divine Truth, in excellency of speech and elegance of manner, may prove an amusement; and persons may flock to it as to a concert. Thus we know it was with Ezekiel's hearers. " Lo, thou art unto them as a very lovely song of one that hath a pleasant voice, and can play well on an instrument, for they hear thy words, but they do them not." If you are with a person whom you dislike, his presence is tolerable in a large company, where you have other attractions—though even then you would rather he was absent; but should the rest withdraw, how embarrassed and miserable would you be with him alone! Some of you seem attached to the House of God; but we often wonder how you would feel, if, upon the separation of the assembly, you were " *detained*" like Doeg " *before the Lord.*"

The *freedom* we enjoy in the exercise, is no inconsiderable recommendation of private devotion. Here we come even to his seat: we reach the secret place of the Most High. Here we are free from the restraints we feel in public. Here we are not condemned as deceivers, or ridiculed as enthusiasts, if we prostrate ourselves before God, or pray like our Saviour " with strong cryings and tears." I know not why we should be ashamed to be seen weeping, yet so it frequently is—but here the eye can pour out tears unto God. Here we may sigh, and pause, and kneel a third time, " saying the same words." Here the mind is affected with those minute but touching recollections and peculiarities which cannot be admitted into public worship. Here we may pray for others, in a way we could not do before them without offence. Would they abide to hear us beseech God to deliver—One of them from the love of money? Another, from a fondness of extravagance? A third, from a hateful and odious temper? Here you can lay open, with proper self-abasement, the secret workings of your own pride, or envy, or carnality. Here you may pour into the bosom of God things which you could not divulge to your dearest friend or relation. Every heart has a bitterness of its own; and this is frequently, what it is least at liberty to communicate. But here no secret is hid; here no complaint is suppressed. Here, " in every thing by prayer and supplication, with thanksgiving, we make known our requests unto God;" and, as the consequence of the full disclosure, we are " careful for nothing;" and " feel a peace that passeth all understanding, keeping our heart and mind through Christ Jesus."

—But ought we to overlook the *promise* which the Saviour has here given us, and with which he would engage us to the performance of this duty? It would be a reflection upon his wisdom and goodness. " Enter into thy closet, and when thou hast shut thy door, pray to *thy Father which is in secret,* and thy Father which seeth in secret, shall reward thee openly."—Let us observe the inducement.

It includes the *Divine Presence.* "Thy Father which *is* in secret." He is everywhere; but he is, it seems, peculiarly in the Closet. Here "he *is* waiting to be gracious, and exalted to have mercy." Here he is clothed in no terror, to make you afraid. Here he is, not as a *Judge* on his tribunal, to arraign you as criminals; nor even as a *Monarch* on a throne of state, to receive you as subjects; but as your *Father*—eager to embrace you as "the sons and daughters of the Lord Almighty." Do children dread to enter a room, where a loved and honoured father is to be found? Would not this be a sufficient attraction to enter it? "When shall I come," says David, "and appear before God?"

It includes his *inspection.* "And thy Father which *seeth* in secret." He is not regardless of you; he is not ignorant of your condition; he knows what is the mind of the Spirit. Your desires are before him, and your groaning is not hid from him. He sees you, but not with eyes of flesh. He is no respecter of persons. He will not fail to notice you, however poor and despised. He views you with approbation. The prayer of the upright is his delight. "Let me see thy countenance, let me hear thy voice; for sweet is thy voice, and thy countenance is comely."

It includes *recompence.* "He *shall reward thee openly.*" He "never said to the seed of Jacob, Seek ye me, in vain." But surely it is enough for a benefactor to be ready to attend to the applications of the distressed, without promising to *reward* beggars for knocking at his door; and to bestow on them, honours that shall distinguish them in public! as if, instead of being urged by their necessities, they had been performing some very meritorious action! The advantage of prayer is all our own: there can be nothing like *desert* in it. And yet, to stimulate us to attend to a course founded entirely in a regard to our welfare, the Lord of all makes himself a debtor to his suppliants; and engages to confer upon them not only a real, but a public and acknowledged recompence. Even *here* he puts a difference between his people and others. Even *now* he induces observers to say, "Verily, there is a reward for the righteous;" "This is the seed which the Lord hath blessed." Even now he can make even a Balaam exclaim, "How goodly are thy tents, O Jacob; and thy tabernacles, O Israel! Let me die the death of the righteous, and let my last end be like his." But if at present any dispensations humble them, any clouds obscure them; they will be exalted in due time; they will soon shine forth as the sun in the kingdom of their Father. "Judge nothing before the time, until the Lord come,

who will bring to light the hidden things of darkness, and make manifest the counsels of the heart, and then shall every man have praise of God."

And now, my dear hearers, upon the ground of this important subject, let me address you with all fidelity and seriousness, For it is not a light thing—it is your life. I remember the observation of an old divine, and it is not too strongly expressed: "It is impossible for a man to *be* godly, who neglects secret devotion, and next to impossible that he should ever *become* so." To which he adds, "You may as well talk of a wise fool, a wicked saint, a sober drunkard, or an honest thief, as of a prayerless Christian!" If this witness be true, what are we to think, even of many who make some pretensions to religion! Their lives are full of action, and void of thought. They visit the temple, and are ever hearing sermons; but they are shy of the Closet. Some of them, in this day of pious and benevolent institutions and exertions, make a figure in public; and their zeal flames at a distance; but it diminishes as it approaches nearer home, and it goes out in a dreadful darkness and coldness between God and their own souls.

In others, a little of this practice of retirement remains, lingering, as the effect of custom or conviction only. But though they do not constantly, they yet frequently neglect private reading, meditation, and prayer. Business, company, the most trifling pretensions, keep them from the duty; and they must be aware, if they would deal honestly with themselves, that whatever they do in this way, is their *task,* and not their pleasure. And need they be told to what character Job alludes, when he asks, "Will he *delight* himself in the Almighty, will he *always* call upon God?"

But some have *wholly* incurred the reproach; "Thou hast not called upon me, O Jacob; thou hast been weary of me, O Israel." Yes—for it was not thus with you once; you have left off to be wise, and to do good. "Apostacy," says Henry, "begins at the closet door." There your irreligion commenced; and ever since this revolt from God, you have been departing more and more from Him. O! what a day was that, when you first left your apartment without prayer! Perhaps you have forgotten it. But, no! How can you forget your hesitation—your strugglings with conscience—the shame and uneasiness you endured, so that you longed and endeavoured as soon as possible to loose the feeling.—And you succeeded. You felt less the day following. At length you obtained a victory over every moral embarrassment. And now you lie down and rise up like the beasts that perish, and feel nothing.

But allow me to ask, Is not this neglect of religious retirement, a proof that the love of

God is not in you? You treat men with attention; but He is not in all your thoughts. You salute your fellow-creatures according to their rank and quality; but you never give Him the glory that is due unto his holy name. You visit your friends and acquaintances, but you never call upon God, though he is not far from any one of you. And have you nothing to do with *Him?* Is he not your Creator? Your Preserver? Your Governor? Your Judge? Have you nothing to hope from Him? Nothing to fear? In his hand your breath is, and his are all your ways. Men deny the depravity of human nature: but we want no other proof of the mortifying truth, than this alienation of your mind from God. Can this be an innocent state? Could this be the condition of man, when God made him upright? No! We do not go, we need not go, to the refuse of society in prisons, and galleys. Setting aside all immorality and profligacy; when we see creatures shunning their Creator; and beneficiaries hating to retain their Benefactor in their knowledge; when we see men, instead of loving God with all their heart, banishing him from his own temple, and forbidding him the bosom that was made for himself—we know they *must* be fallen and perverted, and guilty creatures; and without pardon and renovation can never enter into the kingdom of God. And this is your character; your danger. You are living without God. You are enemies to him. In vain you reckon upon your virtue and safety, because you may be free from the iniquities which disgrace others. Sins of omission expose to condemnation, as well as positive transgressions. They are violations of the same authority. He that forbids, also enjoins. And you show your contempt of God, by neglect as well as by insult. If two persons living together in the same house were never to speak to each other, it would be deemed by all, as much a proof of dislike, as their fighting. Be not therefore deceived. You are wronging your own souls. All they that are far from God shall perish. "The wicked shall be turned into hell, with all the nations that forget God."

Is not, therefore, another cause of your neglect of the Closet, a guilty conscience? You are afraid to enter into solitude. You know that however cheerful you appear, you are far from being happy in reality. You have your occasional forebodings; and it is safer not to look into your condition lest they should be confirmed. You surround yourselves with company, lest, being alone, truth should invade your delusion, or you should be haunted by the ghosts of your own thoughts. The value of your amusements does not consist in the pleasure they yield, but in their power to divert you from reflection. And this power they must soon lose. And its effect at present is limited. It is no easy thing to

keep out light, where there are so many apertures to blind up; or to sleep on, where stillness is impossible. What a life of constraint and uneasiness are you leading! "There is no peace, saith my God, to the wicked."

Another prevention is to be found in creature attraction and worldly cares. You "mind earthly things." Your farm and your merchandise; your rising early, and sitting up late, and compassing sea and land, to carry some temporal interest—these furnish you with excuses; these yield you substitutes; these keep you from seeking those things that are above. We wish not to render you indifferent to your stations in life, or to induce you to undervalue the good things which he gives you to enjoy. But while you are "not slothful in business, be fervent in spirit, serving the Lord." "Labour not," only or principally, "for the meat that perisheth, but for that meat which endureth unto everlasting life." "Seek ye first the kingdom of God and his righteousness, and all these things shall be added unto you." And if you obtain them not in this subordination, you will find them to be nothing but vanity and vexation of spirit. Your table will become a snare. Your prosperity will destroy you.

We have thus again called you to enter your Closet. And, as to many of you, it is probable the application will be again refused. But another call will soon be addressed to you. It will be to die. *That* call you cannot refuse. You live in a crowd—but you must die alone. You now hate silence—but you are hastening to "the house appointed for all living;" and

" Darkness, death, and long despair,
Reign in eternal silence there."

LECTURE III.

THE CHRISTIAN, IN THE FAMILY.

" *Then David returned to bless his Household.'*
2 Sam. vi. 20.

THE human frame is "a body fitly joined together, and compacted by that which every joint supplieth, according to the effectual working of every part." There is nothing in it irregular; nothing defective; nothing superfluous. The eye cannot say to the ear, I have no need of thee; nor the hand to the foot, I have no need of thee. The members are all connected with, all dependent upon, all subservient to each other; and were you to separate them, the body, which is composed of the whole, would be at once disfigured and destroyed.

It is the same with the system of Christianity, as presented in the Scriptures of truth. By separation, it loses both its beauty and its energy: its beauty—for this consists in the fine adjustment of the parts; its energy —for this results from the harmonious operation of the whole. What God therefore has joined together, whether it be, doctrine and duty; or command and promise; or privilege and service; or hope and fear—let not man put asunder.

The zeal of some professors is not always according to knowledge, or such as to evince a "heart right with God." It is not full of "good fruits, without partiality and without hypocrisy." For these are nearly allied. Partiality is always a proof of hypocrisy; for if you are upright before God, and sincerely desirous of pleasing him, you will come to him, not to dictate, but to submit; not to choose, but to say, "Lord, what wilt thou have me to do?" "Then shall I not be ashamed, when I have respect unto all thy commandments."

A Christian is not a perfect character; but he *is* a character. He is always the same; everywhere the same. The same in prosperity and adversity; the same in public and in private; the same in the dwelling-place, as in the temple; the same in the family, as in the Church. If there be any difference, his *immediate* connexions will have the advantage; and looking towards those who have the best opportunities of knowing and observing his religion, he will be able to say, "Our rejoicing is this, the testimony of our conscience; that in simplicity and godly sincerity, not with fleshly wisdom, but by the grace of God, we have our conversation in the world, and more abundantly to you-ward." When Whitfield was asked, whether a certain person was a good man, he replied, "I know not —I never lived with him." And Philip Henry remarks, that "Every man, in religion, is really, what he is relatively."

We have to exhibit the Christian this morning in the FAMILY.

Here it is supposed that he *has* a family. He is not a poor, illiberal, solitary individual: preferring vice, or mopishness, or an escape from expense, care, and trouble, to a state which was designed to complete the happiness of Adam in Paradise; and which Inspiration has pronounced to be "honourable in all." He believes in the wisdom and veracity of God, who has said, "It is not good for man to be alone;" and instead of reflecting upon his parents, and undervaluing and injuring the most amiable part of society, where too they are not even allowed to complain; he forms no leading permanent plan of life, in which marriage is not considered as the foundation. And having entered the condition, he will be anxious to fulfil its duties. He will love his wife, even as himself. He will train up his children "in the nurture and admonition of the Lord." He will behave towards his servants, as one who knows that he has "a Master in heaven," and that there is no respect of persons with God. He will say, with David, "I will behave myself wisely

in a perfect way. Oh! when wilt thou come unto me? I will walk within my house with a perfect heart. I will set no wicked thing before mine eyes. I hate the work of them that turn aside; it shall not cleave to me!"

"Then David returned to bless his household." *Then*—for the period and the occasion are previously marked. The day had been a very pleasing one to David; but it had also proved a very active and busy one. For many hours he had been engaged in bringing up the Ark of God from the House of Obed-Edom into the city of Jerusalem. He had not only attended, to witness all the indications of piety and joy; but had contributed himself, in the sacred performances. And when the symbol of the Divine presence was set in the Tabernacle prepared to receive it; he offered burnt-offerings and peace-offerings before the Lord; and dismissed the multitude with presents, after blessing them in the name of the Lord. But the Monarch does not make him forget the Master; nor does public service hinder domestic. "Then David returned to bless his household."—Let us pass from this instance of excellency, to consider at large,

I. The WAY IN WHICH THE HEAD OF A FAMILY MAY BLESS HIS HOUSEHOLD.

II. To show THE REASONS WHICH SHOULD ENGAGE HIM TO ATTEMPT IT.

III. To ANSWER SOME OBJECTIONS TO THE DUTY. And,

IV. To CONCLUDE WITH SOME ANIMADVERSIONS AND ADMONITIONS RESPECTING IT.

I. If it be asked, HOW the head of a family may BLESS HIS HOUSEHOLD? we would answer, by *Example*,—by *Government*,—by *Discipline*—by *Instruction*—by *Attendance on the Means of Grace*—by the *Performance of Domestic Devotion*.

Some of these particulars, we are aware, in a degree imply and include each other; yet they are distinct enough for the utility of separate remark. Thus we distinguish countries and provinces; though in some places they approximate; and where they unite, the air, and the soil, and the produce, will display resemblance and even sameness.

First, He may "bless his household" by *Example*. I begin with this, because nothing can supply the want of personal religion. He who despises his own soul, will feel little disposition to attend to the souls of others. Destitute of principle, he will be determined only by circumstances; and his exertions, if he makes any, will be partial and rare. Having nothing to animate him from experience, his endeavours will be dull and cold. Where all is merely formal and official, a man will not go far even in the *use* of means; but what probability is there of his *success*, when he *does* use them? Who loves to take his meat from a leperous hand? A drunkard will make a poor preacher of sobriety to servants. A proud and passionate father is a wretched recommender of humility and meekness to his children. What those who are under his care *see*, will more than counteract what they *hear ;* and all his efforts will be rejected, with the question, "Thou that teachest another, teachest thou not thyself? Thou that preachest a man should not steal, dost thou steal? Thou that sayest a man should not commit adultery, dost thou commit adultery?" To what is it owing, that the offspring of many professors are worse than those of other men? Inconsistency. Inconsistency is more injurious than neglect. The one may be resolved into a forgetfulness of principle ; the other shows a contempt of it. You little imagine how early and how effectively children remark things. They notice them when they seem incapable of any distinct observation; and while you would suppose no impression could be *left* on such soft materials, a fixed turn is given to many a part of the future character. You must therefore reverence them, and be circumspect even in your most free and relaxing moments. You must do, as well as teach ; and while you are humble before God, you must be able to say to them, " Be ye followers of me, even as I also am of Christ."

It is commonly observed, that example does more than precept. But the young are peculiarly alive to example; and when example has the advantage of nearness, and constant exhibition ; and unites both authority and endearment; it must prove the most powerful and insensible transformer ; and requires in those who furnish it, and who will necessarily be imitated, that they "abstain from all appearance of evil." We only add here, that they who constitute your moral charge, are not so much affected and swayed by any direct and positive urgings, as by the presence, and exemplification, and sight of " whatsoever things are lovely and of good report." The force of the hot-house is not to be compared with the genial influence of the spring, by which, without violence, and without noise, every thing is drawn into bud and bloom.

Secondly, He may " bless his household" by *Government.* Order is Heaven's first law. God himself is the example of it ; and by nothing does he bless his creatures more, than by the steadiness of the order of Nature, and the regularity of the Seasons. What uncertainty is there in the ebbing and flowing of the tides? What deviations in the changes of the Moon? The Sun knoweth his going down. Even the Comet is *not* eccentric: in traversing the boundlessness of space, he performs his revolutions of fifty or a hundred years, to a moment. And in all the works of God, what seems disorder, is only arrangement beyond our comprehension : for " in wisdom he has made them all."

Hear the Apostle. "Let every thing be done decently and in order." The welfare of your household requires that you should observe times. Every thing should have its season— your business ; your meals ; your devotional exercises ; your rising, and your rest. The periods for these will vary with the condition of families ; but labour to be as punctual as circumstances will allow. It is of importance to peace, and temper, and diligence, and economy. Confusion is friendly to every evil work. Disorder also multiplies disorder. For no one thinks of being exact with those who set at nought all punctuality.

The same principle requires that you should keep every thing in its place. Subordination is the essence of all order and rule. Never suffer the distinctions of life to be broken down. All violations of this kind injure those who are below the gradation, as well as those above it. The relinquishment of authority may be as wrong as its excesses. He that is responsible for the duties of any relation, should claim its prerogatives and powers—how else is he to discharge them? Be kind and affable to servants ; but let nothing divest you of the mistress. Be the tenderest of fathers ; but *be* the father—and no sensible woman will, I am sure, be offended if I add—Be the most devoted of husbands, but *be* the husband.

Thirdly, By *Discipline.* This regards the treatment of offences : "For it must needs be that offences will come :" and what is to be done with them? Here two extremes are to be avoided. The one is severity. You are not to magnify trifles into serious evils ; and instead of a cheerful countenance to wear a gloom ; and instead of commending, to be always finding fault ; and instead of enlivening every thing around you like the weather in spring, to be a continual dropping in a rainy, winter-day. Instead of making home repulsive, let it possess every attraction, and abound with every indulgence and allowance, the exclusions of Scripture do not forbid. Instead of making a child tremble and retreat ; gain his confidence and love, and let him run into your arms. "Fathers," says the Apostle (for this fault lies mostly with our sex), "Fathers, provoke not your children to wrath, lest they be discouraged." The other is indulgence—a foolish fondness, or connivance at things actually wrong, or pregnant with evil. This often shows itself with regard to favourites. And here, ye mothers, let not *your* good be evil spoken of. Do not smother your darlings to death with kisses : and let not your tender bosom be an asylum for delinquents appealing from the *deserved* censures of the father. The success of such appeals, with kind but weak minds, is very mischievous : it makes preferences where there should be an evenness of regard, and tends to check and discourage wholesome reproof; and "he that spareth the rod hateth his son, but he that loveth him chasteneth him betimes." "Chasten thy son while there is hope, and let not thy soul spare for his crying." Here Eli failed: "his sons made themselves vile and he restrained them not." Here also David erred: he had not displeased Adonijah at any time in saying, "Why hast thou done so?" When the head of a family cannot prevent the introduction of improper books; the visits of infidel, or profane companions; the indulgence of ensnaring usages, and indecent discourse; the putting forth of pretensions above his rank; the incurring of expenses beyond his income;—does *he* bear rule in his own house? Is it thus that *he* puts away evil from his tabernacle? Is it thus that *he* blesses his household?

For what is Abraham commended? "I know him, that he will command his children and his household after him, and they shall keep the ways of the Lord to do justice and judgment." Not that he was the tyrant; and terrified his family with the blackness of his frown, or the roughness of his voice. We no more admire a despot in the house, than in the state: but he was decided and firm; not only telling his servants and children what they were to avoid or what they were to perform; but requiring and enforcing obedience by the authority of his station. But *proper* authority requires dignity, as well as power. What can *he* do, whose levities, and follies, and ignorance, and weakness, deprive him of all awe, and all influence, and all impression? Are we to smile or sigh at the thought of some children being in subjection to *their* parents; and of some wives being called upon to reverence *their* husbands? Is there no law to protect females and children? As to children, the case with them is not voluntary; they deserve pity. But no sympathy is due to females who throw themselves into the empire of folly and weakness; and willingly choose a condition, whose duties it is sinful for them to neglect, and impossible for them to perform.

Fourthly, By *Instruction*. "For the soul to be without knowledge, it is not good." And this holds supremely true of religious knowledge. "These words," says Moses, "which I command thee this day, shall be in thine heart: and thou shalt teach them diligently unto thy children, and shalt talk of them when thou sittest in thine house, and when thou walkest by the way, and when thou liest down, and when thou risest up. And thou shalt bind them for a sign upon thine hand, and they shall be as frontlets between thine eyes. And thou shalt write them upon the posts of thy house, and on thy gates." Here observe not only the duty, but the manner in which he has enjoined the performance of it. He would make it a constant, a familiar, an easy, a pleasing exercise—a recreation rather than a task. In another place he says, "When thy son asketh thee in time to come, saying, What mean the testimonies and the statutes and the judgments which the Lord our God hath commanded you? Then thou shalt say unto thy son, We were Pharaoh's bond-men in Egypt; and the Lord brought us out of Egypt with a mighty hand. And the Lord showed signs and wonders, great and sore upon Egypt, upon Pharaoh, and upon all his household, before our eyes: and he brought us out from thence, that he might bring us in, to give us the land which he sware unto our fathers. And the Lord commanded us to do all these statutes, to fear the Lord our God for our good always, that he might preserve us alive, as it is at this day. And it shall be our righteousness, if we observe to do all these commandments before the Lord our God as he hath commanded us." Nothing can be more natural than this recommendation. The curiosity of children is great, and will commonly, if judiciously treated, furnish you with sufficient opportunities to inform them. Their questions will show you the bias of their disposition; the state of their minds; and the nature and degree of the information it is proper to administer; and in various cases it is less necessary to go before them, than to follow. Events too are always turning up; and these will afford a wise parent a thousand hints of natural and seasonable improvement. Yet there are those who though they levy a tax upon every thing their avarice, sagacity, and zeal can find, to promote the temporal interests of their offspring, never seize, and turn to a religious account, any of those occurrences of the day, and of the neighbourhood, whether pleasing or awful, that might so easily be made to speak not only to the understanding, but to the imagination and the heart.

Fifthly, By *securing their attendance on the Means of Grace*. Servants should be allowed opportunities of public worship and instruction, as often as circumstances will permit; and we admire the plan of our forefathers, who disengaged their domestics as much as possible on the Sabbath from the preparations of the table, that they might be at liberty to go themselves, and get food for their souls. Children also should be led to the House of God—though there is a proper time for their "showing unto Israel." In determining this, it is not easy to draw the line. If they are taken too early, besides hindering the attention of those who have the charge of them, there is danger that holy exercises will become irksome by frequent and long detentions, before they can feel any interest in them. Yet an early attendance is valuable, as it tends to render the habit natural; and impressions may be occasionally made, even upon infant minds, sufficient to

E

lead them to inquire, and to aid you much in your endeavours to instruct them at home.

Lastly, By *Domestic Devotion*. This service ought to be performed every morning and evening. It includes prayer. Prayer is not only to be made *for* your family—though this is a duty, and a privilege, and enables you to obtain for your household a thousand blessings; but also *with* them.—It takes in also reading the Scriptures. Mr. Henry goes further: "They," says he, "who daily pray in their houses do well; they that not only pray, but read the Scriptures, do better; but they do best of all, who not only pray, and read the Scriptures, but—sing the praises of God." This exercise is very enlivening, and tends to throw off the formality which adheres perhaps more to domestic worship than either to public or private devotion, as it allows of less variety. If singing be not practicable, a psalm or hymn may be read. It will often produce a good effect, by impressing the minds of servants and children. The whole of the service will help you in performing what we have previously recommended, the duty of teaching and admonishing your families. The psalm or hymn will furnish them with sentiments and sentences. The reading of the word will store their minds with facts and doctrine. While the prayer itself will be no inconsiderable instructer. The very engagement will remind them of the presence and agency of God. Your addressing him for pardon, will convince them of guilt; your interceding for your country, will teach them patriotism; for your enemies, forgiveness of injuries; for all mankind, universal benevolence. Thus a man may bless his household. Let us consider,

II. THE REASONS WHICH SHOULD ENGAGE HIM TO ATTEMPT IT.

For this purpose, let us view Domestic Religion,

First, In reference to *God*. To Him it has—a relation of *responsibility*. We are required to glorify God in every condition we occupy; in every capacity we possess. A poor man is required to serve him; but if he becomes rich, his duty is varied and enlarged; and from the hour of his acquiring wealth, he will be judged by the laws of affluence. A single man is required to serve God as an individual only; but if he enters into connected life, he must serve God as the head of a family, and will be judged by the duties arising from his household-relation. God has given him a talent, and he is to make use of that talent. He has committed to him a trust, and he is to be faithful to that trust. He has made him a steward, and he is to give account of his stewardship. "I assigned you," will God say, "the empire of a family. To qualify you for the office, I furnished you with authority, and influence, and resources. How

have you employed them? Where are the servants and children you were to have trained up for me?"

—A relation of *gratitude*. How much dost thou owe to this kindness and care! Who crowned the wish of thy heart, in granting thee the object of thy dearest choice? Behold thy wife, like a fruitful vine by the sides of thy house; and thy children, like "olive plants round about thy table." Who has supplied not only all thy personal, but all thy relative wants? Whose secret has been upon thy tabernacle? Whose providence has blessed the labour of thy hand? Whose vigilance has suffered no evil to befall thee, and no plague to come nigh thy dwelling? And wilt thou refuse to serve him, with a family which *He* has formed, and secured, and sustained, and indulged? And wilt thou, instead of making thy house the temple of his praise, render it the grave of his mercies?

—A relation of *dependance*. Can you dispense with God in your family? What are all your schemes, all your exertions, all your expectations, without him? "Except the Lord build the house, they labour in vain that build it: except the Lord keep the city, the watchman waketh but in vain. It is vain for you to rise up early, to sit up late, to eat the bread of sorrows: for so he giveth his beloved sleep." How wise is it then to secure the favour of one, who has all things under his control, and is able to make them all work together for your good, or conspire to your destruction. And has he not bound himself by promise and by threatening? "The curse of the Lord is in the house of the wicked; but he blesseth the habitation of the just." What may not be dreaded from the curse of the Almighty? What may not be expected from his blessing? Under the one, the evils of life become intolerable: we sow much, and bring home little; we earn wages to put it into a bag with holes; our table becomes a snare; our successes gender many foolish and hurtful lusts; our prosperity destroys us. Under the other, a little is better than the riches of many wicked; our trials are alleviated; our sorrows are tokens for good; our comforts are enjoyed with a relish which others never taste; the voice of rejoicing and of salvation is in the tabernacles of the righteous. Therefore,

Secondly, View it in reference to *yourselves*. You ought to be concerned chiefly for your *spiritual* welfare; and should value things as they tend to restrain you from sin, and excite you to holiness. If this maxim cannot be denied, let us judge by this rule— the man who performs this duty, and—the man who neglects it. Can *he* give way to swearing and falsehood, who is going to hear *from* God, and to speak *to* him? Can *he* throw himself into a fury, who is just going to hold intercourse with the source of peace and love? *Must* he not guard his temper and conduct, even on the principle of consistency? The other exonerates himself from the reproach of hypocrisy; and because he makes no pretensions to duty, thinks he is justified in living as he pleases. And this it is that restrains many from adopting the practice. They think that it would embarrass them; that it would abridge their liberty; that it would fix upon them the charge of inconsistency. And so far they think justly. But here is their folly; in viewing a freedom from moral motives and restraints as a privilege! and an obligation to urge them to what is right and beneficial in itself, as a hardship and complaint!

And the practice *is* not only right, but every way profitable. While you teach, you learn: while you do good, you are gaining good. Your mind will be tranquillized by a confidence in God, which you alone are justified in reposing, and which you alone *can* repose in Him. How much does your comfort depend on the dutifulness of those that are under you! But how can you look for morality without piety? It is by teaching them to regard God, that you must teach them to regard yourselves, and to be diligent and submissive in their places. It is thus you bind them by sanctions the most powerful, and which operate in your absence, as well as when you are nigh. It is thus you are not only obeyed, but regarded and honoured. Religion, when it is consistently exemplified, always inspires respect and reverence. But what hold have the irreligious on the homage of others? So true it is even here, "They that despise me shall be lightly esteemed." View it,

Thirdly, In reference to the *Family*. By how many ties ought the members of your household to be endeared! "And we *do* love them." But wherein does your love appear? Can you imagine that it only requires you to ask, what shall they eat, and what shall they drink, and wherewithal shall they be clothed? What is the body to the soul? What is time to eternity? Do you wish to do them good? Can any good equal that godliness which is profitable unto all things, having promise of the life that now is, as well as of that which is to come?

Were you to suffer your children to go naked; to perish with hunger; were you to leave them in sickness to die alone; you would be shunned as monsters. But you are far more deserving of execration, if you infamously disregard their spiritual and everlasting welfare. Doubtless Herod was viewed with horror by those who had witnessed the massacre of the infants of Bethlehem: but he was far less cruel than some of you. He slew the children of others; you destroy your own. He only killed the body; you destroy both body and soul in hell. Had you any real love to your children, what would be your feelings

in life, to see them going astray, and verifying, by the evils of their conduct, that the way of transgressors is hard—while conscious that you have done nothing to secure them from it! But what, at death, would you think of a meeting that must take place between you and your children, in the great day! Then they will rise up against you in the judgment, and cause you to be put to death.— "Cursed be the day of my birth! Why died I not from the womb? Why was I not as a hidden untimely birth, as infants that never see light? Thou father, and thou mother, the instruments of my being—to you I am under no obligations. You only consulted your barbarous inclinations—You gave me an existence over which you watched while I could not be guilty; but mercilessly abandoned me as soon as I became responsible— As the creature of a day, you provided for me; but as an immortal, you left me—you made me—to perish. I execrate your cruelty. I call for damnation upon your heads—and the only relief of the misery to which you have consigned me is, that I can reproach and torment you for ever."

From such a dreadful scene, how delightful is it to think what a happy meeting there will be between those who have blessed their households and the favoured subjects of their pious care! Yea, without going forward to this period of mutual and happy acknowledgment, what a joy unspeakable and full of glory must such benefactors feel even now, when they hear a servant saying—"Blessed be God for the hour I entered such a family. I was as ignorant and careless as a heathen —but there the eyes of my understanding were opened, there my feet were turned into the path of peace." Or when they hear a child confessing, "O! what a privilege that I was born of such parents! How early did they teach me to know the Holy Scriptures! How soon they led me to the Throne of Grace; and, by teaching me to pray, furnished me with the best privilege of life! How patiently they watched, and how tenderly they cherished, and how wisely they directed, every pious sentiment and every holy purpose!—And,

" As a bird each fond endearment tries,
To tempt her new-fledged offspring to the skies,
They tried each art, reproved each dull delay,
Allured to brighter worlds, and led the way."

It is thus their children rise up and call them blessed!—Let us view it,

Fourthly, In reference to *Visitants* and *Guests*. These, instead of inducing you to decline the practice, should furnish you with argument in support of it. Wo be to you, if you shrink back from the duty in compliment to the rich, the infidel, the irreligious, or the dissipated—should such ever be found beneath your roof! For "he that is ashamed of me and of my words," says the Saviour, "of him will the Son of man be ashamed, when he comes in the clouds of heaven, with the holy angels."

It is not by concealing your principles, but by owning them verbally and practically, that you must be useful to others, and gain their respect. And here you have an opportunity to confess Him before men; and without going out of your way to effect it. It cannot appear to be sought after, to give offence. It comes, in the regular course of your household arrangement. And nothing is more likely, without effort and without officiousness, to awaken attention; to inform; to admonish. The preacher remembers well the acknowledgment of a man now with God. He moved in superior life; and, from his rank and talents, and extensive and various acquaintance, was likely to have persons frequently at his house who were strangers to his religious economy. He said, his manner was, when the time of domestic service arrived, to inform them that he was always accustomed to worship God with his family: if they disliked the practice, they might remain; if they chose to attend, they might accompany him into the library. He said, he had never known any that refused: and many of them owned they were much struck with the propriety and usefulness of the usage, and resolved, on their return, to adopt it themselves. The lecturer has also known several individuals himself, whose religious course commenced during a visit to a family who thus honoured God, and were thus honoured by Him. It is recorded, I believe, of Sir Thomas Abney, that even when he was lord mayor, and on the evening of the feast, he told the company that he always maintained the worship of God in his house; that he was now withdrawing for the purpose; and should presently return. There are few professors of religion who *could* have done this. They would not have had consciousness enough of their claim to confidence in their integrity. But where the thing was known to be, not the pretence, or show of extraordinary sanctity, but the steady and uniform operation of principle; not an exception from common conduct, but, fine as it was, only a fair specimen of the whole piece; this noble resolution must have produced some impression even in *such* an assembly. Observe it,

Fifthly, In reference to the *Country*. None of us should live to ourselves. Every one should be concerned to benefit and improve a community in which he enjoys so many advantages. But we know that "righteousness exalteth a nation," and that "sin is a reproach to any people." What an enemy then are you, if irreligious, to a country that deserves so much at your hands. However loyally you may talk, you contribute to its danger and disgrace, not only by your personal transgressions, but by sending out into the midst of it so much moral contagion, so many unprincipled and vicious individuals, from your own family. And how much would you befriend it were you to fear God yourselves; and to send forth those from under your care, who will serve their generation according to his will; and induce Him to say, "Destroy it not, for a blessing is in it." Who can imagine the good even *one* of these individuals may effect, by his prayers, his examples, his influence, his exertions! What a blessing did Elkanah and Hannah prove to Israel by their training up such a child as Samuel. And what gratitude do all ages owe to his grandmother Lois, and his mother Eunice, for such a character as Timothy.

Finally, Let us regard it in reference to the *Church.* Baxter thinks that if family religion was fully discharged, the preaching of the word would not long remain the general instrument of conversion. Without being answerable for the extent of this observation, we know who hath said, "Train up a child in the way that he should go, and when he is old, he will not depart from it." We know that among our earlier godly ancestors, religion was a kind of heir-loom, that passed by descent; and instead of the fathers were the children. Families were then the nurseries of the churches: and those who were early "planted in the house of the Lord flourished in the courts of our God, and still brought forth fruit in old age." Even the ministers of the sanctuary were commonly derived from hence; and these domestic seminaries prepared them to enter the more public institutions. And what well-defined and consistent characters did they display. And what just notions did they entertain of divine truth. And how superior were they to those teachers who, brought up in ignorance, and after a profligate course, are suddenly converted; who, impressed before they are informed, are always in danger of extremes or eccentricities; who hold no doctrine in its just bearings, but are carried away disproportionably by some one truth, which first caught their attention; and who often continue crude and incoherent in their notions, and illiberal and condemnatory in their sentiments, through life. They were not always making discoveries, but "continued in the things which they had learned, and been assured of, knowing of whom they had learned them." They were enlightened, but not dazzled. They were refreshed with divine truth, but not intoxicated. They staggered not, but kept on steady in their course; neither turned to the right hand nor to the left. They were not Antinomians: they were not Legalists. None could honour the grace of God more; but they never abused it.

Not only therefore would the Churches of Christ be more filled, but better filled: and though our eye is not evil, because God is good, and so far from wishing to limit the Holy One of Israel, we rejoice in the conversion of any; we reckon, and not without much observation, that the best members and the best ministers of our churches—they who, in their conduct and in their preaching, most *adorn* the doctrine of God our Saviour in all things, are those who are brought from pious families.

III. We were to ANSWER SOME OBJECTIONS TO THE PRACTICE.

But I have been hesitating whether I should pass over this division of our subject; not only because we perceive that we must trespass on your time, but because objections can be raised easily against any doctrine, or practice. The weakest reasoners most frequently advance them; and no wise ones will ever be influenced by them. *They* will look at argument and proof; and if a principle be established by sufficient evidence, they are satisfied, even if there should be difficulties which they must leave unsolved. I will however glance at four or five things.

The *first* regards *Leisure.* "We are so much engaged, that our affairs leave us no time for these exercises." But what time do they require? And is there one of you that does not waste more time every day of his life than is expended in such devotions? And if more time be really necessary, could you not gain more? How do you manage your concerns? Could nothing be saved by more diligence and order? At what time do you rise? Could nothing be saved from late slumberings on the bed, without any injury to health; yea, with the likelihood of improving it? If time falls short for any thing, should it not fall short for things of less moment? Is not the serving of God the "one thing needful?" And cannot He, by his grace and providence, more than indemnify you for every sacrifice you make? Is there not truth in the proverb, "There is nothing got by stealing, nor lost by praying?" Are *you* more employed than David was, who presided in his council, and gave audience to ambassadors, and orders to generals—who reigned over an extensive and distracted empire? Yet he found time for domestic worship; and even on a day of peculiar activity "returned to bless his household."

The *second* regards *Capacity.* "We envy those who are qualified for such a work; but we are unable to perform it, as we wish,—and as we ought." This is perhaps the only instance in which you think and speak humbly of yourselves. But we will not accept of your voluntary humility, till we have obtained from you an answer to a few inquiries. Is it not the want of inclination you feel, rather than of ability? Have you ever fairly made the trial? Have you done every thing

in your power to gain a fitness for the duty? Would not your capacity increase by exercise? Is refinement here necessary? Is not the most imperfect performance preferable to neglect? Suppose you were to do nothing more than, after reading a portion of God's word, to kneel down with your household, and address our Father who is in Heaven in the words which the Saviour himself taught his own disciples? Are there not helps to Family Devotion of which you may avail yourselves? We prefer in this service free prayer to forms; but preference is not exclusion. We love not the contempt with which forms have been treated by some. A Baxter, a Howe, a Watts, a Doddridge, did not ridicule them as "crutches." But, admitting the justness of the depreciating figure, yet surely crutches are a help and a blessing to the lame: and we know who hath said, "Where there is first a willing mind, it is accepted according to what a man hath, and not according to what he hath not."

The *third* regards *Shame.* "We are ashamed to begin!" What! ashamed of your glory? Ashamed of following the great? Ashamed of following a David—a King—who "returned to bless his household?" Of following a Joshua; a hero; a commander; the first man in the commonwealth of Israel; who said, "as for me and my house, we will serve the Lord." Of following Abraham, Isaac, and Jacob, who made it their first care, wherever they came, to build an altar for God? Was his late Majesty ashamed always to worship God with his household morning and evening? Is there not an increasing number of persons in our own day, of high rank and nobility, who keep up, even in their establishments, a custom so laudable and useful? The shame is that you have neglected it so long, not that you are willing to begin it now. Follow the example of a man who was well known to some of us, but whose name we must suppress. He had heard the minister preach in the morning of the Sabbath on Family Worship. The very same evening he called together his wife, and children, and servants, and apprentices; and recapitulated the arguments and motives they had heard, appealed to their reason and conscience whether they were not unanswerable and irresistible. He then said, I condemn myself for the neglect of this duty, in which I have hitherto lived: but as the best proof of repentance is practice, I will now commence it; and, by the help of God, I will omit it no more, as long as I live. Was this weakness? or moral heroism?

The *fourth* regards *false or mistaken orthodoxy.* God forbid we should undervalue divine truth; but there is a highness in doctrine so commonly connected with lowness of conduct, that we have known not a few, whose creed has soon led to the abandonment of family worship; and it is indeed the natural tendency, not of the principles they abuse, but of their abuse of the principles. "The Lord knoweth them that are his. And he will call them in his own due time, and make them willing in the day of his power, without our anxiety." But we are not sure of this. Our exertions may be the very means which he has appointed by which to accomplish the end. And when does He work without means? *He* gives the increase: but Paul plants, and Apollos waters—and what right have we to ask for a moral miracle, by expecting the one without the other?

"Where is the use of it? We cannot give our servants and our children grace." And why not? "If," says James, "a man err from the truth, and one convert him, let him know that he which converteth a sinner from the error of his ways, shall save a soul from death, and hide a multitude of sins." Here it is supposed that *you* may save and convert. "Yes, but not meritoriously or efficiently." How then? "Why only instrumentally." We have no objection to this. Still it seems there is a sense in which *you* may do it. "Yes, under God." This again is right. We never wish to exclude him. But He *is* with us; and by prayer, we secure his assistance.

There is indeed a sense in which you cannot give grace; it is as to the success of means. But for this you are not responsible. This is the Lord's part. But what is yours? Think of another case. The husbandman cannot raise an ear of corn; but he can manure the land, and plough, and sow. And he knows this is indispensable to a crop. And how rarely does he labour in vain! If God promises to communicate his blessing in the use of means, they who refuse them have no right to complain; and they who employ them, have no reason to be discouraged.

Another—But I will answer no more of your objections. You *know* they are excuses. You *know* they are such as you will be ashamed to urge before the Judge of all. You know that your consciences are not satisfied with them even *now*. I will therefore, in the

IV. Place, conclude with SOME ANIMADVERSIONS AND ADMONITIONS.

And "to whom," as says the Prophet, "shall I speak and give warning?"

I must first address those who at present *are unconnected in life.* How powerfully does our subject say to such, "Be ye not unequally yoked together with unbelievers." This will render the performance of family religion in all cases difficult, and in many, impossible. It is lamentable enough, with regard to pious individuals themselves, that while they want every kind of encouragement and assistance, they are allied to those who, instead of helping them, must oppose and in-

jure: but it is also to be deplored, as producing partially or wholly the ruin of domestic godliness. When Peter enforces relative duties, he admits that unless we dwell "as heirs together of the grace of life," our "prayers will be hindered." How can they rule well their own house? How can they seek a godly seed, while, instead of striving together, they thus draw different ways? and, when the one drawing heavenward is the least likely to be successful; the opposite attractions falling in with the depravity of human nature? For evil wants only to be seen or heard; but good must be enforced with "line upon line, and precept upon precept."

But there are those who are already in family alliance, *who are living in the neglect of family devotion.* And this is the case, I fear, with not a few. And yet you would be offended if you were called infidels —but according to the Apostle you have no reason: "He that provideth not for his own, and especially those of his own house, hath denied the faith, and is *worse* than an infidel." Many of you attend regularly the public services of the sanctuary, and we love to see you in the courts of the Lord, and willing to hear his words. But if you gained good in the House of God, you would carry it away, and diffuse it in your own. Yet when you are followed home, there is no more appearance of religion in your habitations, than in the houses of heathens. Heathens! forgive me this wrong. We blaspheme you by the comparison. *You* had, not only your gods for the country, but your household gods: which you regarded as your defenders, and guardians, and comforters; and which nothing could induce you to give up or neglect—

What can I say more? He has threatened to pour out his fury upon the nations that know him not, and upon the families that call not upon his name. But I would rather work upon your ingenuousness, than upon your fears. God has revealed himself under a *domestic* relation, and calls himself "The God of all the families of the earth." And will you refuse him in this endearing character? Will you rob yourselves and your families of your greatest mutual honour and blessedness? An angel, in his intercourse with this world, sees nothing so uninviting and dreary as a house, though rich as a mansion and splendid as a palace, devoid of the service and presence of God! But what so lovely, so attractive as the family altar, "garlanded by the social feelings," and approached morning and evening by the high-priest of the domestic temple, and his train of worshippers? There the master's authority is softened, and he feels respect for the servant who is kneeling at his side, and "free indeed." There the servant's submission is sweetened, and he loves, while he obeys, a master who is praying for his welfare. Here the father, worn down with the labour of the day, is cheered and refreshed. Here the anxious mother hushes her cares to rest. "If any thing in the day has been diverted from its course, now all finds its place, and glides along in its wonted channel. If the relative affections have declined during the day, the evening service, like the dew of heaven, revives and enlivens them. If offences have come, they are easily forgiven, when all are asking for pardon for themselves. Every angry word, every wrong temper, every petulant feeling, flies before the hallowing influence of social devotion."

I must address myself to those *who perform it.* I beseech you, brethren, "suffer the word of exhortation."—Beware of formality. God is a Spirit. He looketh to the heart.—Beware of tediousness and length. "Use not vain repetitions as the heathen do; for they think they shall be heard for their much speaking." "God is in heaven, and thou upon the earth; therefore let thy words be few." God cannot be fatigued: but he knows our frame; he remembers that we are dust.—Beware of lateness. When languor and drowsiness and listlessness prevail, you would bless your households more by suffering them to retire, than engaging them in services irksome to the performers, and insulting to the receiver. "If ye offer the blind for sacrifice, is it not evil? and if ye offer the lame and sick, is it not evil? Offer it now unto thy governor, will he be pleased with thee, or accept thy person? saith the Lord of hosts. But cursed be the deceiver which hath in his flock a male, and voweth and sacrificeth unto the Lord a corrupt thing; for I am a great King, saith the Lord of hosts, and my name is dreadful among the heathen."

I must not overlook those who *are living in religious families.* The lines have fallen to you in pleasant places: you have a goodly heritage. From how many snares are you secured! What opportunities of instruction and improvement do you possess! What pious excitements, and encouragements, and aids do you enjoy! But your responsibility grows with your advantages. To you much is given. From you much will be required. For "to him that knoweth to do good, and doeth it not, to him it is sin." There may be wicked servants in religious families: such an one was Gehazi, who waited upon Elisha. And there may be wicked children in religious families: such an one was Ham, who called even Noah his father! But if you abuse or neglect your means and privileges, your guilt and your condemnation will be greater than those of Pagans. "It shall be more tolerable for Sodom and Gomorrah in the day of judgment than for you"—"There shall be weeping and gnashing of teeth when ye shall see Abraham and Isaac and Jacob in the kingdom of God, and ye yourselves shut out."

Finally, there are some who *reside in irreligious households.* You, we sincerely pity. Whatever temporal advantages you enjoy, they can never compensate for your spiritual privations. How sad, and how awful, to see the Sabbath polluted; the House of God forsaken; every book read, but the Bible. To hear, instead of prayer, profane swearing, and the taking God's name in vain, instead of praise. Or, if no gross immoralities prevail, to witness, lying down and rising up, no acknowledgment of God; but a practical, if not verbal rejection of Him; every thing really saying unto God, "Depart from us, we desire not the knowledge of thy ways."

Surely such a situation, since you have known God, or rather have been known of Him, has not been the object of your choice. But you may have been providentially placed there. You have perhaps been called there, being a servant; or you have been called there, being a child. Be mindful of your danger, and "watch and pray, lest you enter into temptation." Look to Him who preserved saints in Cæsar's household, and Abijah in the family of Jeroboam, that he may secure you. You are much observed. Therefore walk circumspectly. Be harmless and blameless. And not only be without rebuke, but hold forth the word of life—not by stepping out of your sphere—not by talking (though a word fitly spoken, O how good is it!) but by your tempers, your behaviour, your character.

And thus you may be the instruments of introducing religion where you ought to have found it. Not only have wives thus won their husbands without the word, but servants have removed prejudices from their masters and mistresses, and induced them to attend the Gospel. And thus children have conveyed religion to those from whom they ought to have derived it. "Well," said a mother, one day, weeping—her daughter being proposed as a candidate for Christian communion—"I will resist no longer. How can I bear to see my dear child love and read the Scripture, while I never look into the Bible—To see her retire, and seek God, while I never pray —To see her going to the Lord's table, while his death is nothing to me."—"Ah!" said she, to the Minister who had called to inform her of her daughter's desire—wiping her eyes—"Yes, Sir, I know she is right—and I am wrong. I have seen her firm under reproach, and patient under provocation, and cheerful in all her sufferings. While in her late illness she was looking for her dissolution, heaven stood in her face.—O! that I was as fit to die! I ought to have taught her: but I am sure she has taught me. How can I bear to see her joining the Church of God and leaving me behind—perhaps for ever!" From that hour she prayed in earnest, that the God of her child would be her God, and was soon seen walking in company with her in the way everlasting. Is this mere supposition? More than one eye, in reading this allusion, will drop a testimony to the truth of it. "We speak that we do know, and testify that we have seen." May God bless us, and make us blessings! Amen.

LECTURE IV.

THE CHRISTIAN, IN THE CHURCH.

" That thou mayest know how thou oughtest to behave thyself in the House of God, which is the Church of the living God."—1 Tim. iii. 15.

THE connexions of life are many and various; and they have all their appropriate claims and advantages. Some of these relations are natural; some, civil; some, commercial; some, intellectual and literary. But the most important of all alliances are those of a religious quality. The bonds of these are not flesh and blood; but faith and love that are in Christ Jesus. These regard the spirit in man; and fall under the power of the world to come. All other connexions have their sphere only in this life; but these aspire after "new heavens and a new earth, wherein dwelleth righteousness." All other unions, however firm, or however tender, having answered the destinations of Providence, will be dissolved by death; but though Christians die, *they* are still related. The separation between them is only *temporary;* a period of re-union will assuredly and speedily arrive. Yea, it is only *partial:* even now—

> "The saints below, and all the dead,
> But one communion make;
> All join in Christ, their living head,
> And of his grace partake."

You are to view the Christian, this morning, In the CHURCH.

In this state Timothy was when Paul addressed him in the words which we have chosen for our motto—*" That thou mayest know how thou oughtest to behave thyself in the House of God, which is the Church of the living God."*—*Him,* it is true, he addressed as a minister; and his official station demanded a line of conduct becoming it. But every Christian has a place to fill, and a part to act, in the Church of God; and he needs to be informed and admonished concerning it.—Let us,

I. Explain the CONDITION OUR SUBJECT SUPPOSES.

II. The OBLIGATIONS WE ARE UNDER TO ENTER IT.

III. The DUTIES WHICH ARISE OUT OF IT.

I. The CONDITION OUR SUBJECT SUPPOSES.

Now when we speak of the Christian's being in the *Church,* it is necessary to observe two acceptations of the word in the Scripture, as well as in common discourse.

It is sometimes used to comprise *all the redeemed and sanctified people of God.* These, in every age; in every country; under every dispensation, whether Patriarchal, Jewish, or Evangelical; all these, whether residing in earth, or in heaven; all these constitute one church. And of this we read, when it is said, "The church of God, which he hath purchased with his own blood." "We are come to the church of the first-born." "Christ loved the church, and gave himself for it." "That he might present it to himself a glorious church, not having spot, or wrinkle, or any such thing." However distinguished from each other, all *real* Christians, "who worship God in the Spirit, and rejoice in Christ Jesus, and have no confidence in the flesh," belong to *this* church; and to be found in it, is an unspeakable privilege, and constitutes what we mean by "the communion of saints" in the Apostles' Creed—a mutual participation in all their work, honour, and blessedness. But it is not of *this* we *now* speak. *This* is the Church universal; and in this we are necessarily found, as soon as ever we are chosen and called out of the world.

But the word much more frequently means *a particular community, or company of believers associated together for religious purposes.* This coincides with the language of the Nineteenth Article—"A Church is a congregation of faithful men, in which the pure word of God is preached, and the Sacraments are duly administered according to Christ's ordinance in all things that of necessity are requisite to the same." In conformity to this, we read of "the messengers" not of the Church—but "of the churches:" not of the Church—but "the churches which were in Christ." And thus we read of "the seven churches which are in Asia:" of "the churches which were in Galatia;" and of "the churches throughout all Judea, and Galilee, and Samaria:" and what they were may be inferred from their "walking in the fear of the Lord, and in the comfort of the Holy Ghost, and being multiplied." Thus, too, we read of "the church at Philippi," and "the church at Colosse," and so of the rest.

In advancing further, nothing would be more easy than to furnish matter for dispute. My object, however, is not controversial, but practical. It does not require me to undertake the task of attempting to determine the particular form of a Christian church, or the precise mode of administering divine ordinances in it; but only to show, that it is the duty of a Christian to be found in a Church-State;

giving up himself not only to the Lord, but to his people by the will of God; and walking with those who profess to continue steadfastly in the Apostles' doctrine, and in fellowship, and in breaking of bread, and in prayer.

Yet there are some who have here, we will not call them their arguments, but their excuses. To such union, they prefer rambling, or at least detachment. They fix nowhere, or at least commune nowhere. No church is wide enough, or strict enough, or pure enough, or sound enough—for them: no one is completely modified to their taste. Constantine said to such a self-conceited Christian, " Take a ladder, and climb to heaven by thyself." If all were like-minded with some, there would be no such thing as a Church on earth.

I am aware of what I shall incur from certain quarters; but I shall deliver myself with the firmness of conviction. It is not necessary that we should approve of every opinion or usage among those with whom we connect ourselves. It is far better in lesser matters, if we have faith, to have it to ourselves before God; and to exercise forbearance and self-denial, than, for the sake of some trifling difference, to endeavour to originate a new party, or remain destitute of the benefits, and violating the obligations of social Christianity. We should guard against an *undue* attachment to any particular scheme of Church policy, when, though the abettors profess to be governed by the Scripture only, and consider every iota of their system as perfectly clear and binding; others, more numerous than themselves, and equally wise and good, and entitled to the leading of the Spirit of Truth, draw a very different conclusion from the same premises. Mr. Newton, speaking of the several systems under which, as so many banners, the different denominations of Christians are ranged, observes, that " there is usually something left out, which ought to have been taken in, and something admitted, of supposed advantage, unauthorised by the Scripture standard. A Bible-Christian, therefore, will see much to approve in a *variety* of forms and parties: the providence of God may lead and fix him in a more immediate connexion with some *one* of them; but his spirit and affection will not be confined within these *narrow* enclosures. He insensibly borrows and unites that which is excellent in *each*, perhaps without knowing how far he agrees with them, because he finds all in the written word." With regard to myself, though I have a preference, and attach *comparative* importance to the things wherein pious men differ, yet there is no body of Christians, holding the Head, with whom I could not hold communion, and to whom I would not join myself, if circumstances withheld me from my own denomination, rather than remain a religious *solitaire.*

It will be, I presume, committing an un-

pardonable sin with bigots, when I express my persuasion, after all I have read of the claims, whether Episcopalian or Presbyterian, or Independent, to the *only* scriptural standard, that there is no *very* definite plan of Church Government laid down in the New Testament; so that while one mode is canonized, every other is absolutely wrong. Deviation from prescribed orders is sinful; but where there is no law, there is no transgression. " As oft," says the Apostle, " as ye eat this bread, and drink this cup, ye do show the Lord's death till he come?" Now had he told us *how* often we are to do this, we must observe such times only, or oppose the will of God. Is it so, now the thing is left undecided? May there not be a difference in the frequency of its observance, without sin? It is otherwise with the recurrence of the Sabbath: this is determined both by command and example. It would have been criminal in Moses not to have made the snuffers of pure gold; or the holy oil of a mixture of certain ingredients; or the priest's robe of such a quality, such a colour, and such a length: for he had express instructions to do so, and the pattern of every thing was shown him in the Mount. But in what mount has our model of circumstantial regulation been exhibited? What Moses received it? Where do we find a particularity of detail in the Gospels of the Evangelists; or in the Acts, and Epistles of the Apostles? Where do we find many of the materials of angry debate and exclusiveness which have occupied so much time, and spoiled so much temper, in the system of Christianity?—A system designed for every nation, and people, and kindred, and tongue—a system too sublime in its aim to lose itself in minuteness— too anxious to unite its followers in great matters, to magnify little ones—too truly noble, not to be condescending—too tender, not to be tolerant—too impartial, not to say to its subjects, receive one another as Christ also has received you; you that are strong, bear the infirmities of the weak, and not please yourselves.

Now we do not pretend to say, that all who do not thus enter a Christian Church are not in a state of grace. Some, after they are converted, may not have the opportunity. Some are repulsed by the rigidness of admission: they cannot pronounce every Shibboleth of a confession; or express their belief of the divinity of every part of prescribed discipline. —These are to be pitied: the *blame* lies with the exactors of such righteousness. Some, otherwise disposed to come forward, are held back by a sense of unworthiness, or a dread of hypocrisy, or a fear of causing " the way of truth to be evil spoken of," by their acting unbecoming the Gospel. These are to be instructed and encouraged.

But after these concessions, we make no scruple to say, that if a Christian does not be-

F

long to a Christian Church, he is not walking according to God's appointment, and the order of the Gospel; but is living in the loss of privilege, and the omission of duty. It was not thus with the Christians of whom we have accounts in the New Testament. They are represented not as wandering sheep, but a flock having a shepherd and a fold. Not as stones loose and scattered on the ground, but built up a spiritual house. Not as separate and solitary plants and trees, but as a vineyard, a garden watched and watered. Not as rovers and vagrants, in the highways and hedges—but as "fellow-citizens with the saints, and of the household of God."— This brings us to consider,

II. THE OBLIGATIONS WE ARE UNDER TO ENTER THIS STATE.

Let us notice four articles—*Suitability*— *Consolation*—*Safety*—and *Usefulness*.

The first claim is derived from *Suitability*. This state accords with the very constitution of man. He is not only a rational, but a social creature: and so natural are his social feelings, that they can only be rooted up with his very being. Religion therefore does not aim to destroy or injure those propensions; but it sanctifies them. It opens a new sphere for their developement. It presents to them new objects of interest and attachment.

Like attracts like; and when we become godly, our longing is for godly association. Then we pray, "Be merciful unto me, as thou usest to do unto them that love thy name:" then we confess, "I am a companion of them that fear thee:" then, "we take hold of the skirt of him that is a Jew, saying, we will go with you, for we have heard that God is with you:" then, we "choose rather to suffer affliction with the people of God, than enjoy the pleasures of sin for a season." These fall in with our new views, and hopes, and fears, and joys, and sorrows. These are now our fellow-learners, fellow-travellers, fellow-labourers, fellow-warriors—yea, whosoever now, doeth the will of our Father who is in heaven, the same is our brother and sister and mother.

Saul, therefore, upon his conversion, assayed to join himself to the disciples: and every one, when he falls under the same influence, will be like-minded with him. It would be strange indeed, if when we turn away from the vain and the wicked, we should find ourselves in a state of social destitution and abandonment. But God has expressly provided against this repulsion of loneliness. We do not become outcasts. He takes us up. "Wherefore," says he, "come out from among them, and be ye separate, and touch not the unclean thing, and I will receive you, and be a Father unto you; and ye shall be my sons and daughters, saith the Lord Almighty." Ye shall not be homeless and friendless. I will place you in my family. You shall have better relations than those you have resigned; and more valuable connexions than those who have renounced you. When you part with the world, you enter the Church, and this is more glorious than all the mountains of prey. You rise in rank; and so far from being losers, "Verily, I say unto you, there is no man that hath left house, or brethren, or sisters, or father, or mother, or wife, or children, or lands, for my sake, and the Gospel's, but he shall receive an hundredfold now in this time, houses, and brethren, and sisters, and mothers, and children, and lands, with persecutions; and in the world to come eternal life." We therefore

Derive the second claim from *Consolation*. This is the law of Christ: as we "have opportunity, let us do good unto all men; but especially unto them that are of the household of faith." Their members, therefore, have the first claim upon a Christian Church for sympathy and succour. And the privilege arising from thence will appear to be the greater, when it is considered, that the discharge of this duty does not depend upon obligation only. Christians feel themselves disposed, as well as bound to this good work. Their principles lead them to "rejoice with them that do rejoice," and to "weep with them that weep." And is it nothing to belong to a community, who, instead of envying and hating you for your successes, and endowments, and comforts—it is so always with the world—will glorify God on your behalf? Is it nothing to be connected with those who feel it to be their duty and their privilege to guard your reputation, to explore your wants, to soften your cares, to soothe your sorrows; and where, not only the minister and the office-bearers, but all the members, will visit the fatherless and the widows in their affliction, and comfort them that are cast down?

The poor and the needy are too generally overlooked, not to say despised by the world; and from the treatment they receive from others, there is danger of their feeling a kind of self-degradation that makes them regardless of their conduct. But here they have a name and a place. Here they feel an importance, that while it raises them morally, does not injure them in their civil dependance. Here their elevation does not draw them off from their stations; but improves them for every relative duty, by producing self-respect, and augmenting a sense of responsibility. Here their fellow-members, above them in condition, can without envy or uneasiness see their equality with themselves, or even their pre-eminence, in experience. "Let the brother of low degree rejoice in that he is exalted; but the rich, in that he is made low, because as the flower of the grass he shall pass away."

The Church is the only society in which it is either possible or proper to merge the ranks of life. Temporal things divide men, and keep them separate; and they have always a tendency to carry to excess those distinctions which are allowable, and even necessary. However disposed towards each other, the small and the great cannot unite in secular friendship. The master and the servant cannot consort together either in the upper or the lower room. The peasant and the nobleman cannot inhabit the same cottage, or the same mansion. The noble and the vulgar cannot feed together, either at the dinner of herbs or at the stalled ox. But here they all surround the same table. Here all eat the same spiritual meat, and drink the same spiritual drink. Here the rich and the poor meet together. Here all are partakers of the same common salvation. Here all are one in Christ Jesus. Here every disadvantage is compensated. "Also the sons of the stranger that join themselves to the Lord, to serve him, and to love the name of the Lord, to be his servants, every one that keepeth the Sabbath from polluting it, and taketh hold of my covenant; even them will I bring to my holy mountain, and make them joyful in my house of prayer: their burnt-offerings and their sacrifices shall be accepted upon mine altar; for mine house shall be called a house of prayer for all people."

Safety furnishes a third claim. For it is not to be overlooked that this state fortifies individuals against the influence of example, and number, and ridicule, and reproach. It will be allowed that a man ought to do what is right, if no one stands by him. Yet singularity is sometimes a great trial; and to brave all the consequences, in many cases, requires more moral heroism than is always possessed even by one that is upright and sincere. But when he stands in connexion with others; when he sees himself countenanced and supported by those he deems wiser and better than himself; this gives him confidence and courage; and he resembles a soldier who advances boldly with his comrades, when he would hesitate and falter alone. "Two are better than one; because they have a good reward for their labour. For if they fall, the one will lift up his fellow: but wo to him that is alone when he falleth; for he hath not another to help him up. And if one prevail against him, two shall withstand him: and a threefold cord is not quickly broken."

Indecision is as perilous as it is uncomfortable. And therefore the Apostle says, "Resist the devil, and he will flee from you." For while the enemy sees you unfixed and hesitating, he yet hopes to succeed, and this protracts his endeavours: whereas when he finds you determined, he desponds, and departs. How many temptations are cut off, as soon as we cease to halt between two opinions, and proclaim ourselves to be on the Lord's side. And how much circumspection is also hereby induced. He who makes no pretences to a thing, is not judged by it; but a profession of religion is of great value, as it tends to check what is evil, and to bind us to what is righteous, by subjecting us to self-reproach and censure of the others, when we act inconsistently. "Does this temper or conduct become a member of the Church of Christ? Do I wear his livery, and disown him? Have I opened my mouth to the Lord, and can I go back? Are not the eyes of many upon me? And have they not a right to ask, What do ye more than others?"

And let me put it to your conscience, whether this be not one of the reasons which operate to keep you out of the Church. Ye feel yourselves now in a larger place. You have more liberty. You can do your own ways, and find your own pleasures, and speak your own words, on God's holy day. Your tongues are your own: who is Lord over you? And—"I do not profess to be a saint," seems an excuse to prevent or silence all the qualms of the sinner. "I know not," says Doddridge, "a more dreadful mark of destruction upon a man, than a fear to be under an obligation to avoid what is evil, and to cleave to that which is good." A man properly concerned for his spiritual and everlasting welfare, would feel every assistance, every excitement, every motive, in such an important course, a privilege: and such a privilege constitutes a powerful argument on behalf of a Church relation.

Therefore it has a fourth claim. It is *Usefulness*. How much more is a man's zeal drawn forth as soon as he has declared himself in any cause; and he partakes of the spirit of the party. When his vote is solicited for a candidate at the time of an election, though he feels scarcely a preference before, yet as soon as he has avowed himself for either of the applicants, his indifference is destroyed, his fervour is excited, and he is carried along with the proceedings, until he is intensely interested; and his happiness or misery seems suspended on the success. Indeed, whatever we keep concealed within, is likely to lose some of its hold upon us: it is by speaking of it, by pushing it forward, by acting constantly upon it, that we feel more of its impression and influence.

But there is another view to be taken of the subject. We all know how much is to be done by union, even when the parts are inconsiderable in themselves. Thus sands make the mountains. The cable that holds the ship in the storm is composed of small strings. A single soldier that has missed his way, may chance-wise do some little good;

but he is efficient only as acting with a corps; and the war requires an army. If the liberal soul *deviseth* liberal things, how are good schemes to be carried *into effect*, and how are useful institutions to be *supported*, but by union and co-operation? How much often does *one* Christian society accomplish by its collective wisdom, and benevolence, and exertion! Why are the Churches called candlesticks, but because they are instruments, holding forth and diffusing the light of life!

The public worship of God ought always to be considered as an unspeakable benefit to mankind. Amidst the cares and toils and distresses of life, "God is known in his palaces for a refuge." He is "the Father of the fatherless, and the Husband of the widow, in his holy habitation." There the tempted are succoured; and the weak strengthened; and the wandering directed. The sanctuary opens a door for the weary traveller to enter and refresh himself. It awakens, by its administrations, the curiosity of the thoughtful and the attention of the careless; and how often have those who came from no pious motive, been known of all, judged of all, and compelled to exclaim, God is in the midst of them of a truth. While we are anxious for more success to attend the means of grace, we are not aware of the extent and the degree in which they *are* useful. What an injury would be sustained in a neighbourhood if they were given up!

But it is by *Churches* that the ministry of the word and the ordinances of religion are supported and dispensed; and by their means the system of conversion and edification is continued and perpetuated. Individuals die; but thus, as some are removed, others are added. Thus member succeeds member, and pastor succeeds pastor; and, as in the case of a river, change leaves sameness, and permanency is produced by succession.—But we have,

III. To consider THE DUTIES ARISING FROM THE STATE.

These are various as well as important. They relate,

First, To the *Worship*. This a Christian will value as the appointment of Him, who knowing what is in man, ordains what is necessary to him, and delights in the prosperity of his servants. When, therefore, God says, "Seek ye my face," his heart answers, "Thy face, Lord, will I seek." And as he obeys from love, he will never exclaim, "What a weariness is it to serve the Lord! when will the Sabbath be gone?" He calls the Sabbath a delight, and the holy of the Lord, honourable. He loves the habitation of his House. He finds his word and eats it; and it is to him the joy and the rejoicing of his heart. If others can dispense with ordi-

nances, he never rises above his need of them. He feels that something is still wanting to his knowledge, his graces, his comfort; and though he holds communion with God habitually, and wishes in all his ways to acknowledge Him, he sees what an adaptation there is in the means of grace to afford him relief and assistance. His own experience stimulates him,—for he has seen His power and glory in the sanctuary; while the promise justifies his most enlarged expectation—"In all places where I record my Name, I will come unto thee, and I will bless thee." "They that wait upon the Lord shall renew their strength: they shall mount up with wings as eagles; they shall run and not be weary, and they shall walk and not faint."

Cases of prevention will sometimes occur; but he will take heed that they are not excuses. And, as he would not love and serve the creature more than the Creator, he will see that the hinderances are such as would keep him from all other engagements. And if they can be removed by order and skill and diligence in his affairs; or by a little expense in conveyance, saved from vanity and excess; he will remove them. And when the sick relation, or his own bed of languishing, or the painful accident, detains him at home, he will feel himself the prisoner of the Lord, and say, with the royal exile, "When I remember these things, I pour out my soul in me: for I had gone with the multitude; I went with them to the house of God, with the voice of joy and praise, with a multitude that kept holy day." I never believe those, who turning their backs upon the temple, tell us that they pass their time in retired devotion. One duty pleads for another, and prepares for another, and helps another. It is the same with neglect: we may infer one omission from another. It is very questionable too, when they tell us, that the preacher can teach them no more than they know already. It is the remark of an old writer, that "he who will learn of none but himself, is sure to have a fool for *his* master." Besides, novelty of information is not the only or principal object in attending the house of God: but, as Judge Hale said, with regard to himself, "to be impressed and affected; and to have old and known truth reduced to experience and practice."

He therefore regards the means of grace *constantly*. He attends not one part of the Sabbath only, but both parts: and surely two public services cannot be too much for a day dedicated to devotion. Nor will he attend on the Sabbath only, but on the week-day also. He will be thankful for a service which refreshes and nerves his mind amidst the cares and toils of his calling; and he will remember that, as a professor of religion, he has stipulated for his regular attendance, by his joining the Church to which he belongs. Nothing can be more painful to the feelings of a minister, when he comes to water his flock, than to find many of them not at the well. Perhaps, too, he has chosen his subject, and studied it, and prayed over it, with a peculiar reference to the individual then absent. And how often has something been delivered in the absence of that individual, singularly appropriate to his condition or experience; something that might have directed and comforted him to the end of life, and have been remembered in death with pleasure. And thus neglect has been punished with regret.

But you are required to attend the means of divine appointment *spiritually.* Ye are not to think it enough to draw nigh to Him with the mouth, and honour Him with the lip, while the heart is far from him. The Lord looketh to the heart. There is such a thing as an attendance on ordinances, when there is no attention in them; at least none that comes up to the demand, to "worship in spirit and in truth."

And as Paul may plant and Apollos water, but God alone can give the increase, we must attend, in *humbleness* of mind, and never without *prayer,* that the Spirit may help our infirmities, and render the means available to our profit. When the preacher enters upon his work in such an assembly as this, "it is as the smell of a field which the Lord hath blessed :"—And,

Secondly, These duties regard the *Minister,* who is placed over you in the Lord. Add not to his difficulties. He has his trials as a man; and he has his trials as a Christian; and in addition to both these, he has trials peculiar to his office. Could he have foreseen all at the beginning, he would have been disheartened at the entrance; but his work is like John's little book, a bitter sweet, and the sweet comes first. You find it hard enough to manage one temper; what must be the task of governing a multitude, including every diversity! After the engagement of years, he would yield to many a temptation to withdraw, but that necessity is laid upon him. Never successful according to his wishes; and sometimes apparently useless: he is often ready to lay down his commission at his Master's feet; to say, "I have laboured in vain, I have spent my strength for nought and in vain." Bound to engage at the times appointed, and knowing what is expected from him; in his perplexity arising from choice of subjects, in his barrenness of thought, in his unfitness of feeling, in the study which is a weariness to the flesh, and the exhaustion of spirits gendered by intense application; his heart knoweth his own bitterness; death worketh in him, but life in you. Encourage him. Welcome his instructions. Yield to his reproofs. Respect that authority which he has received, not for destruction but edifi-

cation. "Obey them that have the rule over you, and submit yourselves: for they watch for your souls, as they that must give account; that they may do it with joy, and not with grief; for that is unprofitable for you."

A minister must be very mean-spirited if he regards his salary as alms, or benefactions from his people. What they give, they more than have out in services; and "the labourer is worthy of his hire." Has not God ordained, that they who preach the Gospel, should live of the Gospel? And is not this law founded in equity and justice? Would not the same talents the man devotes to the service of the sanctuary, provide for himself and his family, if employed in secular concerns? This is a delicate point for a minister to handle; and he surely would never bring it forward if he could do justice to the part of the subject before us, without it. But he will resign it as soon as possible; and leave it in the words the Holy Ghost teacheth. Let congregations compare themselves with it; and especially those individuals in them who pay more annually to the most menial of their attendants, than to the shepherd of their souls.

"Let him," says the Apostle, "be with you without fear." And again: "Know them that labour among you, and are over you in the Lord, and admonish you; and esteem them very highly in love for their work's sake." He means, not only in reward of their work, but in *aid* of it: for unless you *magnify* his office, you are not likely to be *impressed* by it; and as your regard *for* the preacher declines, so will you profit *by* him. Your relation to him is such, that, if he is degraded, you are disgraced in him; and if he is honoured, you share in his respectability. Ministers are men; and "the best of men are but men at the best." You are not required to approve of their infirmities, or even to be ignorant of them: but surely you will not be suspicious; you will not invite or welcome reflection and insinuation; nor, like too many, speak of him, or suffer him to be spoken of, before children and servants and strangers, with a levity and freedom, far from being adapted to increase or preserve esteem and respect. You will consider his character not only as forming his crown, but as essential to his acceptance and success. "Receive him therefore in the Lord with all gladness; and hold such in reputation."

Thirdly, These duties respect *your Fellow Members.* They are all comprehended in love: and you are required to "love one another out of a pure heart fervently;" to "love as brethren." Has a fellow Christian erred? "Thou shalt not hate thy brother in thine heart: thou shalt in any wise rebuke thy neighbour, and not suffer sin upon him." Has he been overtaken in a fault? "Ye that are spiritual are to restore such an one in the spirit of meekness, considering yourselves lest you also be tempted." Is he declining in zeal, and negligent in duty ? You are to " consider him, to provoke him to love and to good works." Is he oppressed ? You are to bear his " burdens, and so fulfil the law of Christ." Is he in want ? You are to give him such things as are needful. " Now," says the Apostle, " we exhort you, brethren, warn them that are unruly, comfort the feeble-minded, support the weak, be patient toward all men. See that none render evil for evil unto any man ; but ever follow that which is good, both among yourselves and to all men."

Fourthly, Your duty concerns the welfare and prosperity of the *whole Interest*. Not that you are to be exclusively attentive to your *own* community. You are unfit to be a member of *any* Christian Church unless you can say, " grace be with all them that love our Lord Jesus Christ in sincerity." But our conditions and circumstances must regulate not the principle, but the exercises and the expressions of duty. The private affections are not incompatible with the public, but conduct to them ; and the way, the best way, the only way, by which we can promote the good of the whole, is by advancing the good of a part. The man who, in opposing patriotism, pleads that the world is his country, and all mankind his fellow-citizens, has no country, no fellow-citizens. The object for which he pretends to be concerned is too indistinct to impress ; too distant to approach ; too extensive to grasp. To come nearer. If a man were to disregard his family, under pretence that he was acting on a broader, nobler principle, and for an object less selfish and contracted, even the nation at large : he would soon be told that the nation consists of families ; that one of these is committed to his care ; that this he *can* improve ; that this he *ought* peculiarly to regard, even for the sake of the public. " He that provideth not for his own, especially those of his own house, hath denied the faith, and is worse than an infidel." It is much the same here. It is the will of God that we feel a special sympathy with the religious society to which we belong. This demands our immediate attention, and efforts, and sacrifices ; and all the members in their respective places, and by all the influences they can employ, should seek to excel to the edifying of the Church.

Now the first thing that seems to strike us with regard to the prosperity of a cause is the *increase* of its members. There is, however, one kind of accession which a church should not value nor seek after. It is the drawing members from other churches, where they already hear " the truth as it is in Jesus," and enjoy the fellowship of the Gospel. We do nothing, in filling one place, by emptying another, where the same work is carrying on. The transferring of soldiers from one regiment into another, does not increase

the king's army, or add to the defence of the country. The thing is to gain fresh recruits. Our aim should be to make converts, not proselytes. But it is delightful when the inquiry is often made, What shall we do to be saved ?—when sinners are turned from darkness unto light, and the power of Satan unto God : when Zion, surprised at the quality and number of her sons and daughters, exclaims, " who hath begotten me these ? where have they been ?"—and the Lord adds to the Church daily such as shall be saved.

Harmony is included in the welfare of a church. It can only edify itself in love. " For where envying and strife is, there is confusion and every evil work. But the wisdom that is from above is first pure, then peaceable, gentle, and easy to be entreated, full of mercy and good fruits, without partiality, and without hypocrisy. And the fruit of righteousness is sown in peace of them that make peace."

It takes in also *purity*. " Therefore," says the Prophet, " keep peace *and* truth :" and, says the Apostle, " speaking the *truth* in love." The church of Ephesus is commended for not bearing them that are evil. Our concern for the sanctity of our communion is to appear in maintaining godly discipline : in not admitting irreligious characters, whatever recommendations they may otherwise possess ; and in excluding them when they discover themselves to be ungodly after they have been admitted. Improper individuals will occasionally enter the Church : there is no preventing it, unless we were omniscient. But we cannot search the heart ; and our leaning ought always to be on the side of charity : it is better to be mistaken and deceived, than to be suspicious and censorious, or to destroy one for whom Christ died. But when the mask under which the man entered is shifted aside, and his conduct appears sinful, " put away from among you," says the Scripture, " that wicked person." He disgraces you ; and he will contaminate—" a little leaven leaveneth the whole lump."

Some Christians not only individually but collectively do not sufficiently think upon and pursue " whatsoever things are lovely and of good report." A church may be austere and harsh and forbidding : but much of its usefulness depends upon its amiableness. And this will arise from its character for benevolence, and public spirit, and liberality ; and from its joining, with firmness of adherence to essential truth, latitude in things circumstantial ; from its tenderness in receiving the weak, but not to doubtful disputations ; from its readiness to receive all as Christ has received us, to the glory of God.

Towards this prosperity every member should aim and labour to contribute, by his prayers, his conversation, his example, his temper, his influence. And a church thus flourishing; increasing with all the increase of God, in number, and peace, and sanctity, and every moral excellency, is the noblest sight on earth: and full of attraction, and impression, and "a spectacle to the world, to angels, and to men:" it looks forth as the morning, clear as the moon, bright as the sun, and terrible as an army with banners.—Let us conclude.

First, We have been speaking of those that are within. But there are some who are yet *without*, whose condition we lament, and to whom we therefore would address the language of inquiry and invitation, "Come in, thou blessed of the Lord; why tarriest thou without?" And where do we find these? We find them among *you*, whose character and conduct are irreproachable, who constantly attend the preaching of the Cross, who are glad when they say unto you, Let us go into the House of the Lord; who have even the worship of God in your families; and are not strangers to your closets—and yet keep aloof from the table of the Lord, where with his dying breath he is saying, "Do this in remembrance of me." We find them amongst those of you who so often remain as spectators at the holy solemnity, and looking down upon the privileged partakers, sigh and say, "How goodly are thy tents, O Jacob, and thy tabernacles, O Israel!"—yet are restrained from approaching, not by carnality but timidity; and by forgetting that "all the fitness He requireth is to feel your need of Him." We find them among you, my young friends; you, who are shunning the paths of the destroyer; you, whose consciences are awake, whose hearts are tender, whose minds are impressed by divine things, —and who are detained by looking for a change too sudden and too sensible; and for a kind and degree of evidence and assurance by no means necessary.

People talk of the young, and seem to require more satisfactory evidence with regard to them, than with regard to older candidates. But wherefore? Do persons grow more simple and open and undesigning as they advance in life? Who are the members by whom churches have been troubled and disgraced? Not those who joined themselves to the Lord young, and very young too. I never knew a minister who had to repent of encouraging such communicants. And how many youths have I known, who, humanly speaking, would have been excellent and useful characters now, but they were not encouraged when, as our Saviour says, they were not far from the kingdom of God. Their foot was on the threshold of conversion; but no one took them by the hand, to draw them in—but there were enough ready to draw them back: the world laid hold of them; or their convictions, for want of cherishing, died away. Some of them are now

sitting in the seat of the scornful; others, though not the victims of error and vice, are in a state of indifference with regard to the holy communion, which is likely to continue for life. Whereas, had they entered the Church when there was nothing to justify their refusal, they would have been decided; their return into the world would have been cut off; they would have felt identified with a peculiar people; their impressions would have been formed into principles and habits; and the whole man would have been changed from glory to glory as by the Spirit of the Lord.

My young friends, hesitate, we beseech you, no longer. Fulfil ye our joy in verifying the promise, "I will pour water upon him that is thirsty, and floods upon the dry ground; I will pour my Spirit upon thy seed, and my blessing upon thine offspring: and they shall spring up as among the grass, as willows by the water-courses. One shall say, I am the Lord's; and another shall call himself by the name of Jacob; and another shall subscribe with his hand unto the Lord, and surname himself by the name of Israel."

Then will your peace be as a river. You will gain all the succours your age and your condition require. You will become examples to others, in the same period of life: and the young love to follow the young. Your usefulness, early commenced, will advance with your character, and influence, and years: and planted so soon in the house of the Lord, you will flourish in the courts of our God, and bring forth fruit in old age.

Many of you are the children of religious parents. How are they now praying that my attempt to bring you to a decision may be effectual! See you not the tears now dropping from the cheek of thy father—thy mother—at thy side; while each says, "if thy heart be wise, my heart shall rejoice, even mine." Some of us can speak from experience. We only recommend what we have exemplified. We were enabled early to dedicate ourselves unto God; and we have found his yoke easy and his burden light. We have found his ways pleasantness and peace. We have found "godliness profitable unto all things, having promise of the life that now is, and of that which is to come." And, next to the salvation of our souls, we daily praise him for an early conversion. "I bless Thee, O God, for many things," says Beza in his will and testament, "but especially that I gave up myself to Thee at the early age of sixteen."

Wait then no longer. Be encouraged by the assurance, "I love them that love me; and those that seek me early shall find me." If the flower be not blown, offer the bud—

"The flower, when offered in the bud,
    Is no mean sacrifice,"

in his account. And through all the changes

of life, and from the borders of the grave, He will honour this surrender and say, "I remember thee the kindness of thy youth."

Secondly, We see that while Christianity expects us to enter the Church, it does not leave us to ourselves in it, but accompanies us with its social obligations, and requires us to be found in the performance of every part of relative duty. Unless you cultivate the principles and dispositions pertaining to the condition, you have no right to its benefits. Unless you bring forth fruit in the vineyard, you are cumberers of the ground. If in the master's house you are unprofitable, you are wicked servants. Here, as every where else in religion, privilege and duty go together. You had therefore better resign your connexion with the Church, if you are blanks in it. How much more if you are blots! Your relation to the body of Christ stamps upon you a sacred character. It produces a responsibility peculiarly awful. As professors of his religion, you are witnesses for God; and you depose by your actions, as well as by your words—and will you bear a false, or a defective testimony? You are charged individually with a portion of the glory of the Redeemer; and will you not be concerned to carry it unsullied to the grave?

Beware, therefore, lest by any temper or carriage you should cause the adversaries of the Lord to blaspheme, and the way of truth to be evil spoken of. Do not sadden the heart, and slacken the hands of your minister. Do not prove a grief to the strong, and a stumbling-block to the weak among your brethren: but "make straight paths for your feet, lest that which is lame be turned out of the way; but let it rather be healed." "Walk worthy of the vocation wherewith ye are called, with all lowliness and meekness, with long-suffering, forbearing one another in love; endeavouring to keep the unity of the Spirit in the bond of peace. Let no corrupt communication proceed out of your mouth, but that which is good to the use of edifying, that it may minister grace unto the hearers. And grieve not the Holy Spirit of God, whereby ye are sealed unto the day of redemption. Let all bitterness, and wrath, and anger, and clamour, and evil-speaking, be put away from you, with all malice." Thus you will be harmless and blameless, the sons of God, without rebuke, in the midst of a crooked and perverse nation, among whom ye shine as lights in the world, holding forth the word of life. Even then, you may not escape censure and reproach. But you will not be buffeted for your faults; and therefore may take it patiently. Your enemies will find nothing whereof to accuse you, but in the law of your God. You will suffer for righteousness' sake, for well-doing, as Christians: and then you need not be ashamed, but rejoice that you are partakers of Christ's sufferings; that when his glory shall be revealed, ye also may rejoice with exceeding joy.

Thirdly, We may learn that while we are under obligation to make a profession of religion, and come to the table of communion, the Lord's Supper is not a passport to Heaven; and a connexion with a visible Church does not prove our belonging to the invisible. The form of godliness is becoming, and useful, and necessary, as the dress of godliness: but it is nothing, it is worse than nothing, as a substitute for the reality. For, in this case, there is the *utmost* familiarity with divine things; and this prevents, this destroys their impressiveness. The very position of the man screens conscience from alarm, while the terrors of the Lord are addressed to those that are *without*: and as, by his assumption of the character, he passes for a Christian, and is so treated by the world and by his brethren, and is so addressed and encouraged and comforted by the minister, he is in danger of taking it for granted that he is such—when the end of these things is death. "For what is the hope of the hypocrite, though he hath gained, when God taketh away his soul?" He may be discovered and exposed in life; and if not, his name and his place in the Church will soon avail him nothing. The privileges he has enjoyed, instead of affording him any security, will aggravate the awfulness of his condemnation. He not only perishes "from the way," but from the holy hill of Zion—from the sanctuary of God. He falls, at the foot of the altar. He drops into hell, from the table of the Lord, and with the sacred symbols of his body and his blood in his hand and in his mouth. The house of God, in which he pretended to worship; the pew in which he trifled so many hours away, in hearing the word only; the pulpit, and the form of the man of God exerting himself in it; the chalice that never trembled in his unworthy hand—these will be the most dreadful images that will present themselves to the eye of his lost mind. The truths he professed to believe and recommend; the sacred exercises in which he engaged, with those who call on the name of the Lord; his favourite psalms and hymns in which he so often mocked Him with "a solemn sound upon a thoughtless tongue;" his sitting to hear, and to judge of the qualification of candidates; his joining with the Church in reproving, suspending, excommunicating other members with all the grimace of feigned sanctity and zeal—this will be the food of the worm that never dies, and the fire t at never shall be quenched.

Yet in some cases, it would appear that the extent and the continuance of religious delusion may be as wonderful, as the detection will be tremendous. "When once the Master of the house is risen up, and hath shut to the door, and ye begin to stand without, and to knock at the door, saying, Lord, Lord, open unto us; and he shall answer and say unto you, I know ye not whence ye are; then shall ye begin to say"—Not know *us?* Why, " We have *eaten* and *drunk* in thy *presence,* and thou hast *taught* in our streets. But he shall say, I tell you, I know not whence ye are; depart from me, all ye workers of iniquity. There shall be weeping and gnashing of teeth, when ye shall see Abraham and Isaac and Jacob, and all the prophets, in the kingdom of God, and yourselves thrust out. And they shall come from the east, and from the west, and from the north, and from the south, and shall sit down in the kingdom of God. And, behold, there are last which shall be first, and there are first which shall be last."

" But, beloved, we hope better things of you, and things that accompany salvation, though we thus speak." You are poor in spirit. You mourn for sin. You hunger and thirst after righteousness. You love his salvation, and you love his services. You glory in his Cross, and you admire his character, and long to bear the image of the heavenly. Yet you are often ready to shrink back: you often, you always pray, " Search me, O God, and know my heart; try me, and know my thoughts; and see if there be any wicked way in me, and lead me in the way everlasting." Well, be assured of this, that you are more welcome to his house, than you ever feel yourselves to be unworthy. He himself rises up, and in all the freeness and tenderness of his love, invites you to his table; and cries, " Eat, O friends; drink you, drink abundantly, O beloved !"

And we, *fourthly,* conclude by hailing those who are not only members of a Christian church, but are joined to the Lord, and are of one spirit with him. Not resting in the outward and visible sign, you realize the inward and spiritual grace. You discern the Lord's body; and, by the exercise of faith on the Sacrifice of the Cross, your experience tells you that his flesh is meat indeed, and his blood drink indeed. You have a joy in divine things which mere professors and formalists know nothing of. How often, in his word and ordinances, do you sit under his shadow with delight, and find his fruit sweet to your taste. How often, when lying down in green pastures, and feeding beside the still waters, do you exclaim, " Oh! how great is his beauty, and how great is his goodness." While the men of the world consider you as enslaved by superstition, you walk at liberty, because you keep His commandments. While they represent you as given up to dulness and melancholy, you can look them in the face, and say,

> " The men of grace have found
> 　Glory begun below;
> And heavenly fruits on earthly ground
> 　From faith and hope may grow.

G

> " The hill of Zion yields
> 　A thousand sacred sweets,
> Before we reach the heavenly fields,
> 　Or walk the golden streets."

Yes, you are already blessed. But what a prospect is before you! Death has been called a going home—but it is going to church—going from the Church below to the Church above. Your communion on earth has its trials. It is a mixed state of things; and owing to the apostacies of some, and the backslidings of others, and the infirmities of all, you are often sorrowful for the solemn assembly, and the reproach of it is a burden. Yet it is a pleasing emblem, and earnest of the fellowship of heaven; but its defects, as well as its excellences, should lead you to aspire after that world where the Canaanite will be no more in the house of the Lord for ever; and where the spirits of just men are made perfect. " Therefore are they before the throne of God, and serve him day and night in his temple: and he that sitteth on the throne shall dwell among them. They shall hunger no more, neither thirst any more; neither shall the sun light on them, nor any heat. For the Lamb which is in the midst of the throne shall feed them, and shall lead them unto living fountains of waters: and God shall wipe away all tears from their eyes."

Ah! Christian, though you will soon change your place, you will not change your associates. When death lets you go, you will return to your own company. Now were you setting off for a country which you had never seen, would it not be very relieving to think that you would find yourself at home there—many of your connexions being there already—and the rest assuredly coming after? If, Christian, you are at present a stranger to the heavenly world, the heavenly world is not a stranger to you. There is your Father. There is your Saviour. There are the angels who have been your ministering spirits. There are all the saints, your brethren in Christ. There are your dear friends and fellow-worshippers, who have preceded you—while those you leave behind are loosening and preparing to follow.

And can you imagine that your religious acquaintance will not be renewed, and your holy intimacies be completed, there? " I am fully persuaded," says Baxter, " that I shall love my friends in heaven, and therefore know them. And this principally binds me to them on earth. And if I thought I should never know them more, nor therefore love them after death, I should love them comparatively little, as I do all other transitory objects. But I now delight in conversing with them, as believing I shall commune with them for ever." Paul was like-minded. " For what is our hope, or joy, or crown of rejoicing? are not even ye in the presence of our Lord Jesus Christ at his coming? For ye are our glory and joy."

LECTURE V.

THE CHRISTIAN, IN THE WORLD.

" And now I am no more in the world, but these are in the world."—John xvii. 11.

ACCORDING to Isaiah, it is a privilege to "hear a word behind us, saying, This is the way, walk ye in it, when we turn to the right hand, and when we turn to the left." Truth and safety lie in the middle. The pilgrim, ascending the Hill Difficulty, saw a lion on the right hand, and a lion on the left; and was afraid to advance. But he was informed by a voice from above, that these lions were chained; and need only alarm those who approached the sides of the road. The middle was perfectly secure; and keeping in this, though these creatures might look and roar, they could not hurt him. This is another instance of the profound truth, as well as genius, with which Bunyan describes things in his exquisitely simple and admired book. The wisest of men but gives us the same fact, when he represents Wisdom as saying, " I lead in the way of righteousness, in the midst of the paths of judgment." The sentiment may be exemplified in every thing moral and religious. Economy is equally remote from profusion and parsimony. Courage stands between rashness and fear. Patience is equally destroyed by feeling too little or too much: for which reason we are forbidden both to despise the chastening of the Lord, and to faint when we are rebuked of him. The evils to be avoided in all these cases come so near together, that " narrow is the way that leadeth unto life, and few there be that find it."

Let us take this general reflection, and apply it to a particular case. Our Lord said to his disciples—"I have chosen you out of the world." " Ye are not of the world, even as I am not of the world." And they cannot remember and feel this too powerfully ; not only when they assume a profession of religion, but in every stage of their subsequent progress. But though their inheritance is above, their residence is below. Though they are bound for glory, they are now strangers and pilgrims on earth. Though they are not *of* the world, they are *in* it. "I am no more," says the Saviour, "in the world, but *these are in the world*."

They are in the world, in distinction *from heaven*. This is the final abode of the blessed ; and this high and holy place is much more congenial with their views and feelings than the earth, where they are now left. In the natural creation, things are distinguished and separated according to their qualities ; and the Apostle asks, with regard to the Church, " What communion hath light with darkness ; and what fellowship hath righteousness with unrighteousness ; and what part hath he that believeth with an infidel !"

Order, therefore, seems to require that as soon as men are converted, and bear the image of the heavenly, they should go to their own company ; and not remain in " a world lying in wickedness." But were this to be the case, the triumph would be obtained, without the fight ; and the prize would be reached, without running the race : conversion would be always the signal of dissolution ; and religion would enter our families like an undertaker, to carry off our connexions to the grave. But there is *a way ;* and the *end* of this is peace: there is *a course ;* and this is to be *finished* with joy. The Jews imagined they were to possess the land flowing with milk and honey as soon as they were delivered from the house of bondage : but the wilderness was their abode for forty years ; and though this condition was far better than the place from whence they came out, it was not to be compared with their destination. " Ye are not yet come unto the rest and the inheritance which the Lord your God giveth you."

They are in the world, in opposition to the requirements of *Superstition.* This degrading and perverting system very early prevailed, saying, touch not, taste not, handle not : forbidding also to marry, and commanding to abstain from meats, which God hath created to be received with thanksgiving of them which believe and honour the truth ; and inducing the votaries, if not always by precept yet by commendation, to resign their secular callings, and recede from society, and live in cells and dens and caves of the earth—which things have indeed a show of wisdom in will-worship and humility and neglecting of the body, not in any honour to the satisfying of the flesh. But all this was really after the commandments and doctrines of men. Christianity yields it no real countenance. This is not overcoming the world, but refusing the combat. This is not fighting, but fleeing. This is putting the candle under a bushel instead of a candlestick, where it can give light to all that are in the house. But, says the Saviour, " Let your light so shine *before* men, that they may *see* your good works, and *glorify* your Father who is in heaven."

They are in the world, in qualification of a mistake, to which some Christians even now are prone, and which, though it does not carry them into Popery, *withdraws* them, shall I say, *too much, or rather improperly, from the world.* For here we may err, not only in the article of conformity, but separation ; not only in our indulgence, but in our mortification ; not only in our love, but in our aversion. If we are the friends of the world, we are the enemies of God : yet we are to honour all men. If we shun the course, we are not to neglect the welfare of the world. While we decline the wicked as companions, we are to attend to them as patients, and endeavour to recover and save and bless them. The ground that at present does not yield us pleasure, must furnish us with employment; that, cultivating the barren and the briery soil, under the Divine agency, for us—in some few spots at least—the wilderness and the solitary place may be made glad, and the desert rejoice and blossom as the rose. This brings us to the subject of our present meditation—The Christian

In the WORLD.

The theme would fill volumes; and we have only a single Lecture for the discussion of it. But let us do what we can. Let us take five views of the subject. Let us consider the Christian in the World, as

In a sphere of ACTIVITY.
In a sphere of OBSERVATION.
In a sphere of DANGER.
In a sphere of SELF-IMPROVEMENT.
In a sphere of USEFULNESS.

I. In a sphere of ACTIVITY.

God obviously intended us for a life of engagement; and the design is no less conducive to our own advantage individually, than to the welfare of the community in which we live. It is said, that in Turkey the Grand Seignior himself must have been articled to some mechanical trade. Paul had a learned education, yet he was taught the craft of tentmaking; and we see of what importance it was to him in a particular emergency. The Jews proverbially said, that he who did not bring up his son to some employment, taught him to be a thief. Bishop Sanderson said, that the two curses of the day in which he lived were "beggary and shabby gentility." Beggary is too well understood, and too much encouraged; but what his lordship very properly calls shabby gentility, means the pride of family, and the show of finery, and the expensiveness of indulgence, with insufficient means; while all aid derived from any kind of business is declined and contemned. Some, now in easy circumstances, meanly endeavour to conceal the merchandise or trade in which their parents were engaged—though it is pleasing to think the attempt is always vain; as the affectation of these people leads every one to ferret out the secret, and to exclaim, what a pity it is that any should possess property who are ashamed of the honourable way in which it was acquired for them! Of all pride, the most contemptible is that which blushes at trade; especially in a country whose greatness results so much from commerce; and "whose merchants are princes, and whose traffickers are the honourable of the earth." *They* only ought to blush who rise in the morning, not knowing that they have any thing in the world to do, but to eat and drink, and trifle and sleep. An angel

would pray for annihilation, rather than submit to such disgracefulness for a single day. Activity is the noblest life; it is the life of the soul. It is also the most pleasant, and most healthful. No drudgery equals the wretchedness of ennui. The idle know nothing of *recreation*. Peace and content flee from their feelings. Weakness, and depressed spirits, and trembling nerves, and foolish apprehensions, haunt them: so that these people seem referable to the physician, rather than to the divine.

But the thing has a *moral* bearing, and so comes under the notice of the Lecturer. A life of inaction is a disuse of talents, and a perversion of faculties, for which we are responsible. It is the inlet of temptation. Our leisure days are the enemy's busy ones—

"For Satan finds some mischief still
For idle hands to do."

"Behold, this was the iniquity of Sodom—pride, fulness of bread, and abundance of idleness." When was David overcome? Was it not when, instead of commanding his army in the field, he was indulging himself at noon, upon the house-top? Where grossness of vice is not produced, evils, of a less odious quality, but no less anti-christian, are cherished, especially the indulgence of impertinent curiosity, and whisperings, and backbitings, and slanders—"Withal they learn to be idle, wandering from house to house; and not only idle, but tattlers also, and busy bodies, speaking things they ought not." What is the prevention of these vices, and a thousand more? Is the Apostle too severe! "When we were with you, this we commanded you, that if any would not work neither should he eat. For we hear that there are some which walk among you disorderly, working not at all, but are busy bodies. Now them that are such we command and exhort by our Lord Jesus Christ, that with quietness they work, and eat their own bread." Thus Adam and Eve were placed in the garden of Eden—not to live as some of you do; but to dress and to keep it. All through the Old and New Testament, you will find that those to whom God appeared, to communicate information, or bestow prerogative, were all engaged, and following their occupations at the time. If the unemployed think that *He* visits *them*, let them suspect, and inquire whether it be not another being under disguise; for "even Satan also transformeth himself into an angel of light."

Yet is it not sufficient that we are engaged. The Christian must appear in the man of business. He is not only to have a calling, but to "*abide with God* in his calling"—To abide with Him by the moderation of his desires and exertions: not entangling himself in the affairs of this life; diligent in business, but not, by multiplication and complexity, injur ing the health of his body and the peace of his mind, and compelling himself, if not to omit, to curtail his religious duties; if not to neglect the Sabbath, and the sanctuary, and the closet, yet to render himself unable to attend on the Lord without distraction—To abide with Him by invariable conscientiousness: doing nothing but what is conformable to truth and rectitude; not content to keep himself within the precincts of legal obligation, but shunning and detesting in all his dealings, every thing that is mean and overreaching; and exemplifying every thing that is fair and honourable—To abide with Him by a devout temper and habit; that will remind him of the presence of God and his all-seeing eye; that will keep him from planning or achieving any enterprise without dependance upon Heaven; that will not allow him to say, "To-day or to-morrow we will go into such a city, and continue there a year, and buy and sell, and get gain; while he knows not what shall be on the morrow;" but induce him to preface every project with the pious acknowledgment, "If the Lord will, we shall live, and do this or that;" practically owning the agency of his providence in all the contingencies of his affairs; in every failure and disappointment, submitting to his pleasure; in every favourable turn, in every degree of success, not sacrificing unto his own net, and burning incense unto his own drag, as if by them his pasture was made fat, and his meat plenteous; but ascribing all to the blessing of the Lord that maketh rich, and addeth no sorrow with it.

Thus secular life is Christianized, and the bounds of religion enlarged far beyond the district of what we commonly mean by devotion. If the Christian could abide with God only in the express exercises of worship, whether in the closet, the family, or the temple, he could be with Him very little. In all situations, the cares of life demand the vaster part of his time and attention; but he may always walk before the Lord in the land of the living: and whether he eats or drinks, or whatever he does, he may do all to the glory of God. Let him, as often as he has opportunity, repair, for impression, refreshment, and aid, to the means of grace in private and public: but let him also remember, that making the word of God his principle, and the honour of God his aim, he is still serving God, while he is working with his own hands in his secular vocation, and providing things honest in the sight of all men. The spirit of devotion actuates him in the absence of its forms; and this principle, as is reported of the philosopher's stone, turns all it touches into gold. Thus his natural actions become moral; his civil duties become religious; the field or the warehouse is holy ground; and the man of business is " the man of God."

II. In the World, he is in a sphere of Observation.

"Ye are the light of the world: a city that is set on a hill cannot be hid." "Ye are manifestly the epistles of Christ, known and read of all men." "We are a spectacle to the world, to angels, and to men." It is obvious from hence, that as religious characters, you ought not to be concealed; you will not be concealed, you cannot be concealed. Of this I fear you think too little. Did you sufficiently consider, how many eyes are upon you, and the effects that may result from their inspection, you would surely pray, with David, " Teach me thy way, O Lord, and lead me in a plain path, because of mine enemies:" or, as it is in the margin, " because of them that observe me."

In the Church you have observers. The minister who watches for your souls as one that must give an account; the office-bearers; all your fellow-members—all these observe you. But these are good observers, friendly observers: these observe you to consider you, in order to provoke you to love and to good works. But the world furnishes observers of a very different kind, both as to their qualities and their purposes—

—Curious observers. For " you are men wondered at." They think it strange that you run not to the same excess of riot with them. They are amazed at your resigning dissipations, without which they cannot live; and yet profess to be happy ; and to see you bear reproach and persecution; and rejoice that you are counted worthy to suffer. They are staggered at your principles; and they are not perfectly satisfied with their own ; and so resemble Felix, who wished to hear Paul concerning the faith in Christ: and the Jews, to whom the Apostle appealed when he came to Rome—" And they said unto him, We neither received letters out of Judea concerning thee, neither any of the brethren that came showed or spake any harm of thee. But we desire to hear of thee what thou thinkest; for, as concerning this sect, we know that everywhere it is spoken against."

—Malignant observers. Your temper and conduct and pursuits throw censure upon them; and they hate you, because you testify that their deeds are evil. They therefore watch not to commend, but to condemn; not to notice the many good steps you take, but to mark the least halting; and are delighted when they can detect any thing to degrade you down to their level, any thing to justify their insinuations against you, any thing to make them better pleased with themselves, any thing that may help their faith in the hypocrisy of all religion.

—Unjust observers. It is proper enough for them to compare your conduct with your principles, and your practice with your profession; but they do more than this. For you do not profess to be perfect; yet by nothing less than this rule, do they affect to try you. Yea, all irreligious as they are, they exalt themselves into moral censors, and exact more from you than even your religion exacts; for your religion will allow you to be sincere, though you have infirmities; but they will not. Hence they magnify little failings into crimes. Hence they impute the improprieties of a few to the whole body. Hence, instead of judging of your religion by the Scripture, they judge of your religion by you. Hence, they even estimate the Leader by his followers, and the Master himself by the disciple.

This is awful; and it shows what incalculable injury we may do when we walk unworthy of the vocation wherewith we are called. For as the poor Indians said of the Spaniards, what a God must he be, who has such hell-hounds for his servants and children! so, what must many think of Christ, were they to judge of him by the folly and pride, and avarice and implacability of many who are called by his name!

And what inferences, my fellow-Christians, ought you to draw from hence? It is in vain to fret yourselves, and complain of the injustice of the world. You must regulate yourselves accordingly. Yea, you must turn this vile disposition into a blessing. You must walk in the fear of your God, because of the reproach of the heathen your enemies. You are not of the night nor of darkness: you must therefore walk honestly as in the day. You are on a stage: you must therefore be attentive to your movements. "What manner of persons ought ye to be in all holy conversation and godliness!" Never be careless of your reputation. Never adopt the maxim of some indiscreet professors—"I care not what the world thinks or says of me"—You ought to care. You ought to value a good name above great riches. You ought to let no accusation attach to you, but in matters pertaining to the law of your God.

III. In the world he is in a sphere of DANGER.

Our Lord reminds us of this, when he prays not that we might be taken out of the world, but kept from the evil. Hence we are required to pass the time of our sojourning here in fear. And hence we read, "blessed is the man that feareth always."

We are liable to be drawn sometimes beyond the bounds of permission and duty; and so to intermingle with the ungodly as to neglect the command, "Save yourselves from this untoward generation." "Come ye out from among them, and be ye separate, saith the Lord, and touch not the unclean thing." There are companies, and places, and scenes,

to which a Christian may be tempted, but in which he must never be found. We have read in Ecclesiastical History of a damsel supposed to be possessed of the devil. The Bishop approached her, and commanded the unclean spirit to come out of her. But he stoutly replied, "I will not:" adding, as the reason of his refusal, "she is my lawful prize. I took her on my own territory. I found her, not in the temple, but in the theatre." I have no faith in the fact: but the moral of the fable—how much of Ecclesiastical History is no better than fable!—the moral is good, and useful; and teaches us that we have no warrant to look for divine protection when we are on forbidden ground.

We must needs go out of the world, if we would avoid all intercourse with the ungodly. There is scarcely a day in which we are not brought into such contact with them as duty allows and requires. But is there no caution necessary even then? Is there no danger of infection, when we are among the diseased? Has not a heathen told us, that evil communications corrupt good manners? Need you be informed that even the presence of the wicked may chill your religious fervour; and that their conversation may throw doubts into your minds, and leave stains on the imagination, which cannot be easily removed? How insensibly are we drawn to feel and talk and act like others; especially if there be rank to impress, and talent to fascinate, and friendship to allure, and dependance to excite hope, and favours to attach gratitude!

The danger as to the case before us is, not only from what we meet with in the condition, but from what we bring into it. The world is always the same. Its errors, vices, examples, endeavours, frowns, smiles, promises, and threatenings, yield incessant and powerful temptations. Yet an angel is not endangered by them: he has not the senses, the passions, the appetites, the corruptions, on which they can operate. But we are not only rational, but animal creatures. We have not only an immaterial spirit, but a material body accessible to every external impression. We are also fallen creatures, and much of the derangement induced by our depravity, consists in the ascendency of the sensual over the intellectual part of our nature.

And if we are sanctified, we are not completely renewed. And owing to the sin that dwelleth in us, we are in danger from our dress, our food, our calling, our connexions. We are in danger not only from sinful, but lawful things. The piece of ground, the yoke of oxen, the married wife—all these are innocent in themselves; yet they may excuse the acceptance of the invitation to the feast, and become the means of perdition. The knowledge we possess may puff us up with vanity. The applause we meet with may show how drossy we are: for as the fining pot for silver, and the furnace for gold, so is a man to his praise. Owing to our susceptibility of shame, and suffering, the fear of man bringeth a snare, and may drive us back or turn us aside from the path of duty. How perilous is it to have not only an active and sleepless enemy without, but a traitor within, to give him every information and advantage. And with regard to the soul, a man's foes are indeed those of his own household. "Then a man is tempted, when he is drawn away of his own lust and enticed. How apprehensive and cautious should those be who carry gunpowder, while moving in the neighbourhood of sparks. "Can a man take fire in his bosom, and his clothes not be burned? Can one go upon hot coals, and his feet not be burned?"

Be not therefore high-minded, but fear. Some are indeed obliged by their condition and calling to enter further into the world than others; and so are more exposed; but what we say unto one, we say unto all, Watch. "Watch and pray, lest ye enter into temptation." Whose attainments are such as to warrant the dismission, or even the relaxation of his vigilance? Whose standing is so secure as to feel it needless any longer to pray, "Hold thou me up, and I shall be safe?" Are we young? Timothy, with all his faith and godliness, is admonished to flee youthful lusts. Are years beyond the reach of harm? Solomon, after a youth and manhood of piety, is drawn aside in his old age. We may fail even in those qualities and graces wherein we most excel. Abraham, the father of the faithful, staggered through unbelief, and how did it debase him in Gerar! Moses, more meek than any man on the earth, provoked by the perverseness of the murmurers, "spake unadvisedly with his lips." The disciple who disowned the Saviour, even with oaths and curses, was he who had just said, "though I should die with thee, yet will I not deny thee:" and who had just drawn his sword, and in the presence of a number of Roman soldiers had cut off the ear of the High Priest's servant. If any imagines that though these admonitions and warnings are needful for others, they are not necessary for *him*, he is the man who far more than *every* other requires them: for "pride goes before destruction, and a haughty spirit before a fall." It is therefore a great thing, and a thing for which you ought to be thankful to the God of all grace, if, after so long an exposure in an enemy's land, your hearts have not turned back, neither have your steps declined from his ways. Review the hour when you first gave up your ownselves to the Lord and to his people by his will; recall the subsequent vicissitudes of your condition and experience; and exclaim, with wonder and praise,

"Many years have passed since then; Many changes I have seen: Yet have been upheld till now— Who could hold me up but Thou?"

You have had your infirmities; and these ought to humble you. But it is an unspeakable privilege that thus far you have not only been sincere, but without offence; and have not caused the way of truth to be evil spoken of.

"Ah!" say some of you, "such are to be congratulated. Through all the pollutions of a world like this, they have not defiled their garments; and they are ready to walk with their Redeemer in white, for they are worthy. But we are only commencing our religious course. Their warfare may be considered as accomplished: our fight is scarcely begun. The dangers which are behind them, are all before us; and the prospect frequently smites our heart down to the ground." But be not discouraged. Their friend and keeper is with you. He will never leave you nor forsake you. He is able to keep you from falling, and to present you faultless before the presence of his glory with exceeding joy. Look to that grace which is sufficient for you; and be concerned to abstain from all appearance of evil. And the very God of peace sanctify you wholly: and I pray God your body, soul, and spirit may be preserved blameless unto the coming of our Lord Jesus Christ. Faithful is he that calleth you, who also will do it.

IV. In the World he is in a sphere of SELF-IMPROVEMENT.

The Lord takes pleasure in them that fear him. His love to them is infinite. And as he is possessed of unbounded resources to give his friendship effect, it follows that he would not detain them here, unless the condition was compatible with their advantage, and the trials by which they are exercised could be found unto their praise and glory and honour.

When Isaiah would distinguish the guilt of a sinner, he said, "Even in the land of uprightness will he deal unjustly"—and nothing can aggravate a man's wickedness more, than to go on still in his transgressions, when every thing in his situation, every thing ne hears and sees, excites and encourages him to godliness. By the same principle of reasoning it will appear, that the highest religious excellence is that which is displayed in the land of wickedness; and where evil examples and seductions press on every side. Hence the portrait drawn by the sublimest hand that every held a pencil.

——"Abdiel, faithful found
Among the faithless, faithful only he
Among innumerable false, unmoved,
Unshaken, unseduced, unterrified,
His loyalty he kept, his love, his zeal;
Nor number, nor example, with him wrought
To swerve from truth, or change his constant mind,

Though single. From amidst them forth he pass'd
Long way through hostile scorn, which he sustain'd
Superior, nor of violence fear'd aught "

This gave splendour to the faith of those Christians who were saints even in Cæsar's household. This magnified the sanctity of Daniel, and Moses, and Joseph, who lived in the midst of heathenish, and luxurious, and corrupt courts; and yet kept themselves pure. This was the honour of Noah; that when God had explored the whole world, he said, "Thee *have* I seen righteous before me in this generation."

What is virtue untested? "Blessed is the man that endureth *temptation*; for when he is *tried*, he shall receive the crown of life." It is not by the fire-side, or in the circle of his friends, or in the rear of the army with the " stuff," that the hero gathers his laurels; but amidst the confused noise of warriors, and garments rolled in blood. If we were exposed to no frowns and menaces, how could we show the firmness of our religious principles? If we met with no kind of reproach and persecution for the Saviour's sake, how could we evince our belief of his truth and our love to his cause? Were we urged to follow no will but His, how could we obey God rather than man?

Am I offended? What an opportunity have I to prove that I can forgive my brother his trespasses! Am I opposed and injured? Here my patience and meekness are called forth. Here I am in the noblest field of action. I am more than a conqueror. I am not overcome of evil, but overcome evil with good.

Can I pass a day or an hour, and not perceive the goodness and forbearance of that God, who though still insulted by the world which he has made, yet spares it, and is never weary in filling it with plenteousness? Is my soul vexed with the filthy conversation of the wicked; and do I not wonder at the grace of our Lord Jesus Christ, who came into such a world, and resided here for three-and-thirty years, bearing the contradiction of sinners against himself?—Can I view the depravity of others, and know that I am a partaker of the very same nature, and not feel abased, and ashamed, like the martyr, who whenever he saw a sinner in his sins, said, "There goes Bradford, but for the grace of God?"—How can we view the vassalage of the ungodly under the tyranny of their passions, and led captive by the devil at his will, and not remember that we ourselves also were sometimes foolish and disobedient, deceived, serving divers lusts and pleasures; and not ask, who made us to differ from others; and what have we that we have not received?—How can we see the vileness of sin in its ugly tempers and detestable practices, and not be excited to abhor that which is evil and cleave to that which is good?—

How can we contemplate the miseries of the sinner, and not have our faith confirmed in the testimony of the Scripture that assures us the end of these things is death; the way of transgressors is hard; there is no peace to the wicked?—And when we behold them blind and deaf, and madly rushing on to destruction, will not all the compassion of our souls be moved, will not all our zeal be inflamed, to endeavour to save them?

V. In the World he is in a sphere of Usefulness.

We principally mean, religious usefulness. We would not indeed limit your exertions. Do all the good that is in your power. Feed the hungry; clothe the naked; administer to the sick; visit the fatherless and widows in their affliction—But forget not, that charity to the soul is the soul of charity. There is no evil from which you can deliver a fellow-creature to be compared with sin; and there is no good you can obtain for him like that grace whose fruit is holiness, and whose end is everlasting life.

And fix in your minds, my Christian friends, not only the importance of the object, but the possibility of accomplishing it. David did not despair of success when he said, "Then will I teach transgressors thy ways, and sinners shall be converted unto thee." And what says the Apostle James? "Brethren, if any of you do err from the truth, and one convert him; let him know, that he which converteth a sinner from the error of his way, shall save a soul from death, and shall hide a multitude of sins." God works by means; and it is by his people that he principally carries on his cause in the world. They are his witnesses. They are his servants. He first makes them the subjects of his grace, and then the mediums. He first turns them from rebels into friends, and then employs them to go and beseech others to be reconciled unto God. For they know the wretchedness of a state of alienation from Him. They know the blessedness of a return. They have "tasted that the Lord is gracious." Their own experience gives them earnestness and confidence in saying to those around them, "O taste, and see that the Lord is good: blessed is the man that trusteth in him."

Let us enter more fully into this most essential part of our subject.

The persons for whom you are to be concerned are represented as *without*; and your object is to bring them in. They are ignorant, and you must inform them. They are prejudiced, and you must remove their objections. They are full of aversion, and you must subdue this dislike. The Scripture calls this "gaining" them; "winning" them. In order to this, address is necessary, as well as zeal: "He that winneth souls is wise." Hence the Apostle requires you to "walk in wisdom towards them that are without." The question is, what this wisdom includes. Here I wish I had more time to enlarge and particularize. I know nothing concerning which the conduct of many religious people needs more correction. I will therefore venture to exceed a little the limits allotted to this exercise; though, after all, we can only throw out a few hints for your observance.

If then you would bring in those that are without—Show nothing like a contemptuous superiority or distance. Avoid every air of the Pharisee, who says, "Stand by thyself; come not near me; I am holier than thou." Convince them that you love them, and have no object in view but their own welfare. And therefore be kind, and tender, and ready to serve them. Especially be attentive to them in trouble; for nothing affects persons more deeply, than the notice you take of them in distress. It will look disinterested; and will not fail to form in their minds a striking contrast between you and the people of the world, and lead them to say, "How these people differ from others! Other friends drop us in adversity; but then these take us up. They are not meanly governed by advantage; but love their neighbours as themselves."

—Learn to distinguish things that differ. What fisherman would employ the same bait for every kind of fish, and at every season of the year? Who, wishing to convince, would seize the moment of passion and irritation; and not wait the return of calmness and reason? Who, having to reprove, would not administer the rebuke privately, rather than mortify and exasperate by public exposure? "Tell him his fault between him and thee alone: if he hear thee, thou hast gained thy brother." How different are the conditions, the habits, the principles, the tempers of men! And who was it that said, "Let every one of us please his neighbour for his good to edification?" And did not his own example enforce his advice? "Though I be free from all men, yet have I made myself servant unto all, that I might gain the more." "And this I do for the Gospel's sake." "Even as I please all men in all things, not seeking mine own profit, but the profit of many, that they may be saved."

—Never begin in a way of attack. This puts you into the posture of an enemy, and provokes a feeling of defence and resistance. Recommend what is right, rather than oppose what is wrong; and let *them*, by the perception of the one, discover and condemn the other. The best way of effecting the expulsion of evil, is by the introduction of good. What is it to tear people away from their amusements, before any superior source of pleasure be opened to their minds? Their hearts are still after their idols. They only act the hypocrite in their abstinence; and hate the religion that forbids their happiness.

Let something better be substituted, and the soul is even as a weaned child.

—And do not attempt every thing at once. "There is," says Henry, "not only an underdoing, but an overdoing; and such an overdoing, as sometimes proves an undoing." When the disciples of John asked our Saviour, "Why do we and the Pharisees fast oft, but thy disciples fast not?" He said unto them, "Can the children of the bride-chamber mourn, as long as the bridegroom is with them? but the days will come, when the bridegroom shall be taken from them, and then shall they fast. No man putteth a piece of new cloth unto an old garment; for that which is put in to fill it up taketh from the garment, and the rent is made worse. Neither do men put new wine into old bottles; else the bottles break, and the wine runneth out, and the bottles perish: but they put new wine into new bottles, and both are preserved." Now what you have here to consider, is, not so much the imagery of the comparisons, as the principle. His meaning is, that some things, proper in themselves, are yet not seasonable; and that we may do hurt rather than good, by endeavouring to effect too much. Look to his life for an illustration of his doctrine. Did he despise the day of small things? Did he break the bruised reed, or quench the smoking flax? Did not he say to his disciples, "I have many things to say unto you, but ye cannot bear them now?" How unlike him are they who force upon the mind every difficult sentiment, regardless of any preparation made by experience for the reception of it. "How unwise," as an old writer has it, "is the conduct of those who send their pupils to the university of predestination, before they have entered the grammar-school of repentance." How injurious is it, when the tenderness of age requires only milk, to feed babes with strong meat,—yea, and even to furnish them with the bones of controversy.

—Do not attach great importance to little things. This is the way to make people think that your religion consists of whims or trifles; and that your integrity and firmness are but squeamishness and obstinacy. Show, that though you have a tender conscience, you have not a weak one. Show that your convictions are not opinions, but principles. Show that your object is not to make proselytes to your party, but converts to the cause of real Christianity.

—Beware of every thing in your conduct that would prove a scandal. They who see, can get over stumbling-blocks; but who would throw them in the way of the blind? "Make straight paths for your feet, lest that which is lame be turned out of the way; but let it rather be healed." Administer no cause of censure but what your religion itself supplies. You are not answerable for the offence of the Cross. But there are many other offences—and wo to the world because of them! The falls of professors are judgments on the neighbourhood in which they live. What a noble spirit dictated the resolution, "Wherefore if meat make my brother to offend, I will eat no flesh while the world standeth, lest I make my brother to offend." And how far did Ezra carry the delicacy of his religious zeal! There was no real inconsistency between dependance upon God, and the use of means: but he had to deal with a poor ignorant heathen, who might easily misapprehend and pervert the language of his confidence; and therefore, says he, "I was ashamed to require of the king a band of soldiers and horsemen to help us against the enemy in the way, because we had spoken unto the king, saying, The hand of our God is upon all them for good that seek him; but his power and his wrath is against all them that forsake him. So we fasted, and besought our God for this; and he was entreated of us."

——While your religion is impressive by its consistency, let it be attractive by its amiableness. Therefore, think upon and pursue whatsoever things are lovely, and of good report. In excuse for the disagreeable tempers and the repulsive manners of some Christians, it is said, that grace may be sometimes grafted on a crab-stock. Be it so. But instead of excusing the improprieties, the metaphor condemns them. When a tree is grafted, it is always expected to bear fruit according to the scion, and not according to the stock: and "the fruit of the Spirit is love, joy, peace, longsuffering, gentleness, goodness, faith, meekness, temperance: against such there is no law."

——Nothing recommends godliness more than cheerfulness. All men desire happiness; and if while every other candidate for the prize fails, you succeed, your success may determine others to follow your envied course. Hence it is not very desirable that religion should be so often expressed by the word seriousness. Among many people, as soon as ever a man is becoming religious, it is said he is becoming "serious." But does not religion also make him humble, and benevolent, and hopeful, and blessed? Why then should we select, so exclusively for the designation of its influence, an attribute or an effect which is common with many others, but yet the least inviting, and most liable to an injurious construction? I never use it—and if I were obliged to use any other term than religious itself, I would rather say, the man was becoming happy.

It will be allowed that many of these advices are of a negative kind. But there are many ways in which you may positively exert yourselves. Such as—By conversation. By epistolary correspondence. By recommending good books. By bringing persons

H

under the preaching of the word; for "faith cometh by hearing." As soon as Andrew knew the Lord, "he findeth his own *brother* Simon, and saith to him, we have found the Messiah, which is, being interpreted, the Christ; and he brought him to Jesus." As soon as Philip knew him, he findeth his *friend* Nathanael, and saith unto him, "we have found him of whom Moses in the Law and the Prophets did write." As soon as the woman of Samaria knew him, "she left her water-pot, and went into the city, and saith to her *neighbours*, come, see a man that told me all things that ever I did." And how many was she the instrument of inducing to believe on the Saviour of the world!

The opportunities and influences of individuals will be very unequal; but all should seek to obtain the commendation conferred on Mary in the Gospel, "She hath done what she could."

Yet it is not always by direct effort that you will best succeed. A word fitly spoken is valuable; but, in general, it is better for persons to *see* your religion than to *hear* it: it is better to hold forth the word of truth, in your lives, than in your language; and by your tempers, than by your tongues. The relations in which some pious characters are found, peculiarly require the observance of this distinction. Such, for instance, are professing servants. *Their* province of usefulness is not by teaching, and exhorting, and reproving. One of these was recently speaking to the preacher, of her master and mistress, and complained, "Nothing I say to them seems to do them any good." To whom —knowing the *class* of the individual, he replied—"What you *say* to them! But this is not the way in which *you* are to expect to do them good—but by early rising; by neatness, and order, and diligence; by 'not answering again; by not purloining, but showing all good fidelity:' it is thus that you are to 'adorn the doctrine of God your Saviour in all things.'" I am far from ranking wives with servants and dependants. My female hearers, you will bear me witness that I never plead for the degradation of your sex; and I am sure you will not count me your enemy because I tell you the truth. We need not remind you of the language of the Apostle; "I suffer not a woman to teach, nor usurp an authority over the man; but to be in silence." He can only speak comparatively. We know you are well endued with speech; and we delight to hear your readiness and skill. But we yet question whether any talent, even of this kind, be your most advantageous and successful instrument. The love of home; the concern to please; the silent tear; the graceful sacrifice; the willing concession; the placid temper—these, upon men—and we presume you would not have married brutes —these, upon ingenuous and attached husbands, will seldom fail of producing their effect, really if not instantly. "Likewise, ye wives, be in subjection to your own husbands; that if any obey not the word, they also may without the word be won by the conversation of the wives, while they behold your chaste conversation coupled with fear. Whose adorning let it not be that outward adorning of plaiting the hair, and of wearing of gold, or of putting on of apparel; but let it be the hidden man of the heart, in that which is not corruptible, even the ornament of a meek and quiet spirit, which is in the sight of God of great price." There is no eloquence so powerful as the address of a holy and consistent life. It shames the accusers. It puts to silence the ignorance of foolish men. It constrains them, by the good works which they behold, to glorify God in the day of visitation.

—We hope there is no Cain here this morning, who in answer to all this is ready to say, "Am I my brother's keeper?" From this obligation to seek the salvation of others, *none* are exempted. But if some are more peculiarly bound than others, they are those who have been saved from a long and awful course of vice themselves. *You* ought to feel, above others, a claim of gratitude, and of justice. You have had much forgiven, and you should love much. You have been a curse to many; you ought now to be a blessing. Oh! it seems enough to make you shed tears of blood to think that there are some now in hell who ascribe their destruction to you: while others are walking the downward road, urged on and encouraged by your former errors and crimes and influence. Some of these are placed beyond your reach. Others are yet accessible. O! repair to them immediately. They know your former condition: describe to them your present; and acquaint them with the peace and pleasure which have resulted from your conversion. Who can tell what an affectionate and earnest testimony, derived from experience, and accompanied with a change too obvious to be denied, may accomplish?

—But "them that honour me," says God, "I will honour." Let all your attempts therefore be preceded and attended and followed by prayer. This will prepare you for your work; this will encourage you in it. This will preserve you from growing weary in well-doing. This will teach you not to consider any of your fellow-creatures as abandoned; this will keep you from giving over the use of means to reclaim them. Nothing is too hard for the Lord; and prayer brings *him* into the scene; we are workers together with God—"Not by might nor by power, but by my Spirit, saith the Lord."

—And need I say, "whatsoever your hand findeth to do, do it with your might:" do it immediately. While you delay, *they* may be gone, and their condition determined for ever.

While you linger, *you* may be gone, and every possibility of usefulness be shut out. "For what is your life! It is even a vapour that appeareth for a little time, and then vanisheth away." Yet all your opportunities of doing good are limited to this short and equally uncertain duration. In consequence of this, what an inestimable value attaches to the present hour! Awake, my fellow-Christians, and redeem the time. Remember, earth has one privilege above heaven. It is the privilege of BENEFICENCE. The privilege of passing by a transgression, of relieving the distressed, of spreading the Scriptures, of evangelizing the heathens, of instructing the ignorant, of reclaiming the vicious, of seeking and saving them that are lost.—They who are now in joy and felicity, would be ready, were it the will of God, to descend from their glory, and re-enter the body, and traverse the vale of tears again, to be able to do, for a number of years, what at present lies within the reach of every one of you. Is this incredible! They are now perfect in knowledge; and see that "it is not the will of our Father who is in heaven that one of these little ones should perish." Their benevolence is now perfect; they dwell in love, and God dwelleth in them. They are filled with the Spirit of Him who "though he was rich, yet for your sakes became poor, that ye through his poverty might be rich."

Christians! we have thus spoken of your being in the world. Let me now speak of your leaving it. After David had served his generation by the will of God, he fell on sleep, and was gathered to his fathers. Jesus went about doing good; but at last he said, "I have glorified Thee on the earth, I have finished the work which thou gavest me to do." "And now I am no more in the world. Holy Father, I come to Thee." Such is the removal that awaits you all. You will soon be no more in this world—how soon, it is impossible to determine. But as to some of you, from the infirmities of nature and the course of years, the event cannot be very remote, and you need not—you do not deplore it. "Your salvation is now nearer than when you believed." "The night is far spent. The day is at hand."

You are not required to be indifferent to what is passing around you, or insensible to the events that befall yourselves. But you are to feel as Christians; and you are to declare plainly you seek a country. You are not to undervalue a state in which you enjoy many comforts, and are favoured with the means of grace, and are blessed and dignified with opportunities of usefulness; but considered as your portion, and your dwelling-place, the voice cries, and you ought to hear it, "Arise, and depart hence, for this is not your rest, because it is polluted." You are not to be in haste to leave it, while God has any thing for you to do, or to suffer: but while bearing the burden and heat of the day, you may resemble the man in harvest: he does not throw down his implements and run out of the field before the time; but he occasionally erects himself and looks westward, to see when the descending sun will furnish him with an honourable discharge.

"Jesus," the Evangelist tells us, "knew that his hour was come that he should depart out of this world unto the Father." There was something peculiar here. He *knew* the time of his departure, and had his eye upon it, and regulated his measures by it from the beginning—But you must say with Isaac, "I know not the day of my death." Yet you also have *your hour* appointed for this purpose; and appointed by Infinite Wisdom and Goodness. And till it arrives, you are immortal; and friends cannot retard, and enemies cannot accelerate its approach.

—And what will it then be but a departure *out of this world?* This vain world—this vexing world—this defiling world—this tempting world—this world which crucified the Lord of Glory—this world in which you walk by faith, and not by sight; and in which you so often exclaim, " Wo is me, that I dwell in Mesech, and make my tents in Kedar !"

—What will it be but a departure out of this world *to the Father ?*—To *his* world? To *his* abode?—And to *yours* also? For since you are the sons and daughters of the Lord Almighty, your going to the Father is going home. The poet represents the traveller returning at eve, buried in the drifted snow, as "stung with the thoughts of home ;" a home he was not permitted to see. But, Christian, no disaster shall hinder your arriving at your Father's house in peace. And as your home is sure, so it is replenished with every attraction that can draw you forward. When the venerable Mede, whose grey hairs were a crown of glory, being found in the way of righteousness, was asked how he was? resting upon his staff, he cheerfully answered— " Why going home as fast as I can; as every honest man ought to do when his day's work is done: and I bless God I have a good home to go to." God forbid, Christians, that you should be all your lifetime subject to bondage through fear of an event that has so much to render it not only harmless, but desirable. Does the Lord Jesus stand in no relation to you? Is not he your ransom and your advocate? Is not he your righteousness and strength? Has not he abolished death, and brought life and immortality to light through the Gospel? Has not he opened the kingdom of heaven to all believers? Has not he said, "If a man keep my sayings, he shall never see death?" What is dying now, but your hour to depart out of this world unto the Father ?—

" *There* is my house and portion fair ;
My treasure and my heart is there,
And my abiding home :
For me my elder brethren stay,
And angels beckon me away,
And Jesus bids me come."

LECTURE VI.

THE CHRISTIAN, IN PROSPERITY.

" *I spake unto thee in thy Prosperity ; but thou saidst, I will not hear.*"—Jer. xxii. 21.

THE providence of God was presented in vision to Ezekiel, under the image of a vast wheel. The design was to show, that its dispensations were constantly changing, For as, in the motion of a wheel, one spoke is always ascending, and another is descending; and one part of the ring is grating on the ground, and another is aloft in the air; so it is with the affairs of empires, families, and individuals—they never continue in one stay. And not only is there a diversity in human conditions, so that while some are rich, others are poor; and while some are in honour, others are in obscurity and disgrace; but frequently the same person is destined successively to exemplify, in his own experience, the opposite estates of prosperity and adversity. Such characters strike us in the Scripture; they abound in history; they are to be met with in our daily walk; they are to be addressed in every congregation.

But these vicissitudes are great trials of religious principle; and happy is he who can press forward, undismayed by the rough, and unseduced by the pleasant he meets with, in his course: who can preserve the balance of the mind in all the unequal pressures of human life; and who, prepared for each change of circumstances in which he can be placed, is authorized to say, "I know both how to be abased, and I know how to abound; everywhere, and in all things, I am instructed both to be full and to be hungry, both to abound and to suffer need. I can do all things through Christ which strengtheneth me." Such is the Christian—or must I say, such he ought to be? The present exercise brings him before us in the possession of

PROSPERITY.

I need not detain you in specifying the ingredients of this envied state.—It must include health. This is the salt that seasons, and the honey that sweetens every temporal comfort. Yet how little of it do some enjoy! How affecting is the complaint not a few are constrained to utter—"I am made to possess months of vanity, and wearisome nights are appointed unto me : when I lie down, I say, when shall I arise, and the night be gone; I am full of tossings to and fro, until the dawning of the day."—"He is chastened also with pain upon his bed, and the multitude of his bones with strong pain, so that his life abhorreth bread, and his soul dainty meat." While others scarcely know from their own feelings what disease, or indisposition, or infirmity, means.

—It must take in agreeable relations. What are the caresses of the world, if a man be chilled with neglect, or repulsed with frowns, at home? What are the productions of the field and the garden, if, as the Prophet says, "thorns are in our tabernacle?" "Better is a dinner of herbs where love is, than a stalled ox and hatred therewith." What a difference is there, between "a brawling woman in a wide house," and "a wife that is as a loving hind and a pleasant roe!" Job, looking back to the days of his prosperity, says, "when my children were about me." They were united and affectionate and dutiful. What must be the wretchedness of a parent whose offspring are the reverse of all this!—Friendship must not be absent. Who can dispense with this balm of life? Who does not feel his need of another's bosom, if not of another's hand! What is general and indiscriminate society! I must have one whose sympathies lead him to rejoice when I rejoice, and to weep when I weep or my grief is too heavy for me to bear; or my pleasure loses half its relish. "Ointment and perfume rejoice the heart; so doth the sweetness of a man's friend by hearty counsel." Who can be so low and groveling as to have no regard for the opinion and approbation of his fellow-creatures? "A good name is rather to be chosen than great riches; and loving favour rather than silver and gold." "The light of the eyes rejoiceth the heart: and a good report maketh the bones fat."— But the use of the term more directly reminds us of the fruit of our wishes, and the success of our endeavours, in our calling or profession; and the securing and commanding a degree of wealth above competency. For "money is a defence," and screens us from the evils of dependance and embarrassment. "Money answereth all things:" it procures a thousand advantages; and affords not only the necessaries, but the conveniences, and indulgences, and embellishments of life.

Now the portion only of a very few favoured individuals includes all these ingredients; but the greater the confluence of them in number and degree, the better we consider the cup of prosperity replenished.

But can such a cup be seen in the hand of a Christian? In general, indeed, the language of the Scripture befriends the needy and distressed; and what generous mind does not rejoice in this aspect of benevolent preference? Who does not read with pleasure, "I will leave in the midst of thee a poor and an afflicted people, and they shall trust in the Lord their God." "The poor have the Gospel preached unto them." "God hath chosen the poor of this world, rich in faith, and heirs of the kingdom which he hath promised to them that love him." But this is not true of them, *universally* and *exclusively*. We are told that not *many* of the higher ranks in life are called: but the very assertion implies that there are *some*. Our Saviour said to his followers, "If any man will be my disciple, let him deny himself, and take up his cross daily." "In the world ye shall have tribulation." Yet he also said, "Seek ye first the kingdom of God and his righteousness, and all these things shall be added unto you." The Apostle who taught, that "through much tribulation we must enter the kingdom," made no scruple to say, "Godliness has the promise of the life that now is, as well as of that which is to come." Peter, also, who charged Christians not to think it strange "concerning the fiery trial as if some strange thing had happened unto them," confidently asserts, "He that will love life, and see good days, let him refrain his tongue from evil, and his lips that they speak no guile: let him eschew evil, and do good; let him seek peace, and ensue it. For the eyes of the Lord are over the righteous, and his ears are open unto their prayers: but the face of the Lord is against them that do evil. Who is he that will harm you, if ye be followers of that which is good?" And religion, by its natural influence as well as by the blessing of an overruling Providence, tends in various ways to advance the temporal welfare of men.

We have not time to exemplify these remarks: but we mention them the more readily, because some Pietists seem to look upon all the distinctions and endowments of life, as *nearly* sealing their owners unto the day of perdition; and to conclude that their good things here are only pledges of their evil ones hereafter. It is true this was the result, in the case of the rich man in the parable. But it was not so with Abraham, mentioned in the same story—yet Abraham had been very wealthy. We allow that there is enough to alarm the prosperous; but they have no ground for despair. The proprietors of no condition here are under any sentence of reprobation. They that have riches shall hardly enter into the kingdom of God; but with God all things are possible. There is a way to heaven from all the diversities of human life; and there is a passage from the mansion as well as from the cottage, though it is more narrow and perplexing and difficult. In a word: a Christian is never to be known *by* his condition; but he must be always known *in* it; for he belongs to "a peculiar people, zealous of good works."

In confirmation of which, let us proceed to hear what God the Lord has to say concerning us in the estate we are now surveying—*I spake unto thee in thy prosperity*—He is always alive to our welfare, and of this he never leaves himself without witness: and if ever we err in conduct, or fail in character, it is owing to our disbelief of his word, or inattention to it. For the Scripture is not only able to make us wise unto salvation; but "is profitable for doctrine, for reproof, for correction, and for instruction in righteousness, that the man of God may be perfect, throughly furnished unto all good works." Now in your prosperity he requires of you three things:

I. That you should be AWARE OF ITS PERILS.

II. That you should EMPLOY ITS SAFEGUARDS.

III. That you should IMPROVE ITS ADVANTAGES.

O let him not complain—*But thou saidst, I will not hear.*

I. You are required to be AWARE OF THE PERILS OF PROSPERITY.

Here it must be acknowledged we are furnished with a very mortifying view of human nature. The produce of creation, and the bounties of Providence, are good in themselves; and they are the gifts of God; and they ought to induce us to love and serve the Giver. And they would have this effect, were we not in a state of moral perversion and depravity. The goodness of God leadeth to repentance—this is the design of it; this is the tendency of it. But what is the effect? Answer this, ye who suppose that man is so innocent, so amiable, so dignified a creature! You deny that the heart is deceitful above all things, and desperately wicked. You deny that man, as he now comes into the world, is otherwise than he was originally created.—But can you deny that we are evil, *because* God is good? That we are unable to bear gratification uninjured? That what should draw us to God, with the cords of a man and the bands of love, leads us away from him? That the very blessings we receive from him we convert into weapons of rebellion against our Benefactor? Or will you affirm that we *thus* came from our Maker's hand? "Lo! this only have I found, that God hath made man upright; but they have sought out many inventions."

There is one case in which prosperity is peculiarly perilous—when it is not hereditary, but acquired; and when it is acquired, not by degrees, but suddenly. He is most likely to be giddy, who has not been accustomed to elevation. He is most likely to have his health injured, who passes all at once from one climate to another; while, by use, nature may be attempered to almost any extremity. But though prosperity is pecu-

liarly dangerous when it is neither natural nor gradual, it will be easy to prove that it is *never* free from numberless moral hazards.

Let us turn first to the faithful Word. What says David? "Because they have no changes, therefore they fear not God." What says Job? "Their seed is established in their sight with them, and their offspring before their eyes. Their houses are safe from fear, neither is the rod of God upon them. Their bull gendereth, and faileth not; their cow calveth, and casteth not her calf. They send forth their little ones like a flock, and their children dance. They take the timbrel and harp, and rejoice at the sound of the organ. They spend their days in wealth, and in a moment go down to the grave. Therefore they say unto God, Depart from us; for we desire not the knowledge of thy ways. What is the Almighty that we should serve him? and what profit should we have, if we pray unto him?" What is Jeremiah's report concerning Moab? "Moab hath been at ease from his youth, and he hath settled on his lees, and hath not been emptied from vessel to vessel, neither hath he gone into captivity; therefore his taste remained in him, and his scent is not changed." But surely it was otherwise with the Jews? Hear Moses: "He made him to ride on the high places of the earth, that he might eat the increase of the fields; and he made him to suck honey out of the rock, and oil out of the flinty rock; butter of kine, and milk of sheep, and fat of lambs, and rams of the breed of Bashan, and goats, with the fat of kidneys of wheat; and thou didst drink the pure blood of the grape. But Jeshurun waxed fat, and kicked: thou art waxen fat, thou art grown thick, thou art covered with fatness: then he forsook God which made him, and lightly esteemed the Rock of his salvation." Hear Hosea: "According to their pasture, so were they filled; they were filled, and their heart was exalted; therefore have they forgotten me." Are we better than they? Let us appeal to reason, to observation, to experience. How many duties are there which prosperity tends to discourage and hinder! How many evils are there which its influence upon depraved beings is adapted to cherish and increase! What are these? Let us particularize a few of them—for their name is Legion.

—Such is *Unmindfulness of God.* Hence the caution of Moses, "When thou shalt have eaten and art full, then beware lest thou forget the Lord that brought thee forth out of the land of Egypt, from the house of bondage." Hence the prayer of Agar, "Lest I be full, and deny thee, and say, who is the Lord?" The disciples suffered the Saviour to sleep while the vessel was sailing smoothly: but when the wind and the waves threatened, they went to him, saying, "Master, carest thou not that we perish?" It is in affliction we seek him early. It is then we think of his moral agency; and fear that he is come to call our sins to remembrance. It is then we feel our dependance upon him—Then other helpers fail: then we have no substitutes; then we have no diversion—We can dispense with him no longer—we are forced upon Him. "Who is the Lord, that *I* should obey his voice?" said Pharaoh, in all the affluence of his greatness. "Entreat the Lord for me," was the suppliant language of the same haughty monarch, brought down by the judgments of Heaven.

—Such is *Pride.* David remarks this. "Pride compasseth them like a chain." Nebuchadnezzar is an example of it. The king spake and said, "Is not this great Babylon that I have built for the house of the kingdom, by the might of my power, and for the honour of my majesty?"

"Pigmies are pigmies still, though perch'd on Alps:
And pyramids are pyramids in vales."

Yet men estimate their height, not by their figure, but by their elevation. A man is as distinguishable from his circumstances as a steed is from his caparisons; and as the latter would be judged of by his stature, and strength, and gracefulness, and speed, so the former should be valued only by his personal and intrinsic worth. But to make ourselves to be something when we are nothing, we compose ourselves, so to speak, of every thing outward and adventitious; we add houses, and lands, and equipage, and offices, and titles, and attendants; and thus enlarged and magnified, we think ourselves Anakims, while others are but grasshoppers in our sight. Wealth can even give wisdom. It enlarges the understanding of the possessor. It qualifies him to speak and decide; so that his drivellings which were despised before, become oracular. For the world is blameable as the fool himself. The one no more readily receives, than the other pays this vile homage. The image of gold is sure of worshippers, if it be only a golden calf.

—Such is *Self-delusion.* The prosperous seldom hear the truth. They are never reproved. Their failings are often admired. Their faults are even turned into virtues, and imitated, by their dependants. All join to flatter and delude them. Yea, God himself is accessary to their flattery and delusion—not by his design, but by their misconstructions of his conduct. For they are induced to think that they are his favourites, because he not only spares, but indulges them; and conclude that he will not treat them worse in another world than he has done in this.

—Such is *Unwillingness to bear the Cross.* Why did the young man in the Gospel go away sorrowful? "He was very rich." He had much that was amiable, and much that was promising. He engaged our Saviour's

affections; and wished to follow him: but he had too much to leave behind. Why did not the Pharisees, who believed on him, confess him? "They feared lest they should have been put out of the synagogue, for they loved the praise of men more than the praise of God." Eusebius, in speaking of the persecution under Decius, observes, that most of those who apostatized were not from among the poor, but the rich. They who are softened by care, and rendered delicate by indulgence, are little prepared for a rough campaign, and cannot be expected to endure hardness as good soldiers of Jesus Christ.

—Such is *Earthly-mindedness.* Who are so likely to mind earthly things as those who abound with them? Who has so many ties to life? No condition indeed, here, will bear any comparison with the future state of the blessed: yet, according to our present views and feelings, the mansion and the pleasant scenery around, have more power to attract and detain than the desolateness of the poor-house. How little have some to resign! How much have they to urge their departure! How often does the heart's bitterness lead them to sigh, "I loathe it, I would not live alway"—"O! that I had wings like a dove, for then would I flee away and be at rest; I would haste me from the stormy wind and tempest." What uneasiness have others to excite them! How much have they to give up! How deep-rooted are they; and what force is necessary to loosen them from their position! "Ah!" said Johnson to Garrick, as he was walking over his bowers—"these are the things that make us unwilling to die."

—Such is *Worldly Conformity.* They are not the poor, but the rich, who have intercourse with the world. These are they who are tempted to recommend themselves to their friendship; to emulate their pretensions; to adopt their maxims, and manners, and *hours.*

—We may also mention *Self-indulgence.* We are far from pleading for monkish austerities and abstemiousness. Yet a Christian is to deny himself. Yet temperance is a part of godliness. Yet we are forbidden to provide for the flesh to fulfil the lusts thereof. But who is most likely to be profuse in dress and in furniture? Whose table is likely to become a snare? Who is in danger of feasting himself without fear? Whose precious mornings are most likely to be wasted in bed?

—To this we may add *Unfeelingness.* He is most likely to be kind to a stranger who knows the heart of a stranger, having been a stranger in a strange land. Who ever thinks of repairing to the gay and the dissipated in the hour of trouble? What interest will he feel in my grief who never wept himself? The tenderest and most active sympathy flows from experience. What does a king know of the miseries of his subjects? He never looked into their hovel; never tasted their bitter bread. They whose condition or office exempts them from the common vexations and distresses of life, are always the most insensible to the duties and calls of compassion. Only a priest or a Levite *could* have passed by on the other side; and left the poor wounded bleeding traveller to his fate.

After all, we have only presented a few specimens of the dangers of Prosperity. But surely they are enough to keep you from looking with grudging and uneasiness on the condition of those that abound in the world. Surely they are enough to induce you, instead of envying those that rise, to pity them and pray for them; for they are set in slippery places.

Surely we have said enough to excite those who are denied prosperity to be resigned and satisfied. Ah! ye who have had your purposes broken off, even the thoughts of your hearts: ye who have wished to build your nests on high, and to say to your soul, thou hast much goods laid up for many years; take thine ease, eat, drink, and be merry: ye to whom, after all your importunings of his providence, God has said, " Let it suffice; say no more to me of that matter"—Ah! who can tell what you have escaped? Who can tell what you might have been? You might, as Solomon has it, have been talking with your feet, and have swaggered by your neighbours. You might have answered roughly. You might have pleased a tyrant's heart, in making yourselves feared. You might have acted a Diotrephes in the parish or the church. You might have heard with indifference every tale of wo. You might have abandoned the worship of God in your families, and have lost your attachment to his Sabbaths and his house. You might have made your passage your portion; and instead of arising and departing hence, have felt yourselves at home in the body; and, "careful about many things," have overlooked that "good part" which now you have happily chosen, and which shall not be taken away from you.

Let all abandon their eager desires after the world; and, if they must increase, be concerned to increase with all the increase of God. " Seekest thou great things to thyself? seek them not." " Let your conversation be without covetousness; and be content with such things as ye have: for he hath said, I will never leave thee nor forsake thee." " For they that will be rich, fall into temptation and a snare, and into many foolish and hurtful lusts, which drown men in destruction and perdition. For the love of money is the root of all evil; which while some coveted after, they have erred from the faith, and pierced themselves through with many sorrows." The Apostle, in this passage, seems to refer to two classes of persons. First, to those who perish in their worldly things, making shipwreck of faith and a good conscience. These he compares to men at sea who founder, and are seen no more—they are drowned in destruction and perdition. Secondly, to those who are not destroyed but injured. These he compares to travellers, who seeing, as they are going along, some inviting fruit a little out of their road, step aside to gather: but as it is surrounded with thorns and briers, they wound themselves in the attempt. These *err* from the faith, and *pierce* themselves through with *many sorrows.*

For while the prosperity of fools destroys them, the prosperity of wise men may harm them. Saul was lost by his advancement; but David himself was injured; and hence we read of his "first ways." The hero, the conqueror, the king, never equalled the shepherd of Bethlehem.

Upon this principle, if you had to choose, you should not, you would not choose a state so frequently destructive; so commonly hurtful. You would not conclude that you were better than others, and that you should be safe where your brethren have so generally failed. If you did, *you* would be *sure* to yield; for "pride goeth before destruction, and a haughty spirit before a fall."

But the option is not left to yourselves. The Lord chooses your inheritance for you; and in his pleasure you must acquiesce. Only be sensible of the perils of the condition.

II. You are required to employ its SAFEGUARDS.

And, *first*, if you would escape the evils of Prosperity, consider much your *Responsibility.* Never imagine that the things you possess are your own, and that you are at liberty to do what you please with them. They are all in the nature of a trust. You are not the proprietors, but the stewards. When you receive them, a voice cries, "Occupy till I come:" and soon the same voice will say, "Give account of thy stewardship, for thou shalt be no longer steward. Keep your minds alive to the certainty of this account; the extent of this account; the strictness of this account; the nearness of this account—" Behold, the Judge standeth before the door." " Let your moderation be known unto all men: the Lord is at hand."

Secondly, Reflect on the *brevity of your Possessions.* There is a day coming when the heavens shall pass away with a great noise, and the earth, and all the works that are therein, shall be burned up. And then, " to whom will ye flee for help, and where will you leave your glory?"—But this prospect seems very far off; and the distance prevents impression.—Is death then far off? You have only a life-interest in your estate. And "what is your life? It is even a vapour that appeareth for a little time, and then vanisheth away." Then you must part with all for ever. "For we brought nothing with us into the world, and it is certain we can carry nothing out." But how frequently is the continuance of your possessions and enjoyments much shorter than life itself! "Wilt thou," therefore, says Solomon, "set thy heart on that which is not? For riches make to themselves wings and fly away." "Brethren," says the Apostle, "the time is short: it remaineth, that both they that have wives be as though they had none, and they that weep, as though they wept not; and they that rejoice, as though they rejoiced not; and they that buy, as though they possessed not."

Thirdly, Study *the vanity of your Acquisitions.* How little can they contribute to the reality of your happiness! Look at those in the circle of your acquaintance. Do you know any of them, I will not say, that have improved in religion, but that have increased in comfort? As to yourselves; have your contentment, and peace, and pleasure, risen with your circumstances in the world? Can riches profit in the day of wrath? Can any abundance relieve the anguish of a wounded spirit? What a source of perplexity and anxiety is a prosperous estate! "In the midst of his sufficiency he shall be in straits." What an attraction is it of ill-will! What an excitement to envy and slander! The success of a rival; the superior display of a neighbour; yea, even the disregard of an individual seemingly incapable of annoying us—even *his* neglect may spoil the relish of a courtier's bliss, the favourite of the owner of a hundred and twenty-seven provinces. "When he came home he sent and called for his friends, and Zeresh his wife. And Haman told them of the glory of his riches, and the multitude of his children, and all the things wherein the king had promoted him, and how he had advanced him above the princes and servants of the king. Haman said, moreover, Yea, Esther the queen did let no man come in with the king unto the banquet that she had prepared, but myself; and to-morrow am I invited unto her also with the king. Yet all this availeth me nothing, so long as I see Mordecai the Jew sitting at the king's gate."

People often wonder at *your* uneasiness; but the heart knoweth his own bitterness. *You* feel some worm at the root withering the gourd that overshadows you. Perhaps some personal or relative trial preys upon the peace of your mind. Perhaps the dear companion who once walked with you along your flowery path is removed far from you; and, disinclined to retrace the spots once endeared

by social converse, you watch and are alone, as a sparrow upon the house-top. Perhaps, when you sit down at table, David's seat is empty—and tears are your meat day and night. Perhaps the heir, who was to perpetuate your name and inherit your property, now occupies a tomb on which you have inscribed "And Thou destroyest the hope of man." Perhaps an infirmity is entailed upon you for life. Perhaps some disease is gradually undermining your frame. Perhaps your senses are declining; and desire fails: and the days are come wherein you have no pleasure. "Then I looked on all the works that my hands had wrought, and on the labour that I had laboured to do: and, behold, all was vanity and vexation of spirit, and there was no profit under the sun."

Fourthly, Think *how little worldly prosperity has distinguished many of the excellent of the earth.* When you are tempted to glory in wealth, remember what a multitude there is in poor life who would make you shrink into nothing, if you were morally compared with them: and what is gold to godliness? What superior grace and wisdom and usefulness dignified numbers of those servants of the Most High God and benefactors of men, who passed their days in a state of dependance, or ended them in a prison! Read the history, examine the lives of those preachers and writers whose immortal works praise them in all the churches. Take Luther, that great Reformer, who has levied a tax of admiration and gratitude on every age. He has this passage in his last will and testament—"O Lord God, I thank Thee that Thou hast been pleased to make me a poor and indigent man upon earth. I have neither house nor land nor money to leave behind me. Thou hast given me a wife and children, whom I now restore to Thee. Lord, nourish, teach, and preserve them as Thou hast me." The Apostles could say, "Even unto this present hour we both hunger and thirst, and are naked, and are buffeted, and have no certain dwelling-place." And the Lord of glory, the image of the invisible God, had not where to lay his head—And *yet* we think wealth the standard of excellence!

—Again. *Daily realize the assurances of Revelation.* "This is the victory that overcometh the world, even our faith." The influence of a greater good will abolish the impression of a less. The man who walks by sight, is sure to be conquered: the things which are seen are temporal; and he sees no other; these therefore strike and please and engross *him.* But the man who walks by faith, sees things invisible to the eye of sense; and these are eternal: and they are infinite. What is the honour that cometh from man, compared with the smiles of God! What is a handful of shining dust compared with "a far more exceeding and eternal weight of glory?" Can the stars be seen in the shining of the sun? What saved Moses in circumstances far more perilous than those of his birth? "By faith Moses, when he was come to years, refused to be called the son of Pharaoh's daughter; choosing rather to suffer affliction with the people of God, than to enjoy the pleasures of sin for a season." What led Abraham to "sojourn," even "in the land of promise, as in a strange land, dwelling in tabernacles with Isaac and Jacob, the heirs with him of the same promise?" Faith. "For he looked for a city which hath foundations, whose builder and maker is God—These all died in faith, not having received the promises, but having seen them afar off, and were persuaded of them, and embraced them, and confessed that they were strangers and pilgrims on the earth. For they that say such things, declare plainly that they seek a country. And truly, if they had been mindful of that country from whence they came out, they might have had opportunity to have returned. But now they desire a better country, that is, an heavenly: wherefore God is not ashamed to be called their God; for he hath prepared for them a city."

Finally. Forget not *the admonition of the Saviour:* "Watch and pray, lest ye enter into temptation." And what he has joined together let no man put asunder. In vain I invoke God, if I am careless; and expose myself needlessly in dangerous places and company; and leave without a sentinel my senses, and appetites, and passions; and keep not my heart with all diligence; and use not all the means of preservation which are placed within my reach—prayer without watching, is hypocrisy. And—watching without prayer, is presumption. Our strength is in God alone. He will make us know this, not only by the testimony of his word, but by our experience. And we need not be afraid of the growing conviction. When we are weak then are we strong. For He to whom a sense of our weakness will urge us to repair, is able to keep us from falling. Whatever be our inability and danger, if He holds up, we shall be safe. Let not those be discouraged who seek His help. The very exercise of prayer tends to secure you. But you have more to rely upon than the moral influence of the duty. If there be any meaning in the Scriptures, God hears prayer; he grants our petitions; he strengthens us with might by his Spirit in the inward man. "Ask," says the Saviour, "and ye shall *receive,* that your joy may be full."

Thus his grace shall be sufficient for you even in Prosperity. But a Christian should not only be concerned to use the world as not abusing it; he should not only be anxious to avoid the evils of his condition; but to exercise its virtues, and perform its duties, and sanctify its resources.—And the

III. Part of our subject calls upon you to IMPROVE THE ADVANTAGES OF PROSPERITY.

This is to be exemplified in three things. Gratitude. Beneficence. And Enjoyment. The first regards God. The second, our fellow-creatures. The third, ourselves.

First, you are to improve your Prosperity in a way of *gratitude.* God is to be owned as the author of all. The streams of comfort are many, and flow in various channels; but with Him is the fountain of life. "Do not err, my beloved brethren: every good gift and every perfect gift is from above, and cometh down from the Father of lights." The silver and the gold are His. However you have obtained it, whether from inheritance, or the legacies of friendship, or the labour of your own hands, He it is that giveth you power to get wealth. And your prosperity lacketh its firmest support, its loveliest ornament, its sweetest relish, if you do not acknowledge in it the providence of Him, whose blessing alone maketh rich and addeth no sorrow with it. Is this acknowledgment made? And is it real? And is it constant? And is it fervent? What would you think of a dependant who had no claim on your bounty; whom you not only relieved but supported, and supported in affluence; being not only attentive to his necessities, but meeting all his wishes—what would you think of such a dependant, if he should never call upon you; never send to you; never speak of you favourably to others; never think of you—but should take all this goodness as a matter of right, rather than of kindness; and act as if he would have all around him to believe that it was of his own producing or purchasing? How soon would you discontinue your unacknowledged favours; and how hateful would his conduct appear, not only to yourself, but to every one who witnessed it!

Yet how little is God owned! We sacrifice to our own net, and burn incense to our own drag. We ascribe our success to the wisdom of our own understanding; or the power of our own arm; or the interest we have in the favour of our fellow-mortals; or we take it as the effect of chance—while God is not in all our thoughts. "Therefore," says God, "I will return, and take away my corn in the time thereof, and my wine in the season thereof; for she did not know I gave her corn, and wine, and oil, and multiplied her silver and gold, which they prepared for Baal." This is a trying method to bring us to reflection: but it is often necessary. Continued enjoyment seems to give a kind of prescription; at least, it makes us forget our reliance and obligation. We are struck with what is new; while we overlook what is common. Whereas this should be the grand reason for praise; for the claim arises not from our benefits being occasional, but fre-

I   6*

quent and constant. How soon could the great Ruler and Benefactor convince you that he is not obliged to continue what you deem your own; and that he can, as easily as justly, recall what he has given! That this may not be the case, sanctify the Lord God in your thoughts. Think of your desert. Compare your condition with that of others. And while you see that the lines have fallen to you in pleasant places, and that you have a goodly heritage, say, "Bless the Lord, O my soul, and forget not all his benefits." The beginning of some of you was small. You remember a time when you had no inheritance, no not so much as to set your foot on; and had your subsequent enlargement been foretold, you would have exclaimed, with the surprised nobleman, "If the Lord should make windows in heaven, might such a thing be?" Surely *you* will follow the example of Jacob, who said, "Lord, I am not worthy of the least of all the mercies, and of all the truth, which thou hast showed unto thy servant: for with my staff I passed over this Jordan, and now I am become two bands." Surely *you* will retire with David before the Lord, and say, "O Lord God, what is my house, that thou hast brought me hitherto? And this was yet a small thing in thy sight, O Lord God; but thou hast spoken also of thy servant's house for a great while to come: and is this the manner of man, O Lord God?"

Secondly, You are to improve your Prosperity in a way of *beneficence.* In this respect you are favoured above many of your brethren. Their ear is not heavy that it cannot hear; but their hand is shortened that it cannot save. They see wants and miseries which only distress them; for they have only the disposition to relieve. But you can indulge it: you have the power. Value the substance you possess on this account. And remember also, that you have it for this very purpose. In the bestowment, God looked beyond yourselves; and designed to make you not only the subjects of his goodness, but the instruments: not only the recipients, but the diffusers. And how can you neglect to impart relief and comfort to others, while God is perpetually communicating to you; and your condition, as well as your religion, cries, "Freely ye have received, freely give?" This is the way to have your possessions blessed. This is the way also to have them increased. "Give alms of such things as you have, and behold all things are clean unto you." "The liberal soul deviseth liberal things, and by liberal things shall he stand."

Therefore says the Apostle, "Charge them that are rich in this world that they do good, that they be rich in good works, ready to distribute, willing to communicate; laying up in store for themselves a good foundation against the time to come, that they may lay hold on eternal life." The objects of your charity are numberless. Some of these have preferable claims; but none of them are to be excluded. As you have opportunity, you are to do good unto all men, especially unto them that are of the household of faith. There are the fatherless and the widows to visit; and the sick to heal; and the naked to clothe; and the hungry to feed. "The poor you have always with you:" and if you have the ability to succour, and withhold relief, your religion would perplex an inspired Apostle. "Whoso hath this world's good, and seeth his brother have need, and shutteth up his bowels of compassion from him, how dwelleth the love of God in him?" But there are also the careless to awaken; the ignorant to instruct; the vicious to reclaim; and the backsliding to restore. The soul is of supreme importance; and it becomes us peculiarly to aid in supporting those institutions, and exertions, which have in view the spiritual and eternal welfare of men. Even these require much pecuniary assistance; and it is the highest honour that can be conferred upon property that it is employed in carrying on the concerns of the Gospel. These have nobly multiplied in our day; and they occasion frequent applications to your liberality.

But surely you cannot complain of this frequency. It shows the improved state of your beloved country, religiously considered; and Christians should deem those the best times in which the best cause flourishes most. Surely you would not wish to bring back the state of things a century ago, when, for a year together, avarice and selfishness might have escaped these evangelical vexations. Have you not yourselves been accessory to this improvement? Have you not been praying that God's kingdom may come, and that his word may have free course and be glorified? And will you complain or rejoice when those prayers are answered? When you offered them, did you suppose that what you implored was to be carried on by miracles or by means? If by means, did you stipulate in these prayers that God should employ the instrumentality of others, and not require your own? Or, did you not mean to place yourselves at his disposal; and to ask, as the work was going on, "Lord, what wilt thou have me to do?" This must have been your meaning if you prayed sincerely and earnestly; and consistency requires, if you would not be condemned out of your own mouth, every sacrifice in your power. And how much is in the power of some of you! And how would your efficacy be increased, if you would be satisfied with a decent distinction above the vulgar, instead of being splendid; if you would avoid every extravagance and superfluousness in your mode of living; if you would exercise a little of that self-denial, which is the principal test of real benevolence.

Many rules have been laid down, as to the proportion of your estate or income which should be dedicated to beneficence. If conscience was not so often asleep, or if when awake it had any chance of being heard in the same hour with the love of money, the degree might safely be left to every man's own mind. Nothing however can be more just and reasonable than the injunction of the Apostle, "Let every one of you lay by him in store as God hath prospered him." This rule is, we fear, seldom observed. Yea, some, by a perverse process, feel the disposition diminishing as the ability increases. They give not only less in proportion, but less in reality, than they once did. In their contributions, as well as in their qualities, there is a gradation from gold to silver, and from silver to copper. Once they hardly thought it worth while to be covetous. They had little to set up in that character with. But wealth increased, and they soon began to hoard. Nor is it to be supposed that their eagerness to accumulate is declining with age. The less time they have to keep, the harder they are determined to hold; for, as Young says, "there is a dying grasp as well as a dying gasp."

"Of other tyrants short the strife;
But Avarice is king for life:
The despot twists with hard control
Eternal fetters round the soul."

But, with enlarged circumstances, be ye also enlarged. This is the case with a few we have the pleasure to know. Their fortune is a blessing to the neighbourhood and the nation. Their rising in life resembles the rising of the sun: the elevation illuminates and enlivens and fertilizes; and joy springs from its beams. Their wealth is like the dew, raised indeed from the earth, but only to be filtrated from its grossness, and to descend in silent refreshment, and vigour, and life. So it was with Job. He was the greatest man in the east; and he was also the most generous. His substance is mentioned; but it was not his possession, but his use of it, that rendered him so estimable. I envy not the bosom of that man who can hear without emotion his touching and eloquent appeal. "If I did despise the cause of my man-servant, or of my maid-servant, when they contended with me; what then shall I do when God riseth up? and, when he visiteth what shall I answer him? Did not he that made me in the womb make him? and did not one fashion us in the womb? If I have withheld the poor from their desire, or have caused the eyes of the widow to fail; or have eaten my morsel myself alone, and the fatherless have not eaten thereof; (for from my youth he was brought up with me as with a father, and I have guided her from my mother's womb:) if I have seen any perish for want of clothing, or any poor without covering; if his loins have not blessed me, and if he were not warmed with the fleece of my sheep; if I have lifted up my hand against the fatherless, when I saw my help in the gate: then let mine arm fall from my shoulder-blade, and mine arm be broken from the bone." David also had acquired much wealth: but hear his acknowledgment. "Now I have prepared with all my might, for the house of my God, the gold for things to be made of gold, and the silver for things of silver, and the brass for things of brass, the iron for things of iron, and wood for things of wood: onyx stones, and stones to be set, glistering stones, and of divers colours, and all manner of precious stones, and marble stones in abundance. Moreover, because I have set my affection to the house of my God, I have of mine own proper good, of gold and silver, which I have given to the house of my God, over and above all that I have prepared for the holy house, even three thousand talents of gold, of the gold of Ophir, and seven thousand talents of refined silver, to overlay the walls of the houses withal: the gold for things of gold, and the silver for things of silver, and for all manner of work to be made by the hands of artificers. And who then is willing to consecrate his service this day unto the Lord?" Here indeed was accumulation; but the design of it was not for the pleasure of possessing. It was not for his own aggrandizement, or splendour, or indulgence; or for those of his household; but for a moral and religious purpose. It is a sad reflection, especially in our day, for a good man to die wealthy. But if he must die rich, let him die rich towards God. Let him not at his last hour testify only his selfish regards. Let the benefactor appear as well as the man; and the Christian as well as the friend and the relation. While he provides for his own, especially those of his own house, let him not forget the Saviour who loved us, and gave himself for us: and whose cause has claims infinitely above all mortal interests.

Thirdly, You are to improve your Prosperity, in a way of *enjoyment.* I need not say that there is a great difference between possession and enjoyment; and that many who have more than heart can wish, have yet no heart to use it. They are hungry in the midst of food; and are parched with thirst, though the stream is at their lip. Solomon more than once notices this wretchedness; and considers it as one of the sorest evils under the sun. It is worthy of observation that the Latin word for miserable has been applied to designate an individual who possesses, but cannot enjoy. And well may he be called a *miser;* for of all men he is the most mean, and abject, and comfortless. And no one can more oppose the kindness of God in furnish ing us with the supplies of his providence. For He obviously designs to show us, that he is concerned, not for our existence only, but for our happiness. He could have supported us by means of food, as disagreeable to our palate as medicine: but he has rendered our sustenance grateful and inviting; and though eating is necessary to life, no one thinks of eating to avoid death. Our senses might all have been the inlets of pain only, instead of pleasure. Can any one question whether agreeable sounds were intended to delight the ear; or agreeable scents to gratify the smell! Look at the trees in a garden, or an orchard. The fruit could have been produced without the blossom: but in this process his beauty appears in the one, before his bounty is seen in the other: and the eye is charmed as well as the taste. Well therefore does the Apostle say, "He gives us all things richly to enjoy." And there is therefore truth in the remark of the Poet, "To enjoy is to obey." It is falling in with the indications of God's will; for he has given us an express injunction—"In the day of prosperity rejoice."

Religion therefore, instead of being an enemy to the *enjoyment* of this state, enjoins it. And it produces what it requires. We are not afraid to advance it as a maxim capable of demonstration, that in proportion as men are religious, they are prepared to relish prosperity; and that though others may possess more, they will enjoy more; for, even in this sense, "a little that a righteous man hath, is better than the riches of many wicked."

Religion refines and exalts our relish of temporal things. How low and despicable is a life filled up only with sleeping, and eating, and drinking, and trifling! A Christian rises above such an ignoble mode of being. Even in his enjoyments, reason unites with sense; and faith with reason; and devotion with faith. What is material is animated by mind; and what is animal, though its quality be not abolished, loses its grossness by intercourse with intellect and spirit. The earth grows richer by the reflection and touches of all that is heavenly. The rose of Sharon and the lily of the valley acquire a kind of sacredness and divinity in their fragrance and beauty, when they remind us of Him who is altogether lovely: and the charms of creation are hallowed and felt as means of grace, while they bring us into communion with the Creator, addressed and adored in language almost inspired—

" These are thy glorious works, Parent of good—
  Almighty! Thine this universal frame,
  This wondrous fair : Thyself how wondrous then !"

—And thus religion also enlarges as well as improves the enjoyment of prosperity. We readily allow that it forbids licentiousness and excess. But so does reason. So does

health. Yea, so does pleasure itself. The moderate use of the indulgences of prosperity, unspeakably exceeds in enjoyment the intemperate use of the glutton and drunkard. The very restraints which religion imposes are useful and necessary, to give the more lively and potent relish to our participations. For who needs to be informed that the measure of enjoyment corresponds with the strength and freshness of the desire or the appetite? Thus the pleasure of eating depends upon hunger; and where no degree of this is felt, the most delicious viands would be insipid. The full soul loathes the honeycomb, but to the hungry soul every bitter thing is sweet. Thus the unwearied do not welcome repose; but the sleep of a labouring man is sweet. It is therefore easy to see that temperance is the handmaid of enjoyment. By not impairing our appetites and desires, it keeps us from the languor and irksomeness of the dissipated; and by maintaining uninjured the capacities for enjoyment, it really cherishes and increases the resources which excess spoils and destroys.

—But this is not the only way in which religion befriends the enjoyment of prosperity. We must remark its moral influence in rectifying our dispositions and removing the causes of disquietude and dissatisfaction. All outward things affect us according to the state of the mind. It is well known to every man, that a scene which delights us at one time, will be perfectly uninteresting, if not repulsive, at another. The object in this case is the same, but the medium through which it appears, and the feelings in which it is received, are changed. No one can deny but that the agreeable impressions of outward things is impaired by infirmity and sickness of body. But many are not aware, that it may be equally injured by a disorder of the soul. Yet so it is. A pain in the tooth, or in the joint, will no more preclude enjoyment than the workings of jealousy, or suspicion, or envy, or anger, or revenge. Under the corrosion of these evils, a man must be wretched in all the entertainments of a palace, and all the scenery of a paradise. But religion forbids and subdues these self-tormenting, as well as vile tempers. It teaches the man to love his neighbour as himself. It enables him to rejoice in another's welfare. It renders him an Israelite indeed in whom there is no guile; and enables him to confide in others by judging of them from his own feelings of sincerity and harmlessness.—Why is that man so cheerless and uneasy? Is he poor? Has he been robbed of his estate? Look at his portion. What one more thing can he desire? But all will not bend to his humour. All will not respect him as the first man in the neighbourhood. He has the sorrow of the world that worketh death. A Christian does not feel this disease. He is meek and lowly in heart; and finds rest unto his soul.—Here is another dissatisfied and peevish mortal. Nothing pleases him. He reflects upon every one around him. His house is the hospital of ill-nature, and every ward is filled with complaint. What is the cause? He will not own it: but guilt makes him fretful. He is conscious of some duty he has neglected; some sin which he has committed; some restitution which he ought to make; some connexion which he ought to succour. This consciousness makes him uneasy. When censured, he knows he deserves it: when praised, he feels he is unworthy of it. He is a burden to himself. But a good man, says Solomon, shall be satisfied from himself. His rejoicing, though not his dependance, is the testimony of his conscience. He is not free from infirmity; but he can say, with David, "I was upright before Him, and have kept myself from mine iniquity."

Religion makes a man grateful: and gratitude is a lively and cheerful temper: and though to be under obligation to the mean and worthless, or to an enemy, be trying; nothing can be more delightful than to feel and acknowledge what we owe to one we greatly esteem and love, and who is worthy to be praised. David therefore speaks of the "pleasant harp:" and says, "Praise ye the Lord; for the Lord is good: sing praises unto his name; for it is pleasant." And to show what a connexion this exercise has with happiness, we are assured that it will continue in heaven, and perfect the enjoyment of the glorified.

Religion also makes a man beneficent; and this also contributes to his happiness. What do the selfish know of the pleasure of prosperity, compared with those who love to do good and to communicate? Is it not more blessed to give than to receive? Can any gratification be so pure, so cordial, so divine, so fresh and interesting in review, as that which is reflected back into the bosom from the feelings, and tears, and joy, of the partakers of your bounty? What voluptuary from his most studied and costly procurements ever tasted luxury like Job's? "When the ear heard me, then it blessed me; and when the eye saw me, it gave witness to me: because I delivered the poor that cried, and the fatherless, and him that had none to help him. The blessing of him that was ready to perish came upon me: and I caused the widow's heart to sing for joy. I was eyes to the blind, and feet was I to the lame. I was a father to the poor: and the cause which I knew not I searched out."

There is one view more to be taken of the subject; it is, the confidence in God which religion inspires. "Thou wilt keep him in perfect peace whose mind is stayed on thee, because he trusteth in thee." Why do not many enjoy what God has given them? They are anxious and foreboding. They suspend their satisfaction on some future occurrence —they may meet with losses—they may come to want: thus "they are not in quiet from the fear of evil." But the soul of the Christian dwells at ease. He knows not what a day may bring forth; nor does he desire it. He has nothing to do with events. He knows that he is under the providence of his heavenly Father, who is able and engaged to make all things work together for his good.

But this implies the previous adjustment of a case most awfully interesting. Belshazzar's entertainment was destroyed as soon as he saw a handwriting against the wall. Then neither the wine, nor the music, nor the company of a thousand of his lords, had the least power to charm: and though he was ignorant of the meaning of the inscription, he foreboded evil; and the joints of his loins were loosed, and his knees smote one against another. If a man was at the most enchanting banquet, with a sword hanging over his head by a small and rotten ligature, he could not enjoy it; or if he did, it must be by forgetting his jeopardy while yet his danger continued. The sinner is the enemy of God, and the child of wrath; and there is but a step between him and eternal death. The thought of this—the reflection that I must soon, and may every moment exchange all my good things here for the worm that never dies and the fire that never shall be quenched—is surely sufficient to turn all my joy into sadness and horror. To enjoy therefore, in this state, I must forget my exposure. Conscience tells me I have no right to take comfort. I must therefore creep forth and steal, while conscience is asleep. But will it, can it sleep always? How quickly may it be awakened! And then trembling takes hold upon me. My enjoyment, if it deserves the name, depends therefore on delusion; and this delusion is at the mercy of a thousand disturbers. If therefore I am not always in bondage, I am always subject to bondage through fear of death; and there is no peace, saith my God, unto the wicked. But the Christian being justified by faith, has peace with God through our Lord Jesus Christ. His anger is turned away; and as soon as He smiles, every thing smiles. In His favour is life. Tell me, ye who are unpardoned and unrenewed, Can you, you who have no hope of a better world, and no certainty of continuing an instant in this—Can you enjoy the comforts of life, like one who knows that whenever he dies, to die is gain? That he has in heaven a better and an enduring substance? That he has a covenant right to all he possesses? That it comes to him with the good will of his God and Saviour? saying, as he partakes—"Eat thy bread with cheerfulness, and drink thy wine with a merry heart, for God hath accepted thy works?"

"He looks abroad into the varied field
  Of nature, and though poor perhaps, compar'd
  With those whose mansions glitter in his sight,
  Calls the delightful scenery all his own.
  His are the mountains, and the valleys his,
  And the resplendent rivers. His to enjoy
  With a propriety that none can feel
  But who, with filial confidence inspired,
  Can lift to Heaven an unpresumptuous eye,
  And, smiling, say—' My Father made them all !'
  Are they not his by a peculiar right,
  And by an emphasis of interest his,
  Whose eye they fill with tears of holy joy,
  Whose heart with praise, and whose exalted mind
  With worthy thoughts of that unwearied love,
  That planned, and built, and still upholds a world,
  So clothed with beauty for rebellious man ?
  Yes—ye may fill your garners, ye that reap
  The loaded soil, and ye may waste much good
  In senseless riot ; but ye will not find
  In feasts, or in the chase, in song, or dance,
  A liberty like his, who, unimpeach'd
  Of usurpation, and to no man's wrong,
  Appropriates nature as his Father's work,
  And has a richer use of yours than you."

We have seen how religion befriends Prosperity, by raising and increasing its enjoyments. But you ask, can it *preserve?* Yes. It insures the continuance as far as it is good for us.

But we are not going to deny that every thing here is precarious. "Truly light is sweet, and a pleasant thing it is for the eyes to behold the sun: but if a man live many years, and rejoice in them all; yet let him remember the days of darkness, for they be many. All that cometh is vanity." Yes, your treasure on earth moth and rust may corrupt, or thieves break through and steal. Your health may be exchanged for sickness. Your friends may be converted into enemies. Your relations may be carried down to the dust. The soft and delicate hand may be forced to ply the oar of labour. You may not be known of those your bounty has fed. And after the morning sunshine, the noon or the evening of life may set in with dark waters and thick clouds of the sky. Is such vicissitude impossible? Improbable? Unfrequent? Let the day in which we live answer this.

And such desolation religion may not interfere to prevent. Is it then useless? And does it keep aloof when we need its aid? No. When it does not rescue us from the evil day, it prepares us for it. What it does not prevent, it softens. What it does not hinder, it sanctifies. It indemnifies the sufferer by inward supports, and future expectation. It renders every loss a gain. It turns the curse into a blessing.

What will the worldling do in the loss of *his* prosperity? His portion is gone. His hope is wrecked. His heart is desolate. Refuge fails him. He curses God and his king, and looks upward. Or he lies down in his shame, and his soul prefers strangling and death rather than life. His time ends with one hell, and his eternity begins with another. But to the upright there ariseth light in the darkness. God is his refuge and strength: a very present help in trouble. He feels, but

he is not miserable. He is perplexed, but not in despair. He is cast down, but not destroyed. He is laid waste, but he is not resourceless: "Although the fig-tree shall not blossom, neither shall fruit be in the vines; the labour of the olive shall fail, and the fields shall yield no meat; the flock shall be cut off from the fold, and there shall be no herd in the stalls: yet I will rejoice in the Lord, I will joy in the God of my salvation. The Lord God is my strength, and he will make my feet like hinds' feet, and he will make me to walk upon mine high places."

But this falls in with the subject of our next Lecture; which will show us the Christian in Adversity.

LECTURE VII.

THE CHRISTIAN, IN ADVERSITY.

" In the day of adversity consider."
Eccles. vii. 14.

THE condition in which we have recently viewed the Christian is not a very common one. We felt the difficulty; and in the course of the Lecture were often led to make the PROSPEROUS the subjects of reflection, rather than the objects of address. For when a minister enters his pulpit, how few among the godly can he see in his audience, that are set on the high places of the earth, and have the waters of a full cup wrung out unto them, and have more than heart can wish!

But, of this kind, we feel no difficulty, in the present service. We are no more at a loss to find persons to address, than topics to enlarge upon, when we treat of AFFLICTION. The inheritance of grief is as sure to mortals, as the laws of nature are inviolable—" Man is born to trouble as the sparks fly upward." Some parts of his destiny are less exposed, and less painful, than others; but after every concession, life is a warfare, and earth is a vale of tears.

"*I* hang the world in mourning?" It is Solomon, who saw its most favoured aspects, and enjoyed its most envied resources: it is history; it is universal observation; it is individual experience, that proclaims, "All is vanity, and vexation of spirit." Who has purchased an assurance from accident and disease? Who has not enemies that oppose him? Cares that corrode him? Fears that dismay him? Disappointments that confound him? Who does not find in his comforts, the elements of sorrow? In his possessions, the sources of danger? In his distinctions, the excitements of envy and detraction? In his affections, the seeds of anxiety and anguish? In his connexions, the pledges of apprehension and bereavement?

    " E'en roses grow on thorns,
      And honey wears a sting."

Sufferer! You think your case is singular

and you are often urged to exclaim, "*I am
the man that hath seen affliction by the rod
of his wrath.*" "Behold, and see if there be
sorrow like unto *my* sorrow." But this is
the language of self-importance, and ignorance. "For there hath no temptation taken
you, but such as is common to man."

But you ask—"How is it, not with the
man, but with the *Christian?* Has the favourite of Heaven no indulgences, or, at least,
no exemptions on earth? Surely, if they
had it in their power; surely, the friend
would secure the companion of his bosom, and
the father the child of his love, from every
thing hurtful and distressing. If God was
my father and my friend, he *could* by one
violation of his will set me at ease; and
would he suffer me to walk in the midst of
trouble, to be straitened in want, and to pine
away with sickness? If I am his, why am
I thus?" Yet David said, "Many are the
afflictions of the righteous." And our Saviour
says to his disciples, "In the world ye shall
have tribulation." And it is the *Christian*
we are to view, this morning,

IN ADVERSITY.

It is to "the elect according to the foreknowledge of God the Father," that the
Apostle Peter addressed himself, when, to
break the force of their surprise, he said,
"Beloved, think it not strange concerning
the fiery trial which is to try you, as though
some strange thing happened unto you." No.
Religion does not preclude the evil day; but
it prepares us for it; and shows itself to most
advantage, when all other resources *must*
fail.

We have a thousand instructions and admonitions concerning the spirit and demeanour
of the Christian in tribulation: but they may
all be summed up in the words of our text,
"*In the day of adversity consider.*"

We enter upon our subject with one important remark. Whatever the people of the
world may think of it, the religion of Christ
is "a reasonable service." Nothing can be
more distinguishable from groundless belief,
from the enthusiasm of ignorant impulses,
from a mere mass of unintelligible feelings.
It commences in the renewing of the mind.
It is carried on through the medium of thought.
Nothing can be moral that does not arise
from design, and is not influenced by motive.
Spiritual agencies are not like the cures of a
charm, of whose efficiency no account can be
given. They are not like the forced motions
of a machine, insensible of its workings and
results. Neither are they like the operations
of the physical powers in the human body:
these are carried on independently of the
mind and will. The digestive action, the
secretion of the fluids, the circulation of the
blood, go on as well, if not better, when we
are asleep, as when we are awake. This, it

would appear, is too much the notion some
entertain of the work of the Spirit. But this
is the perversion of the language of Scripture. According to the sacred writers, as to
religious influences, we are not only the subjects, but the instruments. What is done in
us, is done by us. God is the author of every
thing good: our progress is from him; but
he does not *carry* us along in the way everlasting, but enables us to *walk.* He works
in us; but it is to *will* and to *do.* We are
not only impressed, but employed. Faith
and repentance are the gifts of God; yet we
believe and repent, and not God.

This being premised, we observe, that religion arises from *consideration.* Therefore,
God, complaining of the Jews, says, "My
people do not consider." Therefore he cries,
"Consider your ways." Therefore David
says, "I thought on my ways, and turned my
feet unto thy testimonies." This extends to
each part of religion, as well as the whole.
The Christian's abhorrence of sin is not a
thoughtless aversion—"How can I do this
great wickedness, and sin against God?" His
godly sorrow is not a thoughtless grief—
"They shall look on him whom they have
pierced, and mourn." His confidence is not
a thoughtless trust—"They that know thy
Name will put their trust in Thee." His
hope is not a presumptuous expectation—He
is "ready to give a reason of the hope that is
in him." His conduct in trouble is not the
result of a natural hardihood, a brutal apathy,
a careless desperation—it is the effect of
thought, scriptural thought, sanctified thought
—"*In the day of adversity consider.*"

Christians! there are many things you
ought to consider in the day of trouble; but
we shall confine your attention to two only.
The DESIGN of Affliction. And the RELIEF
of Affliction.

I. The DESIGN OF AFFLICTION, to regulate
your DUTY. And

II. The RELIEF OF AFFLICTION, to support
your HOPE.

The one will keep you from "despising
the chastening of the Lord;" the other, from
"fainting when you are rebuked of him."

I. Consider the DESIGN OF AFFLICTION.

Without this, you cannot discharge the
duty of the condition. For what is this duty?
It is not only to possess your souls in patience
—it is not only to submit yourselves under
the mighty hand of God—but to acquiesce in
the pleasure of the Almighty. It is not to
say, "This is my grief, and I must bear it;"
but, "Here I am, let him do what seemeth
him good." Nothing less is required of you,
as Christians, than a willing, cheerful resignation. But this can only flow from a knowledge of him that smiteth you. You may
yield, but you cannot acquiesce, without con-

fidence in him. You may, with David, be dumb and open not your mouth, because he doeth it; and you may say, with Watts,

> "Peace, all our angry passions: then
> Let each rebellious sigh
> Be silent at His sovereign will,
> And every murmur die—"

—But you cannot render a voluntary, and cheerful and grateful, resignation, till you see the righteousness, the wisdom, and, above all, the *kindness* of his dispensations towards you. Therefore you are commanded to *hear* the rod—What does it say? "And in the day of adversity *consider*"—consider the ends he has in view in afflicting you. What are these ends? They all show that resignation is the most dutiful and becoming thing in the world. They are all founded in our exigences and advantages: but they are various; and none of them must be lost sight of. For a Christian will often find it necessary to turn to each of them before he can obtain an answer to the prayer, "Show me wherefore Thou contendest with me?" They include Correction—Prevention—Trial—Instruction—and Usefulness.

First, *Correction*. How absurd it is to suppose that God will suffer his children to act improperly, and not reprove them! The very discipline shows that they are not abandoned. It is the language of the paternal heart—"How shall I give thee up, Ephraim? How shall I deliver thee, Israel? How shall I make thee as Admah? how shall I set thee as Zeboim? Mine heart is turned within me, my repentings are kindled together."

No; He "will not cast away his people whom he foreknew:" but this is the law of the house—"If his children forsake my law, and walk not in my judgments; if they break my statutes, and keep not my commandments; then will I visit their transgression with the rod, and their iniquity with stripes."

And these stripes regard sins of omission, as well as of commission. For God enjoins, as well as forbids; and we offend by refusing his orders, as well as by opposing his prohibitions. Yea, further. They regard the state of the heart, as well as the conduct of the life—for "the backslider in heart shall be filled with his own ways." Where no miscarriages have appeared to our fellow-Christians, what a fall is there often in our feelings and our motives! What a decay of devotion! What a coldness of love! What a want of gratitude! What a loss of confidence! What a waste of time! What a misimprovement of privileges!—How does this enlarge the sphere of correction! And when all these calls for the rod are taken into the account, have we any reason to wonder that we are afflicted? Surely the cause for astonishment lies on the other side—that we so often escape; and that our chastisements are not only so few, but so gentle and tender. "I will

bear the indignation of the Lord, because I have sinned against Him." "Surely it is meet to be said unto God, I have borne chastisement, I will not offend any more: that which I see not, teach thou me: if I have done iniquity, I will do no more."

Secondly, *Prevention*. It is proverbially and truly said, that prevention is more than cure. In no case will this better apply, than in our moral failures. Repentance will not always fully recover us as to this world; or hinder the natural effects of our conduct from being entailed upon us for life. David fell by temptation, and was *reclaimed* and forgiven: yet his child died, and the sword never departed from his house; and his sin, in the scandal and mischief, was ever before him. Joseph was assailed by the same foe; but he was *preserved*; and thus sustained his peace of mind, and the approbation of his conduct, and the value of his reputation, and the usefulness of his character, and the benefit of his example. Hezekiah's "heart *was* lifted up;" and as the consequence, "wrath came upon him and upon all Judah." Paul was in danger from the same quarter. From his peculiar privileges he was exposed to high-mindedness; and we know not what injuries might have resulted from it to himself and others; but he was *not* elated. It would seem that he was ignorant of his jeopardy; but he had one to watch over him, who was wiser than himself, and could see effects in their causes. And how did he secure him? "Lest," says he, "I should be exalted above measure, through the abundance of the revelations, there was given to me a thorn in the flesh, the messenger of Satan, to buffet me." What this particularly was, we cannot determine: but it was—and this is sufficient for our purpose—it was a very sharp and painful affliction; and so anguished him, that he "besought the Lord thrice," that is, frequently and fervently, "that it might depart from him."

Ah, Christian, if you could see things as they really are in their moral relations, how many of your sufferings might be explained upon this principle! You have perhaps examined yourself; and though you have always enough in your general unworthiness and imperfections to render you vulnerable to trouble, yet you have been able to discover no one duty that you have knowingly neglected; no one sin that you have knowingly committed; no one idol that you have knowingly adored. But the case was this. You were not vain; but you were becoming so; and it was needful to withdraw the adulation and the incense in time. You were not avaricious; but you were becoming so; and it was necessary to lay waste the gain which made you think of accumulation. You had not worshipped the creature; but the growing fondness would soon have made you kneel, had not the desire of your eyes been taken away with a stroke.

We are little aware, now, of the obligations we are under, for our preservation, to the goodness of God; and the reason is, because the prevention which hinders the injury, hinders the discovery. But there are no blessings for which we shall be more thankful in the world of light, than preserving mercies; and we shall then perceive that the greater part of these were administered by affliction. These often answered the prayer, " Lead us not into temptation, but deliver us from evil." These checked us; but it was in going astray. The hinderance was suddenly interposed; but the danger was immediate, and the next movement would have been into a pitfall. It was sharp as a hedge of thorns; but it was necessary to pierce us back. It was impenetrable as a wall; but it was necessary to make us despair of going on. At first, we felt that we did well to be angry; but a pause was admitted, and the disappointment induced reflection, and we said, " I will go and return to my first husband, for then it was better with me than now."

Thirdly, *Probation.* It is for this reason that afflictions are so often called trials and temptations in the Scripture. They are in the nature of tests applied to our principles and dispositions; they are experiments employed to discover and display the reality and the degree of the evil or good there is in us. Moses tells the Jews, the design of the discipline to which they had been so long subjected in the wilderness was to prove them, and to know what was in their heart, and whether they would keep his commandments or no. And without this process, others would not have believed, nor could they have believed themselves, that they were so unbelieving, so rebellious, so perverse, so ungrateful, as they were now demonstrated to be. Job was charged with not serving God for nought; and the accuser of the brethren said, " Hast thou not made an hedge about him, and about all that he hath on every side? But put forth thy hand now, and touch all that he hath; and he will curse thee to thy face." How was this to be decided? God stripped him of all; of his cattle, of his servants, of his children. But instead of resentment and reviling, he worships, and says, " The Lord gave, and the Lord hath taken away; *blessed* be the name of the Lord." " Skin for skin, yea, all that a man hath will he give for his life," says the defeated but insolent foe: but, " put forth now thine hand and touch his bone and his flesh, and he will curse thee to thy face." And, lo! he is covered with sore biles from the sole of his foot to the crown of his head; and he takes a potsherd to scrape himself withal; and he sits among the ashes. But his lips mutter no reflection upon Providence. And when his wife, amazed at his enduring, asks, " Dost thou still retain thine integrity? Curse God, and die"—what says the sufferer? " Shall we receive good at the Lord's hand, and shall we not receive evil? In all this Job sinned not, nor charged God foolishly." A friend is born for adversity. But this last solace fails him, and his connexions, instead of soothing him, reproach and condemn. But even now he looks up and cries, " Though he slay me, yet will I trust in him."

Was he then perfect in the trial? He bore the proof; and was evinced to be gold. But he was not free from dross. He partially failed in the process—and even cursed the day of his birth. And he, even he, left a complete example to be furnished, by one who was fairer than the children of men; who did no evil, neither was guile found in his mouth; who, when he was reviled, reviled not again; when he suffered, threatened not; but committed himself to Him that judgeth righteously, saying, " Father, if it be possible, let this cup pass from me: nevertheless, not my will, but thine be done." When the Prince of this world came, even in his hour and power of darkness, he found nothing in him: no guilt to accuse him of; no corruption to operate upon. Agitate pure water, and no defilement will appear; but let the sea that has filthiness at the bottom be troubled, and however clean and clear it looks above, its waves will cast up mire and dirt. Afflictions are to the soul, like the rains to the house: we suspected no apertures in the roof, till the droppings through told the tale. The effects of these trials, therefore, are always humbling to the Christian. He is convinced by them that he has much less grace than he imagined: he is often rendered a wonder as well as a grief to himself. " I little thought I was so proud, till I was required to stoop; or so impatient, till I was required to wait; or so easily provoked, till I met with such an offence; or was so rooted to earth, till so much force was exerted to detach me from it."—Such must be the language of every attentive and faithful self-observer, when he reviews the trying scenes through which he has passed. We resemble the birds: they build in the lovely and inviting part of the year; and the foliage hides their nests: but in the winter, when the leaves have dropped off, their nests appear. Our retreats and delights in prosperity are discovered in adversity: and many a passenger can see where we rested, when we made not God our trust. When we have, *with* the Lord, health, and honour, and affluence, and friends; it is not easy to determine whether we are making *Him* or *these* our dependence and our portion. But when these are removed, the case is decided. If we were relying upon them, we sink: but if, while we were using them, we were cleaving to Him, our support·

K 7

will remain; and embracing Him firmer than before, we shall break through every despondence, and say, "Although the fig-tree shall not blossom, neither shall fruit be in the vines; the labour of the olive shall fail, and the fields shall yield no meat; the flock shall be cut off from the fold, and there shall be no herd in the stalls: yet I will rejoice in the Lord, I will joy in the God of my salvation."

Fourthly, *Instruction.* By long usage affliction has been spoken of as a school. It is indeed a dear one; but there is none like it. In this lecture-room the lessons are accompanied with experiments; and the great Teacher, by facts as well as words, says, "There—*There*—See what an evil and bitter thing sin is. See what a poor and vain thing the world is. See how it attracts its votaries to show its emptiness, and elevates only to depress. See what a precarious thing friendship is! See what human helpers can do for you! Men of low degree are vanity, and men of high degree are a lie. Cease from man, whose breath is in his nostrils; for wherein is he to be accounted of? Happy is he that hath the God of Jacob for his help, whose hope is in the Lord his God; which made heaven and earth, the sea, and all that therein is; which keepeth true for ever."

These instances appeal to the conscience, as well as the understanding. They serve not only to explain the subjects, but to quicken our attention. They produce a silence in the mind; a solemnity of soul; a softness of heart, that prepares us to receive divine truth. *Then* "he openeth the ears of men and sealeth their instruction." These are the lessons that make the deepest impression; that are the most easily and firmly remembered; that are the most useful and profitable in their *effects.*

"Blessed," says David, "is the man whom Thou chastenest, and teachest out of thy law." Nor did he speak from reasoning or faith only, but from experience: "It is good for me that I have been afflicted; that I might learn thy statutes." Luther says, "I never knew the meaning of the word till I was afflicted." "We fear," says Bishop Hall, "our best friends: for my part, I have learned more of God and myself in one week's extremity, than the prosperity of a whole life had taught me before."

Lastly, *Usefulness.* Affliction gives a man the tongue of the learned, that he may know how to speak a word in season to him that is weary. It produces that sympathy which arises most powerfully from experience; and which indeed can hardly be found without it. In vain you repair in the hour of trouble to those who never knew what an anguish meant. They will not listen to your tale of wo. It does not interest them—they do not understand it—they are unacquainted with grief. But he who has borne the smart himself, will not, cannot, with a careless mien and an unfeeling heart, listen to a sufferer who cries, "Pity me, pity me, O ye my friends, for the hand of God hath touched me." "Be kind," said Moses to the Jews, "be kind to strangers, for ye know the heart of a stranger; for ye were strangers in a strange land." In this way, the Redeemer himself is not an high priest who cannot be touched with the feeling of our infirmities: he was in all points tempted like as we are: and in that he himself hath suffered being tempted, he is able also to succour them that are tempted.

But nothing strikes like a fact. The oak scathed with lightning attracts the notice of passengers more than all the other trees of the forest. Trouble awakens attention, and draws forth inquiry. The Christian is never so well circumstanced, to "glorify the Lord," as "in the fires." There he can display the tenderness of his care, the truth of his promise, the excellency of the Gospel, the supports of Divine grace. In the review of my own varied intercourse with society, I confess, nothing so vividly and powerfully affects me, as what I recollect to have met with from pious individuals exemplifying the spirit and resources of Christianity under bodily disease, and the losses, and bereavements, and disappointments of life. O when I have visited such a martyr—such a witness for God; when I have found him standing in the evil day like a rock in a raging current with sunshine on its brow: when I have observed him, full of tribulation in the world, and of peace in Christ: mourning more for his sins than his sorrows: afraid of dishonouring his profession by impatience and unbelief: more concerned to have his crosses sanctified, than to have them removed: turning a tearful eye towards the Inflicter, and saying, "I know, O Lord, that thy judgments are right, and that thou in faithfulness hast afflicted me: just and true are all thy ways, O thou King of saints—He hath done all things well:" when I have witnessed religion—and I have witnessed it—accomplishing achievements like these, I have said to it as I withdrew—"I have heard of thee by the hearing of the ear, but now mine eye seeth thee."

As the sky is only decked with stars in the night, so the Christian shines most in the darkness of affliction; and by nothing is he so impressive as by the exercise of the passive graces. And this should reconcile you to the will of God in your sufferings. You are not to be selfish. You are not detached individuals; but parts of a community, civil and religious. And you should think yourselves honoured and happy in serving your generation; and the manner in which you are to serve it, you are to leave to God. People sometimes express a wish to be useful; but it must be in their own way. They wish to do something, but their meaning is to do something that is puolic and striking: originating, perhaps, some institution, or heading some new party—doing something that excites notice and noise. Here the motive *may* be good, but it should be peculiarly examined; for exertions of this kind fall in with the principles of our nature, the love of action and the desire of fame. "But they also serve that wait"—And they also serve that suffer. You may be called to retire rather than to act. You may be usefully employed in the quiet duties of domestic life, or in the soberness and sameness of business. Yea, you may be detached from your callings, and be confined by accident or sickness, and have not only wearisome nights, but months of *vanity* appointed you. So you may deem them—and suppose that you are going to be laid aside, when you are perhaps approaching the most profitable portion of your lives. For there, in the house of affliction, and on the bed of languishing; there, the minister who visits you shall be taught how to preach; your fellow-christians shall be edified; the young convert shall be encouraged and confirmed; the careless neighbour shall be impressed—or, even in the want of human observers, who can tell but other witnesses may look down and adore the displays of divine grace in your sufferings, and glorify God in you. For we are "a spectacle to the world, to *angels*, and to men."

II. In the day of adversity, consider your RELIEF.

This is necessary, to support your hope, and to keep you from being swallowed up of over-much sorrow. You may feel. You must feel. "No chastening for the present seemeth to be joyous, but grievous." It does not depend upon us to be unaffected with certain events. We are made susceptible of pain, and of sorrow: religion cannot require us to attempt to throw off our nature, and to say to our Maker, "Why hast thou made me thus?" There is no giving up what we do not prize; no bearing what we do not feel; no enduring what we do not suffer. Correction is founded on our aversion to misery; and without the sensibility, the discipline cannot answer any of the moral purposes for which it is designed; all of which are included in our being made perfect through suffering.

Yet there is an extreme on the right hand, as well as on the left. As we are not to "despise the chastening of the Lord," so neither are we to "faint when we are rebuked of him." To the upright there ariseth light in the darkness: and he has resources which are not only sufficient to moderate his sorrow, but even to turn his sorrow into joy. This is the high ground we take for a suffering Christian; to "glory also in tribulation;" and to "count it all joy when" he falls "into

divers temptations." We are far from saying that he always can do this actually: but we are not to take his duty from his experience, but to endeavour to bring his experience to his duty. What is not invariably his attainment should be constantly his aim.—To aid you in aspiring after this distinction,

Consider, *First*, That your afflictions are not *peculiar*. "The same afflictions are accomplished in your brethren who are in the world." And will you refuse to drink of the cup they drink of, and to be baptized with the baptism they are baptized with? Is Providence in your case to deviate from the treatment of all the other branches of the household of faith? "Whom the Lord loveth he chasteneth, and scourgeth every son whom he receiveth." To which of the saints in Scripture or in history will you turn, in refutation of this decision? "What son is he whom the Father chasteneth not?" In vain you allege that you are acquainted with persons truly godly who are not afflicted. It is no easy thing to determine who *are* truly godly. Besides. *Have* they not been afflicted? *Will* they not be afflicted? Are you sure they *are not* afflicted even *now?* The rod is not always composed of the same twigs. There are griefs relative as well as personal; mental as well as corporeal; imaginary as well as real; invisible as well as apparent. "The heart knoweth his own bitterness." There are crosses which cannot be displayed. There are groanings which cannot be uttered—He sitteth alone and keepeth silence, because he hath borne it upon him—

"The path of sorrow, and that path alone,
Leads to the land where sorrow is unknown.
No traveller e'er reached that blest abode,
Who found not thorns and briers in his road.
The world may dance along the flowery plain,
Cheered as they go by many a sprightly strain—
Where Nature has her mossy velvet spread,
With unshod feet they yet securely tread:
Admonish'd, scorn the caution and the friend;
Bent upon pleasure, heedless of its end.
But He who knew what human hearts would prove,
How slow to learn the dictates of his love;
That, hard by nature and of stubborn will,
A life of ease would make them harder still;
In pity to the sinners he design'd
To rescue from the ruins of mankind,
Call'd for a cloud to darken all their years,
And said, 'Go, spend them in the vale of tears.'"

Secondly, Consider that they are not *casual*. Do our fellow-creatures oppose and injure us? They always act freely, and often criminally; yet we are not left to the vices and passions of men. They could have no power at all against us except it were given them from above. Nothing in any of our sufferings occurs by chance—there is no such divinity in the universe. Occurrences may be accidental and contingent with regard to us, who are not acquainted with the plan to be executed and developed: but they are not so with regard to Him who sees the end from the beginning, and worketh all things after the counsel of his own will. What takes place without Him? "I form the light, and create darkness; I make peace, and create evil. I the Lord do all these things." And He strikes no random blows. "He performeth the thing that is appointed for us:" and the appointment is made by one who has not only a right to ordain, but who cannot pervert justice; who is too wise to err; and who loved us so as not to spare his own Son, but delivered him up for us all. We are allowed, we are required to cast all our care on him, with the assurance that he careth for us. And is not his attention; his solicitude—how condescending is God in his language!—sufficient to relieve our minds? How delightful is it to sit at the feet of the great Teacher, and hear him discourse on the doctrine of Providence! Here we have nothing of the language of infidel philosophy. *He* does not represent the Supreme Being as occupied with worlds and whole systems; but overlooking individuals, and minute concerns—*He* did not suppose the Supreme Being capable of perplexity and fatigue—*He* did not think any thing too hard for Infinite Wisdom and Power—*He* did not think it beneath God to govern what was not beneath him to create. Among men, an attention to little things prevents an attention to great things; and an attention to great things prevents an attention to little ones; and no one can equally regard all the claims of the province of government he fills, however limited it may be. But, says Jesus, "*He* maketh *His* sun to rise:" and, *He* "sends forth *His* angels;" and, "a sparrow falls not to the ground without your heavenly Father; and the hairs of your head are all numbered." "Are you not of more value than many sparrows?" "Behold the fowls of the air: for they sow not, neither do they reap, nor gather into barns; yet your heavenly Father feedeth them. Are ye much better than they? And why take ye thought for raiment? Consider the lilies of the field, how they grow: they toil not, neither do they spin: and yet I say unto you, that even Solomon in all his glory was not arrayed like one of these. Wherefore, if God so clothe the grass of the field, which to-day is, and to-morrow is cast into the oven, shall he not much more clothe you, O ye of little faith!"

Exclude this doctrine, and God is a God afar off; there is no foundation for confidence; there is no excitement to devotion: in the darkness of my perplexities and difficulties I grope around, and can feel nothing to support me. But by realizing His superintending agency, I bring Him near, and by His presence fill what otherwise would be an awful and irksome void. He hears prayer. His interposition is attainable. By being connected with God, every place is rendered holy, every object interesting; every comfort is enriched; and every trial is softened. This principle I take with me into every allotment, every circumstance; and say, "The cup which my Father giveth me, shall I not drink it? It is the Lord, let him do what seemeth him good. I will cry unto God most high, unto God who performeth all things for me."

Thirdly, Consider that they are not *penal.* When the Israelites came to Marah, they could not drink of the waters, for they were bitter. "And Moses cried unto the Lord; and the Lord showed him a tree, which when he had cast into the waters, the waters were made sweet." If this was not designed to be a type, it yields us a striking allusion.

> "Bitter indeed the waters are
> Which in this desert flow;
> Though to the eye they promise fair,
> They taste of sin and wo."

What is the cure? The Cross—

> "The Cross on which the Saviour hung,
> And conquer'd for his saints,—
> This is the tree, by faith applied,
> That sweetens all complaints.

> "Thousands have found the blest effect,
> Nor longer mourn their lot:
> While on his sorrows they reflect,
> Their own are all forgot."

If the burden of sin be removed, whatever else is laid on us will be felt to be light. And surely he hath borne our griefs and carried our sorrows. The chastisement of our peace was upon him, and by his stripes we are healed. Hence, though his sufferings do not secure us from suffering, they change the nature and design of our afflictions; so that, instead of their being punishments, they are corrections; and are inflicted not by the sword of the Judge, but by the rod of a Father. The believer may sometimes misapprehend them, and, fearful of their being the messengers of justice, may say unto God, Do not condemn me. But the apprehension is groundless. We are chastened of the Lord, that we may not be condemned with the world. For there is no condemnation to them that are in Christ Jesus. He has redeemed them from the curse of the law, having been made a curse for them. And being now justified by his blood, they shall be saved from wrath through him. This is the rest wherewith we are to cause the uneasy to rest; and this is the refreshing. He was angry with us, but his anger is turned away: and he comforteth us. And not only so, but we also joy through our Lord Jesus Christ, by whom we have now received the atonement.

Fourthly, Consider that they are not *unalloyed.* The Apostle seems to enjoin too much when he says, "In every thing give thanks." But there is a reason for it. Take your condition, however trying. Has it no alleviations? Let candour, let gratitude, let truth examine the circumstances of the case. Is there nothing in the time? nothing in the place? nothing in the manner? nothing in the subject of affliction? that serves to soften its pressure? Do you believe that it might not have been worse? "Hath he smitten him, as he smote those that smote him? or is he slain according to the slaughter of them that are slain by him? In measure, when it shooteth forth, thou wilt debate with it. He stayeth his rough wind in the day of the east wind." Take your case, and lay it by the side of your desert. What would you have suffered had he dealt with you after your sins, or rewarded you according to your iniquities? —Place it by the side of the condition of others. You have lost much of your substance; but they have nothing left. You have buried one of your children: the grave has written them childless in the earth. You walk upon crutches: they are bed-ridden. You have months of vanity; but they have wearisome nights, and the multitude of their bones is filled with strong pain.—But O think of the Saviour. Think of his dignity; of his preceding state; of his innocency—We suffer justly, for we suffer the due reward of our deeds; but this man has done nothing amiss. Yet see Him. You suffer partially; he suffered in every part that was capable of passion. You suffer occasionally; and, for hours and days of pain, you have weeks and months of ease and pleasure: his sufferings reached from the manger to the cross: "He was a man of sorrows and acquainted with grief." Your sufferings are unforeseen; his were known from the beginning; and he bore them in prospect before he endured them in reality. And whose tongue can express, whose imagination can conceive, what he endured when he began to be sore amazed and very heavy? when his soul was exceeding sorrowful even unto death? when his sweat was as it were great drops of blood, falling to the ground? when he exclaimed, "My God, my God, why hast thou forsaken me?"

> "Now let our pains be all forgot,
> Our hearts no more repine;
> Our sufferings are not worth a thought,
> When, Lord, compared with thine."

Fifthly, Consider that you are not to bear them *alone*. For he hath said, "I will never leave thee, nor forsake thee." This is a general promise, and necessarily includes every particular case. But knowing the anxieties and forebodings of the heart, he has been pleased to issue particular assurances with regard to the hour of suffering. "I will be with thee in trouble." "When thou passest through the waters, I will be with thee; and through the rivers, they shall not overflow thee: when thou walkest through the fire, thou shalt not be burnt; neither shall the flame kindle upon thee." Herein his conduct forms a contrast with the friendship of others. A friend is born for adversity: but he oftener raises expectations than real-

izes them. And Solomon tells us, "that confidence in an unfaithful man in the time of trouble is like a broken tooth, or a foot out of joint." These are more than useless. You attempt to use them, and they not only fail, but make you writhe with pain. "To him that is afflicted, pity should be showed of his friend; but he forsaketh the fear of the Almighty." Job found it so, and said, "My brethren have dealt deceitfully as a brook, and as the stream of brooks they pass away." Paul found it so: and though the brethren came to meet him, when he was going to Rome, to appeal unto Cæsar, as far as Appii Forum and the Three Taverns, he complains, "at my first answer no man stood by me, but all men forsook me." But he adds, "notwithstanding the Lord stood by me and strengthened me." He is true, whoever is treacherous: whoever fails, He is faithful. To this Latimer testified in his last moments. Being fastened to the stake and the fire just about to be kindled, he turned a heavenly countenance towards his fellow-sufferer, and said, "God is faithful, who will not suffer us to be tempted above that we are able"— While Ridley answered, "Yes, be of good cheer, brother; he will abate the fury of the flames, or give us strength to abide them." Spilsbury had suffered for conscience' sake, and had been released from his confinement. But when apprehended a second time, he said, seeing his wife and children weeping, "I am not afraid to go to prison now—I found God there the first time." In his flight and dreariness, the vision at Bethel was a privilege beyond all Jacob's expectation and thought. Driven from home, and traveling alone; having no guide to direct him, no defender to protect him, no associate to soothe his mind by communion: a forlorn youth, ruminating on his sad condition, and conflicting with those fears which attend uncertain events—he lights on a certain place, and tarries there all night, because the sun was set. The darkness was his curtains, the ground his bed, and a stone his pillow. There he falls asleep, and sees and hears what encouraged him to the last moment of life. But said he in the morning, "Surely God is in this place, and I knew it not." This ignorance and surprise serve to represent the apprehensions of many of the people of God: they seem to think they shall be found deserted in such situations and difficulties. But He is better than their fears; He surpasses even their hopes. He is there, and no sooner do they call, than He answers, "Here I am."

Yea, He is not only with them really, but peculiarly in the day of trouble. "As one whom his mother comforteth," says he, "so will I comfort you; and ye shall be comforted in Jerusalem." The anxious tender mother regards all her offspring: but she is most concerned for the poor weakly sickly child. The knee, the bosom is for *him*: for *him* is the prepared delicacy, and the noiseless room, and the breathless step, and the frequent watching and leaning over the bed of languishing, and the entreated reception of the offensive draught, accompanied with the sincere assurance, "Ah, my darling child, how gladly would I take it for thee." And thus it is with His afflicted people. They have their special privileges. As their day, so their strength is; and as the sufferings of Christ abound in them, the consolation also aboundeth by Christ: and thousands can testify that they have had clearer discoveries, richer communications, and tenderer supports, under their trials, than they ever experienced in seasons of ease and prosperity. What want we more? "God," says the Church, "is our refuge and strength, a very present help in trouble: therefore will not we fear, though the earth be removed, and though the mountains be carried into the midst of the sea; though the waters thereof roar and be troubled, though the mountains shake with the swelling thereof." No creature can be a substitute for Him; but he is more than a substitute for every creature; and his presence peoples and fertilizes and gladdens the gloomiest desert: "I will allure her, and bring her into the wilderness, and *there* will I speak comfortably unto her. And I will give her her vineyards from *thence;* and the valley of Achor for a door of hope: and she shall sing *there*."—The lamp cannot supply the place of the sun; but you have no reason to complain, if you can say, with Mrs. Rowe,

"Thou dost but take the lamp away
To bless me with unclouded day."

If we faint in the day of adversity, it is by losing sight of Him whose grace is always sufficient for us. We resemble Peter. "Come," said our Saviour: "And when he was come down out of the ship, he walked upon the water, to go to Jesus. But when he saw the wind boisterous, he was afraid, and beginning to sink, he cried, Lord, save me." Ah, said Jesus, you should have looked not at the waves but at me. Am not I here? Within sight? Within reach? "And immediately Jesus stretched forth his hand, and caught him; and said unto him, O thou of little faith, wherefore didst thou doubt?" How sublime is the exclamation of Doddridge! but it is founded in reason and truth—make it, Christian, whatever threatens, your own—

"If thou, my Jesus, still art nigh,
Cheerful I live; and cheerful die;
Secure, when mortal comforts flee,
To find ten thousand worlds in thee!"

Lastly, Consider that you are not to endure them *always*. "For there is an end, and thy expectation shall not be cut off." That end is *certain*. Sisera's mother anxiously waited at the window for the arrival of her son, but he never came. The warrior has confidently reckoned upon a victory, which he never obtained; and the mariner has been ready to hail a desired haven, which he never reached. "We looked," said the disappointed Jews, "for light, and behold darkness; for peace, and behold trouble." But, O Christian, there is hope in thy end—a hope that cannot make ashamed. Thy release from sorrow is as sure as the purpose, the promise, the covenant, the oath of God can render it.—That end is *near*. "Yet a little while, and he that shall come, will come, and will not tarry." If your cross be heavy, you have not to carry it far. If life be short, trouble cannot be long. When a few years are come, you will go the way whence you will not return. It may be much less. A few months; a few weeks; a few days more; and all will be peace, all will be quietness, all will be assurance for ever. The sacred writers love to diminish the period. In one place they tell us, "weeping may endure for a *night*, but joy cometh in the morning." In another, that these "light afflictions are but for a *moment*." In a third, that "for a *small* moment we are forsaken." So, and no more is it in the estimation of faith, and compared with eternity.—That end is *blessed* and *glorious*. No power of description or thought can do it justice. It will bring a full developement of all the trying dispensations through which you have passed. You shall no longer walk by faith, but by sight. You shall see that his work is perfect, and his ways judgment. You shall see how the most adverse providences were essential to your welfare; and not only feeling satisfied, but filled with wonder and gratitude, you will be able to say,

"Amidst my list of blessings infinite,
Stands this the foremost, that my heart has bled.
For *all* I bless Thee; *most for the severe*."

What was Canaan to the Jews, after all the bondage of Egypt, and the travels and privations of the desert; what was that land flowing with milk and honey, that rest which the Lord their God gave them; compared with the rest that remains for the people of God—the better, that heavenly country! What a complete, what an eternal discharge! Of all your sufferings, nothing will remain but the remembrance, and this will enhance the deliverance; and "the greater the sorrow, the louder you'll sing." The shadow of care, of sorrow, of fear, shall never flit over those regions of repose and blessedness. "Thy sun shall no more go down; neither shall thy moon withdraw itself: for the Lord shall be thine everlasting light, and the days of thy mourning shall be ended." I could go on repeating Scripture, for it loves to dwell upon this subject; but I will conclude this reference with two passages. The one is, the testimony of the Apostle Paul. He spoke from experience. No one had suffered more; and he had been in the third heaven. But hear him: "I reckon that the sufferings of this present time are not worthy to be compared with the glory that shall be revealed in us." The other is the address of the Angel to John in the Revelation; words which Burns the poet says he could never from a child read without tears—so allied is the tenderness of genius to the sentiments of piety. "He said unto me, what are these which are arrayed in white robes? and whence came they? And I said unto him, Sir, thou knowest. And he said unto me, these are they which came out of great tribulation, and have washed their robes, and made them white in the blood of the Lamb. Therefore are they before the throne of God, and serve him day and night in his temple: and he that sitteth on the throne shall dwell among them. They shall hunger no more, neither thirst any more; neither shall the sun light on them, nor any heat. For the Lamb which is in the midst of the throne shall feed them, and shall lead them unto living fountains of waters: and God shall wipe away all tears from their eyes."

Men and brethren, you have often heard it said, "The end crowns the action." "All is well that ends well." Now religion has this recommendation. We are far from denying its present advantages; for we know from Scripture and observation and experience that it is profitable unto all things, and has promise of the life that now is, as well as of that which is to come. But allowing that it were all gloom, and self-denial, and sacrifice, and suffering, here; yet "mark the perfect man, and behold the upright, for the end of that man is peace." The happiness in which it terminates, infinitely more than indemnifies and recompenses all the hardships and trials of the passage. Even Balaam confessed this; and prayed, "Let me die the death of the righteous, and let my last end be like his."

What a difference between the Christian and others! Both are advancing towards the close of life: but *they* are leaving their good things, and *he* his evil ones. Both will soon bid an eternal farewell; but they to their joys, and he to his sorrows. They at death will plunge into "the blackness of darkness for ever;" while he will reach "the inheritance of the saints in light."

—So reasonable is the Christian's resignation; and so well founded is the Christian's hope, with regard to affliction.

—"But what has such a subject as this to do with me? I am not in trouble." Then I tremble for you. We know of whom David speaks, when he says, "they are not in trouble as other men; neither are they plagued like other men." And we know who has

said, "Because they have no changes, therefore they fear not God." But if you are not afflicted, you soon may. Every thing here is uncertain. How often is the lamp of the wicked put out! Truth whispers, "Truly the light is sweet, and a pleasant thing it is for the eyes to behold the sun: but if a man live many years, and rejoice in them all, yet let him remember the days of darkness, for they shall be many. All that cometh is vanity. Is it not therefore wise to provide against what is possible, what is probable, yea, I will add, unavoidable? "A prudent man foreseeth the evil, and hideth himself; but the simple pass on, and are punished." But are you sure you are not afflicted even now? In the midst of your sufficiency, are you not in straits? In all your successes, do you not feel a cold aching void within, still urging you to ask, "Who will show us any good?" While you walk according to the course of the world, do you not complain of the poverty of its pleasures, and the falseness of its resources? Are you not dissatisfied with all creature enjoyments? Is there not a constant war between your inclinations and convictions? Does not conscience often condemn you? Have you not your forebodings of the future? Do you never think of the infirmities of approaching years; of the house appointed for all living; of the judgment-seat of Christ?

Perhaps at this very moment you are not strangers to a wish that you had never been born. Colonel Gardiner tells us, that "while he was keeping up every gay appearance, and was envied as the happiest of mortals, he would gladly have exchanged conditions with a dog." "There is no peace, saith my God, unto the wicked."

—But here are some, here are many before me who are in trouble. For the days are evil; and the cup is going round; and what family, what individual is not called to taste the bitterness, if not to drink the very dregs? I do not ask you what your trials are; but I must inquire, what are you doing under them? Are you despising the chastening of the Lord, or are you fainting now you are rebuked of Him?—Unsanctified trouble always produces one of these: it always hardens the sufferer against God, or sinks him into despondency.

Is the former of these your case? Are you one of those, who, when he arrays himself against them, instead of submitting, "rush upon the thick bosses of his buckler;" and "fight against God?" Are you like Ahaz, of whom it is said, "In his affliction he sinned yet more and more against God—This is that Ahaz!" It was an awful appeal that Jeremiah made to God, concerning many of his hearers. Must your preacher prefer the same? "O Lord, are not thine eyes upon the truth? Thou hast stricken them, but they have not grieved; thou hast consumed them, but they have refused to receive correction: they have made their faces harder than a rock; they have refused to return." If this be the case, faithfulness requires me to tell you that one of these two consequences will be sure to follow. That is,—either God, provoked by your contempt of his correction, will cease to disturb you, and recalling the instruments of his discipline, will say, "They are joined to idols, let them alone;" or he will turn the rod into a scorpion, and fulfil the threatening, "If ye walk contrary to me, I also will walk contrary to you, and punish you seven times for your iniquity." Thus the blow first affects the man's property. Then it strikes a remoter relation. Then it takes away the desire of his eyes. Then it invades his own person, and shakes him by disorder over the pit—and he recovers—and turns again to folly. At length, having been often reproved, and hardening his neck, he is suddenly destroyed, and that without remedy Are none of you in danger of this? Are there not some of you who have not only been addressed by Him, and frequently addressed; but also have been smitten by Him, and awfully too; so that it would have seemed impossible for you to stand out. "I have overthrown some of you, as God overthrew Sodom and Gomorrah, and ye were as a firebrand plucked out of the burning: yet have ye not returned unto me, saith the Lord. Therefore thus will I do unto thee, O Israel: and because I will do this unto thee, prepare to meet thy God, O Israel." But canst thou stand before Him! Can thy heart endure, or thy hand be strong when He shall deal with thee? How much better to be in subjection to the Father of spirits, and live! Then will his repentings be kindled together. Then will He say, "I have surely heard Ephraim bemoaning himself thus: Thou hast chastised me, and I was chastised, as a bullock unaccustomed to the yoke: turn thou me, and I shall be turned; for thou art the Lord my God. Surely, after that I was turned, I repented; and after that I was instructed, I smote upon my thigh; I was ashamed, yea, even confounded, because I did bear the reproach of my youth. Is Ephraim my dear son? is he a pleasant child? for since I spake against him, I do earnestly remember him still: therefore my bowels are troubled for him; I will surely have mercy upon him, saith the Lord."

There is another extreme. Instead of despising, perhaps you are fainting. You are desponding. You are at your wits' end. You are tempted to curse the day of your birth. Life has lost all its charm—it is a burden too heavy for you to bear. You turn to solitude; but there grief preys upon itself. You think of intoxication; this is drowning misery in madness You glance at infidelity; but annihilation may be a fiction, and the present only the beginning of sorrows. You resolve on suicide; but you cannot destroy yourself. You take the pistol, and shatter to pieces the tabernacle, and your friends are aghast at the ruins; but the inhabitant has escaped, and the spirit feels itself still in the grasp of God. I am far from insulting your grief. I sympathize with you; and rejoice that I can show unto you a more excellent way. "There is One standing among you, whom ye know not." Let me introduce him in all the fulness of his pity and power. He is equally able and willing to relieve you. He is the enemy of sin, but he is the friend of sinners. Cast thy burden upon the Lord: and say, Lord, I am oppressed; undertake for me. He will not, he cannot refuse thy application. For he has said, and is now saying, "Come unto me, all ye that labour and are heavy laden, and I will give you rest." See Manasseh. He was stripped of all, and carried away captive. But his salvation sprang not from his prosperity, but his adversity. "When he was in affliction he besought the Lord his God, and humbled himself greatly before the God of his fathers, and prayed unto him: and He was entreated of Him, and heard his supplication, and brought him again to Jerusalem into his kingdom. Then Manasseh knew that the Lord he was God." Think of the Prodigal. Plenty had ruined him. The famine, and the husks which the swine did eat, made him think of home—"How many hired servants of my father have bread enough and to spare, and I perish with hunger! I will arise, and go to my father." And that father, "while he was yet a great way off, saw him, and had compassion upon him, and ran, and fell on his neck, and kissed him:" and not only clothed and fed, but adorned and feasted him: and said, "Let us eat and be merry: for this my son was dead, and is alive again; and was lost, and is found." Despair not; but follow these examples, and you will be able to say, with the famous Athenian, "I should have been lost, had I not been lost;" and to sing, with many a sufferer before you,

" Father, I bless thy gentle hand;
　　How kind was thy chastising rod,
　　That forced my conscience to a stand,
　　And brought my wandering soul to God!

" Foolish and vain, I went astray
　　Ere I had felt thy scourges, Lord:
　　I left my guide, I lost my way;
　　But now I love and keep thy word."

LECTURE VIII.

THE CHRISTIAN, IN HIS SPIRITUAL SORROWS.

" We hanged our harps upon the willows in the midst thereof."—Psalm cxxxvii. 2.

WE now pass from the condition of the Christian, to his experience. We have contemplated the changes that may take place in his outward circumstances. We have viewed him in his prosperity and in his adversity; and have seen him carrying his religion along with him through all the varying scenes of human life.

But there are similar variations in "the inward man," "the hidden man of the heart." And these changes are no inconsiderable evidences of the reality of a work of grace, in distinction from religious pretensions. The picture of a tree is invariable; but the tree itself has its seasons. At one time it is leafless, and the sap, though not destroyed, retires into the roots. At another, it revives, and buds, and blossoms, and is filled with fruitfulness. I walk in my garden, and see the stones arranged there, always the same. But it is otherwise with the flowers and plants. And the reason is, because the former are dead, while the latter have in them a principle of life. And such is the difference between the form of godliness, and the power: between a man alive to God, and one that hath a name that he liveth, but is dead.

Let us proceed to the part of the Christian's experience which we are pledged to consider this morning. And here, I can easily imagine, that the subject itself will hardly appear necessary to some. They are rather surprised by the very fact we have assumed, as a clear and common verity. Young converts often wonder to hear of the believer's sadness. *They* are often indulged with a peculiar kind and degree of consolation to allure them on, till, whatever difficulties they meet with, they feel themselves too much interested, and too far advanced, to think of retreating. Because, from a regard to their weakness, their enemies are restrained, they seem to conclude that they are destroyed; and because, in the novelty of their views and the liveliness of their feelings, their corruptions are but little noticed, they hope to be vexed with them no more. They therefore wonder to hear older Christians complaining of distraction in duty, and languor of zeal, and weakness of hope, and conflicts with doubts and fears. Thus it was with Israel "in the kindness of their youth." See them on the shore of the Red Sea. They rejoiced in the Lord, and sang his praise, and thought they had only to go forward and possess the pleasant land—ignorant of the wilderness between; and having no foreboding of the drought, and the bitter waters, and the fiery serpents, and the Amelekites and Moabites, and their long detentions, and their being led about, and their being turned back—by all of which the souls of the people were much discouraged because of the way.

But if there are some to whom the intimation of these sorrows is surprising, there are others to whom it will be relieving, if not delightful. For there are some who are dis-

tressed and perplexed, owing to apprehensions that their experience is *peculiar*. They think none ever had such vain thoughts, such dull frames, such woful depressions, as they often mourn over. Therefore in their communings with their own hearts, they are led to ask, "If I am His, why am I thus!" and anxiously turning to others, in whom they repose more confidence than they can place in themselves, say,

> "Ye that love the Lord indeed,
> Tell me, is it thus with you?"

Now these will not rejoice in the deficiencies and distresses of others; but it yields them encouragement to learn, that there are some who can sympathize with them; and that what they feel, is not, though grievous, incompatible with a state of grace; since others, and even those who are far superior to themselves, utter the same sighs and groans.

To return. The Psalm from which the words of our text are taken, is universally admired. Indeed nothing can be more exquisitely beautiful. It is written in a strain of sensibility that must touch every soul that is capable of feeling. It is remarkable that Dr. Watts, in his excellent versification, has omitted it. He has indeed some verses upon it in his Lyrics; and many others have written on the same. We have seen more than ten productions of this kind; the last, and perhaps the best, of which is Lord Byron's. But who is satisfied with any of these attempts?— Thus it begins: "By the rivers of Babylon, there we sat down; yea, we wept when we remembered Zion." These rivers were probably some of the streams branching off from the Euphrates and Tigris. Here it is commonly supposed these captive Jews were placed by their taskmasters, to preserve or repair the waterworks. But is it improper to conjecture that the Psalmist refers to their being here: not constantly, but occasionally; not by compulsion, but choice? Hither I imagine them retiring, to unbend their oppressed minds in solitude. "Come," said one of these pious Jews to another, "come, let us for a while go forth, from this vanity and vileness. Let us assemble together by ourselves under the refreshing shade of the willows by the watercourses. And let us take our harps with us, and solace ourselves with some of the songs of Zion." But as soon as they arrive, and begin to touch the chords, the notes—such is the power of association—awaken the memory of their former privileges and pleasures. And, overwhelmed with grief, they sit down on the grass; and weep when they remember Zion; their dejected looks, averted from each other, seeming to say, "If I forget thee, O Jerusalem, let my right hand forget her cunning. If I do not remember thee, let my tongue cleave to the roof of my mouth; if I prefer

L

not Jerusalem above my chief joy." But what do they with their harps? The voice of mirth is heard no more; and all the daughters of music are brought low. Melody is not in season to a distressed spirit. "Is any afflicted? Let him pray. Is any merry? Let him sing psalms." "As he that taketh away a garment in cold weather, and as vinegar upon nitre, so is he that singeth songs to a heavy heart."—They did not however break them to pieces, or throw them into the stream —but *hanged* them up only. They hoped that what they could not use at present they might be able to resume at some happier period. To be cast down is not to be destroyed. Distress is not despondency.

"Beware of desperate steps: the darkest day,
Live till to-morrow, will have passed away."

"*We hanged our harps upon the willows in the midst thereof.*"—Let us pass from the Jew to the Christian; and let us survey the Christian,

In his SPIRITUAL SORROWS.

He who would preach well, says Luther, must distinguish well. It is peculiarly necessary to discriminate, when we enter upon the present subject. For all the sorrows of the Christian are not of the same kind or descent—Let us consider four sources of his moral sadness.

I. Will be PHYSICAL.
II. Will be CRIMINAL.
III. Will be INTELLECTUAL.
IV. Will be PIOUS.

The *first* source is PHYSICAL.

There are some who understand very little of this. They are blessed with a favoured constitution; and can hardly enter into the feelings of those who pass much of their time under the dominion of a gloomy and depressive temperament that leads them to view every thing through an alarming and dismaying medium; and to draw towards themselves all that is awful and distressing. How affecting is it to hear a man of genius and piety complaining, that in one day, in one hour, he who was such an enthusiastical admirer of the works of nature, had presented to him an universal blank; so that nothing, after, could ever charm him again. We admit that the case of Cowper was extraordinary: but it was so in the degree, rather than in the quality. Others are subject to a measure of the same influence; and while the increased prevalence of this morbid affection produces fixed melancholy, the slighter diffusion of it may be attended with the most trying irritation and depression. We often censure, where, if we knew all, we should only pity. What a conflict have some Christians even in wrestling with flesh and blood! We are fearfully and wonderfully made. We know little of the mechanism of the body; but we

know much less of the chemistry. Who can tell how the nervous juices and the animal spirits are secreted? Who can explain how the fluids blend and temper each other? Who knows how it is that when a particular humour predominates unequally, such a change is resistlessly produced in our mass of apprehensions and feelings? Yet we know the fact. We know that external things affect the body. We know that the body affects the mind. We know that we are the creatures of the season and of the sky. We know that we are not the same in a foggy day, as in a clear one. We know that if there be a suffusion of bile, the world, and the church, and the family are not governed so well now as they were yesterday. Nothing is so agreeable in our condition. Our very religion is doubtful; and God is not the same.

Several things result from this reasoning. Is it not astonishing that many Christians will ascribe every animal variation and effect to the agency of Satan! especially when they know how often, by the aid of a little medicine, all these supposed temptations have been chased away, and every thing restored to its proper hues and attractions again?

It is not necessary for a Christian to be a physician; but it is desirable for him to be able to distinguish between influences purely bodily, and the principles, disposition, and state of his mind. It is difficult to reason with people in this frame, or under this tendency; otherwise we should be amazed at the perplexity and disconsolateness of some excellent characters, and the readiness with which they refuse to be comforted. We have known persons, poor in spirit, hungering and thirsting after righteousness, glorying only in the cross of Christ, and cheerfully going forth to him without the camp, bearing his reproach —yet gloomily concluding that they have no part nor lot in the matter, and that their heart is not right in the sight of God. And wherefore do they write these bitter things against themselves? There is no reason why they *should;* but the cause why they *do,* is to be found in something beyond the preacher's province. And till there is a change in the physical economy, all the succours of religion will be urged in vain.

Good men also should learn from hence to be attentive to their health, and keep the body as much as possible the fit medium of the mind. A man may be a good performer; but what can he do with a disordered instrument? The inhabitant may have good eyes; but how can he see accurately through a soiled window! Keep therefore the glass clean; and the organ in tune. We do not wish you to be finical and fanciful; to live in the shop of an apothecary; or have a medical attendant always dangling at your heels. But be soberly and prudently attentive to the body. Rise early. Take proper exercise

Beware of sloth. Observe and avoid whatever disagrees with your system. Never overburden nature. Be moderate in your table indulgences. Let not appetite bemire and clog the mind. Medical authority will tell you, that where one disorder arises from deficiency, a thousand spring from repletion; and that the Board slays far more than the Sword.—The

Second source is CRIMINAL.

It will be allowed that they who cannot apostatize may backslide: and we know who hath said, "The backslider in heart shall be filled with his own way." "Thine own wickedness shall correct thee; and thy backsliding shall reprove thee: know therefore and see, that it is an evil thing and bitter that thou hast forsaken the Lord thy God." Observe: it is both *evil* and *bitter ;* evil in its nature, and bitter in its consequences. And these bitter effects take in, not only outward troubles, but inward distresses; the corrosions of fretfulness under a feeling of guilt; the reproaches of conscience awakened from its slumbers, and ashamed of its negligence; the perplexities arising from the doubtfulness of our condition; the loss of peace, and a sense of God's favour. What was said of Israel as a people, will apply here to individual experience. "O that thou hadst hearkened to my commandments! then had thy peace been as a river, and thy righteousness like the waves of the sea." You hear much of the hidings of God's face. The expression is perfectly scriptural. "Make thy face," says David, "to shine upon thy servant." His face signifies his favourable regard. This can never be a matter of indifference to the Christian, whether we consider his supreme love to God, or his entire dependence upon Him. He must be miserable under the loss of God's smiles. And as Absalom said, "What do I here in Geshur, unless I see the King's face?" so says the believer—what do I in the closet, or in the house of God, or at his table, with Him? I cannot improve a providence or an ordinance, I cannot enjoy my friends, or myself, without my God. So it was with David —"Thou didst hide thy face, and I was troubled."

But why does he ever hide his face? Is it to display his sovereignty? No; but to testify his disapprobation of our spirit or our conduct. It is of the nature of moral correction. "Behold, the Lord's hand is not shortened, that it cannot save; neither his ear heavy, that it cannot hear: but your iniquities have separated between you and your God; and your sins have hid his face from you, that he will not hear."

There are some who say—quoting the words of Scripture, but mistaking their design—God sees "no iniquity in Jacob, and beholds no perverseness in Israel." Yet we read of "the provoking of his sons and of his daughters." Yet the Lord spake unto Moses and Aaron; because ye believed him not, to sanctify me in the eyes of the children of Israel, therefore ye shall not bring this congregation into the land which I have given them." And no importunity could obtain a relaxation of the sentence. "Sin never hurts a believer!" "He never need be afraid of sin!" And whose inspiration is this language? Where do we learn this doctrine? Did David believe it, after his transgression? Along with the very announcement of his pardon, was he not informed of the sufferings that would still result from his guilt? Did he not continue to confess, "my sin is ever before me?" If not bruised and fractured by his fall, why does he pray, "Make me to hear joy and gladness, that the bones which thou hast broken may rejoice?" If not filled with a dread of Divine abandonment, why does he say, "Cast me not away from thy presence; and take not thy Holy Spirit from me?" If he had not been deprived of the consolation, why does he say, "Restore unto me the joy of thy salvation, and uphold me with thy free Spirit?" If he had not been struck dumb, why does he pray, "Open thou my lips, that my mouth may show forth thy praise?" If he had not impaired the cause of God, why does he pray, "Do good in thy good pleasure unto Zion, build thou the walls of Jerusalem?"

Upon this principle, the chief hope I entertain with regard to some professors of religion is their uncomfortableness. For it would be a sad symptom in their case, if *they* were tranquil and cheerful, and rejoicing in Christ, *while* they are indifferent to the means of grace, and mind earthly things, and display such a worldly conversation and spirit. For I am sure of this, that if they really belong to God, he will rebuke them, and make them look back, with the exclamation, "O that it was with me as in months past, when the candle of the Lord shone upon my head, and when by his light I walked through darkness; while as yet the Almighty was with me." The way to see and enjoy God is to live near him, and to be always endeavouring to please him. The first Christians "walked in the fear of the Lord, and in the comforts of the Holy Ghost." These are inseparable; and all pretensions to the latter without the former, are nothing but delusion. Let me therefore, if the consolations of God are small with thee, ask, "Is there any secret thing with thee?" Thy gourd withers: Is there any worm at the root? You are repulsed, and turn your back on your enemies: Is there any accursed thing in the camp? "Let us search and try our ways; and turn again unto the Lord." Let us do more. Let us fall upon our knees, and pray for Divine examination—"Search me, O God, and know my heart; try me, and know my thoughts; and see if there be any wicked way in me, and lead me in the way everlasting."—The

Third source is INTELLECTUAL.

For the joy of a Christian is not a vain imagination or a groundless persuasion, endangered by inquiry—it flows from knowledge; and the possessor is able to give a reason of the hope that is in him. Hence it will follow, that though a Christian's safety does not depend upon the extent and the degree of his religious information, his comfort will be very much affected by it. Now there are some who are very·defective in their acquaintance with the Gospel; and these, like persons walking in darkness, or at least twilight, are afraid to tread firmly; and are liable to convert harmless objects into spectres of terror. Owing to a want of evangelical instruction from books or teachers, there is in them a prevalence of legality that leads them to look after something in themselves wherein they may glory, or which shall entitle them to pardon and acceptance. Instead of resting in a mediator between *God* and them, they seek after something mediatorial, between *Christ* and them; and thus not coming to *Him*, as they are, they wait till they shall possess certain qualifications, or perform certain conditions. Thus they labour in the fire and weary themselves for very vanity—for

> "If we tarry till we are better,
> We shall never come at all."

They set themselves a mark of attainment; and not being able to reach it, they are cast down. They mistake the degree of their experience for the ground of their hope; and their confidence varies with their frames. And as to their perseverance and final victory, their own vigilance and fidelity usurp their dependence, instead of the everlasting covenant ordered in all things and sure. In the Lord they have righteousness and strength. His grace is sufficient for them: and were they to be only and always looking unto Jesus, their joy might be full and constant; but now they often go mourning all the day.

It is therefore of great importance to have the understanding well informed in "the way of salvation," that we "may know the things that are freely given to us of God." For as the Gospel *is* glad tidings; and all its doctrines are *truths* and *facts;* the more distinctly we hear the one, and the more clearly we discern the other, the more effectual will be our relief, and the full assurance of our hope. Peter admonishes Christians to grow in grace, and in the knowledge of our Lord and Saviour Jesus Christ: and we may consider the latter part of the injunction not only as additional to the former, but as explanatory of its import, and subservient to its per-

formance. The one is necessary to *the* other. We never shall grow in grace, but as we grow in knowledge, and in the knowledge of the Saviour. We are well aware that there may be speculative knowledge without practical; but there cannot be practical without speculative. Every thing in religion is produced and supported and influenced by just views of things. And this is peculiarly the case with the consolation of the Spirit. Hence it is said, "They that know thy name, will put their trust in Thee." Hence, "Blessed is the people that know the joyful sound: they shall walk, O Lord, in the light of thy countenance; in thy name shall they rejoice all the day; and in thy righteousness shall they be exalted." Hence also our Lord said to his disciples, "These things have I spoken unto you, that in me ye might have peace." And again, "These things have I spoken unto you, that my joy may remain in you, and that your joy may be full."

Seek therefore "the riches of the full assurance of understanding." Gain clear and enlarged views of the nature and provisions of the glorious Gospel: of the warrant and command we have to believe on the name of the Son of God: of the ground of our acceptance through the sacrifice and obedience of the Surety of the new covenant: of his ability to save to the uttermost: of the efficacy of his blood to cleanse from all sin: of the perfection of his righteousness to justify the ungodly, and give him a title to endless life: of the prevalency of his intercession within the veil; his changeless heart; his constant presence; his infinite fulness of grace; and our being blessed in Him with all spiritual blessings in heavenly places. Where shall I end? To be led into all this truth, is to be made to lie down in green pastures, and to be fed beside the still waters—to know all this love of Christ which passeth knowledge, is ·to be filled with all the fulness of God.

Thus far, the sorrows which have been spoken of, we have been constrained to pity, or censure, or excuse. They have arisen from constitution, or moral infirmity, or ignorance.—But there are sorrows, which,

Fourthly, Have a PIOUS SOURCE.

These are only experienced by those who are called a peculiar people. But *they* are familiar with them: and they feel them on various accounts. Let us view the Christian taking a fourfold prospect. He looks backward—and inward—and forward—and around him: and at each look he weeps.

First. He looks *backward*, and weeps as he reviews the *past.* Some never review life; we mean, that they never review it for a religious purpose. They may look back occasionally and frequently, to see how they have missed their opportunity for securing some earthly advantage, or how they have been overreached by their fellow-creatures, in order to act a shrewder part in future: but not to become acquainted with their depravity; not to mark how long and how much they lived without God with them in the world.

But grace leads a man to reflect upon his former character and conduct; and to reflect properly. We say properly: for we have heard some professors of religion talk of their former wickedness with no very sorrowful emotions; yea, with a kind of complacency, as if they were relating some remarkable exploits. But how is the Christian affected with the retrospect? "Surely," says God, "I have heard Ephraim *bemoaning* himself thus—Thou hast chastised me, and I was chastised, like a bullock unaccustomed to the yoke—I was *ashamed*, yea even *confounded*, because I did bear the reproach of my youth." How often did Paul, after his conversion, think of his previous state; and with what deep humiliation does he acknowledge his guilt! "When the blood of the martyr Stephen was shed, I was standing by, and consenting unto his death, and I kept the raiment of them that slew him." "I was a blasphemer, a persecutor, and injurious." "I am not worthy to be called an Apostle, because I persecuted the Church of God." "When," says Baxter, "I reflect on my sins, I find it much easier to believe that God will forgive me, than I can forgive myself."

I enter a Christian's retirement. His eyes have been pouring out tears unto God. I ask him, "Why weepest thou?"—"I have been taking a retrospect of the past. I have been examining my former years morally: and every view I take is humiliating and distressing. Time wasted—means neglected—faculties misimproved—injuries done to others by my advice, or example, or influence; and where in many cases the mischief cannot be repaired!—I passed by the Cross; and that which angels desire to look into, was nothing to me. He wooed and awed; blessed and chastised; and I set at nought all his counsel, and would none of his reproof—I violated a thousand resolutions. I resisted and conquered the most powerful conviction. I trampled under foot the Son of God, and did despite unto the Spirit of grace.—For *these* things I weep—"

Secondly. He looks *within*, and weeps as he examines the *present*. Let it be at once conceded, that grace makes the Christian to differ from his fellow-creatures, and from himself. It delivers him from the spirit of the world, and possesses him with the spirit which is of God. It calls him out of darkness into his marvellous light. It turns him from idols to serve the living God, and to wait for his Son from heaven. He is a new creature. Old things are passed away; and

all things are become new. But though he is really sanctified in every part, he is completely renovated in none. The good work is begun; but a thousand deficiencies urge him to pray, "Perfect that which concerneth me: thy mercy, O Lord, endureth for ever; forsake not the works of thine own hands."—Ask him now, why he weeps? And you will hear him say—"The flesh lusteth against the spirit, and the spirit against the flesh, and these are contrary the one to the other, so that I cannot do the thing that I would. For what I would that do I not; but what I hate that I do. For to will is present with me; but how to perform that which is good I find not. I find then a law, that when I would do good, evil is present with me. For I delight in the law of God after the inward man: but I see another law in my members warring against the law of my mind, and bringing me into captivity to the law of sin, which is in my members. O wretched man that I am, who shall deliver me from the body of this death! Instead of advancing, I seem to be stationary—yea, going back in the heavenly life. What ingratitude under benefits! What incorrigibleness under rebukes! What unprofitableness under ordinances! My soul cleaveth unto the dust. What dulness, deadness, distractions, in attending upon the Lord! What little enjoyment in the things of God! The Sabbath returns, and leaves me as it finds me. I hear; but it is almost if not altogether in vain. I pray; but often seem at the throne of grace to forget my errand, and sometimes fall asleep there. I have promises that I cannot believe, and a God I cannot trust. He deserves all the confidence of my heart, and I treat him with the most unworthy suspicions—

"Sure, were not I most vile and base,
  I could not thus my friend requite:
And were not he the God of grace,
  He'd frown, and spurn me from his sight."

—How mistaken are the people of the world! They often charge the Christian with Antinomianism: they suppose that he embraces doctrines which favour licentiousness; and that he loves sin—when, could they witness him alone, where no one sees him and hears him but God, they would find him bewailing evils which are beneath their notice, and even infirmities which never strike their minds, for want of a holy susceptibility. But *his* conscience is so tender, that it resembles the eye which is offended even with a mote. For a Christian feels all the remains of the sin that dwelleth in him. His new principles render it unavoidable. He who longs to advance, groans at every detention and delay; he who pants to excel, is mortified at little deficiencies; he who delights in purity, is offended with the least stain. It may be supposed, that under a perception of his failings, he will be unconcerned, if at the same time he is assured of his safety, and can repose on the certainty and permanency of the Saviour's love. But nothing can be more remote from the truth than this supposition: for it is *then* the Christian feels his imperfections the most painfully. The more he sees of the excellency and goodness of his Benefactor and Friend, the more he laments that he loves him no more, and serves him no better. This is godly sorrow. Thus a good man dying, when observed to weep profusely, said, "I weep, not that my sins may be pardoned, but because I know they are pardoned." This accords with the promise: "I will establish my covenant with thee; and thou shalt know that I am the Lord: that thou mayest remember, and be confounded, and never open thy mouth any more because of thy shame, *when* I am pacified toward thee for all that thou hast done, saith the Lord God."

Thirdly. He looks *forward*, and weeps as he surveys the *future*. Not that he is miserable because God does not admit him into the secrets of his providence, but keeps him ignorant of what a day may bring forth. He knows that all his times are in God's hands, and there he is willing to leave them.

But there are moral hazards sufficient to induce him to pass the time of his sojourning here in fear—not the fear of diffidence as to the truth of God's promises, or of uncertainty as to his final salvation; but a fear of moral circumspection and vigilance. Is there not enough to make him tremble as he moves on —lest he should enter into temptation? Is there not enough to make him apprehensive —that he has to pass through an enemy's country, and that snares are everywhere laid for his feet? Does he not know that he carries within him the remains of unmortified passions—so that every thing he meets with from without may draw him aside? That even things harmless in themselves may occasion his falling? That characters far superior to himself have yielded in the hour of danger—and when no danger has been suspected? Is it not painful to think—that by one wrong step, he may lose his evidences of heaven, distress and injure his brethren, and cause the way of truth to be evil spoken of; and induce the adversaries of the Lord to blaspheme? Is it not painful to think—that after all his professions of attachment, he may yet by his sin pierce the dear bosom on which his soul leans, and grieve the Holy Spirit by which he is sealed unto the day of redemption? Is it not enough to make him sigh— to think that as long as he remains here, he will never appear before One he infinitely loves, without carrying into his presence so much of that which he infinitely hates? Is it not enough to make him groan—being burdened—to think that the leprosy is so inherent and inseparable, that the walls of the house itself must be pulled down and lie under ground for ages, before it can be re-edified, and become an habitation for God through the Spirit?

Fourthly. He looks *around* him, and weeps as he beholds *others*. Fools make a mock at sin; but they that are wise know that it is exceeding sinful, and say, with David, "Rivers of waters run down mine eyes, because they keep not thy law. I beheld the transgressors, and was grieved."

Is he a citizen? He is a patriot. He sighs and cries for all the abominations that are done in the midst of the land. For he knows that righteousness exalteth a nation, and that sin is the reproach of any people.

Is he a minister? O how distressing is it to look down upon those who, after the labour of twenty years, remain the same; yea, who wax worse and worse; to know that he is only preaching them blind and deaf and impenitent: and to think that he is destined to be a swift witness against many that he would gladly save! "I have told you often," says Paul, "and now tell you even weeping, that they are the enemies of the cross of Christ: whose end is destruction, whose God is their belly, and whose glory is in their shame; who mind earthly things." "Give glory to the Lord your God," says Jeremiah, "before he cause darkness, and before your feet stumble upon the dark mountains, and, while ye look for light, he turn it into the shadow of death, and make it gross darkness. But if ye will not hear, my soul shall weep in secret places for your pride; and mine eye shall weep sore, and run down with tears, because the Lord's flock is carried away captive."

Is he a member of a Church? "He is sorrowful for the solemn assembly, and the reproach of it is his burden."

Is he a relation? "How," says he, with Esther, "can I endure to see the destruction of my kindred?"—Of those living in the same house, sitting at the same table, endeared by all the impressions and attractions of breeding and of birth? Can a wife, without anxiety and anguish, see a husband, otherwise amiable and kind, refusing to hear the word of life, and resolved not to receive the love of the truth, that he might be saved? Can a parent, with unbroken heart, see a child in the way to hell, going down to the chambers of death? We sympathize with bereaved fathers and mothers. Yet we ought even to hail those who have buried early hopes, compared with those whose offspring are living, but erroneous and infidel and wicked. Oh! Rachel, "refrain *thy* voice from weeping, and *thine* eyes from tears; for *thy* work shall be rewarded, and *they* shall come again from the land of the enemy. There is hope in thine end, saith the Lord, that thy children shall come again to their own border." "Weep ye not for the dead, neither bemoan him; but weep sore for him that goeth away: for *he* shall return no more, nor see his native country." O ye ungodly! how unreasonable, how unjust are your reflections! You often reproach Christians for their sorrows, when you yourselves, in the various relations of life, occasion a large number of them. For they see the danger you see not, and weep for you when you weep not for yourselves. Have any of you connexions that are godly? And have you grieved them? Resolve immediately to end this cruel persecution. Retire and pray—" O God of my sister, be my God! God of my parents, be my God!" Let not thy father longer repeat in vain, " My son, if thy heart be wise, my heart shall rejoice, even mine." O hasten and ingenuously wipe away the tears of her who has long been saying, " What! my son, and the son of my womb, and the son of my vows!" Yea, let them have joy of thee in the Lord: refresh their bowels in the Lord.

Such are the sorrows which arise from a pious source. These are not only compatible with grace, but spring from gracious principles and dispositions. They are not only found in religious people, but are religious. And we cannot conclude without encouraging and commending them.

We are aware that this is not the way in which they are commonly treated. The subjects of these spiritual griefs are generally despised, or deplored. Commonly, as soon as persons begin to discover any tendency to these sorrows, they are men wondered at; and they are considered as likely to become melancholy or deranged. But the Prodigal lost his senses when he left his father's house, and came to himself when he resolved to return. And what but a carnal mind that is enmity against God, can lead a man to justify cr excuse sorrow in all other instances, and degrade and vilify it here? What is the loss of property to the loss of the soul? What is the burning of a house, or the loss of a limb, to the casting of both body and soul into hell? What evil can we bewail that deserves a thought, compared with sin; in its guilt; in its pollution; the miseries it entails; the God it dishonours; the Saviour it crucifies? Bunyan remarks, that when he was awakened to consider his condition, nothing amazed him so much as to see how much men were affected with their temporal inconveniences and troubles. " These," says he, " had no power now to interest me. All my concern was absorbed in something infinitely more weighty—what must I do to be saved!" And he is a fool, even judged at the tribunal of reason, who does not feel the same difference—if this book be true.

If, however, such persons escape scorn, they are sure to be pitied. They are regarded as strangers to every thing like enjoyment, and are considered as passing all their lives in mopishness and dread. But they no more deserve our commiseration than our contempt. *They* are to be pitied who have their portion in this life, which we spend as a shadow, and possess nothing to carry away with them into another world a few weeks hence—who can speak every language but the language of Canaan—who are familiar with the stars, those orbs of light, and are plunged into the blackness of darkness for ever—who are caressed by worms, but are an abomination to the Lord—who are placed on a stream, and are gladdened with the flowers of the bank, and charmed with the music on board, and are gliding down into the gulf of perdition—*these* we pity; but not those who are weary and heavy laden—not those who are invited by the Saviour to partake of his rest—not those who are poor in spirit, for their's is the kingdom of heaven—not those who hunger and thirst after righteousness, for they shall be filled—not those that mourn, for they shall be comforted.' Though their life may be deemed not only madness, but misery, it *allows* of happiness, and there is a blessedness *arising* from it. We cannot make out this to the comprehension of a natural man. It is a mystery to him, how we "become fools that we may be wise:" how, "when we are weak, we are strong:" how, "though sorrowful, we are yet always rejoicing." Yet so it is. There is pleasure even *in* these sorrows; and there is nothing so painful to a Christian as a hard, unfeeling heart. His weeping moments are his most welcome; and he is never more at home than when looking on Him whom he has pierced, and mourning for him. —This yields him evidence. It is a token for good. It is a proof that he is the subject of that divine agency which takes away the heart of stone, and gives the heart of flesh— that he is the heir of that promise, "they shall come with weeping, and with supplications will I lead them."—Observe the words of the Apostle: "The sorrow of the world worketh death; but godly sorrow worketh repentance unto life, and needeth not to be repented of." Of how many of your griefs are you now ashamed! How unworthy do they now appear of the concern they once gave you! But you will never repent of a tear you shed upon the Bible, or a groan you utter at the foot of the Cross.—It allows, it justifies every hope. He is faithful who promised: and what has he said? "To that man will I look, even to him who is poor, of a contrite spirit, and trembleth at my word." "They that sow in tears shall reap in joy." "He that goeth forth and weepeth, bearing precious seed, shall doubtless come again with rejoicing, bringing his sheaves with him." Yea, the Saviour is appointed "unto them that mourn in *Zion*, to give *them* beauty for ashes, the oil of joy for mourning, the garment of praise for the spirit of heaviness that they might be called trees of righteousness, the planting of the Lord, that he might be glorified." Their comforter is the God of all comfort; and he will soon wipe away all tears from their eyes, and the days of their mourning shall be ended.

But, "wo to you that laugh now, for ye shall mourn and weep." As there is a sorrow connected with joy, so there is a joy that forebodes sorrow; issues in sorrow; is no better than sorrow disguised. Such are the pleasures of sin for a season. Such are all worldly enticements and dissipations. You boast of these. But one who had a much greater experience of them than you, and was much more honest and ingenuous, makes no scruple to say, that "even in laughter the heart is sorrowful, and the end of that mirth is heaviness." He said "of laughter, it is mad, and of mirth, what doeth it?" You may profess nothing like this; but while you wear smiles, the vulture is gnawing within. While you celebrate the day of your birth, you wish you had never been born. What have you to do with pleasure? "There is no peace, saith my God, to the wicked."

Yield no longer to the temptation, which led many, in the days of Malachi, to say, "It is vain to serve God: and what profit is it that we have kept his ordinance, and that we have walked mournfully before the Lord of hosts?" Tell the enemy that he is a liar: that godliness is profitable unto all things, and especially in its griefs. Tell him that this is the high road to safety and satisfaction, for the mouth of the Lord hath spoken it.

And take hold of the skirt of him that is a Jew, saying, "I will go with you, for I have heard that God is with you." "Intreat me not to leave thee, or to return from following after thee: for whither thou goest, I will go, and where thou lodgest I will lodge: thy people shall be my people, and thy God my God: where thou diest will I die, and there will I be buried: the Lord do so to me, and more also, if aught but death part thee and me."

"Blessed are they that keep judgment, and he that doeth righteousness at all times." "Remember me, O Lord, with the favour thou bearest unto thy people: O visit me with thy salvation; that I may see the good of thy chosen, that I may rejoice in the gladness of thy nation, that I may glory with thine inheritance." Amen.

LECTURE IX.

THE CHRISTIAN, IN HIS SPIRITUAL JOYS.

"Then he said unto them, Go your way, eat the fat, and drink the sweet, and send portions unto them for whom nothing is prepared: for this day is holy unto our Lord: neither be ye sorry; for the joy of the Lord is your strength."—Nehemiah viii. 10.

My Brethren: some tell us that religion has nothing to do with the passions. If it were necessary to refute such a notion, we could appeal even to the style of the Scriptures. When an author intends only to convince the judgment, he expresses himself plainly, and merely reasons. But when he means to affect, as well as to inform; when he wishes to strike, and excite, and to carry along the feelings with the convictions; he is never satisfied with simple representation—his language unavoidably avails itself of circumstances, and qualities, and imagery. And can any one deny that this is the mode perpetually employed by all the sacred writers?

But we observe also, that such a view of religion is not adapted to our very nature. Our passions are original parts of our being, and designed to be the impulses of action. And the Christian does not destroy, but sanctifies and employs the man. And what passion is there, for which religion does not find a place and an object? Is it anger? "Be ye angry and sin not." Is it hatred? "Abhor that which is evil." Is it fear? "Be not high-minded, but fear." Is it sorrow? "They shall look on him whom they have pierced, and they shall mourn for him." Is it pity? "Have compassion one for another." Is it love? "O love the Lord, all ye his saints." Is it joy? "We joy in God, through our Lord Jesus Christ, by whom we have now received the atonement."

We are aware that there is a great deal of what may be justly called strange fire offered on the altar of piety. We are not therefore pleading for a zeal without knowledge; but we are not satisfied with a knowledge without zeal. We do not wish for the heat and ravings of the fever, but for the genial warmth and glowing stimulus that pervade the whole system, when the body is in full health; knowing that what is cold and benumbed and unaffected by application and friction, is nigh unto death, or is palsied already. While therefore we acknowledge that there is such a thing as real enthusiasm, the admission shall not drive us to take up with a religion that consists in nothing but speculative opinions, and lifeless ceremonies, and formal duties. Religion is indeed a practical thing; but it is also experimental. It does include doctrinal truths; but in the Christian, these become principles. They descend from the head into the heart; and there grace reigns through righteousness unto everlasting life by Jesus Christ our Lord.

We have viewed the Christian's sadness: we are now to witness his joy. We have seen him hanging his harp on the willows; but he now takes it down, and proves that *the joy of the Lord is his strength.*

The words which introduce our subject were spoken on a very memorable occasion. All the people were gathered together as one man into the street that was before the water-gate; and they spake unto Ezra the scribe to bring the book of the law of Moses, which the Lord had commanded to all Israel. And "upon the first day of the seventh month, Ezra opened the book in the sight of all the people; and when he had opened it, all the people stood up. And Ezra blessed the Lord. And all the people answered, Amen, amen, with lifting up their hands; and they bowed their heads, and worshipped the Lord, with their faces to the ground. So Ezra and his assistants read in the book of the law of God distinctly, and gave the sense, and caused them to understand the reading." The power of God seems to have been peculiarly present. The whole assembly "wept when they heard the words of the law." "Then he said unto them, Go your way, eat the fat, and drink the sweet, and send portions unto them for whom nothing is prepared: for this day is holy unto our Lord: neither be ye sorry: for the joy of the Lord is your strength."

When he says, This day is holy unto our Lord, he means that it was a sacred festival. When he says, Go your way, he means that they should return home, and refresh themselves; for now noon was begun, and they had been standing for hours to hear the reading and expounding of the law. He does not forbid them the delicacies which they had provided for the solemnity, and which were distinguishable from their ordinary meals—Eat the fat, and drink the sweet—But all this was to be accompanied with two things.

First, Liberality towards the indigent and destitute, who would find nothing to regale them, when they returned to their humble dwellings. And send portions unto them for whom nothing is prepared. By the law of Moses, the poor, the fatherless, the widows, and the strangers within the gate, were all to be entertained on these festive occasions; and if they could not provide for themselves, I will not say, their betters, but their superiors were to replenish them. In accordance with the spirit of this statute is the intimation of our Lord to the person who had invited him to his house: "When thou makest a dinner or a supper, call not thy friends, nor thy brethren, neither thy kinsmen, nor thy rich neighbours; lest they also bid thee again, and a recompense be made thee. But when thou makest a feast, call the poor, the lame, the maimed, the blind: and thou shalt be blessed; for they cannot recompense thee: for thou shalt be recompensed at the resurrection of the just."—The very thing that his professed followers are constantly doing!! The same rule is enjoined in religious fasting as well as feasting. "Is not this the fast

that I have chosen? to loose the bonds of wickedness, to undo the heavy burdens, and to let the oppressed go free, and that ye break every yoke? Is it not to deal thy bread to the hungry, and that thou bring the poor that are cast out to thy house? when thou seest the naked, that thou cover him; and that thou hide not thyself from thine own flesh?" Well therefore does the Apostle say, "Let all your works be done with charity." O! what a lovely religion do we profess; and what a Church, what a world shall we have, when those who profess it will throw off, with execration, the detestable habits of avarice and selfishness, hoarding and extravagance; and living according to its admonitions, instead of practically insulting them as they now do, will easily and cheerfully furnish a sufficiency for all the exigencies of sacred and civil beneficence!

Secondly, with Cheerfulness. Neither be ye sorry—Not that sorrow is improper in itself, or absolutely forbidden: but it was now unseasonable, and every thing is beautiful in its time. Joy becomes a feast. And this joy, says Nehemiah, is as important as it is becoming—for the joy of the Lord is your strength—It will strengthen your bodily frame; and what is more, it will renew the strength of your souls, so that you shall mount up with wings as eagles, run and not be weary, and walk and not faint.

Let us contemplate the Christian,

    I. In the DIVINITY; and
    II. In the UTILITY of his JOY.

I. The DIVINITY of it.

—It is the joy of the Lord. So it is called by the Judge of all, in his address at the last day. "Well done, good and faithful servant; enter thou into the joy of thy Lord." Now, this joy enters the Christian; and as he is so contracted a vessel, he cannot contain much; but then, he will enter the joy, and he will find it a boundless ocean. The dawn is nothing compared with the day; yet the one always results in the other: and "the path of the just is as the shining light that shineth more and more unto the perfect day." The dawn also arises from the same sun as the day; and this joy is divine, not only in its completion, but in its progress and even commencement—it is the joy of the Lord.

The joy of the Lord means religious joy. But there is always a reason for the language of Scripture; and we lose much, by not remarking the beauty and energy of "the words which the Holy Ghost teacheth." It is the joy of the Lord in every view he can take of it.

—His, in the authority that binds it upon us as a duty. He has commanded it. He has done this virtually in enjoining many things which necessarily presuppose and require it.

M   8*

But he has expressly enjoined the joy itself; and in terms of peculiar extent and degree— "Rejoice evermore." "Rejoice in the Lord always; and again I say, rejoice." "Rejoice in the Lord, ye righteous; and shout for joy, all ye that are upright in heart."

—His, in the *assurance* which holds it forth as a *privilege.* His purpose could have taken effect without a promise: but in this case we could not have known his thoughts towards us; nor have walked by faith; nor have lived in hope; nor have pleaded his own engagement in prayer. But now we can go to him, and say, "Lord, do as thou hast said. Fulfil the word unto thy servant upon which thou hast caused me to hope." And has he not said, "The redeemed of the Lord shall return and come to Zion with songs and everlasting joy upon their heads: they shall obtain joy and gladness; and sorrow and sighing shall flee away?" "Blessed are the people that know the joyful sound: they shall walk, O Lord, in the light of thy countenance; in thy name shall they rejoice all the day, and in thy righteousness shall they be exalted?" The assurance is also confirmed by an oath. And, "because he could swear by no greater, he sware by himself; that by two immutable things, in which it was impossible for God to lie, we might have a strong consolation who have fled for refuge to lay hold upon the hope set before us."

—His, in the *resemblance* it bears to his own. Christians are "partakers of the divine nature." They are "partakers of his holiness." As far as they are renewed, his views are their views, and his dispositions are their dispositions. When John says, "Whoso hath this world's good, and seeth his brother have need, and shutteth up his bowels of compassion from him, how dwelleth the *love of God* in him?"—by the love of God he means obviously a love like God's. As if he should say, God gave his own Son for his enemies; and this wretch will not give a little of his substance for the relief of one, who is bone of his bone, and flesh of his flesh. Now the same may be said of this joy. Did the joy of the Prodigal himself surpass that of the father, when he said, "Let us eat and be merry: for this my son was dead and is alive again, was lost and is found?" Do we feel the joy of God's salvation? He feels it too; and this salvation is called "the pleasure of the Lord." If it be more blessed to give than to receive, what must be the pleasure of *Him* who "openeth his hand and satisfieth the desire of every living thing?" But you share in this pleasure, in doing good. Is he "ready to pardon;" and does he "delight in mercy?" You may taste the same delight in the exercise of cordial forgiveness. Doth the "Lord take pleasure in them that fear him, in them that hope in his mercy?" So does the Christian.

In them is "all his delight." Does the Lord call his Son his "Elect, in whom his soul delighteth?" And "to them that believe he is precious." What a commendation! To have the same end, and the same way with God! To choose what He chooses! To pursue what He pursues! To relish His happiness! To have His joy fulfilled in themselves!

—His, in the *subject.* The material of it, so to speak, is found in Him, and in him alone. As the dove returned into the ark because she could find no rest for the sole of her foot, so it is impossible for the mind of man to know any true satisfaction till he says, with David, "Return unto thy rest, O my soul, for the Lord hath dealt bountifully with thee." Though, as a fallen creature, he is alienated from the life of God, he retains the same relation to Him, as his portion; and having been made capable of communion with God, and designed for it, he is necessarily miserable without it. He may forget his resting-place; but he can find no substitute for it. He may debase himself into a congeniality with the lowest gratifications; but for happiness he must draw near to God as his exceeding joy. With Him is the fountain of life. And there is enough in Him to bless us, whatever be our wants, or our capacities of enjoyment. And therefore, says the Christian, "My soul doth magnify the Lord, and my spirit rejoices in God my Saviour." In Him I have a shelter from every storm; a support under every load. The eternal God is my refuge, and underneath are the everlasting arms. Am I guilty! "With him there is plenteous redemption." He was angry with me, but his anger is turned away, and he comforteth me. And what comfort can be compared with that which arises from the thought, that I am reconciled unto God by the death of his Son? That I am accepted in the Beloved? Do I want ability to "travel all the length of the celestial road," and a title to heaven when I arrive? "In the Lord have I righteousness and strength." "I will go in the strength of the Lord God; I will make mention of his righteousness, even of his only." All his relations are mine. He is my physician, my friend, my shepherd, my father. All his perfections are mine—his wisdom, his power, his mercy, and his truth. All the dispensations of his providence, all the treasures of his word, are mine. All his grace, all his glory, is mine. "I will greatly rejoice in the Lord, my soul shall be joyful in my God; for he hath clothed me with the garments of salvation, he hath covered me with the robe of righteousness; as a bridegroom decketh himself with ornaments, and a bride adorneth herself with her jewels." Is this exultation excessive? There can be no excess here. As the Lord himself is the source of this joy the joy passeth all understanding. And the meek shall increase their joy in the Lord for ever and ever, because the subject of it is not only perfect, but infinite.

—His, finally, in the *production*. In vain is provision, however suitable and rich, spread within our view, if it be placed beyond our reach. Observe the language of God with regard to Ephraim: "I drew them with cords of a man, with bands of love: and I was to them as they that take off the yoke on their jaws; and I laid meat unto them." The former was as necessary as the latter: while the mouth of the ox was muzzled, the nearness of the food would only tantalize and distress. What we mean by the allusion is this—There may be reasons for rejoicing when yet no joy is experienced: for the mourner may be unable to lay hold of them, and appropriate them to his own use. Asaph saw his safety, but felt his inability to reach it without the aid of him who had provided it. "Lead me to the rock that is higher than I." David therefore says, "Thou shalt make them drink of the river of thy pleasures." And he prays, "Rejoice the soul of thy servant." And he acknowledges, "Thou hast put gladness in my heart." And who can put it there, if *He* does not! Can conscience? Can a Christian friend? Can a minister; even a Barnabas, a son of consolation? "When he maketh peace, then who can make trouble; and when he hideth his face, then who can behold him, whether it be done against a nation or a man only?" Means are to be used; but the agency that renders them effectual is the Lord's. Our sleep would not refresh us without the divine blessing. Our food does not nourish us; but "every word that proceedeth out of the mouth of God."

And if this be true in natural things, is it less so in spiritual? Who then is Paul, and who is Apollos? Neither is he that planteth any thing, nor he that watereth, but God that giveth the increase. He is therefore called the "God of all comfort." And he is so called, not only to forbid our confidence in creatures, but to enlarge our expectations from himself, by bringing an Almighty Creator of succour and refreshment into view, in our difficulties and sorrows. It says, I, even *I*, am he that comforteth you. Is *any* thing too hard for the *Lord*? However dark the scene, if He says, Let there be light, all shall be irradiated. However rough the winds and waves, if He says, Peace, be still, there shall be a great calm. He can turn the shadow of death into the morning. He can plant the hope of glory in the very bosom of despair. What he does not find, he can produce. If there be no pre-existent materials, he can create. *Nothing* hears *His* voice, and yields a world of life and plenty and bliss. He calleth those things which be not, as

though they were. He is the God of all comfort, who comforteth us in all our tribulations.—Let us consider,

II. The UTILITY of this joy.

For it is not only divine, but efficacious; and efficacious, because divine—The joy of the Lord is your *strength*. To know the force of an argument, we apply it. To know the power of an implement, we make trial of it. To ascertain the strength of a man, we compare him with others; we task him with some exertion; we judge by the difficulty of the work which he achieves, and especially by the might of opposition which he overcomes. Let us examine this joy. Let us bring it to six tests—some of them very severe ones. And let us see what it can do for the Christian—in his profession of religion—in his concern to recommend it to others—in the discharge of duty—in his perils—in his sufferings—and in death.

First, let us review the Christian in his *profession* of religion. That this profession is required of us, it is hardly necessary to prove. In one place we are commanded, to "hold fast our profession." In a second, to "hold fast the profession of our faith without wavering." In a third, we are represented not only as "believing with the heart unto righteousness, but as confessing with the mouth unto salvation." In a fourth, our Master tells us, that if we "deny him, he will also deny us;" and that of those who are "ashamed of him and of his words, he will be ashamed when he comes in the clouds of heaven with the holy angels." So necessary is it not only that we should be what we appear, but appear what we are. The religion of Jesus is so perfectly true and excellent, that it will bear any kind of exhibition. And it demands examination. And it is the more beneficial the more it is known.

Now let us see how the joy of the Lord affects this profession. It is the very strength of it. For in proportion as a man possesses it, he feels satisfied with his portion; he glories in his choice: he is ready to avow it. And if it should occasion him some privations or sacrifices which may lead the enemy to reproach him, "Where is now your God?" he feels more than indemnified already; and can say with the Apostle, "for which cause I suffer these things: nevertheless I am not ashamed, for I know whom I have believed, and am persuaded that he is able to keep that which is committed to him against that day." David found God's testimonies his delight and his counsellors; and therefore he could say, "I will speak of thy testimonies also before kings, and will not be ashamed."

There is a great difference between godly sorrow and godly joy. When we feel the former, we naturally seek to elude observation; we retire to weep, and the eye pours out tears unto God. But joy is stirring and manifestative. It says to them that are in darkness, "Show yourselves." To the prisoners, "Go forth"—and they "go forth with joy, and are led forth in peace." We can appeal to the experience of many of you. How long did you carry a wounded and a bleeding conscience, before you laid open the distress to any creature-inspection! It was otherwise when the desire was accomplished. When He commanded deliverance for you; when you were made free indeed; you could no longer conceal your emotions. You then said, "Come and hear, all ye that fear God, and I will declare what he hath done for my soul. I cried unto him with my mouth, and he was extolled with my tongue. I will go into thy house with burnt offerings: I will pay thee my vows, which my lips have uttered, and my mouth hath spoken, when I was in trouble. Thou hast turned for me my mourning into dancing: thou hast put off my sackcloth and girded me with gladness, to the end that my glory may sing praise to Thee, and not be silent: O Lord my God, I will give thanks unto thee for ever." It was the loss of his joy that made David dumb. He therefore prays, "Open thou my lips, and my mouth shall show forth thy praise. Restore unto me the joy of thy salvation; and uphold me with thy free Spirit. Then will I teach transgressors thy ways; and sinners shall be converted unto thee."—Let us therefore observe the Christian,

Secondly, in his *concern to recommend religion* to others. Real godliness shows itself not only personally, but socially. It must begin at home; but it can never end here. *He* will not value the soul of another who despises his own; but an earnestness for our own salvation involves principles that must make us anxious to save all that are around us. We shall therefore say to them, as Moses said to Hobab, "We are journeying towards a place of which the Lord said, I will give it you: come with us, and we will do you good, for the Lord hath spoken good concerning Israel."

Now of this it is easy to see that the joy of the Lord is the strength. It is this that gives us confidence in our addresses. We speak not from conjecture, or from opinion, but experience. "That which we have seen and heard, declare we unto you, that ye also may have fellowship with us; and truly our fellowship is with the Father, and with his Son Jesus Christ." It is this that gives earnestness to our invitations. We have something suitable and valuable to recommend. We do not ask persons to a barren entertainment. We have a rich abundance; and we have found the plenty after we were perishing ourselves; and knowing that others are still in the same condition, we resemble the lepers at Samaria, who said, "this day is a day of good things, and we hold our peace. If we tarry till the morning light, some mischief will befall us; now therefore come, that we may tell the king's household." He is the man to say to others, "O taste and see that the Lord is good," who has himself tasted that he is gracious, and from his own enjoyment can say, "Blessed is the man that trusteth in him."

This also adds conviction and force to our testimony and commendation. Men see what our religion has done for us, and what it can do for them also. Will any thing recommend a master more than the cheerfulness of his servants? When they constantly sing at their work, is it not a proof that they do not find it an irksome, wearisome thing to serve him? All are looking out for happiness; and if they see that you have found what others in every direction miss; that while others, like fools, are running up and down the earth, asking, "Who will show us any good?" your heart is set at rest; while others are full of complaint, you are filled with praise; that while they are enlarging their desires as hell, you learn to be content with such things as you have: troubled, yet not distressed; sorrowful, yet always rejoicing; having nothing, and yet possessing all things—must not this induce them to say, "This is the seed which the Lord hath blessed?" Will not this move them to take hold of the skirt of him that is a Jew, saying, we will go with you, for we have heard that God is with you?

Wo to the world because of offences! says the Saviour. And professors should remember, these offences are various and many. The way of truth may be evil spoken of, not only by your immoral conduct, but by your perverse disposition; and by your unlovely temper; and by your sullenness, and mopishness, and gloom, and fear. Your delicate regard for the honour of the Gospel should lead you to attend to the command of your Lord, "Let not your heart be troubled, neither let it be afraid." But when you are unable to *suppress* sorrowful and desponding feelings, should you not endeavour to *conceal* them? "I was ashamed," says Ezra, "to require of the king a band of soldiers and horsemen to help us against the enemy in the way; because we had spoken unto the king, saying, The hand of our God is upon all them that seek him." Now confidence in God was not incompatible with his asking for such assistance; but it was likely to operate strangely and injuriously on the mind of this pagan monarch: and because it would look like suspicion and apprehension, he avoided the very appearance of evil.

Thirdly, Let us view the Christian in the *discharge of his duties*. These are numerous, and extensive, and difficult; and he is required to be always abounding in the work of the Lord. And here too, the joy of the Lord is his strength. It is well known that fear chills; despondency unnerves; sorrow depresses. But hope is encouragement. It is energy. It is the main spring of action. It sets and keeps the world in motion. Joy inspires; excites; elevates. It renders our work, our privilege. It throws off the dulness and formality in our holy exercises. We not only have life, but have it more abundantly. The absence of this joy is a kind of winter: and then we are not only dark, but barren; not only cold, but lifeless. But the return of it makes the spring; and again the earth teems, and the field and garden are all movement, and the trees are blossom, and the air all song. David understood this, and therefore said, "Then will I run in the way of thy commandments, when thou shalt have enlarged my heart." Bunyan knew this, and therefore he releases his Pilgrim from his burden; and so, not only delights him by the relief, but prepares him for the better and more successful execution of his journey. From this load persons are not all discharged at the same time; and some carry it long: but it is a hinderance, as well as a distress; and favoured is he who is early delivered, and can lightsomely advance in the way everlasting.

Some seem afraid to administer the consolations of the glorious Gospel fully, as if they would have, if not a licentious, yet a paralysing effect on the receiver. But these timid dispensers of divine truth, though they may be well meaning, are not well informed. They are ignorant of the very principles of our nature; and know very little of the comforts of the Holy Ghost—or they would know that these comforts are not opiates, but cordials—that while they refresh, they also animate. If there must be any thing of an extreme (for which however we do not plead,) it would be better for the leaning to be on the side of privilege than of legality, even with regard to practical religion. Such a man, grateful for his indulgences, at the feet of his Benefactor as well as Master, will feel himself much more disposed and bound to dedicate himself to his service; and his language must be, "What shall I render unto the Lord for all his benefits towards me?"

Fourthly, Let us view the Christian in his perils. He is perpetually surrounded with temptations in the world. These flatter him, and would entice him away from God. And these he is to resist, steadfast in the faith. But how is this to be done? By threatening! By constraints! These may indeed induce him actually to refuse the offers and allurements; but not in affection. The joy of the Lord is his strength; and without this, a man will only leave the world as Lot's wife left Sodom—she left it, but her heart was still in the place; and she inwardly sighed, O that I was there! O that I could return, and—not be destroyed! Thus there are some who forsake the world, as far as they are impelled by the fear of hell, or the dread of reproach or shame of inconsistency; but they hate the obligation that keeps them back from their loved indulgences; and, like wasps burnt out of their nests, are angry and resentful towards all around them, for the injuries they have endured. Prohibition, so far from killing desire, has a tendency to increase it; sin takes occasion by the commandment; and that which was ordained to be unto life, proves to be unto death. The Christian is not saved from the world by the law, but by grace. He is not driven out of it against his inclination—he leaves it voluntarily; and gives proof of it: for truly if he were mindful of the country from whence he came out, he would have opportunities to return. He has the same allurements and seductions presented to him, as others. But here is the difference: they are alive to them; but he is dead. He has found something infinitely superior: this, by refining and exalting his taste, has weaned him; and he can no longer relish the mean and ignoble provision of former days. Having found the pure spring, he no longer kneels to the filthy puddle. Having tasted the grapes of Eshcol, he longs no more for the leeks, and garlic, and onions of Egypt. The palace makes him forget the dunghill.

This, this is the way, and the only effectual way of separating the heart from the world; it is to subdue the sense of an inferior good, by the enjoyment of a greater. Who would exchange the green pastures and still waters for barrenness and drought? Who wants lamps, or even stars, when the sun is up!

> " As by the light of opening day
>   The stars are all conceal'd;
> So earthly pleasures fade away
>   When Jesus is reveal'd."

This joy exercises a man of carnal affection: and we are persuaded the efficacy of it is far greater to mortify us to the world, than the influence of afflictions. Losses and disappointments may surprise and confound us, and lead us to lament the uncertainty of every thing below; but they do not make us feel their unsatisfactory and polluted nature. Even under the pressure of their trials, and amidst all their complaints, you will often discern the disposition of the sufferers remaining unchanged. And if not, how soon after, does renewed pursuit succeed deplored deceptions, and men flee to a repetition of similar experiments, till all the mad career is ended! But the experience produced by the sight of the Cross, and communion with God in Christ, will never allow the world to become again the Christian's end, or portion. If by the power of delusion he be drawn astray for a moment, he will soon find that it is not with him as in months past; and he will be sure to feel the wretchedness of what he has chosen, compared with the glory of what he has left. And this feeling will serve to recall him. The *apostate* has no such experience as this to check and turn him. But the *backslider* has: and see the result—"I will go," says the Church, " and return to my first husband, for then it was better with me than now."

Fifthly, We shall see that the joy of the Lord is his strength, if we view the Christian in his *sufferings*. Here we might lead you back, and call to your remembrance the former times. We might show you the glorious army of martyrs tortured, not accepting deliverance, that they might obtain a better resurrection. We might show you Peter and John, after being scourged, departing from the council, rejoicing that they were counted worthy to suffer shame for his name. We might show you the Hebrews taking joyfully the spoiling of their goods; and men, and women, and youths, severing from their friends who hung on their necks, willing to go to prison and to death. I might show you Bradford, who, when the keeper's wife, weeping, said to him, " O Sir, I am come with heavy tidings—you are to be burnt to-morrow: and they are gone into the city to buy the chain:" taking off his hat and laying it upon the ground, and kneeling and raising his hands, he said, " Lord, I thank thee for this honour. This is what I have been waiting for, and longing for."

Such scenes as these, owing to the laws of the land, we are not called to witness. With us, persecution is not national; is not legal. We can sit under our own vine and fig-tree, none daring to make us afraid. Yet there are instances of private and personal wrongs beyond the prevention of law. The carnal mind is enmity against God, and the tongue can no man tame. We have seen servants deprived of their places; and workmen of their employment; and tradesmen of their custom. We have seen wives and children enduring privations, and insults, and outrage. We have seen the follower of the Lamb, bearing his reproach, scorned by his companions, and deserted by his friends—yet acting with decision and consistency, and practically saying, " None of these things move me; neither count I my *life* dear, so that I but finish my course with joy." And why have they not been overcome? Why have they not partially yielded? They were filled with everlasting consolation, and good hope through grace. " The joy of the Lord was their strength."

But afflictions of any kind may supply the place of persecution, and try every religious principle. We talk of martyrs. What martyrs have endured, what some Christians have been called in private life to suffer, month after month, and year after year—a great part of the heart's bitterness perhaps known only to themselves! Yet, under bo-dily anguish, and family bereavements, and the cruelty of connexions, and reductions in life the most humiliating, we have witnessed them—not raging against instruments, not cursing the day of their birth, not impeaching the providence of God, not charging Him unkindly : but looking upward and meekly saying, " I know, O Lord, that thy judgments are right, and that thou in faithfulness hast afflicted me." Not insensible, yet more than resigned—not undervaluing the comforts of which they have been stripped, yet exulting, " Though the fig-tree shall not blossom, neither shall fruit be in the vines; the labour of the olive shall fail, and the fields shall yield no meat; the flock shall be cut off from the fold, and there shall be no herd in the stalls : yet I will rejoice in the Lord, I will joy in the God of my salvation."

Finally, It is hardly needful to say, this joy of the Lord is the Christian's strength *in death*. For what but this *can* be his support then? Then lover and friend must fail him. Then the keepers of the house tremble. Then desire fails. What can nature do here? or nature's light? or nature's religion? But in the multitude of his thoughts within him —and what a multitude of thoughts will beset a dying man!—God's comforts delight his soul. The world passeth away ; but the kingdom of heaven is at hand. The outward man perisheth ; but the inward man is renewed. He looks at his trembling limbs, and feels his fainting heart. His heart and his flesh faileth; but God is the strength of his heart, and his portion for ever. He looks forward, and sees enough to dismay all mortal courage—but says he, " my Shepherd's with me there." " Yea, though I walk through the valley of the shadow of death, I will fear no evil; for thou art with me, thy rod and thy staff they comfort me."

And now what says our subject in a way of practical improvement?

—It says, *Inquire what your joy is*. Is it the joy of the Lord? For there is the joy of the sinner. And we read of the pleasures of sin : these are for a season ; and as they are soon over, so they leave nothing but stains and stings behind. We read of the joy of the hypocrite, and are told that it is but for a moment; because at death he must be detected, and may be laid open much sooner. There is the joy of the Pharisee, who trusts in himself that he is righteous and despises others, and even glories before God. Some are said to rejoice in a thing of nought. Such are all worldlings: for all that cometh is vanity; and honours and riches and power are but, to them, as so many toys or flowers thrown into the vehicle that is conveying the condemned criminal to the place of execution.

Now it matters little which of these joys characterizes you, if you are a stranger to *the* joy of which we have been speaking. But allow me, in reference to your choice, to remind you of the language of Solomon: "Even in laughter, the heart is sorrowful; and the end of that mirth is heaviness. I said of laughter, it is mad, and of mirth, what doth it?" Yes, this is the question—What DOTH it? You have seen what the joy of the Christian can do?—But what doth yours? Does it purify your passions? Does it make you happy alone? Does it afford you any thing like satisfaction? Does it bear you up under the trials of life? Does it raise you above the dread of death and eternity? Has it any constant source? any solid foundation? Is it not the creature of ignorance? Are you not afraid to let in one ray of divine truth upon it? Would not one serious thought of God and of another world strike it dead upon the spot? "I create the fruit of the lips; peace, peace to him that is far off, and to him that is near, saith the Lord; and I will heal him. But the wicked are like the troubled sea, when it cannot rest, whose waters cast up mire and dirt. There is no peace, saith my God, to the wicked. Therefore thus said the Lord God, Behold, my servants shall eat, but ye shall be hungry: behold, my servants shall drink, but ye shall be thirsty: behold, my servants shall rejoice, but ye shall be ashamed: behold, my servants shall sing for joy of heart, but ye shall cry for sorrow of heart, and shall howl for vexation of spirit."

—It says, *See how greatly religion is libelled.* You well know that it is commonly represented as at variance with every thing like pleasure: and nothing can be more injurious than such a representation, especially to the young, who are so alive to happiness. But can any thing be so unfounded and false as this vile and repulsive opinion? Surely God is able to make a man happy; and is it therefore reasonable to suppose that he will suffer one who neglects and hates him to be happier than one who loves and serves him? Has my hoping and believing that death is the gate of life; that heaven is my home; that God is my father; that all things are working together for my good; a tendency to prevent or diminish my enjoyment of the beauties of nature, and the bounties of providence, and the intercourses of life? But if the Scriptures are allowed to decide, and they contain the judgment of the only wise and true God, we know that wisdom's ways "are ways of pleasantness, and all her paths are peace. She is a tree of life to them that lay hold of her, and happy is every one that retaineth her." And in this testimony every partaker of divine grace acquiesces. It would be in vain to appeal to others. They have not made the trial; but these have made it. And these will tell you, that they know nothing of bondage. To them his service is perfect freedom. They find his yoke easy,

and his burden light. They will tell you that they were strangers to real pleasure as long as they were without Christ; but since their knowledge of Him, their common mercies have been sweetened; their very sorrows have been blessed; and they prefer their own lowest estate to all the glory and goodness of the world.

—It says, *What an inducement is here to seek the Lord and his strength, to seek his face evermore!* Joy is a thing to which none are indifferent. All are contriving or labouring to acquire something in which they may rejoice. But here the blessing is. Here is a joy that deserves the name. A joy soft as the ether of Paradise, and pure as the river of life proceeding from the throne of God and of the Lamb—the hidden manna—the bread of heaven—angels' food—yea, more—for

'Never did angels taste above
Redeeming grace and dying love.'

And can you do without this joy? If you can dispense with it while every thing prospers—what will you do, in the day of adversity? If you can dispense with it in the smiles of youth—what will you do, in the decays and privations and depressions of age? If you can dispense with it in the excitements of society—what will you do, in the dreariness of solitude? If you can dispense with it in the attractions of life—what will you do, in the loneliness of death? If you can dispense with it in a world of engrossment and diversions—

"O ye gay dreamers of gay dreams,
How will you weather an eternal night,
Where such expedients fail?"

—But do you not *now* feel your need of it? However successful, however indulged, however amused, do you not *now* feel a void within which this alone can fill—a craving which this alone can relieve—a restlessness which this alone can soothe and calm?—And is it not attainable? Is there not ONE, among all your dissatisfactions and disquietudes, now saying, "Come unto me, all ye that labour and are heavy laden, and I will give you rest. Take my yoke upon you, and learn of me, for I am meek and lowly in heart, and ye shall find rest unto your souls?"

—It says, *Your religion is to be suspected, if you are habitually destitute of joy.* Here we readily exclude all constitutional cases, such as we have admitted in the former Lecture: there is no reasoning from these. We also limit our intimation by observing, that it does not extend to that joy which springs from strong confidence, or the full assurance of hope; though, with regard to this, every one whose heart is right with God will prize it and desire it. But we have known many who have possessed very little of it through life, and yet have given undeniable proof that they are renewed in the spirit of their mind. But this is only one view of the Christian's joy, or rather one kind of it. There are other, and many other sources of sacred delight. There are the pleasures of Divine knowledge; the pleasures of hope; the pleasures of review, in looking back upon the way by which the Lord has led us; the pleasures arising from attendance on the means of grace; the pleasures arising from congeniality with the things of the Spirit, and which makes it our meat to do the will of our heavenly Father; the pleasures arising from the approbation of conscience; and the pleasures of usefulness. There are persons who are ready to exclude themselves from the gladness of God's nation, and yet their eye sparkles with pleasure when they see the prosperity of Jerusalem, and hear that the word of the Lord has free course and is glorified.—But are *they* strangers to the joy of the Lord?

—It says, *Let this joy be a peculiar object of attention to every Christian,*—Let him never forget that it is his strength.

If therefore he has lost it, let him not rest till he has regained it. Let him hasten back to the place where he slept and dropped his roll. Let him repent and do his first works.

Though his state be secure, let him remember that his comfort may vary and decline; and therefore let him guard against every thing that may wound his peace, and grieve the Holy Spirit, and interrupt his communion with God.

Some of you know the worth of this joy from the want, rather than from the experience. You are not strangers to the nature of it; but the degree in which you possess it, is far below your duty and your privilege. Let me beseech you, as you value your own welfare, and the honour of your God, to seek, immediately and earnestly, an increase of it.

And, for this purpose, suffer the word of exhortation. Commune with your own heart, and insist upon a reason for your distress: saying, with David, "Why art thou cast down, O my soul, and why art thou disquieted in me?"—Maintain intercourse with the wise and experienced. Two are better than one. Jonathan went to David in the wood, and strengthened his hand in God. One Christian is frequently to another like the angel to Hagar—she was ready to die of thirst, with water near her; but he opened her eyes and showed her the well. "Retire and read thy Bible, to be gay." Peruse much the Scriptures, which are filled with words good and comfortable. Acquaint yourselves with the method of salvation—the freeness and plenitude of divine grace—the ground of our acceptance—and all the provision made, not only for our safety but consolation.—Pay much attention to the ordinances of God. His ministers are helpers of your joys. He is known in his palaces for a refuge. According to your conduct here, you will be vouchers, both for the promise and the threatening; "Them that honour me, I will honour; and they that despise me shall be lightly esteemed."—Be much in prayer. *Ask,* and ye shall receive, that your joy may be full.—We read of the joy of faith. Look after more of this all-important principle. You can only be filled with all joy and peace, in believing. But, believing, ye shall rejoice with joy unspeakable and full of glory.

Follow these admonitions; and while the joy of the Lord is your strength, you shall not want the strength of the joy. You shall know the truth, and the truth shall make you free. You shall go on singing in the ways of the Lord; and you soon shall reach His presence, where there is fulness of joy; and his right hand, where there are pleasures for evermore. Amen.

LECTURE X.

THE CHRISTIAN, IN DEATH.

"*Mark the perfect man, and behold the upright; for the end of that man is peace.*"— Psalm xxxvii. 37.

You have heard of the manner in which a distinguished writer, and a Secretary of State, expired. "Come," said ADDISON, to a young nobleman of rather infidel principles, as he entered his dying chamber; "Come," said he, taking him softly by the hand; "Come, and SEE HOW A CHRISTIAN CAN DIE."

This has always been admired as a noble expression of composure, and faith, and zeal. And to this the Poet alludes when he says—

"He taught us how to live, and, O! too high
The price of knowledge, taught us how to die."

If we object to any thing in the address, it is not that it came from a character whose religion some may think too undecided; for candour should lead us to conclude that he was what he professed to be—especially at a period so awful—but that the subject of the eulogy should have been the Author. "Let another praise thee, and not thy own mouth; a stranger, and not thy own lips." The exclamation may indeed have been designed, not to glorify the man, but his religion; and to recommend from his own experience what could support and refresh, even when all other succours and comforts failed. Yet we would rather the friend or the minister had laid hold of the approaching observer, and leading him into the room, had said, "COME, SEE HOW A CHRISTIAN CAN DIE."

Such an office your Lecturer has to perform this morning. "*Mark the perfect man, and behold the upright: for the end of that man is peace.*"

Fly, ye profane, or else draw near with awe ;
For here resistless demonstration dwells.
Here tired dissimulation drops her mask,
Here real and apparent are the same.
—You see the man ; you see his hold on heaven.
Heaven waits not the last moment; owns its friends
On this side death ; and points them out to men—
A lecture silent, but of sovereign use.
Life, take thy chance—but O for such an end!"

"*Mark the perfect man, and behold the upright: for the end of that man is peace.*" We premise three remarks.

The *First,* regards the character—The perfect man. This may seem discouraging; but it really is not so. If it intended absolute purity, no creature could claim the title. "Behold, he put no trust in his servants, and his angels he charged with folly." If it intended actual exemption from all moral infirmities, none of the human race, no, not even of the sanctified part of it, could be included. "For there is not on earth a just man that liveth and sinneth not." "In many things," says an Apostle, "we offend all." And our Saviour teaches us to pray for daily pardon as well as for daily bread.

To say that the Christian will certainly be complete hereafter, and that he is complete in Christ now, is true. But the character refers to something present and personal. Bishop Lowth, in his admirable prelections on the Hebrew poetry, remarks how commonly it abounds with parallelisms. The second member of the verse never expresses a new idea, but always repeats the sentiment contained in the first. It may enlarge or enforce or explain it; but never resigns it for another. According to this rule, the character is not only called perfect, but *upright.* And the latter attribute is explanatory of the former—the perfect man *is* the upright—one who is upright in his transactions with his own soul—upright in his dealings with his God—upright in his conduct with his fellow-creatures—one "whose rejoicing is this, the testimony of his conscience, that in simplicity and godly sincerity, not with fleshly wisdom, but by the grace of God, he has his conversation in the world."

The *Second* regards the *subject of attention*—The *end* of this man. Every thing pertaining to his character is deserving of notice: his birth; his relations; his conduct; his condition. But here our eyes are fixed on his death. "*Mark the perfect man, and behold the upright; for the end of that man is peace.*"

The *Third* regards the *testimony* concerning his end—it is *peace.* This word was not used by the Jews as it is with us. With us it always suggests the idea of reconciliation and concord, after variance and strife; or of serenity of mind as opposed to some kind of conflict. With them the term was significant of good at large: prosperity; welfare; happiness. Thus we are commanded to pray for the "peace of Jerusalem." Thus Joseph

says, "God shall give Pharaoh an answer of peace." Thus Artaxerxes superscribes his letter, "Peace, and at such a time." Thus the disciples were to say, as they entered, "Peace be to this house." Thus we are to understand it, as used by Simeon when he took up the Saviour in his arms and blessed God and said, "Lord, now lettest thou thy servant depart in peace." "My desires and hope are accomplished; I am now happy; satisfied with favour, and filled with the blessing of the Lord"—And this is the meaning in the words before us, "*Mark the perfect man, and behold the upright: for the end of that man is peace.*" This accords with our design this morning, which is to view the Christian,

In Death.

There are four things in the dying of the Christian I would call upon you to observe—Its Prospect. Its Experience. Its Influence. Its Issue.

I. The PROSPECT IS NOT ALWAYS PLEASING.

II. The ACTUAL EXPERIENCE IS COMMONLY MUCH INDULGED AND DISTINGUISHED.

III. It is OFTEN PECULIARLY USEFUL BY ITS INFLUENCE.

IV. It is ALWAYS SAFE AND GLORIOUS IN THE ISSUE.

I. It is NOT ALWAYS PLEASING IN ITS PROSPECT.

There are some indeed who are able to look forward to the scene, not only without reluctance and dread, but with resignation and pleasure. They contemplate death as their deliverance; their victory; their triumph. In all their dissatisfactions and trials they seem to say, "Well; all will be soon explained, rectified, completed. When a few years are come, I shall go the way I shall not return." Thus Dr. Gouge was accustomed to say, "I have two friends in the world: Christ and death. Christ is my first, but death is my second." Such a Christian may be compared to a child at school. The little pupil is no enemy to his book; but he likes home; and finds his present condition not only a place of tuition, but of comparative confinement and exclusion. He does not run away; but while he studies, he thinks with delight of his return. He welcomes every messenger *to* him—but far more the messenger that comes *for* him. And though he may be a black servant, he says, "Well, he will take me to my father's house."

But such cheerfulness in the prospect is not invariably nor commonly the feeling of good men. When David says, "Yea, though I walk through the valley of the shadow of death, I will fear no evil," he speaks of this anticipation, as an attainment; and intimates that the fear which he was enabled to defy, was much connected with the event itself.

N 9

Here is a difficulty—not indeed with regard to the unconverted. To them we say, death may well be the king of terrors—and it is. The dread of it prevails more deeply and generally than they are willing to acknowledge. The apprehension of it often makes them superstitious and credulous; and they find a prognostic of their fate in a dream, in the howling of a dog, the croaking of a raven, the ticking of an insect, and a thousand other absurdities. How eager are they to guard against every thing that would accelerate the fatal hour! And how sedulously they strive to keep themselves from every thing that would prove a memento of it! One of the kings of France gave orders that death should never be mentioned in his hearing. Catherine, the Empress of Russia, forbad funeral processions to pass the street near her palace, and required all burials to be performed in the night. Many avoid every reference to their deceased relations and friends, as if in tenderness to their memory; while it really arises from an unwillingness to think of an event to which they are themselves equally exposed. The constant effort of multitudes is to banish the thought from their minds, or to hinder its entrance. The Apostle therefore says, that they are all their lifetime *subject* to bondage, through fear of death. Not always actually in it, but *liable* to it—as their reading, or hearing; a coffin, or an opening grave; an accident, or disease, may urge the subject upon their revolting attention. And it is easy to imagine the wretchedness of such a life: for how hard must it be to keep off from their thoughts a thing that they very much hate and dread; and which daily and hourly occurrences must often obtrude upon them! Yet, as soon as the sentiment is felt, all peace and comfort vanish.

—But the difficulty respects the Christian. Why should *he* be afraid in the prospect? Is not death conquered? and rendered harmless with regard to him? But the serpent may hiss, when it cannot bite. The poisonous fang may be extracted before our eyes, and yet we may feel, at taking the harmless adder into our bosom. There are many Christians whose anxieties and forebodings with regard to death, are only dispelled and destroyed by the event itself. Let us look at the case; and see if we cannot remove a stumbling-block out of the way of God's people. There are several things to be considered—

The fear of death is naturally unavoidable; and must therefore in itself be innocent. The very law of self-preservation necessarily makes every being averse to danger and injury. All the animal creatures have a dread of death. In them, this is merely an impulse, and operates without any distinct apprehension of evil; but in man, this instinctive repulsion has blended with it the result of reasoning, and of local attachment, and social love, and moral responsibility, and reflection, and forecast. Adam and Eve felt this fear in Paradise. To this principle the words were addressed, "In the day thou eatest thereof thou shalt surely die." For this denunciation had been no threatening, had not death been viewed by them as the greatest evil. The apostles themselves, who had the first-fruits of the Spirit, said, "In this we groan, earnestly desiring to be clothed upon with our house which is from heaven: if so be that, being clothed, we shall not be found naked. For we that are in this tabernacle do groan, being burdened; not for that we would be unclothed, but clothed upon, that mortality might be swallowed up of life." What wonder therefore if ordinary Christians feel the same?

And how much is there to excite apprehension! There is the novelty of the case. For, as Joshua said to the Jews, this is a way they have not gone heretofore. Here their own experience affords them no assistance: nor can they derive advantage from the experience of others. No one has returned to "blab the secret out,'" and tell them what it is to die. When they think of the leaving for ever of objects to which they have been long accustomed—The separation from weeping friends—The pains, the groans, the dying strife—The destruction of the body—The consigning of it to the lonely grave—The conversion of it into food for worms—Their immediate access into the presence of Purity and Holiness—The judgment that follows after—Doubts of their acceptance with God—Uncertainties about their future state—Is there not enough here to try all their confidence and courage?

There is one thing more to be taken into the account. Others not only endeavour to avoid thinking of the seriousness of the subject, but, in some measure, they often succeed. By infidelity, and vain reasonings, and dissipations, they may preserve a kind of composure even to the last. Yea, they may amuse themselves even in death itself, as Hume was, joking about Charon and his boat,

"Whistling aloud to keep his courage up."

Yea, they may even bring their principles over to their deluded interest. For though unbelief and diversion do not abate their danger, they affect their apprehension of it, and make them insensible. A man walking upon a precipice is not secure because he is ignorant of his situation; but this ignorance keeps him easy, and laughing, and singing, till he falls off. And thus we are told of the wicked, that they "have no bands in their death; and their strength is firm." But a Christian does not turn away from the subject. He must look at it. He must examine its nature, and bearings, and consequences—and, in doing this he feels much more in the prospect than numbers of those feel, who are ruined by the reality.

Be not therefore ashamed to own your feeling, especially to your fellow Christians and to your Minister. Do not conclude that it is an evidence against the reality or degree of your religion. Do not imagine that it disproves, or renders suspicious your attachment to the Saviour. "O! if I loved him I should long to be with him; and then I should love his appearing; and then I should be able to say, Come, Lord Jesus, come quickly." But you do love him; and you wish to be with him, by wishing full conformity to his image, and the constant beholding of his glory. But you dread the passage. It is thus with the absentee when thinking of his return. His estate, and wife, and children, are in America. And his heart is there also. Yet when he looks on the vast Atlantic, he shudders and shrinks back. But *he* does not from hence question *his* love to them, or his desire to be with them.

We acknowledge however that as believers you stand in a very different condition from others: and you ought to endeavour to rise above the fear of death. And there is enough, if you ever realize it, to produce in your minds a noble confidence. And it does not follow, that what you now feel, you will feel when the season of dissolution arrives.—For,

II. THE DYING OF THE CHRISTIAN IS COMMONLY MUCH INDULGED AND DISTINGUISHED, IN THE ACTUAL EXPERIENCE.

Thus it is said, "The righteous hath hope in his death." The degrees of this hope vary. In some we see this hope contending with fear, and not always able to repel it. In some, it produces a serenity in which the mind is stayed upon God, yet unattended with any higher feeling and pleasure: while some possess and display the full assurance of hope; and have an entrance ministered unto them abundantly into the everlasting kingdom of their Lord and Saviour. Amidst the wreck of nature, *these* are joyful in glory; and shout aloud upon their beds; as if they were already within the vail.

Now we are not going to claim this joy unspeakable and full of glory; or even this perfect peace; or even this supporting confidence; for all Christians in their dying moments. And yet we mean to say, that the highest degree is attainable; and that, in general, they are much more favoured, as to religious consolation, in death than in life. Here we will not speak of things beyond our reach. Were we to say—That the chinks and breaks made in the falling tenement of clay, may let in more light than could enter before—That the believer's nearer approach to the world of glory, may bring him more under its influence and impressions—That when he reaches the borders of the river,

between him and Immanuel's land, he may glance the hills, and hear something of the harmony, and inhale the fragrance blown across—You would say, perhaps, and say justly, all this is figure. But there is truth in the dying privilege of the Christian. And four reasons may be mentioned for his superior indulgence at that solemn hour.

First, *He has now more of that single and entire dependence on the Saviour, which is so friendly to our relief and comfort.* A legal bias is natural to us; and during life, a degree of it prevails, of which the Christian is not himself sufficiently aware. He is searching after something, in which, if he does not glory, he insensibly trusts; and feels his hope varying often with his attainments, as if the one was *founded* on the other. But all this is now over. Now he *must* have immediate consolation. But where is he to find it? When he looks back, he cannot derive it from a well-spent life: and when he looks inward, he cannot derive it from a sense of his present worthiness. He sees more clearly than ever that he is an unprofitable servant. In all his doings his sins do appear. And what can he do now? He *must* look to another; and apply to him *as* he is. He therefore cries,

"A guilty, weak, and worthless worm,
    On thy kind arm I fall:
    Be thou my strength and righteousness,
    My Jesus, and my all."—

And a satisfaction is experienced, which was only hindered *before* by unbelief.

Secondly, *He is then urged to come more conclusively to a judgment concerning his state.* He must, indeed, have often examined himself before; but he never felt so pressing an excitement as he now does. He can *comparatively* neglect it no longer. He now *must* know how matters stand between him and God, for they will soon be found unalterable. And if his condition was an unsound one, the exploring of it would be the way to alarm him, and not to tranquillize. But his state *is* good; and ignorance is the only cause of his suspicion and disquietude. Let this be removed, therefore, and let him see things as they truly are, and his trembling hope is confirmed. *His* fear before was needless, for the house was safe, and able to abide the storm. But now, having been driven to inspect the foundation, he knows its security and permanence; and can rejoice because he *sees* that it is founded on a rock.

Thirdly, *He then needs peculiar support and consolation; and the Lord deals with his people according to the principles of the truest friendship.* He is with them most, when they most require his presence. "I will be with him in trouble." He is always with him; for he hath said, "I will *never* leave thee, nor forsake thee." But the meaning is, that he will be with them then pre-eminently.

And where is the believer who, in passing through life, has not had more of His manifestations and influences and comforts, in his sufferings, than in any other circumstances? But what an hour is here!—when he gathers up his feet into the bed, and turns his face to the wall; and Satan for the last onset comes down, having great wrath, knowing that his time is short! But the Lord he has trusted and served will draw near at his breathing, at his cry. He will whisper into his very soul, "Fear not, for I am with thee; be not dismayed, for I am thy God: I will strengthen thee; yea, I will help thee; yea, I will uphold thee with the right hand of my righteousness." And what is the result? "Whom have I in heaven but thee? and there is none upon earth I desire beside thee. My heart and my flesh faileth; but God is the strength of my heart, and my portion for ever."

Lastly, *He can then safely receive those discoveries and communications which would have made undue impressions before.* For every thing there is a season; and the believer must be prepared for his work, as well as his reward; and for his duty in the way, as well as for his blessedness at the end. Our present conditions and stations are appointed us by the Lord; and while we are in them, their claims must not be despised or neglected. But if we are to regard our natural connexions, and our civil and secular concerns, and the preservation of our health and life; we must be attached to them, and feel a degree of interest in them. Yet there are measures of knowledge and comfort, which would so powerfully affect us, as to draw us away from earth, and make every thing seen and temporal *feel* too low and little to engage us. We see this in Peter. When our Saviour was transfigured, and Moses and Elias appeared with him in glory; Peter was so charmed, that he proposed building tabernacles, to reside there. But, says the Holy Ghost, he knew not what he said. For, to take but one view of the proposal, had it been complied with, what would have become of his house and wife and children? O! Peter, in his ecstasy, had forgotten these. These however must not be forgotten while we continue in our relations to them, and can fulfil their demands. But when we must leave the scene, it is wise and kind to allow us to be dead to it. When we are going, it is well to be loosened from our detentions. When life is ending, and the love of it can no longer be useful, it is a privilege to have our love to it vanquished by something better than life; and to be blinded to every thing we are resigning around us, by a sight of the glory that is to be revealed; and to be rendered deaf to every sound but the voice that cries, "Come up hither."

After all, we may not have perfectly accounted for the higher experience of the Christian in death. But the fact is undeniable. It has been verified in numberless instances. How often have we witnessed it ourselves! How often have we found Christians the reverse of all their previous apprehensions! We have attended them when they have displayed a dignity of sentiment, and expressed themselves with a force of language, to which they had been strangers before. The timorous have become heroical. They whose minds were contracted by ignorance, have burst into the glorious liberty of the sons of God. The illiterate and the vulgar have shown an elevation and refinement of taste, philosophers never knew—and servants and rustics have sung,

> "O glorious hour, O blest abode!
> I shall be near, and like my God
> And flesh and sin no more control
> The sacred pleasure of my soul."

Fear not, therefore, O ye seed of Jacob. Encourage yourselves in the Lord your God; while you say, I wait for the Lord, my soul doth wait; and in his word do I hope. Do not perplex yourselves about a futurity which God has foreseen and provided for. "Take no thought for the morrow, for the morrow shall take thought for the things of itself; sufficient for the day is the evil thereof"— and the good. Your duty has only to do with the present; and the grace you are to seek is grace to help in time of need: active grace for the hour of exertion; and passive grace for the hour of suffering: grace for life, in life; and dying grace, for a dying hour. The Jews were not to live on a hoard. If in their anxious distrustfulness they laid up manna for the ensuing day, instead of affording them a wholesome resource, it bred worms: they therefore gathered it fresh every morning, and it failed them not till they could eat of the old corn of the land. Take another allusion. If you were traveling, and before you could reach your destination you had a trying river to pass, would it not be enough to relieve you to know, that when you came to the brink there would be a boat ready to convey you over? Must it be brought to you now in your journey? Though necessary for the water, would it not rather encumber you on land? Yet so it is; you are not satisfied unless you can take the vehicle along with you. You must *see:* but you are *not* to see—"We walk by faith, and not by sight."

III. The DYING OF THE CHRISTIAN IS OFTEN PECULIARLY USEFUL BY ITS INFLUENCE.

When our Saviour was foretelling the destiny of Peter, he said, "When thou wast young, thou girdedst thyself, and walkedst whither thou wouldest: but when thou shalt be old, thou shalt stretch forth thy hands, and another shall gird thee, and carry thee whither thou wouldest not. This spake he, signifying by what death he should glorify God." He was to die by violence and crucifixion. Ecclesiastical history informs us of numbers who were converted to the faith by the death of those who suffered for the Gospel. The scene naturally tended to raise their curiosity, and fix their attention: and witnessing the firmness of their conviction, and the dignity of their support; and seeing their gentleness and patience; and hearing their prayers for their persecutors and murderers; they became companions of them that were so used. And this led to the remark, that the blood of the martyrs was the seed of the churches.

All are not called to die for the truth's sake; but the effect ascribed to Peter's death will apply to the death of every Christian. Not only is it important to himself, but the glory of God is concerned in it.

" His God sustains him in his final hour.
His final hour brings glory to his God.

The useful death, however, is not that only which abounds with ecstasy and rapture: but also that in which an inferior degree of confidence is blended with patience under suffering, submission to the will of God, humbleness of mind, penitence at the foot of the Cross, a concern to recommend the Saviour's service and to promote his cause. This, if it does not excite so much wonder and discourse, is more exemplary. A death too strikes us where we see a victory over the world; when the individual is willing to depart, though not pressed by the infirmities and pains of age: but in the midst of life; and leaving not a scene of penury and wretchedness behind, but every present attraction and agreeable prospect. We also prize a death preceded by a holy and consistent life. Some religionists are fond of the marvellous and the sudden; and our obituaries are often filled with the triumphant departures of those who began to pray a few days before. This is often peculiarly the case with malefactors. Few of these, if attended by some divines, but in a few hours are quickly ripened for a confident and joyful death. We do not wish to limit the Holy One of Israel in the freeness of his mercy and grace. But wiser people hesitate about these prodigies. They wish for more certainty, more evidence than can be satisfactorily obtained in cases, where the impressions of the condition can scarcely be distinguished from the operation of the principle: and therefore, while they may sometimes indulge a hope, they will rarely be disposed to proclaim it—" Precious in the sight of the Lord is the death of his *saints. Mark the perfect man, and behold the upright: for the end of that man is peace.*"

-Yes, it is peculiarly worthy attention.

How often has the death of the saint proved the life of the sinner; and also helped those much who have believed through grace! A dying minister's end has exemplified, and confirmed, and enforced his doctrine; and he has effected in the sick-chamber what he failed to accomplish in the church. A dying father, disregarded before, has been heard to purpose, when he has summoned his children to his bed, and solemnly addressed them, as Bolton did his family: "See that none of you meet me in an unconverted state at the day of judgment." Or as David admonished Solomon: "I go the way of the world. And thou, Solomon my son, know thou the God of thy father, and serve him with a perfect heart and with a willing mind: for the Lord searcheth all hearts, and understandeth all the imaginations of the thoughts: if thou seek him, he will be found of thee; but if thou forsake him, he will cast thee off for ever." What ingenuousness has ever resisted a dying mother—Heaven in her countenance—her tearful eye—the grasp of her soft hand—her last trembling embrace—her expiring accents—" What my son, and the son of my womb, and the son of my vows—are we here to part for ever?" The husband who refused to hear the word, though urged by beauty, and affection, and tears; when the desire of his eyes is removed—is now won, by the last instances of her lovely conversation made sacred by death: and, while he rears the monument to her memory, resolves to trace her steps, once—how painful now the thought—taken alone!

—How affecting and interesting does grace render the dying of the Christian—not only to his relations and friends, but to all who see or hear it! Not only is the attention then excited, but every thing is adapted to aid impression. Persons are now regarded with peculiar earnestness. They are supposed to be free from the influence of the world. They are regarded as sincere, and entitled to credit. All now is final—it is the last time they can be seen or heard. What a lecture is the event itself! It cries, See, every thing is vanity, the world is passing away. But here is a man that has hold of a better and an enduring substance, and displays a greatness that defies the ravages of death. The outward man perishes, but the inward man is renewed. He is bound, yet free. He is dying, and behold he lives—and not only has life, but has it more abundantly. The way of transgressors is hard, and they say nothing in praise of those things of which they are now ashamed. The people of the world never speak well of it at parting. But here is a man commending the ways of holiness, and bearing testimony to the excellences and goodness of the Master he has served to the last—" Thou hast dealt well with thy servant, O Lord. O taste, and see that the

9*

Lord is good: blessed is the man that trusteth in him." "I have fought a good fight, I have finished my course, I have kept the faith: henceforth there is laid up for me a crown of righteousness, which the Lord, the righteous Judge, shall give me at that day: and not to me only, but unto all them also that love his appearing."

O! such a dying chamber is none other than the House of God, and the gate of heaven. There "is brought to pass the saying that is written, Death is swallowed up in victory." There angels hear the acclamation, "O death, where is thy sting? O grave, where is thy victory! The sting of death is sin; and the strength of sin is the law." Here, weaned from the world, and loosened from life, we have said, "Let us go away that we may die with him." Here a glory has been shed, an influence has been felt, that has impressed the careless, fixed the wavering, emboldened the timid, convinced the ignorant. It has strengthened the saint to live. It has taught the pastor to preach. It has led the infidel to retire, and pray, "Let me die the death of the righteous, and let my last end be like his!"

Upon the principle of this part of our subject, we may make a remark concerning a slow or a sudden death. Unquestionably a sudden death is desirable, with regard to exemption and privilege. For what an indulgence must it be to be spared all the forerunners and attendants of dissolution; and in the twinkling of an eye to pass from earth and to be with God! But it is less preferable on the score of usefulness. We derive nothing from the dying experience and language of such. A Christian is not to choose for himself; and if a lingering death will subserve more the honour of God and the benefit of man, there is enough to induce him to say, "Not my will, but thine be done." Heaven will make amends for all—Yea, the usefulness itself is the sufferer's reward.

And, Christians, let me from hence admonish you to be concerned to serve religion, not only by the life you live, but by the death you die. The Saviour's empire and claims extend to both. "None of us liveth to himself, and no man dieth to himself. Whether we live, we live unto the Lord; and whether we die, we die unto the Lord: whether we live therefore, or die, we are the Lord's." "By faith, Jacob, when he was dying, blessed both the sons of Joseph; and worshipped, leaning upon the top of his staff." Dr. Rivet said, "Let those who come to inquire, see me; I ought to be an example in death as well as in life." Samson, when about to die, prayed that God would strengthen him "this once." This is the last time you can do any thing in the world—It is the last arrow you have in your quiver, says an old writer, and you should take a good aim with this. Cato

is made in the tragedy to complain, that he could die but once for his country. You can die but once, for your family, the church, and the world. O let it adorn the doctrine of God your Saviour in all things.

IV. The DYING OF THE CHRISTIAN IS ALWAYS SAFE AND GLORIOUS IN THE ISSUE.

We *must* take this into the account in doing justice to his end. For there are instances in which the Christian may not be able to express, or enjoy pleasure or hope in death. There are two cases of this kind. The first is, the case of Divine Rebuke for Moral Delinquency. For God, who is of purer eyes than to behold iniquity, has said, "If his children forsake my law, and walk not in my judgments; if they break my statutes, and keep not my commandments; then will I visit their transgression with the rod, and their iniquity with stripes. Nevertheless my lovingkindness will I not utterly take from him, nor suffer my faithfulness to fail." This however is not wrath, but anger. Anger is consistent with love, and springs from it. "As many as I love, I rebuke and chasten." And He sometimes rebukes and chastens, at the last. He hides his face, and they are troubled; and perhaps even their sun goes down under a cloud. But he retains not his anger for ever. Though they are chastened of the Lord, they are not condemned with the world; and though here He humbles them under his mighty hand, he exalts them in due time, for ever.

The other is the case of Constitutional Malady. In this condition our heavenly Bard died; and we have known others who have died under a physical depression, with which religious encouragements have contended in vain. But though their end was not peace in the exit, it was peace in the issue. Their despondency did not affect their right to the tree of life. They condemned themselves; but God delighted in them.

And what an exchange; what a surprise did such sufferers experience! They departed, expecting to awake in torment, and found themselves in Abraham's bosom! They left the world in a momentary gloom, and entered into everlasting sunshine!

For observe, I beseech you, the difference between the delusion of the Infidel, and the mistake of the Christian. "I give," says Hobbs, "I give my body to the dust, and my soul to the Great Perhaps." "I am going to take," says he, "a leap in the dark." And such a man not only takes a leap *in* the dark, but *into* the dark. And from the darkness of ignorance, and doubt, and uncertainty, he plunges into the blackness of darkness for ever. But it is infinitely different with the Christian. He may take this last step in the dark, but he steps into day; perfect and endless day: where it will be said to him, "Thy sun shall no more go down; neither shall thy moon withdraw herself: for the Lord shall be thine everlasting light, and the days of thy mourning shall be ended."

Thus, however he may expire, the result is blessed; and the day of *his* death is better than the day of his birth. It is the day, when, as a weary traveller, he arrives at home: when, as a sea-tossed mariner, he enters his desired haven: when, as a long-enduring patient, he throws off the last feelings of his lingering complaint: when, as an heir of immortality, he comes of age, and obtains the inheritance of the saints in light.—Thus, whatever may be the manner of his death, for *him* "to die is gain." And what gain? Can the tongue of men or of angels express what the Christian by dying gains—In exemption? In residence? In fellowship? In knowledge? In holiness? In pleasure? For when he closes his eye, on the sorrows of life, he "shall not see evil any more." When he leaves this polluted earth, he has a better, even a heavenly country. When the earthly house of this tabernacle is dissolved, he has a building of God, a house not made with hands, eternal in the heavens. When he leaves the wicked world, and the defective Church, he joins the spirits of just men made perfect, and the innumerable company of angels. Now he sees through a glass darkly, then face to face. Now, when he would do good, evil is present with him. Now, the consolations of God are often small with him. Then he will be presented faultless before the presence of His glory with exceeding joy. For when that which is perfect is come, then that which is in part shall be done away. But it doth not yet appear what we shall be.

"In vain my feeble fancy paints
    The moment after death;
    The glory that surrounds the saints,
    When yielding up their breath.

"One gentle sigh their fetters breaks;
    We scarce can say, 'They 're gone!,
    Before the willing spirit takes
    Her mansion near the throne.

"Faith strives, but all its efforts fail,
    To trace her in her flight:
    No eye can pierce within the vail
    Which hides that world of light.

"Thus much (and this is all) we know,
    They are completely blest;
    Have done with sin, and care, and wo,
    And with their SAVIOUR rest."

And is it for *such*, we put on sable attire, and go mourning all the day? Is this thy kindness to thy friend? If you loved them, would you not rejoice because they are gone to the Father? Are they not now, from the most excellent glory, ready to exclaim, "Weep not for us, but for yourselves and children—You are the proper objects of pity, not we. You who are still in the conflict, not we who have gotten the victory. You who are yet in the body, not we who are delivered from the burden of the flesh. You who rise in the morning to cares that perplex you; fears that dismay you; disappointments that vex you; infirmities that depress you; —not we who are for ever with the Lord."

Ah! my Brethren, if all this be true, what reason have we to adore the undeserved and infinite goodness of God? We cannot think too highly of this attribute; and it is well for our consciences that the proofs of it are so numerous and obvious. The earth is full of his riches. In the various seasons, he crowns the year with his goodness. He daily loadeth us with his benefits. He gives us all things richly to enjoy. But what would all these have been, with destruction at the end? Who remembered us in our low estate? Who turned the curse into a blessing? Who converted the avenue to hell into the gate of life? Who caused the spoiler to enrich us? and made the last enemy an inestimable friend?

Let us not also forget the way in which this change is accomplished; the mediation of the Lord Jesus. Here is the mystery, We who were poor could never have been rich, if he who was rich had not for our sake become poor. Because the children were partakers of flesh and blood, he likewise himself took part of the same. He bore our sins in his own body on the tree; and died that we may live. He abolished death, and hath brought life and immortality to light through the Gospel. He therefore says, "If a man keep *my* sayings, he shall not see *death.*" He has indeed to pass through the state; but the bitterness of death is past. *He* has only to finish his course with joy; to fall asleep in Jesus; to depart to be with Christ, which is far better.

—But, my dear Hearers, will this be the case with us? Let us not think the inquiry needless, or incapable of solution. Here people often show their ignorance and presumption. They talk of the desirableness of death; but expose themselves to the censure of the prophet, "Wo unto you that desire the day of the Lord! to what end is it for you? the day of the Lord is darkness, and not light. As if a man did flee from a lion, and a bear met him: or went into the house, and leaned his hand on the wall, and a serpent bit him. Shall not the day of the Lord be darkness, and not light? even very dark, and no brightness?" When some of you wish you were dead, what is it, in reality, but wishing you were damned? You are just as near to hell as you are to death; and the one is as sure as the other. Be not therefore deceived. Whatever privations or sufferings you are now enduring, it is not better for you to die than to live. Much as you complain, these are only the beginning of sorrows, the earnests and foretastes of everlasting lamentation and mourning and wo. What says the voice from heaven? "Write, blessed are the dead that die in the Lord." These are all blessed; but these only. As for those who are not in Him, they are not under grace, but under the law. And, " as many as are under the law are under the curse." His righteousness is not theirs to justify them. His Spirit is not theirs to sanctify them. They have no title to glory. No meetness for it. No capacity for its services. No susceptibility of its joys.

Finally. Let us now turn the medal. We have been speaking of the death of the Christian—but mark the wicked man, and behold the ungodly—What is his end? The answer would seem too awful for declamation; and we should not even present the scene, but to heighten the subject by contrast; and to prevent, if possible, your realizing it in your own experience. We therefore endeavour to save with fear; and knowing the terror of the Lord, would persuade men. And in this work of apparent severity, but real compassion, the sacred writers go before us. " What," says Peter, " shall the end be of them that obey not the Gospel of God?" ' The Lord," says David, " shall laugh at him, for he seeth that his day is coming. For yet a little while and the wicked shall not be; yea, thou shalt diligently consider his place, and it shall not be. I was perplexed and pained at the sight of their prosperity, until I went into the sanctuary of God; then understood I their end. Surely thou didst set them in slippery places: thou castedst them down into destruction. How are they brought into desolation, as in a moment! they are utterly consumed with terrors. As a dream when one awaketh; so, O Lord, when thou awakest, thou shalt despise their image."

Does the dying sinner look back upon the past? " Vanity of vanities," says the reviewer, " vanity of vanities, all is vanity." His life appears a succession of fancies, dreams, and impositions. Nothing seems real—but his sins. These—his neglect of prayer, his forgetfulness of God, the profanation of his Sabbaths, the contempt of his word and commandments—these, in their number and aggravations, revive and reproach —and conscience keeps them in view.

—What satisfaction or relief can the present afford him? Every thing in his outward condition may be agreeable; but what is this to a wounded spirit? Righteousness delivers from death, but riches profit not in the day of wrath. What is honour to one who knows he is ready for the worms? Can flattery soothe the dull cold ear of death? What is the consolation of being praised where we are not—while we are miserable where we are!

What does the future promise? He is separating from every thing he loves, to enter a state in which he has no hope, after which he has no desire, and from which he has no

escape—a state of thought without the possibility of diversion; of passion without the means of gratification; of society without friendship; of enmity without restraint; of accountableness without excuse; of retribution without mercy; of loss without recovery; and of misery without end. Who knoweth the power of thine anger? Even according to thy fear, so is thy wrath. In many cases fear magnifies; and when the evil comes, the reality falls far short of the apprehension. But here the event infinitely exceeds the foreboding. It is a fearful thing to fall into the hands of the living God. No wonder therefore the death of the sinner is represented in the Scripture as the effect of compulsion—" The wicked is driven away in his wickedness." " He shall be driven from light into darkness, and chased out of this world." Some of these scenes are kept secret—perhaps they are misunderstood. They are ascribed to a distempered imagination. The terrified victim is supposed to be in the phrenzy of delirium. Some, by the composing draught, are stupified, who would otherwise drive and keep every attendant from the room. Yet the reluctance, and anguish, and horror, are sometimes known; and make an awful impression for the time. But suppose there is nothing of this; and the sinner dies, as it is often expressed, like a lamb; the delusion is but for a moment. He instantly sees his mistake. But the immutability of his state renders the knowledge as dreadful as it is unavoidable. His disappointment is an unspeakable aggravation of his misery: and the consequences are remediless.

O! that you were wise, that you understood this, that you would consider your latter end! Then surely you would not give sleep to your eyes, or slumber to your eyelids, till you had a good hope through grace, that you were delivered from such a doom.

—But you think the end is not near; and distant things do not impress. You put away the evil day. But can you put it *entirely* away? Yea, can you really put it *far* away? How long do you think of living? Fix the period. Place it at threescore years and ten —place it at fourscore years—It is soon cut off, and you flee away—whither? What will become of you *then*?

But how uncertain is your reaching this period? At what age, in what place, in what condition, in what employment, have not men died? On what are you relying to escape a death which has unexpectedly and prematurely carried so many of your connexions and neighbours down to the dust? On youth? On strength?—What is your life? " It is even a vapour that appeareth for a little time, and then vanisheth away." " Every man at his best state is altogether vanity." O! Thou, in whose hands our breath is, and whose are all our ways, so teach us to number our days, that we may apply our hearts unto wisdom!

And, my Brethren, what is this wisdom? What is the one proper and rational part which creatures, circumstanced as we are, have to act? Is it not to prefer the soul to the body, and eternity to time? Is it not to agree with our adversary while we are in the way with him; lest at any time the adversary deliver us to the judge, and the judge deliver us to the officer, and we be cast into prison? Is it not to flee for refuge to the hope set before us? Is it not to make the concern of Paul supremely and immediately our own—"That I may win Christ, and be found in him, not having mine own righteousness, which is of the law, but that which is through the faith of Christ, the righteousness which is of God by faith: that I may know him, and the power of his resurrection, and the fellowship of his sufferings, being made conformable unto his death?"

LECTURE XI.

THE CHRISTIAN, IN THE GRAVE.

" If I wait, the grave is mine house."
Job xvii. 13.

This was in answer to the opinion and advice of his friends. They had repeatedly intimated, that if he repented and reformed, and prayed to God, he might surely reckon upon a speedy restoration to health, and a peaceful abode, and a prosperous condition. "If thou wouldest seek unto God betimes, and make thy supplications to the Almighty; if thou wert pure and upright; surely, now he would awake for thee, and make the habitation of thy righteousness prosperous. Though thy beginning was small, yet thy latter end should greatly increase." "If thou prepare thine heart, and stretch out thine hands toward him; if iniquity be in thine hand, put it far away, and let not wickedness dwell in thy tabernacles. For then shalt thou lift up thy face without spot; yea, thou shalt be steadfast, and shalt not fear: because thou shalt forget thy misery, and remember it as waters that pass away: and thine age shall be clearer than the noon-day; thou shalt shine forth, thou shalt be as the morning. And thou shalt be secure, because there is hope; yea, thou shalt dig about thee, and thou shalt take thy rest in safety. Also thou shalt lie down, and none shall make thee afraid; yea, many shall make suit unto thee."

Now, says Job, if I were to do this, and wait for the accomplishment of your promises, I should be disappointed. Not that it would be in vain for me to serve God; but he would not appear for me in the way of which you speak. He will not deliver me from my present afflictions in this world; or recover me from the disorder under which I am ready to expire—No. The case is mortal and desperate—"*If I wait, the grave is mine house.*"

This leads us to make two remarks. The first connects itself with a passage which he presently uttered, and which has given rise to much dispute. I refer to his noble confession. There are some who contend, that he means only to express his hope of a temporal redemption, or the revival of his former greatness. But, in answer to this poor and low interpretation, not to observe the solemnity of the introduction, and the grandeur of the sentiment and diction, it is plain, not from a few, but many declarations, that Job entertained no expectation of being restored in this life. "The eye that seeth me, shall see me no more. For now shall I sleep in the dust, and thou shalt seek me in the morning, and I shall not be. My breath is corrupt, my days are extinct, the graves are ready for me. My days are past, my purposes are broken off, even the thoughts of my heart. And where is now my hope? as for my hope, who shall see it?" "*If I wait, the grave is mine house.*" He must therefore have a reference to the most glorious of all events when he says, "Oh that my words were now written! oh that they were printed in a book! that they were graven with an iron pen and lead in the rock for ever! For I know that my Redeemer liveth, and that he shall stand at the latter day upon the earth: and though after my skin worms destroy this body, yet in my flesh shall I see God: whom I shall see for myself, and mine eyes shall behold, and not another; though my reins be consumed within me."

The second remark is, that when Job said, "*If I wait, the grave is mine house,*" he was mistaken. Instead of a speedy dissolution, which he obviously looked for, "the Lord turned his captivity, and gave him twice as much as he had before. And after this, Job lived an hundred and forty years, and saw his sons, and his sons' sons, even four generations." How often, in the risings of his grace and of his providence, does he not only deliver, but surprise his people! The day seemed setting in with clouds and darkness, but at evening time it was light. "We would not, brethren," says Paul, "have you ignorant of our trouble which came to us in Asia, that we were pressed out of measure, above strength, insomuch that we despaired even of life: but we had the sentence of death in ourselves, that we should not trust in ourselves, but in God which raiseth the dead: who delivered us from so great a death, and doth deliver: in whom we trust that he will yet deliver us." David, also, was soon able to refute his own unbelieving conclusion: "I said, in my haste, I am cut off from before thine eyes: nevertheless thou heardest

O

the voice of my supplication when I cried unto Thee." And is there a Christian here, but can acknowledge, to his praise, that he has been better to him than his fears; and done for him exceedingly abundantly above all he was once able to ask or think!

—Yet Job's recovery, with regard to life, was not a *cure*. He was only *reprieved*. The sentence was left suspended over him still—" Dust thou art, and unto dust shalt thou return." And *thus*, the words were true in his case—" *If I wait, the grave is mine house:*" and his house it was. And thus, my dear hearers, the words furnish a motto for each of you. Whatever be the object of your hope, here is your destination. You may wish, and you may wait; but here is the end of all your solicitudes. Whatever is your present abode, here is your last. You may now occupy a strait and mean tenement, or a large and splendid mansion: but you will neither be incommoded with the one, nor delighted with the other, long—Here is the residence to which you are all hastening— hastening even while I speak—*The grave is mine house.* Let two things engage our attention.—Let us,

I. CONSIDER WHAT IS AWFUL AND REPULSIVE IN THE GRAVE,—And,

II. WHAT THE CHRISTIAN CAN FIND TO RELIEVE IT.

I. CONSIDER WHAT IS AWFUL AND REPULSIVE IN THE GRAVE.

———" The grave, dread thing!
Men shiver when thou 'rt named. Nature appalled
Shakes off her wonted firmness. Ah! how dark
Thy long-extended realms, and rueful wastes,
Where nought but silence reigns, and night, dark
    night!"

—This is fine, but Job excels it. "Before I go whence I shall not return, even to the land of darkness and the shadow of death. A land of darkness, as darkness itself; and of the shadow of death, without any order, and where the light is as darkness." What a solemn grandeur pervades this representation! What an evidence does it furnish of Burke's observation, that obscurity is a source of the true sublime; and that, even in poetry, a powerful impression may be made, where no distinct imagery is represented.—Let us take three views of the grave; they are all awful and affecting.

First, We may regard it as *a monument of human guilt*. What error can be named, that is not connected with diminishing apprehensions of sin? Hence we must seize every opportunity of producing the needful conviction, that it is an evil and bitter thing; evil with regard to God, and bitter with regard to ourselves. Men think lightly of it, but it is more poisonous than the gall of asps. They cannot be induced to hate it, and fear it: and yet they may constantly and easily see its hateful and fearful effects. If they will not

believe in the hell that it has prepared for the devil and his angels in another world, they cannot deny the desolations it has produced among the children of men in this. Once all that moved upon the earth was buried in the Deluge. Could you have witnessed the spectacle without horror? But the same sin which then destroyed all the human race at once, acts no less fatally now in killing them all successively and individually. The time is nothing; the execution is the same. Earthquakes, and wars, and pestilence, and famine are of more rare occurrence, and few comparatively can view the effects: but you can all trace the ravages of disease; you can all see men going to their long home, and the mourners going about the streets. Repair to some Golgotha. Enter a churchyard. Throw your eye over the inscribed stones, and the turfed hillocks; think of the undistinguished mass on which you tread—and then ask the question, which Jehu asked when he saw the remains of the sons of Ahab, " Who slew all these?" Why every burying-ground, according to its size, is a jail with so many cells, some holding one, and some more prisoners: and they who are lodged there are not confined in consequence of a debt due to Nature, but to the justice of God. There *is* no grave in heaven; there *was* no grave in Paradise; and there would have been none in all the earth, but for sin. Man was indeed originally capable of dying, as his experience soon evinced; yet no accident without, and no malady within, would have endangered his being, or diminished his vigour, but for sin. While innocent, he was immortal—not from the inherency of any immutable properties of nature, but from the divine appointment and preservation, of which the tree of life in the midst of the garden was either the means or the pledge. " The wages of sin is death." " By one man sin entered into the world, and death by sin, and so death came on all, because all have sinned."

Secondly, We may view it as a *state of extreme degradation*. Of whatever we are invested with, we must be despoiled at the gate of the grave. Even the costly and tempting attire that ministered so much to the vanity of the wearer, and the danger of the beholder, is here stripped off; and if any substitute be allowed, it is the shroud and the winding-sheet—though thousands are denied even these. " We brought nothing with us into the world, and it is certain we shall carry nothing out." " As he came forth of his mother's womb, naked shall he return to go as he came, and shall take nothing of his labour, which he may carry away in his hand." " For when he dieth he shall carry nothing away: his glory shall not descend after him."

What is any condition without society? But the grave forbids all intercourse, all interview. Says Hezekiah, with tears, " I shall behold man no more, with the inhabitants of the world."

Here the man boasts of his relations. There he says to corruption, thou art my father, and to the worm, thou art my mother and my sister.

There all his active functions, and the feelings which they engendered or subserved, have ceased. "The living know that they shall die; but the dead know not any thing. Also their love and hatred, and envy, is now perished; neither have they any more a portion for ever in any thing that is done under the sun." His business, his profession, descends to his successor, or passes to his rival. Even his religious exercises are there abandoned. "In death there is no remembrance of Thee. In the grave who shall give Thee thanks? Shall the dust praise Thee, shall it declare thy truth? Shall thy lovingkindness be declared in the grave?" "Shall thy wonders be known in the dark? and thy righteousness in the land of forgetfulness?"

The body itself, that fine piece of divine workmanship, so fearfully and wonderfully made, is here broken and thrown by as a vessel wherein is no pleasure. The hands have forgotten their enterprise. The cherubic tints have left the cheek, cold and pallid. The bright eye is quenched in darkness; and the tongue that excited so much emotion is muteness itself. Nor is this all. There is enough in the body, even while living, to prevent all glorying in the flesh. It had its humbling appetites and infirmities: it was the seat of diseases which sometimes required all the force of duty and friendship to discharge the offices of humanity. See Job covered with sore boils from the crown of his head to the sole of his foot, sitting among the ashes, and scraping himself with a potsherd. But let the anatomist take off from a human body that translucent veil, the skin; and then observe the hideous and shocking spectacle of flesh, and sinews, and muscles. View the skeleton, when every thing is removed from the dry bones. But see the body in the various stages of decomposition and putrefaction—What an exhibition of expense and finery is that funeral! Why all this pomp and artifice? It is in honour of the deceased. Why then do you not show to the multitude of gazers "the Principal concealed, for whom you make the mighty stir?" You dare not. You have been obliged to enclose, and solder, and coffin him up. What tears bedew the grave at parting! Why then do you part? Why not take and preserve at home "the deceased angel?" You dare not—The form is intolerable. You must bury your dead out of your sight, and shut to the door, and inscribe over it—

How loved, how valued once, avails thee not;
To whom related, or by whom begot:
A heap of dust alone remains of thee;
'Tis all thou art, and all the proud shall be."

Thirdly, We may notice it as *an universal receptacle.* "I know that thou wilt bring me to death; and to the house appointed for all living."

Then, how large its *extent!* Though the memorials of death do not everywhere meet your sight; and particular spaces are properly appropriated for interment; and some of them are very capacious and crowded: yet there is scarcely a spot, that holds not some portion of humanity. You feel as you march over a field of battle: you feel as you walk through a churchyard, especially in the darkness of the night. But are the dead only there? Perhaps some one has been turned to dust beneath the pew in which you are now sitting. Perhaps your house stands, and your garden blossoms, over the remains of some, who were once as active as you. What walk can you take, and not trample on the ashes of those who are gone before?

" What is the world itself? Thy world?—A grave.
Where is the dust that has not been alive?
The spade, the plough disturbs our ancestors:
From human mould we reap our daily bread.
O'er devastations we blind revels keep.
Whole buried towns support the dancer's heel.
As nature, wide our ruins spread; and death
Inhabits all things but the *thought of man!*"

Then, how *numerous its victims!* How soon the power of calculation fails in reckoning up the myriads that do occupy, and will occupy this dark abode! Seven hundred and fifty millions constitute the population of the globe. These in less than a century will be all lodged in the grave. Yet what are these to the multitudes which will follow, and to the immensities that precede!—"Every man shall draw after him, as there have been innumerable before him!"

Then, how *impartial its demands!* Infinitely diversified as the ways of human life are, here they all approximate and unite. The paths of glory lead but to the grave. Here come the nobles with their titles, and princes with their crowns, and scholars with their volumes.

" Why all this toil, the triumph of an hour?
What, though we wade in wealth, or soar in fame,
Earth's highest station ends in—' Here he lies!'
And ' dust to dust' concludes her noblest song!"

"One dieth in his full strength, being wholly at ease and quiet. His breasts are full of milk, and his bones are moistened with marrow. And another dieth in the bitterness of his soul, and never eateth with pleasure. They shall lie down alike in the dust, and the worms shall cover them." There lies the babe that perished in the porch of life; and there the thrice grayheaded Parr. The beautiful and the deformed, the rich and the poor, there meet together. "There the prisoners rest together: the small and the great are there; and the servant is free from his master." "Do not all go to one place? All are of the dust, and all turn to dust again!"

Then, how *painful its separations!* If it be appointed for all living, then must it entomb the friend that is as thine own soul; the child of thy love, the wife of thy bosom, the guide of thy youth. There Mary goes to the grave to weep over Lazarus. There David cries, "I am distressed for thee, my brother Jonathan." Who has not sustained some bereavement? Who has not some spot the dearest on earth, and rendered sacred by a deposit more precious than gold? Thus every man feels an interest in the grave. It is to him the residence not of strangers and foreigners, but of kindred who detach him hence. What do I here, and what have I here? I am related not to the living, but the dead—There lie all that bound me to earth. "Lover and friend hast thou put far from me, and my acquaintance into darkness."

Then, how *personal its claims!* If it be appointed for all living, it must require me. I may escape a thousand other things that befall my fellow-creatures; but I must follow them here. I see, in *their* end, the emblem, the pledge, the certainty of my own. No privilege can exempt me here. I am going the way of all the earth. "*If I wait, the grave is mine house.*"

But surely there is one exception to be found. We read of a peculiar people, and who are not to be numbered among the nations. They are the children of God: and if children, then heirs, heirs of God, and joint heirs with Christ. The Christian, is not *he* free? No. There is no entering heaven but under ground.

Yet, even in those things in which the Christian seems confounded with others, he is really, he is divinely distinguished. The Christian can view the grave with an eye of faith, as well as of sense. He can view it not only in connexion with that sin which has reigned unto death, but in connexion with that grace which reigns through righteousness unto eternal life. Though he cannot escape it, he need not dread it. He is prepared to meet it; to encounter it; to vanquish it; to triumph over it; to insult it; to say, "O grave, where is thy victory?"—Let us pass to the

II. Part of our subject, and consider WHAT THE CHRISTIAN CAN FIND TO RELIEVE THE SCENE.

People seem to have found a kind of satisfaction when entering the grave, from the thought that they are going to join their connexions. Hence, as well as from the pride of distinction, sprang the mausoleums of the great, a kind of family-tomb. Hence, among the Jews, the frequency of sepulchres in their gardens; where they seemed still to retain the departed near them; and maintain a kind of communion with them; and feel soothed at the thought of blending with them; in the exclusive and endearing abode. Hence Ruth said to Naomi, "Where thou diest will I die, and there will I be buried." Jacob said, "I will go down into the grave to my son." "I will lie with my fathers; and thou shalt carry me out of Egypt, and bury me in their burying-place." "And he charged them, and said unto them, I am to be gathered unto my people; bury me with my fathers in the cave that is in the field of Ephron the Hittite." "In the cave that is in the field of Machpelah, which is before Mamre, in the land of Canaan, which Abraham bought with the field of Ephron the Hittite for a possession of a burying-place; there they buried Abraham and Sarah his wife; there they buried Isaac and Rebekah his wife; and there I buried Leah." Nor was this only the language of faith, but of nature. In vain I am told there is no reason in the thing, since there is no conscious community in the grave. There are beautiful insects, too fine for dissection; yet there is in them all the reality of organization. There are sentiments to be felt rather than explained—instincts of the heart; it is nature—it is the God of nature that speaks in them. We often feel most forcibly an impression whose cause is hidden and undefinable. What occurs to the mind in a kind of distinct proposition may be met, and argued, and repulsed: but a principle whose influence is really, yet secretly and unaccountably exerted, resembles those invisible laws in the natural world, whose agency we can neither deny or withstand. To which we may add, that whatever tends to diminish the gloom of the grave, and to render it more inviting, is to be cherished, and not despised.—But we have something superior to all this. There are five things which a Christian should think of with regard to the grave. Jesus himself has been in it. It is a place of repose. It receives only a part of the man. It will not be able to retain this always. It must not only restore it, but restore it improved.

First, When you think of the grave, remember that *Jesus himself has been there.* How far did he, who is all your salvation and all your desire, carry his humiliation! He descended into the lowest parts of the earth. As Jonah was three days and three nights in the whale's belly; so the Son of man was three days and three nights in the heart of the earth. He not only died, but was buried, according to the Scripture. And hereby he not only said, See how certain my death is; but, Are you afraid to enter the grave? I will go in before you, and render it safe and attractive—Yea, the Lily of the Valley, and the Rose of Sharon was laid there, and has left a long perfume. Whenever I am committing the remains of a believer to the tomb, I seem to hear the angels say, "Come, see the place where the Lord lay."

The graves of all his saints he blest,
  And softened every bed;
Where should the dying members rest,
  But with the dying Head?"

Secondly, When you think of the grave, remember, *It is a place of repose.* Hence Job adds, "I have made my bed in the darkness." But who sleeps the less sound for the darkness? The darkness aids our slumber. And who, after the fatigues of the day, dislikes or dreads the refreshment of night? The sleep of a labouring man is sweet. He lies down and forgets his sorrow, and remembers his misery no more.

God has a hiding-place for his people even in *life;* and often says, "Come, my people, enter thou into thy chambers, and shut thy doors about thee; hide thee also for a little season, until the indignation be overpast." But here the clouds return after the rain; and as long as earth is their abode, bonds and afflictions abide them. Therefore, says Job, "O that thou wouldest hide me in the grave; that thou wouldest keep me secret until thy wrath be past; that thou wouldest appoint me a set time, and remember me!" God takes away his people from the evil to come. He foresees it; but they do not. He therefore lays hold of them, and places them in a sheltered retreat. And you often clearly see, after their removal, what some of your connexions would have suffered had they continued here a little longer. Ah! says one, whose purposes are broken off—his very heart desolated within him—Ah! what should *I* have escaped, had I been allowed an earlier retirement. "For now should I have lain still and been quiet; I should have slept: then had I been at rest." Yes—from the snares and vexations of the world; from the reproaches and persecutions of the ungodly; from the perfidy or weakness of friends; from the temptations of the Devil; from the conflicts of flesh and spirit: *there* all will be peace; all will be quietness; all will be assurance for ever. "*There* the wicked cease from troubling, and there the weary are at rest."

Thirdly, When you think of the grave remember *that it has only a partial empire;* it only receives what is *corporeal and mortal.* Here we are not going to enter into metaphysical reasonings. We understand but little of the connexion of spirit with matter: yet why should we doubt the possibility of its existence separate from it? Are we not conscious of some mental operations, in which the body seems to take no share? And when the powers of the body are suspended in sleep, is there not something that sees without eyes, and hears without ears? Do we not even then dream? and often with an amazing degree of activeness?

The heathens seemed to allow that something in man could exist, and would either suffer or enjoy, independently of the body—for of the revival of the body they never had the least notion. But we turn at once to the Scriptures, the only source of satisfactory information in a case like this. "Then shall the dust return to the earth as it was; and the spirit shall return unto God who gave it." Hear the statement of the Apostle: "Absent from the body, and present with the Lord." And his own wish, expressed to the Philippians: "I long to depart to be with Christ, which is far better;" *i. e.* far better for *him;* though to abide in the flesh was more needful for *them.* Now, if he did not believe that his soul would be immediately with Christ, his desire is perfectly unintelligible. For by dying, he would have been no sooner with Christ, than he would by remaining alive, as to time; nor so near, as to enjoyment; for here he had access to him and intercourse with him. How undeniably is this distinction admitted by our Saviour, and made the rule of his most solemn admonitions! "Fear not them which kill the body, but are not able to kill the soul: but rather fear him which is able to destroy both soul and body in hell." "I say unto you, my friends, be not afraid of them that kill the body, and after that have no more that they can do. But I will forewarn you whom ye shall fear: fear him, which after he hath killed hath power to cast into hell; yea, I say unto you fear him." To which we may add his promise to the thief on the cross; which, though often tortured, still refuses to support any other principle: "Verily, verily, I say unto thee, this day thou shalt be with me in Paradise."

This being premised and proved, we observe, that the souls of believers are in their bodies, as the lamps of Gideon in the pitchers: at midnight the pitchers are broken, and the lamps shine forth, and the victory is obtained. This, to drop the metaphor, this is the ground of consolation taken by the Apostle: "And if Christ be in you, the body is dead because of sin; but the spirit is life because of righteousness."

Fourthly, When you think of the grave, remember *that its reign is not only limited as to subject, but as to duration.* Even the body, which it does receive, will not, cannot be retained by it always; therefore the Apostle adds, "But if the Spirit of him that raised up Jesus from the dead dwell in you, he that raised up Christ from the dead shall also quicken your mortal bodies by his Spirit that dwelleth in you."

The grave is called our long home, not because it is far off, for we live in the very neighbourhood; but because our stay there will be long, compared with our stay in our present home. This, indeed, will not apply to all. Some at the last day will have been buried only a year, or a week, or a day. The sexton will be performing his office on some at the very instant: and the reanimated corpse will burst the coffin before it be confined in the grave; and the attendants be all changed in a moment, in the twinkling of an eye. But *you* will lie there till the heavens be no more. *Many* will have been found dwelling there for thousands of years. Yet whatever be the length of the occupancy, it will have an end, and all the inhabitants will be sent forth.

And why should it be thought incredible that God should raise the dead? With God all things are possible. But you say, appearances do not render it probable. We see nothing more of the body we inter; yea, we know it dissolves and returns to dust. Yet was not that oak once an acorn? Did not that beautiful insect once lie in its little mummy grave? But it burst its confinement, and now owns the air and sky. What do men produce from the rudest elements? Show a stranger to the process, a figure of glass; and then place him before the bare materials from which it is deduced. "How are the dead raised up, and with what body do they come? Thou fool, that which thou sowest is not quickened, except it die: and that which thou sowest, thou sowest not that body that shall be, but bare grain, it may chance of wheat, or of some other grain; but God giveth it a body as it hath pleased him, and to every seed his own body." But how decisive is the testimony of the Scripture! The doctrine is found even in the Old Testament. Our Saviour found it in the Pentateuch; and deduced it from the declaration of God at the burning bush: "I am the God of Abraham, and of Isaac, and of Jacob. God is not the God of the dead, but of the living:" for all live unto him—purpose and accomplishment being the same with him. In Isaiah we read, "Thy dead men shall live; together with my dead body shall they arise." Awake and sing, ye that dwell in the dust: for thy dew is as the dew of herbs, and the earth shall cast out the dead." Many have supposed, with much probability, that here is a promise of the resurrection of believers through their union with Christ. But if the evidence of this supposition be not strong enough to bear such an argument, it is undeniable, that the deliverance of the people of God from a state of the lowest degradation and hopelessness, is here held forth by an image taken from the resurrection of the dead. And Ezekiel employs the same image in the vision of the dry bones, raised to union and life. And what can more clearly prove that the doctrine of the resurrection of the dead was in those days a known and popular sentiment? For an image employed to represent any thing in the way of allegory or metaphor, whether in poetry or prophecy, must be generally and well understood, or the end of its appropriation is defeated. In the New Testament, it is more than merely admitted.

It is everywhere affirmed, and reasoned from, as an important principle. And how commonly the notion and belief of it prevailed among the Jews, appears from the language of Martha; "I know that he shall rise again in the resurrection at the last day." And from the defence of Paul before Felix; "And have hope towards God, which they themselves also allow, that there shall be a resurrection of the dead, both of the just and unjust."

Here also we have it in fact and example. Several were raised again: and one of them after he had lain in the grave four days, and the process of corruption must have more than commenced. But Jesus himself arose: and he is not only an instance, but a pledge. If ever an event was proved, it was the resurrection of Christ. But if Christ be preached that he rose from the dead, how say some that there is no resurrection of the dead? But now is Christ risen from the dead, and become the first-fruits of them that sleep. His resurrection is the claim, as well as the proof of ours—"Because I live, ye shall live also." Our nature was revived in his person; and thus we are quickened with Christ, and raised up, and made to sit with him in the heavenly places.

But every man in his own order: Christ the first-fruits; *afterwards* they that are Christ's, at *his* coming. Our Saviour repeatedly said, "I will raise him up at the *last day.*" For this is the period appointed for the resurrection: and the reason of the appointment, in a measure, appears. If each body was raised in succession previously, the order of nature and providence would be perpetually invaded, and miracles would be constantly required. And not only for this reason, but also for the greater honour of the Redeemer, this greatest and sublimest exertion of Almightiness is reserved for the appearing of the Lord Jesus Christ. Then he shall come to be glorified in his saints, and to be admired in all them that believe. *Then*, O Death! he will be thy plagues; *then*, O Grave! he will be thy destruction; and repentance shall be hid from his eyes.

Finally, Remember, to complete your comfort, *that what you resign to the grave will not only be restored, but infinitely improved.* As Egypt was compelled not only to allow the Israelites to depart, but to send them away enriched; and as Cyrus not only gave up the captives from Babylon, but ordered them to be helped with silver and gold, and with goods, and beasts, beside their own free-will offerings to the house of God; so will it be in the resurrection. Believers will not only leave the grave as they entered it—they will be, not only delivered, but exalted; they will not only have life, but have it more abundantly.

I deem this an important part of our subject: you will therefore allow me a little enlargement. Whoever has looked over the early attacks on Christianity will have observed, that the pagan philosophers not only denied the doctrine of the resurrection, but affected to contemn the thing itself. They considered it a bane, rather than a benefit; and represented it as imprisoning us again, and burdening us again, after the soul had been freed from its fetters and load. And some Christians really seem to be almost likeminded. Few appear to consider it a prize; at least, such a prize as Paul did when he said, "If by any means I might attain unto the resurrection of the dead." And the reason is probably this. They now know the disadvantages of the body, and are insensibly led to judge of the future by their feelings at present. And indeed if the bodies raised up were no better than those laid down, the resurrection would excite but little eagerness of desire. But what saith the Scriptures? Do not the sacred writers supremely lead forward your minds to this, and point your highest hope, not to the intermediate state, but to your re-embodied?—"He shall be recompensed at the resurrection of the just." "I am persuaded that he is able to keep that which I have committed to him against that day." Man, in his primeval state, was incarnate: and if hereafter we could attain perfection and happiness without our bodies, what need there be for their re-production from the dust? Yet according to the views and feelings of many, this grandest exertion of divine power seems to be entirely, or almost, unnecessary.

But let us not be wiser than our Maker. However incapable we may be of reasoning convincingly upon the subject, there must be an accession of perfection and happiness to be enjoyed in a state of re-union with the body, unattainable in a separate state. The life of a mere spirit must differ much from its subsistence in a corporeal organization. Without the latter it can hardly connect itself, for want of a medium, with the material universe, the new heavens and the new earth. It must be a stranger to the pleasures that depend on our senses and passions; and also those which arise from imagination. Was it not a privilege for Enoch and Elias to enter heaven embodied? "But their bodies were changed." It is allowed. And ours will be changed also; for flesh and blood cannot inherit the kingdom of God. And what a change must that be that *can* fit us for such a state! We are therefore not to think of our future incarnation by our present. The body then will not be a prison, a burden; it will not be a hinderance, but a help; and will even subserve the soul in knowledge, holiness, benevolence, and enjoyment.

There are two ways by which the Scripture elevates our conceptions of the resurrection body. The first is, to compare, or rather contrast it with the body we now have. "So is the resurrection of the dead. It is sown in corruption, it is raised in incorruption"—Not only incapable of defilement, but of dissolution, of declension, of injury: impassive; immortal. "It is sown in dishonour; it is raised in glory"—No longer composed of base elements, subsisting on gross supplies, subject to the same laws with the beasts that perish, employed in low and degrading toils and pursuits. "It is sown in weakness; it is raised in power"—No longer fatigued with a little exertion, and requiring long insensibilities of sleep, and frequent returns of food, to renew its strength and keep it fit for action; but capable of serving Him in his temple day and night, without languor, and without repose. "It is sown a natural body; it is raised a spiritual body."—Not a spirit, but spiritual. Not spiritual in its essence, but in the refinement of its senses, and indulgences, and functions, and use. For "there is a natural body, and there is a spiritual body."

The second is, to hold forth the conformity it will bear to the body of our Saviour. "And so it is written, The first man Adam was made a living soul; the last Adam was made a quickening spirit. Howbeit that was not first which is spiritual, but that which is natural; and afterward that which is spiritual. The first man is of the earth, earthy: the second man is the Lord from heaven. As is the earthy, such are they also that are earthy: and as is the heavenly, such are they also that are heavenly. And as we have borne the image of the earthy, we shall also bear the image of the heavenly." "It doth not yet appear what we shall be; but this we know, that when he shall appear we shall be like him, for we shall see him as he is." And this likeness takes in the body as well as the soul. What a body was that, which after his resurrection could render itself visible and invisible at pleasure; which walls and doors could not exclude; which moved with the ease and expedition of thought; which ascended up on high without impulsion; which appeared to Saul, and at noonday shone above the brightness of the sun; in which he is now worshipped by all the angels of God; and in which he will judge the world in righteousness, and reign for ever and ever! But this, O Believer, is the model of thy destination. "We look for the Saviour, the Lord Jesus Christ; who shall change our vile body, that it may be fashioned like unto his glorious body, according to the working whereby he is able even to subdue all things unto himself."

—Let this assurance and confidence lead us to bless God for Revelation, and the explicitness of its discoveries. With us the darkness is past, and the true light shineth. And what does it leave undiscovered that is important to our safety, or our welfare, or our comfort? Whatever reasonings and conjectures the Heathen had with regard to a future state, it is well known they gave up the body. No one for a moment ever supposed that the grave could re-open, and the *dead* arise. When Paul was at Athens (where the immortality of the soul was frequently asserted,) and preached unto them Jesus and the resurrection; even the men of science, forgetting the gravity that became their character, "mocked!" and said, "what will this babbler say?" But there is not a peasant or a child in our land of vision, but knows that the *dead*, small and great, will stand before God.

—This prospect should comfort you in the loss of your connexions. You are not forbidden to feel—"Your grief becomes you, and your tears are just." Jesus wept. But "weeping must not hinder sowing." "I would not have you to be ignorant, brethren, concerning them which are asleep, that ye sorrow not, even as others which have no hope. For if we believe that Jesus died and rose again, even so them also which sleep in Jesus will God bring with him."—"But they were so dear!" They were. But they are much dearer now. They have left all their imperfections, and all their sorrows behind—

"They sleep in Jesus, and are blest;
　　How sweet their slumbers are;
From suffering and from sin released,
　　And freed from every care!"

And this is not all. "Martha! Thy brother shall rise again. Rachel! You weep for your child, and refuse to be comforted, because he is not"—"Why was this loved babe born? why was I torn with pain at his birth, and again rent with anguish at his death? What purpose has his brief history answered? What has now become of him?" These and a thousand other inquiries which the busy mind will ask, could never have been answered, but for this book,—never so precious as in the hour of trouble. There the mystery is explained. There, you learn, that a sparrow falleth not to the ground without your Heavenly Father; that the present is only the threshold of existence; that the soul of this infant is now in the Shepherd's bosom; and that his body will not perish, but be seen again, "all heavenly and divine." "Refrain thy voice from weeping, and thine eyes from tears: for thy work shall be rewarded, saith the Lord; and thy children shall come again from the land of the enemy." O ye Children! who are yet spared, and are now responsible for your conduct; let this comfort be put into our hearts with regard to you. Remember your Creator. Live and die in the Lord; and then, though we lose you for a moment, you shall be restored to us, equal to the angels, and be the children of God, being the children of the resurrection. And,

you, Parents! endeared by so much affection, and whose venerable looks remind us of separation; fear not to go in good time. We will rock the cradle of your age; and comfort you on the bed of languishing; and kiss your cold cheeks, and close your eyes, and lay you in the dust—But we shall see you again; and our heart shall rejoice, and our joy no one taketh from us.

—And let this animate you when looking towards your own grave. And surely some of you *must* be thinking of it. Your complaints, your infirmities, your years *must* lead you to ask, How long have I to live? Well! if you are a Christian, you have every reason to think of it with resignation and pleasure. God says to you, as he did to Jacob trembling on the confines of Egypt, "Be not afraid to go down: I will go down with thee; and I will bring thee up again." He will watch over your sleeping dust, and he will bid it rise. If it be trying to part with your companion, the body, remember, it is only for a time; and it will be restored to you in the image of God's Son. Say then, "I am not following cunningly devised fables. I build upon a rock. It is true, sin takes away my health and breath, and lays my body down in the grave. But I hear *Him* saying among the tombs, I am the resurrection and the life: he that believeth in me, though he were dead, yet shall he live; and he that liveth and believeth in me shall never die. At the sound of this, I take courage and go forward. I am not stumbling over a precipice, uncertain where I shall fall, and not knowing that I shall ever rise. I descend into the grave by a gentle flight of steps, leaning on my Beloved and my Friend—I choose to die. It is Thou, my God, my Saviour, who callest me: and I give up my life into thy hand, assuredly persuaded, that thou art able and willing and engaged to return it." This is not empty declamation. I have taken the very language from the lips of a dying saint—I stood by—and after she had surveyed her reduced and wrinkled hands and arms, she ended her address—and life too, a few moments after—with the words of the sweet Psalmist in our British Israel:

"Oft have I heard thy threat'nings roar,
　　And oft endur'd the grief:
And when thy hand hath press'd me sore,
　　Thy grace was my relief.

"By long experience I have known
　　Thy sov'reign pow'r to save;
At thy command I venture down
　　Securely to the grave.

"When I lie buried deep in dust
　　My flesh shall be thy care;
Those with'ring limbs with thee I trust,
　　To raise them strong and fair."

—But what is all this to some of you, my brethren? Let me speak freely; and do not consider me as your enemy because I tell you the truth. Who of you have not frequently been at the grave of a neighbour, a friend, a relation? Sometimes you have been deeply impressed there. But how soon did the impression wear off; and you renewed your pursuit of the world, as eagerly as if you had never heard, never seen, never felt that all was vanity and vexation of spirit.

What do you think of your own grave? Perhaps the thought never enters your mind; or if it does, you deem it an impertinent and hateful intruder; and you drive it from you, as you would a serpent. Some of you have been led down very nearly to the grave, by perilous accident or disease. And how did it appear? Did it not seem an awful thing to enter an invisible and changeless state? Did you not turn your face to the wall and weep? If ever you prayed, was it not then? "O spare me a little, that I may recover strength, before I go hence and be no more." Where now are the confessions and vows of that hour? Perhaps the very scene is rendered disagreeable by your apostacy from your convictions—your endeavour to forget it—and you shun the Christian and the Minister you called in, because they are now witnesses against you.

Here is an awful case. And what can you do? If you wait, the grave is your house—and you know you must enter it. You may play the infidel: you may deny the truth of the Gospel; but it is useless to deny that you are on the borders of the grave—you may reason about it; you may look up and curse God and your King. But you cannot escape. Perhaps you would be shocked to be unburied; but this is not likely to be your case. You may have a good grave—a much better grave than many of your neighbours; and it will afford your body ease; and in this sense, the clods of the valley will be sweet about you. But is there not a spirit in man? Where will your soul be while your body is resting in the grave? Yea, and how is the body to be disposed of at last?

The Lord Jesus will raise *you*, as well as his people; but his agency will have a very different principle. The resurrection of the godly will be performed by him—as their Lord and Redeemer, under the administration of grace: but the wicked will be raised by him as the Ruler and the Judge, under an administration of law; for they are under the law, and not under grace. They refused the ransom, and died in their guilt; and the grave received *them* as criminals in charge bound over to justice—for as many as are under the law, are under the curse; and as they live, and die—so they rise the same.

There is also a difference in the bodies revived. What the bodies of the righteous will be, you have heard; but they that sow to the flesh shall of the flesh reap *corruption*. The evils attached to *your* bodies will not be left in the grave, but will cleave to them

for ever; and they will inherit the seeds of disease and the principles of deformity; and they will have the same raging appetites and passions—but all unindulged.

The conditions following also differ—"And many of them that sleep in the dust of the earth shall awake, some to everlasting life, and some to shame and everlasting contempt." "Marvel not at this; for the hour is coming, in which all that are in the graves shall hear his voice, and shall come forth: they that have done good, unto the resurrection of life; and they that have done evil, unto the resurrection of damnation." Thus both the chief butler and chief baker were released at the same time, and from the same confinement —the one to be advanced, and the other to be executed. The grave, to the believer, is an avenue to heaven. It is the dress-chamber, in which the Church puts on her beautiful garments, to arise and meet the Lord in the air. But to others, it is the condemned cell in which the malefactor is lodged till he is led out to punishment. That can hardly be called a deliverance, that releases a man from a bad condition and consigns him to a worse. It would be well if the bodies of the wicked could remain where by death they are deposited; but this is impossible. The bodies—those bodies which you have so indulged, so pampered, so adorned; the bodies which death delivers to the worms, the resurrection will deliver to the flames!

And where are you now? Take the hemp or the steel, and destroy yourself. Ah! this too is impossible. The soul is instantly before God. You have got rid only of one part of you. And even the part you have demolished will be re-animated, and rendered invulnerable—and you shall seek death, but shall not find it; and shall desire to die, but death shall flee from you.

—But why do I thus address you? It is that, by awakening your consciences from a fatal security, I may in time dispose you to ask, "What must I do to be saved?" I am sure of this, that I would not have enlarged upon your awful condition had I not believed that there is hope in Israel concerning this thing; and that none of you are excluded from it unless those who exclude themselves. The Saviour stands before you in all the combined forms of power and of pity. He is able—he is willing to save unto the uttermost. Seek him while he may be found. Call upon him while he is near. Wait for no qualifications to recommend you to his gracious notice. He requires none. If Paul and Silas were here, they would say, "Believe on the Lord Jesus Christ, and thou shalt be saved." Plead not, as an objection, your unworthiness. This should only increase the earnestness of your application. Behold the number and the character of those who have obtained mercy. Read his word; and hear Him not only allowing, but inviting and commanding you to approach, with the assurance, "him that cometh unto me, I will in no wise cast out." Obey his voice. Commit yourselves into his hands. And you shall never come into condemnation, but shall pass from death unto life. And though, even then, if you wait, the grave is your house, it will only be a peaceful and temporary residence to sleep in; and you will finally enter another house—a building of God, a house not made with hands—eternal in the heavens.

LECTURE XII.
THE CHRISTIAN, IN HEAVEN.

" Who hath brought life and immortality to light through the Gospel."—2 Tim. i. 10.

DID the Heathen then know nothing of life and immortality before? They had their schools and their philosophers. Some of them acquired great distinction and fame. Their sagacity and learning were deep and extensive. They were enriched by a long succession of preceding discoveries and improvements. In the various arts and sciences they much excelled: and he that would see a fine piece of statuary must fetch it from the ruins of Greece and Rome. But, as to the things of God, we are assured by one who was well qualified to judge, "They were vain in their imaginations: their foolish heart was darkened. And professing themselves wise, they became fools."

They had indeed their surmisings concerning a future state; they brought forward some strong probabilities in its favour: and aided in their reasonings by hints of unacknowledged tradition, some fine and worthy sentiments escaped from them. But they never taught life and immortality as a doctrine: they never employed it as a principle and motive. They had no authority to publish it to others: and not one of them was sure of the thing in his own mind. And, as Paley well remarks, "Conjecture and opinion are not knowledge: and in religion, nothing more is known than is proved." Thus the world by *wisdom* knew not God; and if this was the case with the wise and the learned, what was it with the common people, with the old, with children, with the busy and engrossed, who could only eat their bread by the sweat of their brow? The Apostle therefore, speaking of the Gentiles, says, they were left, "if haply they might feel after Him, and find Him"—an expression borrowed from the blind, who grope for their object, and their way, uncertain of success, and in danger of hurting themselves by their own efforts.

But did not the *Jews* know? We make no scruple to say, they did. To them pertained the oracles of God. He gave his word unto Jacob; his statutes and his judgments unto Israel; and dealt not so with any other people. David said, "Thou shalt guide me with thy counsel, and afterward receive me to glory." Jacob, even in death, was "waiting for the salvation of God." How explicit was the profession of Job—"I know that my Redeemer liveth, and that he shall stand at the latter day upon the earth; and though after my skin worms destroy this body, yet in my flesh shall I see God: whom I shall see for myself, and mine eyes shall behold, and not another, although my reins be consumed within me!"

—How then could "life and immortality be brought to light through the Gospel!" We answer: The word Gospel may be taken in two ways. The one more general, for revelation at large; and thus it is to be understood when it is said, "The gospel was preached to the Jews, but the word preached did not profit them." And thus it is to be understood when it is said, "The Scripture, foreseeing that God would justify the heathen through faith, preached before the gospel unto Abraham, saying, in thee shall all nations be blessed." The other is more restricted, and signifies the evangelical dispensation: commencing with the ministry of our Lord, and including not only the discourses which he personally delivered, but all the inspired communications of the Apostles. Now, if we take the word Gospel here in the former sense, the meaning is, that it brought life and immortality to light *really*. But if taken in the latter sense, then the meaning is, that it brought life and immortality to light *pre-eminently*. And it must be confessed that this is the more common acceptation of the term, and so it is required to be taken in the passage before us. The dawn was visible before; but now the day appeared. To the Jews the Sun of righteousness was below the horizon; on us he has risen with healing under his wings: and Christians are all the children of the light and of the day: God having provided some better thing for us, that they without us should not be made perfect. Hence our Saviour said to his disciples—not comparing them with the Gentiles, but with their own nation: "Many prophets and righteous men have desired to see the things that ye see, and have not seen them; and to hear the things which ye hear, and have not heard them. But blessed are your eyes for they see, and your ears for they hear."

Therefore, while for a knowledge of life and immortality we repair to the Scripture *only*, we must look *peculiarly* into the New Testament, where we are furnished with clearer decisions, and ampler representations: and above all, with illustrations and pledges, in a risen and glorified Saviour. Here again the unrivalled excellency of Christianity appears. How unsatisfactory, how cold, how mean, how gross, how absurd, how disgusting, are the intimations of Deism, the Elysian fields of Pagan poetry, the rewards of Hindooism, the Paradise of Mahomedism—when placed by the side of the "life and immortality brought to light through the Gospel!"

Through the discoveries of this Gospel we are going to finish our Series of Lectures, by viewing the Christian, in his final destination. You have seen him—In CHRIST, the source of all his principles, and consolations, and hopes. You have seen him—Withdrawing into his CLOSET, and dealing much with God alone. You have seen him—Leaving his retirement, and stepping into his FAMILY, and with his house serving God. You have seen him—Joining himself to God's people; and walking in the CHURCH in all the commandments and ordinances of the Lord blameless. You have seen him in the WORLD, but not of it. You have seen him—Safe and sanctified in PROSPERITY. You have seen him—Supported and comforted in ADVERSITY. You have seen him—In his SPIRITUAL SORROWS hanging his harp on the willows. You have seen—The JOY of the Lord his strength. You have surveyed him—In the VALLEY of the shadow of DEATH; and have seen that his end is peace. You have seen him though—laid in the GRAVE, not left there; but rising into newness of life. And now you are to view Him—IN HEAVEN. Four things will engage your attention. The

I. REGARDS THE DEGREE OF OUR PRESENT KNOWLEDGE OF THE HEAVENLY WORLD.—The

II. THE MANNER IN WHICH THE SCRIPTURE AIDS US IN CONCEIVING OF A SUBJECT SO VAST AND DIFFICULT.—The

III. ITS PRINCIPAL CONSTITUENTS.—And

IV. THE INSTRUCTIONS AND IMPRESSIONS WE SHOULD DERIVE FROM THE CONTEMPLATION OF THE CHRISTIAN IN THE POSSESSION OF IT.

I. REGARDS THE DEGREE OF OUR PRESENT KNOWLEDGE OF THE HEAVENLY WORLD.

Have you never, my brethren, when perusing the sacred writings, been struck with a kind of contradiction? Here, in one place, you say, I read that "life and immortality *are* brought to light;" and in another, I am told of "the glory that *shall* be revealed." In one, I am assured, that "eye hath not seen nor ear heard, nor have entered into the heart of man the things which God hath prepared for them that love him." And yet in another it is said, "God hath revealed them unto us by his Spirit." But this apparent contradiction supplies us with the fact we are remarking; and the Apostle John has fully expressed it when he says, "It doth not yet appear what we shall be; but this we know, that when he shall appear we shall be like him, for we shall see him as he is." That is, we know something of it; but much, very much, remains concealed. We have some develope-ments in the sacred pages, and in the illuminations of the Holy Ghost—

" Yet we are able only to survey
Dawnings of beams, and glimmerings of day;
Heaven's fuller affluence mocks our dazzled sight;
Too great its swiftness, and too strong its light."

—Of the full disclosure of the heavenly world, there is a moral and a natural prevention. It would not be proper, if it were possible: and it would not be possible, if it were proper. Let us explain.

The only wise God has attempered even our senses to our present condition. The measure in which we possess them, is admirably fitted to the functions and enjoyments of life. It is easy to perceive that if our feeling was more exquisite, it would annoy us; and that if our hearing was increased, it would prove our inconvenience; and that if our eye was to become microscopic, we should be afraid to move. It is precisely the same with our knowledge. This is adjusted in conformity to the claims of our present sphere of action and happiness. We are now in a mixed state, where sorrow is necessary as well as pleasure; and darkness as well as light. Some duties, if they do not entirely result from our ignorance, are enforced by it. Witness the admonition of the Saviour, "Watch, *for ye know not* the day or the hour wherein the Son of man cometh." We are in a course of trial and discipline; where the grand principle of our training is confidence; where we are to walk by faith, and not by sight: for we are to honour God by trusting in him; and to follow the example of our father Abraham, who "by faith, when he was called to go out into a place which he should afterwards receive for an inheritance, obeyed, and went out, not knowing whither he went"—satisfied with his Guide, and the assurance he had received; and leaving all the inquiries which restless curiosity, and proud reasonings, and conferring with flesh and blood, would have gendered, as unworthy a thought.

We may venture to affirm, that if heaven was now fully laid open to our view, it would be so impressive, and engrossing, as to render every thing here insignificant and uninteresting, and loosen and detach us from all our present engagements. St. Pierre tells us of his returning to France, in a ship that had been absent several years in the East Indies. And "when," says he, "the crew approached their native country, they were all eagerness to discern it. Some of them mounted the rigging: some of them employed their glasses. By-and-by an exclamation was heard, 'Yonder it is!' Then they became thoughtful, and listless. But when they drew nearer, and began to discover the tops of the hills and the towers, that reminded them of the spots in which they had been brought up; they knew not how to contain themselves. They dressed themselves in their best apparel: they brought out the presents designed for their connexions. But when the vessel entered the harbour; and they saw their friends and relations on the quay, stretching forth their hands to embrace them,—many of them leaped from the ship, and other hands were employed to bring it to its moorings." Ah! Christians, could you see the better country from which you were born, and to which you are bound—could you behold your connexions there, ready to receive you; your station would soon be deserted, and other agents would be wanted to carry on their concerns.

We go further: and we say that the full disclosure of heaven would not only derange the present order of things, but endanger, injure, and destroy the very beings to whom it was presented. Our physical powers have their limits; and from many instances in the Scriptures, we see the effects of an excess of excitement or impression. Accustomed as she was to grandeur, the Queen of Sheba, at the sight of Solomon's glory, had no more spirit in her. Jacob fainted away when he saw the wagons to convey him to his son Joseph. When the Angel approached Daniel, there was no strength in him, for his comeliness was turned in him to corruption. And though John had often reclined on his bosom; when the Saviour appeared to him, he fell at his feet as dead. No; we have not eyes to see that brilliancy now; we have not ears to endure that melody now; we have not frames to bear up under that weight of glory now. "Flesh and blood cannot inherit the kingdom of God."

The full knowledge therefore is no more practicable, than it is expedient. We have no adequate medium of receiving the communication; and heaven entering the mind now, is like the sun entering the house through a few little crevices, or the sea flowing through the hollow of a straw. There is an amazing force in language, as we see in some most powerful and affecting works: but words, however chosen, can no more express heaven, than paint can do justice to light, or heat, or joy. All our modes of apprehending and feeling, are not refined and exalted enough to take a complete hold of an object so peculiar and spiritual. Even our thoughts, that seem to "leave dull mortality behind," here labour and strive in vain: and one of the sublimest understandings that ever soared, even also when—inspired, could only exclaim, "O! how great is the goodness which thou hast laid up for them that fear thee!"

This, however, is not to be taken absolutely. With all our deficiencies, we are not ignorant of the reality of this glory: nor are we unfurnished with such a *degree* of information concerning it, as our duty and our welfare allow and require.—And we proceed,

II. To observe HOW THE SCRIPTURE AIDS US IN CONCEIVING OF A SUBJECT SO DIFFICULT AND VAST.

It does this four ways.

First, It enables us to conceive of it *negatively*. Thus it tells us what it is not, removing from it every thing we know and feel to be dreadful, or trying, or distressing. And such representations we are prepared to understand and to feel, by a sad and common experience. For often in a world like this, our most lively apprehension of good is the removal of evil; and our most inviting notion of joy is the cessation of grief. Hence the sacred writers assure us, "They shall hunger no more, nor thirst any more. Neither shall the sun light on them, nor any heat. There shall be no more curse. God shall wipe away all tears from their eyes; and there shall be no more death, neither sorrow, nor crying; neither shall there be any more pain; for the former things are passed away."

Secondly, It enables us to conceive of it *figuratively*. Figures are like dress: they are now used for ornament, but they were introduced from necessity. They were originally used not to embellish, but to explain; and we want them for the same purpose still. How can the mind, while incarnate, any more discern than operate, but through the senses, the mediums of all sensation and reflection? How can we reach the distant, but by the intervention of what is near? How can we understand what is difficult, but by the application of what is familiar? How can we hold communion with things unseen and eternal, but by means of those which are seen and temporal? What wonder therefore that the wisdom of God should have levied a tax on all that is inviting in the intercourses of life, and in the productions and appearances of nature, to afford us emblems and illustrations? What wonder that we should read of rivers of pleasure; of trees of life; of robes and crowns; of feastings and mirth; of treasures and triumphs;—and a thousand other images serving to hold forth a little of the better and enduring substance?

Thirdly, It helps us to conceive of it *comparatively*. It is a blessed change Christians now experience in passing from death unto life. Now are they the sons of God; and they have the Spirit of adoption. They have tasted that the Lord is gracious; and they know the things that are freely given them of God. But though the sacred writers view grace and glory as inseparable, and indeed consider them as in the same kind, they remark the difference there is in degree. Here the new creature is in its infancy; there it comes to the measure of the fulness of the stature of Christ. Here we are faithful over a few things; there we are made rulers over many things. Here we are saved by hope:

there we possess the reality. Here we walk by faith; there by sight. Now we have the first-fruits of the Spirit; then the whole harvest. Now we have the earnest; then the inheritance.

The Christian is therefore led from his present experience to his future attainments; and there is no way of his conceiving of heaven so affecting, as to take his best views and frames now, and to imagine them perfect and perpetual. He can learn more from one hour's communion with God, than from all the books he ever read. There are ordinances, in the use of which he is sometimes filled with all joy and peace in believing; and he can say,

> " If such the sweetness of the streams,
> What must the fountain be;
> Where saints and angels draw their bliss
> Immediately from Thee!"

There are spots in his walks rendered sacred by his meeting his Lord and Saviour, and talking with him as a man talketh with his friend. In his vernal or autumnal retreats from the haunts of men, he has sat beneath the branches of his favourite tree, and has felt a perfect sympathy with all that is innocent and beautiful around him; and every thing earthly has been reduced to its just level in his regards; and the world has been conquered, having nothing to tempt and nothing to terrify; and even Death has been frownless; and, ready to be dissolved, he could sing,

> " Oh that the happy hour was come,
> To change my faith to sight!
> I shall behold my Lord at home
> In a diviner light."

Finally, It helps us to conceive of it *positively*. Telling us plainly, "That the upright shall dwell in his presence. That blessed are the pure in heart, for they shall see God. That when He who is our life shall appear, we shall appear with him in glory. The righteous shall go away into life eternal." Yet what does this mean? What does it include?—And what

III. Are THE PRINCIPAL CONSTITUENTS OF THE HEAVENLY STATE?

Here we will not trifle, or pry into things which we have not seen. We shall not therefore enlarge on many topics which have commonly been connected with the subject; and the reason is, either because they are not so explicitly revealed, or because they are not so important in themselves, as those articles which we are going to enumerate.

It has been asked, Are there degrees in glory? We are persuaded there are. All analogy countenances the conclusion. We see diversities and inequalities pervading all the works of God. We know there are gradations among angels; for we read of thrones and dominions, principalities and powers. And though all Christians are redeemed by the same blood, and justified by the same righteousness, we know that there are degrees in grace. We know the good ground brought forth in some places thirty, in some sixty, in some a hundred fold. And the Apostle tells us, "Every man shall receive his own reward according to his own labour." But here we approve of the old illustration—however unequal in size these vessels may be, when plunged into this ocean, they shall all be equally filled.

It has been asked, Shall we know each other in heaven? Suppose you should not; you may be assured of this, that nothing will be wanting to your happiness. But Oh! you say, how would the thought affect me now! *There* is the babe that was torn from my bosom; how lovely then; but a cherub now! There is the friend, who was as mine own soul, with whom I took sweet counsel, and went to the house of God in company. There is the minister—whose preaching turned my feet into the path of peace—whose words were to me a well of life. There is the beloved mother, on whose knees I first laid my little hands to pray, and whose lips first taught my tongue to pronounce the name of Jesus! And are these removed from us for ever? Shall we recognize them no more? —Cease your anxieties. Can memory be annihilated? Did not Peter, James, and John know Moses and Elias? Does not the Saviour inform us that the friends, benefactors have made of the mammon of unrighteousness, shall receive them into everlasting habitations? Does not Paul tell the Thessalonians, that they are his hope, and joy, and crown, at the coming of our Lord Jesus Christ?

Some would ask, Where is heaven? The universe is immense; but what particular part of it is assigned for the abode of the blessed, we cannot determine. It will probably be our present system renovated. May we not infer this from the words of the Apostle Peter—" Looking for and hastening unto the coming of the day of God, wherein the heavens being on fire shall be dissolved, and the elements shall melt with fervent heat—Nevertheless we, according to his promise, look for new heavens and a new earth wherein dwelleth righteousness."

But is it a *place?* Our Lord has a body like our own; and this cannot be omnipresent; and wherever he is corporeally, there is heaven—" *Where* I am, *there* shall also my servants be." Enoch and Elias have bodies; all the saints will have bodies; and these cannot be everywhere. We read of " the hope laid up for us in heaven." Of " entering into the holy place." " And I go," says Jesus to his disciples, " to prepare a place for you." But though it is really a place, we must chiefly consider it as a state. Even now, happiness does not essentially depend on what is without us. What was Eden to Adam and Eve, after sin had filled them with shame, and sorrow, and fear? But Paul in prison was infinitely happier than Cæsar on the throne of the nations.

What then are we allowed to reckon upon as the grand component parts of this exalted state? You may reckon upon

—*Pre-eminent knowledge.* This is a world of action rather than of science; and the wiser men are, the more readily will they confess, that their present knowledge is unspeakably less than their ignorance. In whatever direction they attempt to penetrate, they are checked and baffled. Laboriousness attends every acquirement: and doubts and uncertainties diminish the value of every possession. The difference between the knowledge of Newton and the most illiterate peasant, will be far exceeded by the difference between the knowledge of the Christian on earth and in heaven. "The light of the moon shall be as the light of the sun, and the light of the sun sevenfold as the light of seven days, when the Lord bindeth up the breach of his people, and healeth the stroke of their wound." Now they understand as children, then they will know as men. Now they see through a glass darkly, but then face to face. Now they know in part, then they will know even as they are known. How delightful the thought—amidst my present perplexities and obscurities; and under a sense of the penury of my talents, and in the want of means and opportunities of improvement; that "Messiah cometh who is called Christ; and that when he is come, he will tell us all things."—You may reckon upon

—*Perfect purity.* This announcement has little attraction for those of you who never saw the beauty of holiness, and never abhorred yourselves, repenting in dust and ashes. But O! to a Christian it is worth dying for, to leave behind him the body of this death; this law in the members warring against the law of his mind; this inability to do the things that he would; this presence of evil ever with him; this liableness, this proneness to sin, even in his holy things—tarnishing every duty, wounding his own peace, and vexing and grieving the spirit of his best friend. To be freed from the enemy, and to have nothing in me that temptation can operate upon! To be incapable of ingratitude, and unbelief, and distractions in duty! To be innocent as the first Adam, and holy as the second! What wonder, the Christian exclaims, with Henry, "If *this* be heaven, oh that I was there!"—You may reckon upon

—The most *delightful associations.* We are formed for society. Much of our present happiness results from attachment and intercourse. Who knows not "the comforts of love!" Yea, and who knows not its sorrows also! We must weep when the objects of our affection weep. The arrows that pierce our friends wound us also. We tolerate, we excuse their imperfections; but we feel them. And the thought of absence—separation—death; is dreariness—pain—and anguish. Hence, some have been ready to envy the unrelated, unconnected individual, whose anxieties and griefs are all personal. But it is not good for man to be alone in any condition. It is better to follow the course of Providence; to cherish the intimacies of life; to improve and to sanctify them: and under the disadvantages which now mingle with them, to look forward to a state where the honey will be without the sting, and the rose without the thorn; and attachment and intercourse without the deductions arising from pain, and infirmities, and pity, and fear. In the Revelations, heaven is always presented as a social state. You have now few holy companions; the many are going another way. But, says John, "I beheld, and, lo! a great multitude, which no man could number, of all nations, and kindreds, and people, and tongues, stood before the throne, and before the Lamb, clothed with white robes, and palms in their hands; and cried with a loud voice, saying, Salvation to *our* God which sitteth upon the throne, and unto the Lamb." And you will have access to them all. You will there have the most *endeared* society; for it will include those to whom you were so tenderly related by nature, or pious friendship, and at parting with whom you sorrowed most of all, that you should see their face and hear their voice no more; and also those you left behind you with reluctance and anxiety in a world of sin and trouble. With these, your fellowship, after a brief separation, will be renewed, improved, and perfected for ever. The society will also be the most *dignified;* and without its present embarrassments.— There are now personages so superior, that you seem reduced to nothing at the thought of them. You esteem and admire them; and wish to hear, and see, and mingle with them; yet you shrink from the presence of such genius, wisdom, and goodness. But you will feel nothing of this, when you sit down with Abraham, and Isaac, and Jacob, and Moses, and with prophets, and apostles, and martyrs, and reformers, in the kingdom of God. Nor will *saints* only be your companions: but those glorious beings who never sinned; who excel in strength; who are proverbial for their wisdom; who are your models, in doing the will of God on earth; who are your ministering spirits, invisibly watching over you in your minority—the innumerable company of *angels.* And though they will not be able to say, He hath redeemed *us,* unto God by his blood; they will cry with a loud voice—though you will endeavour to be louder-

"Worthy is the Lamb that was slain, to receive power, and riches, and. wisdom, and strength, and honour, and glory, and blessing."—You may reckon upon

—The most *glorious employment.* 1 should as soon think that heaven was a nursery of vice, as a state of inaction. Indolence is no more irreconcilable to virtue, than perfectly incompatible with happiness.

"A want of occupation is not rest,
A mind quite vacant is a mind distress'd."

All the powers conferred by a wise Creator necessarily imply their application and use: and the more life any being possesses, the more energy and activeness will distinguish him, unless he is in a state of perversion or restraint. But what are the employments of heaven? Dr. Watts has speculated much on this subject. Some of his conjectures are probable, and all pleasing. But we dare not follow him. Of this we are sure, that there will be none of those mean and degrading toils which arise now from the necessities of our nature, or from luxury and pride. Neither will there be any of those religious exercises which pertain to a state of imperfection. Repentance will be hid from our eyes. There will be no more warfare and watchings. Neither will there be any more prayers with strong cryings and tears. Yet it is said, "They serve him day and night in his temple." And their powers will be equal to the work; for neither the fervency nor the duration of the service will produce exhaustion or languor. The common notion of always standing up and singing, is too childish to be entertained. We have no doubt but that there may be stated assemblies for adoration and praise. But Christians are said to be still praising Him now; and they do this, not by acts of worship only, but by performing his will, by filling up their stations in life properly, and promoting the welfare of all around them: and his work even here is honourable and glorious.

—On the *presence* and *sight* of the Saviour, in whom dwelleth all the fulness of the Godhead bodily, you may reckon; and you *will* reckon—and reckon *supremely*—if you are a Christian. "Ah!" says Paul, "I long to depart, and to be with Christ, which is far better." "We are confident, I say, and willing rather to be absent from the body, and present with the Lord." What would every thing be in His absence! Could the place, the company, the harps, be a substitute for him? But here is the consummation—you shall serve "Him, and see his face." You need not envy those who knew him after the flesh; *you* will have access to him; you will see the King, and see him in his beauty. He is now with *you.* He knows your soul in adversity: and comes to you as a friend, and helper, and comforter. But you are now in prison. His visits, when he looks upon you through the bars, and brings you supplies, and communes with you in the cell, are relieving. They solace the confinement; you wish them multiplied; you expect them with joy. But the best of all these visits will be the last, when he will come not only *to* you, but *for* you: when he will open the doors of the dungeon, and knock off the fetters, and take you home to his palace. Then you will be *with him:* you will "walk with" him "in white;" you will "eat and drink at his table in his kingdom;" you will "be for ever with the Lord."—It is hardly necessary to say, that you may reckon upon

—The most *exquisite enjoyment.* This will spring abundantly from all the foregoing sources, and especially the last. It will far transcend every feeling we have had of delight and ecstasy here. The state itself is expressed by it. "Enter thou into the joy of thy Lord."—Jude says, we shall be "presented before the presence of his glory, with exceeding joy." And says David, "In thy presence is fulness of joy, and at thy right hand are pleasures for evermore."—For you may reckon upon

The *perpetuity* of all this. "Permanency," says the Poet, "adds bliss to bliss." But here it is absolutely indispensable even to the happiness itself: for the greater the blessedness, the more miserable we should feel if it were in danger. Who in the possession of such a prize, could exist under the thought of losing it! How careful therefore are the sacred writers never to leave out this *essential* attribute in any of their descriptions! If it be life, it is "eternal" life. If it be salvation, it is "everlasting" salvation. If it be a kingdom, it is a kingdom that "cannot be shaken." If it be a crown, it is a crown of "glory that fadeth not away."

To which we may add, that you may reckon not only on the eternity, but the *increase.* Who could think of being doomed to remain stationary! How irksome would any condition be in which there could be no possibility of advance and improvement! But your faculties will not be confined to a circle of sameness: they will be free: they will break forth on every side. How much more do the angels know now than once; and yet still they desire to look into the Saviour's sufferings and glory. How often will there be new songs in heaven, or fresh exclamations of admiration and praise, from fresh discoveries and displays of the perfections of God, in his works and ways! Every finite being is capable of accession; and in knowing, and doing, and attaining, and enjoying, there will be an infinite progression before us.

If with this account of heaven you are dissatisfied; be assured, the Lecturer is still more so. Who, upon such a subject can speak worthily! I will therefore no longer darken counsel with words without knowledge; but conclude by calling upon you

IV. To BEHOLD THE CHRISTIAN IN HIS FINAL DESTINY, AND TO REMARK THE INSTRUCTIONS AND IMPRESSIONS THAT SHOULD ARISE FROM THE CONTEMPLATION.

Behold him THERE, as a *monument of Divine grace*. What was he *once?* He will not be unwilling to look to the rock whence he was hewn, and to the hole of the pit whence he was digged. He will acknowledge that by nature he was a child of wrath even as others; condemned by the law of God; a fallen, guilty, depraved creature; his powers all defiled and desolate; helpless and ready to perish. But what is he *now?* Redeemed; justified; renewed; quickened together with Christ; raised up and made to sit with him in the heavenly places. And *whence* is all this? It is by his own worthiness, or righteousness, or strength, that he has made himself whole? " This people," says God, " have *I* formed for myself; they shall show forth *my* praise." Here he has placed them to display in their salvation the freeness, the power, and the fulness of his grace—That in the ages to come He might show the exceeding riches of his grace in his kindness towards them by Christ Jesus. And falling in completely with this design, they cast their crowns at his feet, and exclaim, " Not unto us, O Lord, not unto us, but unto thy Name give glory, for thy mercy and thy truth's sake. By the grace of God I am what I am. Not I, but the grace of God which was with me."

—Behold him THERE, and see *the conduct of God towards him in this world explained and vindicated*. It will be acknowledged that though God does much for his people here, yet the relation in which he has been pleased to place himself, implies and requires far more than he *now* performs. A future state of munificent liberality is therefore necessary. To this He appeals, and by this his promises are to be estimated. Hence says the Apostle, " Wherefore God is not ashamed to be called their God, seeing he hath prepared for them a city." Here, while the wicked prospered, and had more than heart could wish, the righteous were poor, and oppressed, and afflicted; plagued every morning, and chastened every moment. And you were ready to ask, If they are His, why are they thus? You were so perplexed at the strangeness of his providence towards them, that your feet were almost gone, and your steps had well nigh slipped. But even then, He told you that his ways are not our ways; he told you that his people were under an economy, a very small part of which falls within your inspection; he told you that the dispensations you complained of were not yet terminated: he said, " Judge nothing before the time, until the Lord come "—But here is the full answer. Look at them now. All that was darkness, is now illuminated: all that appeared disorderly is now arranged: all that seemed evil is now acknowledged good. Now we have the clew, and the difficulties are loosened. Now we have the end, and this justifies the means. We now see by what his dispensations towards them were regulated, and in what they have resulted. They were chastened of the Lord, that they might not be condemned by the world. The trial of their faith was much more precious than that of gold that perisheth, because it was to be found unto praise, and glory, and honour, at the appearing of Jesus Christ. The light afflictions which were but for a moment, have worked out for them a far more exceeding and eternal weight of glory. They themselves are more than satisfied. They acknowledge that He hath dealt well with his servants. They exclaim, He hath done all things well. " Marvellous are thy works, Lord God Almighty; just and true are all thy ways, O thou King of saints."

—Behold the GLORIFIED Christian, and see the *justification of his choice*. Here, his fellow-creatures despised him, or affected to pity. If they allowed him to be sincere, they reproached him as weak, and considered his life a system of restraints, and privations, and sacrifices. Even *then* wisdom was justified of all her children. Even *then* they were conscious that reason itself bore them out in their preference. Even *then* they were not ashamed of their self-denial or sufferings, for they knew whom they had believed; and were persuaded that he was able to keep that which they had committed unto him against that day. Even *then* they rejoiced in the testimony of their consciences, and the secret smiles and whispers of their Lord and Saviour. But the world knew them not. They were princes in disguise. Their titles were refused, and their honours and riches were turned to scorn. And they bore this with firmness and patience—for they saw that their day was coming. And lo! now it is arrived. Now they shine forth as the sun in the kingdom of their Father. Now is the manifestation of the sons of God. Now their enemies return and discern between the righteous and the wicked; between him that serveth God, and him that serveth him not. And O! how changed their sentiments and their language now! " We fools counted their life madness, and their end to be without honour! How are they numbered with the saints, and their lot is among the children of God !"

Contemplate him WHERE he is, and *inquire whether you will be a partaker of the same blessedness*. Is it not astonishing that you can put such a question from you, as if it was the greatest impertinence, from week to week, from year to year, though in the midst of life you are in death, and after death is the judgment? And is it not strange that others can remain in a state of indecision, with only such a peradventure as this to support their peace— *Perhaps* I am in the way to heaven, and *perhaps* I am in the way to hell! What is your real condition with regard to that eternity, on the verge of which you are? Have you a *title* to glory? This results from relationship: "If children, then heirs; heirs of God, and joint heirs with Christ." Have you any *meetness* for the inheritance of the saints in light? Without this you cannot see the kingdom of God—not only for want of permission, but for want of capacity. Threatenings are not necessary to exclude—your disposition bars you out. The excellency of the state cannot make you happy without an adaption to it: your contrariety of temper and taste would make you miserable. "God has wrought us," says the Apostle, "for the selfsame thing." Has he done this for you? Have you any thing in you that is congenial with heaven? Heaven is a holy place. Are you hungering and thirsting after righteousness? It consists in the presence and adoration of Christ. Are you at home now when you are saying, "Unto him that loved us, and washed us from our sins in his own blood, be glory and dominion?" There all religious distinctions will be done away; and the question will be, not where you have worshipped, but only how. Can you now rise above a party, and say, "Grace be with all them that love our Lord Jesus Christ in sincerity?" Many of you *do* not hope for heaven; *do* not desire it. You *cannot* hope for it, you *cannot* desire it—unless you can love and enjoy its ingredients now.

—Let the CONTEMPLATION bring you upon your knees, and be *this your prayer:* "Remember me, O Lord, with the favour thou bearest unto thy people: O visit me with thy salvation; that I may see the good of thy chosen, that I may rejoice in the gladness of thy nation, and glory with thine inheritance." O! how shall I plead with you for this purpose? By what motives can I urge you to make it your immediate and prevailing concern?

Need I remind you of the importance of the object!—Glory! Honour! Immortality! An eternity; an infinity, of blessedness!

—Need you be told that it is placed within your attainment—that you are allowed, invited, commanded, to seek the kingdom of God and his righteousness, with an assurance of success? And if you perish, what an aggravation of your misery will this produce? When an event is unavoidable, you may lament, but you feel no self-reproach. When you suffer innocently, conscience even commends you; you feel a little of the spirit of a martyr; you claim on your side a God of judgment, and believe that in due time he

will appear on your behalf. But here you will be speechless. You will feel that *you* have destroyed yourselves. Your misery will be your greatest *sin*. Every mouth will be stopped; and you will be found guilty before God. Guilty of what? Of transgressing his law. Yes—but still more of neglecting so great salvation, of rejecting the counsel of God against yourselves, and judging yourselves unworthy of everlasting life.

And allow me to ask, for what is it that you are determined to sacrifice this attainable and infinite boon? Are you not spending your money for that which is not bread, and your labour for that which satisfieth not? You condemn the folly of Esau, who for one morsel of meat sold his birthright. You reproach Adam and Eve, who lost the garden of Eden for a taste of the forbidden tree. But you are making a far worse, a far viler exchange. You are sacrificing all the glory of God and the Lamb—I again ask for what? You would be losers if you gained the whole world.—But are you gaining empires? provinces? estates? Are you gaining reputation? The esteem of the wise and good? Health? Peace of mind? Support in trouble? Freedom from fear? Sin ought to yield you much, for it will cost you dear. But the way of transgressors is hard. There is no peace to the wicked. When you lie down in sorrow, how will you answer the question, "What fruit had ye then in those things whereof ye are now ashamed? for the end of these things is death." Remember also the alternative.

—For missing this, there is nothing but a certain fearful looking for of judgment and fiery indignation to devour the adversary. If you are not with the sheep at the right hand, you must be with the goats at the left. If you hear not the sentence, "Come, ye blessed of my Father, inherit the kingdom prepared for you from the foundation of the world," you must hear the doom, "Depart, ye cursed, into everlasting fire, prepared for the devil and his angels."

Lastly, Let us LOOK and hail those who can *make the prospect their own.* We talk of happiness! Can any thing equal the state of those who can humbly and confidently say, "Being justified by faith, we have peace with God through our Lord Jesus Christ, by whom also we have access by faith into this grace wherein we stand, and rejoice in hope of the glory of God." Many are in adversity and tribulation; and yet have no such prospect. All is fighting against them, and they have no refuge. Their thoughts are broken off; even the purposes of their hearts, and their earthly schemes, laid desolate; yet they have nothing better before them. Yea, conscience tells them, this is only the beginning of sorrows; the short preface to a long roll written within and without, with lamentation, and mourning, and wo. But to the upright there

Q   11

ariseth light in the darkness. He sees the storm beginning to clear up; and he knows that no cloud shall return after the rain. "I reckon," says he, "that the sufferings of the present time are not worthy to be compared with the glory that shall be revealed in us." Soon, want will be followed with fulness. Soon, the worm-wood and the gall will be succeeded by the cup of salvation.

> "Yet a season, and we know
> Happy entrance shall be given;
> All our sorrows left below,
> And earth exchanged for heaven."

With this prospect, how superior is he to the envied, the indulged, the successful man of the world! *He* has his portion in this life: but, says the Christian, "As for me, I will behold thy face in righteousness; I shall be satisfied when I awake with thy likeness." His good things are temporal; mine are eternal. He is leaving his; I am advancing to mine. Every hour diminishes the value of his hope; but every moment adds interest to mine.

Nor need the Christian envy the man of claims merely intellectual. Wisdom indeed excelleth folly, as much as light excelleth darkness. Money is a defence; but the excellency of knowledge is, that wisdom giveth life to them that have it. But what wisdom! It was a fine reply of the converted astronomer, who, when interrogated concerning the science which he had been idolizing, answered, "I am now bound for heaven, and I take the stars in my way." How humiliating is it to reflect, that the treasures of learning and science depend upon the brain; that an accident or disease may abolish them; or that, at most, they are limited to the life that now is, and which we spend as a shadow! Whether there be knowledge, it shall vanish away—unless it be the excellency of the knowledge of Christ Jesus our Lord—for this is life eternal.

In much wisdom, also, there is much grief; and he that increaseth knowledge, increaseth sorrow. Some of the most expansive and cultivated minds are the most miserable. Nor is it difficult to account for this. Genius implies a sensibility which strangers intermeddle not with. It is attended with a keenness of feeling, that renders the possessor like a sensitive plant, that shrinks at every touch. He lives in a world of imagination, as well as a world of reality. He views nothing simply and purely. Every thing is dressed up to his conceptions; the beautiful in preternatural tints, and the evil in preternatural horrors. His thoughts are sentiments. He feels intensely; and nothing very intense can continue. Then follows a void which is irksome, and a listlessness which is intolerable, and which are sometimes productive of fatal effects. In Madame de Stael's Memoirs of her Father, we have the following remark: "I have a proof," says Mr. Necker, "of the immortality of the soul in this; that it is at least after a while desirable; and essential to our happiness. By the time we have reached threescore years and ten, we have looked around us, and become familiar with the whole scene; and though not satisfied, we are sated. Then we feel our need of a new residence; a new sphere of activity; and new sources of employment and enjoyment." This is a striking remark; and we may observe, that if at such a period, religion with its motives and promises is not present to the mind, the man, wearied of existence, and feeling every thing here to be vanity, is likely to become the victim of an insupportable oppression, and in a moment of rashness may welcome self-destruction. Have we had no instances of this?

—Here the Christian is guarded; here he is provided for. As this world palls upon him, another opens to his view. This prospect enlivens the solitudes which bereavement and decays of nature have produced. This prospect becomes a substitute for the scenes and charms which have faded and fled. This prospect entertains and engages, now the days are come in which he says, I have no pleasure in them. The outward man perisheth, but the inward man is renewed day by day. His heart and his flesh fail; but God is the strength of his heart, and his portion for ever. He departs: but he leaves what is not his rest, what is polluted, what is nigh unto cursing, and whose end is to be burned —while he enters a creation where every thing that is new, and marvellous, and pure, and attractive, and beautifying, says, Arise and come away. And the hour that obscures and quenches for ever all other glories, immortalizes him.

LECTURE XIII.
THE RESULT.

"Almost thou persuadest me to be a Christian."
—Acts xxvi. 28.

MEN AND BRETHREN,

IN a succession of Lectures I have led you to contemplate the noblest of all characters— THE CHRISTIAN. You have contemplated him in twelve important and interesting positions. You have seen him in CHRIST, the source of all his principles, and consolations, and hopes. You have beheld him retiring into his CLOSET, and dealing with God alone. You have noticed him 'serving the Lord in his FAMILY. You have watched him in the CHURCH, walking in all the commandments and ordinances of the Lord blameless. You have watched him in the WORLD, without being of it. You have viewed him safe and sanctified in his PROSPERITY; and supported and instructed in his ADVERSITY. You have surveyed him hanging his harp on the willows in his SPIRITUAL SORROWS; and exulting in the JOY of the Lord as his strength. You have marked him in the VALLEY of the shadow of DEATH, and seen that his end is peace. You have attended him to the GRAVE, and seen him rising into newness of life. And you have gazed on him as he entered the GLORY of the Heavenly world—

And may I not hope, as the result of the whole, that some serious impressions and excitements have been produced, and that at least here and there a voice is secretly exclaiming, "Almost thou persuadest me to be a Christian?"

These were the words of Agrippa to Paul —"Then Agrippa said unto Paul, Almost thou persuadest me to be a Christian." But what a strange conjunction was here, in the meeting together of two personages, previously so remote from each other, and so differing in condition, and office, and qualities, and pursuits! What procured and produced the intercourse? What were the circumstances accompanying it? What were the consequences that followed it? *"Then* Agrippa said unto Paul, Almost thou persuadest me to be a Christian."

We need not enlarge on Paul. With him we are well acquainted. We know that he was a man of great talent and learning; of a sanguine temper; divinely commissioned; and supernaturally endowed. We know that he was an apostle, and the very chief of the apostles. We know he was engaged in a course, the prosecution of which exposed him to every kind of privation, insult, and suffering: but he could say, "None of these things move me, neither count I my life dear unto myself; so that I may finish my course with joy, and the ministry which I have received of the Lord Jesus to testify the gospel of the grace of God." Yea, he could say, "Therefore I take pleasure in infirmities, in reproaches, in necessities, in persecutions, in distresses for Christ's sake; for when I am weak, then am I strong." And thus even now,

when called forth before this splendid assembly, he does not appear under the advantage of a philosopher, a courtier, or chaplain, but a poor prisoner in fetters, suffering as an evil doer, even unto bonds.

But Agrippa, who was he? He was the youngest son of Herod, that killed James the brother of John with the sword, and, because it pleased the Jews, proceeded to take Peter also; and who, by a very worthy end, was smitten by the angel of the Lord, and was eaten of worms, and gave up the ghost. When the wretched father thus died, Agrippa was at Rome with the Emperor Claudius. Claudius first gave him the dominion of his uncle, King of Chalcis; but afterward, in exchange, he gave him the provinces of Gaulatinus, Traconites, Batanea, Pureas, and Abilene. To all this Nero, the successor of Claudius, added Julias in Parea, and that part of Galilee which included Tarichea and Tiberias. We mention this to show that Agrippa was no inconsiderable sovereign.

Festus being now governor of Judea, Agrippa and his sister Bernice came as far as Cesarea to salute him. During the continuance of the visit, Festus spoke of one Paul who had been apprehended for making a tumult in the Temple, and had recently appealed unto Cæsar. Agrippa, who was acquainted with the customs of the Jews, and had heard some rumours concerning Paul, said, "I have a desire to hear this man myself." "To-morrow," said Festus, "thou shalt hear him." And on the morrow, when Agrippa was come, and Bernice, with great pomp, and was entered into the place of hearing with the chief captains and principal men of the city, at Festus's commandment Paul was brought forth.

Festus having introduced the case with regard to Paul's accusation and appeal, Agrippa said unto Paul, "Thou art permitted to speak for thyself." Here you will observe that Paul was not now upon his trial. His appeal to Augustus had stopped all judicial proceedings against him. Neither was Agrippa sitting before him in the character of a judge. Paul's speech, therefore, was not a legal defence, so much as an explanatory narrative. This he might have declined; but courtesy and prudence, and zeal for his Master, led him to seize the opportunity of address. He therefore stretched forth his hand, and answered for himself—relating his former persecutions of the Christians; the miraculous manner of his conversion as he was journeying to Damascus; his preservation by the providence of God; and the grand, the only subject of his preaching.

And as he thus spake for himself, Festus said, with a loud voice, "Paul, thou art beside thyself; much learning doth make thee mad." But he said, "I am not mad, most noble Festus, but speak forth the words of truth and soberness. For the king knoweth of these things, before whom also I speak plainly; for this thing was not done in a corner. King Agrippa, believest thou the prophets? I know that thou believest." Then

Agrippa said unto Paul, "Almost thou persuadest me to be a Christian."

I cannot proceed without remarking *Three* things with regard to this occurrence :—*First.* It was obviously casual as to the parties. On neither side was there previously the least expectation or design. But it was not accidental with regard to God. He works all things after the counsel of his own will : and, in his arrangements, how much often is suspended on incidents seemingly the most precarious and insignificant! Thus all in the case before us hinged upon a word carelessly spoken in discourse, and the prevalence of a little idle curiosity.

Secondly. It was a distinguished advantage to Paul. It served to verify the promise of the Saviour, "When ye shall be brought before governors and kings for my sake, I will give you a mouth, and wisdom which all your adversaries shall not be able to gainsay or resist." It also afforded him an opportunity to vindicate his character from the calumnies of his countrymen. But, above all, it enabled him to bear witness to the truth and excellency of the Gospel in the presence of a very important and remarkable audience. A faithful preacher has seldom access to the great and princely, nor would Paul have had the advantage which he now improved, but for the persecution he endured. It was thus the wrath of man praised God, and that adverse circumstances turned out rather unto the furtherance of the Gospel.

Thirdly. To Agrippa it was an all-momentous occasion. Nothing before, nothing after, in his history, ever equalled it. It was the most eventful crisis in his life. The kingdom of God was now come nigh him. It was the day of his visitation—And, oh! had he but known the things that belonged to his peace, how immediately, and gratefully, and zealously would he have embraced the accepted time —the day of salvation!

Had it, then, no effect upon his views and feelings! Yes: "Then Agrippa said unto Paul, Almost thou persuadest me to be a Christian." Let us consider this persuasion,

In reference to its OBJECT.

In reference to its DEGREE ; and

In reference to its COMPLETENESS.

I. Let us consider the OBJECT of this persuasion. It was his becoming a Christian— "Almost thou persuadest me to be a *Christian.*"

And what did Agrippa mean by this? He intended a character like Paul. So the apostle took it, and therefore replied, "I would to God that not only thou, but also all that hear me this day, were both almost and altogether such *as I am,* except these bonds." Thou supposest me to be a Christian; so I am. I claim it as a distinction, I glory in it as a privilege. There is nothing I value so much for myself, or so much desire on the behalf of others.

Paul, it must be acknowledged, was not only a real, but a noble specimen of Christi-

anity. Few, if any, ever equalled *him;* yet every Christian essentially resembles him, and should have such a consciousness of it as to be able to say, " I am a Christian ;" and display so much of the excellency of the character as to strike observers, and induce them to wish to become such themselves.

It can hardly be supposed that on such a subject Agrippa should distinguish between pretence and reality; or between a true Christian, and a mere nominal one. The world, at this time, did not think of examining the genuineness of profession. The profession was commonly sincere. Nothing was to be gained by hypocrisy. The cause was so hated and persecuted that even the avowal of it was generally a sure voucher for the existence of the thing. But what was needless then, has become necessary since. For as the offence of the Cross ceases, and Christianity is more diffused and national, and its votaries gain outward respect and influence, profession must be less and less decisive of reality, so that many will have a name to live while they are dead, and assume the form of godliness while they deny the power. Hence the Saviour says, " Not every one that saith unto me, Lord, Lord, shall enter into the kingdom of heaven, but he that doeth the will of my Father which is in heaven." When Paul preached before Agrippa there were no drunken Christians, no swearing Christians, no revengeful Christians, no covetous Christians. But how many are there now, who, while minding earthly things, and walking according to the course of this world, and living in sin, would be surprised if you withheld from them the name of Christians, and indignantly ask whether you think them Pagans, or Turks, or Jews, or Infidels! But persons who are not Infidels, or Jews, or Turks, or Pagans, may not be Christians. As it was of old, "All were not Israel, who were of Israel ;" and "he was not a Jew, who was one outwardly ; neither was that circumcision, which was outward in the flesh ; but he was a Jew, who was one inwardly, and circumcision was that of the heart, in the spirit, and not in the letter ; whose praise was not of men, but of God :"—so now, he is not a Christian who is born in a Christian country, or baptized in his infancy, or confirmed in his childhood, or accustomed to repeat an orthodox creed, or regularly attend on the public worship of God ; but he who has received Christ Jesus the Lord, and is walking in him.

After our text, there is only one passage in the New Testament where the name is expressly applied to a religious character. It is where Peter says, " But if he be a Christian, let him not be ashamed." There is, however, no doubt of its common use after a while ; and we are informed where the title was first appropriated. " The disciples were called Christians first at Antioch." There has been no little dispute whether the name was applied to them by their enemies in a way of reproach, or by a divine interposition. But why should it be supposed that anything extraordinary or particular was necessary in this case? The affair now only took its natural course. There had been always heads and leaders of sects, and it was customary to give their names to their followers. Thus the disciples of Plato were called Platonists; and those of Epicurus, Epicureans; and so of others.

A Christian, therefore, stands in a similar, only a more entire relation to Christ. He is one who derives his religious character and being from Christ. He calls Christ his Master, and his only Master. He embraces and avows his doctrines and principles. He obeys his commands. He conforms himself to his example, and treads in his steps.

If it be said that the acts of obedience and imitation are not always or necessarily implied in the idea of a disciple, like the receiving lessons of instruction; we answer, that it would be strange if a disciple did not resemble his Master as well as learn of him; that it would unavoidably be so if the pupil supremely and entirely loved and honoured him, which is true of every Christian; that in the present instance, conformity is as indispensable as belief; for "if any man have not the spirit of Christ, he is none of his, and he that is joined to the Lord is of one spirit with him;" and that, without obedience to his precepts, we cannot duly regard his tuition, for he always taught and enjoined such practice as a proof of discipleship. "If any man will be my disciple, let him deny himself, and take up his cross and follow me." "Ye call me Master and Lord, and ye say well, for so I am: if I, then, your Lord and Master, have washed your feet, ye ought also to wash one another's feet; for I have given you an example that ye should do as I have done unto you." "Why call ye me Lord, Lord, and *do* not the things which I say? If ye *know* these things, happy are ye if ye *do* them."

The honour and privileges of a disciple must be judged of by the condition and qualities of the master; and when we consider the Christian's master; the dignity of his person; the excellency of his character; the perfection of his knowledge; the patience and gentleness of his teaching; the efficiency of his instructions; and how his words, which are spirit and life, sanctify, and bless, and comfort, it is not wonderful that Peter should exclaim, "Lord, to whom shall we go but unto Thee?" or that we hail those who are sitting with Mary at his feet; or invite others to join them, saying, "Will ye also be his disciples?"

II. We consider this persuasion in reference to its DEGREE—"*Almost* thou persuadest me to be a Christian."

The persuasion went far; and the effect on the mind of Agrippa must have been great, seeing he not only felt the emotion, but could not restrain the expression of it publicly. A thousand things must have made him anxious not to appear to favour the apostle or his cause. A Christian was supposed to be a man without truth or honour; an enemy to Moses and Cæsar; a disturber of the public repose; one who wished to turn the world upside down, one the filth and offscouring of all things. He was the son of a prince who had gloried in hunting down the rising sect, and by his persecutions had ingratiated himself into the favour of the Jews. He knew well that the chief priests and elders had now imprisoned Paul, and sought his condemnation from the Roman governor. He must have felt the pomp of the assembly, and the quality of the persons before him, including leading citizens, military chiefs, and his licentious sister, who would be ready to burst into insult. A few moments before, he had heard Festus, upon the same bench, charging Paul with enthusiasm and phrensy. He was a magistrate and ruler himself, whose words were peculiarly liable to observation; nor could he be aware of the use that might be made of any saying of his by report, among Jews or Romans. And yet, notwithstanding the presence and pressure of all these circumstances, he is unable to restrain himself, and exclaims openly in court, "Almost thou persuadest me to be a Christian."

And does he mean that the apostle's proofs were nearly, but not quite conclusive? and that his reasoning was only sufficient to leave his mind in a state of uncertainty or suspicion? Nothing like it. He is convinced in his judgment. He attempts no reply—he starts no difficulty. He feels the force of truth: he confesses it. But, alas! his office, his honours, his connexions, the pleasures of sin, the love of the world, were too much to be parted with, to go forth to the Nazarene without the camp, bearing his reproach.

We know, indeed, very little of him after this; but no change was effected in his real character; his root, as the Scripture says, became as rottenness, and his blossom went up as the dust. His troops were employed in the siege and destruction of Jerusalem, after which he returned to Rome, where he lived, according to every probability, in incest, died at seventy, and at his end was a fool.

The case is by no means a singular one. We have many instances of a similar nature and issue recorded in the Book of God. When the Jews were rescued from Egypt, and had passed the Red Sea, and saw their enemies dead on the shore, they sang his praise and professed a readiness to obey Him in all that he should command. And ages after, God, referring to this scene, said, "I remember thee the kindness of thy youth and the love of thine espousals when thou wentest after me in the wilderness, in a land that was not sown: Israel was then holiness to the Lord, and the first-fruits of his increase." But, alas! they soon forgot his works and the wonders he had shown them; and their goodness was as the morning cloud and early dew, which soon passeth away.

It was the same when visited with his judgments. "When he slew them, then they sought him; and they returned and inquired after God; and they remembered that God was their rock, and the High God their Redeemer. Nevertheless, they did flatter him with their mouth, and lied unto him with their tongue; for their heart was not right with God, neither were they steadfast in his covenant."

Balaam is an awful instance that a clear head may be connected with a corrupt heart. How strong were his impressions and convictions! "I cannot go beyond the word of the Lord to do less or more." How goodly are thy tents, O Jacob, and thy tabernacles, O Israel! "Let me die the death of the righteous, and let my last end be like his." Yet this man, who seemed more than "almost a saint," this very man, loved the wages of unrighteousness, reconciled his conscience to his covetousness, counselled the seduction of the people he had blessed, and died fighting against the Israel of God.

Is Saul also among the prophets? yes, and the Spirit of the Lord came upon him; and he prophesied; and he had another heart given him—but it was not a new one! He built an altar unto the Lord, and repeatedly acknowledged that he had sinned, and implored forgiveness; yet he continued to pursue David to slay him. He vilely disobeyed in the very command he was sent to execute against the Amalekites, sparing Agag, and preserving for himself the best of the spoil; and at last, deserted of God, he repaired to a witch, for comfort—after having made witchcraft a capital offence, and died on his own sword a self-murderer.

Can we overlook Ezekiel's attendants? They almost idolized him as a preacher. They formed parties to go together to hear him. He was unto them as a lovely song, and as one who had a pleasant voice, and that could play well on an instrument; and they heard his words, but did them not.

Many of the Jews repaired to John's ministry, inquiring of him what they were to do, and numbers of them were even baptized by him in Jordan, confessing their sins. How great the excitement was, may be inferred from our Lord's remark. The kingdom of God is preached, and all men press into it. The kingdom of heaven suffereth violence, and the violent take it by force: yet it was only "for a season they rejoiced in his light."

And Herod reverenced the noble forerunner as a holy and just man, and heard him gladly, and did many things. Yet a criminal passion supplanted all these hopeful beginnings, and the half-converted wretch shut up John in prison, and then sent and beheaded him.

When our Lord in the synagogue of Nazareth read and explained the prophecy of Isaiah, they bare him witness, and wondered at the gracious words which proceeded out of his mouth; but before the hour was ended they took him to the brow of the hill to cast him down headlong. Of those who followed him, not only for the loaves and fishes, but from the impression of his preaching, many went back and walked no more with him; and numbers who witnessed his miracles were convinced of his Divine mission, and they believed on him, but feared to confess him, lest they should be put out of the synagogue, for they loved the praise of men more than the praise of God.

Behold Paul preaching before Felix and his wife Drusilla. And as he reasoned of righteousness, temperance, and judgment to come, what was the effect? 'It was immediately seen in the most unlikely subject. Yes, Felix could not resist the wisdom and spirit with which he spake. He moved, he changed colour, his face became pallid, his limbs shook: "Felix trembled." And yet he said, Go thy way for this time; when I have a more convenient season I will call for thee." Instead of cherishing the conviction, he suffered it to die away—he stifled it. He again, more than once, saw Paul, and heard him concerning the faith in Christ, but without his former feeling. This was gone—gone forever.

As it was then, so it is now: reformation is not renovation; conviction is not conversion; emotion is not principle; impulse is not decision. We are continually seeing how possible it is for men to have impressions which are very powerful, and yet not effectual. Indeed, there are few persons but occasionally, at least, have to resist and get rid of some of these assaults upon their spiritual security and indifference. Man has a conscience, and it is not easy for him to subdue it; he may order it to be silent, but it will sometimes speak; he may stupify it by an opiate; but when it awakes, it will sting as a serpent, and bite like an adder.

He knows he must die certainly, and may die soon; and the thought will now and then occur that it *may* be the entrance into another state of existence, and that after death there may be a judgment.

All God's works proclaim his being and perfections; and God is never far from him: and he says unto God, Depart from us; we desire not the knowledge of thy ways; but this shows that God *does* approach as a reprover and instructer, and how difficult he finds it to keep him off. The difficulty is increased when he lives in a land of vision where God's will is clearly known, and all the means of grace are afforded. He may wish for darkness, but how hard is it to keep out the light where there are so many crevices and apertures, and all is day abroad! He may wish to sleep on, but how hardly can he maintain his slumbers when so many godly noises are around his dwelling!

You are hearers of the word. Has not the preacher sometimes alarmed you so that you have been ready to cry out, What must I do to be saved! At other times have you not been so melted as to shed tears of joy, during which you have said, Lord, I am thine; save me!

You have been exercised with providential dispensations. You have had, perhaps, worldly losses; and when your schemes failed, and your purposes were broken off, even the thoughts of your heart, you said, I will seek a better, and an enduring substance.

Or you have been deprived of the desire of your eyes, or the child of your bosom, and under the bereavement your eye poured out tears unto God.

Or a sudden death of a friend or neighbour cried very loud for the time, "Be ye also ready, for in such an hour as you think not, the Son of man cometh."

A bodily sickness shook you over the grave; and then the minister was called in, and what cries you uttered, and what confessions you made, and what vows you bound yourself by! And you recovered—but soon returned again to folly, and blushed at the remembrance of your fears, and shunned intercourse with the preacher who witnessed your weakness.

Yes; it is awful to think that all such impressions, however they excite and urge, may fail, and indeed will fail, unless *His* agency be implored who works in us to will and to do of his good pleasure. For when the man is almost persuaded to be the Christian, there is much *within* to oppose and hinder the progress of his concern. The sparks are fire, but they fall upon mud or water. The course enjoined is good, but the heart is alienated from the life of God. The pleading is for the spirit, but the leaning is to the flesh. The judgment befriends humility, but the disposition pride.

And how much, also, is there *without* that is unfavourable and hostile! The man is in the world; and the world lieth in wickedness; and all that is in the world, the lust of the flesh, the lust of the eye, and the pride of life, is not of the Father, but is of the world. There is the multitude always doing evil; and how powerful is the influence of general example! And the wicked are not only corrupt, but children that are corrupters; and they are never satisfied to go astray themselves, but make use of every artifice to draw away disciples after them.

When the man is alone, he often thinks justly, and feels morally, and resolves strongly; but no sooner is he in company again than his vows are violated, and his iniquity, like the wind, carries him away. I have hardly ever observed a young man that turned aside from the truth, whose defection I have not ascribed to this cause: "evil communications corrupt good manners"—"a companion of fools shall be destroyed."

Then the cares of this life, and the deceitfulness of riches, spring up and choke the word, and it becometh unfruitful. And is it not also proverbial that "we perish in lawful things?" Here, the engagements not being sinful in themselves, we are off our guard, and thoughtlessly err in the degree; and the oxen, and the piece of ground, and the wife, excuse our negligence in not coming to the feast.

And how many stop short by delays! They mean not to go back; yea, they are determined to go forward; but they wait for a more favourable season. And this death often prevents, or if it arrives, it finds the man with his convictions cooled, and his inclinations deadened, and his heart a proof that God's Spirit does not always strive with man upon the earth.

Let us, then,

III. Consider this persuasion in reference to its COMPLETENESS.

Here we must endeavour to show the desirableness, the importance, the necessity, the absolute necessity there is of your being not only almost, but altogether persuaded to be a Christian.

And let me observe, *How base and dishonourable your indecision is with regard to the Saviour.* Has he no claims upon you? Has his greatness none? His goodness none? Oh! where should we have been if he had been only "almost persuaded" to interfere in our favour, and say, Deliver from going down into the pit; I have found a ransom? He waited not for your importunity, but, self-moved, said, Lo! I come to do thy will, O God. I delight to do thy will; yea, thy law is within my heart. And did he draw back or hesitate as the hour of sacrifice actually drew on? did he not say, I have a baptism to be baptized with, and how am I straitened till it be accomplished? And are you only half disposed to love and follow him who has done and suffered for you what tongue cannot express, or imagination conceive? Is this thy kindness to thy friend? Do you thus requite your infinite Benefactor? Has he not a right to say, My son, give me thine heart! And will he be satisfied with less? Does he not consider a neutral as an enemy? And has he not said, "He that is not for me is against me, and he that gathereth not with me scattereth abroad?" And will he not fulfil his own threatening? "So then because thou art lukewarm, and neither cold nor hot, I will spew thee out of my mouth?"

Consider, also, *How many are interested in your entire determination.* The enemy of souls, all the powers of darkness, all the sinners around you, are hoping that you will not go a step farther; and are eager to keep you easy where you already are. But God, who waits to be gracious, is waiting for your decision, and asking when shall it once be? And angels, who rejoice in the repentance of a sinner, are longing to shout over you. And ministers are praying that they may not watch for your souls in vain. And have you no relations who are saying, How can I endure to see the destruction of my kindred? And is not thy father saying. "My son, if thy heart be wise, my heart shall rejoice, even mine?" And is not thy mother saying, "What, my son, and the son of my womb, and the son of my vows?" ready again, and in a nobler sense, to forget her anguish for joy, that a man is born into the world.

And let me ask, *What keeps you from advancing farther?* Is it the want of more evidence? Have you discovered the insufficiency of the probabilities, and proofs, and demonstrations of the truth of the Gospel? Or is it the apprehension of difficulties? Difficulties we allow there are. But are there not difficulties in the service of sin! Is not the way of transgressors hard! Make a fair comparison, and you will soon find the Saviour's yoke more easy, and his burden more light, than the vassalage of the world. Difficulties there are, but you are not called to meet them in your own strength. His grace is sufficient for you. His strength shall be made perfect in your weakness. His spirit can subdue every aversion, and conquer every corruption. Difficulties there are, but think of the prize of your high calling. Other strivers run for a corruptible crown, but you for an incorruptible. He that overcometh shall inherit all things. Or do you wait *for an assurance of success?* What would you have more than the experience of all who have made the trial! He never said to the seed of Jacob, Seek ye me, in vain. And what says the promise?—and the Scripture cannot be broken:—"Ask, and it shall be given you; seek, and ye shall find; knock, and it shall be opened unto you: for whoso asketh receiveth, and he that seeketh findeth; and to him that knocketh it shall be opened."

Reflect, also, *Upon the uselessness of every thing short of a full surrender to the Lord.* O foolish Galatians, says the apostle, who has bewitched you that you should not obey the truth, before whose eyes Jesus Christ has been evidently set forth crucified among you! Are ye so foolish? Having suffered so many things in vain, if it be yet in vain? And so we may say to you. Why did you begin the work, and employ labour and expense, if you did not intend to finish! Why have you read, and heard, and prayed, and denied yourselves, and bought Bibles, and paid for sittings year after year to no purpose?—for to no purpose it will be, if you go no farther. What says Bunyan!—"So I saw there was a way to hell by the gate of heaven." But it matters not how nigh you go to the kingdom of God if you do not enter it.

Then remember *The wretchedness of indecision.* Nothing is more dissatisfying, yea, distressing, than to be in a strait between two counter-attractions, by which we are drawn now to the one side and now to the other; and the greater the interest depending, the more perplexity and uneasiness will be felt till we are fixed, and can follow our choice with undivided attention. An Infidel must be a stranger to satisfaction while any doubts haunt his mind; for the subject in question is so infinitely momentous, that entire conviction alone can give him ease. The sinner cannot enjoy a wicked course while conscience rebukes him; his peace and pleasure, therefore, require him to get rid of the reprover, or to give up sin. Upon this principle, how many are there in our day who neither enjoy the world nor religion! They lose the world for religion's sake; and they lose religion for the world's sake.

There is no pursuing any thing to advantage unless the heart be in it; neither can it yield us happiness. We must draw nigh to God before we can find it good for us. We must walk in wisdom's ways before we can find them pleasantness and peace. We must enter into the spirit of Christianity before we realize its comforts or benefits.

Finally, Think of *The danger of hesitation.* This will appear from three things.

First, if you stop without a full decision, the impressions you feel will soon diminish and decline. And are not some of you instances of this? You were once easily alarmed; but your tremblings have ceased. You have not, perhaps, assassinated your convictions, but you have starved them. Oh! had you nourished them! Oh! had you yielded to them! what might you now have been!

Secondly, They will leave you worse than they found you. You will be less receptive of pious influence. The heart, too hard before, is now more hardened through the deceitfulness of sin, and familiarity with the means of grace, and the judicial impenitence to which provocation induces God to leave a man, so that in seeing he sees not, and in hearing he hears not; and the savour of life unto life becomes the savour of death unto death. For,

Thirdly, They will increase and aggravate your final condemnation. In themselves these excitements were blessings. They had a merciful design. They were calls of love, but they were not answered; they were visitations of grace, but they were rejected. Therefore, says the insulted Sovereign and Benefactor, "Because I have called, and ye refused; I have stretched out my hand, and no man regarded: but ye have set at naught all my counsel, and would none of my reproof: I also will laugh at your calamity, I will mock when your fear cometh; when your fear cometh as desolation, and your destruction cometh as a whirlwind, when distress and anguish cometh upon you. Then shall they call upon me, but I will not answer: they shall seek me early, but they shall not find me; for that they hated knowledge, and did not choose the fear of the Lord. They would none of my counsel; they despised all my reproof. Therefore, shall they eat of the fruit of their own way, and be filled with their own devices." And, therefore, a thousand times better would it have been for you if you had never known such thoughts and feelings as you have neglected and abused. O how dreadful will it be to see the glory of the saints, and to know that you might have shared it, and were just within reach of it! In a word, though you hover between sin and holiness, religion and the world now, you will not be left in a middle state when you come to die; but be turned into hell with all the nations that forget God. Though enlightened and convinced, you will have your portion in the same misery with the vilest profligate; yea, it will be more tolerable for Sodom and Gomorrah in the day of judgment than for you.

I have now finished the series of reflections on the CHRISTIAN. I know not what effect it *has* produced, but I know what effect it *ought* to have produced; for it has called forth the truth as it is in Jesus; and presented not only a faithful saying, but one worthy of all acceptation. It is therefore not a vain thing; it is your life. It is all your salvation, and should be all your desire.

And can you, my dear hearers, be satisfied with the acknowledgment of this poor, wretched prince—and behold, and wonder, and perish!

If *you* can be satisfied, your *preacher* cannot. He has therefore warned you, and admonished you, and invited you, and again beseeches you not to give sleep to your eyes, or slumber to your eyelids, till you have some reason to conclude you are Christians indeed, and in truth.

And now, may he not deem himself authorized to press for an answer, while he asks, How long halt ye between two opinions? Who is on the Lord's side? Who will consecrate his service this day unto the Lord?

Will any of you, my dear *children?* You remember little Samuel, who, when the Lord called to him, said, "Speak, Lord, for thy servant heareth." The same Lord, though invisible, is not far from any one of you. Go to him by prayer, and say, Lord, receive me graciously, and make me and keep me thine forever. In the days of his flesh he rebuked those who would have hindered them, and said, "Suffer little children to come unto me, and forbid them not, for of such is the kingdom of heaven." Yea, he showed not only his tenderness towards them as infants, but his regard for them as disciples, and therefore said, "Whoso receiveth one of these little ones in my name, receiveth me."

Will any of you, my *youthful* friends? O that *you* would exemplify the language of the prophet, and show that the eye of inspiration saw you, and you, and you, when it pronounced, "One shall say I am the Lord's; and another shall call himself by the name of Jacob; and another shall subscribe with his hand unto the Lord, and surname himself by the name of Israel!" O how lovely would you appear, dedicating to the Lord the best of your time, and the prime of your affections, dressed in all the graces of the Spirit! How useful would you prove in beginning so soon to serve your generation by the will of God! What distinguished regards would you acquire from Him who has said, I love them that love me, and they that seek me early shall peculiarly find me! Thus, if your days should be prolonged till time snows upon you, the hoary head shall

R   11*

be a crown of glory, being found in the way of righteousness: or if a mortal messenger should early call for you (and how many die at your age!), you will the sooner only leave a vale of tears and enter the joy of your Lord.

Or will any of you, my *old* friends? *You* should seriously and earnestly have thought of this a great while ago. How sad and sinful is it, that you have allowed so much of your threescore years and ten to run to waste! Your life is nearly ending, and your work is not even begun! What can you see in looking backward, but guilt; or in looking forward, but gloom? Need I tell you what everything else tells you, that there is but a step between you and death? It is time, it is high time to awake out of sleep; and let me add, with hope and trembling, that it is not too late. You cannot, like Mnason, be an old disciple in grace, but you may be an old disciple in age, and be accepted at the eleventh hour. But to-day, if you will hear his voice, harden not your heart, lest this should be the last call, and you should suddenly be destroyed, and that without remedy.

Or will none of you who are in the *midst of life*, with all its engagements around you? We do not ask you to abandon society, and resign your secular concerns; but we beseech you to remember that you have souls as well as bodies, and that you are heirs of eternity as well as citizens of time. We allow, Be not slothful in business, is a Divine command; but surely no less binding is the added injunction, Be fervent in spirit, serving the Lord. The hand of the diligent maketh rich; but with all your gettings you will be poor and miserable without the one thing needful. Labour, therefore, not only or chiefly for the meat that perisheth, but for that meat which endureth unto everlasting life, and which the Son of man shall give unto you; for him hath God the Father sealed.

And now, O Lord, the source of all success, I turn to Thee! Give testimony to the word of thy grace. Thou knowest how affectionately, faithfully, and earnestly I have again addressed this people: "Count them worthy of this calling, and fulfil in them all the good pleasure of thy goodness and the work of faith with power, that the name of our Lord Jesus Christ may be glorified in them, and they in him, according to the grace of our God and the Lord Jesus Christ. Amen."

THE

DOMESTIC MINISTER'S ASSISTANT;

OR

PRAYERS

FOR

THE USE OF FAMILIES.

PREFACE.

If in the title of this volume the Author has used the word "Minister," in rather an unusual latitude, its adjective will serve to explain and restrict it. The "Domestic" minister intends not the pastor or preacher, not the servant of the Most High God, who officially shows unto men the way of salvation—but he who adopts the resolution of Joshua—As for *me* and my *house*, *we* will serve the Lord.

The preservation and spread of religion should not depend exclusively on a particular order of men, however important their function may be. All Christians, in their respective stations, ought to co-operate with those who are by designation workers together with God.

It ought to be a matter of thankfulness that the number of ministers properly so called, who enter into the spirit of their office, and preach the truth as it is in Jesus, is exceedingly increased. But compared with the field and the vastness of the work, the labourers are yet few. And few they would be found if multiplied a thousand-fold; and we should *still* need the property, the talents, the influence, the example, the exertions, the prayers of *all* the subjects of divine grace.

And can their services be dispensed with *now?* God is not the God of confusion, but of peace: and He has said, Let every thing be done decently and in order. It is his providence that determines the bounds of our habitation, and furnishes the several stations we occupy; and into *these* we are to look for our duties and opportunities. Men are often led out of their own proper sphere of action in order to be useful; but it is ignorance, if not discontent and pride that tempts them astray.

As the stream of a river is most lovely and beneficial when it patiently steals along its own channel, though it makes not so much noise, and excites not so much notice as when it breaks over its banks, and roars and rolls as a flood—so good men are most acceptable and useful in their appointed course. Wisdom will estimate every man by what he is, not out of his place and calling, but in them. *There* we naturally look after him; there we unavoidably compare him with his obligations; there we see him habitually; and there he gains a character, or goes without one.

It is to be feared that some even of the stricter professors of religion have a zeal of God, but not according to knowledge. It blazes at a distance; but it burns dim at home. In a day like the present, there will be many *occasional* calls of public *duty;* but it will be a sad exclamation to make at a dying hour, " My own vineyard have I not kept." In the spiritual still more than in the temporal neglect, " He that provideth not for his own, especially those of his own house, hath denied the faith, and is worse than an infidel."

3

" You wish to serve your generation." It is well that it is in your heart; but let it be according to the will of God. And how does this require you to proceed? From public relation into private, or from private into public? Does it order you to waste time and strength, to go to a *distance*, and begin labouring, where difficulties will be too great, and means too few to allow of your improving the waste back to your own door? Or to begin *near*, to cultivate onward, to clear and fertilize the ground as you advance, so as to feel every acquisition already made, converted into a resource to encourage, support, and assist you in your future toil?

" You long to be useful." And why are you not? Can you want either opportunity or materials? *You* who are placed at the head of families? *You* who are required to rule well your own households, to dwell with your wives according to knowledge, to train up your children in the nurture and admonition of the Lord, to behave towards your servants as remembering that you also have a master in heaven?—Behold O man of God, a congregation endeared and attentive, committed to thy trust. Behold a flock whom you may feed with knowledge and understanding; and before whom you may walk as an example in word, in conversation, in charity, in spirit, in faith, in purity. Behold a church in thy house. Behold an altar on which to offer the morning and evening sacrifice of prayer and of praise.

Here observe these things, without preferring one before another; here teach and exhort, and reprove with all longsuffering and patience; here officiate—and " Ye shall be named the PRIESTS of the Lord; men shall call you the MINISTERS of our God."

The remark of BAXTER is worthy our regard: " If family religion was duly attended to and properly discharged, I think the preaching of the word would not be the common instrument of conversion." And GURNAL says, " The family is the nursery of the church. If the nursery be neglected, what in time will become of the gardens and the orchards?"

The Author will not endeavour to establish the duty of domestic worship. Many excellent things have been written upon this subject; and what he himself could offer in support of the practice is already before the public.*

It is futile to allege as some have done, that there is no positive and express command for it in the Scripture; when nothing could be more easy than to prove the will of God—from the simplest deductions, from the fairest reasonings, and from the most generally acknowledged principles.

The examples of the faithful; the commendations which God has bestowed upon them in his word; his promises and threatenings; the obvious and numberless advantages resulting from domestic devotion, as to personal religion and relative government, with regard to those that preside in the family—and as to instruction, restraints, and motives, with regard to relations, children, and servants:—All this must surely be enough to induce any man capable of conviction, to terminate with a broken heart the mischiefs of neglect; and to swear unto the Lord, and vow unto the mighty God of Jacob—" Surely, I will not come into the tabernacle of my house, nor go up into my bed, I will not give sleep to mine eyes, nor slumber to mine eyelids, until I find out a place for the Lord, an habitation for the mighty God of Jacob."

As to the objections arising from—shame, a want of time, the unfashionableness of the usage, or its interfering with visits or dissipations: all this

---

* See the Introduction to the Author's four volumes of Short Discourses for the Use of Families.

in a being who yet owns himself to be a moral and accountable creature, is unworthy of argument, and would be too much honoured by the attempt of refutation.

There is one thing however which deserves notice. It is the apprehension of inability to perform this duty. With respect to some, if not many, it is no breach of charity to conclude that this is an *excuse* rather than a *reason*. It is disinclination, or at least the want of a more powerful conviction that hinders them from adopting this salutary usage, rather than incapacity. There are few cases in which the old adage is not to be verified. " Where there is a will, there is a way." You feel little difficulty in making known your distresses or your wishes to a fellow-creature: and the Lord looketh, not to the excellency of the language, but to the heart. The facility would be increased by practice and the divine blessing.

And I cannot but earnestly recommend the use of free and extemporaneous prayer, where it is practicable. There is in it a freshness, a particularity, an appropriateness, an immediate adoption and use of circumstances and events, which cannot be found in the best composed forms.

Yet there are those who have only a slender degree of religious knowledge, or discover a natural slowness and hesitancy of utterance, or feel a bashfulness of temper, so that they cannot gain confidence enough even to make a proper trial. And this diffidence is often found, even with persons of education and understanding—Indeed such are more likely to feel difficulty than the vulgar and illiterate, whose ignorance is friendly to fluency, and whose confidence is not perplexed by modes of expression, or embarrassed by the influence of reputation.

Now in cases of inability, or extreme difficulty, surely the greatest zealot for extemporary prayer would recommend forms in preference to neglect.

Besides, there are others—many in the Establishment, and no few out of it—who deem a form more eligible; and it is needless to remark that they have a right to their opinion—and as their practice will of course be regulated by it, it is desirable to aid them in their own way.

And surely in this case, as well as in many others, where we see so much talent, and religion, and even devotional taste, in the opposing advocates, candour requires and compels the concession, that all the arguments, all the advantages, cannot be on *one* side of the question.

Bigotry delights in exclusion; but the meekness of wisdom is satisfied with preference, and freely says, Let every one be fully persuaded in his own mind. The amiable Dr. WATTS observes, " Many a holy soul has found his inward powers awakened and excited to lively religion, in the use of a form, where the wants and wishes of the heart have been happily expressed : and considering the various infirmities that surround human nature, even the wisest and best of men may be glad of such assistance at some seasons."

Several books of prayers have issued from the press; and it is not necessary to undervalue or conceal them, in order to excuse or even justify another effort in the same cause. The great excellency of some of these composures is well known.

Yet it must be confessed that such works, compared with other religious publications, are still very few; and that the far greater part of what we possess is more for personal and private use than domestic. Even in the deservedly popular volume of JENKS, there are only *family* prayers for *one week ;* the rest are all for *individual* service.

1*

But whatever might have been the Author's own opinion of the expediency or necessity of such a work as this—in order to furnish a greater abundance, or to accommodate a difference of tastes, or to excite attention by newness, or to edify more by brevity and simplicity—he can truly aver, that he was principally induced to undertake it at the request of many, urged for years with importunity.

In complying with their desires, he still fears he shall not satisfy their wishes. He unquestionably has not satisfied his own. In the want of that leisure which allows a man to throw his whole soul into the composition of his work, and then to employ all his skill in correcting and completing it, he has done in a few months, at the intervals of much public duty and interruption what he could. Should the effort obtain acceptance, he shall consider it the greatest honour that could have been conferred upon him, that the service of God should ever be performed in words which he has furnished so imperfectly.

He can reckon on some esteemed connexions whose partiality, as it has often admitted him into their circles as a friend, and employed him at their domestic altar as an expositor and intercessor, will retain him as an assistant, in this volume; and thus while absent in body, he will be present with them in spirit. He is also blessed with children, who will not neglect the practice, to which in the order of a happy family they were so early accustomed, and which was never rendered irksome by tediousness; and *they* will—yes he knows they will—train up *their* children in the same holy and lovely usage. And should relationship and endearment serve to render the book the more valued and useful, as a sacred bequest to this descendants, this alone would keep him from thinking he had laboured in vain.

Percy Place, April, 1820

ADVERTISEMENT.

The Author begs leave to offer a few words on the execution of the work itself, here submitted to public attention.

Family prayers ought to be short, especially where reading the Scripture makes a part of the service, and it ought always to make a part. Hence the prayers for the week-days may be read in five or six minutes: those for the Sabbath are commonly a little longer, as families have then more leisure and are more united: those for particular occasions, as they rarely return, and the events are remarkable, are the longest of all.

A prayer is distinguishable from the repetition of a creed, or the annunciation of a system of theology: how much more from the sparring and reflections of controversy! A tincture of the Author's own particular sentiments was hardly avoidable; but he has sought after nothing that would be offensive to Christians who differ from him. And as religious persons accord much more when kneeling than sitting, he ventures to think no one will be unable to join in these forms, who believes in the fall of man, the redemption of the cross, justification by faith, the necessity of divine influence, and of that holiness without which we cannot see the Lord. The Author braves the suspicion of those who are illiberal enough to gauge a man's orthodoxy by the use of an invariable doxology, in the language too which man's wisdom teacheth. Not that he thinks it wrong to close a prayer with a scriptural meaning in human terms; but he prefers the words which the Holy Ghost useth; and where they afford a diversity, why should we be afraid to avail ourselves of it? In this respect the sacred writers would not bear the ordeal of some system-critics.

The Author thinks no one can blame him for using so much of the language of the Scripture: there is a sacredness in it, and it is well known; much of it too has been used devotionally; and contains the adorations, confessions, supplications, and thanksgivings uttered by men of God before us while kneeling at the throne of grace.

Besides being scriptural, he has endeavoured to be very plain and simple in the diction. There is a great difference between addressing men, and addressing God. The least artificial mode of uttering our thoughts in prayer is the best. Prayer admits of no brilliancies; every studied ornament it rejects with disdain. He who feels interested in prayer will forget all critical and elaborate phraseology. And it is an infelicity to be deplored rather than an excellency to be admired, when ingenuity of thought or surprisingness of expression catches and keeps off the attention from devotion. There are young divines who not only err in preaching, by substituting finery for elegance, and the affectation of art for the eloquence of feeling; but in their devotional exercises, too, showing off their tawdriness even in the presence of God, and praying in a strained inflated style, unintelligible to the ignorant, lamented by the pious, and contemned by the wise. The greatest men have always been distinguished by the plainness and simplicity of their devotional language. What a difference is there between the other compositions of Johnson and his prayers! No hard word, no elaborate sentence, no

7

classical, no metaphorical allusion, is to be found in any of the new forms of devotion which he has left us. The same excellency pervades the Liturgy. And it is worthy of remark, that in no prayer recorded in the Bible, is any figure employed, unless as familiar as the literal expression.

This however does not forbid the use of sentences not *directly* of the nature of petition. Prayer is designed not only as an homage to God, but as a moral exercise to affect ourselves; and to accomplish this purpose, we must be informed or reminded. What therefore tends to make us *feel* the things we implore, is not to be considered, as some call it, a preaching or talking in prayer. Read all the prayers given us in the Scripture: there is not one of them which does not contain expressions of enlargement not immediately petitionary, yet conducive to the design.

With regard to appropriateness, JENKS has observed, " That we may as well expect to find a shoe that will fit every foot, as a form of prayer to suit every purpose." Family prayers must be necessarily general, or adapted to the state of a household *devoid of its peculiarities.* No form can be made to include every particular circumstance or occurrence; the very things that would render it suitable to one family, would even hinder the use of it by another. The Author fears whether in a few instances he has not forgotten this.

Yet events and circumstances are perpetually arising, and it is of great importance to notice them *devotionally.* Almost every prayer recorded in the Scriptures arose out of particular occurrences, and was designed to improve them. Here is a difficulty which there is only one way of removing. It is by adding some short addresses applicable to certain events and circumstances, and which the reader may insert in their proper place in the prayer, or use at the end of it. Many of these therefore the Author has supplied in the close of the volume. Many more might have been added, had the prayers been designed for *personal* and *private* use.

In such *multiplied* forms of the same kind, it was not easy to maintain so much diversity as some would wish. Family devotion in itself admits of less variety than either private or public worship. But though similarity will be sometimes found, sameness he believes, with a very few trifling exceptions, has been avoided. This does not extend however to the repetition of the same *scripture* sentences.

The Author has felt what a difference there is between offering and writing a prayer; but he endeavoured as much as possible when he retired to compose, to place himself by thought in the situation of performance; and followed the same mode in writing which he has always found the best in praying, to exclude formality and to gain variety—to yield to the *present* feeling of the mind, whether it leads to indulge *principally* in confession, or in thanksgiving, petition, or intercession.

Some things must be *always* expressed; others can only be admitted *occasionally.* Yet these should not be forgotten. Cases of affliction; the state of public affairs; the nation; the cause of God in the world: these and other things, though not particularized in every exercise, must be noticed so frequently as to keep the mind alive to them.

With regard to the prayers for particular occasions—such as pertain to days of mourning, fasting, or thanksgiving; and those which respect the beginning and end of the year—will draw forth no objection. But as to those which regard religious *festivals,* some will probably condemn the Author on the ground of consistency. On that ground he is willing to be tried. Consistency refers to professed principles: and he avows principles which raise him above any particular body of Christians, while yet he deems it his honour to belong to one of them in preference to all others.

But his attachment to his regiment does not make him an enemy to the army of which it is a part. Let every one of us, says the Apostle, please his neighbour for his good to edification. Why should not the Author wish to be serviceable to members of other communions, as well as to those of his own?

Dr. WATTS, though a firm Pædobaptist, has yet composed and inserted in his excellent book, several hymns adapted to the convictions of those who practise adult baptism by immersion only.

And the late Mr. NEWTON, though an Episcopalian, made no scruple when de sired to draw up a plan for a Dissenting academy.

"Let us stand in the liberty wherewith Christ has made us free. Let not him that eateth, despise him that eateth not; and let not him that eateth not, judge him that eateth, for God hath received him. Who art thou that judgest another man's servant? to his own master he standeth or falleth. One man esteemeth one day above another, another esteemeth every day alike. Let every man be fully persuaded in his own mind. He that regardeth the day, regardeth it unto the Lord: and he that regardeth not the day, to the Lord he doth not regard it." Here every thing non-essential is left, where it ought to be left, to individual *conviction* and *candour*.

Upon these principles, the Author thinks, a Dissenter without superstition may use these forms on these *very days;* especially as he is under no compulsion, and he has nothing to do with the day, but as a season of leisure, and as remind-ing him of some important truth.

A Christian however, if he disregards the seasons, must love the *subjects* con-nected with them; and at some time or other, he may wish more *expressly* to notice them: and this he can do by means of these forms, with the omission of a few words.

It is comparatively easy to be long and diffuse; but to be select and yet full, brief and yet comprehensive—this is the trial.

The Author could have composed a single prayer, far superior to any of these; but the difficulty lay in the number; and the work must be judged of as a whole.

It is hardly necessary to observe, that with a slight alteration, and the substi-tution of the singular number for the plural, most of these prayers will serve for the Closet as well as the Family.

B

CONTENTS.

PART I.

PRAYERS FOR MORNING AND EVENING

PART II.

PRAYERS FOR SELECT OCCASIONS.

PART III.

SHORT DEVOTIONS TO BE USED OCCASIONALLY.

First.—PETITIONS FOR PARTICULAR OCCASIONS.

Secondly.—PIOUS ADDRESSES FOR PARTICULAR SEASONS.

Thirdly.—THANKSGIVINGS FOR PARTICULAR EVENTS

Fourthly.—ACTS OF DEVOTION FOR THE TABLE.

FAMILY PRAYERS.

FIRST WEEK.

SUNDAY MORNING.

O come, let us worship and fall down, let us kneel before the Lord our Maker, for He is our God, and we are the people of his pasture and the sheep of his hand.

Yes, O Lord, we are thine; and Thee we are bound to serve. We grieve to think how many of our fellow-creatures live without Thee in the world; and confess with shame, that other lords have had dominion over *us*: but henceforth by Thee only will we make mention of thy name. We hope Thou hast subdued the insensibility and indifference towards Thyself, so awfully natural to us; and awakened in us the inquiry, Where is God my maker, that giveth songs in the night? We hope we are disposed to acknowledge Thee in all our ways; but we feel our need of the exercises of devotion. We trust we hold communion with Thee every day; but we find week-days to be worldly days; and our allowed intercourse with secular concerns tends to reduce our heavenly impressions, and to make us forgetful of our work, and our rest. We therefore bless Thee for the return of a day sacred to our souls and eternity;—a time of refreshing from the presence of the Lord;—in which, by waiting upon Thee, our hearts are enlarged, and our strength is renewed; so that we can mount up with wings as eagles, run and not be weary, and walk and not faint.

This is the day which the Lord hath made, we will rejoice and be glad in it. O let our minds be withdrawn from the world, as well as our bodies. Let our retirement be devout. Let our meditation be sweet. Let our conversation be edifying. Let our reading be pious. Let our hearing be profitable—and on Thee may we wait all the day!

Afford us the supply of the spirit of Jesus Christ. None can need thy succours more than we. Thou knowest our infirmities—Let thy strength be made perfect in our weakness. Our duties are far above our own power —Let thy grace be sufficient for us. Our dangers are numberless, and we are utterly unable to keep ourselves from falling—Hold Thou us up, and we shall be safe. The burdens we feel would press our lives down to the ground—Lay underneath us thine everlasting arms. Fears alarm us; cares corrode us; losses impoverish us; our very affections are the sources of our afflictions; surely man walketh in a vain show, surely we are disquieted in vain: all, all is vanity and vexation of spirit—While in the world we have tribulation, in Thee may we have peace; and in the multitude of our thoughts within us, may thy comforts delight our souls!

Yet O Lord we would remember, that gratitude becomes us much more than complaint. Our afflictions have been light compared with our guilt; and few compared with the sufferings of others. They have all been attended with numberless alleviations; they have all been needful; all founded in a regard to our welfare; all designed to work together for our good. We bless Thee for what is past; and trust Thee for what is future; and cast all our care upon Thee, knowing that Thou carest for us.

Thou hast commanded us to pray for all men, that we may be bound by our very devotions, as we have opportunity, to do good unto all men, especially unto them that are of the household of faith. May we always cherish and display benevolent dispositions towards our dependents; forgiving dispositions towards our enemies; peaceable dispositions towards our neighbours; and candid dispositions towards our fellow Christians. May we be able to say with our Lord and Saviour, *Whosoever* shall do the will of my Father that is in heaven, the same is my brother, and sister, and mother; and pray with Paul, Grace be with *all* them that love our Lord Jesus Christ in sincerity!

May the goings of our God and King be seen this day in every Christian sanctuary Go with *us* to thy house, and give testimony to the word of thy grace. May it have free course, and be glorified in the hearts and lives of those that shall hear it. May it enlighten the ignorant; awaken the careless, reclaim the wandering; establish the weak;

comfort the feeble-minded; and make ready a people prepared for the Lord!

Remember those who are this day denied our advantages. Be a little sanctuary to them in the midst of their privations; and let them know that Thou art not confined to temples made with hands. And O forget not those who never enjoyed our privileges; never smiled when a sabbath appeared; never heard of the name of a Saviour—and let thy way be known on earth, thy saving health among all nations! Our Father which art in heaven, hallowed be thy name. Thy kingdom come. Thy will be done in earth, as it is in heaven. Give us this day our daily bread. And forgive us our trespasses, as we forgive them that trespass against us. And lead us not into temptation; but deliver us from evil: for thine is the kingdom, and the power, and the glory, for ever and ever. Amen.

SUNDAY EVENING.

Who is like unto Thee, O Lord, among the gods! Who is like Thee, glorious in holiness, fearful in praises, doing wonders! May we approach Thee with the humility which is due to thy greatness, and the hope that becomes thy goodness. For though Thou art high, yet hast Thou respect unto the lowly; and though continually adored by thrones and dominions, principalities and powers, yet Thou despisest not the prayer of the destitute, but wilt hear their prayer. Our fathers cried unto Thee, and were delivered. They trusted in Thee, and were not confounded. And Thou never saidst to the seed of Jacob, Seek ye me in vain.

Behold a company of sinners at thy footstool, earnestly praying to be remembered with the favour Thou bearest unto thy people, and to be visited with thy salvation! We would not overlook the blessings of the life that now is. If we have food, and raiment, and agreeable connexions, and ease, and health, and safe abode, we would bless Thee; for we have no claim to these bounties, and our present condition renders them valuable. But they are not our God;—

Give what thou canst, without Thee we are poor,
And with Thee rich, take what Thou wilt away.

—Thou art the strength of our hearts, and our portion for ever. Whom have we in heaven but Thee? and there is none upon earth that we desire beside Thee.

And praise waiteth for Thee, O God, in Zion. We long to be able with unshaken confidence, to apply the promises of thy grace to ourselves; and to say, Thou shalt guide me with thy counsel, and afterwards receive me to glory. O say to our souls, in language our consciences can understand, I am thy salvation; and give us as a token for good, that we may rejoice in Thee.

Yet O God, we would not rest satisfied with a conviction of our relation to Thee, while we are regardless of improving it. May we walk worthy of the Lord, unto all pleasing, being fruitful in every good work, and increasing in the knowledge of God; strengthened with all might according to his gracious power, unto all patience and long suffering with joyfulness; giving thanks unto the Father who hath made us meet to be partakers of the inheritance of the saints in light. We can never discharge the obligations thy abundant mercy has laid us under: but may we ever show that we are sensible of them; and that our impressed hearts are asking, *What* shall I render unto the Lord for all his benefits towards me? While we hear Thee saying, O do not that abominable thing which I hate, may we be effectually deterred from sin, and induced to watch and pray, lest we enter into temptation. May thy love be shed abroad in our hearts, that none of thy commandments may be grievous. May thy glory be dear to us: may we inquire after thy will with impartiality, and conform ourselves to it with diligence. Uphold us by thy free spirit; and let the words of our mouths and the meditations of our hearts be acceptable in thy sight, O Lord, our strength and our redeemer!

Hitherto we have been compelled to exclaim, My leanness, my leanness! We have been no better in religion than a bruised reed or smoking flax. But it is our mercy, that Thou dost not despise the day of small things; and our encouragement, that Thou givest more grace; that Thou hast promised to perfect that which concerneth us; and commanded us to ask and receive that our joy may be full. May we therefore not only be humble, but active; may we not only shake off sloth, but despondency; may we be strong in the Lord, and in the power of his might; and increase with all—the increase of God, till we are filled with all—the fulness of God!

Thou knowest what is in man, and what is necessary to him. Thou art not only addressing us continually by the voice of creation, and the varying events of thy providence, but Thou hast given us thy word and thine ordinances. We behold our sabbaths, our eyes see our teachers, and our ears hear the joyful sound of salvation by the cross, and the grace of our Lord Jesus. Prophets and righteous men desired to see the things that we see, and did not see them; and to hear the things that we hear, and did not hear them. But blessed are our eyes, for they see; and our ears, for they hear. Yet we would remember, that our responsibility will be answerable to our talents; that our chief danger results from our greatest privileges; and that our very blessings may be converted into a curse. We would therefore fear, lest a promise being left us of entering into thy rest, any of us should seem to come short of it.

Bless this family. May those of us who are at the head of it, walk within our house with a perfect heart, and set no wicked thing before our eyes. May we have a testimony in the bosoms of those who have the best opportunities of observing us, that in simplicity and godly sincerity, not with fleshly wisdom, but by thy grace, we have our conversation in the world, and more especially to themward. May we conduct ourselves towards those who serve us, as knowing that we have a master in heaven, and that there is no respect of persons with God; and may our servants, in fulfilling the duties of their station, serve the Lord Christ. May we train up our children in the nurture and admonition of the Lord; and have the inexpressible satisfaction of seeing them walk in the truth. We ask not great things for them of a worldly nature; only give them health of body, and soundness of mind, and food and raiment convenient and sufficient for them: but O bless them with all spiritual blessings, and number them with thy saints in glory everlasting! Pity those parents whose hearts are bleeding over children of disobedience; and hear all the pious, whose irreligious relations are forcing them often to exclaim, How shall I endure to see the destruction of my kindred!

Hast not Thou made of one blood all the nations of men that dwell upon the face of all the earth? Remember the work of thy hands. Have respect unto thy holy covenant; and let the world know, that Thou hast so loved it, as to give thy only begotten Son, that whosoever believeth in Him should not perish, but have everlasting life.

Hear the prayers which have this day been offered for our native country, for our rightful sovereign, and for the government under which we live. It is a good land which the Lord our God hath given us: Thou hast done great things for us whereof we are glad: May we never grow insensible of our privileges, and provoke Thee by our sins to remove them. May they be continued to the latest posterity; and be sanctified to us and to our children. As thou hast given us such a distinguished rank among the nations, may we be for a name and a praise unto Thee in the whole earth: and as we are so largely the subjects of thy goodness, may we be the instruments too; and from us may the word of the Lord sound out into every land.

Now unto Him that is able to do exceeding abundantly above all that we ask or think, according to the power that worketh in us, unto Him be glory in the church by Christ Jesus throughout all ages, world without end. Amen.

2

MONDAY MORNING.

O Thou God of all grace; the Father of mercies; the hope of Israel, the Saviour thereof in the time of trouble! Why hast Thou revealed Thyself in such lovely characters and endearing relations, but to meet our dejections, to remove our fears, and induce us to say, It is good for me to draw nigh to God!

We come to Thee as criminals to be pardoned, as beggars to obtain relief, and as friends to enjoy communion with the God of love. We bow with submission and gratitude to the method which Thou hast appointed and made known for all intercourse between Thee and us. We approach Thee through Him in whom Thou hast proclaimed Thyself well pleased, pleading the propitiation of his blood, and making mention of his righteousness, and of his only.

But we can have access to Thee through Him only—by one Spirit—that Spirit, the residue of which is with Thee, and which has actuated the souls of thy people in all ages. O give thy Holy Spirit to them that now ask Thee! May He open the eyes of our understanding and convince us of sin. May He humble the pride of our self-righteous hearts, and expel us from every refuge of lies. May He glorify Christ in our wants, desires, dependence, and application; and take of the things of Christ and show them to us. May we be enabled to receive the Lord Jesus in all his blessings and influences; and though now we see Him not, yet believing, may we rejoice with joy unspeakable and full of glory. In all the distresses of conscience, in all the afflictions of life, and in all the dissatisfactions necessarily experienced in creature-enjoyments, may we repair weary and heavy laden, to *Him* who has promised to give us rest. May the vanity of the world wean us from its pursuits; and may the tribulation of the world endear the peace which no storm can either prevent or destroy!

May we arise, and depart hence; may we confess ourselves to be only strangers and pilgrims upon earth; and declare plainly—too plainly to be misunderstood, that we seek a better country even an heavenly. Prepare us for all the allotments of this short, and changing, and uncertain life. May we have a safe passage out of it, and a comfortable passage through it, and a useful residence in it. May we continually illustrate in our character and conduct, the representations Thou hast given of thy people, as the dew of heaven, the salt of the earth, the light of the world. May we never deem it enough to be blameless and harmless; but may our light so shine before men, that they may see our good works and glorify our Father which is in Heaven. May we never be ashamed of Jesus, nor of his words; never be deterred from the prosecution of a known duty, by the fear of man; and never be discouraged from attempting it, by a consciousness of our own weakness. Having thy sanction and presence, may we be strong and courageous; and be steadfast and unmoveable; always abounding in the work of the Lord.

What we know not, teach Thou us. Lead us into all truth. May we see divine things in a divine light, that while they inform our judgment, they may sanctify the heart, and consecrate the whole life to the service and glory of God. Who can understand his errors? Cleanse Thou us from secret faults. Search us, O God, and know our hearts; try us, and know our thoughts, and see if there be any wicked way in us, and lead us in the way everlasting.

Accept of our united thanksgivings for the preservation and refreshment of the past night: and take us under thy guiding and guardian care this day; and whether we eat or drink, or whatever we do, may we do all to the glory of God, through our Lord and Saviour. Amen.

MONDAY EVENING.

We have heard, that to the Lord our God belong mercies and forgivenesses, though we have rebelled against him. Hence we are encouraged to approach Thee. For we are verily guilty, we are deeply guilty. If our depravity has not always broken forth into action, our hearts have been deceitful above all things and desperately wicked; and if our transgressions have not been so gross as those of many of our fellow-creatures, they have been more aggravated, because committed against goodness the most astonishing, light the most clear, and advantages the most distinguishing. And Thou hast seen all, and abhorred all, and couldst easily and righteously have punished us for all. But Thou hast not executed upon us the fierceness of thine anger, because Thou art God and not man. Neither hast Thou treated us with neglect; but Thou hast remembered us in our low estate; and not only without our desert, but without our desire, Thou wast pleased to devise means for our restoration to thy favour, and image, and presence.

We bless Thee for a purpose of grace given us in Christ Jesus before the world began. We rejoice that in the fulness of time he assumed our nature, and became obedient unto death, even the death of the cross: and that as he was delivered for our offences, so he was raised again for our justification, and ascending up on high, entered into the holy place, as a proof of the sufficiency and acceptance of the sacrifice he offered. We rejoice that he has received the whole dispensation of the Spirit, and that in him all fulness dwells. And we bless Thee for the proclamations of the gospel, which hold him forth to our view in all his grace, and glory, and unsearchable riches, that we through patience and comfort of the scripture might have hope.

O Thou God of hope, fill us with all joy and peace in believing thy promises and invitations, that we may abound in hope through the power of the Holy Ghost. May we esteem all things but loss for the excellency of the knowledge of Christ Jesus our Lord; and may we supremely desire to win Christ, knowing that he who hath the Son hath life, and shall never come into condemnation. May we prove that we are joined to the Lord, by being one spirit with him. May our sentiments, tempers, and conduct, be formed after the example which he left us; and may we never consider ourselves Christians, but as we long to be like him, and the life also of Jesus be made manifest in our mortal body. May we never love a world that crucified the Lord of glory; nor suffer those sins to live that caused him to die. May his grace, in becoming poor, that we through his poverty might be rich, make us ashamed of our selfishness; and may his unexampled love, in giving his life a ranson for us, so constrain us, as to render any services or sacrifices for his sake our delight.

May He never be wounded in the house of his professed friends. May we rather die than bring a reproach upon his cause. May all his followers be dear to us. May we recommend him to those who know him not, that they may seek him with us. Let the number of those who love his salvation daily increase; and let the accessions include every member of our household, and all our absent friends. Hasten, O Lord, the blessed hour, when all kings shall fall down before him, and all nations shall serve him—And blessed be his glorious name for ever! And let the whole earth be filled with his glory.

We praise Thee as the length of our days and the God of our mercy. In the morning we committed ourselves to thy care, and Thou hast been with us in our going out and our coming in, and hast kept us in all our ways. Pardon whatever Thou hast seen amiss in us through another period of our time. Accept the charge of us through the approaching night, and grant us the sleep which Thou givest thy beloved: for we hope we desire it not only as creatures, but as Christians; not only to gratify our feelings, but to renew our strength for thy service, and to fit us to glorify Thee in our bodies as well as in our spirits, through our adorable Redeemer. Amen.

TUESDAY MORNING.

O Thou omnipresent and omniscient Jehovah! Thou art about our path, and our lying down. Thou art acquainted with all our ways. There is not a word in our tongue, but, lo! O Lord, thou knowest it altogether. Thou understandest our very thoughts afar off. Yea the darkness hideth not from Thee, but the night shineth as the day: the darkness and the light are both alike to Thee.

Known therefore to Thee are our sins, with every aggravation; and our necessities, with all their circumstances. Yet Thou requirest us to confess our guilt, and to spread our wants before Thee, in order that we ourselves may be suitably affected with them, and be prepared for the promised displays of thy goodness. Every view we take of ourselves convinces us that we lie entirely at thy mercy, and that it is only because thy compassions fail not we are not consumed. We know not the evil there is in one sin; and our iniquities are more in number than the hairs of our head. Thou art our creator: but of the rock that begat us we have been unmindful, and have forgotten the God that formed us. Thou hast nourished and brought up children: but we have rebelled against thee. Thou hast given us laws, founded in a regard to our welfare as well as thine own glory; but we have said with our lives, if not with our lips, Who is the Lord, that we should obey his voice? Thou art the perfection of beauty, the centre of excellency, the source of all blessedness; and Thee we ought to have loved supremely: but we have loved and served the creature more than the Creator; we have loved idols, and after them we have gone. Instead of praying, Lord, lift Thou up the light of thy countenance upon us, we have asked with the multitude, Who will show us any good? Departing from Thee, we have made flesh our arm. We have leaned on broken reeds, and though they have disappointed our hopes, and pierced us through with many sorrows, we have often returned to the same wretched dependence. Thou hast raised up for us a Saviour; and the gospel has presented to our view a plan of redemption and renovation which the angels desire to look into. But we have crowned all our guilt, by neglecting so great salvation, and turning away from Him that speaketh from heaven; and we deserve to be for ever excluded from all the blessings of the cross.

O deal not with us after our desert, but according to our necessity; and where sin has abounded, may grace much more abound. Over all our unworthiness may grace reign through righteousness unto eternal life by Jesus Christ our Lord. It is thy pleasure that we seek Thee. The desires we feel are of thine own producing. We are willing to be saved in thy own way. We love thy salvation; we love it as it is free, and secures to thyself the undivided glory; and we love it as it is holy, and designed to save us from the power as well as the penalty of sin. O

visit us with thy salvation! Shine into our hearts, and give us the light of the knowledge of thy glory in the face of Jesus Christ. Enable us by faith to embrace thy unspeakable gift. May we sit at his feet. May we glory in his cross. May we imbibe his spirit. May we follow his example; and whatsoever we do in word or deed, may we do all in the name of the Lord Jesus.

We extend our wishes beyond the little circle now kneeling in thy presence. We have various absent connexions endeared to our hearts: O place them under thy agency as the God of grace; and keep them under thy care as the God of providence.

We would remember them that are in bonds, as bound with them; and those that suffer adversity, as being ourselves also in the body. Address to the hearts of the afflicted, the promise, I will be with thee in trouble: thy shoes shall be iron and brass, and as thy days so shall thy strength be.

Let glory dwell in our land, and upon all the glory may there be a defence. Do good in thy good pleasure unto Zion; build Thou the walls of Jerusalem. Make bare thine arm in the sight of all the nations; and let all the ends of the earth see the salvation of our God.

May the grace of our Lord Jesus Christ, and the love of God, and the communion of the Holy Ghost, be with us all, now and for evermore. Amen.

TUESDAY EVENING.

O THOU who wast, and art, and art to come, the Almighty! With Thee is the fountain of life. In thy presence there is fulness of joy, and at thy right-hand there are pleasures for evermore. It is our privilege as well as our duty to draw near to Thee. It is the prerogative of our nature, that of all creatures in this lower world, we alone are made capable of knowing, resembling, serving, and enjoying Thee. All our degradation and misery have been produced by our alienation and absence from Thee; and all our happiness and perfection depend upon our reunion and intercourse with Thee. We therefore bless Thee for the revelation Thou hast given us, and by which we learn, that thy thoughts towards us are thoughts of peace and not of evil. We rejoice in a new and living way into the holiest by the blood of Jesus, who has once suffered for sins, the just for the unjust, that he might bring us unto God. We pray that the grand design of his sacrifice may be accomplished in each of us. May we feel that we are brought back from the dreadful distance to which sin had conveyed us, and that we are one with God again: and henceforth may the life that we live in the flesh, be a life of communion with the Father of

S

our spirits and of devotedness to him. May thy service be the employment of our days, and the enjoyment of our hearts. May we love thy commands, and acquiesce in thy dispensations; and then we are at the gate of heaven.

We lament that this has been so little the case with us, since we have known Thee, or rather have been known of Thee. We ought to be ashamed to think, that after all the instructions of thy word, the ordinances of thy house, and the discipline of thy family, our ears are still so dull of hearing, and our hearts so slow to believe; that our souls so cleave unto the dust; that we live so much under the influence of things seen and temporal, and feel so little of the powers of a world to come. How obscure is our knowledge; how weak our faith; how low our hope; how wavering our obedience; how lifeless our worship! O Lord, clothe us with humility; and in this attire help us to present Thee the sacrifice of a broken heart and a contrite spirit, which Thou wilt not despise.

And since Thou art the God of all grace, and hast commanded us to ask and receive that our joy may be full; afford us more of the supply of the spirit of Jesus Christ, to give more decision to our character, and more earnestness to our zeal; that with enlarged hearts in the way of thy commandments we may run and not be weary, and walk and not faint. May we always realise thy presence; and may the thought that thine eye is upon us, operate as a check to sin, an excitement to duty, and a source of consolation. May we bear with firmness and submission the various trials of life and religion, and derive from them all the advantage which they are designed to afford. May we glorify the Lord in the fires, and may every day of trouble afford us an opportunity to prove the truth of thy promise, the tenderness of thy care, and the supports of thy grace. May tribulation work patience, and patience experience, and experience hope.

But how few, how limited, and how light are the afflictions with which we are exercised. How much more reason have we to be thankful than to complain. Bless the Lord, O our souls, and all that is within us bless his holy name. Bless the Lord, O our souls, and forget not all his benefits; who forgiveth all our iniquities; who healeth all our diseases; who redeemeth our lives from destruction; who crowneth us with loving-kindness and tender mercies.

We praise Thee for the protection, the supplies, and the comforts of another day. Take us under thy care for the night on which we have entered. May no evil befall us nor any plague come nigh our dwelling. Refresh our bodies and renew our strength by needful repose; and when we awake, may we be still with God, and rise to love Thee more and serve Thee better than we ever have done, through our Lord and Saviour, to whom be glory for ever and ever. Amen.

WEDNESDAY MORNING.

Again we lift up our eyes unto the hills from whence cometh our help. Our help is in the name of the Lord God who made heaven and earth.

Thou art the author of all existence, and the source of all blessedness. We adore Thee for making us capable of knowing Thee; for possessing us with reason and conscience; and for leading us to inquire, Where is God my maker, that giveth songs in the night! We praise Thee for all the information with which we are favoured to bring us to thyself; especially the revelation of the gospel. Here we look into thy very heart, and see that it is the dwelling-place of pity. Here we see thy thoughts towards us, and find that they are thoughts of peace and not of evil. Here we see Thee waiting to be gracious, and exalted to have mercy. Here Thou hast told our consciences how the guilty can be pardoned, the unholy can be sanctified, and the poor furnished with unsearchable riches.

May we be found in the number of those who not only hear but know the joyful sound, that we may walk in the light of thy countenance, in thy name rejoice all the day, and in thy righteousness be exalted. May we take Thee, the God of truth, at thy word; and believe the record, that Thou hast given to us eternal life, and that this life is in thy Son. And since it is not only a faithful saying, but worthy of all acceptation, that He came into the world to save sinners, to Him may we look alone for salvation, and with all the earnestness the infinite importance of the case requires.

And to Him may we *immediately* repair, remembering how short and uncertain our time is, and filled with holy horror at the thought of closing a life of precious, but neglected privileges with the exclamation, The harvest is past, the summer is ended, and we are not saved. We long for the experience of a present salvation, not only in the comforts, but in the renewings of the Holy Ghost. We desire to have nothing more to do with sin; and pray as sincerely to be restored to thy image, as to be reinstated in thy favour. We implore spiritual graces, as well as spiritual blessings; and pray that we may always value religious duties, as religious privileges. Deliver us from the disposition of the slave, and uphold us in all our goings by thy free spirit; and enable us to run in the way of thy commandments with freedom and delight.

May we cherish simplicity and godly sincerity of character: may we be in reality before God, what we are in appearance before men—Israelites indeed in whom is no guile. May we *be* religious before we profess religion, and leave the world before we enter the church; that we may not be looking back after its forbidden follies and vanities, but with our affections set on things that are above, walk worthy of Him who has called us to his kingdom and glory.

And while we are the partakers of thy grace, may we be also the dispensers of it too. Freely having received, may we freely give. May we feel it to be the sublimest of all satisfactions, and count it the greatest of all rewards, to save a soul from death, and to hide a multitude of sins. And while endeavouring to do good, may we be prepared to bear evil. May we consider Him who endured the contradiction of sinners against himself; and if reviled, revile not again; or if opposed or slighted, never grow weary in well doing.

But we bless Thee that the lines are fallen to us in pleasant places. We are strangers to the sufferings of those who have gone before us; and can not only sit ourselves, but call every man his neighbour under the vine and under the fig-tree. May we avail ourselves of our opportunities; and invite those around us to taste and see that the Lord is good, while it is called to-day, knowing how soon the night cometh wherein no man can work.

O God, count us worthy of this calling, and fulfil in us all the good pleasure of thy goodness, and the work of faith with power; that the Name of our Lord Jesus Christ may be glorified in us, and we in Him, according to the grace of our God, and the Lord Jesus Christ. Amen.

WEDNESDAY EVENING.

O THOU that hearest prayer—Through him who is the great intercessor, let our prayer come before Thee as incense, and the lifting up of our hands as the evening sacrifice. We bless Thee as our creator, the framer of our bodies, and the former of our souls within us. We praise Thee for the blessings of thy providence which encompass us on every side, and are continued to us notwithstanding our unworthiness. Thou hast not only given us life and favour, but thy visitation hath preserved our spirit, and secured our personal and relative comforts.

But above all we thank Thee for thine unspeakable gift. Herein is love, not that we loved God, but that he loved us, and sent his Son to be the propitiation for our sins. Here our hopes find anchorage. Here believing we enter into rest. Here all our woes and wants obtain redress and supplies. O may our souls be united to this Saviour by a divine faith, he the head and we the members, he the vine and we the branches. May we be

his disciples, and learn of him; his soldiers, and war under his banner; his beneficiaries, and live upon his fulness. When we think of our transgressions of thy law, may we remember *him* who is the end of the law for righteousness. When we feel our sin, may we think of *him* whose blood cleanseth from all sin: and when viewing our trials and duties our weakness makes us despond, may we hear the voice that cries, *My* grace is sufficient for thee.

May we be followers of him who was meek and lowly in heart, who pleased not himself, who went about doing good, who said, My meat is to do the will of him that sent me, and to finish his work. Subdue in us the selfishness that is so common to our depraved hearts, and excite in us a disposition to seek after the welfare of others. May sentiments of benevolence and kindness mingle with all our thoughts, words, and actions; may they become more natural, more powerful, more impartial; may we be good to the unthankful and the unworthy, that we may be the children of our Father who is in heaven, for he maketh his sun to shine on the evil and on the good, and sendeth rain on the just and the unjust.

Yet may we especially do good unto them that are of the household of faith. May all who do the will of our heavenly Father be dear to our hearts. May we prefer Jerusalem above our chief joy. Peace be within her walls, and prosperity within her palaces. Let her become a praise in the whole earth. And from the rising of the sun to the going down of the same, may thy name be great among the Gentiles, and in every place may incense be offered unto Thee, and a pure offering. The harvest truly is great, but the labourers are few; command their increase, and abundantly bless those who are already employed.

And may the sincerity of our prayers appear in our exertions and sacrifices. May we honour the Lord with our substance. In our respective stations may we adorn the doctrine of God our Saviour in all things. By every kind of consistent co-operation with our ministers, may we become helpers to the truth: and carrying the effects of the sermons we hear, and dispensing them among those who refuse to hear, win them without the word. May we never hide it in a napkin, because we have only one talent; but use what we have, that more may be given; and be concerned to obtain from the Judge of all, the approving sentence pronounced on Mary, She hath done what she could. May we never despise the day of small things; never grow weary in well doing; but cherish with patience as well as with diligence, every serious conviction, every pious tendency, every godly impression.

And let us not labour in vain nor spend

our strength for nought. May we be the honoured instruments of saving some soul from death; and of producing joy in the presence of the angels of God, over one sinner that repenteth.

Above all, render us successful among those who are more fully under our instruction, influence, and authority. May we rule well our own house; and have the pleasure to see all the members of our family, fellow-citizens with the saints, and of the household of God. Of whom, and through whom, and to whom are all things. To whom be glory for ever and ever. Amen.

THURSDAY MORNING.

O Lord, Thou art good, and Thou doest good. Thou hast revealed thyself as nigh unto all that call upon Thee, to all that call upon Thee in truth. May we who now address Thee, be found the heirs of this promise; nor suffer us to incur the reproach of drawing near to Thee with the mouth, and honouring Thee with our lips, while our hearts are far from Thee. Unite our hearts to fear thy name; and grant that we may worship Thee in the Spirit, and rejoice in Christ Jesus, and have no confidence in the flesh. We remember that we are sinners, and acknowledge the multitude and aggravations of our offences. Conscious not only of the reality, but the greatness of our guilt, we could indulge no hope, hadst not Thou exhibited thine infinite benevolence, and revealed a Mediator, in whom Thou art reconciling the world unto thyself, not imputing their trespasses unto them.

Thou hast not left thyself without witness, in that Thou hast been doing us good, and giving us rain from heaven and fruitful seasons, filling our hearts with food and gladness. But herein is love, not that we loved God, but that he loved us, and sent his Son to be the propitiation for our sins. Blessed be thy name, we have all the certainty we could desire, that with Thee there is mercy. *That* mercy the publican sought, and—found: *that* mercy—has never disappointed any that trusted in it: *that* mercy—at this very moment cries to us, Ask and it shall be given *you*, seek and *ye* shall find. O Lord, we avail ourselves of thine invitation, and plead thy promise! According to the multitude of thy tender mercies blot out our transgressions. Create in us also a clean heart, and renew a right spirit within us.

We hope we are convinced that while many things are desirable and some useful, *one* thing is needful; and that instead of the inquiry, What shall I eat, and what shall I drink, and wherewithal shall I be clothed? the supreme anxiousness of our soul is, What must I do to be saved! O visit us with thy salvation, in the illumination of the mind, and

the sanctification of the life; in all the comforts of the Holy Ghost, and in all the fruits of the Spirit. May we willingly obey all thy commands, and cheerfully submit to all thy appointments. In the annihilation of self-will, and in the temper of implicit devotedness, may we as to every duty say, Lord, what wilt thou have me to do! And as to every event, Here I am, let Him do what seemeth Him good. Grant us piety and wisdom to accommodate ourselves to the allotments of life; and enable us to maintain a Christian temper and behaviour in all the changing scenes of providence, that all things may work together, if not for our gratification, yet for our good.

May we disengage ourselves from the present evil world, and be received and acknowledged as the sons and daughters of the Lord Almighty. May the righteous be our attraction and delight; and though few in number, and despised by the foolish and wicked, may we go with *them*, because God is with them and like Moses, may we choose rather to suffer affliction with the people of God, than enjoy the pleasures of sin for a season.

May we walk by faith, and not by sight. May we weigh both worlds, and may the future and the eternal preponderate. May this be our growing experience as well as profession—As for me, I will behold thy face in righteousness, I shall be satisfied when I awake with thy likeness.

By thy mercies we renew this morning the consecration of ourselves to thy service. Go forth with us into the concerns of the day. Keep us in all our ways. Innumerable are our dangers; but the greatest of all is sin. Uphold our goings therefore in thy word, and let no iniquity have dominion over us. May we abstain from all appearance of evil: and the very God of peace sanctify us wholly: and may our whole spirit, and soul, and body be preserved blameless unto the coming of our Lord Jesus Christ.

And to God only wise, the Father, the Son, and the Holy Ghost, be ascribed all honour and praise for ever and ever. Amen.

THURSDAY EVENING.

O God, thy greatness is unsearchable. Thy name is most excellent in all the earth. Thou hast set thy glory above the heavens. Thousands minister unto Thee, and ten thousand times ten thousand stand before Thee. We feel ourselves in thine awful presence to be nothing, less than nothing, and vanity: nor do we presume to approach Thee because we are deserving of thy notice—for we have sinned—we have incurred thy righteous displeasure—we acknowledge that Thou art justified when Thou speakest, and clear when Thou judgest.

But our necessities compel us; and thy

promises encourage us. Thou art nigh unto them that are of a broken heart, and savest such as be of a contrite spirit. Thou hast provided and revealed a Mediator, who has not only obeyed but magnified the law and made it honourable; and Thou hast made us accepted in the beloved. And we behold an innumerable multitude returning from thy throne successful, rejoicing and encouraging us to go forward. *They* were not, though all guilt and indigence, refused nor upbraided; but freely obtained pardon and holiness and righteousness and strength, and were blessed with all spiritual blessings in heavenly places in Christ.

O look Thou upon us, and be merciful unto us, as Thou usest to do unto those that love thy name! Convince us of sin both in its penalty and in its pollution; and may we mourn over it with a godly sorrow. Give us that faith by which we shall be enabled to believe on the Lord Jesus Christ; and be-lieving may we have life through his name.

And may we not only have life, but have it more abundantly. We often question the reality of our grace; but the imperfections of our religion are too obvious not to be acknow-ledged, and too aggravated not to be deplored. Our souls cleave unto the dust; quicken Thou us according to thy word. Strengthen in us the things that are ready to die. May we not only live in the Spirit, but walk in the Spirit. By holy resemblances may we put on the Lord Jesus Christ. May the same mind be in us which was also in Him; and may we feel it to be our dignity and delight to go about doing good.

And as He suffered for us, leaving us an example that we should tread in his steps; may we learn to suffer like Him. When re-viled, may we revile not again, but commit ourselves to Him that judgeth righteously. Whoever may be the instrument of our grief, may we never lose sight of an over-ruling agency in preparing and presenting it; but be able to say, The cup which my Father giveth me shall I not drink it? In patience may we possess our souls. May we be calm to inquire, wherefore Thou contendest with us. Let not weeping hinder sowing; nor sorrow, duty.

We live in a world of changes, and have here no continuing city—May we seek one to come; and have our minds kept in perfect peace, being stayed upon God. Be with us to the end of our journey; and after honouring Thee by the life we have lived, may we glorify Thee by the death we shall die. When heart and flesh fail, be Thou the strength of our heart and our portion for ever; at death may we fall asleep in Jesus; and in the morning of the resurrection, may He change our vile body, that it may be fashioned like his own glorious body; and so may we be for ever with the Lord

Who can understand his errors? Forgive, O God, the sins of the past day, in thought, word, and deed, against thy divine majesty. We bless thee for our preservation in our going out and our coming in, and in all our ways: and we bless Thee for all the supplies and indulgences which thy good providence has afforded us.

And now, O Thou keeper of Israel, we commit our souls and our bodies to thy all-sufficient care. Suffer no evil to befall our persons, and no plague to come nigh our dwelling. May our sleep be sweet; or if Thou holdest our eyes waking, may we re-member Thee upon our bed, and meditate on Thee in the night-watches.

And with the innumerable company who never slumber nor sleep, and who rest not day and night, we would join in ascribing blessing and honour and glory and power unto Him that sitteth upon the throne, and unto the Lamb, for ever and ever. Amen.

FRIDAY MORNING.

O THOU, whose name alone is Jehovah, the most high over all the earth!—When we con-sider thy majesty and thy purity, and reflect upon our meanness and guilt, how shall we come before the Lord, or bow before the high God? We are unworthy of thy notice, and have rendered ourselves justly obnoxious to the curse of thy holy law: and wert Thou to judge us according to our desert—the most innocent periods of our life, and the devoutest services in which we have ever been engaged, would make us shrink back with dread and despair from thy presence. But we are en-couraged to approach Thee, by the revelation Thou hast given us of thyself as the Lord God gracious and merciful; the invitations and promises of thy word; and the mediation of thy dear Son. We are assured that he put away sin by the sacrifice of himself; and being raised from the dead, entered into the holy place, there to appear in the presence of God for us. We rejoice that we have now an advocate with the Father to plead our cause, and a great high priest over the house of God, to introduce our persons and our services.

May we therefore draw near in full assur-ance of faith, believing that all things are now ready; that we are as welcome as we are needy; and that the blessings we implore are as gracious as they are needful. Yea Thou delightest in mercy, and hast not only permitted, but commanded us to ask and re-ceive that our joy may be full. O let us not refuse to be comforted: let us not reject the counsel of God against ourselves. Suffer us not, after provoking Thee by our rebellion, to offend Thee still more by our unbelief. May we honour thy goodness by our confidence in thy veracity, and come and take of the water of life freely. May we wait for no qualifications to entitle us to those provisions which must be bought without money and without price; but may we come as we are—guilty *to be* justified, unholy *to be* renewed, blind *to be* enlightened, weak *to be* strengthened, and indigent *to be* relieved and enriched. As Thou art presenting to us, in the offers of the gospel, thy unspeakable gift, may we receive Christ Jesus the Lord. May we receive Him immediately without delay, cordially without reluctance, and impartially without exception; feeling our need of, and acquiescing in, all his offices, relations, influences, and blessings.

As thou art well pleased *in* thy beloved Son, may it appear that we are well pleased *with* Him. May we love his salvation, and glory in his cross; may we admire his character, and pant after his likeness. May we judge of our union with Him, by our being new creatures; and of our freedom from all condemnation, by our walking not after the flesh but after the Spirit. May we try our principles by our practice, and our faith by our works. May the origin and certainty of our hope appear in its tendency: may it purify us from sin, wean us from the world, and cause us to live with our conversation in heaven.

Blessed with a well-founded persuasion that when He who is our life shall appear, we shall also appear with Him in glory, may we bear with patience the trials attached to this present time, and weep as if we wept not. And knowing our obligation to thy grace, which has delivered our souls from the lowest hell, and is infallibly conducting us to such a vastness of felicity, may we be principally concerned to walk before the Lord in the land of the living, and to show forth all his praise. Whether therefore we eat or drink, or whatever we do, may we do all to the glory of God.

But we cannot trust in our own hearts: we dare not rely upon our convictions and purposes—they have often betrayed us. We can only serve Thee in thy own strength. We can walk no further than Thou leadest us; we can stand no longer than Thou holdest us. We therefore renounce self-dependence; and desire to be strong in the Lord and in the power of his might. Let thy grace be sufficient for us, in the duties and events of the day into which we have entered. May we abide with God in our respective callings. Whether we are alone, or in company, may we be anxious to gain good, and to do good. May we be serious without gloom, and cheerful without levity, and use the world as not abusing it.

And now unto Him that is able to keep us from falling, and to present us faultless before the presence of his glory with exceeding joy; to the only wise God our Saviour, be glory and majesty, dominion and power, both now and ever. Amen.

FRIDAY EVENING.

O God, the day is thine; the night also is thine. Thou makest the outgoings of the morning and evening to rejoice. The heavens declare thy glory; the earth is full of thy riches, and so is the great and wide sea. Thou art the maker, and sustainer, and proprietor of all things. We are the creatures of thy power, and the beneficiaries of thy bounty. But we have sinned against heaven and before Thee, and are not worthy of the least of all the mercies, and of all the truth which Thou hast showed us. We are of those that rebel against the light; for we have resisted the dictates of our consciences; the demands of thy law; the admonitions of thy providence; and the calls of the gospel of peace. We have made light of those things which angels desire to look into: we have neglected thy great salvation; and we deserve that thy wrath should come upon us as the children of disobedience.

Yet we are in the land of the living, and under a dispensation of hope. We flee for refuge to that dear Saviour who said, Deliver from going down into the pit, I have found a ransom: and who himself bore our sin in his own body on the tree. O that we may be found in Him, and know the power of his resurrection, and the fellowship of his sufferings, being made conformable unto his death. May we not only be justified by his blood, and saved from wrath through Him; but may we derive from Him an influence, that shall subdue our iniquities, and change us into his own image, from glory to glory, as by the Spirit of the Lord.

Deliver us, we pray Thee, from the views and dispositions of men of the world who have their portion in this life. May we never look for that on earth, which can only be found in heaven. Born from above and bound for glory, may we feel the heart of a stranger, and pass the time of our sojourning here in fear. Reminded—and O how often are we reminded!—that here we have no continuing city, may we seek one to come: and in all the changing scenes of time, know in ourselves that in heaven we have a better and an enduring substance.

In our journeyings through a vale of tears, cast us not away from thy presence, and take not thy Holy Spirit from us. Be Thou always within sight or within call—for how often shall we have to address Thee! To thy wisdom we must repair for direction, or we shall every moment go astray. Thy power is our only safety. O thou that savest by thy right hand them that put their trust in Thee, from those that rise up against them, keep us as the apple of thine eye, and hide us under the shadow of thy wing. Be thou our strength in weakness, and our victory in conflict. We dare not say, we never *will* deny Thee, but O grant that we never may! Establish our hearts with grace, and deliver our feet from falling; and may we be sincere and without offence until the day of Christ.

These are great blessings for us to ask—but we are undone for ever without them—and Thou hast encouraged us to hope. We plead thy command and thy promise—'Ask and it shall be given you, seek and ye shall find, knock and it shall be opened unto you.' No suppliant, however unworthy or guilty, was ever rejected or insulted at thy footstool. And we come in the name of Him who made intercession for the transgressors. Him Thou hearest always—and to Him, with the Father, and the Holy Spirit, be praises for ever and ever. Amen.

SATURDAY MORNING.

O God, Thou art great, and greatly to be feared. And Thou art also merciful and gracious; long-suffering and abundant in goodness and in truth. May we so feel our sinfulness as to be humbled in the dust before thee, and filled with self-condemnation and self-despair; but let us not shrink back from thy presence, and be afraid to place our faith and hope in the God of love. Help us to remember, that if we have no claim on the footing of desert, we can plead thy promise and invitation; and that if the blessings we want are infinitely great, they are dispensed as gifts whose freeness delights in the unworthiness of the receiver.

We therefore would neither deny nor palliate our guilt. We know there is evil enough in one sin to plunge us into perdition; but our offences are more in number than the sand; and they have been attended with every aggravation, derivable from light and love, means and mercies. Thou hast called, and we have refused; Thou hast stretched out thy hand, and we have not regarded. How often hast Thou wooed and awed, blessed and chastised us—and yet we refused to return! O Lord, pardon our iniquity, for it is great. Let the free gift be of many offences unto justification of life; and where sin has abounded may grace much more abound.

And as we cannot serve or enjoy Thee, unless our nature be changed as well as our state, O save us by the washing of regeneration, and by the renewing of the Holy Ghost. Deliver us from the dominion as well as the curse of sin; and from the love of it as well as the dominion. May we reckon ourselves to be dead indeed unto sin, but alive unto God through Jesus Christ our Lord. May we view holiness as the beauty and the dignity of the soul, and long after greater degrees of conformity to the will and the image of God. May our hope purify us; and our religious comforts stimulate as well as relieve. May we never slumber, and like the pilgrim lose our roll; never sleep, and like Saul be robbed of our spear and our cruse. May we watch and pray lest we enter into temptation. When we grow indolent and careless, awaken us by lively apprehensions of thy presence, and of the eternal world, on the borders of which we perpetually move; may we feel the infinite importance of improving the few transient periods intervening between us and death; may we daily and hourly answer some of the grand purposes of life and religion. May every place and every company be the better for us. May we diffuse knowledge and happiness by our conversation, example, and influence; and, like our Lord and Saviour, go about doing good.

Whatever advantages we possess, may we never forget that this is not our rest. May we arise and depart hence, not by quitting our stations, or undervaluing the duties attached to them, but by rising above the world as our portion, setting our affections on things above, and having our conversation in heaven. Expecting a succession of encounters in passing through an enemy's land, may we take to us the whole armour of God; and looking for thorns and briers in our marchings through a wilderness, may our feet be shod with the preparation of the gospel of peace.

Fit us for every changing scene: and in all the events that would alarm or perplex us, may our minds be stayed upon God, and our thoughts be established. May we remember that trials from thy hand are blessings in disguise, and that when they come to be unveiled, and we can view them in their designs and effects, they will draw forth our gratitude and praise. Till we can walk by sight, enable us to walk by faith; and may nothing weaken our persuasion, that all thy ways are mercy and truth to thy people, and that all things work together for good to them that love Thee.

We would not forget those that are in affliction—Do not Thou, O God, forget them. Whatever be their losses or distresses, help them to say, Yet the Lord thinketh upon me. May they know, that thy thoughts towards them are thoughts of peace and not of evil, to bring them to an expected end; though it may be by a painful passage. Comfort those who are on beds of languishing. Enter the house of mourning. Be the father of the fatherless, and the husband of the widow, and the friend and helper of the poor and needy—and have mercy upon all men.

Our Father, &c.

SATURDAY EVENING.

O GOD—Thou art glorious in holiness, fearful in praises, continually doing wonders. And it is not one of the least of thy wonderful works that we are yet on this side an awful eternity, and not reaping the due reward of our deeds. We look on each other this evening with astonishment, and exclaim, It is of the Lord's mercies that we are not consumed. Our whole life has been a scene of provocation against thy divine majesty: and if we, with all our ignorance and self-love, can see so much depravity in ourselves, what must have presented itself to *thy* view—O Thou, who knowest all things, in whose sight the very heavens are not clean, and who seest more pollution even in our duties than we ever found in our sins! There is no health in us. We have no works or worthiness to excite thy regard; and if ever we are saved, it must be according to thy own purpose and grace, given us in Christ Jesus before the world began.

We come to Thee in the dear name of Him who loved us and gave himself for us; who magnified the law and made it honourable; who put away sin by the sacrifice of himself, and now ever liveth to make intercession for us. This foundation Thou thyself hast laid in Zion, and thy word assures us, that whosoever believeth on Him shall not be confounded. We hope our dependence upon Him is not a vain reliance, because we love his service as well as his sacrifice, and long to wear his image as well as to be justified by his blood. We hope we are willing to deny ourselves, and take up our cross and follow Him—in the regeneration—and whithersoever he goeth.

O make us partakers of that salvation which, is designed to deliver us from our sins, and to bring us into the glorious liberty of the children of God! Put thy laws into our minds, and write them in our hearts. Render our obedience to thy will holily natural and delightful to us. Rectify all our principles, and give us clear, and consistent, and influential views of divine truth. May we never undervalue or neglect any part of thy revealed will; but regard the practice the gospel enjoins, as well as the doctrine it exhibits; prize its commands as well as its promises, and cultivate such a disposition as will render every religious duty a spiritual privilege.

Sanctify us in every relation, office, transaction, and condition in life. Keep us if we prosper, from being exalted above measure, and if exercised with adversity, suffer us not to be swallowed up of over-much sorrow. May divine grace preserve the balance of the mind in all our varying circumstances, and teach us, in whatsoever state we are, not only to be content, but to glorify God, and be an edifying example to those around us.

May we always be principally concerned for soul-prosperity, and be willing to submit to any means however trying, that thy wisdom shall judge necessary to promote and secure it. May we so pass through things temporal as not to miss those that are eternal at last, or to lose sight of them for a moment now. Too long have our feet and our hands been in the mire; O disengage us, purify us, elevate us: our souls cleave unto the dust, quicken Thou us according to thy word. May none of thy mercies be lost upon us; but may they prove the means of exciting our gratitude, warming our devotion, and encouraging our confidence. May none of our trials be unimproved; but may they all embitter sin, wean us from the world, and endear to us the scriptures, the throne of grace, and the sympathy of that Almighty friend who is touched with the feeling of our infirmities.

Let none of our religious opportunities be unsanctified; may we be thankful for the frequency of their recurrence; may we gladly avail ourselves of them, and instead of resting in the mere outward performance, may we be concerned to worship Thee in spirit and in truth, and to obtain from thy word all the benefits it is intended and adapted to afford.

For this purpose, we implore thy blessing on the solemnities of the Sabbath which is so soon to open upon us. May we in the morning awake with Thee; and begin, go through and end the day, in thy faith, fear and love. May we have satisfactory evidence in our own minds, that we do not wait upon Thee in vain; and may our profiting appear unto all men.

And thus by all the discipline of thy family, and the ordinances of thy house, may we grow in grace, and in our meetness for the inheritance of the saints in light. And when the Saturday evening of life itself shall arrive, and we are called to retreat from every mortal care, may we close the period of toil and trouble by falling asleep in Jesus—and open our eyes on the rest that remains for the people of God—and enter the temple above to go no more out. And may the grace of, &c. Amen.

SECOND WEEK.

SUNDAY MORNING.

O THOU KING eternal, immortal, invisible, dwelling in the light which no man can approach unto, and whom no man hath seen or can see. Thou art incomprehensible, and the highest Archangel cannot find Thee out unto perfection. Yet Thou hast been pleased to reveal thyself; and by means of thy words we behold Thee in every character and relation that can suit our necessities, or encourage our hope. Thy throne is in the heavens, and thy kingdom ruleth over all; and all nations before Thee are as nothing; yet Thou condescendest to regard the things that are done in the earth, and despisest not the prayer even of the destitute. Thou art exalted above all blessing and praise: our goodness extendeth not to Thee—but unless thine be extended to us, we are undone for ever. Without Thee we can do nothing; we *are* nothing. In Thee we live and move and have our being. The way of man is not in himself; it is not in man that walketh to direct his steps. We are universally indigent and dependent: but as Thou art able, so Thou art willing to take the charge of us; and here we are the living to praise Thee, and to acknowledge that goodness and mercy have followed us all the days of our lives.

We bless Thee that Thou hast regarded our souls as well as our bodies, and no less provided for our future interests than our present. When there was no eye to pity us, Thou didst remember us in our low estate; and when there was no arm to rescue, Thou wast pleased to lay help on one that is mighty. Thou hast sent thy own Son into the world, not to condemn the world, but that the world through Him might be saved. To Him may we turn our believing regards, and find in Him the wisdom, righteousness, sanctification, and redemption, which as perishing sinners we need. In all our approaches to Thee, may we have boldness and access with confidence by the faith of Him. May we know that He has borne our grief and carried our sorrow; and be able to rejoice in him as our sacrifice, our sympathizing friend, our almighty helper, and our lovely example. May we drink into his spirit. May we transcribe the excellencies of his character into our own. May we place our feet in the very prints of his steps, and follow him in the regeneration, till we shall be perfectly like him, and see him as he is.

We desire to acknowledge Thee in the dispensations of thy providence; and to own thy agency in all the events that befall us whether pleasing or painful. Thou hast a right to govern us; and thou knowest what will best advance our welfare. May we commit our way unto the Lord, and be able to say at thy foot-stool in unfeigned submission, Here I am, let Him do what seemeth Him good. If darkness veil thy dealings with us, may we trust and not be afraid; believing that what we know not now we shall know hereafter, and that the developement of thy conduct will issue in perfect satisfaction and praise.

We bless Thee for the institutions of religion, in the use of which Thou hast pro-mised to draw near to those who draw near to Thee. We rejoice in another of the days of the Son of man. May we call off our minds from the cares of the world, and attend upon the Lord without distraction. Quicken and elevate our souls, that rising above the formality of devotion, we may come even to thy seat, and enjoy a little of the blessedness of those that have entered the temple above, and are singing the song of Moses and the Lamb. We are going to assemble in the house of prayer—pour upon us the spirit of grace and of supplication, and rank us in the number of those who hunger and thirst after righteousness. We are going to the house of praise—awaken in us every grateful and cheerful emotion, and may we speak to ourselves in psalms and hymns and spiritual songs, singing and making melody in our hearts unto the Lord. We are repairing to the house of instruction—enable us to receive the kingdom of God as a little child. Teach us of thy ways. Lead us into all truth. And let us be neither barren nor unfruitful in the knowledge of our Lord and Saviour Jesus Christ.

For this purpose, let thy presence go with us; and let thy word come to us, not in word only, but in power, and in the Holy Ghost, and in much assurance. Bless all the churches of the faithful; and the ministers of the everlasting gospel, of every name, and of every nation. Clothe thy priests with salvation, and let thy saints shout aloud for joy. Remember our country in all its lawful interests, domestic and foreign. Bless the king as supreme, all subordinate rulers, and all ranks and degrees of men among us. Make us glad according to the days wherein Thou hast afflicted us, and the years wherein we have seen evil. Let thy work appear unto thy servants, and thy glory unto their children, and let the beauty of the Lord our God be upon us. Establish Thou the work of our hands upon us; yea the work of our hands establish Thou it.

Our Father, &c.

SUNDAY EVENING.

WHEN we consider the heavens, the work of thy fingers, the moon and the stars which Thou hast ordained; Lord, what is man that Thou art mindful of him, or the son of man that Thou visitest him? In thy sight the heavens are not clean; and thou chargest thine angels with folly—With what truth therefore *may* we, and with what humiliation *ought* we to exclaim, Behold we are vile!

And yet we believe—help Thou our unbelief—that Thou waitest to be gracious unto us, and art exalted to have mercy upon us. And Christ also has once suffered for sins, the just for the unjust, that He might bring us unto God. Through his obedience unto death, even the death of the cross, it is honourable in Thee to save all that come unto Thee by Him; and thou art faithful and just, as well as gracious and merciful, in forgiving us our sins, and in cleansing us from all unrighteousness.

We bless thy holy name, for a foundation on which the guilty, the depraved, and the helpless can build a hope that maketh not ashamed; for a refuge from the curse of a broken law; for a fountain opened for sin and uncleanness; and for a fulness from which we can receive, and grace for grace. We want to appropriate and realize all the representations given of the Saviour in thy word, and to find him to be in our own experience, what thy people have found him to be in all ages of the world. May our persons and our services be accepted in the Beloved. May we be justified freely by thy grace, through the redemption that is in Christ Jesus. May we be saved by the washing of regeneration, and the renewing of the Holy Ghost. We are weary and heavy laden—give us rest. We are depraved in all our powers—work in us to will and to do of thy good pleasure. We are ignorant—fill us with the knowledge of thy will, in all wisdom and spiritual understanding, that we may approve things that are excellent, and be sincere and without offence till the day of Christ.

Many eyes are upon us—lead us in a plain path because of our enemies. Many watch for our halting—but may we put to silence the ignorance of foolish men, and constrain them, by our good works which they behold, to glorify God in the day of visitation.

Some did run well, but are hindered; they began in the Spirit, but are now walking in the flesh: we tremble for them—and we tremble for ourselves: we pray for them—and we pray for ourselves. Recover and restore them, and keep us by thy power through faith unto salvation. May we never draw back; never turn aside to the right hand or to the left; never stand still; never look back; never seem to come short through unbelief, but be always abounding in the work of the Lord—and so much the more as we see the day approaching.

Though we are ignorant of the future, and know not what a day may bring forth, keep us from being of a doubtful mind. May we be careful for nothing. May we go on our way rejoicing, persuaded that all thy dispensations are designed and adapted to prove that Thou carest for us.

We can even now see much of thy wisdom, righteousness, and kindness, in events that once perplexed and alarmed us; and what we know not now we shall know hereafter. Soon the mystery of providence will be completed and explained. Soon shall we have passed these dark and mournful regions; and then our sun shall no more go down, nor our moon withdraw herself; for God shall be our everlasting light, and the days of our mourning shall be ended.

And till we arrive at heaven our home, may we gratefully avail ourselves of all the advantages afforded us in our journey. We bless Thee for wilderness privileges; for the manna; the streams of the smitten rock; the fiery cloudy pillar; the tabernacle, and the ark. We bless Thee for the sabbath, the sanctuary, and the ministry of the word. We bless Thee for the opportunities we have this day enjoyed in waiting upon thee. Many who love thy salvation, have passed the sacred hours in solitude. Many have had no means of grace to invite their attendance. And many who have been assembled together have not heard the gospel of the grace of God in truth. O let not our privileges increase our guilt, and aggravate our condemnation, so that it shall be more tolerable for Sodom and Gomorrah in the day of judgment than for us. Let not the truths we have been hearing visit us only as weekly guests; but may they be residents in our hearts. May the word of Christ dwell in us richly in all wisdom. And though the exercises in which we have been engaged are transient, may the effects produced by them be deep and durable; may the sabbath pervade the week, and the spirit of devotion actuate us in the absence of its forms; whether we eat, or drink, or whatever we do, may we do all to the glory of God.

Bless, O bless, the rising generation, the sources of future families and communities. When the clods of the valley shall be sweet about us, may they be found a seed to serve thee. Many of them have had the advantage of religious education; they have seen pious examples; they early kneeled at the domestic altar; from infancy they knew the holy scriptures, and have often been alarmed, often melted under the word preached; and frequently have they been ready to subscribe with their own hand, and surname themselves by the name of Israel. O let not these promising appearances and beginnings be destroyed. O let not the wild beast out of the wood carry off the lambs of the flock, but may the Shepherd of Israel gather them with his arm and carry them in his bosom!

Regard all thy professing churches. Bless them with soundness of doctrine, purity and liberality of discipline, and sanctity and amiableness of character in their members; and the Lord add to his people, how many soever they be, an hundred fold. Yea let a little one become a thousand, and a small one a strong nation; and all the families of the earth be blessed in *Him*—who is all our salvation and all our desire—to whom be glory and dominion for ever and ever. Amen.

MONDAY MORNING.

O Thou King of kings and Lord of lords, who only hast immortality, we would adore Thee, and take shame to ourselves; and though allowed to approach thy divine majesty, we would never forget the sentiments of humiliation and contrition which become such creatures as we are. Father, we have sinned against heaven and in thy sight, and are not worthy to be called thy children: we are not worthy of the least of all thy mercies. Yea we have merited thy displeasure; and thy righteousness would be completely acquitted in our destruction.

O for hearts of flesh! Lord produce in us that sensibility of soul which will lead us to feel our vileness, to deplore our guilt, and to cast ourselves at thy feet, abhorring ourselves, and repenting in dust and ashes. And impart to us that faith which will enable us to hope in thy word, and derive strong consolation from the invitations and promises of the gospel. We are come to implore the greatest blessings the God of love can give; but our application is not presumption: we are come to call thee, Abba Father! to enter thy house, to sit down at thy table, to lean on thy arm, to walk with God; but we are not come unbidden or uncalled: Thou hast called us by thy grace; and it is thy commandment that we should believe on the name of thy Son Jesus Christ. Lord, we assent, we submit, we depend, we apply. Since He came into the world to save sinners, we take Him as *our* Saviour; and glory in Him as made of Thee to us wisdom and righteousness, sanctification and redemption.

And O, let our minds be fixed and filled with admiring thoughts of his person and offices; let our hearts be inflamed with a sense of his boundless compassion and love. By the new and living way, which he has not only revealed but consecrated for us, may we come to Thee, and enjoy all the advantages of a state of reconciliation and friendship with God. May the most open and familiar intercourse be maintained between Thee and our souls. To Thee may we commit our way and our works, and in every thing, by prayer and supplication make known our requests unto God. Be Thou always near, to guide us and to defend, to relieve us in trouble, and to help us in duty. And may we walk humbly with our God; wondering at the condescension that deigns to regard our mean affairs, the patience that bears with our manners, and the kindness that employs so many means to advance our everlasting welfare.

We grieve to think that a world so full of thy bounty should be so empty of thy praise. O that men would praise the Lord for his goodness, and for his wonderful works to the children of men. Bless the Lord, all his works; in all places of his dominion, bless the Lord, O my soul.

Again thy visitation hath preserved our spirits. Through the dark and silent watches of the night thou hast suffered no evil to befall us, nor any plague to come nigh our dwelling. And we are not only the living to praise Thee this morning, but the distinguished and the indulged. Many who have seen the light of the day as well as ourselves, are encompassed with want, and pain, and wretchedness, but we have all things richly to enjoy.

Thou takest pleasure in the prosperity of thy servants: may we always take pleasure in the advancement of thy glory. Thou art never weary in doing us good; may we never grow weary in well doing. Thy mercies are new every morning; every morning by thy mercies, may we present our bodies a living sacrifice, holy and acceptable, which is our reasonable service.

And to the God of our salvation, the Father, the Son, and the Holy Spirit, be ascribed the kingdom, the power, and the glory, for ever and ever. Amen.

MONDAY EVENING.

O Thou, in whose presence angels bow, and arch-angels veil their faces, enable us to serve Thee with reverence and godly fear. O Thou, who art a spirit, and requirest truth in the inward parts, help us to worship Thee in spirit and in truth. O righteous Father, we would not come to Thee harbouring the love of any sin in our bosoms; for Thou hast assured us, that if we regard iniquity in our hearts Thou wilt not hear us. We must address Thee as sinners; but we acknowledge our transgression, and our sin is ever before us; we desire to have nothing more to do with idols; we hate every false way; and long to be Israelites indeed in whom is no guile.

Nor would we, O God, appear in thy presence indulging a worldly temper, and seeking after an abundance of those things that afford no satisfaction in the possession, and perish in the using. After all these things do the Gentiles seek, and our heavenly Father knoweth what things we have need of before we ask him, and will administer them as our wants and welfare may require. We are hastening towards an hour which will show us the vanity of all earthly pursuits and possessions. When a few more suns have rolled over us, it will be a matter of indifference whether we have been rich or poor; successful or disappointed in our enterprises; admired of our fellow-creatures or despised! But it will be of eternal moment to us, that we have mourned for sin; that we have hungered and thirsted after righteousness; that we have loved the Lord Jesus Christ in sincerity, and gloried in his cross.

May these objects therefore, however despised of men, engross our chief solicitude. May we labour for that meat which endureth unto everlasting life; may we lay up treasure in heaven; may we seek the honour that cometh from God only. O remember us with the favour thou bearest unto thy people, and visit us with thy salvation. Deliver us from the condemnation of the law, and the bondage of corruption, and bring us into the glorious liberty of the children of God. Justify us freely from all things, and renew us in the spirit of our minds. Produce in us in those principles and dispositions which will render thy service perfect freedom, and make it our meat to do the will of our heavenly Father, and to finish his work.

Expel from our minds all sinful fear and shame, and with firmness and courage may we confess the Redeemer before men, and go forth to Him without the camp bearing his reproach. And may our zeal be according to knowledge. Fill us with all wisdom and spiritual understanding. May we walk circumspectly. May we never take a wrong course or a wrong step. May we venture on nothing without asking counsel of God. Without prejudice may we repair to the scriptures, and kneeling before the divine oracles ask, Lord, what wilt Thou have me to do? May we faithfully study our conditions and connexions in life, and observe every dispensation of thy providence, that we may see how we can honour Thee in our body and spirit, and serve our generation according to the will of God.

Thou hast commanded us to be pitiful and to pray for all men. We would remember that every moment of pleasure to us is a moment of anguish to some; and that while our health and our relative comforts are continued, many are confined to beds of languishing; or sighing, Lover and friend hast Thou put far from me, and mine acquaintance into darkness. In the multitude of their thoughts within them, may thy comforts delight their souls. If not in the suffering, yet in the review of their trials, may they be able to say, It is good for me that I have been afflicted. Let not the prosperity of the successful destroy them; nor the table of the indulged prove a snare. In every state may the voice be heard and obeyed, Arise and depart hence, for this is not your rest.

We know not what a day may bring forth; yet we would not be anxious in prospect of the future, nor perplex ourselves with that care about events, which it is our duty and privilege to cast upon Him who careth for us. We would keep our minds in perfect peace, being stayed upon Thee. Only assure us that nothing can befall us without thy permission, appointment, and administration; only assure us that Thou hast engaged to make all things work together for our good—only say to our hearts, I will never leave thee nor forsake thee. Guide us by thy counsel, and afterward receive us to glory. We implore it in the name of our only Lord and Saviour. Amen.

––––––

TUESDAY MORNING.

O Thou God of Abraham, of Isaac, and of Jacob; the God of all the righteous, and of all that hunger and thirst after righteousness: blessed are the people that are in such a case, yea happy is the people whose God is the Lord. May we be fellow heirs, and of the same body, and partakers of thy promise in Christ by the gospel.

We hope in thy word. There we see Thee, not on a throne of judgment, whose terror would make us afraid, but on a throne of grace, waiting to be gracious, and exalted to have mercy. There we hear Thee saying, not—Depart ye cursed into everlasting fire prepared for the devil and his angels, but—Look unto me and be ye saved, all the ends of the earth, for I am God and there is none else. They that know thy name will put their trust in Thee, for Thou, Lord, hast not forsaken them that seek Thee. How many glorified in heaven, and what numbers now living on earth, are thy witnesses, O God, exemplifying in their recovery from the ruins of the fall, the freeness and riches and efficacy of thy grace. All that were ever saved by Thee, and will through eternity exclaim, Not unto us, O Lord, not unto us, but to thy name give glory, for thy mercy and for thy truth's sake. And after all thy communications, Thou art the same Lord over all, and rich unto all, that call upon Thee. Thou hast the same ear to hear, the same heart to pity, the same hand to deliver.

But thou hast chosen to transact all thy concerns with us through a Mediator. In Him it hath pleased Thee that all fulness should dwell. Him Thou hast exalted at thy own right hand, to be a Prince and a Saviour, to give repentance unto Israel and remission of sins.

To Him therefore may we look; on Him may we entirely depend; and in Him with all the seed of Israel may we be justified and glory. May we know how to derive relief from his sufferings, without losing any of our abhorrence of sin or longing after holiness. May we feel the double efficiency of his blood, in tranquillizing our consciences and cleansing them: may we delight in his service as well as his sacrifice; and under the constrainings of a love that passeth knowledge, may we live not to ourselves, but to Him that died for us and rose again.

In all our approaches to Thee, may we have boldness and access, with confidence by the faith of Him. Give us much of the spirit of grace and of supplication. By a constant readiness for the duty, and a frequent performance of it, may we pray without ceasing; and by guarding against every discouragement, may we pray and not faint.

May we cherish a grateful and cheerful disposition; not murmuring and repining because all our wishes are not indulged, or because some trials are blended with our enjoyments; but sensible of our desert, and impressed with the number and greatness of thy benefits, may we bless the Lord at all times, and may his praise continually be in our mouth. And may our gratitude be real and practical, and increasing with our obligations. Enable us to inquire—Lord, what wilt thou have me to do? Enable us to resolve—I will walk before the Lord in the land of the living; enable us to pray—O that my ways were directed to keep thy statutes.

We commend to thy pity and thy power all those who are any way afflicted in mind, body, or estate. May the young find it good to bear the yoke in their youth; may they that know Thee not, be chosen in the furnace of affliction; and may thy own people find Thee a very present help in trouble. Be favourable to our land. Bless the king as supreme, and all the branches of the royal family. Let those that are at the helm of public affairs be men of understanding, and know what Israel ought to do. May our magistrates be men fearing God and hating covetousness: make our officers peace, and our exactors righteousness. Let not oppression be ever seen on the side of judgment, nor a perverse spirit be mingled in the midst of the people. Let glory dwell in our land, and upon all the glory may there be a defence. May the grace of, &c. Amen.

TUESDAY EVENING.

O Thou that hearest prayer, unto Thee shall all flesh come. Lord, teach us to pray. We have reason to fear that the language of our lips and the feelings of our hearts, in our religious exercises have not always agreed. We have frequently taken carelessly upon our tongues a name never pronounced above without the deepest reverence and humility. We have often desired things which would have proved our injury; and we have deprecated things which have proved some of our chief mercies. We have erred, both on the side of our hopes and fears; we are unfit to choose for ourselves; we are convinced that the way of man is not in himself; it is not in man that walketh to direct his steps. We know not what to pray for as we ought—Let thy Spirit help our infirmities; and produce in us those views and dispositions which will lead us to ask according to thy will, and then we know Thou hearest us.

With regard to temporal blessings, may we never be importunate; may we always refer them to thy fatherly goodness; for Thou knowest that we have need of these things before we ask Thee—But may we seek first, in time and attention, thy kingdom and righteousness. May we value things by their relation to eternity. May we never think we prosper, unless our souls prosper; that we are rich, unless we are rich towards God; that we are wise, unless we are made wise unto salvation. May our spiritual and everlasting welfare be our chief solicitude, and may we be conscious to ourselves, that we would rather be poor and afflicted, and despised—if blessed with much of the life of God in our souls, than to be admired by our fellow men, and be successful in our enterprises, and have more than heart can wish—if these things should prove the means of our forgetfulness of God.

Having found this world to be dreams and lies, vanity and vexation of spirit, may we arise and depart from it; may we seek our happiness in thy favour and image and presence and service. And though we are unworthy to be regarded by Thee, especially after we have so often refused Thee, receive us graciously; justify our persons; renovate our nature, and put thy laws into our minds, and write them in our hearts: and be Thou to us a God, and may we be to Thee a people. Endear to us that Saviour whose unexampled love led him to suffer the just for the unjust, that He might bring us unto God. May we never dare to think of coming to Thee in any other way; but may we always have boldness and access with confidence, by the faith of Him: yea may we joy in God, through our Lord Jesus Christ, by whom we have now received the atonement: and not only so, but may we glory in tribulation also, knowing that tribulation worketh patience, and patience experience, and experience hope.

For blessed be thy name, we live not in a fatherless world; nor are our minutest affairs forgotten before God. The hairs of our head are all numbered. Our losses and trials are not the effects of chance, but events in which thy wisdom and mercy are now concerned and will be hereafter displayed. We know that all things work together for good to them that love Thee; may our character therefore, and not our condition, be the object of our anxiety. May we ascertain that our heart is right with Thee, and be careful for nothing Having given ourselves unto the Lord, may we remember that we have a right from thy holy word to depend upon Thee to provide for us and to manage all our concerns even to the end.

Discharged from the toil and the torment of care, may we feel ourselves at liberty to enjoy the advantages and comforts of our condition in life, and above all to pursue our work as Christians. May we be attentive to duty; may we inquire how we can best promote the welfare of the human race, and glorify Thee in our body and spirit. May holiness to the Lord be inscribed upon all our time and talents and substance. May the inquiry of our grateful hearts every moment be, What shall I render unto the Lord for all his benefits towards me?

Thou hast made the outgoings of another morning and evening to rejoice. Thou hast crowned the day with thy goodness. Let the night witness thy care and kindness; and may we enter on another portion of our time, not only under fresh obligations, but with new desires and resolutions to be for ever thine.

Our Father, &c. Amen.

WEDNESDAY MORNING.

O THOU Most High! enable us to feel and to express becoming regards towards Thee as the creator of the ends of the earth, the preserver of men, the governor of the universe, the judge of all, the Saviour of sinners. Thy greatness is unsearchable, but thy goodness also is infinite. It is because thy compassions fail not that we are not consumed. Thou hast not only prolonged our unworthy lives under numberless provocations, but Thou hast afforded us every needful supply and indulgence. Thy mercies have been new every morning and every moment. Through thy good hand upon us, we have been rescued from the perils of another night; our repose has been unterrified and undisturbed; sleep has refreshed our bodies and renewed our strength; and we find ourselves surrounded at the commencement of another day with all our accustomed privileges.

But O God, we can never be sufficiently thankful, that we have our existence in a Christian country, and where we can hear words by which we may be saved. O how important, how suitable, how encouraging are the discoveries, the doctrines, the promises, the invitations of the gospel of peace! We are lost; but here is presented to us a free, full, and everlasting salvation. We are left without strength; but here we learn that help is laid on One that is mighty. We are poor and needy; but here we behold the unsearchable riches of Christ. We are blind and ignorant; but in him are hid all the treasures of wisdom and knowledge. We thank Thee, O God, for thine unspeakable gift, and we cordially accept of thy mercy extended to us through the mediation of thy dear Son. We rejoice that He has been delivered for our offences, and raised again for our justification; and that He is now exalted at thy own right hand to be a Prince and a Saviour. We abandon every other refuge to hide in, and every other foundation to build upon; and make him our only hope and our only confidence. And while we depend on his death, and make mention of his righteousness only, we admire his example, and desire to be conformed to his image. May we put on the Lord Jesus Christ by holy and accurate imitations, and increasingly resemble Him whose life was beneficence, whose soul was meekness and humility, who pleased not himself; and who, of obedience the most trying and difficult, could say, I delight to do thy will, O my God, yea thy law is within my heart. May his glory fill our minds; may his love reign in our affections; and at his cross and at his tomb may we burn with ardour to live, not to ourselves, but to Him that died for us and rose again.

Let the number of his followers daily increase; and may none of our friends be found among his enemies. Pour thy blessing upon our seed, and thy spirit upon our offspring. Let our sons be as plants grown up in their youth, and our daughters as corner stones polished after the similitude of a palace. May our domestics be the servants of God; may they do his will from the heart, and be prepared for that world where those who serve will be as those who are served, and all the distinctions now necessary will be done away, and none remain but those which arise from character. And whatever be our conditions in life, may we fill them as Christians; may we escape the snares to which they expose us; discharge the duties that grow out of their circumstances; enjoy with moderation and gratitude their advantages; and improve with decision and diligence their opportunities and resources of usefulness. May every place and every company in which we are found be benefited by us.

And whatever may be the opinion of our fellow-creatures concerning us, may we be satisfied and happy in having the testimony that we please God.

We are now going forth into the concerns of another day. Take us under thy protection and influence. Guide us in all our steps. Enable us to realize thy presence and thy providence. Succeed us in all our lawful endeavours, or prepare us for disappointment, and assure us, that we are in the number of those to whom all things are working together for good; and who will for ever acknowledge —Marvellous are thy works, Lord God Almighty; just and true are all thy ways, O Thou King of saints! Amen.

WEDNESDAY EVENING.

GOD over all, blessed for evermore! We desire to acknowledge thy Being and agency, to adore thy perfections, and to admire the works of thy hands. Thou hast made summer and winter. Thou hast appointed the moon for seasons, and the sun knoweth his going down. The day is thine: the night also is thine: and Thou makest the outgoings of the morning and evening to rejoice. To that throne, from which none were ever repulsed or sent empty away, we again approach for mercy and grace to help in time of need. Let our prayer come before Thee as incense, and the lifting up of our hands as the evening sacrifice. Preserve us from formality in these exercises in which we so daily engage; and alarm our fears, lest we should provoke Thee to say, In vain do they worship me.

For this purpose, enable us to realize thine all-seeing eye; to remember with *whom* we have to do, and *what* we have to do with Him. May we deeply feel the guilt of the sins we confess, and hunger and thirst after the blessings we implore. And while we review the numberless blessings we have received from thy hands, may we be more than ever sensible of our unworthiness, that our hearts may be unfeignedly thankful, and that we may be disposed to show forth thy praise, not only with our lips, but in in our lives, by giving up ourselves to thy service, and walking before Thee in holiness and righteousness all our days.

He that is our God is the God of salvation, and unto God the Lord belong the issues from death. We bless Thee this evening as the preserver of men. Another day has been added, by thy good providence, to the season of thy long-suffering, and the time of our preparation for eternity. We lament that the design of our being placed and continued here has been so imperfectly subserved, that in so many things we have offended, and in all come short of the glory of God. If where much is given, much will be required, and the servant who knew his Lord's will and did it not, shall be beaten with many stripes—O Lord, if Thou shouldst mark *our* iniquities, O Lord, who shall stand? We cannot answer Thee for one of a thousand of our transgressions: the review of a single day is enough to plunge us into despair—our only relief is, that there is forgiveness with Thee, and that with Thee there is plenteous redemption.

But while we hope in thy mercy we would not abuse it. We would not sin, that grace may abound; or be evil, because Thou art good. But since Thou art good and ready to forgive, we would the more ingenuously grieve that ever we have offended a Being so worthy of our devotedness, and be the more concerned in future to walk so as to please Thee.

Create in us a clean heart, and renew a right spirit within us. Set a watch, O God, upon our mouth; keep the door of our lips. And in simplicity and godly sincerity, not with fleshly wisdom, but by thy grace, may we have our conversation—in the world, and in the church, and in the family.

We again commend ourselves to thy care: as Thou hast been through the day our sun and our shield, be Thou through the night our shade and our shield. Undisturbed by anxieties, unalarmed by fears, undistressed by pain or indisposition, may we retire and enjoy repose. Remind us, by putting off our garments and lying down to sleep, of putting off the body, and sleeping in the grave, the house appointed for all living. Prepare us for the night of death, the morning of the resurrection, and the day of judgment.

And all we implore is through the mediation of Him who bore the sins of many, and made intercession for the transgressors: to whom, with the Father and the Holy Spirit, be endless praises. Amen.

THURSDAY MORNING.

WE would address Thee, O God, in the language of the publican—which so well becomes us; and say, from our hearts, God be merciful to me a sinner. Sinners we are by nature and practice; sinners thy word proclaims us to be; sinners we hope we feel ourselves to be; and acknowledge that Thou art justified when Thou speakest, and clear when Thou judgest.

Yet Thou hast not left us to despair: nor have we a mere peradventure to encourage us—who can tell if God will return and repent, and leave a blessing behind him that we perish not? We have all the assurance we could desire, that with the Lord there is mercy, and with him plenteous redemption. Conscious of the number and heinousness of our offences, we could not have approached Thee with confidence without a previous token for good. But Thou hast stretched forth the golden sceptre, and said—Touch and live: I will be merciful to thy unrighteousness, and thy sins and iniquities will I remember no more. May we encourage ourselves by a sense of thy all-sufficiency, by faith in thy promises, by views of the experience of others; and ask and receive, that our joy may be full. To that dear refuge in which so many have been sheltered from every storm, may we repair: and in that fountain for sin, always open and free for all, may we be cleansed from every defilement.

Lord, we believe—help Thou our unbelief—that sin is exceeding sinful; it is the abominable thing which thy soul hateth; and this, and this alone, separates between Thee and us. Thou canst not contradict the essential perfections of thy nature: and Thou canst not make us happy *with* thyself, till Thou hast made us holy *like* thyself. O Thou holy God, deliver us from all our iniquities, and make us such creatures as Thou canst take pleasure in, and such creatures as can take pleasure in Thee. While many are asking, Who will show us any good? may the cry of our heart be, Lord, lift Thou up the light of thy countenance upon us. May we consent to the law of God that it is good; may we delight in thy law after the inner man. May we never complain of the strictness of thy demands, but mourn over our want of conformity to them. May we esteem all thy commandments concerning all things to be right, and hate every false way. Put thy Spirit within us, that our practice may spring from principle, and our dispositions be congenial with duty; so that we may resemble Him who could say, My meat is to do the will of Him that sent me, and to finish his work.

We live in a world of changes; but with Thee there is no variableness, nor shadow of turning. May we know that Thou, the eternal God, art our refuge, and that underneath us are thine everlasting arms. Creatures die; friends and relations die. The fathers where are they? And the prophets do they live for ever? But the Lord liveth, and blessed be our rock, and let the God of our salvation be exalted.

May we never forget that we are mortal—ourselves. May we never put the evil day far off. May we frequently and seriously think of a dying hour: may we faithfully inquire, What will be its issue with regard to us, and what preparation have we for it? And may we never rest satisfied, till we are enabled to view it as the period of our release and the end of our conflict; till we can say with Paul, Thanks be unto God who has given us the victory through our Lord Jesus Christ.

Take us this day under thy protection; and make use of us for thy glory. Let thy presence go with us; and do Thou give us rest. Let thy love sweeten our comforts, and thy grace sanctify all our trials. We consecrate ourselves to Thee, body, soul, and spirit. Accept of our persons and services; and enable us to ascribe blessing, and honour, and glory, and power, unto Him that sitteth upon the throne, and unto the Lamb, for ever and ever. Amen.

THURSDAY EVENING.

O God, all thy works praise Thee, and thy saints bless Thee. By thy mercies we again surround this family altar, and engage in the exercises of devotion. May we be concerned to worship Thee, a holy God, in the beauty of holiness; and to worship Thee, who art a Spirit, in spirit and in truth. Such worship alone thy word requires; but such worship thy grace alone can enable us to render. For we know from thy word, and from our own experience we know, that without Thee we can do nothing. All our sufficiency is of thee; do Thou work in us to will and to do of thy good pleasure.

We would call to remembrance our true character and condition before Thee. We would not go about to establish our own righteousness, or seek to deny or extenuate our guilt. We are not only unprofitable servants, but condemned criminals: we confess the number and offensiveness of our transgressions, and acknowledge that we deserve to perish. But we bless Thee for the everlasting consolation and good hope through grace, which the gospel affords; for the news of a Mediator between Thee and us; of a High Priest who has put away sin by the sacrifice of himself; of an Advocate with the Father who ever lives to make intercession for us; and of a Saviour in whom it has pleased Thee that all fulness should dwell.

Produce in us all the feelings of those who are blessed with repentance unto life. Give us that faith by which we can be justified from all things, and have peace with God through our Lord Jesus Christ. To the shadow of the Redeemer's cross may we retreat, and there find security and relief, refreshment and delight. Assure us of an interest in thy favour, which is life; and clothe us with thine image, which is the beauty and dignity of the soul.

We bless Thee for thy Word which we have been reading. May it dwell in us richly in all wisdom. May we yield a suitable attention to its various parts. May we make it, not only our song in the house of our pilgrimage, but the man of our counsel, a light unto our feet, and a lamp unto our paths. May we take it along with us into all the concerns of life; and whether we are rich or poor, whether we are parents or children, whether we are appointed to govern or serve, may we walk by this rule, that mercy and peace may be upon us.

May we ever be willing that the Lord should choose our inheritance for us, and readily and piously accommodate ourselves to the dispensations of thy providence. May we never lean to our own understanding. May we never take a step without asking counsel of the Lord, nor be unwilling to take one at the intimation of thy pleasure. May we never think that Thou art less wise and righteous and good in a cloudy and dark day, than in a shining one; when we cannot trace Thee, may we trust; and walking by faith and not by sight, be fully persuaded that just and right are all thy ways, O thou King of Saints.

Regard those who, under the pressure of affliction, are saying, Brethren, pray for us. Be with them in trouble. Thou knowest the anxieties of thy people, lest by any of their temper or carriage in the evil day, they should injure the religion they profess: let thy grace be sufficient for them: let faith and patience have their perfect work: let them glorify Thee in the fires.

Bless the king, and have respect unto the government under which we live in all its departments. May this Christian country be a country of Christians. Pour out of thy Spirit upon our great men; and let not those who are able to serve the state by their talents injure it by their vices.

May all those who are placed above others in condition, go before them in the profession of truth and the practice of holiness, and be examples to all inferior ranks in society.

And may the grace of, &c. Amen.

FRIDAY MORNING.

O THOU eternal God! with Thee is the fountain of life. Thou art the Father of men and angels. Thou art the Governor of the universe, and the Judge of all. Thou dost from thy throne behold all the dwellers upon earth: and there is not a word on our tongue, or a thought in our heart, but lo! O Lord, Thou knowest it altogether. And Thou art not a God that hast pleasure in wickedness, neither can evil dwell with Thee.

How then can we presume to enter thy presence, who have rendered ourselves guilty before Thee, and have provoked thy righteous displeasure? O wretched creatures that we are! We have wearied thy patience, we have abused thy goodness, we have trampled on thy authority, and we have said unto God, Depart from us! we desire not the knowledge of thy ways. We lie at thy mercy. If Thou pity us not we are undone. But Thou art long-suffering, not willing that any should perish. Hast Thou not sworn by thyself, that Thou hast no pleasure in the death of him that dieth? Hast Thou not delivered up thine own Son for us all! And wilt Thou not with Him also freely give us all things?

Through Him as the way, the truth, and the life, may we return to Thee; and find Thee waiting to be gracious, and exalted to have mercy upon us. Awaken our consciences. Enlighten us in the knowledge of sin and of ourselves. May we feel our personal depravity, misery, and helplessness; and from self-despair, may we be led to value the discoveries of the gospel, and to flee for refuge to lay hold upon the hope set before us. May we rejoice in the suitableness, the all-sufficiency, and the perfect willingness of the Saviour; and find in Him for ourselves individually, wisdom and righteousness, and sanctification and redemption. As our prophet may we receive his instructions. As our High Priest, may we rely on his sacrifice and intercession. As our Prince, may we obey

Him. As our example, may we follow Him: and whatsoever we do, in word or deed, may we do all in the name of the Lord Jesus.

May integrity and uprightness preserve us. May we be Israelites indeed in whom is no guile; and herein exercise ourselves, to have always a conscience void of offence towards God and towards man. May this same mind govern us, and the same spirit actuate us, in prosperity and adversity, alone and in public, in thy house and in our own. May we fulfil our course with diligence and perseverance, and at last finish it with joy. When we have passed the wilderness, and our eyes behold the swellings of Jordan, deliver us from every fear; and give us a dry-shod passage over— an abundant entrance into the everlasting kingdom of our Lord and Saviour.

But, O Lord, we would not reach that felicity alone. May we awaken the attention of others, and induce them to join us in the path of life; ever remembering that if we convert a sinner from the error of his way, we shall save a soul from death, and shall hide a multitude of sins. May we therefore seek every opportunity of usefulness. May we walk in wisdom towards them that are without. May we hold forth the word of life, and adorn the doctrine of God our Saviour in all things—To whom be glory and majesty, dominion and power, both now and for ever, Amen.

FRIDAY EVENING.

O GOD, Thou art greatly to be feared in the assembly of the saints, and to be had in reverence of all them that are about Thee. Thou art King of kings, and Lord of lords: Thou art the blessed and only potentate: Thou only hast immortality—thy greatness is unsearchable: but thy name is Love. Thy compassions never fail; thy mercies are over all thy works; and Thou hast displayed the exceeding riches of thy grace, in thy kindness towards us by Jesus Christ.

We are not only allowed, but even enjoined to seek thy face; and assured, that they who seek the Lord shall not want any good thing. We acknowledge that we have forfeited all claim to thy regard, and are not only unworthy but guilty. We are convinced that if ever we are saved, it must be according to thy mercy, for there is nothing in us from which our recovery can arise, or on which our hope can fix. But thou hast commended thy love towards us, in that while we were yet sinners Christ died for us—died for the ungodly. And thou hast sent the gospel to announce the intelligence, and to certify, that whosoever believeth on Him shall not perish, but have everlasting life.

O Thou God of all grace, as Thou hast given us a Saviour, produce in us that faith by which we shall be enabled to receive Him.

T

and make Him all our desire, all our hope, and all our glory. May we enter Him as our refuge; build on Him as our foundation; walk in Him as our way; follow Him as our guide; and conform to Him as our example.

May we never be ashamed of Jesus or of his words, but go forth to Him without the camp bearing his reproach. May we never draw upon ourselves reflections by unholy or imprudent conduct, nor count it a glory, when buffeted for a fault, to take it patiently; but if we suffer for truth and righteousness' sake, may we rejoice that we are partakers of Christ's sufferings, knowing that when his glory shall be revealed, we also shall rejoice with exceeding joy.

May we never make the multitude our model; never wait for the company and countenance of others, when conviction derived from thy word excites us to advance. Like Caleb, may we have another spirit, and follow the Lord fully; and with Joshua, say to all around us, Choose you whom you will serve—but as for me and my house, we will serve the Lord.

Preserve us from the present evil world. May its smiles never allure, nor its frowns terrify us from the path of duty. May its vices never defile, nor its errors delude us. May we not live looking at the things which are seen and temporal, but as heirs of immortality, may we feel that we are strangers and pilgrims on earth, and declare plainly that we seek a country. And may our title to it daily become more clear, and our meetness for it more perfect, and our foretastes of it more abundant.

May our house be the tabernacle of the righteous; and let it be ever filled with the voice of rejoicing and of salvation. May those who are stationed at the head of the family know their duty towards those who are placed under their care; and may they know their duty to us: and in our several relations may we walk by the rule of thy word, that mercy and peace may be upon us; and that observers may exclaim, Behold, how good and how pleasant a thing it is for brethren to dwell together in unity!

Bless the religious denomination to which we belong, and let every christian church flourish. Wherever we see the grace of God may we be glad, and willingly leave to the author of all good the choice of his own instruments. Bless the king as supreme, and the government under which we live. Regard all the righteous interests of the country, domestic and foreign. Sanctify and perpetuate and extend our religious advantages. Let thy word have free course and be glorified. Let thy way be known on earth, and thy saving health among all nations.

And now unto Him that is able to do exceeding abundantly above all that we ask or think, according to the power that worketh in us, unto Him be glory in the church, by Christ Jesus, throughout all ages, world without end. Amen.

SATURDAY MORNING.

O God, Thou art glorious in holiness, fearful in praises, doing wonders. And it is not one of the least of thy wonderful doings towards the children of men, that we are on this side an awful eternity, and not reaping the due reward of our deeds. Our whole life has been a series of provocations against thy divine majesty. Our offences have not only been countless but aggravated. Conscience has rebuked us; friends have admonished us; the examples of the wise and good have reproached and encouraged us. Thou hast often called us to reflection and repentance by the smart of the rod, and invited and allured us by a profusion of kindnesses. Our iniquities are increased over our head, and our trespass is gone up into the very heaven. And Thou hast seen all our sins, and Thou hast abhorred all; and Thou couldst have easily and justly punished us; yet Thou spared us, and instead of finding ourselves this morning, in the place where even God has forgotten to be gracious, and lifting up our eyes in hopeless torment, we can lift up our eyes unto the hills from whence cometh our help.

In ourselves we are poor and wretched and miserable, but Thou whom we have offended, even Thou hast provided every supply for our souls; and with the announcement we have the invitation, Come, for all things are now ready. O Lord, we thankfully obey thy call; we accept of thy goodness; we acquiesce in all the appointments of the Gospel. We believe the record Thou hast given of thy dear Son—that there is salvation in none other, but that in Him there is plenteous redemption; and apply to Him for all the benefits resulting from every office he sustains in the church. We give up our minds implicitly to his instruction; in the sacrifice he once offered, we trust and glory; we revere; we love his authority, and pray that his grace may reign in us through righteousness unto eternal life. We would not—we will not—love a world that crucified Him. We will not cherish or endure the sin that put Him to grief, or suffer Him to be wounded in the house of his friends. At the same cross which relieves our consciences from a burden too heavy for us to bear, we would learn lessons of self-denial, forgiveness, and submission; we would feel motives to obedience, and find resources for all the exigencies of the divine life.

For we rejoice to think that by his being made a curse for us, the blessing of Abraham comes upon the Gentiles, and that we can receive the promise of the Spirit by faith. For his sake, give thy Holy Spirit to them that now ask Thee—as a spirit of grace and of supplication, of truth and of holiness, of peace and of consolation; and may we not only possess—but be filled with the Spirit.

May we never consider ourselves as detached individuals. May we look not every man on his own things only, but also on the things of others. Never may we ask with Cain, when reproved for unkindness, or urged to beneficence, Am I my brother's keeper? But may we love our neighbour as ourselves. May we do good even to the unthankful and the unworthy; may we teach transgressors thy ways, and be the means of converting sinners unto Thee: and may none of our efforts be rendered fruitless by inconsistency of character and reproachfulness of conduct. May we *be* what we *profess*; and *do* as well as *teach*. May all our connexions *see* as well as *hear* our religion, and be constrained to acknowledge that we are the seed which the Lord hath blessed.

We bless Thee that again we have laid us down in peace and slept, because Thou, Lord, only makest us dwell in safety. Into thy hands we commit our bodies and spirits, for our going out and coming in this day. We are more exposed by day than by night; more surrounded with evil, and more liable to the seductions of sin. May we ever regard sin as our greatest foe, and holiness as our noblest attainment. And whether we are in solitude or society, lead us not into temptation, but deliver us from evil; for thine is the kingdom, and the power and the glory, for ever and ever. Amen.

SATURDAY EVENING.

O GOD, Thou hast made and Thou upholdest all things by the word of thy power. Darkness is thy pavilion. Thou walkest upon the wings of the wind. All nations before Thee are as nothing. One generation passeth away and another cometh; and we are hastening back to the dust whence we were taken. The heavens we behold will vanish away like the cloud that covers them, and the earth we tread will dissolve like a morning dream; but Thou, incapable of change, independent of the vicissitudes of time, and the perishing of worlds, art from everlasting to everlasting, God over all blessed for evermore.

Infinitely great and glorious as Thou art, we are thy offspring and thy care. Thy hands have made us and fashioned us. Thou hast watched over us with more than parental, more than maternal tenderness. Thou hast holden our soul in life, and not suffered our feet to be moved. Thy divine power has given us all things, not only necessary for life but godliness. Bless the Lord, O our soul, and forget not all his benefits, who forgiveth all our iniquities, who healeth all our diseases, who redeemeth our lives from destruction, who crowneth us with lovingkindness and tender mercies; who satisfieth our mouth with good things, so that our youth is renewed like the eagle's.

We raise this evening a fresh Ebenezer, and inscribe it to the God of our salvation. Hitherto hath the Lord helped us. We have passed not only through another day, but through another week. The sun has not smitten us by day nor the moon by night. We have been preserved in our going out and coming in. But thine has been the vigilance that turned aside the evils which threatened us. Thine have been the supplies that have nourished us. Thine the comforts that have indulged us. Thine the relations and friends that have delighted us. Thine have been the means of grace which have edified us; and thine the book which amidst all our enjoyments has told us that this is not our rest; and that in all our successes, one thing is yet needful.

Nothing can equal the number of thy mercies, but our imperfections and sins. These, O God, we would not conceal nor palliate, but confess them with a broken heart and a contrite spirit.

In what a condition would our closet-reviews leave us this evening, were it not for the assurance, that there is forgiveness with Thee, that thou mayest be feared, and with Thee plenteous redemption. Yet while we hope for pardon through the blood of the cross, we pray to be clothed with humility, to be quickened in thy way, and to be more devoted to the things that belong to our everlasting peace.

How soon has the week rolled away! Its days have fled like a dream, a vapour, a shadow—So will all our days flee; so will they all appear when the end arrives. O help us to keep that end in remembrance, and endeavour to view things now as they will appear from the borders of the grave. May we know how frail we are, that we may be cured of the folly of delay and indecision; and so number our days that we may apply our hearts unto wisdom!

May we call the approaching sabbath a delight, the holy of the Lord honourable; and may we honour Thee in not doing our own ways, nor finding our own pleasures, nor speaking our own words. May the private moments of the day be sacred, and the social, innocent and edifying. And may we keep our foot when we go to the house of God, and offer not the sacrifice of fools. Let us not go as thy people go, and sit as thy people sit, and hear thy words, but do them not.

Preserve us from trifling with the things of the soul and eternity, or trusting in those privileges which unimproved will only augment our guilt and our misery.

Thy people the Jews were distinguished

by thy favours above all the families of the earth; but wrath came upon them to the uttermost. The churches of Asia provoked Thee to remove the candlestick out of its place, and they were left in darkness. We have awful examples still nearer. How many who once heard and professed the gospel, have been turned by the abuse of it into apostates and infidels, blasphemers and persecutors—tenfold more the children of hell than before: while numbers who yet maintain the form of godliness, are too hardened to feel the power of it.

While therefore we go to thy house in the multitude of thy mercies, may we in thy *fear* worship towards thy holy temple; for Thou art greatly to be feared in the assembly of the saints. O let us not perish under means designed to save us—O let not the savour of life unto life prove to us only the savour of death unto death.

Make the place of thy feet glorious. Bring us to thy holy mountain, and if we are not made joyful in thy house of prayer—for we would not dictate to thy goodness—convince us, alarm us, humble us, banish the spirit of the world from our hearts, and fill us with all the fulness of God.

So we thy people, and the sheep of thy pasture will give Thee thanks for ever, we will show forth thy praise throughout all generations. Amen.

THIRD WEEK.

SUNDAY MORNING.

O God, we desire with all reverence and humility to approach Thee, as a Being infinitely great and glorious. Thou art the perfection of all excellency, the fountain of all life, and the source of all blessedness. How immense is the family of creatures produced by thy word and depending on thy care. Millions are visible; and myriads of myriads in the air, the earth, and the sea, are invisible: and all these have their wants and their appetites, and are capable of receiving relief and pleasure. And the eyes of *all* wait upon Thee, and Thou givest them their meat in due season; Thou openest thine hand and satisfiest the desire of every living thing.

But *they* never forfeited the care of their Creator, nor swerved from the end of their being: while *we* have revolted from Thee; *we* have joined in alliance with thy foes; and deserve as children of disobedience, that the wrath of God should come upon us. And yet such is the excellency of thy lovingkindness, O Lord, that the *children of men*, unworthy and guilty as they are, are allowed to come and put their trust under the shadow of thy wings.

We bless Thee for the scriptures of truth which make known thy designs concerning us, and assure us that they are thoughts of peace and not of evil. We rejoice in thy word as one that findeth great spoil. We love to peruse its doctrines, promises, and invitations; to contemplate the great mystery of godliness, God manifest in the flesh; and to dwell on the history and experience of those who have obtained mercy. For all who have ever been saved, have been saved by thy grace, and have been thy workmanship. And Thou art the same yesterday, to-day, and for ever: thy hand is not shortened that it cannot save, nor thine ear heavy that it cannot hear.

Bow down thy ear, and hearken to the voice of our supplication: employ thy hand for our deliverance and relief. We are already the creatures of thy power, O make us the subjects of thy grace. We are already the charge of thy providence, O bless us with all spiritual blessings—blessings for our souls and for eternity. Though by nature afar off, may we be made nigh by the blood of Christ: no longer strangers and foreigners, but fellow-citizens with the saints and of the household of God. Bless us we pray Thee with a present salvation—that being justified by faith, we may have peace with God; that the love and power of sin may be subdued in our hearts; that we may be dead to the world, alive to the glory of God, and concerned to serve our generation according to thy will.

May we never be blots or mere blanks in life. May we never cause the way of truth to be evil spoken of: may our liberty never prove an occasion to the flesh, but by love may we serve one another. May every one of us please his neighbour for his good to edification. May we attend not only to what is essential in our religious character, but what is ornamental. May we pursue whatsoever things are lovely and of good report, and render our profession of the gospel not only impressive, but amiable and inviting. May we hold forth the word of life with our tempers as well as our tongues, with our lives as well as our lips, and thus be continually saying to those we meet—We are journeying towards a place of which the Lord said, I will give it you, come with us and it will do you good, for the Lord hath spoken good concerning Israel.

Send out thy light and thy truth; let them lead us, let them guide us to thy holy hill and to thy tabernacles. Bless this day the dispensation of thy gospel by means of preaching. While Paul plants and Apollos waters —it is all that they can do—give Thou the increase. May thy ministers be wise to win souls; and help those much which have believed through grace.

Especially bless thy dear servant on whose labours we are this day to attend. Let him come forth from his sacred retirement in the fulness of the blessing of the gospel of peace; and may he enter the sanctuary as Aaron entered the tabernacle of the congregation when the holy oil was poured upon his head, and the fragrance filled the place—and O let him not prove the savour of death unto death to any that shall hear him. Open our ear to discipline; may we hear for ourselves, hear for our souls; so hear as that our souls may live. And may great grace rest upon all the assemblies of thy people.

Despise not the prisoners of thy providence. Follow those who are unable to follow Thee; and while forbidden to hear the preaching of the word, may they hear the voice of the rod, and have reason to say—It is good for us that we have been afflicted. Make them thankful, that to will is present with them; and that in their hearts are the ways of those who repair to Zion. Prove thyself a very present help in trouble; and render the bed of languishing, the chamber of sickness, the house of mourning—none other than the house of God, and the gate of heaven.

And by all the discipline of thy providence and the ordinances of religion, may we be increasingly prepared for the remaining duties of life, the solemnities of a dying hour, and the services and joys that are beyond the grave.

We implore it through the intercession of Him who has encouraged us to address Thee as—Our Father, &c.

SUNDAY EVENING.

It is a good thing to give thanks unto the Lord, and to sing praises unto thy Name, O Most High; to show forth thy lovingkindness in the morning, and thy faithfulness every night.

We have this evening to acknowledge the blessings, not only of another day, but of another sabbath. We bless Thee that the sabbath was made for man, and that Thou hast hallowed such a portion of our time, for purposes the most important, but which, alas! we are prone to neglect. Thus thou art affording us opportunities to retire, and compare the objects which court our attention; to learn, among all the cares of life, that one thing is needful; and to hear the inquiry—What is a man profited, if he should gain the whole world and lose his own soul? Thus we have moments of abstraction and leisure in which we can more fully investigate our character, examine our condition, and ask for what purpose we entered this mortal stage, and what will become of us when the scene closes.

We thank Thee that the lines are fallen to us in pleasant places, and that we have a goodly heritage; so that we can add to private meditation and devotion the public ordinances of religion, and can sit under our own vine and fig-tree, none daring to make us afraid. We bless Thee that we have not only the scriptures, but the ministry of the gospel; and have this day not only read, but heard the words of eternal life. We hope we have seen thy power and thy glory in the sanctuary, and have found the house of God to be the gate of heaven.

But, O God, the effects we experience while waiting upon Thee though delightful, are as often transitory, and prove like the morning cloud and early dew. Before the lapse of a single day we are compelled to complain, My soul cleaveth unto the dust; and to pray, Quicken Thou me according to thy word. Render therefore the impressions made upon us deep and durable; keep these things for ever in the imagination of the hearts of thy people; and let thy word *dwell* in us richly in all *wisdom.*

May the instructions we receive attend us in every part of our ordinary life, and regulate and excite us in the discharge of all our relative duties, so that whether we are husbands or wives, parents or children, masters or servants, we may adorn the doctrine of God our Saviour in all things. May we be satisfied with no knowledge, no belief, no professions, no feelings in religion—while our hearts are void of thy love, and we are strangers to that grace which bringeth salvation, and teacheth us to deny ungodliness and worldly lusts, and to live soberly, righteously, and godly in the present world.

We take shame to ourselves, not only for our open violations of thy law, but for our secret faults, our omissions of duty, our unprofitable attendances on the means of grace, our carnality in worshipping Thee, and all the sins of our holy things. Our iniquities are increased over our head, and our trespass is gone up into the very heavens—and there *He* is gone also, who is our advocate with the Father and the propitiation for our sins. Behold his hands and his feet; and hear, O hear the voice of the blood of sprinkling that speaketh better things than that of Abel.

Pity those who have this day been deprived of the public means of grace by sickness or infirmity. Let them know that Thou art not confined to temples made with hands; be with them in trouble; and give them their vineyards from thence, and the valley of Achor for a door of hope.

And remember the millions who were never favoured with the advantages we enjoy, and would be grateful for the crumbs that fall from our table. But they never smiled when a sabbath appeared: they never heard of the name of Jesus: they feel guilt, but know nothing of the blood that cleanseth from all sin: they feel depravity, but know nothing of the renewing of the Holy Ghost:

they are bleeding to death of their spiritual wounds, but no one proclaims among them the balm of Gilead and the physician there! O send out thy light and thy truth. Let thy way be known on earth, thy saving health among all nations.

We now commit ourselves with all our connexions into thy hands. Guard us through the defenceless hours of sleep from every evil to which we are exposed. If, as life is always uncertain, it should please Thee to call us hence this night, may we awake in glory and be for ever with the Lord; or if Thou shouldst continue us in being, may we rise in health and comfort, to pay Thee the homage of a grateful heart in a course of cheerful obedience.

In thy favour is life—Do *Thou* bless us and we shall be blessed—safe from every evil, and assured of every good.

And prepare us at length for the rest that remains for thy people; in which we shall join the general assembly and church of the first-born, in ascribing blessing and honour, and glory and power to Him that sitteth upon the throne, and to the Lamb, for ever and ever. Amen.

———

MONDAY MORNING.

O Thou who hast characterized thyself as the hearer of prayer, unto Thee shall all flesh come: and that we may come with acceptance and success, we come in the name of the great intercessor, Jesus Christ the righteous—And Thou eternal Spirit of grace and supplication, do Thou make intercession for us, by making intercession in us according to the will of God.

All they that are far from Thee shall perish; but it is good for us to draw near to Thee. We have found the duty our delight. Devotion has opened a resource, when all other comforts have failed; and in every perplexity, every alarm, every distress, a glorious high throne from the beginning has been the place of our sanctuary. We praise thy name that ordinances have not been unprofitable observances to our souls, but channels through which the God of all grace has replenished us, and means by which we have enjoyed fellowship with the Father and his Son Jesus Christ.

Bless the services in which we were engaged on the past day. Let a savour of divine things be left on our spirits and be diffused in our conversation. And as the face of Moses when he descended from communion with Thee, shone so that the Israelites could not steadfastly behold him for the glory of his countenance, so may it be with us. Let those around us take knowledge of us that we have been with Jesus; and may our profiting appear unto all men. May our light shine before men. May we be *manifestly* the *epistles* of Christ. Instead of confounding our neighbours and friends to determine whether we are settlers, or strangers and pilgrims on the earth, may we declare *plainly* that we seek a country. May we put on as the elect of God, holy and beloved, bowels of mercies, kindness, humbleness of mind, meekness, longsuffering, forbearing one another, and forgiving one another. May we be followers of God as dear children: may we be perfect as our Father who is in heaven is perfect.

At present it is a day of small things with us. We have only light enough to see our darkness; sensibility enough to feel the hardness of our hearts; spirituality enough to mourn our want of heavenly mindedness. But we might have had more; we ought to have had more. We have never been straitened in Thee: Thou hast always placed before us an infinite fulness, accompanied with the command and the promise, Open thy mouth wide; I will fill it.

We confess and bewail not only our deficiencies, but our backslidings also. It is not with us as it was in months past: O recall us to thyself; enable us to feel our first love, and to do our first works. Yea may we forget the things that are behind, and reach forth unto those that are before. May we not only have life, but may we have it more abundantly; and not only be fruitful, but bear much fruit.

May our improvements correspond with our privileges; and our practice with our knowledge. May our wills always bow to the decisions of our judgments; may we choose what we approve; and never condemn ourselves in the things that we allow.

May we never want the threatenings of thy law, and the terrors of hell, to keep us from every evil way. May thy goodness lead us to repentance, and thy love constrain us to all holy obedience.

Let all our churches continue steadfastly in the apostles' doctrine, and in fellowship, and in breaking of bread, and in prayer; and may the Lord add daily to their number such as shall be saved.

Let the dead hear the voice of the Son of God and live. Let those who are asking the way to Zion with their faces thitherward, find a teacher that will say to them, This is the way, walk ye in it, when they turn to the right-hand and when they turn to the left. Let the rich be poor in spirit; and the poor be made rich in faith, and heirs of the kingdom which thou hast promised to them that love Thee. Let the ignorant be enlightened; and let those that are wise become fools that they may be wise.

We bless Thee for all thy former loving kindnesses to this family, and pray that they may be continued to us and sanctified by us. May the outgoings of the morning and evening of another day be made to rejoice. May we continually live under the shadow of thy wing and the influence of thy grace. And let the words of our mouth and the meditations of our hearts be acceptable in thy sight, O Lord, our strength and our redeemer.

And unto Him that is able to do for us exceedingly abundantly above all that we ask or think, according to the power that worketh in us—unto Him be glory in the church by Christ Jesus, throughout all ages, world without end. Amen.

MONDAY EVENING.

Who in the heavens can be compared unto the Lord? Who among the sons of the mighty can be likened unto the Lord? Thy wisdom no difficulty can perplex; thy power no exertion can weaken; thy bounty no communications can exhaust or diminish. Thy goodness waits to be gracious and is exalted to have mercy.

Thou hearest prayer; and to assure our hearts before Thee, Thou hast not only commanded us to seek Thee, but thou hast furnished us with the petitions we are to offer. Thou, even Thou, hast told us to take with us words and turn to the Lord: and say— Take away all iniquity, receive us graciously, so will we render the calves of our lips.

We feel the truth of our character, as drawn in the scriptures; and we acknowledge our desert and our helplessness too. Thy mercy is our only refuge and resource. O be merciful unto us, and bless us, and cause thy face to shine upon us that we may be saved. O visit us with that salvation which is present as well as future; which changes not only our state, but our nature; and which not only admits us into thy family, but makes us new creatures.

As Thou didst in the original creation command the light to shine out of darkness, so do Thou shine in our hearts. Give us the light of the knowledge of thy glory in the face of Jesus Christ; and may we so know Thee as to love Thee supremely, serve Thee as our only Lord, and cleave to thee as our portion for ever. Subdue the rebellion of our wills, that we may submit to thy commands, and acquiesce in thy dispensations without murmurings and disputings. Unite our hearts to fear thy name; and may we be in the fear of the Lord all the day long. Make us Israelites indeed in whom there is no guile. Enable us to maintain a conscience void of offence towards God and towards man. May we be the same when no eye sees us, as we are in the public walks of life. May we enter the closet as well as the temple, and attend to our principles and motives as well as our actions and pursuits.

We mourn over our numberless failures

and backslidings; our incorrigibleness under rebukes; our want of profiting under ordinances; the non-improvement of our talents; and our neglect of opportunities of usefulness. Whatever view we take of ourselves compels us to exclaim—Behold I am vile. Yet while we are humble may we be grateful; and never be backward to acknowledge what Thou hast done for our souls. If we are not like some of thy people, we bless thee that we are not like the rest of the world; if we are not what we ought to be, we are not what we once were. Thou hast made us to differ, and we have nothing which we did not receive from Thee.

And if our religion be imperfect, may it appear to be real and vital by its activity and its tending to growth. May it awaken in us an unconquerable desire to go from strength to strength, and to be renewed day by day.

May our religion always attend us and dignify us in the ordinary scenes of life. May we remember, that greatness consists not in doing great things, but in doing little things with a great mind.

As the events of providence occur, may they always find in us those dispositions which will keep them from injuring us, and which will convert them all into advantages.

In a vale of tears, may we look for a succession of trials; and may we also look for the accomplishment of the promise—I will be with thee in trouble.

May the joy of the Lord be our strength; may it keep us from lusting after the vanities of the world; bear up the heart and mind in the loss of every creature-comfort; and enliven us in the valley of the shadow of death. And before we reach heaven, may we bear the image of the heavenly, possess the earnests of our inheritance, and enjoy the first-fruits of the glorious harvest.

And to God the Father, the Son, and the Holy Ghost, be all honour and glory, for ever and ever. Amen.

TUESDAY MORNING.

O God, Thou art the creator, the upholder, and the proprietor of all things. Thy dominion is everlasting and universal. Thou dost according to thine own will in the armies of heaven, and among the inhabitants of the earth: none can stay thy hand, or say unto Thee, What dost Thou!

We cannot escape from thy presence or control; nor do we desire it. It is our privilege that we are under the agency, not only of omnipotence, but righteousness, wisdom, patience, mercy, and grace. Thou art love. Thou hast loved us with more than parental affection. Thou hast commended thy love towards us, in that while we were sinners Christ died for us. He that spared not his own Son but delivered Him up for us all—how shall He not with Him also freely give us all things? Here may all our fears be banished from our minds; here may we be filled with everlasting consolation and good hope through grace.

Thou hast not only allowed, but commanded us to believe on the name of thy dear Son. O let us not refuse to be comforted; let us not reject the counsel of God against ourselves; but remembering that we are as welcome as we are guilty, may we drink of the fountain of the water of life freely.

But while we know that we *may* come to the Redeemer and *ought* to come—may we never think ourselves interested in the blessings of his salvation unless we *have* come. May there be a real and living union between our souls and Him, that quickened together with Christ, we may be raised up, and made to sit with him in the heavenly places. May we live a life of faith in thy promises, mingled with no jealousy of thy truth nor suspicion of thy power. May we live a life of hope; expecting that Thou wilt be our sun and our shield; that thou wilt give grace and glory; and withhold no good thing from us while we walk uprightly. And may we live a life of love; for he that dwelleth in love dwelleth in God, and God in him. O shed abroad thy love in our hearts, the animating and delightful principle of all obedience. May we love our neighbour as ourselves; and consider every one as our neighbour, who falls within the reach of our knowledge and assistance.

We feel that the work to which we are called is far above our strength. We have tried our purposes and resolutions, and have found them vain. The least temptation has been too powerful for us, when we have gone forth in our own strength. O teach us how to be strong in the Lord and in the power of his might. And at every movement in our journey and our warfare, say to our heart, Fear not, for I am with thee; be not dismayed, for I am thy God; I will strengthen thee; yea I will help thee; yea I will uphold thee with the right hand of my righteousness.

And may we never depart from Thee by making flesh our arm, or the creature our portion. With regard to the world, may our soul be even as a weaned child; but may we draw near to Thee as our exceeding joy, and contemplate with approbation, the period when we shall behold thy face in righteousness, awake up after thy likeness and be satisfied with thy favour.

All which we implore through the mediation of Him who ever liveth to make intercession for us, and to whom, with the Father and the Holy Spirit, be endless praises. Amen.

TUESDAY EVENING

MAY we approach Thee with all the encouragement derivable from a conviction that Thou art the blessed God; happy in thyself, and the source of happiness to thy creatures. The eyes of all wait upon Thee, and Thou givest them their meat in due season; Thou openest thine hand, and satisfiest the desire of every living thing. Thou art our maker and benefactor. Thou hast not only produced us, but sustained; not only supported us, but indulged: yea, Thou hast given us all things richly to enjoy. Thou hast provided for the welfare of our souls as well as our bodies; Thou hast answered the awful question, How shall I come before the Lord and bow before the High God? Thou hast told us what we must do to be saved. May we follow the light of life which Thou hast given us, till it brings us to Him who appears in every attribute, and in every attitude of power and pity to meet all our wants and miseries. And as we draw near, may we hear his gracious voice saying, Him that cometh unto me I will in no wise cast out. May we commit our eternal all into his hands, and being reconciled by his death, may we be saved by his life. May we live by Him, live to Him, live like Him. While we behold Him as rich for our sakes becoming poor, and dying that we may live, may his unexampled love constrain us into all holy obedience and zeal, and render our duty our delight.

May we never wait for the company of others, or feel their approbation necessary to induce us to follow *Him* who is all our salvation, and ought to be all our desire. May we go forth to Him without the camp, bearing his reproach. And if our faith is deemed folly, our hope delusion, our meekness meanness, our zeal madness; may we rejoice that we are counted worthy to suffer shame for his Name, and binding it as a garland around our brow say, If this be to be vile, I will yet be more vile. Thus blessed Redeemer wast Thou treated in the days of thy flesh; thus was thy Name cast out as evil, thy actions misrepresented, and thy spirit blasphemed. O let the servants be willing to be as the master, and the disciples as the Lord.

We hope in thy word; but it is because it assures us that Thou waitest to be gracious, and dost not break the bruised reed nor quench the smoking flax. How poor and pitiable, how maimed and dying a thing, has our religion been under every advantage to promote it. Lord, hide pride from us; enable us to walk humbly with our God, and ask and receive that our joy may be full. Hast Thou not promised to supply all our need from thy riches in glory by Christ Jesus? Thou knowest all our warfare, all our work, all our trials; and Thou knowest the degree and extent of our weakness; and yet Thou hast said, My grace is sufficient for Thee. Lord, we believe; help thou our unbelief. •

While we rejoice in our privileges, we would remember the way in which they have become ours. We have nothing to glory in before Thee. We ourselves also were once foolish and disobedient; and we would ever look to the rock whence we were hewn, and to the hole of the pit whence we were digged. Thou hast made us to differ; and we have nothing but what we have received.

And this encourages us with regard to others. What Thou hast done for us, Thou art able to do for them. And Thou art willing. Thou hast therefore commanded us to pray for all men. O let none of those perish whom we love as our own souls. Keep them as the apple of the eye; hide them under the shadow of thy wing.

Let grace and peace be multiplied to all who have obtained like precious faith with us. And if Thou art pleased to try that faith, may the trial be found unto praise and glory and honour at the appearing of Jesus Christ.

But we would not forget even the ignorant and profligate. Teach transgressors thy ways, and let sinners be converted unto Thee.

Dethrone the God of this world. Destroy the works of the devil. And may our globe, which has so long groaned beneath the curse, be as the smell of a field which the Lord hath blessed. Send out thy light and thy truth, thy servants and thy labourers, and for them may the wilderness and the solitary place be made glad, and the desert rejoice and blossom as the rose.

Amen—Blessing and glory and power and might be unto our God for ever and ever.—Amen.

WEDNESDAY MORNING.

O Thou with whom we have to do! suffer us not to live without Thee in the world.—Thou art our Creator, our Preserver, our Governor—and we believe that Thou wilt be our Judge. It is well for us that we can view thee under another character—the Saviour of sinners; and that before we are called to appear before thy awful tribunal, we are invited and commanded to come boldly to the throne of grace, there to obtain mercy and find grace to help in time of need.

May we readily and thankfully avail ourselves of every opportunity to draw nigh to God, in the temple, in the retirement of the closet, and at the domestic altar; and let not our devotion be bodily exercise only. Quicken our souls to call upon thy name—Detach us from the influence of flesh and sense—Impress us with the power of faith; and produce in us that spirituality of mind which will render our services acceptable to Thee, and delightful and profitable to ourselves.

Though Thou art Most High for evermore, Thou regardest the man that is poor and of a contrite spirit, and that trembleth at thy word. Thou fillest the hungry with good things, while the rich are sent empty away. O bring us, however humbling and painful the process may be, O bring us into that state which attracts thine eye, and prepares for the proofs of thy love! Show us our danger, that we may flee for refuge to the hope set before us. Make us sensible of our disease, and of the eternal death to which it is so rapidly tending, that we may value the physician and cry—Heal me and I shall be healed, save me and I shall be saved, for thou art my praise.

Our deliverance must come entirely from thyself. And Thou hast not forgotten to be gracious. We bless Thee for the purpose of salvation; for the engagements of the everlasting covenant; and for the gift of thy dear Son, the proof and the pledge that Thou wilt also freely give us all things. We thank Thee for the word of truth, which proclaims peace by the blood of the cross; and beseeches us in Christ's stead to be reconciled unto God. O let the message prevail. Let it slay the enmity of our hearts, and lead us to throw down every weapon of rebellion, and mourn over them. With weeping and supplication may we return to Thee from whom we have so deeply revolted. And while with shame and self-abhorrence we confess that other lords beside Thee have had dominion over us, henceforth may we resolve that by Thee only will we make mention of thy Name. With zeal may we engage in that service which is perfect freedom; and with entireness devote ourselves to that work which is honourable and glorious. May we employ every faculty and use every blessing, as those who know that they are not their own, but bought with a price, and are bound to glorify God in their body ·and in their spirit, which are God's.

Work in us to will and to do of thy good pleasure. Uphold us by thy free spirit; and let the joy of the Lord be our strength.

May we be watchful over our ways; may we be jealous over our tempers; and may we keep our hearts with all diligence, knowing that out of them are the issues of life. Divest us of pride, and clothe us with humbleness of mind. Eradicate every root of bitterness, and let the peace of God rule in our hearts.

When we droop, revive us; when we loiter, quicken us; restore us when we go astray; and lead us in the paths of righteousness for thy Name's sake.

Yea though we walk through the valley of the shadow of death may we fear no evil, knowing that Thou art with us, and that thy rod and staff will comfort us.

The Lord bless us and keep us. The Lord make his face to shine upon us and be gracious unto us. The Lord lift up his countenance upon us and give us peace. Amen.

WEDNESDAY EVENING.

O God, Thou art greatly to be feared in the assembly of the saints, and to be had in reverence of all that are about Thee. Those glorious beings that never fell, veil their faces and sink into nothing before the Eternal All, and exclaim, Holy, holy, holy is the Lord of hosts, the whole earth is full of his glory. With what emotions should we enter thy presence, whose foundation is in the dust; and who have contemned thy goodness, defied thy power, trampled upon thy laws, and rendered ourselves worthy of eternal death. Our iniquities are increased over our head, and our trespass is gone up into the very heavens. Enter not into judgment with thy servants: our consciences assure us, that if Thou Lord shouldest mark iniquity, we could not stand.

But there is mercy with Thee, and with Thee there is plenteous redemption: and therefore while a sense of our vileness depresses us, we encourage ourselves in thy word. We know that our recovery can never spring from any cause in us. We have destroyed ourselves, but we cannot save. Yet our condition is not helpless. Help is laid on One that is mighty, and infinitely qualified for his work; and who has shown us in his resurrection from the dead and ascension into heaven, the all-sufficiency and acceptance of his sacrifice on the cross, and proved that by the one offering of himself he hath perfected for ever them that are sanctified.

Informed of this compassionate scheme, may we gratefully fall in with the design; may we unfeignedly believe the record that Thou hast given us of thy Son, embrace Him as our only hope, rejoice in Him as our highest glory; and henceforth may the life that we live in the flesh be by the faith of Him who loved us and gave himself for us.

And while we live by Him, may we live to Him, and may we live like Him. May we never consider ourselves Christians but as we resemble Christ. May our conformity to his principles, temper, and conduct, be hourly growing, and become more apparent not only to ourselves but to others. And may we continue in his word, that we may be his disciples indeed; rooted and built up in Him, and stablished in the truth as we have been taught, and abounding therein with thanksgiving.

May no degree of watching or length of waiting cool our love and zeal. Whatever discouragements we meet with, may we never grow weary in well doing. Yea may we not only persevere, while many draw back, but fear God above many who go forward; and hear the Saviour-Judge saying, I know thy works, and the last to be more than the first.

May we not only *be blessed* but *prove blessings*. May we often look closely at our talents, relations, and circumstances in life, to see how we can be serviceable to the bodies and souls of our fellow-creatures, and especially how we may do good to them that are of the household of faith.

We are continually meeting with wants and miseries which we are utterly unable to remove or release; but we rejoice that in our contracted agency, prayer opens a resource to our benevolence. We can pray; and prayer has power with God and can prevail.

Let the leisure and affluence of the rich in this world afford them means and opportunities of beneficence; may they be ready to communicate; and be rich in good works.

Let the afflictions of the afflicted render sin hateful, wean them from a vain world, endear to them the word of grace, the throne of grace, and the Spirit of grace; and work out for them a far more exceeding and eternal weight of glory.

Let our ignorance of futurity keep us in a state of constant dependence upon thy providential care; and lead us earnestly to seek large supplies of the spirit of Jesus Christ to fit us for all events.

Thou hast redeemed us, O Lord God of Truth; therefore into thine hands we commit ourselves and our interests, beseeching Thee to do for us exceeding abundantly above all we are able to ask or think, through our only Lord and Saviour. Amen.

THURSDAY MORNING.

O God, help us to approach Thee under a very lively conviction of thy abundant mercy, and the exceeding riches of thy grace. We ought to admire thy wisdom, to stand in awe of thy power, and to abase ourselves before thy spotless purity. But it is the discovery of thy goodness alone that can banish our fear, and allure us with humble confidence into thy presence, there to divulge our sorrows and confess our sins.

And O how encouraging is it under a review of our past guilt, and a consciousness of present unworthiness, to know that we have to do with a Being who waits to be gracious, and is exalted to have mercy. We therefore bless Thee, that an attribute so essential to our happiness and hope is not founded on conjecture, or obscurely revealed. Thou hast not left thyself without witness in the seasons of the year, and the bounties of nature and providence. But Thou hast given us thy word, which Thou hast magnified above all thy Name. There we see Thee not sparing thine own Son, but delivering Him up for us all; there we behold the provisions of thy house; there we hear the proclamations of thy servants—Come, for all things are now ready.

Lord make us willing to be saved, and to

be saved in thy own way. Condemned by the law which we have so often transgressed, may we turn for all our relief to the gospel; and perceiving nothing in ourselves, may we find in the hope of Israel, wisdom, righteousness, sanctification, and redemption. May the message which concerns a dying rising interceding Saviour, be received into our very hearts, and become there a well of water springing up into everlasting life. And may we not only receive Christ Jesus the Lord, but also walk in Him; in a state of dependence upon Him, communion with Him, and conformity to Him. May we be followers of Him as dear children; imperfect but still pressing forward; not complaining of labour, but valuing rest; not murmuring under our trials, but thankful for a state—O that we were sure of reaching it!—where our sun shall no more go down, nor our moon withdraw herself, but God shall be our everlasting light, and the days of our mourning shall be ended.

We live in the midst of observation. Many watch for our halting, and wish our good to be evil spoken of. May we walk the more circumspectly, and by well doing may we put to silence the ignorance of foolish men; yea by our good works which they behold, may we constrain them to glorify God in the day of visitation.

We appear not alone in thy presence; but are variously connected in life. Regard those who are dear to us by the claims of nature or friendship. We ask not that Thou shouldst set them upon the high places of the earth, but O number them with thy saints in glory everlasting. O let none of them die without an interest in Christ, and be separated from us in the day when Thou wilt make up thy jewels.

Bless those who are related to us in religious bonds. And such we are delighted to consider *all* the followers of the Lamb, under whatever name, distinctive or reproachful, they may pass among men. May the Lord add to his people how many soever they be, a hundred-fold; and may grace and peace be multiplied unto them.

And forget not we beseech Thee, those to whom we are politically allied. Let the king live before Thee. May all who are in places of public trust be faithful to the public interests. Teach our senators wisdom. May our magistrates be men fearing God, and hating covetousness; terrors to evil doers, and a praise to them that do well: and may all ranks in the community pursue that righteousness which exalteth a nation, that being a holy, we may be a happy people, whose God is the Lord.

So we thy people, and the sheep of thy pasture, will give Thee thanks for.ever; we will show forth thy praise throughout all generations. Amen.

THURSDAY EVENING.

WHEN we enter thy presence, O God, we see Thee in all the glory of thy perfections, seated on a throne of universal and everlasting empire, thousands ministering unto Thee, and ten thousand times ten thousand standing before Thee. Impress our minds with a consciousness of thy greatness—not to drive us back from Thee, but to inspire us with reverence and godly fear in approaching Thee—not to diminish our confidence in Thee, but to lead us to admire the vastness of thy condescension, in deigning to open communications with creatures so mean and vile as we are. Lord, what is man, that Thou art mindful of him? or the son of man, that thou visitest him?

And yet Thou *hast* been mindful of *us;* Thou hast visited us. We have been thy charge from the womb; and Thou hast in all conditions cared for us. We have been constantly fed at thy table, and clothed from thy wardrobe. How often hast Thou drawn the curtain of night around us, and ordered creation to be quiet, while thy children have slumbered and slept. They mercies have been new every morning. Thy goodness has inspired our relations and friends with all the sentiments of tenderness and respect they have ever expressed towards us. And we would not overlook the blessings of the life that now is—

But O Lord, suffer us not to forget—that we want better blessings than these. We want a hope beyond the grave. We are guilty, depraved, dying creatures. We need pardon and holiness, and wisdom and strength, and peace and joy: we want the earnests and foretastes of immortality. And blessed be thy name, what we so much need, and hope we can say, so much desire, Thou hast provided. We thank Thee for thy unspeakable gift. We rejoice that we have our existence in a land of gospel privileges; and where one of the first sounds that entered our infant ears, from a mother's lips, was the name of JESUS. We rejoice that we have been led to view Him, not only as a teacher and an example, but as the Lamb of God that taketh away the sins of the world: and that now in Christ Jesus, we who sometimes were afar off, are made nigh by the blood of Christ, and have boldness and access with confidence by the faith of Him.

May we look after actual and personal benefit from Him, and never be satisfied till we can say, I know whom I have believed, and am persuaded that he is able to keep that which I have committed to Him against that day. Possess us with more of that faith which is the principle and medium of all vital godliness: may we be rich in faith; may we be strong in faith. By faith may we live, and by faith may we walk. May we feel the joy of faith, and do the work of faith. May we abound in hope: may the charity of every one of us towards each other increase; and may we be filled with all the fruits of righteousness which are by Jesus Christ to the glory and praise of God.

We ought to feel a broken heart and a contrite spirit. We grieve to think how insensible we have been to the claims of thy authority, and the endearments of thy love; how little we have credited thy truth, trusted thy promises, feared thy threatenings, obeyed thy commands, or improved any of our advantages. We have had line upon line, and precept upon precept. How numberless have been our admonitions and warnings; and Thou hast said—He that being often reproved, hardeneth his neck, shall suddenly be destroyed, and that without remedy.

We thank Thee, that notwithstanding our desert, this is not at present our doom. As yet we are in the number of those for whom Thou art waiting to be gracious. We are yet in the land of the living. Through another day Thou hast spared us and blessed us. May thy goodness lead us to repentance, and thy longsuffering prove our salvation. Let no evil befall us, and no plague come nigh our dwelling this night; and in the morning may we rise to walk before the Lord in the land of the living, and to show forth all his praise.

We implore it in the name of him who died for our sins, rose again for our justification; and ever liveth to make intercession for us; and to whom, with the Father and Holy Spirit, be ascribed everlasting praises. Amen.

FRIDAY MORNING.

Our voice shalt Thou hear in the morning O Lord; in the morning alone, and in our family will we direct our prayer unto Thee and will look up. How well does it become us to be thankful!—Many during the past night have had no place where to lay their head. Many the victims of disease, have been full of tossing to and fro, until the dawning of the day; so that their bed has not comforted them, nor their couch eased their complaint. Many have been deprived of rest, while watching over their connexions in pain and sorrow. How many have slept the sleep of death, and will not awake till the heavens are no more. Others whose lives are prolonged, have risen to be surrounded with want and wo; and thousands who have all things richly to enjoy, have risen only to live another day without God in the world!

And why is not this the case with us? Thou, O God, hast remembered and distinguished and indulged us. Bless the Lord, O *my* soul, and all that is within me bless his holy name. O magnify the Lord with me, and let us exalt his name *together.*

And thy mercies have been new every morning; yea every morning. All our de-

sires have not been gratified; but it was love that denied us, when the accomplishment of our wishes would have proved our ruin or our injury. We have had our trials, but they have been few compared with our sins; they have been attended with numberless alleviations; and when we have kissed the rod, it has fallen out of thy hand. Thou hast often wiped away our tears, and restored peace to thy mourners. Thou hast never chastened us but for our profit. We already see the design of many of our griefs, and can say, It is good for me that I have been afflicted: and in all other cases, where darkness yet clouds the dispensation, we desire to walk by faith. We believe that Thou hast done all things well, and that thy work is perfect.

But O what do we owe Thee for the word of thy truth, the throne of thy grace, the Son of thy love—thy unspeakable gift! What do we owe Thee, if we have any reason to hope that we are in Christ, and free from all condemnation; and that when He who is our life shall appear, we shall also appear with Him in glory and be for ever with the Lord!

Surely a gratitude becomes us that will not evaporate in a morning acknowledgment with the lip, but such as will keep us in the fear of the Lord all the day long, and lead us to ask, What shall I render unto the Lord for all his benefits towards me? We therefore, by the mercies of God, present our bodies a living sacrifice, holy and acceptable unto Thee, which is our reasonable service.

And now, O Thou author of all good, we come to Thee for the grace another day will require—the grace its duties will require—the grace its events will require; for we know not when we leave our apartments in the morning what a day will bring forth. But we know that we are stepping into a wicked world, and that we carry about us an evil heart; we know that without Thee we can do nothing; and we know that there is nothing with which we shall have any concern in the day, however harmless in itself, but may prove an occasion of sinning and falling, unless we are kept by the power of God. We therefore desire to pray ourselves out of our own keeping, into thy keeping. Hold *Thou* us up and we shall be safe. Preserve our understandings from the subtlety of error; our affections from the love of idols; our senses from the ungovernable impressions of outward objects; our character from every stain of vice; our profession from every appearance of evil; and may the God of peace sanctify us wholly, and may our whole spirit, soul and body, be preserved blameless unto the coming of our Lord Jesus Christ.

May we engage in nothing in which we cannot implore thy blessing, and to which we cannot welcome thy inspection. Prosper us in our lawful undertakings, or prepare us for disappointment. Give us neither poverty nor riches. Feed us with food convenient for us; lest we be full and deny Thee, and say, Who is the Lord? or lest we be poor and steal, and take the name of our God in vain.

May every creature be good to us, being sanctified by the word of God and prayer. Teach us how to use the world, as not abusing it. Enable us to improve our talents, and to redeem our time. May we walk in wisdom towards them that are without, and in kindness towards them that are within; and do good as we have opportunity unto all men, especially unto them that are of the household of faith.

And unto Him that is able to keep us from falling, and to present us faultless before the presence of his glory with exceeding joy—To the only wise God our Saviour, be glory and majesty, dominion and power, both now and ever. Amen.

FRIDAY EVENING.

O Thou incomprehensibly great and glorious Jehovah, the King of kings, and Lord of lords, who only hast immortality—We adore Thee, and abase ourselves. Though we are allowed to approach Thee, we would not be mindless of the views and feelings which so well become those who as creatures are less than nothing, and as sinners are worse than nothing before Thee.

For if we say we have no sin, we deceive ourselves and the truth is not in us: the heavens would reveal our iniquity, and the earth would rise up against us. And why should we endeavour to deny our guilt—since even our thoughts have not been screened from thy gaze, and Thou hast set our most secret sins in the light of thy countenance: and why should we desire it—since we know that if we confess our sins, Thou art faithful and just to forgive us our sins, and to cleanse us from all unrighteousness? From a view therefore of their exceeding sinfulness, we would confess them with a broken heart and a contrite spirit, earnestly longing to be delivered from them, and be led in the way everlasting.

Enable us to remember that blood which cleanseth from all sin; to believe in that grace which can subdue all our iniquities; and to resign ourselves to that agency which can deliver us from the bondage of corruption, into the glorious liberty of the sons of God. While many envy the men of the world who have their portion in this life, may we with Moses choose rather to suffer affliction with the people of God, than enjoy the pleasures of sin for a season. While many seek great things for themselves on earth, things which perish in the using, and afford no satisfaction in the possessing, may the prayer of David become ours—Remember me O Lord with the favour Thou bearest

unto thy people, O visit me with thy salvation, that I may see the good of thy chosen, that I may rejoice in the gladness of thy nation, and glory with thine inheritance!

We sometimes hope that Thou hast already begun a good work in us; and to whom should we go for the continuance, the progress, and the completion, but to Thee, the God of all grace, and who art not only the author, but the finisher of our faith? We rejoice in what Thou hast done for others: in *their* deliverance and elevation we see what Thou art able and willing to do for us. We bless Thee for the promises upon which Thou hast caused us to hope; and in which Thou hast engaged to perfect that which concerneth us. We thank Thee for the means of grace, in the humble and diligent use of which Thou art pleased to draw near to those who draw near to Thee.

May we love the closet as well as the temple; and do Thou sanctify to us, not only the preaching of the gospel, but also the reading of thy word. Believing with a faith unfeigned that it is given by inspiration of God, may we find it profitable for doctrine, for reproof, for correction, and for instruction in righteousness. In every perplexity, may it be the man of our counsel; may we repair to it in every distress; and in the multitude of our thoughts within us may thy comforts delight our souls.

May we have an increasing conviction of our liableness to err, and our exposure to sin, that we may place ourselves under thy guiding and guardian care. As we see the vanity of the world, and meet with trials and disappointments, may we take a firmer hold of that covenant which is ordered in all things and sure; and may *this* be all our salvation and all our desire, when our house is not so with God, and Thou makest it not to grow. May we rejoice in hope, be patient in tribulation, and continue constant in prayer.

May we feel more of the purifying, more of the dignifying, more of the softening influence of the religion we profess. May we have compassion one of another: love as brethren, be pitiful, be courteous. May we never render railing for railing, but contrariwise blessing: may we not be overcome of evil, but overcome evil with good.

May we never incur the curse of the angel of the covenant, for not coming to the help of the Lord. May we deem it an honour to be employed by Thee, and long to be instruments in thy hands. Ready to seize every opportunity of usefulness, and willing to use all our talents in thy blessed service, may we daily ask, Lord, what wilt Thou have me to do?

Bless our country: and as Thou hast placed us at the head of the nations, may we be for a name and a praise unto Thee in the whole earth. Largely have we been the recipients of thy goodness; and freely may we give. Sanction the institutions and efforts by which we are endeavouring to spread the benefits of the gospel. God be merciful unto *us*, and bless *us*, that his way may be known on earth, his saving health among all nations.

O remember the number called in various ways to suffer. Bless their daily rod, as well as their daily bread. May they feel impressions which shall never wear off: may they learn such lessons as shall never be forgotten: may they enjoy such consolations as shall enable them to say, It is good for me that I have been afflicted.

And to God only wise be glory and dominion for ever and ever. Amen.

SATURDAY MORNING.

O THOU everlasting God, the creator of all the ends of the earth, and the father of the spirits of all flesh—We have destroyed ourselves, but in Thee is our help. Our nature is defiled; all the powers of our souls are degraded; we are vile, we are miserable; we are without strength. We condemn ourselves, and confess that we deserve to perish. If ever we are saved, it must be by goodness the most undeserved and astonishing; not only by mercy, but abundant mercy; not only by grace, but the exceeding riches of thy grace.

And such mercy and grace Thou hast been pleased to reveal and to promise and to exemplify. Thou hast told us thy designs, and unlike the forebodings of our guilty minds, they are thoughts of peace and not of evil.

We bless Thee for devising means to rescue us from the perdition of sin, and restore us to a state of happiness and honour and safety, superior to our original condition. We bless Thee for the provisions of the everlasting covenant, and for the constitution of a Mediator between Thee and us. We rejoice that He failed not, nor was discouraged, but accomplished the work that was given Him to do, and said on the cross, It is finished. We exult in the thought that now thy justice is satisfied, thy truth established, thy law magnified, and a foundation laid even in thy own glory for our hope.

May we look after present and personal interest in Christ, and never rest till we can say—Surely he hath borne our grief, and carried our sorrow; the chastisement of our peace was upon him, and by his stripes we are healed. May we know that in Him we have righteousness and strength, and are blessed with all spiritual blessings. While we are justified by his blood, may we be saved by his life. While we glory in his cross, may we bow to his sceptre, and long to have the same mind in us which was also in Him;

knowing that if we have not the spirit of Christ we are none of his.

We are convinced that it is our happiness as well as duty to walk in thy ways, to keep thy statutes, and to submit to thy appointments; but we are equally convinced that thy grace alone is sufficient for us, and that without Thee we can do nothing. We cannot even stand, but as we are upholden by thy free spirit. But with Thee is the residue of the Spirit; and Thou hast engaged to give thy holy Spirit to them that ask Thee: yea Thou hast said, Open thy mouth wide, and I will fill it. Bless us therefore with constant and increasing supplies of grace and strength: work in us to will and to do of thy good pleasure; and fulfil in us all the good pleasure of thy goodness, and the work of faith with power.

May our religion, instead of being an occasional and partial thing, be universal and invariable in its influence and effects. May we be in the fear of the Lord every day, and all the day long. May we hold communion with Thee in thy works as well as in thy word, and in the dispensations of thy providence as well as in the ordinances of thy house.

May we always distinguish between the form of godliness and the power thereof, and between life and a name to live. What is the hope of the hypocrite, though he hath gained, when Thou takest away his soul! O make us Israelites indeed in whom is no guile. Often may we examine ourselves, and inquire whether our religion will bear the eye of God. If we are not right, set us right and keep us right. Search us, O God, and know our heart; try us, and know our thoughts; and see if there be any wicked way in us, and lead us in the way everlasting.

Impress us with a conviction of the vanity of the world, and the brevity and uncertainty of the time of our continuance here; that we may keep the end of life in view, and apply our hearts unto wisdom.

We are ignorant, and liable to a thousand delusions: but Thou knowest what is good for us. To Thee therefore we commit our works and our way; and to Thee we refer the choice of our inheritance.

Only be with us, and keep us in the path that we go, and give us bread to eat, and raiment to put on, so that we come to our Father's house in peace; and the Lord shall be our God.

And may the grace of our Lord Jesus Christ, and the love of God, and the communion of the Holy Ghost, be with us all, now and for ever. Amen.

SATURDAY EVENING.

O GOD, Thou hast been the refuge and the dwelling-place of thy people in all generations. To Thee the poor and the needy have always repaired for succour; and they that know thy name will put their trust in Thee. And to whom should we go but unto Thee? Thou hast the words of eternal life. There is no blessing we can implore, but Thou art *able* to give, and hast *promised* to give, and hast *given* already to a countless multitude, all unworthy and guilty like ourselves. Yea Thou hast not spared thine own Son, but delivered Him up for us all: and wilt Thou not with Him also freely give us all things?

O make us more willing to receive the supply of all our need from thy riches in glory by Christ Jesus. And for this purpose, convince us of sin. Show us our true character and condition in thy sight. Take away the stone out of our hearts, and give us hearts of flesh. May we feel and bewail our folly and ingratitude, our pride and unbelief, the rebellion of our lives, and the corruption of our nature. May we sorrow after a godly sort, and abhor ourselves repenting in dust and ashes. Through the law, may we die unto the law, and despair of obtaining life but from thy own sovereign mercy. May we look with wonder and submission, and gratitude and delight, to the provision which Thou hast made for the glory of thy own name in the salvation of sinners. May we believe in Him whom Thou hast set forth as a propitiation for sin, and as the end of the law for righteousness: may we know Him in the power of his resurrection and the fellowship of his sufferings, and be made conformable unto his death.

Give us that hope which maketh not ashamed. Inspire us with that love which excites to all holy obedience. Pour into our hearts that joy of the Lord which is the strength of thy people; and enable us to say with Paul, The life that I now live in the flesh, I live by the faith of the Son of God, who loved *me* and gave himself for *me*.

And when we cannot pronounce on our own interest in divine things, may we still persevere in duty. May we wait on the Lord, and keep his way; and be humble and earnest suppliants at thy footstool, assured that they who hunger and thirst after righteousness, are blessed, and shall be filled.

Preserve us from that levity and indifference which are so unbecoming creatures who live continually under the eye of God, and are always on the brink of an eternal world.

May we discover nothing like selfishness and unkindness, while professing to be the followers of Him who pleased not Himself; who when rich for our sakes became poor, and went about doing good.

Let us hold ourselves at thy disposal, not only with regard to the duties, but events of life. Whatever preferences we feel, may we submit them all to thy infinite wisdom, and say, Nevertheless not my will but thine be done. If we are called to resign any of our enjoyments, may we remember that it is the absolute proprietor and our best friend who requires them; and yield them up in the spirit of him who when stripped of all could say, The Lord gave, and the Lord hath taken away; blessed be the name of the Lord.

But make us thankful for the continuance of our comforts; and that in a world of such changes and misery our indulgences have been so many and our trials so few.

Especially would we be grateful for the means of grace and the ordinances of religion, which still await us notwithstanding all our unworthiness and provocations. O Lord, teach us to profit by them more than we have done; and as to-morrow is the rest of the holy sabbath unto the Lord our God, may we be in the Spirit on thy own day, and enter it in a state of mind suited to its solemnities, duties, and privileges. May we leave every thing worldly at the foot of the mount, while we go to worship God above. May we experience the blessedness of the man, whose strength is in Thee, and in whose heart are the ways of them. May we go from strength to strength; and at last may every one of us in Zion appear before God.

O Lord God of hosts, hear our prayer; give ear, O God of Jacob. Behold, O God, our shield, and look upon the face of thine anointed. Amen.

FOURTH WEEK.

SUNDAY MORNING.

O Thou Most High! Thine eyes are in every place beholding the evil and the good: thine eyes behold, and thine eyelids try the children of men. We hope we can appear to thy omniscience, and say, In the way of thy appointments we are now waiting for Thee, while our desire is to thy name, and to the remembrance of Thee.

We are sinners, but not insensible of our state. Our iniquities are great and numberless; but with a broken heart and a contrite spirit we pray to be delivered from them, and led in the way everlasting. Our case is desperate in itself, but there is hope in Israel concerning this thing. The combined help of men and angels could not reach our misery: but Thou art adequate to our relief.

Thou art rich in mercy. The blood of Jesus Christ thy Son cleanseth from all sin. The agency of thy Holy Spirit can subdue the most powerful corruptions. Heal us and we shall be healed; save us and we shall be saved: for Thou art our praise. Hide thy face from our sin, and blot out all our iniquity

Create in us also, O God, a clean heart, and renew a right spirit within us. Illuminate our understandings with the light of life. May we know the truth, and may the truth make us free. Give us tender and wakeful consciences; and may they always smite and torment us when we sin against God. May we be consistent and uniform in the whole of our conversation and conduct; the same alone and in company; in prosperity and adversity; esteeming all thy commandments concerning all things to be right, and hating every false way—Israelites indeed, in whom there is no guile.

May we never be satisfied with any present progression in the divine life: but this one thing may we do, forgetting the things that are behind, and reaching forth unto those that are before, press towards the mark for the prize of our high calling of God in Christ Jesus. May we add to our faith virtue; and to virtue knowledge; and to knowledge temperance; and to temperance godliness; and to godliness brotherly kindness; and to brotherly kindness charity: and may all these things not only be in us but abound.

And while we never forget what is necessary to constitute the christian character, may we never neglect what is needful to complete it. May we cultivate the expedient and the lovely. May we be concerned to adorn the doctrine of God our Saviour; to recommend the religion of Jesus to all around us; and to induce observers to say, We will go with you, for we have heard that God is with you.

Enable us to accommodate ourselves to the dispensations of thy providence, with the views and feelings of Christians. May we know how to be abased, and how to abound; may we learn in whatsoever state we are, therewith to be content; yea, in everything may we give thanks, knowing that all the ways of the Lord are mercy and truth to those that trust in Him.

May we feel the ties that unite us to our fellow-creatures, especially to our fellow-christians. By sympathy, and praise and prayer, may we make their mercies and miseries our own; rejoicing with them that rejoice, and weeping with them that weep.

Regard the sons and daughters of distress: and as afflictions are not immutable dispensations, and we are allowed to pray for temporal blessings conditionally, if it be thy pleasure command deliverance for them: or should thy wisdom continue the trial, keep them from sinking or sinning in the evil day; let thy strength be made perfect in their weakness; and in the multitude of their thoughts within them may thy comforts delight their souls.

Be with those who will pass the day in absence from thy dear abode. Though Thou art with thy people in trouble, yet Thou hast taught them by experience to value thy ordinances, and to esteem a day in thy courts better than a thousand. O let them not pass an unprofitable, though a silent sabbath: let their meditation of Thee be sweet; and though not in thy house, may they be in thy Spirit on thy own day.

And make those thankful who are exempted from spiritual privations, and have liberty and health and strength to go into thy house in the multitude of thy mercies.

We bless Thee that this is our privilege. May we know the day of our visitation, and embrace the things that belong to our peace. May we hear with solemnity of mind, knowing that for all these things God will bring us into judgment. May we hear with prayer, remembering that whoever may plant or water, Thou alone canst give the increase. May we be doers of the word, and not hearers only; and may we keep in memory what is preached unto us, that we may not believe in vain.

May we carry into ordinary life the various portions of divine truth which successively engage our attention, and use them as seasons and circumstances render them suitable may its doctrines inform, its warnings caution, its rules guide, and its promises comfort us, till we have received the end of our faith, the salvation of our souls.

Bless the congregation in whose devotions we are to mingle. Let thy minister be clothed with salvation, and let thy saints shout aloud for joy. O Thou holy and beautiful house, where our fathers praised Thee, peace be within thy walls—For our brethren and companions' sakes we will now say, Peace be within thee.

And bless, we beseech Thee, all thy churches and all thy servants of every name. Plead thy own cause. Build up Zion. Establish and make Jerusalem a praise in the whole earth. May many run to and fro, and knowledge be increased: and may all know Thee from the least even to the greatest. Our Father, &c.

SUNDAY EVENING.

QUICKEN our souls to call upon thy name: pour upon us the Spirit of grace and of supplication; and in our enlivened and enlarged experience, may we know that Thou art not only the gracious rewarder, but the Almighty helper of them that diligently seek Thee.

For such, O God, is the ignorance of our minds, the vagrancy of our thoughts, the earthliness of our affections, and the unbelief of our hearts, that without Thee we can do nothing. But the preparation of the heart and the answer of the tongue are from Thee. Thy Spirit helps our infirmities. Thy grace is sufficient for us. Unite our hearts to fear thy name: enable us to come even to thy seat; and may our fellowship be with the God of love.

May we approach Thee, not as the eternal Jehovah only, but as our Father and our Friend, our exceeding joy, the strength of our heart and our portion for ever. May we not only exercise that faith by which we understand the worlds were made by the word of God. May we not only believe in Thee as the God of nature and providence, but in Jesus Christ whom Thou hast sent, and sent to put away sin by the sacrifice of Himself. We feel discouragements resulting from our guilty fears, and find it hard to believe that on our return Thou wilt meet us in peace. We therefore bless Thee for the displaying of the exceeding riches of thy grace, in thy kindness towards us by Christ Jesus: and we rejoice in the blessed intelligence, that God was in Christ reconciling the world unto Himself, not imputing their iniquities unto them.

These glad tidings we have this day been hearing. O Lord, Thou knowest how often we have heard the joyful sound; and Thou knowest the manner in which we have received it. We have reason to fear that many have received it in vain; that their hearing has only added to their guilt; and that their sabbaths have been only employed in treasuring up wrath against the day of wrath. O what would the spirits in prison give for one of our opportunities, one of our offers of mercy! How many now sitting in darkness and in the regions of the shadow of death, would exult at the entrance of that light, against which we shut our eyes, or which we behold with indifference!

Awaken, O Lord, in our consciences the inquiry, How shall we escape if we neglect so great salvation!

May we believe the report we have this day heard; and keep in memory what has been preached unto us, lest we believe in vain. May we hide thy word in our hearts, that we may not sin against Thee. May the truth as it is in Jesus illuminate in us all that is dark, sanctify in us all that is unholy, establish all that is wavering, comfort all that is wretched, and accomplish in us all the good pleasure of thy goodness and the work of faith with power; that the name of our Lord Jesus Christ may be glorified in us, and that we may be glorified in Him.

We sometimes hope Thou hast commenced a good work in us; we hope that we have begun to see the evil of sin, to hunger and thirst after righteousness; that we are asking the way to Zion, with our faces thitherward; and are praying, Remember me, O Lord, with the favour Thou bearest unto thy people.

Command and enable us to go forward. Take us by the hand, and lead us on from strength to strength. Let the dawn break into the perfect day; and the blade become the full corn in the ear.

We live in a world of changes, but Thou art the same: may we know that Thou hast made with us an everlasting covenant ordered in all things and sure. We are pressing through a vale of tears, but we bless Thee for the opening glory at the end of it. Enable us to realize as our own, a better even a heavenly country. Prepare us for every part of our pilgrimage: uphold our goings in thy word; and let no iniquity have dominion over us.

May we rejoice as though we rejoiced not, and weep as though we wept not; and buy as though we possessed not; and use this world as not abusing it.

We would sympathize with those who are in distress. Give to them that mourn in Zion, beauty for ashes, the oil of joy for mourning, and the garment of praise for the spirit of heaviness.

Bless all the institutions which are established to diffuse the Scriptures and to send forth missionaries. Remember those who have gone forth to preach among the Gentiles the unsearchable riches of Christ. Preserve their health, their morals, their spirituality, their zeal: let them be examples of all they teach: and be thou a little sanctuary to them among the heathen. May all the events that take place in the nations of the earth subserve the spread of the Redeemer's empire; and may we exult in the period when the earth shall be filled with the knowledge of the Lord, as the waters cover the sea.

And to God the Father, the Son, and Holy Ghost, be praises for ever and ever. Amen.

MONDAY MORNING.

THE heavens declare thy glory, O God, and the firmament showeth thy handy-work. Day unto day uttereth speech, and night unto night showeth knowledge; and there is no speech nor language where their voice is not heard. We behold displays of thy wisdom, power, and goodness, in all thy works from the largest of them to the least.

But Thou hast magnified thy word above all thy name; and we can never be sufficiently thankful for the revelation of thy will in the scriptures of truth. We bless Thee that this sacred volume has been preserved, and translated, and published, and multiplied, so that we all have it in our possession, and can read in our own tongue the wonderful works of God. Here we see not only thy greatness, but thy grace; and not only thy pity, but thy rectitude; we see mercy and truth meeting together, righteousness and peace kissing each other. Here thou hast shined in our hearts to give us the light of

U

the knowledge of thy glory in the face of Jesus Christ.

For in Him Thou hast reconciled the world unto thyself, not imputing their trespasses unto them. Thou hast made Him to be sin for us who knew no sin, that we might be made the righteousness of God in Him. And Thou hast raised Him up from the dead, and given Him glory, that our faith and hope may be in God. May the hearts thus tenderly wooed be effectually won. At the view of this infinite kindness, may we resign all our unworthy and suspicious thoughts; and placing our confidence in Thee, return and say—Lord, I am thine, save me. Look Thou upon me, and be merciful unto me, as Thou usest to do unto those that love thy name.

We ask not to be enrolled among the rich and the great of this world, but to be numbered with those who are blessed with all spiritual blessings in heavenly places in Christ. The graves are ready for us, and we shall soon be in a state that will render it a matter of indifference to us whether we have been rich or poor, whether we have filled a cottage or a palace—But it will be eternally important to us that we have been justified by thy grace, and sanctified by thy Spirit, and adopted into thy family. May we therefore be wise unto salvation; and make it our present, our supreme, our persevering concern, to obtain those blessings which are spiritual in their nature, eternal in their continuance, satisfying in their possession, and which unerringly indicate that we are the friends of God.

Preserve us from a false estimate of the whole of our character, or of any part of it. May we regard our principles as well as our conduct, our motives as well as our actions. May we never mistake the excitement of our passions, for the renewing of the Holy Ghost. May we never judge of our religion by occasional impressions and impulses, but by our constant and prevailing disposition. May our heart be right with God, and our life such as becometh the gospel.

May we maintain a supreme regard to another and a better world, and feel and confess ourselves to be only strangers and pilgrims in this. How often by bodily infirmities and pains, by relative afflictions, and by dissatisfactions growing out of every enjoyment—how often have we been told—O when shall we be taught—that this is not our rest? O God, not only command, but enable us to arise and depart hence. Afford us all the direction, all the defence, all the support, all the consolation our journey will require. Give us in large abundance the supply of the spirit of Jesus Christ, that we may be prepared for every duty; that we may love Thee in all our mercies; that we may submit to Thee in every trial. May we trust Thee when we walk in darkness and have no light:

and amidst all the changes of the present and the uncertainties of the future, may our minds be kept in perfect peace, being stayed upon God.

Hast Thou not made with us an everlasting covenant ordered in all things and sure? The very hairs of our head—are they not all numbered? Are not all thy ways mercy and truth? Lord, we believe, help Thou our unbelief.

And now unto Him that is able to keep us from falling, and to present us faultless before the presence of his glory with exceeding joy —To the only wise God, our Saviour, be glory and majesty, dominion and power, both now and for ever. Amen.

MONDAY EVENING.

O Lord, Thou art over all by thy providential agency, and rich unto all that call upon Thee in the exercise of thy mercy and grace. With Thee is the fountain of life, and in thy light shall we see light.

Help us to consider the way, the new and living way, in which a fallen creature can approach Thee with acceptance. May we behold the Lamb of God that taketh away the sin of the world. May we contemplate the dignity of *his* person, the perfection of *his* sacrifice, and the prevalency of *his* intercession, who is the great High Priest over the house of God. May we feel the distance between Thee and us done away, and rejoice that now in Christ Jesus, we who sometimes were afar off, are made nigh by the blood of Christ.

A glorious high throne from the beginning has been the place of thy people's sanctuary: and we have found it good to be there. O what a resource is devotion!—When under all the toils that weary us, the cares that corrode us, the infirmities that press us down, the fears that disturb us; in every thing by prayer and supplication, with thanksgiving, we can make known our supplication unto God, and feel a peace which passeth all understanding, keeping our hearts and minds through Christ Jesus!

We were as sheep going astray, but are now returned unto the shepherd and bishop of our souls. Yet we feel the same grace that restored us, to be necessary to preserve us, and to supply us. And hast not Thou promised to lead us, to guard us, to suffer us to want no good thing, to make all grace to abound towards us? And art not thou a faithful God, and able also to perform? Lord, we take Thee at thy word. Do as Thou hast said.

We have tasted that Thou art gracious, and the relish has provoked our desires after more: and they who hunger and thirst after righteousness *are* blessed, and *shall* be filled. Make us to lie down in green pastures, and feed us beside the still waters, where we shall often exclaim, O how great is His goodness, and how great is His beauty!

We often meet with those who have far more grace than we ourselves have: but this only encourages our hope, since they were once poor, and He who supplied them is as rich as ever—and as accessible—and as free. We are continually meeting with duties and trials, which call for more grace than we have in ourselves; but not more than we have in our divine treasury, in whom it hath pleased Thee that all fulness should dwell. To Him therefore may we continually repair, and from his fulness receive, and grace for grace, till every void made by sin be replenished, and we ourselves filled with all the fulness of God. We bless Thee that Thou dost not despise the day of small things; but we aspire after a day of great ones. We are not straitened in Thee, may we never be contracted in ourselves: may our desires be enlarged, and our hopes emboldened: may we honour Thee by the entireness of our dependence, and the greatness of our expectation; and living and walking in the Spirit, may we go from strength to strength, and be changed from glory into glory till we appear perfect before Thee in Zion.

We know not what a day may bring forth; nor would we if it were in our power draw back the veil that hides the future, and learn the times and the seasons which the Father hath put in his own power. But O be Thou with us in all, and prepare us for all. Prepare us for the smiles of prosperity; prepare us for the frowns of adversity; prepare us for those losses in substance, and those bereavements in friends so possible, so probable in a world like this; prepare us for the days of darkness, for they may be many: prepare us for every change, and—prepare us for the change—and when heart and flesh fail us, and we have no more a portion in all that is done under the sun, be Thou the strength of our heart and our portion for ever.

May our very memory be blessed. May those who follow us, praise God that we have ever lived; and may we leave behind us those instructions, examples, and effects, which shall glorify our God on earth, while our spirits have joined the spirits of just men made perfect in heaven.

And may the grace of the Lord Jesus Christ, and the love of God, and the fellowship of the Holy Ghost, be with us all evermore. Amen.

TUESDAY MORNING.

O Thou, whose name alone is Jehovah, the most high over all the earth. We desire to adore the perfections of thy nature, and to admire the works of thy hands. May the united displays of thy greatness and thy goodness impress our minds, and influence our thoughts and affections while we approach Thee.

Heaven is thy throne, and the earth is thy footstool. The universe with all its myriads of creatures was made by thy word and is upholden by thy power: and Thou dost according to thine own will in the army of heaven, and among the inhabitants of the earth: none can stay thy hand, or say unto Thee, what doest Thou?

But Thou art the Father of mercies; the God of all grace; and the God of all comfort. Even we, poor mean dying creatures, are not beneath thy care. Thou hast been mindful of us; Thou hast visited us; and thy visitation hath preserved our spirits. The lines are fallen to us in pleasant places: yea we have a goodly heritage. We live in a land of vision, We have the scriptures in our hands; and our ears hear the joyful sound of the gospel. We know that Thou hast not spared thine own Son, but delivered Him up for us all. We know that He has borne our grief, and carried our sorrow; that his blood cleanseth from all sin; and that whosoever believeth on Him shall not perish but have everlasting life.

We come in His name, and make mention of His righteousness only. We plead the obedience and sufferings of him who magnified the law, both in its precept and penalty, and made it honourable. May we be justified by his blood; may we be saved by his life. May we be joined to the Lord and of one spirit with him. May we deny ourselves and take up our cross and follow Him. May the agency of thy grace prepare us for all the dispensations of thy providence. May we be willing that the Lord should choose our inheritance for us, and determine what we shall retain or lose, what we shall suffer or enjoy.

If indulged with prosperity, may we be secured from its snares, and use its advantages as not abusing them. And may we patiently and cheerfully submit to those afflictions which are necessary to hedge up our way when we are tempted to wander, to excite an abhorrence of sin, to wean us from the present evil world, and to make us partakers of thy holiness. Only assure us, and we shall learn in whatsoever state we are therewith to be content—only assure us that Thou wilt be with us in trouble, and that at the end of the vale of tears we shall enter Emanuel's land, where the inhabitants no more say I am sick; where our sun shall no more go down, nor our moon withdraw itself, but God shall be our everlasting light, and the days of our mourning shall be ended.

May our friends and relations be fellow-heirs with us of the grace of life. Let our house be the tabernacle of the righteous: let our children and servants be a seed to serve Thee, and among none of those who surround this family altar, may there be weeping and wailing and gnashing of teeth, when they shall see Abraham and Isaac and Jacob in the kingdom of God, and they themselves shut out.

Lord, help us all to view our religious opportunities as talents for which we are accountable; to remember that our greatest danger results from our highest privileges; and to fear lest a promise being left us of entering into thy rest, any of us should seem to come short of it.

Thou hast determined the bounds of our habitation; and by the events of thy providence, many of those in whose society we delight are separated from us. When we are absent in body, may we be often present in spirit. We commend our absent friends and kindred to thy covenant care. May no evil tidings concerning them wound our hearts. Spare them in thy mercy; may we often embrace each other in circumstances of health and comfort; or if we have had our last interview on earth, may we all meet in our heavenly Father's house, and be for ever with each other, and for ever with the Lord.

In hope of which, with every other blessing, we devoutly ascribe to the only wise God our Saviour, praise and glory everlasting. Amen.

TUESDAY EVENING.

O Thou King of Glory, we desire to approach thy divine Majesty with reverence and godly fear, and to worship Thee in the beauty of holiness. Every perfection adorns thy nature and sustains thy throne. The heavens are thine; the earth also is thine; the world is thine, and the fulness thereof. Thy power drew the universe from nothing. Thy wisdom has managed all its multiplied concerns, presiding over nations, families, and individuals, and numbering the very hairs of our head. Thy goodness is boundless: the eyes of all wait upon Thee, and Thou givest them their meat in due season: Thou openest thine hand, and satisfiest the desire of every living thing. How precious are the thoughts of thy mercy and grace—and so excellent is thy lovingkindness, that even the children of men put their trust under the shadow of thy wing.

Thou art the blessed and happy God. O teach us to place our happiness in thyself. May we never seek the living among the dead, nor ask with the deluded many, Who will show us any good? but may we prize the light of thy countenance, implore the joy of thy salvation, and passing by the attractions of creatures, be able to say, Whom have I in heaven but Thee, and there is none upon earth that I desire beside Thee.

Thou hast been infinitely more attentive to our happiness, than we ever have been or ever can be. Thou madest man upright, and when by voluntary transgression we fell away from Thee, Thou didst not treat us with the severity or the neglect we deserved. In thy love and pity Thou wast pleased to provide for us a Saviour, who bore our grief and carried our sorrows, and put away sin by the sacrifice of himself.

Apply this redemption to our hearts, by the justification of our persons and the sanctification of our natures. We confess our transgressions—have mercy upon us. We are weary—give us rest. We are ignorant—make us wise unto salvation. We are helpless—let thy strength be made perfect in our weakness. We are poor and needy—bless us with all the unsearchable riches of Christ. Having begun a religious course, may we run and not be weary, and walk and not faint. And though perplexities and trials and dangers await us, yet may we travel on, unchecked and undismayed, knowing that Thou hast said, I will never leave thee nor forsake thee.

Thus far, blessed be thy name, Thou hast led us on, and we have found thee faithful to thy promises. We have had our sorrows; but Thou hast been a very present help in every time of trouble. We have had our fears; but Thou hast not suffered the enemy to triumph over us. We have sometimes been on the verge of despair and have said, I am cast out of thy sight: but we have been enabled to look again towards thy holy temple, and the shadow of death has been turned into the morning. Ebenezer! hitherto hath the Lord helped us. Thy vows are upon us, O God: we will render praises unto Thee. For Thou hast delivered our souls from death: wilt not thou deliver our feet from falling, that we may walk before God in the light of the living?

We would feel the connexions which unite us to others, and by sympathy and prayer and praise, make their miseries and mercies our own. We would rejoice with those that rejoice, and weep with those that weep. Provide support and employment for the poor, and may their hands be sufficient for them. Make the widow's heart to sing for joy; and in Thee may the fatherless find mercy. Visit those that are on beds of sickness, and prepare them for thy pleasure; that if they live it may be to serve Thee; and if they die, it may be to enjoy Thee. Bless the king as supreme. May righteousness and peace be the stability of his times; and the subjects he reigns over be a happy people, whose God is the Lord. Do good in thy good pleasure unto Zion; build Thou the walls of Jerusalem: and may all our churches, like the original disciples, continue steadfastly in the apostles' doctrine, and in fellowship, and in breaking of bread and in prayers.

Protect and refresh us through the night season; and then cause us to hear thy lovingkindness in the morning; for in Thee do we trust: cause us to know the way wherein we should go, for we lift up our souls unto Thee. We implore it through the intercession of thy dear Son and our Saviour.

And blessing and honour, and glory and power, be unto him that sitteth upon the throne, and unto the Lamb, for ever and ever. Amen.

WEDNESDAY MORNING.

O God, Thou art incomprehensible, and in none of thy works and ways can any of thy creatures find Thee out unto perfection. Yet Thou hast not left thyself without witness, nor called us to worship an unknown God. Thou hast been pleased to reveal thyself to us as far as our wants and welfare require, and among other endearing characters we can discern Thee as a God hearing prayer.

Thou never saidst to the seed of Jacob, Seek ye me in vain. A glorious high throne from the beginning has been the place of thy people's sanctuary. And thither would we repair in all our difficulties, necessities, and distresses, and find it good to draw near to God. Possess us with the Spirit of grace, which is always a spirit of supplication. May we live in a prayerful frame of mind, that will always allow of our immediate and pleasing intercourse with Thee: in the ordinary concerns of life may our thoughts and desires often ascend the skies; and in habitual devotion may we find a resource that will soothe our sorrows, sanctify our successes, and qualify us for all our dealings with our fellow-creatures.

We bless Thee that Thou hast made us capable of knowing Thee, the author of all being; of resembling Thee, the perfection of all excellency; and of enjoying Thee, the source of all happiness. Though we are unworthy to share in thy lovingkindness, it is thy pleasure that we seek after it; and Thou hast said, Their hearts shall live that seek God. Therefore look Thou upon us, and be merciful unto us, as Thou usest to do unto those that love thy name. May we be accepted in the Beloved, and know that in Him we have redemption through his blood, even the forgiveness of our sins. May we view Him as the end of the law for righteousness to every one that believeth, and as the source of all that grace by which we are renewed in the spirit of our minds. May we always contemplate our duties in connexion with those promises which insure ability for the performance of them; and while weak in ourselves, may we be strong in the Lord and in the power of his might.

Attend us, O God, in every part of our arduous and trying pilgrimage. We need the same counsel, the same defence, the same comfort we implored at the moment of our setting out—Cast us not away from thy presence, and take not thy Holy Spirit from us. May we live in the Spirit, and may we walk in the Spirit. And may our path be as the shining light, that shineth more and more unto the perfect day.

Let our religion be more obvious to our own consciences, and more perceptible to the eye of those around us. May all that see and hear us take knowledge of us that we have been with Jesus. While He is representing us in heaven, may we represent Him on earth, while He pleads our cause, may we plead his, and be concerned in all things to show forth *his* praise, who is making all things to work together for our good.

Arise, O God, and appear in thy glory. Give the word, and let the company of those that publish the glad tidings of thy kingdom be great. May thy house be filled with inhabitants, and thy table furnished with guests; and let all that love thy salvation say continually, The Lord be magnified.

Be gracious to our absent connexions—our hearts' desire and prayer to God for them is, that they may be saved.

Continue the gentleness of thy goodness to this household.

To the care which has watched over us through another night, we give up ourselves in prospect of the duties and events of the day. Let thy presence go with us, and thy blessing attend us. And whether we wake or sleep, may we live together with Christ.

In whose words we address Thee, as Our Father, &c. Amen.

WEDNESDAY EVENING.

O Thou ever blessed God, we desire to approach Thee, adoring thy perfections and admiring thy works, which are sought out of all them that have pleasure therein. May we feel becoming regard towards Thee as our Creator, the Preserver of men, and the Saviour of sinners.

Thy name is most excellent in all the earth, and Thou hast set thy glory above the heavens. Thy compassions fail not, and therefore we are not consumed. We are filled with wonder at thy condescension in noticing creatures so poor and worthless, and at thy mercy and grace in providing for the deliverance and happiness of creatures so miserable and guilty. We can never sufficiently bless Thee, that we were born in a christian country where the true light shineth, and we can hear words whereby we may be saved. How suitable and encouraging are the discoveries, the invitations, and the promises of the gospel of peace. Here are announced pardon for rebels, liberty for captives, health for the sick, and a free, full and everlasting salvation for them that are lost. Here we are informed that Thou hast not spared thine own Son, budelivered Him up for us all; that He has fulfilled and magnified the law; that his blood cleanseth from all sin; that in Him all fulness dwells; and that whosoever believeth on Him shall not be confounded.

In his beloved name we come, and avail ourselves of the plea which Thou thyself hast afforded us. For his sake be merciful unto us, and bless us, and cause thy face to shine upon us that we may be saved. May we be justified by his blood, and have access into that grace, wherein we shall stand and rejoice in the hope of the glory of God. May thy image be re-impressed upon our souls, in knowledge, righteousness, and true holiness. May thy Holy Spirit take full possession of our hearts, and lead us into all truth, and enable us to walk in all thy commandments and ordinances blameless: may we be fruitful in every good word and work to do thy will. Raise us above the world. May we feel neither its frowns nor its smiles where duty is concerned. May it ever be a light thing with us to be judged of man's judgment. May thy approbation be our only aim, and thy word our only rule; and with Enoch may we all enjoy the testimony, that we please God. Keep us from, or preserve us in, the hour of temptation. May we abhor and avoid whatever would grieve thy Holy Spirit, and cause Thee to hide thy face from us. May we walk in the fear of the Lord, that we may walk in the comforts of the Holy Ghost; and may we always suspect the confidence and consolation which can be enjoyed along with a worldly temper and a careless conversation.

May we have no fellowship with the unfruitful works of darkness, but rather reprove them: yet we may in meekness instruct those who oppose themselves, and be gentle and patient towards all men. And may we *do* as well as *teach*. May we be not only professors of the gospel but examples, displaying in every relation and office and condition of life, its excellency, loveliness, and advantages, that we may put to silence the ignorance of foolish men, and even constrain them to glorify God in the day of visitation.

How well does it become us to be humble! How little have we illustrated our principles, or improved our advantages! How often have we injured, instead of recommending the cause of our Redeemer! How little have we served our generation; and how few are those to whom we have been a blessing! In many things we have offended; and in all come short of thy glory. Pardon our iniquity, for it is great.

Forgive the imperfections, omissions, and sins of another day; and make us thankful for the continuance of its numberless blessings.

Shelter us through the night; and in the morning, with renewed strength and grateful hearts, may we rise to love Thee more and serve Thee better than we have done this day—through our Lord and Saviour. Amen.

THURSDAY MORNING.

O Lord, our God, blessed is the man whom Thou choosest, and causest to approach unto Thee. In thy presence there is fulness of joy, and at thy right hand there are pleasures for evermore. With Thee is the fountain of life, and in thy light alone can we see light.

We therefore entreat thy favour with our whole heart. We acknowledge that we have forfeited all claims to it; and if we had no better ground of hope than our deservings we must sink into despair. For against Thee, Thee only have we sinned, and done evil in thy sight, that Thou mightest be justified when thou speakest, and clear when Thou judgest.

But with Thee there is mercy, and with Thee there is plenteous redemption. We bless Thee for the assurance that Thou hast sent thy own Son into the world, not to condemn the world, but that the world through Him might be saved. We rejoice that neither the number nor heinousness of our transgressions is a bar to that forgiveness which is founded on the sufferings and sacrifice of the cross. The blood of Jesus Christ, thy son, cleanseth from all sin. By the blood of that covenant which he has ratified, send forth thy prisoners out of the pit wherein there is no water. Graciously absolve us from all our guilt; and pronounce our discharge from all condemnation, not only in the court of heaven, but in the court of conscience, that being justified by faith, we may have peace with God, and enjoy the glorious liberty of his children.

But O save us from the hope of the hypocrite which shall perish. Never suffer us to impose upon ourselves in anything that relates to our eternal state. May we never suppose that we are in Christ, unless we are new creatures; or that we are born of the Spirit, unless we mind the things of the Spirit. May we never rest satisfied with any professions of belief, or any outward forms or services, while the heart is not right with God. May we judge of our sincerity in religion by our fear to offend Thee; by our concern to know what Thou wilt have us to do; and by our willingness to deny ourselves, and take up our cross and follow the Lamb whithersoever he goeth.

May nothing render us forgetful of thy glory; may nothing turn us aside from thy commands; may nothing shake our confidence in thy promises. Take from us the evil heart of unbelief—the cause of all our waverings and wanderings. May we believe, that we may be established in our goings, and be always abounding in the work of the Lord.

Prepare us for whatever we have to meet with between this morning and the grave. We know not what lies before us; but Thou knowest, and thy grace can make us sufficient for every service and every suffering.

Let not our temporal occupations ever injure our spiritual concerns, or the cares of this life make us forget or neglect the one thing needful. May we learn the holy art of abiding with God in our callings; of being in the world without being of it; and of making everything not only consistent with religion, but conducive to it.

May we do and may we say nothing by which we shall offend against the generation of thy children. If strong, may we bear the infirmities of the weak, and not please ourselves. If preserved, may we restore a brother that has been overtaken in a fault, in the spirit of meekness, considering ourselves lest we also be tempted.

Bless those who have done us good, and render seven-fold into their own bosom: and forgive those who have done us evil, and enable us to forgive them.

Bless those who are near and dear to us; may they be near and dear to Thee. Bless them in their outward comforts; but above all may their souls prosper.

Be gracious to our native land. Be mindful of our sovereign. Teach our senators wisdom. Bless the ministers of state, and the ministers of the sanctuary. Bless the gates of Zion, and all the dwellings of Jacob. Let thy secret reside in the families of them that fear Thee; and may those that have neglected to call upon thy name, immediately adopt the resolution of Joshua,—As for me and my house, we will serve the Lord.

This morning sacrifice we offer in the all-prevailing name of our adorable Redeemer—And unto Him that loved us, and washed us from our sins in his own blood, and hath made us kings and priests unto God, and to his Father—to Him be glory and dominion, for ever and ever. Amen.

THURSDAY EVENING.

O God, by the return of this hour of devotion, Thou hast again said, Seek ye my face; and our hearts have answered, Thy face, Lord, will we seek.

We value every opportunity of approaching Thee, not only as our duty, but as our unspeakable privilege. We rejoice that there is opened a new and living way into the holiest of all; and that as we enter, we can see Jesus the mediator of the new covenant, and hear the voice of the blood of sprinkling that speaketh better things than that of Abel. We are unprofitable servants. Our obedience, instead of meriting recompense, deserves condemnation for its numerous defects. We

are ashamed even of our devotions; and often question, whether any part of our religion will bear the eye of God.

But it is our encouragement, that if we cannot come to Thee as saints, we may come as sinners, with the assurance that Thou wilt in nowise cast us out. We therefore come as sinners—yet sinners who hate themselves for their abominations and long for deliverance. Hear the groaning of the prisoners, and loose those who are appointed unto death. Heal us and we shall be healed; save us and we shall be saved, for thou art our praise. Save us from the curse of the law which we have violated; save us from the power and love of every sin; save us from an evil heart of unbelief in departing from the living God; save us from the present evil world; save us from our adversary the devil, who goeth about as a roaring lion seeking whom he may devour—that being delivered out of the hand of our enemies, we may serve Thee without fear, in holiness and righteousness before Thee, all the days of our lives.

We sometimes hope Thou hast begun a good work in us, and we take comfort from the assurance that Thou wilt perform it until the day of Jesus Christ. We ought to be humble, but we would not be ungrateful, nor refuse to acknowledge what Thou hast done for our souls; for by thy grace alone we are what we are. Thou hast shown us the evil of sin, and the beauty there is in holiness: Thou hast led us to hunger and thirst after righteousness; we glory in the cross of our Lord Jesus Christ; we long to be conformed to his example; and we have taken hold of the skirt of him that is a Jew, and have said, We will go with you, for we have heard that God is with you.

O Thou, who despisest not the day of small things, perfect that which concerneth us. May we not only have hope, but abound in hope; may we not only have faith, but be rich in faith; may we not only be fruitful, but be filled with all the fruits of righteousness which are by Jesus Christ unto the glory and praise of God.

Let us not be of the number of those who are always learning, and never able to come to the knowledge of the truth. May we have clear and consistent views of divine truth; and may every doctrine we admit into our judgments have a powerful influence over our hearts. May it bring as well as reveal salvation; and teach us to deny ungodliness and worldly lusts, and to live soberly, righteously, and godly in the present world. May the love of God subdue the lust of the flesh, the lust of the eye, and the pride of life, and whatever is not of the Father, but is of the world.

May we love our neighbour as ourselves, and never hide ourselves from our own flesh. May we look not every man on his own things, but every man also on the things of others, and especially the things that are Jesus Christ's.

May we never crucify him afresh and put him to an open shame. May we rather die than cause his worthy name to be blasphemed. May our devoted hearts be hourly asking, What shall I do for him, who when rich for our sakes became poor, and died that we might live? May he obtain the purchase of his blood in our revolted world! May he see of the travail of his soul and be satisfied. Let all kings fall down before Him and all nations serve Him. And blessed be his glorious name for ever, and let the whole earth be filled with his glory. Amen and Amen.

FRIDAY MORNING.

O Thou ever blessed God! It is good for us to draw near to Thee; and if we had no other privilege to be thankful for we ought continually to praise Thee for permission and encouragement to approach the throne of thy grace, there to spread before Thee all our wants and all our desires.

We are not worthy of the blessing; we are not worthy of the least of all thy mercies. We are far gone from the original righteousness in which we were created, and the depravity of our nature has appeared in the disobedience and rebellion of our lives. How early did we discover tendencies to discontent and pride, and envy and revenge. Remember not against us the sins of our youth! nor the multiplied transgressions of riper years—our misimproved time and talents, our abused mercies and means, our wasted and perverted Sabbaths and seasons of grace, our neglect of thy great salvation, and our disregard of the Friend of sinners who loved us so as to die for us.

Our iniquity is increased over our head, and our trespass is gone up into the very heaven. While we confess our guilt may we individually and deeply feel it, and be filled with self-abhorrence and self-despair.

But help us to remember, that there is hope in Israel concerning this thing. Enable us to hear the voice that proclaims, Behold the Lamb of God that taketh away the sins of the world. Through Him may we return to Thee, and find Thee a God ready to pardon sin and able to subdue it. Through Him may we give up ourselves to Thee, as our portion to enjoy and our master to serve for ever. At thy footstool, in the spirit of submission may we ever say, Speak, Lord, for thy servant heareth. May we not only obey, but delight to do thy will, yea may thy law be within our heart.

Conscious of our danger, may we watch; and sensible of our inability to keep ourselves, may we pray—lest we enter into temptation. Hold thou us up and we shall be safe. Pre-serve our understandings from error; our affections from the love of idols; our lips from speaking guile; our conduct from every stain of vice, and our character from the very appearance of evil.

And may we not only be harmless and blameless, the sons of God without rebuke: but may we be exemplary and useful, holding forth the word of life and adorning the doctrine of God our Saviour in all things. If the Saviour has manifested himself to us as he does not unto the world, may we declare that which we have seen and heard unto others, that they also may have fellowship with us; and having tasted that the Lord is gracious ourselves, may we ever be saying to those around us, O taste and see that the Lord is good; blessed is the man that trusteth in Him. And may we walk in wisdom towards them that are without. May our efforts be guided by prudence, as well as animated by zeal. May we distinguish things that differ; and—not by a sacrifice of principle, but by a judicious use of circumstances and opportunities, may we become all things to all men, if by any means we may gain some. And O let our endeavours be successful, that we may be the honoured instruments of converting sinners from the error of their ways, saving souls from death and hiding a multitude of sins.

Especially may our solicitude and exertion be available with regard to our connexions and relations. Let those who are dear to us in the bonds of nature or friendship, become fellow-heirs with us of the grace of life, and fellow-labourers with us in the Lord's vineyard.

Let the rising generation be a seed to serve Thee. Excite them by the command, Remember now thy Creator in the days of thy youth; and encourage them by the promise, I love them that love me, and they that seek me early shall find me.

Regard the aged. Alarm the old in sin; convince them that it is high time, and that it will shortly be too late to seek the things that belong to their everlasting peace. Support those who have long known Thee, and whose gray hairs as a crown of glory are found in the way of righteousness. Cast them not off in the time of old age, and forsake them not when their strength faileth.

Now the God of peace, that brought again from the dead our Lord Jesus, that great Shepherd of the sheep, through the blood of the everlasting covenant; make us perfect in every good work to do his will, working in us that which is well pleasing in his sight, through Jesus Christ; to whom be glory for ever and ever. Amen.

FRIDAY EVENING.

O God, thy command and thy promise, our duty and our privilege, induce us to avail ourselves of every opportunity of approaching the throne of thy grace. We are all in-digence and inability. It is not in the power of men and angels to reach our case, and afford us the blessings we so much need and so much desire. Our only hope is in the name of the Lord God who made heaven and earth.

But Thou art over all and rich unto all that call upon Thee; and Thou Lord hast not forsaken them that seek Thee. We love to reflect upon the displays of thy perfections, and to contemplate what Thou hast done for others, as poor and destitute, as sinful and guilty as we are; and to remember that thy hand is not shortened that it cannot save, nor thy ear heavy that it cannot hear.

Behold a company of suppliants at thy foot-stool, in all the effects of the fall, and let our ruined condition be under thy agency. O Thou God of all grace, work Thou in us to will and to do of thy good pleasure; and vile as we are in ourselves, make us an eternal excellency, the joy of many generations. Our understandings are darkened. Our hearts are hearts of stone. Our very conscience also is defiled. Our affections are earthly and sensual. Open Thou the eyes of our understanding. Give us hearts of flesh. Purify our consciences from dead works to serve the living God. Set our affections on things that are above; and as He who has called us is holy, so may we also be holy in all manner of conversation and godliness.

Deliver us from the bondage of corruption, and bring us into the glorious liberty of thy children; that being made free from sin, and become servants unto God, we may have our fruit unto holiness, and our end everlasting life.

Preserve us from all self-delusion, especially where our souls are concerned. May we never be flattered by the good opinion of our fellow-creatures against the convictions of our own consciences; but remember that if our hearts condemn us, God is greater than our hearts and knoweth all things. May we never substitute mere opinions and outward forms and ceremonies, in the room of that grace which renews the soul and sanctifies the life. Ever keep alive in our minds the belief that in Christ Jesus neither circumcision availeth any thing nor uncircumcision, but a new creature; and in the examinations of our religious state and character, may we look after that kingdom which is not meat and drink, but righteousness and peace and joy in the Holy Ghost.

Inspire us with a well grounded hope of being one day presented before the presence of thy glory; when we shall see Thee without obscurity, approach Thee without sin, serve Thee without imperfection, and enjoy Thee without sorrow. How remote now do we often feel from this exalted state! And how improbable does it frequently seem that we should ever attain it! We have never yet been better than a bruised reed and a smoking flax; and thy patience alone could have borne with our imperfections and perverseness. Yet we trust the root of the matter is found in us: and we bless Thee, if thy grace —by which alone we are what we are—has caused us to loathe sin and abhor ourselves, and to hunger and thirst after righteousness, and to place our happiness in serving and enjoying Thee.

And we pray that our path may be as the shining light that shineth more and more unto the perfect day. Complete that which is lacking in our faith. Lead us into all truth; and establish our hearts with grace. Fill our minds with the sublime and elevating objects of revelation, that worldly things may find no room in our minds; and keep near us all the affecting and awful motives of the gospel, that we may not be able to sin, but in the view of thine all-seeing eye, a burning world, a judgment to come, and the cross of our Lord Jesus Christ.

And the Lord make us also to increase and abound in love one towards another, and towards all men. Let all bitterness and wrath, and anger and clamour, and evil speaking, be put away from us with all malice; and may we be kind one towards another, tenderhearted; forgiving also one another, even as God for Christ's sake hath forgiven us.

Prepare us for all the duties and trials that lie before us. We bless Thee for thy promises, which provide against every want we feel, and for every condition in which we can be found. In God will we praise his word. In God have we put our trust. We will not fear what flesh can do unto us. Thou tellest our wanderings. Put Thou our tears into thy bottle. Are they not in thy book?

We commend ourselves with all our relations and friends this evening, to thy forgiving mercy and providential care. O Thou that givest thy beloved sleep, indulge us with refreshing repose; or if Thou holdest our eyes waking, in the night may thy song be with us, and our prayer unto the God of our life. Guide us by thy counsel through life, and afterwards receive us to glory.

And to the only wise God our Saviour, be glory and majesty, dominion and power for ever and ever. Amen.

SATURDAY MORNING.

O Thou who hast said, I will be sanctified in them that come nigh me, and before all the people will I be glorified; may we have grace whereby we shall serve Thee acceptably with reverence and godly fear. Thou inhabitest eternity; but our age is as nothing before Thee. Thy understanding is infinite.

but we know nothing. Thou art Almighty, but we are crushed before the moth. Thou art of purer eyes than to behold iniquity, but we are vile—what shall we answer Thee? We cannot answer Thee for one of a thousand of our transgressions: and had we followed the forebodings of our consciences we could not have approached Thee.

But Thou hast proclaimed thy name, the Lord God merciful and gracious: Thou hast caused all thy goodness to pass before us; Thou hast opened a new and living way into the holiest of all by the blood of Jesus; and we have boldness and access with confidence by the faith of Him.

We bless Thee that in Him all fulness dwells, and that ignorant and guilty, and depraved and miserable as we are in ourselves, from Him we can derive wisdom, righteousness, sanctification, and redemption. And we rejoice that these blessings are attainable without money and without price, and that we may know they are ours by every title God himself can give, and shall be ours for ever.

And is this the manner of man, O Lord God? O let such undeserved, such infinite goodness melt our hearts, and lead us to throw down the weapons of rebellion and weep over them. May we sorrow after a godly sort, that ever we offended a Being so worthy of all our love and our obedience; and while compelled to acknowledge with a broken heart and a contrite spirit, O Lord, other lords besides Thee have had dominion over us, enable us to say, But henceforth by Thee only will we make mention of thy name. As our reasonable service, to Thee may we dedicate ourselves immediately without delay, and fully without reserve. To Thee may we yield our understanding and our intellectual powers; our wills and our active powers, our senses and our bodily powers; our time, our substance and all our our relative powers: may our words and our actions, and our callings in life, be all holiness unto the Lord.

May we come out from the world, and touch not the unclean thing, and be received and acknowledged as the sons and daughters of the Lord Almighty. And though they are few in number, and the world knoweth them not, may we choose thy people as our companions, and delight in them as the excellent of the earth. With them at thy gates may we daily watch, and wait at the posts of thy doors; with them may we courageously fight the good fight of faith; with them may we patiently labour in thy vineyard.

May we love them all; and as we have opportunity, may we unite with them all in holy communion, and co-operate with them all in schemes of civil and sacred beneficence. We bless Thee for the country and the age in which we live. We bless Thee for the

spirit which has been awakened, and the efforts that are now making to promote the temporal, and above all the spiritual welfare of mankind, by individuals and communities, and combinations of communities. O let them not labour in vain; let the pleasure of the Lord prosper in their hand: let thy work appear unto thy servants, and thy glory unto their children; and let the beauty of the Lord our God be upon us, and establish Thou the work of our hands upon us; yea the work of our hands, establish Thou it.

And prepare us for suffering thy will as well as doing it. May we never look for unmingled felicity, here, but expect to find life, as all who have gone before us have found it, light and darkness, pain and pleasure, good and evil. When we meet with trials, may we never think them strange things, nor murmur and repine under them. Rather may we be thankful that they are so few and alleviated; rather may we rejoice that they are all founded in love to our souls, and designed to make us partakers of thy holiness. Sustain us under them; improve us by them; and assure us in due time of our deliverance from them, and of our entering the rest that remains for the people of God, where all sorrow and sighing shall cease, and all tears shall be wiped from our eyes,

And may the grace of the Lord Jesus Christ, and the love of God, and the communion of the Holy Ghost, be with us all, now and for ever. Amen.

SATURDAY EVENING.

O God! Thou art the God of all the families of the earth; for they are formed by thy will and supported by thy providence. But Thou art in a peculiar manner the God of those families in which thy name is known and loved and honoured. Thy curse is in the house of the wicked, but Thou blessest the habitation of the just. Whatever be the dispositions of others, we desire to say, with increasing resolution and zeal, As for us and our house, we will serve the Lord. Thy yoke is easy, thy burden is light, thy work is honourable and glorious, and in keeping thy commandments there is great reward. Thou art the best of all masters; Thou hast promised to bear with our infirmities, and to suffer us to want no good thing.

Already Thou hast laid us under infinite obligations, as the God of providence and of grace—Thou hast dealt well with thy servants O Lord. Bless the Lord, O our souls, and all that is within us bless his holy name. Bless the Lord, O our souls, and forget not all his benefits.

By thy good hand upon us, we have been conducted through the perils, not only of another day, but another week; a period during which many have been carried down to their graves, and we have been brought so much nearer to our own. Impress us with the lapse of our time, and so teach us to number our days that we may apply our hearts unto wisdom. Many have been involved in perplexities and exposed to want; many have been confined to the house of mourning or the bed of sickness; but we have been indulged with liberty and ease and health and strength; we have seen thy lovingkindness every morning, and thy faithfulness every night; and have had all things richly to enjoy.

But O how little have we been affected by the instances of thy undeserved goodness; how imperfectly have we improved our religious privileges; how negligent have we been in seizing opportunities of doing good to the bodies and souls of our fellow-creatures. How well does it become each of us to exclaim, Behold I am vile; what shall I answer Thee?—wherefore I abhor myself, repenting in dust and ashes.

We stand before Thee this evening in our trespass. Enter not into judgment with thy servants, O Lord. Our only hope is, that to the Lord our God belong mercies and forgivenesses, though we have rebelled against Him. Have mercy upon us, O God, according to thy lovingkindness; according to the multitude of thy tender mercies, blot out our transgressions.

And may a confidence in thy goodness, instead of encouraging us to sin that grace may abound, inspire us with that godly sorrow which worketh repentance unto life. May we hate and forsake every false way. May we be attentive to our condition, and study our character. May we bridle our tongue, and keep our heart with all diligence.

May we often look back and see how at any time we have been ensnared or overcome; and watch and pray in future lest we enter into temptation. And do Thou keep us by thy power; uphold us by thy free spirit; and not only restrain us from sin but mortify us to it.

May sleep refresh our bodies, and fit them for thy service on the ensuing day; and may thy grace prepare our minds. May we leave all the cares of the world for a while behind, that we may attend on the Lord without distraction. May we repair to the hallowed exercises of devotion, as the heart panteth after the water-brooks. May we call the Sabbath a delight; and be glad when they say to us, Let us go into the house of the Lord.

And O Thou God of all grace, do as Thou hast said; fulfil thy word unto thy servants, upon which Thou hast caused them to hope. Bless abundantly the provisions of thy house, and satisfy thy poor with bread. Clothe thy priests with salvation, and let thy saints shout aloud for joy.

And to the God of all grace, the Father, the Word, and the Holy Ghost, be all honour and glory, now and for ever. Amen.

FIFTH WEEK.

SUNDAY MORNING.

O God, Thou art very great, Thou art clothed with honour and majesty; and it becomes us to approach Thee with reverence and godly fear. We can also come before Thee with humble confidence, for thy condescension equals thy grandeur, and thy goodness is thy glory.

If we are unworthy, we rejoice that we are not unwelcome. If we are guilty, Thou art gracious; if we are miserable, Thou art merciful; if we are all indigence, thy riches are unsearchable. By not sparing thine own Son, but delivering Him up for us all, Thou hast shown thy boundless compassion towards a perishing world; and proved that with Him Thou wilt also freely give us all things. Thus a foundation is laid for our hope, a refuge is opened for our safety, and a new and living way is consecrated into the holiest of all for our approach to Thee.

O bless us with that conviction of sin, that brokenness of heart, that self-despair, which will endear to us the gospel message as a faithful saying and worthy of all acceptation; and induce us to say with the apostle, That I may win Christ and be found in Him; that I may know Him, and the power of his resurrection, and the fellowship of his sufferings, being made conformable unto his death. How happy are they that are found interested in Him! They are delivered from the wrath to come; they are justified from all things; they have peace with God; they are heirs of the glory that is to be revealed.

May we feel a holy and increasing concern to know whether these exalted privileges are claimable by us. For this purpose may we frequently and faithfully examine ourselves. May we search after that deadness to the world, that love to the Saviour, that attachment to his house, that devotedness to his service, which characterize the subjects of his salvation.

And may these things not only be in us but abounding. It is an unspeakable blessing if we have life; but it is our duty and privilege to have it more abundantly. It becomes us to be thankful if Thou hast begun a good work in us; but we are allowed to pray that Thou wilt perfect that which concerneth us. According to the riches of thy glory therefore, strengthen us with might by thy Spirit in the inner man; that Christ may dwell in our hearts by faith; that we being rooted and grounded in love, may be able to comprehend with all saints, what is the height and depth, and breadth and length, and to know the love of Christ that passeth knowledge, that we may be filled with all the fulness of God.

May every part of our character and conduct be adapted to make not only a serious but an amiable impression on the minds of those around us; that they may take hold of the skirt of him that is a Jew, saying, I will go with you, for I have heard that God is with you.

May all that we meet with in our passage through life, whether pleasing or painful, instead of injuring the prosperity of our souls, turn to our salvation, through prayer and the continual supply of the Spirit of Jesus Christ.

Send us help this day from the sanctuary and strengthen us out of Zion. We know that thine own appointments were never intended to make us independent of thy agency; without thy superadded blessing the best means will prove in vain. But Thou hast promised to bless the provisions of thy house and to fill thy poor with bread. Thou hast said, In all places where I record my name, I will come unto thee and I will bless thee. And all have found Thee to be faithful to thy word. We have known Thee in thy palaces for a refuge; we have seen thy power and thy glory in the sanctuary; and have often praised Thee with joyful lips.

We therefore bless Thee for the return of these precious advantages. We pity those who are denied them. Sanctify their privations, and compensate the want of ordinances by thine own presence and communications. Enter as an instructer and comforter all the abodes of sorrow. Be the father of the fatherless and the husband of the widow. Guide those who are perplexed; guard those that are tempted; and let all that love Thee, be as the sun when he goeth forth in his might. We ask it through the intercession of Him who has taught us when we pray, to say, Our Father, &c.

SUNDAY EVENING.

O God, the heavens declare thy glory. The earth is full of thy riches. The universe is thy temple. Thy presence fills immensity. It is thy pleasure to produce life, and to communicate happiness. From Thee we have derived all we are and all we own; and in Thee we live and move and have our being continued. Thy good providence has determined the bounds of our habitation, and wisely administered all our affairs.

But above all we bless Thee for the exceeding riches of thy grace, in thy kindness towards us by Christ Jesus. Thanks be unto God for his unspeakable gift, and for

the unclouded revelation of Him in the word of truth. There we behold his person and character, his grace and glory. There we see Him when rich, for our sakes becoming poor, and dying that we may live; delivered for our offences, and raised again for our justification. May we deeply feel our need of this dispensation, in all its parts and in all its influences; and with Peter exclaim, Lord, save—I perish; and with the publican—God be me merciful to me a sinner.

Convince us of the pollution of sin, as well as of its guilt, that we may not only have our fear excited but our aversion; that with Job we may see that we are vile; and abhor ourselves, repenting in dust and ashes. May we feel the necessity of renovation as well as forgiveness, in order to our serving and enjoying Thee in time and eternity. O Thou Holy God, who hast no fellowship with iniquity, subdue in us the love of sin; create in us a clean heart, and renew in us a right spirit.

May we not be in the number of those who are always learning and never able to come to the knowledge of the truth; but may our hearts be established with grace. May we never rest in a mere system of doctrine, however scriptural, that does not bring salvation, or teach us to deny ungodliness and worldly lusts; and to live soberly, righteously, and godly in the present world: looking for that blessed hope, and the glorious appearing of the great God, and our Saviour Jesus Christ. May we live in the Spirit, and may we walk in the Spirit; and instead of relying on our own convictions and resolutions, may we be strong in the Lord and in the power of his might.

In all our duties, conflicts, and trials, may his grace be sufficient for us. To Him who gives rest to the weary and heavy laden, may we repair in all our spiritual distresses, in all our outward troubles, and in all the dissatisfactions experienced in creature-enjoyments. From a world where all is vanity and vexation of spirit, may we retreat to Him who is full of grace and truth; a Friend that loveth at all times; who is touched with the feeling of our infirmities; and who is able to do for us exceeding abundantly above all we can ask or think.

Prepare us for our final hour, and for all the scenes through which we have to pass in the remainder of our pilgrimage. May we know how to be abased, and how to abound. May we learn in whatsoever state we are therewith to be content. May we stand complete in all the will of God.

Do us good by all thy dispensations, and especially sanctify to us all the means of grace. We bless Thee that we have been favoured with another sabbath, and have had opportunities of repairing to the sanctuary, to mingle our prayers and praises with the devotions of thy people, and to hear the words of eternal life. We grieve to think that so much of the precious seed sown by thy servants should fall by the way side, so much upon stony places, and so much among thorns, and that so little fruit is brought forth to perfection. May it appear that we have not received the grace of God in vain; but that thy word in us is like good seed sown in good ground, which springeth up and bringeth forth, in some an hundred fold, in some sixty, and in some thirty.

And suffer us not to confine our religion to extraordinary occasions; but help us to acknowledge Thee in all our ways. May we never limit our devotion to particular seasons, but be in the fear of the Lord all the day long. May we be godly not only on the sabbath, but in the week; not only in the house of God, but in our own. May our piety be not a dress but a habit: not only a habit but a nature—a life—the life of God. And at last by thy grace and guidance, may we enter that world where there is no temple, but the glory of God and of the Lamb is the temple thereof.

But O how can we endure to see the destruction of our kindred! O Lord, let those that are united to us by so many tender ties, be precious in thy sight, and devoted to thy praise. Sanctify and succeed domestic devotion and instruction, discipline and example; and may our houses be nurseries for heaven, from which our churches, as the gardens of the Lord, shall be enriched with trees of righteousness, the planting of the Lord, that He may be glorified.

O let none of those who are amiable and moral, and possess so many attractions, like the hopeful youth in the gospel, fall short of heaven at last.

Where the conscience is tender, and the heart is soft, and the word alarms or delights —let not these promising appearances be blasted, but bring forth judgment unto victory.

Bless all who are connected with us by religious ties. Save thy people, and bless thine inheritance; feed them also, and lift them up for ever.

Regard us as a nation. Inspire all ranks and degrees of men among us with a love to that righteousness which exalteth a nation; and deliver us from that sin which is a reproach to any people.

And as all mankind, of whatever country or condition, are our brethren, bless them with the same civil and religious privileges which this highly favoured island enjoys. Let thy way be known on earth, thy saving health among all nations.

And may the grace of our Lord Jesus Christ, and the love of God, and the communion of the Holy Ghost, be with us all, now and for ever. Amen.

MONDAY MORNING.

O God, thy greatness is unsearchable; but we rejoice to think that thy love passeth knowledge. We have sinned against Thee; but thou art ready to forgive. We have gone far astray from Thee; but thou art more than willing to admit our return. Thou hast even provided the way to accomplish it. Thou hast appointed and made known a Mediator, who has once suffered for sin, the just for the unjust, that he might bring us unto God. In Him we behold Thee reconciling the world unto thyself, not imputing their trespasses unto them. And in Him a multitude which no man can number, redeemed, justified, and renewed, are exulting, My soul shall be joyful in my God, for he hath clothed me with the garments of salvation, he hath covered me with the robe of righteousness, as a bridegroom decketh himself with ornaments, and as a bride adorneth herself with her jewels.

O that it were thus with us! O that we could ascertain our spiritual condition, and read our title clear to the inheritance of the saints in light! Praise waiteth for Thee, O God, in Zion; and we are longing to be able to adore Thee, as the strength of our souls and our everlasting portion. Say to them that are of a fearful heart, Be strong, fear not; Him that cometh unto me, I will in no wise cast out; Whosoever will, let him come and take of the water of life freely :—O say unto our souls, I am thy salvation.

And O Lord, we hope that we are not concerned for our safety only; we trust we not only wish to know that we have the grace of God in truth, but to feel a progression in the divine life; to increase with all the increase of God. We wish to be qualified for our work, to stand complete in the will of our heavenly Father, and to adorn the doctrine of God our Saviour in all things.

Grant us therefore, we pray Thee, more of the supply of the spirit of Jesus Christ; to give more decision to our character, more vigour to our purposes, more elevation to our hopes, more fervour to our devotion, more constancy to our zeal; so that we may run and not be weary, and walk and not faint.

Thou dost not despise the day of small things, nor refuse to encourage a little strength; but Thou hast commanded us to grow in grace, and in the knowledge of our Lord and Saviour: and Thou hast said, To him that hath shall be given; and hast promised, that the feeble among them shall be as David. Be it unto us according to thy word. Fulfil all the good pleasure of thy goodness, and the work of faith with power, that the name of our Lord Jesus Christ may be glorified in us, and we in Him. May we be Christianity embodied and alive. May we be examples of the religion we profess, the most impressive and attracting. May we have a testimony in the bosoms of those who observe us, that we are the seed which the Lord hath blessed; and may every thing around us say to them, Come with us, and we will do you good.

To Thee we desire to submit all our desires, and to Thee would we commit all our concerns, casting all our cares upon Thee, conscious that Thou carest for us. And

Who so fit to choose our lot,
Or regulate our ways—

as a Being who loved us so as not to spare his own Son, who knows what is best for us in every circumstance, and is able to make all things work together for our good.

In every difficulty with which we are called to struggle, may we not only think of thy promises, but also call to remembrance the years of the right-hand of the Most High. We have often been brought low, and Thou hast helped us; and when we have been looking for nothing but darkness, at evening time it has been light. O how does it betray our depravity, that after all thy kindness and care, after all the proofs of thy patience, power, and fidelity, we are yet so little capable of trusting in Thee. We would cry out with tears, Lord, we believe, help Thou our unbelief.

Do us good by all the dispensations of thy providence, especially those of an afflictive kind. And why should we consider them strange things, since Thou hast told us that in the world we shall have tribulation, and that the same afflictions have been accomplished in all our brethren? And why should we desire exemption from them? seeing they are founded in love and intended for our profit. May we ever realize thy design by them, and see thine hand in them: may we believe that Thou wilt be with us in trouble; and look forward with joy to that state where it will be safe for us to be without sorrow, and God shall wipe away all tears from our eyes.

And if we have a portion in this world, keep us from making this world our portion. May we never look for that in the creature which can only be found in the Creator; nor for that on earth which is only to be found in heaven. Among our caresses and indulgences, may we never lose the heart of a stranger, or forget that this is not our rest. May the streams of comfort lead us to the fountain of all good; and may we love and serve our Benefactor in all his benefits.

And thus may we know how to be abased, and how to abound; and in every varying condition, display the principles and dispositions of those who are born from above, and are seeking glory, honour, and immortality.

And to the Father, the Word, and Holy Ghost, be ascribed all honour and praise, world without end. Amen.

MONDAY EVENING.

O Thou, whose name alone is Jehovah, Thou art the Most High over all the earth; and Thou hast set thy glory above the heavens. All thy works praise Thee, O Lord, and thy saints bless Thee. Thou art our fathers' God, and we will exalt Thee: Thou art our own God, and early will we seek Thee, for in thy favour is life.

Open Thou our lips, and our mouth shall show forth thy praise. Thou hast made us, and not we ourselves. Thine eye did see our substance yet being unperfect, and in thy book all our members were written, which in continuance were fashioned, when as yet there were none of them. Thou hast taught us more than the beasts of the field, and made us wiser than the fowls of the air. There is a spirit in man, and the inspiration of the Almighty giveth him understanding. Thy providence has watched over us from the womb, supplied all our wants, arranged all our affairs, and determined the bounds of our habitation.

And O what reason have we to exclaim, The lines are fallen to us in pleasant places, yea we have a goodly heritage! We live in a land of religious privileges. How superior are our advantages to those of thine ancient people the Jews! The Sun of Righteousness, which was below the horizon to them, has risen upon us with healing in his wings, and we are all the children of the day. Let us not therefore sleep as do others; but while we have the light, may we walk in the light lest darkness come upon us.

May we ever be impressed with the conviction, that where much is given much will be required, and that our greatest danger results from our distinguishing advantages—our sabbaths, our sanctuaries, the scriptures of truth, the preaching of the gospel, and all the events which have urged our attention to it.

What more could have been done for us than Thou hast done? And yet how little fruit have we brought forth! How well do we deserve to be cut down as cumberers of the ground and cast into the fire. Yet, O Lord, spare us at the intercession of the Vinedresser: for his sake renew our season of trial; and employ fresh means for our improvement, and accompany them with a divine power. Convince us of our sin and danger. Awaken in us the solemn inquiry, What must I do to be saved? And let not our concern, when awakened, lead us into any refuge of lies, or induce us to build on any false foundation; but may we believe on the Lord Jesus Christ, and find his rest to be glorious.

Produce in us that brokenness of heart, and that self-despair, which will render the faithful saying worthy of all acceptation; and make the Saviour precious to us as He is to all them that believe. May He be delightful to us in all his offices; may we love Him in his commands, as well as in his promises; may we wear his yoke and carry his burden; and find his yoke easy and his burden light. Make us in our views, principles, and dispositions, new creatures; may we shine in all the beauties of holiness; and reflect the praises of Him who hath called us out of darkness into his marvellous light. Explain to us thy secret which is with them that fear Thee; and show us thy covenant in its provisions and stability; and in every distress may this be all our salvation and all our desire.

With affections weaned from the world, and with evidences bright for heaven, all the days of our appointed time may we wait till our change comes: may we die supported by the consolations of the gospel, and surrounded with the glory of God; and have an entrance ministered unto us abundantly into the everlasting kingdom of our Lord and Saviour.

Prepare us for our passage as well as for our end. While we are here may we fulfil the duties, and bear with firmness the trials of our respective stations; may we glorify our Father who is in heaven, and serve our generation according to his will.

Continue thy goodness to us as a family. Remember our absent friends. Let thy ministers enjoy thy presence, and thy churches be filled with thy glory. Let the British empire be under thy care, and ever prove the seat of learning and science; of civil and religious freedom; of social blessedness; and of gospel privileges; and be the source of usefulness to the ends of the earth.

May princes come out of Egypt. May Ethiopia stretch forth her hands unto God. And may all nations whom Thou hast made come and worship before Thee.

For thine, O God, is the power; and thine shall be the glory, through our Lord and Saviour. Amen.

TUESDAY MORNING.

O Lord God of hosts, hear our prayer; give ear, O God of Jacob: behold, O God, our shield, and look upon the face of thine Anointed.

It is in his dear and all-prevailing name we come. We have nothing of our own to plead; no works, no worthiness, no promises. We have all like sheep gone astray. We have been transgressors from the womb. We have knowingly opposed thine authority, and abused thy goodness. We have been un-grateful under thy indulgences, incorrigible under thy rebukes, and have improved none of our religious advantages. We stand before Thee in our trespass, and are condemned by our own consciences as well as by thy word. Yet in the way of thine appointment Thou art waiting to be gracious, and hast said, that whatsoever we ask, believing in his name, we shall receive.

Through Him display thyself in our experience, as a God pardoning and subduing iniquity. Justify us freely from all things; and sanctify us wholly, body, soul, and spirit. May we be thy workmanship, created in Christ Jesus, and prepared unto every good work. We groan within ourselves, longing not only for deliverance from the wrath to come, but from the sin that dwelleth in us; and praying not only for an interest in thy favour, but a participation of thy image.

If thou hast begun the good work in us, carry it on unto the perfect day. Assure us of present assistance and final success, whatever difficulties or oppositions we meet with; that we may go on our way rejoicing, and be strong in the grace that is in Christ Jesus. If we feel little—and O how little do we feel!—of the joys of thy salvation, uphold us by thy free spirit; and enable us to persevere in the path of obedience, and in the use of the means which Thou hast appointed, assured that none of those shall be ever ashamed that wait for Thee. And should we walk in darkness and have no light, may we trust in the Lord and stay upon our God—Yet suffer us to implore that Thou wilt make Thy face to shine upon us, and give us the full assurance of hope—which hope may we have as an anchor of the soul, both sure and steadfast in all the storms of life.

We bless Thee for all that is past. Unless the Lord had been our help, our souls had almost dwelt in silence; but when we said, My feet slipped, thy mercy, O Lord, held us up. But we are still in the body and in the wilderness. We need thine aid as much as ever. We have a growing sense of our ignorance, weakness, and danger. Withdraw not thy presence, and take not thy Holy Spirit from us. Whether we are called to do thy will or to bear it, may we feel that our help is in the name of the Lord who made heaven and earth. If our course conducts us through rough and trying scenes, say to us, Thy shoes shall be iron and brass, and as thy days so shall thy strength be. In view of our encounter with our spiritual foes, clothe us with the whole armour of God; teach our hands to war, and our fingers to fight; and in the midst of the conflict tell our hearts that we shall be more than conquerors through him that loved us.

And may we be concerned that the blessings we ask for ourselves may be imparted to others. Teach us to love our neighbour as ourselves; and may we often examine our conditions in life, our offices, our talents, and our opportunities, to see how we may be serviceable in our day and generation.

Comfort those that mourn in Zion. Let all the afflicted find Thee a very present and an all-sufficient help in the day of trouble. Provide for the poor and needy. Guide those that need instruction; and may integrity and uprightness preserve them while they wait upon Thee.

Sanctify and continue to us, and to our latest posterity after us, all our national blessings, civil and religious; and may our country, by its institutions, character, and usefulness, continue to be a praise in the whole earth.

These are great blessings for such sinful creatures as we are to ask; but Thou hast given us a Name to plead which is above every name. Behold not our guilt, but that blood which cleanseth from all sin; not our unworthiness, but that righteousness with which Thou art well pleased. And accept us in the beloved. Our Father, &c. Amen.

TUESDAY EVENING.

O GOD, we are Thine, and Thee we are bound to worship. We grieve to think how many there are who cast off fear, and restrain prayer before Thee. But whatever be the determination of others, our purpose by thy grace is taken; and as for us and our house, we will serve the Lord.

We would not live a day or an hour without Thee in the world, careless of thy favour or regardless of thy glory. Impress us individually and deeply with a sense of thine omniscience; that Thou art about our path and our lying down, and acquainted with all our ways. Especially may we feel it when we enter thy more immediate presence, and engage in the exercises of devotion. *Then* may we remember that thine eyes are upon us; that thou requirest truth in the inward part; and that nothing can screen even our motives and principles from thy penetration.

Too little we acknowledge has this been our experience in former engagements; we have often been careless, where we should have been full of reverence: we have been strangers to the powers of godliness, while familiar with its forms. Thou hast been nigh in our mouths, but far from our reins. Much of our guilt has originated from our religious means and privileges; from the low estimation in which we have holden them, the slight improvements we have made of them, the little they have contributed to our growth in grace, and in the knowledge of our Lord and Saviour.

Over all this may we sorrow after a godly sort; and may the sincerity of our repentance

be seen in our future alarm and endeavours, and especially in our self-renunciation and dependence upon another—for when we are weak, then and then alone we are strong. May we every moment feel how necessary it is to be more intimate with Him who came, not only that we might have life, but that we might have it more abundantly; whose grace is sufficient for us; whose Spirit helps our infirmities, and can strengthen in us the things that remain, that are ready to die.

We bless Thee for an advocate with the Father, for a propitiation of infinite value; for a fulness that filleth all in all. In Him believing may we rejoice with joy unspeakable and full of glory. And may we know how to obtain relief for a guilty conscience, without feeling reconciled to our imperfections. May we abhor the thought of turning the grace of our God into lasciviousness, or sinning that grace may abound. Because we are not under the law but under grace, may we reckon ourselves to be dead indeed unto sin, but alive unto God through Jesus Christ our Lord—by thy mercies presenting our bodies a living sacrifice, and asking, What shall I render unto the Lord for all his benefits towards me! Through sanctification of the Spirit and belief of the truth, may our affections be set on things that are above; and may this be the growing desire of our souls; O that my feet were directed to keep thy precepts!

We would not seek great things for ourselves, but be content with such things as we have. Deliver us, O Lord, from the love of money which is the root of all evil. May we value our substance, not as the medium of pride and luxury, but as affording us the means of support and usefulness; and may we guide our affairs with discretion, that we may owe no man any thing, and be able to give to him that needeth. Establish in us the royal law: may we love our neighbour as ourselves; and feel it not only our duty but our pleasure, as we have opportunity, to do good unto all men, especially unto them that are of the household of faith.

Bless all the churches of the faithful. Thou hast given them rest; may they walk in the fear of the Lord, and in the comforts of the Holy Ghost, and be edified and multiplied.

Display thy power and thy glory in the sanctuary. Be with thy servants who show unto men the way of salvation. Make them wise to win souls: may they speak the things only that become sound doctrine; may they never expect success as the result of their eloquence and reasonings, but from the excellency of the power that is of God.

Let the king live before Thee; and our highly favoured country be safe and flourishing under the shadow of the Almighty.

Regard our friends and relations. Those that are absent from us, we commend to the are and direction of an ever-present God. Let those that know Thee not be made wise unto salvation: let not those who are endeared by so many ties, be separated from us for ever—How can we endure to see the destruction of our kindred?

Keep us in all places and circumstances. Hide us this night in the secret of thy pavilion, and in the morning encompass us with songs of deliverance.

And now, blessed be the Lord God of Israel, who only doeth wondrous things; and blessed be his glorious name for ever, and let the whole earth be filled with his glory. Amen and Amen.

WEDNESDAY MORNING.

O Thou that hearest prayer, and inhabitest the praises of Israel! with Moses and Aaron among thy priests, and Samuel among them that call upon thy name, we would this morning exalt the Lord our God, and worship at his footstool, for He is holy.

We thank Thee, O Father, Lord of heaven and earth, for all thy inexpressible and inconceivable goodness to the children of men, of which our own history and experience afford such numberless proofs. In thy works of creation we read thy name the Lord God Almighty; in the dispensations of thy providence we acknowledge Thee as the only wise God; but in the gospel of thy grace we behold Thee as the God of love, and so loving the world as to give thine only begotten Son, that whosoever believeth on Him should not perish but have everlasting life. In Him Thou hast provided for our deliverance from all the effects of sin; for the justification of our persons, the sanctification of our natures, and our perseverance in the path of life, till we receive the end of our faith—the salvation of our souls.

We bless Thee, that exposed as we are to the terrors of thy law which we have so often transgressed, here we have a refuge from the storm; and learn that there is no condemnation to them that are in Christ Jesus. We bless Thee, that while we are compelled to exclaim, Unclean, unclean! here is an open fountain, the efficacy of which—for it has often been tried—cleanseth from all sin. We bless Thee, that while in us dwelleth no good thing, and all creatures are cells of emptiness, there is a fulness accessible to all, and incapable of reduction, from which we can receive and grace for grace.

O Lord, we ask not for worldly riches or honours, but pray that we may be blessed with all spiritual blessings in heavenly places in Christ. We envy not those whom the multitude admire; they will soon be cut down as the grass, and wither as the green herb; but look Thou upon us, and be merciful to us, as Thou usest to do unto those that fear thy name. They are happy now, and are inviting and encouraging us to taste and see that the Lord is good. May a vital union be immediately established between Him and us —He the head, and we the members; He the vine, and we the branches; He the shepherd, and we the sheep of his pasture; He the chief corner-stone, and we also as lively stones built up a spiritual house, an habitation of God through the spirit.

Let us not walk as other gentiles, in the vanity of our minds, and having our understandings darkened; but may we estimate things according to the testimony of thy word, and feel a persuasion that to obtain salvation by our Lord Jesus Christ, is a concern in comparison with which every other interest is a shadow and a dream.

And O Lord save us from presumption. Keep us from suspending our attention to the things of eternity on a more convenient season, or any future period which may never arrive; but reflecting upon the shortness and uncertainties of life, and knowing how frail we are, may we seek the Lord while He may be found, and call upon Him while He is near. May we immediately begin to live the life of the righteous, that we may die the death of the righteous, and that our last end may be like his.

And O save us from the delusion of those who go far, but not far enough in religion; who are convinced but not converted; who have another heart, but not a new one; and who with all their light and zeal and confidence, have not the spirit of Christ, and therefore are none of his. May we judge of our Christianity not only by our dependence upon Christ, but our love to Christ, and by our conformity to Christ. May we know that He dwelleth in us and we in Him, because He hath given us of his Spirit.

Let our religion not only be real but progressive; let us not only hold on our way, but wax stronger and stronger. May we live and may we walk in the Spirit. May we profit by every correction, and be injured by no indulgence.

Accept of our personal and combined acknowledgments, that Thou hast been our salvation in the night watches; and that we are not only the living to praise Thee this morning, but have all things richly to enjoy.

Bless the word which we have been reading. Let not the cares of this life, or the deceitfulness of sin render it unfruitful. May thy word abide in us and operate. May it attend us in all the businesses of the day, that we may not sin against Thee; and that whether we eat or drink, or whatever we do, we may do all to the glory of God—

To whom be glory in the church, by Christ Jesus, throughout all ages, world without end. Amen.

WEDNESDAY EVENING.

O Thou that inhabitest eternity, and with whom a thousand years are as one day. If we were angels we should veil our faces as we approach Thee, and exclaim, Holy, holy, holy is the Lord of hosts, the whole earth is full of his glory. With what emotions then should *we* enter thy presence, who are but sinful dust and ashes! Give us grace whereby we may serve Thee acceptably, with reverence and godly fear.

May we always combine thy majesty with thy mercy, that we may not trifle before Thee, or incur the reproach of the hypocrite and the formalist, who draw nigh unto Thee with their mouth, and honour Thee with their lips, while their heart is far from Thee. And may we always connect thy goodness with thy greatness, that we may draw near in full assurance of faith. May our consciences at this moment believe that Thou art good, and ready to forgive, and plenteous in mercy to all that call upon Thee.

And do Thou have mercy upon us, O God, according to thy lovingkindness, according to the multitude of thy tender mercies. Thou art under no obligation to save us! we lie as guilty at thy sovereign disposal. Thou hast a right to exercise thy mercy in thine own way; and Thou hast sent thine own Son into the world, not to condemn the world, but that the world through *Him* might be saved. Thou hast made Him to be sin for us who knew no sin, that we might be made the righteousness of God in Him. We bow, O God, to thine appointment; and gratefully comply with thy command, for this is thy commandment, that we believe on the name of thy Son Jesus Christ our Lord. We would flee to no other refuge; we would wash in no other fountain; we would build on no other foundation; we would receive from no other fulness.

May the life that we henceforth shall live in the flesh, be by the faith of Him who loved us and gave himself for us. In his name may we rejoice all the day, and in his righteousness may we be exalted.

May we feel a growing conformity to the image of thy Son, and like Him, learn obedience to the things we suffer. May the law of the Spirit of life in Christ Jesus make us free from the law of sin and death.

In all our dealings with our fellow-creatures, may we do justly; in all cases requiring relief and compassion, may we show that we love mercy; and with regard to all the dispensations of thy providence and grace, may we walk humbly with our God.

May we be strong and of good courage to to follow our convictions, regardless of the opinions of others, and obey God rather than man. Having obtained the knowledge of thy will from thy word, may we go forth and be steadfast, unmoveable, always abounding in the work of the Lord. And let us not be slothful, but followers of them who through faith and patience inherit the promises.

O how great is the goodness which in thy promises and in thy kingdom Thou hast laid up for them that fear Thee!—Number us with them; and enable us to say, Thou hast given me the heritage of them that fear thy name. This assurance, O God, we want, to animate us in duty; to support us under our trials; and to raise us above the fear of death and the dread of eternity. For we know that we are not to live here always, nor to live here long. Dangers surround us; within us are sown the seeds of disease; our breath is in our nostrils; and there is but a step between us and the grave. How soon is another day gone! and how solemnly does it remind us, That all our days are as a shadow! Great God, so teach us to number our days, that we may apply our hearts unto wisdom. Amidst all the uncertainties of time, may we know in ourselves that in heaven we have a better and an enduring substance; and when the earthly house of this tabernacle is dissolving, may we see prepared to receive us a building of God, a house not made with hands eternal in the heavens.

We feel our weakness and our wants. We depend on all the elements for our subsistence, and there is no creature but can be our help or our hurt. We need day by day our supplies of food. We labour for a few hours, and we feel ourselves exhausted, and require weary nature's sweet restorer balmy sleep. We would not say to Him that made us, Why hast thou made me thus? but bless Thee for a season of repose and refreshment; for the promise we have that when we lie down, Thou wilt make us to dwell in safety; and for a state where we shall feel no languor and need no rest; where there shall be no night, and they need no candle, neither light of the sun; for the Lord God giveth them light, and they shall reign for ever and ever. Receive and bless us in the name and for the sake of our adorable Redeemer. Amen.

THURSDAY MORNING.

O Thou, who wast, and art, and art to come, the Almighty. Thou art the creator of all the ends of the earth. Thou art our maker, and not only the framer of our bodies, but the former of our souls. For there is a spirit in man, and the inspiration of the Almighty giveth him understanding. May we remember that Thou madest us upright, but that we have sought out many inventions. Let us not forget what we are, what we deserve, and what we want in our present state.

Nor let us be ignorant of the provisions of thy mercy and grace; nor of Him in whom t hath pleased Thee that all fulness should dwell. In all our outward troubles, and in all our spiritual distress, He is the hope and the consolation of Israel. May we receive the record, that Thou hast given to us eternal life, and that this life is in thy Son. To Him may we always look for relief, and to Him *only*; persuaded that there is none other name given under heaven among men, whereby we must be saved. We know from thy word, that he came by water and by blood; as these were not served in their effusion from the cross, may they never be separated in our creed and our experience. May we be equally convinced of the guilt and the pollution of sin; may we alike feel our need of the Prince and the Saviour, and implore of Him repentance as well as forgiveness. May we love holiness and be pure in heart. O that our feet were directed to keep thy statutes! O that we had the same mind in us which was also in Christ Jesus, and were enabled to tread in his steps, who has gone before us in every path of duty and trial!

As long as we are in the world, keep us from the evil; and may we be always alive and awake to discharge every obligation resulting from our condition in life and the particular events of thy providence.

We would not be at our own disposal, but rejoice to think we are under the care of one who is too wise to err, and too kind to injure. However ignorant of the future, we will trust and not be afraid; and begin even in this vale of tears, the song we hope for ever to sing—Marvellous are thy works, Lord God Almighty, just and true are all thy ways, O Thou King of saints.

Thou hast been pleased again to renew our time and our strength and our comforts, help us to renew our purposes and resolutions to obey and serve Thee. In all our ways may we this day acknowledge Thee, and do Thou direct our paths. Let thy presence go with us, and thy free spirit uphold us.

May we scandalize none by our temper or conduct, but recommend and endear the religion we profess to all around us. May we decline no opportunity of usefulness that our circumstances may present. May we not withhold good from him to whom it is due, when it is in the power of our hand to do it. May we dread the sentence, Whoso stoppeth his ears at the cry of the poor, he also shall cry himself and not be heard. May we therefore be merciful, ready to communicate, feeling the grace of our Lord Jesus Christ, who when rich for our sakes became poor, that we through his poverty might be rich.

Let those who are advanced in years be anxious to bring forth fruit in old age. Let those who are in the midst of life abide with God in their calling; and while they are not slothful in business, may they be fervent in spirit, serving the Lord. And O preserve the young from the snares and temptations of youth. May they be sober-minded. If sinners entice them, let them not consent. With the infidel and the vicious, and the despiser of the sabbath, may they not go, lest they learn of their ways, and get a snare to their souls. Let them say, I am a companion of all them that fear Thee, and choose that good part which shall not be taken away from them.

Bless us as a nation, in our sovereign, senators, and magistrates; in all the dependencies and interests of the country; in all its civil and sacred institutions. Let glory dwell in our land, and upon all the glory may there be a defence.

We rejoice that Thou wilt have all men to be saved and come to the knowledge of the truth; and that Jesus Christ gave himself a ransom for all to be testified in due time.

Call in the Jews with the fulness of the Gentiles. Say to the north, give up, and to the south, Keep not back; bring my sons from far, and my daughters from the ends of the earth. Bless all those who by their exertions and sacrifices are proving the sincerity of their prayers for the spread of the Redemer's cause; and let many run to and fro, and knowledge be increased, till all shall know Thee, from the least even to the greatest.

Our Father, &c. Amen.

———

THURSDAY EVENING.

GIVE ear to our words, O Lord; consider our meditation; and enable us to approach Thee with becoming conceptions of thy nature, relations, and designs.

Thou inhabitest eternity; but our age is as nothing before Thee. Thou dwellest in the heaven of heavens, and this cannot contain Thee; but we dwell in houses of clay, whose foundation is in the dust. Thy power is almighty; but we are crushed before the moth. Thy understanding is infinite, but we know nothing as we ought to know. Thou art of purer eyes than to behold evil, and canst not look upon iniquity; but we are vile—What shall we answer Thee? We cannot answer Thee for one of a thousand of our iniquities; and had we listened to the language of our guilty consciences alone, we could not have entered thy sacred presence.

But Thou hast called us to thy footstool; Thou hast shown us a new and living way into the holiest by the blood of Jesus; and we have boldness and access with confidence by the faith of Him. We therefore draw nigh in full assurance of faith, believing that we are as welcome as we are unworthy, and that the blessings we are come to implore are as free as they are great and numberless. O receive us graciously. Be merciful to our un-righteousness. Adopt us into the household of faith; and say to our souls, I am thy salvation.

We have often feared that we have no part nor lot in the matter; and that our heart is not right in the sight of God. We have often questioned whether we know any thing of the new creature; whether we have ever exercised repentance towards God, and faith towards our Lord Jesus Christ. And what if after all our advantages, we should perish; and after all our profession, have a name only that we live while we are dead! O Lord, decide our doubts, and bear witness with our spirits that we are the children of God.

We would not deceive ourselves in a business of everlasting moment; but if we are in a *state* of grace, enable us to know it, for our own comfort and the glory of thy great name.

And, O Lord, we pray that we may *grow* in grace. If we have the reality of religion, how far are our works from being found perfect before God! Strengthen in us the things that remain that be ready to die; and help us to reach after the higher attainments and privileges of the divine life. May we be followers of God as dear children, and feel it the joy of our lives to be holy as Thou art holy, and merciful as Thou art merciful. May thine eye be more to us than the inspection of all our fellow-creatures; and thy approbation be dearer than the applause of a thousand worlds.

May no grace of the Spirit be wanting or weak in us; may no duty of our calling be neglected, or carelessly performed. May our faith be a strong faith, our hope a lively hope, our charity a fervent charity, our conversation a conversation becoming the gospel of Christ. May we stand complete in all the will of God; and may our light so shine before men, that they may see our good works and glorify our Father who is in heaven.

May we long to serve our generation according to thy will; may wisdom select and regulate our means, and a blameless and lovely consistency of character give weight to our endeavours. And may all our works begin, continue, and end in Thee. On Thee may we depend for light to know, and disposition to choose, and strength to perform, and submission to suffer, and patience to wait.

And when we have done all, may we acknowledge that we are unprofitable servants, and confess that we deserve condemnation for the defects of our obedience, rather than a reward for its excellency. And looking off from our duties as well as our sins, to find a foundation for our hope, may we rejoice in Christ Jesus, and have no confidence in the flesh. And may our persons and services be accepted in the beloved—To whom be glory and dominion for ever and ever. Amen.

FRIDAY MORNING.

WE would lift up our hearts, with our hands, unto God in the heavens. Behold before Thee a company of highly-indulged but sinful beings. If we say we have no sin, we deceive ourselves, and the truth is not in us. None of our fellow-creatures know half so much of our depravity as we ourselves know; and our knowledge is ignorance compared with thy wisdom.

Thou readest the heart. Thou viewest actions in their principles and motives. Thou seest more defilement in our duties than we ever saw in any of our sins. In thy sight the heavens are not clean; and Thou chargest thine angels with folly. And if we hate ourselves, and are ready to flee from ourselves because of our abominations, how wonderful is it that Thou dost not abhor us, and swear in thy wrath that we shall not enter into thy rest.

But, be astonished, O heavens, and wonder, O earth! instead of such a deserved exclusion, Thou hast even devised means that thy banished be not expelled from Thee—means the most astonishing and glorious, and which the angels desire to look into. For Thou hast so loved the world, as to give thine only begotten Son, that whosoever believeth on Him should not perish but have everlasting life. In Him mercy and truth meet together, righteousness and peace kiss each other; and thy honour is not only secured, but prominently displayed, even in our escape from thine own threatenings. In Him the enslaved can find redemption, the guilty pardon, the unholy renovation. In Him are everlasting strength for the weak, and unsearchable riches for the needy; in Him we find all the treasures of wisdom and knowledge for the ignorant; in Him all fulness dwells.

We bless Thee for the provision which thine infinite goodness has made for our everlasting welfare; and for the gospel of our salvation which makes it known; and which not only reveals it to our view, but proposes it to our hope, and presses it upon our acceptance.

O Lord, at thy gracious call we hear, we look, we come, we apply, we receive. We not only submit to the scheme of mercy, but we acquiesce in it; we glory in the cross of our Lord Jesus Christ; we joy in God through our Lord Jesus Christ by whom we have now received the atonement. We bless Thee that in this grace we *stand:* Thou hast rendered the blessings as secure as they are glorious; and we are persuaded that neither death, nor life, nor angels, nor principalities, nor powers, nor things present, nor things to come, nor height, nor depth, nor any other creature, shall be able to separate us from the love of God which is in Christ Jesus our Lord.

Yea for ever blessed be thy name, Thou

hast not only provided for our safety, but our prosperity. Thou hast not only promised that the righteous shall hold on their way, but wax stronger and stronger. Thou dost not despise the day of small things; but Thou givest more grace; and hast commanded us to ask and receive that our joy may be full.

And now, O Lord, what shall we render for all thy benefits towards us? We can never discharge the obligations we are under, but we pray that we may be sensible of them; and though we can make no adequate, may we make suitable returns; and ever ask from the heart, as well as with the lip, Lord, what wilt Thou have me to do?

And may we show forth thy praise. May we speak well of thy name. May we be concerned to bring others to love and serve Thee; and to share with us in all the good which Thou hast spoken concerning Israel.

O let our children be thy children, our friends thy friends, our servants thy servants.

May our neighbours, and our enemies too, be visited with thy salvation.

Dwell in our families. Let thy goings be seen in our sanctuaries. Let the people praise Thee, O God, yea let all the people praise Thee. Let the whole earth be filled with thy glory.

Bless the Lord, ye his angels that excel in strength, that do his commandments hearkening unto the voice of his word. Bless ye the Lord, all ye his hosts, ye ministers of his that do his pleasure. Bless the Lord, all his works, in all places of his dominion. Bless the Lord, O my soul. Amen, and Amen.

FRIDAY EVENING.

AGAIN, O Lord of all, we desire to bow in thy presence. May we approach Thee with all the encouragements that can be derived from thy character as the God of love. We are not left to feel after Thee in the darkness of nature; nor to worship Thee as the unknown God. We cannot find Thee out unto perfection; but we know that Thou art good and ready to forgive, and plenteous in mercy unto all them that call upon Thee.

For Thou hast given us thy word, which Thou hast magnified above all thy name; and Thou hast favoured us with the gospel, which has turned the dawn of Judaism into perfect day : so that on us who were sitting in darkness and the shadow of death, has risen a great light, the light of life.

But we acknowledge how ungratefully we have received the benefit, and how little we have improved our privileges to the purposes for which they have been given. We have made light of these things though angels desire to look into them; we have neglected the great salvation; we have turned away from

Him that speaketh from heaven. And all that Thou hast kindly employed to enforce the messages of thy word we have disregarded; for we have contemned the examples of the good, the admonitions of friendship, the reproaches of conscience, the rebukes of thy providence, and the strivings of thy Holy Spirit; and well do we deserve that the kingdom of God should be taken away from us. O let us not confess our sins without feeling and lamenting them, but with a broken heart and a contrite spirit, with self-abhorrence, self-condemnation, and self-despair.

And under a deep impression of our guilt, may we seek relief alone from Him who is the hope and the consolation of Israel. Viewing Him as dying for the ungodly, may we believe in his name. May we know that He bare our sins in his own body on the tree, and that by his stripes we are healed. And may we find in Him, not only righteousness but strength. May He impart to us, not only forgiveness of sins, but repentance unto life. May we never separate in our regards, what He has joined together in the scripture ; nor suppose that we are justified by his blood, unless we are sanctified by his Spirit.

We believe we can never be happy in sin, and we do not desire it: Lord, deliver us from it, and lead us in the way everlasting. Make us holy like thyself, that we may be made happy in thyself. We are naturally disqualified for all communion with a holy God; work in us to will and to do of thy good pleasure; produce in us those principles and dispositions which will attach us to thyself as our exceeding joy; and enable us to say, Whom have I in heaven but Thee? and there is none upon earth that I desire beside Thee.

Under all our ignorance, weakness, fears, and depressions, may thy Spirit help our infirmities with supplies of wisdom, strength, and comfort.

May we faithfully study our character, and be always willing to come to the light, that if evil our deeds may be reproved. May we peculiarly observe ourselves under the operation of those events which are designed to try us; that we may judge of the reality and degree of our grace. May we often review life, and see how we have at any time been ensnared or overcome, that we may in future become more wise and circumspect. And while we watch, may we also pray lest we enter into temptation. May we never trust in our own hearts, nor depend upon any past experience or present resolution, but be strong in the grace that is in Christ Jesus.

Thus far Thou hast helped us. Hitherto our enemies have not triumphed over us. And though we have seen many decline from their profession, we hope if Thou wert to ask, Will ye also go away? we should be able to say, with more conviction and affection than ever, Lord, to whom should we go but unto Thee! Thou hast the words of eternal life. Thou hast been with us in trouble; and many a shadow of death hast Thou turned into the morning. We can now discern thy wisdom and kindness in dispensations which once perplexed and dismayed us: and what we know not now we shall know hereafter.

Never leave us nor forsake us; but support and lead us through all these dark and sorrowful regions; and enable us with confidence to hail the hour when our sun shall no more go down, nor our moon withdraw herself; for the Lord shall be our everlasting light, and the days of our mourning shall be ended.

We implore it through the intercession of Him who gave himself for our sins, that He might deliver us from this present evil world according to the will of God and our Father; to whom be glory for ever and ever. Amen.

SATURDAY MORNING.

LET not the Lord be angry, while we, who are but dust and ashes, take upon us to speak unto the living God. Pardon our unworthiness—help our infirmities; and hearken unto the voice of our cry, our King and our God, for unto Thee will we pray.

Thou art good to all; and we have largely shared with thy creatures the bounties of thy providence. But O remember us with the favour Thou bearest unto thy people. We bless Thee for characterizing them; and we bless Thee that Thou hast placed the distinction in no high and discouraging attainments: for Thou takest pleasure in them that *fear* Thee; in them that *hope* in thy mercy. May these dispositions be found in each of us. May we dread thine anger, revere thy perfections, stand in awe of thy majesty, and tremble at thy word. And hide not thy mercy from us: enable us to trust in it and to plead it; and with a broken heart and a contrite spirit may we earnestly cry, God be merciful to me a sinner. In how many ways do we need the exercise of it! But Thou art rich in mercy; Thou art abundant in mercy; Thou delightest in mercy.

We are all so many proofs of this. Because thy compassions fail not we are not consumed. Our forfeited lives have not only been continued, but crowned with thy goodness. Thou hast provided for our souls as well as for our bodies; and we hear a thousand voices inviting us to the feast, and saying, Come, for all things are now ready. Thanks be unto God for his unspeakable gift: we bless Thee for a Saviour, who died for our sins, and rose again for our justification, and is now ascended far above all heavens that He might fill all things.

May we be made the partakers of Christ and not only of his righteousness but of his Spirit; that we may be not only pardoned but renewed; and not only have a title to heaven but a meetness for it. No longer alienated from the life of God, may our meditations of Thee be sweet, and may we draw near to Thee as to our exceeding joy. May we confide in thy promises, and rely on thy constant protection and care. May we be devoted to thy service, and find it perfect freedom. May we love obedience: may thy law be within our heart.

Let thy cause be dear to our souls. We pray that thy word may have free course and be glorified. Let thy church not only be multiplied in number, but increased in knowledge and sanctity and peace and concord and joy, so that it may be a praise in the whole earth. Let the light of the moon be as the light of the sun, and the light of the sun be sevenfold, as the light of seven days. For brass, bring gold; and for iron, silver; and for wood, brass; and for stones, iron.

Thou dost not stand in need of us; but in thy condescension and wisdom Thou art pleased to make use of means, and we desire the honour and happiness of being instruments in thy hand. Lord, what wilt Thou have us to do! We would value every day afforded us as a new period of usefulness. May we be anxious to accomplish all we can to alleviate human wo, and to advance the temporal and spiritual welfare of all around us.

And may we not only be zealous, but persevering. May we never be discouraged, never grow weary in well-doing. While many go back after following the Saviour, may we cleave to him with purpose of heart, and at last hear Him say, Ye are they who have continued with me in my temptation, and I appoint unto you a kingdom, as my Father also hath appointed unto me.

We would not forget the afflicted. Hear the sighing of the needy; cause the widow's heart to sing for joy; and in Thee may the fatherless find mercy. Remove indisposition and disease from those who are exercised thereby, or assure them of that world where the inhabitant no more says, I am sick.

Be with us all through the changing scenes of life, and at the hour of dissolution: when heart and flesh fail be Thou the strength of our heart and our portion for ever. If death should be sudden, let it not find us unprepared; if it should be awful in the apprehension, let it be safe in the result; and if we cannot depart in triumph, may we expire in humble hope.

And through eternal ages may it be our privilege to unite with those who are singing, Unto Him that loved us, and washed us from our sins in his own blood, and hath made us kings and priests unto God, and to his Father

—to Him be glory and dominion for ever and ever. Amen.

SATURDAY EVENING.

O LORD God of Hosts: Thou hast established thy throne in the heavens, and thy kingdom ruleth over all. It is a source of joy to our minds, and of encouragement to our hopes, that the Lord God Omnipotent reigneth. In thy greatness we see thy all-sufficiency to accomplish all that Thou hast promised, to confer upon us all we need, and to do for us exceeding abundantly above all we can ask or think.

It is therefore good for us to draw near to Thee; and it is our mercy to know that we can approach Thee with confidence of acceptance and success; founded not on any worthiness or works of our own, but on thine own grace in the appointment of a Mediator, who has put away sin by the sacrifice of himself, and opened a new and living way into the holiest of all by his own blood.

We have no other name to plead, and we need no other. Behold, O God, our shield, and look upon the face of thine Anointed; and for his sake, who groaned in the garden and died upon the cross, and now appears in thy presence for us, pardon our iniquity, for it is great: cleanse us from all unrighteousness; deliver us from the power of darkness; and translate us into the kingdom of thy dear Son.

May we no longer be strangers and foreigners, but fellow-citizens with the saints and of the household of God; and because we are sons, send forth the spirit of thy Son into our hearts, crying, Abba, Father. May our intercourse with Thee be free and delightful and constant; and not on peculiar occasions only, but in every thing by prayer and supplication with thanksgiving, may we make known our requests unto Thee. May we live in thy presence.

May we walk with God, and walk humbly with God; sensible of our deficiencies and desert; admiring thy condescension and patience; and bowing to all thy dispensations without murmuring or repining.

May we walk circumspectly, not as fools but as wise, redeeming the time. May we be zealous in the discharge of all those duties, the performance of which depends on a season so fleeting and precarious. May we consider one another, and provoke one another to love and to good works; not forsaking the assembling of ourselves together as the manner of some is, but exhorting one another, and so much the more as we see the day approaching.

Enable us to realize the universality and perfection of thy agency in all our affairs; and since all thy ways are mercy and truth, may we learn in whatsoever state we are therewith to be content; yea in everything may we give thanks.

May we not only submit to our trials, but be grateful for them. They are designed for our profit, that we may be partakers of thy holiness. They evince a care of which we are unworthy, and which we have never properly repaid. Lord, what is man, that Thou shouldst magnify him; that Thou shouldst set thy heart upon him; that Thou shouldst visit him every morning, and chasten him every moment. So impatient and wayward and foolish have we been under thy hand, that we have forfeited all claim to the rod, and deserve to be stricken no more. It would be just in Thee to say, They are joined to idols, let them alone. But, O Lord, abandon us not to ourselves; treat us not with neglect. Employ whatever means are necessary to save and sanctify our souls. Try us as Thou pleasest; only while we are chastened of the Lord, let us not be condemned with the wicked.

Humble us under a view of our depravity through another day and another week, which is now hastening to join the days and weeks before the flood. Who can understand his errors? In many things we all offend. Hide thy face from our sins. Heal our backslidings, and receive us graciously; so will we render the calves of our lips.

On the coming day, let thy good Spirit lead us to thy holy hill and to thy tabernacle. May we go unto the altar of God as to our exceeding joy, and taste the blessedness of those that dwell in thy house and are still praising Thee. Teach us to value properly the means of grace, and be concerned to derive from them the benefit they are designed to afford. May we remember our accountableness for them. May we remember that they never leave us as they find us; but always prove the savour of life unto life, or of death unto death.

Let not our attendance add to our sin and condemnation. Let us not sing without devotion, pray without desire, and hear in vain; but be found in the number of those who know the joyful sound, and walk in the fear of the Lord, and in the comforts of the Holy Ghost.

And may those who will not be able to hear the word, hear the rod, and hear it saying, As many as I love I rebuke and chasten. Let meditation and reading and pious conversation, and above all thy special presence, be substitutes for public ordinances. Thus send portions to those for whom nothing is prepared; and let them that tarry at home divide the spoil. And have mercy upon all men, as we implore it through the mediation of the ever blessed Redeemer. In whose words we address Thee—Our Father, &c. Amen.

SIXTH WEEK.

SUNDAY MORNING.

O God, Thou hast made, and Thou upholdest all things by the word of thy power. The day is thine, the night is also thine; and by thy wise and kind appointment they are also rendered ours—The night to wipe off from our minds the cares of the day; to refresh our wearied bodies; and to renew our natural strength—and the day to summon us to new activities, and to afford us opportunities to glorify our heavenly Benefactor, to serve our generation, and to acquire knowledge, holiness and everlasting life.

To these duties every morning calls us; but *this* is the day which the Lord hath made more peculiarly for his own honour and our improvement; and therefore we will rejoice and be glad in it. It brings to our remembrance the creation of the world, when God rested from all his works which He had made, and pronounced them to be very good. And there is none like unto Thee, O Lord, among the gods, neither are there any works like unto thy works: they proclaim thy eternal power and godhead, so that we should be without excuse were we not to glorify Thee as God. But Thou hast said, Behold, I create new heavens and a new earth, and the former shall not be remembered nor come into mind. We adore Thee therefore as the God and Father of our Lord Jesus Christ, who having finished the work that was given him to do, entered into his rest: we call to our minds a risen Saviour, who has obtained eternal redemption for us; who dieth no more; who must reign till all his enemies are made his footstool.

May we enter into *his* rest and find it to be glorious. May we cease from all the wretched attempts to deliver and save ourselves; and believe in the name of the only begotten Son of God; that being justified by faith we may have peace through the blood of the cross; and standing in his grace rejoice in hope of the glory that shall be revealed.

We feel our depravity as well as our guilt; and therefore we pray, not only that Thou wilt forgive us our sins, but cleanse us from all unrighteousness. Create in us a clean heart; renew in us a right spirit; and in simplicity and godly sincerity, not with fleshly wisdom but by thy grace, may we have our conversation in the world.

We rejoice that the tabernacle of God is with men; and we bless Thee that Thou hast said, Let them make me a sanctuary that I may dwell among them. We are now to repair from the retirement of the closet and the family altar, to the habitation of thy house, and to mingle with the multitude that keep holy-day. We are unworthy to behold the beauty of the Lord, and to inquire in his temple; and are we unfit for services which require a spirituality to which we are naturally averse? Our encouragement is in the all-sufficiency of thy grace; and therefore blessed be thy name, we go with a lively hope derived from thy own promise, In all places where I record thy name, I will come unto thee and I will bless thee. Save now, O Lord we beseech Thee; O Lord we beseech Thee send now prosperity.

We cast our eyes over a world lying in wickedness; and our compassion and zeal are awakened. How many are perishing with hunger, while there is bread enough and to spare in our Father's house. How many are suffering under the miseries of this life, and the fears of another, but they have no comforter. The captive exiles hasten that they may be loosed, and that they may not lose their life in the pit; and by their condition, if not by their consciousness of it, are saying, Come over and help us. O send out thy light and thy truth, that all nations whom Thou hast made may come and worship before Thee and glorify thy name. We bless Thee that so many Societies have been formed for this noble purpose; and that so many have counted the cost, and have gone forth to preach among the Gentiles the unsearchable riches of Christ. And we bless Thee for the smiles with which Thou hast crowned their efforts. Thou hast risen up out of thy place. Thou hast made bare thy arm in the sight of all the nations. Kings of armies do flee apace, and she that tarries at home divides the spoil—and princes shall come out of Egypt; and Ethiopia shall soon stretch forth her hands unto God; and all the ends of the earth shall see his salvation, for the mouth of the Lord hath spoken it.

God save the king; and render him equal to all the importance and responsibility of his exalted station: and may he reign not only over a great and mighty empire, but over a moral and holy people, whose God is the Lord. Clothe thy priests with righteousness; let thy saints shout aloud for joy; let thy poor be satisfied with bread. Let the blind and the lame come to Jesus in the temple and be healed. May private trials subserve the designs of public instruction; and thy own presence make the chamber of sickness and the dwelling-place of sorrow, the house of God and the gate of heaven. And prevent us, O Lord, in all our doings by thy most gracious favour: and further us with thy continual help; that in all our works begun, continued, and ended in Thee, we may glorify thy holy name; and finally obtain everlasting life, through Jesus Christ our Lord: to whom be glory for ever and ever. Amen.

SUNDAY EVENING.

Praise waiteth for Thee, O God, in Zion,

and to render it is the noblest exercise of which our nature is capable. And it is infinitely thy due from all thy creatures; and all thy works display thy attributes and fulfil thy designs. The sea and the dry land; the winter's cold and the summer's heat; the morning light and the evening shade, all are full of Thee. Thy paths drop down fatness. Thou givest us richly all things to enjoy. Thou art the King of kings, and the Lord of lords. Empires rise and fall, and fade and flourish at thy pleasure. But while all thy works praise thee, O Lord, thy saints bless Thee. And how many of these are there in thy house above. And how many are there even in this world which lieth in wickedness; and how does it delight us to think that their multitude is so greatly increasing. The Lord add to his people how many soever they be, a hundred fold!

But O number us with thy saints in glory everlasting. We turn from men of the world who have their portion in this life, the grovellers of mortality, and long to be remembered with the favour Thou bearest unto thy people. If we know our own hearts, we would choose rather to suffer affliction with the people of God than enjoy the pleasures of sin for a season; and esteem the reproach of Christ greater riches than the treasures of Egypt. How goodly are thy tents, O Jacob, and thy tabernacles, O Israel! May we die the death of the righteous, and may our last end be like theirs. And, O Lord, we pray to resemble them, not only in their future allotment, but in their present condition and character. With them we would sit at the great Teacher's feet and receive of his words. With them we would run the race that is set before us, looking unto Jesus. With them we would fight the good fight of faith, and lay hold on eternal life.

May our religion never be an undecided thing in our own minds: may we know that the root of the matter is found in us; and may others know it too. May our principles be evinced in their operation and effects. May we not only believe with the heart, but confess with the tongue, and hold forth the word of life by our lives as well as by our lips. May our understandings be more informed in divine things: our affections more holy and heavenly; our principles more confirmed; our motives more simple and pure; our hearts more right with God. Till the day dawn, and the shadows flee away, may there be an open and unrestrained intercourse between Thee and our souls. Till the full fruition comes, may we enjoy the earnests of our inheritance, and the first-fruits of the Spirit. Till we walk by sight, may we walk by faith. Till we finish our course with joy, may we pursue it with diligence, and in every intermediate part display the resources of the Christian, and adorn the doctrine of God our Saviour in all things.

Not only by the word but by the rod, teach us to profit. May we learn obedience by the the things we suffer: and however grievous any dispensation may be to flesh and blood, may we be able to say with a sufferer of old, I know that this shall turn to my salvation. We forget not the sons and daughters of affliction: O do Thou remember them in the displays of thy power, and the tenderness of thy pity.

Our goodness extendeth not to Thee, but may the poor and the needy, and the ignorant and the vicious find that it ever extends to them: and that Thou art pleased to make us not only the subjects of thy goodness, but the instruments of thy mercy. Bless the throne, the government, and the country. May the British empire be under thine eye continually, and ever prove the seat of knowledge and freedom, of social order and happiness, of gospel privileges and genuine godliness, of benevolence and usefulness.

Let better days arrive than the world has ever yet witnessed. Let the gospel break in upon those who are lying in the shade of death and hell: and where the illumination has begun, may the light of the moon be as the light of the sun, and the light of the sun be sevenfold as the light of seven days. Bind up all the breaches of thy people, and heal the stroke of their wounds. Bless thy church universally: and revive and enlarge the portion of it with which we are connected, and have been again engaged in the exercises of devotion. Behold us as a family; and may the good will of Him that dwelt in the bush, ever reside in this house to secure and to bless.

Regard us as individuals, at the close of another Sabbath. How many have this day been awakened to the resolution, I will arise and go unto my Father. How many have had their faith and hope in God established. How many have obtained supplies to prepare them for their re-entrance into the duties and trials of life. But we fear it is not so with us. We mourn over our unprofitableness, and tremble at our condition. We have again met together, if not for the better for the worse. O let us not provoke Thee to withdraw the means of grace from us, or to withhold the influence which can alone render them effectual. We know the Word we hear will judge us in the last day; may we judge ourselves by it now, that we may not be condemned with the wicked. Enter not into judgment with thy servants, for in thy sight shall no flesh living be justified. Our Father, &c.

MONDAY MORNING.

O Lord, open Thou our mouth, and our lips shall show forth thy praise. We adore and bless Thee, not only as our Creator, and

Preserver, and Benefactor, but also as our condescending Teacher. None teaches like Thee. Thou hast opened before us the volume of Nature, and there we can read and consider the works of the Lord which are great and useful, sought out of all them that have pleasure therein : but we have also spread before us the fuller and clearer pages of revelation. In these we see what Thou wilt have us to do ; and it is inscribed with such plainness that he may run that readeth. And here we learn not only what Thou requirest of us, but what Thou hast done for us and promised to us. Here we commune with Thee as the God of all grace, and the Father of mercies ; the God and Father of our Lord Jesus Christ. In the fulness of time Thou wast pleased to send forth thy Son, made of a woman, made under the law to redeem them that were under the law ; and he bore our sins in his own body on the tree ; and having made peace by the blood of his cross, he was exalted at thy own right hand to be a prince and a Saviour, to give repentance unto Israel and forgiveness of sins.

O Lord, we would cheerfully and thankfully avail ourselves of the provisions of thy love ; and while others go about to establish their own righteousness, we would submit ourselves to the righteousness which is of God. May we renounce every other refuge for our souls, every other foundation for our hope ; and rejoice in Christ Jesus ; and have no confidence in the flesh.

It delights us to think how many are already made the partakers of this life-giving Saviour ; but we pray for a participation of him ourselves. O bless us with a present experience of his salvation, in our deliverance from sin, in our bearing the image of the heavenly, in our enjoying his presence, and in our being upheld by his free Spirit. And O bless us with a conscious experience of his salvation. Let us not live from day to day, uncertain what we are and whither we are going ; but bear witness with our spirits that we are thy children, and enable us to say, I know that my Redeemer liveth. And bless us with a growing experience of this salvation : if already enlightened, may we see greater things than these ; if already quickened together with Christ, may we have life more abundantly : renew us day by day in our inward man ; and lead us on from strength to strength in the way everlasting, till we shall appear perfect before Thee in Zion.

O for more of that abiding in Jesus without which we cannot bring forth fruit ! O for a deeper sense of our obligations to him, that we may surrender ourselves to his will, and feel it the joy of our hearts to serve him ! While faith justifies our souls, may obedience justify our faith, and prove it to be of the operation of the Spirit. May our faith work by love, love to Him that died for us and rose

again : and love to all our fellow-creatures, but especially to them that are of the household of faith. May we love them notwithstanding differences of opinion and imperfections of character ; and love them out of a pure heart fervently.

Be the friend of our friends ; the father of our children ; the master of our servants. Bless this family. May thine eye and thy heart be here continually. May all the members of the household make thy word the rule of their conduct, submitting themselves one to another in the fear of God, and by love serving one another. Some of our connexions are far off from us ; but we rejoice to think that they are near Thee, and that thou art a very present help in trouble. Keep them as the apple of the eye ; hide them under the shadow of thy wing ; and may all grace abound towards them. Let the young be soberminded, and flee youthful lusts. Let the hoary head be a crown of glory, being found in the way of righteousness. We pray for the afflicted ; and we pray still more for the prosperous and indulged.

Bless the services of the past Sabbath. Let us not lay aside our religious concern with the day appointed to excite and increase it : may we retain a savour of the things of God through all the unhallowing avocations of the week. We often hear thy word : let us not resemble a man beholding his natural face in a glass : for he beholdeth himself, and goeth his way, and straightway forgetteth what manner of man he was. But may we look into the perfect law of liberty and continue therein, that being not forgetful hearers, but doers of the word, we may be blessed in our deed. And to God only wise, be glory for ever and ever. Amen.

MONDAY EVENING.

O GOD, Thou dost according to thine own will in the army of heaven, and among the inhabitants of the earth : none can stay thy hand, or say unto Thee, What doest Thou ! We are the creatures of thy power ; Thou art the Father of our spirits ; and it is thy inspiration that giveth them understanding. We are entirely the care of thy providence ; Thou hast holden our souls in life, and not suffered our feet to be removed : and having obtained help of Thee we continue to this day.

But, O God, we are sinners in thy sight ; and if we say we have not sinned, we make thee a liar, and thy word is not in us. Far from wishing to deny or excuse our offences, we throw ourselves at thy footstool, confessing that our iniquities are increased over our head, and our trespass is gone up into the very heavens. We have erred and strayed from thy ways like lost sheep. We have followed too much the devices and desires of our own hearts. We have offended against thy holy laws. We have left undone the things we ought to have done; and we have done the things we ought not to have done; and there is no health in us.

For these things we mourn; we abhor and condemn ourselves, and acknowledge that Thou art justified when Thou speakest, and clear when thou judgest. Nothing can rescue our guilty minds from the horrors of despair, but an assurance from thyself, that Thou art not only good, but ready to forgive, and plenteous in mercy unto all them that call upon Thee. And blessed be thy Name, Thou hast given us a full revelation of thy reconcileableness to thy revolted subjects: and we know that Thou hast sent thy only begotten Son to be the propitiation for sin; and we see opened before us through Him, a wide and a welcome way to thyself.

And thou hast assured us that there is salvation in no other: and that no man cometh unto the Father but by Him. O help us to hear the voice that proclaims, Behold the Lamb of God that taketh away the sin of the world: give us the eye of faith to see him; and the hand of faith to receive him; and the appetite of faith, the hungering and thirsting of faith that we may feed upon him, and know from our own experience as well as the testimony of thy word, that his flesh is meat indeed and his blood drink indeed. He is the hope of Israel, the consolation of Israel: may we repair to him, as the deliverer from the fall, and find in him the light, the life, the riches, the honours of eternity; and rejoice in him with joy unspeakable and full of glory.

Too long have we joined in the cry of folly, Who will show us any good? Too long have we observed lying vanities and have forsaken our own mercies. But convinced of our madness, no longer would we spend our money for that which is not bread, and our labour for that which satisfieth not. May we hearken diligently unto Thee our heavenly Inviter, and eat that which is good, and let our soul delight itself in fatness. And so much the more as our time advances, and every moment we seize for reflection tells us that more of our opportunities are fled for ever. For Thou hast made our days as a hand's-breadth, and our age is as nothing before Thee, and verily every man at his best estate is altogether vanity. O that we were wise, that we understood this, that we considered our latter end! O teach us, thou Almighty Instructer, teach us to live as dying creatures; to live with our conversation in heaven; to live looking for that blessed hope and the glorious appearing of the great God and our Saviour Jesus Christ. May we not only believe that there is a better country, even a heavenly; but may we seek after it, and seek after it in the all-sufficiency of thy grace; and never be satisfied till we know that we have an inheritance among all them that are sanctified, and feel in ourselves those principles and dispositions which evince, not only that the blessedness is promised to us, but begun in us. May thy Spirit help our infirmities, and prepare us for every part of our passage homeward: for the successes and comforts with which we may be indulged; for the disappointments and troubles with which we may be tried; for the various duties we have to discharge; and for all the opportunities of usefulness our stations in life may furnish. Help Thou our unbelief—The hinderance of all our religious excellence and proficiency: increase our faith; and fill us with all joy and peace in believing.

Forgive the sins of another day. And may we now lay us down in peace and sleep: for Thou, Lord, only makest us dwell in safety: and with the returning day, continue thy care over us, and enable us to renew our dedication of ourselves to Thee.

The grace of our Lord Jesus Christ be with us all. Amen.

TUESDAY MORNING.

O Thou Creator and Preserver of all mankind, again we come before Thee in the multitude of thy mercies, and would call on our souls and each other to bless and praise thy holy name. Preserve us, in this exercise of devotion, not only from hypocrisy but formality. Enable us to remember what Thou art, into whose presence we have entered, and what we are who have taken upon us to speak unto the living God. How wise, how great, how holy art Thou! But we are dust and ashes; unworthiness and vileness.

In what more becoming attire can we approach Thee than clothed with humility? In how many things have we offended; in all we have come short of thy glory. When we compare ourselves with thy law, we see that we are carnal, sold under sin; and that in us dwelleth no good thing. When we examine our hearts we find there an aggregate of vanity, frowardness, insensibility, disorderly affections, backwardness to duty, proneness to evil that causes us to loathe ourselves, and exclaim, Behold I am vile. When we look well into our lives; when we survey our relations and offices; our trials and our mercies; our opportunities and our means: and when we consider how often Thou hast called, and we have refused; how much Thou hast excited us, and how we have rebelled and vexed thy Holy Spirit; we cannot but fall upon our knees and cry, Enter not into judgment with us—God be merciful to us sinners—Save, Lord, or we perish.

O lead us to the cross, and enable us to pray believing in the name of thy dear Son.

All hope in, all help from ourselves we reject for ever. What things have been gain to us, these we count but loss for Christ: yea doubtless and we count all things but loss for the excellency of the knowledge of Christ Jesus our Lord. Behold us in Him. Accept of his ransom as our discharge. Let his sufferings be the chastisement of our peace; and by his stripes may we be healed.

We know there is salvation in none other: but Him Thou hast sealed, Him Thou hast anointed; He is mighty to save; able to save to the uttermost them that come unto Thee by Him. May we therefore rejoice in hope; and have faith in those promises and invitations which he has given us in the gospel, and which must include ourselves, because they are addressed to all the ends of the earth and cry, Whosoever will, let him take of the water of life freely. O let these assurances enter our consciences, and live and operate there, till for them the wilderness and the solitary place shall be made glad, and the desert rejoice and blossom as the rose.

The world passeth away and the lusts thereof; every thing earthly in which we can trust is found to be vanity and vexation of spirit. How often has our heart bled, and our very life been smitten down to the ground. So much the more we desire in heaven a better and an enduring substance. Thy love in Christ Jesus our Lord is firm and changeless: nothing can separate us from it; nothing can make us miserable in the enjoyment of it. Say unto our soul, I am thy salvation, that we may have the satisfying persuasion that whatever may befall us, or however we may be tried here, in a little time the days of our mourning shall be ended, and we shall enter the rest that remains for the people of God.

And while the period of our pilgrimage is lengthened out, leave us not nor forsake us, O God of our salvation; but afford us those supplies and influences of thy Holy Spirit, which shall keep us from evil, and enable us to walk worthy of the vocation wherewith we are called, and prove a blessing to all around us.

Make us grateful for the continuance of thy care and kindness; for the security and repose of the past night; and for all the advantages and comforts that meet us at our entering on another day. Be with us in all the duties and occurrences of a new and unknown portion of our time. Include in thy regards, as the God of providence and of grace, all our relations and friends, and for us and for them do exceeding abundantly above all we can ask or think: and to Thee be glory in the church by Christ Jesus throughout all ages world without end. Amen.

TUESDAY EVENING.

O God, Thou inhabitest the praises of Israel. The spirits of just men made perfect, and the innumerable company of angels are perpetually serving Thee in thy house above. We desire to join in their adorations, and rejoice to think that the sacrifices of a broken heart and a contrite spirit, O God, Thou wilt not despise. Thou art a God that hidest thyself, and by no searching can we find Thee out unto perfection; but we know that Thou art Almighty; that Thou art about our path and our lying down, and acquainted with all our ways. We know that Thou art of purer eyes than to behold iniquity, and therefore we could not stand before Thee; but we also know, for Thou hast proclaimed thy name, that Thou art merciful and gracious. We know that it is possible for Thee to save the very chief of sinners, in harmony with every attribute of thy nature. We know that Thou hast not spared thine own Son, but delivered him up for us all; and wilt Thou not with him also freely give us all things? Yea, Thou *hast* given us all things freely with Him. What can we need as perishing sinners that is not to be found in Him?

May we never be so ignorant of the worthiness of his character and the worthlessness of our own, as to think of appearing before Thee in our own claims, but may we win Christ, and be found in Him, not having our own righteousness which is of the law, but that which is of God by faith. May we know Him, and the power of his resurrection; and the fellowship of his sufferings being made conformable unto his death.

And, O Lord, teach us often to consider what fallen and miserable creatures we were in ourselves; and in what a fearful condition we should have been found for ever, had we been left to ourselves; that the view of thine undeserved goodness, and a sense of the unspeakable benefits we have received from Thee, may so fill our minds and hearts that we may henceforth resolve to yield ourselves unto God, as those that are alive from the dead, and our members as instruments of righteousness unto God. And while others lie down and rise up, go out and come in, and God is not in all their thoughts, may we never live a day, or an hour, or a moment without Thee. May we realize thy presence, thy perfections, thy providence. May we *walk* with God, and may we be *workers* together with God. May we keep the same end in view with himself. May we study and labour to promote it by all the opportunities and means placed within our reach; and whether we eat or drink, or whatever we do, may we do all to the glory of God.

And in all this do Thou enable us, for we

are not sufficient of ourselves to think any thing as of ourselves; and to every good work we are naturally disinclined. Open therefore the eyes of our understanding, and show us not only the truth, but the beauty and glory of divine things. Take from us the heart of stone; put thy Spirit within us; and cause us to walk in thy statutes, and delight in thy law which we have loved. And when Thou hast brought us into the way of holiness and peace, uphold us by thy grace, and establish, strengthen, settle us. Let us not be slothful or barren in our Christian profession; but filled with all the fruits of righteousness, that we may put to silence the ignorance of foolish men, and by our good works which they behold, constrain them to glorify our heavenly Father. Draw out of our hearts the love of the present evil world, and set our affection on things that are above; things which will at once fill, and purify, and ennoble the mind. May we faint not at our tribulations, remembering that they are for our profit and glory, and that he who sends them has promised to be with us in trouble. When burdened, may we cast our burden upon the Lord: and when careful, cast all our care upon him who careth for us.

May we be diligent and faithful in our several callings; and by no injustice or wicked policy may we provoke Him whose blessing alone maketh rich and addeth no sorrow. May we never feast ourselves without fear, nor refuse in the midst of abundance, to stretch forth our hands to the sons and daughters of want. And as the elect of God, holy and beloved, may we put on bowels of mercies, kindness, humbleness of mind, meekness, longsuffering, forbearing one another, and forgiving one another: and above all these things, may we put on charity which is the bond of perfectness.

Now unto Him that is able to keep us from falling, and to present us faultless before the presence of his glory with exceeding joy: to the only wise God our Saviour, be glory and majesty, dominion and power, for ever and ever. Amen.

WEDNESDAY MORNING.

WE bow our knee before the God and Father of our Lord Jesus Christ, of whom the whole family in heaven and earth is named. Our exigencies are great, but Thou art able to supply them all from thy riches in glory. Our sins are more in number than the hairs of our head, but Thou art merciful and gracious. None however unworthy and guilty, ever sought Thee in vain; and from the experience of a multitude which no man can number, Thou hast obtained the character of a God hearing prayer; and unto Thee shall all flesh come.

Behold, O God, a company of suppliants at thy footstool, hopeless in ourselves but encouraged by thy promises, and taking hold of thy strength that we may make peace with Thee. Look upon the face of thine Anointed. Behold his obedience unto death, even the death of the cross. Hear the blood of sprinkling that speaketh better things than that of Abel. By his poverty may we be made rich; and by his stripes may we be healed. And may we thereby be healed, not only as to the wounds of a bleeding conscience, but as to the moral maladies of our nature, and be saved not only by a deliverance from the wrath to come, but by the washing of regeneration and the renewing of the Holy Ghost. May the darkness of death give place to the light of life in our understandings. May the rebelliousness of our wills be exchanged for submission to thy commands and acquiescence in thy dispensations, without murmurings or disputings. Thou hast claims to us, arising not only from creation but redemption: may we glorify Thee in our bodies and in our spirits which are doubly thine. Let our Father, who seeth in secret, meet us in the closet as well as in the temple; and find us often examining our principles and our motives as well as our actions. Let us not confine our devoutness to the morning and evening hour of prayer; but be in the fear of the Lord all the day long.

Though our religion is at present very imperfect, may it show itself to be vital by its activities and its tendencies. Let the weak say, I am strong, strong in the Lord, and in the power of his might; strong for our way, for our work and for our warfare.

May we never forget the experience we have had of our innate and remaining depravity in the various passages of our life and our religion, that we may be kept humble, and vigilant, and prayerful; that we may never trust in our own hearts, and never lean to our own understandings. And may we never forget the experience we have had of thy patience, and wisdom and power, and faithfulness, and care, that we may be grateful, and encourage ourselves in the Lord our God. We have never served Thee for nought; we have never sought Thee in vain; we have never confided in Thee and been confounded. Thou hast often made us ashamed of our fears; Thou hast often surpassed our hopes. At many an evening-tide it has been light; and many a shadow of death Thou hast turned into the morning. Thou hast already enabled us to see how our welfare has resulted from events which once discouraged us: and where darkness yet hangs on any of thy dispensations, we hear Thee saying, What I do thou knowest not now, but thou shalt know hereafter. O for faith to believe; and patience to suffer, to wait, and to submit! We pray not that

Thou shouldst take us out of the world, but keep us from the evil. We ask not for the accomplishment of all our wishes, for we often know not what we ask; but we pray that whatever may be denied us, we may be blessed with all spiritual blessings in heavenly places in Christ. May the joy of the Lord be our strength. And let all those that put their trust in Thee rejoice: let them ever shout for joy, because Thou defendest them: let them also that love thy name be joyful in Thee.

We love the communion of saints, and would be mindful of them in our prayers. Bless those with whom we are more immediately connected in the fellowship of the gospel. And bless thy church universal! may peace be within her walls, and prosperity within her palaces. Abba, Father, all things are possible to Thee. Take to thyself thy great power and reign; and let the exclamation be heard from earth and from heaven, Hallelujah, for the Lord God omnipotent reigneth! The kingdoms of this world are become the kingdoms of our Lord and of his Christ, and he shall reign for ever and ever. Even so; Amen.

WEDNESDAY EVENING.

O God, thy greatness is unsearchable, and thy ways are past finding out. Before Thee we are nothing, less than nothing and vanity, worse than nothing and iniquity. With shame and sorrow we acknowledge our degraded and perishing condition. For sin has forfeited thy favour, stripped us of thy image, banished us from thy presence, and exposed us to the curse of thy holy law. And from this condition we have no power to deliver ourselves: and we lie down in despair unless a resource be found in thyself from whom we have so deeply revolted, and who for our sins are so justly displeased.

But Thou, even Thou, without our desert, without our desires, and ages before our existence, wast pleased to accomplish a plan extending from everlasting to everlasting, honourable to all thy perfections, and which the angels desire to look into. And the word which announces all the glory of this goodness is nigh us; and invites and beseeches us to partake of all the fulness of God. O let us not turn away from Him that speaketh from heaven, and reject the counsel of God against ourselves: but as convinced and self-despairing sinners may we receive it as a faithful saying and worthy of all acceptation; and find it to be the power of God to salvation. And as the cross of our Lord Jesus Christ is the centre of all the parts, and the source of all the blessings of the gospel, may we repair to it, and there be relieved from a burden too heavy for us to bear; and there be crucified to the world; and there become dead indeed unto sin but alive unto God. There may we sink into the deepest humiliation; there may we find motives to patience, self-denial, active benevolence: there may hope lift up its head; and faith lay hold on eternal life; and love bind us to live not unto ourselves, but to Him that died for us and rose again.

Enable us to rejoice in Him whom Thou hast sent, not only as a Redeemer, but the Sanctifier. We want holiness; and not only the reality of the principle and the practice, but the increase. May we be more thankful for thy mercies, more humble under thy corrections, more zealous in thy service. Make us more constant in duty, more watchful against temptation, more contented in our stations, more exemplary in our conduct, more useful in our day and generation. May we do justly, and love mercy, and walk humbly with our God.

Teach us to be ready for affliction. In health may we think of sickness; and in our brightest hours may we remember the days of darkness, for they may be many. We know that Thou wilt bring us to death and to the house appointed for all living: may we also know that when this earthly house of our tabernacle shall be dissolved, we have a building of God, a house not made with hands, eternal in the heavens. We must all stand before the judgment-seat of Christ: may we labour that whether present or absent we may be accepted of Him.

O Thou whose mercies are over all thy works, have pity upon all men. Smile upon our country, and fill our churches with thy glory. Bless all the magistrates of the land, and all the ministers of thy word. Be a father to the fatherless; plead the cause of the widow; comfort the feeble-minded; support the weak; be the guide of the young, and the solace of the old. In a peculiar manner regard all those who are near and dear to us; be their sun and their shield; give them grace and glory, and withhold no good thing from them.

In how many dangers hast Thou preserved us, and by how many comforts hast thou indulged us through another day. Let the night also praise Thee, and the morning rejoice; as we implore it through the intercession of Him, in whose words we address Thee as Our Father, &c.

THURSDAY MORNING.

O Thou great and only Potentate; the sovereign Ruler of heaven and earth; whose mercies are over all thy works: we desire to come before thy presence with thanksgivings. We bless Thee for all thy amazing goodness to the children of men, and of which we have so largely shared ever since we have had a being. Thou hast made summer and winter, and each of these revolutions subserves our welfare. The day is thine, the night also is thine, and both these seasons are full of thy care and kindness. We see thy bounty in the relations that train us up, in the laws that defend us, in the houses that shelter us, in the fuel that warms us, in the food and raiment that comfort us; in the continuance of our health, our members, our senses, and our understandings—Thou givest us all things richly to enjoy.

But all these benefits Thou hast eclipsed, as the stars disappear before the rising of the sun. O lead us to adore the wisdom that planned, and the grace that purposed the redemption of the world by our Lord Jesus Christ. O blessed for ever be that abundant mercy that laid help on one that is mighty, and one that is as willing as he is able to save unto the uttermost them that come unto God by him. Make us deeply sensible of our need of the influences and blessings he has to impart. May we value, as weary and heavy laden, the rest he has promised, and sigh in our bondage for the liberty wherewith he makes us free indeed. Give us a full interest in that blood which cleanses from all sin; the complete imputation of that righteousness which can justify the guilty, and give them a title to life everlasting; and the entire possession of that Spirit which can renovate our nature, and make us meet for the inheritance of the saints in light.

May we not only discern the all-sufficiency of the Saviour, but by appropriation render it our own, and be able to exclaim with Thomas, My Lord and my God!

And may we not only be replenished ourselves, but concerned also that our fellow-creatures may be partakers of the benefit. Thou hast commanded us to pray for others, and we rejoice in the command as an evidence of thy benevolence, and as the resource of our own. We are perpetually meeting with wants which we cannot relieve, and distresses which we cannot remove: but we can implore and gain the attention of Omnipotence; prayer has power with Thee and prevails; and success depends not on our rank or our talents. Thou despisest not the prayer of the destitute, but wilt hear their prayer.

Sanctify the afflictions of the afflicted; turn the curse into a blessing; and let the effects of sin be the fruits to take away sin. Preserve the prosperous from the folly that will destroy them; may they possess as if they possessed not, and rejoice as if they rejoiced not; and ever use this world as not abusing it. Reward those who have done us good or wished us good; and forgive those who have injured or wished to injure us. May all our dear connexions be bound up in the bundle of life with the Lord our God.

Compass our country with thy favour as with a shield. Establish the throne in righteousness. Bless all the branches of the royal family, and all the nobles of the land; and may they remember that in the heraldry of heaven nothing is great but what is good. May the king's counsellors never be ashamed to ask counsel of Thee: and let our magistrates be the ministers of God for good; a terror to evil-doers, and a praise to them that do well.

And may he who said, I, if I be lifted up from the earth, will draw all men unto me, reign from sea to sea, and from the river to the ends of the earth. May all kings fall down before him, and all nations serve him. And blessed be his glorious name for ever, and let the whole earth be filled with his glory. Amen and Amen.

THURSDAY EVENING.

O God of all grace; the heavens declare thy glory, and the firmament showeth thy handy work. Day unto day uttereth speech, and night unto night showeth knowledge. There is no speech nor language where their voice is not heard. We adore Thee for making thy ways known unto Moses; thine acts unto the children of Israel. At sundry times and in divers manners Thou spakest in times past unto the fathers by the prophets; but Thou hast in these last days spoken unto us by thy Son. At His feet may we sit, and receive of his words; and be led into all truth.

May we admit the testimony that we are fallen, guilty, depraved, perishing creatures; and be driven to that self-despair which will urge us to seek after the hope of the gospel, and endear us to that Saviour in whom is all our help found. All we like sheep have gone astray; we have turned every one to his own way; but Thou hast laid on Him the iniquity of us all. Surely he hath borne our grief and carried our sorrow: the chastisement of our peace was upon Him, and with his stripes we are healed. It is well for us that He died for the ungodly; that He makes intercession for the transgressors; and that from the pitiableness of his great goodness he is now saying, Him that cometh unto me, I will in no wise cast out. We have nothing to recommend us, and we want nothing. We have no money, and we are called to buy without money and without price.

While we love the freeness of his salvation, we also rejoice in the holiness of it. Our sins are our worst enemies, and never does he appear more worthy the name of Jesus, than when engaged to save us from them. May he accomplish in us the new creation; and uphold us with his free Spirit; for where the Spirit of the Lord is, there is liberty. Put thy fear into our hearts, that we may never depart from Thee. We know that only as we walk in the fear of the Lord can we walk in the comforts of the Holy Ghost. We have made the trial, and can say from experience, that no joy can be compared with that which arises from serving and fearing the Lord.

May we therefore feel more dedicated to Him in all the obedience of faith: and while we live, may we increasingly live unto the Lord, and when we die, die unto the Lord, that living and dying we may be only and entirely the Lord's.

We bless Thee for the exceeding great and precious promises upon which Thou hast caused us to hope. They provide for every exigency we feel, and every evil we fear. May we be more familiarly acquainted with them: may we take them as our heritage for ever; and make them our song in the house of our pilgrimage. May they yield us such satisfaction that our hearts may be kept from straying after forbidden pleasures; that the world may lose its power of allurement; that we may learn in whatsoever state we are therewith to be content.

May thy providential will bound all our wishes; for we know not what is good for us in this vain life which we spend as a shadow: but Thou knowest. To thine unerring care therefore, we resign all our concerns, remembering that Thou art able to make all things work together for our good: and hast proved thy regard for our welfare in not sparing thine own Son, but delivering Him up for us all.

We are in a vale of tears, in a world of tribulation, and among creatures that prove reeds and broken cisterns: in the multitude of our thoughts within us, may thy comforts delight our souls. And since we are daily told that this is not our rest, may we arise and depart; may we seek a better country; and lay hold on eternal life. Make us sensible of our weakness, that we may be strong in the grace that is in Christ Jesus. Secure us from all those temptations which in every state of life arise from a wicked world and a wicked heart. May we, under the belief of thy all-seeing eye and thy awful tribunal, discharge faithfully the duties arising from our various relations in life.

As a family, may we keep sin from our tabernacle, and dwell together in unity and love. We present Thee our evening sacrifice of thanksgiving for the preservations, the supplies, and the indulgences of the day; and into thy hands we commit our spirits and our bodies for the night. Cover us with thy feathers, and under thy wing may we trust: and in every future period may thy truth be our shield and buckler. And to the blessed and only Potentate, the King of kings and Lord of lords, be honour and power everlasting. Amen.

FRIDAY MORNING.

O LORD God Almighty. Thou dwellest in light inaccessible to men and angels. Thou hidest thyself behind the elements of thy own creation. None can find Thee out unto perfection. Possess our minds with the grandeur of thy nature and perfections. There is no searching of thy understanding: it is infinite. There is no staying of thy arm: it is almighty. Thy agency extends through all space; and all worlds hang on thy care. One day with Thee is as a thousand years, and a thousand years are as one day. The most elevated beings Thou hast made are continually crying, Holy, holy, holy is the Lord of Hosts, the whole earth is full of thy glory. Thy wisdom is a holy wisdom; thy power is holy; thy mercy is holy. Thou art holy in all thy ways, and righteous in all thy works.

How then, O God, can we stand before Thee! How numberless and how aggravated have been our offences! How often have we said, if not by our words, yet by our disposition and conduct, Depart from us, we desire not the knowledge of thy ways.

O how have we loved darkness rather than light; how have we observed lying vanities, and forsaken our own mercies; how have we trampled under foot the Son of God. Thy providence has restrained us; but we have done evil as we could. We have had our religious convictions and excitements; but we flattered Thee with our lips, and lied unto Thee with our tongue; for our heart was not right with God, neither were we steadfast in his covenant.

And why are we not beyond the reach of hope? Why are we not exclaiming, The harvest is past, the summer is ended, and we are not saved? It is because thy compassions fail not, that we are not consumed. O let us not add to all our iniquities impenitence; but let thy goodness lead us to repentance. Let us not seal up our doom for ever by despair; but grievously as we have offended, may we come to thy footstool, renouncing, condemning, loathing ourselves for our abominations, but hoping in that grace which flows to the chief of sinners through the obedience and sufferings of thy dear Son. May we receive the atonement; and know the blessedness of the man whose transgression is forgiven, and in whose spirit there is no guile.

If Thou hast begun a good work in us, perfect that which concerneth us. Strengthen us in the name of the Lord, that we may run and not be weary, and walk and not faint.

O Thou hope of Israel, the Saviour thereof in the time of trouble, why shouldst Thou be as a stranger in the land, and as a wayfaring man that turneth aside to tarry for a night? What will become of us if we are left to ourselves? But Thou hast said, I will never leave thee nor forsake thee. May we therefore say, The Lord is my helper, and I will not fear.

May we live out of the world, as to its spirit and maxims and manners, but never may we refuse to enter it as the sphere of action and of usefulness. At every call of duty may we be alive and awake. May we leave Thee to determine the nature of our service, without murmuring and disputing; as we have opportunity may we do good unto all men; and especially unto those that are of the household of faith.

We are now in the wilderness, but, blessed be thy name, all is not briers and barrenness. We are not without the bread from heaven, and the streams of the rock, and the pillar, and the tabernacle, and the ark. We are sometimes discouraged because of the way, but the way, though winding and trying, is safe and short. Jordan often dismays us, but the feet of our High Priest, standing himself in the waters, will open for us a passage; and beyond it there is a better, even a heavenly country. Many have reached it, and some we once called and still call our own; and we believe that through the grace of the Lord Jesus Christ, we shall be saved even as they. While we live may our lives be exemplary; and when we die, may our end be peace. May we give diligence to make our calling and election sure; that doing these things we may never fall; and so an entrance may be ministered unto us abundantly into the everlasting kingdom of our Lord and Saviour—To whom be glory and dominion for ever and ever. Amen.

FRIDAY EVENING.

O Thou Most High, we bow before Thee. It becomes us to lie very low in thy presence. We are nothing compared with Thee as creatures. Yet we would not despise ourselves as we are the work of thy hands; or because we do not occupy the rank and possess the powers of angels. We acquiesce in thy sovereign pleasure which has placed us where we are, and made us what we are: yea we thank Thee that in this embryo stage of our endless being, we are rendered capable of so much knowledge and improvement; that we can bear thy own image, and not by subserviency only but by design, can be workers together with God, and advance his cause and his glory.

But so much the more deplorable is the confession we are constrained to make; the crown is fallen from our head; wo unto us, for we have sinned. We mourn over the depravity of our nature; that we are alienated from the life of God through the ignorance that is in us; that the heart is deceitful above all things and desperately wicked; that the carnal mind is enmity against God, for it is

W

not subject to the law of God, neither indeed can be.

O how glorious is the grace that was mindful of us in this desperateness, and devised means for our rescue. Thou wouldst not at an infinite expense have provided salvation for us, had we not been entirely lost; and Thou wouldst not have laid help on one that is mighty, could we have been our own deliverers. We bless Thee for the designs of thy goodness, and for the accomplishment of them by the Son of thy love; that he came between and laid his hands upon us both; that he made peace by the blood of his cross; that he opened the kingdom of heaven to all believers; that he received gifts for the rebellious also, that the Lord God might dwell among them; that in Him surely we have righteousness and strength.

May we be found in Him, that we may be freed from all condemnation, and possessing a new source of influence, may we walk not after the flesh but after the spirit. And may we mind the things of the spirit; may we savour the things that be of God; may we call the Sabbath a delight; may we love the habitation of thy house; may we find thy word and eat it, and may it be to us the joy and the rejoicing of our heart.

Spare around us, if it please Thee, our outward comforts, though we are unworthy of the least of them; but keep us from abusing them, from idolizing them, from being satisfied with them, without the hope of having in heaven a better and an enduring substance. May we never act, never feel as those who make flesh their arm, and the world their portion, and earth their rest; but may we declare plainly that we are heirs of immortality, and that our utmost anxiety is to lay hold on eternal life.

Thou dost not afflict willingly, nor grieve the children of men, but Thou art concerned for our profit; and thy regard for our welfare often compels Thee to adopt a painful discipline. May we be concerned to gather from it the peaceable fruits of righteousness. Let tribulation work patience, and patience experience, and experience hope. How many hast Thou allured and brought into the wilderness, and given them their vineyards from thence, and the valley of Achor for a door of hope. May we be also thy witnesses, and be able to testify that it is good for us that we have been afflicted.

These returning periods remind us of the progress of our time. We lament over opportunities now alas gone, and gone for ever, in which we could have glorified our Saviour, and been blessings to those around us. How few remain; and these how short and uncertain! Enthrone and keep divinely alive in each of our souls the conviction, I must work the work of Him that sent me while it is day: the night cometh wherein no man can work.

Regard this household. May all the members of it be the charge of thy providence, and the subjects of thy grace; and in their several stations may each daily ask, Lord, what wilt thou have me to do? Bless all the families of Israel. Favour all the churches of the faithful, however denominated among men. Rule and govern thy church universally in the right way. And let all the dispensers of thy truth, both by their preaching and living, set it forth and show it accordingly. Let the king live before Thee, and his subjects be the happy people whose God is the Lord. And from the rising of the sun to the going down of the same, may thy name be great among the gentiles, and in every place incense be offered unto Thee, and a pure offering. Our Father, &c.

SATURDAY MORNING.

O THOU whose name alone is Jehovah. From everlasting to everlasting Thou art God. One generation passeth away, and another cometh; and Thou hast appointed us bounds which we cannot pass: and every day upon which we enter, brings us nearer the end of our course. But thou art the same, and thy years shall have no end. Verily Thou art a God that hidest thyself, yet Thou art the God of Israel, the Saviour: and by means of thy word we know that Thou art not far from any one of us, and that Thou art not only able to relieve all our wants, but willing to hear our supplications: yea, Thou hast commanded us to ask and receive, that our joy may be full.

O these wretched hearts of ours, these evil hearts of unbelief, in departing from the living God instead of trusting in Him! How full of suspicions are we; how backward to approach Thee in full assurance of faith, though we know Thou art pacified towards us, and waiting to be gracious, and exalted to have mercy upon us. Work in us, O God, to will and to do: fulfil in us all the good pleasure of thy goodness, and the work of faith with power. May we believe the record that Thou hast given to us eternal life; and knowing that this life is in thy Son, and that he who hath the Son hath life, may we receive Him as He is presented to us in the Gospel; and having received him continue to walk in Him.

May we feel far more powerfully than we ever have felt the importance of religion; may we regard it as the one thing needful. If ever we are negligent, or if ever we trifle, may it be in the concerns of time and sense; not in those which pertain to the soul and eternity, and for which the Lord of all bled and died.

And may we feel more of the power of godliness, in subduing the corruptions of our nature; in loosening us from the present evil world; in supporting us under the trials of life; in enabling us to abide with God in our callings; and in exercising ourselves always to have a conscience void of offence towards God and towards man.

In all our affairs may we learn to distinguish between duty and anxiety. May we diligently and dependently use the means which Thou hast appointed; but cast all care upon Him who careth for us. May our character rather than our circumstances, chiefly engage our attention; remembering that if we seek the Lord, we shall not want any good thing; and if we love Him, all things will work together for our good.

Give us compassionate hearts that we may feel the distresses of others, and never refuse our aid when it is in the power of our hand to give. Is any afflicted? Teach him to pray; and let him find Thee a very present help in trouble. Awaken the careless and especially alarm those that are at ease in Zion. Preserve the awakened from those betrayers and murderers of souls who never cry, Believe on the Lord Jesus Christ, and thou shalt be saved. Meet those who are asking the way to Zion with their faces thitherward, with the assurance, I will lead thee, I will guide thee, I will direct thee with mine eye. Say to them that are of a fearful heart, Be strong; restore them that have gone astray, and help them much who have believed through grace.

We forget not the millions of our fellow-creatures who are sitting in darkness and in the regions of the shadow of death; and to every empire, every province, every village, say, Arise, shine, for thy light is come, and the glory of the Lord is risen upon thee. Raise up and send forth many more labourers; for the harvest truly is great. May those who remain at home aid in this blessed cause by their property and their prayers; and in their own spheres of action, may they be careful to hold forth the word of life, not only by a verbal testimony, but by an actual exemplification.

To Thee, the God of our mercy, we afresh dedicate this morning the lives which Thou hast spared, the strength which Thou hast renewed, and the comforts which Thou hast continued. May we be in the fear of the Lord all the day long: and whether we eat or drink, or whatever we do, may we do all to thy glory: through our adorable Redeemer Amen.

SATURDAY EVENING.

O THOU, in knowledge of whom standeth our eternal life, and whose service is perfect freedom, cleanse the thoughts of our heart by the inspiration of thy Holy Spirit, and give us grace whereby we may serve Thee acceptably with reverence and godly fear.

Thou art our hiding-place; Thou art our resting-place; Thou art our dwelling-place; the home of the soul, and our everlasting portion. By sin we revolted from Thee, and Thou couldst have justly left us to the natural and penal consequences of the fall; but in thy love and pity Thou wast pleased to devise means that thy banished should be restored to Thee. Thou hast sent thy only begotten Son into the world, that we might live through him; and he has once suffered for sins, the just for the unjust, that he might bring us unto God.

Having therefore boldness and access with confidence by the faith of him, we draw near and cry, God be merciful to us sinners. Thou hast been merciful to us in the bounties of thy Providence, and thy mercies have been new every morning; but O impress us with the conviction that the body is nothing to the soul, and that time is nothing to eternity. When a few more of these weekly periods have rolled away, our flesh will be laid beneath the cold stone or the green turf, and our spirits will be returned to God who gave them; and the solemn decision will have passed, He that is holy, let him be holy still, and he that is filthy, let him be filthy still. O bless us with the heritage of Jacob; remember us with the favour Thou bearest to thy people. Absolve us from all condemnation; and let the spirit of life in Christ Jesus make us free from the law of sin and death. Deliver us from the power of darkness, and translate us into the kingdom of thy dear Son; that kingdom which is not meat and drink, but righteousness, peace and joy in the Holy Ghost.

In how many ways have we borne the image of the earthly; O let us evermore bear the image of the heavenly. May the humility and benevolence, the devotion and zeal, the patience and submission which adorned his lovely character, be in a measure our attainment now: and pressing after a fuller conformity to him, may we rejoice in the assurance that we shall be one day perfectly like him and see him as he is.

Enable us to hold communion with Thee in all the dispensations of thy providence, and display the Christian in all the varying events of life. Man is born to trouble; regard us in all our sorrows. Though our afflictions are the effects of sin, they are taken up, and employed by thy wisdom and goodness for our profit: and though no chastening seemeth for the present to be joyous but grievous, nevertheless afterward it yieldeth the peaceable fruit of righteousness. Be it unto us, O Lord, according to thy word. May we learn obedience by the things we suffer; and may every adversity turn to our salvation through prayer and the supply of the Spirit of Jesus Christ.

Though ignorant of the future, and not knowing what a day might bring forth, may we be fearful of nothing, and careful for nothing. May we commit our way and our works unto Him who has been with us in six troubles; and has promised that He will never leave us nor forsake; whose grace will be sufficient for us while we live, and whose hand shall wipe away all tears from our eyes when we die.

May we feel more of the tender and benevolent agency of the gospel. May it make us long for the salvation of souls; and rejoice in the belief that Jesus gave himself a ransom for all, to be testified in due time.

Already the lines have fallen to us in pleasant places. Blessed are our eyes for they see, and our ears for they hear. Yet the blessing may be converted into a curse; and Thou hast commanded us to fear, lest a promise being left us of entering into thy rest, any of us should seem to come short of it.

We would now dismiss the cares of the world with the week. May we rise in the morning with refreshed bodies and renewed strength, and be in the Spirit on thine own day. And do Thou send out thy light and thy truth, that they may lead us and guide us to thy holy hill and to thy tabernacles. Our Father, &c.

L

FORMS OF PRAYER

FOR

SELECT OCCASIONS.

CHRISTMAS DAY.

MORNING.

O God, Thou art worthy of universal and everlasting adoration. Thy nature is incomprehensible, thy perfections are infinite, and thy ways are past finding out. Thou art the Creator and upholder of all things. All thy works praise Thee, O Lord, and thy saints bless Thee; and were we to hold our peace the stones would immediately cry out and reproach our ingratitude. All our lives have been full of thy undeserved goodness.

But we are called this morning to behold the exceeding riches of thy grace, in thy kindness towards us by Christ Jesus. Herein is love; not that we loved God, but that He loved us, and sent his Son to be the propitiation for our sins.

May we contemplate this matchless event with all those views and affections which its importance demands. May those who observe the day, observe it unto the Lord. May our festivity be becoming the occasion, harmless and holy. Let us not disgrace the season by reviving those works of the devil which the Son of God was manifested to destroy; nor rest satisfied with the mere remembrance of his advent, as founded in truth and attended with wonders, but inquire for what end He was born, and for what cause He came into the world. And since we are informed that He came to seek and to save that which was lost; and suffered the just for the unjust, that He might bring us unto God; may we deem the report not only a faithful saying, but worthy of all acceptation; and may it be in us as a well of water springing up into everlasting life.

May none of us disregard Him, from ignorance, worldly-mindedness, presumption, self-righteousness, or despondency. As our prophet, may we repair to his feet for instruction. May we look to his sacrifice, and find relief for our burdened consciences. May we acknowledge his authority and obey his commands. In all our approaches to Thee, may we make mention of his righteousness only, and in his strength go forth into all the duties and trials of life.

May we never feel miserable even in a vale of tears, while we think of the Consolation of Israel; but rejoice in him with joy unspeakable and full of glory.

Reflecting upon his grace in becoming poor, that we through his poverty might be rich, may all selfishness and uncharitableness be extirpated from our hearts; may we love one another as he has loved us; and may we delight to go about doing good.

May no coldness, no indifference ever approach our spirits, whenever we are engaged in serving a master who has all the claims of a benefactor; yea who died for us and rose again.

To Him may we consecrate all our faculties and possessions; and on our time and our substance, our souls and our bodies, may there be inscribed, holiness unto the Lord. May we grieve to hear his name blasphemed, and weep to see his laws transgressed.

May his cause lie near our hearts; and may we long for the time when He shall be known and adored from the rising of the sun to the going down of the same; when to Him shall every knee bow, and every tongue confess; and the glad tidings of great joy shall be to all people—Unto *you* is born a Saviour which is Christ the Lord.

Through his mediation we address Thee; and in his words we conclude our imperfect supplications—Our Father, &c.

CHRISTMAS DAY.

EVENING.

Though Thou art exalted above all blessing and praise, yet, O God, we love to explore thy ways, to admire thy works, and to adore thy perfections. Thy understanding is infinite, thy power is almighty, thy mercy endureth for ever. Thy goodness transcends all our conceptions, as far as the heavens are higher than the earth.

We call on our souls and each other, this evening, to praise and magnify thy holy name. We bless Thee for our creation, and the degree we .iold in the rank of being. We bless Thee for our preservation, and for all the supplies which have rendered life supportable; and all the . indulgences which have rendered it comfortable. But above all, we thank Thee for thine unspeakable gift. For Thou hast surpassed all thy works and crowned all thy benefits by remembering us in our low estate, and laying help on one that is mighty.

And we have again heard the intelligence, that God so loved the world, that He gave his only begotten Son, that whosoever believeth on Him should not perish but have everlasting life. Convince us of our need of this dispensation of mercy and grace; and may we acquiesce in it, not with coldness of assent, but with gladness of heart. May we exclaim with the angels—glory to God in the highest, on earth peace, good-will towards men: and with the multitude of disciples, shout—Hosanna, blessed is He that cometh in the name of the Lord.

Though the world knew him not, and his own received Him not, and He is still despised and rejected of men—may we receive Him as all our salvation and all our desire.

May we rejoice to view Him in a nature which leads Him to call us brethren; in which as our example, He can go before us in the duties of obedience and submission; in which he can sympathize with us in all our wo; and in which He has suffered for sins, the just for the unjust, that He might bring us unto God.

May we look to Him for all we want, and live a life of faith upon his fulness. In Him may we know that we have redemption through His blood; that we have righteousness and strength; that we have all the treasures of wisdom and knowledge.

May we connect with his work *for* us in the flesh, his work *in* us by the Spirit. While we are reconciled by his death, may we be saved by his life: and remember that his name is Jesus, because He saves his people from their sins.

As He came not only that we might have life, but have it more abundantly, may our expectations be large and our desires importunate. May He dwell in our hearts by faith, that we being rooted and grounded in love, may be able to comprehend with all saints what is the height and depth, and breadth and length, and know the love of Christ, which passeth knowledge, and be filled with all the fulness of God.

Once in the end of the world hath He appeared to put away sin by the sacrifice of himself; and unto them that look for Him will He appear a second time without sin unto salvation. O prepare us for that solemn day! May we believe in Him as a Saviour before we meet Him as a judge; that when the tribes of the earth shall wail because of Him, we may lift up our heads with joy, knowing that our redemption draweth nigh; and say with the church, Lo! this is our God, we have waited for Him, He will save us; this is the Lord, we have waited for Him; we will rejoice and be glad in his salvation.

Make thy ministers wise and zealous and successful in the dispensation of thy word; and let signs and wonders be done in the name of thy holy child Jesus.

Bless the king and endue him with all that grace which shall render him equal to his station, and add a lustre to his crown.

We are a sinful people; but Thou hast not dealt with us after our desert; and Thou hast not left us without witness. Thou hast in the midst of us a people for thy name; and we pray that our beloved country may be a growing part of the empire of the Prince of Peace.

May the root of Jesse stand for an ensign to the people; to it may the Gentiles seek; and let his rest be glorious. May he come down like rain upon the mown grass, as showers that water the earth. In his days may the righteous flourish; and abundance of peace so long as the moon endureth. Let all nations be blessed in Him; all generations call Him blessed.

And blessed be his glorious name for ever: and let the whole earth be filled with his glory. Amen.

LAST EVENING OF THE OLD YEAR.

O GOD, Thou hast been our refuge and dwelling-place in all generations. Before the mountains were brought forth, or ever Thou hadst formed the earth and the world, even from everlasting to everlasting, Thou art God. A thousand years in thy sight are but as yesterday when it is past, and as a watch in the night. But as for man, his days are as grass; as a flower of the field so he flourisheth; for the wind passeth over it and it is gone, and the place thereof knoweth it no more.

We appear before Thee, to close in thy presence another of the revolutions of our fleeting existence, earnestly praying that the season may not pass away without suitable and serious reflections. O let us not imagine in spite of scripture and observation, and reason and feeling, that we have many of these periods left to notice; but say with Job, When a few years are come, I shall go the way whence I shall not return. It may be only a few months—or weeks—or days—or hours—for we know not at what *hour* the Son of man cometh. But we know that our life is a vapour that appeareth for a little time, and then vanisheth away; we know the frailty of our frame, and the numberless diseases and disasters to which we are exposed: So teach us to number our days, that we may apply our hearts unto wisdom.

What numbers of our fellow-creatures, and many of them much more likely to have continued than their survivors, have during the past year been carried down to their long home. But we have been preserved, and are the living to praise Thee this day. Blessed be the God of salvation, to whom belong the issues from death, that we are yet in the regions of hope, that we have yet an accepted time and a day of salvation, and that our opportunities of doing good as well as of gaining good are still prolonged. Yet are they all diminished by another irreparable loss; and the reduced remainder, with every trembling uncertainty attached to it, calls upon us to say with growing seriousness and zeal, I must work the works of Him that sent me while it is day—the night cometh wherein no man can work.

Thou hast commanded us to remember all the way which Thou hast led us in the wilderness. The scene of our journeying has indeed been a wilderness; but the hand that has conducted us is divine, and a thousand privileges not derivable *from* our condition have been experienced *in* it.

Thou hast corrected us—but it is of the Lord's mercies we are not consumed.

We have had our afflictions—but how few have they been in number, how short in continuance, how alleviated in degree, how merciful in design, how instructive and useful their results!

With regard to our severest exercises we are compelled to acknowledge, Thou hast not dealt with us after our sins, neither hast Thou rewarded us according to our iniquities. It is good for me that I have been afflicted.

But O, what a series of bounties and blessings present themselves to our minds, when we look back upon the year through which we have passed: and to what, but to thine unmerited goodness in the Son of thy love, are we indebted for all? Health, strength, food, raiment, residence, friends, relations, comfort, pleasure, hope, usefulness,—all our benefits have dropped from thy gracious hand; and there has not been a day, or an hour, or a moment, but has published thy kindness and thy care.

Especially would we acknowledge thy goodness in continuing to us the means of grace. Whatever has been denied us, we have had the provisions of thy house. The toils and trials of the week have been refreshed and relieved by the delights of the Sabbath. Our eyes have seen our teachers; our ears have heard the joyful sound of the gospel; and our hearts have often said, Lord, it is good for us to be here.

And O that every moment of the past year could, if called upon—and it *will* be called

upon—bear witness to our gratitude, love, and obedience. O that it was not in its power to convict us of the most unworthy requitals of thy goodness. To Thee, O Lord, belong glory and honour, but to us shame and confusion of face. O who can understand his errors? O how many duties have we neglected or improperly performed. How little have we redeemed our time or improved our talents. How little have we been alive to thy glory, or sought, or even seized, when presented, opportunities of serving our generation. How unprofited have we been under the richest means of religious prosperity; and when for the time we ought to be able to teach others, we have need to be again taught ourselves which be the first principles of the oracles of God.

God be merciful to us sinners. Pardon our iniquity, for it is great. Cleanse us from all unrighteousness, and work in us to will and to do of thy good pleasure. Let us not carry one of our old sins with us into the new year unforgiven, unrepented of, unbewailed, unabhorred. With a new portion of time may we have new hearts, and become new creatures.

If this year we should die—and in the midst of life we are in death—may death prove our eternal gain. And if our days are prolonged, may we walk before the Lord in the land of the living and show forth all thy praise. The number of our months is with Thee. In thy hand our breath is, and thine are all our ways. Prepare us for all, and be with us in all, and bring us safely through all into the rest that remains for thy people, for the sake of our Lord and Saviour: in whose words we call Thee—Our Father, &c Amen.

FIRST MORNING OF THE NEW YEAR.

OF old Thou hast laid the foundation of the earth: and the heavens are the work of thy hands. They shall perish, but Thou shalt endure; yea all of them shall wax old like a garment; as a vesture shalt Thou change them and they shall be changed: but Thou art the same, and thy years shall have no end. Through all the successions of time, which with us constitute the past, the present, and the future, I AM is thy name; and this is thy memorial in all generations. We desire, O God, with the profoundest reverence, to contemplate the eternity of thy nature. May our minds be filled with elevation and grandeur at the thought of a Being with whom one day is as a thousand years, and a thousand years are as one day; a Being, who, amidst all the revolutions of empire and the lapse of worlds, feels no variableness nor shadow of turning. How glorious, with immortality attached to them, are all thy attributes! and how secure are the hopes and happiness of all those who know thy name, and put their trust in Thee!

May we rejoice, that while men die, the Lord liveth; that while all creatures are found broken reeds and broken cisterns, He is the Rock of ages, and the fountain of living waters. O that we may turn away our hearts from vanity; and among all the dissatisfactions and uncertainties of the present state, look after an interest in that everlasting covenant which is ordered in all things and sure. May we seek after a union with thyself, as the strength of our heart and our portion for ever, and be partakers ourselves of the immutability we adore; for Thou hast assured us that while the world passeth away and the lusts thereof, he that doeth the will of God abideth for ever.

We thank Thee that Thou hast revealed to us the way in which a fallen and perishing sinner can be eternally united to thyself, and that Jesus is the way, the truth, and the life. In his name we come. O receive us graciously. Justify us freely from all things. Renew us in the spirit of our minds; and bless us with all spiritual blessings in heavenly places in Christ.

By the lapse of our days and weeks and years, which we are called upon so often to remark, may we be reminded how short our life is, and how soon we shall close our eyes on every prospect below the sun. Suffer us not to neglect the claims of eternity in the pursuit of the trifles of time: but knowing how frail we are, may we be wise enough to choose that good part which shall not be taken away from us; and before we leave the present evil world, may we secure an inheritance in another and a better. May thoughts of death and eternity so impress our minds, as to put seriousness into our prayers and vigour into our resolutions; may they loosen us from an undue attachment to things seen and temporal; so that we may weep as though we wept not, and rejoice as though we rejoiced not.

And remembering that the present life, so short, so uncertain, and so much of which is already vanished, is the only opportunity we shall ever have for usefulness, may we be concerned with a holy avarice to redeem the time. May we be alive and awake at every call of charity and piety. May we feed the hungry and clothe the naked; may we instruct the ignorant, reclaim the vicious, forgive the offending, diffuse the gospel; and consider one another, to provoke one another unto love and good works, not forsaking the assembling ourselves together, as the manner of some is, but exhorting one another, and so much the more as we see the day approaching.

As we have entered on a new period of life, may we faithfully examine ourselves, to see what has been amiss in our former temper or conduct; and in thy strength may we resolve to correct it. And may we inquire for the future, with a full determination to reduce our knowledge to practice, Lord, what wilt Thou have me to do?

Prepare us for all the duties of the ensuing year. All the wisdom and strength necessary for the performance of them must come from thyself; may we therefore live a life of self-distrust, of divine dependence, and of prayer; may we ask and receive, that our joy may be full; may we live in the Spirit, and walk in the Spirit.

If we are indulged with prosperity, let not our prosperity destroy us or injure us. If we are exercised with adversity, suffer us not to sink in the hour of trouble or sin against God. May we know how to be abased without despondence, and to abound without pride. If our relative comforts are continued to us, may we love them without idolatry, and hold them at thy disposal; and if they are recalled from us, may we be enabled to say, The Lord gave, and the Lord hath taken away, blessed be the name of the Lord.

Fit us for all events. We know not what a day may bring forth; but we encourage ourselves in the Lord our God, and go forward. Nothing can befall us by chance. Thou hast been thus far our helper: Thou hast promised to be with us in every condition; Thou hast engaged to make all things work together for our good; all thy ways are mercy and truth. May we therefore be careful for nothing, but in everything by prayer and supplication with thanksgiving, may we make known our requests unto God; and may the peace of God that passeth all understanding, keep our hearts and minds through Christ Jesus.

Bless, O bless, the young! May each of them, this day, hear Thee saying, My son, give me thy heart; and from this day may they cry unto Thee as the guide of their youth. Regard those who have reached the years wherein they say, We have no pleasure in them. If old in sin, may they be urged to embrace, before it be for ever too late, the things that belong to their peace; and if old in grace, uphold them with thy free Spirit, and help them to remember that now is their salvation nearer than when they believed.

Bless all the dear connexions attached to us by nature, friendship, or religion. Grace be to them, and peace be multiplied.

Let our country share thy protection and smiles. Bless all our rulers and magistrates.

Bless all our churches and congregations. Bless all thy ministers; may thine ordinances in their hands be enlivening and refreshing, and thy word effectual to wound and to heal.

May this be a year remarkable for the conversion of souls and the extension of the gospel. Bless all missionary societies; and let the circling months see the banners of the Redeemer carried forward, till all nations are subdued to the obedience of faith. Our Father, &c. Amen.

GOOD FRIDAY.

MORNING.

O Thou, King eternal, immortal, and invisible! though Thou art past finding out unto perfection, we rejoice that we are not called to worship an unknown God. Thou hast not left thyself without witness. We bless Thee for the revelation which Thou hast given us; and that in thy word we can view Thee as the Father of mercies and the God of all grace. All thy works and ways correspond with the names Thou hast assumed, and demand and justify our confidence in Thee. We praise Thee for the displays of thy goodness in the productions of nature and the bounties of thy providence; but above all, for thine inestimable love in the redemption of the world by our Lord Jesus Christ; for the means of grace, and for the hope of glory.

Herein Thou hast commended thy love towards us, in that while we were yet sinners Christ died for us.

We find ourselves this morning at the foot of his cross, where angels are desiring to look into these things—And if they who need no repentance, study the sufferings of Christ and the glory that should follow, how much more should we, to whom they are not only true and wonderful and sublime, but all-important and infinitely interesting! Help us, O Lord, to turn aside and see this great sight; and not suffer a dying Saviour to address us in vain—Is it nothing to you, all ye that pass by! Behold and see if ever there was sorrow like unto my sorrow.

Here may we see the value of our souls in the price paid for their deliverance; and instead of neglecting them for the vanities of time and sense, may we regard them according to the estimation in which they were holden by Him who gave his life a ransom for many. Here may we contemplate the evil of sin, and abhor it; here look upon Him whom we have pierced, and mourn for Him. Yet remembering that He was not only slain by us, but for us, may we rejoice in our tears; and by believing enter into rest.

With humble and holy confidence may we be enabled to say, Surely He hath borne our griefs and carried our sorrows; the chastisement of our peace was upon Him, and with his stripes we are healed.

May we never degrade his death, by fearing that it will not be available for guilt so great and aggravated as ours, even if we depend upon it, and plead it before God; but be fully persuaded that his blood cleanseth from all sin, and that by the one offering up of himself he hath perfected for ever them that are sanctified.

Yet, O God, never suffer us to sin that grace may abound. May we never crucify the Saviour afresh, and put him to an open shame. May He never be wounded in the house of his professing friends. Rather may we live only and wholly for Him who died for us, and adorn the doctrine of God our Saviour in all things.

May our old man be crucified with Him, and the body of sin be destroyed, that henceforth we may not serve sin. May we be planted together in the likeness of his death. As He suffered for us, leaving us an example that we should follow his steps, may we learn of Him submission, and meekness and forgiveness of injuries: when reviled, may we revile not again; when suffering may we threaten not, but commit ourselves to Him that judgeth righteously.

Like Him, in all the afflictions of life may we look to the hand that prepares and presents them, and say, The cup which my Father hath given me, shall I not drink it?

Whatever be the cross we are required to bear, may we look before us, and see Him carrying a much heavier; carrying it for us, and carrying it without a murmur.

Convert and pardon all those who by their lives or doctrine are the enemies of the cross of Christ. Have mercy upon the descendants of those who shed his blood; and let his dying prayer be answered, Father, forgive them, for they know not what they do.

As Thou hast made his soul an offering for sin, may he see his seed, and prolong his days, and the pleasure of the Lord prosper in his hand. May He see of the travail of his soul and be satisfied; and by his knowledge may He justify many, having borne their iniquities.

Yea, having been lifted up from the earth, may He draw all men unto Him. May all kings fall down before Him, and all nations serve Him; and in all the earth which He has purchased with his own blood, may there be one Lord, and his name one.

And when He who made himself of no reputation, but took upon Him the form of a servant, and became obedient unto death, even the death of the cross, shall come in his glory, with all the holy angels, may we be enabled to say, Even so, come Lord Jesus; and unite with those who will be eternally employed in saying—

Unto Him that loved us, and washed us from our sins in his own blood, and hath made us kings and priests unto God, and to his Father, be glory and dominion for ever and ever. Amen

GOOD FRIDAY.

EVENING.

O Thou, whose name alone is Jehovah, the Most High over all the earth: we desire to adore thy perfections, and to admire thy works, which are sought out of all them that have pleasure therein.

Thou art the only wise God. Thy power is almighty. Whither can we go from thy presence, or whither can we flee from thy spirit? Thou art holy in all thy ways. And such is thy purity, that even the heavens are not clean in thy sight.

How shall we come before the Lord, or bow before the high God? We have no offering of our own to bring. No man can redeem his brother, or give to God a ransom for him. The blood of bulls and of goats could not take away sin. The law itself made nothing perfect—but the bringing in of a better hope did, by the which we draw nigh to God.

Yes, blessed be thy name, Thou hast shown us what is good; and we behold the Lamb of God, who is the propitiation for our sins, and not for ours only, but also for the sins of the whole world.

Here a foundation is laid for our hope, in connexion with the highest glory of all thy perfections; and we rejoice to think that while pleading for salvation by the blood of the cross, we ask Thee not to deny thyself, or to trample on thy holy law: for here thy law is magnified and made honourable; here all thy attributes are developed and harmonized: mercy and truth meet together, righteousness and peace kiss each other.

Here weary and heavy laden may we come for relief, and find rest unto our souls. May we take fresh views of this adorable sacrifice under a sense of our constant unworthiness and desert; and in all our approaches to Thee may we have boldness and access with confidence by the faith of Him.

May we not only rely upon his cross, but glory in it. Yea may we joy in God through our Lord Jesus Christ, by whom we have now received the atonement. And may we be able, individually, to say, I am crucified with Christ; nevertheless I live, yet not I, but Christ liveth in me; and the life that I now live in the flesh, I live by the faith of the Son of God, who loved me and gave himself for me.

We are thankful that as He atoned for our guilt, so He procured for us the grace of life, that the blessing of Abraham might come on the gentiles, and that we might receive the promise of the Spirit through faith. May we never separate the pardon and sanctification which Thou hast joined together. May we prove that He gave himself—not only for our sins, but that He might deliver us from this present evil world; yea, that He might redeem us from all iniquity, and purify unto himself a peculiar people zealous of good works.

And O that in every future moment of our existence, we may be constrained to live not to ourselves, but to Him that died for us and rose again. As He so loved us, may we also love one another; and never deem anything too great to do or to suffer, while endeavouring to seek and to save that which is lost.

May the hearts which are too hard to be broken by terror, be melted by love, and gained by confidence. May none of those who are desirous of returning to Thee be discouraged by a fear of rejection, but calling to remembrance and belief the infinite proof which Thou hast already exhibited of thy benevolence, thus judge—He that spared not his own Son, but delivered Him up for us all, how shall He not with Him freely give us all things.

Smile upon our sovereign and our country. Let all the churches of the faithful be edified and multiplied. Bless all the ministers of the everlasting gospel, and may they increasingly determine to know nothing, save Jesus Christ and Him crucified.

Increase the number of those who love his salvation; and as he gave himself a ransom for all, may it be testified in due time; that He may have the heathen for his inheritance, and the uttermost parts of the earth for his possession, and reign King of kings, and Lord of lords.

In his words we conclude our devotions: Our Father, &c. Amen.

EASTER SUNDAY.

MORNING.

When we consider the heavens, the work of thy fingers, the moon and the stars which Thou hast ordained; Lord, what is man that Thou art mindful of him, or the son of man that Thou visitest him. We are not worthy of an audience at thy footstool; we are not worthy of the least of all thy mercies; our sins have even called aloud for vengeance.

But Thou hast not executed upon us the fierceness of thine anger; because Thou art good as well as great; and thy goodness constitutes thy greatness. Thou hast turned our very fall into an occasion of improving our condition, by advancing us to the possession of greater blessings than we originally enjoyed; so that we not only have life, but have it more abundantly.

For this purpose the Son of thy love was manifested; and in the fulness of time we behold Him assuming our nature, and coming into our world, not to be ministered unto, but to minister, and to give his life a ransom for many. We rejoice to see, in his release from the prison of the grave, the evidence of the all-sufficiency and acceptation of the sacrifice He offered on the cross. O help us to consider Him as a risen Saviour; and may we feel the power of his resurrection, in establishing our faith, enlivening our hope, and securing our sanctification. May we not only believe his resurrection, but partake of it and resemble it; that like as Christ was raised from the dead by the glory of the Father, even so we also might walk in newness of life, reckoning ourselves to be dead indeed unto sin, but alive unto God through Jesus Christ our Lord.

And if risen with Christ, may we give evidence of it, and act becoming it in seeking those things that are above.

May we never leave our spiritual and everlasting condition undecided and unknown: may we never be satisfied till we are able to say, Blessed be the God and Father of our Lord Jesus Christ, who according to his abundant mercy hath begotten us again unto a lively hope by the resurrection of Jesus Christ from the dead—to an inheritance incorruptible, undefiled, and that fadeth not away, reserved in heaven for us.

In all our difficulties and dangers, may we rejoice that He who was dead is alive again, to plead for us, to defend us, and to supply; and has the keys of hell and of death.

In all the afflictions of life, in the decay of nature, and when looking into the horrors of the grave, may we with humble and holy confidence be able to say, I know that my Redeemer liveth, and shall stand at the latter day upon the earth; and though after my skin worms destroy this body, yet in my flesh shall I see God.

Are we called to mourn over the loss of our dear and pious connexions? Let us not sorrow as those who have no hope; but comfort one another with these words—That Jesus died and rose again, and them that sleep in Jesus will God bring with Him.

We glory in the victory which our risen Saviour has obtained, not only over death and the grave, but the powers of darkness. We rejoice that He has set judgment in the earth, and that the isles are waiting for his law; that his word is translating into every language, and his servants entering every clime. We hail what he has done, as a pledge of his universal triumph. And though we yet see not all things actually put under Him, we see Him, for the suffering of death, crowned with glory and honour; and in possession of all the resources necessary to accomplish the benevolent designs of his heart: and He must reign till *all* his enemies are made his footstool.

Through Him, as the once-suffering but now exalted Saviour, we address Thee, as Our Father, &c. Amen.

EASTER SUNDAY.

EVENING.

O Thou ever blessed God, we rejoice to think Thou hast determined to get thyself honour in this apostate part of thy empire, not by the merited infliction of thy justice, but the displays of thy goodness. For thou hast said, mercy shall be built up for ever, a monument higher than the heavens, more durable than eternity, and inscribed to the praise of the glory of thy grace, wherein Thou hast made us accepted in the Beloved.

We bless Thee for the appointment and revelation of the one only Mediator between Thee and us; by whose death sinners are reconciled, and by whose life they are saved. Thou hast laid on Him the iniquity of us all. Surely He hath borne our griefs and carried our sorrows; the chastisement of our peace was upon Him, and with his stripes we are healed.

Establish in our minds a full persuasion that He was delivered for our offences, and raised again for our justification; and may we above all things be concerned to know, not only that He has risen again, but that we are quickened together with Christ, and raised up, and made to sit with Him in the heavenly places. May we hold communion with Him as a living and reigning Saviour, able to carry on our cause, and save unto the uttermost all that come unto God by Him.

Is He not head over all things unto his body the church? Is He not exalted to be a Prince and a Saviour? Has he not assured us that because He lives, we shall live also! May we view Him as the first-fruits of them that sleep; and believe that as in Adam all die, even so in Christ shall all be made alive. May we view his resurrection, not only as the pledge, but the model of our own; knowing that He shall not only change our vile body, but fashion it like *his* own glorious body, according to the working whereby He is able even to subdue *all* things unto himself.

Thou hast appointed a day in which Thou wilt judge the world in righteousness by that man whom Thou hast ordained; and Thou hast given assurance of it unto all men, in that Thou hast raised Him from the dead. O save us from the wrath of the Lamb. May we tremble at the thought of appearing before Him, if we have neglected his salvation, despised his precious blood, and resisted his Holy Spirit.

Let not the head stone of the corner be a stone of stumbling and a rock of offence; but as He is chosen of God and precious, may He be precious to us. And while He is living for us in heaven, may we be living for Him on earth. May we esteem it our highest honour to be like Him, and feel it our greatest pleasure to serve Him.

And let all the house of *Israel* know assuredly, that Thou hast made that same Jesus whom their fathers crucified, both Lord and Christ. May the veil be taken from their heart, and may they behold as in a glass his glory.

As a nation, be merciful unto us and bless us. May this Christian country be a country of Christians; and let all who name the name of Christ depart from iniquity.

Bless all those who preach Jesus and the resurrection. May they preach with the Holy Ghost sent down from heaven. May their sound go into all the earth, and their words unto the ends of the world.

As yet, after all we have read and heard and experienced, we know but little of the value of the gospel; but we know enough to induce us to be thankful for our religious advantages, to sympathize with those who are without Christ, and to pray that in Him all the families of the earth may be blessed, and all generations call Him blessed.

Now the God of peace, that brought again from the dead our Lord Jesus, that great Shepherd of the sheep, through the blood of the everlasting covenant, make us perfect in every good work to do his will, working in us that which is well-pleasing in his sight, through Jesus Christ: to whom be glory for ever and ever. Amen.

WHITSUNDAY.

MORNING.

O GOD, Thou hast established thy throne in the heavens, and thy kingdom ruleth over all: and all nations before Thee are as nothing. Yet blessed be thy name, it is only in comparison with thy infinite greatness that they are nothing—not in reference to thy condescension and kindness and care. Even as individuals we have been the charge of thy providence; goodness and mercy have always attended us, and having obtained help of Thee we continue to this day. Thou hast been mindful of our souls as well as our bodies; yea Thou wast pleased to form a purpose of grace in our favour, and devise means the most glorious to deliver us from the degradation and misery and perdition of sin, and to make us partakers of the hope of eternal life.

We bless Thee for the dispensation of religion under which it is our exalted privilege to live. How superior are our advantages, to those enjoyed by many of thy people in earlier ages. The law was given by Moses, but grace and truth came by Jesus Christ. Prophets and righteous men desired to see the things which we see, and did not see them; and to hear the things which we hear, and did not hear them; but blessed are our eyes for they see, and our ears for they hear. Instead of a portion of revelation, we have the sacred

M

scriptures complete. Instead of the blackness and darkness and tempest of Sinai, we have the milder glories and the small still voice of Zion. We have not received the spirit of bondage again to fear; but the spirit of adoption, whereby we cry, Abba, Father.

We praise Thee for the establishment of the glorious gospel which at the first began to be spoken by the Lord, and was confirmed unto us by them that heard Him; God also bearing them witness, with signs and wonders, and with divers miracles and gifts of the Holy Ghost, according to his own will. We rejoice, that though his supernatural agency has ceased with its necessity, the ministry of the Spirit continues, and that his saving influences are confined to no period of the church. All that have been enlightened and renewed since the fall, have been the subjects of his operation; and with Thee is the residue of the Spirit.

We rejoice that as there is no blessing we so much need, so there is no blessing we are so much encouraged to implore: for thy truth has said, If ye, being evil, know how to give good gifts unto your children, how much more shall your Father which is in heaven give his Holy Spirit to them that ask Him.

O Thou God of all grace, fulfil the word unto thy servants, upon which Thou hast caused us to hope. Impart unto us thy Holy Spirit, to open the eyes of our understanding, to sanctify our affections, to comfort our hearts, to glorify Christ, by taking of the things of Christ, and showing them to us.

May we never commit the sin against the Holy Ghost. Never quench the Spirit. Never resist the Holy Ghost. Never grieve the Holy Spirit. But may we pray in the Holy Ghost, and worship God in the Spirit, and be led by the Spirit, and be filled with the Spirit.

May we always view thy commands in connexion with thy promises, and our duties and trials in connexion with our resources. Great is our work, great is our warfare, and far greater than we have ever yet felt it to be is our weakness. But our sufficiency is of God; and Thou hast said, I will never leave thee, nor forsake thee. Not by might nor by power, but by my Spirit, saith the Lord.

Let the goings of our God and our King be seen in the sanctuary; and when thy truth is dispensed, let it come to those who hear it, not in word only, but in power and in the Holy Ghost, and with much assurance.

And bless not only the gates of Zion, but all the dwelling-places of Jacob. May every family contain a church in the house. Pour thy blessing upon our seed, and thy Spirit upon our offspring; and may the rising race grow up the ornaments, examples, and benefactors of their day and generation.

To Thee we commend our rightful sovereign, with all in authority under him and over us; and implore thy favourable regards to the privileged country in which we live. Humble us before Thee for our sins, especially our neglect and abuse of our religious advantages. Withdraw not from us the blessings we have forfeited; and inflict not upon us the judgments we have deserved. But spare us according to the greatness of thy mercy.

And from our land of vision, may the light break forth upon all those who are in darkness and the region of the shadow of death.

Bless all missionary exertions. Let the various societies employed in this work of faith and labour of love view each other with pleasure and rejoice in each other's success; and if not in immediate and personal co-operation, yet in accordance, and tendency, and design, may they stand fast in one spirit, with one mind, striving together for the faith of the gospel. Let those who remain at home hold forth the word of life in their own circles, and be concerned to evangelize the districts in which they reside. But O, let there not be a deficiency of those who offer themselves to the help of the Lord among the heathen, and that say, Lord, send me. Let it be said, as it was in the beginning of the gospel—The Lord gave the word, great was the company of them that published it.

And be with those that are already engaged. We know that Paul can only plant, and Apollos water; but Thou canst give the increase.

Pour thy Spirit from on high, and the wilderness shall become a fruitful field. Our Father, &c. Amen.

WHITSUNDAY.

EVENING.

O Thou Author of peace and lover of concord, in knowledge of whom standeth our eternal life, and whose service is perfect freedom; cleanse the thoughts of our hearts by the inspiration of thy Holy Spirit, and give us grace whereby we may serve Thee acceptably, with reverence and with godly fear.

We adore Thee as the Creator of all things, visible and invisible. Thou art the maker of our earth; and Thou art the maker of man upon it: and Thou madest man upright in the possession of thy image and the enjoyment of thy presence. But man, being in honour, abode not. Our first father sinned; and we have borne his iniquity. We have gone astray from the womb; and in numberless instances have evinced ourselves to be the degenerate offspring of a fallen original—and there is no health in us. As transgressors of thy law, we are under the curse; and did our deliverance depend upon ourselves, we must lie down in endless despair. We admit in all its extent the testimony of thy word against us, but admire with gratitude the developement of a plan of mercy and grace divinely appropriate to all our wants and woes, and uniting the highest display of thy highest glory with the salvation of sinners.

Adored be the benevolence that led the Son of thy love, before the foundation of the world, to say, Lo! I come to do thy will, O God; thy law is within my heart. Blessed be the day when the angels saw Him who was rich for our sakes becoming poor, that we through his poverty might be rich. Blessed be the hour, when the Prince of Life bore our sins in his own body on the tree; and having obtained eternal redemption for us, ascended up on high, leading captivity captive, and receiving gifts for men, even the rebellious also, that the Lord God might dwell among them. We rejoice that Christianity was originally preached, with the Holy Ghost sent down from heaven; and in the demonstration of the Spirit was so firmly established, that the gates of hell can never prevail against it. We praise Thee that at so early a period the Sun of Righteousness, in the knowledge of the gospel, arose with healing under his wings upon this distinguished island, and said, Arise, shine, for thy light is come, and the glory of the Lord is risen upon thee. And O what reason have we to be thankful if this gospel has come to us, not in word only, but in power, and in the Holy Ghost, and in much assurance.

For we bless Thee, that though miracles have ceased, yet thy Spirit is insured to thy people to the end of the world, as the source of light and life, and peace and joy; giving testimony to the word of thy grace, and working in the souls of men to will and to do of thy good pleasure.

O Thou Author of all good, save us, we beseech Thee, by the washing of regeneration and the renewing of the Holy Ghost. May we be found in the number of those who are born of the Spirit, and give evidence of it by our walking after the Spirit, and our minding the things of the Spirit. Instead of judging ourselves by dreams, fancies, and impressions, may we prove what is acceptable unto the Lord, and remember that the fruit of the Spirit is in all goodness, and righteousness, and truth.

We desire, O God, to acknowledge our entire dependence upon Thee. Whatever time we have been engaged in Thy service, we are still in the body, and feel our need of the continuance of those counsels, supports, and consolations, which have ever been afforded us. Cast us not away from thy presence, and take not thy Holy Spirit from us.

In all the dangers to which we are exposed, uphold us by thy free Spirit; and may we not think it enough to be preserved from falling, but may we go forward, and be always abounding in the work of the Lord. Strengthen us with might by thy Spirit, in the inner man, for every purpose of the Christian life; and may we be satisfied with no attainment, till we are filled with all the fulness of God.

Awaken the careless; convince of their error and guilt all those who deny or vilify the work of thy grace; and plant in their consciences the conviction, that if any man have not the spirit of Christ he is none of his.

Pour the spirit of grace and of supplication upon all our congregations. Bless the ministry of the gospel, and make it the ministration of the Spirit, and the power of God to salvation to every one that believeth.

But how can they believe in Him of whom they have not heard? And how can they hear without a preacher? How many are there, who by the wretchedness of their condition, if not by their actual desire, are saying, Come over and help us!

Hast Thou not commanded us to pray that thy kingdom may come? Hast not Thou promised that the earth shall be full of the knowledge of the Lord, as the waters cover the seas?

May we encourage our expectation by reviewing what Thou hast already accomplished, and remembering that Thou art a God of truth, and—the Almighty. May we therefore realize in our minds the delightful period when the heathen shall cast their idols to the moles and to the bats; when Mahometanism and antichrist shall perish; when the Jews shall look upon Him whom they have pierced, and mourn; and among Protestants, every plant which our heavenly Father hath not planted, shall be rooted up.

But why are thy chariot wheels so long in coming? Why does the whole creation groan and travail in pain together until now? How many would say, Lord, now lettest Thou thy servant depart in peace, according to thy word—could their eyes see thy salvation, which Thou hast prepared before the face of all people; a light to lighten the gentiles, and the glory of thy people Israel.

While using the means, may we trust in thy wisdom as well as thy faithfulness: and hear the voice saying, I the Lord will hasten it—in his time.

And to God the Father, the Word, and the Holy Ghost, be ascribed the kingdom, power, and glory, both now and for ever. Amen.

THE EVENING AFTER A FUNERAL.

O Thou Father of mercies, and God of all comfort—Thou hast often invited us to thyself by a profusion of kindnesses; and it manifests our depravity, that we think of Thee so little in the hour of ease and prosperity. But we are now before Thee in affliction and distress. Yet we rejoice to know that Thou art a very present and an all-sufficient help in trouble.

Thou takest away, and who can hinder Thee, or say unto Thee, What doest Thou? Thou hast a right to do what Thou wilt with thine own. Thou art a sovereign, and the reasons of thy conduct are often far above out of our sight: but thy work is perfect, thy ways are judgment. All thy dispensations are wise, and righteous, and kind—kind, even when they seem to be severe.

May we hear thy voice in thy rod, as well as in thy word; and gathering from the corrections with which we are exercised the peaceable fruit of righteousness, be able to acknowledge with all our suffering brethren before us, It is good for me that I have been afflicted.

It is not the Scripture only that reminds us of our living in a dying world, but all observation and experience. Man is continually going to his long home, and the mourners daily go about the streets. And we are all accomplishing as an hireling our day, and in a little time our neighbours, friends, and relations, will seek us—and we shall not be. Our days are swifter than a weaver's shuttle, and are spent without hope. Thou hast made our days as an hand's breadth, and our age is as nothing before Thee: verily every man at his best state is altogether vanity. For our days are not only few, but full of evil. Anxieties perplex us; dangers alarm us; infirmities oppress us; disappointments afflict us; losses impoverish us; we are consumed by thine anger, and by thy wrath are we troubled—O shut not thy merciful ear to our prayers; but spare us, O Lord, most holy; O God, most mighty; O holy and most merciful Saviour: Thou most worthy Judge eternal, suffer us not at our last hour, for any bitter pains of death, to fall from Thee.

We acknowledge, O God, with shame and sorrow, that the state of degradation and mortality in which we groan was not our original condition. Thou madest man upright; but he sought out many inventions. Our first father sinned, and we have borne his iniquity. By one man sin entered into the world, and death by sin; and so death hath passed upon all men, for that all have sinned.

And we bless Thee that this is not our final state. By the discoveries of faith, we see new heavens, and a new earth wherein dwelleth righteousness. We see the spirits of just men made perfect. We see our vile bodies changed, and fashioned like the Saviour's own glorious body; and man the sinner raised above the angels who never sinned.

We bless Thee for this purpose of grace, formed before the world began, and accomplished in the fulness of time by the Son of thy love, who hath abolished death, and brought life and immortality to light by the gospel; and who among the ravages of the grave, says—I am the resurrection and the life: he that believeth in me, though he were dead, yet shall he live; and whosoever liveth and believeth in me shall never die.

May it be our immediate and supreme concern to win Christ, and be found in Him; knowing that there is no condemnation to them that are in Christ Jesus; and that blessed are the dead that die in the Lord.

So teach us to number our days, that we may apply our hearts unto wisdom—that wisdom which will lead us to prefer the soul to the body, and eternity to time; that wisdom which will lead us to secure an interest in a better world, before we are removed from this.

O let not the trifles of time induce us to neglect the one thing needful. While each of us is compelled to say, I know Thou wilt bring me to death, and to the house appointed for all living, may we be enabled also to say, I know whom I have believed, and am persuaded that He is able to keep that which I have committed to Him against that day.

And O let not the solemnities we have this day witnessed be ever forgotten; for often our most serious impressions have worn off, and our goodness has been as the morning cloud, and as the early dew that soon passeth away.

Thou hast permitted death to invade our circle, and hast turned our dwelling into a house of mourning. May we find that it is better to be in the house of mourning than in the house of mirth. By the sadness of the countenance may the heart be made better, more serious to reflect, and more softened to take impression.

With the feelings of the creature may we blend the views and the hopes of the Christian. May we remember that Thou hast bereaved us, not as an aggressor, but as a proprietor; resuming what was lent us for a season, but never ceased to be thine own. May we therefore be dumb, and open not our mouth, because Thou hast done it; or if we speak, may it be to acknowledge and pray—I know, O Lord, that thy judgments are right, and that Thou in faithfulness hast afflicted me; let thy loving-kindness be for my comfort, according to thy word unto thy servant.

We bless Thee for thy goodness to the deceased, and that we are not called to sorrow as those who have no hope. We ascribe whatever excellency was found in them to thy grace; and desire to be followers of them, as far as they also were of Christ.

Forgive us in whatever instances we failed in our duty towards them. Let the prayers they offered for us while on earth be answered; may we hold communion with them in our living Redeemer; and look forward to a period of renewed and improved intercourse, in which we shall be for ever with each other, and for ever with the Lord.

Now unto Him that is able to keep us from falling, and to present us faultless before the presence of his glory with exceeding joy—To the only wise God our Saviour, be glory and majesty, dominion and power, both now and ever. Amen.

FAST-DAY.

MORNING.

Holy, holy, holy is the Lord of hosts, the whole earth is full of thy glory. O for such an impression of thy holiness as Isaiah had, when, penetrated with a sense of his own sin, and the sin of the nation, he exclaimed, Wo is me, for I am a man of unclean lips, and I dwell among a people of unclean lips. Banish all insensibility and indifference from our minds, and unite our hearts to fear thy name.

We lament that the world in which we live, formed to show forth thy praise, was so early defiled by sin; that all flesh corrupted its way before God, and every imagination of the thoughts of the heart was only evil continually. We adore thy awful but righteous displeasure, in bringing the flood upon the world of the ungodly and taking them all away.

Yet even this tremendous desolation did not hinder the renewed human race from rebelling against Thee; and a long succession of private and public calamities proclaims the desperate depravity of our nature, and the evil of sin. Our world is the empire of death, a vale of tears; and tempests and earthquakes, and war, and pestilence and famine, scatter the tokens of thy wrath, for Thou distributest sorrows in thine anger.

Thy judgments are now abroad in the earth—may the inhabitants thereof learn righteousness. They have reached and invaded us—may we lay them to heart, and be suitably impressed with the afflicting circumstances of the country to which we belong.

We have been equally distinguished by privileges and guilt; and it is impossible for us to review the one, without being reminded of the other. An innumerable multitude of natural, providential, and religious benefits, have distinguished our portion. The lines have fallen to us in pleasant places, yea we have a goodly heritage. At an early period the gospel visited our shores, and has continued in the midst of us to this hour. We have lived under the administration of laws, just, mild, and beneficent. We have enjoyed civil and religious freedom. The scriptures have not been withholden from us, nor have our teachers been removed into a corner-but our eyes have seen our teachers; and, sitting under our own vine and fig-tree, none has dared to make us afraid. In our dangers Thou hast appointed salvation for walls and bulwarks; the earth has yielded to us her increase; and God, even our own God, has blessed us.

It is impossible for us to express or conceive the obligations we are under to love and serve Thee.

But we know—and O help us to feel—how unworthily and ungratefully we have behaved ourselves towards our adorable Benefactor. We are a sinful nation, a seed of evil-doers; children that are corrupters. The whole head is sick, and the whole heart is faint: from the crown of the head even to the sole of the foot, there is no soundness, but wounds and bruises and putrefying sores. O Lord, righteousness belongeth unto Thee, but unto us confusion of faces, as at this day, to our princes and our rulers.

We do not wonder at the scourge under which we are now groaning. We cannot complain of thy severity—we deserve to be turned into hell, with all the nations that forget God.

But Thou art the Almighty. Thou hast all hearts in thy hand, and all events at thy disposal.

And we have heard that to the Lord our God belong mercies and forgivenesses, though we have rebelled against Him. We are proofs ourselves, that thy compassions fail not—hence though corrected, we are not consumed; and though guilty, we are yet allowed and invited to enter thy presence.

With deep humiliation, not unmingled with hope, may we approach the throne of thy grace, at this time of need. O be merciful unto us and bless us, and cause thy face to shine upon us that we may be saved. For the sake of thy dear Son, who died the just for the unjust, by whose name we are called —behold a country prostrate at thy footstool; and hear the voice which will issue to-day from so many temples and closets, saying, Spare thy people, O Lord, and give not thine heritage to reproach.

Remove, if it please Thee, the blow of thy heavy hand, in the calamity which we are deploring; and after giving us such a deliverance as this, may we no more break thy commandments. Or if Thou hast determined to continue the correction, O correct us, but with judgment, not in thine anger, lest Thou bring us to nothing.

Aid thy people in the private and public devotions of the day. Pour out a spirit of grace and of supplication, that we may sorrow after a godly sort. May thy ministers be faithful and fearless: may they cry aloud, and spare not; but lift up their voice like a trumpet, and show thy people their transgression, and the house of Jacob their sin.

And let the word that is to be spoken be quick and powerful, sharper than any two-edged sword, piercing even to the dividing asunder of soul and spirit, and of the joints and marrow, and be a discerner of the thoughts and intents of the heart.

Our Father, &c. Amen.

FAST-DAY.
EVENING.

O GOD, Thou hast established thy throne in the heavens, and thy kingdom ruleth over all. We prostrate ourselves before Thee, deeply impressed with a sense of the vastness of thy agency and dominion. Thou changest the times and the seasons: Thou removest kings, and settest up kings. Empires rise and fall, and fade and flourish, at thy bidding; and all nations are in thy hand but as clay in the hand of the potter.

But none of thy dispensations are arbitrary. Whatever Thou doest, is done, because O Father it seemeth good in thy sight: and thy judgment is always according to truth. Thou art holy in all thy ways, and righteous in all thy works—And Thou art good even in wrath. Thou rememberest mercy; and dost not afflict willingly, nor grieve the children of men.

Therefore it is that we have been this day humbling ourselves in thy presence.

For we acknowledge that we have been deeply guilty. Thou hast nourished and brought up children, but we have rebelled against Thee. The ox knoweth his owner, and the ass his master's crib; but we have not known, we have not considered. Thou hast given us our corn, and wine, and oil, and multiplied our silver and gold; and we have prepared them for Baal. Because of swearing, the land has mourned. Pride has compassed us about as a chain. Discontent has rebelled against thine appointments. How has the love of money, which is the root of all evil, abounded among us. How have thy sabbaths been profaned, and thine ordinances disregarded. How has the gospel been undervalued, neglected, despised!

And all our transgressions have been more aggravated than those of any other people, because Thou hast favoured us unspeakably more than all the families of the earth.

Therefore Thou couldst easily and justly have destroyed us: but Thou hast not stirred up all thy wrath. In all that is come upon us for our evil deeds, Thou hast punished us less than our iniquities deserve. Yet Thou hast testified thy displeasure; and visited us with thy judgments: so that when we looked for light and peace, we have seen darkness and trouble.

O let us not be inattentive to the design of thy dealings, or insensible under thy rebukes. O let it not be said of us, as it was of the

Jews, The harp and the viol, and the tabret and pipe, and wine, are in thy feasts, but they regard not the work of the Lord, neither consider the operation of his hand. Thou hast stricken them, but they have not grieved; Thou hast consumed them, but they have refused to receive correction: they have made their faces harder than the rock; they have refused to return.

In the way of thy judgments, O Lord, may we wait for Thee. Thou hast said, Is any afflicted? Let him pray. Call upon me in the day of trouble, and I will deliver thee, and thou shalt glorify me. Fulfil the word unto thy servants, upon which Thou hast caused us to hope. And O let not the calamity be removed only, but above all sanctified: let it appear that we have heard the rod, and Him that appointeth it: and be able to say, It is good for us that we have been afflicted.

For which purpose, bless, we beseech Thee, the word of thy grace which has been spoken; and grant that the professed humiliation of the day may be real—for Thou lookest to the heart. And let it also be universal: may it extend from the highest to the lowest; may it pervade the court and the country; may it enter every church and every family—Let none of us lose sight of ourselves in the public calamity. May each individual retire and ask, What have I done?—and what wilt Thou have me to do? And though other lords have had dominion over us, henceforth by Thee only may we make mention of thy name.

Regard the king as supreme, and the government under which we live. Bless his majesty's confidential advisers; the hereditary and constituted nobility of the realm; the representatives of the people; and the magistracy of the land—may all be wise in counsel, exemplary in conduct, and faithful to their trusts.

And thus may we be reformed and not destroyed. Thus may we be a holy, that we may be a happy people, whose God is the Lord. Return, O Lord, how long? and let it repent Thee concerning thy servants. O satisfy us early with thy mercy; that we may rejoice and be glad all our days. Make us glad according to the days wherein Thou hast afflicted us, and the years wherein we have seen evil. Let thy work appear unto thy servants, and thy glory unto their children. And let the beauty of the Lord our God be upon us; and establish Thou the work of our hands upon us; yea the work of our hands establish Thou it.

And to the Father, the Son, and the Holy Spirit, be rendered the kingdom, power, and glory for ever and ever. Amen.

FOR A DAY OF THANKSGIVING.
MORNING.

O God, Thou art very great, Thou art clothed with honour and majesty: Thou coverest thyself with light as with a garment Thou walkest upon the wings of the wind When we reflect on the glory of thy majesty we are filled with wonder at the vastness of thy condescension. For Thou condescendest even to behold things that are in heaven. What then is man that Thou art mindful of him, or the son of man that Thou visitest him!

We rejoice that we are under the governance of a Being, who is not only almighty, but perfectly righteous, and wise, and good; that all things in our world are appointed and arranged by thy paternal agency; that thy providence numbers the very hairs of our head, and that a sparrow falleth not to the ground without our heavenly Father.

Hitherto hath the Lord helped us. We bless Thee for personal mercies. If we are called, it is by thy word. If we are renewed, it is by thy Spirit. If we are justified, it is freely by thy grace, through the redemption that is in Christ Jesus. It is in Thee we live and move and have our being. Thy goodness has been always near us, to hear our complaints, to soothe our sorrow, and to command deliverance for us. And numberless are the instances of lovingkindness that now, from ignorance or inattention, elude our notice; the discovery of which will awaken our songs, when we mingle with those who dwell in thy house above and are still praising Thee.

We thank Thee for relative benefits; for blessings on our families, blessings on our churches, and blessings on our country. We confess that we are not worthy of the least of all thy mercies, and of all the truth which Thou hast showed unto thy servants. Sins of every kind and of every degree have reigned among us; have spread through all ranks and orders; and continued notwithstanding all warnings and corrections: and if Thou hadst dealt with us after our sins, or rewarded us according to our iniquities, we should long ago have had no name nor place among the nations of the globe.

But to the Lord our God belong mercies and forgiveness, though we have rebelled against Him. All thy dispensations towards us have said, with a tenderness that ought to penetrate our hearts—How shall I give thee up, O England! Our privileges, never properly improved, and forfeited times without number, have been continued. We still behold our sabbaths, and our ears still hear the joyful sound. Our constitution, liberties, and laws, have not been subverted or impaired. Thou hast given us rains and fruitful seasons; Thou hast filled us with the finest of the wheat: our garners have been affording all manner of store; our oxen have been strong to labour; our sheep have brought forth thousands and ten thousands in our streets. Thou hast spread thy wing, and sheltered us from the pestilence that walketh in darkness, and the destruction that wasteth at noonday. Civil discord has not raged in our provinces; our shores have not been invaded; we have not heard the confused noise of warriors, or seen garments rolled in blood—it has not come nigh us. Our enemies have often threatened to swallow us up, but the Lord has been on our side, and they have not prevailed against us. We are this day called upon to acknowledge thy goodness in (————).

God is the Lord who hath showed us light; bind the sacrifice with cords, even to the horns of the altar. After giving us such a deliverance as this, may we no more break thy commandments. May we never convert our blessings into the instruments of provocation, by making them the means of nourishing pride and presumption, wantonness and intemperance: and compel Thee to complain —Do ye thus requite the Lord, O foolish people, and unwise? Is not He thy Father that hath bought thee? Hath He not made thee and established thee?

For this purpose meet with us in thy house; and may the goings of our God and our King be seen in the sanctuary. Be with the preacher and with the hearers; and let the words of his mouth, and the meditation of their hearts, be acceptable in thy sight, O Lord, our strength and our Redeemer. May public instruction awaken the ardour of our feelings. May our gratitude not only be lively, but practical and permanent. And by all thy mercies may we present our bodies a living sacrifice, holy and acceptable unto Thee, which is our reasonable service.

Bless the Lord, ye his angels, that excel in strength, that do his commandments hearkening unto the voice of his word. Bless ye the Lord, all ye his hosts; ye ministers of his that do his pleasure. Bless the Lord, all his works, in all places of his dominion: bless the Lord, O my soul. Amen

---

FOR A DAY OF THANKSGIVING.

EVENING.

O God, Thou art good, and Thou doest good. Thou art good to all, and thy tender mercies are over all thy works.

We have thought of thy lovingkindness this day, in the midst of thy temple; and are again surrounding this domestic altar to exclaim O that men would praise the Lord, for his goodness, and for his wonderful works to the children of men.

We lament to think that a world so filled with thy bounty, should be so alienated from thy service and glory. We mourn over the vileness of our ingratitude, and abhor ourselves repenting in dust and ashes.

O Thou God of all grace, make us more thankful. In order that we may be more thankful may we be more humble; impress us with a deep sense of our unworthiness, arising from the depravity of our nature, and countless instances of unimproved advantages, omitted duties, and violated commands. May we compare our condition with our desert, and with the far less indulged circumstances of others. May we never be inattentive to any of thy interpositions on our behalf; but be wise and observe these things, that we may understand the lovingkindness of the Lord.

How many blessings, temporal and spiritual, public and private, hast Thou conferred upon us. Thy mercies have been new every morning, and every moment.

Our afflictions have been few and alleviated, often short in their continuance, and always founded in a regard to our profit. Thy secret has been upon our tabernacle; and we have known Thee in thy palaces for a refuge. The lines have indeed fallen to us in pleasant places, yea we have a goodly heritage. Thou hast not dealt so with any people. It is a good land which the Lord our God has given us—a land distinguished by knowledge; dignified as the abode of civil and religious freedom: endeared by the patriot's zeal, and the martyr's blood, and the ashes of our forefathers: a land the Lord careth for, and upon which his eye has been from the beginning even to the end of the year.

Thou hast been a wall of fire round about us by thy providential protection, and the glory in the midst of us by the gospel of our salvation, the ordinances of religion, and the presence of thy Holy Spirit.

What shall we render unto the Lord for all his benefits towards us! Because Thou hast been our help, therefore under the shadow of thy wing may we rejoice. Because Thou hast heard our voice and our supplication, therefore may we call upon Thee as long as we live; and in every future difficulty and distress, make Thee our refuge and our portion.

Enable us to bless Thee at all times; may thy praise continually be in our mouth; and may we show forth thy praise, not only with our lips, but in our lives.

Being delivered from the peril and calamity (of ————) with which we have been exercised, may we serve Thee without fear, in holiness and righteousness, all the days of our lives.

We dare not trust our own hearts. We have often resembled thy people of old, who in the hour of deliverance and indulgence sang thy praise, and said—All that the Lord commandeth us will we do; but soon forgot his works and the wonders which he had showed them. Keep these things for ever in the imagination of our hearts; and not only draw us, but bind us to thyself with the cords of love and the bonds of a man.

And with all our calls to gratitude and joy

X

may we remember that we have also reason for sorrow and humiliation. O give us that repentance which is unto life. Reform as well as indulge us; and pardon as well as spare. Let not our prosperity destroy us, nor our table become a snare. Let us not, by our perverse returns, provoke Thee to visit us with heavier inflictions; and turn the rod into a scorpion. May our ways please the Lord, that we may hope for a continuance of thy favour, and know that all things shall work together for our good.

Do good in thy good pleasure unto Zion. Build Thou the walls of Jerusalem. And as the churches have rest, may they walk in the fear of the Lord, and in the comforts of the Holy Ghost, and be multiplied.

Let the king live before Thee; and on his head may the crown flourish. Bless all the branches of the royal house: preside over our national councils; impart wisdom to those who conduct our public affairs: and may all the various classes in the community pursue that righteousness which exalteth a nation, and forsake that sin which is a reproach to any people.

Regard the services in which we have been engaged with the thousands of our Israel: accept the poor and imperfect thanksgivings we have offered; and let thy word which has been dispensed in aid of the devotion of the day, accomplish all the good pleasure of thy goodness—through Jesus the Lord, our righteousness and strength; and in whose words we address Thee as—

Our Father, &c. Amen.

PETITIONS

FOR

PARTICULAR OCCASIONS.

FOR RAIN.

ARE there any of the vanities of the gentiles that can cause rain? Or can the heavens give showers? Art not Thou He, O Lord our God? Therefore will we wait upon Thee, for Thou hast made all these things.

Thou visitest the earth and waterest it; Thou greatly enrichest it with the river of God which is full of water. Thou makest it soft with showers; Thou blessest the springs thereof. Thy paths drop fatness. They drop upon the pastures of the wilderness, and the little hills rejoice on every side.

We have been made to feel the worth of this blessing by the want of it; and it would be easy for Thee to continue the privation, till the heavens over us were brass, and the earth under us iron; and the husbandman be ashamed for the wheat, and for the barley, because the harvest of the field is perished, and because joy is withered away from the sons of men.

But O deal not with us after our desert. Turn not a fruitful land into barrenness. Command thy rain to descend. Cause the grass to grow for the cattle, and herbs for the service of man, and bring forth food out of the earth.

FOR FAIR WEATHER.

—How numberless are our wants and dangers! Our hopes are destroyed, not only by the deficiency, but the excess of our supplies. Stop, we pray Thee, the bottles of heaven, which have so long been pouring down water upon us; and cause thy sun not only to rise but to shine. Give us the clear shining after rain, that the earth may yield her increase in maturity, and opportunity be afforded for the wholesome in-gathering of grass for the cattle, and grain for the use of man; that there may be no complaining in our streets, but that we may eat in plenty, and be satisfied and praise the Lord.

And O let us not forget our souls, in our mindfulness of the body; nor expend all our concern upon the meat that perisheth, but be above all things anxious to secure the meat which endureth unto everlasting life, and which the son of man will give, for him hath God the Father sealed.

IN VIEW OF JOURNEYING.

O GOD, thou hast called thyself the Preserver of men, and the length of our days. We are therefore encouraged to commit ourselves to thy guardian care, in the journey before us.

Many have parted with the hope of soon embracing each other again, but instead of returning to their own dwelling, they have been conveyed to the house appointed for all living. We pray, with submission to thy pleasure, that this may not be our experience. Give thine angels charge concerning us to keep us in all our ways. Let no evil befall our persons, and no plague come nigh our dwelling. May we know also that our tabernacle is in peace, and visit our habitation and not sin.

Yet uncertain what a day may bring forth, may we be prepared for every event of thy providence; and wherever, in dying, we go *from*, may it be our happiness to know where we are going *to*, and rejoice in the prospect, that when all our wanderings and partings are ended, we shall unite in our heavenly Father's house, and be for ever with the Lord.

FOR A NEW-MARRIED PARTY.

BLESS those who have just entered a state honourable in all. May they remember the vows they have left at the altar, and in the discharge of their personal and relative duty may they make their word their rule, that mercy and peace may be upon them. May the husband love his wife even as himself, and the wife see that she reverence her husband; and both walk together as heirs of the grace of life, that their prayers be not hindered.

Preserve them from the evils which destroy or diminish the welfare and comfort of the condition in which Thou hast placed them; and may they enjoy all the happiness derivable from prudence, temper, accommodation, real godliness, and the divine blessing.

May they expect to discern infirmities in one another, but may they be always most deeply conscious of their own. And let them not look for unattainable, by looking for unmingled bliss on earth; but remember that this is not our rest, and be prepared for difficulties, trials, changes, and final separation.

FOR A WOMAN APPROACHING THE TIME OF TRAVAIL.

—REGARD thine handmaid, who is looking forward to an important hour. Be not Thou far from her when trouble is near. May her mind be kept in perfect peace, being stayed upon the God of her salvation. Bring to the birth, and give strength to bring forth. Soften the pains of labour, as well as command deliverance; and in due time may she remember no more her anguish, for joy that a child is born into the world. And may the root and the branch abide under the shadow of the Almighty.

FOR ONE UNDER SICKNESS.

—THINK, O God, for good upon the afflicted, especially him (or her) whom we now commend to thy compassionate regard. Comfort him upon the bed of languishing, and make all his bed in his sickness.

If the sickness be unto death, prepare him for the solemn event, and be with him in it. But we are allowed to implore deliverance, with submission; nothing is too hard for the Lord; Thou canst heal as well as wound: we therefore pray, if it be thy good pleasure, that Thou wilt put efficacy into the means, rebuke the disorder, renew the strength, and prolong the days of thy servant.

Above all, let the dispensation be sanctified to the sufferer, and his connexions; and may all have reason to acknowledge in the review, It is good for me that I have been afflicted.

FOR A YOUTH GOING FROM HOME.

(If with a view to Business.)

—O GOD, Thou appointest the bounds of our habitations, and arrangest all our individual concerns; and it is thy pleasure, not only that we should part at death, but often separate in life. When absent from each other in body, may we be present in spirit; and may our natural affection be strengthened and sanctified by inquiry and correspondence, and divine remembrance at the throne of grace.

Regard the member of our family who is now leaving the parental roof and the parental wing. In all his ways may he acknowledge Thee, and be Thou the guide and the guard of his youth. Secure him from the paths of the destroyer and the evils of the world. May uprightness preserve him. In the situation he will be called to fill, may he be dutiful and obliging, and diligent and faithful. May he always remember that the eye of God is upon him; and be not only amiable but pious; and be in favour with God as well as man.

(If with a view to a School.)

—O THOU God of providence and grace, we commend to thy care the dear child about to leave our abode for a season in order to receive needful instruction. Let his (or her) life be precious in thy sight. May he redeem his time, and acquire the improvement that will fit him for usefulness in his day and generation. And O let him be made wise unto salvation; and let the beauty of the Lord our God be upon him; that he may be a useful and ornamental member in thy church below, and hereafter a pillar in thy temple above, never more to go out.

FOR A SERVANT COMING INTO THE FAMILY.

—AND, O Thou, with whom there is no respect of persons, bless the servant that has just entered our household. May she (or he) be diligent in her station; may she rise early, be attentive to punctuality, and neatness, and cleanliness; pleasing well in all things, not answering again; not purloining, but showing all good fidelity; that she may adorn the doctrine of God our Saviour in all things. May she cheerfully conform to the religious order of the family, be thankful for its daily worship, and improve every spiritual privilege.

And while our servants know and observe their duty to us, may we never neglect our duty to them, but remember that we also have a Master in heaven.

FOR CHILDREN IN ORDINARY CIRCUMSTANCES.

(All the petitions need not be used at the same time.)

—O GOD, Thou art the lovely Father of

all mankind. Thou hast implanted in us the parental instincts; and commanded us to train up our children in the nurture and admonition of the Lord. We feel our awful responsibility, and often exclaim, Who is sufficient for these things? But Thou givest wisdom to the ignorant and power to the faint. Aid, O aid us, in discharging the duties we owe to those whom Thou hast given us and continued to us.

We give them up to Thee, who art able to fulfil all our petitions. Rescue them from the numberless accidents and diseases to which they are exposed. Let their tempers be lovely, and meek, and kind. Let their manners be simple and engaging. May they be respectful towards their superiors, obliging towards their equals, and condescending towards their inferiors.

—Let not envy and pride and censoriousness render them disdainful to others and wretched to themselves. May they speak evil of no one. Upon their tongue may there dwell the law of kindness. May they hate and abhor lying—with all deceit and hypocrisy.

—May they be always willing to receive instruction; and be diligent in acquiring all the knowledge and improvement that may render them the blessings and ornaments of society.

—Keep them from evil company. If sinners entice them, may they never consent; but early may they take hold of the skirt of him that is a Jew, saying, I will go with you, for I have heard that God is with you.

—Let our sons be as plants grown up in their youth, and our daughters as cornerstones, polished after the similitude of a palace.

—Pour thy blessing upon our seed, and thy Spirit upon our offspring; that one may say, I am the Lord's, and another call himself by the name of Jacob, and another subscribe with his own hand, and surname himself by the name of Israel.

—We seek not great things for them as to this world—but O let them live in thy sight; let them be numbered with thy saints in glory everlasting; let them be blessed with all spiritual blessings in heavenly places in Christ.

Instead of multiplying riches, and leaving them incentives to pride, and vanity, and idleness, and sensuality, and augmenting a thousand fold all the difficulties of their salvation—may we lay up for them treasure in heaven; may we be concerned to leave behind us a large inheritance of prayers and instructions and examples—with the blessing of God, that maketh rich, and addeth no sorrow with it.

—If their parents should be taken away from them—when father and mother forsake them, may the Lord take them up. If they should be deprived of their father—be Thou the father of the fatherless. If they should be deprived of their mother—as one whom his mother comforteth, so do Thou comfort them.

—Should they be removed from us in early life, may the heavenly Shepherd gather the lambs with his arm, and carry them in his bosom; and may we be prepared to resign them. And if, as we submissively implore, their lives should be prolonged—may they grow up, and prove our comfort and honour, serve their generation according to thy will, and walk before Thee in the land of the living.

FOR CRIMINALS IN PRISON.

—Behold, in the greatness of thy mercy, those who are bound in affliction and iron, because they rebelled against the word of God. May they be led to reflect upon the evil of sin, in the degradation and misery to which it has reduced them. Give them repentance unto life; that they may acknowledge that Thou art just in all that is brought upon them, and be more concerned to obtain deliverance from the wrath to come, than exemption from the hand of civil justice. If after lengthened confinement they should be released, let them be rescued from the bondage of corruption, and partake of the glorious liberty of the sons of God; and if appointed unto death, O hear the sighing of the prisoner, and though the flesh be destroyed, let the spirit be saved in the day of the Lord Jesus.

While we feel an abhorrence of sin, may we always display compassion for sinners, and be thankful that we have been exempted, by the favourableness of our condition in life, by pious relations, by education, by thy restraining and thy sanctifying grace, from so many temptations by which we might have been conquered. Who made us to differ from another? And what have we that we did not receive?

FOR A FRIEND AT SEA.

—The sea is thine as well as the dry land. All the elements obey thy voice. We commend to thy kind and almighty care, our friend who is now on the perilous ocean. Give to the winds and the waves commandment to save him. O Thou that art the confidence of all the ends of the earth, and of them that are far off upon the sea, encourage and tranquillize his mind by holy reliance on thy Providence. May he not only see, but improve the works of the Lord, and his wonders in the deep. And should the waters thereof roar and be troubled, and vain be the help of man, hear him in his distresses; make the storm a calm; and bring him to his desired haven.

ADDRESSES

PARTICULAR SEASONS

SPRING.

—Thou art the fountain of life. In Thee we live, move, and have our being; and the prerogative of that being is, that we are able to contemplate thy perfections, and rise from thy works—to thyself.

Thou sendest forth thy Spirit, and renewest the face of the earth; and from apparent death, all nature starts into re-animated vigour and joy. In what myriads of productions art Thou displaying afresh the wonders of thy wisdom, power, and goodness—the whole earth is full of thy riches.

While we partake of the general sympathy and delight, may we join with all thy works to praise Thee. And O Thou God of all grace, bless us with the renewing of the Holy Ghost in all the powers of our souls. May old things pass away, and all things become new in Christ. May the beauty of the Lord be upon us; and the joy of the Lord be our strength.

May the young remember that they are now in the spring of life, and that *this* spring once gone returns no more. May they therefore eagerly seize and zealously improve the short but all-important season, for the cultivation of their minds, the formation of their habits, the correction of their tempers, their preparation for future usefulness, and their gaining that good part which shall not be taken away from them.

SUMMER.

—We hail Thee in the varying aspects of the year, and bless Thee for all their appropriate influences and advantages. O let us not view them and enjoy them as men only, but as Christians also; and ever connect with them the blessings of thy grace.

How wise and useful and necessary are these intermingled rains and sunbeams! May Jesus, as the Sun of Righteousness, arise upon us with healing under his wings; may he come down as rain upon the mown grass, and as showers that water the earth.

When we walk by the cooling brook, may we think of that river the streams whereof make glad the city of God.

When we retire from the scorching warmth of the day into the inviting shade, may we be thankful for a rest at noon, a shelter from the heat, the shadow of a great rock in a weary land.

May thy servants behold the moral fields, that are already white unto harvest, and be all anxiety to save the multitudes that are perishing for lack of knowledge.

The harvest truly is great, but the labourers are few; we therefore pray that Thou wilt send forth labourers into thy harvest.

He that gathereth in summer is a wise son; he that sleepeth in harvest is a son that causeth shame. Now is our accepted time, now is our day of salvation. O let us not waste our precious privileges, and in a dying hour exclaim,—The harvest is past, the summer is ended, and we are not saved.

AUTUMN.

—How fleeting, as well as varying, are the seasons of the year! How insensibly have the months of spring and summer vanished! Nature has no sooner attained its maturities, than we behold its declension and decay. The fields are now shorn of their produce; the beauties of the garden are withered; the woods are changing their verdure, and the trees shedding their foliage—we also never continue in one stay. Many of our connexions and comforts have already dropped away from us; and the remaining are holden by a slender tenure—while we ourselves do all fade as a leaf—and in a little time our places will know us no more.

Blessed be the God and Father of our Lord Jesus Christ, for the announcement of an inheritance that fadeth not away. O for a hope full of immortality—for a possession of that good part which shall not be taken away from us!

WINTER.

O Thou God of nature and providence; manifold are thy works, in wisdom hast Thou made them all; and all are full of thy goodness. The welfare of thy creatures requires the severity of winter as well as the pleasures of spring. We adore thy hand in all. Thou givest snow like wool; Thou scatterest the hoar frost like ashes. Thou sendest abroad thine ice-like morsels: who can stand before thy cold?

But we bless Thee for a house to shelter us; for raiment to cover us, for fuel to warm us; and for all the accommodations that render life, even at this inclement season, not only tolerable but full of comfort.

—Not more than others we deserve,
Yet God has given us more.—

May we be grateful; and may we be pitiful. May we reflect on the condition of those who are the victims of every kind of privation and distress—and waste nothing—hoard nothing—but hasten to be the ministers of mercy, and the disciples of Him who went about doing good.

O let the rich *now* deservedly prize their wealth, and use it as the instrument of usefulness. May they be willing to communicate, ready to distribute; and enjoy the blessing of him that is ready to perish, and make the widow's heart to sing for joy.

A TIME OF THUNDER AND LIGHTNING.

—With Thee is terrible majesty. Thou lookest on the earth, and it melteth; Thou touchest the mountains, and they smoke. Thou thunderest in the heavens, and all nature shudders at thy voice. How vain now is the help of man! Who can resist thy will! We feel ourselves to be nothing, less than nothing, and vanity. Our very houses are no protection now! O Thou, to whom belong the issues from death, defend our persons and our dwelling. May we always stand in awe of Thee, and sin not. May we know that this awful God is ours, our Father and our Friend; and may we have boldness in that day, when the heavens being on fire shall be dissolved, and the elements melt with fervent heat, and the earth also, and all the works that are therein, shall be burnt up.

THANKSGIVINGS

PARTICULAR EVENTS.

FOR RAIN AFTER A LONG DROUGHT.

—Thou hast never left thyself without witness, but hast been continually doing good, even to the unthankful and unworthy, in giving them rain from heaven, and fruitful seasons, filling their hearts with joy and gladness. We acknowledge that the heavens over us might have been brass, and the earth under us iron. We have justly deserved the calamity; and thy power, without a miracle, could have inflicted it. But though Thou hast tried our patience, and awakened our fears, Thou hast not forgotten to be gracious. We praise Thee for sending us the seasonable and plentiful rain, by which Thou hast refreshed and revived the drooping fields, so that the earth promises to yield her increase.

FOR FAIR WEATHER AFTER MUCH RAIN.

O God, Thou art good, and doest good. Thou hast again surpassed our deserts, and been better to us than our fears. Thou hast caused the clear shining after rain; so that in the meadows the hay appeareth, and in the fields Thou art preparing of thy goodness for the poor. Thou preservest man and beast. May we feel our entire dependence upon Thee, and by prayer and praise give Thee the glory that is due unto thy holy name.

FOR A GOOD HARVEST.

—Again Thou hast crowned the year with thy goodness. The grain might have perished in the earth, or have failed of maturity for want of the showers and of the sunshine. But Thou wast pleased to bless the springing thereof; and we saw, first the blade, then the ear, and after that the full corn in the ear. We hailed the valleys standing thick with corn, and heard the little hills rejoicing on every side. In due time the mower filled his hands, and the binder of sheaves his bosom; and the appointed weeks of harvest have been afforded us to gather in the precious produce. O that men would praise the Lord for his goodness, and for his wonderful works to the children of men! For he satisfieth the longing soul, and filleth the hungry soul with goodness.

We have again witnessed thy faithfulness and truth in the promise—While the earth remaineth, seed-time and harvest, and cold and heat, and summer and winter, and day and night shall not cease. May we learn to trust Thee in all thy engagements.

And make us thankful that as we have no famine of bread, so we have no famine of hearing the word of the Lord. With regard to the soul, as well as to the body, Thou fillest us with the finest of the wheat.

FOR PEACE.

—O Thou that stillest the noise of the seas, the noise of their waves, and the tumult of the people; we bless Thee that Thou hast made peace in our borders, and called us to adore Thee, as the repairer of the breach, the restorer of paths to dwell in.

We lament the evils of war, both natural and moral; and confess with shame, that ever since man became an apostate from Thee, he has been an enemy to his brother, and that from the death of Abel our earth has been a field of blood. O let thy word be speedily accomplished. Let the nations learn war no more, but beat their swords into ploughshares, and their spears into pruning-hooks; and only emulate each other in husbandry, and commerce, and science, and religion.

O Thou Prince of Peace, preside in every privy council. May all public teachers recommend peace. In private life, may we follow peace with all men; and cherish the principles and the dispositions which will prepare us for that world, where we shall enter into peace, and the sound of war will be heard no more.

FOR A SAFE RETURN FROM A JOURNEY.

—As the keeper of Israel Thou hast been

with us, not only in the house, but by the way. We might have been injured by wicked and unreasonable men. We might have been left groaning under the pain of bruised limbs or fractured bones. Our lives might have been spilt like water on the ground, which cannot be gathered up again; and the first tidings that reached our friends might have plunged them into anguish.

But all our bones can say, Who is a God like unto Thee? Thy secret too in our absence has been upon our tabernacle, and secured it from all evil. O that it may be the tabernacle of the righteous; and be ever filled, not only with the voice of rejoicing but of praise.

And be with us in all the future journey of life. Guide us by thy counsel. Uphold us by thy power; and supply all our wants, till we come to our Father's house in peace.

FOR RECOVERY FROM SICKNESS.

—ALL our times are in thy hand. All diseases come at thy call, and go at thy bidding. Thou redeemest our life from destruction, and crownest us with lovingkindness and tender mercies. We bless Thee that Thou hast heard prayer, and commanded deliverance for our friend and thy servant, who has been under thine afflicting hand. He (or she) was brought low, but Thou hast helped him: Thou hast chastened him sore but not delivered him over unto death. May he not only live but declare the works of the Lord.

As Thou hast delivered his eyes from tears, his feet from falling, and his soul from death, may he daily inquire, What shall I render unto the Lord for all his benefits towards me? and resolve to offer unto Thee the sacrifices of thanksgiving, and to call upon the name of the Lord.

And may we ever remember that a recovery is only a reprieve: that the sentence which dooms us to the dust is only suspended; and that at most, when a few years are come, we shall go the way whence we shall not return. May we therefore secure the one thing needful, and live with eternity in view.

FOR SAFE DELIVERY IN CHILD-BIRTH.

—WE bless Thee on the behalf of thine handmaid, who is now saying, I love the Lord, because he hath heard my voice and my supplication. Thou hast been with her in the hour of pain and peril, and made her the joyful mother of a living and well-formed infant. Complete thy goodness by the re-newal of her strength, and her ability to appear again in all the duties of her important station.

Let the impressions produced by recent mercies be rendered as durable as they are lively. May she remember, and pay Thee the vows which her soul made when in trouble.

May the life spared, and the life given, be dear in thy sight and devoted to thy glory; and may every addition made to the world of creatures be found an accession to the church of the living God.

FOR THE RETURN OF A FRIEND FROM SEA.

—WHAT shall be done unto Thee, O thou Preserver of men! We offer to Thee the sacrifice of praise, the fruit of our lips, giving thanks to thy name, for thy goodness towards our friend and thy servant, whom Thou hast delivered from the dangers of the pitiless deep. Thou wast with him when trouble was nigh; and at thy command were the issues from death. Others have found a watery grave, till the sea shall give up her dead; but he has returned alive and in comfort. Many are weeping over the loss of those for whom they long anxiously waited; but we have embraced the desire of our eyes; and in the multitude of thy tender mercies we pay Thee the vows of renewed intercourse.

ACTS OF DEVOTION FOR THE TABLE.

BEFORE MEAT.

O GOD, the eyes of all thy creatures wait upon Thee, and Thou givest them their meat in due season. Bless to our use the bounties of thy providence, by which Thou hast spread another table for us in the wilderness. Let them refresh, nourish, and strengthen our frail bodies, that we may be the better able to serve and glorify Thee, through our Lord and Saviour. Amen. Or thus:—

Forgive our sins, and sanctify to us the comforts with which we are now indulged. May we eat, and be satisfied, and praise the Lord, through the mediation of thy dear Son and our Redeemer. Amen.

AFTER MEAT.

WE adore Thee, O God, as the giver of every good and perfect gift. We bless Thee for the meat that perisheth, but above all for that meat which endureth to everlasting life.

Feed us and lift us up for ever, through our Lord and Saviour. Amen. Or thus :—

What shall we render unto the Lord for all his benefits towards us! Let thy goodness lead us to repentance, induce us to pity and release the destitute, and constrain us to present our bodies a living sacrifice, holy and acceptable, through Jesus Christ our Lord. Amen. Or thus :—

Add to the bounties of thy providence the better blessings of thy grace; and may we be found in the number of those that shall eat bread in the kingdom of God, for the Redeemer's sake. Amen.

END OF THE FAMILY PRAYERS.

Date Loaned

Demco 292-5

CPSIA information can be obtained
at www.ICGtesting.com
Printed in the USA
LVOW04s0621141117
556231LV00010B/290/P

9 781277 075472